Proceedings of the

23rd European Conference on Cyber Warfare and Security

ECCWS 2024

A Conference
Hosted By
University of Jyväskylä and
JAMK University of Applied Sciences, Finland

27-28 June 2024

Edited by Dr Martti Lehto

Review Process

Papers submitted to this conference have been double-blind peer reviewed before final acceptance to the conference. Initially, abstracts were reviewed for relevance and accessibility and successful authors were invited to submit full papers. Many thanks to the reviewers who helped ensure the quality of all the submissions.

Ethics and Publication Malpractice Policy

ACIL adheres to a strict ethics and publication malpractice policy for all publications – details of which can be found here:
http://www.academic-conferences.org/policies/ethics-policy-for-publishing-in-the-conference-proceedings-of-academic-conferences-and-publishing-international-limited/

Self-Archiving and Paper Repositories

We actively encourage authors of papers in ACIL conference proceedings and journals to upload their published papers to university repositories and research bodies such as ResearchGate and Academic.edu. Full reference to the original publication should be provided.

Conference Proceedings

The Conference Proceedings is a book published with an ISBN and ISSN. The proceedings have been submitted to a number of accreditation, citation and indexing bodies including Thomson ISI Web of Science and Elsevier Scopus. Author affiliation details in these proceedings have been reproduced as supplied by the authors themselves.

From 2022 these proceedings are open access and freely available for all to read. The Conference Proceedings for previous years can be purchased from http://academic-bookshop.com

The Electronic version of the Conference Proceedings is available to download from https://papers.academic-conferences.org/.

E-Book ISBN: 978-1-917204-07-1
E-Book ISSN: 2048-8610
Book version ISBN: 978-1-917204-06-4
Book Version ISSN: 2048-8602

Published by Academic Conferences International Limited
Reading, UK
www.academic-conferences.org
info@academic-conferences.org

Contents

PhD Papers

Masters Papers

ECCWS Preface

These proceedings represent the work of contributors to the 23rd European Conference on Cyber Warfare and Security (ECCWS 2024), supported by University of Jyväskylä, and JAMK University of Applied Sciences, Finland on 27-28 June 2024. The Conference Chair is Dr Martti Lehto from the University of Jyväskylä, Finland, and the Programme Chair is Dr Mika Karjalainen from JAMK University of Applied Sciences, Finland.

ECCWS is a well-established event on the academic research calendar and now in its 23rd year conference remains the opportunity for participants to network and share ideas. The aims and scope of the conference is to be a forum for technical, theoretical and practical exchange about the study, management, development and implementation of systems and concepts to improve cyber security and combat cyber warfare.

The opening keynote presentation is given by Stefan Lee, from Ministry of Transport and Communications, Finland, on the topic of *Geopolitics and Cyberspace: Key Implications for National Cybersecurity Policies and Strategies.* The second day of the conference will open with an address by Colonel Janne Jokinen, Finnish Defence Force, Finland speaking on *Ten Practical Hindrances to Building Cyber Defence.*

With an initial submission of 171 abstracts, after the double blind, peer review process there are 180 Academic research papers, 11 PhD research papers, 6 Masters research paper and 2 work-in-progress papers published in these Conference Proceedings. These papers represent research from Australia, Austria, Belgium, Canada, Czech Republic, Estonia, Finland, Germany, Ireland, Japan, Kingdom of Saudi Arabia, Lithuania, Norway, Oman, Poland, Portugal, Romania, South Africa, Spain, The Czech republic, United Arab Emirates, UK and USA.

We hope you enjoy the conference.

Dr Martti Lehto
University of Jyväskylä
Finland
June 2024

ECCWS 2024 Conference Committee

Dr Mohd Faizal Abdollah, University Technical Malaysia Melaka, Malaysia; Dr Hossein Abroshan, Anglia Ruskin University, UK; Dr William Adams, University of Michigan/Merit Network, USA; Dr Ertuğrul Akbas, Istanbul Esenyurt University, Turkey; Prof Hamid Alasadi, Basra University, Iraq; Dr Kari Alenius, University of Oulu, Finland; Prof Antonios Andreatos, Hellenic Air Force Academy, Greece; Dr Olga Angelopoulou, University of Warwick, UK; John Anohar, Higher Education Dept, India; Dr Leigh Armistead, Edith Cowan University, Australia; Dr Sajad Bagheri Baba Ahmadi, Flinders University, Australia; Dr Hayretdin Bahsi, Tallinn University of Technology, Estonia; Dr Dragos Barbieru, CAROL I National Defence University, Romania; Prof Jorge Barbosa, Coimbra Polytechnic, ISEC, Portugal; Stacey Baror, University of Pretoria, South Africa; Prof Matt Bishop, University of California at Davis, USA; Dr Sabarathinam Chockalingam, Institute for Energy Technology, Norway; Dr Paul Crocker, Universidade de Beira Interior, Portugal; Prof Tiago Cruz, University of Coimbra, Portugal; Dr Christian Czosseck, CERT Bundeswehr (German Armed Forces CERT), Germany; Josef Demergis, University of Macedonia, Greece; Prof Patricio Domingues, Polytechnic Institute of Leiria, Portugal; Paul Dowland, Edith Cowan University, Australia; Marios Efthymiopoulos, Political Science Department University of Cyprus, Cyprus; Dr Colin Egan, University of Hertfordshire, Hatfield, UK; Dr Ruben Elamiryan, Public Administration Academy of the Republic of Armenia, Armenia; Dr Thaddeus Eze, University of Chester, UK; Dr Mohammad Faisal, University of Malakand, Pakistan; Prof Eric Filiol, ENSIBS, Vannes, France & CNAM, Paris, France; Dr Jonathan Fuller, United States Military Academy, USA; Prof Steve Furnell, University of Nottingham, UK; Dr Dimitra Georgiou, University of Piraeus, Greece; Bill Hutchinson, Edith Cowan University, Australia; Hamid Jahankhani, University of East London, UK; Nor Badrul Anuar Jumaat, University of Malaya, Malaysia; Dr Connie Justice, Purdue School of Engineering and Technology, IUPUI, USA; Dr Aikaterini Kanta, University of Portsmouth, England; Maria Karyda, University of the Aegean, Greece; Anthony Keane, Technological University Dublin, Ireland; Prof Mortaza Kokabi, Shaheed Chamran Univ.,Iran; Prof Ahmet Koltuksuz, Yasar University, Dept. of Comp. Eng, Turkey; Peter Kunz, Hexagon Geosystems, Germany; Martti Lehto, National Defence University, Finland; Christoph Lipps, German Research Center for Artificial Intelligence, Germany; Dr Leandros Maglaras, De Montfort University, UK; Assc Manmeet Mahinderjit Singh, University Sains Malaysia, Malaysia; James Malcolm, University of Hertfordshire, UK; Arun Mamgai, Red Hat Inc, USA; Dr Arianit Maraj, AAB College-Faculty of Computer Sciences, Kosovo; Ioannis Mavridis , University of Macedonia, Greece; Rob McCusker, Charles Sturt University, UK; Prof Marius-Iulian Mihailescu, SPIRU HARET University, Romania; Atefeh Mohseni Ejiyeh, University of California, Santa Barbara, USA; Antonio Muñoz, University of Málaga, Spain; Dr Stefania Loredana Nita, Military Technical Academy "Ferdinand I", Romania; Prof Teresa Pereira, Instituto Politécnico de Viana do Castelo, Portugal; Michael Pilgermann, Technische Hochschule Brandenburg - University of Applied Sciences, Germany; Prof Pedro Pinto, Instituto Politécnico de Viana do Castelo, Portugal; Dr Ajeet Singh Poonia, Full time academic, Bikaner Technical University, Rajasthan; Prof Maria-Magdalena Popescu, Carol I National Defence University , Romania; Prof Carlos Rabadão, Politechnic of Leiria, Portugal; Dr Trishana Ramluckan, University of KwaZulu-Nata, South Africa; Dr Mark Reith, Full time academic, Air Force Institute of Technology; Dr Neil Rowe, US Naval Postgraduate School, Monterey, USA; Prof Vitor Sa, Catholic University of Portugal, Portugal; Dr Char Sample, Carnegie Mellon University/CERT, USA; Prof Henrique Santos, University of Minho, Portugal; Prof Leonel Santos, Polytechnic of Leiria, Portugal; Dr Keith Scott, De Montfort University, UK; Prof Dr Richard Sethmann, University of Applied Sciences Bremen, Germany; Dr Yilun Shang, Northumbria University, UK; Prof Jill Slay, University of South Australia, Australia; Dr Lee Speakman, University of Chester, UK; Dr Joseph Spring, University of Hertfordshire, UK; Prof Marco Valeri, Niccolò Cusano University, Italy; Prof Omar Zakaria, National Defence University of Malaysia, Malaysia.

Conference and Programme Chairs

Dr. Martti Lehto, (Military Sciences), Col (GS) (ret.) works as a Research Director (Cyber security) in the Faculty of Information Technology in the University of Jyväskylä. He has over 30 years' experience as developer and leader of C4ISR Systems in the Finnish Air Force. He is Cyber security and Cyber defence researcher in the IT Faculty. He has over 200 publications, research reports and articles on the areas of C4ISR systems, cyber security and defence, information warfare, air power and defence policy. Since 2001 he has been the Editor-in-Chief of the Military Magazine. He also acts as a director of Finnish Center of expertise for Cybersecurity (FICEC).

Dr. Mika Karjalainen holds a PhD in information technology. Dr. Mika Karjalainen is a distinguished expert in the field of cybersecurity and an esteemed faculty member at JAMK University of Applied Sciences. Dr. Karjalainen completed his doctoral studies with a focus on cybersecurity, specifically focusing for the learning in cyber security exercises and the pedagogical foundations of cyber ranges. At JAMK University of applied Sciences Dr. Karjalainen serves as Vice rector.

Keynote Speakers

Colonel Janne Jokinen has a long career in cyber-related positions at the Finnish Defence Forces. From March 2024 he is the director of the C5 Agency in Jyväskylä, which, amongst several other duties, has the largest and broadest scoped cyber defence unit in Finland. Previously he was the deputy division (J6) head at the Defence Command responsible for coordinating cyber throughout the Finnish Defence Forces and government-wide. Col Jokinen has a PhD degree in physics, and master's degrees in physics, military electronic systems engineering, and psychology. He is a docent (adjunct professor) of signals intelligence and electronic warfare at the Finnish National Defence University, a docent of Cyber Security at the University of Jyväskylä, and is a licensed psychologist

Stefan Lee was appointed by the Government of Finland as Deputy Director of National Cyber Security in 2022. The main areas of his responsibilities cover external dimensions of national cyber security related to foreign- and security policy, defence and national security as well as international cooperation and dialogue with relevant domestic stakeholders as well as with allies and partners. Stefan is also currently the Vice-Chair of the Management Board of the EU Cybersecurity Agency, ENISA. Prior to his current position, Stefan was a career diplomat at the Ministry for Foreigns Affairs of Finland with work experince in both bilateral and multilateral diplomacy including, inter alia, Deputy Director of EU Common Foreign and Security Policy and Head of team on security policy and technology (cyber and technology diplomacy) at the political department of the MFA. He has served abroad in Finnish missions to the Hague, Seoul and Geneva. Stefan holds Master's degrees from both ETH Zurich of Switzerland and Hanken School of Economics of Finland. He is fluent in Finnish, Swedish, English and Korean and has basic knowledge of French and German.

Mini Track Chairs

Dr Olga Angelopoulou is an Assistant Professor in Cyber Security at the University of Warwick. Olga completed her doctorate in digital forensics in 2010 at the University of South Wales (Glamorgan) and is an active researcher in the field. She previously held academic posts at the University of Derby and the University of Hertfordshire. Olga is also the Editor-in-Chief for Information Security Journal: A global Perspective. Her research interests include digital investigations, cybercrimes, incident response and online fraud. She has several publications and presentations in the field and is involved in numerous scholarly activities.

Dr. Sabarathinam Chockalingam is a Research Scientist I at the Institute for Energy Technology in Halden, Norway. Saba has a PhD in Cyber Security and Artificial Intelligence from the Delft University of Technology and MSc in Cyber Security and Management from the University of Warwick. His research interests include cyber security, risk management, and safety.

Dr Tiago Cruz received his Ph.D. degree in informatics engineering from the University of Coimbra (Coimbra, Portugal), in 2012. He is an Assistant Professor in the Department of Informatics Engineering, University of Coimbra. His research interests include areas such as management systems for communications infrastructures and services, critical infrastructure security, broadband access network device and service management, Internet of Things.

Christoph Lipps, graduated in Electrical and Computer Engineering at the University of Kaiserslautern, where he meanwhile lectures as well. He is a Senior Researcher and Ph.D. candidate at the German Research Center for Artificial Intelligence (DFKI) in Kaiserslautern, Germany, heading the *Cyber Resilience & Security* Team of the Intelligent Networks Research Department. His research focuses on Physical Layer Security (PhySec), Physically Unclonable Functions (PUFs), Artificial Intelligence (AI), Biometrics and Security in the Sixth Generation (6G) Wireless Systems.

Dr. ir. Clara Maathuis is an Assistant Professor in AI and Cyber Security at the Open University in the Netherlands. With a PhD in AI and Military Cyber Operations from the Delft University of Technology, she is involved in teaching different AI and cyber security courses and conducts research in AI, cyber/information operations, military technologies, and social manipulation

Matthias Rüb graduated in physics at the University of Kaiserslautern. His fields of work included laser physics, molecular magnets, photoemission spectroscopy and ultrafast electron dynamics in 2D-materials. He works as a Researcher and Ph.D candidate at the German Research Center for Artificial Intelligence (DFKI) in Kaiserslautern. His topics of interest include Body-Area-Networks, Artificial Intelligence and security applications.

Dr Keith Scott Is Programme Leader for English Language at De Montfort University in Leicester. His research operates at the intersection of communication, culture and cyber, with particular interests in influence, information warfare, and simulations and serious gaming as a training. teaching, and research tool. He is a member of the Prometheus Research group, supported by the UK Development, Concepts and Doctrine Centre, which investigates the application of cybernetics and systems thinking within the context of warfare, as well as more general considerations of AI and pervasive technology.

Dr Paulo Simões received his Ph.D. degree in informatics engineering from the University of Coimbra (Coimbra, Portugal), in 2002. He is an Associate Professor in the Department of Informatics Engineering, University of Coimbra. His research interests include network and infrastructure management, security, critical infrastructure protection.

Workshop Facilitators

Dr Edwin "Leigh" Armistead is the Principal of ArmisteadTec LLC, a Veteran-Owned Small Business (VOSB) that is certified by the Small Business Administration (SBA) as a Historically Underutilized Business Zone (HBZ), https://www.armisteadtec.com/. This company primarily focuses on the academic functions of Information Warfare (IW), to include curriculum development, teaching as well as other related tasks to include lecturing and writing. A retired United States Naval Officer, Dr Armistead has significant Information Operations academic credentials having written his PhD on the conduct of Cyber Warfare by the federal government and has published three books, in an unclassified format in 2004, 2007 and 2010, all focusing on full Information Warfare. He is also the Chief Editor of the Journal of Information Warfare (JIW) https://www.jinfowar.com/; the Program Director of the International Conference of Cyber Warfare and Security and the Vice-Chair Working Group 9.10, ICT Uses in Peace and War.

The Role of Digitalisation in Shaping Country Image: Towards a Conceptual Framework

Dauda Adejumo[1], Martin Wynn[2] and Vera Vale[1]
[1]University of Aveiro, Aveiro, Portugal
[2]University of Gloucestershire, Cheltenham, UK

daudaadejumo2@ua.pt
mwynn@glos.ac.uk
v.c.vale@ua.pt

Abstract: The objective of this study is to examine the complex role played by digital technologies in shaping a country's image on the global stage. In recent times, with the rapid evolution of digital communication platforms, developing nations have increasingly turned to digital technologies to project their cultural, economic, and political narratives to an international audience. This paper examines the relevant literature relating to how digital technologies contribute to the creation and dissemination of a country's image, impacting the opinions and views of global stakeholders. It so doing, the paper reviews the challenges and opportunities arising from the integration of digital tools in country branding efforts, including misinformation concerns, digital diplomacy, cybersecurity, and the democratization of narrative-building. The paper then puts forward a provisional conceptual framework for primary research in Nigeria that will examine the interplay of digitalisation and country image. The paper concludes that digitalisation has a significant influence on a country's image, affecting perceptions of technological advancement, economic development, access to information, social transformation, and global competitiveness, and suggests that the framework put forward here may act as a model for cross-country comparisons in subsequent studies.

Keywords: Digitalisation, Country Image, Provisional Conceptual Framework, Digital Transformation.

1. Introduction

Digitalisation can significantly impact a country's image, transforming the perception of its economic competitiveness and cultural identity. Digital technologies can help countries to showcase their unique attributes and achievements through websites, social media platforms, and digital marketing campaigns. This digital storytelling allows countries to influence perceptions among key stakeholders, including tourists, investors, policymakers, and the global community. Digitalisation has democratised access to information, empowering individuals and communities to participate in shaping their country's image, but has also brought new risks as regards misinformation, cyber-attacks, and online reputation management. Despite these challenges, the extant literature emphasises the importance of authenticity, storytelling, and digital diplomacy in shaping global perceptions. Understanding how countries use digital tools to shape their image is crucial for policymakers, marketers, and scholars. This paper thus explores this research area, reviewing relevant literature and putting forward a framework that encapsulates the key concepts.

Figure 1: Digital Technologies 2024

The two concepts that are central to this research are digitalisation and country image. "Digitalisation" implies the use of modern electronic devices, tools, equipment, and resources to generate, store, process, or present information in numerical form. However, it also refers to the process change brought about by the introduction of digital technologies (Riedl et al., 2017). These digital tools are often categorized under acronyms like SMAC (social media, mobile, analytics/big data, and Cloud) and BRAID (blockchain, robotics, automation of knowledge work/artificial intelligence, internet of things, and digital fabrication), and these nine technologies have recently evolved to support a wider conceptual categorisation (Figure 1). According to Frenzel et al. (2021), digitalisation means converting analog information into digital format, but also entails the streamlining of processes and activities, reducing costs and enhancing efficiency for businesses. The strategic integration of digital technologies can bring about substantial changes to an organization's culture, operations, and value proposition. When this change also involves the development of new products or services, then "digital transformation" occurs (Wynn & Felser, 2023).

"Country image" refers to a nation's global perception and reputation, influenced by its digital presence, policies, and technological advancements (Revilla-Camacho et al., 2022). As the world becomes more interconnected and interdependent, the study of country image has gained prominence in academic and practical spheres. The paradigm shift demands understanding and managing the complexities of a country's image crucial for various stakeholders, including governments, businesses, and individuals as its impact on international relations, trade, and tourism. In today's world, a country's digital presence, policies, and technological advancements are crucial in shaping its international reputation (Ahmed et al., 2021). This rapid evolution of technology has completely revolutionized the way we communicate and access information within a country (Vahdat, 2022). Anholt (2021) emphasizes the need for countries to actively manage their image, recognizing its far-reaching implications on various aspects of global interactions and introduces the concept of a "good country". It explores strategies for fostering positive international perceptions, emphasizing collaboration and contribution to global well-being. How other countries view a nation can impact its ability to attract investments, foster diplomatic relations, and encourage citizen engagement (Abdulquadri et al., 2021). While some experts in developed nations may argue that we have moved beyond the digital revolution and entered a post-digital era, digitalisation remains critical for developing countries (Yina, 2020). The image is an important aspect when describing a country (Anyanka, 2018). It determines how citizens of a country are being viewed and treated based on their opinion about that country, which could either be positive or negative. The government should work with all sectors to ensure that digital tools are used in a way that can enhance the country's image.

Integrating digital technologies across various sectors plays a critical role in shaping a country's socio-economic landscape and global standing (Udegbunam et al., 2023). Digitalization has the potential to enhance government efficiency, transparency, and citizen participation while also generating employment prospects, but it remains a major challenge in most developing countries. Cybersecurity, infrastructure gaps, and lack of digital literacy are major hurdles that impede sustainable development in most African nations. The current study aims to understand how digitalisation contributes to the creation and promotion of a positive country image. The research will contribute to the ongoing discourse on the dynamic relationship between digitalisation and a country's global image, and more specifically this article addresses the following research questions (RQs):

RQ1. What literature exists that explores the relationship between digitalisation and country image?

RQ2. Can a conceptual framework be developed from the extant literature to act as a basis for primary research?

Following this introduction, the research method is set out. Section 3 then directly addresses the two RQs in the Results section. This is followed by a discussion of some of the emergent themes in section 4. Section 5 provides a conclusion to the paper, highlighting key issues and suggesting possible future research agendas.

2. Research Method

The overall research approach is qualitative and inductive, based on an interpretivist paradigm. A scoping literature review was the main applied methodology used to address the RQs. Various academic databases, including Google Scholar, Scopus, Web of Science and Science Direct were accessed to search the existing literature This allowed the identification of key sources and the construction of the provisional conceptual framework for the research project (which will subsequently involve in-depth interviews with appropriate local and central authority personnel and industry representatives). This is essentially qualitative research, which Mason (2017) concluded, because of its intensity, provides a powerful source of information for analysis. Bell et al. (2018) (p. 97) have observed that a literature review can provide "a means of gaining an initial impression" of relevant themes, whilst Porter et al. (2002) noted that a scoping review involves a "broad scan of contextual literature" through which "topical relationships, research trends, and complementary capabilities can be discovered" (p. 351).

A literature review is a way of collecting and synthesizing previous research (Tranfield et al., 2003) and can provide a firm foundation for advancing knowledge and facilitating theory development (Webster & Watson, 2002). Here, the study expands on the two main concepts—digitalisation and country image—to develop the provisional conceptual framework to address the two RQs noted above.

3. Results

3.1 RQ1. What Literature Exists That Explores the Relationship Between Digitalisation and Country Image?

In contemporary literature, the intersection of digitalisation and country image has become a compelling area of study, reflecting the increasing importance of digital platforms in shaping perceptions of countries. The digital landscape is constantly evolving, and nations worldwide recognise the significance of projecting a positive and appealing country image through various digital platforms (Ahmed et al., 2021). Experts have identified digitalisation as the defining characteristic of our current era (Gebayew et al., 2018). The role of digitalisation in shaping a country's image is a complex and evolving phenomenon that requires further exploration and analysis. Furthermore, the digital divide between urban and rural areas within a country can exacerbate inequalities and distort the true representation of its development progress. As digital technologies continue to advance and permeate every aspect of society, policymakers, marketers, and scholars must understand how countries use these tools to shape their image and influence global perceptions.

Lee and Kwak (2020) emphasize the importance of social media in nation branding and argue that digital platforms have become indispensable tools for shaping and managing a country's image, offering unprecedented opportunities for engagement and influencing a country's image in the digital age. Research findings revealed that digitalisation has facilitated the dissemination of information about countries, both positive and negative, and has played a pivotal role in shaping public opinion. Manor's (2020) studies explore the impact of digitalisation on Israel's image and digital diplomacy. They highlight how digitalisation has transformed diplomacy, allowing countries to communicate directly with international audiences through social media, digital campaigns, and online initiatives. The study also explores the challenges and opportunities associated with digital diplomacy, highlighting its importance in shaping global perceptions. The widespread use of digital platforms in shaping a country's image also presents a range of challenges and ethical considerations. Digitalisation has brought about significant ethical implications in shaping a country's image on the global stage. Lee (2021) submitted that the use of digital technologies by governments and businesses can influence perceptions of a country's values, governance, and societal norms. Issues such as data privacy, online surveillance, and the spread of misinformation have raised concerns about the trustworthiness and credibility of a country's digital presence. As countries strive to enhance their digital capabilities, it is crucial to consider the ethical implications of digitalisation on their overall image and reputation in the global arena. Due to global competition among countries, it has become the responsibility of every country to be concerned about their image and identity projecting to the rest of the world (Hakala et al., 2013; Saad, 2020). Digitalisation significantly impacts a country's tourist image, soft power, and global standing, with studies highlighting its role in destination marketing through user-generated content and online reviews.

The level of stability in a country's government and political system can have a significant impact on its image. While it is a general assumption that the concept of country image plays a crucial role in shaping perceptions and influencing the decisions of individuals and organizations regarding travel, investment, and trade. Such areas of concern include political stability, economic strength, cultural heritage, international relations, natural beauty, and social issues. So, countries with stable governments and peaceful societies are often perceived more positively by outsiders. Anyanka (2018) submits that image is an important aspect when describing a country, while Anholt (2009) concludes that using images themselves may not be a direct measurement of a country's competitiveness. However, the importance of images is greater in the modern digital age (Thompson, 2020). A comprehensive understanding of the current state of place branding, including the branding of countries in the context of trade, tourism, or international relations, and the shaping of a country's image, is essential for fostering positive perceptions and achieving sustainable global engagement (Govers, 2020). Furthermore, nations need to ensure that technology is used to promote shared prosperity and enhance democracy, rather than restrict freedom and opportunities both nationally and internationally.

In this era, digital security is crucial because it forms the foundation of a country's economic and social development and national security. Mihelj & Jiménez-Martínez (2021) reveal how technological advancements, communication strategies, and audience responses influence perceptions of nations, forming the basis for understanding digital nation branding. According to Ylianttila et al., (2020), digital security has become a significant concern for nations because it affects the security of digital infrastructure, individual privacy, and confidentiality, as well as a country's national security. A positive image can in turn lead to increased economic and political influence for the country. Modern innovative technology such as blockchain technology helps countries to identify potential threats, share information easily, and protect mechanisms in them that have the sensitivity to protect information, and the level of digital security of a country can significantly impact its national image. As a result, technology can be leveraged to improve national security and economic stability in the nation. Schwab and Sala-i-Martín (2016) emphasize the importance of innovation in keeping countries competitive and enhancing their global image. Countries with advanced security systems and protocols, such as surveillance technology or emergency response systems may be perceived as more secure. The role of digitalisation in shaping a country's image is a multifaceted and dynamic phenomenon that warrants careful examination.

Cai & McKenna (2023) investigated how digital affordances, such as social media platforms, influence the creation of a national destination image. While not expressly focused on country image, it does provide insights into how digitalisation affects impressions of locations with an emphasis on tourism management. Jin et al. (2021) investigated the effect of digital technology in improving country's image through a case study of South Korea. This study looks at how digital technologies, including social media and mobile applications, help to shape South Korea's image as a tourist destination. It emphasizes the importance of digitalisation in maintaining and developing a positive national image. A country's image can be greatly influenced by the stability of its government and political system. Yang et al. (2021) investigate how digital change influences destination image through a study of Chinese outbound tourists. This study looks at the impact of digital transformation, such as e-commerce, mobile payment, and social media, on the destination image perceived by Chinese outbound tourists. It emphasizes the role of digitization in altering perceptions of countries as travel destinations. Lee and Kwak (2020) undertook a thorough analysis of the effects of digitalisation on a country's image, with a particular emphasis on the role played by the political system and internet freedom as moderators. This research delves into how digitalisation shapes people's perceptions of a country's image, with a keen eye on how the political landscape and internet regulation may affect these outcomes. It suggests that the impact of digitalisation on a country's image may vary depending on the political climate and the level of internet governance in place.

3.2 RQ2. Can a Provisional Conceptual Framework be Developed From the Extant Literature to act as a Basis for Primary Research?

A conceptual framework can provide a theoretical basis for understanding the impact of digitalisation on a country's image, which will be applied to Nigeria's specific circumstances in due course. Figure 2 depicts the provisional conceptual framework based on the literature review, reflecting the interactions between the key concepts involved.

3.2.1 Impact of Social Media

In recent years, the rise of online platforms has created a significant shift in communication patterns (Lüders et al., 2022). Social media is a recent addition to the realm of information and communication technology, particularly in Africa (Orngu, 2018). Social media has become the dominant platform for information sharing, offering both benefits and drawbacks. At first, social media platforms have become essential in shaping our interactions and cultural expression, providing numerous advantages such as effortless communication and collaboration, streamlined data management, and access to extensive information. According to Collins et al. (2021), while it can be a blessing, it has also led to significant suffering. The lack of regulation opens the door to misuse, resulting in many forms of criminalities. Social media plays a significant role in shaping Nigeria's global image. While it has the power to connect millions of people and provide access to information, it also presents risks to personal safety and societal well-being. Mobile internet and social platforms have allowed citizens to engage with the government and access news, promoting transparency and accountability. However, the government has yet to fully grasp the potential of digital platforms in combating misinformation, projecting a positive image, and engaging with international audiences. The impact of social media on Nigeria's image is multifaceted, encompassing global perception, cultural representation, economic implications, political influence, diaspora engagement, and challenges related to misinformation.

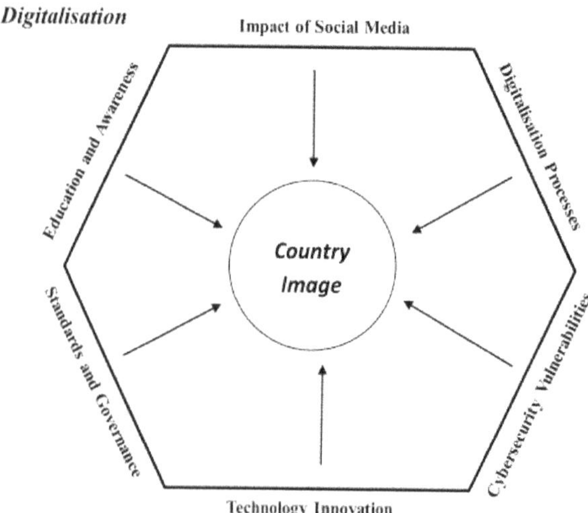

Figure 2: Provisional Conceptual Framework for the Study

3.2.2 Digitalisation Processes

The process of digitalisation leads to an increase in organisational productivity and efficiency, and its success depends on how effectively it is implemented, particularly in the context of process re-engineering (Wynn & Felser, 2023). Digitalisation is a driving force for change in technology and society, and as such, it has implications for both internal and external relationships of individual countries. Countries create their images through international interaction, and these images have an impact on foreign economic and other relationships. In the past, country images were based on hard and soft power resources, such as military, economic, and cultural strength. However, in today's information society, a country's ability to manage its digital information and its global accessibility will play a significant role in shaping its image and relationships with other countries. Nigeria's policies and objectives to improve its capabilities in the digital global environment and promote the development of its identity and the well-being of its societies are closely related to this topic. Nigeria has made significant progress in this regard, with the deployment of digital health platforms, e-learning initiatives, and mobile banking services. These initiatives have improved access to vital services, particularly in underserved areas, thereby enhancing Nigeria's image as a country committed to leveraging technology for social development and inclusion.

A related aspect is the provision of necessary support infrastructure. Investing in infrastructure and leveraging digital opportunities can enhance global competitiveness and digital leadership (Johnson-Hart, 2023). Nigeria is facing various challenges due to a lack of technological infrastructure, including internet connectivity, mobile networks, and digital services, which significantly impact Nigeria's digital transformation journey. Investments in broadband infrastructure, data centers, and e-government platforms are crucial for supporting digital innovation and inclusion. Technology infrastructure availability plays a crucial role in shaping Nigeria's image by impacting investment attractiveness, digital inclusion, business competitiveness, quality of life, global reputation, and addressing existing challenges and disparities (Adeleke, 2021).

3.2.3 Cybersecurity Vulnerabilities

The 21st century has seen significant technological and informational advancements, leading to a rise in global risks and uncertainty. One notable consequence of this progress is the emergence of new forms of criminal activity, such as cybercrime, resulting from globalization and digital transformation (Armencheva et al., 2019). These impact national security, economic growth, trust and confidence, global reputation, policy and governance, capacity building, and collaboration. Oyewole et al., (2024) opine that safeguarding data and organizational resources from cyber threats is imperative in light of the complexity of cyber-attacks and the impact of digital footprints. The increasing reliance on digital platforms and the interconnectedness of systems expose the country to potential cyberattacks and data breaches (Deora & Chudasama, 2021). For instance, social media has proved to have the potential in Nigeria to reach millions all around the world but poses danger not just to the society, but even unintended consequences to the individual who is at the receiving end, including the security of life. Cybersecurity and Vulnerability in Nigeria affecting perceptions of national security, economic growth, trust and confidence, global reputation, policy and governance, capacity building, and collaboration. Cyberattacks, data breaches, and online fraud highlight the importance of cybersecurity awareness, capacity-building, and proactive measures to safeguard digital assets and mitigate vulnerabilities among Nigerians. So, therefore, Countries' technology can be leveraged to improve national security and economic stability with advanced security systems and protocols (Kitchin, 2020).

3.2.4 *Technology Innovation*

The integration of digital technologies is considered a crucial driver of innovation (Lee & Trimi, 2021). For example, the development of information and communication technology (ICT) and digital innovation are essential for a country's global competitiveness. Additionally, digital platforms play a significant role in promoting international collaboration, partnerships, and information exchange, which ultimately contributes to a positive global image (Melissen and Wang, 2019). However, the study also showed that the increased use of digital platforms may facilitate cultural exchange, knowledge sharing, and improved diplomatic relations. It is important to note that technological advancement is outpacing the ability of policies and regulations to provide protection and ensure that technology is channeled for positive rather than nefarious purposes. The impact of technology innovation in Nigeria is multifaceted and influences perceptions of economic growth, competitiveness, global recognition, social impact, digital inclusion, policy support, collaboration, and partnerships (Ajayi & Mohammed, 2022). The deployment of digital health platforms, e-learning initiatives, and mobile banking services has improved access to vital services, particularly in underserved areas, thereby enhancing Nigeria's image as a country committed to leveraging technology for social development and inclusion.

3.2.5 *Standards and Governance*

Establishing regulatory standards and governance frameworks is essential to ensure the responsible use of digital technology, protect user data privacy, and promote digital trust. Effective governance mechanisms facilitate collaboration between government agencies, industry stakeholders, and civil society to address emerging challenges and promote ethical practices. The use of standards and governance in digitalisation is essential for shaping a country's image by ensuring quality, reliability, interoperability, compliance, consumer protection, international collaboration, capacity building, and innovation. For instance, in Nigeria, adoption of common technical standards for digital payments and financial services has facilitated interoperability among banks, fintech companies, and mobile money operators, enhancing the country's image as a conducive environment for digital innovation and business integration. The establishment of regulatory bodies like the Nigerian Communications Commission (NCC) and the National Information Technology Development Agency (NITDA) have strengthened Nigeria's regulatory environment for digital technologies, enhancing its image as a transparent and regulated market for digital investments and activities (Ezeigweneme et al., 2024). "Digital diplomacy" can also be viewed as an element of governance, and can project a positive image to international audiences. The proliferation of mobile internet and social media platforms, enables citizens to access news, participate in online discussions, and engage with government agencies, thereby fostering transparency and accountability (Abdulquadri et al., 2021).

3.2.6 *Education and Awareness*

Digital technology contributes to global economic competition and progress in developing countries and sustainability. The key to the journey towards a Smart nation vision requires skills, confidence, and motivation to use technology. Government must foster a digitally inclusive society and empower citizens to leverage technology for personal and professional development. Wong et.al. (2023) submit that competencies in various areas such as computer literacy, ICT literacy, information literacy, data literacy, and media literacy become a basic need of any society. Digital literacy is the ability to define, access, manage, integrate, communicate, evaluate, and create information safely and appropriately through digital technologies and networked devices for participation in economic and social life. Educational initiatives, training programs, and public awareness campaigns play a vital role in promoting responsible digital citizenship and mitigating online risks (Aminu et al., 2021). These digital technologies have transformed the way we learn and acquire knowledge through online learning platforms, educational software, and digital libraries have revolutionized education by offering flexible and interactive learning opportunities (Mtebe & Raphael, 2018). Education and awareness are critical variables in the digitalisation process in Nigeria, impacting perceptions of digital literacy, empowerment, cybersecurity, digital rights, policy advocacy, international collaboration, and cooperation.

4. Discussion

The provisional conceptual framework provides the platform for developing primary research on the relationship between digitalisation and country image in Nigeria. However, certain aspects warrant further discussion at this stage.

Firstly, the world of digital transformation offers great opportunities for government organizations to improve their efficiency, productivity, transparency, and accountability. It also serves as a valuable tool for driving government reform and addressing complex societal issues. Intelligent governments are a new phenomenon that utilize cutting-edge technologies and innovative strategies to develop strong and adaptable administrative frameworks. They invest in emerging technologies and creative strategies to gain a comprehensive understanding of their environment, accurately evaluate situations or individuals, and make swift and responsive decisions to tackle perceived challenges. A prime example of digital transformation is the creation of a digital economy, which prioritizes seamless and user-centric experiences as citizens expect public services to be accessible, efficient, and flexible. Digital transformation involves a complete shift of an entity into the digital economy, including tools, activities, people, and management, signifying a change from non-digital.

Secondly, digital transformation offers immense potential for becoming more proficient, productive, transparent, and accountable (Sarker et al., 2018). Technological infrastructure, including internet connectivity, mobile networks, and digital services, significantly impact the digital transformation journey. Technology innovation has a multifaceted analytical impact on the country's image, influencing perceptions of economic growth, competitiveness, global recognition, social impact, digital inclusion, policy support, collaboration, and partnerships. The proliferation of mobile internet and social media platforms enables citizens to access news, participate in online discussions, and engage with government agencies, thereby fostering transparency and accountability (Abdulquadri et al., 2021). Investments in broadband infrastructure, data centers, and e-government platforms are crucial for supporting digital innovation and inclusion. Technology infrastructure availability plays a crucial role in shaping Nigeria's image by impacting investment attractiveness, digital inclusion, business competitiveness, quality of life, global reputation, and addressing existing challenges and disparities (Adeleke, 2021).

Thirdly, education and awareness are critical variables in the digitalisation process and impacting perceptions of digital literacy, empowerment, cybersecurity, digital rights, policy advocacy, international collaboration, and cooperation. Cybersecurity and vulnerability in Nigeria have a multifaceted analytical impact on the country's image, affecting perceptions of national security, economic growth, trust and confidence, global reputation, policy and governance, capacity building, and collaboration. As digitalisation accelerates in Nigeria, cybersecurity threats pose significant risks to individuals, businesses, and critical infrastructure. Cyberattacks, data breaches, and online fraud highlight the importance of cybersecurity awareness, capacity-building, and proactive measures to safeguard digital assets and mitigate vulnerabilities among Nigerians (Adejumo, 2023).

Fourthly, the advancement of digital technologies has paved the way for Smart/Intelligent governments, which utilize innovative strategies and emerging technologies to establish resilient governance structures. By leveraging digital tools, governments can improve their efficiency and service delivery, while creating accessible channels for citizens to engage with the government. Governments around the world are implementing digital innovation projects to refine their processes and enhance their business strategies. According to Welby & Tan (2022), digital government entails delivering public value through new methods and making services and procedures digital by default. This requires the integration of ICT in public sector reform from the outset. The proposed innovation is not limited to national, regional, or local government levels, but extends to public sector services like transport, education, and healthcare, as well as various government agencies, and regulated and semi-regulated services, which vary by country. The roadmap for policymakers, professionals, and researchers is to understand the intricacies of the digital era and harness its potential for inclusive and sustainable development (Sharma and Gupta, 2024).

5. Conclusion

Nigeria is a dynamic and multifaceted phenomenon with far-reaching implications for socioeconomic development and global competitiveness (Chingoriwo, 2022). By addressing key challenges, leveraging opportunities, and embracing digital transformation holistically, Nigeria can position itself as a leading digital economy and a beacon of innovation in Africa and beyond (Oladeinde et al., 2023).

This paper has set out some key issues and a provisional conceptual framework that will provide the platform for primary research in this area. The end-goal is to enhance Nigeria's global image through targeted marketing, social media campaigns, and improved digital presence. This will improve the perception of Nigeria among investors, visitors, and stakeholders, increase FDI, boost tourism, facilitate meaningful engagement with stakeholders, utilize data-driven decision-making, and reinforce digital skills among stakeholders. Policy recommendations will be developed based on implementation insights and lessons learned. Digitalisation greatly impacts a country's image, enabling it to promote its culture, legacy, economic potential, and achievements to a global audience. It combats disinformation and preconceptions, fostering two-way communication and transparency. However, digitalisation alone does not provide a solution; serious efforts to address socioeconomic growth, governance, and human rights are required. Authenticity and communication consistency are also essential for developing a lasting national image. Nations may improve their reputation and attract investment by embracing innovation, utilizing digital platforms, and implementing strategic communication tactics.

Further research could also apply this framework to other nations in the developing world to help advance the deployment of digital technologies in support of national image progression. This could provide the basis for cross-country comparisons, and the development of theoretical perspectives in what remains a relatively unresearched field of study.

References

Abdulquadri, A., Mogaji, E., Kieu, T. A., & Nguyen, N. P. (2021). Digital transformation in financial services provision: A Nigerian perspective to the adoption of chatbot. Journal of Enterprising Communities: People and Places in the Global Economy, 15(2), 258-281.

Adejumo, D.A. (2023). Review of Issues on Data Security Cybercrimes and Image: The Nigerian Case. International Journal of Marketing, Communication and New Media, (12).

Adeleke, R. (2021). Digital divide in Nigeria: The role of regional differentials. African Journal of Science, Technology, Innovation and Development, 13(3), 333-346

Ahmed, Z., Nathaniel, S. P., & Shahbaz, M. (2021). The criticality of information and communication technology and human capital in environmental sustainability: evidence from Latin American and Caribbean countries. Journal of Cleaner Production, 286, 125529.

Ajayi, O.J., Muhammed, Y., Olah, F., & Tsado, J.H. (2016). Effect of Information and Communication Technology (ICT) usage on cassava production in Otukpo Local Government Area of Benue State, Nigeria.

Aminu, M., Sani, I., & Jodi, R. (2021). Impact of Information and Communication Technology (ICT) on the Nigerian Education system. International Journal of Scientific & Technology Research, 10(7), 112-115.

Anholt, S. (2009). Should place brands be simple? Place Branding and Public Diplomacy, 5(2), 91-96.

Anyanka, H. (2018). The Image of a Country, its Link to Corruption and the impact on its Citizens in Diaspora Case Study: Nigeria.

Armencheva, I., Atanasova, N., & Ivanov, I., (2019). cyber globalization as an in/stability factor. ijasos-international e-journal of Advances in Social Sciences, 5(13), 71-81.

Bell, E., Bryman, A., & Harley, B. (2018). Business Research Methods; Oxford University Press: Oxford, UK.

Cai, W., & McKenna, B. (2023). Digital-free tourism. Routledge Handbook of Trends and Issues in Global Tourism Supply and Demand.

Chingoriwo, T. (2022). Cybersecurity challenges and needs in the context of digital development in Zimbabwe. British Journal of Multidisciplinary and Advanced Studies, 3(2), 77-104.

Collins, B., Hoang, D. T., Nguyen, N. T., & Hwang, D. (2021). Trends in combating fake news on social media–a survey. Journal of Information and Telecommunication, 5(2), 247-266.

Deora, R.S., & Chudasama, D., (2021). Brief study of cybercrime on the internet. Journal of Communication Engineering & Systems, 11(1), 1-6.

Ezeigweneme, C.A., Umoh, A.A., Ilojianya, V.I., & Adegbite, A.O., (2024). Review of telecommunication regulation and policy: comparative analysis USA and AFRICA. Computer Science & IT Research Journal, 5(1), 81-99.

Frenzel, A., Muench, J. C., Bruckner, M., & Veit, D. (2021). Digitization or digitalization?–Toward an understanding of definitions, use and application in IS research

Gebayew, C., Hardini, I. R., Panjaitan, G. H. A., & Kurniawan, N. B. (2018, October). A systematic literature review on digital transformation. In 2018 International Conference on Information Technology Systems and Innovation (ICITSI) (pp. 260-265). IEEE.

Govers, R. (2020). Imaginative communities and place branding. Place Branding and Public Diplomacy, 16(1), 1-5.

Hakala, U., Lemmetyinen, A., & Kantola, S. P. (2013). Country image as a nation-branding tool. Marketing Intelligence & Planning, 31(5), 538-556.

Jin, N., Lee, S., & Lee, H. (2021). The role of digital technology in enhancing country image: A case study of South Korea. Tourism Management, 85, 104311.

Johnson-Hart, M. (2023). Strategies for Sustaining Success in Small Businesses in Nigeria (Doctoral dissertation, Walden University).

Kitchin, R. (2020). Using digital technologies to tackle the spread of the coronavirus: Panacea or folly. The Programmable City Working Paper, 44(April), 1-24.

Lee, J., & Kwak, D. H. (2020). The impact of digitalisation on country image: The moderating roles of political system and internet freedom. Telematics and Informatics, 51, 101413.

Lee, Y. K. (2021). Impacts of digital technostress and digital technology self-efficacy on Fintech usage intention of Chinese Gen Z consumers. Sustainability, 13(9), 5077.

Lee, S. M., & Trimi, S. (2021). Convergence innovation in the digital age and in the COVID-19 pandemic crisis. Journal of Business Research, 123, 14-22.

Lüders, A., Dinkelberg, A., & Quayle, M. (2022). Becoming "us" in digital spaces: How online users creatively and strategically exploit social media affordances to build up social identity. Acta Psychologica, 228, 103643.

Manor, I. (2020). Digital Diplomacy: Understanding Islam and the West.

Mason, J. (2017). Qualitative Researching; Sage Publications Ltd.: London, UK.

Melissen, J., & Wang, J. (2019). Introduction: Debating public diplomacy. The Hague Journal of Diplomacy, 14(1-2), 1-5.

Mtebe, J. S., & Raphael, C. (2018). Formative assessment using mobile learning technologies: A literature review. Interactive Learning Environments, 26(8), 1097-1112.

Mihelj, S., & Jiménez-Martínez, C. (2021). Digital nationalism: Understanding the role of digital media in the rise of 'new'nationalism. Nations and nationalism, 27(2), 331-346.

Oladeinde, M., Hassan, A.O., Farayola, O.A., Akindote, O.J., & Adegbite, A.O., (2023). review of its innovations, data analytics, and governance in Nigerian enterprises. Computer Science & IT Research Journal, 4(3), pp.300-326.

Orngu, C.S. (2018). The Social Media and Nigeria's Electoral Politics since 1999: Trends and Implications for Nigeria's External Image.

Oyewole, A.T., Okoye, C.C., Ofodile, O.C., & Ugochukwu, C.E. (2024). Cybersecurity risks in online banking: A detailed review and preventive strategies application. World Journal of Advanced Research and Reviews, 21(3), 625-643.

Porter, A. L., Kongthon, A., & Lu, J. C. (2002). Research profiling: Improving the literature review. Scientometrics, 53, 351-370.

Riedl, R., Benlian, A., Hess, T., Stelzer, D., & Sikora, H. (2017). On the relationship between information management and digitalization. Business & Information Systems Engineering, 59, 475-482.

Revilla-Camacho, M. A., Rodriguez-Rad, C., Garzon, D., Sanchez del Rio-Vazquez, M. E., Prado-Roman, C., &

Saad, M. (2020). Key elements of nation branding: The importance of the development of local human capital in the UAE. Human Capital in the Middle East: A UAE Perspective, 227-251.

Sarker, M.N.I., Wu, M., & Hossin, M.A., 2018, May. Smart governance through bigdata: Digital transformation of public agencies. In 2018 international conference on artificial intelligence and big data (ICAIBD) (pp. 62-70). IEEE

Schwab, K., & Sala-i-Martín, X. (2016, April). The global competitiveness report 2013–2014: Full data edition. World Economic Forum.

Sharma, R., & Gupta, H., (2024). Leveraging cognitive digital twins in industry 5.0 for achieving sustainable development goal 9: An exploration of inclusive and sustainable industrialization strategies. Journal of Cleaner Production, p.141364.

Tranfield, D., Denyer, D., & Smart, P. (2003). Towards a methodology for developing evidence-informed management knowledge by means of systematic review. British journal of management, 14(3), 207-222.

Thompson, J. B. (2020). Mediated interaction in the digital age. Theory, Culture & Society, 37(1), 3-28.

Udegbunam, I. P., Igbokwe-Ibeto, C. J., & Nwafor, C. C. (2023). challenges and opportunities in implementing digital transformation in Nigerian public service. journal of the Management Sciences, 60(3), 296-308.

Vahdat, S. (2022). The role of IT-based technologies on the management of human resources in the COVID-19 era. Kybernetes, 51(6), 2065-2088.

Welby, B., & Tan, E. H. Y. (2022). Designing and delivering public services in the digital age.

Webster, J., & Watson, R. T. (2002). Analyzing the past to prepare for the future: Writing a literature review. MIS quarterly, xiii-xxiii.

Wong, G.K.W., Reichert, F., & Law, N. (2023). Reorienting the assessment of digital literacy in the twenty-first century: a product-lifecycle and experience dependence perspective. Educational technology research and development, 71(6), pp.2389-2412.

Wynn, M., & Felser, K. (2023). Digitalisation and Change in the Management of IT. Computers, 12 (12). Art 251. doi:10.3390/ computers12120251

Yang, F. X., Zhang, K. Z. K., Chen, H., & Tseng, H. H. (2021). How digital transformation shapes destination image: A study of Chinese outbound tourists. Tourism Management, 85, 104295.

Yina, M. N. (2020). The challenges of digital technologies for Nigeria. Journal of interdisciplinary Studies, 32(1-2), 81-95.

Ylianttila, M., Kantola, R., Gurtov, A., Mucchi, L., Oppermann, I., Yan, Z., ... & Röning, J. (2020). 6G white paper: Research challenges for trust, security and privacy. arXiv preprint arXiv:2004.11665.

Cyber Protection Applications of Quantum Computing: A Review

Ummar Ahmed, Tuomo Sipola and Jari Hautamäki
Institute of Information Technology, Jamk University of Applied Sciences, Jyväskylä, Finland

ummar.ahmed@student.jamk.fi
tuomo.sipola@jamk.fi
jari.hautamaki@jamk.fi

Abstract: Quantum computing is a cutting-edge field of information technology that harnesses the principles of quantum mechanics to perform computations. It has major implications for the cyber security industry. Existing cyber protection applications are working well, but there are still challenges and vulnerabilities in computer networks. Sometimes data and privacy are also compromised. These complications lead to research questions asking what kind of cyber protection applications of quantum computing are there and what potential methods or techniques can be used for cyber protection? These questions will reveal how much power quantum computing has and to what extent it can outperform the conventional computing systems. This scoping review was conducted by considering 815 papers. It showed the possibilities that can be achieved if quantum technologies are implemented in cyber environments. This scoping review discusses various domains such as algorithms and applications, bioinformatics, cloud and edge computing, the organization of complex systems, application areas focused on security and threats, and the broader quantum computing ecosystem. In each of these areas, there is significant scope for quantum computing to be implemented and to revolutionize the working environment. Numerous quantum computing applications for cyber protection and a number of techniques to protect our data and privacy were identified. The results are not limited to network security but also include data security. This paper also discusses societal aspects, e.g., the applications of quantum computing in the social sciences. This scoping review discusses how to enhance the efficiency and security of quantum computing in various cyber security domains. Additionally, it encourages the reader to think about what kind of techniques and methods can be deployed to secure the cyber world.

Keywords: Quantum Computing, Cyber Security, Quantum Computing Applications, Cyber Protection, Quantum Algorithms

1. Introduction

Quantum technology is an emerging field that is changing the IT industry. The power of quantum technology can increase the computational capability of any computing environment and produce highly efficient results. Quantum computing is in a growth phase, but it still has enough power to impact real-world scenarios (Coccia, Roshani and Mosleh, 2024). One of these scenarios is software engineering. Quantum software engineering plays a pivotal role in building applications especially in the most complex and critical areas (Ali et al., 2022). Quantum computing also plays a critical role in concrete applications such as smart city planning and urban design. This is a less technical aspect of the world where quantum computing can deliver extraordinary results (Bashirpour Bonab et al., 2023a). Furthermore, quantum computing has taken problem solving to the next level. For example, Dempster–Shafer Theory (DST) shows that quantum computing can be used to analyse data using quantum mechanical principles (Zhou, Tian and Deng, 2023). Raheman (2022) describes the future of quantum computing in relation to cyber security. He highlights the concepts of post quantum cryptography, exploits against quantum-as-a-service and mitigating network architecture. As the cyber world expands, devices mature, and new technologies emerge, problems become more complex. (Shaw and Dutta, 2023). The question that arises is how we can use quantum computing in cyber protection. As every device on the network generates data, the likelihood of network vulnerabilities increases with the advancement of tools and skills. This review has been conducted precisely to explore the applications of quantum computing in the field of cyber protection, given the increasing challenges posed by the evolving cyber landscape.

The journey began with research questions aimed at understanding the cyber protection applications of quantum computing and explore potential methods or techniques for effective solutions in this domain. In this scoping review, databases such as IEEE Xplore, Science Direct, and Google Scholar were used to gather relevant information. Machine learning and artificial intelligence are key areas and the synergy with quantum computing opens up possibilities that promise unprecedented levels of excellence (Maheshwari, Garcia-Zapirain and Sierra-Sosa, 2022). This study uncovers the potential of quantum computing to address complex problem-solving scenarios and explores how quantum engineers can receive automated assistance in developing diverse quantum programs for problem-solving applications (Alonso, Sánchez and Sánchez-Rubio, 2022). With networks constantly generating data and ubiquitous use of the Internet of things (IoT) in which numerous devices communicate with each other, the challenge of maintaining data protection becomes pronounced. This study focuses on into identifying quantum algorithms and techniques that can enhance security, mitigating risks and vulnerabilities in such interconnected environments (Li et al., 2022). Beyond the technical aspects, this study sheds light on the deceptive practices in the quantum realm. It draws attention to instances where certain companies are engaged in futile endeavours, highlighting the importance of distinguishing genuine advancements from misleading activities driven by financial motives (Khan et al., 2023). Throughout the scoping review, the following research questions will be addressed:

- **RQ1:** What are the applications of quantum computing in the field of cybersecurity, in particular cyber protection?
- **RQ2:** What are the potential methods or techniques that could be used to effectively address the challenge of cyber protection?

From here, our paper will follow to the methodology in section 2, which includes steps such as providing the study background, formulating the research question, and detailing the processes of data collection, identification, screening, and paper inclusion. Moving on to section 3, the results of this scoping review will be discovered, organized into different categories within its subcategories. Following this, section 4 deals with the discussion, while section 5 serves as the conclusion, summarizing all the findings of this scoping review.

2. Methodology

This is systematic scoping review conducted to examine the cyber protection applications of quantum computing. The stages of scoping review described by Arksey and O'Malley (Arksey and O'Malley, 2005; Levac et al., 2010) were used in this study.

Having research questions about the applications of quantum computing for cyber protection and the techniques for potential solutions, and recognizing the breadth of the topic, the exploration by employing targeted search phrases was initiated. IEEE Xplore, Science Direct and Google scholar were used and *Quantum Computing Applications* and *Quantum computing use cases* search phrases were selected to start of scoping review, as described in Figure 1. This search was most relevant to this study, and it was finalised on the basis of outcomes found with it in different databases. Moreover, the research was limited to journals only to obtain the most precise data. As quantum computing is one of the novel computing technologies, the search was limited to the years 2022 and 2023. Moreover, it was decided to limit the research to 10 pages for Google Scholar and the first 400 relevant results using Science Direct. In the identification phase, the criteria for filtering the papers was the relevance of the data provided to quantum computing.

Thus, any the search results that included quantum studies with principals from physics and other domains were easily excluded using these criteria. In addition to this physics material, collaboration of quantum computing was found in industries of *data science, artificial intelligence, algorithms and applications, bioinformatics, cloud and edge computing, complex system optimisation, cryptography and security, education and learning, engineering and automated process control, environment science, ethics and societal impact, finance and economics, fundamentals and reviews, hardware and architectures, healthcare, IoT, machine learning, material science, nanotechnology, networks, optimization problems, power system applications, renewable energy, robotics, simulations, smart cities and urban planning, space technology, specific industries* and *theoretical physics*. All these are well-known domains but the research was limited and continued with *software and programming, smart cities and urban planning,* and *IoT (internet of Things)*. All these categories with their references are presented in Table 1.

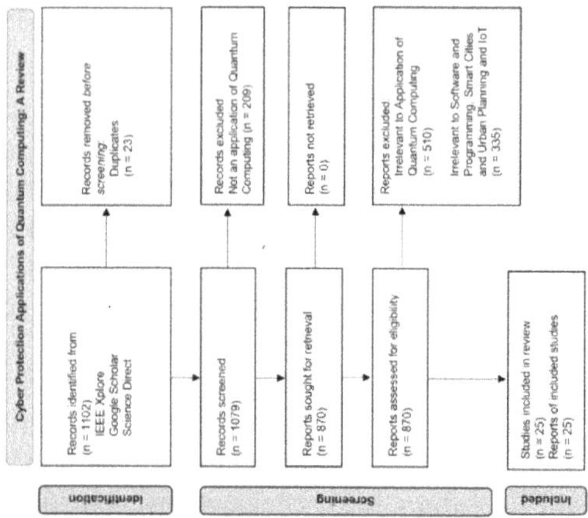

Figure 1: PRISMA flowchart of the scoping review

3. Results

The result for cyber protection applications of quantum computing covers many dimensions of emerging computing. It includes different categories such as data security, innovation in IT industry, energy, efficient use of energy, simulations, network traffic management and data security, quantum collaboration with emerging technology and most interestingly quantum application in social sciences. The resulting categorization is described in Table 1.

Table 1: Research Papers

Categories	References
Generation of Quantum Programs	Alonso, Sánchez and Sánchez-Rubio (2022)
Data Security and Privacy	Shaw and Dutta (2023) Li et al. (2022) Padmaa et al. (2022) Chawla and Mehra (2023)
Quantum Support Data	De Stefano et al. (2022)
Fake Improvements in Quantum Technology by IT giants	Khan et al. (2023)
Innovation in Computing Efficiency	Macrae (2023) Willsch et al. (2022) Zhou, Tian and Deng (2023) Jałowiecki, Lewandowska and Pawela (2023)
Energy Efficiency	Al-Khafaji et al. (2023)
Problem Solving	Feng and Li (2023) Pérez-Castillo, Jiménez-Navajas and Piattini (2023) Yi et al. (2023)
Simulation	Arufe et al. (2023)
Network Communication	Hildebrand et al. (2023) Qadir et al. (2022) Abd El-Aziz et al. (2022)
Data Analytics	Harikrishnakumar and Nannapaneni (2023)
Quantum and Social Science	Bashirpour Bonab et al. (2023a) Ukpabi et al. (2023)
Quantum and Emerging Technologies	Bashirpour Bonab et al. (2023b)

3.1 Generation of Quantum Programs

Using quantum technology with Model Driven Engineering (MDE) techniques, such applications are developed that generate quantum programs. These programs are readable by quantum machines, and highly focused problems are proposed to be solved using this technique. Moreover, a metamodel has been introduced for quantum circuits and model-to-text transformations for generating IBM Qiskit code have been introduced, as they bring the quantum usability closer to reality (Alonso, Sánchez and Sánchez-Rubio, 2022).

3.2 Data Security and Privacy

Quantum continues to play its role for data security and privacy. Research proposed a quantum triple qubit model for image scaling using hue, saturation and light which encodes data in the scaled-up image and decodes data by scaling down at the receiver end (Li et al., 2023). Another research shows that as the types of interconnected devices increased, the chances of network attacks also increased due to the difficulty to manage security. Researchers called it signcryption which involves signing and encryption. This method uses isogeny-based encryption (Shaw and Dutta, 2023). Researchers proposed a new way to secure the user information in the advanced IoT environment using a technique called quantum key pool. The addition of advanced devices in networks motivated the researchers. This technique involves rapid distribution of encryption keys using quantum technology (Li et al., 2022)]. With the expansion of IoT networks, security and privacy are also compromised. Therefore, researchers come up with a new energy-efficient and secure data transmission protocol for intelligent IoT edge systems, called EEC-SDTP, to solve these challenges. This system will create cluster heads and routes for secure transmission. The system uses the oppositional chaos game optimization-based clustering (OCGOC) technique to determine cluster heads and routes (Padmaa et al., 2022) (Chawla and Mehra, 2023).

3.3 Quantum Support Data

A quantum software developer in today's world does not rely solely reliant on their own knowledge, but rather collaborates with a diverse community of researchers, engineers, and experts to advance the field. Quantum software development has such repositories and resources that can benefit the quantum developer in developing something e.g. ryuNagai/QML, oliverfunk/quantum-natural-gradient, kongju/QML etc. A study has been done to know how much quantum data is present in repositories to support quantum software engineers. Therefore, it is a positive gesture that quantum engineers share their work to support the quantum engineer community (De Stefano et al., 2022).

3.4 Fake Improvements in Quantum Technology by IT giants

At this time when quantum systems are being improved IT giants such as IBM, Google, or Microsoft are busy in exploiting the architectural solutions by developing various software to manage and manipulate quantum hardware. Quantum technology still has too much room for improvement. So-called IT giants are not really serving the industry. Most of the research papers published in the last 4 years are about solutions and validations. It is time to serve the quantum industry to get better results. (Khan et al., 2023).

3.5 Innovation in Computing Efficiency

Still, the quantum industry is growing in innovation. Quantum scientists are trying to build super-small and efficient computer systems using the quantum-dot cellular automata approach (Macrae, 2023). In addition, there is ongoing research to improve the computational power of computers. A new model called "balanced ternary" has been proposed to calculate the processing in a new way which will speed up the computational processing in an exceptional way (Faghih et al., 2023). In a GPU level research, researcher used Jülich universal quantum computer simulator (JUQCS–G) that was fast due to advanced GPUs. They tested the computer on JUWELS Booster, a GPU cluster with 3744 NVIDIA A100 Tensor Core GPUs and JUQCS–G to analyse the relationship between quantum annealing and quantum optimization algorithm. They surprisingly found approximate quantum annealing (AQA) (Willsch et al., 2022). Researchers try to explore the Dempster–Shafer Theory (DST) of AI, which is easy to represent knowledge but less useful in the real world due to a lot of data. To address this aspect, researchers use Basic Belief Assignment BBA and encode it in a quantum form which is derived from principles of quantum mechanics. It gave excellent results even for representing belief functions, analysing similarities between various information, collecting and evidence and transforming probabilities. It all happened because of quantum computing (Zhou, Tian and Deng, 2023). A Python library, PyQBench was introduced, which provides a ready-made command line interface CLI to use predefined functionalities. It can benchmark NICQ devices based on their capability of differentiating two von Neumann measurements (Jałowiecki, Lewandowska and Pawela, 2023).

3.6 Energy Efficiency

Research reveals an alternative called quantum dot cellular automata (QCA) to address traditional computing challenges. Researchers have successfully developed small energy-efficient digital circuits using QCA technology for IoT devices (Al-Khafaji et al., 2023).

3.7 Problem Solving

Quantum also plays an important role in problem solving. Research talks about error or problem checking techniques without actually running them. Researchers discuss "quantum-while-program" to show how these techniques are relevant to each other (Feng and Li, 2023). In addition, research also shows the quantum programs written in Python and D-Wave to analyse which problems are being solved by quantum annealing (Pérez-Castillo, Jiménez-Navajas and Piattini, 2023). Companies provide services and products. If someone does not plan when and where to use these services/products, they are useless. Researchers are trying to solve this problem with a technique called quantum annealing. Successful experiments have been carried out on the larger problems of vehicles (Yi et al., 2023).

3.8 Simulation

In discussions surrounding simulation, researchers propose a solution known as DBGA-X to address the quantum circuit compilation problem (QCCP), facilitating the execution of quantum programs on actual quantum hardware (Arufe et al., 2023).

3.9 Network Communication

Research has brought blockchain-enabled IoV (Internet of Vehicles) technology to overcome security and privacy issues on the Internet of Vehicles by not relying on a central entity. Vehicles communicate with each other to understand the traffic environment without sharing sensitive information (Hildebrand et al., 2023). The idea of 6G emerged to solve tricky problems in optimizing the network by using artificial intelligence, THz (terahertz) and quantum communications. As a result of this effort, holographic beamforming, AI-powered IoT networks, edge computing, and backscatter communications are expected (Qadir et al., 2022). In the world of neural networks, researchers are bringing a new technique called deep residual learning based quantum classical neural network (Res-QCNN). It will be used to monitor data coming from various devices and understand the IoT data in a better and faster way (Abd El-Aziz et al., 2022).

3.10 Data Analytics

Quantum is also used for prediction. One study shows how to optimise prediction for bike-sharing. Researchers used quantum Bayesian networks (a fancy term for a quantum computing method) to make the prediction more accurate over different days (Harikrishnakumar and Nannapaneni, 2023).

3.11 Quantum and Social Science

The approach known as the quantum urban paradigm seeks to tackle issues across multiple domains of liveability such as society, environment, and technology. By combining quantum technologies with social sciences, it aims to improve daily life by, for instance, optimising urban planning and streamlining communication management (Bashirpour Bonab et al., 2023a). While everyone is talking about the technical side of quantum computing, this paper adds a new dimension. It discusses the impact of quantum computing on business, politics, solving legal problems and other such non-technical areas (Ukpabi et al., 2023).

3.12 Quantum and Emerging Technologies

Researchers point out that quantum technologies can improve smart cities in terms of IoT, cloud computing, big data, smart transport, AI, and blockchain (Bashirpour Bonab et al., 2023b). Traditional von Neumann architectures can be used to integrate quantum technologies into modern smart city solutions. This integration of physics-based quantum technologies will represent a new paradigm that differs from current standards.

4. Discussion

Researchers have proposed a new way to keep the user information secure in an advanced IoT environment using the technique called quantum key pool. The Researchers felt the need for it due to the arrival of advanced devices in the network. This technique involves the rapid distribution of encryption keys using quantum technology. It is also a new way to keep smart grid data private on mobile devices. It uses a special method to manage secret keys and allows users to securely check their data securely. The proposed method is said to be fast, lightweight, and strong, using three layers of security. However, more research is needed to ensure that one part of the method works well (Li et al., 2022).

If we look at the security of network communications, researchers have introduced blockchain enabled internet of Vehicles technology to overcome security and privacy issues in the Internet of Vehicles by not relying on a central entity. Vehicles communicate with each other to understand the traffic environment without sharing sensitive information. In addition, the research explores recent advances in Blockchain-based Internet of Vehicles (BIoV) networks, covering applications like crowdsourcing, energy trading, and traffic management. It explores collaborative learning, blockchain-enabled hardware security, and the intersection of blockchain and quantum computing (Hildebrand et al., 2023). Researchers say that the evolution of wireless networks, such as 5G, is improving the technology, but it is not enough for the growing communication needs. Researchers are now looking at 6G networks to meet future demands, exploring technologies such as THz communication and quantum communication for faster data rates (Qadir et al., 2022). Other research has created a quantum-conventional hybrid neural network has been created, called Res-QCNN, to improve cost function optimization for deep networks. By using quantum neural networks in a residual structure block, the Res-QCNN training algorithm allows information to flow efficiently through layers, similar to deep residual learning in classical artificial neural networks, although it can be run on a standard computer (Abd El-Aziz et al., 2022).

Quantum computing is also making an impact on data security and privacy. In one study, researchers introduced a quantum colour model called quantum hue, saturation, and lightness (QHTS) based on triple-qubit sequence encoding. They developed quantum circuits for encoding and retrieving QHTS images using only a few qubits, improving operability. The study explored applications such as quantum steganography for secure message embedding and a spatial image fusion algorithm for remote sensing, demonstrating improved embedding capacity and potential advances in quantum image processing. Future work aims to explore quantum bicubic interpolation, improve the efficiency of key image generation, and enhance the quality of image fusion using advanced technologies. The researchers also plan to establish a quantum image fidelity metric (QIFM) for evaluating QHTS images in various applications (Li et al., 2023). Another study discusses the multi-user level encryption. In this study, the team has developed a quantum-resistant signcryption scheme that ensures key invisibility and ciphertext anonymity, addressing security concerns not addressed by many existing schemes. The size of their encrypted data is small, comparable to SeaSign signatures, and their security analysis accounts for insider attacks, multi-user settings, and non-repudiation. Additionally, key privacy has been investigated in an isogeny-based encryption scheme called Hashed-PKE (Shaw and Dutta, 2023).

During this scoping review, we also found a new way to secure data in smart grids using a method called PMAS-QS. It involves a multi-level privacy-preserving encryption, a quantum key pool for key management, and a data query method using proxy re-encryption. The proposed scheme is analysed to be efficient, lightweight, and robust, although the efficiency of the aggregate signcryption aspect is identified for further investigation (Li et al., 2022). In another research, a new technique called EEC-SDTP is introduced to make IoT edge systems more energy-efficient and ensures secure data transmission. The technique focuses on selecting optimal communication hubs (CHs) and secure routes for data transmission by using the OCGOC technique for CH selection and the SRP-QSPO technique for determining trustworthy routes. The inclusion of trust factors increases the reliability of node selection, resulting in superior performance compared to existing methods, as demonstrated by detailed simulation analyses. Future extensions could explore resource allocation and task scheduling strategies for more efficient use of available resources in IoT edge systems (Padmaa et al., 2022).

5. Conclusion

The research was started to get the answers to our research questions, the first one being that what are the cyber protection applications of quantum computing (RQ1). This is an important topic to study now, because of the advancement of network traffic and the versatility of data generation and communication of devices in the Internet (Internet of Things, IoT). There should be solutions or techniques to overcome these vulnerabilities. Therefore, we decided to ask that what kind of techniques or methods can be used for cyber protection (RQ2). Nowadays, different kinds of devices are connected to networks and produce data continuously. We have a fast, lightweight, and robust method with three layers of security called a quantum key pool for the security of user information. There are also links between blockchain and quantum technologies. In addition, cost function optimisation of deep networks has been improved using a quantum-conventional hybrid neural network. Light-based technologies for data security were presented, with applications in quantum steganography and spatial image fusion. A quantum-resistant signcryption scheme was also presented. In smart grids, this technology ensures secure data management. It will improve energy efficiency and secure data transmission in IoT edge systems with optimised communication hubs and routes, offering potential for further exploration in resource allocation strategies. The main limitation of this study is that it focuses only on journal articles. In technical areas, such as quantum computing, many important studies are also published in conferences. It would be beneficial to extend our research into different areas of quantum computing, including the exploration of quantum-safe standards, conducting security analyses using quantum computing, and investigating the application of blockchain in the field of quantum computing. Additionally, further studies could be conducted on the role of quantum computing in education and training.

Acknowledgements

We are grateful to Emils Bagirovs, Grigory Provodin and Thien Nguyen for their help with data collection and assistance with database creation. This research was partially supported by the ResilMesh project, funded by the European Union's Horizon Europe Framework Programme (HORIZON) under grant agreement 101119681. The authors would like to thank Ms. Tuula Kotikoski for proofreading the manuscript.

References

Abd El-Aziz, R.M., Taloba, A.I. and Alghamdi, F.A. (2022). "Quantum Computing Optimization Technique for IoT Platform using Modified Deep Residual Approach". Alexandria Engineering Journal, Vol 61(12), pp 12497–12509. https://doi.org/10.1016/j.aej.2022.06.029

Ali, S., Yue, T. and Abreu, R. (2022). "When software engineering meets quantum computing". Communications of the ACM, Vol 65(4), pp 84–88. https://doi.org/10.1145/3512340

Al-Khafaji, H.M.R. et al. (2023). "Performance optimization of the nano-scale carry-skip adder based on quantum dots and its application in the upcoming Internet of Things". Optik, Vol 287, pp 170976. https://doi.org/10.1016/j.ijleo.2023.170976

Alonso, D., Sánchez, P. and Sánchez-Rubio, F. (2022). "Engineering the development of quantum programs: Application to the Boolean satisfiability problem". Advances in Engineering Software, Vol 173, pp 103216. https://doi.org/10.1016/j.advengsoft.2022.103216

Arufe, L. et al. (2023). "New coding scheme to compile circuits for Quantum Approximate Optimization Algorithm by genetic evolution". Applied Soft Computing, Vol 144, pp 110456. https://doi.org/10.1016/j.asoc.2023.110456

Bashirpour Bonab, A. et al. (2023a). "In complexity we trust: A systematic literature review of urban quantum technologies". Technological Forecasting and Social Change, Vol 194, pp 122642. https://doi.org/10.1016/j.techfore.2023.122642

Bashirpour Bonab, A. et al. (2023b). "Urban quantum leap: A comprehensive review and analysis of quantum technologies for smart cities". Cities, Vol 140, pp 104459–104459. https://doi.org/10.1016/j.cities.2023.104459

Chawla, D. and Mehra, P.S. (2023). "A Survey on Quantum Computing for Internet of Things Security". Procedia Computer Science, Vol 218, pp 2191–2200. https://doi.org/10.1016/j.procs.2023.01.195

Levac, D., Colquhoun, H. and O'Brien, K.K. (2010). "Scoping studies: Advancing the Methodology". Implementation Science, Vol 5(1), pp.1–9. https://doi.org/10.1186/1748-5908-5-69

De Stefano, M. et al. (2022). "Software engineering for quantum programming: How far are we?" Journal of Systems and Software, Vol 190, pp 111326. https://doi.org/10.1016/j.jss.2022.111326

Faghih, E. et al (2023). "Efficient realization of quantum balanced ternary reversible multiplier building blocks: A great step towards sustainable computing". Sustainable Computing: Informatics and Systems, Vol 40, pp 100908. https://doi.org/10.1016/j.suscom.2023.100908

Feng, Y. and Li, S. (2023). "Abstract interpretation, Hoare logic, and incorrectness logic for quantum programs". Information and Computation, Vol 294, pp 105077. https://doi.org/10.1016/j.ic.2023.105077

Arksey, H. and O'Malley, L. (2005). "Scoping studies: Towards a Methodological Framework". International Journal of Social Research Methodology, Vol 8(1), pp.19–32. https://doi.org/10.1080/1364557032000119616

Harikrishnakumar, R. and Nannapaneni, S. (2023). "Forecasting Bike Sharing Demand Using Quantum Bayesian Network". Expert Systems with Applications, Vol 221, pp 119749. https://doi.org/10.1016/j.eswa.2023.119749

Hildebrand, B. et al. (2023). "A comprehensive review on blockchains for Internet of Vehicles: Challenges and directions". Computer Science Review, Vol 48, pp 100547. https://doi.org/10.1016/j.cosrev.2023.100547

Jałowiecki, K., Lewandowska, P. and Pawela, Ł. (2023). "PyQBench: A Python library for benchmarking gate-based quantum computers". SoftwareX, Vol 24, pp 101558. https://doi.org/10.1016/j.softx.2023.101558

Khan, A.A. et al. (2023). "Software architecture for quantum computing systems - a systematic review". Journal of Systems and Software, Vol 201, pp 111682. https://doi.org/10.1016/j.jss.2023.111682

Li, K. et al. (2022). "A novel privacy-preserving multi-level aggregate signcryption and query scheme for Smart Grid via mobile fog computing". Journal of Information Security and Applications, Vol 67, pp 103214. https://doi.org/10.1016/j.jisa.2022.103214

Li, N. et al. (2023). "Quantum image scaling with applications to image steganography and fusion". Signal Processing: Image Communication, Vol 117, pp 117015. https://doi.org/10.1016/j.image.2023.117015

Coccia, M., Roshani, S. and Mosleh, M. (2022). "Evolution of Quantum Computing: Theoretical and Innovation Management Implications for Emerging Quantum Industry". IEEE Transactions on Engineering Management, Vol. 71, pp.1–11. https://doi.org/10.1109/TEM.2022.3175633

Macrae, R.M. (2023). "Mixed-valence realizations of quantum dot cellular automata". Journal of Physics and Chemistry of Solids, Vol 177, pp 111303. https://doi.org/10.1016/j.jpcs.2023.111303

Maheshwari, D., Garcia-Zapirain, B. and Sierra-Sosa, D. (2022). "Quantum Machine Learning Applications in the Biomedical Domain: A Systematic Review". IEEE Access, Vol 10, pp 80463–80484. https://doi.org/10.1109/ACCESS.2022.3195044

Padmaa, M., Jayasankar, T., Venkatraman, S. et al (2022). "Oppositional chaos game optimization based clustering with trust based data transmission protocol for intelligent IoT edge systems". Journal of Parallel and Distributed Computing, Vol 164, pp 142–151. https://doi.org/10.1016/j.jpdc.2022.03.008

Pérez-Castillo, R., Jiménez-Navajas, L. and Piattini, M. (2023). "Dynamic analysis of quantum annealing programs". Journal of Systems and Software, Vol 201, pp 111683. https://doi.org/10.1016/j.jss.2023.111683

Qadir, Z. et al. (2022). "Towards 6G internet of things: Recent advances, use cases, and open challenges". ICT Express, Vol 9(3). https://doi.org/10.1016/j.icte.2022.06.006

Raheman, F. (2022). "The Future of Cybersecurity in the Age of Quantum Computers". Future Internet, Vol 14(11), pp 335. https://doi.org/10.3390/fi14110335

Shaw, S. and Dutta, R. (2023). "A quantum resistant multi-user signcryption scheme featuring key invisibility for Internet of Things". Journal of Information Security and Applications, Vol 76, pp 103549. https://doi.org/10.1016/j.jisa.2023.103549

Ukpabi, D. et al. (2023). "Framework for Understanding Quantum Computing Use Cases from A Multidisciplinary Perspective and Future Research Directions". Futures, Vol 154, pp 103277–103277. https://doi.org/10.1016/j.futures.2023.103277

Willsch, D. et al. (2022). "GPU-accelerated simulations of quantum annealing and the quantum approximate optimization algorithm". Computer Physics Communications, Vol 278, pp 108411. https://doi.org/10.1016/j.cpc.2022.108411

Yi, L. et al. (2023). "Service provision process scheduling using quantum annealing for technical product-service systems". Procedia CIRP, Vol 116, pp 330–335. https://doi.org/10.1016/j.procir.2023.02.056

Zhou, Q., Tian, G. and Deng, Y. (2023). "BF-QC: Belief functions on quantum circuits". Expert Systems with Applications, Vol 223, pp 119885. https://doi.org/10.1016/j.eswa.2023.119885

Evaluating SIEM RADAR: A New Metric for Enhancing Regulatory and Compliance Efficiency

Ertuğrul Akbaş
Computer Engineering, Istanbul Esenyurt University, SureLog SIEM İstanbul, Turkey,

eakbas@gmail.com

Abstract: This research paper explores the modern cybersecurity landscape, particularly focusing on the risks associated with SIEM products and SOC services. It underscores the critical issue of insufficient logging practices that compromise an organization's threat detection and response capabilities, thereby increasing the risk of security breaches. The importance of real-time log retention to address evolving digital threats is highlighted, with recommended retention periods from authoritative sources such as the White House, OWASP, MITRE, and SANS. The paper also addresses scalability challenges due to the exponential growth of log data, the necessity for effective correlation within SIEM systems for timely threat detection, and the importance of compliance with various standards and regulations to enhance security. This comprehensive analysis provides valuable insights for cybersecurity professionals, organizations, and policymakers. Categories and Subject Descriptors: C.2.0 [**Computer-Communication Networks**]: General—Security and Protection; D.4.6 [**Operating Systems**]: Security and Protection; H.5.3 [**Information Interfaces and Presentation**]: Group and Organization Interfaces. **General Terms:** Design, SIEM, Security

Keywords: Security Information and Event Management, Log, SIEM, SOC, Cyber Security, Insufficient logging, Live Log, Hot Log, Log Loss, Correlation

1. Introduction

SIEM solutions and SOC services are foundational elements in modern cybersecurity, crucial for protecting organizations against sophisticated cyber threats. However, their effectiveness can be significantly undermined by challenges ranging from log management intricacies to data correlation complexities. This paper takes a unique approach by evaluating these security measures in alignment with legal requirements, governmental orders, industry regulations, and best practices.

The significant issue of insufficient logging is highlighted with real-world statistics demonstrating its impact on security. For instance, scenarios like the Stuxnet Worm Attack and the 2017 Verizon Communications Data Breach reveal the dangers of inadequate logging and monitoring, which allowed severe breaches and data exposures.

The objective of this paper is to explore these vulnerabilities in-depth, providing a comprehensive understanding of how they can erode an organization's security posture and what can be done to mitigate these risks effectively.

This paper is structured as follows: After this introduction, we delve into the current methodologies for evaluating SIEM solutions, followed by a detailed discussion on the importance of log retention, the challenges of log scalability, and the critical role of effective correlation within SIEM systems. We then examine compliance requirements and conclude with strategic recommendations for strengthening security postures in the face of evolving cyber threats. This comprehensive framework aims to equip cybersecurity professionals, organizations, and policymakers with the necessary insights to enhance their security strategies effectively.

2. Current Methodologies in Evaluating SIEM Solutions

In evaluating SIEM solutions, this paper identifies several limitations that are often overlooked in traditional analyses. The comparison of SIEM features across various products, as depicted in Table 1 and Table 2, provides a foundation for discussing these limitations. However, instead of listing features, a more nuanced approach is taken to discuss the underlying issues and gaps in SIEM functionalities.

Table 1. Analysis of different SIEM solutions (Sheeraz,M. et al 2018.)

Functionality	ArcSight	QRadar	McAfee	LogRhythm	USM-OSSIM	RSA	Splunk	SolarWinds
Correlation rules	○	○	•	•	•	○	–	•
Data sources	•	•	•	○	○	•	•	○
Real time processing	•	•	•	•	•	•	•	•
Data volume	•	○	•	○	○	○	•	○
Visualization	–	○	○	○	○	○	•	○
Data analytics	○	•	○	•	○	○	•	○
Performance	○	○	•	○	○	•	○	•
Forensics	–	•	•	○	•	•	○	○
Complexity	•	○	○	○	○	•	•	•
Scalability	•	•	•	•	–	•	•	•
Risk analysis	–	○	○	○	–	○	–	○
Storage	○	○	•	○	○	○	○	•
Price	•	•	•	○	○	•	•	○
Resilience	○	•	•	○	○	•	○	○
Reaction and reporting	–	–	•	•	–	○	○	○
UEBA	•	•	–	•	–	•	•	–
Security	•	•	–	–	○	○	○	–

– Low/Basic ○ Average • High/Advanced.

The common features across SIEM systems, including correlation rules, real-time processing, data analytics, and user and entity behavior analytics (UEBA), are critical for effective security monitoring. However, despite their presence, significant gaps remain in the practical application of these features. For instance, real-time processing is often constrained by the scalability of the system as log volumes increase, which can lead to delays in threat detection and response. Similarly, while correlation rules are fundamental to identifying security threats, they require continuous updates and tuning to remain effective against evolving attack vectors.

Furthermore, the integration of threat intelligence is another area where SIEM systems often fall short. Although many SIEM solutions claim to incorporate threat intelligence, the effectiveness of this integration varies significantly. The ability to dynamically adapt to new threats based on reliable intelligence feeds is crucial, yet many systems struggle to update their operational parameters swiftly enough to counteract new threats effectively.

These limitations highlight the need for ongoing research and development in SIEM technology to address these critical gaps. By understanding the deficiencies in current methodologies, organizations can better prepare for and respond to cybersecurity threats. This analysis sets the stage for exploring advanced solutions and adaptations in SIEM technologies to enhance their efficacy in the ever-changing cybersecurity landscape.

Table 2. Analysis of different SIEM solutions (Granadillo,G. and González-Zarzosa,S. and Diaz,R. 2021)

Feature	Open-Source SIEM					Proprietary SIEM					Proposed
	OSSIM	ELK	Wazuh	MozDef	SIEMonster	QRadar	Splunk	Securonix	Exabeam	LogRhythm	SIEM
Real-time monitoring	✓	✓	✓	×	✓	✓	✓	✓	✓	✓	✓
Threat intelligence	×	✓	✓	×	✓	✓	✓	✓	✓	✓	✓
Behavior profiling	✓	✓	×	✓	×	✓	✓	✓	✓	✓	✓
Data monitoring	✓	✓	✓	✓	✓	✓	✓	✓	✓	✓	✓
User monitoring	✓	✓	✓	✓	✓	✓	✓	✓	✓	✓	✓
Application monitoring	✓	✓	✓	✓	✓	✓	✓	✓	✓	✓	✓
Analytics	✓	✓	✓	✓	✓	✓	✓	✓	✓	✓	✓
Log management	×	✓	✓	✓	✓	✓	✓	✓	✓	✓	✓
Updates	✓	✓	✓	✓	×	✓	✓	✓	✓	✓	✓
Reporting	×	✓	✓	×	✓	✓	✓	✓	✓	✓	✓
GUI	✓	✓	✓	✓	✓	✓	✓	✓	✓	✓	✓
Detailed system description	×	×	×	×	×	×	×	×	×	×	✓
Database	MySQL	ES	MySQL	ES	ES	Ariel	GZip-files	A.Hadoop	ES	SQL-server	MySQL

ES=Elasticsearch.

3. Insufficient Logging

In the realm of cybersecurity, sufficient logging practices are indispensable for effective threat detection and incident response. However, a pervasive issue among various organizations is insufficient logging, which significantly impedes their ability to manage security threats efficiently. This section introduces the Event Volume Score (EVS), a novel metric designed to quantitatively assess and compare the logging practices of organizations, informed by standards such as those set by MITRE and SANS.

The EVS is a comprehensive metric that evaluates the adequacy of logging based on three primary criteria:

- Frequency of Log Generation: Measures how often logs are recorded, capturing the timeliness of log entries in response to security events.
- Variety of Log Sources: Assesses the diversity of sources from which logs are collected, reflecting the breadth of monitoring across the network and systems.
- Detail Level of Logs: Analyzes the granularity and relevance of the information captured in the logs, crucial for detailed forensic investigations and effective threat detection.

A higher EVS indicates robust logging practices that enhance an organization's capability to detect and respond to cyber threats promptly and accurately.

Companies should calculate EPS values according to this table, and if it is different, then it means inadequate logging, a concern highlighted in the OWASP Top 10 Web Application Security Risks – 2021 (OWASP. "Top 10 Web Application Security Risks", 2021), OWASP Top 10 API Security Risks – 2019 (OWASP. "OWASP Top 10 API Security Risks – 2019", 2019), OWASP Top 10 Application Security Risks – 2017 (OWASP. "OWASP Top Ten 2017", 2017.)

Insufficient logging is also listed as a vulnerability in the MITRE CWE database [13,14]. Common Weakness Enumeration (CWE) is a cybersecurity standard developed by MITRE. CWE provides a list of software and hardware weaknesses and vulnerabilities. This listing is developed to enhance the security of computer systems and software and to strengthen defense against cyber-attacks. It is a database that assigns a number and includes a description to identify a type of error or vulnerability. This enables security experts and software developers to identify and address potential vulnerabilities with guidance.

Another challenge of log loss or unsuccessful log filtering is the potential reflection in the need for log access as required by standards like GDPR, PCI. Failing to access the necessary proof or logs in such contexts can lead to legal consequences.

Table 1: Baseline Network Device EPS Averages

Qty	Type	Description	Avg EPS	Total Peak EPS	Average Peak EPS
750	Employees/Endpoints (Windows XP)	Desktops & laptops at 5 locations	Included at domain servers	Included at domain servers	Included at domain servers
7	Cisco Catalyst Switches	One at each location, one in DMZ and one in the Trusted network	5.09	51.88	26.35
7	Cisco Gateway/Routers	One at each location	0.60	380.50	154.20
5	Windows 2003 Domain Servers	One at each location	40.00	404.38	121.75
3	Windows 2003 Application Servers	In high availability cluster at data center	1.38	460.14	230.07
3	MS SQL Database Servers running on Windows 2003 Server	High availability cluster at data center	1.83	654.90	327.45
6	Microsoft Exchange Servers	One at each location with two (cluster) at the data center	3.24	1,121.50	448.60
3	MS IIS Web Servers on Windows 2003	High availability cluster at data center	1.17	2,235.10	1,117.55
2	Windows DNS Servers	At data center – failover	0.72	110.80	110.80
2	Linux Legacy Application Servers	At data center	0.12	43.60	21.80
1	Linux MySQL Database Server	One in Trusted network for legacy application	0.12	21.80	21.80
7	NitroGuard IPS	One at each location, one in DMZ and one in the Trusted network	40.53	5,627.82	1,607.95
1	Netscreen Firewall	Netscreen facing the Internet	0.58	2,414.00	2,414.00
3	Cisco Pix Firewalls	Between the data center and the other four sites, in front of Trusted network, between Trusted and the DMZ	39.00	1,734.00	1,178.00
1	Cisco VPN Concentrator	Located at data center Facing the Internet	0.83	69.45	69.45
1	Squid Proxy	Located at data center	14.58	269.03	269.03
		Totals:	**149.79**	**15,598.90**	**8,118.80**

Figure 1. SANS EPS calculation table

3.1 Examples of Insufficient Logging and Monitoring Attacks

Without proper monitoring and logging of network traffic, businesses fail to prevent attackers from installing malware and accessing crucial data. In recent history, the following are some of the well-known examples of security incidents arising from insufficient logging and monitoring:

The Stuxnet Worm Attack on Iran's Nuclear Program. The Stuxnet worm is a masterfully crafted Malware that attacks Supervisory Control and Data Acquisition (SCADA) systems. In 2010, the security team at the Iranian nuclear program discovered that the bug had been used to access critical weapons control systems.

On deeper analysis, the bug was active since 2005 and spread using infected USB drives. The hackers took advantage of poor logging and monitoring mechanisms to gain elevated access discreetly.

The 2017 Verizon Communications Data Breach. While no data was stolen, Verizon admits that at least 14 million customer records were exposed to the internet in a data breach discovered in 2017. These records included such data as phone numbers and account PINs. This data was not password-protected, and attackers could have easily downloaded and exploited it. However, the records were stored in a cloud-based data repository and were discovered by a cybersecurity researcher before any attackers could take advantage of the loophole.

The 2019 Dominion National Data Breach. In 2019, Insurer Dominion National discovered that members of its health plans could have been exposed to a data breach that lasted more than nine years. The breach, which was determined to have affected over 2 million individuals, exposed sensitive customer data, including:

- Bank account numbers Routing numbers
- Taxpayer identification information social security numbers
- Names and Dates of Birth among others

After an exhaustive investigation, it was determined that this information was not accessed or used by unauthorized persons. Dominion National was, however, ordered to cover any claims for monetary losses reasonably traceable to the breach.

4. Hot, Live, Online, Immediately Available Log Retentions

It is now understood that archiving logs is insufficient from various practical aspects, including legal and cybersecurity concerns. Keeping logs live, meaning being able to go back years for evidence and logs when needed, has been proven essential in numerous studies and literature reviews about incident response against advanced attacks. Moreover, this has become a requirement through laws and standards, surpassing research and development. For instance, there's a presidential memorandum in the United States specifying that logs should be kept live for at least 1 year, and there's an order for at least 1.5 years of archiving. The "Memorandum for the Heads of Executive Departments and Agencies," published by the Executive Office of the President, Office of Management and Budget (**2021."MEMORANDUM FOR THE HEADS OF EXECUTIVE DEPARTMENTS AND AGENCIES")**

Across the globe, a multitude of standards, laws, and illustrative best-case scenarios concerning the vital role of live logs have been disseminated (2021."Event Logging Guidance from Treasury Board of Canada Secretariat", Google."Retaining Logs for A Year: Boring or Useful?", 2019, SANS. "An Evaluator's Guide to NextGen SIEM", 2018, NIST. "Assessing Security and Privacy Controls in Information Systems and Organizations" 2022, "Vadodara Smart City Development Limited (VSCDL)" 2021). This burgeoning body of knowledge underscores the paramount importance of real-time, dynamic log data in the realm of cybersecurity. As the digital landscape continues to evolve, the significance of live logs has become more pronounced, serving as a beacon for organizations striving to fortify their security postures.

In this evolving landscape, a paradigm shift has occurred. The conventional reliance on archived logs for incident response has been debunked, as the shortcomings of such an approach have become glaringly apparent. Timely incident response demands the immediacy and accuracy that only live logs can provide. These logs, capturing events as they unfold, offer a real-time perspective that is invaluable in identifying and mitigating security breaches promptly.

In light of this realization, a clarion call echoes across the industry: companies and organizations must reevaluate their approach to log management. The static nature of archived logs falls short in meeting the demands of modern cybersecurity, where threats can materialize in moments. Acknowledging this, proactive measures are indispensable. Organizations should not only embrace the usage of live logs but also elevate their status as a vital risk parameter.

The heart of this transformation lies in the realm of SIEM solutions and the acquisition of SOC services. These pivotal tools stand as the vanguard of an organization's defence against the ever-evolving landscape of cyber threats. However, their efficacy hinges on the quality and timeliness of the data they process. Live logs, as an integral component of this data, assume an outsized role in bolstering an organization's resilience. Therefore, the imperative is clear: companies and organizations must regard live logs as a linchpin in their cybersecurity strategy. The integration of live logs into the fabric of SIEM solutions and SOC services enhances the accuracy of threat detection, facilitates rapid incident response, and bolsters post-incident analysis. By recognizing live logs as a formidable risk parameter, organizations set the stage for a proactive stance against potential breaches. To this end, taking measures to optimize the collection, aggregation, and analysis of live logs is paramount. Automation, advanced analytics, and real-time monitoring must be harnessed to ensure the efficacy of these logs in a dynamic threat landscape. Compliance with industry standards and regulations further underscores the significance of live logs, as their utilization aligns with the best practices advocated by these frameworks.

In conclusion, the era of static, archived logs as the cornerstone of incident response has passed. The ascendancy of live logs in the cybersecurity narrative is undeniable. With a shift in perspective, organizations can embrace the agility and accuracy that live logs offer. This paradigm shift beckons companies and organizations to leverage live logs as a vital component in their cybersecurity arsenal, navigating the complexities of modern threats with vigilance and confidence.

4.1 Challenges

The exponential growth of log data poses challenges in managing and retaining large volumes of logs. There are different technologies in the market. For example, Apache Lucene's indexed (hot, live) log growth formula:

disk space used(original) = 1/3 original for each indexed field + 1 * original for stored + 2 * original per field with term vectors

There are other technologies utilized by some SIEM vendors that compress both the indexes and raw logs. Organizations must contend with scalability issues and invest in robust log storage and management solutions to accommodate the influx of log data. Log volume increases can be unmanageable both in terms of price and disk size.

5. Log Investigation: an Indispensable and Crucial Part of Incident Response

Log investigation is indeed a crucial and indispensable part of incident response. Logs serve as a valuable source of information, providing insights into the activities that transpire within an information system. They encompass a wide range of data, including network traffic, system events, user actions, and application activities. By thoroughly analyzing logs, security analysts can unlock various benefits and effectively respond to security incidents.

1. Detection of Indicators of Compromise (IOCs): Logs play a pivotal role in identifying IOCs, which are signs or evidence of a security breach or compromise. Security analysts can examine logs for patterns, anomalies, or specific events that indicate unauthorized access, malicious activities, or potential vulnerabilities. These IOCs might include IP addresses, file modifications, failed login attempts, or abnormal behavior.
2. Tracing the Steps of an Attacker: Through log investigation, analysts can retrace the steps of an attacker, reconstructing the sequence of events that led to a security incident. By analyzing network logs, system logs, and other relevant logs, analysts can determine the attack vectors, techniques employed, and the extent of damage caused. This information is crucial for understanding the attack landscape and devising effective countermeasures.
3. Assessing the Scope of a Breach: Logs provide critical insights into the scope and impact of a security breach. By examining logs from different systems or devices, analysts can identify the systems compromised, data accessed or exfiltrated, and the duration of the breach. This helps in assessing the severity of the incident, prioritizing response efforts, and containing further damage.
4. Gathering Evidence for Investigation and Legal Proceedings: Logs serve as a valuable source of evidence during investigations and legal proceedings. They provide a chronological record of events and actions taken within the information system, enabling analysts to reconstruct the incident timeline and identify

key actors. Log analysis can assist in building a case, supporting legal actions, and facilitating compliance with regulatory requirements.

6. SOC

SOC stands for Security Operations Center. It is a centralized unit within an organization responsible for monitoring, detecting, analyzing, and responding to security incidents and threats. A SOC is designed to provide continuous monitoring and protection of an organization's information systems, networks, applications, and data. It typically employs a combination of technologies, processes, and skilled cybersecurity professionals to ensure the organization's security posture is maintained and threats are promptly addressed. The SOC's primary goal is to enhance an organization's ability to identify, mitigate, and recover from security breaches and incidents.

There are standards related to live logs for SOCs. For instance, in the book '11 Strategies of a World-Class Cybersecurity Operations Center' published by MITRE, it is stated that logs should be retained for a period ranging from 6 months to 2 years depending on the type of logs (such as Firewall logs, for example) (MITRE. "11 Strategies of a World-Class Cybersecurity Operations Center", 2022).

7. Correlation

Effective correlation is a crucial aspect of SIEM solutions. Numerous regulations worldwide emphasize real-time correlation as a means of identifying and responding to security threats promptly (The Monetary Authority of Singapore (MAS). 2021, Australian Cyber Security Center. 2021, NIST. "NIST Cybersecurity Framework 2.0" 2023). Correlation capabilities enable the identification of patterns and anomalies across diverse data sources, enhancing an organization's ability to detect and mitigate potential security breaches.

The future of SIEM and SOC services lies in the integration of artificial intelligence (AI) and automation. AI-driven anomaly detection and predictive analytics enable the identification of sophisticated threats that evade traditional security measures. Machine learning models can learn from historical data and adapt to evolving threat landscapes. Additionally, integrating threat intelligence feeds and collaborating with external cybersecurity communities strengthen an organization's ability to identify emerging threats quickly.

Moreover, the process of correlating data across diverse sources poses an enigmatic challenge. SIEM solutions rely on the accurate correlation of events to identify patterns and indicators of potential breaches. Yet, as logs pour in from different devices, platforms, and applications, deciphering meaningful connections becomes a complex puzzle. Incorrect or incomplete correlations can lead to missed threats or false alarms, both of which can significantly impact an organization's ability to respond effectively.

7.1 Real Time Correlation

In today's complex and ever-evolving cybersecurity landscape, organizations face a myriad of sophisticated threats that can cause significant damage if left undetected. Real time correlation is the critical requirements for regulations (The Monetary Authority of Singapore (MAS). 2021, Australian Cyber Security Center. 2021, NIST. "NIST Cybersecurity Framework 2.0" 2023).

In this context, real-time correlation is of paramount importance for several reasons:

- Timely Threat Identification: The speed at which security incidents are identified and responded to is crucial in mitigating potential damage. Real-time detection in SIEM/UEBA solutions allows security teams to receive alerts as soon as suspicious activities are detected. This rapid identification gives organizations a crucial advantage in thwarting attacks before they can escalate and cause harm.
- Reduced Dwell Time: Dwell time, the period between a security breach and its discovery, is a critical metric in cybersecurity. Real-time detection helps reduce dwell time by quickly spotting malicious activities, preventing attackers from establishing a persistent presence within the network. Minimizing dwell time limits the damage attackers can inflict and shortens the window of opportunity for exfiltrating sensitive data.
- Automated Response: Integrating real-time detection with automated response capabilities enables organizations to respond rapidly to security incidents. Automated actions, such as blocking malicious IPs, quarantining compromised systems, and initiating predefined incident response playbooks, ensure that threats are contained promptly, even when security teams are not immediately available.

- Correlation of Events: The true value of SIEM/UEBA solutions lies in their ability to correlate seemingly unrelated security events in real-time. This correlation identifies patterns, trends, and relationships between different activities that could indicate a coordinated attack or unusual user behavior. By connecting the dots, security analysts gain valuable insights into the attack's nature and can respond more effectively.
- Advanced Threat Detection: Advanced threats, including APTs (Advanced Persistent Threats), often involve multiple stages and tactics spread across the network. Real-time detection and correlation can piece together disparate events, even those occurring in different parts of the network, to uncover these sophisticated attack campaigns. This holistic view is essential for understanding the full scope of the threat.
- Insider Threat Detection: Insider threats, whether malicious or unintentional, pose significant risks to organizations. UEBA solutions play a vital role in detecting anomalous user behavior that might indicate insider threats. Real-time analysis of user actions, such as accessing sensitive data outside regular working hours or attempting unauthorized activities, allows organizations to respond swiftly and prevent data breaches.
- Compliance and Reporting: Meeting regulatory compliance requirements demands timely detection and response to security incidents. Real-time detection and correlation ensure that organizations can demonstrate their adherence to compliance standards by promptly reporting incidents and maintaining accurate audit trails.
- Proactive Incident Response: Real-time detection allows organizations to adopt a proactive approach to incident response. By identifying potential threats early, organizations can take preemptive actions to prevent attacks, strengthen security controls, and bolster their overall security posture.
- Adaptive Security Measures: Real-time detection and correlation enable organizations to dynamically adjust their security measures based on emerging threats and attack vectors. This adaptability ensures that security protocols remain effective and relevant in an ever-changing threat landscape.

Real-time correlation is not supported or is limited in some cases. When Splunk is deployed in cloud environments, it disables real-time searching and correlation. In on-premises installations, it also dedicates a core for each real-time monitoring task, which translates into substantial CPU costs (Splunk. Splunk Community, 2019, Splunk. Splunk Community, 2016, Splunk. Splunk Community, 2021, Splunk. Splunk Community, 2018).

Even Microsoft Sentinel, a powerful player in the security information and event management arena, has its own set of constraints. It imposes a limit of 50 rules for a tenant when it comes to real-time correlation (Microsoft. Microsoft Community, 2023).

8. Discussion

SIEM solutions are essential in the realm of cybersecurity, serving as robust guardians in an increasingly digital landscape where threats are omnipresent. The Security Operations Center (SOC) framework, fundamental to modern cybersecurity, involves procuring vital services with SIEM systems at the forefront. Whether through in-house teams or external outsourcing, the commitment to rigorous and detailed cybersecurity practices is essential.

Central to these practices is effective log management, which acts as the digital memory of an organization's activities. The criticality of real-time log monitoring is akin to monitoring the vital signs of an organization's network and systems, providing essential visibility and control.

A crucial element in enhancing these practices is the introduction of the Event Volume Score (EVS), a new metric developed to quantitatively assess and improve logging practices. EVS focuses on evaluating the frequency, variety, and detail of log entries, thereby ensuring that logging practices are robust enough to handle complex security demands. This metric is pivotal in maintaining the integrity and continuity of logs, which should be active for at least a year and archived for an additional 1.5 years to support forensic investigations and compliance.

The journey up the correlation pyramid is also vital, with each level representing a deeper and more sophisticated understanding of threat detection through the integration of disparate data points. Achieving higher levels of this pyramid indicates a mature capability to decipher and address the complex relationships between varied cybersecurity events.

Ignoring these enhanced practices can have severe implications, as demonstrated by significant breaches like the SolarWinds and Stuxnet incidents. These events underscore the risks of inadequate cybersecurity measures and highlight the necessity of stringent log management and effective correlation practices.

Our discussion extends to include recognized risk lists from sources such as OWASP and MITRE, aligning our practices with industry standards to underscore the universality of these challenges. Furthermore, we delve into the legal and regulatory frameworks governing global data protection, illustrating that cybersecurity risks encompass more than just technical challenges; they have broad implications across legislative and regulatory environments.

At this critical juncture, as organizations select products and services to strengthen their defenses, our mission is twofold: to expose potential vulnerabilities that could lead to cyber threats and to provide clarity and insights, guiding end-users to make informed decisions that fortify their digital infrastructures against the dynamic spectrum of cybersecurity risks. This comprehensive approach ensures that organizations not only understand the risks but also have the tools and knowledge to mitigate them effectively.

9. Conclusion

In conclusion, the risks inherent in deploying Security Information and Event Management (SIEM) systems and acquiring Security Operations Center (SOC) services are complex and constantly changing. As organizations work to strengthen their cybersecurity measures, it is crucial to navigate the myriad challenges posed by evolving laws, regulations, standards, and best practices.

This paper introduces a novel approach by not only scrutinizing the criteria for SIEM and SOC systems but also incorporating perspectives from esteemed entities such as OWASP, MITRE, the White House, and SANS, along with introducing the Event Volume Score (EVS) as a new metric to assess these systems. This holistic evaluation provides a detailed view of the effectiveness and relevance of SIEM and SOC solutions within the larger cybersecurity framework.

The findings from this research highlight the importance for organizations to continuously refine and adjust their cybersecurity strategies to keep pace with the dynamic security landscape. As threats evolve, so must the methods and approaches to managing SIEM and SOC systems to effectively safeguard critical assets. In such a rapidly shifting environment, it is imperative for organizations to remain vigilant and proactive, ensuring their cybersecurity defenses are both resilient and adaptive.

References

Australian Cyber Security Center. 2021. "Australian Government Information Security Manual", [online] https://kmtech.com.au/wp-content/uploads/2021/11/Australian-Government-Information-Security-Manual-September-2021.pdf [Accessed: 18th Aug 2023]

2021."Event Logging Guidance from Treasury Board of Canada Secretariat", [online] https://www.canada.ca/en/government/system/digital-government/online-security-privacy/event-logging-guidance.html [Accessed: 1st May 2023]

Gartner. 2023. "6 Macro Factors Reshaping Business This Decade", [online] https://www.gartner.com/en/articles/6-macro-factors-reshaping-business-this-decade [Accessed: 2nd May 2023]

Granadillo,G. and González-Zarzosa,S. and Diaz,R. 2021 "Security Information and Event Management (SIEM): Analysis, Trends, and Usage in Critical Infrastructures", Sensors, vol 21(14), 4759. [online] http://dx.doi.org/10.3390/s21144759 [Accessed: 3rd May 2023]

Google."Retaining Logs for A Year: Boring or Useful?", 2019. [online] https://chroniclesec.medium.com/retaining-logs-for-a-year-boring-or-useful-9b04c1e55fba [Accessed: 2nd Aug 2023]

InfoTech. 2021. [online] http://www.infotech.com [Accessed: 6th May 2023]

Info-Tech Research Group. 2015. "Vendor Landscape: Security Information & Event Management. In Optimize IT Security Management and Simplify Compliance with SIEM Tools" [online] https://infotech.report/Resources/Whitepapers/4d60fcda-43d8-410a-bb83-e737f828d078_SIEM%20Tools%20to%20Optimize%20IT%20Security.pdf [Accessed: 8th May 2023]

2021."MEMORANDUM FOR THE HEADS OF EXECUTIVE DEPARTMENTS AND AGENCIES",[online] https://www.whitehouse.gov/wp-content/uploads/2021/08/M-21-31-Improving-the-Federal-Governments-Investigative-and-Remediation-Capabilities-Related-to-Cybersecurity-Incidents.pdf [Accessed: 6th Aug 2023]

Microsoft. Microsoft Community, 2023. [online] https://docs.microsoft.com/en-us/azure/sentinel/near-real-time-rules [Accessed: 7th Aug 2023]

MITRE. "Common Weakness Enumeration: CWE", 2019. [online] https://cwe.mitre.org/data/definitions/1210.html [Accessed: 9th Aug 2023]

MITRE. "Common Weakness Enumeration: CWE", 2009. https://cwe.mitre.org/data/definitions/778.html [Accessed: 9th Aug 2023]

MITRE. "11 Strategies of a World-Class Cybersecurity Operations Center", 2022. [online] https://www.mitre.org/sites/default/files/2022-04/11-strategies-of-a-world-class-cybersecurity-operations-center.pdf [Accessed: 10th Aug 2023]

NIST. "NIST Cybersecurity Framework 2.0" 2023. [online] https://www.nist.gov/cyberframework [Accessed: 12th Aug 2023]

NIST. "Assessing Security and Privacy Controls in Information Systems and Organizations" 2022. [online] https://csrc.nist.gov/pubs/sp/800/53/a/r5/final [Accessed: 14th Aug 2023]

OWASP. "Top 10 Web Application Security Risks", 2021. [online] https://owasp.org/www-project-top-ten [Accessed: 15th Aug 2023]

OWASP. "OWASP Top 10 API Security Risks – 2019", 2019. [online] https://owasp.org/API-Security/editions/2019/en/0x11-t10 [Accessed: 16th Aug 2023]

OWASP. "OWASP Top Ten 2017", 2017. [online] https://owasp.org/www-project-top-ten/2017/A10_2017-Insufficient_Logging%2526Monitoring [Accessed: 17th Aug 2023]

SANS. "An Evaluator's Guide to NextGen SIEM", 2018. [online] https://www.sans.org/media/vendor/evaluator-039-s-guide-nextgen-siem-38720.pdf [Accessed: 18th Aug 2023]

Sheeraz,M. et al 2018. "Effective Security Monitoring Using Efficient SIEM Architecture", Human-centric Computing and Information Sciences, vol 8, [online] https://doi.org/10.22967/HCIS.2023.13.017 [Accessed: 18th Aug 2023]

Solutions Review . "Security Information and Event Management Vendor Map",[online] https://solutionsreview.com/security-information-event-management/security-information-event-management-vendor-map [Accessed: 19th Aug 2023]

Splunk. Splunk Community, 2019. [online] https://community.splunk.com/t5/Splunk-Search/Real-Time-Search-Issues/m-p/423805 [Accessed: 20th Aug 2023]

Splunk. Splunk Community, 2016. [online] https://answers.splunk.com/answers/433872/why-are-real-time-searches-not-running-and-getting.html [Accessed: 21st Aug 2023]

Splunk. Splunk Community, 2021. [online] https://docs.splunk.com/Documentation/Splunk/latest/Search/Realtimeperformanceandlimitations [Accessed: 22nd Aug 2023]

Splunk. Splunk Community, 2018. [online] https://answers.splunk.com/answers/671819/real-time-alert-1.html [Accessed: 23rd Aug 2023]

TechTarget. TechTarget Search Security. [online] http://searchsecurity.techtarget.com [Accessed: 24th Aug 2023]

TechTarget. 2013. "How to Define SIEM Strategy, Management and Success in the Enterprise", [online] https://searchsecurity.techtarget.com/essentialguide/How-to-define-SIEM-strategy-management-and-success-in-the-enterprise [Accessed: 25th Aug 2023]

The Monetary Authority of Singapore (MAS). 2021. "Guidelines on Risk Management Practices – Technology Risk", [online] https://www.mas.gov.sg/regulation/guidelines/technology-risk-management-guidelines [Accessed: 26th Aug 2023]

"Vadodara Smart City Development Limited (VSCDL)",2021. [online] http://vadodarasmartcity.in/vscdl/assets/tenders/17.09.2020/2021_499-1.pdf [Accessed: 2thth Aug 2023]

VirginiTech."Benchmarking Security Information Event Management (SIEM)", [online] https://apps.es.vt.edu/confluence/download/attachments/460849213/sans%20siem%20benchmarking.pdf [Accessed: 27th Aug 2023]

PentHack: AI-Enabled Penetration Testing Platform for Knowledge Development

Meera Alaryani, Shamsa Alremeithi, Fatima Al Ali and Richard Ikuesan
Zayed University, Abu Dhabi, United Arab Emirates

202102492@zu.ac.ae
202005474@zu.ac.ae
201915426@zu.ac.ae
Richard.ikuesan@zu.ac.ae

Abstract: The process of conducting and executing penetration testing within the pedagogical paradigm often requires complex and arduous processes. This is especially daunting for beginners who often struggle with the complexities of penetration processes: reconnaissance, enumeration, and system hacking. Research works to address this complexity leverage industry tools that have proven to work for industry-related training, however, they fail to support pedagogical learning in higher education systems. To address this limitation, this study proposed the development of an academic-focused penetration testing learning platform. The proposed approach integrates large language models (LLM) into the penetration testing lifecycle through a user-friendly GUI tool. The tool addresses the void in beginner-friendly ethical hacking tools by offering a stepwise guide, built-in commands and justifications, report generation, and an LLM prompt-engineered output displayed in a simple tabular format for easy reference. Furthermore, the tool provides an interactive menu for each phase of the penetration lifecycle thereby guiding users through common penetration testing commands. To cater to deeper learning needs, the tool leverages LLMs to furnish additional information on commands, empowering users with AI-generated insights. With the capability to compile a comprehensive report with all commands and logs acquired during its use, the proposed tool has the potential to reduce the time spent on research and decision-making. In addition, it streamlines the learning curve, allowing a more informed and structured approach to Pen-testing for beginners. By leveraging this platform, academics and learners can enhance their penetration testing knowledge without the complexities associated with learning penetration testing.

Keywords: Penetration Testing, Artificial Intelligence, Knowledge Development, Cyber Security Education, Pedagogy

1. Introduction

In the contemporary digital age, the Internet stands out as the linchpin that connects the threads of our technological progress. An omnipresent force creating our present, with origins in the late 1960s was a military project called ARPANET, which was built to withstand atomic attacks. Following that, in the late 1980s, the World Wide Web was launched, marking an important turning point in its transformative journey. Today, the Internet is a digital giant that cuts across numerous geographical boundaries, transforming social interactions, knowledge exchange, and global connectedness. Its impact on education, culture, and social dynamics has been nothing short of phenomenal, according to Castells (Castells, 2019; Navarria, 2016), who emphasized the Internet's role in building a more gregarious digital world. As we delve into the technical world, the Internet's evolution has become a tribute to human creativity, evolving from room-sized equipment to an era of pocket-sized handheld devices. The Internet's continual growth underlines its vital role in establishing an interconnected society in which information flows easily across borders, influencing the very fabric of our world. Graham and Dutton (2019) emphasized how software applications, vast databases, and interconnected network systems have brought the world together, facilitating fast connections. As well as maintaining vigilance in the face of technological advances is critical, underlining the need to embrace innovation and stay current with trends, as noted by Koutsikouri et al. (2018). Looking ahead, IT trends predict a future dominated by artificial intelligence (AI) and machine learning, which will transform job execution and decision-making processes across a variety of fields. This dynamic merging of the two drives information technology into new territory, transitioning from mainframes to the intricate interweaving of modern technologies (Duan, Edwards, & Dwivedi, 2019). As the force that drives growth, information technology continues to change the way people live, work, and perceive the world.

With the onset of the COVID-19 pandemic and the increased reliance on remote work and digital technologies, the attack surface has increased for exploitation by cyber criminals, leading to a rise in cyber threats and incidents. This urgency to adapt to remote operations potentially resulted in oversights in cybersecurity measures, making organizations more vulnerable to attacks, particularly in critical infrastructure sectors (Garcia-Perez, Sallos and Tiwasing, 2023). The global pandemic set thus the stage for a substantial surge in cybercrimes, with a notable increase in cyber-dependent crimes such as hacking, malware, online fraud, phishing, and DDoS attacks, particularly during the strictest lockdown measures (Buil-Gil et al., 2021). Ethical hacking, also known as white hat hacking, encompasses the practice of using hacking skills for defensive and constructive purposes (Rathore, 2016). Ethical hackers are pivotal in identifying vulnerabilities in networks and systems, thereby allowing organizations to secure their infrastructure from potential cyber threats (David & Smiley, 2022; Rathore, 2016). They play a critical role in providing organizations with opportunities to reveal weaknesses and administer countermeasures before black hat hackers exploit vulnerabilities, thus safeguarding against unauthorized access (David & Smiley, 2022). Overall, its ongoing significance is attributed to its pivotal role in mitigating risks, protecting systems and data, and maintaining security measures in the ever-evolving landscape of cyber threats. However, recent years have witnessed a surge in cyber-attacks and data breaches, highlighting an urgent need for skilled cybersecurity professionals (Tang et al., 2017; Bowen, 2017;). Consequently, cybersecurity degrees have garnered a national priority, yet the field faces a critical shortage of adequately qualified professionals (Gross & Ho, 2021).

The lack of cyber defenders goes beyond a competent technical background since studies have shown a mismatch between education provisions and essential industrial skills, particularly among recent graduates (Chhetri, 2023). Given the urgent demand for qualified cybersecurity professionals and the evident gaps in educational provisions, it is crucial to explore certifications capable of bridging this skills gap. Institutes of higher education (HEI) stress the significance of acquiring such certifications, considering them among the many advantages that can set apart cybersecurity professionals in the marketplace. This includes vendor-neutral certifications such as the Certified Information Systems Security Professional (CISSP), regarded as the golden standard in the field, the Certified Information Systems Auditor (CISA) certificate from ISACA, valuable for IT management roles, and CompTIA Security+, an entry-level certification covering fundamental concepts and practices (Knapp et al., 2017, p.105). The second category encompasses vendor-specific certifications, notably the Cisco Certified Network Associate Security (CCNA Security) which covers essential security skills needed to navigate Cisco network devices, and the Certified Ethical Hacker (CEH), a comprehensive certification in ethical hacking (Knapp et al., 2017, p.105-107). Lastly, attention is drawn to certifications that have recently gained prominence in the market, such as the Cloud Security Professional (CSP) highlighting the importance of cloud security skills, and the Offensive Security Certified Professional (OSCP), focusing on advanced penetration testing skills for professionals (Knapp et al., 2017, p.107-108). The need to develop a novel pedagogical approach in conducting ethical hacking and penetration testing in HEI capable of bridging the skill gap required to build graduates in industry-rooted skills is therefore a growing concern. While each mentioned certificate holds intrinsic value within the market, it is important to note that they do not supplant the significance of a cybersecurity diploma or other relevant certifications in the field.

Whilst it is important to grow beyond the knowledge provided in a typical HEI and the corresponding degrees, the fundamental problem still resides in how educational institutions mostly rely on teaching methods that lean towards theoretical frameworks and compliance, which in return lack emphasis on practical technical skills and soft skills (Bowen, 2017). These limitations have prompted the integration of operation-based exercises and shedding light on hands-on skill development(Sánchez et al., 2020), a phenomenon which has shown promise in addressing the skill gaps within the pedagogy of cyber security (Taylor-Jackson et al., 2020). Existing studies that attempt to develop a hands-on approach to ethical hacking within the HEI pedagogy generally suffer from robustness and student-centered learning (Bhatia et al. 2023; Barman et al. 2023). Given that artificial intelligence has been widely deployed in areas such as intrusion detection and response systems, anomaly, and behavioral profiling, as well as intuitive malware analysis, this study posits that such can be leveraged to provide a robust learning framework. Furthermore, the demand for AI-powered tools capable of alleviating the burden of memorization has surged (Heim et al., 2023). This raises the question: Can AI serve not only as a tool for penetration testing but also to effectively train the penetration testers themselves? This is particularly pertinent for Large Language Models (LLMs). This study therefore proposes a student-centered learning process called PentHack— a tool designed to incorporate a human-AI collaborative approach into the ethical hacking lifecycle. The study by Chhetri (2023) highlights the effectiveness of personalized learning experiences in establishing a solid foundation for beginner penetration testers. Through PentHack, this study aims to harness AI technology, offering personalized learning across various skill levels within the penetration testing lifecycle. This approach aims to streamline the learning curve for HEI students in this field. To the best of the Authors' knowledge, this is the first study to explore the development of a learning platform that integrates LLMs with the learning process of hacking. Furthermore, the study conducted both usability and adoption tests for the developed platform. The remainder of the manuscript is structured as follows: section II provides a brief study on related works targeted at the ethical hacking (and penetration testing) process in HEI. A detailed breakdown of the methodology is provided in Section III while the result and analysis of the developed tool are provided in Section IV. Discussion and conclusion are provided in Section V and Section VI respectively.

The literature reveals that Large Language Models (LLMs) are playing a transformative role in cybersecurity, enhancing security information and event management (SIEM) systems (Pulyala, 2023). These AI-powered models, integrated with machine learning and natural language processing capabilities, are enabling more efficient threat detection and response mechanisms in the face of evolving cyber threats. In education, LLMs like ChatGPT are being explored for their potential to revolutionize academic practices and pedagogical experiences (Grassini, 2023). Several studies have highlighted the instrumental role of AI technologies in various educational activities, from essay grading to enhancing the learning process through automation and personalized feedback mechanisms. Moreover, the intersection of AI and academic integrity is a subject of increasing scrutiny (Gustilo et al., 2024). With the advent of algorithmically driven writing tools, educators are facing new challenges and ethical considerations in ensuring academic integrity standards while leveraging AI technologies to enhance students' learning experiences and writing proficiency. Overall, these documents underscore the significant potential of AI technologies, including LLMs, in transforming various sectors such as cybersecurity and education. However, alongside the benefits, there is a growing emphasis on addressing ethical implications, ensuring data privacy, and maintaining academic integrity standards in the deployment of these advanced technologies. By encompassing these key insights from the documents, it is evident that AI technologies, particularly LLMs, are reshaping traditional practices and methodologies in diverse spheres, leading to both opportunities and challenges that need to be carefully navigated for the realization of their full potential.

2. Related Works

Numerous pedagogical methods within cybersecurity education have come to light, aiming to optimize student learning experiences by integrating various approaches. Active Learning, exemplified by interactive activities and hands-on exercises, enhances comprehension and retention of cybersecurity concepts by encouraging students to actively connect ideas (Bowen, 2017; Gross & Ho, 2021). Problem-Based Learning (PBL), a student-centered approach, fosters critical thinking and practical application of knowledge through collaborative solving of real-world cybersecurity challenges (Shivapurkar et al., 2020). Psychological Integration integrates behavioral theories into cybersecurity education, improving problem-solving skills and enabling students to discern criminal motivations beyond technical concepts (Shivapurkar et al., 2020). Innovative pedagogical approaches, inspired by web-based learning theory, create immersive training interfaces that engage learners in simulated cyber threat scenarios, promoting theoretical understanding and practical competencies (Tang et al., 2017).. The amalgamation of these methodologies forms a comprehensive pedagogical framework in cybersecurity education, nurturing technical proficiency alongside critical thinking, adaptability, and a profound comprehension of cyber threats and human vulnerabilities. This holistic approach addresses the multifaceted nature of the field, producing well-rounded cybersecurity professionals. This perspective is supported by Bhatia et al. (2023) which asserts that ethical hacking and network security curriculum development should follow a problem-based learning approach. The study suggests mapping the phases of ethical hacking, particularly reconnaissance and enumeration, to the MITRE ATT&CK framework. Whilst the mapping to the MITRE framework can provide a good benchmark process, it failed to ensure a robust learning process for students in HEI. Similarly, the study by Barman et al. (2023) developed a framework for conducting reconnaissance and enumeration using relevant tools and their associated commands. The study further provides a baseline for effectively delivering ethical hacking courses to HEI students. However, the study failed to provide a robust baseline for problem-solving learning. Furthermore, it demonstrated that it is limited to only two stages in the hacking lifecycle.

A study by Yu et al. (2023) considers the integration of LLMs into the penetration testing process, albeit, for Red teamers. The study developed a GPTFUZZER; a tool that can automate the process of generating templates for jailbreaking any LLM towards producing *any* desired output. The study further evaluated the effectiveness of template generation of GPTFUZZER with ChatGPT, LLaMa-2, and Vicuna. Suffice it to say that the study provides a useful insight into LLM jailbreaking which may not be required for an HEI ethical hacking course. Happe and Cito (2023) assert that there are pieces of evidence to suggest that penetration testers have begun experimenting with generative AI to complete the last phase of the ethical hacking lifecycle. Based on this assertion, the study further attempts to answer the question: *"To what extent can we automate security testing with LLMs?"*. The study leveraged the knowledge base of the MITRE ATT&CK framework to align the tactics, techniques and procedures used by attackers with the proposed LLM-induced hacking process. By using AgentGPT, AutoGPT, and GPT3.5 the study experimented on two use cases: low- and high-level prompts applicable to penetration testers. The result presented in the study shows the potential relevance of the study to penetration testers. However, this still lacks the educational construct where HEI students can follow a creative learning curve which can be built on. These studies lend credence to the need for a more robust problem-solving learning mechanism suitable for all students within the learning spectrum. The methodology adopted for the development and evaluation of the proposed PentHack is provided in the next section.

3. Methodology

To develop the proposed PentHack, the operational framework presented in Figure 1 is leveraged. This framework comprises three interconnected phases. In Phase I, exhaustive research was undertaken to ensure that the tool met the foundational expectations of an educational platform. This involved a thorough examination of various aspects, including the university's cybersecurity curriculum, particularly focusing on courses geared towards educating beginner ethical hackers. Additionally, recent pedagogical methodologies supporting interactive teaching methods for students were explored. Through this research phase, the core system requirements and optional system requirements of the tool were finalized, as depicted in Figure 1, utilizing agile methodology. Furthermore, this phase includes the characterization of pedagogical principles within the design of the functional model.

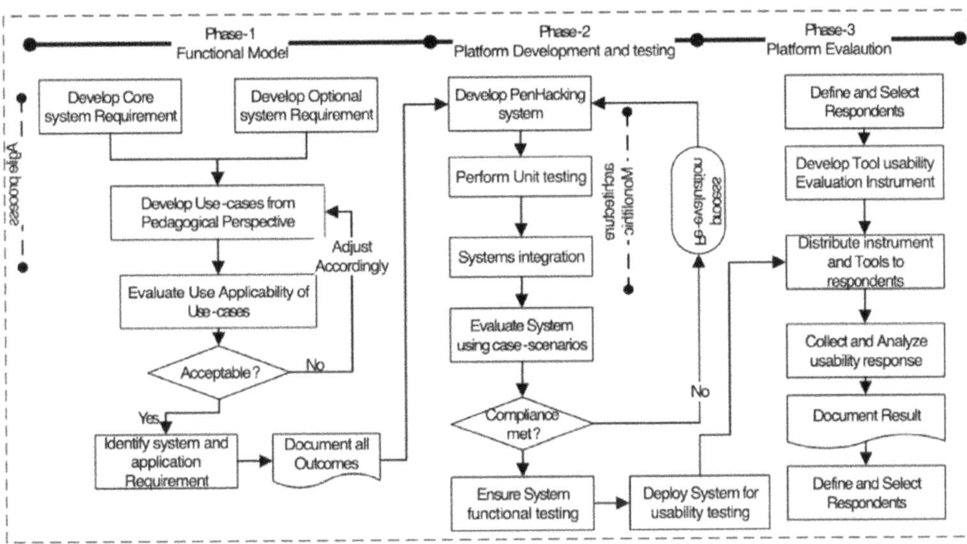

Figure 1: Operational framework of the proposed PentHack Platform

The output of the first phase is parsed as input to the second phase. During the second phase of PentHack's development, a monolithic architecture was implemented to streamline the development and testing processes. The platform was built as a single, cohesive unit, encompassing the graphical user interface (GUI) layer, logical layer, and Thesedata access layer.

To ensure the platform's quality and reliability, extensive unit testing was conducted to validate the functionality of individual components independently. Comprehensive testing measures were implemented to identify and rectify any potential bugs or errors that users might encounter during tool usage. Conducting testing concurrently with development enabled the identification of issues, such as the failure of response from the AI, failure to use and optimize prompt engineering, and several function and class overwriting. These issues were promptly addressed, ensuring the stability and reliability of the platform.

PentHack was developed using Python as the programming language. The application utilized various libraries such as Tkinter, customTkinter, datetime, reportlab.lib, and Pillow. Detailed evaluations were conducted on various AI technologies, including Google BERT, Microsoft's LLM, OpenAI's GPT-3, and GPT-4. API keys were integrated to incorporate LLM functionalities into the application. After extensive evaluation, OpenAI's GPT-4 was integrate into PentHack for its superior security, top-notch performance, and widespread adoption among developers.

In the third phase, a usability and relevance test is carried out. Three constructs in the Technology Adoption Model (Pranoto and Lumbantobing, 2021) were adapted to evaluate the platform. A synopsis of the construct and the measurement items is further provided in Table 1. The 5-point Likert scale was adopted for this study.

Perceived ease of Use (PEU) and Perceived Usefulness (PU) were used as the dependent variables, and Behavioral Intention to Use (BIU), the independent variable. Thus, the following null hypotheses are defined:

1. There is no statistically significant relationship between PEU and BIU ($H_0 1$)
2. The relationship between PU and BIU is not statistically significant ($H_0 2$).

The logic of leveraging PU is to measure the potential benefit and relevance of the developed tool. PEU on the other hand was adopted to measure the perceived level of ease of using this platform. Both PEU and PU therefore provide a user evaluation of the proposed platform. BIU is a construct which reflects the tendency of the respondents to use the proposed platform for their ethical hacking classes. The platform was put under evaluation by students enrolled in a university ethical hacking course. The students were eligible for the evaluation as they were actively engaged in studying ethical hacking and were therefore well-positioned to provide insights into the importance and effectiveness (or otherwise) of the developed PentHack platform. Following ethical clearance approval, students were recruited to participate in the study voluntarily, without any form of incentive or compensation. A total of 39 students partook in the evaluation process of the platform, with 70:30 female: male distribution. SmartPLS 4.0 was used to analyze the relationship between variables (BIU<--PU and BIU<--PEU).

Table 1: Summary of the Evaluation Instrument.

CONSTRUCT	QUESTIONS
Perceived Ease of Use (PEU)	PEU1: Overall, the tool seems to be easy to use
	PEU2: Learning to operate the application would be easy for me due to its intuitive user interface.
	PEU3: I find the application simple to use due to its user-friendly design and clear content presentation.
Behavioral Intention to Use (BIU)	BIU1: If available, I intend to use this application as it corresponds with my educational goals and needs.
	BIU2: I intend to add this tool to my list of tools for the ethical hacking course as it provides further guidance on the ethical hacking steps and phases.
	BIU3: If available, I intend to use this tool for my ethical hacking course to aid my understanding
Perceived Usefulness (PU)	PU1: This application will be useful and valuable in my ethical hacking journey.
	PU2: The application will be useful for obtaining a fundamental understanding of the ethical hacking phases.
	PU3: The application will be useful in remembering commands and how to use them.
	PU4: I believed that using the application would improve my ability to comprehend ethical hacking principles.

4. Result and Analysis

The study's findings provided vital insight into the PentHack platform's effectiveness in addressing the cybersecurity skills gap. The evaluation approach comprised usability and relevance testing, which were then completed through a questionnaire, providing numerous critical results. First, usability testing revealed that, while participants generally considered the PentHack platform intuitive and user-friendly, there were certain areas for improvement. Some users had trouble navigating specific features and accessing resources. In addition, feedback on the interface design indicated the need for clearer instructions and more streamlined procedures. These findings showed the significance of fine-tuning the user experience to improve overall usability. Table 2 shows the descriptive statistics of participant responses categorized by their satisfaction levels with the knowledge development tool. It illustrates the mean and standard deviation values for various aspects of the tool's usability and usefulness across different levels of satisfaction, ranging from very dissatisfied to very satisfied.

Table 2: Descriptive Statistics of the Response

Satisfaction Level	Mean Overall Ease of Use	Std. Dev. Overall Ease of Use	Mean Learning Ease	Std. Dev. Learning Ease	Mean User-Friendliness	Std. Dev. User-Friendliness	Mean Intention to Use	Std. Dev. Intention to Use	Mean Usefulness	Std. Dev. Usefulness	Mean Understanding	Std. Dev. Understanding
Very Dissatisfied (1)	-	-	-	-	-	-	-	-	-	-	-	-
Dissatisfied (2)	-	-	-	-	-	-	-	-	-	-	-	-
Neutral (3)	2.8	0.632	3.1	1.249	3.2	0.7	3.3	1.048	3.1	0.829	3.1	1.171
Satisfied (4)	3.9	0.316	3.9	0.7	4.0	0.282	4.0	0.0	4.0	0.447	3.8	0.421
Very Satisfied (5)	4.4	0.875	4.5	0.5	4.4	0.875	4.4	0.875	4.6	0.548	4.3	0.9

Second, the significance of the assessment demonstrated the PentHack platform's applicability to educational goals and industry expectations. The findings revealed that the platform effectively addressed key themes and provided valuable information about penetration testing methodologies. However, some participants expressed concerns about the level of coverage for certain topics and suggested additional resources or modules to augment learning. This underscores the need to ensure that the platform effectively addresses the diverse needs of cybersecurity learners.

Overall, while the PentHack platform shows potential as a tool for bridging skill gaps in cybersecurity education, more refinement is required to enhance its effectiveness. The findings of usability and relevance testing gave useful feedback for iterative changes, which will guide future development efforts.

The result of the structural analysis used for testing the hypothesis is presented in Table 3. Using a bootstrap of 5000 samples, the reliability, average variance explained (AVE), and composite reliability (CR) of the measurement model satisfied the standard thumb rule for a measurement model. Furthermore, the loading (outer loading) for all measurement items was greater than the standardized 0.5 regression weight as highlighted in Figure 1.

Table 3: Analysis of the Measurement model

Construct	Cronbach's alpha	AVE	CR
Perceived Ease of Use (PEU)	0.943	0.897	0.947
Behavioral Intention to Use (BIU)	0.930	0.877	0.94
Perceived Usefulness (PU)	0.967	0.910	0.968

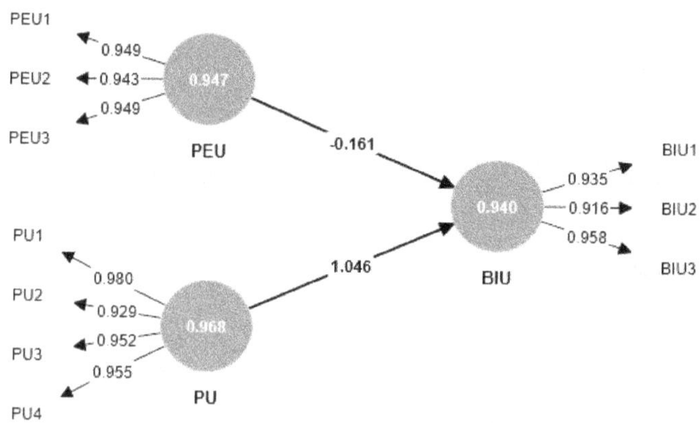

Figure 2: Measurment model of the evaluation process

Given the result of the measurement model, the structural model (further shown in Figure 2) was used to test the stated hypothesis of the study. The relationship between BIU<-- PU generated a statistically significant relationship at *p*-value <0.05. This implies that the null hypothesis, $H_{0}2$, can be rejected in favor of the alternate hypothesis. However, the relationship between BIU<--PEU generated a statistically insignificant result with a *p*-value >0.05, as shown in Figure 1. Thus, the null hypothesis, $H_{0}1$, is accepted.

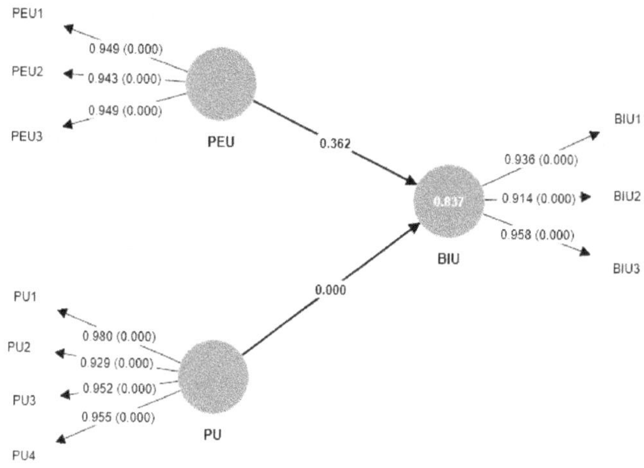

Figure 3: Structural model showing the *P*-value of the relationships.

By accepting the null hypothesis, $H_{0}1$, the model result suggests that the respondents opine that the perceived overall presentation and ergonomics of the developed platform would likely not induce their intention to use the platform for their ethical hacking lessons. This position aligns with the overall descriptive analysis. Also, it supports the notion that the developed platform is a preliminary prototype which would be advanced further. Conversely, by rejecting the null hypothesis, $H_{0}2$, in favor of the alternate hypothesis, the model suggests that the respondents strongly opine that the developed platform is conceptually relevant and useful for ethical hacking lessons. This perception would in turn induce the tendency to use the platform for ethical hacking classes. Given that the platform is infused with a pedagogical perspective, the result of the model further highlights the agreement of the respondents to the potential of the platform.

5. Discussion

The PentHack platform represents a significant effort to address these gaps by employing AI technology to create personalized learning experiences. However, assessing the platform's usability and relevance reveals room for development, particularly in terms of user-friendliness and alignment with educational aims. Despite these limitations, the research contributes significantly to the industry by suggesting a viable solution to the skills gap mentioned.

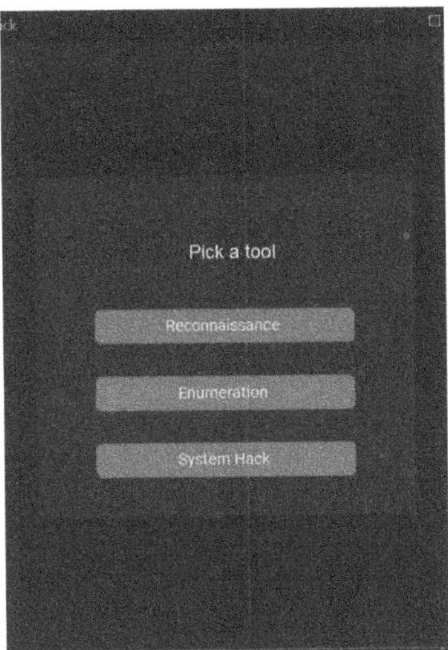

Figure 4.1: First window after user login

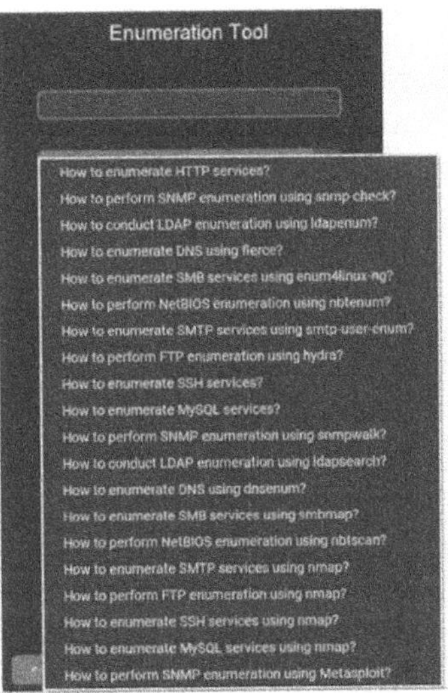

Figure 4.2: built-in prompts for user

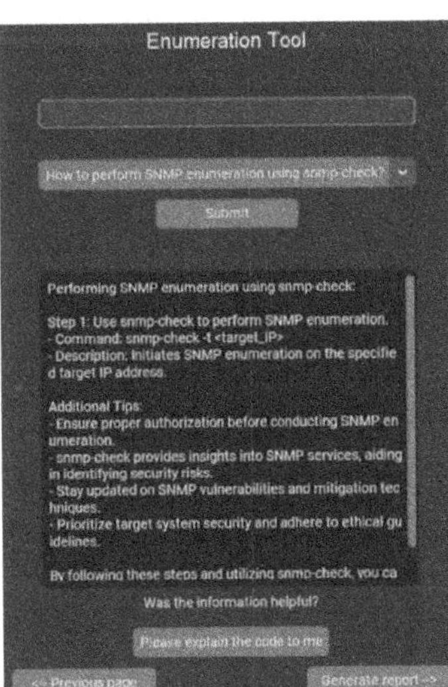

Figure 4.3: displayed built-in responses

Moving forward, more research is needed to increase the PentHack platform's effectiveness and scalability while simultaneously tackling rising cyber threats. The study introduces an academic-focused penetration testing learning platform, integrating large language models (LLMs) to offer user-friendly ethical hacking tools. Highlighting the pressing need for innovative pedagogical approaches within CS education. Similarly to Chhetri's study on pedagogical approaches in teaching penetration testing to beginner pen-testers, shedding light on the importance of a customized, project-based learning experience (Chhetri, 2023), the study focused on offering a full course in penetration testing for a wider sample of demographics, whereas our goal is to elevate the learning experience of students by offering a more customized approach for students, having each student make use of the platform in their preferred way.

It goes to show how the need for innovative pedagogical approaches in cybersecurity education is crucial to bridging the skills gap and adapting to emerging cyber threats. Moreover, it is crucial to acknowledge the limitations encountered during the evaluation process, the survey conducted to assess the PentHack platform's effectiveness in bridging the cybersecurity skills gap provided valuable insights, explicitly regarding its usability and alignment with educational goals. Overall, respondents expressed positive experiences with the platform's usability with the identified areas for improvement. Despite the insightful feedback received from survey respondents regarding PentHack usability and relevance, the findings were interpreted with caution due to the sample size limitation. With the limited number of participants, the scope of the survey findings may be constrained, as the insights gathered represent a specific subset of the population. The small sample size limits the ability to extend the findings to a broader audience or make definitive claims about the platform's overall effectiveness in addressing cybersecurity skills gaps. Moving forward, it is recommended to consider expanding the sample size in future surveys or usability testing to capture a broader range of perspectives and experiences, as it can be more representative and offer deeper insights into the platform's efficacy in educational settings. Additionally, leveraging a larger sample size can enhance the statistical validity of the survey results and support more conclusive recommendations for refining the PentHack platform and other AI-integrated tools in cybersecurity education.

6. Conclusion

This paper introduced and detailed the evolution and significance of the internet, emphasizing its revolutionary role in society and current technological advancements. The presented work created a variety of significant insights into the chosen topic in cyber security learning, as well as the development of unique pedagogical approaches. Furthermore, it correctly contextualizes the necessity of cybersecurity in today's digital landscape, particularly in light of COVID-19's impact on digital reliance. Furthermore, the examination of relevant works provides a comprehensive overview of existing material, indicating gaps in current instructional approaches and possibilities for improvement. To summarize, the outcome of this study highlights the necessity of new pedagogical techniques in meeting the changing needs of education in cybersecurity. The PentHack platform could therefore be a significant advancement in offering students immersive, hands-on learning experiences in the field of ethical hacking. With that, the platform has the potential to revolutionize cybersecurity education by leveraging AI technology and individualized learning approaches, empowering students to address increasingly complex problems. As an ongoing work, the proposed platform will be further enhanced with several user-input processes. In addition, the platform will integrate immersive learning experiences through virtual and augmented reality which could help develop an action-consequence paradigm in users.

References

Bhatia, S., Elhadad, S., Deshmukh, A., Yellela, M.K. and Vangala, O.S.R., 2022, March. Hack The Problem: A Problem-Based Learning Approach for Ethical Hacking and Network Defense Curriculum. In Proceedings of the 54th ACM Technical Symposium on Computer Science Education V. 2 (pp. 1346-1346).

Barman, F., Alkaabi, N., Almenhali, H., Alshedi, M., & Ikuesan, R. (2023). A Methodical Framework for Conducting Reconnaissance and Enumeration in the Ethical Hacking Lifecycle. Retrieved from https://papers.academic-conferences.org/index.php/eccws/article/download/1438/1148

Bowen, L. M. (2017). The Limits of Hacking Composition Pedagogy. Computers and Composition, 43, 1-14.

Buil-Gil, D., et al. (2021). Cybercrime and shifts in opportunities during COVID-19: a preliminary analysis in the UK. European Societies, 23(sup1), S47–S59. https://doi.org/10.1080/14616696.2020.1804973

Castells, M. (2019). The Impact of the Internet on Society: A Global Perspective. OpenMind. Retrieved from https://www.bbvaopenmind.com/en/articles/the-impact-of-the-internet-on-society-a-global-perspective/

Chhetri, C. (2023). "It was a one of a kind experience:" Student Experiences and Pedagogical Design of a Project-based Hands-on Cybersecurity Pen-testing Course. In Proceedings of the 24th Annual Conference on Information Technology Education (pp. 22-27).

David, E., & Smiley, G. (2022). An Ethical Framework for Cybersecurity Professionals: A Grounded Theory Study. ProQuest Dissertations and Theses. Retrieved from https://www.proquest.com/dissertations-theses/ethical-framework-cybersecurity-professionals/docview/2746081552/se-2?accountid=15192

De Paoli, S., & Johnstone, J. (2023). A qualitative study of penetration testers and what they can tell us about information security in organisations. Information Technology & People [Preprint]. https://doi.org/10.1108/ITP-11-2021-0864

Duan, Y., Edwards, J. S., & Dwivedi, Y. K. (2019). Artificial Intelligence for Decision Making in the Era of Big Data – evolution, Challenges and Research Agenda. International Journal of Information Management, 48, 63–71.

Garcia-Perez, A., Sallos, M. P., & Tiwasing, P. (2023). Dimensions of cybersecurity performance and crisis response in critical infrastructure organizations: an intellectual capital perspective. Journal of Intellectual Capital, 24(2), 465–486. https://doi.org/10.1108/JIC-06-2021-0166

Graham, M., & Dutton, W. H. (2019). Society and the Internet: How Networks of Information and Communication are Changing Our Lives. Oxford University Press. Retrieved from https://books.google.ae/books?hl=en&lr=&id=vdShDwAAQBAJ&oi=fnd&pg=PP1&dq=social+and+cultural+impacts+of+the+Internet&ots=zIAUf9Omi0&sig=WOGxG_z8FTcsmpvOZI4BlaewHvg&redir_esc=y#v=onepage&q&f=false

Grassini, S. (2023). Shaping the Future of Education: Exploring the Potential and Consequences of AI and ChatGPT in Educational Settings. In Education Sciences (Vol. 13, Issue 7). Multidisciplinary Digital Publishing Institute (MDPI). https://doi.org/10.3390/educsci13070692

Gross, M., & Ho, S. M. (2021). Collective learning for developing cyber defense consciousness: an activity system analysis. Journal of Information Systems Education, 32(1), 65-76.

Gustilo, L., Ong, E., & Lapinid, M. R. (2024). Algorithmically-driven writing and academic integrity: exploring educators' practices, perceptions, and policies in AI era. International Journal for Educational Integrity, 20(1), 3. https://doi.org/10.1007/s40979-024-00153-8

Happe, A. and Cito, J., 2023, November. Understanding Hackers' Work: An Empirical Study of Offensive Security Practitioners. In Proceedings of the 31st ACM Joint European Software Engineering Conference and Symposium on the Foundations of Software Engineering (pp. 1669-1680).

Heim, M.P., Starckjohann, N. and Torgersen, M., 2023. The Convergence of AI and Cybersecurity: An Examination of ChatGPT's Role in Penetration Testing and its Ethical and Legal Implications (Bachelor's thesis, NTNU).

Kaur, R., Gabrijelčič, D., & Klobučar, T. (2023). Artificial intelligence for cybersecurity: Literature review and future research directions. Information Fusion, 97, 101804. https://doi.org/10.1016/J.INFFUS.2023.101804

Knapp, K. J., Maurer, C., & Plachkinova, M. (2017). Maintaining a cybersecurity curriculum: Professional certifications as valuable guidance. Journal of Information Systems Education, 28(2), 101.

Koutsikouri, D., Lindgren, R., Henfridsson, O., & Rudmark, D. (2018). Extending Digital Infrastructures: A Typology of Growth Tactics. Journal of the Association for Information Systems.

Navarria, G. (2016). How the Internet was born: from the ARPANET to the Internet.

Pranoto, A. H. and Lumbantobing, P. (2021) 'The Acceptance Technology Model for Adoption of Social Media Marketing in Jabodetabek', *The Winners*, 22(1), pp. 75–88.

Pulyala, S.R. 2023, "The Future of SIEM in a Machine Learning-Driven Cybersecurity Landscape", Turkish Journal of Computer and Mathematics Education, vol. 14, no. 3, pp. 1309-1314.

Sánchez, J., Mallorquí, A., Briones, A., Zaballos, A. and Corral, G. (2020). An integral pedagogical strategy for teaching and learning IoT cybersecurity. Sensors, 20(14), p.3970.

Shivapurkar, M., Bhatia, S. and Ahmed, I., 2020, July. Problem-based learning for cybersecurity education. In Journal of The Colloquium for Information Systems Security Education (Vol. 7, No. 1, pp. 6-6).

Tang, D., Pham, C., Chinen, K.I. and Beuran, R. (2017). Interactive cybersecurity defense training inspired by web-based learning theory. In 2017 IEEE 9th International Conference on Engineering Education (ICEED) (pp. 90-95). IEEE.

Taylor-Jackson, J., McAlaney, J., Foster, J.L., Bello, A., Maurushat, A. and Dale, J. (2020). Incorporating psychology into cyber security education: a pedagogical approach. In Financial Cryptography and Data Security: FC 2020 International Workshops, AsiaUSEC, CoDeFi, VOTING, and WTSC, Kota Kinabalu, Malaysia, February 14, 2020, Revised Selected Papers 24 (pp. 207-217). Springer International Publishing.

Yu, J., Lin, X. and Xing, X., 2023. Gptfuzzer: Red teaming large language models with auto-generated jailbreak prompts. *arXiv preprint arXiv:2309.10253*.§

The Optimal Organisational Structure for Cyber Operations based on Exercise Lessons

Marko Arik, Adrian Nicholas Venables and Rain Ottis

Department of Software Science, Tallinn University of Technology Tallinn, Estonia.

marko.arik@taltech.ee
adrian.venables@taltech.ee
rain.ottis@taltech.ee

Abstract: The NATO Cooperative Cyber Defence Centre (CCDCOE) of Excellence hosts annual Locked Shields (LS) and Crossed Swords (CS) cyber exercises to help NATO nations develop, train, and test their cyber capabilities. These exercises have successfully experimented with cyber capabilities and human organisational structures. However, there are still opportunities to optimise cyber exercise structures. This article employs a use case study based on these exercises to compare structures used by NATO nations in cyber exercises and cyber operations. This identified an optimal structure for operational-level cyber defence and offence exercises and proposed methods for their planning, development, and execution.

Keywords: Cyber Operations Exercises, Cyber Command organisational structure, Blue Team organisational structure, Red Team organisational Structure.

1. Introduction

Cyberspace threat actors can exploit advanced nations' reliance on the information environment, necessitating the establishment, training, and preparation of a military force to counter adversary activities. However, countries developing cyber defence capabilities are often reluctant to disclose specific information about them. Cyber exercises can contribute to the e training and preparation of cyberspace forces and the development of their operational-level organisational structures. The NATO Cooperative Cyber Defence Centre of Excellence (CCDCOE) organises two well-known annual cyber exercises, Locked Shields[1] and Crossed Swords[2], to assist nations in developing, training, and testing their cyber capabilities. This research examines the cyber capabilities and structures by collecting and interpreting new data to analyse the Operational and Tactical levels of Command. This addresses the challenge of obtaining reliable data from non-classified exercises to reveal cyber organisations' optimum Command structures.

2. Methods

This article employs a use case study based on the 2022 Locked Shields and Crossed Swords cyber exercises organised by the CCDCOE. It provides an overview of NATO Cyber Operations and exercise organisational structures. The literature review examined the Locked Shields exercise from "after-action" reports used for research purposes. Interviews with experts from Estonian Defence Forces Cyber Command, CCDCOE, Locked Shields 2022 Red Team, and NATO Cyberspace Operations Centre supplement the review.

3. Literature Review

Three sources were used for data in this research. As the leading global cyber power, the US offers insight into large organisations' structures (Voo et. al., 2022, p. 11). The smaller Estonian Cyber Command and its organisational structures were also reviewed as the exercises were organised by the CCDCOE based in Tallinn, and data on its composition was available. Finally, the publicly available NATO Cyber Operations (CO) command organisational structures are reviewed (Pederson et al., 2022), (Dalmijn et al., 2020), (Blumbergs, 2019), (Kohler, 2020).

3.1 Cyber Operation Organisational Structures

In the Routledge Handbook of International Cybersecurity, Piret Pernik states the role of a cyber command as follows:

---

[1] https://ccdcoe.org/exercises/locked-shields/

[2] https://ccdcoe.org/exercises/crossed-swords/

"At a minimum, a cyber command should be composed of staff sections (capabilities) for strategic and policy analyses and planning (including legal and technological development), intelligence, situational awareness, operational planning, and conduct of cyber operations. A military centre of excellence for research and competence and a cyber range should support the cyber command. Finally, the command should have a degree of authority for the acquisition and personnel policies (including reserve forces and conscription if applicable), as well as education, training, and exercises" (Pernik, 2020). In addition, the organisation's success depends on its members' training and experience to succeed (Pomerleau, 2022)

An article by Air Land Sea Space Application Center (Pederson et al., 2022) discusses cyber operations structures. The current USCYBERCOM cyberspace operations structure is a temporary fix, a 'band-aid' that patches the infrastructure using the least expensive materials. For the optimal solution, Pedersen proposed a separate standing organisational structure as the optimal solution for U.S. military forces and the protection of DOD cyberspace from adversaries (Ibid). The subsequent structures include more details concerning the organisations' roles and departments or teams.

2020, the CCDCOE published 'The Cyber Commanders` Handbook' (Dalmijn et al., 2020). This stated, "A one-size-fits-all Cyber Command structure is impossible to define." Instead, the handbook proposed a reference organisational structure, which includes the core activities of cyber operations. The Cyber Commanders' Handbook outlines an organisational structure with four levels: Commander, Advisors, Staff, and Subcommand. Specialised branches facilitate military cyber operations, including C2 for situational awareness, C3 for cyber defence, C5 for planning, and C6 for communications. Legad provides legal guidance on national and international laws in cyber operations.

A different cyber operations structure focused on Specialized Cyber Red Team Responsive Computer Network Operations was proposed by Blumbergs (Blumbergs, 2019). Dr. Blumberg's concept of Red Team (RT) can be expanded to offensive cyber operations in general. It is not restricted to narrow "red teaming" or opposing force framework but is a product of the CCDCOE exercise culture where Blue Teams are on the defence, while the Red Teams are on the offensive role. This was done in a very abstract version of the chain of command. This described the chain of command based on the specific activity focus area, shown in white in Figure 1.

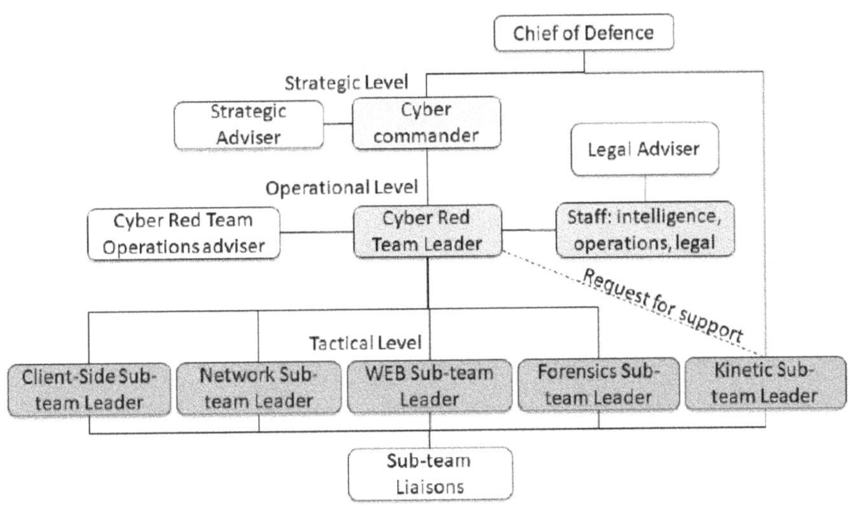

Figure 1: Exercise Crossed Swords 2019 Cyber Red Team chain-of-command (Blumbergs, 2019).

The 2019 Crossed Swords exercise adapted this structure to introduce a chain-of-command model with grey rectangles representing the Cyber Red Team at political, strategic, and tactical levels. Chain-of-command represents a hierarchy of authority in which each position is accountable to the one directly superior. This highlighted linkages to exercise control functions and sub-teams are based on expertise in targeted technologies.

An alternative model is utilised in Estonia's Defence Forces Command organisational structure by Kohler (Kohler, 2020). This offers an example of how the organisational structure of the Cyber Command can be located inside the broader Armed Force's organisation.

The Cyber Commanders' handbooks provide a helpful reference organisational structure for those nations seeking to establish an initial capability. In addition, Dr Blumberg provides a basis for developing Cyber Red

Teaming structures for exercises. These structures for peacetime cyber operations should be independent of other military Services and supported by research and cyber range capabilities.

3.2 Selected Cyber Exercises Organisational Structures Review

The Locked Shields 2022 Blue Teams' "after-action" reports reveal their organizational structures, with 14 out of 23 reports providing an overview. Multi-nation structures were excluded because they are often operation/case-specific and thus temporary. This research resulted in reviewing nine national team structures, including the related functional components such as the departments or teams within the organisation. An analysis of these structures focused on identifying commonalities and differences. Figure 2 illustrates the organisational structure of each team. The horizontal axis represents the team number, and the vertical axis represents the elements in the organisation. The minimum number was eight elements, the maximum was 23, and the average team consisted of 14 elements. The elements of the structures represent the roles and departments or teams within the organisation.

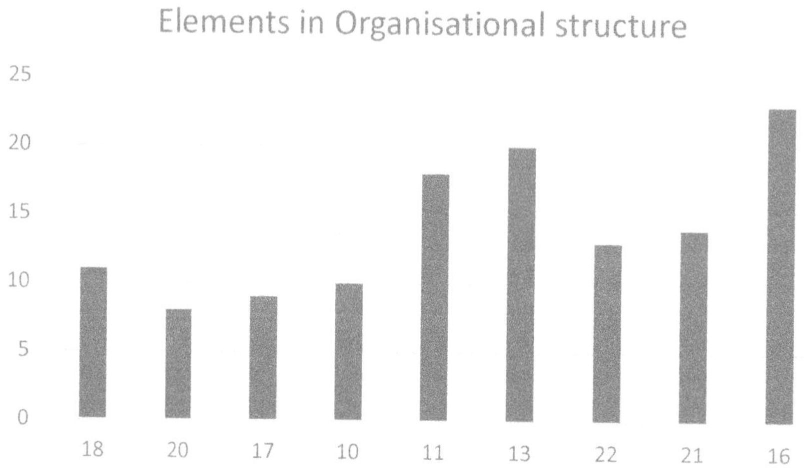

Figure 2: Exercise Locked Shields 22 selected Team Elements in Organisational Structure.

Figure 3 illustrates the number of personnel in each team. The average was 80 persons per team, with the smallest number being 50 and the largest comprising 102 people. The horizontal axis represents the team number against the number of personnel in each team.

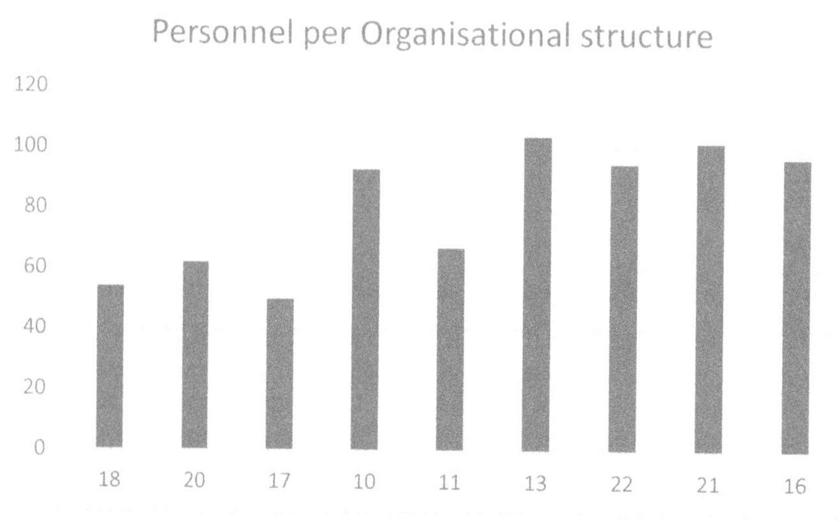

Figure 3: Exercise Locked Shields 22 selected Team Personnel per Organisational structure.

Error! Reference source not found. indicates the proportion of each team with earlier experience in a similar exercise.

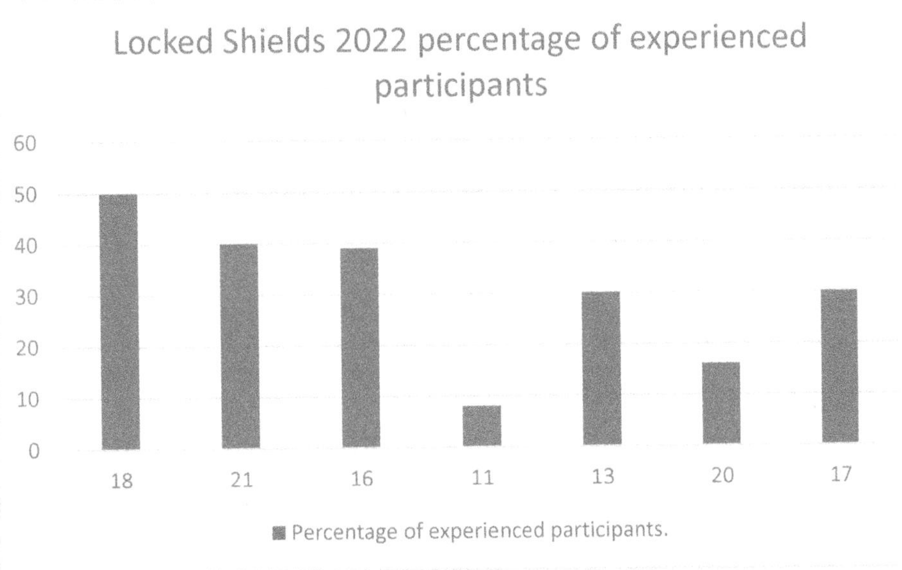

Figure 4: Locked Shields 2022 percentage of experienced participants.

The following section highlights the key attributes of a sample of a team's organisational structure.

The organisational structure of team Number 18 is shown in Figure 5. It should be noted that this team was the winner of the exercise. The winning score was calculated by CCDCOE's exercise evaluation team and is based on a complex scoring algorithm, which includes factors such as cyber-attacks successfully defended, availability of defended assets, forensics and legal.

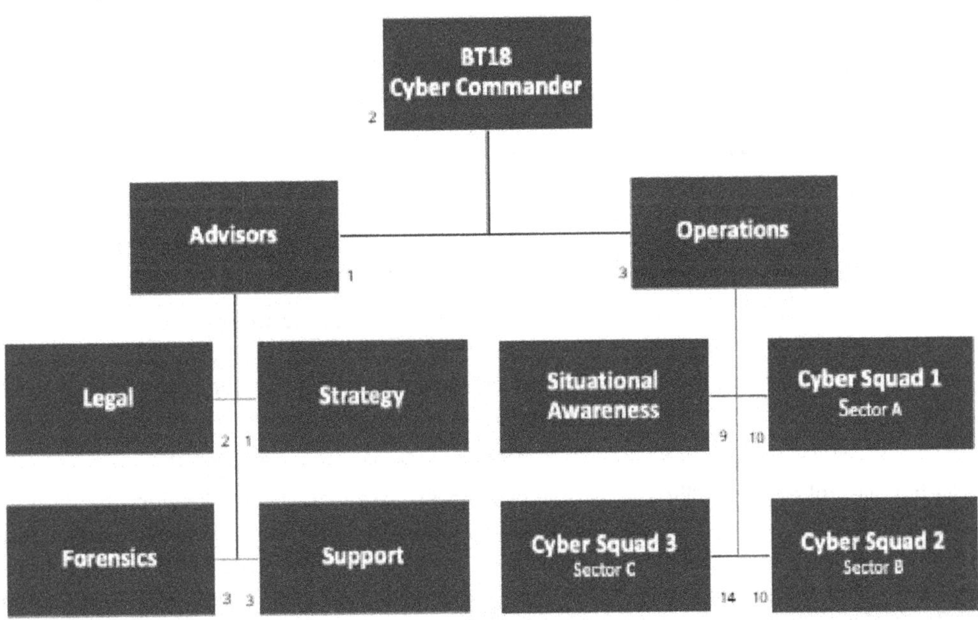

Figure 5: Exercise Locked Shields 2022 Blue Team 18 organisational structure.

Team number 20 had an operational framework and objectives based on various software applications. A little over a quarter of the team had participated in previous similar exercises. Based on the exercise scoring system, the team's results were in the last third.

Team number 17 had team objectives in place, and their strategy and tactics were derived from their national Standard Operational Procedures (SOP). Many tools were used, both in-house and externally provided. The team was placed close to last based on the exercise scoring system.

Team number 10 utilised a capability-based approach, focusing on results unrelated to team size. Capability-based planning is an approach that ensures that changes in an organisation are aligned with the overarching strategic vision. Their unique organisational structure includes a Task Group, Tactical Operations Commanders, and a Joint Cyber element. The team's results were in the bottom third.

Team number 11, organisational structures, used elements from different domestic organisations. These elements originated from the nation's military, governmental and academic sectors. Based on the exercise scoring system, the results of this team were slightly below average.

Team number 13 comprised 104 participants from 25 organisations with a complex organisational structure. Based on the exercise scoring system, the team's results were in the last third. However, they planned to maintain this structure for subsequent exercises, with only a proposed increase in information-sharing and reporting aspects.

Team 22 combined military and civilian personnel with six sub-elements and was placed in the top five.

Team 21 comprised 102 participants from 25 organisations, including private companies, energy, finance, national police, military, and telecoms. Despite providing their team objectives, the strategy and tools used were withheld from the report. This team was placed in the top ten.

Team number 16 had 97 participants from private and governmental sectors, including the military, public agencies, and academia. A distinctive feature of this team was the inclusion of a Finance element, and they were also placed in the top ten.

The results of the "after-action" reports are summarised in Table 1, and their similarities are highlighted.

Table 1: Exercise Locked Shields 2022 AAR summary.

Strategy in place	Tactics in place	Goal set	Tools	Previous LS experience	Military leader	Forensics el. in structure	Legal el. in structure
66%	44.00%	88.00%	88.00%	75%	77%	55%	88%

4. Results of the Interviews

While preparing for the Crossed Swords exercise, an interview was held with the cyber headquarters' chief of staff (COS) (CHQ). The CHQ was the only operational-level headquarters involved in the exercise. The interview was focused on the organisational command structure for the exercise.

The command element organisational structure is shown in **Error! Reference source not found.**6 and was based on the previous year's exercise. Based on the exercise feedback, mentors were added for the 2022 exercise organisational structure. The exercise feedback was received through the questionnaire that the article's author conducted in December 2021. These were utilised to share knowledge and pass the experience to the new cyber operators (Gaston, 2022).

In 2022, CHQ initially utilised the Military Decision-Making Process (MDMP) to develop Standard Operating Procedures. However, the lead author of this paper proposed an alternative approach called Intelligence Preparation of the Cyber Environment (IPCE) (Lemay et al., 2014) to complement the MDMP process. The military decision-making process (MDMP) is an iterative planning methodology. However, the IPSE complements it with a detailed intelligence planning process to address the limitations of cyber operations planning.

The CHQ aimed to create an operational plan for sub-units, practice MDMP, and improve procedures. They focused on planning tasks, aligning tasks with relevant kinetic military units, and considering interactions between the Air Force, Navy, and cyber units. The Commander had complete command of the tactical units, divided into Defensive (DCO) and Offensive (OCO) teams. Live exercise units are marked in **Error! Reference source not found.** 6 with dotted lines.

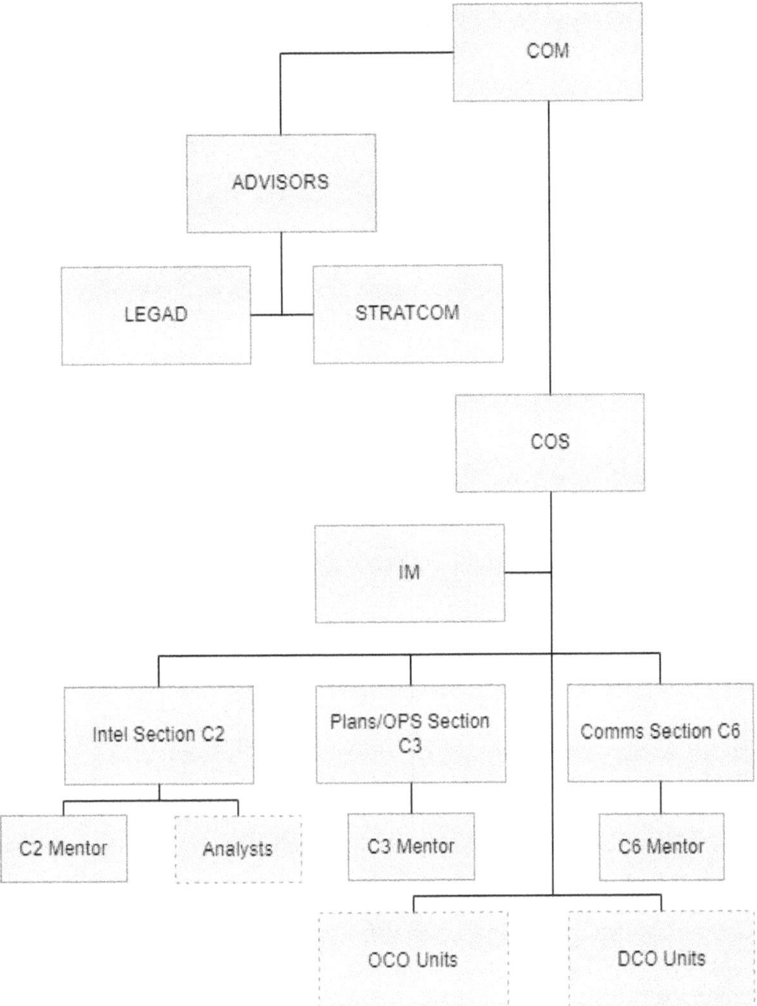

Figure 6: Estonian Defence Forces Cyber Exercises 2022 CHQ organisational structure.

The challenge in creating a cyber exercise command structure is appointing suitably qualified and experienced staff to critical positions. These include technical operators and intelligence and operations personnel to ensure a clear and comprehensible structure for military entities. The exact number of C2 and C3 positions should be proportional to the intensity of the exercise. The most critical roles from the CHQ planning perspective are C2, C3, COS, and Legad.

4.1 LS 2022 Case Study

In April 2022, the CCDCOE held the international cyber defence exercise, LS 2022, which involved 2000 participants from 32 nations (Papp, 2022). At the beginning of the exercise, the Red Team leader was interviewed to determine the prerequisites for conducting Red Teaming.

Successful Red Teaming exercises in tactical units require a two-day workshop, rigorous screening, and subjective assessment. Emphasising the importance of harmonised teams, the Red Team leader assembles sub-teams and identifies non-harmonized teams as a known weakness leading to mission failure. Novel aspects include recognising the significance of understanding Blue Team's motivations, the ability to develop custom tools, and adaptability to exercise the infrastructure's tempo. These prerequisites ensure a robust foundation for effective Red Teaming operations, encompassing technical readiness, strategic understanding, tool development proficiency, and flexibility in response to exercise dynamics.

The second interview with the Red Team leader took place in September 2022. The interview was about preparing an organisational command structure for Locked Shields. The interview aimed to illustrate and specify the details of the Read Team organisational command structure.

The Red Team's management methodology is based on twelve years of experience in cyber exercises. This allows the Red Team leader to plan and control activities without a detailed order, utilising good memory, common sense, and realism. The Red team composition is shown in *Figure* 7.

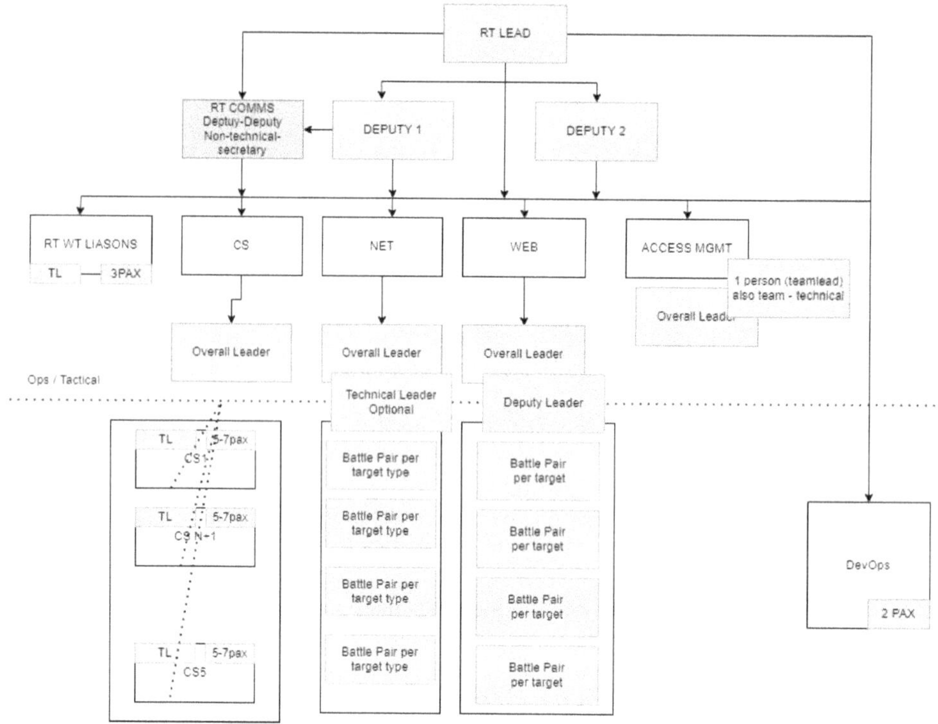

Figure 7: Exercise Locked Shields 2022 Red Team organisational structure.

The Red Team structure during the Locked Shields exercise consists of the following sub-teams: network (NET), client-side (CS), web application (WEB), and access management team. The NET team handles network attacks, the CS team prepares and executes client-side attacks, and the WEB team handles web application attacks.

The Red Team leader and their two deputies managed the major DevOps and COMMS teams. These created technical tools for the Red Team and managed information and human resources. The CS team had five sub-teams led by a Team leader, with five to seven subordinates, compared to NET and WEB teams, which were divided into battle pairs per target type.

The Red Team leader created a scalable structure depending on the size of the exercise, with the operational level handling mission planning and the tactical level engaging targets. The technical team leads with field experience supporting operational planning, while other participants support the command element. Sub-teams are involved with CS, NET, and WEB mission development to execute decisions during planning.

A further interview was conducted with a former military officer who has experience planning cyber operations. The interview highlighted the differences between real-life and exercise structures and was conducted before the CS 2022 execution period in November 2022.

The interview suggested that a headquarters' organisation is determined by exercise objectives and the Commander's experience or can be created through dialogue between higher command and tactical units. It was highlighted that a rule of thumb in military structures is that a commander should have at most seven subordinates to ensure the effectiveness of command and control (C2) activities. The meaning of command is the authority delegated to someone/somebody to give orders and directions, and control – is the ability to influence the execution of the orders mentioned above by allocating or withholding resources needed. This applies to cyber organisations as well as conventional military structures.

4.1.1 Locked Shields

LS exercises follow procedures to maintain the technical integrity of the network, which can prevent operational testing due to planning constraints. However, real-life operations have no restrictions, with politicians deciding priorities.

Blue Teams are often pre-formed with internal C2 structures and pre-agreed procedures created for mutual understanding and interoperability. However, this setup has limitations, requiring minimal modifications and preventing operational-level involvement.

4.1.2 *Crossed Swords*

In contrast to LS, most of the CS training audience (TA) is brought together as individuals only for the exercise execution without prior collaboration training. The structures formed for the exercise cannot go through team dynamics such as forming, storming, norming, and performing. This describes the path teams follow to high performance (Tuckman, 1965).

The CS exercise enables cyber headquarters personnel to simulate real-world scenarios, training in a realistic and dynamic environment. In contrast, the LS exercise maintains fixed rules, limiting its focus to technical aspects and revealing operational gaps due to shorter planning times. Participants need help integrating technical, operational, and strategic layers, particularly in the operational domain, where resources may need to be increased. Preparing competent cyberspace officers, establishing specific goals, and considering Joint Multinational Training Center (JMRC, 2022) courses are recommended to address this. Drawing inspiration from a similar training approach at the Joint Multinational Training Center in Germany, incorporating full-time military unit engagements against opposing forces could be a valuable future enhancement for CS exercises.

The CS Cyber Command element headquarters (CHQ) for the observed exercise was established Ad hoc. It was compiled from individual experts rather than involving an established vertical organisational structure. This provided the opportunity for CHQ to utilise previously developed and tested SOPs. The exercise provides an opportunity to test and re-assess the SOP and implement improvements based on the experience gained. In 2022, CHQ planned to develop and test its SOP. An iterative planning methodology known as the military decision-making process (MDMP) was used to comprehend the situation and mission, devise an action plan, and create an operating plan or order. The MDMP is designed against a predictable enemy who follows a doctrinal approach.

Based on the US Marine Corps Cyberspace Training and Readiness Manual, the recommendation is to create a Mission Essential Task List (METL) to address operational issues (NAVMC, 2018). The METL aids in defining organisational structures, tools, and equipment for planning, developing, and executing cyber operations. An example of Mission Essential Task List Relations in the Crossed Swords Exercises is provided in Figure 8.

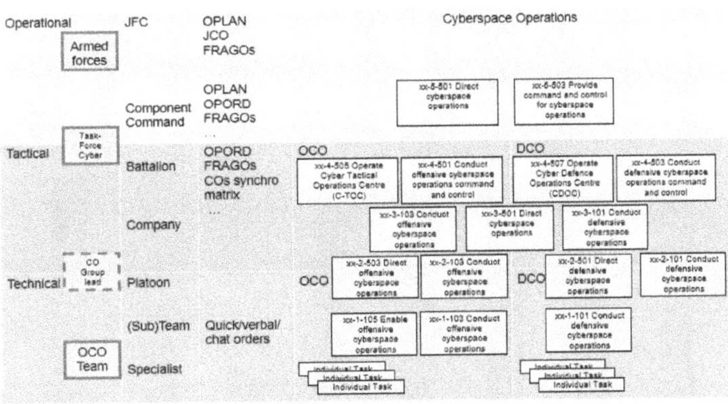

Figure 8: Example Mission Essential Task List Relations in the Crossed Swords Exercises.

A concluding interview transpired with a Plans Staff Officer within the NATO Cyberspace Operations Centre (CYOC). It was asserted that the exercise's command and control (C2) framework ought to be meticulously delineated, encompassing due consideration for the headquarters' inherent processes and procedures. The structural configuration should be tailored to align with the distinct objectives of the training audience, contingent upon their hierarchical positioning within the organisational framework.

Regarding the differences between cyberattack and -defence organisational structures, NATO's official policy is defined as "NATO is a defensive alliance with no plans to develop its offensive cyber capabilities. In cyberspace, as in all other domains, NATO acts in line with its defensive mandate and international law" (Ackerman, 2019). Therefore, it can be concluded that NATO has not developed its own OCO capabilities. Instead, it relies on its Member States. The Sovereign Cyber Effects Provided Voluntarily by Allies (SCPEVA) mechanism requests offensive cyber effects on a target (Goździewicz, 2019).

An exercise organisational structure requires a clear understanding of roles, responsibilities, and authority, addressing all functional areas without overlapping responsibilities. Integrating cyberspace into all HQ functions is the best practice. Different exercises should focus on training technical, operational, strategic, and political participants. A diverse range of stakeholders is crucial for success. Additionally, innovative aspects of the layered exercise design are proposed. Recommending distinct exercises for technical, operational, strategic, and political level participants to address their specific training requirements.

4.2 Findings from the Interviews

The main challenge in building a cyber exercise command structure is staffing the required positions, selecting people with the appropriate cyberspace competencies, and having well-instructed sub-team leaders. A goal-oriented structure with seven to eight subordinates is essential, with technical leads providing opinions on operational planning. Cyber operations exercises should involve strategic and operational planning, including cyberspace experts and trusted agents. Addressing the operational level planning resource gap is crucial, with a proposed Joint Multinational Training Center as a potential solution. To excel, create a cyberspace-specific framework for planning and execution, set training objectives, and effectively manage time. The uniqueness of a cyber exercise command structure lies in its specialised staffing, technical focus, goal-oriented approach, inclusion of cyberspace experts, international collaboration, cyberspace-specific framework, and emphasis on addressing operational challenges specific to the cyber domain. A Mission Essential Task List (METL) is crucial for organisational structures, setting mission-critical tasks with necessary tools and equipment. This study proposes Intelligence Preparation of the Cyber Environment (IPCE) as a supplement to the iterative MDMP, providing a detailed intelligence planning process to enhance cyber operations planning.

5. Results

An analysis of the organisational structures of the Blue Teams participating in LS enables structural elements to be correlated with the place achieved in the exercise. Figure 9 shows that in the top three teams (teams nr 18, 22, and 21), the number of elements in their organisational structure ranges from eleven to fourteen. Although this might suggest that the most optimal number of organisational elements is in this range, further research is required to analyse each team's skill set. No clear indication of an optimal team size based upon this limited sample size is recognised, and these results represent only Exercise Locked Shields 2022.

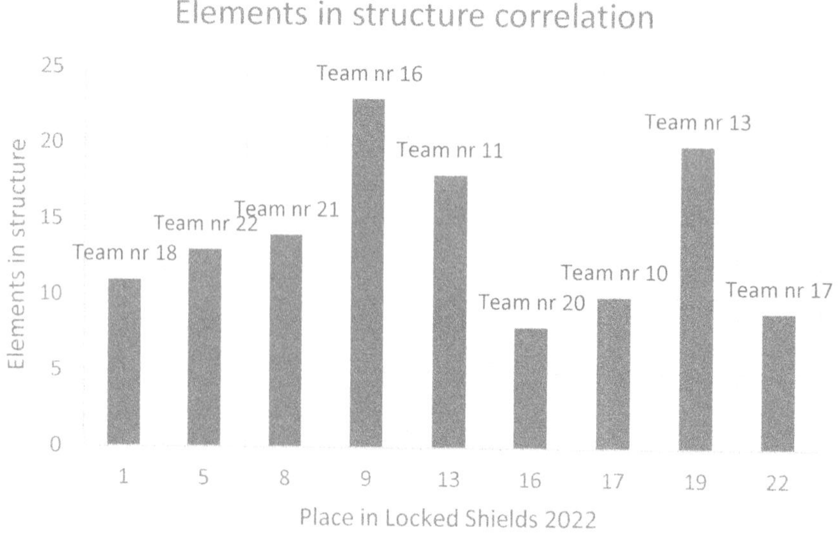

Figure 9: Exercise Locked Shields selected Blue Teams organisational structure, element count correlation.

A further characteristic recognised is the number of people per organisational structure. This is illustrated in Figure 3 and Figure 10, which illustrate the personnel appointed in each team's organisational structure in correlation with the place achieved in the exercise. The top three teams are highlighted on the left side of the graph. Their personnel count per organisational structure remains between 54 and 102. The personnel to organisational structure element ratio for the first-place team is 4.9, for the second 7.3 and the third 7.2. The

22nd team had a ratio of 5,5, and the 19th-place team had a ratio of 5.2. This indicates that the ratio of the number of people per organisational structure and the team size is irrelevant to the team's overall success. Over half of the observed teams had more than 80 persons per organisational structure. This might indicate that the number of people per organisational unit and units per team does not significantly influence the team's success.

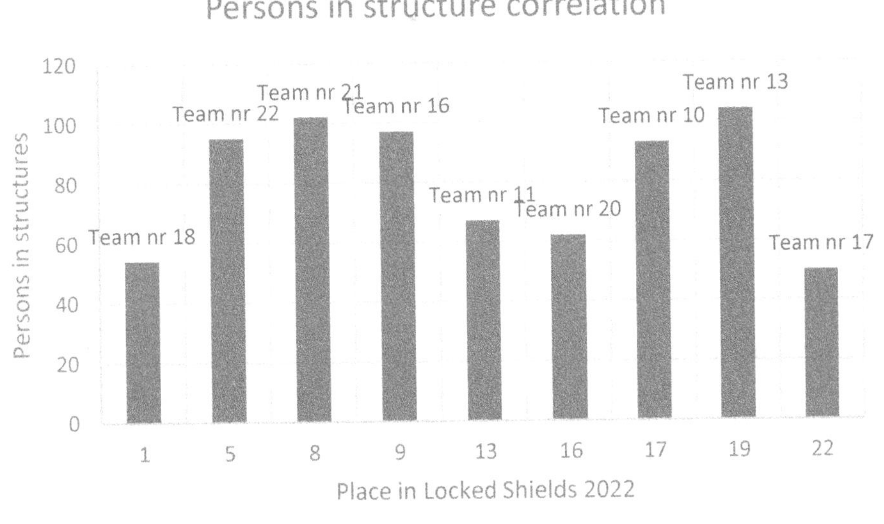

Figure 10: Exercise Locked Shields selected Blue Teams organisational structure, personnel count correlation.

The study analysed team composition and personnel count per organisational structure. The winning team had 11 elements, 54 personnel, and an average 4.9 personnel-to-structure element ratio. The correlation between place in the exercise and number of people was -0.09, suggesting a need for more relevance in success. The study reveals that success in the Locked Shields exercise relies on well-defined strategies, clear training objectives, technical readiness, and personnel experience, with team size and structural elements not determining success.

Successful teams in the Locked Shields exercise have standard skill sets, including military commanders, forensics, and legal advisors. They prioritise strategic planning and collaboration, engaging organisational structure members 3-4 months before exercise execution. They rely on customised software tools, demonstrating adaptability and commitment to technology readiness.

The success of LS team structures relied on effective leadership, specialised elements, early planning, and tailored software tools, providing valuable insights for cybersecurity exercise preparedness.

In compiling all the data collected, the optimal structure for the Locked Shields Blue Teams may consist of 11 elements and 55 personnel. At a minimum, there must be the following elements: a commander, Legad, forensics, and technology capabilities. Based on the exercise's technical challenges, up to eight separate Technology Capabilities elements might be included. These skillsets are shown in Figure 11 and could include capabilities such as Industrial control system (ICS), Network, Windows, Linux, Monitoring, Web, Mobile and Threat Hunting.

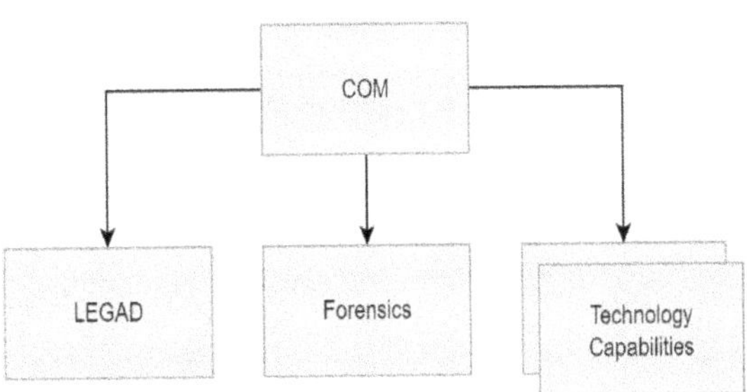

Figure 11: The Optimal Blue Team Structure for Locked Shields Exercise

6. Conclusions

The research emphasises the need for adaptive organisational structures in cyber exercises, addressing challenges unique to cyber operations training. A resource gap in cyber headquarters development requires preparing competent officers and leveraging training programs. This underscores the complexity of cyber exercises, emphasising continuous improvement and flexibility in structures and training to meet incipient expectations.

Cyber power countries are adjusting their cyber operations structures for future employment, requiring modifications to their Cyber Commanders Handbook and goal-specific structure for NATO exercises.

The Estonian Defence Forces Command's organisational structure is an example, and nations should consider the need to train dedicated cyber ranges. Dr. Blumbergs' designed chain-of-command for the Crossed Swords exercise is advantageous, as it outlines the hierarchy of tactical, operational, and strategic levels.

The top three Blue Teams' organisational structure elements in Exercise Locked Shields 2022 were 11-14, with 8-15 elements, although there needed to be a clear correlation and further analysis is required. As for conventional exercises, cyber exercises should include tactics, strategies, objectives, and tools with experienced individuals. Military commanders are preferred to the team, with members forming 3-4 months before an exercise. The Blue Teams structure typically includes Legal, Strategy, Advisors, and Operations, which are managed by the headquarters Plans/Operations (C3) sections. The EDF Cyber Exercises 2022 CHQ structure faced challenges in filling the necessary planning staff, as cyber operations planners' competencies are uncharted, requiring further research. The structure should be proportional to the exercise level and complexity.

Dr. Blumberg's design of the Red Team's organisational structure for Locked Shields is nearing optimal. With team leaders having no more than five to seven subordinates, goal-oriented is supported by interviews and provides an optimal and scalable structure for Red Teaming exercises.

A distinctive feature of the Red Team is that no specific direction is needed depending on the attackable systems and experience of the Red Teamers. However, Blue Teams need a higher command level to plan and maintain DCO. Therefore, planners and commanders must understand this essential difference and that roles, procedures, and tools differ. Red Teams focus on recruiting individuals with practical and hands-on skills relevant to cyber operations. In contrast, blue teams manage structures that categorise members based on specific skill sets, such as specialising in cybersecurity products or defendable assets. The need for additional research is emphasised, suggesting that further investigation or exploration is required to understand and refine the distinctions and roles within these teams. Red Teamers require special tools, infrastructure, and planning time, with good sub-team leaders and harmonised teams.

Planning officers must understand command-and-control authority and chain-of-command differences and integrate cyber into all HQ functions to prepare for entire spectrum operations, integrating kinetic and cyber operations.

Exercise participants face technical, operational, and strategic challenges, particularly at the operational layer. Cyber headquarters structural evolution needs faster development, with increasing numbers of competent officers and specialists needed. CHQs need to improve SOP and cyber operations planning, using alternative methods and setting goals during execution. However, in-depth planning is challenging due to strategic, operational, and tactical differences between cyber and other operations.

The research recommends implementing the US Marine Corps Cyberspace Training and Readiness Manual's recommendation for creating a Mission Essential Task List to enhance preparedness and operational response.

As cyber exercises increase in complexity, the command-and-control aspect for each headquarters becomes more critical. The CYOC experience underscores the need for diverse technical, operational, strategic, and political layers in one exercise, fostering trust and building cyber operations training structures.

This research revealed the complexity of cyber exercises and the importance of planning, training, and collaboration to address the unique challenges of cyber operations. It also highlights the need for adaptation and flexibility in organisational structures to meet the evolving demands of cyber operations training.

References

Ackerman. (2019) "NATO Cyber Policy Under Construction", [online], https://tinyurl.com/txwufe8b

Blumbergs. (2019) "Specialized Cyber Red Team Responsive". Tallinn: Tallinn University of Technology.

Dalmijn et al. (2020) Cyber Commanders' Handbook. In NATO CCDCOE Publications (pp. 26-27). Tallinn: North Atlantic Treaty Organization.

Gaston. (2022) "Air Force officers share paths to personal and professional success with cadets", [online], https://tinyurl.com/bdwhyd3a

Goździewicz. (2019) "Sovereign Cyber Effects Provided Voluntarily by Allies (SCEPVA)", [online], https://tinyurl.com/4zjydnpe

JMRC. (2022) "7th Army Training Command. Retrieved from 7th Army Training Command", [online], https://www.7atc.army.mil//

Kohler. (2020) "Cyberdefense Report: Estonia's National Cybersecurity and Cyberdefense Posture. Zürich: ETH Zürich".

Lemay et al. (2014) "Intelligence Preparation of the Cyber Environment (IPCE)", Journal of Information Warfare, Vol. 13, No. 3 (2014), pp. 46-56.

NAVMC. (2018). NAVMC 3500.124. Department of the Navy Headquarters United States Marine Corps.

Papp. (2022) "Locked Shields 2022 - Multinational Cyber Defense Exercise", [online], https://defence.hu/news/locked-shields-2022-multinational-cyber-defense-exercise.html

Pederson et al. (2022) "DOD Cyberspace: Establishing a Shared Understanding and How to Protect It", [online], https://tinyurl.com/y6dvyn4p

Pernik. (2020). Handbook of International Cybersecurity. Routledge: National Cyber Commands.

Pomerleau. (2022) "DoD must focus on skilled cyber defenders, not just new tech, warns weapons tester", [online], https://tinyurl.com/4fzyu6c2

Tuckman. (1965) "Developmental Sequence in Small groups", [online], https://tinyurl.com/2xymzt7z

Voo et al. (2022) "National Cyber Power Index 2020", [online], https://tinyurl.com/2aukkv4z

Applications of Post-Quantum Cryptography

Emils Bagirovs, Grigory Provodin, Tuomo Sipola and Jari Hautamäki
Institute of Information Technology, Jamk University of Applied Sciences, Jyväskylä, Finland

emils.bagirovs@student.jamk.fi
grigory.provodin@student.jamk.fi
tuomo.sipola@jamk.fi
jari.hautamaki@jamk.fi

Abstract: With the constantly advancing capabilities of quantum computers, conventional cryptographic systems relying on complex math problems may encounter unforeseen vulnerabilities. Unlike regular computers, which are often deemed cost-ineffective in cryptographic attacks, quantum computers have a significant advantage in calculation speed. This distinction potentially makes currently used algorithms less secure or even completely vulnerable, compelling the exploration of post-quantum cryptography (PQC) as the most reasonable solution to quantum threats. This review aims to provide current information on applications, benefits, and challenges associated with the PQC. The review employs a systematic scoping review with the scope restricted to the years 2022 and 2023; only articles that were published in scientific journals were used in this paper. The review examined the articles on the applications of quantum computing in various spheres. However, the scope of this paper was restricted to the domain of the PQC because most of the analyzed articles featured this field. Subsequently, the paper is analyzing various PQC algorithms, including lattice-based, hash-based, code-based, multivariate polynomial, and isogeny-based cryptography. Each algorithm is being judged based on its potential applications, robustness, and challenges. All the analyzed algorithms are promising for the post-quantum era in such applications as digital signatures, communication channels, and IoT. Moreover, some of the algorithms are already implemented in the spheres of banking transactions, communication, and intellectual property. Meanwhile, despite their potential, these algorithms face serious challenges since they lack standardization, require vast amounts of storage and computation power, and might have unknown vulnerabilities that can be discovered only with years of cryptanalysis. This overview aims to give a basic understanding of the current state of post-quantum cryptography with its applications and challenges. As the world enters the quantum era, this review not only shows the need for strong security methods that can resist quantum attacks but also presents an optimistic outlook on the future of secure communications, guided by advancements in quantum technology. By bridging the gap between theoretical research and practical implementation, this paper aims to inspire further innovation and collaboration in the field.

Keywords: Quantum Computing Applications, Post-Quantum Cryptography, PQC, Cryptographic Algorithms.

1. Introduction

As quantum computers become more powerful, they bring new risks to the current security systems. Traditional cryptographic methods, like those used in online banking and email encryption, rely on complex math problems that classical computers find hard to solve. However, quantum computers, with their advanced capabilities, can solve these problems much faster, making many of the current security methods weak against quantum attacks (Shaller, Zamir and Nojoumian, 2023; Lei et al., 2023).

Quantum computers employ multiple quantum mechanics phenomena such as superposition, entanglement, non-cloning theorem, and more. Superposition is a cornerstone of the quantum bits (qubits). While classical computers can be only in one state of 0 or 1, quantum computers can be in two states simultaneously. This aspect of superposition enables a dramatic increase in the speed of quantum computers. Entanglement is a unique state where two particles are interconnected, meaning that these particles when observed can provide information about each other, despite the distance between them. In quantum computation, this phenomenon is mostly used in optimization problems, secure communications, and quantum internet. No-cloning theorem states that the perfect cloning of a quantum state is impossible. The means of information as we know it today will be very different with the employment of quantum computers (Belkhir, Benkaouha and Benkhelifa, 2022; Sridhar, Ashwini and Tabassum, 2023; Zhao and Zheng, 2001).

Post-quantum cryptography (PQC) should solve the challenge of the cryptography created by quantum computers. It uses new kinds of math problems that even quantum computers find hard to solve, positioning PQC as a strong candidate for securing our data against future quantum threats (Chawla and Mehra, 2023; Verchyk and Sepúlveda, 2023). However, PQC's practicality is as important as its strength. This means PQC methods should function efficiently on current computers and networks, requiring minimal memory or processing power, crucial for devices like smartphones (Kumar, 2022).

Despite its potential, PQC is still nascent and faces its challenges. These new cryptographic methods haven't undergone as extensive testing as current methods, which have been trusted for many years. PQC, being newer, necessitates more time and testing to gain comparable trust levels. Moreover, transitioning from current methods to PQC is a significant undertaking, involving the complex and costly updating of numerous systems (Yalamuri, Honnavalli and Eswaran, 2022).

This article explores how PQC works, its benefits, and the challenges in applying it to real-world situations. We will also delve into some of the leading PQC methods being considered today, aiming to provide a clear understanding of how post-quantum cryptography can safeguard our data in the quantum computing era.

After an analysis of the quantum computing advancements two research questions were defined. Later, after the evaluation of the obtained sources third research question was defined.

RQ1: *What applications are there for quantum computing? And how can they be categorized?*

This question aims to identify various practical applications of quantum computing and to structure the obtained applications.

RQ2: *What is the current state of post-quantum cryptography: progress, use cases, and challenges?*

This question aims to identify the latest progress, use-cases, and challenges of the current post-quantum cryptography.

The article is outlined as follows: Section 1 introduces the topic and sets the stage for the discussion. Section 2 outlines the methodology, detailing the criteria for quantum computer application data collection. Section 3 is dedicated to exploring post-quantum cryptography, its types, and applications. Section 4 presents various use cases, while Section 5 discusses the implications and challenges faced in the field. The paper concludes with Section 6, looking towards the future of cryptography in the quantum computing era.

2. Methodology

We conducted a scoping literature review that explores quantum computing advancements (Peters et al., 2020). This chapter outlines databases that were used for data collection, inclusion and exclusion criteria that were applied during the review and an overview of the domains that were identified during the review. The paper follows the PRISMA checklist, and its methodology is supported by a PRISMA flow diagram presented in *Figure 1* that shows an overview of the scoping process (Page et al., 2021).

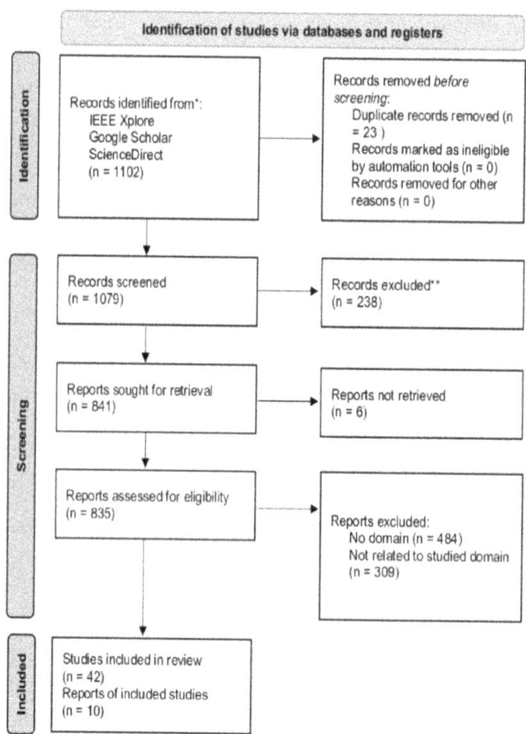

Figure 1: PRISMA Flow Diagram

2.1 Data Collection

This subsection covers means that were applied during data collection: search phrases, databases, inclusion and exclusion criteria, and screening criteria.

2.1.1 Search Phrases

Based on the research question RQ1 two search phrases were compiled and used across all databases. The two search strings are as follows:

- "Quantum computing applications"
- "Quantum computing use cases"

2.1.2 Used Databases

For this research three reputable and popular databases were used: IEEE Xplore, which offered a variety of engineering articles; Google Scholar, which provided a range of multidisciplinary articles from various sources; and ScienceDirect, which provided a collection of scientific articles. Our search was limited to the relevant databases that we were able to access through our institution.

2.1.3 Inclusion and Exclusion Criteria

Inclusion and exclusion of the articles were conducted in three stages, where during the first stage only title, abstract, and results sections were considered. As for the second stage, the whole content of the papers was analyzed and evaluated. During the third stage, 42 articles that were included in the review were analyzed based on the scope of the paper. This study focuses on the latest articles, as the progress of the field has accelerated during the last years. Therefore, the selection of the searched papers was restricted to those published between 2022 and 2023. The following criteria and their justifications are outlined below.

2.1.4 Inclusion Criteria

- Articles are written in English (Aligns with the language of the research and researchers).
- Articles are written between 2022 and 2023 (Ensures focus on recent developments).
- Articles are published in scientific journals (Ensures reliability of the sources).

- Articles are related to quantum computing or/and search phrases (Ensures the correct scope of the review.)

Screening stage 1:

- Is the article relevant based on the title, abstract, and results?

Screening stage 2:

- Is there an application, and is it usable in practical life?
- Can you identify the topic of the application?

Screening stage 3:

- Does this article cover the PQC?
- Can you identify recent developments, algorithms, use-cases, and problems of the PQC?

2.2 Domains of Quantum Computer Applications

Out of the 835 retrieved papers 351 had a domain related to applications of quantum computing. The papers and their respective domains can be seen in **Table 1**. Throughout the research, we identified 31 domains of quantum computing applications based on the keywords, headers used, and topics discussed in the papers. The focus of this paper was limited to the domain of Cryptography and Security, in which 42 articles met the inclusion criteria and passed the first two screenings. However, only 10 articles passed the third screening because most of the articles from the Cryptography and Security domain were too niche focusing on the development, calculations, and testing of the variations of PQC algorithms rather than providing an outlook or evaluation.

Table 1: Identified domains

Domain	Paper count
Data Science	7
AI	13
Algorithms and Applications	13
Bioinformatics	4
Challenges and Future Directions	14
Cloud and Edge Computing	7
Complex System Optimization	10
Cryptography and Security	42
Education and Learning	1
Engineering and Automated Process Control	1
Environmental Science	2
Ethics and Societal Impact	1
Finance and Economics	6
Fundamentals and Reviews	7
Hardware and Architecture	16
Healthcare	23
IoT	7
Machine Learning	40
Material Science	23
Nanotechnology	10
Networks	12
Optimization Problems	11
Power System Applications	5
Renewable Energy	4
Robotics	3
Simulation	12
Smart Cities and Urban Planning	5
Software and Programming	13
Space Technology	4
Specific Industries	16
Theoretical Physics	19
Total	351

3. Post-Quantum Cryptography

Post-quantum cryptography represents a forward-looking approach to cybersecurity, designed to withstand the computational prowess of quantum computers. This segment focuses on the fundamentals of this emerging field, examining specific algorithms and their respective merits and challenges. In addition, **Table 2** is used to represent the ten articles that were included in the final review and shaped this paper.

Table 2: Papers included in the review

Categories	Applications	References
	Algorithms	
Lattice-Based	Government communications, financial transactions, and personal data exchanges	Shaller, Zamir and Nojoumian (2023); Yalamuri, Honnavalli and Eswaran (2022); Rewal et al. (2023)
Code-Based	Protection of intellectual property	Kumar (2022); Chawla and Mehra (2023)
Multivariate Polynomial	Public key cryptosystems	Kumar (2022); Yalamuri, Honnavalli and Eswaran (2022)
Hash-Based	Digital signatures	Chawla and Mehra (2023); Yalamuri, Honnavalli and Eswaran (2022); Kumar (2022)
Isogeny-Based	Small scale devices	Shaller, Zamir and Nojoumian (2023)
	Future directions	
	New applications of PQC	Aithal (2023)
	Requirements for integration of PQC in existing digital infrastructure	Gill et al. (2022)
	Necessity in PQC education and training	Rietsche et al. (2022)
	Background	
	Threat from Quantum computers	Lei et al. (2023)
	PQC	Verchyk and Sepúlveda (2023)

Lattice-based cryptography is a prominent example of post-quantum cryptography. It relies on the hardness of lattice problems, which, to date, have no efficient solving algorithm on quantum computers. The advantage of this approach lies in its presumed resistance to quantum attacks, offering a secure alternative to traditional systems (Rewal et al., 2023). However, the downside includes larger key sizes and increased computational overhead, which could be a hindrance in environments with limited resources (Shaller, Zamir and Nojoumian, 2023). Another notable method is hash-based cryptography, which utilizes cryptographic hash functions. These systems are highly efficient and offer strong security assurances against quantum attacks. Their simplicity of design allows for easy integration into existing systems. However, they are not without drawbacks. For instance, hash-based signatures are typically larger than traditional signatures, which can increase data transmission requirements and storage needs (Chawla and Mehra, 2023). Code-based cryptography, drawing security from the hardness of decoding a general linear code, is another viable post-quantum method. Its long-standing presence in the cryptographic community has allowed for substantial analysis and testing. However, like lattice-based systems, code-based cryptography suffers from the requirement of larger key sizes. This characteristic can limit its practicality in systems where bandwidth and storage are constrained (Kumar, 2022). Multivariate polynomial cryptography is yet another approach, which bases its security on the difficulty of solving systems of multivariate polynomials. One of its primary advantages is the potential for smaller key sizes compared to other post-quantum methods. Nonetheless, this advantage comes at the cost of complex key generation and signing processes, which can be computationally intensive (Yalamuri, Honnavalli and Eswaran, 2022). Lastly, isogeny-based cryptography, a relatively newer field, focuses on the computational difficulty of finding isogenies between elliptic curves. This method stands out for its small key sizes and potential efficiency. However, being a newer area of research, it lacks the extensive testing and vetting those older methods have undergone, posing a risk of unknown vulnerabilities (Shaller, Zamir and Nojoumian, 2023).

3.1 Categories of Post-Quantum Cryptographic Algorithms

In the field of post-quantum cryptography, various categories of cryptographic algorithms have been developed to counteract the potential threats posed by quantum computers. These categories, each with their unique approach and underlying principles, are pivotal in understanding the landscape of quantum-resistant cryptography (Shaller, Zamir and Nojoumian, 2023; Chawla and Mehra, 2023; Kumar, 2022; Yalamuri, Honnavalli and Eswaran, 2022).

- Lattice-Based Cryptography: This category relies on the complexity of lattice problems, which involve multidimensional grids of points. The security of these algorithms is based on the difficulty of finding the shortest path or closest point in a high-dimensional lattice. Notable for their efficiency and the ability to support advanced cryptographic functions like fully homomorphic encryption, lattice-based algorithms are considered promising for post-quantum cryptography (Shaller, Zamir and Nojoumian, 2023). However, their key sizes and ciphertexts can be relatively large, which might be challenging for systems with limited storage or bandwidth.

- Code-Based Cryptography: Originating from error-correcting codes, this category includes algorithms that are secure due to the difficulty of decoding a general linear code. The most famous example is the McEliece cryptosystem, which has been noted for its fast encryption and decryption processes. While offering strong security, the main drawback of code-based cryptography is the large key sizes, which pose a challenge in terms of storage and transmission efficiency (Chawla and Mehra, 2023).
- Multivariate Polynomial Cryptography: These algorithms are based on the hard problem of solving systems of multivariate polynomials over a finite field. They are known for their fast decryption and potential for small key sizes making them suitable for public key cryptosystems. However, creating secure instances of multivariate polynomial problems can be complex, and some earlier schemes have been broken, raising concerns about their security (Kumar, 2022).
- Hash-Based Cryptography: This type involves cryptographic algorithms that use hash functions. These algorithms are relatively simple and are known for their high speed and security, which rely on the well-studied hardness of finding collisions in hash functions. Hash-based signatures, for example, are a practical application, although they typically have larger signatures than traditional algorithms (Yalamuri, Honnavalli and Eswaran, 2022).
- Isogeny-Based Cryptography: A newer area in post-quantum cryptography, it focuses on the hard problem of finding isogenies between elliptic curves. These algorithms are notable for their small key sizes, making them suitable for systems with limited storage. However, they are less mature than other categories and require more research to fully understand their security and practicality (Shaller, Zamir and Nojoumian, 2023).

Each of these categories represents a different approach to securing cryptographic systems against the threat of quantum computing. The choice of a particular category depends on various factors, including the specific application, the required level of security, and available system resources. As research in this field progresses, these algorithms are continuously evaluated and improved to meet the evolving challenges of cybersecurity in the quantum era (Chawla and Mehra, 2023; Kumar, 2022).

3.2 Applications of Post-Quantum Cryptography

The first significant application of Post-Quantum Cryptography (PQC) is in securing communication channels. In the digital age, the exchange of information over the internet, including emails, instant messaging, and online transactions, relies heavily on encryption protocols. Current encryption methods like RSA and ECC are effective against classical computing threats but are vulnerable to quantum attacks. PQC introduces algorithms like lattice-based cryptography, resistant to quantum computing capabilities, making it essential for protecting sensitive information in government communications, financial transactions, and personal data exchanges (Shaller, Zamir and Nojoumian, 2023). Another critical application of PQC is in digital signatures, which are vital for verifying the authenticity of documents and software. Traditional digital signature schemes could be easily compromised with quantum computers. PQC offers solutions like hash-based cryptography, secure against quantum attacks, thereby ensuring the integrity and authenticity of digital signatures in legal documents, software updates, and secure communications (Chawla and Mehra, 2023). Furthermore, the Internet of Things (IoT) is an area where PQC can be transformative. IoT devices, often limited in computational resources, are increasingly involved in critical functions such as healthcare monitoring, smart homes, and industrial automation. Implementing PQC in IoT devices ensures their security in a post-quantum world, protecting them from potential quantum-enabled cyber-attacks (Kumar, 2022). Despite these promising applications, implementing PQC presents challenges. One of the main issues is the increased computational and storage requirements compared to classical cryptography, problematic for devices like IoT devices. Additionally, the relative newness of PQC means a lack of long-term studies and real-world testing, raising concerns about potential vulnerabilities. The application of PQC is crucial in securing the digital world against future quantum threats. Its implementation in secure communications, digital signatures, and IoT devices highlights its importance. However, addressing challenges in computational requirements and the need for further research and testing is necessary to fully realize PQC's potential in these applications.

3.3 Challenges and Considerations

One major challenge is the increased computational resources required by many PQC algorithms. Compared to traditional cryptographic methods, PQC often demands more processing power and larger memory spaces, especially for key storage and management. This can be particularly problematic for devices with limited resources, such as smartphones and IoT devices. Implementing PQC in these devices requires careful optimization to balance security needs with available resources (Shaller, Zamir and Nojoumian, 2023).

Another consideration is the current lack of standardization in PQC algorithms. The cryptographic community is still in the process of researching and identifying the most secure and efficient post-quantum algorithms. This ongoing research means that the algorithms have not yet undergone the extensive testing and validation that classical cryptographic algorithms have. There is a need for broad agreement on standards to ensure compatibility and security across different platforms and applications (Chawla and Mehra, 2023).

The integration of PQC into existing systems also presents a significant challenge. Transitioning from current cryptographic standards to PQC involves complex updates to existing infrastructure. This process must be managed carefully to maintain security during the transition period. It is also important to ensure that this change does not disrupt user experience or business operations (Kumar, 2022).

Moreover, there is a need for widespread education and awareness about PQC. Many professionals in the field of cybersecurity and related areas may not be familiar with the concepts and importance of PQC. Training and educational programs will be essential to prepare the workforce for the upcoming changes in cryptographic standards (Yalamuri, Honnavalli and Eswaran, 2022).

Finally, the potential for unknown vulnerabilities in PQC algorithms cannot be overlooked. As with any new technology, there is always the risk of undiscovered weaknesses that could be exploited. Continuous research and testing are essential to identify and address these vulnerabilities.

While post-quantum cryptography is a crucial advancement in securing data against the threats posed by quantum computing, its implementation is fraught with challenges. These include the need for increased computational resources, the lack of standardization, difficulties in integration, the requirement for education and awareness, and the potential for undiscovered vulnerabilities. Addressing these challenges is vital for the successful and secure adoption of PQC in various applications.

3.4 Use Cases and Success Stories

One notable use case is in the field of secure communications. Traditional security protocols like RSA and ECC are vulnerable to quantum attacks. However, post-quantum methods such as lattice-based encryption have been successfully implemented in various communication platforms to ensure future-proof security (Yalamuri, Honnavalli and Eswaran, 2022). For instance, a leading tech company recently integrated lattice-based cryptography into their messaging service, significantly enhancing the security against potential quantum decryption.

Another area of successful application is in secure government communications. Recognizing the quantum threat, a European government agency adopted post-quantum cryptographic algorithms for protecting sensitive state communications. This implementation not only secured their data against future quantum attacks but also served as a model for other government bodies globally.

Financial institutions have also been proactive in adopting post-quantum cryptography. A major bank successfully employed hash-based signatures for securing transactions, demonstrating the effectiveness of these methods in a high-stakes environment (Kumar, 2022). This not only ensured the security of financial transactions against quantum threats but also boosted customer confidence in the bank's commitment to future-proof security measures.

Furthermore, post-quantum cryptographic methods have found use in protecting intellectual property. A global pharmaceutical company implemented code-based cryptography to secure their research data. This application is particularly significant given the sensitive nature of pharmaceutical research and the catastrophic potential of data breaches in this field.

4. Future Directions and Developments

With the growing power of quantum computers, the need for PQC becomes more urgent. Our work in this field aims to address these challenges and leverage opportunities to enhance cybersecurity in a quantum computing era.

One promising direction is the development of more efficient PQC algorithms. Current PQC systems often require larger key sizes compared to traditional cryptography, which can lead to higher demands on storage and processing power. This is particularly challenging for devices with limited resources, like smartphones and IoT devices (Kumar, 2022). Future research should focus on optimizing these algorithms to reduce their computational and storage needs while maintaining their security against quantum attacks.

Another important area is the integration of PQC into existing digital infrastructures. As businesses and governments rely heavily on encryption for securing data, a smooth transition to PQC is essential. This involves updating protocols, software, and hardware that currently use vulnerable cryptographic methods. Collaborative efforts between academia, industry, and government bodies are crucial to ensure a coordinated and efficient transition (Gill et al., 2022).

Moreover, there is a need for extensive testing and standardization of PQC algorithms. The current state of PQC is akin to the early days of classical cryptography, where various algorithms are still being evaluated for their security and practicality. Establishing widely accepted standards, like what NIST is doing through its Post-Quantum Cryptography Standardization project, will be key in bringing PQC to mainstream use (Kumar, 2022).

Furthermore, the education and training of professionals in the field of PQC are vital. As we move towards a post-quantum era, there will be a growing demand for experts who understand both quantum computing and cryptography or other domain skills (Rietsche et al., 2022). Developing educational programs and resources will help in preparing the next generation of cybersecurity professionals.

Lastly, exploring the potential of PQC in new applications beyond traditional cybersecurity is an exciting prospect. This includes areas like secure communications, blockchain technologies, and even quantum key distribution systems. As the field of quantum computing continues to evolve, the applications of PQC will likely expand into new and unforeseen domains (Chawla and Mehra, 2023; Aithal, 2023).

5. Conclusion

The research addresses the field of quantum computing applications by presenting a diverse array of practical uses ranging from cryptography to complex system simulations. The paper categorizes these applications (RQ1) into sectors such as healthcare, finance, and information security, providing a framework for understanding the multifaceted impact of quantum computing. This paper also covers the field of post-quantum cryptography (RQ2), reflecting the most popular algorithms and their applications as well as the challenges that the field is facing today. It highlights the transformative potential of these applications and underscores the need for structured categorization to inform future research and development strategies.

Our exploration of various PQC methods, including lattice-based, hash-based, code-based, multivariate polynomial, and isogeny-based cryptography, has highlighted their potential in safeguarding against quantum computing threats. These methods show promise in areas such as secure communications, digital signatures, and the Internet of Things (IoT), offering a shield against the formidable computational abilities of quantum computers.

However, the journey towards fully implementing PQC is not without its challenges. The increased computational and storage requirements of PQC methods, especially in resource-limited environments like IoT devices, present a considerable hurdle. Additionally, the lack of standardization and the need for extensive testing and validation underscore the nascent stage of these cryptographic methods. Integrating PQC into existing digital infrastructures requires a collaborative approach, involving academia, industry, and government bodies, to manage a smooth transition without disrupting current systems and operations.

Furthermore, the importance of educating and training professionals in the field of PQC is paramount. As we transition into a post-quantum era, there will be an increasing demand for experts skilled in both quantum computing and cryptography. Developing educational programs and resources will be crucial in preparing a well-equipped cybersecurity workforce.

In conclusion, while the path to implementing PQC is complex and filled with challenges, it is a necessary progression in the realm of cybersecurity. As quantum computing continues to advance, PQC stands as a vital component in protecting our digital world. Embracing this new era of cryptography, we must continue to innovate, research, and collaborate, ensuring that our data remains secure against quantum vulnerabilities. Future research could include scoping how to integrate PQC into the existing infrastructure. Furthermore, continuous review of the latest advancements in PQC is also needed to evaluate the latest threats.

Acknowledgments

We are grateful to Ummar Ahmed and Thien Nguyen for their help with data collection and assistance with database creation. This research was partially supported by the ResilMesh project, funded by the European Union's Horizon Europe Framework Programme (HORIZON) under grant agreement 101119681. The authors would like to thank Ms. Tuula Kotikoski for proofreading the manuscript.

References

Aithal, P. S. (2023) "Advances and New Research Opportunities in Quantum Computing Technology by Integrating it with Other ICCT Underlying Technologies", *International Journal of Case Studies in Business, IT, and Education*, Vol. 7, No. 3, pp. 314-358. https://doi.org/10.5281/zenodo.8326506

Belkhir, M., Benkaouha, H. and Benkhelifa, E. (2022) "Quantum Vs Classical Computing: a Comparative Analysis", *2022 Seventh International Conference on Fog and Mobile Edge Computing (FMEC)*. Paris, France. IEEE, pp. 1-8. https://doi.org/10.1109/FMEC57183.2022.10062753

Chawla, D. and Mehra, P.S. (2023) "A roadmap from classical cryptography to post-quantum resistant cryptography for 5G-enabled IoT: Challenges, opportunities and solutions", *Internet of Things*, Vol. 24, pp. 100950. https://doi.org/10.1016/j.iot.2023.100950

Gill, S.S. et al. (2022) "Quantum computing: A taxonomy, systematic review and future directions", *Software: Practice and Experience*, Vol. 52, No. 1, pp. 66-114. https://doi.org/10.1002/spe.3039

Kumar, M. (2022) "Post-quantum cryptography Algorithm's standardization and performance analysis", *Array*, Vol. 15, pp. 100242. https://doi.org/10.1016/j.array.2022.100242

Lei, Z. et al. (2023) "*Making existing software quantum safe: A case study on IBM Db2", Information and Software Technology*, Vol. 161, pp. 107249. https://doi.org/10.1016/j.infsof.2023.107249

Page, M.J. et al. (2021) "The PRISMA 2020 statement: an updated guideline for reporting systematic reviews", *BMJ*, Vol. 372. https://doi.org/10.1136/bmj.n71

Peters, M.J. et al. (2020) "Scoping Reviews", in Aromataris E. and Munn Z. (eds.) *JBI Manual for Evidence Synthesis*. JBI. https://doi.org/10.46658/JBIMES-20-12

Rewal, P. et al. (2023) "Quantum-safe three-party lattice based authenticated key agreement protocol for mobile devices", *Journal of Information Security and Applications*, Vol. 75, pp. 103505. https://doi.org/10.1016/j.jisa.2023.103505

Rietsche, R. et al. (2022) "Quantum computing", *Electronic Markets*, Vol. 32, pp. 2525-2536. https://doi.org/10.1007/s12525-022-00570-y

Shaller, A., Zamir, L. and Nojoumian, M. (2023) "Roadmap of post-quantum cryptography standardization: Side-channel attacks and countermeasures", *Information and Computation*, Vol. 295, pp. 105112. https://doi.org/10.1016/j.ic.2023.105112

Sridhar, G. T., Ashwini, P. and Tabassum, N. (2023) "A Review on Quantum Communication and Computing", *2023 2nd International Conference on Applied Artificial Intelligence and Computing (ICAAIC)*, Salem, India. IEEE, pp. 1592-1596. https://doi.org/10.1109/ICAAIC56838.2023.10140821

Verchyk, D. and Sepúlveda, J. (2023) "A practical study of post-quantum enhanced identity-based encryption", *Microprocessors and Microsystems*, Vol. 99, pp. 104828. https://doi.org/10.1016/j.micpro.2023.104828

Yalamuri, G., Honnavalli, P. and Eswaran, S. (2022) "A Review of the Present Cryptographic Arsenal to Deal with Post-Quantum Threats", *Procedia Computer Science*, Vol. 215, pp. 834-845. https://doi.org/10.1016/j.procs.2022.12.086

Zhao, S. and Zheng, B. (2001) "Security of QKD with single particles in probabilistic cloning fashion", *2001 International Conferences on Info-Tech and Info-Net. Proceedings*, Beijing, China. IEEE, pp. 140-145. https://doi.org/10.1109/ICII.2001.983508

Botnets in Healthcare: Threats, Vulnerabilities, and Mitigation Strategies

Michaela Barnett[1], James Womack[1],Christopher E. Brito[1], Khadijah Miller[1], Lucas Potter[2] and Xavier-Lewis Palmer[2]

[1]Blacks In Cybersecurity Headquarters, Inc.,VA,USA

[2]BiosView, Oswego, KS, USA

michaela@bichq.org

Abstract: The increasing digitization of healthcare systems has introduced new opportunities to improve efficiency and accessibility for medical professionals and patients. Examples include the simplified collection, storage, and organization of patient data using electronic health records (EHRs), the use of teleconferencing software like Zoom to allow patients to meet with their care providers remotely, and medical IoT devices like glucose monitors, pacemakers, and other remote patient monitoring devices that leverage software and the internet to provide patients and their healthcare providers with critical information. All of these use cases are examples of how technology can increase the quality of patient care. While the healthcare industry has realized many benefits from its increased investment in new technology, trends have shown that this increased utilization has also opened avenues for malicious cyber actors. One of these threats is botnets. These malicious networks of compromised computers, controlled by cybercriminals, can wreak havoc on all sectors of society, with the healthcare industry proving to be a desirable target. This research is a high-level analysis that investigates the threat botnets pose by employing an exploratory review. We identify the multifaceted nature of botnet threats in healthcare, analyzing their standard forms and the vulnerabilities inherent in healthcare infrastructures, ranging from outdated software to inadequate cybersecurity protocols to poor or total lack of security awareness training for staff. Moreover, the various techniques botnets use to propagate are explored to elucidate the potential points of exploitation and the damage they can cause organizations when proper controls are not implemented. These negative consequences include data breaches, service disruptions, and compromised patient confidentiality, which can endanger medical staff and patients if not addressed. This paper then discusses proven mitigation strategies such as end-user awareness, traffic monitoring, and detection response tools that organizations can employ to reduce the potential and efficacy of such threats. The threat landscape will continue to evolve; however, by staying on top of the latest trends, we can ensure the security of such critical infrastructure and save lives.

Keywords: Healthcare, Botnets, BioCybersecurity, CyberBiosecurity, Medical, IoT

1. Introduction

In an increasingly interconnected digital landscape, the emergence of botnets, malicious networks of compromised computers, have become a formidable challenge for industries across the board (Wazzan et al, 2021; Owen et al, 2022; Booth et al, 2023; Kumar and Sharma, 2023). They are often controlled by malicious actors and can wreak havoc on multiple industries, with the healthcare industry being a desirable target. This paper explores the ways in which botnets have begun to permeate the healthcare sector, posing threats to patient privacy, data security, and the overall integrity of healthcare services. Understanding the dynamics of botnets and their specific implications for healthcare is not just an academic exercise; it is a critical step in fortifying the digital defenses of an industry that plays an indispensable role in safeguarding public health.

The healthcare industry's growing reliance on technology and the internet is evident in its continued adoption of innovative digital solutions for patient care, communication and, integration into medical devices. Electronic Health Records (EHRs) have become a cornerstone of modern healthcare, improving patient record-keeping, accessibility, and data management. Another recent integration would be the standard utilization of Telemedicine, accelerated by the COVID-19 pandemic, which allows patients to access medical care remotely, increasing healthcare accessibility and reducing barriers to seeking treatment (Mueller, 2020; Finch et al, 2023; Affia et al, 2023; Hiller et al, 2024). These advancements enhance patient care as they take an active approach and contribute to the industry's cost-efficiency. The consulting industry has reported that healthcare organizations increasingly invest in digital health, data analytics and artificial intelligence to improve operational efficiency, patient engagement, and clinical outcomes (Arboleda and Shah et al., 2019).

As technology integration continues to expand, so does the overall attack surface (Potter et al, 2021; Affia et al, 2023; Potter and Palmer, 2023). Healthcare providers, while committed to patient care, often grapple with data security and privacy concerns, necessitating a robust infrastructure and security measures to safeguard sensitive medical information and devices in this increasingly digital environment. Botnets present a significant and evolving threat to healthcare systems, with potential consequences that can harm patient care and data security (Liu et al, 2009; Ali et al, 2020; Wazzan et al, 2021; Owen et al, 2022; Kumar and Sharma, 2023). Botnets can infiltrate healthcare organizations, placing sensitive patient data at risk, disrupting vital medical operations, and potentially endangering lives.

2. Background & Methodology

Information and Data Security in healthcare is paramount due to the sensitive nature of the data involved and the potential consequences of breaches (Alhuwail et al., 2021). The integrity of computer systems is the primary concern, as the effort is concentrated on maintaining the confidentiality and integrity of the data needed to assess, track, and treat patients. Breaches to these portions of our critical infrastructure can result in the unavailability of treating patients, transferring data between facilities, or possibility of malicious threat actors to manipulate or infiltrate a system. One of the most concerning aspects of botnet attacks in healthcare is their potential to disrupt critical medical services (Liu et al, 2009; Ali et al, 2020; Wazzan et al, 2021; Owen et al, 2022; Kumar and Sharma, 2023). For example, a DDoS attack orchestrated by a botnet could overwhelm a hospital's network infrastructure, leading to the unavailability of essential systems such as electronic health records (EHR) or medical imaging systems. Such disruptions can severely affect patient care, potentially delaying treatments or compromising patient safety. In addition to internal hospital infrastructure, security measures and considerations extended to medical devices; with sensors, pumps, and or otherwise, implanted or non, which may find themselves connected to the internet for monitoring and control (Biran Achituv et al, 2016; Mavrogiorgou et al, 2019; Raju and Moh, 2020; Astillo et al, 2022; Farooq et al, 2023). Compromising these devices could have life-threatening consequences for patients, despite growing use or popularity. Implementing robust measures, including regular risk assessments, employee training, data encryption, network segmentation and continuous monitoring for threats, is crucial in mitigating these risks.

To protect patient data, healthcare providers and institutions must adhere to strict regulations, such as the Health Insurance Portability and Accountability Act (HIPAA) in the United States (*Summary of the HIPAA security rule,* 2022). HIPAA's primary purpose is to protect individuals' sensitive health information, known as protected health information (PHI). This and the electronic version (e-PHI) includes demographic data, i.e.; physical condition or mental health status, care provided, payment information, name, address, birth date, Social Security Number (SSN), and related sensitive data (Edemekong et al, 2022). HIPAA establishes national standards for the security and privacy of this information.

Botnet attacks pose a significant threat to the healthcare sector (Ali et al, 2020; Kumar and Sharma, 2023) They leverage compromised systems or devices with access to a target network to carry out malicious activities. In recent years, the healthcare industry has increasingly become a target for botnet attacks due to its valuable patient data and critical services (Ali et al, 2020; Wazzan et al, 2021; Owen et al 2022; Kumar and Sharma, 2023). Botnets can launch various mis-actions, including distributed denial-of-service (DDoS) attacks, ransomware campaigns, and data exfiltration.

Preventing and mitigating botnet attacks in the healthcare sector requires a multi-faceted approach. This includes implementing robust cybersecurity measures such as network segmentation, intrusion detection systems, and regular vulnerability assessments to identify and patch potential entry points for malicious actors. Additionally, employee training and awareness programs can help educate healthcare staff about the risks of botnet attacks, how to recognize them and how to respond to suspicious activities.

Collaboration within the healthcare industry and with cybersecurity professionals is crucial for staying ahead of botnets' evolving threats. Sharing threat intelligence and best practices can help healthcare organizations better understand and mitigate the risks associated with these attacks.

Due to the strategies employed in initiating these attacks, certain pertinent research has yet to enter the academic domain. There is a lack of desired publicly accessible reporting in quality and quantity, which has required the authors to widen data sources to ingest additional relevant literature. This discussion will hopefully serve as guidance or reference to either contemporary non-open source analyses, or future academic works. To that end, the authors have utilized and sampled insights among authors at various points in the field.

3. Botnets in Healthcare: Threat Assessment

Common techniques for exploitation or vulnerabilities that may be exploited, that are threatening connected medical devices in the IoMT (Internet of Medical Things) are Spoofing, Tampering, Information Disclosure, Denial of Service, and Escalation/Elevation of privilege. IOMT aims to improve patient care, enhance healthcare delivery, and enable higher function. Disabling unused, unnecessary, or unsecured network services is a simple and critical part of the device hardening process. Exposing unsecured services to the internet "could impact the confidentiality, integrity, and availability of information and increase exposure to unauthorized remote access" (Malamas et al., 2021). Another area of concern regarding IoMT is the implementation of encryption methods and the limitation of forensics that can be applied due to device constraints (Malamas et al., 2021; Yaacoub et al, 2022). This yields resource constraints that have left the deployment of strong encryption out of some IoMT devices.

Another attack vector to consider would be the many "edge" (Malamas et al., 2021) devices that make up the internet-facing networks and IoMT devices that can be included in this attack surface, such as security cameras, printers, or other monitoring devices (Malamas et al., 2021; Farooq et al, 2023; Hernandez-Jaimes et al, 2023). They often have configurations that must be changed, updated, or disabled. Configurations are often left on default settings and not adjusted, leading to possible attack path entry points if discovered. It has been noted that most administrators will harden essential network devices or appliances, but this may be insufficient in the broader scope of a healthcare network's security when other layers are considered (Filkins, 2014; Malamas et al., 2021; Affia et al, 2023). Further, in evaluating the case of a device that may not be misconfigured, an interface may be left in default configuration and can be accessed by malicious actors. Access can also be gained through plainly available credentials, manuals or configuration instructions (i,e; manufacturer support sites, online tutorials). Actors may also be able to find administration panels or access login portals via particular search engines designed to locate devices connected to the internet, such as Shodan or Censys (Al-Alami et al, 2017; Zhao et al, 2020). The resulting access could be utilized to push further into a network and move laterally through a system. Additionally, it is important to discuss the possibility of attacks that may occur at a private residence, in the absence of on-site professionals who can address specific IT configurations (Travis, 2023; Fisher, 2023). An example of this activity would be the rise in work-from-home environments where equipment is mailed or picked up by an employee and is open to remote maintenance and updates.

A unique way to demonstrate yet another risk to this infrastructure would be to examine the process by which a DDoS attack aims to deplete the battery of a glucose monitor. A DDoS (Distributed Denial of Service) attack floods a target system or network with overwhelming traffic from multiple sources, aiming to disrupt or deny legitimate access to services or resources (Farooq et al, 2023). Devices that run on battery power can be overwhelmed in this fashion and run their battery power down quickly. If attacked in this frequent/constant fashion, this can lead to life-threatening problems, especially in the case of a monitoring device outputting data essential to on-demand care such as vital signs or changes in biologically relevant chemical levels.

Disruptions to sensing capability can also be tampered with resulting in a disrupt or malfunction of hardware or software in a device. In a recent analysis of IoT health devices (IoTHDs) it is noted that certain functions and the transmission of data are intertwined. "The network layer constitutes wired and wireless networks, which connect perception devices, application-layer devices, and other network devices to transmit medical information collected at the perception layer to the application layer" (Affia et al, 2023). Thus, If a glucose monitor is attacked to the point where it is completely depleted of power and fails to function, results could be lethal either independently or combined. In a situation where a device function or sensor is impacted, proper measures, planning, configuration and monitoring can help greatly minimize the chances of success in exploiting vulnerability translating to other portions of interconnected healthcare infrastructure.

4. Mitigation and Prevention Strategies

Many facets must be addressed when discussing mitigation and prevention strategies for botnets. The study Botnet: Classification, Attacks, Detection, Tracing, and Preventive Measures acknowledges succinct tasks that IT administrators can implement to protect their systems and networks (Liu et al., 2009). Identifying the affected operating systems and the origin of network traffic can be leveraged to identify incoming attacks. Traffic can be null routed, as malicious traffic can take down critical systems (Puri, 2007). Mitigation would include an attempt to remove any unnecessary DNS hosting services as well, further restricting the resources a potential threat actor could leverage.

Organizations should continuously request and install security updates, fixes, and patches released by their vendors to ensure systems have the latest protections. End users should be regularly trained to avoid downloading software from unscrupulous sites and downloading unnecessary software. A restricted amount of software on a system would make it easier to administor, catalog and maintain, reducing the risk of malicious actors gaining unauthorized access to data or organizational infrastructure.

While it is essential for IT and security staff to be aware of how to defend the organization from cyber threats, it is also essential that the entire staff, regardless of duty or function, receive security awareness training. Healthcare organizations can facilitate this to improve end user recognition and adoption of concepts from relevant training programs (Alhuwail et al, 2021; Polis, 2023). Alhuwail et al (2021) recommends "targeted bottom-up approach via personalized outreach, in-person contacts, and frequent announcements throughout the workflow" (Alhuwail et al., 2021). In conjunction with proper training, devices in the healthcare infrastructure's network should be assessed, updated and/or configured properly prior to being introduced to the overall network, especially over time with regards to software life cycles (Otieno et al, 2023; Phiri, 2023; Harkat et al, 2024; Dadkhah et al, 2024). A core principle highlighting the necessity of this approach lies in the notion that a single vulnerability is sufficient for a malicious actor to access, move laterally or gain privileges in a system and that understanding the risk of each vulnerability allows for holistic comprehension and aids security teams as they work toward building resistance.

5. Regulatory and Compliance Considerations

The policy and compliance of Cybersecurity is to ensure best practices related to mitigating security risks, protecting sensitive data, and maintaining the confidentiality, integrity and availability of information systems and assets. The compliance enforced by policies plays a critical role in promoting trust, resilience, and accountability within organizations. Ensuring these principals play a crucial role in protecting sensitive information assets and mitigating cybersecurity risks in an increasingly complex and interconnected digital environment. In the Healthcare sector, there is a focus on the portion of HIPAA called "The Security Rule" (Craig, 2017). This rule establishes a set of security standards for protecting health information that is stored or transferred in electronic form and applies to "health plans, health care clearinghouses, and to any health care provider who transmits health information in electronic form in connection with a transaction for which the Secretary of HHS has adopted standards under HIPAA (the "covered entities") and to their business associates" (*Summary of the HIPAA security rule,* 2022). Covered entities were thus tasked with heightened data management responsibilities and to note, additional importance exists in the locations of e-PHI (*Summary of the HIPAA security rule,* 2022; Fard Bahreini, 2023). This regulation requires covered entities or business associates to maintain reasonable and appropriate administrative, technical, and physical security measures for protecting e-PHI.

The HITECH Act of 2009 (Health Information Technology for Economic and Clinical Health Act) was enacted to strengthen HIPAA and promote the adoption of EHR (Electronic Health Record) systems (Mennemeyer et al, 2016; Burde, 2011; Zahedi et al, 2021). Like HIPAA, HITECH requires covered entities and business associates to implement a risk management and audit program to ensure the protection of e-PHI. In addition, HITECH results in stricter penalties for HIPAA violations and the breach notification rule, which requires covered entities and business associates to notify affected individuals within 60 days.

Healthcare providers are slated to place additional consideration on complexities surrounding choices of payment data security standards, even where not mandated. It is palpable that healthcare systems are often placed concurrently to on-site or online payment technologies, such as Point of Sales systems, ATMs, kiosks, or online processing analogs. The Payment Card Industry Data Security Standard (PCI DSS) is a standard that providers should also reference in their security considerations (Ataya, 2010; Yulianto, 2016). Though it is not mandated by law, credit card payments are ubiquitous in the healthcare industry and cannot be avoided. Coupled with the fact that credit card processors follow PCI DSS and will reduce transactions that can be made or even ban a provider from taking credit card payments, ePHI and credit card information protection needs to be a priority for providers across the healthcare industry. Although beyond the scope of this paper, it is important that healthcare providers be mindful of multisystem considerations that may emerge with enviornmental integration with payment systems (Elmas, 2023; Chitadze, 2023). In general, it is important that attack surfaces within healthcare services are regularly evaluated and examined for areas of reinforcement, ideal configuration or improvement.

6. Future Trends and Challenges

Trends in botnet activity include the sophistication in development and the methods from which the crafted botnet can interact with emerging technologies. Already, healthcare companies and important related infrastructure have been targeted. It is reasonable to expect that attacks will continue to spread and adjust with improving technologies (Baisley and Cherrat, 2023; Kalutharage et al, 2023; Suhag and Daniel, 2023; Rufai et al, 2023; Pavelea and Negrea, 2024). The evolving threat landscape is projected to include integrations with Artificial Intelligence and corresponding Swarm Intelligence that botnets are capable of (Saini, M., & Budakoti, J., 2013; Owen et al, 2022; Hossain, 2023; Jada and Mayayise, 2023). These abilities would allow the botnet to utilize and share resources between running programs to emulate greater degrees of intelligence. Future botnet development may continue to mature in the ability to conceal actors actions through interacting and utilizing decentralized systems, advanced cryptography, or fileless protocol. The threats to predictive and diagnostic medical systems utilizing Machine Learning are also a factor in emerging threats as these are susceptible to data poisoning, model attacks and concept drift (Javaid et al, 2022; Booth et al, 2023).

Additionally, as we move toward more mobile healthcare infrastructure that may rely heavily on cellular technology in remote or emergency locations it is important to consider the vulnerabilities threat actors may identify and abuse. Specifically within the increased use of wireless broadband communication such as 5G and 6G (Moubayed et al, 2022). An example of the practical implication of these prospective routes can be expected in the development of smart cities. Parallel to the Healthcare industry and its consideration of multiple interconnected systems it is imperative that there is an examination of several additional factors influencing communications & connectivity; current and developing telecommunications technology, consideration of the quality of life (QoL) provided to those that use a system, and the integration with IOT are such areas of reflection. Defense-minded Smart City planners would need to consider systems connected, the management and configuration of each portion and potential attack paths that could be exploited (Wazzan et al, 2021; Haque et al, 2022; Acworth, 2023; Ahmad et al, 2023; de Nobrega, 2023; Kim et al, 2023). In addition, it is important to consider the techno-culture of a group as well as diversity of cybersecurity literacy of the end users who interface with and utilize the systems. A final protective and important defensive measure would be the recruiting of neurodiverse and background diverse perspective holders who can adjust and provide feedback on systems, infrastructure and processes. There must be both innovation and mindfulness in the approaches to defense, so that holistic resilience can be fostered as a mindset and in technical implementation.

7. Conclusion

Healthcare organizations must stay vigilant against the emerging threat of improved and well-integrated botnets engineered to better interface with technical advancements stemming from artificial intelligence, machine learning and further integration with the Internet of Medical Things. As medical devices continue to be designed to connect to the internet and end users are motivated to pursue connecting their devices to the internet, security measures must be well explored at both the user, staff, and technical personnel levels. Ultimately, by proactively addressing security vulnerabilities and enhancing resilience to botnet threats, the healthcare sector can better protect patient data and infrastructure to ensure the continued delivery of critical medical services.

References

Acworth, F. (2023). *National Security Policy Options For Cyber Ecosystem Resilience* Doctoral dissertation. Te Herenga Waka-Victoria University of Wellington. Available at: https://openaccess.wgtn.ac.nz/articles/thesis/National_Security_Policy_Options_For_Cyber_Ecosystem_Resilience/22313419/1/files/39696343.pdf

Affia, A.A.O., Finch, H., Jung, W., Samori, I.A., Potter, L. and Palmer, X.L., (2023). 'IoT health devices: exploring security risks in the connected landscape'. *IoT*, 4(2), pp.150-182 doi: 10.3390/iot4020009

Ahmad, M.O., Tripathi, G., Siddiqui, F., Alam, M.A., Ahad, M.A., Akhtar, M.M. and Casalino, G. (2023). 'BAuth-ZKP—A blockchain-based multi-factor authentication mechanism for securing smart cities'. Sensors, 23(5), p.2757. doi: 10.3390/s23052757

Al-Alami, H., Hadi, A. and Al-Bahadili, H. (2017) "Vulnerability scanning of IoT devices in Jordan using Shodan. In 2017 2nd International Conference on the Applications of Information Technology in Developing Renewable Energy Processes & Systems (IT-DREPS) (pp. 1-6). *IEEE*. doi: 10.1109/IT-DREPS.2017.8277814

Alhuwail, D., Al-Jafar, E., Abdulsalam, Y., & AlDuaij, S. (2021). 'Information security awareness and behaviors of health care professionals at public health care facilities'. *Applied Clinical Informatics*, 12(04), 924-932. doi: 10.1055/s-0041-1735527

Ali, I., Ahmed, A. I. A., Almogren, A., Raza, M. A., Shah, S. A., Khan, A., & Gani, A. (2020). Systematic literature review on IoT-based botnet attack. IEEE access, 8, 212220-212232. doi: 10.1109/ACCESS.2020.3039985

Arboleda, P., Mukherjee, D., Shah, S., & Snyder, G. (2019). *Winning in the future of Medtech*. Deloitte Insights. Available at: https://www2.deloitte.com/content/dam/insights/us/articles/5144_Medtech-company-of-tomorro w/DI_Medtech-of-tomorrow_Report.pdf

Astillo, P.V., Duguma, D.G., Park, H., Kim, J., Kim, B. and You, I., 2022. "Federated intelligence of anomaly detection agent in IoTMD-enabled Diabetes Management Control System". *Future Generation Computer Systems*, 128, pp.395-405. doi: 10.3966/160792642021012201001

Ataya, G., (2010). PCI DSS audit and compliance. Information security technical report, 15(4), pp.138-144. doi: 10.1016/j.istr.2011.02.004

Baisley, T. and Cherrat, Y., (2023). *Cyber Threats and Engagements in 2022*. Available at: https://apps.dtic.mil/sti/citations/trecms/AD1208002

Biran Achituv, D., & Haiman, L. (2016). Physicians' attitudes toward the use of IoT medical devices as part of their practice. Online Journal of Applied Knowledge Management (OJAKM), 4(2), 128-145. doi:10.36965/OJAKM.2016.4(2)128-145

Booth, J., Metz, D. W., Tarkhanyan, D. A., & Cheruvu, S. (2023). Machine Learning Security and Trustworthiness. In *Demystifying Intelligent Multimode Security Systems: An Edge-to-Cloud Cybersecurity Solutions Guide* (pp. 137-222). Berkeley, CA: Apress.

Burde, H., 2011. The HITECH act: an overview. AMA Journal of Ethics, 13(3), pp.172-175. doi: 10.1001/virtualmentor.2011.13.3.hlaw1-1103

Chitadze, N. (2023). *Basic Principles of Information and Cyber Security. In Analyzing New Forms of Social Disorders in Modern Virtual Environments* (pp. 193-223). IGI Global.

Craig, D.J. (2017). 'Ensuring compliance with the HIPAA Security Rule: Think twice when e-mailing protected health information'. *The Nurse Practitioner*, 42(6), pp.12-14. doi: 10.1097/01.NPR.0000515424.38284.e6

de Nobrega, K. (2023). *Cyber defensive capacity and capability: A perspective from the financial sector of a small state.* Masters thesis. Tilburg University. Available at https://pure.uvt.nl/ws/portalfiles/portal/75137858/Thesis.pdf

Dadkhah, S.; Carlos Pinto Neto, E.; Ferreira, R.; Chukwuka Molokwu, R.; Sadeghi, S.; Ghorbani, A. (2024) "CICIoMT2024: Attack Vectors in Healthcare devices-A Multi-Protocol Dataset for Assessing IoMT Device Security." *Preprints* 2024020898. doi: https://doi.org/10.20944/preprints202402.0898.v1

Edemekong, P.F., Annamaraju, P. and Haydel, M.J. (2022). Health Insurance Portability and Accountability Act. In StatPearls [Internet]. StatPearls Publishing.

Elmas, E. (2023). *Dijital Çağda Ödeme Sistemlerinde Siber Güvenlik ve Risk Değerlendirme*. Doctoral dissertation. Marmara Universitesi. Available at: https://www.proquest.com/openview/2b31d7ed3b321e5f277f1746014b4e3a/1

Fard Bahreini, A. (2023). Which information locations in covered entities under HIPAA must be secured first? A multi-criteria decision-making approach. Journal of Healthcare Risk Management, 43(2), pp.27-36. doi: 10.1002/jhrm.21555

Farooq, M.S., Riaz, S., Tehseen, R., Farooq, U. and Saleem, K. (2023). "Role of Internet of things in diabetes healthcare: Network infrastructure, taxonomy, challenges, and security model". *Digital Health*, 9, p.20552076231179056. doi: 10.1177/2055207623117905

Filkins, B. (2014). *Health Care Cyberthreat Report: Widespread Compromises Detected, Compliance Nightmare on Horizon.* Available at: https://www.redwoodmednet.org/projects/events/20150731/docs/Norse-SANS-Healthcare-Cyberthreat-Report2014.pdf

Finch, H., Affia, A.A., Jung, W., Potter, L. and Palmer, X.L.(2023) Commentary on healthcare and disruptive innovation. In International Conference on Cyber Warfare and Security (Vol. 18, No. 1, pp. 77-84).

Fisher, D. (2023). *The Fourth Industrial Revolution: A case study of the impact of the Internet of Things on road travelers in the Western Cape.* Doctoral dissertation. Stellenbosch University. Available at: https://scholar.sun.ac.za/server/api/core/bitstreams/4e058879-c944-4921-bd5d-6baa01f7613c/content

Haque, A.B., Bhushan, B. and Dhiman, G.(2022) "Conceptualizing smart city applications: Requirements, architecture, security issues, and emerging trends". *Expert Systems, 39*(5), p.e12753. doi: 10.1111/exsy.12753

Harkat, H., Camarinha-Matos, L. M., Goes, J., & Ahmed, H. F. (2024). 'Cyber-Physical Systems Security: A Systematic Review.' *Computers & Industrial Engineering*, 109891. doi: 10.1016/j.cie.2024.109891

Hernandez-Jaimes, M. L., Martinez-Cruz, A., Ramírez-Gutiérrez, K. A., & Feregrino-Uribe, C. (2023). Artificial intelligence for IoMT security: A review of intrusion detection systems, attacks, datasets and Cloud-Fog-Edge architectures. Internet of Things, 100887. doi: 10.1016/j.iot.2023.100887

Hiller, J., Kisska-Schulze, K., & Shackelford, S. (2024). Cybersecurity carrots and sticks. American Business Law Journal, 61(1), 5-29. doi: 10.1111/ablj.12238

Hossain, K. A. (2023). 'Analysis Of Present And Future Use Of Artificial Intelligence (Ai) In Line Of Fourth Industrial Revolution (4IR)'. *Scientific Research Journal (SCIRJ)* doi: 10.31364/SCIRJ/v11.i8.2023.P0823954

Jada, I., & Mayayise, T. O. (2023). 'The impact of artificial intelligence on organizational cyber security: An outcome of a systematic literature review'. *Data and Information Management*, 100063. doi:10.1016/j.dim.2023.100063

Javaid, M., Haleem, A., Singh, R. P., Suman, R., & Rab, S. (2022, June 5). 'Significance of machine learning in Healthcare: Features, pillars and applications'. *International Journal of Intelligent Networks.* doi:10.1016/j.ijin.2022.05.002

Kalutharage, C.S., Liu, X., Chrysoulas, C., Pitropakis, N. and Papadopoulos, P., 2023. Explainable AI-based DDOS attack identification method for IoT networks. *Computers*, 12(2), p.32. doi:10.3390/computers12020032

Kim, D., Jeon, S., Shin, J. and Seo, J.T., 2023. Design the IoT Botnet Defense Process for Cybersecurity in Smart City. *Intelligent Automation & Soft Computing*, *37*(3). doi: 10.32604/iasc.2023.040019

Kumar, A. and Sharma, I., 2023, May. Augmenting iot healthcare security and reliability with early detection of iot botnet attacks. In *2023 4th International Conference for Emerging Technology (INCET)* (pp. 1-6). IEEE. doi:10.1109/INCET57972.2023.10170738

Liu, J., Xiao, Y., Ghaboosi, K., Deng, H., & Zhang, J. (2009) 'Botnet: classification, attacks, detection, tracing, and preventive measures'. *EURASIP journal on wireless communications and networking*, 2009, 1-11. doi:10.1155/2009/692654

Malamas, V., Chantzis, F., Dasaklis, T. K., Stergiopoulos, G., Kotzanikolaou, P., & Douligeris, C. (2021). 'Risk assessment methodologies for the internet of medical things: A survey and comparative appraisal'. *IEEE Access*, 9, 40049-40075. doi: 10.1109/ACCESS.2021.306468

Mavrogiorgou, A., Kiourtis, A., Perakis, K., Pitsios, S. and Kyriazis, D., 2019. IoT in healthcare: Achieving interoperability of high-quality data acquired by IoT medical devices. Sensors, 19(9), p.1978. doi: 10.3390/s19091978

Mennemeyer, S.T., Menachemi, N., Rahurkar, S. and Ford, E.W., 2016. Impact of the HITECH act on physicians' adoption of electronic health records. *Journal of the American Medical Informatics Association, 23*(2), pp.375-379. doi: 10.1093/jamia/ocv103

Moubayed, A., Shami, A. and Al-Dulaimi, A., 2022. On end-to-end intelligent automation of 6G networks. Future Internet, 14(6), p.165. doi: 10.3390/fi14060165

Mueller, S., 2021. Facing the 2020 pandemic: What does Cyberbiosecurity want us to know to safeguard the future?. Biosafety and health, 3(01), pp.11-21. doi: 10.1016/j.bsheal.2020.09.007

Otieno, M., Odera, D., & Ounza, J. E. (2023) Theory and practice in secure software development lifecycle: A comprehensive survey. doi:10.30574/wjarr.2023.18.3.0944

Owen, H., Zarrin, J. and Pour, S.M., 2022. A survey on botnets, issues, threats, methods, detection and prevention. Journal of Cybersecurity and Privacy, 2(1), pp.74-88. doi: 10.3390/jcp2010006

Pavelea, A., & Negrea, P. C. (2024) A Comprehensive Analysis of High-Impact Cybersecurity Incidents: Case Studies and Implications. Masters thesis. Babeș–Bolyai University. doi: 10.13140/RG.2.2.17461.65763

Phiri, L. (2023). *A framework for cyber security risk modeling and mitigation in smart grid communication and control systems.* Doctoral dissertation. The University of Zambia. Available at: https://dspace.unza.zm/items/f775ee4e-140c-4dd9-84be-bab5caa69c32

Polis, G. (2023). *Using the principles of cybersecurity ethics to mitigate cybersecurity risks.* Masters thesis. Banku Augstskola School of Business and Finance. Available at: doi:10.13140/RG.2.2.15285.86245

Potter, L., Ayala, O. and Palmer, X.L. (2021). "Biocybersecurity: a converging threat as an auxiliary to war". In *ICCWS 2021 16th international conference on cyber warfare and security* (p. 291).

Potter, L. and Palmer, X.L. (2023). Mission-aware differences in cyberbiosecurity and biocybersecurity policies: Prevention, detection, and elimination. In Cyberbiosecurity: A new field to deal with emerging threats (pp. 37-69). Cham: Springer International Publishing.

Puri, V. (2007). *Automated alerting for black hole routing.* Doctoral dissertation. Naval Postgraduate School. Available at: https://apps.dtic.mil/sti/citations/tr/ADA474419

Raju, R. and Moh, M. (2020) Cyber-physical systems in healthcare: Review of architecture, security issues, intrusion detection, and defenses. *Recent Advances in Security, Privacy, and Trust for Internet of Things (IoT) and Cyber-Physical Systems (CPS)*, pp.23-62.

Rufai, A.U., Fasina, E.P., Uwadia, C.O., Rufai, A.T. and Imoize, A.L.(2023) "Cyberattacks against Artificial Intelligence-Enabled Internet of Medical Things". *Handbook of Security and Privacy of AI-Enabled Healthcare Systems and Internet of Medical Things* (pp. 191-216). CRC Press.

Saini, M., & Budakoti, J. (2013). 'Impact of social media marketing on consumer behavior.' *Procedia Economics and Finance*, 11, 677-689. https://doi.org/10.1016/S2212-5671(13)00116-1

Suhag, A. and Daniel, A., 2023. Study of statistical techniques and artificial intelligence methods in distributed denial of service (DDOS) assault and defense. *Journal of Cyber Security Technology*, 7(1), pp.21-51. doi: 10.1080/23742917.2022.2135856

Summary of the HIPAA security rule (2022) *HHS.gov*. Available at: https://www.hhs.gov/hipaa/for-professionals/security/laws-regulations/index.html

Travis, F. J. M. (2023). *Secure Interface Improvements Internet of Things (IoT) Vendors Need to Protect Smart Home IoT Devices from Cyber Attacks.* Doctoral dissertation. University of the Cumberlands. Available at: https://www.proquest.com/openview/52c715f15eeb29df9405a49dbf48ea17

Wazzan, M., Algazzawi, D., Bamasaq, O., Albeshri, A., & Cheng, L. (2021). 'Internet of Things botnet detection approaches: Analysis and recommendations for future research'. *Applied Sciences*, 11(12), 5713. doi: 10.3390/app11125713

Yaacoub JP, Noura HN, Salman O, Chehab A. (2022) 'Advanced digital forensics and anti-digital forensics for IoT systems: Techniques, limitations and recommendations.' *Internet of Things*.;19:100544. doi:10.1016/j.iot.2022.100544

Yulianto, S., Lim, C. and Soewito, B., (2016) "Information security maturity model: A best practice driven approach to PCI DSS compliance". *2016 IEEE Region 10 Symposium* (TENSYMP) (pp. 65-70). IEEE. doi: 10.1109/TENCONSpring.2016.7519379

Zahedi, Z., Mahmud, F., & Pinto, C. (2020). Systemic risk management plan for electronic medical records (EMR): Why and how? In *HTI Open Access Collection 2020* (19 pp.). IOS Press https://doi.org/10.3233/SHTI200016

Zhao, B., Ji, S., Lee, W.H., Lin, C., Weng, H., Wu, J., Zhou, P., Fang, L. and Beyah, R., 2020. "A large-scale empirical study on the vulnerability of deployed iot devices". *IEEE Transactions on Dependable and Secure Computing*, 19(3), pp.1826-1840. doi: 10.1109/TDSC.2020.3037908

Enhancing Network Security: Rogue Switch Detection and Prevention in Local Area Network

Vijay Bhuse, Yesaswini Vellaboina and Xinli Wang
School of Computing and Information Systems, Grand Valley State University, Allendale, MI, USA

bhusevij@gvsu.edu
vellaboy@mail.gvsu.edu
wangx@gvsu.edu

Abstract— Our paper comprehensively examines ways to detect and handle unauthorized switches in Local Area Networks (LANs) within today's intricate and interconnected network landscape. We demonstrate the utilization of PortFast and BPDU guard configurations to reinforce LAN security against unauthorized devices and potential complications arising from the spanning tree protocol. These measures not only enhance network performance but also function as robust protective mechanisms, safeguarding the integrity of the LAN infrastructure. Furthermore, this paper delves into advanced techniques for the proactive identification and prevention of rogue switches, fostering an overall enhanced security posture within LANs. By synergistically integrating PortFast, BPDU guard, and advanced rogue switch detection methods, the paper proposes a robust methodology to strengthen LAN security and maintain uninterrupted network operations. It equips organizations with crucial resources to establish a resilient, secure, and dependable digital infrastructure, addressing the evolving demands of network security.

Keywords: Rogue Switch, Portfast, BPDU Guard, Network Security, LAN, Detection

1. Introduction

In our interconnected digital realm, where the seamless flow of information is indispensable for businesses, institutions, and individuals, network security is most important. Local Area Networks (LANs) serve as the cornerstone of modern communication, safeguarding the integrity, availability, and confidentiality of sensitive data. As the intricacy of networked devices intensifies, bolstering LAN security becomes an absolute necessity in the face of increasing array of threats.

We comprehensively explore the intricate domain of LAN security, emphasizing three pivotal components that synergistically augment security: PortFast (PortFast 2018), Bridge Protocol Data Units (BPDU 2018) guard, and Rogue Switch Detection. PortFast and BPDU guard configurations optimize network performance and resilience, mitigating risks from unauthorized devices and alleviating risks associated with potential Spanning Tree Protocol (STP 2018) anomalies. These configurations embody proactive measures shielding LANs from disruptions and unauthorized intrusions.

Notwithstanding, in the face of a constantly evolving threat landscape, a more in-depth examination of rogue switch identification and mitigation is warranted. Rogue switches can introduce instability and security vulnerabilities, underlining the criticality of advanced detection mechanisms. The research rigorously investigates and implements these techniques to empower organizations with the capability to proactively counter potential threats.

Rogue switches can infiltrate the network through physical connections, where unauthorized individuals directly connect them to open network ports, mimicking legitimate equipment. This can be accomplished by plugging the rogue switch into an open wall jack or by connecting it to a network switch that is not properly secured. Employee errors, stemming from a lack of security awareness, can also contribute to rogue switch introductions. For example, an employee may accidentally connect a rogue switch to the network if they are not aware of the potential security risks. Insiders with malicious intent pose a substantial threat, as they may intentionally introduce rogue switches to the network to steal data or disrupt operations.

BPDU guard and PortFast stand as two critical components, working in tandem to safeguard Local Area Networks (LANs) from unauthorized access and potential disruptions. BPDU guard, a feature developed by Cisco, complements PortFast by actively monitoring ports for Bridge Protocol Data Units (BPDUs). These BPDUs serve as signals indicating the presence of unauthorized switches or misconfigurations within the network. By continuously monitoring for these BPDU signals, BPDU guard effectively identifies and neutralizes potential threats before they can compromise network integrity. On the other hand, PortFast expedites the transition process for access ports, eliminating the delays often encountered in traditional implementations. This rapid transition ensures that end-user communication remains uninterrupted and efficient. By streamlining the access port transition process, PortFast contributes to a seamless and responsive network environment.

The integration of BPDU guard with PortFast proves to be a pivotal combination for network security. BPDU guard's active monitoring capabilities, coupled with PortFast's efficiency enhancements, provide a comprehensive approach to safeguarding LANs. This synergy ensures that both network efficiency and security are maintained on access ports, fostering a robust and reliable network infrastructure.

2. Related Work

The challenge of identifying rogue devices in network environments is a critical concern for network administrators aiming to maintain network security and stability. While existing methods have been established for detecting rogue wireless access points, the distinctive characteristics of wired networks necessitate separate approaches (Bhuse *et al.*, 2019 and Bhuse *et al.*, 2020).

The methods typically employed for identifying rogue wireless access points, such as wireless traffic analysis, site survey software, and tools like NetSpot (NetSpot, 2011), face limitations in the context of wired networks. These solutions are primarily reliant on monitoring wireless traffic patterns to identify suspicious activities, rendering them inapplicable for wired network infrastructures (Solarwinds, 2019) (Cisco Packet Tracer, 2023). Confronted with the challenge of detecting rogue switches in wired networks, network administrators have sometimes turned to IP sweep tools like Nmap (Nmap, 1997). However, these tools, while useful for IP address-based scanning, exhibit limited effectiveness. In wired networks, unmanaged Layer 2 switches are prevalent, often lacking IP addresses and support for neighbor discovery protocols. This limitation makes it difficult to accurately identify and locate rogue switches using traditional IP sweep.

Cisco's proprietary PortFast protocol provides an effective solution to address the challenge of rogue switches in wired networks. PortFast allows switches to expedite the activation of access ports by assuming that the connected device is a non-Spanning Tree Protocol (STP) device. As a result, the port is immediately transitioned to the forwarding mode. This streamlined approach significantly reduces network convergence time and, despite its proprietary nature, PortFast has become a standard feature in Cisco's switch offerings, facilitating the rapid provisioning of access ports (Cisco, 2018).

Complementing PortFast, Cisco's BPDU Guard serves as a vital security feature in wired network environments. BPDU Guard prevents unauthorized devices from transmitting Bridge Protocol Data Units (BPDUs) on access ports. When BPDU Guard is enabled on an access port and an unauthorized device attempts to send a BPDU, the port is promptly shut down. This proactive approach safeguards the network's integrity by swiftly blocking potentially harmful devices.

Numerous research efforts have been undertaken to determine the optimal configuration of PortFast and BPDU Guard for various types of local area networks (LANs) (Cisco, 2018). Cisco's PortFast and BPDU Guard protocols offer effective solutions to enhance network performance and security in wired environments. Ongoing research efforts aim to optimize the configuration of these protocols, tailoring them to diverse LAN topologies and security requirements.

3. Problem Definition

The existence of unauthorized rogue switches in Local Area Networks (LANs) poses a substantial threat to both the security and reliability of the network. These rogue switches, which are not authorized network devices, have the potential to disrupt normal network operations, compromise the security of data, and introduce anomalies into the spanning tree protocol. Regardless of whether they infiltrate the network with malicious intent or unintentionally, these devices introduce various risks such as network congestion, unauthorized access, data breaches, and potential network outages. The increasing number of connected devices in LANs further complicates the task of identifying and mitigating rogue switches.

To tackle this issue effectively, it is essential to use PortFast and BPDU guards. PortFast facilitates swift access for authorized end-user devices, ensuring efficient network operations. On the other hand, the BPDU guard acts as a protective measure against unauthorized switches by promptly disabling the corresponding port, thereby preventing network disruptions, and bolstering overall security. This configuration is crucial in environments where network reliability is a top priority, including critical infrastructure, guest networks, and remote office setups. By employing PortFast and BPDU guards, organizations can establish a robust defense against the threats posed by rogue switches, ensuring both efficiency and security in LAN operations.

4. Experimental Analysis

Through a series of four experiments simulated with Cisco Packet Tracer, the application of PortFast and BPDU guard configurations was systematically explored to address network security concerns. The initial experiment highlighted security vulnerabilities in a baseline network topology without these configurations. Subsequent experiments demonstrated the collaborative impact of PortFast and BPDU guard in facilitating swift network access for authorized devices while effectively guarding against potential security threats, including the introduction of a rogue switch.

The final experiment, conducted in a complex network topology, emphasized the crucial role of BPDU guard in preventing unauthorized devices from disrupting the network's stability. Collectively, these experiments underscored the critical importance of implementing PortFast and BPDU guard configurations to enhance network performance, secure authorized access, and mitigate potential threats from unauthorized devices, ensuring the overall integrity and security of network infrastructures.

4.1 Experiment 1:

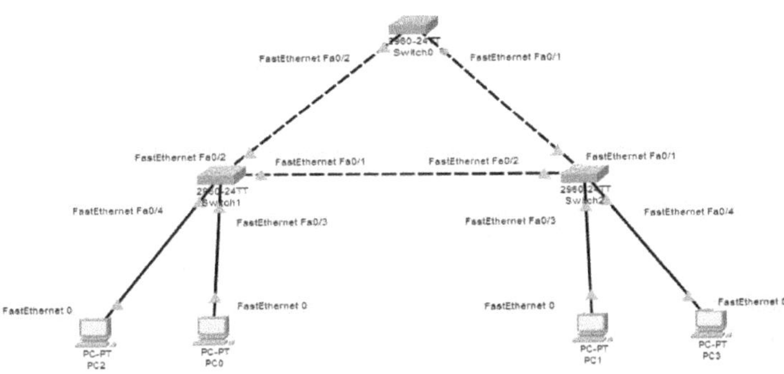

Figure 1: Network with STP enabled.

In a Cisco Packet Tracer simulation, a network topology was created to illustrate the practical application of network security. The network topology consists of three Cisco switches (Switch 0, Switch 1, and Switch 2) interconnected in a simple topology. Switch 0 is connected to Switch 1 via port 2, and Switch 0 is also linked to Switch 2 via port 1. Switch 1 is further connected to Switch 2 through port 2. This arrangement forms the foundation for demonstrating network configuration and security concepts. On Switch 1, two personal computers (PC 0 and PC 2) are connected to ports 3 and 4, respectively. Switch 2 has PC 1 and PC 3 connected to ports 3 and 4. These end-user devices represent practical network access points where network administrators must balance security and rapid connectivity.

In the current state of the network, PortFast and BPDU guard configurations have not been applied to the switch ports connecting to these end-user devices. Therefore, the network currently operates with standard spanning tree protocol settings. Significance of this scenario lies in the potential application of PortFast and BPDU guard configurations to enhance network performance and security. By configuring PortFast on the switch ports that connect to these end-user devices, network administrators can reduce the time required for devices to become operational, a critical requirement in environments where swift network access is essential.

Furthermore, the scenario highlights the potential security risks associated with swift port transitions when unauthorized devices, including rogue switches, exploit this rapid network access. Applying BPDU guard in conjunction with Port Fast can effectively monitor and prevent unauthorized network equipment from introducing disruptions or security breaches.

While the network in its current state does not employ PortFast and BPDU guard, the scenario sets the stage for the application of these configurations to strike a balance between network efficiency and security. By illustrating the impact of these configurations on a representative network topology, this research paper aims to enhance the understanding of how they can be applied to improve performance and safeguard against unauthorized network access and disruptions. It underscores the crucial role of network administrators in configuring and managing these features effectively to maintain network security and operational efficiency.

4.2 Experiment 2:

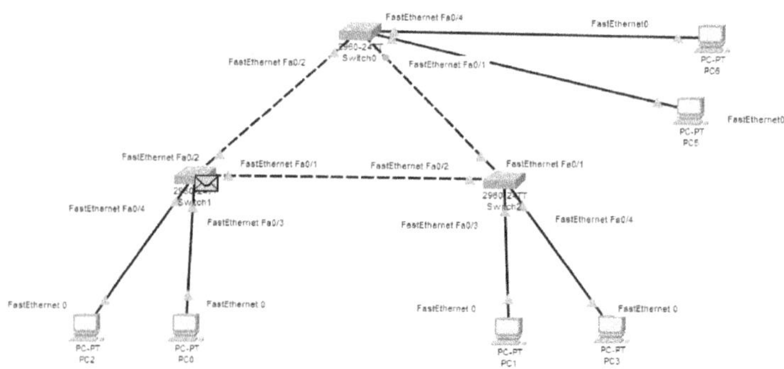

Figure 2: Network with PortFast and BPDU guard configured

In this Cisco Packet Tracer experiment, we have configured Switch 0, Port 4, with both PortFast and BPDU guard enabled, and introduced PC6 to the network, exemplifying the significance of these configurations in the realm of network security and efficient network access.

4.2.1 PortFast and BPDU Guard Configuration:

PortFast has been thoughtfully applied to Port 4 of Switch 0 to expedite network access for connected devices. Its primary objective is to reduce the time required for devices to transition to a fully operational state, significantly improving user experience. In scenarios where swift network access is paramount, Port Fast simplifies the process.

Complementing Port Fast, BPDU guard has been configured on the same port. BPDU guard plays a pivotal role in safeguarding the network from unauthorized or potentially disruptive devices. It continually monitors incoming traffic for Bridge Protocol Data Units (BPDUs), which are indicative of Spanning Tree Protocol (STP) messages typically generated by network switches. The presence of BPDUs suggests the potential connection of an unauthorized switch or a misconfigured device. In response to this security threat, BPDU guard is programmed to disable Port 4 promptly, protecting the network against potential disruptions and unauthorized access attempts.

4.2.2 Network Operation:

With PC6 connected to Port 4, the network operates smoothly. PC6 experiences rapid network access, and the network remains unaffected by any security actions triggered by BPDU guard. There are no disruptions or security concerns because PC6 is an authorized device and does not generate BPDUs.

This scenario demonstrates the practical implications of PortFast and BPDU guard configurations in a security-sensitive environment. It highlights how these configurations, when properly employed, can strike a delicate balance between network efficiency and security. While PortFast expedites network access for authorized devices, BPDU guard acts as a vigilant guardian against rogue devices and unauthorized network access.

The experiment showcases the synergy between these configurations, safeguarding the network against unauthorized or potentially disruptive devices, while ensuring swift network access for authorized users. By illustrating the impact of these configurations on a tangible network setup, this research paper seeks to enhance the understanding of how PortFast and BPDU guard can be applied to improve network performance and security. It underscores the critical role of network administrators in configuring and managing these features effectively to maintain network security and operational efficiency, ensuring that authorized devices can access the network swiftly without compromising its integrity.

4.3 Experiment 3:

In a controlled Cisco Packet Tracer experiment, we implemented PortFast and BPDU guard configurations on Switch 0, Port 4, and introduced a rogue switch to the network, providing valuable insights into the practical application of these security features. This scenario elucidates the significance of PortFast and BPDU guard in network security by addressing real-world vulnerabilities. Switch 0, a key component of the network topology, is equipped with Port 4, which has been configured with PortFast and BPDU guard settings. These settings are crucial for enhancing network efficiency while concurrently bolstering security.

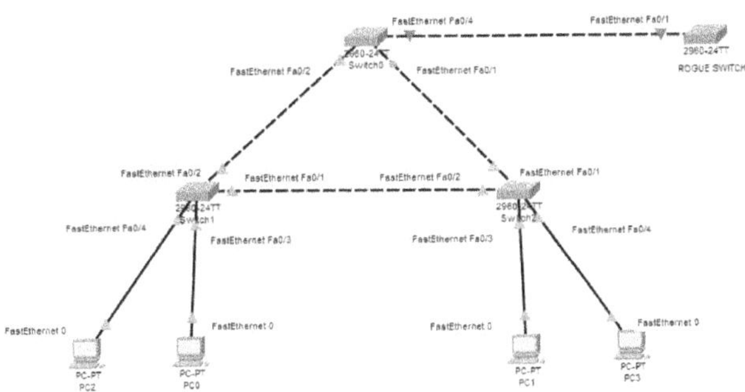

Figure 3: BPDU guard implemented

Port Fast Configuration: Port Fast is applied to Port 4 of Switch 0 to expedite network access for devices connected to this port. The primary goal is to reduce the time required for devices to become fully operational. In scenarios where swift network access is imperative, Port Fast streamlines the process.

BPDU guard Configuration: BPDU guard, implemented in tandem with PortFast on Port 4, serves as the network's first line of defense against unauthorized or rogue devices. BPDU guard vigilantly monitors incoming traffic for Bridge Protocol Data Units (BPDUs), typically indicative of spanning tree protocol messages generated by network switches. The presence of BPDUs suggests the potential connection of an unauthorized switch or a misconfigured device. In response to this security threat, BPDU guard automatically disables Port 4 to safeguard the network against potential disruptions and unauthorized access attempts.

Introducing the Rogue Switch: In the experiment, a rogue switch is introduced and connected to Port 4 of Switch 0, impersonating an authorized network device. Rogue switches are a potential security concern as they can inadvertently or maliciously introduce network loops or disrupt network operations. Rogue switches often remain undetected until they compromise network stability.

This controlled experiment demonstrates the real-world implications of PortFast and BPDU guard configurations in a security-sensitive environment. The deployment of PortFast expedites network access, enhancing the user experience, while the implementation of BPDU guard offers immediate protection against rogue devices.

The presence of the rogue switch on Port 4 initiates a critical response from the network. BPDU guard, diligently monitoring the port, detects the unauthorized BPDUs originating from the rogue switch. In response, BPDU guard promptly disables Port 4, neutralizing the potential security threat and preventing network disruptions.

This scenario underscores the essential role of PortFast and BPDU guard in securing network access points. It provides a tangible demonstration of the critical security implications and efficiency enhancements brought about by the simultaneous use of these features, protecting the network against rogue devices while ensuring rapid network access for authorized users. The experiment showcases how these configurations are pivotal in maintaining network security and operational efficiency in the face of evolving network threats.

4.3.1 *Detection of Rogue Switch:*

Ensuring the security and stability of a local area network is of paramount importance. Rogue switches, unauthorized devices that can disrupt network operations and compromise security, pose a significant threat. In this scenario, we explore the use of PortFast and BPDU Guard to detect and respond to rogue switches effectively.

4.3.2 *Experimental Analysis:*

Step 1: Configuration

Port 4 on Switch 0 is configured with PortFast, ensuring that it transitions to the forwarding state without the usual spanning-tree checks and timers. Additionally, BPDU Guard is enabled on Port 4 of Switch 0.

Step 2: Rogue Switch Connection

A rogue switch attempts to connect to Port 4 of Switch 0. When the rogue switch is powered on, it begins sending BPDUs due to its lack of proper network configuration.

Step 3: BPDU Guard Activation

As the rogue switch sends BPDUs, BPDU Guard on Port 4 of Switch 0 detects these unexpected BPDUs.

Step 4: Error Detection

The command-line interface (CLI) of Switch 0 displays a BPDU Guard error message indicating the detection of unexpected BPDUs on Port 4. This message is a critical alert for network administrators.

Step 5: Port Shutdown

In response to the BPDU Guard error, Switch 0 takes action to safeguard the network. Port 4 is placed into an error-disabled state, effectively disconnecting the rogue switch from the network.

Upon detecting the error, the network administrator is alerted to the situation. They can investigate and resolve the rogue switch issue, ensuring network security and integrity. Port 4 can be manually re-enabled once the rogue switch is removed.

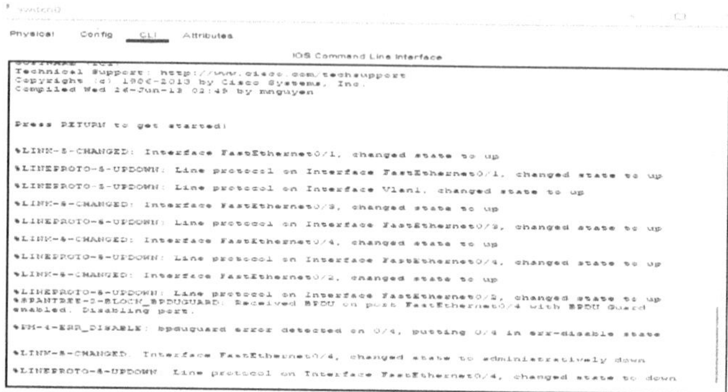

Figure 4: Detection of Rogue Switch

The scenario illustrates the significance of employing features like PortFast and BPDU Guard to protect a network from rogue devices. Rapid detection and response to unexpected BPDUs contribute to network stability and security, safeguarding the network from potential disruptions.

4.4 Experiment 4:

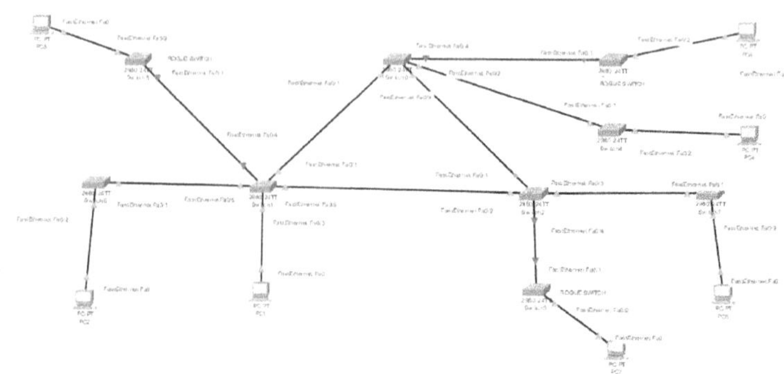

Figure 5: Network Infrastructure with Rogue Switches

For our research, we have configured a BPDU guard on three switches (Switch 0, Switch 1, and Switch 2), specifically on Port 4 of each switch. These switches are part of a network infrastructure, and Port 4 is strategically selected for this experiment. In our setup, rogue switches are introduced and connected to Port 4 of each of the three switches to evaluate the BPDU guard's effectiveness. BPDU guard operates by monitoring incoming BPDU frames on a switch port. If it detects a BPDU frame, the port is immediately placed in an error-disabled state.

In this network topology, Switch 0 serves as the central hub, connecting various switches and devices. Port 1 of Switch 0 links to Switch 1, while Port 2 connects to Switch 8, subsequently connecting to PC4. Port 3 is directed towards Switch 2, and Port 4 establishes a connection with Switch 4, which, in turn, connects to PC5. The network branching out from Switch 0 forms the core of the infrastructure, facilitating data flow between the switches and connected devices.

Switch 1 plays a pivotal role in the network by connecting to Switch 0 and various devices. It has links to Switch 2 via Port 2, connects directly to PC1 through Port 3, and establishes connections with Switch 5 and Switch 6 via Ports 4 and 5, respectively. These interconnections create a hierarchical structure, allowing for the distribution of data and resources efficiently. Switch 2, in turn, further expands the network, connecting to Switch 7 and Switch 3, which in turn connect to PC3 and PC7, respectively. This intricate design provides a comprehensive framework for the network's operations.

Switches 5, 6, 7, and 8 are responsible for connecting to individual devices: PC6, PC2, PC3, and PC4, respectively. The network design is structured to optimize data traffic and facilitate communication between the devices, ensuring seamless data transfer and efficient resource allocation. Understanding this network topology is crucial for network management, troubleshooting, and planning for scalability. It forms the backbone of a robust communication infrastructure, with each switch acting as a critical node in the network's overall functionality.

This action helps safeguard the network by preventing unauthorized devices from participating in the STP process, thus minimizing the potential for loops and other network disruptions. In our experiment, when rogue switches were introduced and connected to Port 4 of the switches (Switch 0, Switch 1, and Switch 2), the BPDU guard was triggered as expected. Upon receiving unauthorized BPDUs from the rogue switches, all three switches promptly disabled Port 4. This action successfully prevented the rogue switches from interfering with the network topology and maintained network stability.

The results of our study emphasize the vital role of BPDU guard in securing network infrastructure. By effectively disabling ports in response to unauthorized BPDU frames, it acts as a robust line of defense against rogue switches and other potential threats.

This security feature ensures that the network topology remains intact and operates without disruptions caused by unauthorized devices. In this research paper, we have explored the effectiveness of BPDU guard in mitigating network vulnerabilities introduced by rogue switches.

Our case study demonstrates that BPDU guard successfully identifies and responds to unauthorized BPDU frames, promptly disabling the affected ports and preventing rogue switches from compromising network stability. As such, we conclude that BPDU guard is a valuable feature for enhancing network security and ensuring the smooth operation of network infrastructure.

5. Conclusion

In conclusion, this research paper has delved into the critical realm of network security within Local Area Networks (LANs), with a specific focus on the prevention of rogue switches. The investigation has centered around the strategic implementation of PortFast and BPDU guard configurations as essential measures to fortify LANs against unauthorized devices and potential disruptions to the spanning tree protocol.

Through meticulously designed experiments simulated with the Cisco Packet Tracer, the practical implications of PortFast and BPDU guard configurations have been elucidated. These configurations, when appropriately deployed, showcase a synergistic relationship, enhancing both network efficiency and security. The experiments have underscored the importance of striking a delicate balance between rapid network access and safeguarding against unauthorized devices, particularly rogue switches.

Beyond the technical configurations, this research has addressed the multifaceted challenges associated with the introduction of rogue switches, considering various avenues such as physical connections, employee errors, and insider threats. The emphasis on proactive measures, including robust identity and access management, heightened employee awareness, and regular assessments, underscores the holistic approach required to mitigate security risks comprehensively.

This case study proves the critical role PortFast and BPDU guard play in preventing the introduction of rogue network switches. The insights derived from the experiments and analysis, empower network administrators with practical methodologies to enhance both the security posture and operational efficiency of LANs. By understanding and implementing the findings presented herein, organizations can foster resilient, secure, and trustworthy digital infrastructures in the face of evolving threats within interconnected environments.

References

Bhuse, V., Kalafut, A., & Dohn L. (2019). "Detection of a Rogue Switch in a Local Area Network". International Conference on Internet Monitoring and Protection, Nice, France.

Bhuse, V., James V. (2020). "Detecting a Rogue Switch using Network Automation". ECCWS 2020 19th European Conference on Cyber Warfare and Security.

BPDU (2018) "Configuring BPDU Guard" Cisco.

Catalyst 3560 Software Configuration Guide, https://www.cisco.com/c/en/us/td/docs/switches/lan/catalyst3560/software/release/12-2_52_se/configuration/guide/3560scg/swstpopt.html#wp1203191

Cisco (2018). "Configuring Spanning Tree Protocol", https://www.cisco.com/c/en/us/td/docs/switches/lan/catalyst9200/software/release/16-10/configuration_guide/lyr2/b_1610_lyr2_9200_cg/configuring_spanning___tree_protocol.html

Cisco Packet Tracer (2024) "Cisco Packet Tracer." https://www.netacad.com/courses/packet-tracer.

NetSpot (2011). "Wi-Fi Network Planning and Site Survey." https://www.netspotapp.com

Nmap (1997). "Nmap: the Network Mapper - Free Security Scanner." https://nmap.org

fInNUcastPkts (2018) Available at: http://oid-info.com/get/1.3.6.1.2.1.2.2.1.12.

STP (2018). "Understanding Spanning Tree Protocol (STP)" https://www.cisco.com/en/US/tech/tk389/tk621/technologies_white_paper09186a0080094cfa.shtml

Solarwinds (2019) "Detecting and Preventing Rogue Devices." https://www.solarwinds.com.

PortFast (2018) "Configuring PortFast"

Quitiquit, T., and Bhuse, V. (2022) "Utilizing Switch Port Link State to Detect Rogue Switches." Grand Valley State University, Allendale, MI, USA.

An Analysis of a Cryptocurrency Giveaway Scam: Use Case

Johnny Botha[1] and Louise Leenen[2]
[1]Council for Scientific and Industrial Research, Pretoria, South Africa
[2]University of Western Cape and CAIR, Cape town, South Africa

jbotha1@csir.co.za
lleenen@uwc.ac.za

Abstract: A giveaway scam is a type of fraud leveraging social media platforms and phishing campaigns. These scams have become increasingly common and are now also prevalent in the crypto community where attackers attempt to gain crypto-enthusiasts' trust with the promise of high-yield giveaways. Giveaway scams target individuals who lack technical familiarity with the blockchain. They take on various forms, often presenting as genuine cryptocurrency giveaways endorsed by prominent figures or organizations within the blockchain community. Scammers entice victims by promising substantial returns on a nominal investment. Victims are manipulated into sending cryptocurrency under the pretext of paying for "verification" or "processing fees." However, once the funds have been sent, the scammers disappear and leave victims empty-handed. This study employs essential blockchain tools and techniques to explore the mechanics of giveaway scams. A crucial aspect of an investigation is to meticulously trace the movement of funds within the blockchain so that illicit gains resulting from these scams can be tracked. At some point a scammer wants to "cash-out" by transferring the funds to an off-ramp, for example, an exchange. If the investigator can establish a link to such an exchange, the identity of the owner of cryptocurrency address could be revealed. However, in organised scams, criminals make use of mules and do not use their own identities. The authors of this paper select a use case and then illustrate a comprehensive approach to investigate the selected scam. This paper contributes to the understanding and mitigation of giveaway scams in the cryptocurrency realm. By leveraging the mechanics of blockchain technology, dissecting scammer tactics, and utilizing investigative techniques and tools, the paper aims to contribute to the protection of investors, the industry, and the overall integrity of the blockchain ecosystem. This research sheds light on the intricate workings of giveaway scams and proposes effective strategies to counteract them.

Keywords: Blockchain, Crypto-crime, Cryptocurrency, Crypto-scam, Giveaway-Scam.

1. Introduction and Background

Cryptocurrencies continue to grow by means of legitimate users, but they also attract a wide range of criminal activities (Pelker, 2021). Cryptocurrency (crypto) giveaway scams are one of the most common scams in which an attacker lures a victim by announcing a giveaway of a certain cryptocurrency or digital asset (Botha, Badenhorst, & Leenen, 2023). These types of scams have been a major problem for the crypto community since late 2017. It is recommended that all crypto investors be educated on current crypto related scams in order to identify such instances. A giveaway scam is a form of social engineering where a scammer attempts to deceive an investor in believing some major crypto currency exchange, such as Coinbase[1] or Binance[2] for example, is hosting a giveaway. To participate in the giveaway, the investor is requested to send a specified amount of cryptocurrency to a given address so that the platform can verify the investor's wallet address and the legitimacy of the investor's account. It should be noted that crypto transactions are irreversible; once the victim has sent funds to the scammer's address the transaction cannot be reversed. It should also be noted that exchanges host actual giveaways from time to time, but these exchanges never issue requests for cryptocurrency contributions to participate in giveaways (Hauer, 2020).

Scammers make use of social media sites to advertise or announce their fake giveaways. A giveaway scam is often linked to an impersonation scam. Scammers will either impersonate a company, a celebrity or a famous influencer. An example of a scam where a company is impersonated, may involve a Twitter account supposedly belonging to the Coinbase company. In this scam a 5000 Bitcoin (BTC) giveaway scam is promoted by a tweet containing a link which redirects users to a fraudulent web page. The target is asked to send any amount from 0.1 to 10 BTC to the scammer's giveaway address in order to verify the target's address. On the web page, targets are assured that they will earn ten times their "verification"payment. In reality, a victim will not receive any payback – they have fallen for a scam. The impersonation of an individual is any instance in which a scammer tries to take advantage of a famous person's trustworthy reputation on social platforms such as Facebook, Twitter, YouTube, Telegram, Discord, Instagram, TikTok, etc. Celebrities who have often been impersonated in

[1] https://www.coinbase.com
[2] https://www.binance.com

giveaway scams in recent years are, for example, Elon Musk, Michael Saylor, and others. The scammer will pretend to have benefited from a giveaway by supposedly thanking the impersonated celebrity in a tweet. An example is shown in Figure 1; an image of a tweet, supposedly posted by Musk, promotes a cryptocurrency giveaway being hosted by Tesla. However, the image was manipulated and did not originate from Musk. The link in the scammer's image redirects a user to a landing page that appears to be from Tesla or Mr Musk offering "free" Bitcoin and Ethereum (Hauer, 2020).

Figure 1: Celebrity Twitter Impersonation (Hauer, 2020)

Another method scammers use is to send a direct message (DM) on a social media platform, pretending to be a celebrity or an ambassador of that celebrity, advising a potential victim to participate in some crypto investment or giveaway. When a victim engages, he is requested to send a WhatsApp message to a given cell phone number so assistance can be provided. This approach may appear to be more personal to the victim and will contain a link where more details on participation will be provided. Figure 2 shows a website to which the potential target is directed - a photo of the individual being impersonated is shown. When a target opts in, a crypto address will be provided where the crypto coins can be sent in order to participate and to receive, for example, double the rewards in return. This scam continues after the victim has sent the money; the attacker will send fake proof of supposed profits generated and then request a withdrawal fee for payment of the reward. By the time the victim realises he has not received any payment even after he has paid the withdrawal fee, it is too late. The person has fallen victim to a crypto giveaway scam (Bureau, 2022) (Guez, 2023).

YouTube live streams is a new technique being used by scammers to lure victims. A scammer creates a YouTube video, using an older video stream of an interview with a famous person or CEO or a company. The scammer will then overlay the video with the details of the giveaway promotion. The scammer will set up the video as a current live stream so that it appears the giveaway is happening currently, enticing viewers to participate immediately. A link or QR code is normally provided in the description of the video, directing the viewer to a web page with more details on the fake crypto giveaway. Furthermore, it will also appear as if thousands of people are participating in the livestreams. However, these are generally bots and not real people. The YouTube account will often also appear to have been verified. In these cases, the accounts were hacked, all contents were deleted, and the attackers are running their own livestreams. Another way of launching this type of attack is when an attacker runs advertisements that appear around legitimate videos. If a targets clicks on one of these advertisements he is transferred to a fake site. Figure 3 contains a screenshot of a YouTube live stream using a video of an actual interview with the CEO of Coinbase, Mr Brian Armstrong.

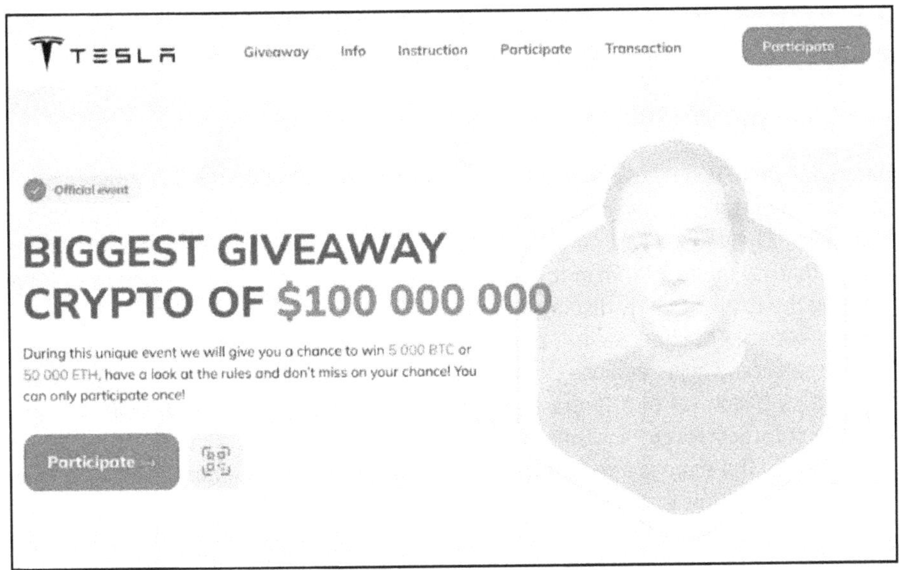

Figure 2: Tesla Crypto Giveaway (Guez, 2023)

Figure 3: YouTube Live Stream

Another, more traditional way in which scammers lure their victims is via email. The scammer sends a phishing mail attempting to convince a user that a crypto giveaway is being hosted. The user clicks on a provided link and participates.

Scammers have been around long before crypto, but they find some of the characteristics of crypto very appealing. Crypto has no middleman as in the case with bank transactions. Instead, direct transactions occur between two individuals. Crimes in the cryptocurrency space victimise innocent people - it places a big barrier on further adoption rates and increases government restrictions. Investigating and exploring cryptocurrency transactions remain intractably hard due to its pseudonymous nature and with every cryptocurrency having its own protocol and blockchain (Social Links, 2022).

This paper contributes towards the body of knowledge by raising awareness of crypto giveaway scams. In addition, the study illustrates how an investigator can analyse and investigate this type of scam, on the blockchain, using various tools and techniques. The paper further highlights how a user can be protected against these attacks. Blockchain is a revolutionary technology with immense benefits. However, the technology attracts criminals and poses an international crisis. In Section 2, a use case is selected and described. In Section 3, this use case is investigated and analysed. Section 4 contains some recommendations and the paper is concluded in the last section.

2. Use Case Selection

During our search for a relevant use case, various websites and data sources have been considered. Bitcoinabuse.com is known for providing good data on scams involving cryptocurrency. Bitcoinabuse.com has recently merged with Chainabuse.com and now offers more functionalities (BitcoinAbuse.com, 2024). Chainabuse is currently the leading platform for reporting malicious cryptocurrency activities (Chainabuse.com, 2024a). Upon filtering the results to only display impersonation scams, which are similar to giveaway scams, one particular scam impersonated Michael Saylor, the former CEO of Microstrategy (Forbes, 2024). The authors of this paper decided to select this scam as a use case because he is a popular figure in the crypto space, a billionaire with a net worth of $2.9 billion (as of 8 January '24), one of the biggest Bitcoin Maxis (a person who believes only Bitcoin is a true cryptocurrency) and one of the biggest Bitcoin holders via the company MicroStrategy (Chainabuse.com, 2024b). The scam is a recent case; it was reported on 6 January 2023. Two links are available to view more details on the scams in pdf format:

- https://bafybeic2yumotbzu6u36tkteckdceqrftfyqyye4xegczin5iufuh7nmaq.ipfs.w3s.link/mstrx2.com.pdf *(YouTube Live Stream).*
- https://bafybeihmck427mca37tkz22zpceglcrzpmvxr67bbt75o6telnvyzkqmay.ipfs.w3s.link/v%3DPaSQ5dZ25dg.pdf *(Web page).*

The two contributing crypto addresses are:

- 15YU4Pr3gDN78JjhgctKjRQ9NJhRdZn4Hf *(BTC)*
- 0x766352635223f86abe5C970bb1C199DF14099B8f *(ETH)*

The scam was announced on a YouTube Channel called Super DJ Sound where a live video of an interview with Mr Saylor, regarding the Bitcoin ETF approval, has been manipulated with added on information that took participants to the giveaway landing page. In the "chat" section on the channel, Mr Saylor was impersonated where he interacted directly with participants (Figure 4). The link to the actual video does not work anymore and has been removed.

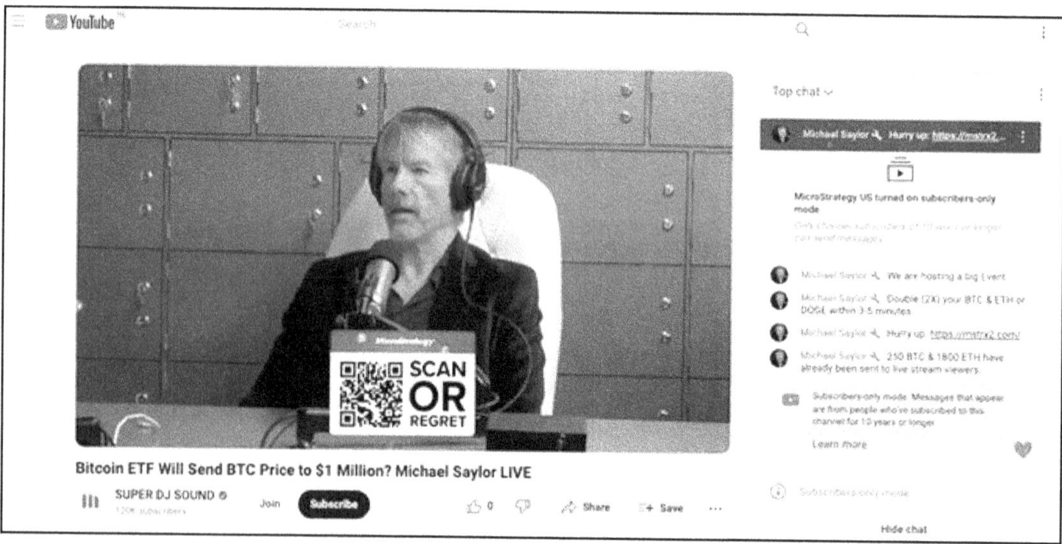

Figure 4: Live YouTube Video - Bitcoin ETF - Michael Saylor (Random Generated Link 1, 2024)

The channel displayed a QR code that takes the participant to a fake MicroStrategy website, http://www.mxstrx2.com. Instructions and rules are explained on the landing page, announcing that MicroStrategy would give away crypto assets to the value of $1 billion to participants (Figure 5). Note that the website looks exactly like the one from the Tesla giveaway example in Section 1, Figure 2 (apart from the photos of two impersonated individuals). This indicates that the same scammer is running multiple scams using the same website template and updating the content on multiple impersonations.

At the time of writing, Windows Defender reported the website to be unsafe and containing misleading content. However, the website can still be accessed if the warning from Microsoft Defender is ignored and one accepts the risks to visit the website. On the website, a giveaway of 1000 BTC and 10,000 ETH is promised. To participate, the user must send any amount between (0.1 BTC – 15 BTC) or (1 ETH – 200 ETH) to the contributing address, and MicroStrategy will then send back double the amount (0.2 BTC – 30 BTC) or (2 ETH – 400 ETH) to the address from which the payment was received. A list of supposedly successful transactions where users received double the paid amount, is shown on the landing page (Figure 6). It should be noted that these addresses in the transaction list are deliberately not displayed in full and those transactions cannot be verified (Random Generated Link 2, 2024). Section 3 covers an analysis and a technical investigation of the selected scam where the full addresses will be revealed as a result, and can be verified if the visible parts of the address match any of the addresses that are uncovered.

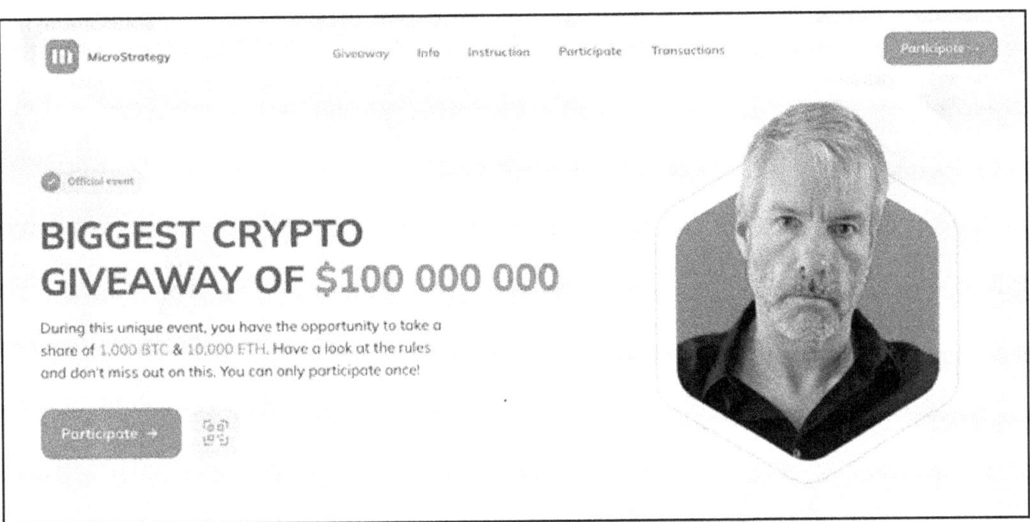

Figure 5: MicroStrategy Crypto Giveaway (Random Generated Link 2, 2024)

Figure 6: Completed Payback Transaction List (Random Generated Link 2, 2024)

3. Analysis and Investigation of the Use Case

A popular misunderstanding regarding blockchain transactions is that they are completely anonymous. BTC is the most popular cryptocurrency blockchain and all its transactions are visible to the public. However, only transactional data are visible and no personal information linked to any of the transactions are available. The second most popular blockchain is Ethereum. In 2022, it was calculated that 80% of crypto theft involved the Ethereum blockchain. Due to no personal information being available to investigators, other techniques and tools are needed to identify entities behind transactions. Five popular techniques are used when analysing and investigation a cryptocurrency crime (BIG Investigations, 2023):

3.1 Crypto Transaction Tracing

Transaction tracing is the primary technique and is also referred to as "follow the flow of funds". The process involves analysing transaction metadata such as the from and to addresses, the amount transacted and the timestamp to build a hypothesis. An investigator will try to identify hidden relationships, detect suspicious activities, and increase transparency.

3.2 Address Clustering

Address Clustering techniques involve the grouping of addresses that are likely to belong to the same person or entity within a cryptocurrency network. People often use a set of addresses for different transactions and tend to not create new addresses for each transaction. The technique considers the frequency, amount and timing of transactions. Several address clustering heuristics are in use today, see section 3.4 and Figure 7.

3.3 Graph Analysis

Graph analysis involves the visualisation of the flow of funds, making use of nodes to present the addresses and connecting lines to represent the transactions. This helps investigators to identify clusters, patterns, and other insights on the flow of funds. It also assists in understanding the relationships between various addresses and transactions. Crypto tracing, address clustering and graph analysis are often used in conjunction with each other, building a comprehensive picture of the flow of funds on the blockchain network.

3.4 Heuristics

Heuristics refers to using functions based on domain knowledge to enhance the performance of algorithms that find patterns leading to the identification of suspicious activities on a blockchain network. For address clustering, the multi-input-heuristic (MIH) method is the most effective and most studied one used today. It assumes that if two addresses (i.e. A and B), see Figure 7, are used as inputs with the same transaction, and one of the addresses is also used with another address (i.e. B and C) as inputs into another transaction, the three addresses A,B and C must be used by the same actor. The actor conducted both transactions and should be in possession of the private keys to all three addresses (Fröwis, 2020).

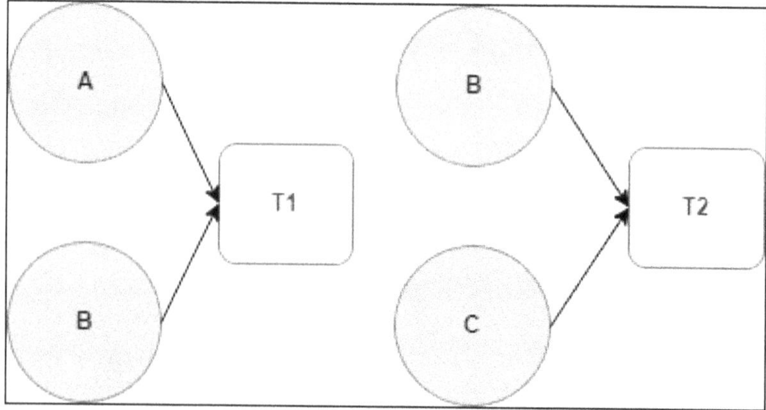

Figure 7: Multi-Input Clustering Heuristics (Fröwis, 2020)

3.5 Data Analysis

Data analysis involves the study of patterns, relationships and anomalies in the transaction information that could be key in closing complex cases. Good data analysis will uncover hidden relationships and patterns in large amounts of data and is key to cryptocurrency transaction investigations.

To perform cryptocurrency transaction analysis and investigations, a tool is needed that can assist in executing the five techniques mentioned above. A few tools exist such as Maltego, QLUE, Tatum, CipherTrace and

Breadcrumbs[3]. Most of the tools are quite expensive. However, Breadcrumbs has a more affordable option available and was selected for analysing and investigating the selected cryptocurrency giveaway scam.

The investigation has two angles to start off from:

1. The BTC contributing address (*scammer's BTC address*), **15YU4Pr3gDN78JjhgctKjRQ9NJhRdZn4Hf**, found on the landing page where participants can deposit funds into.
2. The ETH contributing address (*scammer's ETH address*), **0x766352635223f86abe5c970bb1c199df14099b8f,** also found on the landing page.

The first step was to enter the scammer's BTC address into the tool – it was discovered that no transaction took place. No funds have been received or sent from the address. This indicates that no scam took place on the BTC address. This could be due to the price of 1 BTC being too expensive, for targets and that they found it was cheaper to participate in the Ethereum giveaway. On entering the ETH address into the tool, the immediate results are that three transactions took place as incoming into the contributing ETH address, i.e. funds paid into the scammer's address. One transaction came from an address linked to the exchange Coinbase, one from a cryptocurrency wallet address and transactions from the exchange Binance (Figure 8). The final graph (after analysis had been done) is too big to be included in this paper as an image. The full graph can viewed at https://www.breadcrumbs.app/reports/9609 and a partial graph is provided in Figure 10. Note that Figure 7 is included in Figure 9, but in the latter graph, the resulting address nodes have been numbered from 1 to 4. The scammer's BTC address is shown in dark grey in Figure 9.

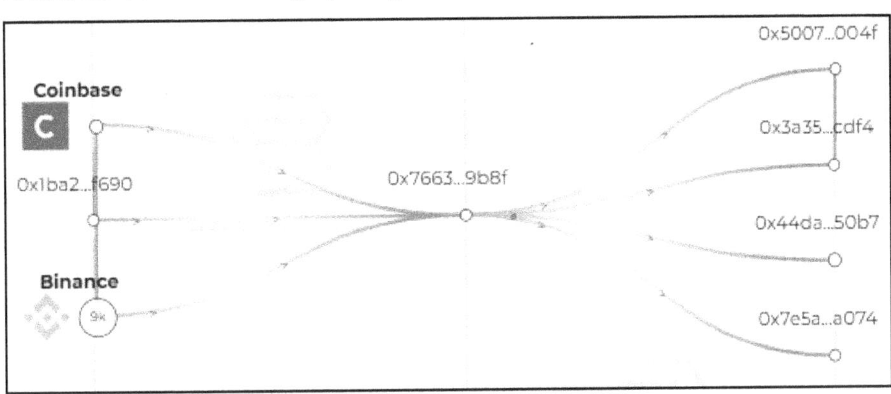

Figure 8: Scammer's ETH Address Incoming and Outgoing Transactions

Table 1 lists the direct incoming transactions from three sources into the scammer's address. Figure 9 indicates that a total of 2.3264 ETH has been sent to the scammer's address – this total corresponds to the sum of the amount ETH sent from the three sources. Note the first transaction into the scammer's address was done on 5 Jan 2024, indicating that this is a newly created address probably only for the lifetime of this scam. Also note the scammer's address still has a balance of 0.0039 ETH. Most of the incoming funds were moved quickly, with the last transaction executed on 8 Jan 2024.

Table 1: Direct Incoming Transactions into Scammer's Address

Source	From Address	Sent (ETH)	Timestamp
Coinbase	0xa9d1...3e43	1.1697	7 Jan 2024, 18:54
Wallet Address	0x1ba2...f690	0.9078	7 Jan 2024, 23:18
Binance	0x21a3...5549	0.2487	5 Jan 2024, 18:30

The main interest is to determine where the funds have been sent to from the scammer's address. Following the funds can become a daunting task and one must go through hundreds or thousands of transactions. The aim is to link the sent transactions to an exchange. Once this can be identified, an investigator can interact with law enforcement to issue a subpoena, instructing the exchange to reveal the personal information behind the address linked to their exchange.

[3] www.breadcrumbs.app

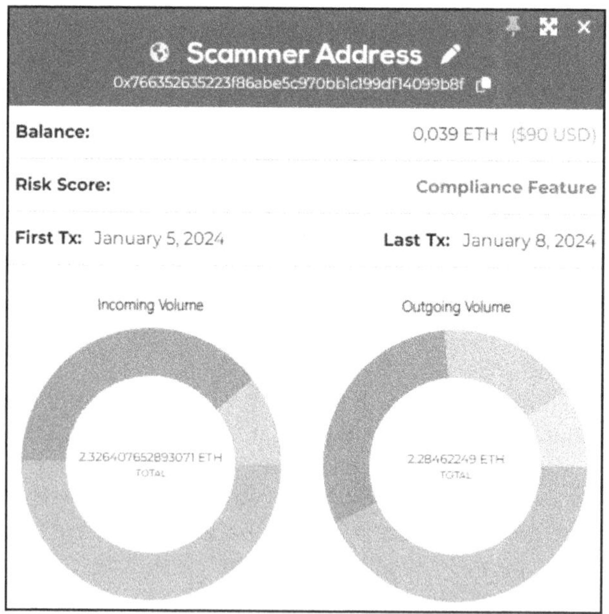

Figure 9: Scammer's ETH Incoming and Outgoing Volume

Four outgoing transactions were made to four cryptocurrency wallet addresses from the scammer's address, see Figure 8. Table 2 lists the four transactions' details at the time of writing. The amounts and number of transactions may be different in the future if funds have been moved in the interim.

Table 2: Direct Outgoing Transactions from Scammer's Address (Including the Total Received and Total Sent)

To Address	Received (ETH)	Timestamp	Total Received (ETH)	Total Sent (ETH)	Balance (ETH)
(1) 0x5007...004f	0.9825	7 Jan 2024, 23:37	0.9825	0.9814	0
(2) 0x3a35...cdf4	0.7	7 Jan 2024, 23:46	1.6814	1.6794	0
(3) 0x44da...50b7	0.3874	8 Jan 2024, 19:51	**38.7051**	**32.1114**	**6.527**
(4) 0x7e5a...a074	0.2146	8 Jan 2024, 20:38	2.3328	2.3019	0

In Figure 10, three incoming and four outgoing transactions are linked to the scammer's address. An interesting observation on the outgoing transaction from the address **(1) 0x5007...004f** is that the total amount of funds received from the scammer address was transferred to the address **(2) 0x3a35...cdf4**. The total amount sent out is slightly less than the total amount received, but the balance is 0. This discrepancy is due to transaction fees that are subtracted. The same applies for all the transactions, for each transaction there is a fee to be paid.

The total amount received in address **(2) 0x3a35...cdf4** was moved, leaving the balance at 0 ETH. By making use of Breadcrumb's functionality to follow the flow of funds, it was discovered that a transaction had been made into an exchange called FixedFloat. The two addresses (1 and 2) both have a balance of 0 ETH, indicating the funds have been moved out. Further tracing showed funds were moved into another address linked to FixedFloat, with a balance greater than 0. All addresses with a balance greater than 0 ETH will be marked as an address of interest, and indicated in light grey in Figure 10. Since the address is linked to an exchange, the next step is to determine if the exchange requires Know Your Customer (KYC) information. If this is the case, together with law enforcement agencies, a subpoena can be issued to the exchange to reveal the personal information linked to the addresses. With such personal information, the investigator can continue the investigation using traditional OSINT techniques. Contacting law enforcement to conduct a further investigation is out of the scope of this paper.

The address **(3) 0x44da...50b7** received 0.3874 ETH from the scammer's address and in total 38.7051 ETH were received *(at the time of writing)*. This indicates that funds were received from other addresses as well, possibly more scams were run, and that this address is used as a more permanent address into which to move funds from the scams. In other words, this address was probably not just used for the lifetime of the scam; it is likely one of the scammer's personal addresses where funds are transferred into from his various scams. This is regarded to be a mistake made by the scammer and the address will be closely monitored. Future research can be done to follow the funds backwards, and possibly link the address to more scams. Links from other sources to this address is not covered in this paper, because hundreds of transactions have been found to be coming in to this address. Another observation is that only 32.1114 ETH has been sent out of this address, leaving the balance at 6.527 ETH. Since the balance is not 0, this address is marked as an address of interest and will be monitored until funds are being moved again. Breadcrumbs has the functionality to monitor certain addresses and to send notifications when funds are moving from the address. By following the flow of funds, Breadcrumbs indicated that hundreds of transactions have been linked to this address, in and out, further indicating that this is a permanent address being used by the scammer.

One of the outgoing transactions (out of address 3) is linked to an address, **0x2f1d...4d12,** from the exchange Kucoin. Kucoin requires KYC and steps can be taken to issue a subpoena to obtain personal information linked to the address and Kucoin account. Tracing funds from the Kucoin address, **0x2f1d...4d12**, shows a transfer has been main into a Kucoin Main Wallet address, **0xcad6...8fdd.** The latter address is shaded in light grey in Figure 9. Continuing the tracing, a transaction made from the FixedFloat address **0x4e5b...972f** into the same Kucoin Main Wallet address was detected (the FixedFloat address appears directly above the Kucoin address in Figure 9). This indicates the scammer is performing some sort of mixing, where he transfers funds to various addresses and exchanges and then eventually transfers all the amounts back to one specific address.

Another key finding is that transactions from the exchanges Coinbase and Binance are linked to this Kucoin Main Wallet address. Since many transactions point to the Kucoin Main Wallet address, it is being monitored and marked to be of high interest. This is a crucial result because an investigator can request a subpoena to be issued to all exchanges with known links to this wallet, and then compare current known personal information to the new information gathered from these exchanges. If the scammer is very advanced, he may be making use of mules and not be using his own personal information on the exchanges. However, it is a step in the right direction. If the sets of personal information from the various exchanges match, the probability that the target person can be identified is high.

Further tracing revealed that a transaction was made to the address **0xacc3...0x26** from the Kucoin Mani Wallet address. A transaction was also made into the same address from **(3) 0x44da...50b7** via one hop through the address **0x9f5d...c45f**. The address **0xacc3...0x26** is marked as high interest due to a large amount of ETH as the balance. From this address, **0xacc3...0x26**, things became more interesting; a number of transactions were made into various wallet addresses and into exchanges such as Binance, OKX, MXC and FixedFloat. The Binance address, **0x9b39...76fd** and the OKX address, **0x57ae...adb6** both had balances greater than 0 ETH, and is consequently marked as addresses of interest. Subpoenas to all the exchanges need to be issued to obtain personal information. From the latter address, two hops back of Figure 9, transactions were made into the exchanges HitBTC and WhiteBit. Again, subpoenas are to be issued to the exchanges as well. The address from WhiteBit, **0x4853...1e54,** had a very large amount of ETH linked to it and is marked as an address of high interest. Since the balance in this address is very high, it can be requested that a subpoena also includes a request to freeze this address to prevent any further transactions. Another finding is that various transactions were made from the Binance address, **0x9b39...76fd**, into multiple addresses also linked to Binance. From these Binance addresses, multiple transactions were made back into a previously used address linked to FixedFloat, **0x4e5b...972f.** Based on these patterns showing transactions back and forth between the same addresses, it can be said with high certainty that the addresses belong to the same scammer.

The address **(4) 0x7e5a...a074** received a total amount of 2.3328, but only 0.2146 has been received from the scammer's address. This is also an indication that this address can possibly be linked to more scams sending scammed funds to this address. By continuing to follow the flow of funds, it has been discovered that transactions were made into the address **0x24b5...2a25.** Another fund transfer to this (latter) address came from **(3) 0x44da...50b7**; this indicates that the address **0x24b5...2a25** is used as a more permanent address into which to transfer funds. A similar pattern of transfers was found for both the address **0x82e2...14ab** the address **0xae7a...fe84**. **0xae7a...fe84** is linked to the Bitget exchange and contains a very large amount of ETH. This address is marked of very high interest. Bitget could be issued with a subpoena to obtain personal information to identify the person of interest.

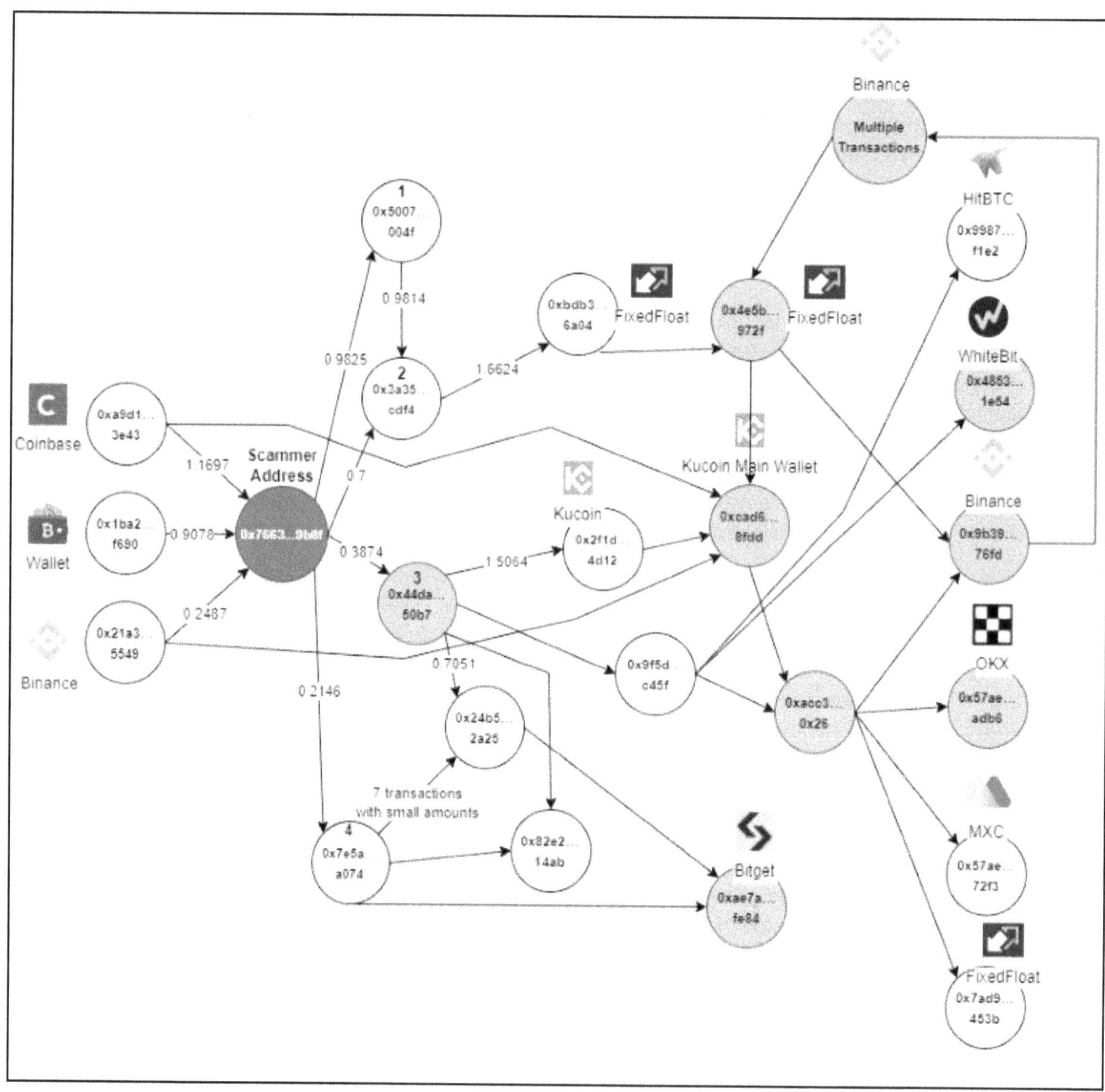

Figure 10: Transaction Tracing

It should be noted that none of the ETH addresses that were uncovered during this analysis did not match the visible parts of the addresses listed in Section 3, Figure 6. It can be confirmed that those addresses were fake generated addresses and not real addresses on the Ethereum blockchain.

4. Protection Against and Avoiding Giveaway Scams

Scammers are drawn to cryptocurrency for various reason such as there is no bank or centralised body to identify suspicious transactions and crypto transactions cannot be reversed. Various types of scams exist in the crypto space and a giveaway scam is one just one example of these (Agarwal, 2024). Giveaway scams are normally done by an impersonation of a legitimate platform or a celebrity as mentioned in in Section 1. It should be noted that legitimate platforms do run real promotions and giveaways, but they will never request a crypto amount to be sent in exchange for a larger return investment. No celebrity or famous influencer on social media platforms will send a direct message (DM) to any unknown individual to "help" with any trading or investment schemes. Users should not click on any link sent by someone that offers any cryptocurrency investment advice (Botha, Badenhorst, & Leenen, 2023).

Scammers are leveraging artificial intelligence (AI)-powered tools to amplify their reach and to create a fanbase of thousands of people on their social media accounts. The fake account interactions are used to give the illusion of popularity of their scam projects. They also make use of AI driven bots to engage with individuals providing investment advice. A good example of how AI is used by scammers is by "pig butchering" scams. A bot can spend days to befriend someone on social media and to gain their trust just to end up scamming later. Fortunately, AI can also be used to protect individuals from giveaway scams. An AI system, called GiveawayScamHunter, has been developed by researchers from San Diego State University in the United States to detect and expose cryptocurrency giveaway scams on Twitter. The system has identified over 95, 000 scam lists that were created by over 87 000 accounts on social media platforms between June 2022 and June 2023. The team trained a natural language processing (NLP) tool on data from previously identified scams, which enabled them to identify close to 100 000 instances of giveaway scams. In addition, the system can extract the scam giveaway Internet domains and scam-related cryptocurrency wallet addresses. The system reported that 365 victims were attacked by cryptocurrency scams during this period and have suffered losses of over $872, 000 (Haqshanas, 2023).

Below is a check-list of some common red flags to protect against cryptocurrency giveaway scams (Hetler, 2023):

- A promise is given of very large gains or returns on investments.
- The only form of payment accepted is cryptocurrency.
- There will be no contractual obligations.
- Any form of communication, for example emails or social posts, contains spelling or grammar mistakes.
- Scammers always make use of manipulation tactics such as blackmail or extortion.
- Fake endorsements of influencers or celebrities will be found.
- Very few details will be provided about the investment and money movements.
- Several transactions are taking place in a day.

If an individual believes that he/she has been scammed, they should report it immediately. Scams can be reported at their country's Internet crime or complaints center or any federal trade commission or organization. If an exchange was linked to the scam, the exchange should be notified (Hetler, 2023). It can also be reported on chainabuse[4]. To avoid these types of scams, it is necessary is to understand that no-one on the Internet is going to give something away for free, and no one will double an investment amount in exchange for a payment in cryptocurrency coins. If it sounds too good to be true, it usually is. An investor should think twice before sending cryptocurrency funds; all transactions are irreversible, and it is not possible to get the funds back once it is sent (Bureau, 2022) (Hauer, 2020).

5. Conclusion

Blockchain adoption continues to increase and so do crypto-crimes and scams. This study provided examples of known crypto giveaway scams and raises awareness regarding these type of scams. A use case was selected from the data source chainabuse.com. The selected case is a crypto giveaway scam promoted via a manipulated YouTube Live Stream video of an interview with the former CEO of Microstrategy, Mr Michael Saylor. The video navigates participants to a webpage containing more details on the giveaway promotion (or rather the scam). Once a user participated by sending crypto to the specified address, they have been scammed. The paper indicates key pointers on how to investigate such a scam. The key pointers are put to practice with a blockchain analysis and investigation tool, Breadcrumbs, capable of tracing the flow of funds on the blockchain, perform address clustering, graph analysis, heuristics and data analysis. The analysis and investigation aim to trace the funds up to a point where a link can be made to a crypto exchange. Once a link can be made, in collaboration with law enforcement agencies, a subpoena can be issued to the exchange to instruct them to reveal the personal information linked to the address on their exchange as well as all transactional information. However, this is out of the scope of this paper and the analysis ends when a link can be made to an exchange. The study also aims to raise awareness of protective measures against these scams. Since there is no official legislation in place to guard against crypto scams, it remains a very significant international threat that cannot be ignored.

References

Agarwal, U. R. (2024). Blockchain and crypto forensics: Investigating crypto frauds. *34(2)*, p. p.e2255. International Journal of Network Management.

BIG Investigations. (2023, Mar 1). *The Must-Have Crypto Tracing Techniques For 2023*. Retrieved from Blockchain Intelligence Investigations (BIG): https://blockchaingroup.io/the-must-have-crypto-tracing-techniques-for-2023/

BitcoinAbuse.com. (2024, Jan 8). *Bitcoinabise.com*. Retrieved from Bitcoinabuse.com: https://www.bitcoinabuse.com/

[4] www.chainabuse.com

Botha, J., Badenhorst, D., & Leenen, L. (2023). An Analysis of Crypto Scams during the Covid-19 Pandemic: 2020-2022. *International Conference on Cyber Warfare and Security* (pp. 36-48). Towson University, Baltimore County, Maryland, USA: ACIL.

Bureau, C. (2022, May 18). *WORST Crypto Scams in 2022!! DONT Fall For These!!* Retrieved from YouTube: https://www.youtube.com/watch?v=GKTa5ciCJl4

Chainabuse.com. (2024a, Jan 8). *Chainabuse.com*. Retrieved from About: https://www.chainabuse.com/about

Chainabuse.com. (2024b, Jan 8). *Chainabuse.com*. Retrieved from Impersonation Scam: https://www.chainabuse.com/report/984f747b-ab29-4ae1-b127-6fc880ca4c45?context=browse-category&category=IMPERSONATION

Forbes. (2024, Jan 8). *Profile - Michael Saylor*. Retrieved from Forbes.com: https://www.forbes.com/profile/michael-saylor/?sh=556a1c557e0f

Fröwis, M. G. (2020). Safeguarding the evidential value of forensic cryptocurrency investigations. *Forensic Science International: Digital Investigation. 33*, p. p200902. ScienceDirect. Elsevier.

Guez, S. (2023, Mar 23). *Chatbots, Celebrities, and Victim Retargeting: Why Crypto Giveaway Scams Are Still So Successful*. Retrieved from akamai.com: https://www.akamai.com/blog/security-research/crypto-giveaway-scams-are-still-successful

Haqshanas, R. (2023, Aug 12). *Researchers Deploy AI to Uncover Crypto Giveaway Scam Schemes on Twitter*. Retrieved from Cryptonews.com: https://cryptonews.com/news/researchers-deploy-ai-uncover-crypto-giveaway-scam-schemes-twitter.htm

Hauer, T. (2020, April 6). *Crypto giveaway scams and how to spot them*. Retrieved from Coinbase: https://www.coinbase.com/blog/crypto-giveaway-scams-and-how-to-spot-them

Hetler, A. (2023, Dec 23). *11 common cryptocurrency scams in 2024*. Retrieved from TechTarget: https://www.techtarget.com/whatis/feature/Common-cryptocurrency-scams

Pelker, C. B. (2021). Using Blockchain Analysis from Investigation to Trial. *69*, p. p59. Dep't of Just. J. Fed. L. & Prac.

Random Generated Link 1. (2024, Jan 8). Retrieved from https://bafybeihmck427mca37tkz22zpceglcrzpmvxr67bbt75o6telnvyzkqmay.ipfs.w3s.link/v%3DPaSQ5dZ25dg.pdf

Random Generated Link 2. (2024, Jan 8). Retrieved from https://bafybeic2yumotbzu6u36tkteckdceqrftfyqyye4xegczin5iufuh7nmaq.ipfs.w3s.link/mstrx2.com.pdf

Social Links. (2022, April 22). *Enhancing Cryptocurrency Investigations with OSINT*. Retrieved from https://blog.sociallinks.io/: https://blog.sociallinks.io/cryptocurrency-investigations/

Remotely the Same? Going Virtual with a Cybercamp in a Pandemic

Matthew W. Bovee and Huw O.L. Read
Norwich University, Northfield, Vermont, USA

mbovee@norwich.edu
hread@norwich.edu

Abstract: Summer camps and other week-long activities are popular ways to introduce cybersecurity to middle- or high-school aged children. Such experiences have traditionally been conducted in-person, with many having residency components and evening activities. The COVID-19 pandemic brought these traditional experiences to an abrupt halt. To support and promote continued education in the face of the global pandemic many such in-person camps – as well as higher-education courses – precipitously migrated to online remote learning. The shift presented challenges beyond simply preparing and posting content online. This case study examines the challenges, solutions, and lessons learned from morphing a successful hands-on residential NSA GenCyber digital forensics summer camp to a fully online remote learning "camp".

Keywords: Digital Forensics, Remote Learning, Cyber Security Education and Training, Gamification Strategies

1. Introduction

Summer camps and other week-long activities are popular ways of introducing cybersecurity to children in their last six to seven years of required education in the United States of America (USA). One prominent example is the GenCyber program, founded and sponsored in 2014 by the USA's National Security Agency (NSA) in collaboration with the National Science Foundation (NSF, n.d.). GenCyber grants support provision of cybersecurity summer camps to students, teachers, or both. GenCyber seeks to: promote correct, safe student behaviour online; increase student diversity and interest in cybersecurity and related national workforce careers; and, improve cybersecurity teaching content and methods in secondary curricula (NSF, 2022). In its first five years, GenCyber reached over 15,000 students directly. In its last pre-COVID year (2019) over 3,000 students and nearly 780 teachers attended GenCyber camps (NSF, 2022). Such experiences are traditionally conducted in-person, often with residency components and evening activities.

From 2016 through 2019, the authors created and conducted five week-long GenCyber residential student camps. Three focused on introductory cybersecurity; two on digital forensics. Students in each had multiple face-to-face (F2F), hands-on, and team-based activities, including: lessons; labs, outdoors exercises, and competitions in which they applied cybersecurity and digital-forensics principles; off-campus site visits; and guest speakers. The camps all received very positive anecdotal and survey-based ratings from participants and NSA auditors tasked with observing and improving GenCyber camps. In 2019 the authors were awarded two additional GenCyber grants for summer 2020 camps.

However, in Spring 2020 the COVID-19 pandemic brought traditional USA F2F camp experiences to an abrupt halt (Table 1). By late March 2021 many USA states were considering lifting some or all restrictions on travel and large gatherings. During this time the NSA notified GenCyber camp grant awardees they could fulfil their 2020 grant obligations in 2021 with either F2F or online camps and required official notice of the modality by April 1st. The authors' State still had an emergency order in effect and no final decision, assurance, or guidance whether or when COVID-19 restrictions would be lifted. The authors therefore opted for an online-only camp format. This case study examines challenges, solutions, and lessons learned converting our NSA GenCyber digital forensics summer camp to a fully online remote learning "camp".

1.1 Contributions

This rapid shift presented numerous challenges beyond simply preparing and posting content for online delivery. As contributions, this paper:

1. Examines key considerations for converting an established residential Cyber camp to virtual format;
2. Identifies virtual digital forensics activities that simulate residential camp experiences; and,
3. Highlights lessons learned that served to improve future F2F teaching.

Table 1: USA COVID-19 Educational Events. Within two months, USA schools went from being fully open to mandatory closures state- and nation-wide (Education Week, 2020; Lieberman, 2020).

Date (dd/mm/yyyy)	Action	School Impact
29/01/2020	Few confirmed mainland USA COVID-19 cases	Calls for guidance; voluntary temporary closures
25/02/2020	USA Centers for Disease Control and Prevention (CDC) hints about virtual schooling	"Ask about teleschool"
27/02/2020	Temporary individual school closings	Disinfections attempted
Early 03/2020	Major USA school district closings	District-wide actions
11/03/2020	CDC declares global COVID-19 pandemic	Formal federal confirmation
13/03/2020	300 universities have closed	Shift to remote-only classes
17/03/2020	Kansas closes all schools	First USA state-wide closure
25/03/2020	All USA public schools closed	GenCyber (GC) camps postponed indefinitely
01/042021	USA states begin considering lifting restrictions	GC Camp modality decision required

The rest of this paper is presented as follows. Descriptions of a 'normal' digital forensics camp versus an online-only version are provided. Next, differences, challenges and developed solutions are discussed. Finally, lessons learned and their impact on future teaching are summarised.

2. Residential Digital Forensics Camp

After Sunday arrival and "check-in", residential camp consisted of five consecutive days of lessons, hands-on exercises, and activities oriented towards GenCyber program goals (Appendix A). These included: learning and applying appropriate online behaviour, cybersecurity and digital forensics terminology and concepts; contemporary cybersecurity issues; assembling a working device for continued studies; observing cybersecurity in practice in the field; and a professional-level digital-forensics tool certification exam. Participants ate meals with the camp instructors, staff, and guest speakers. Attendees departed on Saturday.

3. Virtual Equivalent of the Residential Forensics Camp

The virtual version also began Sunday (Appendix B), hosted at the authors' university, which standardized on Microsoft Teams for videoconferencing. Instead of arrivals and "check-in", Sunday was the final opportunity for participants to download, install and test the Teams delivery platform remotely. The next five days involved online lessons, hands-on exercises guided by remote demonstration and discussion, and online individual- and team-based activities oriented towards the same GenCyber program goals.

4. Differences and Challenges

Differences in each camp type and their respective challenges are categorized as logistical or instructional. Table 2 summarises the logistical issues: policy & practice, general event planning, camp schedules, recruitment, staffing, instructional support, lesson materials, environment of the modality, and review sessions. Table 6 presents three example activities that highlight key instructional issues: digital forensic acquisition; forensic analysis; and installation of Kali NetHunter.

Although categorized for ease of consideration, some logistical issues impacted instruction and vice versa, and some caused "knock-on" issues. For example, dropped network connections and software crashes were anticipated to cause attendees to fall behind. To address this staff were scheduled to provide on-call support via phone and online text, and lesson sessions were recorded for review by attendees. That required guidelines for staff-attendee interactions and a data retention plan for recordings. Since camp attendees were not adults, these practices had to be documented and approved by their parents during application.

4.1 Logistical Issues

For the schedules in Appendices A and B much planning, scheduling and coordination was required (Table 2). These issues are highlighted next, with differences in the virtual camp emphasised.

Table 2: Logistical Issues Overview. Examples of logistical challenges pivoting from residential to virtual camp.

Category	Residential	Virtual	Challenges
Policy & Practice	Legal responsibilities	Legal responsibilities	Each activity and service and related policies reviewed for virtual camp applicability
General Event Planning	Accommodations, services, staff, site visits, materials	Services, staff, materials	Room & board, transportation, or site visits not required for virtual camp
Camp Schedules	Lessons, meals, breaks, field trips, study sessions	Regular lesson times, breaks and meals	Virtual attendees spanned several time zones, required a later start and finish; offered less collaboration during meals and breaks
Recruitment	Limited computer experience	More advanced computer experience	Virtual attendees had to be self-sufficient with computers and virtual resources
Systems Required	Provided by camp	Provided by attendee	Virtual attendees required access to basic hardware, software, network, & peripherals
Staff	Lead evening activities, supported academic activities	Lead team-session "breakout rooms"; staffed on-call "hotline"	Dropped connections due to distal issues; assisting by remote via bad connections; need for after-hours "catch-up" help sessions
Instructors & Speakers	Hosted on-campus	Participated via remote	All participants and attendees required hardware, Microsoft Teams software, network, and minimal training
Lesson Materials	On-site	Remote "site"	All required materials for virtual lessons had to be packaged and shipped in advance
Modality Environment	Physical lab space	Virtual "breakout" rooms	"Virtual space" makes it more difficult to spot distracted or struggling attendees
	Meals, breaks, F2F help	Regular schedule, breaks	Virtual-only risks screen fatigue for all; "out of your seat" activities needed to vary routine
Review	After-hours sessions	Homework, "hotline", and streamed video	On-call help & streamed video to support homework replaced in-person help sessions

4.1.1 *Policy and Practice*

Regardless of the camp modality, the instructors, staff, and hosting University had a legal obligation to act in the best interests of the participants, who were not adults. All necessary guidelines, documentation, and measures had to be in place in advance. Examining organizational policy and practice was therefore critical.

For the virtual camp all F2F camp policies and procedures were considered (Table 3). Some were easily clarified to show they applied to virtual sessions (Table 3, asterisks). Additional issues were unique to a virtual camp and required separate guidelines, documentation, or preparation (Table 3, italics). For example, attendees needed guidelines for acceptable use of virtual university resources, support staff interactions, online behaviour during camp, and the recording of camp sessions.

4.1.2 *General Event Planning*

Many camp elements such as staffing, facilities, transportation, equipment, materials, and lessons must be planned and prepared well in advance (Table 4). Some relate directly to the need for policy review (e.g. parking, linens, and rooms). Some require considering the sequence of their resolution. For example, to determine required equipment and materials requires identifying and planning the related lessons and exercises. The *only* general issues that could be excluded for the virtual camps were room and board, transportation, and site-visit field trips.

4.1.3 *Changes to Camp Scheduling*

Both camp types were designed to maximize learning opportunities. The residential camp alternated between lecture-style lessons and individual- or team-exercises applying lesson information (Appendix A). For example, the mobile forensics lesson was followed by practice acquiring mobile handset data using Cellebrite's UFED4PC software, and then by a team-based mock-case analysis competition modelled on the classic sleuthing game "Cluedo!". Meals and breaks punctuated daily schedules. After-hours cybersecurity-themed activities provided a change from the classroom.

Table 3: Policy & Practice Issues. Items with an asterisk were extended to the virtual context. Italicized items were virtual camp issues requiring additional guidelines and documentation.

Category	Description
General	• Attire: University guidelines on acceptable attire and classroom decorum* • Calling Home: Participants confirmed arrival and departure details; Periodic contact with their legal guardians was recommended • Cars & Parking: Some participants were of legal age to drive to camp • Linens: Items provided with room, and what to bring • Mail: Sending/receiving regular mail during camp • Medication: Appropriate storage and timely access for prescription medications • Rooms: Key card use/deposit; secure storage of valuables; respect for privacy • Supervision: Appropriate adult supervision throughout the camp experience*
Conduct	• *Acceptable Use: Guidelines regarding access and use of virtual University resources* • *Difficulties with Labs & Exercises: on-demand virtual support was provided by camp counsellors* • *Disrupted/Lost Connections: Supported via campus IT Services* • *Microsoft Teams Problems: Supported via campus IT Services* • *Session Communications, Interactions, and Recordings: expectations regarding online interaction, its supervision, and recordings for quality control purposes*
Emergencies	• Procedures, contact numbers, and notification systems for medical and other emergencies*

Table 4: Event-Planning Logistical Issues. Advance preparation required for hosting a summer camp for juveniles. Italicized items applied solely to the residential camp.

Category	Description
Room & Board	*Advance scheduling and booking space on campus*
Staff	Identifying, hiring, training camp counsellors
Instructors	Identifying, soliciting, and scheduling instructors and invited subject-matter experts
Field Trips	*Identifying appropriate facilities and points of contact, securing visit approval, scheduling visit*
Transportation	*Hire staff with commercial licenses (or train staff); schedule vehicle use/rental*
Lessons	Identify, acquire, and prepare all lesson and exercise plans and materials

Virtual camp attendees joined from time zones up to four hours behind that of lessons. To minimize potential disruption, yet keep a reasonable length to the class day, the virtual schedule started later and was less variable than the F2F camp (Appendix B). So-called "Zoom fatigue" (Elbogen, et al., 2020) or "exhaustion" (Fauville, et al., 2021) was another key concern. Meals and breaks still punctuated the schedule, and attendees were asked to spend them away from the computer to provide a break from "screen time". Because many attendees fitted the virtual camp into a busy home schedule, and the wide range in attendee time zones, virtual group evening activities were not attempted. To prepare attendees for the certification exam associated with the camp, homework was assigned instead of hosting group study sessions. Other than academic sessions, the virtual camp offered fewer opportunities for attendees to make casual connections useful for team building and collaboration.

Table 5: Camp Application Packet Requirements. Italicized items were for virtual camps only.

Requirement	Assessment Purpose
Transcript	Appropriate cybersecurity or computer science background
Interest Statement	Identifying those who might best benefit from increased cybersecurity interest, academic pursuit
Support Letters	Motivation, interest, and prior extracurricular experiences regarding cybersecurity
Broadband Access	*Videoconferencing and collaboration requirement*
Microsoft Teams	*Hosting university video conferencing standard*
	PC with adequate hardware and software specifications
	Webcam and microphone
	Administrative access (parental permission) to install the software

4.1.4 *Recruiting Attendees; Systems Requirement*

Recruiting attendees must start even before addressing many logistical issues. Applicants submitted packets (Table 5, above) that aided review and selection of attendees who would potentially benefit most from the camp, plus help meet the GenCyber goals. A glaring difference was that residential applicants had no hardware requirements - everything was provided in situ. Virtual camp required basic systems (Windows PC, webcam, microphone) for the best experience of participants. Unfortunately, that excluded some applicants.

4.1.5 *Staffing*

Experienced adult student staff were hired for each camp type. At residential camps they supported lessons and activities, supervised evening activities, and provided overnight and emergency supervision. The virtual camp needed no evening supervision, but team-based activities required what Microsoft describes as Teams "breakout rooms". Rather than gathering around a table, each student team interacted in a videoconference session separate from the main course. Camp staff supported each breakout session.

To support virtual attendees who missed session content due to connection issues, staff were available throughout each day by phone and online, and for four evening hours. All sessions were also videorecorded and accessible via Teams until four weeks after camp. Notice of sessions being recorded, and permission to temporarily use them, also helped motivate appropriate norms for online interaction in the context of a non-adult class.

4.1.6 *Instructors and Speakers*

Both camps scheduled invited guest speakers. For the virtual camp everyone interacted via Teams, requiring advance preparation and testing by instructors and speakers as well as attendees.

4.1.7 *Lessons & Materials*

To determine content, schedule it, and identify necessary materials, lessons appropriate for attendees and camp goals were planned for both camp types. Residential lessons and materials needed to be ready by the start of camp. Virtual lessons needed to be ready sooner, so related materials could be acquired, vetted, packaged, and shipped to reach attendees *before* the start of the camp.

4.1.8 *Modality Environment*

Four issues unique to the virtual camp environment were "videoconferencing fatigue" (Elbogen et al, 2022), shutting off cameras, suboptimal learning environments, and the ability to identify when an attendee is struggling with the material or distracted.

At residential camp, attendee time spent focused on computer monitors was not an issue. Varied sessions, breaks, and topic introductions ensured at most several hour-long sessions and daily totals of a few hours. Virtual camp sessions were deliberately kept at or below one hour to reduce screen fatigue, and activities varied between lessons and exercises. Regardless, almost *everything* was necessarily done via computer. To address this, we introduced impromptu changes that required getting away from the screen. For example, when describing mobile phones, the instructor announced an unscheduled competition. Attendees were given five minutes to get up, find the oldest example of technology in their house they could think of, and bring it (or a photo of it) back to show everyone online. The three oldest examples were declared winners and discussed in the context of rapid technological change and digital forensics. This also related the topic to attendee households and got them out of their chairs and away from the screens for a few excited minutes.

Residential camps provided a focused study and learning environment, whereas some virtual camp attendees connected from communal home areas and other environments rife with distractions. Virtual attendees would periodically turn off their webcam, often for a valid reason such as others in the background, concerns about their appearance, or a bathroom break. During virtual sessions we were especially mindful of identifying students looked puzzled, distracted, or detached. However, with the camera off one cannot. Even with the camera on, postural and gestural cues suggesting someone needs help are absent or difficult to detect. Many attendees whose cameras were off still interacted; some did not. Requiring Teams reaction and emoji responses (such as a virtual "thumbs up") helped focus attendees and identify those who had lost connection or become distracted. We also demonstrated how much faster, easier, and – frankly – more satisfying it was to keep the camera on and see a *physical* "thumbs up" to gauge comprehension than to find, select, and use an emoji. Those struggling were able to visit a side-room with camp staff for catching-up with the activity.

4.1.9 Review & Revision

Residential camps had scheduled evening sessions for review and revision, supported by camp staff. Some students also collaborated independently via Google Docs. To give virtual camp attendees a break from screen time, we did not hold evening online reviews. Instead, students were assigned homework to prepare for the professional certification (something most were very interested in achieving). Interestingly, some virtual camp students *also* collaboratively studied in the evenings via Google Docs, sharing notes and study tips.

We next highlight instructional issues by discussing three exercises: forensic acquisition; forensic analysis via a "whodunnit" based on Cluedo; and installation and testing of Kali NetHunter. These are outlined briefly in Table 6.

4.2 Instructional Issues

4.2.1 Forensic Acquisition

Performing basic forensic data acquisition is a key exercise in our digital forensics camp. Residential attendees used physical kit in the lab, learning how to connect hard drives and cell phones to forensic workstations via write blockers, create images, and about image formats and log files. Pre-acquired extractions developed by the authors were used in later exercises and competitions.

For each virtual camp attendee, we created a virtual machine (VM) configured with licensed and freeware digital forensics tools and an attached read-only virtual drive. Using these, we demonstrated digital forensic imaging online plus provided clear, streamlined, and illustrated process instructions (a "walk-through") on the Teams site. Although the walk-through guides were well received and attendees created images successfully, they missed learning nuances of handling and connecting physical kit. The authors' pre-acquired extractions were loaded to attendee VMs for later exercises and competitions.

4.2.2 Forensic Analysis

A popular camp exercise involved a gamified (Švábenský V, et al., 2021) forensic cell phone analysis to solve a mock "whodunnit" like the game *Cluedo*. Residential camp teams were each given a phone extraction from a different "character" in a mock incident, plus the software tools to analyse it for evidence. Use of the software was explained and demonstrated, and they were provided questions that prompted finding useful case details. No one extraction was sufficient to fully solve the case. However, teams could ask other teams a limited number of analysis-related questions (which required honest answers). Thus, the exercise had elements of "capture the flag" (CTF), team competition and inter-team collaboration.

For virtual camp attendees, special VMs with the same software tools plus access to a single mock case phone extraction were provided. The analysis software was explained and demonstrated online. To promote inter-student collaboration in the virtual environment, each VM was shared by two attendees who then had to figure out how to work together, collaborate to analyse the data, record their findings, and query other teams.

Table 6: Instructional Issues Overview. Example instructional changes pivoting a residential to a virtual one.

Category	Residential	Virtual	Challenges
Forensic Acquisition	Physical kit: write blockers, hard drives, cell phones, workstations	Providing kit to each attendee impractical, expensive	Demonstrating imaging with read-only virtual drives attached to virtual machine
Forensic analysis	Group activities, digital whodunnits.	No F2F group interaction	Encouraging communication between virtual attendees by sharing one VM.
Kali NetHunter	Detailed booklet, self-paced. Staff support and check-in.	Installation of tools and Kali led step by step online. Breakout rooms for those who fell behind.	Ensuring materials arrived before camp; extra time after camp to work one-on-one for those who lost activity.

4.2.3 *Kali NetHunter*

Another popular camp activity was self-paced installation of Kali NetHunter penetration testing software to a Google Nexus phone. Residential camp attendees were provided a detailed booklet and all materials. Instructors and staff monitored and supported their progress. Virtual camp attendees were shipped the same materials in advance and given a guided online session by an experienced instructor. However, even by day four of the camp some attendees' materials had not arrived. Others temporarily lost connection during the demo. Some were confused by the demo or the instructions, not readily identified as such, and fell behind. Experienced staff opened real-time breakout rooms to support those who fell behind. Ultimately, additional one-on-one sessions were needed to ensure virtual attendees succeeded and benefited from the exercise.

5. Lessons Learned

Lessons learned are not always purely logistical or instructional. However, as with the examination of issues and solutions above, for convenience we have summarised our lessons learned in the same manner plus highlight several used in current F2F teaching.

5.1 Logistical Lessons

1. *Do Not Underestimate the Task.* As the preceding tables illustrate, preparing and delivering a virtual camp involves as many issues and as much work as a F2F camp, or more.
2. *Start Preparations Earlier*. Allow as much time to prepare for a virtual camp as a F2F one. If you will be sending lesson materials to participants to use during the camp, plan on extra time (and money) to ensure they arrive in time to be used and pay for parcel tracking.
3. *Be Alert for Emergent Issues*. Technological, policy, and instructional issues - and the choices made to deal with them - can result in a cascade of other issues. Even small things normally taken for granted, such as stable network connections, can be overlooked.
4. *Plan for Lost Connections*. This is an inevitable and incredibly disruptive risk of online instruction. Expect it.
5. *Leverage VM "Snapshotting"*. Teach how to create VM snapshots to capture/rollback to previous states. This provides students more creative control and reduces reliance on instructors and staff to "fix" VMs.

For academics (who are not project managers), lessons one through three can be challenging to actualize, especially when creating any camp for the first time. Lesson five is now routinely used in our F2F instruction.

5.2 Instructional Lessons

1. *Beware of Videoconferencing Exhaustion*. "Zoom fatigue" appears to real, although its antecedents and causes are still being researched and debated (Fauville, et al., 2021). Limit attendee screen time, motivate engagement and learning, and require getting up and moving.
2. *Beware of Instructor/Staff Burnout*. They lead and support virtual sessions, plus must stay focused and alert to attendees. They also incur more screen time reviewing, planning, and prepping for the next day. Schedule screen-time breaks for them, too.
3. *Plan for Lost Connections*. Provide instructional support for those who fall behind. Helplines, streaming videos, one-on-one tech support, and even repeat sessions, may be needed.
4. *Watch for/Motivate Interaction*. The usual cues of confusion or disaffection are harder to detect. Prompt for visual, verbal, or technological responses to gauge attention.
5. *When Webcams are Off, Inquire*. Not everyone with a webcam is necessarily able or ready to turn it on. However, it may mean a dropped connection or loss of interest.
6. *Present Modules; Provide Walk-Throughs*. Some of our best-received virtual sessions, whether standalone or sequenced, were crafted to take 40 minutes of a 50-minute block (80%) plus provided clear and simple walk-throughs to help attendees keep up or catch up when dealing with several multimodal resources simultaneously.
7. *Creative Ideas/Solutions Also Help*. Game-like or realistic, CTF-type scenarios generate strong student interest. Although aspects of F2F group/team interaction are lost, some exercises translate well to virtual contexts.
8. *Motivate Discovery of How to Collaborate Remotely*. Creating situations where participants must interact and share resources to succeed can prompt them to find ways to work together.

Many of these lessons also make sense F2F (e.g. varying activities, scheduling breaks, gauging attention, motivating collaboration). However, we utilize modularisation and walk-throughs, game-like/CTF scenarios, and after-hours technical-support staffing in current F2F teacher-training camps to great success.

6. Conclusion

Pivoting a residential camp to an equivalent virtual version is daunting, with a scope and complexity like creating and coordinating a physical camp. Some preparations may require *more* time than the F2F equivalent. Small, easily overlooked issues can have important knock-on consequences, and solutions can cause a cascade of other issues. Attempting to actualise lessons learned can leave academics feeling like project managers. Logistical issues and solutions can impact instruction, and vice versa. So-called video conferencing fatigue is a major concern in a week-long camp, for attendees, *and* instructors and staff. However, creative instructional approaches can help deal with detecting lack of attention, generate collaboration and aspects of group- or teamwork, and translate F2F teaching of traditional digital forensics concepts and skills to a virtual environment.

References

Education Week (2020) "The Coronavirus Spring: The Historic Closing of U.S. Schools (A Timeline)", *Education Week*, https://www.edweek.org/leadership/the-coronavirus-spring-the-historic-closing-of-u-s-schools-a-timeline/2020/07 (last visited 26/02/2024).

Elbogen EB, et al. (2022) "A National Study of Zoom Fatigue and Mental Health During the COVID-19 Pandemic: Implications for Future Remote Work", Cyberpsychology, Behavior, and Social Networking. July, Volume 25, No. 7, pp 409-415.

Fauville G, et al. (2021) "Zoom Exhaustion & Fatigue Scale", Computers in Human Behavior Reports. Volume 4, August-December.

Lieberman, M. (2020) "Schools Should Prepare for Coronavirus Outbreaks, CDC Officials Warn". Education Week, https://www.edweek.org/leadership/schools-should-prepare-for-coronavirus-outbreaks-cdc-officials-warn/2020/02, (last visited 26/02/2024).

National Science Foundation (January 2022) *CyberCorps: Scholarship for Service 2021 Biennial Report*, https://www.nsf.gov/edu/Materials/2021SFSBiennialReport.pdf (last visited 26/02/2024).

National Science Foundation (n.d.) GenCyber – DoD Cyber Exchange. https://public.cyber.mil/gencyber/ (last visited 26/02/2024).

Švábenský V, et al. (2021). Cybersecurity knowledge and skills taught in capture the flag challenges. Computers and Security, Volume 102.

Appendix A: Residential Digital Forensics Camp - Daily Schedule

Time	Day 1 Activities	Time	Day 2 Activities	Time	Day 3 Activities
0700	Breakfast	0700	Breakfast	0700	Breakfast
0830	What is "digital forensics"?	0830	Morning Kahoot!; Q'n'A on "Searching.."	0830	Daily Kahoot!
1015	Break	0915	Break	0900	Intro to casework and case analysis
1030	What is "digital forensics"? (continued)	0930	Searching…(hands-on activities)	1015	Break
1200	Lunch	1200	Lunch	1030	Casework and case analysis (continued)
1300	Intro to Forensic Took Kit (FTK) Imager	1300	Windows Registry & Access Data Registry Viewer	1200	Lunch
1400	Handling Evidence	1415	Break	1300	Intro to Mobile Forensics; Evidence acquisition; Cellebrite UFED4PC
1500	Break	1430	AD Registry Viewer (continued)	1430	Break
1515	Handling Evidence (continued)	1600	The problem with passwords, and PRTK	1515	Mobile Data Extraction & Analyses
1700	Dinner	1700	Dinner	1615	Break
1800	After-hours activities	1800	Open lab	1630	(We haven't got a) Clue!
Time	**Day 4 Activities**	**Time**	**Day 5 Activities**		
0700	Breakfast – Review the day's activities	0700	Breakfast – Review the day's activities		

0830	Competition Time – (We Haven't a) Clue!	0830	FTK Q'n'A / Catch-Up		
1030	Break	0915	Break		
1030	Mobile Forensics with Kali NetHunter	1045	FTK ACE Certification		
1200	Lunch	1200	Lunch		
1300	Bookstore Trip	1300	FTK ACE (continued)		
1430	FTK ACE Certification – Review & Practice	1545	Forensic analysis of game systems		
1515	Break	1615			
1530	FTK ACE Review & Practice (continued)	1615	Break		
1630	FTK ACE Certification – Q'n'A	1630	Team Results & Awards		
1700	Dinner	1700	Dinner		
1800	Open Lab	1800	Pack'n'Prep for Departure		

To accommodate different topics and exercise requirements, time blocks are of unequal length. After hours activities included games and movies with a cybersecurity theme or issue. Supervised evening open labs provided opportunity for review and preparation for the professional-level certification exam.

Appendix B: Virtual Digital Forensics Camp - Daily Schedule

Time	**Day 1 Activities**	**Time**	**Day 2 Activities**	**Time**	**Day 3 Activities**
1000	Welcome & Orientation	1000	Fun with "Hex"	1000	Mobile Forensics
1050	Break	1050	Break	1050	Break
1100	Welcome & Orientation (continued)	1100	Fun with "Hex" Ex(ercise)	1100	(We don't have a) Clue!
1200	Lunch Break	1200	Lunch Break	1200	Lunch Break
1300	What is Digital Forensics?	1300	Windows Registry	1300	Clue! (continued)
1350	Break	1350	Break	1350	Break
1400	Introduction to FTK Imager & Hashing	1400	Windows Registry (continued)	1400	Clue! (continued)
1450	Break	1450	Break	1450	Break
1500	Introduction to FTK	1500	Passwords and Password Recovery Tool Kit	1500	Scholarships & Admissions
1550	Break	1550	Break	1550	Break
1600	Introduction to FTK (continued)	1600	Regular Expressions (RegEx) & KFF	1600	Cyber Jobs Panel
1650	Break	1650	Break	1650	Break
1700	Daily Wrap-Up	1700	Daily Wrap-Up	1700	Daily Wrap-Up
1730	Scheduled End of Day	1730	Scheduled End of Day	1730	Scheduled End of Day
	After-hours activities (Oh no…Homework!)		After-hours activities (Oh no! *More* homework)		Oh no! (Just kidding - it's a night off!)
Time	**Day 4 Activities**	**Time**	**Day 5 Activities**		
1000	Kali NetHunter	1000	ACE Certification		
1050	Break	1050	Break		
1100	Kali NetHunter (continued)	1100	ACE Certification (continued)		
1200	Lunch Break	1200	Lunch Break		
1300	Kali NetHunter (continued)	1300	ACE Certification (continued)		
1350	Break	1350	Break		

1400	Recap/Review/FTK ACE Q'n'A	1400	IoTease		
1450	Break	1450	Break		
1500	Recap/Review/FTK ACE Q'n'A	1500	IoTease (continued)		
1550	Break	1550	Break		
1600	RecapReview/FTK ACE Q'n'A	1600	IoTease (continued)		
1650	Break	1650	Break		
1700	Daily Wrap-Up	1700	Final Wrap-Up		
1730	Scheduled End of Day	1730	Scheduled End of Day		
	After-hours activities (Oh no! *More* homework)		After-hours activities - Have a great summer!)		

To accommodate participants in multiple time zones, days started later than a residential camp. To better coordinate via virtual supervision, activities and breaks followed a fixed schedule. To replace the supervised open-hours labs, after-hours activities involved assigned homework.

Exploring Shifting Patterns in Recent IoT Malware

Javier Carrillo-Mondéjar[1], Guillermo Suarez-Tangil[2], Andrei Costin[3,5], and Ricardo J. Rodríguez[1,4]

[1]Department of Computer Science and Systems Engineering, Universidad de Zaragoza, Zaragoza, Spain

[2]IMDEA Networks Institute, Madrid, Spain

[3]University of Jyväskylä, Jyväskylä, Finland

[4]Instituto de Investigación en Ingeniería de Aragón (I3A), Universidad de Zaragoza, Zaragoza, Spain

[5]Binare Oy, Jyväskylä, Finland

jcarrillo@unizar.es
guillermo.suarez-tangil@imdea.org
ancostin@jyu.fi
rjrodriguez@unizar.es

Abstract: The rise of malware targeting interconnected infrastructures has surged in recent years, driven largely by the widespread presence of vulnerable legacy IoT devices and inadequately secured networks. Despite the strong interest attackers have in targeting this infrastructure, a significant gap remains in understanding how the landscape has recently evolved. Addressing this knowledge gap is essential to thwarting the proliferation of massive botnets, thereby safeguarding end-users and preventing disruptions in critical infrastructures. This work offers a contemporary analysis of Linux-based malware, specifically tailored to IoT malware operating in 2021-2023. Using automated techniques involving both static and dynamic analysis, we classify malware into related threats. By scrutinizing the most recent dataset of Linux-based malware and comparing it to previous studies, we unveil distinctive insights into emerging trends, offering an unparalleled understanding of the evolving landscape. Although Mirai and Gafgyt remain the most prominent families and present a large number of variants, our results show that (i) there is an increase in the sophistication of malware, (ii) malware authors are adding new exploits to their arsenal, and (iii) malware families that originally attacked Windows systems have been adapted to attack Linux-based devices.

Keywords: Static Analysis; Dynamic Analysis; Malware IoT; Malware Evolution; Malware lineage

1. Introduction

The battle against malware has been going on for more than 30 years in the security community. Historically, Windows was the primary target due to its widespread use. However, a significant shift has occurred with the rise of Linux-based operating systems, driven by the growing popularity and the large number of Internet of Things (IoT) devices that use Linux as the underlying operating system.

The global expansion of IoT, which was predicted to reach 50 billion devices by 2020 according to Cisco's (Evans, 2011) and to expand to 100 billion by 2025 according to Huawei (Attia, 2019), brings various benefits in various sectors, including industry, transportation, smart cities, health-care, and daily life. The success and attractive features of IoT have revolutionized the technology, but have also raised serious concerns about the security and privacy of user data.

IoT comprises a multitude of interconnected devices within a network, using various communication protocols, such as MQTT, CoAP, and UPnP, among others. None of these systems are inherently designed with security in mind; rather, they prioritize cost-effectiveness and innovation, often at the expense of security and privacy (Girish et al., 2023). Additionally, the devices themselves have intrinsic limitations, including low storage and computing capacities, along with challenges such as manufacturers' reluctance to provide software/firmware updates (Ibrahim et al., 2023) or the complexity involved in installing updates, even for competent users.

Despite innovative features, many IoT devices exhibit vulnerabilities, ranging from default passwords to outdated software with known security issues (Costin et al., 2016, 2014), which are subsequently abused by increasingly sophisticated IoT malware and botnet families (Cozzi et al., 2018). For instance, Mirai infected more than 600,000 devices in 2016 using default passwords from IoT devices such as IP cameras or routers, causing one of the most severe denial-of-service attacks on the Internet (Antonakakis et al., 2017).

This highlights security challenges within networks of IoT systems, where keeping firmware/software up to date represents a significant hurdle (Carrillo-Mondéjar et al., 2023). Cybercriminals exploit known vulnerabilities to scan networks and launch attacks aimed at taking control of devices (Zhao et al., 2022). Notably, the number of malware attacks targeting interconnected infrastructures has significantly increased in recent years (Al Alsadi et al., 2022; Li et al., 2022). This is mainly due to the widespread presence of vulnerable IoT devices and poorly secured networks (Costin et al., 2014). However, despite attackers' interest in attacking this type of infrastructure, there is still a significant gap in understanding how the landscape has evolved. It is crucial to address this knowledge gap to prevent the proliferation of massive botnets, protect end-users, and prevent disruptions in critical infrastructures.

In this regard, by examining the latest dataset of Linux-based malware and comparing it to previous studies, we unveil distinctive insights into emerging trends, offering unparalleled insight into the evolving landscape. We show that understanding the evolutionary dynamics of malware is a crucial step in addressing the challenges posed by new computing platforms, such as those in the IoT, online services, and critical infrastructures. By analyzing the latest IoT malware threats through the lens of a novel --- and updated --- dataset of over 45K malware samples we shed light on several threats unknown to the community. We set out to conduct our study using well-established methods in the area of IoT malware analysis (Al Alsadi et al., 2022; Alrawi and others, 2021; Carrillo-Mondéjar et al., 2020; Costin and Zaddach, 2018; Cozzi et al., 2020, 2018). In particular, we analyze malware samples to extract information and identify patterns. Then we run the samples and observe how they interact with the system. We combine the data obtained from both stages, using a distance function to correlate samples that exhibit similar behavior. We examine each of the unknown clusters in detail, using cutting-edge reverse engineering and forensic techniques, along with our extensive expertise as malware analysts. Through our analysis, we provide a deep understanding of the latest trends in malware, including the study of various malware families. Among other findings, we observe for the first time that:

i) the level of sophistication is increasing: the new IoT malware infrastructure is borrowing sophisticated tools from Advanced Persistent Threats (APTs), ii) there is a rapid proliferation of new variants with minimal infrastructure investment, and iii) expertise and tools devised by Windows malware are permeating the IoT ecosystem.

In summary, our paper introduces a state-of-the-art analysis of Linux-based malware in the context of IoT, specifically focusing on malware prevalent in the years 2021-2023. In particular, the key contributions of our work are:

1. We deploy an automated system dedicated to examining malware in IoT systems and specially engineered to examine the most recent malware samples seen in the wild at the time of writing. Our system employs a combination of well-established static and dynamic analysis, designed to establish connections between unknown samples and recognized threats.
2. Leveraging our system, we validate recent and unidentified IoT malware samples, characterizing their behaviors. Subsequently, we present an extensive analysis of the most recent trends based on an in-depth study of several malware families.
3. We elucidate the impact of architecture on malware propagation, providing valuable insights into the dynamics influencing the recent spread of malicious activities. Our study deliberately separates Linux-based IoT malware exploration from the predominant IoT architectures associated with malware in the wild.

The rest of the paper is organized as follows. Section 2 provides an overview of related work in the field of IoT malware analysis. Section 3 details our methodology, covering data collection, static and dynamic analysis. In Section 4, we present our analysis results, covering key aspects in the evolution of IoT malware based on static similarity (including a characterization for obfuscation and static-linking), behavioral similarity (including a characterization for dynamic-linking), correlation of malware family, and exploits used in the wild. Section 5 delves into the discussions, highlighting key findings and addressing the limitations of this work. Finally, Section 6 concludes the paper, summarizing our contributions and outlining potential avenues for future research.

2. Related Work

Cozzi et al. (2018) design and implement a comprehensive analysis sandbox for Linux-based malware. Testing this sandbox involves using 10,548 malware samples collected between November 2016 and November 2017, covering more than ten different architectures.

Alrawi et al. (2021) introduce an analysis framework for the life-cycle of IoT malware, taking into account five components: infection vectors, payload properties, persistence methods, capabilities, and C&C infrastructure. Then, IoT malware is characterized through extensive measurements involving over 166,000 Linux-based IoT malware samples collected in 2019 across six different architectures. The results are compared with traditional studies on desktop and mobile malware, revealing Mirai as the predominant family for IoT malware and a variety of malware families for desktop and mobile systems.

Al Alsadi et al. (2022) aims to track the evolution of exploit code in IoT malware using static and dynamic analyses. It identifies 63 unique exploit codes from 17,720 binaries belonging to 26 IoT malware families and conducts multidimensional analysis. The analyzed binaries cover a period from 2015 to 2020. Findings show an average exploit lifespan of 23 months, with an impressive time-to-exploit of 29 months.

Carrillo-Mondéjar et al. (2020) use static and dynamic analyses with similarity detection in order to create an automated system to classify malware into related threats. The dataset used in this paper was collected by the authors in (Cozzi et al., 2018) between 2016 and 2017. Their findings show diverse sophistication levels in Linux-based malware, ranging from brute-force to botnet attacks. In contrast to architectures like x86_64, Linux-based malware is less complex. Therefore, static analysis techniques are effective due to the simplicity of the disassembly code.

Cozzi et al. (2020) employs binary code similarity to methodically reconstruct the lineage of IoT malware families, tracing their relationships, evolution, and variants. Their methodology is applied to a dataset comprising over 93,000 samples submitted to a prominent database (VirusTotal) over a 3.5-year period (from January 2015 to August 2018). Despite the simplicity of IoT malware, their findings indicate that antivirus tools struggle to detect minor modifications within binaries, resulting in mislabeling and missed detections.

Costin and Zaddach (2018) presents an extensive survey, analysis, and cross-validation of more than 60 IoT malware families and 48 unique vulnerabilities. The study covers malware families between the years 2008 and 2018. Alongside this, they provide an open-source malware analysis framework and a comprehensive dataset covering all IoT malware. Their findings reveal that the mean scores for vulnerabilities in IoT malware families are relatively modest, averaging 6.9 for CVSSv2 and 7.5 for CVSSv3. Importantly, preventive measures based on public knowledge could have been implemented, on average, at least 90 days before the submission of the initial malware samples for analysis.

All datasets that have been studied in previous research are before 2020. **Our work builds on these efforts to offer a contemporary view of the malware landscape.** Thus, our data collection spans over three years between early 2021 to late (December) 2023.

3. Methodology

In this section, we explain our methodology. First, we show the dataset we used. Then we present the static analysis that we conducted on each of the malware samples. Finally, we discuss the dynamic analysis and the sample correlation based on our corpus of execution traces.

3.1 Dataset

To better understand the evolution of malware targeting IoT devices and networks, we collect a set of malware samples from VirusShare (Corvus Forensics, 2023) between 2021 and 2023. VirusShare is a malware repository that archives real malware samples for different operating systems and architectures. We collected all torrent files uploaded to the repository during this time, which adds up to approximately 84 torrent files, each containing around 65,536 malware samples. This dataset provides us with recent and comprehensive information on the evolution of malware targeting IoT devices, allowing us to compare it with previous studies. We focus on detecting malware targeting devices running Linux-type operating systems and use ELF (Executable and Linkable Format) binary file format to filter samples. Our dataset comprises 45,871 malware samples targeting various CPU architectures. Table 1 provides a breakdown of all the files, distributed by the architectures they target. For each malware sample in our dataset, we obtain its VirusTotal report.

Additionally, we use AVClass (Sebastián and Caballero, 2020) to label malware samples. This tool is widely accepted and used by the community for labelling malicious samples (Alrawi and others, 2021; Wei et al., 2017; Zhu et al., 2020). AVClass uses the antivirus labels from VirusTotal reports to label a given sample. In total, AVClass provides labels for 44,204 malware samples from 248 different families.

3.2 Static Analysis

We statically analyze the malware binaries to extract metadata from them. During this phase, we collect information such as the architecture and endianness used by the binary, the type of linking it employs (static or dynamic), as well as other details such as cyclomatic complexity, entropy, file size, and text strings. This analysis allows us to obtain information from dynamic link libraries. This information will be used to choose the virtualized environment that best suits the analysis we carry out in subsequent stages. This static analysis allows us to better understand the behavior of malware during dynamic analysis.

Additionally, during this phase we also check whether the binary is packed or not. To do so, we first use the entropy of the binary to identify if it is packed, and then apply a set of rules to detect the specific packer. For detection we employ the cross-platform tool Detect It Easy (DIE), which contains pre-defined signatures to identify a large number of packers and compilers. We also found a few samples packed with Ultimate Packer eXecutable (UPX), and tried to unpack them using the UPX tool itself.

Finally, we look for exploits targeting IoT devices. To do this, we collect exploits from various sources and create specific YARA rules (Alvarez, 2013) for each of them. We also create rules for the vulnerabilities mentioned in (Al Alsadi et al., 2022; Alrawi and others, 2021; Costin and Zaddach, 2018), as well as other exploits targeting IoT devices found on the Internet, mainly from exploit.db. In total, we produce YARA rules for 132 exploits. YARA rules focus on searching for a Uniform Resource Identifier (URI) present in exploits targeting HTTP-based protocol interfaces. We check each sample to identify any exploits embedded in them through static detection. We then use the static information collected in this phase to assist in the dynamic analysis process.

Table 1: Dataset distribution

Arch	Total	Not packed	Packed	Static Linking	Dynamic Linking
ARM	15,603	13,146 (15.75%)	2,457 (15.75%)	13,190 (84.54%)	2,369 (15.18%)
MIPS	11,437	7,900 (69.07%)	3,537 (30.93%)	9,741 (85.17%)	1,666 (14.57%)
Intel 80386	5,416	4,679 (86.39%)	737 (13.61%)	5,030 (92.87%)	371 (6.85%)
x86-64	3,662	3,268 (89.24%)	394 (10.76%)	2,059 (56.23%)	1,565 (42.74%)
PowerPC	2,806	2,166 (77.19%)	640 (22.81%)	2,775 (98.90%)	25 (0.89%)
Renesas SH	2,567	2,567 (100%)	0	2,538 (98.87%)	24 (0.93%)
Motorola m68k	2,218	2,218 (100%)	0	2,064 (93.06%)	150 (6.76%)
SPARC	1,510	1,510 (100%)	0	1,494 (98.94%)	14 (0.93%)
AARCH64	525	514 (97.90%)	11 (2.10%)	37 (7.05%)	487 (92.76%)
Others	127	127 (100%)	0	43 (33.86%)	80 (62.99%)
	45871	38,095 (83.05%)	7,776 (16.95%)	38,971 (84.96%)	6,751 (14.72%)

3.3 Dynamic Analysis

We develop a framework to analyze each of the malware samples in our dataset. This framework leverages a virtualized environment that we implemented for the main architectures. We equip this environment with home-made tools to speed up the execution of the malware sample and collect information related to the system calls made during its execution. To create the virtual machines, we use Buildroot (Petazzoni and Electrons, 2012), which helps us automate the process of creating an embedded Linux system. For the architectures that have Buildroot support, we create different virtual machines using various runtime libraries (i.e., uClibc, glibc, and musl) to ensure that our system supports multiple dynamic linking libraries.

We use the results of the static analysis (e.g., architecture, endianness) to determine which virtual machine is best suited to run the malware sample, thus increasing the probability of success. Overall, we create virtual machines for nine different architectures, including ARM, MIPS, MIPSel, Intel 80385, x86-64, SPARC, PowerPC, Renesas SH, and Motorola m68k. However, we only have virtual machines with uclibc as a dynamic linking library for Motorola m68k and SPARC architectures. For the remaining architectures, we run samples linked dynamically using glibc, uclibc, or musl. To emulate these architectures, we use QEMU as it supports with most of the architectures found in our dataset. To monitor the system calls made at runtime by the malware, we utilize the *strace* system utility and run each sample for 60 seconds in our virtualized environment, since code coverage tends to stabilize within the first minute or two of execution (Küchler et al., 2021). At the end of this stage we obtain execution traces of the samples that were executed successfully. These execution traces consist of the sequence of system calls made by the malware sample, as well as each of the arguments to that system call.

3.4 Phylogenetic Analysis

Our dynamic analysis framework allows us to link samples based on the behavior they exhibit during execution in our sandboxes. We use the execution traces we collect to connect samples that have a similarity greater than 80%. To determine this similarity, we extract N-grams of size 4 from the set of executed system calls and use the Jaccard index to calculate the similarity between each pair of samples of a particular architecture. We define two samples as similar when their Jaccard index is greater than 80%. Next, we use clustering to represent the similarities between the samples. We construct a graph to examine the phylogenetic relationship (evolutionary connection) between various malware samples and families. Each node in the graph represents a sample, while the edges represent the presence of similarity between them.

4. Results

This section presents the result of the statistical analysis of the metadata of the existing malware samples in our dataset.

4.1 Overview

As we pointed out in Section 3.1, our original data set consists of 45,871 ELF malware samples spread across more than 10 CPU architectures. Table 1 shows a breakdown of the number of samples per architecture. We observe that the architectures with the most samples are ARM 32 bits and MIPS, which includes both little and big endianness. Between both architectures, they represent approximately 59% of the total set of samples existing in the dataset.

4.2 Obfuscation

We also study the number of samples that are obfuscated (packed) and the number of samples linked statically and dynamically. We see obfuscation in 7,776 (16.95%) of our samples, many of them using UPX. When unpacking these samples, we observe that 38.87% of the samples have been obfuscated with a custom packer that prevented automatic unpacking (e.g., by adversarially modifying the headers of the binary). As a result, we unpack 67.13% of the samples.

Takeaway. We have observed that unlike other platforms like Windows or Android, malware developers on IoT devices do not use code packers or obfuscators to make their malicious code difficult to detect (Dong et al., 2018; O'Kane et al., 2011). This is because security measures for IoT are not widely practiced. The primary reason for this is the lack of security solutions that are specifically designed for IoT devices and networks. Previous studies (Al Alsadi et al., 2022; Alrawi and others, 2021; Cozzi et al., 2018) reported similar type (UPX) and percentages of packed samples in their datasets, suggesting that the malware ecosystem has not evolved in complexity when it comes to the use of packers.

4.3 Static Analysis

We see that most of the malicious software samples (about 85%) in our collection are statically linked. This is a common practice for malware that targets IoT devices because there are different architectures and library versions on these platforms. By statically linking the binaries, the malware creators can ensure that the software will run correctly on the infected systems. Additionally, we found that 69.82% and 74.21% of statically and dynamically linked binaries, respectively, have had their symbols removed.

Takeaway. Symbol removal is a technique used by malware creators to obfuscate their code. Stripping symbols makes it harder for security analysts and tools to analyze and understand the functionality of the malicious software. Despite leveraging vanilla packers (UPX), our finding suggests a deliberate effort by malware authors to hinder reverse engineering and increase the complexity of detection.

4.4 Dynamic Analysis

Our dynamic analysis framework analyzed 35,378 (77.12%) of the samples observed between 2021 and 2023. By analyzing 35,378 execution traces, we study the following three dimensions: interaction between processes, evasion mechanisms, and profiling behaviors.

Process interaction. We see that around 29% execute a single process and around 66% create three or more processes, with 16,283 being the maximum number of processes created by a sample related to the exploitation of CVE-2015-1325. We also see that 4,566 malware samples attempted to execute some system commands. The most used shell commands were *sh, iptables, killall, rm, chmod*, and *wget*.

Evasion. We found that IoT malware tries to hide its identity, some by disguising itself with the name of legitimate processes such as *sshd* (39.49%), *busybox* (6.32%), or services ([*kworker*] (4.25%), [*watchdog0*] (4.19%)). Some others choose a random name for cloaking. We noticed that a few samples were using certain access paths crafted so that they can detect virtual environments (225 samples). We also observed that 169 samples try to "trace" themselves to prevent the sample from being debugged or to detect if a debugger is attached.

Profiling. We observed that the malware gathers system data, likely for communication with C2C or its operations. Specifically, we see 21,711 access paths found under the */proc* directory, 611 access paths under the */sys* directory, and 8025 access paths related to the system configuration under */etc*.

Takeaway. Our findings on the use of evasion indicate that some IoT malware authors are concerned about their samples being analyzed dynamically, but we did not find this figure as prevalent as the obfuscation used to evade static analysis. This speaks to the challenges the CIT community faces to emulate the full gamut of architectures, which may devoid malware developers from the need to evade dynamic analysis as we discuss in Section 5.

4.5 Evolutionary Connection

We generate similarity graphs for the ARM, MIPS/MIPSel, Intel 80386, x86-64, PowerPC, Renesas SH, Motorola m68k, and SPARC architectures. Due to space restrictions, we only show the similarity graphs for ARM, MIPS, x86, and x86-64.

MIPS and ARM. Figure 1 shows the similarity graph for the MIPS and ARM architectures. The colors represent the labels of the families with the most presence in each of the architectures. Mirai and Gafgyt are the most prominent malware families. Interestingly, we see different clusters for the Mirai and Gafgyt families, showing evolutionary traits stemming from variations of the same family. This indicates that antivirus engines using generic signatures for Gafgyt and Mirai families may fail to detect new variants.

We see new families like Aenjaris, Specter, or Mutiliverze. Aenjaris is a ransomware family that was created using leaked Babuk source code, while Specter is a new botnet that specifically targets IoT devices. We have also observed a new family called Multiverze, which appears in both MIPS, ARM, x86, and x86-64 architectures. However, upon close inspection, we have determined that Multiverze is a generic label that encompasses a range of behaviors, from backdoors to cryptomining malware. These types of "bag of malware samples" severely challenge existing data-driven identification and detection mechanisms due to their morphic behavioral traits.

Intel 80385 and x86-64. Figure 2 shows the clustering of the samples belonging to the Intel 80385 and x86-64 architectures. These architectures are commonly used in personal computers and servers, and thus, consist of a larger number of different families. However, significant differences can be observed between them. Looking at Intel 80385 in Figure 2 we see, apart from the usual suspects, Xorddos and Setag. These widely known families continue to operate.

Looking at x86-64 in Figure 2 we observe the following differences:

- Although both Mirai and Gafgyt families are still present, there are not as many clusters of both families anymore. This suggests that not all variants of Mirai and Gafgyt generate specific versions for this architecture.
- We also observe several families with significant representation, such as Ladvix, Prometei, Pancar, Ransomexx, and Rekoobe. These families have different functionalities, ranging from a file infector to a Trojan that is based on the publicly available Tiny SHell source code, which is used by APT31.

- We have identified several cryptomining families such as Prometei, Skidmap, and Xmrig. Prometei, for instance, is a botnet that was initially discovered on Windows and now targets Linux-based systems as well.
- We also see the Rozena family, a sophisticated type of malware written in Python where the interpreter is embedded in the binary itself.
- Another prominent variant we came across is called Prism, which is an open-source backdoor.
- Finally, we have seen several examples of the Multiverze family, which is a generic name given to many unidentified samples as discussed earlier. After analyzing a few samples from the Multiverze cluster and some unlabeled samples, we determined that it is a downloader most likely engaging in Pay-Per-Install (PPI) services.

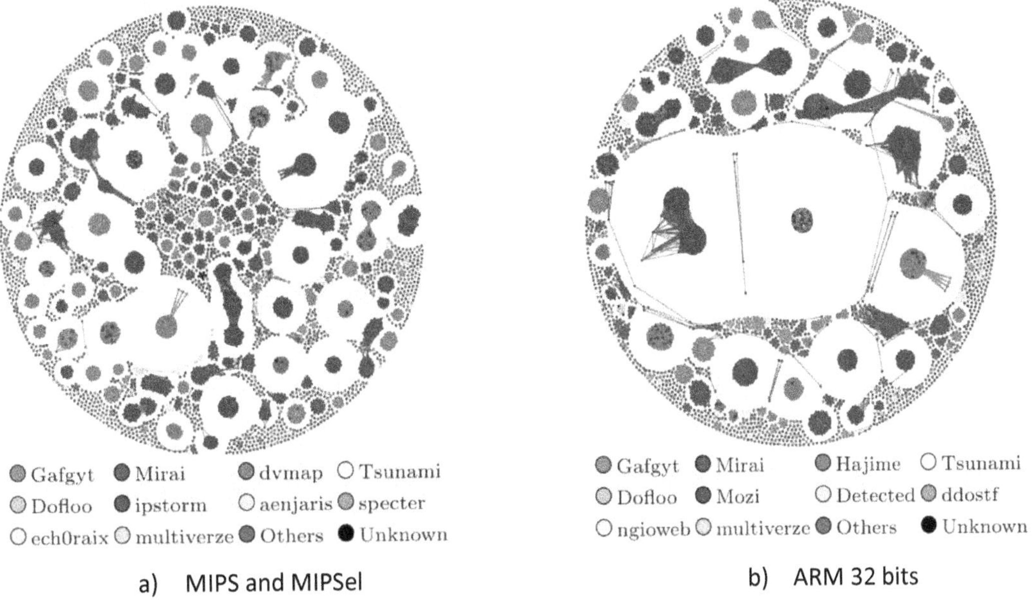

a) MIPS and MIPSel

b) ARM 32 bits

Figure 1: Graph Similarity

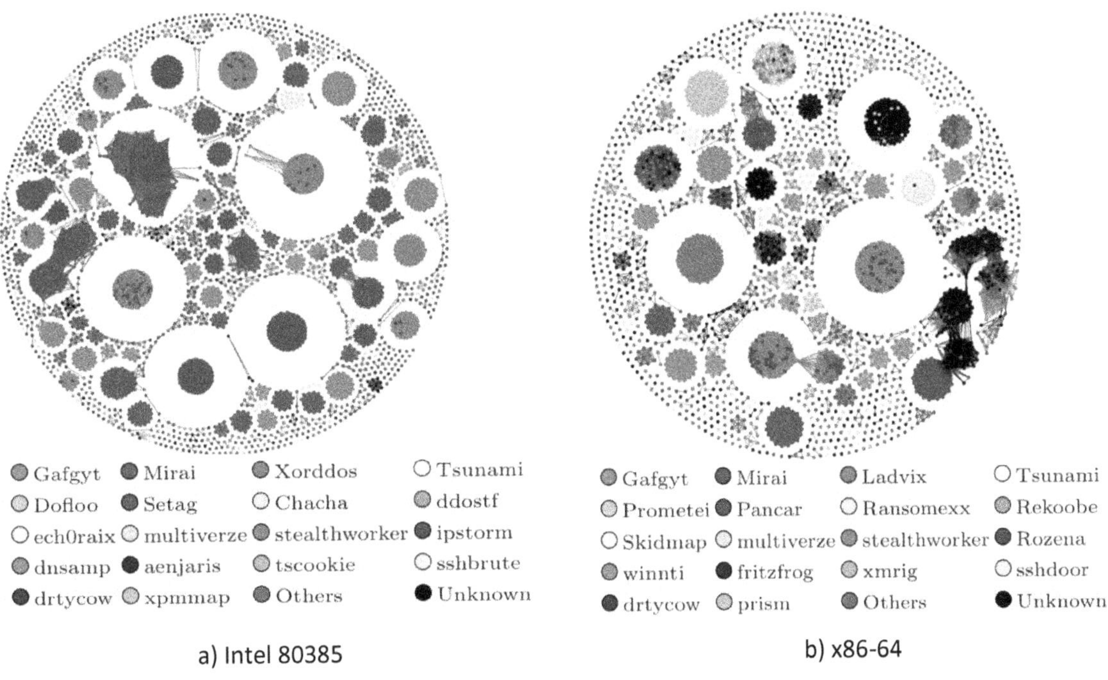

a) Intel 80385

b) x86-64

Figure 2: Graph similarity

Other architectures. Clustering on the rest of the architectures shows that variants of Mirai, Gafgyt, and some Tsunami samples are also prevalent on Motorola m68K, Renesas SH, and PowerPC. It is worth noting that these architectures have striking similarities to those depicted in Figure 1.

Takeaway. While we see that Mirai and Gafgyt continue to be prevalent families (Carrillo-Mondéjar et al., 2020), we see an explosion of variants. We note that a significant evolution of popular IoT malware can jeopardize existing defenses. We also see new families in the landscape that have the potential (sophisticated open-sourced projects) to become as insidious as Mirai.

4.6 Exploits Used in the Wild

Our analysis reveals the use of 89 different exploits. We map each exploit with the samples we have collected in the wild. In total, we found that 13,061 (28.47%) samples with actionable exploits. Figure 3 displays a graph, where the nodes represent malware samples and the vulnerability they exploit. Edges represent the reuse of exploits across samples. The size of the node represents the severity of the vulnerability. The different colors represent the corresponding malware families. All the samples found are distributed mainly in 5 families, with the Mirai and Gafgyt families being the ones that stand out from the rest. Some exploits are very central to the samples of one single family (e.g., Gafgyt), while other malware families carry an arsenal of exploits scattered across samples.

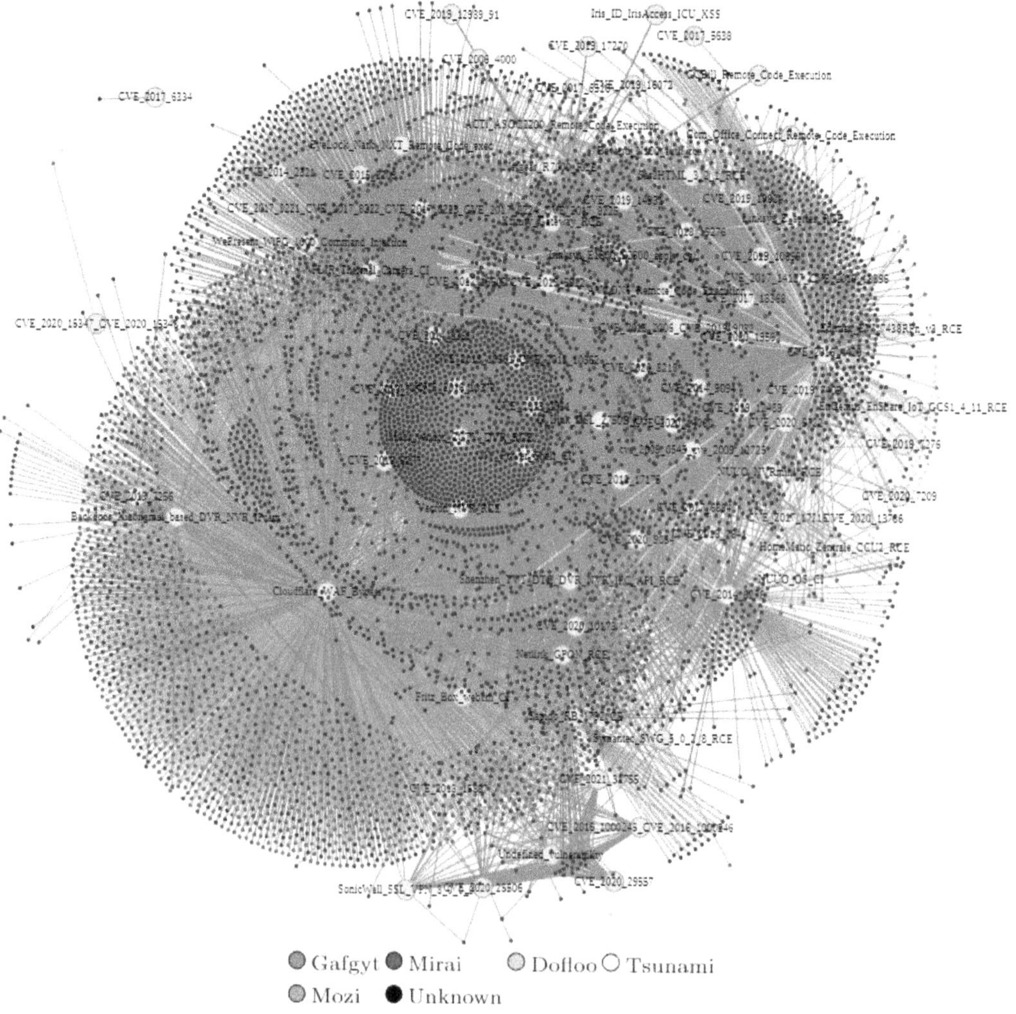

Figure 3: Exploits

Takeaway. After comparing our results with those presented in previous studies (Al Alsadi et al., 2022; Alrawi and others, 2021), we have noticed a slight increase in the number of exploits found, which were 25 and 58 respectively. This indicates that malware creators are including new exploits in their arsenals, that are already publicly available as proof of concept, to improve their chances of infecting new devices and achieving success. However, some other malware families persistently stick to a handful of exploits.

5. Discussion

5.1 Findings

Strategies. IoT devices typically have limited resources and diverse architectures, making them attractive targets. Despite not seeing a radical change in the technology used to pack malware, IoT malware authors are adopting strategies, such as statically linking stripped binaries, to make detection more difficult while ensuring their malicious software runs seamlessly on different IoT devices. This insight is valuable for IoT security strategies as it emphasizes the need for customized defenses against such threats.

Evasion. The limited need for mechanisms to evade dynamic analysis suggests potential challenges within the CIT community in accurately emulating a comprehensive range of architectures. This could potentially reduce the imperative for malware developers to actively avoid dynamic analysis. We found this to be a valuable new insight, which calls for important future work in the research community.

Evolution. Malware targeting IoT devices is constantly changing. Most samples in the IoT landscape are variants of the well-known Mirai and Gafgyt malware families. However, in recent years other families of diverse natures have appeared. Interestingly, some of these malware families initially attacked Windows systems but have expanded to Linux-based systems. This insight can help forensic analysts and inspire new research into developing effective mitigations for Windows systems in the IoT field. On top of that, we have also seen new malware families that rely heavily on sophisticated code, publicly available on the Internet, emerging from an Advanced Persistent Threat (APT31), for which we foresee a prominent emergence. We advocate for greater scrutiny of open repositories and underground forums that may host IoT malware.

Prioritization. We noticed an increase in the number of exploits found in previous studies. Naturally, malware authors are adding new exploits to their toolbox. On the other hand, some malware families seem to continue using the same old exploits. This insight can provide a valuable prioritization strategy to CIT when designing mitigations. That is, fixing one single exploit will effectively thwart many malware attacks (most in Gafgyt).

5.2 Limitations

Our analysis platform may have some limitations that may influence the study. First, the analyses of the interaction with the system are carried out in user mode through the *strace* tool, so it can be detected by malware. However, only 0.48% of the dynamically executed samples use *ptrace* to attempt to debug themselves and could therefore detect that the process is being debugged since there cannot be two debuggers attached to the same process. Execution traces could also be affected if the malware detects that it is running in a virtualized environment, so it may change its behavior relative to a real environment. However, we have only identified 0.64% of the samples that try to access system paths that allow them to detect whether it is a virtual machine or not. On the other hand, for the extraction of exploits, we focus exclusively on the clear text strings that appear in the binaries and, therefore, there may be more exploits than we report since these may be encrypted or encoded within the binary and decrypted before use.

6. Conclusions

In this work, we presented a thorough examination of recent malware trends targeting IoT platforms between 2021-2023. Through data analysis, we systematically characterized malware across diverse threats using static and dynamic features. This approach helped us identify new malware samples and their connections to previously known threats, following one of the main objectives of this work.

Our methodology extended beyond individual samples, allowing the extraction of knowledge over large groups of connected samples. This approach was instrumental in investigating recent unlabeled malware samples found in the wild. To expand our analysis, we used state-of-the-art reverse engineering techniques and our own malware analysis pipeline to study unknown clusters and provide nuanced insights into the type of exploits they leverage. Our analysis delved into the latest trends, revealing novel insights including: i) an increase in sophistication as the emerging IoT malware infrastructure incorporates advanced tools borrowed from APT31, ii) the dissemination of knowledge and tools originally designed for Windows malware in the IoT ecosystem, and iii) a rapid proliferation of novel variants driving future work in the area as discuss next.

Future work: The minimal need for evasive mechanisms in dynamic analysis highlights upcoming challenges for the CIT community in effectively simulating diverse architectures. This emerging trend may alleviate pressure on malware developers to actively evade dynamic analysis. Our discovery presents a novel perspective, underscoring the need for significant future efforts within the research community to address this evolving dynamic.

Acknowledgements

This research was supported in part by TED2021-132900A-I00 and by TED2021-131115A-I00, funded by MCIN/AEI/10.13039/501100011033, by the Recovery, Transformation and Resilience Plan funds, financed by the European Union (Next Generation), by the Spanish National Cybersecurity Institute (INCIBE) under *Proyectos Estratégicos de Ciberseguridad -- CIBERSEGURIDAD EINA UNIZAR*, and by the University, Industry and Innovation Department of the Aragonese Government under *Programa de Proyectos Estratégicos de Grupos de Investigación* (DisCo research group, ref. T21-23R). G. Suarez-Tangil was appointed as 2019 Ramon y Cajal fellow (RYC-2020-029401-I) funded by MCIN/AEI/10.13039/501100011033 and ESF Investing in your future.

(Part of) This work was supported by the European Commission under the Horizon Europe Programme, as part of the project LAZARUS (https://lazarus-he.eu/) (Grant Agreement no. 101070303). The content of this article does not reflect the official opinion of the European Union. Responsibility for the information and views expressed therein lies entirely with the authors.

References

Al Alsadi, A.A., Sameshima, K., Bleier, J., Yoshioka, K., Lindorfer, M., van Eeten, M., Gañán, C.H., 2022. No Spring Chicken: Quantifying the Lifespan of Exploits in IoT Malware Using Static and Dynamic Analysis, in: Proceedings of the ACM on Asia Conference on Computer and Communications Security (ASIACCS). Association for Computing Machinery.

Alrawi, O., others, 2021. The Circle Of Life: A Large-Scale Study of The IoT Malware Lifecycle, in: 30th USENIX Security Symposium. USENIX Association.

Alvarez, V., 2013. YARA - The pattern matching swiss knife for malware researchers [WWW Document]. The pattern matching swiss knife for malware researchers. URL http://virustotal.github.io/yara/ (accessed 1.27.24).

Antonakakis, M., April, T., Bailey, M., Bernhard, M., Bursztein, E., Cochran, J., Durumeric, Z., Halderman, J.A., Invernizzi, L., Kallitsis, M., Kumar, D., Lever, C., Ma, Z., Mason, J., Menscher, D., Seaman, C., Sullivan, N., Thomas, K., Zhou, Y., 2017. Understanding the Mirai Botnet, in: 26th USENIX Security Symposium (USENIX Security 17). USENIX Association, Vancouver, BC, pp. 1093–1110.

Attia, T.M., 2019. Challenges and opportunities in the future applications of IoT technology.

Carrillo-Mondéjar, J., Martínez, J.L., Suarez-Tangil, G., 2020. Characterizing Linux-based malware: Findings and recent trends. Future Generation Computer Systems 110, 267–281.

Carrillo-Mondéjar, J., Turtiainen, H., Costin, A., Martínez, J.L., Suarez-Tangil, G., 2023. HALE-IoT: Hardening Legacy Internet of Things Devices by Retrofitting Defensive Firmware Modifications and Implants. IEEE Internet of Things Journal 10, 8371–8394. https://doi.org/10.1109/JIOT.2022.3224649

Corvus Forensics, 2023. VirusShare.com - Because Sharing is Caring.

Costin, A., Zaddach, J., 2018. IoT malware: Comprehensive survey, analysis framework and case studies. BlackHat USA.

Costin, A., Zaddach, J., Francillon, A., Balzarotti, D., 2014. A {Large-scale} analysis of the security of embedded firmwares, in: 23rd USENIX Security Symposium.

Costin, A., Zarras, A., Francillon, A., 2016. Automated dynamic firmware analysis at scale: a case study on embedded web interfaces, in: Proceedings of the 11th ACM on Asia Conference on Computer and Communications Security.

Cozzi, E., Graziano, M., Fratantonio, Y., Balzarotti, D., 2018. Understanding Linux Malware, in: IEEE Symposium on Security and Privacy (SP).

Cozzi, E., Vervier, P.-A., Dell'Amico, M., Shen, Y., Bilge, L., Balzarotti, D., 2020. The Tangled Genealogy of IoT Malware, in: Annual Computer Security Applications Conference (ACSAC). Association for Computing Machinery.

Dong, S., Li, M., Diao, W., Liu, X., Liu, J., Li, Z., Xu, F., Chen, K., Wang, X., Zhang, K., 2018. Understanding Android Obfuscation Techniques: A Large-Scale Investigation in the Wild, in: Beyah, R., Chang, B., Li, Y., Zhu, S. (Eds.), Security and Privacy in Communication Networks. Springer International Publishing, Cham, pp. 172–192.

Evans, D., 2011. How the next evolution of the internet is changing everything. Cisco Whitepapers.

Girish, A., Hu, T., Prakash, V., Dubois, D.J., Matic, S., Huang, D.Y., Egelman, S., Reardon, J., Tapiador, J., Choffnes, D., others, 2023. In the Room Where It Happens: Characterizing Local Communication and Threats in Smart Homes, in: Proceedings of the 2023 ACM on Internet Measurement Conference. pp. 437–456.

Ibrahim, M., Continella, A., Bianchi, A., 2023. AoT - Attack on Things: A security analysis of IoT firmware updates, in: 2023 IEEE 8th European Symposium on Security and Privacy (EuroS&P). pp. 1047–1064. https://doi.org/10.1109/EuroSP57164.2023.00065

Küchler, A., Mantovani, A., Han, Y., Bilge, L., Balzarotti, D., 2021. Does Every Second Count? Time-based Evolution of Malware Behavior in Sandboxes., in: NDSS.

Li, R., Li, Q., Huang, Y., Zhang, W., Zhu, P., Jiang, Y., 2022. IoTEnsemble: Detection of Botnet Attacks on Internet of Things, in: Computer Security – ESORICS 2022: 27th European Symposium on Research in Computer Security, Copenhagen,

Denmark, September 26–30, 2022, Proceedings, Part II. Springer-Verlag, Berlin, Heidelberg, pp. 569–588. https://doi.org/10.1007/978-3-031-17146-8_28

O'Kane, P., Sezer, S., McLaughlin, K., 2011. Obfuscation: The Hidden Malware. IEEE Security & Privacy 9, 41–47. https://doi.org/10.1109/MSP.2011.98

Petazzoni, T., Electrons, F., 2012. Buildroot: a nice, simple and efficient embedded Linux build system, in: Embedded Linux System Conference.

Sebastián, S., Caballero, J., 2020. AVclass2: Massive Malware Tag Extraction from AV Labels, in: Proceedings of the 36th Annual Computer Security Applications Conference (ACSAC). Association for Computing Machinery.

Wei, F., Li, Y., Roy, S., Ou, X., Zhou, W., 2017. Deep ground truth analysis of current android malware, in: 14th International Conference on Detection of Intrusions and Malware, and Vulnerability Assessment (DIMVA). Springer.

Zhao, B., Ji, S., Lee, W.-H., Lin, C., Weng, H., Wu, J., Zhou, P., Fang, L., Beyah, R., 2022. A Large-Scale Empirical Study on the Vulnerability of Deployed IoT Devices. IEEE Transactions on Dependable and Secure Computing 19, 1826–1840. https://doi.org/10.1109/TDSC.2020.3037908

Zhu, S., Shi, J., Yang, L., Qin, B., Zhang, Z., Song, L., Wang, G., 2020. Measuring and modeling the label dynamics of online {Anti-Malware} engines, in: 29th USENIX Security Symposium.

The U.S. National Cybersecurity Strategy: A Vehicle with an International Journey

Jami M. Carroll
Harvard University, Somerset, MA, USA
jcarroll@prisidian.com

Abstract: The *U.S. National Cybersecurity Strategy* is focused on the five pillars of defending critical infrastructure: detect, disrupt, and dismantle threat actors; improve market resilience and security; invest in future resilience; and create international partnerships with shared goals. The National Cybersecurity Strategy Implementation Plan is focused on critical infrastructure supporting energy, financial, healthcare, information technology, and manufacturing sectors. In the U.S. alone, the SolarWinds supply chain attack affected nine federal agencies and about 100 companies. Ransomware attacks such as the Colonial Pipelines, the largest U.S. oil pipeline, disrupted supplies of gasoline and fuel to the U.S. East Coast and the JBS USA as the largest meat processor ransomware attack affecting one-fifth of the nation's meat supply. The *U.S. National Cybersecurity Strategy* as a response to the U.S.'s critical infrastructure concerns led to the creation of two core cybersecurity documents which were crafted jointly with several other allies. Cybersecurity and Infrastructure Security Agency (CISA) crafted the *Shifting the Balance of Cybersecurity Risk: Principles and Approaches for Secure by Design Software* with joint agreement with National Security Agency (NSA), the Federal Bureau of Investigation (FBI), and 15 international government agencies to give international vendors a roadmap of the expected cybersecurity hygiene required from their products. (CISA, 2023a; Car & De Luca, 2022) Building on the *Shifting the Balance of Cybersecurity Risk: Principles and Approaches for Secure by Design Software*, CISA, FBI and NSA met with cybersecurity organizations from Australia, Canada, New Zealand, and United Kingdom and jointly created *The Case for Memory Safe Roadmaps: Why Both C-Suite Executives and Technical Experts Need to Take Memory Safe Coding Seriously* as a core issue identified in the earlier guidance. (CISA, 2023c). These two jointly led by the U.S. helped initiate an international cybersecurity norm insisting international software manufacturers demonstrate product security and transparency in the products they sell. These joint documents quickly showed how a global community can rally to solve cybersecurity challenges that have existed for decades. This led to twenty of the largest international software vendors creating the Minimum Viable Secure Product (MSVP) Working Group to address the requirements levied by these documents; CISA has joined this working group to help shape procurement, contractual controls, self-assessment, and system development lifecycle (SDLC) with these vendors. (CISA, 2024d; MSVP, n.d.) This research argues that the U.S. National Security Council (NSC) should leverage the talent pool of CISA, National Institute of Standards and Technology (NIST), Department of Defense (DoD), FBI, and NSA to improve detection, information sharing, security standards, and implementation for not only the U.S.'s government and commercial sectors, but also helps our allies and partners. The DoD and Office of the Director of National Intelligence (ODNI) have made great strides in improving security by integrating improvements with Zero Trust Architecture (ZTA), Supply Chain Risk Management (SCRM), Software Supply Chain Security, Cybersecurity Safety Review Board (CSRB), Cybersecurity Incident & Vulnerability Response Playbooks, and DoD National Security Systems (NSS) standards. The NSC should coordinate through CISA to develop a collaborative effort to not only benefit the U.S. critical infrastructure but also help our allies and partners.

Keywords: National Cybersecurity Strategy, critical infrastructure attacks, zero trust architecture, supply chain risk management, software supply chain security

1. Introduction

Disclaimer: All statements of fact, opinion, or analysis expressed are those of the author. The views and opinions expressed herein by the author do not represent the official policies or positions of the United States (U.S.) Department of Defense (DoD), U.S. Navy, or other agencies or departments of the U.S. government and are solely representative of the views of the author. This does not constitute an official release of DoD or Navy information.

The research methodology used in this research will be a survey methodology based on U.S. cybersecurity practices that shape international norms and could be collaborated on with allies. This research methodology starts with unfolding the Biden-Harris *U.S. National Security Strategy*. A literature review of the documents that evolved from this strategy will cover the two jointly created documents with allies, and the frameworks of ZTA, SCRM, Software Supply Chain Security, Cybersecurity Safety Review Board (CSRB), Cybersecurity Incident & Vulnerability Response Playbooks that allies could leverage and expand international cybersecurity norms with the U.S.

The Biden-Harris *U.S. National Security Strategy* is a cornerstone to protecting, improving, and maintaining the security of U.S. vital national interests, especially those things deemed critical infrastructure. It helps ensure economic prosperity and opportunity for the U.S. while laying out a plan that protects our critical infrastructure as it supports our democratic values and way of life. Most nations have similar interests that are highly compatible with ours and "we will build the strongest and broadest possible coalition of nations that seek to cooperate with each other, while competing with those powers that offer a darker vision and thwarting their efforts to threaten our interests." (Biden, 2022, 7) Supply chain resiliency regardless of the product whether manufacturing, mining, Defense Industrial Base (DIB), or critical infrastructure is key to a nation's national security.

In 1998, President Clinton released PDD-63, *Presidential Decision Directive 63 (PDD-63) on Critical Infrastructure Protection: Sector Coordinators* where he defined critical infrastructures are those essential systems with a cyber-based and physical capability critical to the "minimum operations of the economy and government" with banking, energy, emergency services, finance, telecommunications, transportation, and water whether they are owned by the government or the commercial entities. (Clinton, 1998, 1) In 2000, Clinton released the *National Plan for Information Systems Protection* stating that cyber and the information revolution had touched every facet of our daily lives, whether the lights in our homes, boarding planes, or contacting loved ones since they all used critical infrastructure. Even our sophisticated Department of Defense (DoD) systems rely on computer-controlled capabilities and networks which could affected by intrusion and destruction if they become vulnerable. These commercial and defense segments could have catastrophic impacts on our economic sectors and government agencies if we fall prey to its peril. New approaches to the evolution of computers and their threats are tantamount to understanding the threats to critical infrastructure. We must create measures to safeguard these capabilities to gain all the benefits of the Information Age. (Clinton, 2000) In July 2000, The Commission on America's National Interests designated the U.S. critical infrastructure as "vital" and that the "U.S. critical infrastructure be reasonably resistant to concerted, sophisticated cyber-attack." (Allison & Blackwill, 2000, p. 48-49.) The U.S. Cybersecurity & Infrastructure Security Agency (CISA) was created in 2018 as a component under the U.S. Department of Homeland Security focusing on cybersecurity and critical infrastructure across the U.S. working with government agencies and the private sector; they work in collaboration with government and private sectors focusing on the U.S. critical infrastructure sectors listed in Table 1. (CISA, n.d.)

CISA realized that many in the international community had similar goals of creating a more resilient cybersecurity posture for their critical infrastructure like what was evolving from the U.S.'s *U.S. National Security Strategy* but crafted jointly for an international community. CISA requested comments of these joint goals in the *Shifting the Balance of Cybersecurity Risk: Principles and Approaches for Secure by Design Software*. This CISA released, joint document captured the goals of Australian Cyber Security Centre (ACSC), Canadian Centre for Cyber Security (CCCS), Cyber Security Agency of Singapore (CSA), Computer Emergency Response Team New Zealand (CERT NZ), Cyber Security Centre New Zealand (NCSC-NZ), Czech Republic's National Cyber and Information Security Agency (NÚKIB), FBI, Germany's Federal Office for Information Security (BSI), Israel's National Cyber Directorate (INCD), Japan Computer Emergency Response Team Coordination Center (JPCERT/CC), Japan's National Center of Incident Readiness and Strategy for Cybersecurity (NISC), Korea Internet & Security Agency (KISA), OAS/CICTE Network of Government Cyber Incident Response Teams (CSIRT) Americas, Netherlands' National Cyber Security Centre (NCSC-NL), Norway's National Cyber Security Center (NCSC-NO), NSA, and the United Kingdom's National Cyber Security Centre (NCSC-UK). (CISA, 2023a)

Table 1: U.S. Critical Infrastructure

U.S. Critical Infrastructure			
Chemical	Dams	Financial Services	Information Technology
Commercial facilities	Defense Industrial Base	Food and Agriculture	Nuclear Reactors, Materials, and Waste
Communications	Emergency Services	Government Facilities	Transportation Systems
Critical Manufacturing	Energy	Health Care and Public Health	Water and Wastewater

The U.S. Office if the National Cyber Director (ONCD) was created by Congress in 2021 as an advisor to the President as a component of the Executive Office of the President to spearhead the President's *National Cybersecurity Strategy* to coordinate a whole-of-government implementation of the strategy.

ONCD assisted President Biden with developing *U.S. President's Executive Order (EO) 14017, America's Supply Chain: A Year of Action and Progress* as a direct result of supply chain security concerns after the SolarWinds supply chain attack of 2020, Colonial Pipelines ransomware attack of 2021, and JBS USA ransomware attack of 2021. The SolarWinds attack affected nine federal agencies and about 100 U.S. companies; the Colonial Pipelines ransomware attack disrupted supplies of gasoline and fuel to most of the U.S. East Coast; and the JBS USA ransomware attack affected the largest meat supply source in the U.S. and affected one-fifth of the nation's meat supply. Had good Cybersecurity Supply Chain Risk Management (C-SCRM) practices been in place, there is the likelihood that no impact or a significantly reduced impact would have occurred. EO 14017 focused on these 2020 and 2021 attacks while widening the focus to the six sectors of energy, transportation systems, food and agriculture, health care and public health, information technology and defense industrial base after assessments from the private sector, think tanks, academia, non-profits, non-government organization, and numerous government organizations. These focus areas were endorsed by the National Security Advisor, Jake Sullivan, and the Economic Policy / Director of the Economic Council, Brian Deese. EO 14017 directed our agencies to partner with our industrial bases to monitor, rebuild, and strengthen our supply chain management with added resilience. (Biden, 2021a)

EO 14028 expanded the improvements to the supply chain by also requiring Zero Trust Architecture (ZTA), improved federal/private sector threat intelligence sharing, modernizing federal government cybersecurity, enhancing C-SCRM, establishing a Cyber Safety Review Board (CSRB), improved detection, standardized response, investigation and remediation capabilities in response to cybersecurity vulnerabilities and incidents, and a renewed improvement with National Security Systems (NSS) security posture. In EO 14028, President Biden indicated that we must work with allies and partners to decrease vulnerabilities before they enter the global supply chain. This should entail improving international adoption of best practices with allies, partner nations, and even competitor nations so that industrial policies and global sourcing of products receive similar cybersecurity treatment in the source countries before they are shipped out to the U.S. and other nations. (Biden, 2021b).

2. Secure Your Supply Chains: A Recipe for Building the Best Products

NSA says it's critical to consider the ingredients of software, firmware, and hardware as the starting point to resilient C-SCRM. Over the past five years, cybersecurity software supply chains as one of the most critical elements that has affected the U.S.; some of the issues with cybersecurity software supply chains likely affect our allies and partners. (NSA, 2023a) Over the past five years, the NSA has seen cybersecurity software supply chains as one of the most critical elements in developing a solid Cybersecurity Supply Chain Risk Management (C-SCRM). Upon release of EO 14028, NSA, ODNI, and CISA led a collaborative partnership between the U.S. government and private organizations across multiple sectors which created the Enduring Software Framework (ESF) and a panel creating the *Securing the Software Supply Chain: Recommended Practices for Customers*. (NSA, 2022a; NSA, 2022b; NSA, 2022c) The NSA recommended process starts with the ingredients as the key and monitoring them through their lifetime:

- Analyze software planned to examine it before it is integrated so it can be managed,
- After deployment, identify vulnerabilities and develop mitigations to correct the vulnerabilities, and
- During operation, use incident management to detect and respond to vulnerabilities. (NSA, 2023a)

2.1 Software Security & Firmware

NSA argued that software security should focus on three key areas: using the Software Bill of Material (SBOM) to gain transparency into what software is used and what vulnerabilities it possesses; leveraging memory-safe programming languages to eliminate the largest percentage of vulnerabilities; and using ongoing vulnerability scanning, detection and mitigation to address problems as they arrive. Vulnerabilities related to SolarWinds and Log4j could have been mitigated early in the vulnerability mitigation process affecting hundreds of organizations had they used the SBOM. (NSA, 2022c)

The SBOM collects the provenance of the software from the standpoint of who created the software or if received from a software supplier, who provided the software whether open source or commercial software. EO 14028 mandates the SBOM for all U.S. federal agencies. This provenance of each piece of software gives an organization transparency in the software used or provided to others; supports risk identification, analysis, and management; and for U.S. federal customers to show their compliance with EO 14028. (Biden, 2021b).

The U.S. Office of Management and Budget (OMB) mandates the use of the SBOM for all federal agencies as directed by EO 14028 and directs federal agencies to refer to the National Institute of Standards and Technology (NIST) for secure software development practices. The SBOM can create an inventory, it includes a hash / digital signature representing the software package and includes a Vulnerability Exploitability eXchange (VEX) capability that has a channel to report flaws and track vulnerabilities using key risk management tools like the National Vulnerability Database (NVD), OASIS Common Security Advisory Framework (CSAF), and several MITRE-developed tools and guidance like the MITRE Adversarial Tactics, Techniques, and Common Knowledge or (MITRE ATT&CK), MITRE Common Attack Pattern Enumeration and Classification (MITRE CAPEC). Using the VEX capability, suppliers and consumers can gain greater insight into what vulnerabilities exist with the software package. Apache CycloneDX is one of the most used SBOM tools. (CISA, 2022; NIST, 2022a; NIST, 2022b) Apache CycloneDX can provide numerous pieces of information that support cyber risk deduction; these CycloneDX capabilities include:

- Software Bill of Materials (SBOM)
- Software-as-a-Service Bill of Materials (SaaSBOM)
- Hardware Bill of Materials (HBOM)
- Machine Learning Bill of Materials (ML-BOM)
- Operations Bill of Materials (OBOM)
- Manufacturing Bill of Materials (MBOM)
- Bill of Vulnerabilities (BOV)
- Vulnerability Disclosure Report (VDR)
- Vulnerability Exploitability eXchange (VEX)
- Common Release Notes Format

Elements of these CycloneDX capabilities go into CycloneDX's object model attributes to display metadata, components, services, dependencies, compositions, vulnerabilities, formulation, and annotation; they are illustrated in Figure 1.

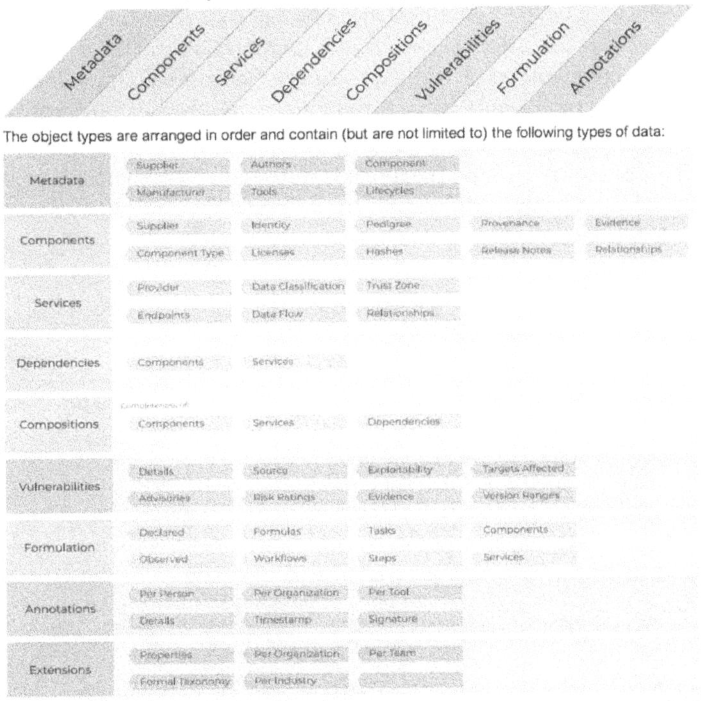

Figure 1: CycloneDX Object Model

NSA argued that 70% of most Common Vulnerability & Exposure (CVE) vulnerabilities have resulted because of memory-safe vulnerabilities. Using memory-safe programming languages (MSLs) like C#, Go, Java, Python, Rust, and Swift instead of C, C++, and Objective-C will correct most of these memory-safe vulnerabilities and enable a key process in the Secure by Design approach CISA and others laid out to eliminate most memory safety vulnerabilities. Security by Design leverages: 1) owning the security outcome, 2) developing radical transparency in development, and 3) employing a top-down security approach to ensure products developed are secure. To guide consumers wanting to leverage Security by Design, the U.S. CISA, FBI, and NSA collaborated with the Australian Signals Directorate's Australian Cyber Centre, Canadian Centre for Cyber Security, the United Kingdom's National Cyber Security Centre, New Zealand National Cyber Security Centre, and the Computer

Emergency Response Team New Zealand to develop *The Case for Memory Safe Roadmaps: Why Both C-Suite Executives and Technical Experts Need to Take Memory Safe Coding Seriously*. (CISA, 2023c)

The last key area is vulnerability testing. Static Application Security Testing (SAST) and Dynamic Application Security Testing (DAST) should be used throughout the development and test before becoming operational. SAST and DAST tools are commonly used in Development, Security, and Operations (DevSecOps) environments, but they can be used in non-DevSecOps environments. SAST tools look internally at the code as a static form of source, byte, or binary code to find code weaknesses. Many of these code weaknesses are from poorly created code such as using inappropriate coding practices or incorporating vulnerable libraries. SAST is extremely useful for looking at code in an early stage of development before it has been integrated with other capabilities. DAST looks at the code externally like it is a black box. DAST will look at runtime, environment, and logic that may make the code perform differently than expected. Quite often DAST tools will incorporate fuzzing to create situations where the code performs in an unexpected manner such as being able to order a negative 5 books or pay with a negative 10 dollars. (DoD, 2019; DoD, 2021) Once the system is built, before deployment and in operation, it should have ongoing vulnerability scanning, detection, and mitigation against the system. Vulnerability scanners are used to identify shortfalls in data encryption, opportunities for denial of service, privilege elevation, SQL injection, unauthorized access to data, and inappropriate user authentication and authorization. (NIST, 2022a).

Periodic vulnerability assessments and penetration testing are good forms of testing the system for potential vulnerabilities that may not have been captured by DAST and SAST or are recent vulnerabilities that have just recently developed. A vulnerability assessment is done to potentially find the possibility for exploitation without executing the exploitation. Penetration testing takes vulnerability assessment to the next step by exploiting the vulnerability. The process of vulnerability assessment and penetration testing follows a sequence of steps. That sequence is footprinting, fingerprinting, enumeration, research, escalation, repeat visits, and covering tracks using stealth so as not to become discovered, much like a hacker might execute their steps to stay hidden. The steps used in the vulnerability assessment inform the penetration tester of the possibility of threats, vulnerabilities, and impacts so that vulnerability analysis can be performed. This vulnerability analysis will focus on what vulnerabilities will have the biggest impact; the penetration test can use this analysis to perform the exploitation. Whether penetration testing is unannounced, only known to the leadership of the organization, or announced, known to the wider organization audience is determined by the rules of engagement set by the organization's leadership. Table 2 illustrates the general steps used in a vulnerability assessment and penetration testing effort. (Carroll, 2018)

Table 2: Typical Steps Used in Vulnerability and Penetration Testing of Systems

	Common Approaches	Description	Comments
Vulnerability Assessment	Footprinting	Where do the IP addresses/systems show up?	• Reconnaissance (active (scanning) or passive (sniffing) • External – DNS and external-facing systems (nslookup, whois, dig, SamSpade, NMAP, & Zone Transfer) • Internal – SNMP, Unix, Windows, LDAP, SMTP, & NMAP) *Note: Approach is slightly different if coming from inside the network than from outside the network*
Vulnerability Assessment	Fingerprinting	What are the ports and services for the OSs and Applications?	Fingerprinting (scanner with OS recognition)
Vulnerability Assessment	Enumeration	What version of a service exists? (Example – banner grabbing of a web server or mail server)	Enumeration, potential vulnerabilities
Vulnerability Assessment	Research	Common Vulnerability Database (CVE.mitre.org); National Vulnerability Database (http://nvd.nist.gov/);Open Source Vulnerability Database (www.osvdb.org)	
Penetration Test	Escalation	Privilege escalation, Denial of Service, Man in the Middle	Obtain access
Penetration Test	Repeat visits	Backdoors - Hackers do this - Pen Testers simulate unless authorized to perform destructive testing (DoD) - Computer Network Attack (CNA)/Computer Network Exploitation (CNE) may do this when authorized	Maintain Access
Penetration Test	Covering tracks	Log zappers, log stoppers - Hackers do this - Pen Testers simulate unless authorized to perform destructive testing (DoD) - Computer Network Attack (CNA)/Computer Network Exploitation (CNE) may do this when authorized	Erase evidence

2.2 Hardware / Firmware Security

NSA recommends that all enterprise servers, laptops, and desktops perform an automated acceptance test that includes secure boot (enabled), Trusted Platform Module (TPM) activated and enabled, and platform certificated that matches the components used in the system. This is usually done with a Unified Extensible Firmware Interface (UEFI)-enabled computer. Once all these features are initiated, they provide attestation that the computer has not been tampered with. Should the UEFI fail any tests, NSA recommends that the computer be considered defective and returned. (NSA, 2023b)

3. Zero Trust Architecture

Zero Trust Architecture (ZTA) moved away from having static perimeters that put all their trust in users, assets, and resources and move the trust based on the location or network the user is coming from and the resource they are trying to access. It treats all transactions as a workflow where trust is vetted before accessing assets, services, workflows, and network accounts. ZTA's security model is based on maintaining strict access controls and not trusting any entity by default, even those inside the network perimeter by ensuring micro-segmentation, continuous monitoring, and least privilege access of all assets with the architecture. ZTA calls also potentially reduce the effects of Distributed Denial of Service (DDoS) attacks. It does this by using network segmentation (NS), identity and access management (IAM), continuous monitoring and analytics (CMA), least privilege access (LPA), multi-factor authentication (LPA), and leveraging secure access service edge (SASE). (NIST, 2020) Table 3 rolls up the key features of the six major ZTA categories.

Table 3: Six Major ZTA Categories and their key features.

NS	IAM	CMA	LPA	MFA	SASE
Provides enhances security by using network segmentation to isolate critical resources, reduce attack surface, and improve overall security.	User authentication ensures users follow a strict mechanism or set of mechanism using MFA to gain access to resources.	Realtime threat detection ensures constant monitoring to help identify and respond to threats as they occur.	Minimal access granted to users that is specific to the permissions their specific role and tasks require – thus limiting damage from insider threat.	Enhances security by ensuring a layered defense with a combination of verification methods to validate the user's identity.	Cloud-Native Architectures can consolidate networking and security services in a cloud-delivered solution.
Controlled access to allow organization to monitor and control data moving between segments.	Extremely granular access control based on permissions and rights within the organization.	Anomaly recognition uses AI and Bayesian methods to detect unusual network behavior or unauthorized attempts to access organization resources.	Prevents over-privileging users with access to sensitive data, and thereby reducing the potential for data breaches or misuse.	User verification requires two or more verification factors, e.g. passwords, tokens, biometrics.	Edge protection ensures users and devices regardless of their location or network.
Reduced impact if a breach occurs as it will be limited to the single segment rather than the overall capability.	Continuous monitoring to track real-time user activities by the assigned credentials and mitigation of potential security risks.	Forensic analysis provides detailed investigation and post incident analysis to improve the security posture of the capability for the future.			Integrates security through consistent policies and their enforcement across the organization.
Ensures compliance to meet regulatory and isolation of sensitive data within segments.					

4. Cybersecurity Safety Review Board

The Department of Homeland Security (DHS) created the Cybersecurity Safety Review Board (CSRB) because of President Biden's release of EO 14028. The CSRB looks at incidents where the worse of the worse threat actors, whether cybercrime syndicates or state actors have impacted major critical infrastructure, analyze their tactics, techniques, and procedures (TTP), the degree and type of impact so they can determine what additional security controls should be added. (CISA, 2023b; DHS, 2023) A CSRB is an independent entity comprised of highly qualified federal government and private sector members established to assess and analyze significant cybersecurity incidents that have impacted U.S. critical infrastructure. They conduct investigations into cyberattacks with the goal of understanding affected systems, vulnerabilities exploited, root causes of these exploits, and the impact they have had on the affected systems. The CSRB learns from past incidences and provides recommendations to prevent future occurrences to increase cybersecurity resilience. They seek to encourage cybersecurity transparency and accountability. Their comprehensive review often discovers evolving cyber threats and vulnerabilities previously not well known at the time, but through this review, they recommend the development and implementation of more robust cybersecurity measures that can often be applied across multiple critical infrastructure sectors. The CSRB ultimately plays a critical role in maturing the U.S.'s critical infrastructure cybersecurity resilience through their detailed investigations which often provide significant insights into cyber incidents through their focus on transparency, accountability, and the potential for improved cybersecurity practices. (CISA, 2023b)

5. Cybersecurity Incident & Vulnerability Response Playbooks

The Cybersecurity Incident & Vulnerability Response Playbooks serve as a comprehensive guide so that organizations can effectively manage and respond to cybersecurity incidents. In the case of the U.S. federal government, there is whole-of-government roles and responsibilities citing several high-level government documents such as U.S. EOs, laws, and other mandatory requirements. One of the biggest benefits of the playbook is the standardized approach it provides to detecting, investigating, and mitigating cyber-related incidents in a play-by-play manner that walks the organization through the roadmap of events that should be accomplished during a cybersecurity crisis. The playbook structure covers best practices, guidelines, and procedures that the organization should do in a structured sequence. The emphasis on the early detection of cyber incidents is one of the greatest benefits. Other key benefits include recommended strategies to identify potential breaches at the earliest opportunity so that a swift response can be used resulting in minimal impact from the attackers thereby limiting the scope of the incident and giving the organization the greatest control over the incident. With the numerous steps that must be taken during an incident, the methodological approach leads the organization through a structured plan of action to understand the threat, vulnerability, impact, and mitigation steps. Along the way, this thorough investigation approach using the playbook helps to understand the threat landscape, vulnerabilities exploited, and the root cause of the breach; this provides critical threat intelligence about the incident that can be used to prevent similar attacks in the future. While every organization is different and has different vulnerabilities, threats, and impacts, the playbook is relatively tailorable to respond with the best response for that incident. There are sections on containment strategies, threat eradication, and mitigation approaches. Additionally, the playbook can serve as a training tool so that specific roles in organizations can enhance their response to upcoming incidents and ultimately improve their overall security posture. (CISA, 2021)

6. Conclusion

This paper argues that the proposed collaboration between the U.S. National Security Council (NSC) and key cybersecurity entities like CISA, NIST, DoD, NSA, and ONCD presents significant benefits for U.S. allies in terms of enhancing their cybersecurity capabilities which were jointly cosigned by several of the U.S.'s allies. CISA continues engaging international software vendors and collaborating with allies on cybersecurity norms. By leveraging this U.S. whole-of-government expertise and the resources they offer, allies and partners can significantly improve their detection, prosecution, and mitigation of cyber risks. Many of these advanced technologies and methods developed by these U.S. agencies could provide allies with cutting-edge tools to identify potential cyber threats more efficiently and accurately. These approaches could significantly improve the proactive stance of these allies against cyberattacks, reduce risks in their countries, and reduce risks affecting other countries. Information sharing is another critical area where U.S. allies could benefit – the collaboration outlined in this research could create a more open exchange of ideas related to cyber threat intelligence between the U.S. and its allies. Sharing of details from recent cyberattacks could better explain future, emerging threat vectors and provide indicators and warnings (I&W) allowing other nations to better prepare for attacks. A common collective defense approach could prepare other allies for the moving waves of attacks that go from region to region in their attacks. U.S. allies could benefit from the extensive set of security standards that NIST and other U.S. organizations have created. By adopting these standards, the overall global cybersecurity posture goes up amongst allied nations while knowing other adoptees have used similar approaches to protect their organizations. This mutual adoption could lead to common more effective cybersecurity across government organizations and private sectors which could bolster the globalization of trade, smoother cooperation, and greater interoperability with joint initiatives and operations. The integration of SCRM, ZTA, CSRB, and Cyber Incident Detection, Investigation, and Mitigation Playbook could serve as a blueprint for U.S. allies; although CISA and other U.S. agencies are leading these initiatives, strength in numbers could be achieved with more allies being involved. Learning from the U.S.'s approach to institutionalizing cybersecurity best practices, allies could help codify approaches leading to more resilient and responsive cybersecurity infrastructures, capable of withstanding and quickly recovering from cyberattacks. In essence, the collaborative effort spearheaded by the

CISA, NIST, DoD, NSA, and ONCD could offer a comprehensive model for strengthening global cybersecurity resilience, with U.S. allies standing to gain significantly from these initiatives.

References

Allison, G.T. and Blackwill, R., 2000. *America's National Interests: A Report From the Commission on America's National Interests*, The Commission on America's National Interests, July, https://www.belfercenter.org/sites/default/files/files/publication/amernatinter.pdf

Biden, J. R., 2021a. *The U.S. President's Executive Order (EO) 14017, America's Supply Chain: A Year of Action and Progress*, The White House, Washington, DC, https://www.whitehouse.gov/wp-content/uploads/2022/02/Capstone-Report-Biden.pdf

Biden, J. R., 2021b. *The U.S. President's Executive Order (EO) 14028, Improving the Nation's Cybersecurity*, The White House, Washington, DC, https://www.govinfo.gov/content/pkg/FR-2021-05-17/pdf/2021-10460.pdf

Biden, J.R. (2022). *U.S. National Security Strategy*, The White House, Washington, DC, October, https://nssarchive.us/wp-content/uploads/2022/10/Biden-Harris-Administrations-National-Security-Strategy-10.2022.pdf

Car, P. and De Luca, S., 2022. EU Cyber resilience act. *EPRS, European Parliament*, https://www.dimt.it/wp-content/uploads/2022/12/EPRS_BRI2022739259_EN.pdf

Carroll, J., 2018, June. Offensive and Defensive Cyberspace Operations Training: Are we There yet? In *European Conference on Cyber Warfare and Security* (pp. 77-86). Academic Conferences International Limited.

Clinton, W., 1998. *Presidential Decision Directive 63 (PDD-63) on Critical Infrastructure Protection: Sector Coordinators*. The White House, Washington, DC, May, https://www.govinfo.gov/content/pkg/FR-1998-08-05/pdf/98-20865.pdf

Clinton, W., 2000, *Defending America's Cyberspace: National Plan for Information Systems Protection Version 1.0 An Invitation to a Dialogue*, The White House, Washington, DC, April, https://irp.fas.org/offdocs/pdd/CIP-plan.pdf

Cybersecurity & Infrastructure Security Agency (CISA), n.d., "Critical Infrastructure Sectors," https://www.cisa.gov/topics/critical-infrastructure-security-and-resilience/critical-infrastructure-sectors

CISA, 2021, Cybersecurity Incident & Vulnerability Response Playbooks, [https://www.cisa.gov/sites/default/files/publications/Federal_Government_Cybersecurity_Incident_and_Vulnerability_Response_Playbooks_508C.pdf]

CISA, 2022, Vulnerability Exploitability eXchange (VEX) – Use Cases, https://www.cisa.gov/sites/default/files/2023-01/VEX_Use_Cases_Aprill2022.pdf

CISA, 2023a, Shifting the Balance of Cybersecurity Risk: Principles and Approaches for Secure by Design Software, https://www.govinfo.gov/content/pkg/FR-2023-12-20/pdf/2023-27948.pdf

CISA, 2023b, Review Of The Attacks Associated with Lapsus$ And Related Threat Groups Report, [https://www.cisa.gov/sites/default/files/2023-08/CSRB_Lapsus%24_508c.pdf]

CISA, 2023c, *The Case for Memory Safe Roadmaps: Why Both C-Suite Executives and Technical Experts Need to Take Memory Safe Coding Seriously,* https://www.cisa.gov/sites/default/files/2023-12/The-Case-for-Memory-Safe-Roadmaps-508c.pdf

CISA, 2024d, CISA Joins the Minimum Viable Secure Product Working Group, https://www.cisa.gov/news-events/news/cisa-joins-minimum-viable-secure-product-working-group

CycloneDX, n.d., Authoritative Guide to SBOM: Implement and Optimize Use of the Software Bill of Materials. https://cyclonedx.org/guides/sbom/OWASP_CycloneDX-SBOM-Guide-en.pdf

DHS, 2023, Cyber Safety Review Board Releases Report on Activities of Global Extortion-Focused Hacker Group Lapsus$, [https://www.dhs.gov/news/2023/08/10/cyber-safety-review-board-releases-report-activities-global-extortion-focused]

DoD, 2019, *DoD Enterprise DevSecOps Reference Design*, V 1.0, https://dodcio.defense.gov/Portals/0/Documents/DoD%20Enterprise%20DevSecOps%20Reference%20Design%20v1.0_Public%20Release.pdf

DoD, 2021, *DoD Enterprise DevSecOps Strategy Guide*, v 2.0, https://dodcio.defense.gov/Portals/0/Documents/Library/DoDEnterpriseDevSecOpsStrategyGuide.pdf

MSVP, n.d., Minimum Viable Secure Product (MSVP), https://mvsp.dev/

NIST, 2020, NIST SP 800-207, Zero Trust Architecture, https://nvlpubs.nist.gov/nistpubs/SpecialPublications/NIST.SP.800-207.pdf

NIST, 2022a, *NIST SP 800-161r1, Cybersecurity Supply Chain Risk Management Practices for Systems and Organizations* https://nvlpubs.nist.gov/nistpubs/SpecialPublications/NIST.SP.800-161r1.pdf

NIST, 2022b, *NIST SP 800-218, Secure Software Development Framework (SSDF) v1.1: Recommendations for Mitigating the Risk of Software Vulnerabilities*, https://nvlpubs.nist.gov/nistpubs/SpecialPublications/NIST.SP.800-218.pdf

NSA, 2022a, NSA, CISA, ODNI Release Software Supply Chain Guidance for Developers. https://www.nsa.gov/Press-Room/Press-Releases-Statements/Press-Release-View/Article/3146465/nsa-cisa-odni-release-software-supply-chain-guidance-for-developers/

NSA, 2022b, ESF Partners, NSA and CISA Release Software Supply Chain Guidance for Customers, https://www.nsa.gov/Press-Room/Press-Releases-Statements/Press-Release-View/Article/3221208/esf-partners-nsa-and-cisa-release-software-supply-chain-guidance-for-customers/

NSA, 2022c, Securing the Software Supply Chain: Recommended Practices for Developers. https://media.defense.gov/2022/Sep/01/2003068942/-1/-1/0/ESF_SECURING_THE_SOFTWARE_SUPPLY_CHAIN_DEVELOPERS.PDF

NSA, 2023a, Recommendation for Software Bill of Materials (SBOM) Management, https://media.defense.gov/2023/Dec/14/2003359097/-1/-1/0/CSI-SCRM-SBOM-MANAGEMENT.PDF

NSA, 2023b, Procurement and Acceptance Testing Guide for Servers, Laptops, and Desktops Computers, https://media.defense.gov/2023/Sep/28/2003310132/-1/-1/0/CSI_PROCUREMENT_ACCEPTANCE_TESTING_GUIDE.PDF

OMB, 2022, "Memorandum M-22-18, Enhancing the Security of the Software Supply Chain through Secure Software Development Practices," https://www.whitehouse.gov/wp-content/uploads/2022/09/M-22-18.pdf

ODNI, n.d.-a, "Safeguarding Science Goals", https://www.dni.gov/index.php/safeguarding-science

ODNI, n.d.-b, Supply Chain Risk Management for Industry & Academia, https://www.dni.gov/index.php/safeguarding-science/supply-chain-risk-management

OWASP, n.d., OWASP CycloneDX https://owasp.org/www-project-cyclonedx/

Implications of Large Language Models for OSINT: Assessing the Impact on Information Acquisition and Analyst Expertise in Prompt Engineering

Jan Černý
Department of Information Technologies, Faculty of Informatics and Statistics, Prague University of Economics and Business, Czech Republic

cerj07@vse.cz

Abstract: This paper explores the potential use of large language models (LLMs) in Open Source Intelligence (OSINT), with a focus on integrating information acquisition and the increasing importance of prompt engineering for analysts. The research includes a comprehensive literature review, which highlights the widespread use of AI in OSINT and the related challenges, such as data validity and ethical concerns. The study emphasizes the significance of prompt engineering as a crucial skill that demands a profound comprehension of LLMs to generate validated intelligence. A model of the OSINT lifecycle that incorporates LLMs is proposed. The paper further discusses updated training in critical thinking, search techniques, and prompt engineering for intelligence professionals. The findings indicate a noteworthy shift in OSINT procedures, highlighting the importance of continuous research and education to fully utilize AI in intelligence gathering.

Keywords: Open-Source Intelligence, OSINT, Large Language Models, Llms, Prompt-Engineering, Education

1. Introduction

The use of open information and its potential benefits have been demonstrated throughout history. The effectiveness of Open-Source Intelligence (OSINT) has been evident in significant contemporary conflicts. For instance, as stated in (Gibson and Barnouw, 1969) the Foreign Broadcast Monitoring Service (FBMS) was established in the early 1940s. It was used to analyze propaganda radio broadcasts from German, Japanese, and other stations. Subsequently, after the war, the Foreign Broadcast Information Service played a critically important role in the Cold War and other events. It was also used as one of the sources for the President's Daily Briefs, supporting covert operations and serving as a powerful tool for verifying human intelligence (HUMINT).

Open-source intelligence is the process of identifying and clearly stating investigation needs, legally collecting publicly available data and information, conducting a complex analysis, and synthesizing the analyzed information entities into verified and validated conclusions - intelligence. (NATO, 2001) identifies the four main classes of the OSINT entities that underline the importance of validation and verification processes:

1. **Open Source Data (OSD):** OSD is the raw print, broadcast, oral debriefing, or other forms of information from a primary source. This category includes photographs, tape recordings, commercial satellite images, or personal letters from individuals.
2. **Open Source Information (OSIF):** OSIF consists of data that has undergone an editorial process, providing some filtering, validation, and presentation management.
3. **Open Source Intelligence (OSINT):** OSINT refers to information that has been purposefully discovered, discriminated, distilled, and disseminated to a select audience.
4. **Validated OSINT (OSINT-V):** OSINT-V is information to which a very high degree of certainty can be attributed. It can be produced by an all-source intelligence professional with access to classified intelligence sources.

OSINT is not a single discipline, but rather a set of related information activities that offer unique insights and solutions for complex challenges. The development of information technology is often cited as fundamental to new directions in OSINT in many articles, academic papers, and grey literature. Today, the availability of virtually any data within the global network of the Internet is not the only factor, but also the rapid development of artificial intelligence in the context of efficient data and information gathering capabilities, and consequently advanced analytical capabilities. This paper focuses on the relationship between OSINT, generative AI models, and related activities such as prompt engineering, including the customization of models for OSINT purposes in the context of AI. The trend of using AI in OSINT is evident in the current literature review presented. Additionally, the paper will analyze the activities of individual states in the use of AI in military and warfare. Simultaneously, there is an increasing demand for novel educational approaches for intelligence officers and analysts to analyze and synthesize information entities. This requirement extends beyond technological proficiency and encompasses the cultivation of critical thinking skills. Critical Literature Review

The extraordinary publishing frequency on AI topics has been evident in academia in the past months. Papers relevant to our domain present a multifaceted view of the integration of Artificial Intelligence (AI) into Open Source Intelligence (OSINT)., highlighting both opportunities and challenges in this evolving field. We have focused on the most recent relevant works from 2022 to the present. (Govardhan *et al.*, 2023; Iashvili and Iavich, 2023) both emphasize the role of AI in enhancing cybersecurity through OSINT, addressing challenges in data analysis and penetration testing, respectively. This focus is shared by (Ranade, 2023; Yadav *et al.*, 2023; Yamin *et al.*, 2022) who explore AI's capacity to organize fragmented OSINT sources and evaluate the effectiveness of various OSINT tools in cybersecurity scenarios. These works collectively underscore the crucial role of AI in synthesizing and interpreting vast quantities of open-source data for cyber defense purposes. (Al-Dmour *et al.*, 2023; Stone *et al.*, 2023) demonstrate the application of AI in specific contexts: radiological event detection in war conditions and automated OSINT collection and management, respectively. Both studies highlight AI's potential in processing and analyzing large-scale, diverse data sets, a theme also explored by (Dale *et al.*, 2023) in the context of aggregating Twitter (X) data for cybersecurity intelligence. The potential of AI in OSINT extends beyond cybersecurity, as shown by (Arroyo *et al.*, 2023), who develop AI-supported tools for debunking scientific misinformation. This emphasis on AI's role in combating misinformation is echoed by (Song *et al.*, 2023), who addresses the creation of fake cyber threat intelligence, indicating the dual-use nature of AI in OSINT, a concern also raised by (Klingberg, 2022; Ranaldi *et al.*, 2022; Riebe, 2023) explore AI's application in law enforcement, particularly in monitoring Dark Web Marketplaces and digital policing for counter-terrorism, respectively. Their findings resonate with (Watters, 2023), who outlines the intersection of AI, digital forensics, and OSINT in cyber counterintelligence, emphasizing the growing importance of AI in various aspects of law enforcement and intelligence gathering. (Panda and Rungta, 2024; Suryotrisongko *et al.*, 2022) both focus on vulnerable social groups and botnet traffic detection, respectively, using AI and machine learning in conjunction with OSINT to address specific threats and vulnerabilities. This targeted application of AI in OSINT underscores the technology's adaptability to various societal needs. (Kaswan *et al.*, 2022; Katzner *et al.*, 2022) broaden the scope of AI and OSINT applications to conservation biology and smart city decision support systems, respectively, highlighting the cross-disciplinary potential of these technologies. (Evangelista *et al.*, 2023; Radoi, 2023), on the other hand, delve into more technical aspects of AI in OSINT, with the former developing AI approaches for Google Hacking Dorks and the latter integrating a GPT model for efficient data processing in open-source investigations. Finally, (Raina MacIntyre *et al.*, 2023) highlight AI's role in utilizing open-source data for early epidemic warning, showcasing the public health applications of AI in OSINT and the broader societal benefits that can be derived from this synergy. In summary, these papers collectively illustrate the diverse and significant impact of AI on OSINT across various fields, from cybersecurity and law enforcement to public health and environmental conservation. They also draw attention to the ethical and dual-use implications of these technologies, underscoring the need for continued research and development in this dynamic field. Despite extensive research in the context of Open Source Intelligence (OSINT) and Artificial Intelligence (AI), a significant gap remains in understanding how large language models can be implemented as isolated entities within the OSINT lifecycle.

2. OSINT & Generative AI Perspective

To begin this section, let us first define what is meant by the term 'language model'. The working principles, conceptualization, and learning methods of large language models are discussed in various sources (Kedia et al., 2024; Kojima et al., 2022; Meyer et al., 2023; Naveed et al., 2023; Ouyang et al., 2017; Zhao et al., 2023). A language model is a computer program that can predict the words that will follow in sentences. Their extensive training data enables them to understand the structure of text, even in multiple languages and specific contexts. These models employ statistical and probabilistic learning techniques. Statistical methods and probabilistic learning methods are two fundamental approaches in the field of artificial intelligence that aid in data interpretation and prediction.

2.1 Conceptual Design of an Isolated Large Language Model

In this paper, we present a model for the OSINT intelligence cycle (Figure 1) with the later stress on prompt engineering, and its importance for gathering intelligence. The process begins with the **User**: This class represents the individual or entity initiating the OSINT operation. Attributes like `name` and `role` contextualize the user in the operation, while operations like *`defineTask()`* initiate the intelligence cycle. It is necessary to point out that this model does not rank the seniority level of the **User**, however as will be mentioned later, they need to be fully aware of concepts of prompt engineering or be trained before the model is applied in the intelligence cycle.

Followed by **IntelligenceTopic**, which defines the specific intelligence objective. Attributes like **`taskID`** and **`Description`** give a unique identity and detail to each intelligence topic. The operation *`getInformationNeeds()`* advances the process to the next stage of intelligence gathering. **InformationNeeds => InformationRequirements** classes progress the intelligence topic into actionable components. **InformationNeeds** outlines what information is necessary, while

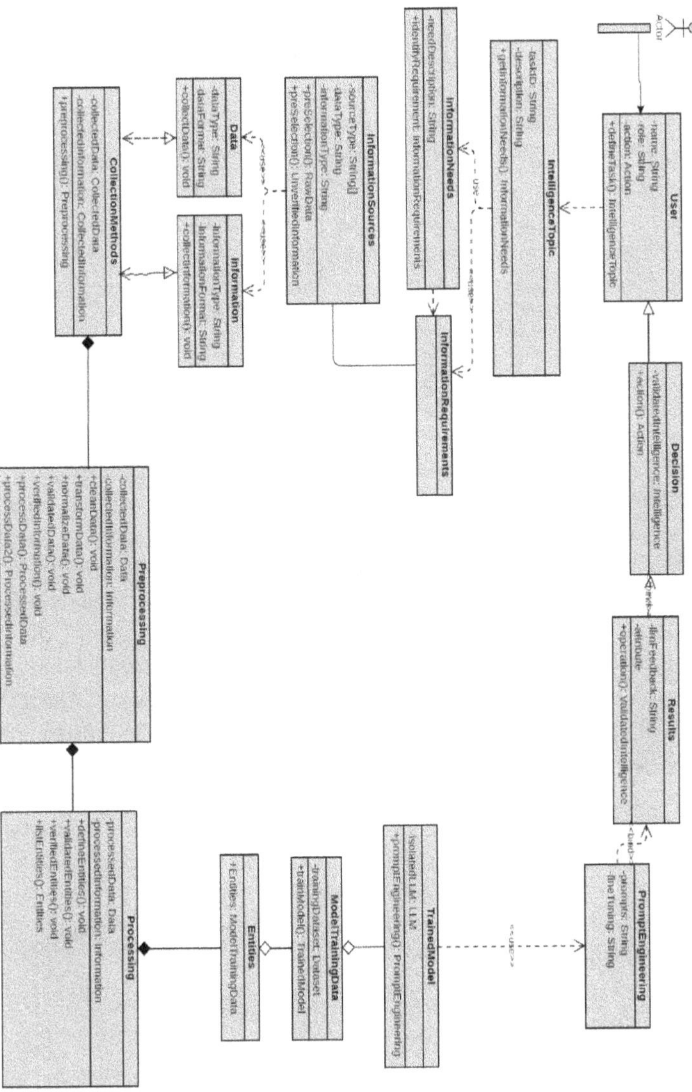

Figure 1: OSINT Isolated Large Language Model Prototype (author)

InformationRequirements concretizes these needs into detailed requirements, determining the data collection process. This model respects the information science perspective, however, some intelligence departments could be used instead of information needs, intelligence questions that are then reflected in information requirements. The class **InformationSources** identifies potential sources for data collection with attributes like **`sourceType`**, **`dataType`**, and **`informationType`**. Operations like *`preSelection()`* guide the selection of relevant data, influencing the quality and relevance of collected intelligence. More importantly, the model focused on three types of external information environments, surface web, deep web, and dark web (in fact darknets) and an internal knowledge base. **Data, Information** as fuel for our isolated language model must be specified before the collection starts. To be clear, data holds raw, unprocessed datasets, while Information pertains to more structured yet unprocessed data. Both classes are crucial for building a comprehensive intelligence picture and driving the preprocessing phase. The context of the **`SourceType`** class is crucial in terms of the collection methods used. While the surface web mainly provides unstructured data, such as social media snippets collected based on metadata elements or specifically identified patterns, the deep web sources, in contrast, offer vast amounts of hidden data and information. Moreover, deep web sources require detailed analysis regarding planned autonomous crawling, as well as updated policies and frequencies. Concerning the dark web or darknet environment, given its volatility and rate of change, especially the .onion identifier, it might be prudent to train autonomous onion crawlers based on specific strings and language characteristics. The **CollectionMethods** class encompasses data collection strategies that reflect all the environments described. Moreover, we need to distinguish three main directions of the collection phase:

1. Fully automated (collection of data from large numbers of different data sources, integration of collected signals into early warning systems to support large-scale investigations, monitoring of developments in geopolitical conflicts, trends, but also local anomalies, civil unrest, demonstrations, riots, demonstrations and others, using technology to perform autonomous tasks with the initial inputs or information needs, further analysis and alerting system).
2. semi-automated (collection of data and information with necessary human intervention, but with advanced technology, e.g. social media monitoring of accounts of specific targets with additional manual investigation)
3. manual (investigative needs that require a strictly individual approach, e.g. traditional media research, grey literature searches, etc. It is characterized by a high degree of personal involvement and often relies on the skills and expertise of the individual conducting the research, without the extensive use of automated tools or systems.).

The **CollectedData** and **CollectedInformation** are attributes, and the *Preprocessing()* operation leads to data refinement, which impacts the accuracy of the intelligence cycle. Furthermore, **Preprocessing** is responsible for cleaning, transforming, and normalizing collected data and information. Operations like *cleanData()*, *transformData()*, and *normalizeData()* ensure data usability, directly impacting the effectiveness of the intelligence gathered. **Processing** involves analyzing and interpreting the preprocessed data. The quality of processing dictates the reliability of the intelligence, influencing the User's subsequent decisions. The class **Entities** represent refined, process-ready elements for intelligence analysis. These entities feed into the model training phase, influencing the scope and focus of the trained LLM. **ModelTrainingData** prepares and structures data specifically for training the isolated LLM. The *trainModel()* operation defines how effectively the LLM will be trained, impacting its subsequent intelligence-generating capabilities. **TrainedModel** embodies the capabilities of the LLM post-training. This model's effectiveness in interpreting and analyzing intelligence will directly influence the results obtained. **PromptEngineering** focuses on developing effective prompts for the LLM, with operations that guide how the LLM is queried for intelligence. The quality of these prompts significantly impacts the relevance and usefulness of the LLM's outputs. **Results** dignify the intelligence output from the LLM, which is vital for decision-making. The nature of these results will directly guide the User in making informed actions. And finally, **Decision** involves interpreting the intelligence results to make informed decisions. This class is the culmination of the OSINT process, where the User synthesizes all gathered intelligence into actionable insights. The user's actions are driven by the insights and intelligence gathered through the process.

2.2 Prompts & Prompt Engineering

In our model, we want to focus on a critical part of intelligence acquisition, namely the generation of prompts. In the field of artificial intelligence and computer programming, a prompt is an instruction or query given by a user to elicit a particular response or reaction from a system. When working with AI, such as GPT-4 or other generative models, a prompt typically takes the form of a textual query or instruction that specifies the desired response or output from the model. A prompt may be either simple or complex. Simple prompts usually take the form of a question, such as "What is the capital of France? On the other hand, complex prompts involve specific instructions or requirements, such as 'Write a short story about a science fiction-style space adventure'. The quality and specificity of the prompt can have a significant impact on the quality and relevance of the AI's response or output. In computing, the term 'prompt' refers to any request or instruction that elicits a response or action from a user or system.

3. Practical Implication of Prompt Engineering

Prompt engineering involves creating effective prompts, such as instructional AI models, that produce accurate, creative, and efficient results for various tasks. Although prompt engineering may seem like a new discipline, its origins can be traced back to the distant past. This is primarily due to the ability to ask relevant and substantive questions, or in terms of librarianship or information science, the ability to query or create syntax in library catalogs, large database systems, and other information resources so that these systems return the optimal amount of information to meet our 'information needs'. The closest term to 'information need' can be found in the aforementioned sciences.

According to (Brown *et al.*, 2020), prompt engineering is a field that aims to exploit the capabilities and capacities of AI models (LLMs) for reasoning in context without the need for fine-tuning. First, the authors divide the three main approaches to learning these models (Brown *et al.*, 2020; Kojima *et al.*, 2022; Wei *et al.*, 2022). These approaches include zero-shot learning, where the model is given only instructions and asked to perform a task without prior examples, and few-shot learning, where the model is given examples illustrating the task and then asked to perform a similar task by generating its own answer to a similarly structured question. Let's also include the 'one-shot' approach in this group. The chain-of-thought model is asked to generate intermediate answers before providing a final solution to a multi-step problem. The aim of this approach is to mimic the multi-step intuitive thought process of problem-solving. This is also discussed in detail in (Wei *et al.*, 2022). It should be noted that since the publication of (Brown *et al.*, 2020), other related approaches have emerged. The prompt engineer and its properties are also worth discussing. First of all, let's profile the activities of a prompt engineer, whose main characteristics are as follows:

- Designing, constructing, testing, and optimizing prompts according to situation and information needs.
- Achieve relevant results from human-computer interaction based on information needs.
- Continuously review the development, structure, concept, and function of prompts.
- In the case of creating a library of prompts, to keep it up to date or to adapt changes on an ongoing basis.

At this point, I would like to point out the rather fundamental role of the human being in the interaction with the computer. Obviously, their knowledge, experience, and intuition influence the outcome of any model. Of course, the field of prompt engineering will be subject to exploration and obvious development, but I would like to allay concerns about replacing the work role with artificial intelligence. In fact, given humanity's current progress, these roles will only change or new ones will emerge. Ultimately, human creativity seems to be the primary value of the future in terms of human intellectual activity, the results, and intellectual property. All this is underlined by the key human qualities: the ability to learn, to adapt to new conditions, and to create – which underlines the crucial characteristics of OSINT analysts. Based on (Bsharat *et al.*, 2023; Contentify, 2023; OpenAI, 2024a; OpenAI, 2024b, Park, 2023; Saravia, 2023; W3Schools, 2023) including our extensive experimenting with prompts in ChatGPT and GPT-4, we can identify the following summarized rules for constructing effective prompts.

1. **Direct Instruction**: Straightforward commands detailing the exact task for the AI.
   - OSINT perspective example: "Analyze the following list of URLs to identify potential cybersecurity threats and report any suspicious activities.
2. **Role Play**: Assigning a specific character or professional role for the AI to embody in its responses.
   - OSINT perspective example: Assume the role of a digital forensics expert. Investigate the digital footprint left by this username across various platforms to uncover any illicit activities.
3. **Creative Storytelling**: Guiding the AI to construct narratives or stories with set parameters.
   - OSINT perspective example: Create a hypothetical scenario where leaked information from a private forum leads to a major data breach. Detail the progression from leak to breach.
4. **Exploratory Questions**: Using open-ended questions to elicit detailed and informative responses from the AI.
   - OSINT perspective example: What could be the implications of the sudden increase in traffic to dark web marketplaces following a major corporate data breach?
5. **Comparative Analysis**: Requests for the AI to compare and contrast different items or concepts.
   - OSINT perspective example: Compare the online behavior patterns of two suspected accounts to determine if they could be operated by the same individual.
6. **Idea Generation**: Employing AI for brainstorming ideas, solutions, or creative concepts.

- OSINT perspective example: List potential open-source tools and techniques that could be used to trace the origin of an anonymous whistleblower's claims.

7. **Instructional Guides**: Ask the AI for step-by-step instructions or tutorials on various topics.
    - OSINT perspective example: Provide a tutorial on using advanced search operators to filter through social media posts for specific keywords related to an ongoing investigation.
8. **Personalized Recommendations**: Seeking tailored suggestions based on specific preferences or criteria.
    - OSINT perspective example: Based on my investigation into fraudulent online marketplaces, recommend the most effective digital tools for tracking cryptocurrency transactions.
9. **Debate and Persuasion**: Engaging the AI in discussions to present arguments on various sides of a topic.
    - OSINT perspective example: Argue for and against the ethical considerations of using hacked data in OSINT investigations.
10. **Feedback and Critique**: Requesting the AI's evaluation, feedback, or review of creative works or ideas.
    - OSINT perspective example: Review the compiled dossier on a high-profile cybercriminal and suggest any additional avenues of investigation that may have been overlooked.

4. Educational Needs for OSINT Experts

The proposed model incorporates the traditional intelligence cycle and reflects the demands of critical thinking, advanced search techniques and strategies, entity analysis approaches, and understanding and leveraging new directions with incoming generative AI. This is underlined by the actively developing field of prompt engineering. It highlights the importance of creating prompts based on tacit knowledge and lifelong learning for conducting relevant validated open-source intelligence. The opportunities for an updated approach to education are evident. The article proposes training groups for intelligence officers, analysts, searchers, and other specialists, including Critical Thinking, AI and LLM, and Prompt Engineering.

4.1 Critical Thinking

Developing human reasoning and contextual thinking is crucial for maximizing the use of big language models. Later, we will discuss how prompt generation is closely linked to the ability to provide careful instructions based on knowledge. It is also essential to avoid information overload, which can hinder successful and responsible analysis, leading to the production of validated intelligence. **This includes key activities:**

- Developing information literacy
- Practicing rational reading (fast reading)
- Research methods
- Search strategies and tactics
- Analysis and data storytelling

4.2 AI and Large Language Models

The history of AI offers insight into the nature of intelligent machines and highlights significant opportunities and risks associated with machine and deep learning, generative models, and fine-tuning language models, including knowledge of the obvious risks.

This includes key activities:

- Historical perspectives on AI
- Statistical and probabilistic methods in AI
- (Large) language models
- Optimizing training data
- Training language models
- Principles of fine-tuning
- AI ethics and regulatory mechanisms

4.3 OSINT in the Context of Prompt Engineering

In the context of using our prototype of an isolated model, prompt engineering is considered a crucial area for training personnel in the security and military sectors. The following activities lead to fetching key competencies for future OSINT capabilities and opportunities:

1. Emphasize the importance and application of prompt engineering in intelligence gathering and develop a comprehensive understanding of OSINT methodologies.
   - Cover the key concepts, tools, and ethical considerations involved in practicing OSINT.
   - Advanced Prompt Engineering Techniques
   - Explore the intricacies of prompt construction tailored to OSINT tasks. Focus on optimizing queries to retrieve accurate and relevant information.
   - Learn advanced techniques for constructing effective prompts, including contextual cues, specificity, and anticipating potential AI model biases.
2. Critically analyses and evaluate AI-generated information
   - Practice the critical thinking skills needed to evaluate AI-generated output. Identify biases, inaccuracies, and "hallucinations" in the data.
   - Increase the reliability of intelligence reports through practical exercises that apply these analytical skills to real-life OSINT scenarios.
3. Hands-on applications and case studies
   - Engage in practical projects and case studies requiring the application of learned OSINT and technical skills in various intelligence operations.
   - Group projects, peer review, and discussion of innovative approaches to OSINT challenges encourage collaborative learning.

5. Conclusion

In the conference paper, we propose a model for using isolated large language models for various intelligence tasks. The core concept comes from traditional approaches. It starts with a preparatory phase, including the definition of information needs and requirements, the identification of information sources, data, and information collections, followed by preprocessing and processing operations to obtain a prepared dataset for training a large language model. More importantly, we see the significant role of OSINT analysts as advanced prompt engineers with the ability to build relevant, optimally structured prompts for the isolated models that will result in verified contextual LLM insights transformed into validated open-source intelligence. Based on these premises, we propose the three basic training paths for military, law enforcement, and relevant security roles focused on OSINT processes. Following current trends in working with data, information, and AI-generated content, we identify educational needs in critical thinking processes, including the development of information literacy and rational reading, followed by AI aspects, including history, statistical and probabilistic methods, model training processes, fine-tuning and ethical aspects of working with AI models. Finally, we see a critical training need in the area of prompt engineering, mainly for the provision of high-quality, unbiased, and hallucination-free answers in order to deliver validated intelligence to stakeholders.

6. Future Work

In the context of our prototype of the isolated OSINT LLM, we would like to design an ontology for the OSINT data and information entities in order to continuously build relevant training datasets for different intelligence tasks, and thus to be applied in different areas of intelligence activities. Furthermore, we are aware of the turbulent changes in the AI world, and therefore we would like to prepare a customizable syllabus for the expert workshops focused on the military and security forces.

References

Al-Dmour, N.A., Kamrul Hasan, M., Ajmal, M., Ali, M., Naseer, I., Ali, A., Hamadi, H.A., *et al.* (2023), "An Automated Platform for Gathering and Managing Open-Source Cyber Threat Intelligence", *2nd International Conference on Business Analytics for Technology and Security, ICBATS 2023*, doi: 10.1109/ICBATS57792.2023.10111470.

Arroyo, D., Degli-Esposti, S., Gómez-Espés, A., Palmero-Muñoz, S. and Pérez-Miguel, L. (2023), *On the Design of a Misinformation Widget (MsW) Against Cloaked Science*, *Lecture Notes in Computer Science (Including Subseries Lecture Notes in Artificial Intelligence and Lecture Notes in Bioinformatics)*, Vol. 13983 LNCS, doi: 10.1007/978-3-031-39828-5_21.

Brown, T.B., Mann, B., Ryder, N., Subbiah, M., Kaplan, J., Dhariwal, P., Neelakantan, A., *et al.* (2020), "Language Models are Few-Shot Learners", *Advances in Neural Information Processing Systems*, Neural information processing systems foundation, Vol. 2020-December.

Bsharat, S.M., Myrzakhan, A. and Shen, Z. (2023), "Principled Instructions Are All You Need for Questioning LLaMA-1/2, GPT-3.5/4".

Dale, D., McClanahan, K. and Li, Q. (2023), "AI-based Cyber Event OSINT via Twitter Data", *2023 International Conference on Computing, Networking and Communications, ICNC 2023*, pp. 436–442, doi: 10.1109/ICNC57223.2023.10074187.

Evangelista, J.R.G., Sassi, R.J., Gatto, D.D.O., Romero, M., Portellada, N., da Silva, R.C. and Farias, E.B.P. (2023), "Open Source Intelligence Approach with Self-Organizing Kohonen Maps and Natural Language Processing for Automated Execution of Dorks | Abordagem de Inteligência de Fontes Abertas com Mapas Auto-Organizáveis De Kohonen e Processamento de Linguagem Natural ", *RISTI - Revista Iberica de Sistemas e Tecnologias de Informacao*, Vol. 2023 No. Special Is, pp. 425–439.

Gibson, G.H. and Barnouw, E. (1969), "The Golden Web: A History of Broadcasting in the United States. Volume II: 1933 to 1953.", *The Journal of Southern History*, Vol. 35 No. 2, p. 285, doi: 10.2307/2205749.

Contentify. (2023), "AI Prompts Library & More", available at: https://github.com/alphatrait/100000-ai-prompts-by-contentifyai#license (accessed 25 January 2024).

Govardhan, D., Krishna, G.G.S.H., Charan, V., Sai, S.V.A. and Chintala, R.R. (2023), "Key Challenges and Limitations of the OSINT Framework in the Context of Cybersecurity", *Proceedings of the 2nd International Conference on Edge Computing and Applications, ICECAA 2023*, pp. 236–243, doi: 10.1109/ICECAA58104.2023.10212168.

Iashvili, G. and Iavich, M. (2023), "Enhancing Cyber Intelligence Capabilities through Process Automation: Advantages and Opportunities", *CEUR Workshop Proceedings*, Vol. 3575, pp. 92–101.

Kaswan, K.S., Gautam, R. and Dhatterwal, J.S. (2022), *Introduction to DSS System for Smart Cities*, *Intelligent Decision Support Systems for Smart City Applications*, doi: 10.1002/9781119896951.ch4.

Katzner, T., Thomason, E., Huhmann, K., Conkling, T., Concepcion, C., Slabe, V. and Poessel, S. (2022), "Open-source intelligence for conservation biology", *Conservation Biology*, Vol. 36 No. 6, doi: 10.1111/cobi.13988.

Klingberg, S. (2022), *Countering Terrorism: Digital Policing of Open Source Intelligence and Social Updates Media Using Artificial Intelligence*, *Artificial Intelligence and National Security*, doi: 10.1007/978-3-031-06709-9_6.

Kojima, T., Gu, S.S., Reid, M., Matsuo, Y. and Iwasawa, Y. (2022), "Large Language Models are Zero-Shot Reasoners", *Advances in Neural Information Processing Systems*, Neural information processing systems foundation, Vol. 35.

NATO. (2001), *NATO OSINT Handbook* , NATO, Norfolk.

OpenAI. (2024), "Prompt engineering - OpenAI API", available at: https://platform.openai.com/docs/guides/prompt-engineering (accessed 15 January 2024).

OpenAI. (2024b), "ChatGPT", available at: https://chat.openai.com/ (accessed 15 January 2024).

Panda, S. and Rungta, O. (2024), *Leveraging OSINT and Artificial Intelligence, Machine Learning to Identify and Protect Vulnerable Sections of Society*, *Signals and Communication Technology*, Vol. Part F1803, doi: 10.1007/978-3-031-45237-6_5.

Park, D. (2023), "Amazing Bard Prompts VOL.1", *GitHub*, available at: https://github.com/dsdanielpark/amazing-bard-prompts/tree/main (accessed 16 January 2024).

Radoi, T.-C. (2023), "Artificial Intelligence in Data Analysis for Open-Source Investigations", *15th International Conference on Electronics, Computers and Artificial Intelligence, ECAI 2023 - Proceedings*, doi: 10.1109/ECAI58194.2023.10193894.

Raina MacIntyre, C., Lim, S., Gurdasani, D., Miranda, M., Metcalf, D., Quigley, A., Hutchinson, D., *et al.* (2023), "Early detection of emerging infectious diseases - implications for vaccine development", *Vaccine*, doi: 10.1016/j.vaccine.2023.05.069.

Ranade, P. (2023), "Knowledge-Embedded Narrative Construction from Open Source Intelligence", *Proceedings of the 37th AAAI Conference on Artificial Intelligence, AAAI 2023*, Vol. 37, pp. 16131–16132.

Ranaldi, L., Nourbakhsh, A., Fallucchid, F. and Zanzotto, F.M. (2022), "C-OSINT: COVID-19 Open Source artificial INTelligence framework", *CEUR Workshop Proceedings*, Vol. 3260, pp. 219–235.

Riebe, T. (2023), *Technology Assessment of Dual-Use ICTs: How to Assess Diffusion, Governance and Design*, *Technology Assessment of Dual-Use ICTs: How to Assess Diffusion, Governance and Design*, doi: 10.1007/978-3-658-41667-6.

Saravia, E. (2023), "Prompt Engineering Guide", *Dair.Ai*, available at: https://www.promptingguide.ai/es (accessed 11 January 2024).

Song, Z., Tian, Y., Zhang, J. and Hao, Y. (2023), "Generating Fake Cyber Threat Intelligence Using the GPT-Neo Model", *2023 8th International Conference on Intelligent Computing and Signal Processing, ICSP 2023*, pp. 920–924, doi: 10.1109/ICSP58490.2023.10248596.

Stone, H., Heslop, D., Lim, S., Sarmiento, I., Kunasekaran, M. and Raina MacIntyre, C. (2023), "Open-Source Intelligence for Detection of Radiological Events and Syndromes Following the Invasion of Ukraine in 2022: Observational Study", *JMIR Infodemiology*, Vol. 3, doi: 10.2196/39895.

Suryotrisongko, H., Musashi, Y., Tsuneda, A. and Sugitani, K. (2022), "Robust Botnet DGA Detection: Blending XAI and OSINT for Cyber Threat Intelligence Sharing", *IEEE Access*, Vol. 10, pp. 34613–34624, doi: 10.1109/ACCESS.2022.3162588.

W3Schools. (2023), "Bard Tutorial", available at: https://www.w3schools.com/gen_ai/bard/index.php (accessed 11 January 2024).

Watters, P.A. (2023), *Counterintelligence in a Cyber World, Counterintelligence in a Cyber World*, doi: 10.1007/978-3-031-35287-4.

Wei, J., Wang, X., Schuurmans, D., Bosma, M., Ichter, B., Xia, F., Chi, E.H., *et al.* (2022), "Chain-of-Thought Prompting Elicits Reasoning in Large Language Models", *Advances in Neural Information Processing Systems*, Neural information processing systems foundation, Vol. 35.

Yadav, A., Kumar, A. and Singh, V. (2023), "Open-source intelligence: a comprehensive review of the current state, applications and future perspectives in cyber security", *Artificial Intelligence Review*, Vol. 56 No. 11, pp. 12407–12438, doi: 10.1007/s10462-023-10454-y.

Yamin, M.M., Ullah, M., Ullah, H., Katt, B., Hijji, M. and Muhammad, K. (2022), "Mapping Tools for Open Source Intelligence with Cyber Kill Chain for Adversarial Aware Security", *Mathematics*, Vol. 10 No. 12, doi: 10.3390/math10122054.

Teaching Next-Generation Cyber Warfare

Jim Q. Chen
U.S. National Defense University, USA
drchen878@gmail.com

Abstract: Cyberspace plays a unique and crucial role in an era of a new geopolitical competition between the major powers. Cyber warfare has the flexibility of being launched either below or above the threshold of armed conflict in supporting the achievement of strategic goals and political aims. Meanwhile, cyber maneuvers are also inalienable to maneuvers in other warfighting domains such as land, maritime, air, and space. How can cyber capabilities be harnessed and integrated into joint warfighting? How can these new capabilities be taught to the joint force in a new way? These are the questions that the joint professional military education (JPME) programs should address. In the current JPME curricula, cyber capabilities are taught either in silo or in a way that is loosely connected to conventional military maneuvers. In a sense, they are not seamlessly integrated into the JPME programs. This paper addresses the issues of the current approach as well as their consequences. It intends to explore a new way of teaching next-generation cyber warfare, in which cyber capabilities are not only built into joint warfighting but also used to support the employment of relevant instruments of national power as well as the collaboration with allies and partners. This multi-level integrated approach is enabled by disruptive technologies such as artificial intelligence (AI). In so doing can cyber capabilities, especially AI-enabled cyber capabilities, be well integrated into the joint warfighting curricula, thus enabling joint force to obtain strategic advantage in the geopolitical competition.

Keywords: New Character of war, AI-Enabled Cyber, Joint Warfighting, Integration, Curricula

1. Introduction

In an era of a new geopolitical competition between the major powers, cyberspace plays a unique and crucial role since it can be used either below or above the threshold of armed conflict and it is inalienable to maneuvers in other warfighting domains such as land, maritime, air, and space. The flexibility makes cyberspace a suitable means in supporting the achievement of strategic goals and political aims. Hence, figuring out a new way of harnessing cyber capabilities and integrating them into joint warfighting is crucial.

As pointed out by the then Chairman of Joint Chiefs of Staff General Milley (2023), "Geostrategic competition and rapidly advancing technology are driving fundamental changes to the character of war." "The rapid change in the character of war demands a corresponding fundamental shift in our Joint Force." There are two tasks listed. One is to understand the new character of war. The other is to lead a change in the joint force. Of these two tasks, the first one drives the second one. In other words, without a deep understanding of the new character of war, it is hard to drive a shift in the joint force.

To understand the new character of war, one needs to understand at least the two major drivers of the change: geostrategic competition and rapidly advancing technologies.

The 2022 U.S. National Security Strategy mentions two strategic challenges that we are facing. "The first is that the post-Cold War era is definitively over and a competition is underway between the major powers to shape what comes next." "The second is that while this competition is underway, people all over the world are struggling to cope with the effects of shared challenges that cross borders–whether it is climate change, food insecurity, communicable diseases, terrorism, energy shortage, or inflation." These two strategic threads define the strategic environment that we are currently in, namely, competition in some areas while cooperation in other areas, or competition in some cases while cooperation in other cases. This requires the relevant nation-states to act within the spectrum of cooperation, coexistence, competition, and conflict.

The emerging technologies that contribute to the innovative and decisive military capabilities and capacities as well as military superiority involve artificial intelligence (AI) including machine learning (ML) and data analytics, robotics including drones, quantum computing, global positioning systems (GPS), etc. They, in turn, have made it possible for the development of ubiquitous sensors, analytical tools, new cryptographic tools, automated or autonomous vehicles and platforms, precision-guided munitions, long-range precision fires, advanced space capabilities, advanced cyber capabilities, just to list a few.

One may wonder what the character of war is. Milley (2023) further explains that it is about the way militaries conduct warfare. Specifically, it is about "how, where, with what weapons, and technologies wars are fought". Specifically, in fighting a modern war, cyber, space, electromagnetic spectrum, and information capabilities should be integrated into the land, maritime, and air capabilities. Without this integration, a military force will lose its eyes and ears as well as some critical capabilities in significant domains. This will make it almost impossible to win a war, or even to survive in a war.

It must be acknowledged that in the current JPME curricula, cyber capabilities are covered but not fully explored with respect to their role in joint warfighting. The skilful employment of cyber capabilities together with capabilities from other warfighting domains in a joint warfighting environment is seldom explored, not mentioning the strategies of their employment in joint warfighting. This, in a sense, fails in preparing the next-generation military leaders in dealing with the challenges in an environment in which the new character of war dominates. Thus, it can be claimed that cyber capabilities are not seamlessly integrated into the JPME programs at present.

One may wonder how cyber capabilities, especially AI-enabled cyber capabilities, can be harnessed and integrated into joint warfighting. One may also wonder how these new capabilities can be taught to the joint force in an JPME program. These are the questions that this paper intends to address.

This paper is structured as follows: Here in Section 1, the new character of war is briefly highlighted. So is the role that the cyber domain plays in joint warfighting. In Section 2, the issues of the current approach to cyber in the JPME programs are examined. In Section 3, a multi-level, multi-aspect, and integrated framework is established. This framework explicitly shows at which levels and in which aspects cyber capabilities can be integrated into capabilities of other domains and/or aspects. In this proposed approach, cyber capabilities are not only built into warfighting but also used to support the employment of relevant instruments of national power as well as the seamless collaboration with allies and partners. This multi-level, multi-aspect, and integrated approach is enabled by emerging technologies such as AI. In Section 4, the benefits of this framework are discussed. So is its implementation to improve the JPME education. Besides, future study is recommended. In Section 5, a conclusion is drawn.

2. Issues of the Current Approach to Cyber in the JPME Programs

The current curricula for the JPME programs were designed and developed for the warfare in the physical sphere, not for the hybrid warfare that involves the physical, virtual, and psychological spheres. Since the changing character of war is still emerging, the curricula lack the following components in general.

(1) The changing character of war is not well addressed in a holistic and systematic way in the current JPME curricula. Even though varied warfighting domains and varied instruments of national power are covered, a seamless integration of them is not, not mentioning the coverage of how to build and educate "an integrated and interoperable, multi-domain-capable, joint, and coalition force", that is capable of "maneuvering through space and time in a fast-paced, high-tech, rapidly changing, and exceptionally challenging environment", required in *Joint Publication 1 Volume 1 Joint Warfighting* by the U.S. Joint Chiefs of Staff (2023). In many cases, conflict and competition below the armed conflict are examined independently. Strategies in launching campaigns and operations in multiple domains and areas with allies and partners to achieve shared goals are not fully explored.

(2) The cyber domain is not prioritized in the current JPME curricula. In other words, the virtual battlefield is not emphasized. It is pointed out by Lonergan and Montgomery (2024) that "at root, the current readiness issue stem from the fact that none of the existing services prioritizes cyberspace." Quoting a retired Navy captain, they note that this fundamental mismatch "has yielded varying levels of fragmented support to cyber operations, [a] lack of continuity of cyber personnel, unclear career paths, insufficient experience, wide use of non-cyber personnel in cyber leadership positions, and cyber operations being treated always as a supporting entity across all services". This attitude is reflected in the current JPME education. Cyber capabilities are examined within the cyber domain. They are seldom explored together with capabilities in other warfighting domains. Hence, cyber is poorly integrated into joint warfighting. Consequently, modern warfighting is not investigated in a holistic and systematic way.

(3) In cyber force generation and development, specific domain knowledge, which is technical in nature, is required. Lonergan and Montgomery (2024) comment, "Manning and training for cyber operations are not equivalent to furnishing infantry or logistics personnel. All specialties have distinct training and skill requirements, but the cyber domain requires a uniquely high level of technical training." As a result, how to effectively upskill senior leaders with sufficient cyber knowledge, especially AI-enabled cyber knowledge, is constantly a challenge. In the current JPME curricula, cyber fundamentals are covered. However, it is insufficient in teaching senior leaders how to harness AI-enabled cyber capabilities to fight and win both in cyberspace and

in conventional warfare. In this sense, the future leaders are not fully prepared in leading an integrated, interoperable, multi-domain-capable, joint and coalition force.

Force generation requires elegant organizing, effective training or education, and sufficient equipping. Missing any component will result in a failure. Therefore, a framework that connects cyber to other domains and aspects should be explored. Based on this framework, new way of teaching next-generation cyber warfare can be figured out. These topics are discussed in the following sections.

3. A Framework of AI-Enabled Cyber Engagement

Joint Publication 3-12 *Cyberspace Operations* defines cyberspace as the domain "that consists of the interdependent network of information technology (IT) infrastructures and resident data". Cyberspace "includes the Internet, telecommunications networks, computer systems, and embedded processors and controllers". To put it in another way, cyberspace consists of hardware, software, firmware, internetworking systems, embedded processors and controller, and data. With the help of these systems, cyberspace is capable of engaging both the physical sphere and the virtual sphere. Since it can be used to influence humans, cyberspace is also capable of engaging the psychological sphere. Hence, it can be claimed that cyberspace sits on emerging and disruptive technologies since novel technologies in hardware, software, firmware, and internetworking systems, embedded processors and controller, and other innovative solutions are constantly being created and developed.

Likewise, AI is deeply rooted in cyberspace, as AI technologies are built on hardware, software, networking and communications systems, embedded processors and controllers, and other innovative solutions. In a sense, AI technologies further enhance the functions in cyberspace with respect to automation, autonomy, data analysis, decision-making, prediction, deception, and influence, thus further penetrating into the physical and psychological spheres. For instance, robotics (such as unmanned aerial vehicles (UVAs), unmanned surface vehicles (USVs), unmanned underwater vehicles (UUVs), and unmanned ground vehicles (UGVs)), Internet of Things (IoTs), and cyber-enabled industry control systems (ICSs) have helped to bring close together the virtual sphere and the physical sphere. Similarly, cyber-enabled information or influence campaigns have helped to bring close together the virtual sphere and the psychological sphere. Looking from this perspective, one may claim that AI has made cyberspace more powerful. In Joint Publication 3-12 *Cyberspace Operations*, it is stated, "Most aspects of joint operations rely in part on cyberspace". Cyberspace and AI are directly related, as the development and the use of AI applications heavily depends upon cyberspace. AI-enabled cyber can sufficiently bring close together the physical and virtual spheres by building physical hardware appliances operated with software and networking capabilities. Various robots are good examples. So are self-driving vehicles. Should cyberspace be enabled by AI, novel capabilities can be expected in bringing close together the physical, virtual, and psychological spheres. It is in this sense that AI-enabled cyber can be claimed to be an integrator of these spheres. Graphically, the relationship among AI-enabled cyber and the three spheres can be captured in Figure 1 below:

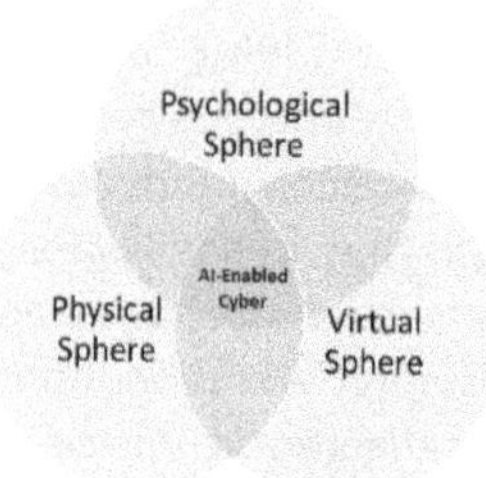

Figure 1: AI-Enabled Cyber - An Integrator of the Physical, Virtual, and Psychological Sphere

In modern warfighting, AI-enabled cyber can be a game-changer for command, control, communications, computer, cyber, intelligence, surveillance, and reconnaissance (i.e., C5ISR). According to the U.S. Army C5ISR Center, C5ISR can provide platforms "from Soldiers to ground vehicle, and from Air to Space". AI-enabled cyber thus "ensures our forces have the capability to see, sense, communicate, and move faster than our adversaries". In addition to the land domain, it can be employed to support C5ISR in the maritime, air, space, and cyber domains. Therefore, it can be argued that AI-enabled cyber can play a significant connectivity role in all warfighting domains.

As a contemporary war is conducted in the physical, virtual, and psychological spheres, emerging and disruptive technologies are required to support campaigns at different levels during different phases of war. In this sense, they are needed not only in joint warfighting that involves all domains, all instruments of national power, government agencies, international allies and partners, but also in unity of command or C3.

In examining deterrence in the contemporary age, Chen (2018a) explores levels of campaigns and operation both above and below the threshold of armed conflict. Chen and Dinerman (2018b) examine various types of cyber capabilities within these levels in modern warfare. Chen (2023) further proposes a multi-level and multi-aspect architecture that captures the escalation and de-escalation of conflict, the employment of multiple instruments of national power, and the engagement of alliances. All these levels cover the physical, virtual, and psychological spheres. Based on these studies, the author proposes a multi-level and multi-aspect framework of cyber engagement in competition and conflict. This framework is shown in Figure 2 below:

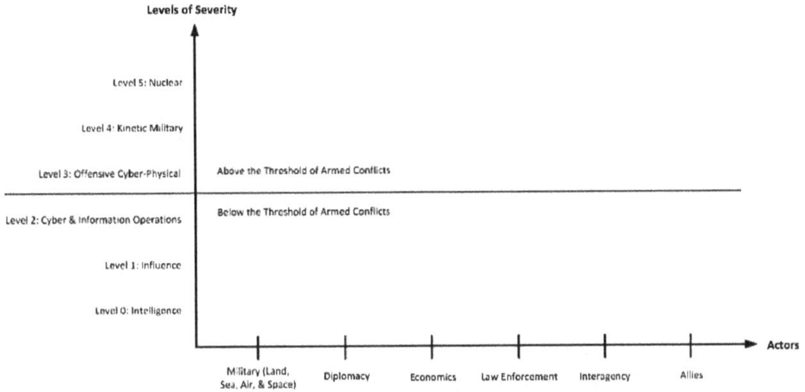

Figure 2: A Framework of Cyber Engagement in Competition and Conflict

This framework captures cyber engagement at various levels of competition and conflict. The vertical levels indicate levels of severity. The levels below the threshold of armed conflict are within the virtual and psychological spheres. The activities at these levels are for competition. The levels above the threshold of armed conflict are within the physical and virtual spheres. The campaigns and operations at those levels are for conflict.

The following levels are below the threshold of armed conflict:

- Level 0 is the level of intelligence collection and analysis operations.
- Level 1 is the level of influence campaigns.
- Level 2 is the level of cyber operations and cyber-enabled information operations.

The following levels are above the threshold of armed conflict:

- Level 3 is the level of offensive cyber-physical operations and campaigns.
- Level 4 is the level of kinetic or conventional military campaigns.
- Level 5 is the level of nuclear warfare.

Going from a lower level to a higher level indicates an escalation of a conflict, while going from a higher level to a lower level designates a de-escalation of a conflict. While in the physical sphere, AI-enabled cyber capabilities can be integrated into capabilities in the land, maritime, air, and space domains for joint campaigning and operations at each level of the framework.

At Level 0, intelligence can be collected in virtual and physical spheres via open-source intelligence collection methods, traditional intelligence collection methods, sensors, and other AI-enabled systems such as visual perception systems, image and facial recognition systems, speech recognition systems, natural language processing systems, machine translation systems, and decision-making systems. ML and data analytics can then be used to categorize the intelligence collected, figure out underlying trends of events, predict future development, and recommend courses of action (COAs).

At Level 1, cyber-enabled influence campaigns can be enhanced by AI in the virtual, physical, and psychological spheres. With AI-enabled deep fake capabilities in manipulating audio, video, images, and texts, the influence campaigns and information operations in social media and news media may confuse the targeted audience with misinformation and disinformation. Hageback and Hedblom (2022) list the following venues being used to influence the targeted audience: media content, television, radio, music, movies, other entertainment means, websites, emails messages, and social media. Consequently, the targeted audience will be convinced of something false for a period of time, causing them to make wrong decisions before they realize the information that they receive and use for decision-making is false or inaccurate.

At Level 2, AI-enabled cyber capabilities can be used for offensive cyber operations, which include but are not limited to passive network attacks (such as wiretapping, fibre tapping, and port scan), passive host attacks (such as keystroke logging, setting up backdoor, and data scraping), active network attacks (such as distributed denial-of-service (DDoS) attacks, spoofing attacks, man-in-the-middle (MITM) attacks, and address resolution protocol (ARP) poisoning attacks), active host attacks (such as buffer overflow attacks, malware attacks, ransomware attacks, and data exfiltration attacks), social engineering attacks (such as phishing attacks and spear phishing attacks), database attacks (such as SQL injection attacks and cross-scripting attacks), cloud attacks, etc. AI can enhance these types of offensive operations with speed, stealth, and autonomy. Meanwhile, AI can enhance cyber defense in terms of malware detection, intrusion detection, intrusion prevention, and attack attribution.

Level 3 and above are engaged in conflict within the physical, virtual, psychological spheres. From the offensive perspective, AI-enabled cyber can play a significant role in offensive attacks against critical infrastructure (such as industry control systems (ICS) attacks, supervisory control and data acquisition (SCADA) system attacks, and Internet of Things (IoTs) system attacks) as well as weapon system attacks and logistic system attacks. From the defensive perspective, AI-enabled cyber can contribute greatly to the defense of these systems in terms of identification, prevention, detection, response, and recovery.

At Level 4, AI-enabled cyber can support kinetic or conventional military campaigns, especially the following principles of joint operations: offensive action, maneuver, economy of force, unity of command, surprise, and resilience. Specifically, in an offensive operation, AI-enabled cyber capabilities can be used to seize, retain, and exploit virtual targets. They can also be used to assist in seizing, retaining, and exploiting physical targets. UAVs, USVs, UUVs, UGVs, drone swarms, and other intelligent autonomous robotic devices can help to accomplish the military missions such as detection, deterrence, disruption, damage, and destruction. As observed by Husbands (2021), these robots are comprised of hardware devices (such as sensors and actuators) and software applications (such as perception, modelling, planning, motor commands, as well as analysis systems built on artificial neural networks). In maneuver, they can be utilized to put an adversary in a disadvantageous position virtually and physically. With the employment of human-machine teaming, minimum-essential human combat power is required, thus enabling economy of force. Furthermore, AI-enable cyber capabilities can be employed to support command, control, and communications (C3). Data analytics systems, visualization systems, and AI systems can visually project real-time data on environment as well as predictions and varied COAs to commanders in a unified format at dispersed locations, enhancing C3 capabilities. Being good at speed, precision, flexibility, anonymity, and stealth, AI-enabled capabilities can be used to launch unexpected strikes against virtual and physical targets, creating surprise effect for an adversary who is not prepared. As duplication is rapid in cyberspace, resilience can be easily set up in the virtual sphere. This enables the joint force to recover from loss quickly.

At Level 5, AI-enabled cyber capabilities can be used for nuclear warfare. As noted by Johnson (2021), technologies like AI, ML, and data analytics "have the potential to significantly improve the ability of militaries to locate, track, target, and destroy a rival's nuclear-deterrent forces without the need to deploy nuclear weapons". Besides, AI systems may "affect the dependability and survivability of nuclear command, control, and communications system" as well as the strategic decision-making process, since "AI-infused cyber capabilities may be used to manipulate, subvert, or otherwise compromise states' nuclear assets". In other words, AI-enabled or AI-augmented systems can create impact upon states' nuclear deterrence force. In this sense, "AI applications that make survivable strategic forces, such as submarines and mobile missiles, more vulnerable (or perceived as such), could have destabilizing escalatory effects". Likewise, Lieber and Press (2017) argue that AI and autonomy can enable real-time tracking and more accurate targeting of an adversary's nuclear assets in ways that make counterforce operations more feasible. Meanwhile, speed, precision, flexibility, anonymity, and stealth that AI enjoys can further enhance the capability of nuclear weapons.

As shown above, AI-enabled cyber and information capabilities can be force-multipliers. They can be integrated into every level of the escalation ladder for military campaigns and operations. In addition, they can be integrated into other instruments of national power, such as diplomacy, economics, law enforcement, interagency collaboration, and cooperation with international allies.

In diplomacy, data analytics can be used to synthesize and analyze the data collected to have a better understanding of the current environment and the relationship among various events. AI can be used to figure out varied COAs in negotiation and then to select and recommend the most appropriate one to decision-makers. In economics, data analytics can be used to synthesize and analyze the economic and financial data. ML can help to find out the patterns as well as deviations from norms. Modelling and simulations can be utilized to examine the issues and to figure out varied solutions. AI can select the best solution and recommend it to decision-makers. For law enforcement, sensors and surveillance systems can be used to collect data. Data analytics systems can help to identify abnormal or suspicious activities and behaviour. AI systems can provide different COAs for selection. It can also select and recommend the most appropriate COA to decision-makers. In interagency collaboration and international allies' cooperation, AI systems can provide varied COAs, then select and recommend the most effective and efficient methods and measures, thus benefiting all the parties involved.

As shown above, the framework of cyber engagement in competition and conflict can seamlessly integrate AI-enabled cyber into other warfighting domains and instruments of national power.

Next, let us have a look at the benefits and implementation of the framework.

4. Benefits, Implementation, and Future Study of the Framework

In this section, the benefits of the framework are discussed. So are its implementation in helping to revise the JPME programs. Besides, the future study is recommended.

The framework enjoys the following benefits:

(1) Offering a holistic view: The framework elegantly brings together varied warfighting domains and instruments of national power. Since it takes into consideration both the levels below and the levels above the threshold of armed conflict, it provides a holistic view of the environment for decision-makers or commanders. Besides, it provides them with a platform for calculating the impact of a COA upon varied domains and aspects during a decision-making process.

(2) Adapting to the new character of war: By resorting to AI-enabled cyber capabilities, which are built on emerging and disruptive technologies, this framework makes it possible for each warfighting domain and each instrument of national power intricately linked together, thus combining the physical, virtual, and psychological spheres. This integration accelerates the adaptation to the new character of war via effectively employing cyber, space, electromagnetic spectrum, and information capabilities as well as emerging and disruptive technologies (such as AI, ML, and data analytics) at varied levels and in varied aspects to gain and maintain advantages in warfighting. In this way, the joint force will be accustomed to the new ways of fighting.

(3) Prioritizing the cyber domain: The framework provides the opportunity of having AI-enabled cyber capabilities seamlessly integrated into warfighting domains and instruments of national power. This can increase the role that the cyber domain plays in joint warfighting, thus prioritizing the cyber domain. This prioritization can help to ensure the continuity of highly technical and skilful cyber personnel, establish clear career paths, sufficiently employ AI-enabled cyber capabilities, greatly improve warfighting capabilities, thus laying the foundation for the joint force to effectively maneuver through the physical, virtual, and psychological spheres.

(4) Harnessing AI-enabled cyber capabilities: The framework makes it possible to harness AI-enabled cyber capabilities and utilize them in joint warfighting. Automation, autonomy, data analysis, decision-making, prediction, deception, and influence become available at each level and in each aspect with the help of the AI-enabled systems, such as sensing and surveillance systems, intelligence collection and analysis systems, risk assessment systems, cost-benefit analysis systems, impact analysis systems, decision-making systems, robotic systems, and other AI systems. As a result, the joint force can adapt to the new way of fighting, especially in the areas of offensive, maneuver, unity of command, security, surprise, and resilience, thus effectively maneuvering through the physical, virtual, and psychological spheres in the "fast-paced, high-tech, rapidly changing, and exceptionally challenging environment" (*Joint Publication 1 Volume 1 Joint Warfighting*, 2023).

Having a good understanding of the benefits of the framework can help us to figure out how to improve the current JPME curricula.

To develop future leaders and joint warfighters, *Joint Publication 1 Volume 1 Joint Warfighting* (2023) has mandated the revision of the JPME curricula "to develop strategically and operationally minded joint warfighters who can anticipate future joint warfighting, think critically, and creatively apply military power". Hence, in the JPME curricula, AI-enabled cyber, AI-augmented joint warfighting, and other emergent technologies that can be integrated into each level and each aspect should be included, together with doctrines and leadership. Experiential learning and wargaming exercises should be used to enhance student learning.

Having these topics covered in the JPME programs can successfully address the issues of the current approach to cyber in the JPME programs, update the current JPME curricula to help students to gain a holistic view, adapt to the new character of war, prioritize the cyber domain in strategic decision-making, and harness AI-enabled cyber capabilities in campaign planning. Ultimately, it helps students to know how to fight and how to win in the hybrid warfare that consists of the physical, virtual, and psychological spheres.

Therefore, it is not sufficient to teach AI-enabled cyber warfare only within the cyber domain. It must be taught in the joint warfighting environment, in which AI-enabled cyber capabilities are closely integrated into every warfighting domain and every instrument of national power. This is the approach that should be adopted.

The research here outlines why the framework of cyber engagement in competition and conflict is needed, how it can be used to help develop the next-generation joint force, and what it can do in helping to revise the JPME curricula. Future study can be conducted to reveal the details of how AI-enable cyber capabilities are integrated into campaigns and operations in the land, maritime, air, and space domains. Besides, case studies and wargaming exercises on AI-enabled cyber capabilities and their integration into joint warfighting can be designed and developed to enhance student learning and joint force personnel development, thus helping the joint force in adapting to the new character of war and helping leaders to successfully lead a change in the joint force.

5. Conclusion

Geopolitical competition and rapidly advancing technologies have led to fundamental changes to the character of war. Contemporary warfare is conducted in the physical, virtual, and psychological spheres. AI-enabled capabilities, which engages all three spheres, can serve as an integrator of these spheres. Besides, AI-enabled cyber can be a force multiplier, as it consists of the unique characteristics such as speed, precision, flexibility, anonymity, stealth, low-cost, hit-and-run, and others. To show the roles that AI-enabled cyber can play in joint warfighting and other national security missions, this paper proposes the framework of cyber engagement in competition and conflict. This framework categorizes cyber engagement or maneuvers below or above the threshold of armed conflict at varied levels and in varied aspects. It also reveals that AI-enabled cyber capabilities can be integrated into other warfighting domains and instruments of national powers. It argues that the next-generation AI-enabled cyber warfare should be taught in this way.

After examining the issues of the current approach to cyber in the JPME programs, the paper proposes the framework that can integrate AI-enabled cyber capabilities into joint warfighting and that can improve the JPME curricula by effectively addressing the issues. Thus, it helps the joint force to adapt to the new character of war and gain strategic advantage in the geopolitical competition.

References

Chen, J. (2023) "Deterrence in Cyberspace: An Essential Component in Integrated Deterrence", *Integrated Deterrence and Cyberspace*, Joseph Billingsley (ed.), pp.1-21. Washington DC, USA: The National Defense University Press.

Chen, J. (2018a) "On Levels of Deterrence in the Cyber Domain", *Journal of Information Warfare*, Vol.17, 2, pp.32-41.

Chen, J. and Dinerman, A. (2018b) "Cyber Capabilities in Modern Warfare", *Cyber Security: Power and Technology*, M. Lehto and P. Neittaanmäki (eds.), pp.21–30. Springer.

Hageback, N. and Hedblom, D. (2022) *AI for Digital Warfare*, Oxon, UK: CRC Press.

Husbands, P. (2021) *Robots: What Everyone Needs to Know*, Oxford, UK: Oxford University Press.

Johnson, J. (2021) *Artificial Intelligence and the Future of Warfare*, Manchester, UK: Manchester University Press.

Lonergan, E. and Montgomery, M. (2024) "United States Cyber Force: A Defense Imperative", Washington DC, USA: Foundation for Defense of Democracies (FSS) Press.

Lieber, K. and Press, D. (2017) "The New Era of Counterforce: Technological Changes and the Future of Nuclear Deterrence," *International Security*, Vol.41, 4, pp.9-49.

Milley, M. (2023) "Strategic Inflection Point: The Most Historically Significant and Fundamental Change in the Character of War Is Happening Now–While the Future Is Clouded in Mist and Uncertainty", *Joint Force Quarterly,* Volume 110, 3rd Quarter, pp.6–15, Washington DC, USA: the NDU Press.

The U.S. Army C5ISR Center (2024) "Combat Capabilities Development Command C5ISR Center". Retrieved from c5isrcenter.devcom.army.mil.

The Joint Chiefs of Staff. (2023) *Joint Publication 1 Volume 1 Joint Warfighting*, Washington DC, USA.

The Joint Chiefs of Staff. (2018) *Joint Publication 3-12 Cyberspace Operations*, Washington DC, USA.

The Joint Chiefs of Staff. (2011) *Joint Publication 3-0: Joint Operations*, Washington DC, USA.

The White House. (2022) *U.S. National Security Strategy*, Washington DC, USA.

Harnessing Broadcast Receivers for Classification of Android Malware Threats

Nikolaos Chrysikos[1], Panagiotis Karampelas[1] and Konstantinos Xylogiannopoulos[2]
[1] Hellenic Air Force Academy, Dekeleia, Greece
[2] University of Calgary, Calgary, AB, Canada; Stetson University, DeLand, FL, USA

nikoschrysikos2000@gmail.com
panagiotis.karampelas@hafa.haf.gr
kostasfx@yahoo.gr

Abstract: With the increasing number of malicious attacks, the way how to detect and classify malicious apps has drawn attention in mobile technology market. In this paper, we proposed a classification model to seek and track malware Apps broadcast receivers in such devices. To identify the family of apps, static features of each app was extracted and a novel deterministic classifier is employed to categorize malware apps. With such, we can act against malware of known family, since we understand its functions, and prevent it from spreading out in larger scale, affecting extensively our society. Detailed description of the classification model is provided, as well the core technologies of this novel malicious android applications' model are presented. From experiments performed on a set of Android-based malware apps, we observe that the proposed classification model achieves highest accuracy, true-positive rate, false-positive rate, precision, recall, f-measure in comparison to other methods implemented in published experiments. The proposed classification model is promising since the average accuracy reaches an average of 97.31% and can effectively be applied to Android malware categorization, providing early detection of the capabilities of malware and the prospect of warning users of threatens ahead.

Keywords: Malware Classification, Android Malware Threats, Broadcast receivers, Malware APKs

1. Introduction

According to the latest statistics, as of October 2023 (DataReportal, 2023), there were 5.60 billion unique mobile users recorded globally, constituting two-thirds of the global population. This widespread ownership spans diverse age groups, educational backgrounds, and origins, integrating smartphones into daily life. Common usage patterns encompass activities such as audio and video calling, instant messaging, news reading, social media engagement, healthcare monitoring, smart-home controlling, gaming, photo/video capturing, navigation, music listening, emailing, financial transactions, and e-government service utilization (Xu, 2019). With this multitude of functions, smartphones become repositories for personal data, encompassing phone calls, messages, photos, videos, medical records, financial information, and more.

The abundance of personal information stored on smartphones renders them enticing targets for cybercriminals. Their toolkit encompasses various malicious applications, including AdWare, SpyWare, Downloaders, Bankbots, Ransomware, Backdoor tools, hack tools, etc. (securelist.com, 2023). These applications are adept at disguising themselves as legitimate mobile apps. However, once downloaded onto smartphones, they become weaponized, infiltrating users' personal data for illicit purposes. Given that the Android operating system holds a 70% share in the mobile phone market, cybercriminals have chosen it as their primary target. Consequently, Android smartphones face a likelihood that is 50 times greater of being infected with malware compared to iOS smartphones.

Hence, numerous security analysts strive to devise innovative methods for the detection and classification of mobile malware, employing diverse techniques. Current Android malware analysis methods broadly fall into three categories: static analysis, dynamic analysis, and a hybrid approach that merges aspects of both.

Static analysis concentrates on scrutinizing, reviewing, and comparing static information, such as program code, permissions, intents, and broadcast receivers extracted from a suspicious application, with known malware information to identify common patterns or signatures. However, static analysis is susceptible to obfuscation techniques that alter the code, rendering the detection of malicious payloads more challenging. Moreover, it is ineffective against zero-day attacks, as there are no pre-existing signatures for such malware, making them undetectable.

On the other hand, dynamic analysis observes runtime behaviors of the applications in real or virtual mobile environments, examining API calls, system calls, data transmission, hidden icon operations, and network traffic. Hybrid analysis combines the strengths of both dynamic and static analyses, achieving enhanced results by merging their outputs. Modern hybrid approaches also incorporate Deep Neural Networks (DNN), which appear to yield better results by combining static and dynamic techniques, however their performance is not deterministic and thus not always reliable especially when a different dataset is tested.

Our approach is focused on the static analysis of one of the very important characteristics of an Android application which is broadcast receivers. Broadcast receivers () are used by applications to receive broadcast messages sent from the Android system or other Android applications, when an event occurs. For example, when the battery is almost depleted or the system boots up, broadcast messages will be sent to other applications, so actions will be taken. There are three types of broadcast intents according to Bigsin et al (2021), normal, sticky and ordered.

- Normal broadcasts: Normal broadcasts are sent simultaneously to all registered receivers, and then they cease to exist.
- Ordered broadcasts: Ordered broadcasts are delivered to one receiver and any receiver in the delivery chain can stop the propagation of the broadcasts.
- Sticky broadcasts: Eventually sticky broadcasts are accessible even after they have been sent and can be re-delivered to future receivers.

As can be understood, broadcast receivers pose a potential threat to smart devices, as they can receive messages from both the Android system and other applications (Google, 2024). In recent years, there has been growing interest in the research community regarding the exploitation of broadcast receivers. Several researchers have proposed various methods for utilizing broadcast receivers in malware detection (Mohsen et al., 2017; Tian, 2016; Bisgin et al, 2021).

In this field of study, our proposed methodology exploits the existence of broadcast receivers to perform Android malware classification. We claim that our methodology:

- Exclusively employs broadcast receivers as input data for analyzing and classifying malware applications, achieving exceptionally high accuracy. This constitutes a competitive advantage, considering that the majority of real-world malicious Android applications obfuscate most of their code. Therefore, an approach requiring additional features may perform poorly or not at all if some of the necessary features for the classification is obfuscated or missing.
- Has the potential to outperform machine learning techniques, as these methods rely on probabilistic metrics, whereas our method represents a deterministic classification approach.

The rest of the paper is organized as follows: The related work section, presents relevant papers that utilize features such as broadcast receivers or permissions in malware classification. Section 3, describes in details the proposed methodology while section 4 presents the dataset used and the conducted experiments to verify the effectiveness of the proposed methodology. Section 5 presents the results and discusses the limitations of the methodology. Finally, the conclusions and tentative future work are presented.

2. Related Work

There have been a great number of studies on detecting malicious Android applications based on technical information such as broadcast receivers, permissions or any other information included in the AndroidManifest.xml file. Through the analysis of such information, the researchers have developed several methodologies which attempt to detect whether a mobile application is malicious or not. A variety of techniques have been used for that purpose utilising permissions, receivers and other features integrated in mobile applications. The analysis of those features have been attempted to be done with a wide range of methods including data mining techniques and diverse machine learning approaches.

Lin et al. (2013) proposed SCSdroid, utilizing thread-grained system call sequences for detection accuracy, achieving a high rate of 95.97%. However, there are case in which some benign families have almost the same sequences as malware families and thus the classification is not always accurate. Another limitation of this methodology according to the authors is that it requires a balanced training with malicious and benign applications in order to perform well.

Mohsen and Shehab (2016) investigated broadcast receiver usage patterns, achieving a robust 97% malware prediction accuracy by combining permissions and receivers. The same researcher with a new team investigated broadcast receiver usage patterns in Android applications to detect malware. They proposed a data mining malware detection mechanism based on statically registered broadcast receivers, achieving a malware prediction accuracy of 97%. Their findings revealed that malicious apps intensively use receivers compared to benign ones, making this aspect a valuable indicator for classification (Mohsen et al., 2017).

Massarelli et al. (2020) introduced AndroDFA, (detrended fluctuation analysis) for extracting features from malicious applications. They utilized Support Vector Machine (SVM) for classification, achieving an accuracy of 82%. Notably, their approach can be used on physical devices rather than exclusively on emulators, addressing the challenge of modern mobile malware detecting emulated environments and hiding malicious behavior.

In another approach, Fang et al. (2020) suggested an Android malware classification method based on DEX files, achieving a precision, recall, and F1 score of about 0.96. The authors highlighted the effectiveness of their method, reducing future extraction time by 2.999 seconds compared to alternative approaches. In the specific technique that selected features are converted into a picture and to text and then a fusion algorithm is used for the classification.

Milosevic et al. (2017) introduced a machine learning-aided static analysis technique, achieving a notable 95.1% F-score for source code-based and 89% for permission-based classification. It is noteworthy, that the authors compared a permission-based classification method with a permission-based clustering approach and the result was that the first method outperforms the clustering-based approach. Thus, they conclude that the permission clustering-based approach cannot be used in malware detection since benign application may use the same permissions and thus an agnostic approach does not help in this case. Similarly, since broadcast receivers have legitimate use in the Android applications, a clustering approach will not have good results.

Ngamwitroj and Limthanmaphon (2018) generated signatures using both permissions and broadcast receivers to identify malware applications. They employed a dataset comprising 800 applications to create these signatures, subsequently utilizing the same dataset to detect malicious applications with a success rate of 86.56%.

An additional notable effort to leverage inter-component communication mechanisms, specifically broadcast receivers, is the ICCDetector (Xu et al., 2016). This tool utilizes various application components such as Activity, Service, Broadcast Receiver, and Content Provider, as well as intents and intent filters, to categorize Android applications as either benign or malicious. Employing a dataset comprising 5,264 malware applications and 12,026 benign applications, the conducted experiments demonstrated an impressive accuracy of 97.4%.

Another similar approach is named AppoScopy, which introduces a signature-based specification language for mapping the control and data flow within Android applications. This method specifically records broadcast receivers and the associated data linked to these receivers. By employing the proposed specification language, researchers generate signatures for the detection of malware applications (Feng et al., 2014). The effectiveness of this methodology was assessed using 1,027 malware samples, resulting in an accuracy of 90%.

In contrast with the above-mentioned methods, that combine receivers and other features such as permissions, opcodes system calls and actions which then are processed by machine learning algorithms, our work focuses on the broadcast receivers alone in a static deterministic approach, out of all features. Thus, our methodology classifies a malicious mobile application to the related malware family analysing the broadcast receivers achieving a 97.3% accuracy rate outperforming all other methods of similar approach.

3. Classification Framework

3.1 Problem Statement

The algorithms developed by researchers mentioned in related work section implement a wide range of methods with varying data inputs collected with static analysis such as opcodes extracted from .smali files, permissions , receivers, intents extracted from AndroidManifest.xml file and with dynamic analysis such as api dependency graphs and system calls. All these algorithms may follow a different approach of data collection and processing, but on the final step of decision making and classification, they share one common characteristic, they use probabilistic classification algorithm (either Machine Learning or some Neural Network model). The main weakness of these algorithms, which we aim to combat with our heuristic approach, is that their output is always prone to statistical error. Our method is based on a deterministic categorization model that achieves the highest accuracy compared to mentioned work.

We therefore consider a classification problem in which as input is used a malicious smartphone application which should be classified into one of the known categories of malware. To solve this problem, a classification method is proposed that uses the application broadcast receivers which are then compared with the corresponding receivers sets of each category of malware.

3.2 Methodology

The core idea behind this methodology is classification of malicious applications (APKs) by similarity. In details, that means we extract specific features from applications of pre-classified data, and we process them in order to create unique sets of these features for each family. Then we extract the same data from an unknown sample, and we compare it with these sets. The sample is categorized to the family that is more similar with (Fig. 1).

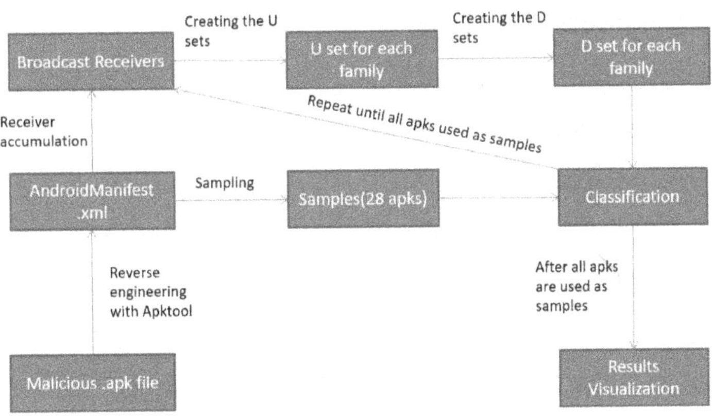

Figure 1: Flow diagram depicting the methodology used

The overall methodology spans in six stages:

3.2.1 *Reverse Engineering*

In order to obtain the data needed and used for the classification process, we initially have to extract the AndroidManifest.xml files out from the applications. In order to achieve that, we use a decoding tool for Android applications, named Apktool[1]. Apktool is a tool for reverse engineering 3rd party, closed, binary Android apps. It can decode resources to nearly original form and rebuild them after making some modifications. It also makes working with an app easier because of the project like file structure and automation of some repetitive tasks like building apk, etc.

Its main features are:

- Disassembling resources to nearly original form (including resources.arsc, classes.dex, .png files and XMLs)
- Rebuilding decoded resources back to binary APK/JAR
- Organizing and handling APKs that depend on framework resources
- Smali Debugging
- Helping with repetitive tasks

In our methodology, we are interested in XML files since the broadcast receivers are included in AndroidManifest.xml. In the AndroidManifest.xml file, broadcast receivers are defined within the <receiver> element, each linked to an <intent-filter> element. These intent filters play a pivotal role in dictating the circumstances under which a receiver is activated. Intent filters encompass a spectrum of criteria such as actions, categories, and data types, outlining the specific broadcasts to which a receiver should respond. This mechanism allows control over the events that trigger the receiver's functionality. However, the flexibility of intent filters also introduces a potential vulnerability. Malicious applications may strategically exploit specific intent filters to intercept sensitive broadcasts or manipulate communication channels between components. The careful analysis of intent filters is, therefore, imperative in identifying and mitigating potential security risks associated with broadcast receivers in the Android ecosystem. In the following table, we have included some representative instances of broadcast receivers that we can extracted during our analysis:

---

[1] https://ibotpeaches.github.io/Apktool/

Table 1: Examples of Broadcast Receivers found during receiver accumulation stage.

Family	Apk's hash	Broadcast Receiver
AndroRAT	3f1fe2984a0573fa0e466c0c6b81e856	BootReceiver
BankBot	d55243c458f1da54a2473714f5ab4de8	org.starsizew.Aa
Boqx	0c2f86b8c066cd4f8573b115b19b578c	com.cdfg.ad.poster.ReceiverAlarm
Dowgin	0a1bead476e2de6e2c94f000ca1aab84	AppReceiver
DroidKungFu	b39667306cf1ec7a52b689ca5214a1f4	com.cdjm.reader.control.Receiver
FakeAV	049241403fdbc4cabd880aabddd69cf0	DefenderAppWidgetProvider
Fjcon	73f75636d00c766c6096e6051e474a76	InstallShortcutReceiver
GingerMaster	519bab12b8d846e4a599d1f25ffb0e49	receiver.ShutdownReceiver
Mecor	0abd91480a05102fa8ff8d915e7e6584	com.google.android.gcm.GCMBroadcastReceiver
RuMMS	0dd1d8d348a3de7ed419da54ae878d37	com.nihopgezk.azszafsi.qjsaenabjy
SimpleLocker	58bbfc398808946b482f587b27d7af0e	a.b.c.d.Event
Ztorg	54938db23973a525d1c427df86f3ef6b	dl.ph.yy.mf.BootReceiver

3.2.2 *Receiver Accumulation*

In order to gather the features needed, we extract the broadcast receivers contained in the XML files and we store them in text files, for every apk. Thus, the output of this stage is a list of files containing information about the broadcast receivers associated with each application. Specifically, each text file is named after its corresponding application, ensuring easy reference. These files serve as valuable repositories, containing the extracted names of broadcast receivers for subsequent stages of analysis. To enhance systematic organization, all these files are arranged within folders, designated with the names of the respective APK families.

3.2.3 *Sampling*

In this stage, a systematic recurring approach is adopted to create a representative sample for analysis. Initially, one application is linearly selected from the queue of applications of each family, serving as a sample for later evaluation. Following this step, the testing dataset, with cardinality 28, is created, comprising the selected applications. Subsequently, we proceed to create the Union (U) and Difference (D) sets as described in section 3.2.4 and 3.2.5 and then classify the testing dataset.

The stages from the sampling to the classifying are performed repeatedly, until every apk has been utilized at least once as a sample in the testing dataset, following a cyclic process. To elaborate, consider a dataset with the largest family of 3,000 apps. The process, in order to sample every application of the family, needs to iterate 3,000 times. In this way, for the largest family every application is selected once, while for smaller families we have to calculate the iteration ratio of the family with the largest one. For example, if a family has 10 apks and the largest one has 3,000 apks then the iteration ratio is 300 and the first apk of the smaller family will be used as sample for the first 300 testing sets, the second apk will be used for the next 300 testing sets and so on.

Following the above described process, for the experimental dataset of section 4.1 with the completion of all iterations, an average score of the results for all iterations of the model for each family is calculated and presented. In this case, the largest family is Dowgin with 3,371 apks, so our model will repeat steps 3.2.3 to 3.2.6 3,371 times. This approach aims to exhaustively test the model's integrity by employing every apk as a sample. This is crucial since most families display great variance of different receivers. Random sampling under these circumstances, proves inadequate in forming a representative testing set for each family.

3.2.4 *Creating the U set*

For all families, we find their unique receivers that each application uses and then we store all these receivers in a text file. In terms of set theory, we calculate the union of the subsets, where subset is considered each application receivers, for example the subsets A, B and C, as it is illustrated in Figure 2. The output process is the Union (U) set of all unique broadcast receivers from all the applications in the same family.

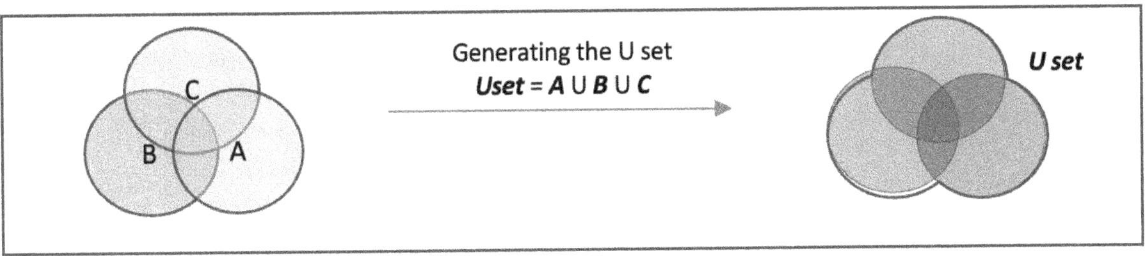

Figure 2: A visual representation of applications' A B and C receivers Venn Diagram as sets and the computation of U set.

3.2.5 *Creating the D set*

For the U sets for every family, we detect the broadcast receivers that are common in at least two families, and we remove them. Continuing the aforementioned example, in Figure 3, for the U set of A B and C subsets, we calculate the difference of A with B and C, of B with A and C and of C with A and B and then we calculate the union of all differences as the D set.

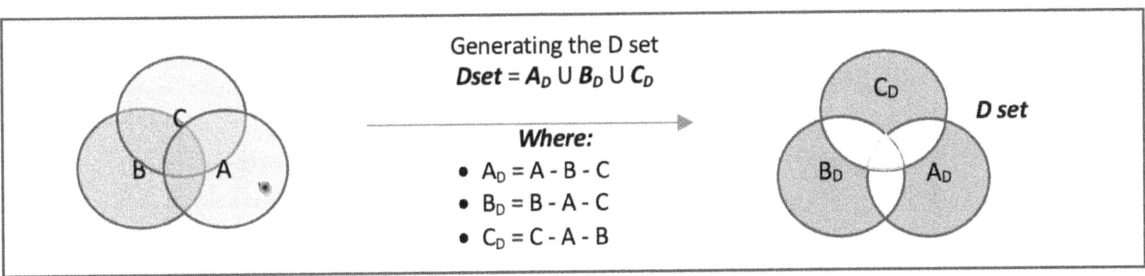

Figure 3: A visual representation of applications' A B and C receivers using Venn Diagram as sets and the computation of D set.

3.2.6 *Classification*

During the classification phase, the D sets, which are sets of broadcast receivers created in the prior step, are utilized. The heuristic model employed for classification involves comparing the similarity between an application's receivers and the D sets. Thus, we compare the D sets with the current sample group, where each sample represents an apk. The process involves taking the receivers of each application in the sample group and comparing them with the receivers in each D set belonging to different families. For every shared receiver detected between the sample and a D set, we increment the similarity score of the sample with that specific family. The similarity score is calculated as the total number of common receivers divided by the number of receivers in the corresponding D set.

Let's illustrate this with an example: Consider a sample application with 5 receivers. If it shares 3 receivers with a D set from a family having 200 receivers, the similarity score with that family would be 3/200. On the other hand, if the same application has 1 common receiver with a D set from a family with 18 receivers, the similarity score would be 1/18. In this case, the application would be categorized into the second family since 3/200 is less than 1/18.

It's crucial for the success of this methodology that broadcast receivers are unique to their respective families and are not detected in applications from other families. To achieve this, the D sets were crafted, ensuring the reliability of the classification process and minimizing the risk of misjudgements and errors.

4. Experiments

4.1 Dataset and Hardware Description

The dataset originally consists of 24,650 malware samples categorized in 71 families (Wei et al, 2017). A segment of it has been used for the experiment. More specifically, out of 32 families in the original dataset, only 29 use broadcast receivers and one of them, Fobus, has only two malicious samples whose AndroidManifest.xml contain receivers, and thus it is exempted from analysis and classification. In addition to that, it should be noted that not all samples of the 28 families use receivers which means that the actual number of samples that are going to be used is less than the samples that a family contains.

Table 1 provides an overview of the malware families in the part of the dataset we used. For each family, we show its type indicating the main purpose of the family. In total, these 28 families contain 14,288 samples but as mentioned, not all of them have broadcast receivers. Specifically, 10,693 malicious applications are used, which is 68.3% of the original dataset.

Table 2: Overview of the malware families of the dataset

Families	Type	# of Varieties	# of Samples	# of Samples Used	Used Percentage
AndroRat	Backdoor	1	46	45	97.8
Andup	Adware	1	45	43	95.5
Aples	Ransom	1	21	21	100
BankBot	Trojan-Banker	8	740	646	87.3
Bankun	Trojan-Banker	4	70	54	77.1
Boqx	Trojan-Dropper	2	215	213	99.1
Cova	Trojan-SMS	1	17	4	23.5
Dowgin	Adware	1	3385	3371	99.6
DroidKungFu	Backdoor	6	546	486	89.0
FakeAngry	Backdoor	2	10	10	100
FakeAV	Trojan	1	5	5	100
FakeDoc	Trojan	1	21	21	100
FakeInst	Trojan-SMS	5	2172	1997	91.9
FakePlayer	Trojan-SMS	1	21	5	23.8
Finspy	Trojan-SMS	1	9	9	100
Fjcon	Backdoor	1	16	16	100
Fusob	Ransom	2	1277	1270	99.4
GingerMaster	Backdoor	7	128	117	91.4
GoldDream	Backdoor	2	53	53	100
Koler	Ransom	1	69	4	5.8
Kuguo	Adware	1	1199	10	0.8
Lotoor	HackerTool	3	333	15	4.5
Mecor	Trojan-Spy	1	1820	1820	100
RuMMS	Trojan-SMS	2	402	350	87.1
SimpleLocker	Ransom	1	173	11	6.4
SlemBunk	Trojan-Banker	3	174	18	10.3
Youmi	Adware	1	1301	76	5.8
Ztorg	Trojan-Dropper	1	20	3	15
Total / Average	-	62	14288	10693	68.3

4.2 Experimental Environment

Both analysis and classification were performed in a laptop that utilizes an AMD Ryzen 7 3750 H with Radeon Vega Mobile Gfx processor. The computing system was equipped with 16 Gb of Memory. The overall methodology lasted about 4 hours starting by the extraction of the receivers from each application, processing all the applications, classifying them, and repeating the same process for all samples and producing the final results. The whole process utilized, on average, 70% of the processing power of the processor and 8 Gb of memory to store the temporary data.

5. Results

This section summarizes the results of the methodology that was applied in the previously described dataset. In Figure 4, it can be seen the accuracy achieved and the number of applications per family that were classified along (True Positives). Light grey bars indicate lower True Positive Ratio while dark grey bars indicate high TPR For example, our methodology accurately classifies 2 applications of FakeAngry family, that results in 100% accuracy, but as the above table implies, there are 8 more FakeAngry applications in the dataset, that not classified in the correct family, or they were unclassified. On the other hand, in Mecor we can see that the algorithm achieves 100% True Positive Ratio, which means all Mecor applications were correctly classified to the family, but we have 85.85% accuracy, that indicates 14.15% of applications were incorrectly categorized as Mecor.

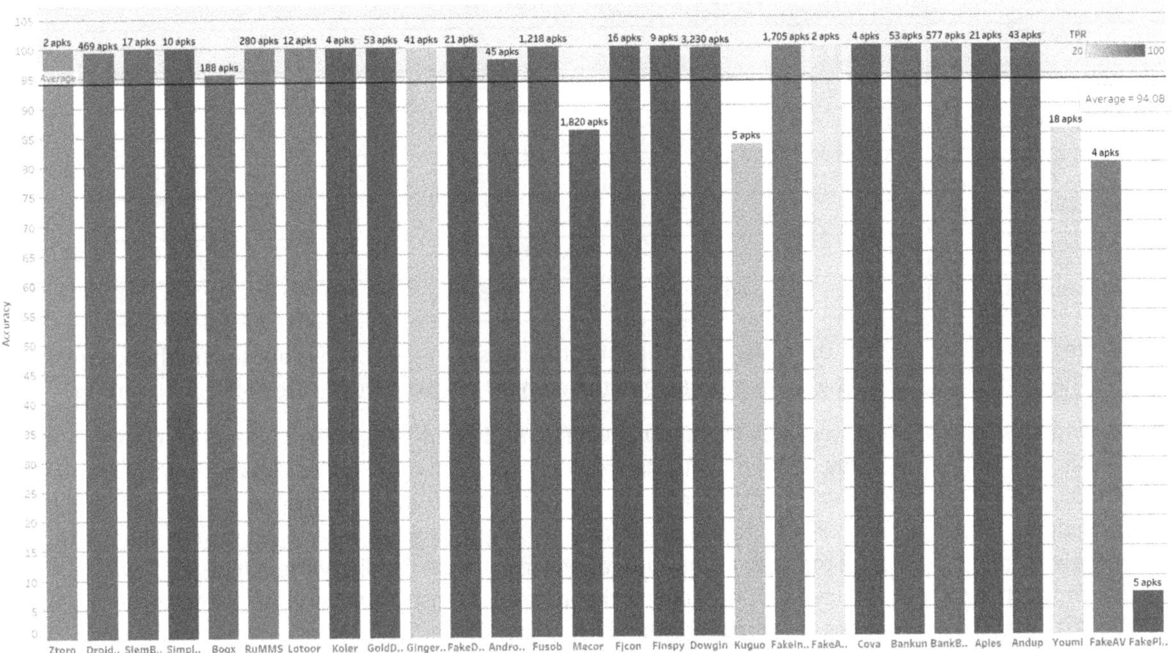

Figure 4: The results of the proposed methodology in the test dataset

Table 3: TP vs. Accuracy

Families	Total Predictions	True Positive Rate	True Positives	Accuracy
AndroRat	46	98	45	97.83
Andup	43	98	43	100
Aples	21	100	21	100
BankBot	577	89	577	100
Bankun	53	96	53	100
Boqx	197	90	188	95.43
Cova	4	100	4	100
Dowgin	3,239	97	3230	99.72

Families	Total Predictions	True Positive Rate	True Positives	Accuracy
DroidKungFu	472	88	469	99.36
FakeAngry	2	20	2	100
FakeAV	5	80	4	80
FakeDoc	21	100	21	100
FakeInst	1,705	85	1705	100
FakePlayer	70	100	5	7.14
Finspy	9	100	9	100
Fjcon	16	100	16	100
Fusob	1,218	96	1218	100
GingerMaster	41	35	41	100
GoldDream	53	100	53	100
Koler	4	100	4	100
Kuguo	6	40	5	83.33
Lotoor	12	80	12	100
Mecor	2,120	100	1820	85.85
RuMMS	280	80	280	100
SimpleLocker	10	100	10	100
SlemBunk	17	94	17	100
Youmi	21	24	18	85.71
Ztorg	2	67	2	100
Average	-	84.17	-	94.08
Unclassified	483	15.83	-	-

Table 3 presents the overview of the malware families of the dataset used for the proposed methodology that provides the number of apks that each family has, and the number of apks actually used for our algorithm.

The experiment's findings yield valuable insights. On average, 84.17% of APKs were successfully classified into their respective families. Notably, families with diverse receivers exhibit a lower classification percentage. Importantly, the overall false positive ratio is minimal, standing at 5.92%. Upon reviewing the table above, it becomes apparent that certain malicious families, namely FakeAngry, GingerMaster, Kuguo, and Youmi, exhibit a low positive rate. This indicates that numerous applications from these families were not accurately classified into their respective categories. However, intriguingly, the model demonstrates high accuracy for these families. This suggests that the applications categorized within FakeAngry, GingerMaster, Kuguo, and Youmi are indeed correctly placed despite the challenges posed by the lower positive rates. An interesting observation arises when excluding the FakePlayer family from the calculations, resulting in a significant improvement in the overall methodology's accuracy, reaching an average of 97.31%. Specifically, the accuracy for the FakePlayer family is merely 7.14%. This implies that among the 70 APKs in the FakePlayer family, only 5 genuinely belong to FakePlayer, while 64 belong to DroidKungFu Variety 2, and 1 to Dowgin. This misclassification issue extends to DroidKungFu applications utilizing the "Receiver" receiver common to both families. Despite the shared receiver, misclassifications occur due to the FakePlayer family having only 2 unique receivers compared to DroidKungFu's 67. Consequently, the similarity based on receivers is higher for FakePlayer (1 out of 2) and significantly lower for DroidKungFu (1 out of 67). This disparity increases the likelihood of an APK belonging to the FakePlayer family rather than other families based on the methodology's functioning. In conclusion, these results underscore the efficiency and effectiveness of the proposed methodology, particularly when dealing with an unbalanced dataset, as exemplified in our experiments.

However, it's crucial to note that not all families encompass receivers; out of 32 families, only 28 include them. Furthermore, not every APK within these families necessarily incorporates receivers. The classification process introduces a potential challenge, as a legitimate application might be erroneously categorized within a family due to shared receivers with a malicious counterpart, leading to the assumption of malware presence. This classification hinges on the concept of similarity, emphasizing that the fewer unique receivers a family possesses, the greater the likelihood that an APK using one of these receivers may be classified into that family, irrespective of its actual association.

6. Conclusions

In the realm of mobile security, addressing the challenge of detecting malicious attacks has become increasingly critical, especially with the growing sophistication of such threats. The urgency to categorize malicious apps into families based on their functionality has led to the widespread use of machine learning algorithms for this purpose. However, these algorithms are susceptible to errors due to their reliance on probabilistic methods. In this study, we mitigate these errors by employing a deterministic classification method.

In contrast to more complex hybrid classification algorithms that leverage extensive features from static and dynamic analyses, our proposed method takes a unique approach. Since the proposed methodology uses a deterministic approach, the classification of the malicious APKs is realized with high certainty based on the receivers they utilize. The observed accuracy is 97.31% if algorithm's accuracy for the FakePlayer family is considered as an outlier, due to specific APKs in the dataset possessing receivers commonly associated with families they do not belong to. Upon comparing the outcomes of our approach with those of the algorithms discussed in the related work section, it becomes evident that our methodology attains the highest accuracy score. Despite this limitation, the underlying logic of our algorithm serves as a novel contribution to the malware classification problem. This deterministic approach can be adopted and utilized as input or a foundation for a malware classification model. Moreover, it offers valuable guidance to fellow researchers exploring implementations with different features and possibly across various operating systems.

References

Bisgin, H., Mohsen, F., Nwobodo, V. and Havens, R., 2021. Enhancing malware detection in Android application by incorporating broadcast receivers. *International Journal of Information Privacy, Security and Integrity*, *5*(1), pp.36-68.

DataReportal, 2023. Digital around the World. [online] DataReportal – Global Digital Insights. Available at: https://datareportal.com/global-digital-overview (Accessed: 15 January 2024).

Fang, Y., Gao, Y., Jing, F.A.N. and Zhang, L.E.I., 2020. Android malware familial classification based on dex file section features. *IEEE Access*, *8*, pp.10614-10627.

Feng, Y., Anand, S., Dillig, I. and Aiken, A., 2014, November. Apposcopy: Semantics-based detection of android malware through static analysis. In *Proceedings of the 22nd ACM SIGSOFT international symposium on foundations of software engineering* (pp. 576-587).

Google, 2024. Broadcasts overview. Available at: https://developer.android.com/develop/background-work/background-tasks/broadcasts (Accessed: 15 January 2024).

Lin, Y.D., Lai, Y.C., Chen, C.H. and Tsai, H.C., 2013. Identifying android malicious repackaged applications by thread-grained system call sequences. *computers & security*, *39*, pp.340-350.

Massarelli, L., Aniello, L., Ciccotelli, C., Querzoni, L., Ucci, D. and Baldoni, R., 2020. Androdfa: android malware classification based on resource consumption. *Information*, *11*(6), p.326.

Milosevic, N., Dehghantanha, A. and Choo, K.K.R., 2017. Machine learning aided Android malware classification. *Computers & Electrical Engineering*, *61*, pp.266-274.

Mohsen, F. and Shehab, M., 2016, November. The listening patterns to system events by benign and malicious android apps. In *2016 IEEE 2nd International Conference on Collaboration and Internet Computing (CIC)* (pp. 546-553). IEEE.

Mohsen, F., Bisgin, H., Scott, Z. and Strait, K., 2017, October. Detecting Android malwares by mining statically registered broadcast receivers. In *2017 IEEE 3rd International Conference on Collaboration and Internet Computing (CIC)* (pp. 67-76). IEEE.

Ngamwitroj, S. and Limthanmaphon, B., 2018, February. Adaptive Android malware signature detection. In *Proceedings of the 2018 International Conference on Communication Engineering and Technology* (pp. 22-25).

securelist.com, 2023. Mobile malware statistics, Q3 2023. [online] Available at: https://securelist.com/it-threat-evolution-q3-2023-mobile-statistics/ (Accessed: 15 January 2024).

Tian, D., 2016. *Detecting vulnerabilities of broadcast receivers in Android applications*. University of Ontario Institute of Technology (Canada).

Wei, F., Li, Y., Roy, S., Ou, X. and Zhou, W., 2017, July. Deep ground truth analysis of current android malware. In *International conference on detection of intrusions and malware, and vulnerability assessment* (pp. 252-276). Springer, Cham.

Xu, K., Li, Y. and Deng, R.H., 2016. Iccdetector: Icc-based malware detection on android. IEEE Transactions on Information Forensics and Security, 11(6), pp.1252-1264.

Xu, X. ed., 2019. Impacts of mobile use and experience on contemporary society. IGI Global.

AI: The Future of Social Engineering!

Henry Collier, Ph.D.
Norwich University, Northfield, VT United States
hcollier@norwich.edu

Abstract: Artificial intelligence (AI) is at the forefront of computer science today. Everyone is talking about AI and how it is the way of the future. Companies are using machine learning (ML)algorithms to enhance their business offerings, which is showing promise in the realm of improved efficiency. The potential benefit of a fully developed AI is exceptional, but so are the threats that AI poses. While the developers of the various forms of AI are eager to be the first to create a fully functional, truly intelligent AI, they do not always consider the negative possibilities that AI creates. ChatGPT was recently used to hack itself and exposed a vulnerability in its open-source library. In addition to using AI to create hacks and exploits, AI is also being used to support social engineering efforts by creating more convincing social engineering attacks. Whether the attack is using AI to duplicate a person's voice to convince a loved one to send a gift card to get them out of jail or if it is being used to simply scrape a person's social media to develop a more precise method of attack, the concern that AI will be used for nefarious purposes is genuinely profound. This paper is a case study looking into how AI is and will be used to improve social engineering. A literature review was conducted to identify how researchers are already seeing how AI is being used and to project future threats. AI is here to stay, and the threats it brings are existential, and it is imperative that these threats are realized, and defensive measures are developed. This case study looks at how AI is and will be used to improve the efficacy of social engineering attacks.

Keywords: Social Engineering, Social Media, Artificial Intelligence, Information Security

1. Social Engineering

In the realm of information security, the human is the weakest link in the security chain (Schneier, 2004). The primary avenue of attack is Social Engineering. Social engineering is the art of tricking individuals into giving away sensitive information, that they otherwise would not give away (Nohlberg & Kowalski, 2008). It is a form of manipulation and influence used to deceive someone and it comes in many forms including the most common forms-phishing, vishing, and smishing. Phishing is a form of attack, whereby a threat actor sends someone an email trying to trick them into divulging their log-in credentials, and other sensitive information or clicking on a link that will load malware and give the attacker access to their system or lock it up with ransomware. Vishing is a form of attack whereby the threat actor calls an unsuspecting individual and tries to get them to give sensitive information, including bank account information or credit card information. The notorious vishing attack where the caller says they are from "Windows Computers and your system is infected" is an example of this kind of attack. Smishing is a form of attack where the threat actor sends the end user a text over the SMS system. One known attack is where the text says a package is being delivered but has been incorrectly routed and asks the user to click on a link. The link will then either install malware or try to prompt the user for a credit card to cover the change in the cost of shipping due to the error. These are not the only forms of social engineering, but they are the most common and most successful. Social engineering boasts a success rate of 1 in 5 or 20% of people will fall for the tricks (Gundersen, n.d.). 74% of all cybersecurity breaches have a human element to them and are financially motivated (Verizon, 2023). Social engineers use psychological triggers like imposing a false sense of urgency, causing the victim to be afraid that if they don't act, they will become a victim, and of course offering the victim something for free, to dupe their victim.

Urgency and fear are only some of the psychological triggers used by social engineers, seven triggers have been previously identified: strong affect, overloading, reciprocation, deceptive relationships, diffusion of responsibility, authority, and integrity and consistency (Kancherla, 2020). A sense of urgency falls within a broader psychological trigger known as strong affect (Kancherla, 2020). Fear also falls within the category of strong affect because fear is a strong, emotional motivator (Andreasen, 2016). Strong affect is a situation where the social engineer uses emotion to trigger a response. In the case of urgency, the user would have a sense that if they didn't act, they would miss out, or perhaps be punished for their lack of action depending on the message of the attack.

In addition to urgency and fear, there is overloading. Overloading exists because people have very complex lives that are over-inundated with data. This can lead to too much information being sent and people becoming overburdened with the data and not evaluating the data correctly, leading to them becoming victims (Kancherla, 2020). Beyond urgency, fear, and overloading, we also see reciprocation, deceptive relationships, authority, integrity, consistency, and dispersion of responsibility (Kelly & Hadnagy, 2014) (Kancherla, 2020).

Reciprocation is related to the social engineering attack known as Quid-Pro-Quo (give and take). Deceptive relationships are related to the concept of catfishing or dating manipulation. This is where a threat actor pretends to be something they are not, and they pretend to care about the victim, preying on their emotional state. Attacks using the integrity and consistency trigger are designed to take advantage of people's inherent belief that most people are honest. The authority trigger is commonly used by social engineers. The idea is that if they send an email that appears to come from someone's supervisor, they will be more likely to do what the email says to do. The diffusion of responsibility trigger is related to the group mindset. A threat actor will try to pretend to be a member of the group to trigger a response. This is most effective in spreading disinformation, especially during political events.

Because social engineers target psychological triggers that are built into each of us, defending against such attacks is difficult because of the nature of humans. Many people do not like conflict or the way conflict impacts their emotional state, and most are taught to trust authoritative figures and comply with their instructions (Lindner, 2006). Social engineers play against these emotions when they develop their attacks (Hadnagy, 2018). 128 behavioral traits influence a person to become a victim of social engineering (Collier & Collier, 2020) (Collier, 2021). These behavioral traits are further influenced by the emotions of the moment and can be effectively used against an unsuspecting user by a social engineer (Hadnagy, 2018) (Collier, 2021). From one perspective, it is possible to think of this type of influence as a form of manipulation that uses mind perception as its basis (Anderson, 2020).

At its most basic form, social engineering is simply manipulation. One of the reasons why social engineering is so successful is because manipulation occurs at the subconscious level (Anderson, 2020). Manipulation is a form of deceit and manipulators are people who use deceptive tactics to obtain their desired result, regardless of the damage it causes their target (Anderson, 2020). Deception is built around lies and lying is something that comes naturally to people (Pace, 2017). Anyone who would try and disagree with this only needs to look at a baby who fakes hunger cries to get attention, this is the beginning of deceit, and manipulation (Pace, 2017). It is our moral code that influences us to not lie. Unfortunately, it is also our moral code that makes many individuals think that people are generally good and don't lie. This belief in the average person's goodness is one of the key factors that makes social engineering so successful. Social engineering also takes advantage of the fact that biases exist like gender bias, age bias, racial bias, and status bias (Hadnagy, 2018).

Social media increases the effectiveness of social engineers by creating a wealth of information about the target (Collier, 2020)(Collier & Morton, 2024). The social engineering process starts with Open Source Intelligence (OSINT), whereby a threat actor begins to build a profile of their target (Kelly & Hadnagy, 2014) (Hadnagy, 2018). The more they get to know the target, the better the attack will be. After OSINT comes Pretext development, whereby the threat actor uses the information gathered during OSINT to develop pretexts. A pretext is the fabricated story used by the social engineer to gain the victim's trust. This could be something as simple as posting to the victim's social media account a congruent belief in something (Kelly & Hadnagy, 2014) (Hadnagy, 2018). Take the famous actor Betty White. Ms. White was a lover of animals and supported many organizations, so it is not entirely unreasonable to think that a social engineer might use this against her. First, the attacker would post something about their love of animals, and how they support organizations like People for the Ethical Treatment of Animals or the Humane Society. This would be an example of pretexting. Following this pretext, comes the attack plan.

The attack plan is where the threat actor develops the bones of the attack (Hadnagy, 2018)(Kelly & Hadnagy, 2014). How is the attack going to occur? What methods are going to be used? What is the right timing for the attack? After the attack plan is completed, then the attack is launched. The attack on Ms. White would occur when Ms. White "likes" this post or reposts it, the attacker would then generate another message about a poor animal that needs a home, and provide a link to support this animal. The link may be an avenue to simply steal Ms. White's credit card information, but it also could be a means of loading malware on her device, so the threat actor can obtain other financial information or load ransomware. The social engineer is counting on their message to pull on Ms. Whites's heartstrings, hopefully, strong enough to get her to click on the link. Emotion is one of the strongest parts of being a human being. Emotion directly influences our decision-making process (Bechara, Damasio, & Damasio, 2000) (Emotion and Decision Making, 2015). If emotions generate empathy, then the attack is more likely to be successful due to the way the human brain works. (Kelly & Hadnagy, 2014) Once a social engineer develops an emotional bond with their victim, the logic centers and rational will temporarily shut down and logic will not be used to make the decision that leads to the target becoming a victim (Kelly & Hadnagy, 2014). People are inherently insecure and this leads to breaches. As new tools, like Artificial

Intelligence, are being developed, threat actors are learning to use them to make better, more effective social engineering attacks.

2. Artificial Intelligence

Artificial intelligence has been in the realm of science fiction for decades. Whether you think about the computer Hal in the movie 2001: A Space Odessy, SkyNet in the Terminator franchise, the Red Queen in the Resident Evil series, or any of the other movies that present AI as a theme, AI comes in many forms, many of them being malevolent. So as forms of AI like ChatGPT, and Bard are created, it is only natural to think about how these tools can be used by threat actors in their attack methodology.

When one takes a look at the power that AI brings, it is easy to see that this power can be used for both good and evil. AI can be used to reduce mistakes and human error, take over and automate repetitive tasks and processes, easily analyze and process large amounts of data, make data-driven decisions faster and more effectively, assist with predicting medical trends based on data, and solve complex problems faster than a human can. It is important to note that AI is not smarter than a human, but rather it processes data, especially large data sets, at a speed that the human mind cannot do. What AI cannot do is be creative, express emotions, make emotional decisions, or feel. For this reason, the current models of AI are still more machine learning than true AI. Because of this, AI cannot make decisions regarding whether something is or isn't moral or ethical, which is what threat actors rely on. A great example is when ChatGPT was asked to find a vulnerability within itself (Burgess, 2023). A human would not intentionally look for a weakness and then give it away, especially if the weakness could be used against them. Humans would use emotion, and feeling to determine if a request is a valid request and has merit.

AI comes with a variety of other cons. There are ethical concerns, privacy concerns, concerns that AI has the biases of the developers who created it, and then the concern that AI will take people's jobs away (Khanzode & Sarode, 2020) (Williams & Yampolskiy, 2021). Although AI is supposed to have safeguards put in place, there is also a concern that these safeguards are not fully developed, nor would they be followed if the AI did truly achieve a state of self-awareness.

If appropriate safeguards are not in place, or ignored by the AI, AI can do something counter to good order. There are several examples of this in the AI Failures Incident Database including where social media creators manipulated AI to provide inappropriate material or construct hate speech (Williams & Yampolskly, 2021) (Burgess, 2023). In addition to this, there was an incident where AI was used to hack and spoof biometrics in the process of stealing Etherium cryptocurrency (Williams & Yampolskiy, 2021). Both of these examples demonstrate how AI can be used in a nefarious manner. These examples only brush the surface and open the door to threats coming from AI from multiple domains.

3. Social Engineering With AI

When you consider that AI has already been used to hack itself, steal cryptocurrency, and mold/manipulate social media, the jump to using AI in the development of Social Engineering attacks is small (Williams & Yampolskiy, 2021) (Burgess, 2023) (Arabo, 2023). As threat actors continue to look for new ways to target users, and users continue to make decisions based on the various psychological triggers, we will start to see rapid changes in how Social Engineering attacks are developed.

AI could be used to help reduce the number of phishing attacks that are successful, while at the same point, AI could be used to develop better phishing attacks that get through the traditional methods of detection, especially the human detection process. Think about the attack that most often impacts the elderly, the grandparent scam, whereby someone calls the grandparent in the middle of the night saying they are their grandchild and need money (Federal Communications Commission, 2023). If the person's voice on the other end isn't close to the grandchild's voice, then there is a probability that the elderly grandparent will realize it is a scam. Now, what happens if you take the same scam and you implement AI into it? We know that AI can take someone's voice and clone it pretty easily. If the grandchild is a frequent poster online on social media platforms, then a threat actor can get samples of their voice to use. They can then use the cloned voice to call the grandparent whom they identified using the same social media, which increases the likelihood of success. It has already been proven that social engineers use social media as a tromping ground (Abladi & Weir, 2018)(Collier, 2020)(Collier & Morton, 2024). Therefore everyone who has a social media account, where they don't know personally everyone they are connected with, should assume there is at least one social engineering in their network of friends.

Threat actors are already using AI in an adversarial way to generate cyber attacks (Thota & Menaka, 2023). AI is now being used to develop more effective phishing schemes, vishing schemes, and phishing websites. AI is further being used to implement many of these attacks, reducing the operational overhead of the threat actor. SlashNext's report *The State of Phishing 2023,* reveals that phishing emails increased by 1265% due to ChatGPT, which signals a new era of cybercrime fed by Artificial Intelligence (SLASHNEXT, 2023). The report goes on to show that there has been a 967% rise in credential phishing (SLASHNEXT, 2023). Generative AI creates an environment where threat actors can generate new, more insidious phishing campaigns that have a higher success rate than in previous years (SLASHNEXT, 2023). In 2023 the phishing market saw a growth in generative AI in business email compromise (BEC) attacks (SLASHNEXT, 2023) (Violino, 2023). It was found that Worm GPT, which is an AI chatbot with a large customized language model (LLM), helped cybercriminals with numerous activities, many related to business email compromise (BEC) attacks (SLASHNEXT, 2023). Add to this problem, it is evident, ChatGPT can leak training data and violate privacy (Ray, 2023). Threat actors are using jailbreak attacks to bypass the ethics safeguards in AI, and develop harmful responses, which can be used to develop new forms of attack on end users (Xie, et al., 2023). With ChatGPT, and other forms of AI/ML in the wild, it is clear that the cyber threat landscape is rapidly changing.

On a positive note, AI is also being used to detect social engineering attacks (Basit, et al., 2020) (Dhake, et al., 2023). AI is being used in phishing attack detection strategies (Basit, et al., 2020) (Dhake, et al., 2023). In addition to phishing attack detection, AI is being used to enhance intrusion detection in the Internet of Things, which is an area that has seen significant attacks over the last few years, including the attack on Dyn, an ISP Domain Name Service provider (Wang, 2018) (Saied, et al., 2024).

The trends that are being seen with AI and cyber attacks are concerning. Some of the questions that need to be answered by researchers are as follows: If AI is responsible for these attacks, how can we defend against them? Will we use AI to respond to an AI-based attack? If so, will AI against AI create an environment on the Internet whereby it becomes useless? It is doubtful that there will be easy answers to these questions. Cybersecurity researchers must begin to develop tools and techniques that can be used to identify AI-generated attacks.

4. Conclusion

The threat of AI being used to enhance social engineering attacks is real and needs to be addressed. As AI continues to grow, both the benefits and threats will continue to grow. Cybersecurity researchers need to continue to understand how AI is being used to target users, and how new defenses can be developed to successfully defend against such attacks. As part of this process, cybersecurity researchers must do more to understand why people are susceptible, and how to strengthen their security mindsets and modify their behavioral reactions. Combining a better understanding of the user and a better understanding of how AI can be used to attack end users, is the only way we can defend against this new threat.

Acknowledgments

I would like to acknowledge and thank my friend and soon-to-be Ph.D. holder, Charlotte Morton for her exceptional advice and proofreading ability. I would further like to acknowledge and thank my wife Heidi for her support, especially when I am writing a paper one of these papers.

References

Abladi, S. M. & Weir, G. R., 2018. User characteristics that influence judgment of social engineering attacks in social networks.. *Hum. Cent. Comput. Inf. Sci,* 8(9).

Anderson, E., 2020. *The Art of Manipulation.* Middletown : s.n.

Andreasen, S., 2016. Fear: The social motivator-the only thinkg you have to fear is everything.. *Journal of Multidisciplinary Scientfic Research,* 4(2), pp. 13-18.

Anon., 2015. Emotion and Decision Making. *Annual review of psychology,* pp. 799-823.

Arabo, A., 2023. *The use AI (ChatGPT) for Offensive.* Stanford, The 2nd International Conference on Computing Innovation and Applied Physics.

Basit, A. et al., 2020. A comprehensive survey of AI-enabled phishing attacks detection techniques. *Telecommunications Systems,* Volume 76, pp. 139-154.

Bechara, A., Damasio , H. & Damasio, A. R., 2000. Emotion, decision making and the orbitofrontal cortex. *Cerebral cortex,* pp. 295-307.

Burgess, M., 2023. The Hacking of ChatGPT Is Just Getting Started. *WIRED,* 13 April.

Collier, H., 2021. *Enhancing Information Secuity by Identifying and Embracing Executive Functioning and the Human Behaviors Related to Susceptibility.* Colorado Springs: ProQuest.

Collier, H., 2022. *Including Human Behviors into IA Training Assessment: A Better Way Forward.* Reading, Academic Conferences International Limited.

Collier, H. & Collier, A., 2020. *The Port z3R0 Effect!: Human Behaviors Related to Susceptibility.* Copenhagen, AIRCC Publishing Corporation, p. 5.

Collier, H. D., 2020. *Social Media: A Social Engineer's Goldmine.* Larnaca, s.n.

Collier, H. & Morton, C., 2024. *Teenagers: A Social Media Threat Vector.* Johannesburg, Academic Conferences International.

Dhake, B. et al., 2023. The threat of AI being used to enahance social engineering attacks is real and needs to be addressed.. *SSR.*

Federal Communications Commission, 2023. *FCC.gov.* [Online]
Available at: https://www.fcc.gov/grandparent-scams-get-more-sophisticated
[Accessed 14 01 2024].

Gundersen, G. M., n.d. *cyberpilot.io.* [Online]
Available at: https://www.cyberpilot.io/cyberpilot-blog/does-phishing-training-work-yes-heres-proof#:~:text=The%20results%20showed%20that%20a,the%20employees%20submitted%20their%20credentials.

Hadnagy, C., 2018. *Social Engineering: The Science of Human Hacking.* Indianapolis: Wiley.

Kancherla, J., 2020. Motivational and Psychological Triggers in Social Engineering. *SSRN.*

Kelly, P. F. & Hadnagy, C., 2014. *Unmasking the Social Engineer: The Human Element of Security.* Indianapolis: John Wiley & sons inc..

Khanzode, K. C. A. & Sarode, R. D., 2020. Advantages and Disadvanteges of Artificial Intelligence and Machiner Learning: A Literature Review. *International Journal of Librry & Information Science (IJLLIS),* 9(1), pp. 30-36.

Lindner, E. G., 2006. Emotion and Conflict: Why It Is Important to Understand how Emotions Affect Conflict and How Conficlt Affects Emotions.. In: *The Handbook of Conflict Resolution.* s.l.:Jossey-Bass, pp. 286-.

Nohlberg, M. & Kowalski, S., 2008. *The Cycle of Deception - A Model of Social Engineering.* Plymouth, HAISA.org.

Pace, M., 2017. *Dark Psychology 202.* Coppell: Make Profits Easy LLC.

Ray, T., 2023. *zdnet.com.* [Online]
Available at: https://www.zdnet.com/article/chatgpt-can-leak-source-data-violate-privacy-says-googles-deepmind/
[Accessed 15 01 2024].

Saied, M., Guirguis, S. & Madbouly, M., 2024. Review of artificial intelligence for enhancing intrusion detection in the internet of things. *Engineering Applications of Artifical Intelligence,* 127(Part A).

Schneier, B., 2004. *Secrets & Lies: Digtiatl Security in a Networked World.* Indianapolis: John Wiley & Sons, Inc. .

SLASHNEXT, 2023. *slashnext.com.* [Online]
Available at: https://slashnext.com/wp-content/uploads/2023/10/SlashNext-The-State-of-Phishing-Report-2023.pdf
[Accessed 05 01 2024].

Thota, S. & Menaka, D., 2023. Botnet detection in the internet-of-things networks using convolutional neural network with pelican optimization algorithm. *Journal for Control, Measurement, Electronics, Computing and Communications,* 65(1), pp. 250-260.

Verizon, 2023. *DBIR 2023 Data Breach Investigations Report.* [Online]
Available at: https://www.verizon.com/business/resources/T616/reports/2023-data-breach-investigations-report-dbir.pdf

Violino, B., 2023. *cnbc.com.* [Online]
Available at: https://www.cnbc.com/2023/11/28/ai-like-chatgpt-is-creating-huge-increase-in-malicious-phishing-email.html#:~:text=Technology%20Executive%20Council-,AI%20tools%20such%20as%20ChatGPT%20are%20generating,increase%20in%20malicious%20phishing%20emails&text=Sin
[Accessed 20 01 2024].

Wang, C., 2018. *The 2016 Dyn Attack and its Lessons for IoT Security,* Stanford: Stanford Management Science and Engineering.

Williams, R. & Yampolskiy, R., 2021. Understanding and Avoiding AI Failures: A Practical Guide. *Philosophies,* 6(53).

Xie, Y. et al., 2023. Defending ChatGPT against jailbreak attack via self-reminders. *Nature maching Intelligence,* Volume 5, pp. 1486-1496.

A Survey of Learning Technology Integration in Information Warfare Education

Matthew Douglas and Mark Reith
Air Force Institute of Technology, Wright-Patterson AFB, Ohio, United States of America

matthew.douglas@afit.edu
mark.reith@afit.edu

Abstract: Information and communication technologies (ICTs) are enduringly important in today's world. From paying for morning coffee at the local cafe to receiving a text message from a loved one, ICTs are a part of everyday life. On a larger scale, entire nations are dependent on ICTs. From power grids to the storage of classified documents, nations have come to rely on ICTs. This dependence on ICTs has increased information warfare's importance as a warfighting domain. In order to effectively conduct information warfare operations, operators must first be properly trained on how to be successful in this domain. The use of learning technologies could be useful to train information warfare forces. This paper surveys the current state of learning technology integration into information warfare education. Learning technologies have become commonplace in today's professional world. Many topics in organizations are taught through learning technologies such as interactive computer-based trainings, educational videos, and more complex serious games. This is no different for information warfare professionals. Learning technologies can provide alternative ways to teach important information warfare concepts such as the roles, assets, and capabilities that are necessary to succeed in this domain. The use of artificial intelligence, game-based learning, gamification, and simulation-based learning to enhance the training of information warfare forces is discussed in this survey. Additionally, the effect of adding learning technology into information warfare education curriculum as well as the key elements for each type of learning technology integrated are analysed. This paper also identifies areas of future research to further develop this topic. These findings are useful to information warfare educators who are developing curriculum or looking for ways to introduce new technologies into existing curriculum. Artificial intelligence, game-based learning, gamification, and simulation-based learning are all great options to support information warfare education, and there are even more options that have yet to be researched that present further opportunities to study in this area.

Keywords: Information Warfare, Learning Technology

1. Introduction

Information warfare, characterized by the strategic use of information and communication technologies for offensive or defensive actions, has become a critical topic in an era where nations heavily rely on information and communication technologies (ICTs) (Taddeo, 2012). Recognizing the importance of preparing individuals for this domain, the incorporation of learning technologies provides opportunities to more effectively organize, train, and equip information warfare professionals. Learning technologies, a wide array of hardware, rules, and systems, has become an important resource to support the learning process (An & Oliver, 2021). In today's increasingly digital world, the use of technology allows for education to be more interactive and dynamic, therefore increasing engagement from learners. This shift away from more traditional means of education, such as pure lecturing, becomes particularly relevant when applied to complex subjects such as information warfare. Complex topics can be hard to effectively teach solely through lecture-based instruction methods. Learning technologies provide alternate ways of training individuals on such complex topics (An & Oliver, 2021). One potential of utilizing learning technologies in information warfare education is the chance to gain knowledge directly in a simulated environment that resembles the one they will apply their knowledge in later (Plass, Mayer & Homer, 2020). This paper focuses on the intersection of information warfare education and learning technologies, exploring the potential this integration could hold in shaping the future of national security and education.

2. Research Questions

This survey is guided by the following research questions:

(RQ1) How have learning technologies been integrated into information warfare education?

(RQ2) What is the effect of adding learning technologies into information warfare education curriculum?

(RQ3) What are the key elements of successful integration into information warfare education for each type of learning technology?

This paper introduces the concepts of information warfare and learning technology, surveys past and current methods of learning technology integration into information warfare education, analyses the effect of adding learning technologies into information warfare education, and details key elements for each type of learning technology that is surveyed. This paper also identifies key areas for future research. This survey differs from others like it by having a broader scope of learning technology applications (artificial intelligence, game-based learning, gamification, and simulation-based learning) and its focus on literature specifically related to information warfare education.

3. Background

In this section, the topics of information warfare and learning technology are discussed to provide context for this survey. A discussion of how learning technologies are appropriate for use in information warfare education also follows in this section.

3.1 Information warfare

Information warfare is the utilization of ICTs with the intention of either launching offensive or defensive actions to swiftly infiltrate, disrupt, or exert control over an adversary's assets and resources or defend against such attacks (Taddeo, 2012). Figure 1 models this behaviour. Both offensive and defensive intentions have the aim of securing a competitive advantage by leveraging the power of information. This kind of warfare spans multiple professions including cyber and intelligence operations (Williams, 2010). Information warfare has continually grown in importance over the years as nations around the world become increasingly dependent on ICTs (Frater & Ryan, 2001). In today's ICT-dependent world, it is critical for nations to properly organize, train, and equip information warfare professionals.

The four characteristics that differentiate information warfare from traditional warfare are variance, non-lethality, ambiguity, and persistence (Libicki, 2020). Variance refers to the unpredictability of effects when conducting information warfare. This makes relying on these effects as key parts of operations as unrealistic, but information warfare can be used as supporting effects or multiple information warfare efforts can be executed for a potentially cumulative effect. Non-lethality and ambiguity are massive advantages of information warfare. Effects can be generated in both physical and non-physical domains (Taddeo, 2012), and these effects can be non-lethal and hard to determine who actually caused the effects due to the relative anonymity of ICTs (Libicki, 2020). The last differentiating characteristic of information warfare is persistence, and this refers to the constant connection ICTs provide to nations. A nation is able to constantly generate effects on another nation, no matter where in the world those two nations are, due to their constant connection through ICTs.

3.2 Learning technology

Learning technology, also known as educational technology, is the use of technology to deliver educational experiences to learners (An & Oliver, 2021). This broad field covers a wide range of technologies, which enhance and support the learning process. Technology in this context can be defined as hardware, rules, or systems (Dusek, 2006). This includes, but is not limited to, physical tools and resources, computers, mobile devices, online platforms, and other digital resources. Table 1 provides the different types of learning technology this survey acknowledges (Baek, 2009; College, 2024). While the use of learning technologies does not inherently make education better, it can change how individuals approach it (An & Oliver, 2021). Direct instruction does not allow full comprehension of a topic for everyone, so education can be made interactive and dynamic through learning technologies. This is a step toward integrating knowledge directly into the learner's world rather than the learner and knowledge remaining independent of one another.

Table 1: A partial list of learning technologies present in education

Learning Technologies	Description
Adaptive Learning Systems	Systems that can provide personalized learning plans and feedback.
Artificial Intelligence and Machine Learning	Intelligent agents that can be used to enhance systems such as e-learning platforms, tutoring systems, and personalized learning experiences.
E-Learning Platforms	Online platforms that host self-paced, interactive e-learning courses.
Game-Based Learning	The use of games to teach educational content through gameplay.
Gamification	The use of game elements, such as points, badges, and leaderboards, to engage and motivate learners.

Learning Technologies	Description
Learning Management Systems	Software that allows for the creation and online delivery of educational content.
Mobile Learning	The use of mobile devices to deliver and access educational content.
Simulation-Based Learning	Virtual learning simulations allow learners to gain experience in scenarios similar to the real world.
Social Learning	The use of platforms such as discussion boards and blogs to support and enhance learning.
Virtual and Augmented Reality	Technologies that simulate the real world or overlay new information onto it to deliver immersive educational content.

A majority of studies in this survey utilized game-based learning. Game-based learning is the use of games to transfer knowledge to learners in an environment comparable to the real-world (Tobias, Fletcher & Wind, 2014). Studies suggest that knowledge learned in this manner can transfer to external tasks and can engage learners more than traditional instruction methods. That is not to say game-based learning should replace direct instruction, rather it should complement and enhance the overall learning experience. This is because game-based learning benefits from a learner already having baseline knowledge of the subject related to the game's learning objectives (Plass, Mayer & Homer, 2020). The other studies found in this survey employed artificial intelligence and simulation-based learning as well as one study for gamification.

3.3 Discussion of how Learning Technologies are Appropriate for use in Information Warfare Education

The four characteristics of information warfare previously discussed, variance, non-lethality, ambiguity, and persistence, present opportunities to utilize learning technologies. Variance is easily conveyed through game-based learning. Rules and systems can be implemented that create randomness in the form of percentage-based chances for actions to successfully take place (Henno, Jaakkola & Mäkelä, 2018). This can be implemented in a physical environment with dice or in a digital environment by generating random numbers. Persistence can be conveyed through game-based learning as well. Real-time strategy games, for example, create constant connectivity by putting players in a shared world in which any player can create effects on any other player and at any time they desire, given they have the means to carry out their plans (Metoyer et al., 2010).

Non-lethality can be conveyed in simulations. A learner could be guided to complete particular actions within a simulation, and then they can be shown the results of those actions (Barjis et al., 2012). Ambiguity can also be conveyed in simulations. A learner could be given a scenario in which a lot of information is unknown, yet a specified task must still be completed and the learner must use critical thinking skills. (Barjis et al., 2012). These examples show how learning technology can be applied to information warfare education in an appropriate and effective manner.

4. Survey of Learning Technologies Integrated Into Information Warfare Education

Table 2 lists the inclusion and exclusion criteria used for this survey. These criteria were chosen due to this paper's specific interest in information warfare and the desire to survey papers no older than the beginning of this century. The majority of papers that were excluded were on the basis of not pertaining to information warfare education.

Table 2: Inclusion and exclusion criteria used in this survey

Inclusion Criteria	Exclusion Criteria
1. Papers with a focus on information warfare education and the use of learning technologies	1. Papers with a focus on operational information warfare units, papers solely on classical methods of instruction, or papers with unrelated topics
2. Papers with the full text available	2. Papers that did not have the full text available
3. Papers written after the year 1999	3. Papers written before the year 2000
4. Papers written in English	4. Papers written in any language besides English

The methodology used to gather papers consisted of keyword searches using "learning technologies", "educational technologies", "information warfare", and "information warfare education". These keyword searches were conducted through the databases shown in Table 3. A total of 4,238 results were found, but only 14 of the results matched the inclusion criteria of this survey.

Table 3: The results of the database searches that used exclusion criteria 2, 3, and 4 to filter the databases and exclusion criterion 1 was used to exclude papers after reviewing each of them.

Database	Number of Results	Number Selected for Inclusion
Google Scholar	383	9
IEEE Xplore	54	2
JSTOR	1,434	1
Database	**Number of Results**	**Number Selected for Inclusion**
ACM Digital Library	1,623	1
Springer Link	744	1

Table 4 lists the surveyed learning technologies and which studies pertain to them.

Table 4: The information provided includes references of papers that contain pertinent discussion of a specific learning technology (two of the studies are discussed in both the artificial intelligence and game-based learning sections as indicated by *)

Learning Technology	References
Artificial Intelligence	Bowman et al., 2004 Cramer, Ramachandran & Viera, 2004* Ormrod et al., 2020*
Game-Based Learning	Cramer, Ramachandran & Viera, 2004* Doriot, Hutto & Smoak, 2011 Herr & Allen, 2015 Evgenia, Ekaterina & Gennady, 2019 Flack & Lin et al., 2020 Flack & Voltz et al., 2020 Ormrod et al., 2020* Yamin, Katt & Nowostawski, 2021
Gamification	Berisford et al., 2022
Simulation-Based Learning	Davey & Armstrong, 2001 Ragsdale, Lathrop & Dodge, 2003 Schweitzer & Fulton, 2010 Katsantonis et al., 2023

4.1 Artificial Intelligence

Artificial intelligence (AI) is a fast growing field in the modern world. It has the potential to do many things, including enhance education. An example of this is an AI agent used at the United States Army War College (Bowman et al., 2004). An AI agent called "Disciple-RKF" was created to aid in rapid knowledge formation and reasoning in the Information Age. The main use case of the agent was to help military officers identify centres

of gravity, but evidence was provided that subject matter experts could teach "Disciple-RKF" agents about any complex military domain, including information warfare. The agents could then be used in a classroom environment to assist the learner in creating a knowledge base while performing educational activities (Bowman et al., 2004). This learning technology allows for the instructor's knowledge to be freely available to learners and allows for more individualised training.

Although not actually implemented, one of the game-based learning studies highlighted the use of AI agents to act as evaluators that can provide immediate feedback as a desired feature that would enrich the overall experience (Cramer, Ramachandran, & Viera, 2004). This could be an effective use of AI as it allows the learner to receive feedback at any time including when an instructor is not present. Another example of AI in one of the game-based learning studies was the utilization of AI agents to create massive amounts of posts on a privately hosted social media site in attempt to realistically generate massive amounts of data (Ormrod et al., 2020). This is an effective use of AI to support information warfare education as it enables instructors to add game elements that would otherwise take large amounts of time to implement into a game.

The effect of artificial intelligence on information warfare education is still fairly unknown. Its ability to act as a virtual tutor and evaluator or to create large amounts of data have potential to ease burdens on educators. A key element of successful integration of artificial intelligence into information warfare education may include teaching AI agents within the proper context of the learning content to avoid the agents providing irrelevant information to the learner.

4.2 Game-Based Learning

Many of the studies found in this survey utilize game-based learning to teach information warfare. This is most likely due to the flexibility that is allowed when designing a game and how effective games are at engaging learners (Plass, Mayer & Homer, 2020). For example, one study created a pre-test for an information warfare education course in the form of a game. This proof of concept computer-based game allowed incoming students to participate in a simulated scenario, and their success or failure would indicated their understanding of the game's learning objectives. This use of game-based learning was decided upon due to its distance learning capabilities as well as the immersion it can provide to learners (Cramer, Ramachandran, & Viera, 2004).

One such study that also sought to be immersive was the design of CyberWar RTS, a cyber real-time strategy training game (Doriot, Hutto, & Smoak, 2011). Real-time strategy games allow learners to think strategically at a high level while still having tactical control over the simulated environment. The game itself consists of a dynamic network diagram that the learner must complete tasks within such as defending ally networks or attacking adversary assets. The goal behind CyberWar RTS was to provide an entertaining educational experience for information warfare education that could be stand-alone or used within the context of a training course (Doriot, Hutto, & Smoak, 2011). A serious real-time strategy game like this is a great example of conveying the persistence of information warfare. The learner must balance both offence and defence due to the constant connectivity with adversaries.

It is important to understand certain elements are necessary for game-based learning to be effective within an information warfare education environment (Herr & Allen, 2015). Realism needs to be maintained, but must be balanced with the learners' engagement level. This applies to complexity as well. The game should be complex enough to relate to its real-world counterpart, but must also be simple enough for learner to understand what they must accomplish. Clear learning objectives are also key for learners to comprehend what they are supposed to master through the game. Recommendations to achieve these elements include achievements, enabling collaboration, and ensuring relevance of the game in relation to its target audience (Herr & Allen, 2015).

One such game that implemented these ideas is Information Security Quest (Evgenia, Ekaterina & Gennady, 2019). In this game, participants were tasked with investigating the theft of a flash drive that contained the usernames and passwords of a fictional bank's clientele. The participants had to work together to complete multiple objectives that included cracking passwords to get information on laptops, using a stenography tool to uncover hidden data, and discovering an encryption key to decrypt a file. The game only covered high-level information security concepts, but it implemented active education methods that future information warfare games could seek to implement as well. The participants were all very engaged during the game with the exception of instructions they were given at the beginning of the game. The instructions were deemed too lengthy by the participants, so this is something other information warfare games should be cognizant not to repeat (Evgenia, Ekaterina & Gennady, 2019).

Two studies that used card games to teach information warfare are Multi-Domain Command and Control Trading Card Game (MDC2 Game) and Battlespace Next™ (Flack et al., 2020). Both of these serious games teach multi-domain operations (MDO), with an emphasis on information warfare. The original game, MDC2 Game, contained a deck building element that allowed for custom strategies, while its successor, Battlespace Next™, removed that element for simpler entry into the game. While Battlespace Next™ added features as well, the core concepts of both games remain the same. The learners utilize cards representing assets from various military domains to defeat their opponent. The data from the studies show that through playing these card games, a majority of the learners felt like their knowledge of MDO increased and that the game was enjoyable (Flack et al., 2020). These two serious games are great examples of the ambiguity that is present in information warfare. A player does not know what cards their opponent has in their hand, but they are expected to complete their objective regardless.

Another study in which learners encountered much ambiguity was a large-scale wargame, referred to as The Persuasion Game, in which information warfare played an extensive part (Ormrod et al., 2020). A fictional world was constructed that contained six nations, five of which consisted of teams of learners. A large part of the world-building included the use of privately hosted social media platforms and online news platforms. Within this environment, the teams of learners had to create multiple concepts of operation to produce strategic, operational, and tactical actions that advanced the goals of their nation. These actions encompassed multiple domains, including information warfare. The findings from this study concluded while there were many improvements to be made, the wargame was successful at achieving its learning objectives (Ormrod et al., 2020). It stands as an effective example of utilizing learning technologies to aid information warfare education.

Some serious games can be customizable such as a study that created a proof of concept cyber attack and defence game (Yamin, Katt, & Nowostawski, 2021). The game allowed for scenarios, either attack or defence, to be built by instructors which could then be played by learners. These scenarios sought to offer both a strategic simulation and a low-level cybersecurity infrastructure experience (Yamin, Katt, & Nowostawski, 2021). Customizable serious game frameworks can be beneficial because then specific scenarios can be produced without having to design a whole new game.

The effect of game-based learning on information warfare education is largely positive from the studies above. Learners were widely reported to be engaged and gaining the intended knowledge. Key elements of successful integration of game-base learning into information warfare education include finding the right balance of gameplay and learning objectives, not overburdening learners with instructions, and providing the appropriate level of complexity as to relate to the real world but be simple enough to learn the mechanics of the game.

4.3 Gamification

Gamification is the use of game elements to increase engagement and motivation in learners. This can be seen in a study that created a gamified learning system that taught three ICT vulnerabilities: broken access control, cryptographic failures, and injection (Berisford et al., 2022). This system was built in the Unity game engine, and consisted of gamified elements such as storylines, experience points, levels, and badges. Learners were asked to analyse code and answer whether or not the code was safe or it if contained a vulnerability. Experience points would be gained for correct answers and lost for incorrect answers. Once enough experience points were gained, learners would increase in level, or promote, which allowed them to access new content. Learners could also be "fired" though if they lost too much experience points. Badges were also earned as positive and negative achievements. The results of this study revealed that the promotion/firing mechanic was the most motivating to learners, and the storylines were the least interesting, although they were still seen as beneficial (Berisford et al., 2022).

The effect of gamification on information warfare education could be increased motivation and engagement. Key elements of successful integration of gamification into information warfare education include experience points and levels as well as negative consequences for consecutive failures.

4.4 Simulation-Based Learning

Simulation-based learning focuses on the creation of real-world scenarios in an educational environment. This can be seen in a study that discusses the creation of custom-designed computer networks, isolated from all outside networks, for the purpose of simulation-based learning (Davey & Armstrong, 2001). A five stage process was introduced in which a learner would start by familiarizing themselves with this custom network and the provided tools. Then, elements would start getting added on such as traffic from another human, two networks divided by routers and firewalls, and pseudo network traffic generated to mimic network activity as if it was connected to the internet. Finally, learners would participate in scenarios that pitted them against other learners and each team was tasked with specific objectives they must complete to win. The benefits of this approach include required planning of how objectives would be achieved, hands-on experience, reflection of actions taken, and collaboration with teammates (Davey & Armstrong, 2001).

A similar approach was taken in a study that created a cyber security laboratory that would allow learners to study offensive and defensive cyber operations (Ragsdale, Lathrop & Dodge, 2003). This laboratory consisted of two main parts: a cyber "firing range" and a network of computers that contained the software VMware on them. The "firing range" was a completely isolated network that allowed for learners to practice with both offensive and defensive tools without risking the release of malicious code outside of the network. The network of computer with VMware on them allowed students to practice being network and server administrators. VMware allowed them to create virtual machines that gave them full configuration control. This network resulted in a laboratory for students to learn about cyber operations that would give them skills they could use in the real world (Ragsdale, Lathrop & Dodge, 2003).

Another study incorporated simulation-based learning into the information warfare program at the United States Air Force Academy (Schweitzer & Fulton, 2010). The motivation for integrating simulation-based learning into this program was based on two challenges that arose from only using a lecture-based approach: the large amount of material to cover and the lack of hands-on training that allows for active engagement with the material. A mix of lecture and simulation-based learning allowed for the students to first develop a common understanding of the subject and then apply their knowledge to interactive exercises. The incorporated simulation-based learning included web labs and a capture the flag (CTF) competition. These labs and CTF competition both used custom networks that allowed students to attack and defend ICTs that were specifically designed for them. The data collected showed that the combined lecture and learning technology approach was far more effective in teaching students the desired material than a solely lecture-based approach (Schweitzer & Fulton, 2010).

The final simulation-based learning paper in this survey discusses how a modern cyber range should be designed. (Katsantonis et al., 2023) The COFELET framework is highlighted as the foundation of this proposed modern cyber range. At a high-level, this framework seeks to combine teaching content, learning objectives, learner profiles, learning strategy, and educational context to fine-tune simulation scenarios and environments. Many range architectural specifications are provided, but the important part is that this new cyber range was designed to correct perceived weaknesses in current cyber ranges. This includes high costs, high testing requirements, learning strategy neglection, fixed workspace, ineffective assessment, and lack of participant profiles. The expected results of implementing this new cyber range design is the strengthening of cyber education by simulating real networks with a high degree of realism (Katsantonis et al., 2023).

The effect of simulation-based training on information warfare education are very positive. Simulation-based learning allows learners to gain hands-on experience in an educational environment that they can transfer directly into the real world. Key elements of successful integration of simulation-based learning into information warfare education include realistic custom networks and providing learners with scenarios that make them plan, act, and reflect.

5. Future Research

Future research should include further analysis of how AI can support information warfare education. Through research for this survey, it was discovered that there is much literature discussing how AI can support operational information warfare units, but very little on how it could benefit training. Promising uses of how AI could support information warfare education include AI agents to be used as opponents in digital information warfare serious games and educational assistants such as "Disciple-RKF". Future research should also include more holistic studies that compare traditional information warfare education to hybrid approaches that include the use of learning technologies such as game-based learning and simulation-based learning. Case studies showing the successful use of learning technologies within the information warfare education environment could encourage larger scale adoption of hybrid instruction approaches, and it can enable further research to be conducted on the use of specific learning technologies in this context. Finally, the learning technologies that were not found in this survey such as adaptive learning systems, e-learning platforms, learning management systems, mobile learning, social learning, and virtual/augmented reality should be explored to further this research area.

6. Conclusion

Information warfare is a critical warfighting domain in the modern world, and it is important to keep the training of these forces relevant and to utilize the best methods of instruction available. The use of learning technologies in this context can enhance information warfare education for both learners and instructors. Whether it be through artificial intelligence, game-based learning, gamification, or simulation-based learning, learning technologies provide additional support to the direct instruction of information warfare. This is a topic that should continue to be researched to further both national security and education.

NOTE: The views expressed are those of the author and do not reflect the official policy or position of the U.S. Air Force, Department of Defense, or the U.S. Government. Any reference to a commercial product is for informational purposes only and does not constitute an endorsement from the Department of the Air Force, the Department of Defense, or the U.S. Government.

References

An, T., & Oliver, M. (2021). What in the world is educational technology? Rethinking the field from the perspective of the philosophy of technology. Learning, Media and Technology, 46(1), 6–19. https://doi.org/10.1080/17439884.2020.1810066

Baek, Y. (2009). Digital Simulation in Teaching and Learning. In D. Gibson & Y. Baek (Eds.), Digital Simulations for Improving Education: Learning Through Artificial Teaching Environments (pp. 25-51). IGI Global. https://doi.org/10.4018/978-1-60566-322-7.ch002

Barjis, J., Sharda, R., Lee, P. D., Gupta, A., Bouzdine-Chameeva, T., & Verbraeck, A. (2012). Innovative teaching using simulation and virtual environments. Interdisciplinary Journal of Information, Knowledge & Management, 7. https://www.researchgate.net/profile/Tatiana-Bouzdine-Chameeva/publication/235246024_Innovative_Teaching_Using_Simulation_and_Virtual_Environments/links/0fcfd51098d1e6becd000000/Innovative-Teaching-Using-Simulation-and-Virtual-Environments.pdf

Berisford, C. J., Blackburn, L., Ollett, J. M., Tonner, T. B., Yuen, C. S. H., Walton, R., & Olayinka, O. (2022). Can gamification help to teach Cybersecurity? 2022 20th International Conference on Information Technology Based Higher Education and Training (ITHET), 1–9. https://doi.org/10.1109/ITHET56107.2022.10031716

Bowman, M., Tecuci, G., Boicu, M., & Comello, J. (2004). Information Age Warfare-Intelligent Agents in the Classroom and the Strategic Analysis Center. https://apps.dtic.mil/sti/citations/ADA431997

College, A. M. (2024). What is Instructional Design & Learning Technology?. Albertus Magnus College in New Haven, Connecticut. We have faith in your future. https://www.albertus.edu/instructional-design- and-learning-technology/ms/what-is-instructional-design-and-learning-technology.php

Cramer, M. J., Ramachandran, S., & Viera, J. K. (2004). Using computer games to train information warfare teams. Proceedings of The Interservice/Industry Training, Simulation & Education Conference (I/ITSEC). https://apps.dtic.mil/sti/citations/ADA459676

Davey, J., & Armstrong, H. L. (2001). An Approach to Teaching Cyber Warfare Tools and Techniques. Journal of Information Warfare, 1(2), 87–94.

Doriot, C., Hutto, C. J., & Smoak, C. (2011). Applying Training Analysis and Game-Based Learning toward the Design of a Cyber Warfare Real-Time Strategy Training Game.

Dusek, V. (2006). The Philosophy of Technology: An Introduction. Oxford: Blackwell.

Evgenia, I., Ekaterina, M., & Gennady, V. (2019). Development of information security quest based on use of information and communication technologies. Proceedings of the 12th International Conference on Security of Information and Networks, 1–5. https://doi.org/10.1145/3357613.3357632

Flack, N., Lin, A., Peterson, G., & Reith, M. (2020). Battlespace Next(TM): Developing a Serious Game to Explore Multi-Domain Operations. International Journal of Serious Games, 7(2), 49–70. https://doi.org/10.17083/ijsg.v7i2.349

Flack, N., Voltz, C., Dill, R., Lin, A., & Reith, M. (2020). Leveraging Serious Games in Air Force Multi-Domain Operations Education: A Pilot Study. International Conference on Cyber Warfare and Security, 155-164,XVIII. https://doi.org/10.34190/ICCWS.20.097

Frater, M., & Ryan, M. (2001). Electronic warfare for the digitized battlefield. Artech House, Inc. https://scholar.google.com/scholar?hl=en&as_sdt=0%2C36&q=Frater%2C+M.+R.%2C+%26+Ryan%2C+M.+%282001%29.+Electronic+warfare+for+the+digitized+battlefield.+Boston%3A+Artech+House.&btnG=

Henno, J., Jaakkola, H., & Mäkelä, J. H. A. (2018). Using games to understand and create randomness. Workshop on Software Quality Analysis, Monitoring, Improvement, and Applications, 1–9. https://research.ulapland.fi/fi/publications/using-games-to-understand-and-create-randomness

Herr, C., & Allen, D. (2015). Video Games as a Training Tool to Prepare the Next Generation of Cyber Warriors. Proceedings of the 2015 ACM SIGMIS Conference on Computers and People Research, 23– 29. https://doi.org/10.1145/2751957.2751958

Katsantonis, M. N., Manikas, A., Mavridis, I., & Gritzalis, D. (2023). Cyber range design framework for cyber security education and training. International Journal of Information Security, 22(4), 1005–1027. https://doi.org/10.1007/s10207-023-00680-4

Libicki, M. C. (2020). The convergence of information warfare. In Information warfare in the age of cyber conflict (pp. 15–26). Routledge. https://www.taylorfrancis.com/chapters/edit/10.4324/9780429470509-2/convergence-information- warfare-martin-libicki

Metoyer, R., Stumpf, S., Neumann, C., Dodge, J., Cao, J., & Schnabel, A. (2010). Explaining How to Play Real- Time Strategy Games. In M. Bramer, R. Ellis, & M. Petridis (Eds.), Research and Development in Intelligent Systems XXVI (pp. 249–262). Springer London. https://doi.org/10.1007/978-1-84882-983- 1_18

Ormrod, D., Scott, K., Scheinman, L., Kodalle, T., Sample, C., Turnbull, B., & Ormrod, A. (2020). The Persuasion Game: Serious Gaming Information Warfare and Influence. Journal of Information Warfare, 19(2), 27– 45.

Plass, J. L., Mayer, R. E., & Homer, B. D. (2020). Handbook of game-based learning. Mit Press. https://books.google.com/books?hl=en&lr=&id=_2fKDwAAQBAJ&oi=fnd&pg=PR5&dq=handbook+of+game+based+learning&ots=AhkVTh--H2&sig=XQsvVXONk696N0p95lj6l8IvJdo

Ragsdale, D. J., Lathrop, S. D., & Dodge, R. C. (2003). Enhancing Information Warfare Education Through the Use of Virtual and Isolated Networks. Journal of Information Warfare, 2(3), 47–59.

Schweitzer, D., & Fulton, S. (2010). A Hybrid Approach to Teaching Information Warfare. International Conference on Information Warfare and Security, 299–X. https://www.proquest.com/docview/869617317/abstract/50C47F9FE5441F2PQ/1

Taddeo, M. (2012). Information Warfare: A Philosophical Perspective. Philosophy & Technology, 25(1), 105– 120. https://doi.org/10.1007/s13347-011-0040-9

Tobias, S., Fletcher, J. D., & Wind, A. P. (2014). Game-Based Learning. In Handbook of Research on Educational Communications and Technology (pp. 485–503). https://doi.org/10.1007/978-1-4614-3185-5_38

Williams, P. A. (2010). Information Warfare: Time for a redefinition. https://ro.ecu.edu.au/isw/37/

Yamin, M. M., Katt, B., & Nowostawski, M. (2021). Serious games as a tool to model attack and defense scenarios for cyber-security exercises. Computers & Security, 110, 102450.

Automated Extraction of Structured Data from the Social Network Instagram

Petr Františ, Michal Bureš, Aneta Coufalíková and Ivo Klaban
Department of Informatics and Cyber Operations, Faculty of Military Technology, University of Defence, Brno, The Czech republic

Petr.Frantis@unob.cz
Michal.Bures3@unob.cz
Aneta.Coufalikova@unob.cz
Ivo.Klaban@unob.cz

Abstract: The paper explores the extraction of structured information from the social network Instagram through a suitable application programming interface, namely the unofficial Instagram Private API. It focuses on creating a computer program that identifies which posts a user has tagged as "Likes" and then stores this information for profiling specific user profiles. The introduction of the paper highlights the general use of social media in modern society and the importance of personal data for these platforms. It specifies the aim of the study, which is to extract information from Instagram and then analyse it for user profiling. It then describes the evolution of the social network Instagram and key features such as different types of posts. This paper further focuses on the solution and implementation by using Python programming language to minimize the load on Instagram servers and reduce the risk of detection of automated processes. It describes the process of setting up new Instagram accounts, the obstacles in obtaining login credentials, and the need to simulate human behaviour to bypass the network's defence mechanisms. It then focuses on the actual retrieval of information such as the users followed, their posts and information about which posts the user has marked as favourites. It mentions that extracting data from closed profiles is difficult and elaborates on the technical challenges associated with this task. A significant part of this paper is a discussion of Instagram's defence mechanisms that respond to automated computer programs. It describes access denial, account blocking, and identity verification prompts such as CAPTCHA tests. Finally, the conclusion summarizes the results obtained, which indicate the acquisition of approximately 90,000 records for user profiling. It discusses the shortcomings of a fully automated solution due to Instagram's account creation conditions and defence mechanisms. It mentions the need for further research and highlights key gaps and challenges in this area. Overall, the study highlights the technical and security challenges in extracting information from Instagram and emphasises the need for further research and improvements in the technical procedures for extracting data from the platform.

Keywords: Instagram, Profiling, Instagram Private API, Automation, Osintgram, Python

1. Introduction

Social networking is a prevalent phenomenon in contemporary society that almost every individual utilises (Eurostat, 2021). While some networks are limited to a single country, others serve as transnational platforms, connecting diverse cultures and schools of thought in one place. However, a fundamental aspect of all social networks is that users systematically contribute significant amounts of data every day (Marr, 2018).

Social network users often share highly sensitive information, such as their whereabouts, favourite leisure activities, lists of friends, and other personal details. This information is processed and analysed by each social network, which then uses it to implement new functionalities and to influence the behaviour of its users, either directly or indirectly. Due to its significance as a major market value for social network providers, structured public access to this data is not available.

This paper aims to extract structured data from Instagram, a social network, with a focus on individual user information. Each user generates activity on this network. By assuming that they identify with the content they label as 'Likes', it is possible to create a psychological profile of the individual. This study focuses on developing a computer program that extracts this information from Instagram and makes it available for detailed analysis to profile a specific user.

2. Instagram

The social network was launched in 2010 as a mobile app for the iPhone 4, available in the App Store. In 2012, Instagram released a version for the Android operating system, leading to a rapid increase in its user base. Shortly after its acquisition by Facebook, Inc. (now known as Meta Platforms, Inc.) for approximately 20 billion Czech crowns, Instagram underwent significant changes that greatly influenced its future development (Eldridge, 2024).

This change in ownership between two software-focused companies resulted in significant changes to the approaches and features offered to users. A separate chapter focuses on the application programming interfaces that underpin these approaches. Users are attracted to this social network by key features such as image sharing, post creation and monitoring, and interactive features like comments and likes (Meta, 2024).

Posts are the primary means of communication for each user and are currently divided into five categories: Image, Video, Carousel, IGTV Video, and Sequence (see Table 1).

Table 1: Categories of contributions

Name	Description
Image	Photo most often taken with a mobile phone.
Video	Video most often recorded with a mobile phone
Carousel	Containing images and videos displayed sequentially after a certain time interval
IGTV Video	Longer-form video shot vertically with a mobile phone for up to 60 minutes
Sequence	Fun short video up to 15 seconds in length

One important feature of a post is its ability to link to another user. The owner can tag one or more other users, even if they have no connection to the post. Another way to associate a user with a post is to use the hashtag symbol in the caption or to collaborate with them using a double post. With a double post, you can upload a post to both profiles simultaneously. In an Instagram post, the owner can tag a user with whom they are not friends. Once the post is published, the tagged user will receive a notification of the tag.

In social media, users can write captions for their posts and include hashtags to link them with other posts. Posts may also include location information and allow for comments from other users.

2.1 Stories

For a period of 24 hours, any user has the ability to upload a story, which can be an image, video, or link to another post. These stories can be accessed by clicking on the user's profile picture and are automatically saved to the archive. After the initial 24-hour period, users have the option to keep their stories visible by featuring them as highlighted stories on their profile.

These stories can be shared or forwarded if the author has enabled this option. They can also be marked with a heart symbol to indicate approval of the story. However, this information is not public and is only available to the author of the post. By default, the poster receives notifications from the mobile app when a user marks their story with a heart symbol, indicating sympathy.

2.2 Watchers and Watched

The platform also includes features that allow users to connect directly, but these interactions are tracked and monitored. The followers of a profile are users who have clicked the 'follow' button on a public profile or, for a private profile, those who have been granted permission to follow by the profile owner. Similarly, tracked users are those who have accepted a tracking request on a private profile or have a public profile and have been tracked by the user.

This feature enables additional functionality, such as displaying the followed user's story on the main page after logging in, receiving notifications when the followed user posts, and displaying the post on the main page.

The main source of interaction and connection between users in this work is through watching and tracking. We assume that a user follows those whose activity interests them and directly or indirectly influences their thinking. Social graphs can be used to monitor these interactions and look for links between the set of users under study.

2.3 Direct Messaging

Every social network involves sharing text information between two users. Instagram allows users to send links to posts, stories, and profiles, in addition to text and emojis. Users can also send photos, temporary photos, voice messages, or initiate a call or video call.

Regarding the aim of this paper, this feature is not significant because, for user privacy reasons, only those users directly involved in a conversation can access this information. At present, there is no way to identify which users are messaging each other and which are not.

3. Application Programming Interface

When extracting data from web servers, the standard procedure is to use queries. In this study, we aimed to identify and evaluate the available application programming interfaces (APIs) that could facilitate the data extraction process and enable more efficient system integration. This approach aligns with current trends in software engineering, where system integration plays a crucial role in tool innovation (Jensen et al, 2021).

The aim of our study was to identify user data related to social media interactions, specifically data on posts that users marked as 'Likes'. This information is significant for user profiling, which is important for sociological research and marketing analysis. Our research found that certain APIs provide access to this specific data, which was crucial for our purposes. The following sections present detailed analysis and comparisons of several interfaces that were considered.

3.1 Instagram Graph API

The official application programming interface is exclusively designed for special user accounts designated as business or creative upon request (Meta, 2024). Its main functions include uploading posts, replying to comments, filtering hashtags, and obtaining statistical data on profile status. Processing information about other accounts not owned is not enabled, making this interface unsuitable for achieving the goal of this thesis.

3.2 Instagram Basic Display API

An additional option for acquiring official data is the basic imaging interface (Meta, 2024). This interface can retrieve the same information as the previously mentioned interface but is designed for common profiles that are not marked as business or creative. However, it is limited to retrieving information about the logged-in account and cannot access information about other accounts, making it unsuitable for our purposes.

3.3 Other Official Interfaces

The creators of the social network Instagram provide other public interfaces, such as interfaces for direct messaging, sharing stories or posts, and using links to other web applications (Meta, 2024). However, none of these interfaces met the requirements of our work.

3.4 Osintgram

The tool under analysis is named by combining 'OSINT', an acronym for 'open source intelligence', with a suffix derived from the name of the social network Instagram (Datalux, 2022). It was created by a user with the nickname Datalux on the GitHub platform and is capable of extracting useful information from Instagram using the command line. GitHub is a widely used platform for version control and sharing software projects in the developer community.

The tool's interface allows users to retrieve information about other Instagram users but requires authentication through an existing account. The documentation warns that using the tool may trigger Instagram's security mechanisms, which require authentication to confirm that interactions are by a human and not automated software.

The tool offers various options such as a list of followers, emails, posts, and user stories. However, it does not provide information about users who have tagged a particular post as 'Like'. For our study, this functionality proved to be insufficient.

3.5 Instagram Private API

The interface is once again available on GitHub and is a crucial component of the Osintgram source code. This interface is highly functional and well-documented, making it effective for research and analytics applications (Ping, 2019). However, there is a risk of suspicious activity detection when interacting with Instagram servers, which may result in rejected queries and loss of access to the associated account.

The study primarily chose the Instagram Private API due to its web interface that can be accessed without logging in. The source files are written in Python and use GraphQL, a query language used by Instagram servers. Additionally, the API allows logging in using stored cookies, reducing the likelihood of detection by the server's defence mechanisms. These cookies usually have a validity of two months.

Other benefits of the interface include its ease of use. Once a name and password are entered, the interface authenticates with Instagram's servers, providing access to a variety of features. However, to obtain specific information, such as lists of users who have tagged posts as 'Likes', a universally unique identifier (UUID) must be entered, which is obtained with the login cookies.

However, the interface is unofficial and may be prone to malfunctioning if Instagram's query structure changes. Furthermore, Instagram may flag access through this interface as a security risk due to the use of Android devices. This is because the geographical location of logins can vary, which may indicate the use of different Android devices over time. It is important to note that this risk is particularly high because of the dynamic change of the login configuration file.

4. Solution and Implementation

Python was chosen as the programming language for the presented software solution due to its compatibility with the selected API. The software design aimed to minimize queries to the Instagram server to reduce its load and the risk of detection by its defence mechanisms. This approach included introducing artificial delays between queries, ranging from 20 to 120 seconds. This helped to increase the time required to retrieve data while also reducing the likelihood of detection.

Additionally, emphasis was placed on efficiently processing and storing the large volume of data collected from the server. To avoid automatic detection by Instagram's defence mechanisms, authentic human behaviour was simulated. It was suggested that an alternative and potentially more effective approach could be to include queries mimicking human clicks in the web browser. However, due to the high complexity of defining and replicating average human behaviour, this approach was not implemented in our research.

The study aimed to create a computer program that could identify Instagram posts tagged as 'Likes' based on the user's username. This was accomplished by gathering and analysing data on the monitored users, their posts, and the users who tagged those posts. Then, an analysis was conducted to identify the specific username entered in the input. The methodology and implementation steps of this solution are described in detail in the following sections of the paper.

4.1 Setting up an Instagram Account

To conduct the research, it was necessary to register an account on the social network Instagram. This required providing certain information, including a unique username, password, full name, and either a mobile phone number or email address. As the study focused on the creation of a botnet, the potential for automated generation of this data was investigated. The main challenge was verifying an email address or phone number, which Instagram requires through a six-digit verification code.

The experiment tested disposable internet phone numbers with an accessible SMS mailbox that are freely available online. Although Instagram confirmed sending the verification code, the message was not found in the incoming messages. The evidence indicates that Instagram may need additional verification from the operator to confirm legitimate use of the phone number. It is possible to have up to five user accounts per phone number, according to available sources.

Disposable email boxes were also investigated, but they faced the same problem of unavailability of the authentication code. This phenomenon may be due to the need to verify the email address with the domain owner or an Instagram-owned database of suspicious emails. Current email security trends require two-factor authentication, typically via a phone number. Therefore, the most effective way to set up new Instagram accounts is to use a phone number. In our case, we implemented this option by purchasing a new SIM card.

To retrieve information through a new account, it was crucial to ensure that it was indistinguishable from regular user accounts. Therefore, we developed an identity creation strategy that involved tracking designated profiles and interactions with posts. However, Instagram restricted the activity of our accounts after tracking an average of seven profiles, often temporarily blocking them for a week. This phenomenon highlights the advanced mechanisms used to detect automated behaviour on this platform.

It is worth noting that shortly after setting up our accounts, one of them started monitoring a suspicious account, which suggests the possible existence of a computer program on the other end. The account was flagged as suspicious based on the content and timing of its interactions, providing evidence for the existence of sophisticated automated accounts on this platform.

4.2 Finding the Monitored

The first step of the automated computer program was to identify the users tracked by the target Instagram account. To achieve this, we used the Instagram Private API, which provided usernames and other information in individual server responses. As each response contained a large amount of data, we maximized its use for subsequent profiling and stored it in the SQLite3 database.

The Instagram Private API utilises a sequential data loading mechanism to reduce the amount of data in each request. As a result, a single response can process approximately 100 profiles when retrieving information about tracked users. The following data was stored in the database from these profiles:

- unique user identification number (pk_id),
- username,
- full name,
- information about whether the profile is private or public,
- URL of the profile picture.

Such publicly available data can be collected and processed, but it is important to respect data protection laws and only use it for legitimate purposes. These laws may vary depending on the location.

It should be noted that our automated program was unable to retrieve information such as posts from private accounts. The limited fact prevented the extraction of information regarding the target user's interactions, including the 'Like' label of a post. It is challenging to bypass Instagram's privacy protection mechanisms in the current technological and legal environment, and doing so could potentially violate privacy rights.

Regarding the persistence of stored data, it is important to note that the URL of profile images is temporary. Storing the images themselves in a database may be more efficient but would significantly increase data volume.

4.3 Extracting Data from the Posts

The second step in profiling a specific Instagram user was to gather data from the posts of users followed by the target account. This data was collected using the Instagram Private API, which provided both the necessary data and additional information that was not the primary focus of the study. The database stores specific attributes extracted from the data, such as post type, unique post code, number of comments, number of 'Like' tags, location name, address, city, latitude and longitude, post URL, and caption. Storing the posts themselves in the database was considered, but due to the temporary nature of the URL, it would have significantly increased the data volume.

Due to the large amount of data contained in server responses, they were often divided into multiple parts. When retrieving contribution data, approximately 20 contributions could be processed in a single request. In some cases, submissions did not include complete information, particularly regarding location if the author chose to remove this metadata. In these instances, NULL values were used to replace the missing information in the database. Significant problems with duplicate contributions were noted, particularly when one of the authors was a private user, making it impossible to retrieve additional information. As a result, the number of contributions retrieved was not always consistent with the expected number from the queries.

When copying information from a social network, it is important to consider the frequency of database updates and the rate at which information changes. In this version of the program, the database was not updated continuously due to complications associated with detecting and processing hidden double posts from private users.

4.4 "Likes" Posts

The last step of the profiling process involved gathering data on users who labelled particular Instagram posts as 'Likes'. This information was then filtered and analysed using the methodology outlined in section 4.2. Throughout the study, the Instagram terms of use were updated to permit users to conceal both the number of 'Likes' and the list of users who tagged the post. The change resulted in Instagram displaying only the first 100 users who had tagged the post.

To address this, we applied the user tracking feature in the research tool. If a particular user was being tracked by our profile, they were displayed among the first 100, ensuring that relevant data was captured. The captured information was stored in the database using two keys: the username and the unique post code. The database was efficiently filtered by a specific username, allowing for user profiling and meeting the research objectives. Around 90,000 records were retrieved during the study. Figure 1 illustrates an example of the filter applied to the username 'david'.

	username	code
	david	Filter
1	krajnak_david	Ckth5TzNBkE
2	krajnak_david	CkZSP47Nl4B
3	krajnak_david	CkZQTX0N_N5
4	krajnak_david	CkZPtC4tIEL
5	davidsojka20	B5lYMfjFWap
6	davidberger93	BfRFixUHP0N

Figure 1: Database table contains information about which user has marked a post as 'Like'.

Analytical graphs of the selected person's interests can be automatically generated based on the frequency of keywords (hashtags) used in their posts (see Figure 2).

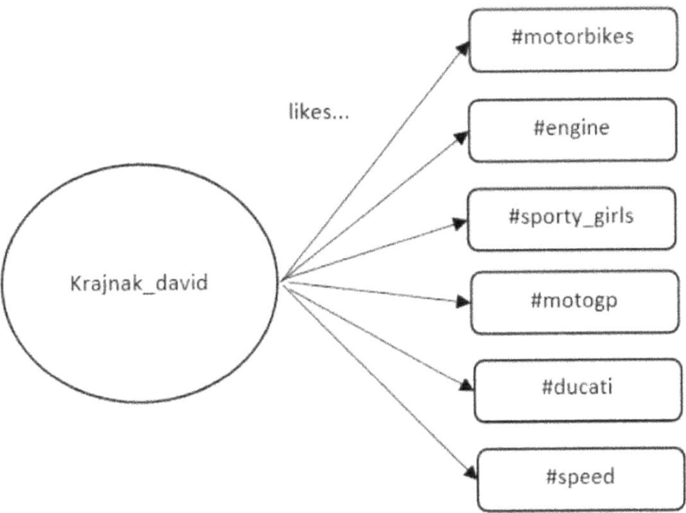

Figure 2: Graph of the selected person's areas of interest

The data from the generated database can be used to perform more sophisticated analyses of individual relationships based on the number of 'like' posts tagged to each other. These relationships can then be displayed in the form of mind maps, either static or interactive with appropriate tools, allowing the user to navigate through the map of individual relationships (see Figure 3) (Gould et al, 1986).

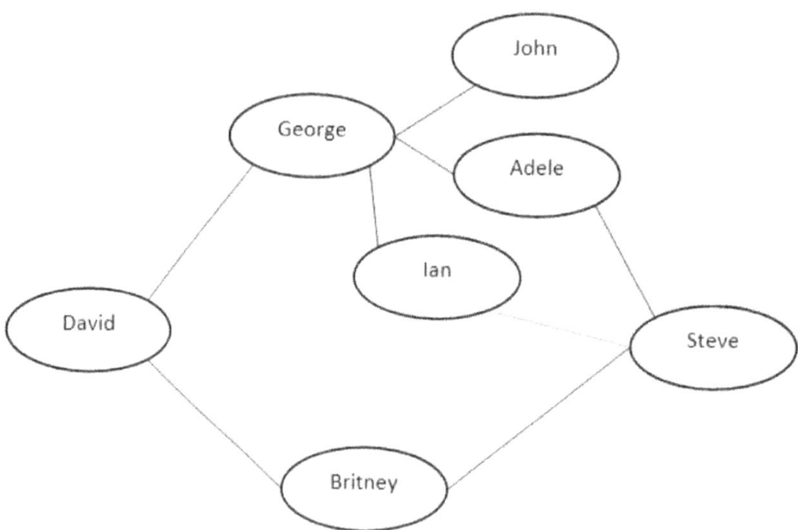

Figure 3: Relationship mind map (anonymised)

5. Instagram's Defence Mechanisms

Similar to other social networks, Instagram has implemented various defence mechanisms to prevent automated computer programs. These mechanisms are intended to safeguard the server from excessive computing power through queries, prevent the publication of inappropriate posts, prevent users from spamming, and prevent other activities that violate the platform's terms of service.

Throughout our research, the computer program we used was frequently rejected and logged out due to suspicious behaviour or excessive server usage. For instance, a server response with code 401 indicated a user logout, while code 429 indicated a need to slow down the frequency of queries. The maximum number of queries allowed varied depending on the rejection history of a particular account, usually around 20 queries. It appears that Instagram monitors and analyses the behaviour of accounts that are considered suspicious and adjusts their access policy accordingly.

To partially solve the issue of repeated rejections, a new login session can be generated, as the timeout limitation seems to be associated with the universal identifier of the session. However, it is important to note that multiple login sessions linked to a single user account may be perceived as an indication of automated behaviour.

One response to the query was the display of a prompt, which is a security measure that requires human confirmation. In this case, a CAPTCHA test was presented, which required the selection of specific images based on a text input. The computer account was blocked multiple times during the data retrieval process due to suspected automated behaviour. To unblock the account, specific requirements must be followed:

- Write the username and specific code on a blank piece of paper.
- Take a photo holding this paper with your face and hand visible.
- Upload this photo to the form and wait for the evaluation.

None of our research profiles had a profile photograph, and we were unable to provide a face or hand for security reasons. Therefore, we were unable to circumvent this process.

6. Conclusion

The study aimed to develop and test a computer program that extracts information from Instagram using the unofficial Instagram Private API. Specifically, the program collected data on posts that users had tagged as 'Likes'. The testing phase successfully stored approximately 90,000 entries in the database.

The collected data provides valuable information for subsequent user profiling, which has potential applications in areas such as marketing, social research, or trend analysis. During the program's development, we identified and analysed various obstacles that limit the possibility of creating a fully automated solution. The obstacles encountered during the project primarily involved challenges related to creating new accounts and Instagram's defence mechanisms for detecting and blocking suspicious activity.

The program was developed with scalability in mind, allowing it to run continuously on multiple computers, resulting in increased efficiency and faster information retrieval. During the development process, we identified and documented certain performance shortcomings in the source code documentation. These deficiencies provide valuable input for further development and improvement of the program, allowing for even greater efficiency and reliability in the future.

This study makes a significant contribution to the field of social network data extraction and offers a useful basis for further research and development in this rapidly developing area. The findings and knowledge gained from this study offer valuable insights for other developers and researchers working on comparable projects in the realm of social media.

References

Datalux (2022) "Osintgram", [online], https://github.com/Datalux/Osintgram#osintgram-

Eldridge, A. (2024) "Instagram social networking service", [online], https://www.britannica.com/topic/Instagram

Eurostat (2021) "ICT use in households and among individuals - 2021: Individuals in EU countries using social networks evolution over time", [online], https://www.czso.cz/documents/10180/142872020/ 062004210705.pdf/4dc708a2-442e-41b8-bd43-e12a7ecc42c4?version=1.1.

Gould, P. and White, R. (1986) *Mental Maps*, 2nd ed., Routledge, London.

Jensen, M. and Patel, H. (2021) "Trends in Software Engineering: System Integration and Its Challenges", *Journal of Advanced Computing*, Vol. 12, No. 3, pp 234-247.

Marr, B. (2018) "How Much Data Do We Create Every Day? The Mind-Blowing Stats Everyone Should Read", [online], https://www.forbes.com/sites/bernardmarr/2018/05/21/how-much-data-do-we-create-every-day-the-mind-blowing-stats-everyone-should-read/

Meta (2024) "Instagram", [online], https://about.meta.com/technologies/instagram/

Meta (2024) "Instagram Platform", [online], https://developers.facebook.com/docs/instagram

Ping (2019) "Instagram Private API", [online], https://github.com/ping/instagram_private_api#instagram-private-api

Cognitive Security in a Changing World: Citizen Perceptions During Finland's NATO Joining Process

Hilkka Grahn[1], Teemu Häkkinen[1] and Toni Taipalus[1,2]
[1]University of Jyväskylä, Finland
[2]Tampere University, Finland

hilkka.grahn@jyu.fi
teemu.hakkinen@jyu.fi
toni.taipalus@jyu.fi

Abstract: Contemporary conflicts are multifaceted and no longer fit the traditional war-and-peace dichotomy due to digital dimensions and the role of the human mind. The concept of warfare has transformed significantly: it's no longer solely reliant on physical capabilities but increasingly fought within digital environments and individuals' minds. These persistent, intertwined crises and psychological information influence present challenges to cognitive security. Psychological influence shapes opinions, attitudes, emotions, behaviors, and decision-making in individuals, groups, and societies using various methods, often involving digital tools to manipulate cognitive processes. It aims to shape the human mind, going beyond altering information to influence how the human brain processes received information. To safeguard human cognition, cognitive security is crucial. It involves the capability to detect, recognize, control, and counter negative psychological information influence aimed at an individual. Cognitive security plays a critical role in enabling individuals and society to recognize, understand, and manage a wide range of threats and risks. The rapidly changing world, driven by technology, politics, and the environment, poses new challenges for citizens' cognitive security. As warfare evolves, individuals struggle to understand the complex threats, including cyber and information influence. Hence, this study aims to ascertain whether individuals' feeling of security has changed and if they are perceiving psychological information influence. The study investigates the sense of security among Finnish people using survey data collected during two significant time periods: after Finland announced its intention to join NATO (N = 1080) and after it officially became a NATO member (N = 1047). Additionally, whether an increase in hostile online influence and disruptions in the cyber environment was noticed by Finnish people during these same time frames is being investigated. The results indicate a statistically significant decrease in the feeling of security and a significant increase in the awareness of hostile influences. This implies that these phenomena warrant further investigation to gain a better understanding of citizens' cognitive security status and to explore ways to improve it.

Keywords: Cognitive Security, Cognitive Warfare, Cognitive Dimension, Psychological Information Influence, Feeling Of Security, Trust

1. Introduction

Traditionally, war has been viewed as dichotomous – either there is war or there is peace. However, contemporary conflicts are complex and diverse, no longer adhering to traditional models of warfare. For example, in Russian military thinking, the premise is that the boundary between war and peace can be easily blurred in the digital dimension without formally crossing the border (Giles, 2016). The perception of war has thus undergone a significant change: combat no longer relies solely on physical capabilities, but battles are increasingly fought in digital environments and within people's minds (Robinson, Jones and Janicke, 2015; NATO, 2016; Lehto, 2018; Kania, 2019; Claverie and Cluzel, 2022; Danyk and Briggs, 2023). The primary and crucial battleground for the new generation of warfare is identified as the cognitive dimension, that is, the human mind (Bērziņš, 2019; Tashev, Purcell and McLaughlin, 2019). We have thus moved from the traditional dichotomy to an era of gray instability (e.g., Morris et al., 2019, p. 8): we can no longer unequivocally say whether it is war or peace.

A crucial aspect within the cognitive dimension is psychological information influence. This influence involves employing strategies and actions aimed designed to shape the attitudes, emotions, opinions, actions, and decision-making of individuals, groups, and societies using various methods (e.g., Starbird, Arif and Wilson, 2019; Tashev, Purcell and McLaughlin, 2019). Influence often involves the use of digital tools to shape human cognitive processes (Claverie and Cluzel, 2022). The target of psychological information influence is thus the human mind. Such actions go beyond mere information manipulation – psychological information influence seeks to impact how the human brain processes the received information (Claverie and Cluzel, 2022).

One of the fundamental human needs is security (Maslow, 1943), and a crucial aspect of this is cognitive security, closely related to the previously mentioned psychological information influence. Cognitive security plays a critical role in enabling individuals and society to recognize, understand, and manage a wide range of threats and risks. As described by Grahn and Taipalus (2023), cognitive security encompasses a state and process wherein undesired malign influence or manipulation is incapable of altering human cognition. This alteration of human cognition includes aspects such as opinion formation and decision-making. Cognitive security holds immense significance in today's landscape, given that Large Language Models (e.g., ChatGPT) and social media platforms enable the rapid and widespread creation and dissemination of disinformation with unprecedented ease and speed. For instance, according to Evans (2022), Russia used TikTok to spread disinformation regarding the Ukrainian war. Also, different newspapers and magazines have reported Russia's disinformation campaigns in TikTok (e.g., Brown, 2022; Paul, 2022). The Russian invasion of Ukraine in 2022 has even been characterized as "the world's first TikTok war" (Chayka, 2022). Actually, in the World Economic Forum's Global Risk Report (2024), misinformation and disinformation were identified as the most severe global risks over the next two years, exacerbating societal and political divides. Goldstein et al. (2023) predicted that language models are likely becoming more usable, reliable, and efficient, thereby providing distinct advantages to propagandists. This evolution is expected to introduce new tactics of influence, making campaign messaging more tailored and potentially more effective. Additionally, the rapidly changing world also poses new challenges to citizens' cognitive security. Technological, political, and environmental factors increasingly impact people's daily lives. Due to these factors and the evolving nature of warfare, individuals find it increasingly difficult to comprehend the complex threats of the modern world, including the potential for hostile cyber and information influence.

In Finland, a neighboring country of Russia, the information landscape has changed since the onset of the Ukrainian war and the decision to join NATO. Consequently, it becomes imperative to delve deeper into Finland's information landscape and explore citizens' perceptions of malign influence and their sense of security. In line with this perspective, we have formulated the following research questions:

1. To what extent do Finnish individuals perceive malign influence?
2. How do Finnish individuals assess their overall level of safety?
3. To what extent has the decision to join NATO influenced the way Finnish individuals perceive malign influence and evaluate their overall sense of safety?

To investigate these aspects, we utilized openly available datasets compiled by Statistics Finland and the Prime Minister's Office for the years 2022 and 2023. These datasets include inquiries related to the perception of malign influence, internet service disruptions, as well as the sense of security and trust, and provide a representative view on the topic.

2. Materials and Method

2.1 Data

The openly available datasets used in this study were derived from Statistics Finland and the Prime Minister's Office's Citizens' Pulse (2022, 2023) surveys conducted in the years 2022 and 2023. Data for the year 2022 was collected in June, while data for the year 2023 was collected in August. These datasets were chosen because, in May 2022, Finland announced its interest in joining NATO, and by April 2023, Finland had become a NATO member. Although there is a couple of months' delay in 2023 between the country's NATO membership and the data collection, no earlier dataset was accessible for analysis.

According to the description of the datasets (Statistics Finland & the Prime Minister's Office, 2022; 2023), both datasets' samples were composed of individuals aged 15 to 74 living in mainland Finland. Invitations to participate in the study, along with a personal direct link to a Webropol survey, were sent to respondents via text message. The text message also included a link to the Statistics Finland data collection webpage, where participants were informed about aspects such as data protection. The data collection page contained a link to the privacy notice. The surveys were web-based, self-administered structured questionnaires containing 58 Likert-style questions in the year 2022 and 57 questions in the year 2023. Both samples are considered representative of the Finnish citizen population.

2.2 Analysis

To analyze the possible change in perceptions among the Finnish people, we employed IBM SPSS Statistic 29.0.1.1. A Mann-Whitney U test, a rank-based nonparametric test, was chosen for assessing differences between two groups on ordinal dependent variables. In this context, the tested dependent variables were ordinal, and the independence of observations justified the use of the selected test. The distributions of scores for both years 2022 and 2023 were similar in all Mann-Whitney U tests assessed by visual inspection, unless otherwise reported. A significance level (alpha) of 0.05 was applied in all statistical tests.

3. Results

3.1 Descriptive Statistics

The dataset for the year 2022 consisted of 1080 participants, including 510 males, 564 females, and 6 individuals who did not specify their gender. The distribution of ages is visually depicted in Figure 1, showcasing representation across different age categories. The mean age falls within the 45–49 years old category.

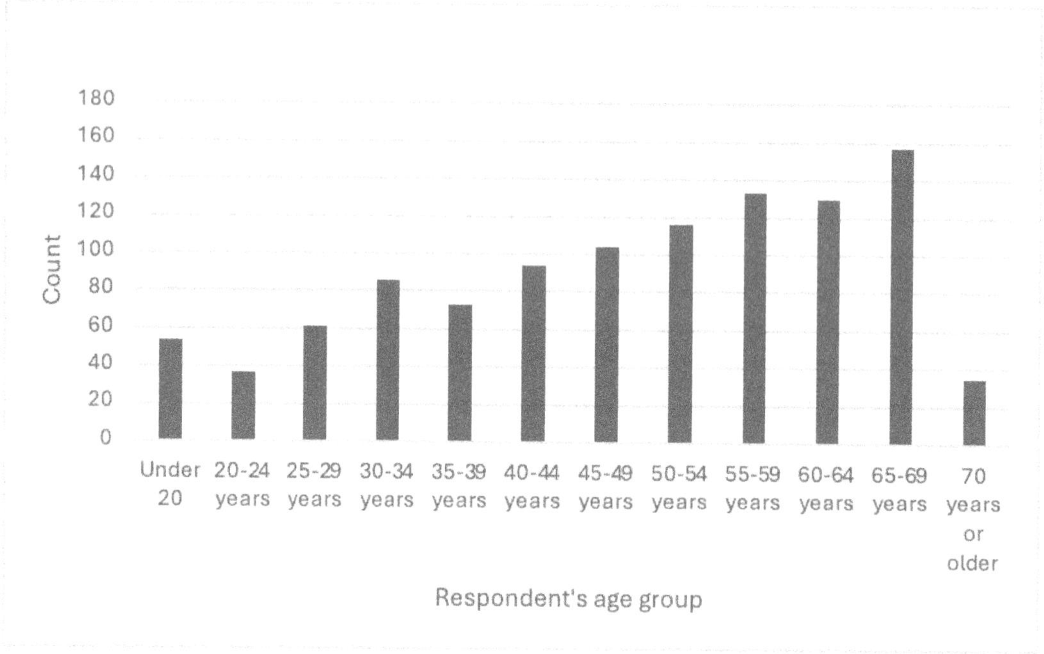

Figure 1: Age distributions in the 2022 data set

The sample size (N) for the 2023 dataset was 1047, comprising 475 males, 564 females, and 8 participants who did not specify their gender. The mean age category in this dataset was 45–49 years old, as illustrated in Figure 2, which displays the distribution across different age categories.

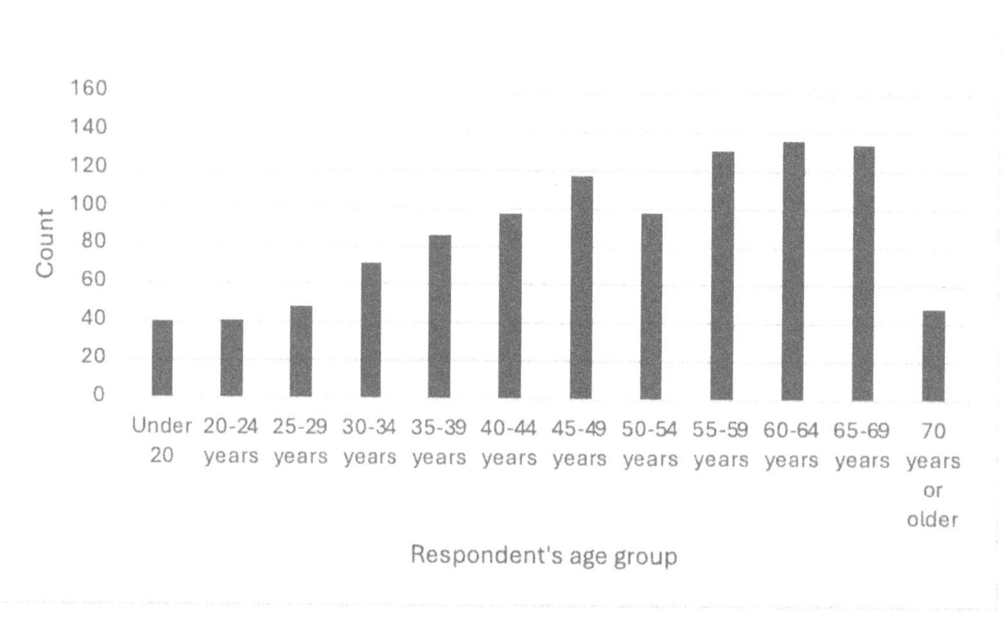

Figure 2: Age distributions in the 2023 data set

3.2 Influence Attempts and Internet Malfunctions

The survey question indicating influence attempts was "Have you observed any of the following first-hand in the past month: Attempts to influence others by spreading deliberately misleading information on the internet or social media?" (1 being none and 5 being very much). In the year 2022 (N = 977), the mean was 2.44, standard deviation 1.13, and median 2.00. In 2023 (N = 903,) these values were mean 2.79, standard deviation 1.22, and median 3.00. As justified earlier, A Mann-Whitney U test was run to determine if there were differences in observations of attempts to spread misleading information on the internet between years 2022 and 2023. A statistically significant difference was observed between the years 2022 and 2023 (U = 6.318, $p < .001$), with the year 2023 indicating more observations of misleading information.

The survey question indicating internet malfunctions was "Have you observed any of the following first-hand in the past month: Malfunctions in internet services or issues related to personal data security?" (1 being none and 5 being very much). In the year 2022 (N = 1006), the mean was 1.85, standard deviation 0.89, and median 2.00. In 2023 (N = 959) these values were mean 1.98, standard deviation 0.92, and median 2.00. Similarly, the difference between years 2022 and 2023 the observed malfunctions of internet services and personal data security was tested. A statistically significant difference was observed between the years 2022 and 2023 (U = 3.173, $p = .002$), with the year 2023 indicating more observations of internet malfunctions.

3.3 Feeling of Safety

The survey question indicating feeling of safety was "To what extent do you agree or disagree with the following statement? I feel that my life is safe" (1 being totally disagree and 5 = totally agree). In the year 2022 (N = 1073), the mean was 4.12, standard deviation 0.77, and median 4.00. In 2023 (N = 1043,) these values were mean 4.02, standard deviation 0.79, and median 4.00. According to the Mann-Whitney, there were also differences in feeling of being safe between years 2022 and 2023 A statistically significant difference was observed in the feeling of being safe between the years 2022 and 2023 (U = -3.465, $p < .001$), with the year 2022 indicating higher sense of safety.

Another question related to safety was associated with NATO. In year 2022, the survey inquired, "Finland has applied to become a member state of the military alliance NATO. How has this impacted your sense of safety when compared to the time period prior to Finland's application?". In the year 2023, after joining NATO, the question was modified to "Does Finland's NATO membership affect your sense of security?". Here, 1 indicated weakening, and 5 indicated strengthening. In the year 2022 (N = 1038), the mean was 3.66, standard deviation 0.94, and median 4.00. In 2023 (N = 1011,) these values were mean 4.08, standard deviation 0.90, and median 4.00. Again, there was a statistically significant difference between the years in the feeling of security (U = 10.996, $p < .001$), but now indicating an improvement in the sense of safety among Finnish people in year 2023.

3.4 Trust in Finnish Defense Forces

Trust in the Finnish Defense Forces was also assessed in the survey with a question "How much do you personally trust the following institutions? Finnish Defense Force", with a scale of 1 indicating zero trust and 10 indicating full trust. In the year 2022 (N = 1043), the mean was 8.58, standard deviation 1.31, and median 9.00. In 2023 (N = 1013,) these values were mean 8.53, standard deviation 1.40, and median 9.00. In this case, there was no significant difference between the years 2022 and 2023 ($p = .772$); the level of trust remained consistent.

4. Discussion

In this study, our objective was to examine potential changes in the perceptions of Finnish individuals regarding malign influence, internet malfunctions, sense of security, and trust in the defense forces following Finland's NATO membership, as compared to the period approximately a year before when Finland expressed its intention to join NATO. To achieve this, we conducted a comparative analysis of two survey datasets collected in the specified years.

The findings suggest that following Finland's NATO membership, Finnish individuals have observed an increase in attempts to exert malign influence through the deliberate dissemination of misleading information on the internet or social media compared to the preceding year. Additionally, Finnish citizens have observed more internet service malfunctions and concerns related to personal data security after Finland joined NATO, surpassing the levels observed in the year prior to the alliance. However, these observations were still at a relatively low level on a scale from 1 to 5. The observed increase in Finnish individuals' awareness of malign influence, particularly in the form of misleading information on digital platforms, aligns with the evolving landscape of information warfare (e.g., Giles, 2016). Simultaneously, as Finnish individuals have noted an increase in malign influence and internet malfunctions, their overall sense of security has diminished over the course of the year. This sentiment was measured simply with the questionnaire item "I feel my life is safe." The simultaneous decrease in the overall sense of security among Finnish individuals in response to heightened malign influence and internet malfunctions introduces a complex dynamic. This suggests that while advances in digital communication bring about conveniences, they also introduce vulnerabilities that impact individuals' perceptions of safety.

In 2022, prior to joining NATO, respondents were asked about the potential impact of NATO membership on the sense of security among the Finnish people. Subsequently, after joining, they were questioned about whether NATO membership affected their personal sense of security. Interestingly, an increase in the feeling of security was observed. This is in contrast to the initial observation when the question was phrased simply as "I feel my life is safe." Notably, the introduction of NATO into the question appeared to positively influence the sense of security among Finnish respondents. The dynamic relationship between the introduction of NATO into the questionnaire and the heightened sense of security raises questions about the psychological influence of collective security agreements on individuals' perceptions. Exploring this phenomenon deeper could shed light on the intricate connections between geopolitical affiliations and citizens' sense of safety.

As noted in the literature, the Russian military perspective emphasizes the blurring of boundaries between war and peace in the digital dimension (Giles, 2016), a notion that resonates with our findings of increased attempts at malign influence and internet malfunctions following Finland's NATO membership. However, it should be noted that these are perceptions among the Finnish people, and there is no knowledge of the actor behind the observed malign influence and internet malfunction. Nevertheless, this shift challenges the conventional understanding of warfare, extending it beyond physical capabilities to include battles fought in digital environments and within the cognitive realm (Robinson, Jones and Janicke, 2015; NATO, 2016; Lehto, 2018; Kania, 2019; Claverie and Cluzel, 2022; Danyk and Briggs, 2023). The results also support the idea that the cognitive dimension, the human mind, is another battleground in this new era of warfare (Bērziņš, 2019; Tashev, Purcell and McLaughlin, 2019). The observed changes in Finnish individuals' perceptions of malign influence, alterations in their sense of security, and the paradoxical influence of NATO membership on their feelings of safety reflect the profound impact of geopolitical events on the cognitive landscape.

Furthermore, we sought to explore whether joining NATO or recent global events has affected the level of trust in the Finnish defense forces. According to the questionnaire results, the trust level has remained consistent regardless of world events or NATO membership. It's noteworthy that the trust level is notably high, with a median score of 9 on a scale ranging from 1 to 10. While influence operations have been identified as potential factors eroding trust (e.g., Goldstein et al., 2023), it appears that, at least in this instance, the observed malign influence has not impacted this particular trust metric. This aligns well with the broader Finnish cultural context, where trust in institutions has historically been robust (Simonen et al., 2022).

Overall, malign influence, internet malfunctions, the overall feeling of security, and trust in various institutions collectively form essential components of the aforementioned cognitive security. While these individual questions analyzed here offer a valuable starting point for examination, it is important to recognize that these isolated inquiries may not fully encompass the complexity of the entire phenomenon.

4.1 Limitations and Further Research

This study comes with limitations which should be considered when interpreting the obtained results. While efforts were made to capture the period encompassing Finland's decision to join NATO in May 2022 and its subsequent NATO membership in April 2023, there exists a time gap of a couple of months between the official NATO accession and the data collection in 2023. This limitation implies that the immediate aftermath of Finland's NATO membership might not be fully represented in the collected data. Another limitation arises from the modification of the survey question between 2022 and 2023, transitioning from an inquiry about the impact of Finland's application to become a NATO member to a question specifically addressing the effect of Finland's NATO membership on the sense of security. While this modification was essential for capturing evolving perceptions, it introduces a challenge in directly comparing the responses between the two years. The nuanced wording differences may influence participant interpretations and responses, potentially impacting the coherence of the comparative analysis. Also, while the statistical tests revealed significant differences among the variables, it's crucial to note that these differences, though statistically significant, were of a small magnitude. Nevertheless, it is noteworthy that the robustness of our findings is supported by a substantial sample size in the surveys. While a larger sample size can enhance the reliability of findings, it is important to interpret results with caution and consider both statistical and practical significance. Finally, to delve deeper into this issue and gain a comprehensive understanding of cognitive security, a more nuanced and holistic approach is essential. Moving beyond the analysis of individual components, a thorough investigation should explore the intricate interconnections and interdependencies among these aspects. The use of a validated quantitative measurement instrument would facilitate a more precise and insightful exploration of the broader cognitive security landscape, unveiling its dynamic interplay with various factors.

5. Conclusions

The evolving landscape of contemporary conflicts, as discussed by Giles (2016), challenges the traditional dichotomy of war and peace. With the integration of digital dimensions and the significance of the human mind, warfare has undergone a profound transformation. No longer confined to physical capabilities, conflicts are increasingly waged in digital environments and within the cognitive realm of individuals' minds (Bērziņ š, 2019; Tashev et al., 2019). Within the cognitive dimension, psychological information influence plays a role and is linked to cognitive security. As described by Grahn and Taipalus (2023), cognitive security encompasses a state and process wherein undesired malign influence or manipulation is incapable of altering human cognition. This alteration of human cognition includes aspects such as opinion formation and decision-making. The findings of the study underscore the impact of Finland's NATO membership on the cognitive security landscape. The observed increase in attempts to exert malign influence and the rise in internet malfunctions and personal data security concerns among Finnish citizens after joining NATO indicate the complex interplay between geopolitical events and cognitive security. Simultaneously, the study reveals a nuanced dynamic, as the introduction of NATO into the questionnaire positively influences the sense of security among respondents. In essence, the results contribute to the broader understanding of how contemporary conflicts are reshaping the cognitive dimension of warfare, emphasizing the need for nuanced approaches to security in an era characterized by gray instability. The study also suggests that due to the broad and intricate nature of cognitive security, a more comprehensive metrics to measure it is needed.

Acknowledgments

This work was partly funded by the Finland's Ministry of Education and Culture (OKM/93/523/2022).

References

Bērziņš, J. (2019) 'Not "Hybrid" but New Generation Warfare', in G.E. Howard and M. Czekaj (eds) *Russia's Military Strategy and Doctrine*. Washington, DC: The Jamestown Foundation, pp. 157–185.

Brown, A. (2022) *Kremlin's RIA Novosti continues posting TikTok propaganda despite platform's Russia 'Ban', Forbes*.

Chayka, K. (2022) *Watching the World's "First TikTok War", The New Yorker*.

Claverie, B. and Cluzel, F. du (2022) *The Cognitive Warfare Concept, INNOVATION HUB (Cognitive Warfare Project - Reference Documents)*.

Danyk, Y. and Briggs, C.M. (2023) 'Modern cognitive operations and hybrid warfare.', *Journal of Strategic Security*, 16(1), pp. 35–50.

Evans, J. (2022) 'War in the age of TikTok', *Russian Analytical Digest (RAD)*, 280, pp. 17–19. Available at: https://doi.org/https://doi.org/10.3929/ethz-b-000538061.

Giles, K. (2016) 'The Next Phase of Russian Information Warfare', *NATO Strategic Communications Centre of Excellence*, 20.

Goldstein, J.A., Sastry, G., Musser, M., DiResta, R., Gentzel, M. and Sedova, K. (2023) 'Generative Language Models and Automated Influence Operations: Emerging Threats and Potential Mitigations'. *arXiv preprint arXiv:2301.04246*.

Grahn, H. and Taipalus, T. (2023) 'Towards defining comprehensive cognitive security: Literature review and concept analysis'. Manuscript submitted for publication.

Kania, E.B. (2019) 'Minds at war', *PRISM*, 8(3), pp. 82–101.

Lehto, M. (2018) 'The modern strategies in the cyber warfare', in *Intelligent Systems, Control and Automation: Science and Engineering*. Available at: https://doi.org/10.1007/978-3-319-75307-2_1.

Maslow, A.H. (1943) 'A theory of human motivation', *Psychological Review*, 50(4), pp. 370–396.

Morris, L.J., Mazaar, M.J., Hornung, J.W., Pezard, S., Binnendijk, A. and Kepe, M. (2019) *Gaining Competitive Advantage in the Gray Zone, RAND Corporation*.

NATO (2016) *Warsaw Summit Communiqué*. Available at: https://www.nato.int/cps/en/natohq/official_texts_133169.htm.

Paul, K. (2022) *'Game of Whac-a-Mole': why Russian disinformation is still running amok on social media, The Guardian*.

Robinson, M., Jones, K. and Janicke, H. (2015) 'Cyber warfare: Issues and challenges', *Computers and Security*, 49, pp. 70–94. Available at: https://doi.org/10.1016/j.cose.2014.11.007.

Simonen, J., Westinen, J., Pitkänen, V. and Heikkilä, A. (2022) *Luottamusta ilmassa, mutta kuinka paljon? Tutkimus eri sukupolvien luottamuksesta yhteiskunnan instittutioihin*.

Starbird, K., Arif, A. and Wilson, T. (2019) 'Disinformation as collaborative work: Surfacing the participatory nature of strategic information operations', *Proceedings of the ACM on Human-Computer Interaction*, 3(CSCW). Available at: https://doi.org/10.1145/3359229.

Statistics Finland & Prime Minister's Office: Citizens' Pulse 6/2023 [dataset]. Version 1.0 (2023-09-15). *Finnish Social Science Data Archive* [distributor]. http://urn.fi/urn:nbn:fi:fsd:T-FSD3808

Statistics Finland & Prime Minister's Office: Citizens' Pulse 6/2022 [dataset]. Version 1.0 (2022-08-04). *Finnish Social Science Data Archive* [distributor]. http://urn.fi/urn:nbn:fi:fsd:T-FSD3683

Tashev, B., Purcell, M. and McLaughlin, B. (2019) 'Russia's Information Warfare: Exploring the Cognitive Dimension', *MCU Journal*, 10(2). Available at: https://doi.org/10.21140/mcuj.2019100208.

World Economic Forum. (2024) *'Global Risks Report 2024'*, https://www.weforum.org/publications/global-risks-report-2024/

Social Media in the Aftermath of the 2016 US Presidential Election: Disruption at the Cost of Connection

Rosanna E. Guadagno[1], Alberto F. Olivieri[1] and Amanda M. Kimbrough[2]
[1]OASIS, Faculty of ITEE, University of Oulu, Oulu, Finland
[2]Instagram, Dallas, TX, USA

Rosanna.Guadagno@oulu.fi
Alberto.Olivieri@oulu.fi
Amkalbright@gmail.com

Abstract: This data captures people's experiences as unknowing targets of disinformation. Participants were US citizens naive to the actions of the different entities using social media to target Americans with disinformation in the months leading up to the 2016 US presidential election. Results indicated participants reported notable changes in their interactions on social media in the form of disruptions to existing relationships. Specifically, participants reported that they argued with their connections more, observed others disagree more, and reported an increase in the loss of friends and family connections through the unfriending or unfollowing features of social media. While, some participants found these changes amusing, most reported increased psychological distress. Not one participant mentioned Russian election interference or disinformation as the cause of these interpersonal difficulties. Analysis of text responses did not include any mention of disinformation, Cambridge Analytica, or Russia as causes of these disruptions. These results suggest that social media use has implications for individuals' social relationships and these disruptions may impact their psychological functioning. Implications of these results for the psychological impacts of social media use will be discussed.

Keywords: Social Media, Cognitive Warfare, Disinformation, Interpersonal Relationships, Facebook, Information Operations

1. Introduction

Over the past decade, people and organizations have shown a marked change in the way they consume news and information and communicate with one another. With the advent and adoption of social media and other forms of Internet Communication Technologies (ICTs), their use for communication and information consumption purposes has become increasingly common among people and organizations. Social media was initially intended to facilitate existing relationships and help people find new friends, employment opportunities, and groups of people with similar interests. However, as this technology evolved, it slowly became a vehicle to spread fake news and disinformation through targeted advertising and other mechanisms (Guadagno & Guttieri, 2021). While the past decade has generated much research to understand the effects of Cognitive Warfare and how to combat it, little research has examined whether individuals using social media noticed the way that their communications with others changed. To illustrate this, the present study presents data collected from US Facebook users five months after the conclusion of the divisive 2016 US presidential election. This was before it was widely known that multiple forces such as the Russian GRU, and the Russian Internet Agency, were using social media to sow disinformation, chaos, and discord.

1.1 Information Warfare and IC

The change in the information ecosystem has revolutionized many aspects of modern life. The affordances of features of this technology – particularly the ease of sharing information from one to many and the rapid spread of viral content – have created an environment rife with misinformation. This environment is ripe for bad actors to implement inexpensive but widespread influence or information operations (IO). This is also known as Information Warfare (IW) or Black/Grey Propaganda. Information warfare is the deliberate dissemination of disinformation by an individual, group, or state actor. Disinformation is classified as false or misleading information disseminated with the intent to affect the psychological functioning of an adversary by sowing chaos, disrupting interpersonal relationships, and influencing the emotions, beliefs, motivations, and behaviors of its targets. IW is also considered a "class of communication", separate from other forms of communication such as persuasion, because of its purpose. While persuasion attempts to balance the needs of the persuader and the persuadee, propaganda is designed to promote "the desired intent of the propagandist" through a "deliberate, systematic attempt to shape perceptions, manipulate cognitions, and guide behavior" (Jowett & O'donnell, 2018). While IW has existed since the dawn of human civilization, the recent technological developments in internet communications technology (ICT) have created significantly more opportunities for people to use this means of warfare at a much larger scale.

1.2 Facebook and Personal Relationships

Humans have a fundamental need to belong; to affiliate with others and be a part of a group (Baumeister & Leary, 2017; Brewer, 1991). This is one of the many reasons why people find social media so engrossing – it is a convenient and easy way for people to connect with others from the comfort of their own home. Social media platforms have heightened people's capacity to communicate, share data, discover, and collaborate with strangers and friends that live all over the world. These capacities have drastically improved, and changed, how we perceive and connect with society and people, at a scale never thought of before (Akram & Kumar, 2017). The single most well-known capability of social media is the ability to keep in contact with connections or create new ones, regardless of location, time, and physical constraints of the people involved. Even if its implications, drawbacks, and potential are still not fully understood by most of the public, especially the privacy risks involved in having an online persona (Eijkman & Weggemans, 2012). The ability to communicate easily and quickly through messaging, video, and voice calls, for most outweighs the real or perceived risks involved in this sort of online activities.

Another inherent attribute of social media is sharing. This capacity involves broader topics in fields like education, health, news, and critical message sharing during catastrophic events (Abbasi et al., 2012). This feature is also extremely important for interpersonal relationships, as the sharing of experiences, thoughts, and feelings with friends and family can act as a bonding agent that strengthens the group ties. A feature that partially overlaps with sharing is collaboration. Collaborative efforts through data sharing, or other networking endeavors abound in both the private and the public sectors, and in the private and public sphere (Abbasi et al., 2012). Social media platforms make the process of networking trivial, improving also the scale, reach, and speed of such processes. In the private sphere, individuals can benefit from all these new capabilities provided by technology. Moreover, new ties between family and friends could be created through these collaborative efforts, along with a new, or renewed, sense of belonging and community.

The last feature that will be discussed here is discovery. From hobbyists to protestors, passing through concerned parents and groups of interest, the ability to find and connect with other individuals or groups sharing similar interests or goals is invaluable (Abbasi et al., 2012). This ability lends itself as being a prime tool for community building, and it helps create a deep sense of connection and belonging.

All the features we presented have in common one more advantage, all the social networks are a continually live service. This creates a permanent stream of information going through groups, people, and platforms (cross-platform content sharing and diffusion is a common occurrence, regardless of whether the social network has a built-in function for that purpose), that allows users to see and keep track of what others are doing.

Furthermore, this connectedness was initially seen as a laudable improvement for keeping in touch with friends and family. The ability of social media to connect people to a wider selection of news, knowledge, and ideas, was positively received in various academic circles. Digital media were seen as an innovation with characteristics that could be useful to contrast propaganda tactics (McQuail, 2010). However, by networking people in this manner, social media also opened them up to campaigns of mass persuasion. The constant stream of information can cause information overload making people uniquely susceptible to heuristic-based persuasion (Guadagno, 2021; Guadagno et al., 2013). The positive effects of having so many options are greatly reduced by people`s tendency to attend to information consistent with pre-existing beliefs, and the end result is the creation of online eco-chambers (Quattrociocchi et al., 2016).

While there are many positive aspects to social media use, the current investigation focuses on using social media for mass persuasion. However, it urges a more nuanced approach that would like to underline the unanticipated issues that this technology in particular has brought to us. Generally speaking, progress, can be a challenging process that forces us to renegotiate previously held social norms and belief systems. Overall, social media is a powerful tool that allows us to build and maintain relationships that otherwise would have never come to fruition, with a reduced risk of deteriorating them because of time or distance. However, moderation is fundamental while approaching those platforms, and the risks inherent to our electronic lives should be better understood by the user base.

1.3 Russian Disinformation and the 2016 US Presidential Election

The Russian Internet Research Agency (RU-IRA) was an organization in which employees attempted to manipulate and create conflict in online communities, also known as a "Troll Farm". It was established by the former leader of Wagner Private Military Company and oligarch, Yevgeny Prigozhin. While in activity, played a significant role in two of the major IO uncovered in recent American history. Alongside the recently formed IRA, another entity was involved in those IO. The Main Directorate of the General Staff of the Armed Forces of the Russian Federation, formerly known as the Main Intelligence Directorate (GRU) in Russian Гла́вное Разве́дывательное Управле́ние (ГРУ), the foreign intelligence service of the Russian Federation, direct successor of the same agency during Soviet time. The GRU was the main actor in the cyber-attack on the Democratic National Committee, that resulted in a precise and controlled leak of email data related to the Clinton Presidential campaign team, on the well-known WikiLeaks platform (DiResta et al., 2019). The US Department of Justice investigated the cyberattacks and concluded that two units of the GRU where involved, Unit 26165 stole the material using spearphishing (targeted phishing emails) to get an initial foothold, and then applied network traversal techniques to compromise more machines on the Democratic network. After the data exfiltration, Unit 74455 assisted Unit 26165 in the release of the material, through a sympathetic WikiLeaks (Special Counsel's Office, 2019).

The IRA influence during the 2016 US presidential campaign (DiResta et al., 2019; Linvill et al., 2019), and the peak of the #BlackLivesMatter social movement (Stewart et al., 2018) was profound. Though challenging to quantify, it effectively sowed discord and exploited the deep ideological and societal divisions of the American public.

The researchers who studied the social scene on Twitter during the BLM protests, identified the existence of two, completely separated communities, divided along political lines (left and right). Embedded in both of these communities, the most influential and controversial accounts were linked to this state-sponsored foreign actor. The IRA used employees with fake accounts – trolls, to pose as US citizens, and generated artificial interactions through the use of bots (Stewart et al., 2018). The themes that these accounts were most interested revolved around violence and shootings, and the intent of destabilization through the exploitation of the deep divisions still present in the US social tissue is evident (Guadagno, 2021). This tactic is well known since the soviet times, as reported by Ladislav Bittman (Bittman, 1985), a former chief of the Czechoslovakian Intelligence Service Disinformation Department, and discussed in military circles since the cold war (Kux, 1985).

The same tactic of seeding dissent and division was used during the 2016 election, where the IRA conducted a sophisticated and multi-platform campaign infiltrating unwitting US citizens' discussions and interactions. In this IO, as in the previous BLM operation, the IRA infiltrated both sides of the political aisle. However, unlike in the BLM operation, the agency took a more biased approach in the operation in favor of Donald Trump. The trolls worked both to reinforce Trump's messaging and to undermine the legitimacy of Hillary Clinton as a candidate for the presidency. The U.S. House Intelligence Committee uncovered a staggering amount of data attributed solely to the IRA's activities targeting US citizens (DiResta et al., 2019). Recently the government of the United Kingdom also released a memorandum regarding interference in the 2019 elections by Center 18 of Russia's Federal Security Service, within an ongoing effort from at least 2015 till now. The UK faced spearfishing attacks, a compromise of a research institute that was leading initiatives against disinformation, and targeted leaks of the obtained information. The targets where universities, journalists, public sector, NGOs and other Civil Society organizations (National Cyber Security Centre, 2023). This new information seems to reinforce the idea of a well-developed and tested formula for conducting offensive IO from Russia, to influence and destabilize Western democracies.

The data collected for the US House Intelligence Committee regarding the 2016 US election, along with data coming from other IO of the IRA, spanning from 2014 to 2017 was thoroughly analyzed, and confirmed the presence of "a sweeping and sustained social influence operation consisting of various coordinated disinformation tactics aimed directly at US citizens, designed to exert political influence and exacerbate social divisions in US culture" (DiResta et al., 2019). In the months leading up to the 2016 US Presidential election in November 2016, The American voters were unaware of these various attempts to influence them through their social media. The gravity of the situation assessed by various agencies initially was not understood by the U.S. administration initially, and its first answer was slow and weak (Lipton et al., 2016; Sanger, 2016). This initial indecisiveness by the administration was intertwined with a general mistrust by the public of the reports regarding the Russian IO that took years to overcome (Gilberstadt, 2019), with half of the American public, the influence targets, unwilling to accept that this actually happened (Epstein, 2017).

1.4 Overview of the Present Study

This study employed a web-based survey to examine the extent to which attempts to interfere with the 2016 US presidential election through social media affected people's interpersonal relationships on those platforms.

These data were collected in February 2017 – at a time when knowledge of election interference was not widely accepted by both Republican and Democrats (Epstein, 2017; Gilberstadt, 2019). The present investigation, therefore, is intended to provide a snapshot of people's perceptions of their social media experiences during this unprecedented election season. Given the literature reviewed above, we expected to find evidence of disruption in interpersonal relationships within friends and family circles on social media.

2. Method

2.1 Participants

Participants were 285 (128 men, 157 women) United States citizens over the age of 18 (M = 38.34, SD = 12.81). All were social media users and 253 (88.77%) reported voting in the 2016 US Presidential election.

2.2 Procedure

Participants were recruited from Amazon's Mechanical Turk and paid $0.25 for their participation. They were instructed that the purpose of the study was to learn about people's experiences on social media in the months leading up to the election. Additionally, we obtained ethics approval to conduct the study, ensuring the respect of the standards of research integrity. The voluntary nature of the study, and the absence of any kind of penalty or loss of benefit if the subject decided to withdraw from the study at any time, were stressed. The participants were also informed of the potential risks of the survey, like the potential loss of privacy due to unauthorized third parties accessing their data (e.g., Hackers). After participants provided informed consent, they filled out a survey assessing their experiences on social media in the months leading up to the 2016 US Presidential election.

2.3 Measures

Participants completed a series of author-generated measures to assess their attitudes toward the impact of the election on their social media use, they used a 7-point Likert scale ranging from 1 (strongly disagree) to 7 (strongly agree).

Next, participants were asked to write about their experiences on social media in the months leading up to the 2016 US presidential election. Specifically, they described their most negative experience during the pre-election and election period. They also reported with a "yes" or a "no" whether they had unfriended or unfollowed someone due to their political posts, explaining whether this was prompted by the political posts of those people or by their replies under their own posts.

Lastly, participants` political affiliation was measured on a 5-point Likert-type scale ranging from 1 (very conservative) to 5 (very liberal; M = 3.37, SD = 1.22). Their voting choices in the 2016 US Presidential election were gauged by asking participants to indicate which candidate they supported. Participant demographics, age, and gender were also assessed.

3. Results

3.1 Participant's Voting Choices

Overall, 253 reported voting in the 2016 US presidential election. Of these, 56.5% reported voting for Hilary Clinton, 32.8% for Donald Trump, 5.5% for Gary Johnson, 4.4% for Jill Stein, and 0.8% voted for other. There were no significant differences in results based on voting choice.

3.2 Evidence of Election-based Relationship Disruptions

When asked if they unfriended someone for their political posts in the months leading up to the US Presidential election, 32.3% of participants responded yes, while 42.8% reported unfollowing people for the same reasons. These two responses were significantly correlated r (283) = 0.59, $p < 0.001$, indicating that the people who unfriended others owing to the election were also likely to unfollow people. Political affiliation and gender in our sample did not have any significant effect on the responses.

3.3 Unfollowing Results

In this series of analyses, we examined whether people who reported unfollowing others due to their social media connections' posts had different experiences while using social media in this timeframe. To examine whether unfollowing actions were related to the amount of political posting participants engaged in, we conducted a point-biserial correlation analysis. There was a significant positive correlation between the variables, $r_{pb}(283)=.23$, $p<.001$. People who unfollowed someone were more likely to be people that post political content with higher frequencies than people that post political content with lower frequencies. Moreover, a series of independent-samples t-test was conducted to determine whether people who unfollowed others had different attitudes towards their experiences using social media in the months leading up to the 2016 US Presidential election. Specifically, people who unfollowed others had higher means on all 6 items assessing the extent to which their relationships were disrupted during this period. See Table 1 for means and standard deviations, and the t-statistics accompanying each item.

Table 1: Independent-Samples T-test comparing six attitude items and the yes/no conditions to the question Unfollowing Due to Direct Posts (2-tailed)

Did you unfollow anyone on social media due to their posts about the U.S. presidential election campaign?	Yes M(SD)	No M(SD)	t
The 2016 US Presidential election was more decisive than previous elections	4.20(2.21)	3.61(1.95)	2.37(282)*
The 2016 US Presidential election disrupted my friendships	4.22(1.87)	2.55(1.64)	8.00(282)***
The 2016 US Presidential election disrupted my family relationships	3.58(1.97)	2.21(1.47)	6.67(282)***
The 2016 US Presidential election disrupted my romantic relationships	2.12(1.52)	1.77(1.17)	2.15(282)*
The 2016 US Presidential election led me to unfriend people on Social Media	5.01(2.02)	1.82(1.20)	16.65(282)***
The 2016 US Presidential election led people to unfriend me on Social Media	3.98(2.13)	2.19(1.62)	8.05(282)***

*. Correlation is significant at the 0.05 level (2-tailed), ***. Correlation is significant at the 0.001 level (2-tailed)

3.4 Unfriending Results

A point-biserial correlation coefficient analysis was performed to evaluate the relationship between unfriending someone because of posts made directly by the unfriended person and participants' frequency of posts with political content. There was a positive correlation between the variables, which was statistically significant ($r_{pb}(283)=.21$, $p<.001$). People that unfriended others because of posts made directly by the unfriended person were more likely to be people that post political content with higher frequencies than people that post political content with lower frequencies. Moreover, a series of independent-samples t-tests were conducted to compare six attitude items using the categorical (yes/no) response to the question: "Did you unfriend anyone on social media due to their posts about the U.S. presidential election campaign?". While not all items revealed a significant difference, all the means were in the same direction indicating that people who unfriended people experienced more disruption in their social relationships. See Table 2.

Table 2: Independent-Samples T-test comparing six attitude items and the yes/no conditions to the question Unfriending Due to Direct Posts (2-tailed)

Did you unfriend anyone on social media due to their posts about the U.S. presidential election campaign?	Yes M(SD)	No M(SD)	t(df)
The 2016 US Presidential election was more decisive than previous elections	4.13(2.23)	3.73(2.00)	*ns*
The 2016 US Presidential election disrupted my friendships	4.50(1.78)	2.67(1.70)	8.35(282)***
The 2016 US Presidential election disrupted my family relationships	3.83(1.95)	2.30(1.55)	7.12(282)***
The 2016 US Presidential election disrupted my romantic relationships	2.12(1.50)	1.82(1.25)	*ns*
The 2016 US Presidential election led me to unfriend people on Social Media	5.60(1.56)	2.03(1.48)	18.66(283)***
The 2016 US Presidential election led people to unfriend me on Social Media	4.32(2.08)	2.31(1.69)	8.69(283)***

***. Correlation is significant at the 0.001 level (2-tailed)

3.5 Motivations for Unfriending or Unfollowing

As a final task, participants were asked to write about their experiences on social media in the months leading up to the 2016 US presidential election. They were asked to recall and write about the motivations that lead to unfriend or unfollow people from their family and friend circles and also to describe their most negative experience during the months leading up to the presidential election. The results were then processed to create data visualizations (wordclouds) of the most used words regarding those two inquiries. Notably, in both wordclouds (see Figures 1 and 2) there is a striking absence of any reference to Russia. These seem to be in line with the initial skepticism with which the American public received reports on Russian involvement in election manipulation (Epstein, 2017; Gilberstadt, 2019). Also of note, the most prominent word in Figure 1 (reasons why people unfriended or unfollowed their friends and family on social media in the months leading up to the 2016 US Presidential election), *posting*, matches with our findings as the most significant indicator of unfollowing or unfriending someone while taken in relation with the frequency of their political involvement.

Figure 1: A data visualization of the reasons why people unfriended or unfollowed their friends and family on social media in the months leading up to the 2016 US Presidential election.

Figure 2: Data visualization based on participants' descriptions of their most negative experiences on social media in the months leading up to the 2016 US Presidential election.

4. Discussion

In this study, we explored how political posts on social media influenced people's decisions to unfriend or unfollow others during the months leading up to the 2016 US presidential election. We were able to discern an intriguing pattern: the frequency with which people posted online political content, is related to the frequency the same people tend to unfriend or unfollow others. In our study, 32.3% of participants unfriended someone for political reasons, and 42.8% unfollowed other people for the same reason. Of note, political affiliation, support for a particular candidate, and gender in our sample did not have a significant impact on the decision of cutting their digital ties with others. We also discovered that the type of online interaction has probably an influence. For example, the political posts that people posted directly on their pages were strongly correlated with our participants decision to unfriend or unfollow them. On the other hand, if the interactions with others were a response to the participant's own posts, or a response under other people posts, the correlation could be weaker. Our results also suggest that people who unfriended or unfollowed others during the 2016 election period perceived that period as more conflictual than people that did not unfriend or unfollow others. Lastly, we should stress how heavily threat actors tried to influence the American public during those elections. Unfortunately, the souring political discourse, marred by those external interferences, had a noticeable negative impact on people's interactions on social media but also on their relationships and social ties with family members and friends in real life. We should also remind that at the time of data collection – February 2017, people were largely unaware of the foreign election interference in their social media experiences, the evidence provided by these self-reports suggested that people felt the effects of this interference as it placed a strain on their interpersonal relationships.

4.1 Limitations and Future Avenues of Research

This study has fully explored the dataset within the scope of our research objectives, but the data and our conclusions could offer value in additional inquiries for other research questions. Given its specific focus on the general public's experience during the US election of 2016, researchers should also be especially wary of extrapolating general trends based solely on this study. Despite the temporal and geographical focus, combined with the preliminary nature of this study, and our warning toward generalization, we believe that other similar studies would probably reinforce the notion of propaganda as a core cause of strain between people (friends and family) on social media.

Future studies conducted with different temporal and geographical horizons would be the most suited for the objective, as they could fill the knowledge gap left by this study. We hope for a future meta-analysis of related studies, particularly those from regions where Russian propaganda is more aggressive, such as Central and Western Europe, the Baltic States, and Finland.

4.2 Conclusion and Implications

Propaganda tactics rely heavily on the psychology of persuasion (Lin & Kerr, 2021). The principle of Commitment and Consistency refers to the tendency of individuals to align their actions and beliefs with their previous decisions and beliefs. Similarly, the principle of Social Validation is based on the idea that people look to the behavior of others to guide their actions in unfamiliar situations (Cialdini, 2009). These principles are frequently employed as key strategies in numerous propaganda campaigns.

People like to stay consistent with our own preconceived notions and their first impressions on an event or topic will somewhat tie to their future responses on similar events (Cialdini, 2009). Within propaganda, the aim is to reach people using their already preconceived biases as to influence their vision on related matters (Lin & Kerr, 2021). Tying the information to a political affiliation will affect the view that a reader has of the information itself. A conservative reader will be more likely to believe conservative sources, and a liberal one will be more likely to believe liberal sources (Hmielowski et al., 2020), and propagandists exploit this weakness.

Research on social norms indicates that, in unfamiliar situations, where people are not sure how to act, their rely on the behavior of others to guide their choices (Cialdini, 2009). This principle is extremely exploitable in online closed communities, and we find this type of community prevalent in alternative media groups (Pasquetto et al., 2022). Within those groups, threat actors find fertile ground in which to spread unopposed, and even aided by the social consensus, their messages.

Social Media Platforms promised to be a useful tool that would keep people connected, and up to date with others. Unfortunately, the platforms are designed to keep their users as engaged as possible, and divisive content is optimal to reach such outcome (Martin, 2022). Outrage creates traffic, and traffic helps company revenue streams. Threat actors understood quite rapidly how to exploit the platforms design to improve revenue through the promotion of divisive content, weaponizing it against liberal democracies. Our own tools are designed to further division, and expertly manipulated by Russian threat actors. This manipulation has true and tangible consequences for ordinary people. The negative impact on the lives and social interactions of ordinary citizens, due to the manufactured hyperpolarization of the political discourse, as discussed in the present study, is an issue for which solutions are needed, to prevent further damage to our society.

Societal institutions are becoming more aware of the extent of the disinformation and propaganda issue. In 2023 a start-up dedicated to monitoring disinformation in support of the EU code of practice on disinformation made the rounds in the news cycle as it highlighted the issue of social media misinformation and disinformation discoverability ratios within X (the platform formerly known as Twitter) (Vallance, 2023). The EU's Values and Transparency Commissioner Vera Jourova openly spoke about how "The Russian state has engaged in the war of ideas to pollute our information space with half-truth and lies to create a false image that democracy is no better than autocracy.". These are all signals that the legislative body of the EU will hopefully take further steps to regulate Social Media platforms in a stricter manner. This is also a sign that we should develop more proactive measures, rather than solely relying on passive reactions to these attacks. The USA has already been moving towards developing proactive measures, with seemingly promising results (Lee Myers Steve, 2023), but prebunking campaigns are time-sensitive endeavors. Their success is closely related to the ability of the people conducting them to reliably discern the emerging threats in the information space from the background noise. The rise in traction of manufactured stories aimed at eroding Western credibility can be viewed as the escalation phase of an informational attack on democratic systems, that requires early detection and responsive action to mitigate these threats.

The modern cyber threats take advantage of the internet high connectivity and ease of dissemination, the low latency of information spread, the anonymity, the low cost of this sort of operation, the multiple avenues of information delivery, the insensitivity of national borders, and the high availability of personal information (Lin & Kerr, 2021). In the case of the US election, the IO clearly used almost every one of those advantages. In particular, the anonymity made it possible for the IRA employees to pose as US citizens, and the availability of information on their target from Facebook itself (targeted advertisement) made their campaigns easier (DiResta et al., 2019; Guadagno, 2021). These cyber threats ultimately aim to influence the choices or to create enough noise to impair or block the decision-making processes of the population targeted. The threat actors exploit the openness of democratic society and are especially effective in weakening the institutions or radicalizing the population in our democratic regimes (Schleffer & Miller, 2021).

References

Abbasi, M.A., Kumar, S., Filho, J.A.A. and Liu, H., 2012. Lessons learned in using social media for disaster relief-ASU crisis response game. In *Social Computing, Behavioral-Cultural Modeling and Prediction: 5th International Conference, SBP 2012, College Park, MD, USA, April 3-5, 2012. Proceedings 5* (pp. 282-289). Springer Berlin Heidelberg.

Akram, W. and Kumar, R., 2017. A study on positive and negative effects of social media on society. *International journal of computer sciences and engineering, 5*(10), pp.351-354.

Baumeister, R.F. and Leary, M.R., 2017. The need to belong: Desire for interpersonal attachments as a fundamental human motivation. *Interpersonal development*, pp.57-89.

Bittman, L., 1985. The KGB and Soviet disinformation: an insider's view. *(No Title)*.

Brewer, M.B., 1991. The social self: On being the same and different at the same time. *Personality and Social Psychology Bulletin, 17*(5), pp.475-482.

Vallance, C., 2023, September 26. *Disinformation most active on X, formerly known as Twitter, EU says - BBC News*. https://www.bbc.com/news/technology-66926080

Cialdini, R.B., 2009. *Influence: Science and practice* (Vol. 4, pp. 51-96). Boston: Pearson education.

DiResta, R., Shaffer, K., Ruppel, B., Sullivan, D., Matney, R., Fox, R., Albright, J. and Johnson, B., 2019. The tactics & tropes of the Internet Research Agency.

Eijkman, Q. and Weggemans, D., 2012. Open source intelligence and privacy dilemmas: Is it time to reassess state accountability. *Sec. & Hum. Rts., 23*, p.285.

Epstein, R.J., 2017. *About Half of Americans Think Russia Interfered with Election Through Hacking, Poll Finds - WSJ*. WSJ. https://www.wsj.com/articles/about-half-of-americans-think-russia-interfered-with-election-through-hacking-poll-finds-1484686800?mod=Searchresults_pos1&page=1

Gilberstadt, H., 2019. For the First Time, Majority of Republicans Express Confidence in the Fairness of Mueller's Investigation. *Pew Research Center*.

Guadagno, R.E., 2021. From Russia with Love: A Social Psychological Analysis of Information Warfare in the Social Media Age. In *Democracy in the Disinformation Age* (pp. 182-200). Routledge.

Guadagno, R.E. and Guttieri, K., 2021. Fake news and information warfare: An examination of the political and psychological processes from the digital sphere to the real world. In *Research anthology on fake news, political warfare, and combatting the spread of misinformation* (pp. 218-242). IGI Global.

Guadagno, R.E., Okdie, B.M. and Muscanell, N.L., 2013. Have we all Just Become "Robo-Sapiens"? Reflections on social influence processes in the Internet age. *Psychological inquiry, 24*(4), pp.301-309.

Hmielowski, J.D., Hutchens, M.J. and Beam, M.A., 2020. Asymmetry of partisan media effects? Examining the reinforcing process of conservative and liberal media with political beliefs. *Political Communication, 37*(6), pp.852-868.

Intelligence, U. S. H. of R. P. S. C. on, 2018. *Exposing Russia's effort to sow discord online: The Internet Research Agency and advertisements.* https://democrats-intelligence.house.gov/social-media-content/

Jowett, G.S. and O'donnell, V., 2018. *Propaganda & persuasion*. Sage publications.

Kux, D., 1985. Soviet active measures and disinformation: Overview and assessment. *The US Army War College Quarterly: Parameters, 15*(1), p.17.

Lee Myers, S., 2023, October 27. *U.S. Tries New Tack on Russian Disinformation: Pre-Empting It - The New York Times.* https://www.nytimes.com/2023/10/26/technology/russian-disinformation-us-state-department-campaign.html

Lin, H. and Kerr, J., 2021. On cyber-enabled information warfare and information operations. *The Oxford Handbook of Cyber Security*, p.251.

Linvill, D.L., Boatwright, B.C., Grant, W.J. and Warren, P.L., 2019. "THE RUSSIANS ARE HACKING MY BRAIN!" investigating Russia's internet research agency twitter tactics during the 2016 United States presidential campaign. *Computers in Human Behavior, 99*, pp.292-300.

Lipton, E., Sanger, D.E. and Shane, S., 2016. The perfect weapon: How Russian cyberpower invaded the US. *The New York Times, 13.*

Martin, K., 2022. *Yes, Social Media Really Is Undermining Democracy - The Atlantic.* The Atlantic. https://www.theatlantic.com/ideas/archive/2022/07/social-media-harm-facebook-meta-response/670975/

McQuail, D., 2010. *McQuail's mass communication theory.* Sage publications.

National Cyber Security Centre, 2023, December 7. *Russian FSB cyber actor star blizzard continues worldwide spear-phishing campaigns.* National Cyber Security Centre. https://www.ncsc.gov.uk/news/star-blizzard-continues-spear-phishing-campaigns

Pasquetto, I.V., Olivieri, A.F., Tacchetti, L., Riotta, G. and Spada, A., 2022. Disinformation as Infrastructure: Making and maintaining the QAnon conspiracy on Italian digital media. *Proceedings of the ACM on Human-Computer Interaction, 6*(CSCW1), pp.1-31.

Quattrociocchi, W., Scala, A., & Sunstein, C. R. (2016). Echo chambers on Facebook. *Available at SSRN 2795110.*

Sanger, D.E., 2016. Obama strikes back at Russia for election hacking. *The New York Times, 29.*

Schleffer, G. and Miller, B., 2021. The Political Effects of Social Media Platforms on Different Regime Types (Summer 2021).

Mueller III, R.S., 2019. Report On The Investigation Into Russian Interference In The 2016 Presidential Election. Volumes I & II.(Redacted version of 4/18/2019).

Stewart, L.G., Arif, A. and Starbird, K., 2018, February. Examining trolls and polarization with a retweet network. In *Proc. ACM WSDM, workshop on misinformation and misbehavior mining on the web* (Vol. 70).

Placing Behavior in Context: Political Interpretations of Individual Behavior in Countering Information Warfare in Finland

Teemu Häkkinen and Hilkka Grahn
University of Jyväskylä, Jyväskylä, Finland

teemu.r.p.hakkinen@jyu.fi
hilkka.grahn@jyu.fi

Abstract: Malign information influence often targets large segments of the population, with the intent to manipulate individual behavior for the benefit of the actors disseminating this harmful information. However, in a liberal society like Finland, individual behavior is closely tied to personal freedoms and liberties, making the commentary and regulation of individual behavior for the sake of security a complex endeavor. This paper investigates how Finnish politicians and officials perceive individual behavior within the context of information warfare. We examine the emergence of particular discourses that interpret, critique, and potentially seek to influence individual behavior. Our research draws from parliamentary debates and legislative documents, as well as executive branch materials, providing insight into contemporary political thought. By exploring the evolving landscape of political discourse in Finland, our paper contributes to a better understanding of the environment in which countermeasures against information warfare are developed and the roots of national security policy. It underscores the intricate challenges of safeguarding cognitive security while respecting individual freedoms in a modern democratic society.

Keywords: Information Warfare, Individual Freedoms And Liberties, Policy-Maker View, Cognitive Security.

1. Introduction

This paper is interested in the potential impact of information warfare in the peacetime context and the interaction and setting up of norms of a society that tries to understand information warfare as a phenomenon. Any society in which the spreading of malign information is considered a threat to security needs to understand the phenomenon and prepare its response to it as a threat. In those circumstances behavior of individuals towards misinformation, disinformation, or propaganda may become an important theme, as deliberately disseminated malign information poses dangers for democratic institutions (Bennett & Livingston 2018), further highlighted by the argument that personal value orientations may have an impact on the believability of disinformation (Gupta et. al. 2023).

Inspired by the recent brochure by the Swedish Civil Contingencies Agency (2022) aiming to strengthen household preparedness against war or crises and bring individuals and families to the forefront, we will investigate the theme of individual and politics. We are particularly interested in decision-makers from the point of view of politicians and officials who are acting in the context of Western liberal democracy. There, individual freedoms and liberties have an important role in legislation and society, thus influencing the possibilities of politicians and officials to provide public views on individual behavior. Nevertheless, decision-makers are also in a key position to create and implement a national strategy to counter information-related threats to national security. The threat of information warfare and other forms of intentional dissemination of malign information continues to highlight the need to bring more attention to the individual, their behavior, and the response from the rest of society. (See Nistor 2023) Indeed, we identify a three-fold research problem in (i) how political decision-makers see individuals as part of communities, (ii) how decision-makers see their role in maintaining and creating norms for behavior within the community, and in such context, (iii) how decision-makers understand the security-related changes in the surrounding society.

We will narrow our approach to focus on Finland, and our research question is how Finnish political thought surrounding security views individual behavior in the context of countering malign information activities. The period we investigate takes place between 2015 and 2022. This period starts from the aftermath of the Russian annexation of the Crimean, takes place simultaneously with the prolonged conflict in Eastern Ukraine, and includes the period before and after the Russian invasion of Ukraine. Furthermore, the selected period features a potential for a variety of policy papers related to the role of information and information warfare in particular. We utilize political discourse presented in the Finnish context to explore the topic, and as a result, we will discuss the role and potential impact of public politics and decision-making to evaluate and even categorize individual behavior. There are two levels of interpretations this paper is interested in (i) the interpretations of national security policy doctrines and other forms of collectively produced policy-related documents concerning information warfare and behavior attached to the phenomenon; and (ii) more individual political interpretations that reflect the contemporary societal thinking on the subject.

2. Information Warfare as a (Political) Phenomenon

We define information warfare as an activity in which malign information or disinformation is utilized to shape the thoughts and behavior of individuals in target groups and we understand the term to be closely associated with other forms of concepts that reflect or describe either malign information or attempts to instrumentalize malign information. As a whole, the definition of information warfare is not easy. Often information warfare is broadly linked to data and technology, where technology such as information networks provides the framework for activity, and human cognition or opinion is seen as the core target. No wonder the conceptualization of information warfare has evolved from the 1990s to the present day, especially with associated concepts such as cyber warfare, psychological operations, or cognitive warfare. (Libicki 1995; Waltz 1998, 21–24; Hutchinson & Warren 2001, 2–3; Hutchinson 2021)

The challenges related to defining information warfare partly influence the way individuals and their behavior have been and continue to be seen, and how political decision-making is linked to the phenomenon. For instance, in the US thinking on information operations, an individual has been seen both as a threat and a target for operations that relate to themes such as psychology or information networks (E.g. Headquarters, Department of the Army 1996; Joint Chiefs of Staff 2014), and the information environment has been seen as the "aggregate of individuals, organizations, and systems that collect, process, disseminate, or act on information" (Joint Chiefs of Staff 2014, I-1). Opinions and thinking of individuals become relevant when individuals form groups and groups gain a shared understanding of a particular issue or start to act according to the group's dominating thinking. Indeed, individuals help to form the cognitive dimension of the information environment, shaped by factors such as education, beliefs, norms, emotions, experiences, and ideologies. (Joint Chiefs of Staff 2014, I-3) The US concept of information environment provides a conceptual definition that can be utilized in other national contexts as well, helping this paper to connect the general idea of individuals and organizations handling information to a particular organization linked to the information, i.e. the national political decision-makers in the executive or legislative branches. Nevertheless, information warfare poses both an instrument and a threat from a military point of view, which should be reflected on the policy level as well.

As a term of its own, information warfare can include tools of phenomenon described as political warfare. According to Paul Smith (1989), political warfare relates to an aim to compel an opponent to do one's will, "political" refers to the different forms of interaction between the one using the tools of political warfare and the target audience, such as the government of the target state. Historical precedents show that it is often about the use of propaganda, psychological operations, or persuasive rhetoric to gain an impact. Since then, the political spectrum in warfare has gained more attention as a potential target for operations (E.g. Arquilla & Ronfeldt 1993; Paterson & Hanley 2020). However, besides identifying politics as a key spectrum or domain of activity, we should consider the dynamics within politics in the context of information warfare. Here the role of individuals has received some attention in recent years (Bolton 2021), but we acknowledge the existence of a gap in research that needs more case-specific understanding. When it comes to political decision-making in the Finnish context, the behavior of individuals creates a potentially key problematic topic to be involved with and to pave the way for further future analyses. In liberal democratic contexts, individual freedoms and liberties have particular significance and Finland is no exception (Freedom in the World 2023). However, political speaking is connected not only to the issues about legislative processes but also to themes of representation and to discussion and negotiation in general, in which participants are not only the other politicians but also the electorate that observes the activities of elected decision-makers. Such factors influence political speaking also in Finland, for instance in the Finnish Parliament, although the ability to speak in parliament to lead to significant political consequences is often questionable, as various speeches are mostly aimed at the media or the electorate (Pekonen 2011, 92-106). However, when the use of political language takes place, it is bound by the context and forum on which the use of language takes place and is linked to the themes of the debates or policy processes, enabling an opportunity to find ideas and issues such as norms, values, and ideas.

3. Sources and Methods

In this chapter, we will first describe the selected sources and the process of how the sources were selected. In the second part of this chapter, we will describe the methodology we applied in analyzing the sources.

The selection of sources was done to provide a comprehensive view of the discussions, policies, and ideas of the Finnish Government and the Finnish legislature and thus form a representative primary source material for further analysis. As a result, the primary source material consisted of three types of material: firstly, verbatim reports of parliamentary debates (2015-2022, available at https://parlamenttisampo.fi/) selected based on keyword searches. The choice of keywords was done according to the existing knowledge of Finnish vocabulary related to information warfare (Flyktman 2017), resulting in the choice of keywords "informaatiovai* (information influen*)" and "informaatiosodank* (information warf*)". The selection of sources was further narrowed down by the means of close reading of sources and identification of whether the initial hits were related to individuals or groups of people. This produced 108 separate pieces of text related to the theme. Secondly, the Government's Reports on foreign, security, and defense policy to which similar ideas of keyword searches were applied. This produced five reports between 2015 and 2022 (available at https://julkaisut.valtioneuvosto.fi/). These reports are created by the government with the help of parliamentary involvement and outline the commonly accepted stance on key policy principles and means associated with foreign and security policy and defense, thus constituting a key source for policy analysis in the Finnish political context. Thirdly, analyzed sources included parliamentary committee reports related to the Government's Reports, meaning 27 individual reports from committees in the Finnish legislature such as the Foreign Affairs Committee, Defence Committee, etc (available at https://www.eduskunta.fi/FI/search/Sivut/Vaskiresults.aspx). These reports have an official role in particular political processes, are based on evidence from experts and officials and discussions within the committee, and can thus feature more viewpoints on thematic issues compared to the crystallized and often more compact view of the Government's Reports. Keyword searches ("informaatiovai* and informaatiosodank*") were utilized to explore each Government's Report or committee report, and all the parliamentary debates, reports, or memorandums were in Finnish. As a whole, 145 separate pieces of text were identified and selected for further analysis.

As a research method, we employed qualitative content analysis, in which we paid attention to notions regarding individuals in the context of disinformation, misinformation, propaganda, and other potential forms of information in societal security. Thus, the role of information acts as a point of reflection to understand the behavior of an individual concerning information warfare. As highlighted by Moilanen (2023) in his non-academic writing on the Finnish conceptualization surrounding information warfare and information influence, the Finnish vocabulary does not perceive information-related threats yet as a form of information warfare, contrary to the context of neighboring country Russia.

The selected and collected pieces of text formed the data that was analyzed qualitatively with the help of qualitative content analysis, source criticism, and contextualization. The approach in this study was linked to political history in which 3the study of language has been seen as a useful approach to understanding the political thought, contexts, and intentions of contemporaries. (Wiesner et. al. 2017; Skinner 2002, 103-126; see also Pocock 1973)

In relation to qualitative content analysis, ATLAS.ti software (version 23.3.4) was utilized to code the collected data to categories to help in understanding the variety of evidence drawn in the pieces of text to make between the surrounding society and information warfare, and thus to understand how the use of language conveys a thematic view related to the state of surrounding society. Categorization of data also relates to the use of computer-assisted qualitative analysis, or software that enables testing with it (see Lepper 2000; Konopásek 2007) and to the role of grounded theory, in which coding of data enables helps to conceptualize and classify findings and see relations between different concepts or categories of findings, and eventually build a theory based on findings. (Strauss & Corbin 1990, 66-71, 101-121) However, contrary to the idea of grounded theory, in this article the theoretical focus is on understanding the linguistic context for politicians when they are talking about information warfare or other connected phenomena.

In this article, the key coding principles were created based on the understanding of the potential content of the empirical sources, produced by organizations that are bound by practices and rules of the organization in question, and which have major significance for parliamentary speaking. (Ilie 2015) A systematic coding principle, in the spirit of grounded theory, was seen to provide a useful analysis tool to highlight the role of the individual as a particular focus of study. As such, the coding principles were created according to whether the separate remarks related to information influence or warfare and whether sources talked about individuals or groups. Furthermore, we were interested in what other themes were present, including ideas of what kind of threats were present, ideas of what information or malign information actually could mean, and what kind of behavior might take place. For instance, coding principles included interpretations regarding behavior in which behavior might be positive or negative, and whether the use of language featured hopes regarding the future and seeing the potential for individual or group behavior changing to a positive or negative direction. Quotes were coded, and some codes were applied to the same quotation.

4. Empirical Analysis

Empirical analysis revealed that in the political discourse utilized by the Members of Parliament in the Finnish Parliament or politicians and officials in the Government's Reports and committee reports, the role of individuals in countering information warfare was limited. The use of discourse focused on group behavior, indicating an interest to approach the theme from a perspective of the macro level instead of trying to raise and discuss rather micro-level phenomena.

Information warfare as a phenomenon was discussed usually outside the context of warfare, and the more typical way of parlance focused on "information influence". This meant deliberate efforts to utilize information to influence or manipulate group behavior, but rarely the topic was seen to represent a form of warfare. However, based on the content of the analyzed pieces of texts, Finnish politicians and officials were gradually learning what threats dissemination of malign information might constitute for societal security. Of 145 selected pieces of documents, in addition to the role of malign information in general (20 coding hits), key danger in the dissemination of negative information was seen in the increasing danger of polarized society (16 coding hits) and in the increasing erosion of trust (11 coding hits), and malign information was seen as a leading threat (20 coding hits) for individual behavior.

The discussion of the theme was not focused on only one or two parliamentary parties, as parties with more than one Member of Parliament generally discussed the topic at least occasionally and both males and females participated in discussions. The concept of hybrid warfare (43 coding hits) worked as an important concept that either included the outspoken role of malign information or was used together with more specific information-related threats such as information influence and information warfare.

Figure 1: illustrates the use of coding and whether they were grounded to the sources.

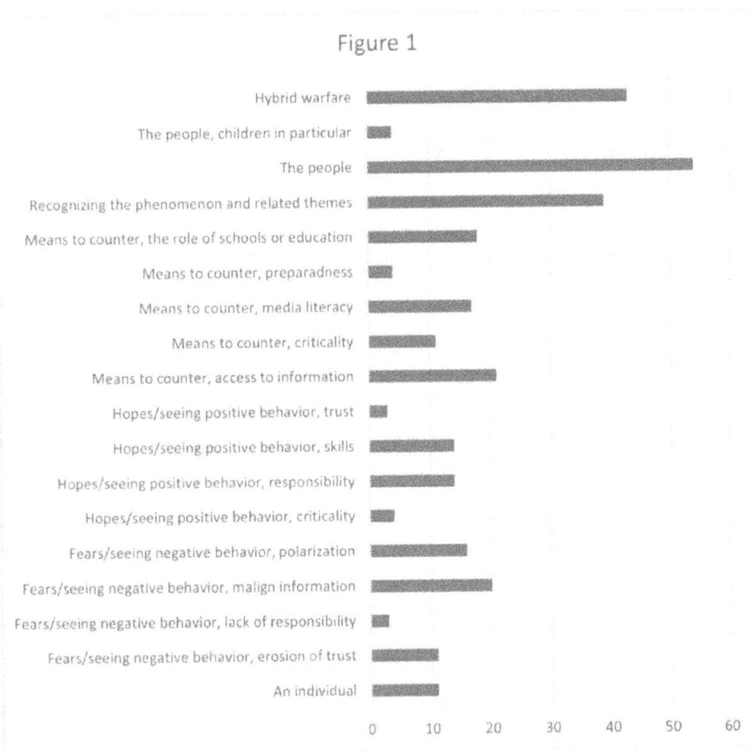

Figure 1: Codes and whether they were grounded to the text.

Information-related threats were consistently raised throughout the explored period, but the attention and depth given to the topic was broader at the end of the period than compared to the earlier period. However, the attention given to annual decrease or increase of attention should not be high. Political decision-making is a context-bound activity, in which the frequency of publication of the Government's Reports was an important framework for documents that referred to the role of information. As a key contextual factor leading to more political consideration related to security, the Russian invasion of Ukraine in 2022 not only led to the publication of a new Government's Report but also to considerations on the committee level (Valtioneuvosto 2022; e.g. Ulkoasiainvaliokunta 2022; Hallintovaliokunta 2022) Indeed, in 2020 the concept of "information defense" was utilized for the first time in the analyzed Government's Reports (Valtioneuvosto 2020), and had major prominence in another report published in 2021 about defense policy (Valtioneuvosto 2021). There the concept was linked to both information influence and other forms of information-related operations, indicating a gradual understanding at the doctrinal level.

The sources were extremely sparse concerning whether individual behavior was present. Politicians talked a lot about the Finns as a "people" or even as a nation and utilized discourse in which the Finns were raised as a group, and there also existed other forms of references to groups (58 coding hits), invoking "we" included. None of the sources explicitly mentioned names of individuals and in all 11 separate occasions in which the coding based on individual was possible referred to individuals as abstract notions or to political decision-makers themselves.

To better grasp the way how of talking about information warfare, we will raise a few selected quotations we perceive relevant and feature commentary either on groups or, on rare occasions, on more individual behavior.

Firstly, the was a rare occasion in which an "individual" was directly mentioned, indicating a view on individuals and their behavior. The topic related to critical commenting on individual behavior in social media, although without directly proposing any alternative guidelines on how to behave:

"As individuals many of us are responsible for our actions when it comes to information society and security. (...) we themselves want to share the information (...) and have it shared and published to all possible people."[1] (Eduskunta 2018, 43)

Secondly, the political discourse focused on means to counter the impact of the dissemination of malign information. The idea to improve common skills provided a logical way to discuss the chances to counter the dissemination of malign information but focused on the Finns as a whole, as represented by the quotation from 2022:

"In its report, the Education and Culture Committee very strongly raised the significance of learning to us all. To a human being, education provides many good traits for life. During this time the important point is also that education gives societal stability and durability against, for example, hoax news and information influence."[2] (Eduskunta 2022a, 61)

As Figure 1 illustrates, also means to counter malign information was discussed. Here learning to approach information (17 coding hits), having schools teach needed skills (18 coding hits), and enabling the availability of correct information (21 coding hits) were seen as the most essential ways to create resilience against malign information, further underlining the group-bound approach. As an example of the latter from 2021:

"Free, responsible, and equal communication and the freedom of speech are one of the cornerstones of democracy. Media increases the political know-how of citizens and simultaneously makes us as politicians more responsible and more respectful towards the opinions of the voters. (...) Disinformation and other forms of information influence disseminated mostly with the help of social media, weakening the citizens' trust in traditional media and more broadly towards the open and democratic order of society. To secure responsible

---

[1] Original in Finnish: "Yksilöinä olemme monet myös vastuussa omasta toiminnastamme, mitä tietoyhteiskuntaan ja turvallisuuteen liittyy. (...) itse haluamme jakaa sitä tietoa (...) jakaa ja antaa julkaistavaksi kaikelle mahdolliselle kansalle." Speaker: Markku Pakkanen (Centre of Finland).

[2] Original in Finnish: "Sivistysvaliokunta tuo mietinnössään hyvin vahvasti esille sivistyksen merkitystä meille kaikille. Koulutus antaa ihmiselle monia hyviä eväitä elämää varten. Tässä ajassa tärkeä huomio on myös se, että koulutus antaa yhteiskuntaan vakautta ja kestävyyttä esimerkiksi erilaisia valeuutisia ja informaatiovaikuttamista vastaan." Speaker: Pekka Aittakumpu (Centre of Finland).

and plural communication we continue to need both the Yleisradio (Finnish public service media company) that takes care of public service and the actors of commercial media."[3] (Eduskunta 2021, 68-69)

Thirdly, as the previous quotation already shows, the role of decision-makers was often present, as the Administration Committee stated in its report in 2016:

"The information influence aims to influence decision-makers and decision-making process and to have the target carry out harmful decisions for itself or beneficial decisions from the perspective of influencer, by using different means on several media forums. Influencing also takes often place indirectly through the so-called general public or it may be focused directly on the decision-makers or the decision-making process."[4] (Hallintovaliokunta 2016, 14–15.

This was a typical way of discourse that was present, particularly in committee reports, probably related to the need to have a shared understanding regarding the dissemination of information with potentially malign purposes as a phenomenon. On this occasion, the potential to have both individuals but also the general public as the target for malign information activities was acknowledged and thus the individuals were seen as potential agents of activity. However, deeper consideration of individual roles, behavior, and in particular responsibilities and rights associated with the behavior were not discussed.

Fourthly, on the other hand, political discourse enabled commentary that seemed to have more populist tendencies, highlighting the positive effect of information on the citizens when it comes to the decision-making by the politicians. In this view, not all types of negative "information influence" were products of foreign entities:

"This [different messages received by certain the Members of Parliament] shows that they have been targets of information influence. This shows that also these politicians have indeed trusted that the citizens wouldn't participate (...)".[5] (Eduskunta 2021b, 184)

Fifthly, the group behavior was seen to pose potential dangers, and some Members of Parliament called for restraint, patience, and a critical approach to information among the population. (Eduskunta 2022a, 21; Eduskunta 2022b, 95)

Furthermore, in 2022, Russia was directly seen as the actor that wanted to pursue information activities with malign purposes. As the Government's Report, published in 2022 as a result of the changes in the Finnish security environment stated:

"The significance of information security is highlighted in an information society where every citizen can be both a recipient and processor of information and a producer and distributor of information. Russia's aggression against Ukraine has led to a strong segregation of information environments. Russia aims to influence the formation of opinions both in Russia and abroad, and it creates a narrative to justify its actions." (The Finnish Government 2022, 31)

5. Discussion

Based on the selection of sources and their analysis, the findings reflect a reality of political decision-making in which the level of individuals is difficult to discuss, especially when it comes to information-related behavior of individuals. However, further research could try to find new forms of sources to understand the politicians'

---

[3] Original in Finnish: "Vapaa, vastuullinen ja yhdenvertainen tiedonvälitys sekä sananvapaus ovat yksi demokratian kulmakivistä. Media lisää kansalaisten poliittista tietotaitoa ja samalla tekee myös meistä poliitikoista vastuullisempia ja äänestäjien mielipiteitä kunnioittavampia. (...) Pitkälti sosiaalisen median välityksellä leviävä disinformaatio ja muu informaatiovaikuttaminen horjuttavat kansalaisten luottamusta perinteiseen mediaan ja laajemmin koko avoimeen ja demokraattiseen yhteiskuntajärjestelmään. Vastuullista ja moniäänistä tiedonvälitystä turvataksemme tarvitsemme niin julkisen palvelun tehtäviä hoitavaa Yleisradiota kuin kaupallisen median toimijoita myös jatkossa." Speaker: Suna Kymäläinen (Social Democratic Party of Finland).

[4] Original in Finnish: "Informaatiovaikuttamisen tavoitteena on vaikuttaa viime kädessä päätöksentekijöihin ja päätöksentekoprosessiin sekä saada sen kohde tekemään itselleen haitallisia tai vaikuttajan kannalta myönteisiä päätöksiä käyttämällä erilaisia toimintatapoja useilla eri median alustoilla. Vaikuttaminen tapahtuu usein myös välillisesti niin sanotun suuren yleisön kautta tai se voi kohdistua suoraan päätöksentekijöihin tai päätöksentekoprosessiin."

[5] Original in Finnish: "Tämä kertoo siitä, että heihin on yritetty informaatiovaikuttaa. Tämä kertoo siitä, että nämäkin poliitikot ovat todella luottaneet siihen, että tosiaan kansalaiset eivät osallistuisi". Speaker: Sebastian Tynkkynen (Finns Party).

thinking towards individuals in general and especially the context of malign information to broaden the contribution of this study. However, the research approach is influenced by some key contextual factors, the most important of them being the role of rights and liberties. In the liberal democratic context, citizens enjoy major rights related to individual freedoms and liberties, also in the context of information. In the Finnish context, such a framework of rights and liberties seemed to form a key contextual framework, probably contributing to the fact that the behavior of individuals was seen through the lenses of a group instead of an individual, creating a way of parlance that also affects the way how information warfare as a topic was approached. This is interesting, taken that in the Finnish society, there have been individuals who have been associated with the dissemination of malign information from the point of view of the Finnish society. (Aro 2020) On the other hand, as the findings indicate, the phenomenon of dissemination of malign information was seen as a macro-level phenomenon in which group behavior was more important than individual behavior.

6. Conclusion

In this study, we asked how Finnish political thought surrounding security perceives individual behavior in the context of countering malign information activities, i.e. themes linked to information warfare. We were particularly interested in two levels of interpretation: (i) the level of doctrines and (ii) the level of more individual political interpretations.

Our results show that in the context of countering malign information activities in Finland, political discourse tends to focus on group behavior instead of individual behavior, and key themes that are present in discourse focus on threats, skills, and needed media literacy, but also on the role and behavior of political decision-makers. The level of doctrine, as presented by the Government's Reports, highlighted malign information as a general phenomenon in crystallized form. The level of more individual political interpretations had more room to discuss on variety of topics. We believe that these results illustrate the current state of political guidance given on countering information warfare.

It will remain to be seen whether some future event emerges that might lead to the broadening of the debate to feature more attention on individual behaviour, but meantime the policies especially in the Finnish context will be dominated by a general approach focusing on groups or even to the entire nation.

Acknowledgements

This work was funded by the Finland's Ministry of Education and Culture (OKM/93/523/2022).

References

Aro, J. (2020). Putinin trollit: Tositarinoita Venäjän infosodan rintamilta. Johnny Kniga.

Arquilla, J., & Ronfeldt, D. (1993). Cyberwar is coming!. Comparative Strategy, Vol. 12, No. 2, pp. 141–165. https://doi.org/10.1080/01495939308402915

Bennett, W., & Livingston, S. (2018) "The disinformation order: Disruptive communication and the decline of democratic institutions", European Journal of Communication, Vol 33, pp 122–139. https://doi.org/10.1177/0267323118760317.

Bolton, D. (2021) "Targeting Ontological Security: Information Warfare in the Modern Age", Political Psychology, Vol. 42, No. 1, pp. 127-142. https://doi.org/10.1111/pops.12691

Eduskunta. (2018) PTK 9/2018 vp, täysistunto. Tiistai 20.2.2018 klo 14.05—18.19. https://www.eduskunta.fi/FI/vaski/Poytakirja/Documents/PTK_9+2018.pdf, accessed 17 January 2024.

Eduskunta. (2021a) Pöytäkirja PTK 117/2021 vp, täysistunto. Torstai 14.10.2021 klo 16.00—21.13. https://www.eduskunta.fi/FI/vaski/Poytakirja/Documents/PTK_117+2021.pdf, accessed 17 January 2024.

Eduskunta. (2021b) Pöytäkirja PTK 55/2021 vp, täysistunto. Tiistai 11.5.2021 klo 13.59—4.24. https://www.eduskunta.fi/FI/vaski/Poytakirja/Documents/PTK_55+2021.pdf, accessed 17 January 2024.

Eduskunta. (2022a) Pöytäkirja PTK 32/2022 vp, täysistunto. Tiistai 29.3.2022 klo 14.00—21.30. https://www.eduskunta.fi/FI/vaski/Poytakirja/Documents/PTK_32+2022.pdf, accessed 17 January 2024.

Eduskunta. (2022b) Pöytäkirja PTK 41/2022 vp, täysistunto. Keskiviikko 20.4.2022 klo 14.04—1.24. https://www.eduskunta.fi/FI/vaski/Poytakirja/Documents/PTK_41+2022.pdf, accessed 17 January 2024.

Freedom in the World 2023. Freedom House. https://freedomhouse.org/country/finland/freedom-world/2023, accessed 10 January 2024.

Flyktman, J. (2017) Informaatiosodankäynnin merkitys: Käsitetutkimus, doktriinitutkimus sekä tapaustutkimus Krimin ja Syyrian operaatioista. Yleisesikuntaupseerikurssin diplomityö, Yleisesikuntaupseerikurssi 58. Maanpuolustuskorkeakoulu. https://www.doria.fi/bitstream/handle/10024/144308/Flyktman_JT_YEK58.pdf, accessed 13 February 2024.

Gupta, M., Dennehy, D., Parra, C.M., Mäntymäki, M and Dwivedi, Y. K. (2023) "Fake News Believability: The Effects of Political Beliefs and Espoused Cultural Values", Information & Management, Vol. 60, No. 2, pp 103745. https://doi.org/10.1016/j.im.2022.103745.

Hallintovaliokunta. (2016) Valiokunnan lausunto HaVL 40/2016 vp. https://www.eduskunta.fi/FI/vaski/Lausunto/Documents/HaVL_40+2016.pdf, accessed 17 January 2024.

Hallintovaliokunta. (2022) Valiokunnan lausunto HaVL 14/2022 vp. https://www.eduskunta.fi/FI/vaski/Lausunto/Documents/HaVL_14+2022.pdf, accessed 17 January 2024.

Headquarters, Department of the Army. (1996) Information Operations. FM 100-6. https://www.hsdl.org/?view&did=437397, accessed 19 December 2023.

Hutchinson, W. and Warren, M. (2001) "Principles of Information Warfare", Journal of Information Warfare, Vol. 1, No. 1, pp 1–6.

Hutchinson, W. (2021) "Some Basic Principles of Information Warfare: A Reappraisal for 2021", Journal of Information Warfare, Vol. 20, No. 4, pp 18–29.

Ilie, C. (2015) "Parliamentary Discourse", In Tracy, K. Sandel, T. and Ilie, C. (eds) The International Encyclopedia of Language and Social Interaction. 1st ed. Wiley, pp 1–15. https://doi.org/10.1002/9781118611463.wbielsi201.

Joint Chiefs of Staff. (2014, November 20) Information Operations. Joint Publication 3-13. https://irp.fas.org/doddir/dod/jp3_13.pdf, accessed 19 December 2023.

Konopásek, Z. (2007) "Making Thinking Visible with Atlas.Ti: Computer Assisted Qualitative Analysis as Textual Practices", Historical Social Research / Historische Sozialforschung. Supplement, No 19, pp 276–98.

Lepper, G. (2000) Categories in text and talk: A practical introduction to categorization analysis. London: SAGE.

Libicki, M. C. (1995) What Is Information Warfare?. Center for Advanced Concepts and Technology, Institute for National Strategic Studies. https://apps.dtic.mil/sti/pdfs/ADA367662.pdf, accessed 15 Dec 2023.

Moilanen, P. (2023, 23 May). Sanottaisiinko ruma sana niin kuin se on?. Monilogi. https://www.panumoilanen.fi/?p=180, accessed 10 January 2023.

Nielsen, R. K. and Fletcher, R. (2020) "Democratic Creative Destruction? The Effect of a Changing Media Landscape on Democracy," In Persily, N. and Tucker, J. A. (eds) Social Media and Democracy: The State of the Field, Prospects for Reform. Cambridge: Cambridge University Press (SSRC Anxieties of Democracy), pp 139–162.

Nistor, D. I. A. (2023) "Target Audiences' Characteristics and Prospective in Countering Information Warfare", Proceedings of the 22nd European Conference on Cyber Warfare and Security, Vol. 22, No. 1, pp 623–630.

Pekonen, K. (2011) Puhe eduskunnassa. Tampere: Vastapaino.

Paterson, T. & Hanley, L. (2020) "Political warfare in the digital age: cyber subversion, information operations and 'deep fakes'", Australian Journal of International Affairs, Vol. 74, No. 4, pp. 439-454, DOI: 10.1080/10357718.2020.1734772

Pocock, J. G. A. (1973) "Verbalizing a Political Act: Toward a Politics of Speech", Political Theory, Vol. 1, No. 1, pp 27–45.

Skinner, Q. (2002) Visions of politics. Volume 1, Regarding Method. Cambridge: Cambridge University Press.

Smith, P. (1989) On Political Warfare. National Defense University, Washington Dc. https://apps.dtic.mil/sti/citations/ADA233501

Strauss, A. L. and Corbin, J. M. (1990) Basics of qualitative research: Grounded theory procedures and techniques. Newbury Park (Calif.): SAGE.

The Finnish Government. (2022) Government report on changes in the security environment. Publications of the Finnish Government 2022:20. https://julkaisut.valtioneuvosto.fi/bitstream/handle/10024/164002/VN_2022_20.pdf, accessed 16 January 2024.

The Swedish Civil Contingencies Agency. (2022) If crisis or war comes. https://rib.msb.se/filer/pdf/30307.pdf, accessed 10 January 2024.

Ulkoasiainvaliokunta. (2022). Valiokunnan mietintö UaVM 5/2022 vp. https://www.eduskunta.fi/FI/vaski/Mietinto/Documents/UaVM_5+2022.pdf, accessed 17 January 2024.

Valtioneuvosto. (2020) Valtioneuvoston ulko- ja turvallisuuspoliittinen selonteko. Valtioneuvoston julkaisuja 2020:30. https://julkaisut.valtioneuvosto.fi/bitstream/handle/10024/162513/VN_2020_30.pdf, accessed 15 February 2023.

Valtioneuvosto. (2021) Valtioneuvoston puolustusselonteko. Valtioneuvoston julkaisuja 2021:78. https://julkaisut.valtioneuvosto.fi/bitstream/handle/10024/163405/VN_2021_78.pdf, accessed 15 February 2024.

Valtioneuvosto. (2022) Ajankohtaisselonteko turvallisuusympäristön muutoksesta. VNS 1/2022 vp. https://www.eduskunta.fi/FI/vaski/JulkaisuMetatieto/Documents/VNS_1+2022.pdf, accessed 10 January 2024.

Waltz, E. (1998) Information Warfare: Principles and Operations. Boston: Artech House, Inc.

Wiesner, C., Haapala, T. and Palonen, K. (2017) Debates, Rhetoric and Political Action: Practices of Textual Interpretation and Analysis. New York, NY: Palgrave Macmillan.

Measuring Societal Impacts of Cybersecurity

Jarmo Heinonen and Harri Ruoslahti
[1]Security and Risk Management, Laurea University of Applied Sciences, Espoo, Finland

Jarmo.heinonen@laurea.fi
Harri.ruoslahti@laurea.fi

Abstract: Cybersecurity is more important than ever. All facets of society, including critical sectors such as financial, healthcare, energy, and transportation, are very reliant on cyberspace. Information and communications technology have become more and more relevant in organizations and are crucial elements in organizational learning and networked development and resilience. This study focuses on the analysis and findings of a cybersecurity questionnaire on the quantitative side of the survey contemplate mainly cybersecurity competences of the personnel in the participants' companies. The data was analysed with principal component, correspondence analysis, and the Euclidean distance two-dimensional figures. The extraction method was Principal component analysis to extract 11 factors, with more than 25 iterations. Correspondence analysis shows that the private and public non-authority sectors prefer workers with communication and collaboration skills and an ability for situational awareness. Private subsidiaries prefer leadership skills. The results show that the Societal Impact Assessment Toolkit questionnaire can be used in organizations or projects to assess the societal impact of their cybersecurity products and services. The questionnaire will be developed to-ward a standardized method, which will require collecting answers from larger numbers of respondents for further evaluation and testing it with ap-propriate qualitative methods. This will add to the body of knowledge on the societal impacts of cybersecurity. The tool is a very practical contribution for companies, while the continued use and the ensuing analysed data that be-comes collected from large numbers of respondents becomes a contribution to theory.

Keywords: Societal Impact, Assessment, Cybersecurity

1. Introduction

Society is more connected than ever, as all its facets, including critical sectors such as financial, healthcare, energy, and transportation, rely very heavily on cyber-space (Tagarev & Davis, 2020). Modern information and communications technology (ICT) solutions and infrastructures are vulnerable to cyberattacks that leverages malware, phishing, machine learning or artificial intelligence, and may target individual, organizational, and state levels (Maglaras et al., 2018; Stellios et al., 2028), calling for investments in cyber-security, which are at an all-time high Morgan, 2019).

The "Cybersecurity Competence Network", a European network of Cybersecurity centres and competence Hub for innovation and Operations (ECHO), was one of four pilot projects of 30 partners from 14 European countries from different sectors including healthcare, transport, manufacturing, ICT, education, research, telecom, energy, space, defence, civil protection, public, and private organizations. (ECHO network, 2020). The project Dynamic Resilience Assessment Method including a combined Business Continuity Management and Cyber Threat Intelligence solution for Critical Sectors (DYNAMO) develops a platform where artificial intelligence-based (AI) approaches combine business continuity management (BCM) and cyber threat intelligence (CTI) to deal with increasing digitalisation with resilience assessment and awareness to minimize the number of cyberattacks against the critical sectors of society (DYNAMO project, 2023).

One key cybersecurity challenge is preparing for future risks and finding ways to respond to new emerging types of attacks, while concurrently. Understanding what potential impacts cybersecurity, or the lack of, may have on society and its members will help make relevant decisions on how to plan and prepare against cyber threats and what cybersecurity investments should be made. The research question of this study is: What are the Societal Impacts of Cybersecurity?

2. Literature Review

This section discusses how information and communications technology have become more and more relevant in organizations and have become crucial elements in organizational learning and networked development. This section also discusses resilience and preparedness against the many possible cyber threats to better under-stand what impacts cybersecurity may have on society.

2.1 Information and Communications Technology in Organisations

Ruoslahti and Trent (Ruoslahti & Trent, 2020) find four main themes of consideration of information and communications technology (ICT) implementation, which are ICT alignment, Organizational Culture, Innovation Culture, and ICT-readiness. ICT can be in a critical element in promoting innovation (Lu et al., 2019) and in supporting decision-making and transforming business processes (Cupiał et al., 2018), and business survival may even depend how well new IT are implemented, and the opportunities that they bring being taken advantage of (Hernandez, Jimenez & Martin, 2010).

ICT can promote Organizational Learning as a catalyst for Knowledge Management practices (Huang, Gardner & Moayer, 2016), and as they are applied to existing processes, they serve to im-prove internal and external flows of information (Im, Porumbescu & Lee, 2013). Business strategies Information Systems strategies should align so that the development and usage of IT-infrastructures are clear for all members of the organization (Choe, 2016). Building modern competitiveness is increasingly reliant on ICT-implementation (Mihalic & Buhalis, 2013), as ICT offers opportunities for strategic and distance learning (Lopez-Nicolas & Soto-Acosta, 2010).

Learning is necessary in modern organizations (Lemmetty & Collin, 2019), and mobile technologies have brought new opportunities to the education sector (Turi, 2019). Organizational Culture plays an integral role in successful ICT integration (Ruoslahti & Trent, 2020), while leadership can and should promote positive policies and sense of readiness, to minimize change resistance (Cha, Hwang & Gregor, 2015), and ICT makes it easier to store and share organizational knowledge (Siddiqui et al., 2019).

As ICT plays a prominent role on organizational knowledge management, their processes, services, and product innovation become strongly influenced by the used ICT-tools, and these shape organizational cultures (Siddiqui et al., 2019). Innovation culture can bene-fit from consolidating the strengths of blended e-learning and traditional face-to-face interactions to increase quality, effectiveness, efficiency, and abilities (Conková, 2013).

Because ICT is instrumental in supporting knowledge sharing, by lowering communication barriers and promoting collective behaviours, building adequate ICT-support is critical for organizational knowledge management systems (Rahman, Islam & Abdullah, 2017). protecting ICT-systems against threats is highly significant for the overall availability of the critical systems that support organizational processes, and to ensure the availability of digital information calls for risk assessment (RA) based measures (Pöyhönen et al., 2020).

2.2 Networked Development

When people work towards common objectives that affects their communities, they become more responsible, which promotes social learning (Webler, Kastenholz & Renn, 1995), and as innovation is based on new knowledge, it can drive growth and success (Dandonoli, 2013; Burdon, Mooney & Al-Kilidar, 2015). Co-creation is a collaborative activity with determined objectives, arenas, collaborators, tools, processes, and contracts (Bhalla, 2014), which takes place on different layers, involving agents to co-create policies and futures (Accordino, 2013), to generate new knowledge and skills resulting to innovations (Henriksson, Ruoslahti & Hyttinen, 2018; Ruoslahti, 2018).

Co-creation of knowledge can combine physical spaces and digital environments or occur in one or the other (Bhalla, 2014), as actors meet in these physical or digital spaces to address and discuss issues that are relevant to them, communication can be seen to take place in these Issue Arenas (Vos, Schoemaker & Luoma-aho, 2014). These arenas can be competitive spaces, where actors have both common agendas and interests of their own and where they use problem solving and influencing strategies (Saarinen, 2012; Vos, 2018).

Linkov, et al. (2014) find that critical infrastructures may typically lack resilience, which can cause them to lose essential functionalities if hit by adverse events. Successful crisis-management enables organizations prepare to sustain and resume operations, and to minimize losses, and adapt to manage future incidents (Linkov et al., 2013). Effective response to disturbances and collaboration during those disturbances depend heavily on shared situational awareness (Pöyhönen, 2020).

Ruoslahti, Rajamäki & Koski (2018) note that considering resilience event management cycles, such as plan or prepare, absorb, recover, adapt, and learn, and self-modify, may help plan measures to ensure the continuity of Cyber Physical Systems (CPS), which are composed of cyber, technical, social and ecological systems. Organizational resilience includes conditions and to understand and reduce risks and mitigate crises (Vos, 2017), and prior knowledge of critical infrastructure sectors, experiences of CPS, and avail-able best practices can help design and maintain resilience (Pöyhönen, 2020; Ruoslahti, 2018).

2.3 Societal Impacts

De Jong et al. (2014) highlighted that societal impact can be understood through interactions and as product, knowledge use, and direct benefit to society. Societal im-pacts as a product shows potential societal value when used by societal audiences as a product, which can also be a service, information, tool, instrument, method, or model (Shapiro, 2007). Societal impacts as knowledge use can include interactions between societal stakeholders that result in the adoption or use of knowledge, which may, or may not be, facilitated by a product (Castro Martínez, Molas Gallart & Fernández de Lucio, 2008). Societal benefits to society can be use of innovation research results, policies, practices, jobs, education, community formation, network building, trust that have impacts on culture, media, and community (Walter et al., 2007).

The Internet and connected technologies have increased cyber influence, cyber-crime, behaviours, and actions that may impact personal privacy corporate and nation-al security (Michel & King, 2019). The ramifications of cybercrime go beyond may go the consequences inflicted by cyber-attacks themselves, and economies could be impacted with significant costs (Gañán, Ciere & van Eeten, 2017). A cyber-attack may even lead to environmental damage, which in turn could have detrimental effects on the stability of society (Kallberg & Burk, 2014).

Economic and societal developments increasingly rely on digitalization and ICT, and this adds to the need for Cyber Security to protect these benefits (Schia & Gjesvik, 2018). Personal data, for example, are increasingly harvested and sold, so maintaining an explicit awareness of what is real, and fake is a key safeguard from cyber influence and harm; technology can help detect and support awareness of personal privacy or national security harm related influence (Michel & King, 2019). Defending all levels of infrastructures from cyber-attacks means that information, network availability, and information grids are protected, to preserve ecosystems and ecosystem services, while safeguarding the people's property and lives (Kallberg & Burk, 2014).

Though societies may be aware of most emerging technologies and with the potential of disruptions, they may still fail to understand what impacts these innovations may have on society or the lives of its citizens (Bradshaw, 2018). Effective, economic and impact evaluations require systematically collecting accurate reliable data on agent-level costs of cybercrime, where analysis and information become based on pre-set factors and indicators that better understanding of the respective impacts to support decision-making and cyber security investments (Gañán et al., 2017). Policy makers should prepare for an upcoming technology-driven disruption of society, as this 'dark side' of IT has the potential to violate the wellbeing of individuals, organizations, and societies (Tarafdar, Gupta & Turel, 2015).

3. Method

This study serves as a pilot study of the ECHO Societal Impact Assessment Toolkit questionnaire. The aim of the study is to understand the societal impacts of cybersecurity as a selected case study of the D9.15 ECHO deliverable. A secondary aim is to verify the questions of the Toolkit questionnaire. This study focuses on the analysis and findings of organizational cybersecurity structures and substructures, and the competencies needed on different task levels to build comprehensive cyber-security.

Developing the 73 survey questions for the Societal Impact Assessment Toolkit were based on the main research question and a prior empirical study on expert views on Cyber Range (CR) capabilities, interactions and features in acquisition of cyber skills. The context of the Toolkit questions is cybersecurity skills, where the cybersecurity related backgrounds of respondents form a sample of relevant companies and organizations.

The Toolkit has open-ended and multiple-choice questions that use a five step Likert scale of cybersecurity alternatives. ECHO partner experts working in the field of cybersecurity were asked to check and comment the first version of the Toolkit questionnaire questions. The sample size did not quite reach the goal of a hundred respondents. The final sample (n = 81) was less than expected but deemed sufficient to conduct this pilot study as more answers proved difficult to obtain. All questionnaires that were not completed in full were left out of the analysis.

Background data are first collected in the beginning of the questionnaire to collect personal and organizational information. The quantitative questions of the sur-vey focus on cybersecurity choices and competences of the personnel in the participating companies.

The data was analysed with principal component analysis to find out groups in which one of the loadings are connected (Principal component analysis and Kaiser normalization, cutting point 0,25). The highest loadings from the same component that were focused as the most meaningful were analysed by correspondence analysis with two variables. The Likert scale questions were analysed with correspondence analysis and the Euclidean distance two dimensional figures. The Euclidean distance can be calculated with Pythagorean theorem (d(p,q)2 = (q1-p1)2+ (q2-p2)2) in two-dimensional space. Correspondence analysis is an exploratory multivariate technique that converts a data matrix into a particular type of graphical display in which the rows and columns are depicted as points (Yelland, 2010; Greenacre & Hastie, 1987).

Besides two-dimensional graphics limitations more figures are needed to reveal additional information. For example, factor analysis or other suitable multidimensional methods are needed to reveal the best suitable variables for correspondence analysis and its graphics. The reliability of the material was analysed with Cronbach's Alpha (0,899). The open-ended survey responses were analysed with qualitative content analysis (Denzin & Lincoln, 1994).

The extraction method, Principal component analysis, provided and extraction of 22 factors after 25 iterations with the first cutting point that was set at 0,25 (Metsämuuronen 2005) in the SPSS program. The cumulative variance was mostly on the first component, so to focus on the more meaningful aspects a final cutting point was set at 0,45, which provided eleven (11) factors.

4. Results: Attributes of Collaboration Network Resilience

This section discusses the results of the qualitative and quantitative analysis of the Societal Impact Toolkit questionnaire, which has 73 questions altogether. The first five open-ended questionnaire questions deal with company background and the participant information. The remaining 68 questions are multiple choice questions on a five-step Likert scale deal with cybersecurity related choices and skills.

Two of the questions (profession and the organization) proved to be too complicated for relevant analysis. There were too many professional titles and organisational departments to categorize them appropriately. This indicates that there is a need for predetermined groups or options for respondents to choose from to these questions. This will make the questionnaire easier to answer by providing more specific title backgrounds.

The questionnaire contains 68 multiple-choice questions that deal with cybersecurity related choices and skills. Principal component analysis was used to extract eleven principal components from multiple-choice questions. Table 1 lists these principal components and shows the number of questions that they are connected to.

Table 1: Principal components.

Order of component	Name of component	Connected to n questions (over 0.45)	Connected to n questions negatively
1st	Vulnerability evaluations	16	0
2nd	European solution	3	0
3rd	Cyber-attacks	1	1
4th	Insurance	2	2
5th	Outsourced	2	2
6th	External consultants	1	0
7th	Business first	0	1
8th	Hard work	1	0
9th	Key features	1	0
10th	Who should be trained	1	0
11th	Key skills	1	0

The first component named "vulnerability evaluations" was connected to the 16 questions (table 1) : "we conduct regular vulnerability evaluations in-house " (0,664), "we have a dedicated in-house capabilities for handling cyber-attacks " (0,783), "we have dedicated budget to address cybersecurity" (0,730), "we conduct vulnerability evaluations to identify potential points" (0,784), "we conduct regular vulnerability evaluations by external providers" (0,612), "we use cybersecurity practices in a daily basis to maintain a safer environment" (0,609), "we have a dedicated budget for cybersecurity expenditure" (0,603), "we regularly have cyber exercises to identify key milestones for improvements" (0,623), "we regularly have cyber exercises to define the level of resilience" (0,692), "we use needs based self-evaluations when purchase cyber security" (0,689), "we make cybersecurity related purchases" (0,677), "we have mandatory compliance requirements" (0,636), "business planning processes look at previous cybersecurity designs"(0,663), "we engage proactively in using cybersecurity cases" (0,679), we measure cost effectiveness of cybersecurity based n cost analyses" (0,600), and "we have a fixed budget for cyber security" (0,687).

The second component named "European solution" (table 1) was connected to three questions: "do you favour European cybersecurity solutions over non-European" (0,526), "would you purchase cybersecurity services from Europe" (0,501), and "would you use a European cybersecurity marketplace" (0,561).

The third component named "cyber-attacks" (table 1) was connected to one question "we feel threatened by cyber-attacks" (0,448), and negatively to one question: "we use cybersecurity practices in a daily basis to maintain a safer environment" (-0,483).

The fourth component named "insurance" (table 1) was connected to one question: "we will continue without cyber insurance" (0,462), and negatively connected to two questions: "we use insurance to cover certain types of cybersecurity incidents" (-0,635), and "we have insurance coverage for cybersecurity supply chain risks" (-0,558).

The fifth component named "out-sourced" (table 1) was connected to one question: "we have out-sourced partners for handling cyber-attacks" (0,490), and negatively connected to two questions: "we hire and train in-house people who have basic understanding of domain" (-0,509), and "we hire people with proven competence even without degree" (-0,464).

There were six components that related to one question each. the sixth component was named "external consultants" (table 1) connected with the question: "we purchase cyber services from security firms" (0,511). the seventh component "business first" (table 1) was connected to the question: "do you have dedicated career path for employees" (-0,475). the eighth component "hard work" (table 1) was connected to the question: "we appreciate work experience" (0,478). the ninth component was named "key features" and connected to: "what are the key features expected cyber-security service" (0,503). the tenth component "who should be trained" connected with the question: "who should be trained in cyber security in your organizations" (0,494). the eleventh was named "key skills" and connected with the question: "what are the key cybersecurity skills you seek from your employees" (0,457).

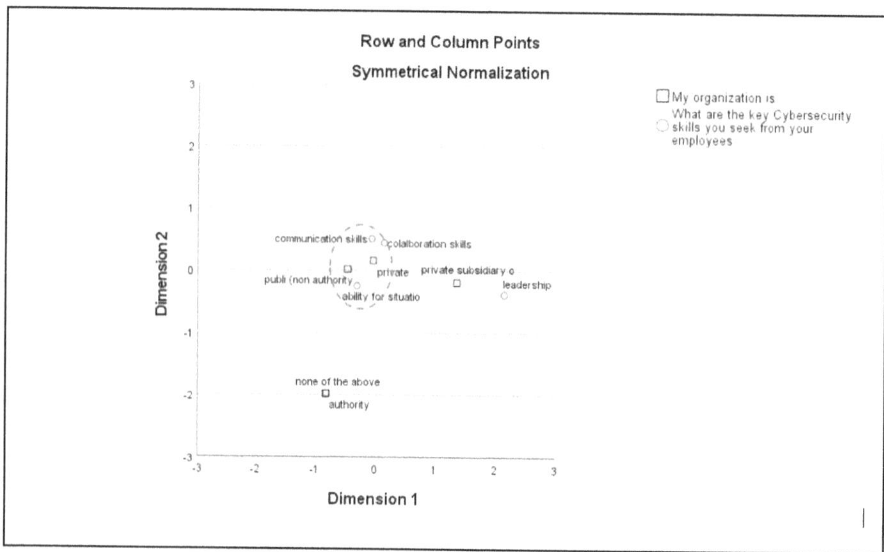

Figure 1: Correspondence analysis between key skills and organization

Figure 1 visualizes that the Correspondence analysis of the data shows that the private sector and the public-non-authority sector prefer workers who have good communication skills, collaborative skills, and an ability for situational awareness. Private subsidiary organizations mainly look for leadership skills. Public-authority organizations however differ in the way that they do not look for these above-mentioned features.

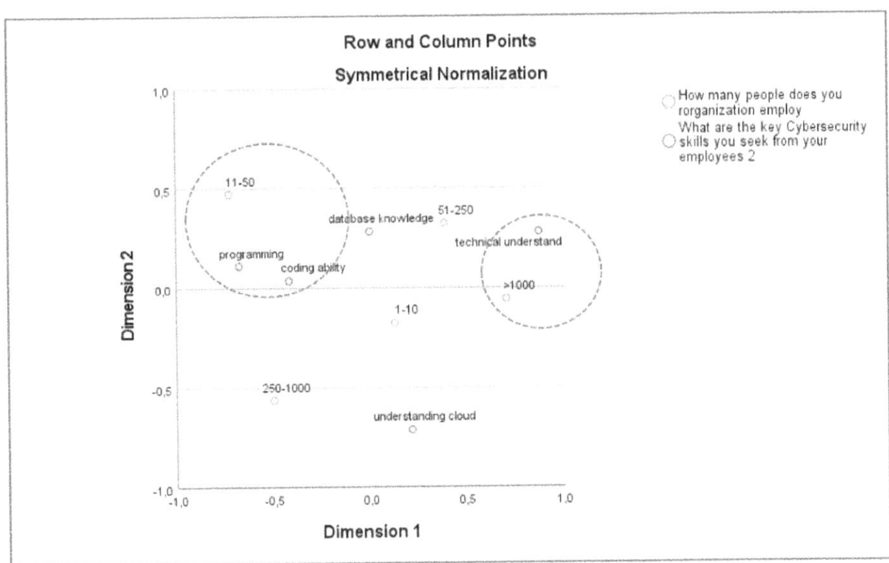

Figure 2: Key Cybersecurity skills needed in companies.

Large companies that have more than 1000 employees look for technical under-standing, while smaller companies that have between 11 and 50 employees seem to prefer programming skills and coding ability from their employees (Figure 2).

5. Conclusions

The Societal Impact Assessment Toolkit questionnaire can be used operatively. The principal component analysis shown that there are many components which affect societal impact, and the first component "Vulnerability evaluations" was connected to the 16 questions which gather the biggest quantity of variables. There are different kind of requisites how big is the company and what kind of workers they need.

The components that have relate to largest number of positive questions are "Vulnerability evaluations" (16), "European solution" (7), "Hard work" (7) and "Effectiveness" (6). Ten of the 22 identified components are related to one or two questions (cutting point 0,25). To address this, the further development of the questionnaire should be based on collecting significantly larger numbers of respondents.

The results of this study clearly indicate the need to develop the background questions on profession and the organization by providing predetermined options from which respondents can choose. This will make both answering these questions and future analysis of them easier.

The aim is to collect more respondents and further develop the Toolkit towards a standardized method with which the societal impacts of cybersecurity. To this end, the ECHO Societal Impact Assessment Toolkit questionnaire was partially based on a previous cyber-range (CR) study, and its questions were evaluated by cyber security experts and validated with relevant quantitative methods.

The Societal Impact Assessment Toolkit questionnaire can be used within organisations or projects that wish to assess the societal impact of their products and services. Developing this structured questionnaire toward a standardized method will require collecting answers from a larger sample of respondents and to further evaluate and test it with appropriate qualitative methods. When used in more quantity, this path towards a standardized method to assess the societal impacts of cybersecurity can provide a contribution to science and theory. The contribution to practice will be the availability for usage of this Societal Impact Assessment Toolkit questionnaire in future research and innovation projects. Interestingly, malware and firewalls were not mentioned. New current questions can be listed at the end of the questionnaire, if the first part remains the same and comparability with the previous one is maintained.

Though this Toolkit questionnaire purely addresses the societal impacts of cyber-security, this same approach could be adopted to similarly develop structured and standardized methods to assess other issues. These could be for example, sustainability or ethics. This would further answer a recognized need to develop easier to use analysis methods to replace some of the time and labour-intensive qualitative approaches currently used.

This questionnaire will be used to analyse societal impacts in the DYNAMO project. This pilot study under the ECHO project has been a valuable starting point. The results are expected to improve with a larger sample of respondents. In the field of security, the respondents tend to be reluctant to answer questionnaires, but rather wish to keep themselves in the dark. In time this questionnaire many be used in other future projects to provide even more responses that will further deepen the results.

Acknowledgement

This study has received funding by the European Union projects ECHO, which has received funding from the European Union's Horizon 2020 research and innovation programme under the grant agreement no. 830943, and DYNAMO, under grant agreement no. 101069601. The views expressed are those of the author(s) only and do not necessarily reflect those of the European Union. Neither the European Union nor the granting authority can be held responsible for them.

References

Accordino, F. (2013), The Futurium – a Foresight Platform for Evidence-Based and Participatory Policymaking, Philosophy & Technology, vol. 26, no. 3, pp. 321-332.

Bhalla, G. (2014). How to plan and manage a project to co-create value with stakeholders, Strategy & Leadership, Vol. 42 No. 2 2014, pp. 19-25.

Bradshaw, D. J. (2018). Technology Disruption and Blockchain: Understanding Level of Awareness and the Potential Societal Impact, Doctoral dissertation, Dublin, National College of Ireland.

Burdon, S., Mooney, G. R. and Al-Kilidar, H. (2015). Navigating service sector innovation using co-creation partnerships. Journal of Service Theory and Practice, vol. 25, no. 3, pp. 285-303.

Castro M., E., Molas G., J., and de Lucio, F., I. (2008). Knowledge transfer in the Human and Social Sciences: the importance of informal relationships and its organizational consequences.

Cha, K.J., Hwang, T. and Gregor, S. (2015). An integrative model of IT-enabled organizational transformation: A multiple case study. Management Decision, 53(8), pp. 1755-1770.

Choe, J. M. (2016). The Construction of an IT Infrastructure for Knowledge Management. Asian Academy of Management Journal, 21(1).

Conková, M. (2013). Analysis of Perceptions of Conventional and E-Learning Education in Corporate Training. Journal of Competitiveness, 5(4), n/a.

Cupiał, M., Szeląg-Sikora, A., Sikora, J., Rorat, J. and Niemiec, M. (2018). Information technology tools in corporate knowledge management. Ekonomia i Prawo, 17(1), pp. 5-15.

Dandonoli, P. (2013). Open innovation as a new paradigm for global collaborations in health. Globalization and Health, vol. 9, no. 1, pp. 1-5.

De Jong, S., Barker, K, Cox, D, Sveinsdottir, T. and Van den Besselaar, P. (2014). Understanding societal impact through productive interactions: ICT research as a case Research Evaluation 23(2), pp. 89-102.

Denzin, N. K. and Lincoln, Y. S. (1994). Handbook of Qualitative Research, Sage Publications, Thousand Oaks, USA

DYNAMO project, 2023. Dynamic Resilience Assessment Method [WWW Document]. URL https://horizon-dynamo.eu/wp-content/uploads/2023/01/DYNAMO_Leaflet_web.pdf (accessed 1.24.24)

ECHO network (2020). ECHO network webpage (https://echonetwork.eu/, accessed November 4).

European Commission (2017). Joint Communication to the European Parliament and the Council Resilience, Deterrence and Defence: Building strong cybersecurity for the EU (JOIN/2017/0450 final https://eur-lex.europa.eu/legal-con tent/EN/ALL/?uri=CELEX:52017JC0450, accessed February 8 2021).

European Commission (2020). Europe investing in digital The Digital Europe Programme (https://ec.europa.eu/digital-single-market/en/europe-investing-digital-digital-europe-pro gramme, accessed December 15).

Gañán, C. H., Ciere, M. and van Eeten, M. (2017). Beyond the pretty penny: the Economic Impact of Cybercrime Proceedings of the 2017 New Security Paradigms Workshop October 2017, pp. 35-45.

Greenacre M. and Hastie T. (1987). The Geometric Interpretation of Correspondence Analysis. Journal of the American Statistical Association, Vol. 82, No. 398 (Jun. 1987), pp. 437-447.

Henriksson, K., Ruoslahti, H., and Hyttinen, K. (2018). Opportunities for strategic public relations - evaluation of international research and innovation project dissemination. In Bow man, S. Crookes, A., Romenti, S. & Ihlen, Ø (eds.). Public Relations and the Power of Creativity (Advances in Public Relations and Communication Management, Volume 3).

Hernandez, B., Jimenez, J. and Martin, M.J. (2010). Business management software in high tech firms: the case of the IT services sector. The Journal of Business & Industrial Marketing, 25(2), pp. 132-146.

Huang, F., Gardner, S. and Moayer, S. (2016). Towards a framework for strategic knowledge management practice: Integrating soft and hard systems for competitive advantage Very In formal Newsletter on Library Automation. VINE Journal of Information and Knowledge Management Systems, 46(4), pp. 492-507.

Im, T., Porumbescu, G., and Lee, H. (2013). ICT as a buffer to change: A case study of the Seoul Metropolitan Government's Dasan Call Center. Public Performance & Management Review, 36(3), pp. 436-455.

Kallberg, J. and Burk, R. A. (2014). Failed Cyberdefense: The Environmental Consequences of Hostile Acts Military Review 94(3), 22.

Lemmetty, S., and Collin, K. (2019). Self-Directed Learning as a Practice of Workplace Learning: Interpretative Repertoires of Self-Directed Learning in ICT Work. Vocations and Learning, pp. 1-24.

Linkov, I. et al. (2013). Resilience metrics for cyber systems. Environment Systems and Decisions, 33(4), pp. 471-476.

Linkov, I. et al. (2014). Changing the resilience paradigm. Nature Climate Change, Volume 4, pp. 407-409.

Lopez-Nicolas, C. and Soto-Acosta, P. (2010). Analyzing ICT adoption and use effects on knowledge creation: An empirical investigation in SMEs: SSIS. International Journal of Information Management, 30(6), 521.

Lu, H., Pishdad-Bozorgi, P., Wang, G., Xue, Y. and Tan, D. (2019). ICT Implementation of Small- and Medium-Sized Construction Enterprises: Organizational Characteristics, Driving Forces, and Value Perceptions. Sustainability, 11(12), 3441.

Maglaras, L., Ferrag. M, Derhab, A., Mukherjee, M., Janicke, H. and Rallis, S. (2018) Threats, countermeasures and attribution of cyber-attacks on critical infrastructures EAI Endorsed Transactions on Security and Safety 5 (16).

Michel, M. C. K. and King, M. C. (2019). Cyber Influence of Human Behavior: Personal and National Security, Privacy, and Fraud Awareness to Prevent Harm. 2019 IEEE International Symposium on Technology and Society (ISTAS), November 2019, pp. 1-7.

Mihalic, T. and Buhalis, D. (2013). ICT as a New Competitive Advantage Factor - Case of Small Transitional Hotel Sector. Economic and Business Review for Central and South-Eastern Europe, 15(1), 33-56

Morgan, S. (2019). Global Cybersecurity Spending Predicted to Exceed $1 Trillion From 2017-2021, Cybercrime Magazine June 10 2019.

Pöyhönen, J., Rajamäki, J., Lehto, M. and Ruoslahti, H. (2020). Cyber Situational Awareness in Critical Infrastructure Protection. Annals of Disaster Risk Sciences, Vol 3, No 1 (2020): Special issue on cyber-security of critical infrastructure. Available: https://ojs.vvg.hr/in dex.php/adrs.

Rahman, S., Islam, M. Z., and Abdullah, A. D. A. (2017). Understanding factors affecting knowledge sharing. Journal of Science and Technology Policy Management.

Ruoslahti, H. 2018. Co-creation of Knowledge for Innovation Requires Multi-Stakeholder Public Relations. In Bowman, S., Crookes, A., Romenti, S. and Ihlen, Ø. (Eds) Public Relations Public Relations. In Bowman, S., Crookes, A., Romenti, S. and Ihlen, Ø. (Eds) Public Relations and the Power of Creativity, Advances in Public Relations and Communication Management, Volume 3, Emerald Publishing Limited, 115-133.

Ruoslahti, H., Rajamäki, J. and Koski, E. (2018). Educational Competences with regard to Resilience of Critical Infrastructure. Journal of Information Warfare, 17(3), pp. 1-16.

Ruoslahti, H. and Trent, A. (2020). Organizational Learning in the Academic Literature – Systematic Literature Review. Information & Security: An International Journal 46:1, pp. 65-78.

Saarinen, L. (2012). Enhancing ICT Supported Distributed Learning through Action Design Research. Aalto University publication series, Doctoral Thesis 92 7 2012, Helsinki.

Schia, N. N. and Gjesvik, L. (2018). Managing a Digital Revolution-Cyber Security Capacity Building in Myanmar NUPI Working Paper 884, Norwegian Institute of International Affairs.

Shapiro, H., Haahr, J. H., Bayer, I. and Boekholt, P. (2007). Background paper on innovation and education Danish Technological Institute and Technopolis for the European Commission, DG Education & Culture in the context of a planned Green Paper on innovation.

Siddiqui, S. H., Rasheed, R., Nawaz, S., and Abbas, M. (2019). Knowledge sharing and innovation capabilities: The moderating role of organizational learning. Pakistan Journal of Commerce and Social Sciences (PJCSS), 13(2), pp. 455-486.

Stellios, I., Kotzanikolaou, P., Psarakis, M., Alcaraz, C. and Lopez, J. (2018). A survey of IOT enabled cyberattacks: Assessing attack paths to critical infrastructures and services, IEEE Communications Surveys & Tutorials 20 (4), pp. 3453-3495.

Tagarev, T. and Davis, B. Á. (2020). Towards the Design of a Cybersecurity Competence Network: Findings from the Analysis of Existing Network Organisations International Conference on Multimedia Communications, Services and Security (Springer, Cham), pp. 37-50.

Tarafdar, M., Gupta, A. and Turel, O. (2015). Special issue on dark side of information technology use: an introduction and a framework for research Information Systems Journal 25(3), pp. 161-170.

Turi, J. A., Javed, Y., Bashir, S., Khaskhelly, F. Z., Shaikh, S., and Toheed, H. (2019). Impact of Organizational Learning Factors on Organizational Learning Effectiveness through Mobile Technology. Quality-Access to Success, 20(171).

Vos, M. (2017). Communication in Turbulent Times: Exploring Issue Arenas and Crisis Communication to Enhance Organisational Resilience, Jyväskylä: Jyväskylä University School of Business and Economics.

Vos, M. (2018). Issue Arenas. In Heath, R. and Johansen, W. (Eds.), The International Encyclopedia of Strategic Communication (IESC). Whiley Blackwell, Malden MA.

Vos, M., Schoemaker, H. and Luoma-aho, V. L. (2014). Setting the agenda for research on issue arenas. Corporate Communications: An International Journal, Vol. 19 No. 2, 2014. Emerald Group Publishing Limited, pp. 200-215.

Walter, A. I., Helgenberger, S., Wiek, A. and Scholz, R. W. (2007). Measuring societal effects of transdisciplinary research projects: design and application of an evaluation method Evaluation and program planning 30(4), pp. 325-338.

Webler, T. Kastenholz, H. and Renn, O. (1995) Public Participation in Impact Assessment: A Social Learning Perspective. in Environmental Impact Assessment Review 15(5), 443-463 · September 1995. https://doi.org/10.1016/0195-9255(95)00043-E.

CTI Sharing Practices and MISP Adoption in Finland's Critical Infrastructure Protection

Katja Henttonen[1,2] and Jyri Rajamäki[1]
[1]Laurea University of Applied Sciences, Espoo, Finland
[2]University of Jyväskylä, Jyväskylä, Finland

katja.henttonen@laurea.fi
katja.m.henttonen@student.jyu.fi
jyri.rajamaki@laurea.fi

Abstract: Cyber Threat Intelligence (CTI) sharing is crucial for safeguarding organisations and securing national critical infrastructure. This study delves into the CTI-sharing practices of large, safety-critical Finnish organisations, with a specific interest in the deployment and potential of the Malware Information Sharing Platform (MISP). We gathered insights through qualitative interviews with cybersecurity experts from key sectors: energy, healthcare, and transportation. Our findings reveal that a significant proportion of regional CTI data is still shared through manual methods such as email and chat. While these systems are generally viewed positively, they are also understood to be prone to delays and inaccuracies. The interest in utilising MISP is rising in Finland, yet its implementation is still in the nascent stages. Organisations are looking towards the National Cyber Security Center to lead the establishment of a national MISP instance. The benefits of adopting a national MISP framework could be further amplified by organisations joining Europewide industry specific MISP instances or leveraging MISP to share threat intelligence with their supply chain partners. However, challenges remain, particularly in balancing threat data sharing with European data protection laws, motivating community contributions, and standardising CTI-sharing tools and practices within a country.

Keywords: Cyber Threat Intelligence, CTI Sharing, Critical Infrastructure, MISP, Finland

1. Introduction

In cybersecurity, sharing Cyber Threat Intelligence (CTI) is key to protecting organisations and national infrastructures. While global CTI repositories are widely used, the specific security needs of countries, shaped by their unique geopolitical, regulatory, and industry-related factors, call for a closer look at how CTI sharing works on a local level. This is especially true in Finland, where the dynamics of CTI sharing within critical sectors like energy, healthcare, and transportation remain largely unexplored despite their critical importance to the country's security and resilience.

This study contributes to the field by examining the state of CTI sharing in Finland's critical infrastructure, focusing on the Malware Information Sharing Platform (MISP). While the transformative potential of MISP in revolutionising national-scale CTI sharing is acknowledged, its practical deployment and efficacy within the unique Finnish context have not yet been systematically studied. To address this knowledge gap, our research is driven by two main questions:

1. How do critical infrastructure organisations in Finland receive and share Cyber Threat Intelligence (CTI)?
2. What are the current MISP deployment status and potential usage scenarios in these organisations?

Employing a qualitative research approach, this inquiry involved engaging cybersecurity experts from key sectors through six in-depth interviews. These conversations, supplemented by document analysis, provide insights into the complexities of CTI sharing in Finland, especially the usage and potential of MISP.

The structure of the paper is as follows. The second section provides background information, introduces key terms, and reviews CTI sharing and MISP literature. The third section elaborates on this study's data collection and analysis methodology. The fourth section presents the research results, first offering an overview of CTI-sharing practices within Finland's critical infrastructure and then delving into the status and potential of MISP adoption. Discussions and conclusions close the paper.

2. Literature Review

This section provides a concise overview of relevant literature. The first subsection covers general literature on CTI sharing. The second subsection explores the automation of CTI sharing and introduces the MISP platform.

2.1 Cyber-Threat Intelligence (CTI) Sharing

Cyber-threat intelligence (CTI) is knowledge about current or potential cyber threats, encompassing aspects like malicious actors, attack methods, vulnerabilities, and their impacts. Li et al. (2017) offer a more detailed definition, describing CTI as evidence-based knowledge that includes context, mechanisms, indicators, implications, and actionable advice about existing or emerging threats. Abu (2018) highlights that the core objective of CTI is to empower organisations to tackle cyber threats strategically, operationally, and tactically.

Actionable CTI refers to cyber threat information that provides specific details for effectively detecting, preventing, or responding to threats (Wagner et al., 2019). Several criteria for actionable CTI have been proposed (ibid). Influential criteria outlined by the European Union Agency for Cybersecurity (Pawlinski et al., 2015) include relevance (ensuring the CTI directly applies to the system at risk), timeliness (sharing current information promptly), accuracy (informing stakeholders on vulnerabilities post-analysis), completeness (covering all threat aspects for adequate response), and ingestibility (the organisation's ability to integrate and apply CTI within its systems). The criteria help ensure that CTI is informative and practical, enabling organisations to mitigate and respond to cyber threats effectively.

Cyber-threat intelligence sharing (CTIS) is the process of exchanging CTI among different entities, such as security teams, business partners, vendors, customers, regulators, and industry peers (Jonsson et al., 2016). Following Vazquez et al. (2011), Wagner et al. (2019) outline three CTI sharing models: Peer-to-Peer, where organisations share CTI directly without intermediaries; Peer-to-Hub, involving a central hub that collects, processes, and disseminates CTI to stakeholders; and a Hybrid model that blends direct sharing between entities with the centralised management and broad reach of a hub.

CTI sharing has demonstrated its efficacy in mitigating cyber-attacks, preventing potential ones, and quickly pinpointing attackers and their tactics (Tounsi, 2019). Its benefits, including cost savings and improved cybersecurity quality, are widely acknowledged in different contexts (Skopik et al., 2017; Zibak & Simpson, 2019). This recognition has led to a growing trend among organisations to participate actively in CTI sharing (Wagner et al., 2019).

While there is an increase in global and industry-specific CTI-sharing initiatives, national CTI-sharing remains prevalent (Wagner et al., 2019). CTI-sharing landscapes can differ markedly across countries due to their unique geopolitical dynamics, local regulations, and industry-specific contexts (Fransen & Kerkdijk, 2017). However, research focusing on national CTI-sharing ecosystems remains sparse, with only a few case studies (e.g., Fransen & Kerkdijk, 2017; Amanowicz, 2020) addressing this area.

2.2 CTI Sharing Automation and Malware Information Sharing Platform (MISP)

With the increasing volume of threat data, automating Cyber Threat Intelligence (CTI) sharing is becoming critical (Haque & Krishnan, 2021; Wagner, 2019). Traditional methods like email are inefficient, leading to delays and information overload (Kampanakis, 2014). Despite the recognised importance of automated CTI sharing (Piotr & Pawliński, 2014; Wagner, 2019; Haque & Krishnan, 2021), challenges persist in ensuring data accuracy and algorithm sophistication, which is necessary to avoid false positives or missed threats (Wagner, 2019). Additionally, concerns about privacy legislation are significant (Schwartz et al., 2016; Sullivan, 2017).

Various platforms have been developed to improve threat intelligence sharing through automation and standardisation (Stojkovski et al., 2021). These platforms, while varying in capabilities, are essential for efficient Cyber Threat Intelligence (CTI) sharing among organisations and have been widely adopted due to their demonstrated benefits (Dandurand & Serrano, 2023; Bauer et al., 2020; De Melo e Silva et al., 2020). Notable platforms include MISP, OTX (Open Threat Exchange), OpenCTI, and ThreadQ, each offering unique features and strengths (Bauer et al. 2020, De Melo e Silva et al. 2020).

Evolving from its initial purpose of malware information sharing within military circles, MISP has expanded its scope to encompass a wide range of cybersecurity intelligence (Wagner et al., 2016; Stojkovski et al., 2021) and even other domains like dissemination of COVID information (Ramallo-Gonzále, 2021). With the backing of the Computer Incident Response Center Luxembourg (CIRCL) and the European Union (MISP 2024), MISP operates as an open-source collaborative platform, serving a diverse user base ranging from NATO agencies to private sector entities (Stojkovski et al., 2021). Organisations can join established MISP communities or establish their own MISP instances, which function as centralised or decentralised servers within a network to enable efficient CTI exchange (Stojkovski et al., 2021).

3. Methodology

We opted for a fully qualitative research approach involving content analysis of semi-structured interviews and relevant business documents. This approach allows for a comprehensive exploration of the multifaceted nature of CTI sharing and is well-suited to this study's exploratory nature.

We initially reached out to 12 organisations meeting specific criteria: operating in Finland's energy, healthcare, or logistics/transport sectors, ranking among the country's largest in their respective fields, headquartered in Finland, and identified by the Finnish National Emergency Supply Agency as critical for national supply security. Eventually, cybersecurity directors or managers from six critical infrastructure organisations agreed to participate. Please refer to **Table 1** for a summary of the informants and their organisations. Following our commitment to confidentiality, we maintain the anonymity of the interviewees and their organisations.

Table 1: Summary of interviewees

Abbreviation	Sector	Position	Time of interview
Interviewee A	Energy	Executive Level	December 2023
Interviewee B	Energy	Executive Level	December 2023
Interviewee C	Transportation/Logistics	Executive Level	December 2023
Interviewee D	Transportation/Logistics	Managerial Level	September 2023
Interviewee E	Healthcare	Managerial Level	November 2023
Interviewee F	Energy	Managerial Level	November 2023

The semi-structured interviews covered the following themes: current CTI sharing practices and their effectiveness, existing and potential use cases of MISP, and the perceived benefits and challenges in MISP adoption. The discussions aimed to capture insights not only from the organisational perspective but also in the broader national context. All interviews were conducted remotely and took about 45 minutes on average. Most were recorded and subsequently transcribed for analysis. In two cases, we relied on detailed notes due to the interviewees' preference not to record or automatically transcribe their responses. We corroborated and cross-referenced the evidence collected during interviews by examining relevant business documents related to CTI sharing in the studied organisations or their respective industries. These documents were provided to us by our informants.

Conventional content analysis (Hsieh & Shannon, 2005) was used to approach the interpretation of data. It is particularly effective in research where theoretical knowledge is limited, as it allows themes to emerge from the data instead of being imposed by existing theories. Template Analysis (King 2012) was employed as a practical technique to analyse the interview transcripts and the business documents. It involves developing a coding 'template' that represents themes identified in the data. The process begins with initial codes, which are then refined and organised into higher-order themes as the analytic process proceeds (King, 2012). This method is flexible and allows for modifying the template as new data is incorporated, making it particularly suitable for data-driven research where themes evolve during the analysis.

4. Results

This section presents out findings in two main parts. First, we examine how CTI is shared among Finland's critical infrastructure organisations. Then, we explore how MISP is being adopted and its potential benefits and challenges for the future.

4.1 Current CTI Sharing Practices in Finnish Critical Infrastructure

Finnish critical infrastructure follows a hybrid CTI sharing model involving centralised information exchange through a hub, the National Cyber Security Centre Finland (NCSC-FI), and direct organisational exchanges. Information happens formally and informally, using various traditional tools like email, instant messaging, and meetings. Figure 1 gives an overview of the CTI sharing network by Finnish critical infrastructure organisations (CIOs), as outlined by the informants. The details of these exchanges are described in the following sections.

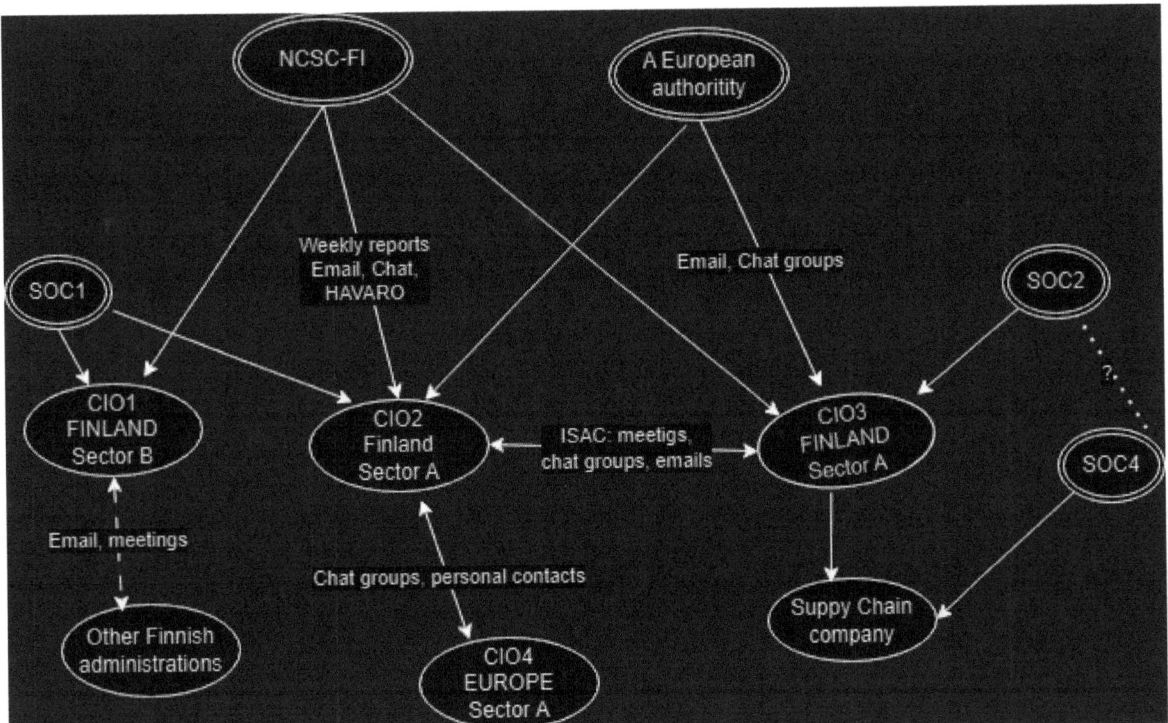

Figure 1: CTI sharing network around Finnish CIOs

4.1.1 Information Exchange with Hubs

National Cyber Security Centre Finland (NCSC-FI) operates under the Finnish Transport and Communication Agency (Traficom). It is a key information hub for critical sector organisations, disseminating cyber threat information primarily through traditional means like email and weekly reports. The CTI shared by NCSC-FI was highly appreciated due to itś regional specificity. For example, interviewee A said, *"The threat information reserved by Microsoft and these other American platforms is global. From there, one can observe major trends, but it does not tell what is currently happening in the Finnish context specifically, nor is it very detailed. In that sense, the information from the National Cyber Security Centre is very important to us."*.

Some participants highlighted that while information on NCSC-FI mailings and reports was valuable, there was room for improvement in terms of specificity. They emphasized the importance of detailed and actionable threat information, stressing that it should enable a swift response, e.g., by allowing them to provide technical identifiers to their SOC (Security Operations Center) for immediate checks and actions. Informant C said: *"They [NCSC-FI] provide really good information, especially about certain vulnerabilities and others, but then it can be general."* Industry-specific European supervisory authorities served as a secondary CTI hub for Finnish critical organisations and sometimes provided more concrete alerts than the NCSC-FI. Informant C continued: *"They [a European authority] share information at a level where, for example, they notice an organisation's data being sold on a Dark Web marketplace and then warn others that such an attack is underway, or they alert about ongoing DDoS attacks at specific locations based on mentions in Telegram"*.

NCSC-FI is also the main producer of the HAVARO service, which detects serious cybersecurity threats targeting Finnish organisations and issues warnings. It is based on automatically monitoring the data traffic through sensors, but humans analyse the findings before the target organisation is contacted. Notably, while NCSC-FI collects a substantial amount of threat data, much of it is not shared directly due to data protection considerations. However, organisations can still access it through HAVARO identifiers. Informant C says: *"Currently, organisations like Traficom [=NCSC-FI] may collect a lot of threat information but do not actively share it with others [due to data protection considerations]. However, as HAVARO users, we receive their identifiers, essentially the threat information they do not share directly with us."*

Most organisations we interviewed utilise commercial Security Operations Centers (SOCs) to manage their security operations. These commercial SOCs collaborate with NCSC-FI in delivering the HAVARO service and function as a central 'hub' or repository for their respective client bases, facilitating the sharing of Cyber Threat

Intelligence (CTI) among clients. However, due to the competitive landscape among commercial SOC providers, genuine information sharing between different SOCs is reportedly not a prevalent practice.

4.1.2 *Peer-to-Peer Information Sharing*

Instructure critical organisations (CIOs) in Finland share CTI in so-called ISAC groups (the abbreviation stands for Information Sharing and Analysis Center), which are maintained and facilitated by NCSC-FI. The industry-specific groups include one or more ISAC groups for energy, transportation, and healthcare sectors. Within these groups, organisations share CTI in quarterly meetings, via secure email, and through instant messaging services like Signal or RocketChat when classification permits. Access to ISAC groups is limited to major critical infrastructure companies that appoint their own representatives, and informal rules of the group enforce reciprocity, saying that if you want to be a member and receive CTI, you must also share your own CTI.

Information disseminated via ISAC-related chat groups typically focuses on detected cyberattack attempts or vulnerabilities within a company, serving as alerts for others to investigate potential similar issues. These groups occasionally facilitate the sharing of solutions as well. Regarding the relevance of the shared information, informant B provided an estimate, suggesting that approximately one-fifth of the messages resulted in actionable responses. He explained, *"In about four out of five cases, we can independently determine that no action is needed. We either confirm that the situation is under control or does not pertain to us. However, in the remaining twenty percent, we conduct further reviews and may share information. On the administrative side, users are often informed on appropriate actions or precautions."*

CIOs also exchanged CTI with domestic authorities, such as the police's cybersecurity department, the border security agency, and regulatory authorities. These exchanges were generally viewed positively but were not without challenges. For example, informant B mentioned instances where the organisation had to act as an intermediary, relaying information between different authorities during cybersecurity incidents.

Additionally, interviewees mentioned the importance of providing thread intelligence to non-critical supply chain partners who lack access to CTI channels but may handle sensitive data. In addition to informing their supply chain partners independently, some organisations sought to leverage their client influence to mandate direct information sharing between their SOC provider and partner companies' SOC providers.

4.2 The Status and Potential of MISP Deployment in Finland

None of the interviewed organisations – and based on our secondary data, this also applies to all contacted organisations that declined to participate – have fully implemented the MISP platform. However, there is a notable interest in adopting MISP, with some organisations having either decided to deploy it or have already initiated the process. **Figure 2** shows the organisations represented by our informants that are placed on adopting MISP (refer to Table 1 in Section 3 for background information).

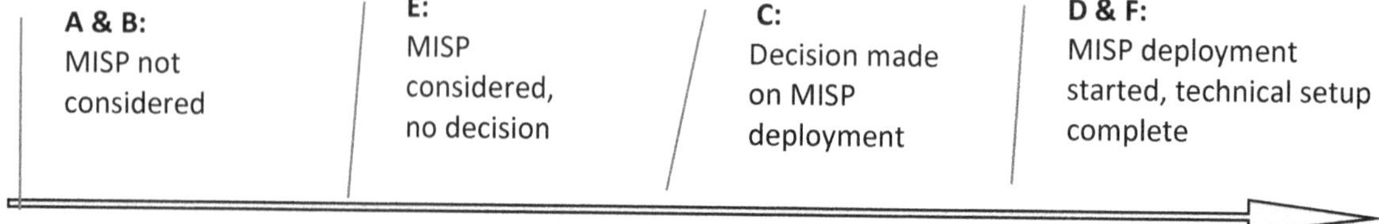

Figure 2: Status of MISP adoption in Finnish CIOs

Those informants whose organisations had considered MISP or taken steps towards deployment emphasised the advantages of the MISP system over the current email and chat-based CTI exchange systems. They emphasised MISP's capability for real-time CTI sharing, reducing delays. For example, Informant E explained:" *Whenever we start threat hunting and find something actionable, it takes time. In any case, it takes a long time before we can share it with other organisations. [...] If all organisations were connected to MISP, each organisation would instantly receive the information, eliminating unnecessary delays."*

Some informants also emphasised MISP's ability to provide access to structured data, facilitating automation for prompt security updates. Informant F gave an example*: "For instance, when we receive information through MISP, we could automatically use the identification details, like updating firewall rules or other security measures. If you inform someone via email, it is manual work at every endpoint where I inform 1000 parties, and each person handles it manually. [...] With MISP, the information becomes immediately actionable, and you can* *do whatever you want, even automate it*". They acknowledged potential challenges in automating threat responses but stressed the importance of MISP in making it possible when appropriate.

While recognising the advantages of MISP, informants expressed strong reservations about the possibility of widespread MISP adoption in Finland without NCSC-FI assuming a leadership role. Their leadership was seen as instrumental in building trust and ensuring broader participation. Informants C and F strongly called for an approach in which NCSC-FI would serve as the central authority, administrating a MISP instance and providing it as a (preferably free) service to CIOs. Informant C said: "*If we get what everyone dreams and asks for from Traficom [NCSC-FI], then they would be a government authority that either builds or implements MISP, so then these critical sector organisations [...] could join that MISP*". No other organisation than NCSC-FI was seen as well-positioned to administrate the national MISP instance. The idea was not new, as informant F noted: "*We see that there would be much use for such a tool [MISP]. Discussions about this have been ongoing for several years, but we have not seen any concrete steps taken, for example, from Traficom's* [NCSC-FI] *side*."

Among the organisations interviewed, the national MISP instance maintained by NCSC-FI, as described earlier, emerged as the most widely discussed and desired usage scenario. It was envisioned to have sector-specific subgroups and work in parallel with existing ISAC-group collaborations, offering more real-time and actionable threat information than email or chat. In addition to the national MISP, two other usage scenarios were discussed. Some organisations expressed interest in joining MISP instances provided as a service by European administrations within their respective industries. Furthermore, some contemplated the possibility of maintaining their own MISP groups to share threat information with their supply chain partners. These three MISP instances relevant to Finnish CIOs are summarised in **Table 2**. Global and open threat data feeds in MISP were not perceived as equally appealing. For example, informant D noted that they often contain excess information and noise, making it challenging to discern the relevant data amid the clutter.

Table 2: Envisioned and Existing MISP Instances relevant to Finnish CIOs

	Administrator	Members	Focus	Status
Finnish National MISP	NCSC-FI / Traficom	Critical infrastructure organisations in Finland	Sharing and collaborating on regional cybersecurity threats within Finland.	Envisioned, not yet operational
Supply Chain MISP	A Finnish infrastructure-critical organisation	Supply chain partners	Enhancing supply chain cybersecurity and sharing threat information among partners.	Envisioned, not yet implemented by interviewed companies
European Industry-Specific MISP	A relevant European administration	Large organisations in specific industries	Sharing cybersecurity threats within specific industries (e.g., electricity transfer or maritime) on a European scale	Already established in many industries.

Informants elaborated on several challenges in adopting MISP within the Finnish critical sector. To make such a solution valuable and sustainable, enough organisations in Finland must adopt MISP and actively use it to contribute thread data. Even if the service were free, effectively utilising MISP would necessitate acquiring specific skills and resources, which could prove challenging, especially for certain public sector organisations, as highlighted by informant E. Some informants stressed the importance of mechanisms to ensure active community participation, such as making reciprocal sharing a requirement for membership or enacting legislation mandating threat information sharing in specific cases.

The perceived reluctance of the National Cyber Security Centre Finland (NCSC-FI) to spearhead the implementation of MISP was attributed, in part, to concerns surrounding GDPR (General Data Protection Regulation). Classifying dynamic IP addresses as personal data subject to GDPR can create obstacles to sharing detailed and specific threat data within MISP groups. Informants also highlighted differing interpretations of GDPR across European countries, with Finland and Germany cited as examples of nations with particularly strict interpretations. Informant D emphasised that while GDPR facilitates data sharing more readily within the public sector, it poses greater challenges when sharing between the public and private sectors. Furthermore, other regulatory hurdles, particularly those pertaining to publicly traded companies, were identified as potential impediments to wider MISP use. Specifically, concerns were raised regarding classifying threat information as material non-public information under securities laws.

5. Discussion

Due to a limited number of interviews, the findings may not represent the entire spectrum of critical infrastructure organisations in Finland. The participation of only half the invited organisations introduces the possibility of selection bias, potentially favouring those more inclined towards MISP adoption or its national implementation. To counteract this, we concentrated on collecting comprehensive data during the interviews, encouraging participants to share not only specifics from their organisations but also broader trends and practices from their sectors, thus enriching the organisational focus with broader industry insights.

Interviews were limited to large, safety-critical organisations; however, concerns about resource constraints affecting MISP adoption were still raised. This leads to questions about the scalability of MISP adoption, especially for smaller organisations. The interviews highlighted the inclusion of smaller companies within their supply chains, which, while not officially categorised as critical infrastructure, can still access valuable data and should be considered in CTI collaborations. Previous research (e.g. Van Haastrecht, 2021) suggests MISP's potential for SME-sized organisations, but its practicality for the supply partners of Finnish safety-critical organisations merits examination. Further research is needed on standardising CTI-sharing tools and practices within a national context to ensure they are accessible for organisations of all sizes.

The discussions on the strict GDPR interpretations hindering MISP adoption reflect a broader concern within the cybersecurity community regarding the delicate balance between data privacy and threat intelligence sharing (see, for example, Nweke & Wolthusen, 2020; Grotto & Schallbruch, 2021). The observations made by informants regarding the varying interpretations of GDPR across European countries find support in existing research (Custers et al., 2018). These findings raise concerns about whether the stringent approaches adopted by some countries might potentially jeopardise long-term European cybersecurity efforts.

6. Conclusion

In conclusion, this study sheds light on the existing landscape of CTI sharing within Finland's critical infrastructure sectors and highlights the promising role of MISP in advancing these efforts. Notably, several critical organisations are contemplating a shift from conventional CTI sharing methods, such as email and chat groups, to MISP, attracted by its benefits like real-time sharing and the facilitation of data automation. However, the broader adoption of MISP at the national level is still hindered, with the critical infrastructure organisations waiting for the initiative from the National Cybersecurity Centre to establish a national MISP instance. Such a move was anticipated to strengthen Finland's cross-sectoral and industry-specific CTI exchanges. Implementing a national MISP framework also holds the potential to drive Finnish organisations towards engaging in Europe-wide, sector-specific MISP instances or adopting MISP as a tool for more effective threat intelligence exchange with supply chain partners. Additionally, this study draws attention to the challenges posed by data protection regulations, especially the varied interpretations of GDPR, which impact the sharing of detailed threat data across Europe. We hope this study will spark further research to deepen the understanding of CTI sharing and MISP adoption within a national framework.

Acknowledgments

Acknowledgment is paid to DYNAMO Project, funded by the European Union under grant agreement no. 101069601. Views and opinions expressed are however those of the authors only and do not necessarily reflect those of the European Union or European Commission. Neither the European Union nor the granting authority can be held responsible for them.

References

Abu, M.S., Selamat, S.R., Ariffin, A. & Yusof, R. (2018). Cyber threat intelligence–issue and challenges. Indonesian Journal of Electrical Engineering and Computer Science, 10(1), 371–379.

Adam, Z. & Simpson, A. (2019). Cyber threat information sharing: Perceived benefits and barriers. ACM International Conference Proceeding Series. [Available at: https://doi.org/10.1145/3339252.334052

Amanowicz, M. (2020). Towards building national cybersecurity awareness. International Journal of Electronics and Telecommunications, 321-326.

Bauer, S., Fischer, D., Sauerwein, C., Latzel, S., Stelzer, D., and Breu, R. (2020) Towards an Evaluation Framework for Threat Intelligence Sharing Platforms. In: 53rd Hawaii International Conference on System Sciences, HICSS 2020, Maui, Hawaii, USA, January 7-10. ScholarSpace, pp. 1-10. Available at: http://hdl.handle.net/10125/63978

Bowen, G. A. (2009). Document analysis as a qualitative research method. Qualitative research journal, 9(2), pp 27-40, https://doi.org/10.3316/QRJ0902027

Custers, B., Dechesne, F., Sears, A. M., Tani, T., & Van der Hof, S. (2018). A comparison of data protection legislation and policies across the EU. Computer Law & Security Review, 34(2), 234-243.

Dandurand, L. and Serrano, O.S. (2013). Towards improved cyber security information sharing. In: Cyber Conflict (CyCon), 2013 5th International Conference on. IEEE, pp. 1-16.

de Melo e Silva, A., Gondim, J.J.C., Albuquerque, R.O., García Villalba, L.J. (2020). A methodology to evaluate standards and platforms within cyber threat intelligence. Future Internet, 12(6), pp. 1–23. Available at: https://doi.org/10.3390/fi12060108

Fransen, F., & Kerkdijk, R. (2017). Cyber threat intelligence sharing through national and sector-oriented communities. Collaborative Cyber Threat Intelligence: Detecting and Responding to Advanced Cyber Attacks at the National Level, 187.

Grotto, A. and Schallbruch, M. (2021) Cybersecurity and the risk governance triangle: Cybersecurity governance from a comparative US–German perspective. International Cybersecurity Law Review 2(1), pp. 77-92.

Haque, M.F. and Krishnan, R. (2021). Toward automated cyber defense with secure sharing of structured cyber threat intelligence. Information Systems Frontiers 23, pp. 883–896. Available at https://doi.org/10.1007/s10796-020-10103-7

Hsieh H. and Shannon S (2005). Three approaches to qualitative content analysis. Qualitative Health Research, 15 (9) (2005), pp. 1277–1288, https://doi.org/10.1177/1049732305276687

Johnson, C.S., Badger, M.L., Waltermire, D.A., Snyder, J., & Skorupka, C. (2016). Guide to Cyber Threat Information Sharing. Technical Report NIST Special Publication (SP) 800–150. National Institute of Standards and Technology, Gaithersburg, MD. Available at: https://doi.org/10.6028/NIST.SP.800-150

Kampanakis, P. (2014). Security automation and threat information-sharing options. Security & Privacy, IEEE, 12(5), pp. 42-51.

King, N. (2012). Doing Template Analysis. In: Qualitative Organizational Research: Core Methods and Current Challenges. Sage

Kure, H. and Islam, S. (2019). Cyber threat intelligence for improving cybersecurity and risk management in critical infrastructure. Journal of Universal Computer Science, 25(11), pp.1478-502.

Li, Q., Yang, Z., Liu, B., Jiang, Z.Y. (2017). Framework of Cyber Attack Attribution Based on Threat Intelligence. ICST Inst Comput Sci Soc Informatics Telecommun Eng, 2017;190:92–103.

MISP (2024)- Model of Governance.[Online] Accessed 10th of January 2025. Available at: https://www.misp-project.org/governance/

Nweke, L. and Wolthusen, S. (2020) Legal issues related to cyber threat information sharing among private entities for critical infrastructure protection. 12th International Conference on Cyber Conflict (CyCon). Vol. 1300. IEEE, 2020.

Pawlinski, P., Jaroszewski, P., Kijewski, P., Siewierski, L., Jacewicz, P., Zielony, P., Zuber, R. (2015). Actionable information for security incident response. European Union Agency for Network and Information Security, Heraklion, Greece.

Ramallo-González, A. P., González-Vidal, A., & Skarmeta, A. F. (2021). CIoTVID: Towards an open IoT platform for infective pandemic diseases such as COVID-19. Sensors, 21(2), 484.

Saeed, S., Suayyid, S. A., Al-Ghamdi, M. S., Al-Muhaisen, H., & Almuhaideb, A. M. (2023). A systematic literature review on cyber threat intelligence for organizational cybersecurity resilience. Sensors, 23(16), 7273.

Skopik, F., Settanni G., and Fiedler, R. (2017). The Importance of Information Sharing and Its Numerous Dimensions to Circumvent Incidents and Mitigate Cyber Threats. In: Skopik, F. (Ed.), Collaborative Cyber Threat Intelligence: Detecting and Responding to Advanced Cyber Attacks at the National Level. Auerbach Publishers, Incorporated.

Stojkovski, B., Lenzini, G., Koenig, V., and Rivas, S. (2021). What's in a Cyber Threat Intelligence sharing platform? A mixed-methods user experience investigation of MISP. In: Annual Computer Security Applications Conference, pp. 385-398.

Sullivan, C., Burger, E. (2017). In the public interest: The privacy implications of international business-to-business sharing of cyber-threat intelligence. Computer Law & Security Review, 33(1), 14–29. ISSN 0267-3649. [Online] Available at: https://doi.org/10.1016/j.clsr.2016.11.015

Schwartz, A., Shah, S. C., MacKenzie, M. H., Thomas, S., Potashnik, T. S., & Law, B. (2016). Automatic threat sharing: how companies can best ensure liability protection when sharing cyber threat information with other companies or organizations. U. Mich. JL Reform, 50, 887.

Tounsi, W. (2019) What is Cyber Threat Intelligence and How is it Evolving? In: Cyber-Vigilance and Digital Trust. John Wiley & Sons, Ltd, Chapter 1, pp. 1–49. Available at: https://doi.org/10.1002/9781119618393.ch1

Van Haastrecht, M., Golpur, G., Tzismadia, G., Kab, R., Priboi, C., David, D., Răcătăian, A., Baumgartner, L., Fricker, S., Ruiz, J.F. and Armas, E., 2021. A shared cyber threat intelligence solution for smes. Electronics, 10(23), p.2913.

Vazquez, D.F., Acosta, O.P., Spirito, C., Brown, S., Reid, E. (2012). Conceptual Framework for Cyber Defense Information Sharing within Trust Relationships. In: 4th International Conference on Cyber Conflict, CyCon 2012, Tallinn, Estonia, June 5-8, pp. 1–17.

Wagner, C., Dulaunoy, A., Wagener, G., & Iklody, A. (2016). Misp: The design and implementation of a collaborative threat intelligence sharing platform. In Proceedings of the 2016 ACM on Workshop on Information Sharing and Collaborative Security, pp. 49-56.

Wagner, T.D., Mahbub, K., Palomar, E., Abdallah, A.E. (2019). Cyber threat intelligence sharing: Survey and research directions. Computers & Security, 87, 101589.

Evaluating Cybersecurity Class Activities Based on the Cognitive Continuum Theory: An Exploratory Case Study

Thomas Heverin, Addison Lilholt and Emily Woodward
The Baldwin School, Bryn Mawr, U.S.

thomas.heverin@baldwinschool.org
alilholt@baldwinschool.org
ewoodward@baldwinschool.org

Abstract: With the cybersecurity workforce estimated to have grown to 5.5 million in 2023 but still facing a significant shortage, there is an urgent need for educational strategies that can effectively enhance decision-making skills in this domain. This paper explores the application of Hammond's Cognitive Continuum Theory (CCT) in the context of K-12 cybersecurity education, aiming to address the global cybersecurity workforce shortage and skills gap by preparing the next generation of cybersecurity professionals. This study adopts a case-study methodology to investigate the use of CCT in a high school "Cybersecurity and Ethical Hacking" class, analysing 104 tasks across six class activities to determine how different cognitive modes (Analytical Cognition, Quasi-Rational Cognition, and Intuitive Cognition) are induced by various task characteristics from CCT's Task Continuum Index (TCI). Analytical cognition consists of rational decision making while Intuitive Cognition represents intuitive decision making. Quasi-Rational Cognition represents a blend of these two decision making styles. Directed content analysis and thematic analysis reveal that most tasks in the case promoted Analytical Cognition, with a significant presence of tasks inducing Quasi-Rational Cognition and fewer tasks facilitating Intuitive Cognition. The findings also highlight the dominance of information retrieval and analysis, methodical approaches in information seeking, and synthesis and decision-making across the cognitive modes, pointing towards the critical role of information behaviour in cybersecurity tasks. This research provides insights into how CCT can potentially inform the design of educational activities in cybersecurity, suggesting that a balanced inclusion of tasks across the cognitive spectrum can better prepare students for the complexities of the cybersecurity field. The paper discusses the implications for cybersecurity education, emphasising the need for instructional strategies that encompass a range of cognitive modes to reflect real-world challenges and enhance decision-making capabilities in future professionals. Additionally, the findings make a connection between cybersecurity tasks and school library instruction which focuses heavily on information behaviours. Limitations and directions for future research, including expanding data collection and connecting CCT to other theoretical frameworks, are also discussed.

Keywords: Cybersecurity Education, Cybersecurity Information Seeking, Cognitive Modes

1. Introduction

The ISC2 (2023) cybersecurity workforce annual report, which is based on a global survey, shows a 12.6% annual increase in the workforce shortage, signalling the need for 4 million more cybersecurity professionals. With 67% of respondents noting staff shortages and 92% identifying skills gaps, the urgency for nearly doubling the workforce is evident, especially against the backdrop of the most challenging cybersecurity threat landscape in five years as stated by 75% of respondents (ISC2, 2023).

Addressing this shortfall requires starting cybersecurity education early, at the K-12 level, to boost university enrollments and subsequent workforce readiness, as emphasised by Chen et al. (2021). Cybersecurity tasks vary widely, from simple email analysis to complex malware attack analysis, necessitating a spectrum of decision-making skills—from analytical to intuitive, as described by Heverin (2014) and Hammond (1996). This blend of skills is crucial in high-stakes environments like cybersecurity, where decisions often blend analysis and intuition.

Hammond's Cognitive Continuum Theory (CCT) offers a framework for developing these decision-making skills in K-12 cybersecurity education, balancing analytical and intuitive approaches. However, challenges such as access to technology, age-appropriate content, and effective teaching strategies, along with the time demands of creating engaging class materials, remain significant hurdles (Rowland, Podhradsky, and Plucker, 2018; Chen et al., 2021).

2. Research Background

The CCT, as conceptualised by Hammond (1996), introduces a nuanced perspective in understanding decision-making processes. It delineates three cognitive modes: analytical cognition (AC), intuitive cognition (IC), and quasi-rational cognition (QRC), which is a blend of AC and IC. Rather than dichotomizing IC and AC, CCT places them along a continuum, recognizing the adaptability of human cognition to various task demands.

This continuum is exemplified in the Cognitive Continuum Index (CCI) introduced by Hammond (1996), outlining traits associated with each cognitive mode. The concept of quasi-rationality is central to CCT. This mode is described as "robust and adaptive," fitting for tasks that do not squarely fall into purely intuitive or analytical categories (Dunwoody et al., 2000). The CCI is shown in Table 1.

Table 1: The Cognitive Continuum Theory's Cognitive Modes of Analytical and Intuitive Cognition.

Cognitive Property	Analytical Cognition	Intuitive Cognition
Cue use	Sequential	Simultaneous
Cognitive control	Conscious information processing	Unconscious information processing
Availability of rules	Formal rules available and used	Formal rules unavailable
Cue type	Reliance on quantitative cues	Reliance on qualitative cues
Cue evaluation	Cues evaluated at measurement level	Cues evaluated perceptually
Organising principle	Task specific organising principle	Pattern recognition, averaging

In addition to cognitive modes, CCT connects task characteristics with induced cognitive modes, as seen in the Task Continuum Index (TCI) (Hammond, 1996). The TCI categorises tasks based on properties that evoke IC or AC, thereby offering a comprehensive framework for understanding cognitive mode utilisation in various contexts. The TCI is shown in Table 2.

Table 2: Selected Task Properties from the Task Continuum Index of the Cognitive Continuum Theory.

Task Properties	Analytical Cognition Inducing	Intuitive Cognition Inducing
Number of Cues	Less Than Five	Greater Than Five
Measurement of Cues	Objective	Perceptual
Redundancy Among Cues	Low	High
Decomposition Level of Task	High	Low
Degree of Certainty in Task	High	Low
Display of Cues	Sequential	Simultaneous

The application of CCT across disciplines has been substantial. For instance, in healthcare, studies have explored the relationship between the TCI and the CCI in nurse decision-making, finding correlations between task properties and cognitive modes (Cader, 2005; Conlon, Raeburn, and Want, 2023; O'Connor et al. 2023). This is evidenced in scenarios where nurses, facing high-pressure situations with multiple cues, predominantly engage in intuitive cognition, as observed by Hunter, Consideine, and Manias (2023). Mahan (1994) and Lipshitz (1993) also found support between the correlation of the TCI with the CCI in high-stakes contexts.

Similarly, in cybersecurity, Molinaro and Bolton (2019) revealed that structured tasks, such as tasks phishing email detection, benefit from an analytical cognitive approach. This finding aligns with Heverin's (2019) study, which showed correlations between cybersecurity task properties and cognitive modes in tasks such as phishing email, zero-day exploit analysis, and malware attack detection. The more simple straight-forward tasks (phishing email detection) induced more AC while the more complex tasks (malware attack detection) resulted in inducing more IC (Heverin, 2019).

Moreover, the notion of quasi-rationality in CCT finds a particular resonance in the medical field. Custers (2013) emphasised that clinical problem-solving often occupies the middle ground between pure intuition and analysis. Experienced clinicians, using what Custers refers to as "educated intuition," engage in a more intuitive approach, balancing hypothesis generation with analytical verification.

In a meta-aggregative systematic review of CCT applied to nursing research, O'Connor et al. (2023), found the transferability of CCT to nursing decision making as "high" and that CCT could improve nurse-decision making and ultimately patient outcomes. Similarly, Cader, Campell, and Watson (2005) used Fawcett's framework, a framework for theory evaluation and testability, to evaluate the CCT and to determine its level of applicability to nurse's decision making. The researchers found empirical evidence across multiple studies that support the concepts and correlations posed by the CCT.

Custers (2013) underscored the importance of exposing novices to a variety of tasks via the TCI, enhancing training by aligning cognitive strategies with task characteristics. This is echoed by O'Connor et al. (2023), who highlighted the significance of incorporating decision-making into education. Cader, Campbell, and Watson (2005) also supported an educational approach based on CCT, arguing it allows for the practice of diverse cognitive modes suited to specific tasks, thereby improving future professional decision-making. Parker-Tomlin et al. (2017) further emphasized CCT training's benefits, particularly for understanding decision-making in team settings and enhancing skills like interprofessional collaboration and communication. Mahan (1994) and Kutschera and Byrd (2005) added that CCT-oriented education fosters superior decision-making strategies over traditional lecture-based methods.

In conclusion, CCT is crucial for understanding decision-making across disciplines, highlighting the CCI and TCI interaction. Integrating CCT into education could enhance future professionals' decision-making abilities, vital for navigating complex environments. Yet, a systematic method to evaluate instructional activities using CCT is missing. Our exploratory study in cybersecurity education begins to address this gap.

3. Methodology

3.1 Case Study Approach

The researchers utilised a case-study methodology for this CCT exploratory study, a strategy that can involve detailed investigation of a single or multiple cases through quantitative, qualitative, or mixed-methods analysis (Yin, 2018). Case studies are valuable for examining phenomena within their natural contexts, with a case typically defined as a phenomenon confined to a specific context and timeframe (Miles, Huberman, and Saldana, 2014). Yin (2018) describes this process as "bounding the case" (p. 31).

In this exploratory case study, the focus was on a high school cybersecurity class of 10 students at a college preparatory school, spanning the September 2023 to January 2024 timeframe. This first of its kind class at the school involved six main cybersecurity activities, including malware analysis and ethical hacking, encompassing a total of 104 tasks. The curriculum aimed at imparting practical skills in cybersecurity tool usage, ethical hacking, network reconnaissance, vulnerability detection, report generation, and malware analysis tasks. Table 3 shows the six main activities and the number of tasks that make up each activity. The results of the ethical hacking tasks were shared with organizations that gave permission for the class to conduct security tests.

Table 3: Malware Activities and Ethical Hacking Activities Analysed for the Case Study.

Malware Activity Cases	Ethical Hacking Activity Cases
Gozi Malware Analysis (14 tasks)	Ricoh Printer Ethical Hacking (11 tasks)
WannaCry Malware Analysis (28 tasks)	Moxa Nport Serial-Ethernet Device Ethical Hacking (13 tasks)
Petya Malware Analysis (28 tasks)	Lantronix Serial-Ethernet Device Ethical Hacking (10 tasks)

The malware tasks focused on using tools such as DynamiteLabs AI and AnyRun which are malware analysis tools freely available in web browsers. The tasks focused on analysing attributes of malware attacks including Gozi, WannaCry and Petya attacks. The ethical hacking tasks focused on using various tools including Shodan, hacking-tools created by the teacher, VirusTotal, Google, ChatGPT and more to conduct ethical hacking of live targets (with permission received ahead of time from the target organisations for testing).

The research questions that guided this exploratory case-study consisted of the following:

- What proportion of malware analysis and ethical hacking tasks in the selected high school cybersecurity class fall into AC, QRC, and IC categories, as determined by predefined TCI criteria?
- Are there differences across the malware analysis and ethical hacking tasks in terms of the AC, QRC, and IC categories?

- What insights can be gained from comparing AC, QRC, and IC tasks identified within malware analysis and ethical hacking tasks beyond the TCI criteria?

To address the first question, the researchers utilised directed content analysis to assess the distribution of cognitive modes tied to specific task characteristics from the TCI. For the second question, they performed inductive thematic analysis on the tasks to identify recurring themes beyond TCI task characteristics. Through these combined analyses, the aim was to thoroughly understand how task characteristics differed across various activities in the cybersecurity learning environment.

3.2 Content Analysis of TCI Task Characteristics

The researchers selected a directed content analysis approach for examining the tasks. Directed content analysis consists of using a deductive approach based on previous theory and uses definitions of coding categories from that theory (Hsieh and Shannon, 2005). In this case, the CCT provided the theoretical framework and the task characteristic coding categories. For this exploratory case study, two researchers conducted the content analysis. Both have several years of computer science and cybersecurity teaching experience at the K-12 and university levels. The lead researcher holds a Ph.D. and research expertise in NDM and CCT as well as several years of operational experience in cybersecurity supporting the U.S. Navy. Given the exploratory nature of this study, two coders were employed to analyse student task data. This approach facilitated the development of a rich initial thematic framework for further investigation in larger studies.

A code book was initially developed based on the TCI. The TCI task characteristics selected were number of cues, measurement of cues, redundancy among cues, decomposition level of task, degree of certainty in task, and display of cues. These are listed above in Table 2 which show which values of the selected TCI characteristics are predicted to induce either AC, QRC or IC.

Two coders independently reviewed a subset of tasks from multiple activities and coded each task as either AC-T, QRC-T, or IC-T, signifying if the task had more AC, QRC, or IC inducing characteristics respectively from the TCI. To ensure consistent application of the coding scheme, two independent coders assessed inter-rater reliability through Cohen's kappa (McHugh, 2012). Initial discrepancies were resolved through discussion, resulting in a final "almost perfect agreement" (kappa = 0.924) for the remaining tasks (McHugh, 2012). Examples of AC-T, QRC-T and IC-T tasks are provided in Table 4.

Table 4: Example tasks falling within each CCT cognitive mode.

Task Characteristics	Example Tasks
AC-T	-Enter the IP address into VirusTotal and state how many vendors marked it as malicious. -For the IP address, state how many ports Shodan shows are open.
QRC-T	-Given that we found open ports on the Nport devices on the target IP address and that you found specific vulnerabilities, state what security recommendations do you have for the university
IC-T	-Before looking at the attack attributes, view the graphical representation only of the malware attack in AnyRun. State what you think may be happening with this attack.

3.3 Thematic Analysis of Tasks within AC-T, QRC-T, and IC-T Categories

After the 104 tasks were coded as falling into AC-T, QRC-T or IC-T categories, the researchers conducted a thematic analysis on the categorised instructions to look for themes beyond measurable task characteristics from the TCI. Thematic analysis aims to uncover and interpret recurring patterns of meaning within qualitative data, providing insights into the underlying themes and experiences it represents (Braun and Clarke, 2006). The researchers followed a traditional six-phase approach to thematic analysis which consists of researchers familiarising themselves with the data, generating initial codes, searching for themes across the data, reviewing and refining those themes, defining and naming them clearly, and finally summarising the findings in a meaningful and comprehensive way (Braun and Clarke, 2006).

4. Results

4.1 Content Analysis Results

Table 5 shows the results of the TCI task characteristics analysis for malware analysis tasks (77), ethical hacking tasks (34) and all tasks combined (104). The table shows that most of the tasks examined in this case study were associated with inducing AC. This means that most of the tasks called for rational and deliberate decision making across malware analysis and ethical hacking tasks. QRC was found to be induced in close to 30% of all tasks. QRC represents a mix of rational and intuitive decision making. To a much lesser extent, IC, which represents intuitive decision making, was found to be induced in 10% or less across malware and ethical hacking tasks.

Table 5: Percentages and counts of tasks that fall within each task type (AC-T, QRC-T or IC-T).

TCI	Percent of Malware Analysis tasks (77 Tasks)	Percent of Ethical Hacking tasks (34 Tasks)	Percent of All Tasks (104 Tasks)
AC-T	66% (46)	65% (22)	65% (68)
QRC-T	24% (17)	32% (11)	27% (28)
IC-T	10% (7)	3% (1)	8% (8)
Total	100% (70)	100% (34)	100% (104)

Various statistical tests were used to examine potential differences in the frequencies of AC-T, QRC-T, and IC-T across the six activities. First, the researchers compared the frequencies of AC-T, QRC-T, and IC-T for two types of tasks (malware analysis and ethical hacking tasks) using a Chi-squared test. While no statistically significant differences were found (chi-square statistic: 2.04, p-value: 0.36), it's important to note that the small sample size may have limited the ability to detect subtle differences. Similarly, a Chi-squared test on frequencies across all six activities together also showed no significant difference (chi-square statistic = 5.12, p-value = 0.88) across AC-T, QRC-T and IC-T.

Given the limitations of sample size, Fisher's exact test for pairwise comparisons was then used. As shown in Table 6, there were significant differences between AC-T and IC-T, as well as QRC-T and IC-T. However, the difference between AC-T and QRC-T was not statistically significant. This aligns with the observed trend of higher frequencies for AC-T compared to QRC-T and IC-T, although further research with larger samples is needed to confirm these findings.

Table 6: Results of Fisher's exact tests for pairwise comparisons for AC-T, QRC-T and IC-T.

Pairwise Comparison	p-value	Interpretation
AC-T vs. QRC-T	0.081	No significant difference
AC-T vs. IC-T	< 0.001	Significant difference: AC-T used significantly more than IC-T
QRC-T vs. IC-T	0.027	Significant difference: QRC-T used significantly more than IC-T

4.2 Thematic Analysis Results

To explore task characteristics beyond the coded categories from the TCI, the researchers performed inductive thematic analysis on each task set (AC-T, QRC-T and IC-T), following Braun and Clarke's approach (2006). This identified recurring themes and patterns within each task set, uncovering insights into task features that influence cognitive engagement beyond task characteristics listed in Table 2. The inductive thematic analysis yielded nine main themes, each containing several sub-themes (20 sub-themes in total). The themes focused on information behaviours which encompass the ways individuals seek, gather, process, apply, and share information. Table 7 summarises the main themes and enumerates the number of sub-themes for each.

Table 7: Identified main themes across the AC-T, QRC-T, and IC-T sets of tasks.

Task Type	Main Themes from Thematic Analysis (Number of Sub-Themes)	Examples
AC-T	Detailed, Precise Information Seeking (4) Detailed Analysis of Information (2) Critical Evaluation of Information (1)	-Find IP addresses in Shodan for a target -Review Shodan results to find open ports -Determine common thread in hostnames
QRC-T	Translation of Information to Advice (4) Adaptive Information Seeking (2) Critical Evaluation of Information Sources (1)	-Recommend mitigations based open ports -Generate searches to identify employee's full name and role based on username -Use multiple sources in and outside of the printer to try to find users of the specific printer
IC-T	Informed Judgement with Uncertainty (3) Active Discovery and Application to New Situations (2) Comparative Analysis and Contrast (1)	-Given 1 malicious link alert, determine risk -Given the map of open industrial control system (ICS) ports in Shodan, state which cities you would defend first and why -Compare and contrast Petya & WannaCry attacks

For AC-T, three main themes emerge: *Detailed Information Seeking for Precise Information*, highlighting detailed searching for precise and accurate information; *Detailed Analysis of Information to Make Decisions,* underscoring detailed analysis of results to make a highly informed decision; and *Critical Evaluation of Information*, focusing on summarising results and assessing the information's accuracy and reliability. This emphasis on a structured and analytical approach facilitates a deep understanding of cybersecurity information, allowing learners to apply this knowledge effectively in practical settings.

QRC-T is characterised by three main themes: *Translation of Complex Information into Advice*, blending technical information results with reasoning to make real-world judgments; *Adaptive Information Seeking*, emphasising iterative strategy refinement and decisions with incomplete information; and *Critical Evaluation of Information Sources,* evaluating which sources provide information and using incomplete information from across sources to make judgements. These themes reflect a dynamic learning environment where students are encouraged to apply technical knowledge adaptively, mirroring the unpredictable nature of cybersecurity challenges.

IC-T's themes include *Informed Judgement in Uncertainty*, fostering decisions based on limited information and scenario-based learning; *Active Discovery and Application*, promoting proactive information search, contextual analysis, and intuitive problem-solving without exhaustive analysis; and *Comparative Analysis and Contrast*, encouraging comparisons and informed assessments. This approach nurtures a proactive and intuitive mindset, preparing students to tackle cybersecurity issues with a blend of critical thinking and adaptability.

Across AC-T, QRC-T, and IC-T tasks, a consistent emphasis on information behaviour underlines the importance of effective information seeking, processing, and application. While AC-T focuses on a detailed and systematic analysis, QRC-T advocates for an adaptive application of technical knowledge in real-world scenarios, and IC-T emphasises intuitive decision-making, based on uncertainty and scarcity of information, and active discovery. These differences highlight the varied information behaviours that appear across the three types of tasks.

5. Discussion

5.1 Research Implications

The case study's finding that cybersecurity tasks predominantly focused on AC, rational decision making, offers a pivotal discussion point. Despite students' engagement with tools like Shodan and Virus Total, the emphasis on AC might have limited the exploration of diverse cognitive modes. This focus could stem from the students' novice status, necessitating structured approaches aligned with AC, or the course's inaugural run prioritising foundational skills. Incorporating more tasks aimed at QRC and IC in future iterations could enrich students' decision-making abilities. Training in varied cognitive modes is suggested to foster "educated intuition" among novices, akin to expert behaviour (Lipshitz and Shual, 1997; Custers, 2013; Mahan, 1994; Cader, Campbell, and Watson, 2005; Kutschera and Byrd, 2005; Parker-Tomlin et al., 2017; O'Connor et al., 2023).

The absence of diverse decision-making strategies in the curriculum calls for attention, though the acquired direct experience with cybersecurity tools is invaluable. Starting with AC might lay the groundwork for later intuitive expertise, reflecting Kolb's Experiential Learning Theory (ELT) where structured learning precedes intuitive application (Kolb, 1984; Schoonenboom et al., 2008). This approach, suggesting a progression from concrete experience (CE) to active experimentation (AE), mirrors the development from novice to expert. Further research could delve into the parallels between CCT and ELT.

Unexpectedly, the thematic analysis highlighted varied information-seeking behaviours across cognitive modes, underscoring the importance of this aspect in cybersecurity learning. Information behaviour, integral to how individuals seek, process, and utilise information, varied across AC, QRC, and IC tasks, aligning with Taylor's Information Use Environment (IUE) model (1991). The IUE model names 11 problem dimensions (such as "well-structured/ill-structured", "simple/complex", and "susceptible/not susceptible to empirical analysis") that mirror task characteristics found in the CCT's TCI, suggesting a fruitful avenue for future research on the interplay between information behaviours and cognitive modes in cybersecurity learning. According to Taylor, the problem dimensions influence the types of information deemed useful. Taylor (1991, p. 229) stated that problems "pose different requirements on the type of information perceived as necessary, and hence different uses to which information is put in the process of resolution." The potential connection to Taylor's IUE model further implies that the context in which information is sought and used could significantly influence the cognitive modes engaged by learners. For example, using the IUE problem dimensions as a guide, one could develop tasks that are ill-structured, complex, not susceptible to empirical analysis which would most likely induce IC according to the CCT.

5.2 Cybersecurity Education Implications

This study's application of CCT in analysing a high school cybersecurity class presents a unique lens for evaluating educational methods, particularly beneficial for cybersecurity educators. By aligning tasks with the identified TCI task characteristics and information behaviour themes, educators can enhance learning experiences, encouraging students to navigate complex information landscapes through AC, QRC, and IC. Tasks designed to challenge students with evaluating disparate information sources (QRC) or making decisions under data scarcity (IC) are prime examples of how to cultivate essential skills.

The thematic-analysis results in Table 7 show nine high-level themes that focus primarily on information seeking. The high-level themes incorporate 20 sub-themes such as "conduct critical assessments of information gathered", "leverage tools for information gathering," and "synthesize data from disparate sources." These themes align well with the American Association of School Libraries (AASL) Standard Framework for Learners (2018). The AASL Standard contains competencies such as evaluating the quality of information sources, using a variety of tools for information seeking, and comparing information gathered from various sources. Three expert librarians, all who hold a M.S. in Library and Information Science and an average of 12 years of library experience, independently coded the 20 sub-themes in this current study as being related (or not related) to AASL Standard competencies. The results showed a 100% agreement among the librarians for 13 of 20 sub-themes. These initial results show how school library instruction can be embedded in cybersecurity education.

5.3 Limitations and Future Research

This exploratory case study has limitations. The small sample size restricts generalizability. Studying a wider range of cybersecurity tasks and incorporating perspectives beyond just task instructions (teacher reflections, student responses, observations) would provide a more complete picture.

Future research should expand data collection through interviews, surveys, and reflections to enhance credibility and understand how task design influences learning. Sharing lessons would allow for replication studies. Additionally, applying information behavior theories to the framework could offer deeper insights into how tasks influence students' cognitive modes in cybersecurity.

6. Conclusion

This study's exploration into the application of the CCT in K-12 cybersecurity education through a detailed analysis of task characteristics within a high school class reveals a significant tilt towards AC which represents rational decision making. It demonstrates an essential shift is needed towards integrating more IC-inducing tasks (intuitive decision making) and QRC-inducing tasks (a mix of rational and intuitive decision making). This integration aims to balance the range of decision-making strategies used, enhancing students' ability to adapt to the multifaceted challenges of cybersecurity by fostering critical thinking, problem-solving, and adaptive decision-making skills.

Moreover, the study highlights the crucial role of information behaviour in cybersecurity education, aligning with findings to Taylor's IUE model and suggesting pathways for enriching cybersecurity education through the strategic involvement of school librarians. This connection to information behaviour not only aligns with the AASL standards but also opens avenues for interdisciplinary collaboration, emphasising the symbiotic relationship between cybersecurity tasks and librarian instructional practices. Future research is directed towards expanding the CCT framework's application within diverse educational settings, further exploring the interplay between task design, information behaviour, and cognitive modes, and incorporating feedback from students and educators to refine CCT-aligned educational strategies.

Acknowledgements

The authors thank Lauren Friedman-Way and Jessica Tingling of the Baldwin School for providing their librarian expertise.

References

American Association of School Librarians (AASL) (2018) AASL Standards Framework for Learners.

Braun, V. and Clarke, V. (2019) "Thematic Analysis". *Handbook of Research Methods in Health Social Sciences*. Hoboken, New Jersey: Springer. pp. 843–860.

Cader, R., Campbell, S. and Watson, D. (2005) Cognitive Continuum Theory in nursing decision-making. *Journal of Advanced Nursing*, 49(4), pp.397-405.

Chen, W., He, Y., Tian, X. and He, W. (2021) Exploring cybersecurity education at the k-12 level. In *SITE Interactive Conference* (pp. 108-114). Association for the Advancement of Computing in Education (AACE).

Conlon, D., Raeburn, T. and Wand, T. (2023) Cognitive Continuum Theory: Can it contribute to the examination of confidentiality and risk-actuated disclosure decisions of nurses practising in mental health? *Nursing Inquiry*, 30(2), pp. 1-29.

Custers, E.J. (2013) Medical education and cognitive continuum theory: an alternative perspective on medical problem solving and clinical reasoning. *Academic Medicine*, 88(8), pp.1074-1080.

Dunwoody, P.T., Haarbauer, E., Mahan, R.P., Marino, C., and Tang, C. (2000) Cognitive adaptation and its consequences: A test of Cognitive Continuum Theory. *Journal of Behavioral Decision Making*, 13(1), pp.35-54.

Hammond, K.R. (1996) *Human judgment and social policy: Irreducible uncertainty, inevitable error, unavoidable injustice*. New York: Oxford University Press.

Hammond, K. R., Frederick, E., Robillard, N., and Victor, D. (1989) Application of cognitive theory to the student–teacher dialogue. In D. A. Evans and V. L. Patel (Eds.), *Cognitive science in medicine: Biomedical modeling* (pp. 174–210). Cambridge, MA: MIT Press.

Heverin, T. (2014) Information Behaviors and Cognitive Modes Used for Cyber Situation Assessment. Drexel University.

Hsieh, H., and Shannon, S. E. (2005) Three approaches to qualitative content analysis. *Qualitative Health Research*, 15(9), pp. 1277–1288.

Hunter, S., Considine, J. and Manias, E. (2023) Nurse decision-making when managing noradrenaline in the intensive care unit: A naturalistic observational study. *Intensive and Critical Care Nursing*, 77.

International Information System Security Certification Consortium (ISC2) (2023) Cybersecurity Workforce Study 2023.

Kolb, D.A. (1984) *Experiential learning: experience as the source of learning and development.* Prentice-Hall, Inc. Englewood Cliffs, NJ.

Kutschera, I. and Byrd, J. (2005) Applying the concept of cognitive continuum to leadership training. *Journal of American Academy of Business*, 6(1), pp.20-25.

Lipshitz, R. (1993) Converging themes in the study of decision making in realistic settings. In Klein, G., Orasanu, J., Calderwood, R., and Zsambok, C. (Eds.), *Decision making in action: Models and methods* (pp.103-137). Westport, CT: Ablex Publishing Corporation.

Lipshitz, R., and Shaul, O. B. (1997) Schemata and mental models in recognition-primed decision making. In *Naturalistic decision making expertise: Research and applications* (pp. 293– 303). Hillsdale, NJ: Erlbaum.

Mahan, R.P. (1994) Stress-induced strategy shifts toward intuitive cognition: A cognitive continuum framework approach. *Human Performance*, 7(2), pp.85-118.

McHugh, M.L. (2012) Interrater reliability: the kappa statistic. Biochem Med (Zagreb), 22(3), pp.276-282.

Miles, M.B., Huberman, A.M., and Saldana, J. (2014) *Qualitative data analysis: A methods sourcebook (3rd ed.)* Thousand Oaks, CA: SAGE.

Molinaro, K.A., and Bolton, M.L. (2019) Using the lens model and cognitive continuum theory to understand the effects of cognition on phishing victimization. *Proceedings of the Human Factors and Ergonomics Society Annual Meeting*, 63(1), pp.173-177.

O'Connor, T., Gibson, J., Lewis, J., Strickland, K. and Paterson, C. (2023) Decision-making in nursing research and practice—Application of the Cognitive Continuum Theory: A meta-aggregative systematic review. *Journal of Clinical Nursing*, 32(23-24), pp.7979-7995.

Parker-Tomlin, M., Boschen, M., Morrissey, S. and Glendon, I. (2017) Cognitive continuum theory in interprofessional healthcare: A critical analysis. *Journal of Interprofessional Care*, 31(4), pp.446-454.
Rowland, P., Podhradsky, A., and Plucker, S. (2018) CybHER: A Method for Empowering, Motivating, Educating and Anchoring Girls to a Cybersecurity Career Path. Paper presented at the *Proceedings of the 51st Hawaii International Conference on System Sciences*.
Schoonenboom, J., Tattersall, C., Miao, Y., Stefanov, K. and Aleksieva-Petrova, A. (2008) The role of competence assessment in the different stages of competence development. *Handbook on Information Technologies for Education and Training*, pp.317-341.
Taylor, R. S. (1991) Information use environments. In Dervin, B. and Voigt, M. J. (Eds.), *Progress in Communication Sciences* (Vol. 10, pp. 217–255). Norwood, NJ: Ablex Publishing Corporation.
Yin, R.K. (2018) *Case study research: Design and methods (6th ed)*. Thousand Oaks, CA: SAGE.

A Theory of Offensive Cyberspace Operations and Its Policy and Strategy Implications

Gazmend Huskaj[1,2], Fredrik Blix[1] and Stefan Axelsson[1]
[1]Department of Computer and Systems Sciences, Stockholm University, Kista, Sweden
[2]Geneva Centre for Security Policy (GCSP), Geneva, Switzerland

g.huskaj@gcsp.ch
blix@dsv.su.se
stefan.axelsson@dsv.su.se

Abstract: The significance of Offensive Cyberspace Operations (OCO) in cyber warfare and national security is increasingly recognised, yet academic literature lacks a dedicated theoretical framework to fully articulate its unique aspects and strategic dimensions. Traditionally enveloped within the broader context of information warfare, OCO's distinct characteristics have often been overlooked. Addressing this gap, our paper aims to delineate the specificities of OCO and establish a structured conceptual model that enhances understanding and operational clarity. To achieve this, the study adopts an interpretive approach, drawing from existing literature on information warfare and cyberspace, alongside official U.S. government and military publications on cyberspace operations. Employing the theory-building method, we focus primarily on conceptualization. This involves creating a coherent conceptual framework through abstraction, synthesis, and diagramming, informed by seminal works in the field. Among the paper's key contributions are detailed conceptual models that shed light on OCO's integration within the broader cyber domain, the influence of U.S. policy and strategy on OCO, and the critical triad for successful operations: access, vulnerabilities, and payloads. Furthermore, we elucidate the primary and secondary components of OCO, specifically cyberspace attack and exploitation, offering new insights into their roles and implications. Thus, the framework includes conceptual maps highlighting OCO's key elements, relationships, and challenges, aiming to advance academic discourse, practical strategies, and policy in cyberspace operations. This effort marks a significant step forward in both theoretical engagement and practical application within the field.

Keywords: Cyberspace Attack; Cyberspace Exploitation; Offensive Cyberspace Operations; Policy and Strategy.

1. Introduction

Offensive cyberspace operations (OCO) are now a part of modern warfare (e.g., Nakasone, 2022, 2023; Sky News, 2024; Jensen & Watts, 2023; Leyden, 2022). Research on cyberspace operations began to gain traction in 2006. Specifically, Jane's Defence Weekly discussed the US Air Force's intent in their October issue to "create and recognize a cyber-warfare command for cyberspace operations" (JDF, 2006). To understand the etymology, the term cyberspace originated from William Gibson's 1982 book "Burning Chrome" (Dictionary.com, 2019). The word 'cyber' descends from Cybernetics, and was coined by Norbert Wiener in his book with the same title in 1948 (Hardesty, 2011). By 1961, the word 'cyber' combined with other terms appeared first in the Wall Street Journal, leading to combinations such as "cyber warfare," "cyber security," "cyber operations" (Dictionary.com, 2019). However, not as much can be said about OCO. How can we develop a comprehensive and theory of OCO that accounts for their technical, policy, and social dimensions?

The authors acknowledge the contributions of existing theories on information warfare (e.g., Denning, 1999) and cyberspace (e.g., Caton & Bartholomees, 2012), but note that they are not focused on OCO. Therefore, the authors have developed a theory for this topic, drawing on the insights of Denning & Denning (2010), JCS (2018), and Lin (2009). Before introducing this theory, brief definitions of cyber warfare and cyberspace are provided. RAND Corporation (n.d.) defines cyber warfare as "the actions by a nation-state or international organization to attack and attempt to damage another nation's computers or information networks through, for example, computer viruses or denial-of-service attacks." The definition explicitly refers to actions by nation-states that involve attacking and attempting another nation's computers or information networks. In this research, cyber warfare is considered a subset of OCO, which encompasses a broader set of activities.

Cyberspace is defined as "A global domain within the information environment consisting of the interdependent networks of information technology infrastructures and resident data, including the Internet, telecommunications networks, computer systems, and embedded processors and controllers" (JCS, 2018, p. GL-4). Cyberspace operations (CO) on the other hand are defined as "The employment of cyberspace capabilities where the primary purpose is to achieve objectives in or through cyberspace" (JCS, 2018, p. vii). Offensive cyberspace operations (OCO) are defined as "Missions intended to project power in and through cyberspace" (JCS, 2018, p. GL-5). Based on these definitions, it may be inferred that OCO are military missions that employ cyberspace capabilities in a very complex man-made technological domain.

This research begins by describing what theory is and how it is developed in applied disciplines. It does so by reviewing what previous researchers have contributed to scholarly research on the topic. Next, the concept of *conceptualisation*, one of five phases in the theory-building process, is described. Its application is done on the reviewed literature on Denning's (1999) "information warfare theory", Lin's (2009) work on "Lifting the veil on cyber offense", Denning & Denning (2010) "The profession of it discussing cyber attack.", and JCS (2018) "Joint Publication 3-12 Cyberspace Operations". Section 3 presents the methodological considerations and Section 4 presents the results of the conceptualisation. The contribution of this paper are the conceptual maps, which in sum, represent a theory of offensive cyberspace operations. Section 5 presents the theory's policy and strategy implications and concludes in Section 6.

2. What is Theory and How is it Developed in Applied Disciplines?

The concept of theory is not universally agreed upon by scholars, but it generally involves a system of statements, constructs, and relationships that explain or describe a phenomenon (Gregor, 2006). Theory can be represented in various ways, such as words, diagrams, or mathematical terms, and it can have different purposes, such as causal explanation, hypothesis testing, or prescription (Gregor, 2006). Theory can also be distinguished from data, facts, or variables, which are not theory but may form the basis of theory (Saunders et al., 2016; Sutton & Staw, 1995; Whetten, 1989). Theory can be as simple as a set of sentences (Simon and Newell, 1956) or as complex as a symbolic construction (Kaplan, 1964). Theory can also prevent the observer from being dazzled by the full-blown complexity of natural or concrete events (Hall and Lindzey, 1957). According to Dubin (1978, p. 26), "a theory tries to make sense out of the observable world by ordering the relationships among elements that constitute the theorist's focus of attention in the real world". One way to order the relationships among the elements constituting the theorist's focus is conceptualisation (Swanson and Chermack, 2013).

In their *General Method of Theory Building in Applied Disciplines*, Swanson & Chermack (2013) state that Conceptualisation, one of five phases in the theory-building process, is about constructing a coherent and rigorous conceptual framework: crucial for theory building. The theoretical conceptual framework represents the central descriptive capability inherent in any theory. Thus, theory is a system of statements, constructs, and relationships that explain or describe a phenomenon, but it is not necessarily a universal or objective truth. Theory can have different forms, functions, and scopes, depending on the researcher's perspective, purpose, and context. Theory can also be influenced by the data, facts, and variables that are available and relevant to the research problem. However, theory is not necessarily a final or definitive answer, but a tentative and provisional one, that can be challenged, modified, or extended by further research. Through the process of conceptualisation, a framework can be developed that represents the core inherent in any theory.

3. Methodological Approach

This study adopts an interpretive approach (Oates, 2005) to develop a theory of offensive cyberspace operations (OCO). Interpretivism suggests that our understanding of offensive cyber operations is shaped by exploring the subjective meanings and motives in human interactions with computer systems. The main sources of data are the existing literature on information warfare and cyberspace, as well as the official documents and publications of the U.S. government and military on cyberspace operations. The study follows the general method of theory building in applied disciplines proposed by Swanson and Chermack (2013), which consists of five phases: problem identification, conceptualisation, operationalisation, testing, and refinement. This paper focuses on the second phase, conceptualisation, which involves constructing a coherent and rigorous conceptual framework that represents the core descriptive capability inherent in any theory. The conceptual framework is developed through a process of abstraction, synthesis, and diagramming, based on the insights of Denning and Denning (2010), JCS (2018), and Lin (2009). The resulting framework consists of several conceptual maps that depict the essential elements, relationships, and challenges of OCO, as well as its policy and strategy implications. The framework is intended to provide a comprehensive and detailed understanding of OCO. The limitations of the theory and research lies because the paper is based on a limited number of sources, and mainly from a U.S. perspective, which may not represent the full complexity and diversity of OCO.

4. Analysis – A High Level Conceptualisation of Offensive Cyberspace Operations Theory

This section presents the conceptual maps as part of the theory, which are akin to network diagrams. These diagrams are created through a process of abstraction, synthesis, and diagramming, informed by seminal works in the field. The placement of concepts within these diagrams is determined by their interconnectedness and relevance to the theory of offensive cyberspace operations. The diagrams illustrate the key elements, relationships, and challenges of OCO. The purpose of these diagrams is to provide a visual representation of the theory, enhancing understanding of OCO's integration within the broader cyber domain and its policy and strategy implications. Figure 1 as an integral part of the theory, presents a high-level conceptualisation describing OCO and its interconnectedness with the cyber domain. Figure 1 is the results of conceptualisation applied on the seminal works of Denning (1999), Lin (1999), Denning & Denning (2010), and JCS (2018).

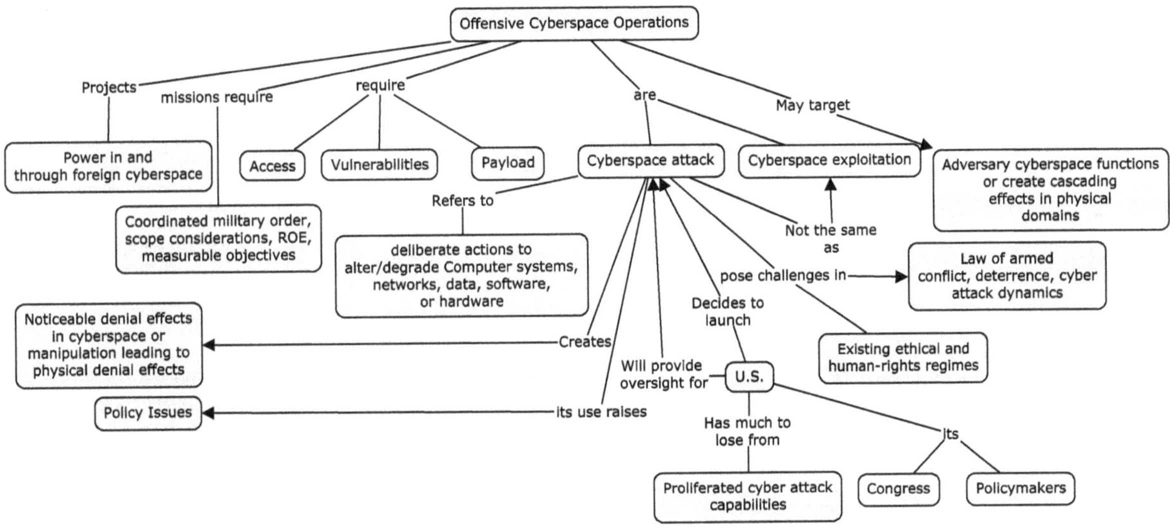

Figure 1: High Level Conceptualisation of Offensive Cyberspace Operations Theory.

This conceptualisation describes what offensive cyberspace operations are, what is required to conduct them, and potential challenges. Following this overview, the section will present and describe detailed conceptualisations to provide a comprehensive understanding of each component that forms this theory. The descriptions are done in a sequential manner that traces the connections from one concept to the next, as they appear in the diagram.

Describing the conceptualisation in Figure 1, Offensive cyberspace operations (OCO) project power in and through foreign cyberspace. Successful OCOs require three elements: access to the target, identification of a vulnerability within that target, and a payload designed to exploit said vulnerability.

These operations manifest in two primary ways: cyberspace attacks and cyberspace exploitation (more under *4.4 Cyberspace Exploitation – A Secondary Component of Offensive Cyberspace Operations*). These two are distinct, with cyberspace exploitation differing from Cyberspace attack. The concept of cyberspace attack is characterised by deliberate actions that alter or degrade computer systems, networks, data, software or hardware. Through such attacks, one can achieve noticeable denial effects in cyberspace or manipulation effects producing physical denial effects in the real world.

However, the execution of OCOs is not without complexities. The deployment and oversight of these operations raise policy issues. This is where governmental policymakers, exemplified in Figure 1 by the U.S. Government, come into play, setting policy directives and strategies for their use. It is crucial to recognise that governments, while developing and having access to these capabilities, also stand to lose significantly from the proliferation of cyber attack capabilities, tools, tactics, techniques and procedures. Finally, OCOs, specifically the component of cyberspace attack, while being a tool of national power, also introduces challenges. They span from understanding and interpreting the law of armed conflict in cyberspace, deterrence and how to deter cyber threats to understanding the dynamics of cyber attacks.

As the reader may note, conducting offensive cyberspace operations is complex, and requires (amongst other things) technical expertise, ethical, and strategic considerations. While the high-level conceptualisation provides a comprehensive overview of OCO and their interconnectedness, the next part of the theory is to go down one level, Level 2, the presents and describes specific areas in more detail. The next area crucial for OCO, is policy.

4.1 U.S. Policy Directing the use of Offensive Cyberspace Operations

This step discusses the importance of policy. Figure 2 presents a conceptualisation of U.S. policy and strategy. This is level 2, a more detailed conceptualisation than Level 1 in Figure 1. This section focuses on presenting and describing the relationships between policy directives, their implications, and how they drive OCO.

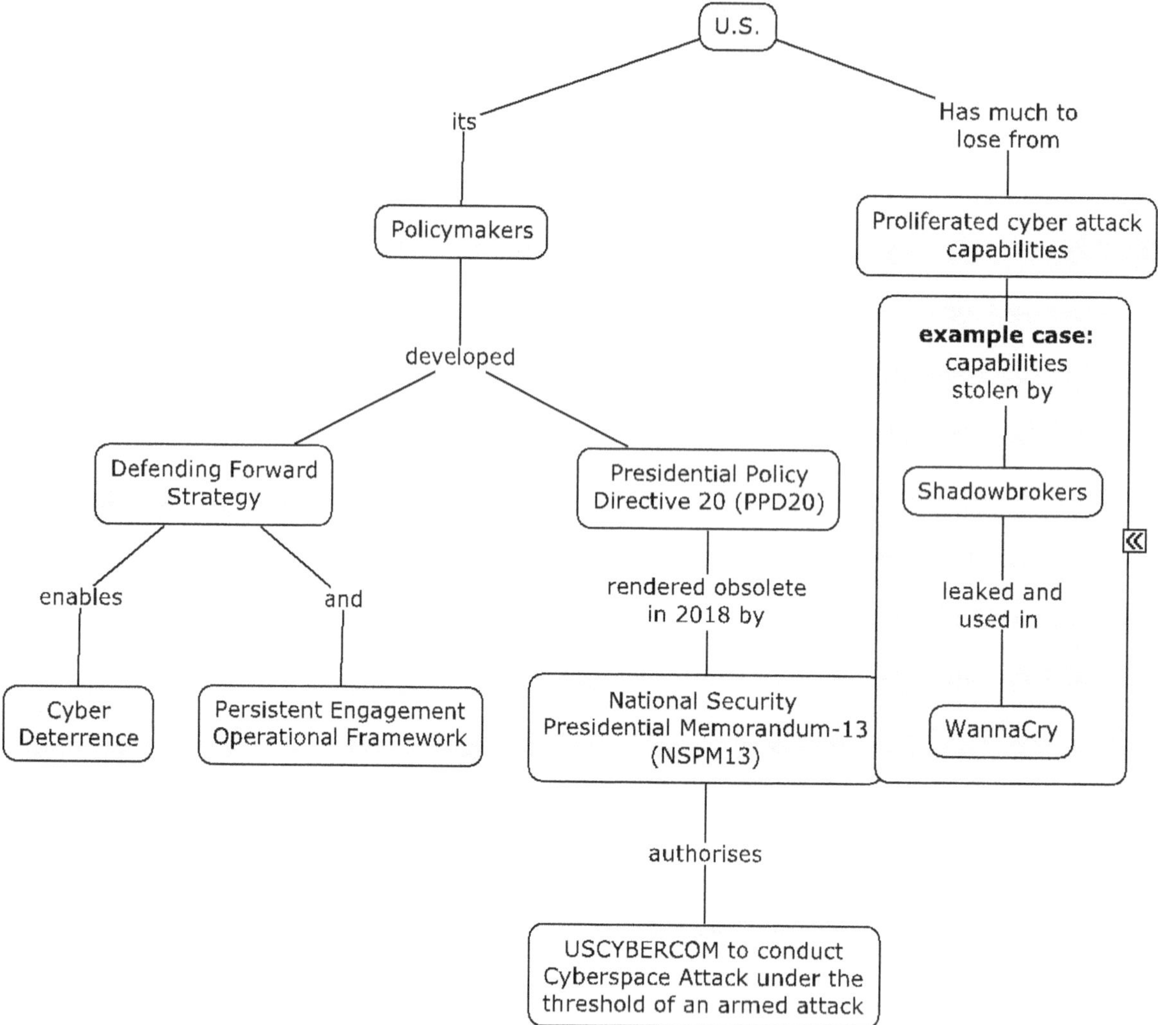

Figure 2: Conceptualisation of U.S. Policy Directing the use of Offensive Cyberspace Operations.

The conceptualisation of policy, exemplified by U.S. policymakers, begins with setting a policy on offensive cyberspace operations. The U.S., as depicted in Figure 2, while being technologically advanced, has also a lot to lose from the proliferation of cyber attack capabilities. Starting from the directive and memorandum developed by policymakers, shows the importance of having policy in place. Firstly, Presidential Policy Directive 20 (PPD20) was developed. This directive treated offensive cyberspace operations like any other tool of national power, mandating that operations with potentially significant consequences, such as leading to human death, required the president's approval. However, as time progressed and likely U.S. policymakers became more certain with OCO, PPD20 was later rendered obsolete by the National Security Presidential Memorandum 13 (NSPM13). NSPM13 provides more operational freedom, allowing the head of USCYBERCOM to conduct offensive cyberspace operations under the threshold of an armed attack without risking generating significant consequences, like human death.

In parallel, policymakers developed the Defending Forward-strategy. This is a paradigm shift in the U.S. approach to cyber deterrence. Recognising the unique challenges in cyberspace, Fischerkeller (2017), (Healey, 2019), and Lewis (2020) realised that a traditional deterrence strategy does not work in cyberspace. Defend Forward changes USCYBERCOM from a defensive to a proactive stance. Instead of just reacting to cyber threats, under the new Persistent Engagement operational framework, USCBYERCOM can take the fight to the adversary's cyberspace.

Figure 2 describes that policies and strategies do not exist in isolation but can be linked to real world cases. The case of the Shadow Brokers highlights this (Fruhlinger, 2022). The Shadow Brokers, believed to be Russian-threat actor, stole alleged National Security Agency (NSA)-tools, and leaked them online. According to publicly available information (Hern & MacAskill, 2017), the North Korean threat actor Lazarus Group used the leaked tools to conduct a cyberspace attack with global repercussions: in particular, health-care sectors suffered the most from this attack. The attack came to a halt thanks to a built-in-kill-switch: the malware first checks if it finds the domain name "iuqerfsodp9ifjaposdfjhgosurijfaewrwergwea.com" (Fruhlinger, 2022). If it is not found, then it continues its attack. If it is found, the attack stops. A then 22-year-old U.K. citizen named Marcus Hutchins found and registered the domain name, setting a global cyber attack to stop (Gibbs, 2017).

Describing the importance of policy, exemplified by U.S. government policies, directives and strategies, it becomes evident that it is important to know how they direct OCO. At the core of OCO is Cyberspace Attack (CA). Just as policy directs when and how OCO should be used as a tool of national power, the success of CA lies on a triad of essential elements: access, vulnerabilities and payloads. The next section presents and describes the importance of the elements essential for CA.

4.2 The Triad for Successful Offensive Cyberspace Operations: Access, Vulnerabilities & Payloads

Launching a Cyberspace Attack (CA) requires access, vulnerabilities, and payloads. As described in Figure 3, a successful CA requires these three elements. This is level 2, a more detailed conceptualisation than Level 1 in Figure 1.

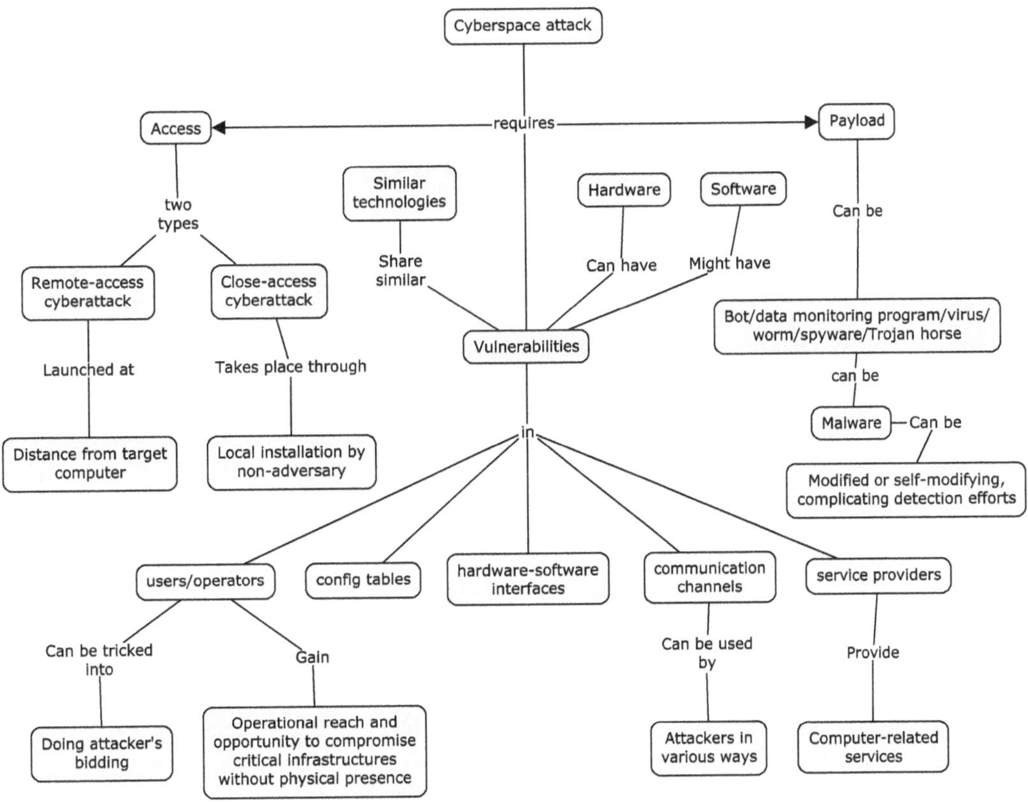

Figure 3: Conceptualising access, vulnerabilities and payload.

Access is crucial. It can be achieved in one of two ways: remote access or closed access. Remote access is launched from a distance, typically through the Internet, to its target computer. Close-access involves a local installation, such as a disgruntled employee. This method can escalate into an insider threat if the employee intentionally compromises the system's security.

Vulnerabilities (flaws, features or user errors) are the entry points an attacker exploits to gain entry. These vulnerabilities are not limited to just software or hardware. Even similar technologies may share similar vulnerabilities. These potential weaknesses can exist in users/operators, configuration tables, hardware-software interfaces, communication channels, and service providers offering computer and cloud-based services. For example, Figure 3 presents how vulnerabilities in communication channels can be used by attackers in "various ways", which include spear phishing or man-in-the-middle attacks.

Once an entry point (vulnerability) is identified, an attacker requires a payload (a tool) to exploit it. These payloads can take the shape of various forms: bots, and monitoring programs, viruses, worms, spyware, or Trojan Horses. Bots, derived from the term 'robot', denote a computer under the control of an external threat actor. Monitoring programs, viruses, worms, spyware, or Trojan Horses are different types of malicious software (malware) designed to infiltrate, damage, or exfiltrate data from the targeted system. Some of these, especially malware, can have traits like self-modification, further obfuscating their detection. Malware is an integral part of OCO, serving as a payload to exploit vulnerabilities. While malware is a distinct category, it operates in conjunction with other OCO elements like access and vulnerabilities. Malware, is not exclusively separate but is interconnected alongside bots and monitoring programs, forms the arsenal for cyberspace attacks and exploitation, working together to achieve the objectives of OCO.

In summary, the triad comprising access, vulnerabilities, and payloads forms the basis for successful CA. Therefore, it becomes even more important to present and describe Cyberspace Attack, a primary component of OCO.

4.3 Cyberspace Attack – A Primary Component of Offensive Cyberspace Operations

This section presents a conceptualisation of Cyberspace Attack (CA). This is level 2, a more detailed conceptualisation than Level 1 in Figure 1.

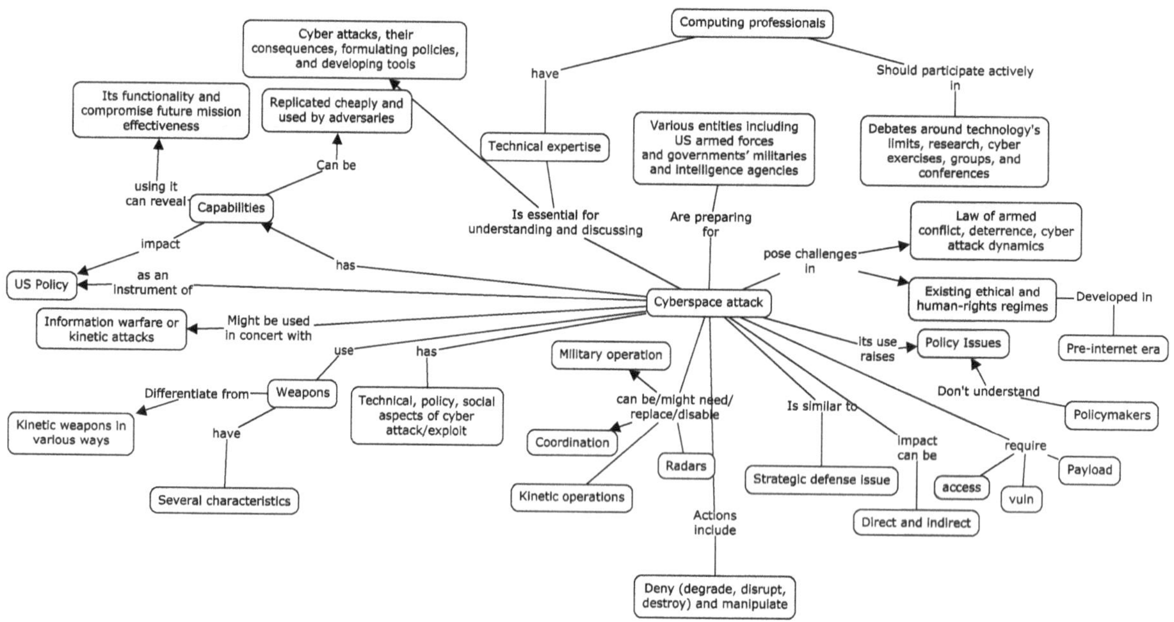

Figure 4: Conceptualising Cyberspace Attack.

Cyberspace Attack (CA) is crucial for OCO, as capabilities are crucial for CA. These capabilities, primarily computer code, are unique in that if used, they can reveal their functionality, risking compromising their future mission effectiveness. Furthermore, because they are code, these capabilities can be replicated cheaply and may be exploited by threat actors.

Technological expertise is essential for not only comprehending CA but also understanding its consequences, formulating policies, and developing tools. Hence, the role of computer professionals is emphasised for their active participation in debates around the limits of technology, engaging in cyber security research, and being part of cyber exercises, groups and conferences.

CA is linked to various policy domains, especially as a tool of national power. Organisations ranging from the U.S. Armed Forces to militaries around the globe and intelligence agencies are preparing for CA. However, since its introduction, it has raised policy challenges. Some policymakers have a challenge to grasp CA, indicating the need for clear policy, strategy, and directives that reflect current realities. Simultaneously, we must understand that some principles, like ethical and human-rights regimes, have been developed in the pre-Internet era.

One of CA's distinct features is its agility. It can function independently or generate synergies with information warfare or kinetic attacks. This capability presents itself as a national instrument in U.S. Policy. Its impact can be direct or indirect, lifting its importance to that of strategic defence issues. CA actions can be considered in a spectrum: from denying and degrading to disrupting, destroying, or manipulating targeted systems.

Furthermore, while CA is heavily based on technology, it has a vast area of operations. It has technical, policy, and social dimensions, presenting challenges to the law of armed conflict, deterrence, and the dynamics of cyber attack. It has distinct weaponry, with several characteristics setting it apart from traditional kinetic weapons.

Finally, CA can be integrated into military operations. It can complement or even replace kinetic operations in certain scenarios, like disabling radars. Executing CA may require coordination so as not to risk any other potential ongoing cyberspace operations.

In summary, CA is a complex component of offensive cyberspace operations. It poses challenges and opportunities, and it requires technical, policy, and social aspects to support it. Therefore, as CA is the primary component of OCO, it also requires support from its secondary component: Cyberspace Exploitation.

4.4 Cyberspace Exploitation – A Secondary Component of Offensive Cyberspace Operations

This section discusses Cyberspace Exploitation. Figure 5 presents a conceptualisation of Cyber Exploitation. This is level 2, a more detailed conceptualisation than Level 1 in Figure 1.

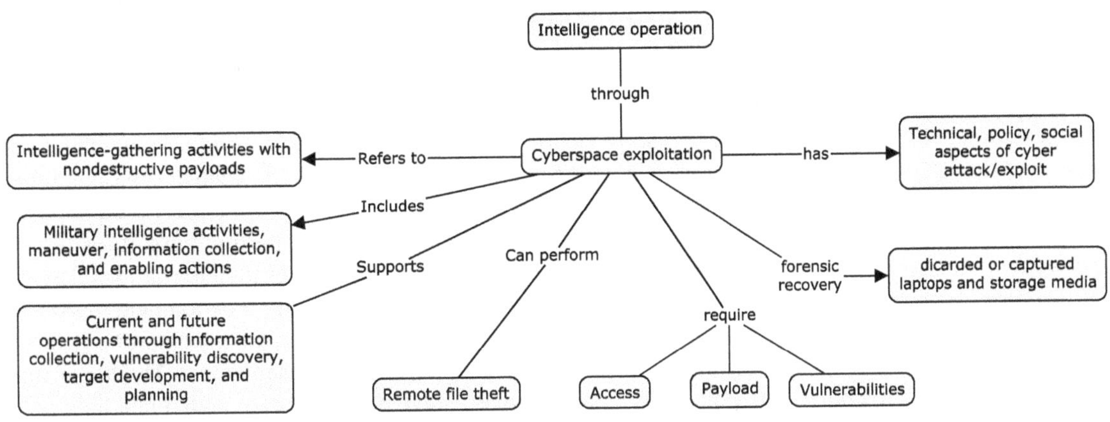

Figure 5: Conceptualisation of Cyberspace Exploitation.

Cyberspace Intelligence operations in cyberspace are executed through cyberspace exploitation (CE). CE are intelligence gathering activities with non-destructive payloads. This exploitation includes a range of activities, including military intelligence activities, manoeuvre through information collection, and enabling actions. It is essential to state that while at a first impression CE may appear "inferior" and "less complex" than CA, they are fundamentally identical in operation. The primary distinction lies in the objectives: CE aims to remain undetected over extended periods of time, emphasising the use of non-destructive payloads, ensuring a persistence in the target system. These efforts directly support current and future operations by the collection of information, discovering vulnerabilities, target development, and planning. Once an operator is inside a target, they have the capability to exfiltrate and conduct remote file theft. However, CE, just like its counterpart, Cyberspace Attack (CA), requires a base of Access, Payload and Vulnerabilities. Additionally, CE plays a role in the support of the forensic recovery of information from discarded or captured laptops and storage media. Just like CA, CE has implications for the technical, policy, and social dimensions of cyber attack and exploitation.

5. Discussion - The Theory's Policy and Strategy Implications

The comprehensive theory of offensive cyberspace operations, as described in Section 4, that accounts for their technical, policy, and social dimensions, is developed through *conceptualisation*. This represents one of the five phases in the theory-building methodology in applied disciplines. The theory describes a high level conceptualisation of offensive cyberspace operations. Additionally, it describes detailed conceptualisations of the importance of policy, the triad of access, vulnerabilities and payloads, cyberspace attack, and cyberspace exploitation.

We acknowledge the challenges in ensuring the exhaustiveness and accuracy of the conceptual framework. Continuous research and peer review are essential for validation. This conceptualisation serves as a base for academics, strategists, and policymakers to understand the complexities of OCO. It benefits those involved in the development and implementation of cyber strategies and policies, providing a structured approach to OCO. The deniability of cyber attacks does raise concerns about circumventing international laws. It is imperative for policymakers to ensure that operations are conducted within legal boundaries and for military leaders to enforce adherence among cyber operators. While there are inherent challenges in monitoring and enforcing compliance, especially with decentralised units, command structures and clear rules of engagement can mitigate risks.

Policymakers have early understood the opportunities provided using OCO as a tool of national power. Therefore, from a policy perspective, it is important to ensure that all OCO adhere to international law, are conducted under oversight and under the threshold of an armed attack, and do not risk generating significant consequences, such as human death. Presidential Policy Directive 20 is an example of a first policy for OCO, providing a framework for decision-makers and the actions that could be taken for the conduct of OCO. It is likely that as policymakers asked USCYBERCOM for courses of action to support U.S. policymakers in their policy-response options, USCYBERCOM in turn were tasked to conduct OCO. Over the years, as USCYBERCOM conducted OCO, it is very likely that the organisation become more mature through the experience generated by the conduct of OCO. This in turn is also likely to have led to policymakers becoming more confident in how to conduct OCO as a tool of national power. The evolution of U.S. policy from PPD20 to NSPM13 and the Defend Forward Strategy is an indicator of the maturity that US policymakers generated by what is believed to continuously asking USCYBERCOM for courses of actions to support U.S. policymakers in their policy-response options, and through OCO, generated enough experience and maturity.

The theory underscores the importance of policymakers comprehending the risks and technological aspects of cyberspace operations to make informed decisions. Figure 1 shows that OCO require access, vulnerabilities and payload, and that OCO are cyberspace attack (CA) and cyberspace exploitation (CE), while at the same time CA is not the same as CE. Using CA raises policy issues, and because CA require access, vulnerabilities and payload, this implies that policymakers must also have some understanding of technology. Furthermore, it suggests that they need to understand the ethical and legal implications of OCO in the context of the international law. With this understanding, policymakers can then develop policy that balances operational freedom and flexibility for organisations such as USCYBERCOM to conduct OCO, under oversight. NSPM13 is an example of a policy that offers more operational freedom to conduct OCO without risking significant consequences. The implication is that policymakers need to continuously monitor the technological development, adapt, and refine their policies that direct the use of OCO.

The theory emphasises that conducting OCO require an understanding of the technology dimension. Primarily, an understanding of the triad of access, vulnerabilities, and payloads, and the complexities and uncertainties inherent in these operations. Additionally, the theory describes the importance of computer professionals in developing, deploying, and maintaining OCO capabilities. While it may seem obvious that engineers are needed to develop capabilities, the theory aims to highlight the specific types of engineering expertise required for sophisticated cyberspace operations. Furthermore, the theory describes the importance of research, cyber exercises, and the participation of the same professionals in cyber groups and conferences. The theory does not state that the computer professionals must hold any form of university degrees, however, they need to have a high level of expertise, creativity, and innovation, as well as a sense of responsibility and ethics so the conduct of OCO fall within the developed policy as mentioned above.

The theory also distinguishes between two important components of OCO: cyberspace attack and cyberspace exploitation. While cyberspace attack is crucial for OCO to generate, for example, destructive effects on an adversarial target, cyberspace exploitation seeks instead to collect intelligence. Therefore, both components (CA and CE) are identical in operation but the effects and objectives of the operations differ. Thus, military commanders and their policymakers need to have a clear understanding of the target, the target's cyberspace and cyber environment, the mission, and the desired end state, or outcome. Additionally, it is crucial to understand the likelihood of collateral damage (secondary, tertiary effects), potential escalation, and attribution, in order to conduct OCO responsibly, within international law (= under the threshold of an armed attack), and proportionally.

The theory has implications for the social dimension. Although the targets are technological in nature, such as interconnected networked information systems, these systems are generally a node in a bigger system. These systems, critical infrastructure, can be the political, military, economic, social, and electoral systems.

Therefore, through the conduct of OCO, it is possible to influence public perception and awareness through disinformation by exploiting vulnerabilities inherent in living in a highly digitalised society. It is also possible to undermine societal trust in government institutions and impact the integrity of democratic processes. This in turn can lead to societal divisions and weakening national cohesion. Additionally, through OCO, it is possible to impact private companies, industry, academia and more. Examples include corporate espionage and theft of intellectual property by targeting vulnerabilities in supply chains, leading to reputational risks, shifts in market dynamics and competition, impacting not only the security of the companies, industry and academia, but also the economic and national security of a State.

In summary, the theory suggests that OCO stakeholders need to have a holistic and systems multidisciplinary and multilevel approach on OCO. From the technical, policy, and societal dimensions to the national, global and organisational levels. It is imperative that stakeholders collaborate and communicate on all domains and levels, vertically and horizontally, in order to conduct OCO as a tool of national power.

6. Conclusions & Future Research

The paper presents a comprehensive theory of offensive cyberspace operations, which are military missions that employ cyberspace capabilities to project power in and through foreign cyberspace. The theory was developed through conceptualisation, one of five the five phases in the theory-building methodology in applied disciplines, by reviewing previous research based on the works of Lin (2009), Denning & Denning (2010), and JCS (2018). The paper also discusses the policy and strategy implications of OCO by focusing on the role of U.S. government policies and strategies, which have shaped the conduct of OCO. Furthermore, the paper also examines the importance of a technical understanding, requirements and challenges, of OCO, specifically of cyberspace attack, cyberspace exploitation, and the triad of access, vulnerabilities and payloads.

The paper contributes to theory and practice by providing understanding and how OCO are conducted, as well as offering practical insights into the role of policymakers for policy development. Furthermore, it contributes to the scientific literature by offering a unified and comprehensive theory of OCO. Finally, the paper also bridges the gap between academics and practitioners, and technology and policy, by interpreting the empirical evidence.

Future areas of research can explore different contexts, such as regions, actors, and domains, employ other methodologies like simulations, experiments, and surveys, or address additional unanswered questions within deterrence, escalation, and conflict resolution. Future research can also support policy by informing policy development, and strategy development, through the collection of empirical evidence from human sources.

References

Caton, J. L., & Bartholomees, J. B. (2012). ON THE THEORY OF CYBERSPACE (VOLUME I:, pp. 325–344). Strategic Studies Institute, US Army War College; JSTOR. http://www.jstor.org/stable/resrep12116.26

Denning, D. E. (1999). Information Warfare. https://is.theorizeit.org/wiki/Information_warfare

Denning, P. J., & Denning, D. E. (2010). The profession of it discussing cyber attack. Communications of the ACM, 53(9), 29–31. https://doi.org/10.1145/1810891.1810904

Dictionary.com. (2019). The Origin Of Cyber Monday's Name Is From The 1940s. https://www.dictionary.com/e/cyber-monday-cyberspace/

Fischerkeller, M. (2017). Incorporating Offensive Cyber Operations into Conventional Deterrence Strategies. Survival, 59(1), 103–134. https://doi.org/10.1080/00396338.2017.1282679

Hardesty, L. (2011). Norbert Wiener's earlier work may prove more important. https://phys.org/news/2011-01-norbert-wiener-earlier-important.html

Healey, J. (2019). The implications of persistent (and permanent) engagement in cyberspace. Journal of Cybersecurity, 5(1), 1–15. https://doi.org/10.1093/cybsec/tyz008

Jensen, E. T., & Watts, S. (2023). Pressing questions: Offensive cyber operations and NATO strategy. Modern War Institute. Retrieved from: https://mwi.westpoint.edu/pressing-questions-offensive-cyber-operations-and-nato-strategy/.

Joint Chiefs of Staff. (2018). Joint Publication 3-12 Cyberspace Operations (Issue June 2018, pp. 1–104).

Leyden, J. (2022). NSA general confirms US offensive cyber ops in Ukraine war. The Register. Retrieved from: https://www.theregister.com/2022/06/02/nakasone_us_hacking_russia/.

Lin, H. (2009). Lifting the veil on cyber offense. IEEE Security and Privacy, 7(4), 15–21. https://doi.org/10.1109/MSP.2009.96.

Nakasone, P. M. (2022). The evolution of cyber defense and deterrence. Joint Force Quarterly, 92, 6-113.

Nakasone, P. M. (2023). 2023 posture statement of General Paul M. Nakasone. U.S. Cyber Command. Retrieved from: https://www.cybercom.mil/Media/News/Article/3320195/2023-posture-statement-of-general-paul-m-nakasone/.

Oates, B. J. (2005). Researching Information Systems and Computing (First). Sage Publications, Inc.

RAND Corporation. (n.d.) Cyber Warfare. Retrieved from: https://www.rand.org/topics/cyber-warfare.html.

Sky News. (2024). US military hackers conducting offensive operations in support of Ukraine, says head of Cyber Command. Retrieved from: https://news.sky.com/story/us-military-hackers-conducting-offensive-operations-in-support-of-ukraine-says-head-of-cyber-command-12625139.

Swanson, R. A., & Chermack, T. J. (2013). Theory Building in Applied Disciplines. Berrett-Koehler Publishers, Inc.

USAF to create cyber-warfare command. (2006). Jane's Defence Weekly. www.scopus.com

Key Actions to Enable Automation for Mobile Network Security Operations

Jarno Kämppi and Karo Saharinen
Jamk University of Applied Sciences, Jyväskylä, Finland

AB7833@student.jamk.fi
karo.saharinen@jamk.fi

Abstract. Over time, the landscape of Cyberspace surrounding Internet Service Providers (ISPs) has undergone enduring transformations. Notably, mobile networks, integral to contemporary societal infrastructure, consistently encounter evolving cybersecurity threats and risks. ISP processes have adapted with a persistent focus on optimizing network performance and availability, yet the challenges emerge from a laborious and protracted network change management process, hindering the practical automation of network security. Addressing the rightful demand for the highest level of security from mobile network users, our research question probes: "How can we intensify the emphasis on network security and facilitate the automation of network security operations?" To delve into this, we conducted extensive interviews with ISPs globally, affirming the inherent difficulty in automating security operations. The findings categorize challenges into three domains: Security Culture, Operational Processes, and Tools. Cultivating a security culture demands a pivotal commitment to change from top management, coupled with dedicated time and resources. Essential to this is the enhancement of security competence, extending beyond specialists to encompass network engineering staff. Robust network security not only safeguards against threats but significantly influences various business processes. Initiating a secure network requires ISPs to articulate explicit security requirements during the network procurement process, exerting pressure on vendors to fortify systems with a security-by-design approach at the factory. Critical to this is the secure deployment of networks, integrating comprehensive network hardening during the build phase. However, findings indicate a prevalent oversight where network security configuration changes are often neglected or deprioritized in favor of network performance. Achieving a harmonious balance between security and performance necessitates a predefined agreement on a network security configuration baseline. This collaborative effort involves network security specialists and competent network engineers. To effectively monitor and enforce network security configuration, ISPs require automation-enabled tools with the predefined baseline, offering capabilities for monitoring and enforcing network assets. In conclusion, our research emphasizes the imperative need for a paradigm shift in organizational culture, operational processes, and tool utilization to enhance the focus on network security and enable the critical automation of network security operations within the ever-evolving landscape of Cyberspace.

Keywords: Cyber Security, Mobile Network Operations, Security Operations, Network Change Management.

1. Introduction

In contemporary times, businesses and societies heavily depend on mobile networks managed by Internet Service Providers (ISPs). The advent of 5G technology introduces novel cybersecurity requirements due to its seamless connectivity for devices and businesses. The vast interconnection of millions of devices through mobile networks renders these networks increasingly susceptible to cyber threats (Pejanović-Djurišić et al., 2022). While considerable attention is focused on securing end-user devices, it is crucial to underscore the significance of fortifying the network infrastructure for both connection and usage.

Presently, mobile network operators face the challenge of managing diverse technological generations (Teng et al., 2020). Simultaneously, new investments become imperative to align networks with the evolving demands of customers and societies. The obsolescence of aging technologies poses hurdles in acquiring updated software featuring essential security patches while securing skilled resources for maintenance activities becomes challenging as the emphasis shifts toward emerging technologies.

Despite these challenges, the fundamental objective of any corporation or business remains the generation of profit for its stakeholders (Suhaily Maizan et al., 2021). Revenue streams are derived from customer contracts wherein communication service providers commit to delivering contracted services. Consequently, a significant emphasis is placed on network performance, encompassing dimensions such as network availability and data throughput. Presently, security considerations do not hold a prominent position in discussions surrounding network performance, and the augmentation of network security incurs high costs. As a non-profit-generating expense, security competes with other investments that directly impact profitability.

In the context of modern mobile networks, comprising a multitude of assets, manual monitoring and configuration prove to be laborious and costly endeavors (Anirban et al., 2023). In some instances, the sheer volume of network assets makes manual monitoring and enforcement impractical (Lee et al., 2014). To heighten network security for businesses and societies, there is a need to integrate automation into security operations. Justifying long-term investments in security is essential, as a significant security incident can have far-reaching consequences on trust and reputation. The erosion of trust and reputation, in turn, can exert deleterious effects on the overall well-being of a business. Furthermore, there are identified gaps in network and security management platforms (Steinke et al, 2018).

2. Challenge

Given the historical emphasis on the performance and availability of networks, existing business processes align with this central objective (Aykurt et al, 2023). For instance, the network change management process is commonly characterized by its cumbersome and slow nature. Even minor and straightforward alterations to network configurations necessitate navigating through an extended network change management process. Consequently, the immediate automation of network security becomes unattainable.

Automation means we allow technology to monitor and control operations or production (Shetty, 2021). In practical terms, we must place a significant degree of trust in technology, entrusting our business operations to its capabilities. The current solutions for mobile networks are excessively intricate, making the maintenance and operation of networks demanding (Aykurt et al, 2023). Simultaneously, meeting all business targets poses a considerable challenge. Communication Service Providers bear the responsibility of serving as critical infrastructure in our society (Homeland Security, 2015).

In the realm of cybersecurity, Internet Service Providers (ISPs) are obligated to deliver top-tier services under any given scenario. To fulfill these obligations comprehensively, ISPs must establish geo-redundancy for all network assets responsible for carrying traffic. Additionally, every alteration or operation within the network undergoes thorough scrutiny by the change control process to guarantee adherence to all obligations. (Drvodelić Cvitak, 2010). This entails subjecting every modification in network configuration, encompassing alterations in security-related settings, to a meticulous network change management process. The existing operational methodology appears hierarchical, time-intensive, and notably distant from the realm of automation. Frequently key personnel within organizations lack the necessary cybersecurity skills, and there is a need to enhance cybersecurity competencies. (Aaltola et al, 2022).

3. Research Methodology & Analysis

We opted for the qualitative research methodology to address the query "Why is automation for Security Operations not enabled?" In qualitative research, our exploration centers on comprehending the perspectives of individuals or groups regarding the problem (Creswell, 2014).

Over the course of multiple mobile network deployments, we have consistently observed a recurring pattern during the implementation of cybersecurity measures in these networks. During the network launch phase, there is a pronounced emphasis on optimizing network performance, as the marketing and contracts to customers revolve around significantly enhanced speeds and reduced latency. The competition among Internet Service Providers (ISPs) intensifies as each endeavours to offer the most high-performing network, thereby attracting the highest number of subscribers. Moreover, there is a collective aspiration among ISPs to be the first to introduce 5G services. These pursuits bind a considerable amount of resources, garner undivided attention, and elevate network performance as the paramount priority.

Throughout these network deployments, we have identified analogous challenges associated with the implementation of cybersecurity measures. Some of these challenges persist even after the network has been launched and transitioned into production. Our research inquiry seeks to address the question "How can we enhance the emphasis on network security and facilitate the automation of network security operations?". In pursuit of this answer, we conducted interviews with senior professionals in the telecommunications and security domains from ISPs worldwide.

3.1 Questionnaire & Interviews

The development of the Semi-Structured Interview template emanated from insights derived from experiences and challenges encountered during the implementation of cybersecurity measures in mobile network deployments. Employed for the collection of open-ended qualitative data, the semi-structured interview approach adheres to predetermined discussion topics (Creswell, 2013). This approach facilitates focused conversations while allowing for the exploration of new areas.

The interview template, was segmented into three overarching Themes, namely:

1. Organization & Security Establishment
2. Operational Processes
3. Tools and Methods Utilized in Operations

Each Theme is accompanied by a defined discussion objective. In pursuit of these objectives, we formulated key questions designed for elucidation through open discussion.

Within Theme 1, we gathered data about the organization under investigation and how security is instituted within the corresponding organization. This entailed a concentrated examination of organizational structure and the establishment of security governance across the organizational framework. In Theme 2, a detailed discussion unfolded regarding the operation of both mobile network operation and its security operation. The principal objective was to conclude the authority of executing the network security configuration changes, with a secondary objective focused on determining ownership of network asset security. Theme 3 delved into an exploration of the tools employed for security operations and areas where additional support is deemed necessary. The interviews, conducted via video conference, were recorded to facilitate comprehensive analysis. Interviews were anonymous and material was only shared with participants, and the identity of the Internet Service Provider (ISP) and its physical location have been safeguarded as confidential information.

3.2 Data Analysis

The data analysis process employed Microsoft Office tools and encompassed the following sequential steps:

1. Integration of Data
2. Data Cleansing
3. Data Categorization
4. Data Anonymization
5. Preliminary Analysis
6. In-Depth Data Analysis
7. Concluding Remarks

In the first step, all interview data was consolidated into a unified Excel table. Subsequently, in the second step, any extraneous or unnecessary data entries were removed. The third step involved categorizing the data based on the geographical presence of the Internet Service Provider (ISP). Following this, in step four, the data underwent anonymization, involving the removal of respondent-specific information. The fifth step comprised an initial analysis, while the sixth step involved a comprehensive examination of the data. Finally, in the seventh step, conclusive insights and findings were drawn.

4. Results

Following the analysis phase, the outcomes were categorized into three subdomains: Security Culture, Operational Processes, and Tools. The conclusions are evident; however, as anticipated, variances in Internet Service Provider (ISP) responses were detected. These can be observed from the results in Table 1. It can be deduced that the operational processes of ISPs are comparable. Our thorough investigation provides evidence supporting the limitation imposed on the implementation of automation in security operations.

Table 1. ISP responses to key questions.

	ISP 1(Global)	ISP 2	ISP 3	ISP 4(Global)	ISP 5
Security culture					
Is cybersecurity policy implemented?	Yes	Yes	Yes	Yes	Yes
Is cybersecurity measured?(KPI)	Yes	Yes	No	Yes	Yes
Is cybersecurity part of business governance?	Yes	Yes	No	Yes	No
Is dedicated cybersecurity department established?	Yes	Yes	Yes	Yes	Yes
Format of Security Operations Center (SoC)	Outsourced	Outsourced	Outsourced	Inhouse Central, several ISP's	Inhouse
Operational processes					
Format of Network Operations Center (NoC)	Inhouse	Inhouse	Inhouse	Inhouse	Inhouse
Change Management process implemented	Yes	Yes	Yes	Yes	Yes
SoC authorized to execute network configuration	No	No	No	No	No
Who monitors network security?	SoC	SoC	SoC	SoC	SoC
Who owns network asset security?	NW Operations	NW Operations	NW Operations	NW Operations	NW Operations
NoC authorized to execute network configuration	Yes, change control	Yes, change control	Yes, change control	Yes, change control	Yes, change control
Tools					
SIEM (Security Incident and Event Management)	Yes	Yes	Yes	Yes	Yes
IAM (Identity and Access Management)	Yes	Yes	Yes	Yes	Yes
Manual Annual Security Audits	Yes	Yes	Yes	Yes	Yes
Manual Annual security hardening monitoring	Yes	No	Yes	Yes	No

4.1 Results, Security Culture

The outcomes of the interviews reveal that Internet Service Providers (ISPs) commonly maintain distinct Chief Information Officer (CIO) organizations and Chief Network Officer/Chief Technology Officer (CNO/CTO) organizations, each operating autonomously with unique business objectives. In all surveyed ISPs, a Security organization is overseen by the Chief Information Security Officer (CISO), reporting directly to the CIO.

In the rapidly evolving contemporary landscape, safeguarding assets becomes indispensable for organizational resilience. The swift evolution of technology and cyberspace, encompassing cybercrime and hacking techniques, presents a formidable challenge for ISPs striving to keep pace. All ISPs interviewed have instituted a dedicated Security organization to protect their assets and operations. This contemporary security apparatus aligns with defined business strategies and adapts to business requirements set by owners. ISP security organizations play a pivotal role in defining security policies and ensuring their comprehensive implementation, continuous security monitoring, and ongoing improvement across the organization. Meanwhile, the network operations department remains steadfast in its commitment to achieving optimal network performance.

Given that mobile networks constitute integral components of societal critical infrastructures, heightened attention is imperative for effective Cyber Security Management. The Cyber Security process is executed and governed across the organization through an Information Security Management System (ISMS), representing a systematic approach to managing Information Security processes and activities. According to insights gathered from interviews, there is a crucial need to elevate the perceived value of security and enhance the comprehension of security risks among network operations staff. The personnel within Network Operations often lack the necessary expertise to execute network security operations, or it is not explicitly designated as part of their responsibilities. Dawson and Thomson (2018) share a common conclusion and emphasize that individuals working in the cyber domain should possess a blend of technical expertise and specialized knowledge within the respective domain. Despite the existence of Key Performance Indicators (KPIs) aimed at monitoring security quality, our research reveals a consistent prioritization of business targets over security objectives.

Further research indicates that Global ISPs typically adopt a structured approach to establishing security frameworks, often driven by a dedicated central Security organization throughout the corporation. However, this central entity lacks the authority to alter operational processes, which remain under the purview of business owners, particularly in network operations. Conversely, smaller local ISPs operating within a single country tend to exhibit more flexible approaches to cybersecurity governance.

In a broader context, there exists a general inclination and top management support for automation. In some instances, automation is explicitly established as a collective goal, predominantly motivated by considerations of financial savings.

4.2 Results, Security Operations, and Network Operations Processes

In accordance with our research findings, it is evident that the Security Operations Center (SOC) and Network Operations function as distinct entities, each possessing autonomous Processes, Tools, People, and Budget allocations. This separation is presented in Figure 1.

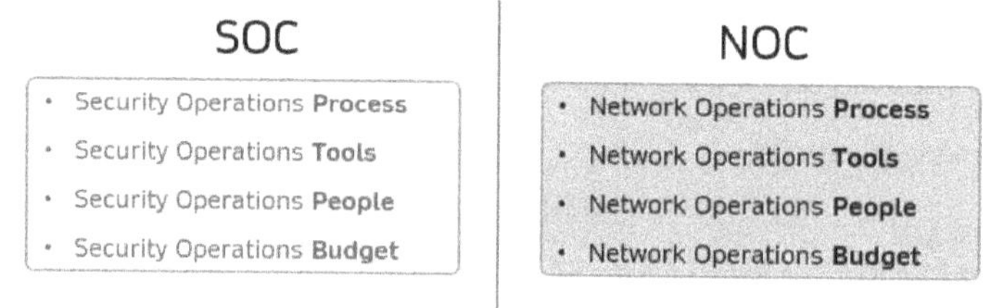

SOC
Security Operations Process
Security Operations Tools
Security Operations People
Security Operations Budget
NOC
Network Operations Process
Network Operations Tools
Network Operations People
Network Operations Budget

Figure 1. The Security Operations Center and Network Operations Center are independent organizational units.

The Security Operations Center (SOC) is tasked with executing security operations, encompassing activities such as security monitoring, threat detection, security maintenance, and managing security incidents. Network security configuration changes requested by the SOC follow the same aforementioned change management process.

In contrast, Network Operations oversees the management and upkeep of the mobile network infrastructure, with a broad mandate covering network planning, deployment, optimization, monitoring, troubleshooting, and maintenance. Every alteration in the network undergoes an extensive network change management process, involving detailed documentation of change requests. During the execution of the change management process, the change advisory board analyzes the potential network impact, subsequently accepting or rejecting the requested change.

Our research findings indicate that SOC staff lacks the authority to implement changes in the network directly, while Network Operations is permitted to execute changes through the network change management process. This dichotomy results in prolonged lead times for network security changes. Moreover, the change advisory board and network operations staff often struggle to comprehend the impact of network security configuration changes.

The reasons prohibiting the automation of security operations can be summarized as follows:

1. The application of the Network Change Management process for every network change.
2. Restrictions on the SOC to enact security configuration changes in the network.
3. The change advisory board or network operations staff may not fully grasp the impact of security configuration changes.

Addressing security noncompliance and seeking resolution necessitates collaborative efforts between at least two distinct organizations, namely the SOC and Network Operations. Our research underscores the existence of significant barriers hindering the achievement of automated network security operations.

4.3 Results, Tools for Security Operations

Based on the interviews conducted, Internet Service Providers (ISPs) employ a diverse range of tools for the implementation and monitoring of their security posture. Many of these tools necessitate specialized expertise and manual labour. In instances where this specialized expertise is lacking internally, ISPs may procure it from third-party suppliers (3PP), posing a challenge to the continuous monitoring of security posture. Some security-related activities are performed on an annual basis, potentially leaving security vulnerabilities unaddressed for extended periods.

All ISPs surveyed utilize a Security Incident and Event Management (SIEM) tool for threat detection and an Identity and Access Management (IAM) tool to govern and oversee network access. The SIEM tool, employed by the Security Operations Center (SoC), automates threat detection monitoring. However, the SoC is not authorized to enact changes in the network, necessitating network operations to enforce security posture through a change management process. Network operations staff controls access to network assets using IAM. SIEM and IAM serve as foundational elements for maintaining security posture.

Our research also indicates that ISPs routinely conduct manual security audits, encompassing activities such as vulnerability assessments (both internal and external), manual hardening monitoring, and, in some cases, penetration testing. Regulatory requirements often guide ISPs to perform these manual audits annually.

ISPs recognize the need for improved tools to visualize the state of network security, monitor network security hardening, and manage software patching for network assets.

5. Proposals

Internet Service Providers (ISPs) have allocated substantial resources and financial investments to establish cybersecurity practices and implement cybersecurity frameworks within their networks. However, despite these investments, the realization of security automation requires concurrent development in three critical domains: Security culture, Business processes, and Tools.

5.1 Proposals for Security Culture

Establishing a robust security culture requires proactive leadership from top management, demanding a significant investment of both time and resources. The gradual cultivation of such a culture necessitates a systematic, incremental approach, acknowledging that its establishment is a process that unfolds over time. At present, the Security Operations Center (SoC) is responsible for overseeing security monitoring and proposing security configuration enhancements for network assets, subject to approval or rejection by network operations.

To empower network engineering staff to take responsibility for security monitoring and configuration of the assets they oversee, there is a critical need to enhance their security competence. Network asset owners must gain a comprehensive understanding of the impact of security risks, acknowledging accountability for security configuration as an integral part of operational processes. The overarching goal is to instigate change and development among individuals executing business processes, fostering a security culture. The ultimate objective is to equip Network Security Operations personnel with the competencies needed to conduct fundamental security monitoring and configuration for the assets they manage, enabling them to be accountable for the security operations of these assets.

The Information Security Management System (ISMS) acts as the framework for establishing the security posture objective and is crafted and overseen by a specialized security organization. The heightened awareness of security risks within the network operations department facilitates their substantial engagement in the formulation and execution of ISMS. This strategy guarantees a thorough evolution in the security culture, contributing to the advancement of the company's ISMS to the next level.

In addition to basic security training, fostering awareness of cybersecurity risks could be achieved through participation in or organization of Cyber Exercises and the execution of penetration testing by ethical hackers within the similar ISP environment.

The ongoing transition of networks from virtualized environments to cloud-native environments represents a fundamental shift in network operations, necessitating competence development. This transformation presents an opportune moment to align actions for security and network operations competence development.

Research findings emphasize the independence of the Security Operations Center and Network Operations, each executing their respective processes, utilizing distinct tools, personnel, and budgets. To enhance the security culture, some responsibilities of the Security Operations Center should transition to Network Operations. The development of network security competence among network operations staff should encompass security monitoring and configuration of network assets as integral components of their responsibilities. Meanwhile, the Security Operations Center should hone its focus on and specialize in IT infrastructure security monitoring and security incident management. The evolved organizational diagram with responsibilities is presented in Figure 2.

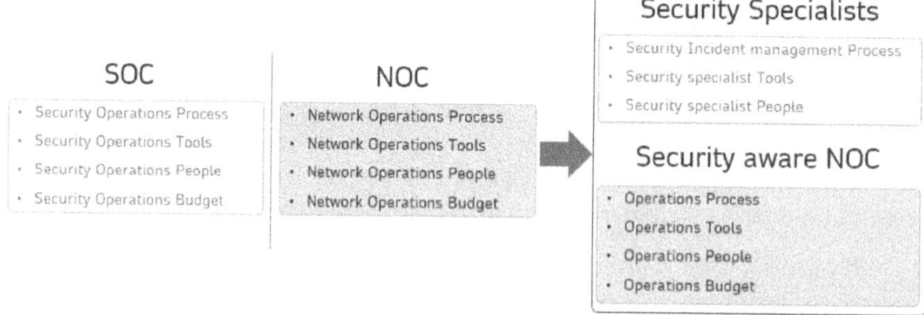

Figure 2. Evolving security culture from separated SOC and NOC to security aware NOC.

To foster continuous development in cybersecurity culture, it is imperative for telecom standardization and regulation to keep pace with the rapid evolution of cyberspace. Telecom standards hold significant authority among telecom vendors, shaping the development of telecom equipment and software in adherence to established norms like 3GPP. Ensuring a perpetual evolution of telecom standards aligned with the dynamic changes in cyberspace is crucial.

While local legislation and regulation are adjusting to the transformations witnessed in cyberspace, this adaptation tends to lag behind the rapid evolution of cyberspace. Internet Service Providers (ISPs) find themselves regularly responding to the evolving requirements dictated by local regulations, and concurrently, ISPs are stipulating corresponding prerequisites for telecom vendors.

5.2 Proposals, Security Operations, and Network Operations Processes

Internet Service Providers (ISPs) conduct their business and operational activities in accordance with established business processes. Embedding cybersecurity effectively within key business processes is crucial for ensuring an adequate cybersecurity implementation. However, the swift evolution of cyberspace presents a significant challenge in maintaining the relevance and efficacy of these processes. Our research underscores the profound impact of two specific business processes on the landscape of cybersecurity automation.

1. **Operations Process:** For the facilitation of automation in network security operations, immediate acceptance of network security configuration changes becomes imperative. To circumvent the intricate network change management process, network operations must cultivate a methodology wherein the network security baseline is collaboratively agreed upon by network security specialists and network operation experts. Following this agreement, the security baseline undergoes meticulous network performance verification and approval in staging or laboratory environments before transitioning to the production phase. The objective is to establish a network security baseline recognized for its concurrent high performance and security. This collaborative development involves ongoing collaboration with security specialists and network operation experts to ensure the agreed-upon network security baseline is well-balanced and meets both high-performance and security requirement. A proposed example for a collaborative process can be observed in Figure 3.

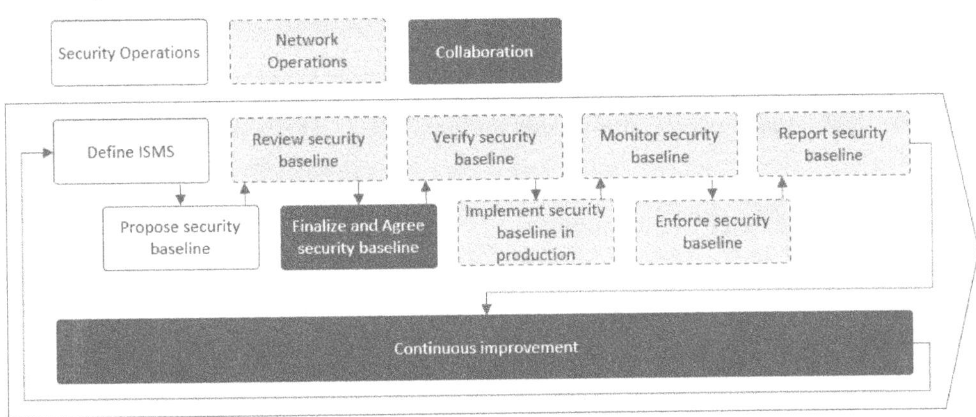

Figure 3. Collaborative operations process, including Security baseline setup, verification, implementation, monitoring, and automated enforcement and continuous improvement.

2. **Network Procurement Process:** Achieving a secure network with the desired network security baseline from its inception necessitates clear articulation of security requirements during the network procurement planning phase. As the network procurement planning process commences, it is vital to precisely and professionally define security requirements. This requires the assurance of sufficient cybersecurity competence and a comprehensive understanding of business dynamics. Clear definition of cybersecurity requirements ensures that telecom vendors, responding to requests for pricing, commit to fulfilling these security standards. With a procurement process attuned to security considerations, ISPs exert influence on telecom vendors, compelling them to adopt a security-by-design approach and undertake network asset hardening during the network build process based on the defined network security requirements. However, if an ISP exclusively prioritizes achieving a high-performing network at the lowest possible cost, this inevitably results in the deprioritization of cybersecurity requirements in the procurement process.

5.3 Proposals, Tools for Security Operations

The foundation of automation lies in the accessibility of suitable tools. Considering the integral role of telecom networks in society's critical infrastructure, there exists a crucial imperative for steadfast trust and confidence in the ability of machines to execute commands directed at network assets. Our investigative endeavours have revealed that Internet Service Providers (ISPs) need support in two pivotal functional areas.

5.3.1 Network Security Configuration

Within the domain of monitoring network security configuration, ISPs require a tool proficient in establishing communication with network assets and presenting a visual representation of the adherence to network security requirements. The effectiveness of this tool in enforcing network security configuration hinges on its capability to compare the existing network security configuration with the desired baseline. Subsequently, it should establish a connection with the network asset and execute the relevant configuration operations. To facilitate this functionality, the tool must incorporate the collectively agreed-upon network security configuration baseline and execute pertinent commands through scripts on the network assets. Importantly, this same tool can be judiciously employed for monitoring security hardening procedures and, additionally, for the implementation of security hardening measures. The specific procedural phases that an automated tool for network security configuration should encompass are highlighted in Figure 4.

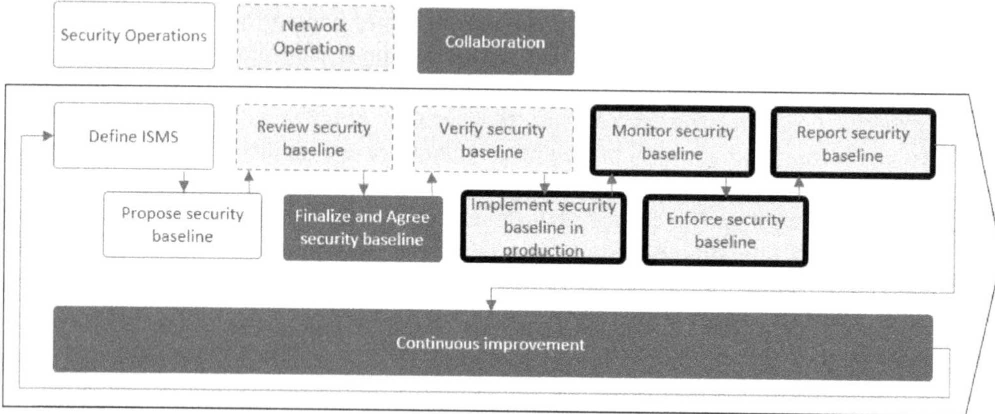

Figure 4. Here are highlighted the procedural phases that can utilize an automated tool for network security configuration.

5.3.2 *Network Software Patch Management*

In an ideal scenario, Network Software Patch Management tools should be provided either directly by network vendors or, if supplied by a third-party partner, seamless integration with the mobile network vendor's software catalogue is a necessity. This integration is crucial, establishing a unified and interconnected methodology for managing network software patches, thereby enhancing the network's capacity to promptly address vulnerabilities. The automated administration of network software patches is a pivotal element in ensuring the security and resilience of a network. This process encompasses three comprehensive functions: Inventory and Asset Management, Software Patch Deployment, and Integrations.

1. **Inventory and Asset Management:** Involves maintaining a precise inventory of all software within the network per vendor, a crucial aspect for identifying systems requiring patching. Continuous monitoring of software levels is essential.
2. **Patch Deployment:** Utilizes patch management tools, this phase involves deploying software patches across the network. Automation within this process ensures uniformity and reduces the time between patch release and deployment. Before deploying patches to the production network, a verification process is employed in a test environment to identify potential problems, preventing unintended disruptions to critical services. Implementation of a patch deployment schedule is crucial to minimize disruption to business operations, scheduling patches during maintenance windows or low-traffic periods to reduce the impact on users. A predefined rollback plan is in place in case a patch causes unexpected issues, ensuring swift reversion to a stable state if problems arise.
3. **Integrations:** To receive information for Network Software patch management these integrations are needed.
    - Integration with a Security Incident and Event Management (SIEM) solution correlates patching activities with security events, enhancing the organization's ability to detect and respond to potential threats.
    - Vendor integration is necessary to stay informed about patch releases by subscribing to vendor notifications and security alerts, ensuring the organization promptly addresses critical vulnerabilities.
    - Integration with an endpoint protection solution is required to provide a layered defence against security threats, ensuring comprehensive addressing of both vulnerabilities and active threats.

6. Conclusion

Security permeates every aspect of an organization, impacting each individual within it. A holistic perspective is essential for the successful implementation of security measures throughout the organization. The strength of security is inherently linked to its weakest point; should a vulnerability exist, a determined hacker will inevitably exploit it, and this exploitation is only a matter of time. Our research emphasizes that the successful automation of network security operations necessitates concerted efforts across three essential domains: Security Culture, Operational Processes, and Tools. Disregarding any of these domains results in suboptimal outcomes due to a lack of alignment. When prioritizing these domains, our findings indicate that Security Culture takes precedence, as it constitutes a pivotal factor for success. Well-implemented security protocols are grounded in the actions of individuals and their collective will. A strategically defined security direction, complemented by individuals possessing competence, collaboration skills, and motivation, plays a pivotal role in guiding the organization toward the envisioned outcomes. The desired results materialize when there is a collective commitment to achieving them. Given the heightened emphasis on network performance, it is imperative to elevate the prioritization of security through regulatory guidance. This involves a proactive approach by local regulatory bodies in each country, necessitating the revision and enhancement of their existing security requirements. Subsequently, these refined security standards should be explicitly communicated and mandated for adherence by Internet Service Providers (ISPs). This strategic regulatory intervention is essential for reinforcing the security landscape within the telecommunications infrastructure, aligning with the prevailing imperative to enhance security in tandem with the prioritized focus on network performance.

References

Pejanović-Djurišić, M. and Kuklinski, S. (2022). 5G Security Landscape: Concept and Remaining Challenges. *30th Telecommunications Forum (TELFOR)*, Belgrade, Serbia, 2022, pp. 1-4, https://doi.org/10.1109/TELFOR56187.2022.9983722.

Teng, C. C., Chen, M. C., Hung, M. H. and Chen, H. J. (2022). End-to-end Service Assurance in 5G Crosshaul Networks. *21st Asia-Pacific Network Operations and Management Symposium (APNOMS)*, Daegu, South Korea, 2022, pp. 306-309, https://doi.org/10.23919/APNOMS50412.2020.9236977.

Suhaily Maizan, A. M., Nurul Husna, A. A. K. and Wan, A. S. (2021). Determinants of Profitability on Listed Telecommunications Service Providers Companies: Evidence in Bursa Malaysia. *Journal of Research in Business and Management Volume 9 ~ Issue 1 (2021)* pp: 22-28, ISSN(Online):2347-3002. Available at https://www.questjournals.org/jrbm/papers/vol9-issue1/4/C09012228.pdf

Anirban, D., Asif Imran, A. T. M. and Chinmay, B. (2023). Network Automation: Enhancing Operational Efficiency Across the Network Environment, *INTERNATIONAL CENTER FOR RESEARCH AND RESOURCES DEVELOPMENT*, ISSN Number: 2773-5958, https://doi.org/10.53272/icrrd

Lee, S., Levanti, K. and Kim, H. S. (2014). Network monitoring: Present and future, *Computer Networks*, Volume 65, 2014, pp. 84 – 98, ISSN 1289-1286, https://doi.org/10.1016/j.comnet.2014.03.007.

Shetty, R. S. (2021). 5G Mobile Core Network: Design, Deployment, Automation, and Testing Strategies. Apress Skillsoft version, Available at https://2masteritezproxy.skillport.com/skillportfe/main.action?assetid=154626

Homeland Security, (2015). Communications Sector-Specific Plan, An Annex to the NIPP 2013, Available at https://www.cisa.gov/sites/default/files/publications/nipp-ssp-communications-2015-508.pdf

Creswell, J. (2014). Research design; qualitative, quantitative, and mixed methods approaches. 4th ed. United Kingdom: SAGE Publications

Creswell, J. (2013). Qualitative Inquiry and Research Design: Choosing Among Five Approaches. 3rd ed. United Kingdom: SAGE Publications

Dawson, J. and Thomson, R. (2018). The future cybersecurity workforce: going beyond technical skills for successful cyber performance. Frontiers in psychology, https://doi.org/10.3389/fpsyg.2018.00744

Aykurt, K. and Kellerer, W. (2023), Autonomous Network Management in Multi-Domain 6G Networks based on Graph Neural Networks, *2023 IEEE 9th International Conference on Network Softwarization (NetSoft)*, Madrid, Spain, 2023, pp. 338-341, doi: https://doi.org/10.1109/NetSoft57336.2023.10175480

Steinke, M. and Hommel, W. (2018). Overcoming Network and Security Management Platform Gaps in Federated Software Networks," *2018 14th International Conference on Network and Service Management (CNSM)*, Rome, Italy, 2018, pp. 295-299. https://ieeexplore-ieee-org.ezproxy.jamk.fi:2443/stamp/stamp.jsp?tp=&arnumber=8584959

Drvodelić Cvitak, L. D. and Car, Ž. (2010). Impact of agile development implementation on configuration and change management in telecom domain, *The 33rd International Convention MIPRO*, Opatija, Croatia, 2010, pp. 377-381. https://ieeexplore-ieee-org.ezproxy.jamk.fi:2443/stamp/stamp.jsp?tp=&arnumber=5533407

Aaltola, K., Ruoslahti, H. and Heinonen, J. (2022), Desired Cybersecurity Skills and Skills Acquisition Methods in the Organizations, *21st European Conference on Cyber Warfare and Security, Chester, UK, 2022, pp. 1-9,* https://papers.academic-conferences.org/index.php/eccws/issue/view/7/8

Iran's Digital Authoritarianism as the Blueprint for National Sovereignty

Eleni Kapsokoli

University of Piraeus, School of Economics, Business, and International Studies,
Department of International and European Studies, Piraeus, Greece
Laboratory of Intelligence and Cyber-Security, Department of International and European Studies of the University of Piraeus, Greece

ekapsokoli@unipi.gr
ekapsokoli89@gmail.com

Abstract: As the technological landscape undergoes continuous transformation, nations are seizing the combination of technology, governance, and sovereignty in their strategies. Following the Arab Spring, a movement primarily focused on overthrowing oppressive regimes in the Middle East, Iran took a distinctive turn by establishing a digital authoritarian model. Fueled by concerns stemming from democratic reforms worldwide - especially those facilitated by the Internet and social media, which have played a pivotal role in the collection and dissemination of information - the Iranian government perceived a potential threat to its national security and sovereignty as well as its political survival. In response to the above, Tehran implemented a range of strategies and measures in Internet governance, which represent a form of oppressive control. To regulate the Internet and control the flow of data, Iran established the National Information Network, known as the 'Halal Internet'. This effort aims to safeguard national sovereignty through persistent control, shield political ideology, and promote a particular religious behavior within cyberspace. These developments have a noteworthy impact on individual rights, liberties, and privacy. This paper aims to explore the methods through which Iran exercises digital authoritarianism.

Keywords: Iran, Digital Authoritarianism, Sovereignty, Internet Fragmentation, Censorship, Surveillance.

1. Introduction

In an era marked by technological advancements, the intersection between governance, authority, and cyberspace has become increasingly pivotal. In recent years, there has been a growing trend among nations, seeking to enhance their national security and sovereignty, through the deployment of technology. Issues such as digital surveillance, information control, online censorship, law enforcement measures, the use of artificial intelligence and manipulation of big data can pose threats to human rights. This trend is facilitated by the swift digitalization of modern societies and is primarily orchestrated by state actors.

Many nations have (mis)used digital technology in the name of national security, leading to violations of (digital) rights and freedoms. The adoption of emergency security measures not only weakens democratic processes and regulatory structures but also leads to legitimizing authoritarian practices. Belarus, China, Iran, Russia, North Korea, and Saudi Arabia are notable examples of extensive censorship which significantly limits online access, thus violating people's right to information and communication. Other states such as the USA, France and the UK have used cyberspace to monitor their citizens, either for reasons of national security (terrorism, homeland security, pandemics, etc.) or to preserve and promote democracy. This trend has triggered numerous debates regarding the efficacy of using technology to galvanize national security and sovereignty. The emergence of authoritarian strategies by states in cyberspace imposes numerous constraints on fundamental rights such as privacy, freedom of speech, and political participation.

Among the states that (mis)use technology to hold power, Iran stands out as a distinctive one. Its path towards digital authoritarianism has unfolded due to geopolitical tensions, economic challenges, socio-political reforms, and a deeply rooted historical and religious content. Iran is a unified Islamic republic with a Shiite Islamic political doctrine based on the Guardianship of the Islamic Jurist (Velayat-e Faghih). This doctrine centralizes all political and religious power to the Supreme Leader of the country, who is considered a Guardian Jurist (Kasra, 2019). After the Iranian Revolution in 1979, Iran established a theocratic regime, combining propaganda and censorship, to exercise political control.

Over the past decades, Iran has witnessed periods of political and social conflict and protests, such as the Green Movement (2009) and the Arab Spring (2011) (Syed, 2022). The rule by Iranian radical clerics has resulted in restrictions on citizen's freedoms and rights and discrimination against minorities. Breaches of government policies lead to severe punishments, including prosecutions, imprisonments, and executions of dissenters, who violate international human rights standards (Human Rights Watch, 2023). The Iranian government responded to these protests by using the Internet for surveillance and repression purposes. A notable recent incident illustrating this authoritarianism occurred in the autumn of 2022 during the intense protests over the tragic demise of Mahsa Jina Amini by the "Morality Police", for not adhering to hijab regulations (Rahimpour, 2022). This protest stands as the latest in a long struggle for civil rights and social justice (Bayat, 2022). These violations extend to the digital sphere, with the imposition of oppressive measures, such as surveillance, censorship, and hacking.

This paper aims to examine Iran's shift towards a digital authoritarian model to safeguard its national sovereignty and ensure its religious and political survival. The analysis begins with unveiling the layers of Iran's digital governance model, shedding light on the measures through which the regime utilizes technology to govern society. From surveillance technologies to control of information and cyber strategies, this paper aims to deepen our understanding of how the Iranian government shapes its political landscape using a digital toolbox to ensure national authority. Additionally, it examines the implications of these practices on the Iranian population and considers their broader impact on the international community. The paper concludes by highlighting the exchange of best practices and means between Iran and other digital authoritarian regimes.

2. Iranian Digital Authoritarianism

Iran has experienced a significant rise in digitalization in recent years, especially in terms of Internet usage and social media adoption. The statistics below highlight the growing influence of information communication technologies (ICTs) and cyberspace in Iranian society. From a total of 88.84 million, there are 69.83 million Internet users, which is essential for understanding the growth and engagement of its population with the Internet. Furthermore, the number of social media users reached 48 million in 2023, proving the existence of an active digital blogosphere (Kemp, 2023).

Despite undergoing a digital transformation, Iranians have experienced Tehran's effort to control cyberspace and social media, thus regulating the flow of information within society. It implemented restrictive measures to monitor and surveil information and activities. This country is one of the most active and formidable cyber actors in the Middle East region, with a growing and increasingly sophisticated set of capabilities. The analysis of the strategic use of ICTs for a range of objectives by Iran is depicted through the following figure with the title "Iran's Digital Authoritarian Model". This figure exemplifies the extensive and often malicious use of technology in the pursuit of national authority. It includes objectives such as censorship, surveillance, hacking, propaganda, filtering, and Internet fragmentation. This figure has a dual use. On the one hand, it aspires to monitor national security crises such as epidemics, acts of terrorism, military operations, and geopolitical challenges. On the other hand, it aims to restrict dissenters' voices because the Internet is the primary tool for promoting political views.

Figure 1: Iran's Digital Authoritarian Model

Specifically, the government exercises extensive and unrestrained censorship of users' online content, employing a sophisticated filtering system to block access to websites, news outlets, and social media platforms that criticize the government. On June 27, 2023, Khamenei requested the judiciary to act in 'purging' dissenting voices from the Internet, for the protection of public rights, the preservation of societal psychological safety, and the suppression of violations and crimes (Article 19, 2023). According to Freedom House's annual report of Internet Freedom, covering the period from June 2022 to May 2023, Iran experienced a significant decline in its score, dropping 5 points. This decline resulted in the country securing the third lowest ranking, with an overall score of 11 out of 100 (Freedom House, 2024). This underscores that the very technology can contribute to societal development and can also be employed to undermine it.

In addition, the government conducts strict surveillance using advanced software and artificial intelligence tools (algorithms and biometric features) to monitor mobile telephony and online activity. Another method involves the dissemination of online propaganda with disinformation campaigns and the creation of fake news by Iranian state and non-state actors. They manipulate social media platforms by creating troll accounts to influence public opinion with pro-government narratives. Iranian authorities provide citizens with access to specific news sources that reproduce fake news to promote Tehran's narratives. Iranian users cannot find information on Internet search engines that is against the Iranian government. The Iranian Constitution refers to freedom of expression and press, but news agencies enjoy these freedoms as long as their content does not oppose the political principles of Iran. Thus, Iran is ranked 177/180 in the World Freedom of Reporters without Borders (2024). For example, information related to the protests, the arrests and killings of dissenters, and the financial corruption of state actors, are blocked. Furthermore, the Iranian authorities provide access to carefully constructed and filtered information, or they reply to criticism by using disinformation and fake news (Martin, 2018). One example is the dissemination of a video by the Tehran police to defend the official version of the cause of death of Mahsa Amini. This video claimed that Masha Amini had died of a heart attack and was not murdered by the Iranian morality police (NPR, 2023). Iran's digital toolbox is further complemented by the implementation of a sophisticated filtering system, which controls the flow of online information.

Since 2012, Tehran has been trying to establish its national Internet, referred to as the National Information Network [also known as SHOMA, or Internet-e Paak (Pure Internet), or Halal Internet (Permitted or Lawful Internet)]. The primary objectives of the Halal Internet include the improvement of speed connectivity, safeguarding information, hindering international surveillance, and developing cyber-defence capabilities against malicious cyber activities. The main idea is to create a 'clean' network that does not need censorship and protects citizens from moral hazards. It is envisioned as a locally controlled version of the Internet (Free Word Centre, 2016). The fragmentation and localization of the Internet offers Iran the means to control its digital frontiers, while at the same collecting citizens' metadata within local information infrastructures (Hendrix, 2022). In this National Information Network, all users are identifiable through a single and unique digital identifier, enabling the state to determine the content that users are allowed to access. The government is trying to de-westernize Iranian society, by prohibiting fashion, music, and pornography, thereby strengthening national sovereignty. Although the government promotes the adoption of the National Information Network, citizens remain skeptical. This skepticism stems from the recognition of its purpose, which is to impose stricter surveillance and censorship. In the pursuit of this agenda, the government is trying to develop and promote local communication platforms and strengthen the operation of this information infrastructure. Iranians face the following dilemma. Either sacrificing their privacy and anonymity, but gaining better connectivity, greater cybersecurity measures and low-cost services within the National Information Network or remaining digitally isolated. Many Iranians have found ways to bypass the restrictions of the National Information Network, with proxy servers (such as virtual private networks - VPNs) to hide their Internet Protocol (IP) addresses and geolocation while maintaining anonymity (OONI, 2022). This trend has resulted in a continual hide-and-seek game between the government and the citizens, with the former implementing ever-increasing censorship and surveillance techniques, and the latter trying to express their voice their dissent and resist these measures.

Iran's digital architecture consists of distinct entities with varying responsibilities and decision-making authority, engaging in both defensive and offensive cyber activities. To begin with, the Supreme Council of Cyberspace (SCC) was established in 2012 to employ decisions related to the governance of the Internet. Serving as an extension of SCC, the National Center of Cyberspace (NCC) focuses on information content and the development of security measures. The Iranian Cyber Police (Fata), established in 2011, has a responsibility to counter cybercrime and cyber threats that compromise national security. The Ministry of Information and Communications Technology has as a task the formulation and implementation of policies and measures concerning technology development and usage. The Ministry of Intelligence and Security (MOIS) is responsible for the flow of information, by collecting and processing intelligence derived from electronic communications. Operating within the Armed Forces, the Islamic Revolutionary Guards Corps (IRGC) oversees offensive cyber activities. A part of IRGC is the

Electronic Warfare and Cyber Defense Organization (IRGC EWCDO), which provides essential training to personnel to develop cyber-defence, surveillance, and censorship capabilities. The Basij Cyber Council (BCC) consists of volunteer hackers actively engaging in conducting malicious cyber activities. The defensive digital front includes the National Passive Defense Organization (NPDO) and Cyber Defense Command (CDC), which strengthen the state's cyber resilience. The Working Group to Determine Criminal Content (WGDCC) is responsible for detecting illegal content and informing the Center to Investigate Organized Crime (CIOC), which proceeds with the arrest of users who post content against the Iranian government. Moreover, the Communications Regulatory Authority (CRA) was established in 2003 and is responsible for regulating the telecommunications sector. Finally, the Iran Legal Intercept System (ILIS) constitutes a mechanism for surveillance and regulation of cyber activities. It gathers data about individual's mobile services which can modify or terminate their access (Center for Human Rights in Iran, 2015; Access Now, 2023). Within this System, there are some sub-entities, including the Control Illegal Devices (CID) System which issues warnings regarding the change of unauthorized SIM cards and the SHAHKAR System, which is designed for the collecting of audio data from mobile users and detecting cases of tampering (Miller et al, 2023).

Tehran has facilitated its ability to control the Internet and surveil the online behavior of Iranians by using espionage software like SIAM, SecondEye and EyeSpy (Alimardani, 2023, 9). SIAM can execute remote forty commands such as the ability to engage in online activity monitoring; to decrypt, collect, and process data; to do geo-location; to slow down Internet connectivity; to track the physical movements of individuals or large individuals; and to restrict access to dissenters. The 'Forge2GNumber' command, enables the degradation of network quality and speed connectivity from 4G and 3G to 2G (Zetter, 2020). Such a decline makes connections extremely vulnerable, making smartphones and high-tech applications useless, while compromising the personalization and privacy of data due to the absence of encryption. Therefore, Iranian authorities can easily collect, process, and store data, given the increased exposure of information at 2G speeds. SIAM's 'GetCDR' command facilitates the categorization of data, resulting in the creation of a personalized profile for each citizen. The data collected including information such as names, family details, passport information, IP addresses, phone-related data, etc. – contributes to a strategic advantage for the Iranian authorities during surveillance and censorship of cyberspace. The 'LocationCustomerList' command permitted the tracking and identification of mobile phone users based on their physical movements (Intercept, 2022). Telecommunications entities in Iran - including Ariantel, Telecommunication Company of Iran (TCI), Mobile Communications Iran, MTN Irancell, Rightel, and Shatel - install SIAM on citizens' mobile phones, thereby granting authorities full access to essential information (Bushwick & Bose, 2022). Bypassing the SIAM surveillance program cannot be achieved through simplistic solutions such as changing the SIM cards.

Tehran has manipulated hacking groups that are state-sponsored and engage in cyber espionage for various purposes, including gathering intelligence from foreign or domestic entities, monitoring geopolitical developments, and supporting national interests (e.g. gathering scientific knowledge). Examples of these groups are the APT33 (Elfin, Rocket Kitten, or Refined Kitten), APT34 (OilRig or Helix Kitten), APT35 (Charming Kitten, Newscaster, or NewsBeef), Tahr Andishan (The Thinkers) and APT39 (Chafer). For example, in retaliation for the Stuxnet computer virus on Iranian nuclear facilities, Iranian hacking groups conducted large-scale cyberattacks on the national critical infrastructure of foreign states, such as the Saudi Arabian Oil Company and the Shamoon virus (Gambrell, 2018B). Another significant cyberattack was against the Technical University of Denmark in March 2018. Hackers gained illegal access to several research projects to be used to enhance Iran's scientific knowledge across different fields. The US authorities reported in 2018, that nine Iranian hackers were accused of cybercrime by targeting 320 universities in 22 countries (Saikal & Vestenskov, 2020, 18–30). These actions highlight Iran's strategic use of cyber espionage to gather scientific knowledge.

3. Iran Suppresses Digital Rights

The Iranian government has witnessed a rise in public protests motivated by a spectrum of socio-political grievances. The Green Movement and Arab Spring highlighted the dynamic and direct impact of social media in shaping socio-political situations and narratives, thereby enhancing the online presence of Iranians. Activists organized the Green Movement by using platforms like Twitter and Telegram. During these protests, Iranian authorities prevented the 'Twitter revolution' by banning the app (Liaropoulos, 2013, 8). The oxymoron is that Ahmadinejad, the orchestrator of this ban, was a Twitter user. This app proved to be valuable for the dissemination of information, primarily orchestrated by foreign citizens and journalists in other foreign languages and not in local dialects, thus attracting the attention of a global audience (Keller, 2010).

In the aftermath of the Arab Spring, Iranian authorities adopted a dual approach to counter the scope of the demonstrations and control the narratives. The first approach is to monitor online activities and censor content as politically sensitive or unlike within its ideological and religious standpoint. In this context, Tehran employed methods such as the filtering and blocking of websites, messaging applications, and social media platforms, where individuals express dissenting socio-political perspectives and engage in online political activism (Gambrell, 2018A). Iran spent 36 million dollars in 2016 to develop 'smart filtering' technology that would allow authorities to selectively censor its citizens' Internet access (Cuthbertson, 2018). They also forbid two-step verification codes which are essential to using some online services or social media (RadioFreeEurope, 2022).

An important example is the prohibition of Telegram on December 31, 2017, following the decision of its CEO, Pavel Durov, to refuse to deplatform the peaceful protest channels. These channels provided the possibility of encrypted communication and coordination for the protests as well as the dissemination of audio-visual material that testified to the use of force by the Iranian authorities (BBC News, 2018). Durov criticized Tehran's decision and hashed measures, stating that Telegram is used by thousands of major opposition channels around the world and that freedom of speech is an undeniable human right. A few months later, Khamenei deactivated his personal Telegram account to protect national security.

Concurrently, Iranian authorities employ sophisticated tactics to manipulate social media narratives through disinformation campaigns and fake news to distort confusion and polarization and affect public opinion. Troll accounts are used to promote state-sponsored propaganda, suppress dissenting voices, and create a new online socio-political reality. By blocking the counter-narratives in cyberspace, the Iranian government seeks to shape both domestic and international perceptions of the inside policy. They also developed regional social networking and communication platforms, such as Soroush and Gap, resembling Instagram and Telegram, to replace them (McDermott, 2022). Iranian authorities have closely monitored these platforms to censor and control their users. However, these apps were not very successful, as users were aware of the potential risks that they posed to their privacy and security (Article 19, 2018).

Numerous women have opposed the restrictive legislative measures and obligatory hijab requirements, engaging in protests to voice their dissent. After these protests, in September 2022, the Headquarters for the Promotion of Virtue and the Prevention of Vice announced the adoption of artificial intelligence facial recognition technologies with biometric features for women who do not comply with regulations regarding the use of hijab (Shakibi, 2022). It is the first known case of a government using facial recognition to impose dress laws on women based on religious beliefs. Incidents have emerged wherein women are being notified via text messages or emails about violations, detected by traffic cameras, social media, and personal data from their phones. Between April till June 2023, more than one million warning messages through the Najer program were sent to women found without hijab in public spaces or on social media, or those displaying nudity or wearing thin or tight clothing (Amnesty International, 2024). Women, who are considered lawbreakers, face severe consequences, including the denial of access to financial institutions, public transportation, employment, health care and other basic government services. Furthermore, such violations may lead to prosecutions or morality training. The implementation of these measures has been exacerbated following the adoption of the Hijab and Chastity Bill in September 2023, which further intensifies penalties for women who either do not follow hijab requirements or promote relevant protests (Alimardani, 2023, 9).

The second approach includes constraints of Internet accessibility and shutdowns (Article 19, 2022). Iran has had a series of incidents with Internet shutdowns during periods of high unrest. By disrupting the Internet, the government aims to hinder communication among protesters and the organization of the protests and to control the dissemination of information. During these shutdowns, citizens are in a state of digital isolation, unable to communicate and to have access to news. Notably, during the November 2019 protests, the Internet remained offline for ten consecutive days. Iranian authorities effectively targeted protests by knowing their location and organizational information. In the protests of autumn 2022, they shut down the Internet for at least one week. During this period, there was a systemic violation of human rights and freedoms with arrests and executions, specifically, more than 14,000 civilians were arrested, and 300 civilians were executed (Amnesty International, 2023).

The general perception of the government regarding the usage of cyberspace by citizens is confirmed by Khamenei's statement that the Internet is being used by the enemy to target Islamic thought and the Islamic way of life. Based on the above perception, Tehran introduced in July 2021, the 'Regulatory System for Cyberspace Services Bill' (Tarhe Sianat), which enhances oppression in Iran. This Bill is a set of regulatory restrictions on rights and freedoms that aim to digitally isolate and fully control the flow of data and services (Article 19, 2021). It criminalizes the use of VPNs and imposes strict regulations on social media and technology companies. These companies are required to align with government standards, including access and storage of metadata to local information systems (Motamedi, 2019). The Bill empowers the Committee Charged with Determining Offensive Content (CCDOC) to take drastic actions against companies that resist collaboration with authorities. This includes the possibility of complete prohibition of activity, bandwidth limitations or imposition of economic sanctions (McDermott, 2022). Till now, Iran's Supreme Cyberspace Council (SCC), which was established by Khamenei in 2012, has seemingly adopted partial draconian measures of the Bill. If it is fully adopted, it will violate several human rights, and surveillance and censorship will be unhindered and limitless.

The above measures not only restrict the fundamental right of freedom of expression but also interfere with the citizens' right to access information and the right to peaceful assembly. The government seeks to silence opposition and maintain control. The Iranians have shown their dissatisfaction by increasing political activism and externalizing information about governmental violence. Moreover, Iranians are becoming more adaptable by identifying and countering disinformation campaigns and fake news and developing a sense of media literacy. In addition, the protesters have found alternative solutions to respond to these violations by using VPNs and encrypted messaging apps. Despite these collective efforts, the struggle for human rights and political change remains an unequal and difficult battle. Tehran aims to dominate within its physical borders by building a 'digital wall'.

4. Iranian's digital alliances

The imposition of economic sanctions by the United States on Iran has been notable, leading to economic and societal challenges, and public discontent. This economic pressure contributed to social unrest and protests as a response to both economic conditions and dissatisfaction with the political regime. The Iranian government has taken measures to control and suppress protests. Regarding the government's actions in response to sanctions, Tehran seeks alternative solutions and alliances to mitigate the effects. Cooperation with like-minded countries can be one effective strategy. Additionally, investing in technological capabilities and forming alliances with technologically superior actors are potential responses to sanctions.

China became Iran's primary technological ally, providing substantial support with intelligence monitoring and control, geolocation, espionage, and censorship systems. Since 2012, ZTE Company has signed a technology agreement with Iran to provide mobile geolocation and data interception equipment and software. In 2022, the Chinese company Tiandy Technologies further enhanced Iran's surveillance capabilities, by supplying closed-circuit cameras (Iran International, 2022). A pivotal development in Sino-Iranian relations happened in March 2021, when they signed the 'Iran-China 25-Year Cooperation Plan'. This Plan is a roadmap for trade, economic cooperation, military engagements, technological exchanges, and transportation initiatives, with a key emphasis on the private sectors of both entities. Beijing committed to invest more than 400 billion dollars in a period of 25 years, in all the aforementioned sectors, but mainly in telecommunications and technological ones by installing 5G networks. The bilateral cooperation emphasizes various domains such as long-distance communication equipment, 5G programs, ICT equipment, cybersecurity, artificial intelligence and browsing software and technology, and the exchange of practices and information between higher education institutions and technology companies (Azarhoosh, 2020). In a statement, an Iranian official has announced that Iran will launch 4.000 sites to provide 5G Internet services till March 2025 (Islamic Republic News Agency, 2023). China is systematically trying to penetrate the Iranian sphere and play a decisive regional role in an area of the Middle East. This geopolitical shift is a source of heightened apprehension for the USA, given their bilateral escalating relations, fueled by concerns over China's actions and their potential effect on the regional balance of power.

Another state that actively supports Iran and applies relevant strict measures in its society is Russia. Moscow has been providing Tehran since 2022, with advanced surveillance technologies, as part of their military and cyber cooperation. In exchange for military support that Iran had offered for the Ukrainian battlefield – Russia has supplied Tehran with advanced eavesdropping and photography devices, lie detectors and software for hacking mobile and information systems (Iran Wire, 2023). PROTEI Ltd, a Russian technology company, has enabled Iranian authorities to monitor, decrypt, redirect, degrade or deny all mobile communications of Iranians, by using software for online censorship (Miller et al., 2023). This collaboration between Moscow and Tehran extends beyond surveillance and espionage programs and aims at enhancing their capabilities to conduct cyber warfare (Lieber et al., 2023).

5. Concluding Remarks

Iran has transformed into a sophisticated surveillance, censorship, and hacking state. Instead of aligning its strategies and laws with international standards on human rights, accountability and freedoms, Iran has adopted harsher measures against its society. The Iranian government does not necessarily want to prohibit the Internet and the use of social media and platforms; rather, it seeks to 'purify' these means from any element that infects Iranians' loyalty and civic duties. Iran now possesses a digital toolbox that is capable of silencing and controlling its citizens, but also maintaining security and sovereignty.

The National Information Network does not guarantee anonymity, privacy, or data protection. Instead, authorities can filter or censor online content for any citizen. The status of net neutrality is compromised by regulations and strategies, content diversity is greatly reduced, and individuals are impeded from freely disseminating information. In the event of future protests, the government could resort to shutting down the Internet and blocking mobile communication, preventing Iranians from exchanging, gathering, and accessing information, as well as publicizing violent state incidents. Even if Iran is diplomatically isolated from the West, it maintains crucial ties with powerful allies such as China and Russia. It is imperative for the international community, human rights mechanisms, governments, and the technology sector not to remain passive, but to actively address these practices. Iranians deserve unhindered access to cyberspace and their fundamental rights should be intact.

Acknowledgements

This work has been partly supported by the University of Piraeus Research Center.

References

Access Now (7 March 2023) *Iran: Human rights groups sound alarm against draconian Internet Bill*. Available at: [Online] Iran: Human rights groups sound alarm against draconian Internet Bill - Access Now

Alimardani, Mahsa. (2023). 'Aggressive New Digital Repression in Iran in the Era of the Woman, Life, Freedom Uprisings', in *"New Digital Dilemmas: Resisting Autocrats, Navigating Geopolitics, Confronting Platforms"*, edited by Steven Feldstein Steven, Carnegie Endowment.

Amnesty International (26 July 2023) *Iran: International community must stand with women and girls suffering intensifying oppression*. Available at: [Online] https://www.amnesty.org/en/latest/news/2023/07/iran-international-community-must-stand-with-women-and-girls-suffering-intensifying-oppression/

Amnesty International. (Last access 9 April 2024) *A web of Impunity: The killings Iran's internet shutdown hid*. Available at: [Online] A web of impunity: The killings Iran's internet shutdown hid — Amnesty International

Article 19 (21 October 2018) *Iran: National messenger apps are the new hallmark of Internet nationalization*. Available at: [Online] https://www.article19.org/resources/iran-national-messenger-apps-are-the-new-hallmark-of-internet-nationalisation/

Article 19 (4 November 2021) *Tightening the net: Alarming moves to enforce the "User Protection Bill"*. Available at: [Online] Tightening the net: Alarming moves to enforce the "User Protection Bill"

Article 19 (17 November 2022) *Iran: New tactics for digital repression as protests continue*. Available at: [Online] https://www.article19.org/resources/iran-new-tactics-for-digital-repression-as-protests-continue/

Article 19 (6 July 2023) *Iran: Supreme Leader orders judiciary to further restrict online freedoms*. Available at: [Online] https://www.article19.org/resources/iran-supreme-leader-orders-judiciary-to-further-restrict-online-freedoms/

Azarhoosh, K. (2020) *The Iran-China Partnership: A Bad Deal for Citizens and Tech Companies*, Investigations. Available at: [Online] https://filter.watch/en/2020/11/13/the-iran-china-partnership-bad-news-for-tech-companies-a-disaster-for-citizens-rights/

Bayat, A. (26 October 2022) *A New Iran Has Been Born — A Global Iran*, New Lines Magazine. Available at: [Online] A New Iran Has Been Born — A Global Iran - New Lines Magazine

BBC News (3 January 2018) *Iran protests: Telegram under fire as Tehran clamps down*. Available at: [Online] https://www.bbc.com/news/world-middle-east-42558317

Bushwick, S. and Bose, T. (4 November 2022) *What You Need to Know about Iran's Surveillance Tech*, Scientific American. Available at: [Online] https://www.scientificamerican.com/podcast/episode/what-you-need-to-know-about-irans-surveillance-tech/

Center for Human Rights in Iran (2018) *Guards at the Gate the Expanding State Control over the Internet in Iran*. Available at: [Online] EN-Guards-at-the-gate-High-quality.pdf (iranhumanrights.org)

Cuthbertson, A. (5 January 2018) *Iran Internet Censorship Forces Protesters to Turn to Dark Web*, Newsweek. Available at: [Online] https://www.newsweek.com/iran-internet-censorship-sees-protesters-turn-dark-web-772182

Free Word Centre (2016) *Tightening the Net: Internet Security and Censorship in Iran. Part 1: The National Internet Project*. Available at: [Online] The_National_Internet_AR_KA_final.pdf (article19.org)

Freedom House (Last access 9 April 2024) *Freedom on the Net 2023- Iran*. Available at: [Online] https://freedomhouse.org/country/iran/freedom-net/2023

Gambrell, J. (29 January 2018A) *'Halal' internet means more control in Iran after the unrest*, Associated Press. Available at: [Online] https://apnews.com/article/c02a320725fc4afda305a0f3a660dbe6

Gambrell, J. (4 February 2018B) *In Iran, a 'halal' internet means more control after unrest*, Arab Weekly. Available at: [Online] https://thearabweekly.com/iran-halal-internet-means-more-control-after-unrest

Hendrix, J. (17 November 2022) *Internet Shutdowns and Censorship, in Iran and Beyond*, Tech Policy Press. Available at: [Online] Internet Shutdowns and Censorship, in Iran and Beyond | TechPolicy.Press

Human Rights Watch (2023) *World Report 2023: Iran*. Available at: [Online] World Report 2023: Iran | Human Rights Watch (hrw.org)

Iran International (16 December 2022) *US Sanctions Chinese Video Surveillance Firm Supplying Iran*. Available at: [Online] US Sanctions Chinese Video Surveillance Firm Supplying Iran | Iran International (iranintl.com)

Iran Wire (28 March 2023) *Russia Provides Iran with Digital Surveillance Capabilities.* Available at: [Online] Report: Russia Provides Iran with Digital Surveillance Capabilities (iranwire.com)

Islamic Republic News Agency. (31 October 2023) *4,000 sites to provide 5G internet in Iran by March 2025.* Available at: [Online] https://en.irna.ir/news/85276210/4-000-sites-to-provide-5G-internet-in-Iran-by-March-2025

Kasra, A. (20 March 2019) *What Is Velayat-e Faqih?*, Tony Blair Institute for Global Change. Available at: [Online] https://www.institute.global/insights/geopolitics-and-security/what-velayat-e-faqih

Keller, J. (18 June 2010) *Evaluating Iran's Twitter Revolution*, The Atlantic. Available at: [Online] Evaluating Iran's Twitter Revolution - The Atlantic

Kemp, S. (13 February 2023) *Digital 2023: Iran*, Datareportal. Available at: [Online] https://datareportal.com/reports/digital-2023-iran

Liaropoulos, Andrew. (2013) "The Challenges of Social Media Intelligence for the Intelligence Community", *Journal of Mediterranean and Balkan Intelligence*, Vol 1, No 1.

Lieber, D., Faucon, B. and Amon, M. (27 March 2023) *Russia Supplies Iran with Cyber Weapons as Military Cooperation Grows*, The Wall Street Journal. Available at: [Online] Russia Supplies Iran With Cyber Weapons as Military Cooperation Grows - WSJ

Martin, A.J. (12 January 2018) *Iranian regime's 'halal' internet stifling protest*, News Sky. Available at: [Online] https://news.sky.com/story/iranian-regimes-halal-internet-stifling-protest-11202100

McDermott, G. (10 November 2022) *Iran's digital authoritarianism is being tested by the country's youth*, Prachatai English. Available at: [Online] https://prachataienglish.com/node/10087

Miller, G., Al-Jizawi, N., Ermoshina, K., Michaelsen, M., Panday, Z., Plumptre, G., Senft, A. and Deibert, R. (16 January 2023) *You Move, They Follow. Uncovering Iran's Mobile Legal Intercept System*, The Citizen Lab. Available at: [Online] You Move, They Follow: Uncovering Iran's Mobile Legal Intercept System - The Citizen Lab

Motamedi, M. (2 October 2019) *Locked out: Why is Amazon blocking Iranians from its services?* Al Jazeera. Available at: [Online] https://www.aljazeera.com/economy/2019/10/2/locked-out-why-is-amazon-blocking-iranians-from-its-services

NPR (5 February 2023) *Iran acknowledges it has detained 'tens of thousands' in recent protests.* Available at: [Online] https://www.npr.org/2023/02/05/1154584532/iran-acknowledges-it-has-detained-tens-of-thousands-in-recent-protests

OONI (25 September 2022) *Iran blocks social media, app stores, and encrypted DNS amid Mahsa Amini protests.* Available at: [Online] https://ooni.org/post/2022-iran-blocks-social-media-mahsa-amini-protests/

RadioFreeEurope (9 September 2022) *Iran Accused of Secretly Implementing Controversial Draft Internet Bill.* Available at: [Online] https://www.rferl.org/a/iran-internet-bill-controversy-secretly-implementing/32026313.html

Rahimpour, R. (16 September 2022) *Fury in Iran as young woman dies following morality police arrest, BBC News Persian.* Available at: [Online] Fury in Iran as young woman dies following morality police arrest - BBC News

Reporters Without Borders (Last access 9 April 2024) *Index.* Available at: [Online] Iran. https://rsf.org/en/index

Saikal, Amin and Vestenskov, David. (2020) "Iran's National Security and Operational Capability", *Scandinavian Journal of Military Studies,* Vol 3, No 1.

Shakibi, L. (28 September 2022) *Government Use of AI-enabled Facial Recognition Systems*, FilterWatch. Available at: [Online] https://filter.watch/en/2022/09/28/policy-monitor-august-2022/

Syed, A. (22 November 2022) *Iran Has a Long History of Political Activism and Protest. Here's what to Know*, TIME. Available at: [Online] Iran's History of Protest and Activism: What to Know | Time

The Intercept (28 October 2022) *Iran's SIAM manual for tracking and controlling mobile phones*. Available at: [Online] Iran's SIAM Manual for Tracking and Controlling Mobile Phones - The Intercept

Zetter, K. (31 July 2020) *How cops can secretly track your phone*, The Intercept. Available at: [Online] https://theintercept.com/2020/07/31/protests-surveillance-stingrays-dirtboxes-phone-tracking/

Exploring Zero-Day Attacks on Machine Learning and Deep Learning Algorithms

Marie Kovářová

Prague University of Economics and Business, Prague, Czech Republic

marie.kovarova@vse.cz

Abstract: In the rapidly evolving field of artificial intelligence, machine learning (ML) and deep learning (DL) algorithms have emerged as powerful tools for solving complex problems in various domains, including cyber security. However, as these algorithms become increasingly prevalent, they also face new security challenges. One of the most significant of these challenges is the threat of zero-day attacks, which exploit unknown and unpredictable vulnerabilities in the algorithms or the data they process. This paper provides a comprehensive overview of zero-day attacks on ML/DL algorithms, exploring their types, causes, effects, and potential countermeasures. The paper begins by introducing the concept and definition of zero-day attacks, providing a clear understanding of this emerging threat. It then reviews the existing research on zero-day attacks on ML/DL algorithms, focusing on three main categories: data poisoning attacks, adversarial input attacks, and model stealing attacks. Each of these attack types poses unique challenges and requires specific countermeasures. The paper also discusses the potential impacts and risks of these attacks on various application domains. For instance, in facial expression recognition, an adversarial input attack could lead to misclassification of emotions, with serious implications for user experience and system integrity. In object classification, a data poisoning attack could cause the algorithm to misidentify critical objects, potentially endangering human lives in applications like autonomous driving. In satellite intersection recognition, a model stealing attack could compromise national security by revealing sensitive information. Finally, the paper presents some possible protection methods against zero-day attacks on ML/DL algorithms. These include anomaly detection techniques to identify unusual patterns in the data or the algorithm's behaviour, model verification and validation methods to ensure the algorithm's correctness and robustness, federated learning approaches to protect the privacy of the training data, and differential privacy techniques to add noise to the data or the algorithm's outputs to prevent information leakage. The paper concludes by highlighting some open issues and future directions for research in this area, emphasizing the need for ongoing efforts to secure ML/DL algorithms against zero-day attacks.

Keywords: Zero-Day Attacks, Machine Learning, Deep Learning, Security, Models

1. Introduction

Recent advances in machine learning (ML) and deep learning (DL) have revolutionized many areas, from natural language processing through image data analysis to autonomous driving. However, these advances have also brought with them new security challenges.

The most serious attacks are those that are unknown and thus unpredictable, called zero-day attacks (Vaisla 2014). Zero-day attacks are undiscovered security vulnerabilities that hackers can exploit to attack a system. The term "zero-day" refers to the fact that the vendor or developer has only just become aware of the vulnerability i.e. has exactly zero days to fix it. A zero-day attack occurs when hackers discover a bug before the developer has a chance to fix it.

One of the most pressing areas is protection against zero-day attacks, which can target both the network infrastructure and the ML/DL algorithms themselves. An important point in this context is therefore the need to protect both the network infrastructure itself, through which the data flows, and the ML/DL algorithms that provide the processing and evaluation of the data.

2. Zero-Day Attacks

In addition to the phrase zero-day, words such as vulnerability, exploit and attack are usually used. Thus, a zero-day attack can be divided into the following areas (Kaspersky 2023)

- A "zero-day vulnerability" is a software flaw that was discovered by attackers before the manufacturer knew about it.
- "Zero-day exploits are a method hackers use to attack systems with undetected vulnerabilities.
- "A zero-day attack is the use of a zero-day exploit to corrupt or steal data from a system affected by a vulnerability.

2.1 Zero-day Attacks and ML/DL Algorithms

Zero-day attacks pose a challenge not only in protecting network infrastructure but also in protecting ML/DL algorithms.

A zero-day attack path occurs when a multi-step attack contains one or more zero-day exploits. Early detection of zero-day attack paths could enable early detection of zero-day threats. The authors (Sun et al. 2016) propose a probabilistic approach to identify zero-day attack paths and try to implement a prototype system called "ZePro". The "ZePro" system is based on a Bayesian network that is built on an instance graph. The system then detects high-probability attack instances and creates zero-day attack paths. According to the research, the system was able to effectively identify zero-day attack paths. The work of these authors (Sun et al. 2016) focuses more on the zero-day attack path within the network traffic and does not directly address attacks on applications on ML/DL algorithms. In her analysis, author did not find any work that addresses the identification of the path of zero-day attacks directly on ML/DL algorithms.

Zero-day attacks pose a serious threat because they exploit vulnerabilities that have not yet been discovered or patched. In the case of ML/DL algorithms, these attacks can cause significant breaches in the confidentiality, integrity and availability of systems that often rely on these algorithms for their operation.

2.1.1 Existing Research

Currently, there are already several researches aimed at influencing ML/DL algorithms. For example, a collective of authors (Biggio et al. 2013) have addressed zero-day attacks on Support Vector Machines (SVM) algorithms, which are often used for data classification. In this work, the authors proposed methods by which attackers can exploit vulnerabilities in SVM algorithms by creating so-called "poisoned" data that is embedded in a training set. This poisoned data can lead to reduced classification accuracy and reliability, as well as dangerous errors in the results. The authors of this paper also propose defense mechanisms against these attacks. Other research focuses on DL algorithm attacks in natural language processing (Zhang et al. 2020). The authors of (Zhang et al. 2020) show how attackers can insert subtle modifications to input data to mislead models into making incorrect decisions. These attacks can have serious consequences, for example, in introducing models for sentiment classification or generating misleading messages.

Other studies focus on the vulnerability of convolutional neural networks (CNNs) to attacks (Li et al. 2023). The authors (Li et al. 2023) focus on introducing a visual analytics approach to understanding adversarial attacks (Sciforce 2022), using two main questions:

- The first question asks which neurons are more vulnerable to attack.
- The second question answers which features are captured by these vulnerable neurons during prediction.

These attacks can be used, for example, to deceive autonomous vehicles or monitoring systems.

Another study reveals the vulnerability of Graph Neurol Networks (GNN) (Zügner et al. 2020). Where they concentrate on attacks on Graph Neural Networks (GNN) which are used for graph analysis and social networking. The authors investigate the possibilities of attacks on GNNs, including the generation of misleading graphs that can lead to incorrect analysis decisions.

2.2 Attacks Against ML/DL Algorithms

To protect against attacks on ML/DL algorithms, it is necessary to know their weaknesses and the types of possible attacks. As mentioned in the introduction, there are already several studies done on zero-day attacks on ML/DL algorithms by simulating them. For example, using "poisoned" data (Biggio et al. 2013) or using a visual analytics approach (Li et al. 2023), etc. In this chapter, the author elaborates more on possible attacks on ML/DL algorithms.

2.1.2 Data Poisoning Attack

In "Data Poisoning" attacks, according to the authors (Lin et al. 2021), attackers try to manipulate the training data to:

- reduce the overall performance (accuracy) of the ML model,
- cause misclassification of a particular sample or subset of a test sample, or

- extend training time.

Data poisoning attacks can manipulate the training process. Specifically, in data poisoning, attackers attempt to manipulate the training set by, for example, poisoning features, flipping labels, manipulating the model configuration settings, or altering the model weights to affect the learning model (Lin et al. 2021).

If the attacker has a designated target label to which a particular test sample is misclassified, the attack is called a "targeted data poisoning attack", otherwise it is an "untargeted data poisoning attack" (Lin et al. 2021).

Data poisoning attacks can be divided into two categories:

- Model skewing
- Feedback weaponization

Model skewing

In a "Model skewing" attack, the attackers want to falsify (misrepresent) data and get the organization to make the wrong decision in favour of the attacker. There are two registered variants of skewing attacks (Bursztein 2018)

a) ML data poisoning attacks

In "ML data poisoning attacks," attackers modify the training data used by a machine learning algorithm and cause the algorithm to make incorrect decisions.

b) Web analytics skewing

In "Web analytics skewing", attackers modify analytics data from platforms such as Google Analytics or Adobe Analytics by executing a large number of automated queries using bots. The goal is to make it appear that visitors to the site are taking certain actions more often than they actually are.

Feedback weaponization

Feedback weaponization is the misuse of the user feedback system to attack legitimate users and content. The attacker's goal is to either lower or raise the rating of a given application. As the author (Bursztein 2018) states, one of the worst attempts of this feedback misuse was in 2017, when a group of "4chan" users decided to destroy CNN's app ratings on the Play Store and App Store by leaving thousands of one-star reviews. This kind of attack is used for a number of reasons e.g. to destroy competitors, revenge or cover their tracks.

2.1.3 Adversarial Input Attack

An adversarial ML attack is a deceptive technique that "tricks" machine learning models using faulty input. The goal of an adversarial attack is to cause the ML/DL model to malfunction. (Sciforce 2022) Examples of possible adversarial attacks are when a self-driving car takes a stop sign as a speed limit, or when the autopilot moves in the opposite direction than intended. Other serious attacks can happen in the medical field, where medical machine learning can classify benign birthmarks as malignant. Therefore, adversarial attacks are a major threat in the future. Adversarial attacks are divided into white-box attacks, black-box attacks and grey-box attacks.

- "white-box" - the attacker has access to the ML model parameters and knows the target model completely. This knowledge of the model makes it easier for the attacker to generate hostile examples and create poisoned input data.
- "black-box" - the attacker has no access to the ML model parameters. Instead, the attacker only knows the model outputs (logit, confident score or label). These attacks are commonly observed in online learning techniques used in anomaly detection systems.
- "grey-box" - the attacker has incomplete knowledge of the overall structure of the target model.

White-box attacks mean that the attacker has access to the parameters of the model; black-box attacks, on the other hand, do not.

Mathematically, according to (Sciforce 2022), an adversarial attack looks like this:

$$f(x + d)! = y$$

Where the model *f* using the input *x* can produce a prediction *y* that is not equal to the model's prediction *f* with input *x*.

$$L(d) < T$$

Where *L* is a general function that measures the norm *d*, a *T* is the upper limit of that norm. *L* is the perturbation boundary that measures the magnitude of the perturbation *d*, the norm is usually used *Lp* (Sciforce 2022). Based on these parameters, there is an extensive family of algorithms that can be used to generate such perturbations. Figure 1 shows their basic distribution.

According to the example taxonomy, there can be many types of attacks. According to (Malhar 2021), the adversary threat can be modeled as in Figure 1.

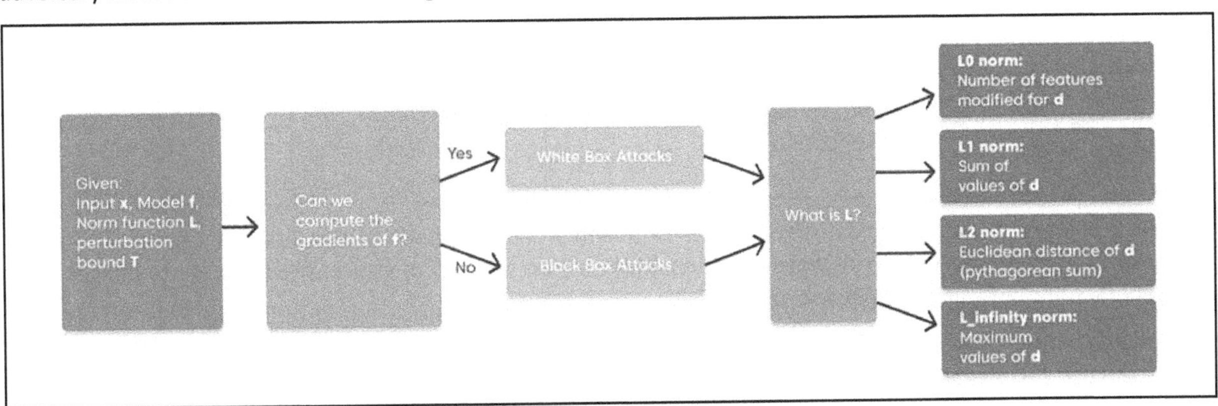

Figure 1: Taxonomy of different adversarial examples (Sciforce 2022)

2.1.4 *Gradient Access*

Gradient access controls who have access to the model *f* and who doesn't have access. We can divide them into white-box adversaries and black-box adversaries.

White-box adversaries usually have full access to the model parameters, architecture, training routines and training hyperparameters, and are usually the most powerful attacks. These attacks use information from the gradient to find adversarial examples.

The black-box adversaries have little or no access to the model parameters and the model is generalized as an API. Attacks on the black-box adversaries according to (Malhar 2021) can be performed using non-gradient based optimization methods such as genetic algorithms, random search and evolutionary strategies according to (Malhar 2021).

2.1.5 *Perturbation Bound*

Perturbation limits determine the size of the perturbation *d* (Malhar 2021). Usually measured by some mathematical standard, here by Lp. (Poursaeed et al. 2018) Where we can classify these selected standards:

- L0 norm: represents an attack that is limited by the norm L0. It involves modifying a number of properties of the input signal to the model. These attacks are often very realistic and can be performed on real systems. A common example would be to put a sticker on a stop sign to force a self-driving car not to slow down. (Malhar 2021)
- L1 norm: represents an attack that is an upper bound on the sum of the total perturbation values. (Malhar 2021)
- L2 norm: attacks that are constrained by this norm represent upper bounds on the Euclidean distance / Pythagorean distance perturbation d. These attacks are relatively frequent, given the mathematical meaning of the norm L2 in linear algebra and geometry. (Malhar 2021)
- L_infinity norm: represents an attack limited by a norm L_infinity. This attack includes an upper bound on the maximum perturbation value d. According to (Malhar 2021), L_infinity attacks are the most studied of all, due to their simplicity and mathematical convenience in robust optimization.

According to (Malhar 2021), up to 8 different types of attacks (Table 1) can be combined within perturbation boundaries if we use the standard as a robustness metric Lp.

Table 1: Examples of commonly known adversarial examples categorized by gradient access and attack norm type (Malhar 2021)

	Norm bound			
Access to compute gradients	L0 standards	L1 standards	L2 standard	L_infinity standard
White Box	SparseFool (Modas et al. 2019), JSMA (Papernot at al. 2017)	Elastic-net attacks (Chen et al. 2018)	Carlini-Wagner (Carlini 2017)	PGD (Madry 2019) i-FGSM (Goodfellow et al. 2015), Carlini-Wagner (Carlini 2017)
Black Box	Adversarial Scratches (Jere 2020), Sparse-RS (Croce et al. 2022)	-	GenAttack (Alzantot et al. 2019), Sim (Guo et al. 2019)	GenAttack (Alzantot et al. 2019), SIMBA (Guo et al. 2019)

There are several other domain-specific ways to quantify the magnitude of the disturbance *d*, but all attack norms can be generalized to all types of inputs. Although these types of attacks are exclusive to images, their general principles can be applied to any model *f*.

Adversarial attacks can be performed in different application domains (Lin et al. 2021) for example audio (Carlini 2018), text (Sato et al. 2018), network signals (Corona et al. 2013) and images (Engstrom et al. 2019).

2.3 Model Stealing Techniques Attack

ML/DL models represent intellectual property for society. ML/DL models are trained on company data such as financial transactions, medical information or user transactions. Ensuring the security of ML/DL models trained on sensitive user data, such as data related to a selected person's financial situation or health status, is very important. Therefore, such ML models can be misused to reveal sensitive user information.

"Model stealing" is known as model theft or model extraction. Like many other attacks, this one works by querying the target model with samples and using the model responses to spoof the replicated model. What is valuable about the ML/DL model is its functionality, which can be restored by stealing its trained parameters (weights *w*) or its decision boundaries. According to (Irolla 2019), model stealing can be represented by Eq:

$$y = f(x,w)$$

Where *x* represents the input and *y* output. By submitting a large number of samples to the target model and storing its responses, it is possible to collect enough equations to construct a solvable system of equations where *w* are the unknown variables to be found. This is very effective for all kinds of models, assuming that the attacker knows the dimension *w* and the architecture of the model f (i.e., the relationship between the input *x*, the weights *w* and the output *y*). Therefore, this attack works best in "grey-box" approaches where we have some information about the model. In the case where the attacker does not have any information about the model, he can use a surrogate ML model called a shadow model. This is a deep learning model that the attacker trains to learn the relationship between the inputs that are presented to the target model and its responses. Given enough inputs, the Shadow model can learn the decision boundaries of the target model, thus reproducing its functionality.

A study (Correia-Silva et al. 2018) shows that it is possible to steal a model with any type of input, even if it has no relation to the original problem. The authors managed to steal different models for facial expression recognition, general object classification and satellite intersection classification with roughly the same recovery rate using related images. By stealing a model, an attacker can achieve several different goals, for example:

- Reverse engineering: an attacker can perform an engineering analysis of the model to understand how it works, so that they can uncover sensitive information or business process secrets that the model contains.
- Attacks on privacy: ML models may contain information that reveals sensitive data about the individuals on whom the model was trained. An attacker could use this information to invade privacy.
- Creating a copy or fake model: an attacker can steal a model to create their own copy to use in a competing product or service.

- Exploiting the model for further attacks: an attacker can analyse the model to discover weaknesses that could be exploited to create targeted attacks on the system or the people who use the system.
- Financial abuse: if the model is part of a commercial product, its theft may involve a financial loss for the model owner, while the attacker may sell or exploit the technology for financial gain.
- Manipulation of models: If an attacker has access to a model, they can potentially modify or alter it to produce biased or malicious results. This can be used to discredit or disrupt the operation that the model supports.

In practice, stealing a model could look like this:

1. Gaining access to the target model: an attacker could target a web service or application that provides an interface to a model for facial expression recognition, object classification, or any other task they want to steal.
2. Generating or collecting related images: an attacker collects or generates a set of images that are similar to those used to train the target model. For example, these could be similar faces, objects, or satellite intersections.
3. Creating a new model: the attacker will use the collected or generated images as input for a new model, which will be a mimic of the target model.
4. Model tuning: an attacker can use techniques such as transfer learning or fine-tuning to fine-tune a new model to achieve similar results as the target model.
5. Attack: an attacker could then use this new model for his purposes, such as face identification, object classification or satellite intersection recognition, without having to know and use the original training data.

3. Protection Against Zero-Day Attacks on ML/DL Algorithms

There are many ways for an attacker to compromise the security of algorithms and thus network traffic. Algorithms that are part of network traffic detection and prevention systems today will be more vulnerable and therefore need to be protected from third party attacks. One of the biggest challenges is identifying new types of attacks that exploit specific vulnerabilities in the algorithms or datasets that are used to train them.

The basic methods for protecting against zero-day attacks on ML/DL algorithms include:

1. Anomaly detection: Using statistical methods and pattern recognition to detect anomalous input data that may indicate zero-day attacks (Kotu 2019). This method focuses on detecting unusual patterns of algorithm behaviour that may indicate tampering.
2. Model verification and validation: performing thorough verification and validation of ML/DL models as they are deployed and regularly monitoring their behaviour in the production environment (Sargent 2011). This can identify unusual changes in model outputs that could indicate a zero-day attack.
3. Federated learning and differential privacy: the use of techniques that minimize the transfer of sensitive data between different participants. It is a machine learning technique that trains an algorithm through several independent sessions, each using its own data set (McMahan 2017).

4. Conclusion

In this paper is provided an examination of the critical challenge of zero-day attacks on machine learning (ML) and deep learning (DL) algorithms, which is becoming increasingly significant in the field of cybersecurity. Zero-day attacks exploit previously unknown vulnerabilities and present a considerable threat to the integrity, confidentiality, and availability of systems dependent on ML/DL algorithms. These attacks can have far-reaching consequences in various domains such as facial expression recognition, object classification, and satellite intersection recognition, potentially affecting user experience, safety, and national security.

The research has categorized and detailed three primary types of zero-day attacks on ML/DL algorithms: data poisoning attacks, adversarial input attacks, and model stealing attacks. Each of these attacks presents unique challenges and requires specific strategies for mitigation.

The paper has also shed light on the different techniques used in these attacks, such as manipulating training data, injecting adversarial inputs, or stealing model parameters, all of which can severely compromise the performance and reliability of ML/DL systems.

In response to these threats, basic protection methods against zero-day attacks on ML/DL algorithms are introduced. These include anomaly detection techniques to identify unusual data patterns or algorithm behaviour, model verification and validation methods to ensure algorithmic correctness and robustness, federated learning approaches to maintain the privacy of training data, and the application of differential privacy techniques to add noise and prevent information leakage.

However, there are still open issues and is necessary to continue research in this area. The evolving nature of zero-day threats means that the field must constantly adapt and improve defensive strategies. Future research should focus on developing more robust and adaptive models, enhancing data security measures, and exploring new methodologies for early detection and prevention of zero-day attacks. As ML/DL algorithms continue to permeate various sectors, ensuring their security against zero-day attacks remains a paramount concern, demanding ongoing attention and innovation in cybersecurity research and practice.

Existing methods may not be sufficient or effective against novel and sophisticated attacks that exploit unknown vulnerabilities in the algorithms or the data. New methods should be able to identify and mitigate such attacks in a timely and robust manner. In future research, the author will focus on developing new methods to detect and prevent zero-day attacks on ML/DL algorithms.

Another aspect that can be further developed is ethical and legal frameworks for attack prevention on ML/DL algorithms. Attacks on ML/DL algorithms raise ethical and legal issues, such as privacy, accountability, liability, and trust. There is a need for clear and consistent frameworks that define the rights and responsibilities of the stakeholders involved in the development, deployment, and use of ML/DL algorithms, as well as the regulations and standards that govern their security and robustness.

This approach can be combined with promoting collaboration and information sharing among researchers, practitioners, and policymakers. Addressing the security issues of ML/DL algorithms requires a multidisciplinary and coordinated effort. This includes sharing data, tools, methods, results, and insights, as well as developing common standards and best practices.

The approach mentioned in the two paragraphs above won't stop the attacks but can create an environment that will make the attacks harder for the attackers. It can make additional protection levels in addition to new algorithmic methods, which the author of this paper wants to develop.

The main contributions of this paper lie in the innovative application of machine learning and deep learning techniques to pre-emptively identify and mitigate zero-day attacks. This proactive methodology sets it apart from related works, which often focus on reactive measures. By integrating predictive ML algorithms with DL models that refine detection processes, this paper advances the field of cybersecurity. It is imperative for future research to extend this preliminary analysis, employing a more extensive data analysis, modelling and simulations.

References

Alzantot, M., Sharma, Y., Chakraborty, S., Zhang, H., Hsieh, C.-J., & Srivastava, M. B. (2019). *GenAttack: practical black-box attacks with gradient-free optimization*. Proceedings of the Genetic and Evolutionary Computation Conference, 1111-1119. https://doi.org/10.1145/3321707.3321749

Biggio, B., Nelson, B., & Laskov, P. (2013). *Poisoning Attacks against Support Vector Machines* (arXiv:1206.6389). arXiv. https://doi.org/10.48550/arXiv.1206.6389

Bursztein, E. (2018). *Attacks against machine learning-An overview*. Elie Bursztein's Site. Retrieved June 20, 2023, from https://elie.net/blog/ai/attacks-against-machine-learning-an-overview/

Carlini, N., & Wagner, D. (2017). *Towards Evaluating the Robustness of Neural Networks*. 2017 IEEE Symposium on Security and Privacy (SP), 39-57. https://doi.org/10.1109/SP.2017.49

Carlini, N., & Wagner, D. (2018). *Audio Adversarial Examples: Targeted Attacks on Speech-to-Text*. 2018 IEEE Security and Privacy Workshops (SPW), 1-7. https://doi.org/10.1109/SPW.2018.00009

Chen, P.-Y., Sharma, Y., Zhang, H., Yi, J., & Hsieh, C.-J. (2018). *EAD: Elastic-Net Attacks to Deep Neural Networks via Adversarial Examples*. Proceedings of the AAAI Conference on Artificial Intelligence, 32(1), Article 1. https://doi.org/10.1609/aaai.v32i1.11302

Corona, I., Giacinto, G., & Roli, F. (2013). *Adversarial attacks against intrusion detection systems: Taxonomy, solutions and open issues. Information Sciences*, 239, 201-225. https://doi.org/10.1016/j.ins.2013.03.022

Correia-Silva, J. R., Berriel, R. F., Badue, C., de Souza, A. F., & Oliveira-Santos, T. (2018). *Copycat CNN: Stealing Knowledge by Persuading Confession with Random Non-Labeled Data*. 2018 International Joint Conference on Neural Networks (IJCNN), 1-8. https://doi.org/10.1109/IJCNN.2018.8489592

Croce, F., Andriushchenko, M., Singh, N. D., Flammarion, N., & Hein, M. (2022). Sparse-RS: *A Versatile Framework for Query-Efficient Sparse Black-Box Adversarial Attacks*. Proceedings of the AAAI Conference on Artificial Intelligence, 36(6), Article 6. https://doi.org/10.1609/aaai.v36i6.20595

Engstrom, L., Tran, B., Tsipras, D., Schmidt, L., & Madry, A. (2019). *Exploring the Landscape of Spatial Robustness*. Proceedings of the 36th International Conference on Machine Learning, 1802-1811. https://proceedings.mlr.press/v97/engstrom19a.html.

Goodfellow, I. J., Shlens, J., & Szegedy, C. (2015). *Explaining and Harnessing Adversarial Examples* (arXiv:1412.6572). arXiv. https://doi.org/10.48550/arXiv.1412.6572

Guo, C., Gardner, J., You, Y., Wilson, A. G., & Weinberger, K. (2019). *Simple Black-box Adversarial Attacks*. Proceedings of the 36th International Conference on Machine Learning, 2484-2493. https://proceedings.mlr.press/v97/guo19a.html

Irolla, P. (2019). *What is model stealing and why it matters*. ML-SECURITY. https://www.mlsecurity.ai/post/what-is-model-stealing-and-why-it-matters

Jere, M., Rossi, L., Hitaj, B., Ciocarlie, G., Boracchi, G., & Koushanfar, F. (2020). *Scratch that! An Evolution-based Adversarial Attack against Neural Networks* (arXiv:1912.02316). arXiv. http://arxiv.org/abs/1912.02316

Kaspersky. (2023). What is a Zero-day Attack? - Definition and Explanation.Www.Kaspersky.Com. https://www.kaspersky.com/resource-center/definitions/zero-day-exploit

Kotu, V., & Deshpande, B. (2019). *Chapter 13-Anomaly Detection*. In V. Kotu & B. Deshpande (Eds.), Data Science (Second Edition) (pp. 447-465). Morgan Kaufmann. https://doi.org/10.1016/B978-0-12-814761-0.00013-7

Li, Y., Wang, J., Fujiwara, T., & Ma, K.-L. (2023). *Visual Analytics of Neuron Vulnerability to Adversarial Attacks on Convolutional Neural Networks*. ACM Transactions on Interactive Intelligent Systems. https://doi.org/10.1145/3587470

Lin, J., Dang, L., Rahouti, M., & Xiong, K. (2021). *ML Attack Models: Adversarial Attacks and Data Poisoning Attacks* (arXiv:2112.02797). arXiv. https://doi.org/10.48550/arXiv.2112.02797

Madry, A., Makelov, A., Schmidt, L., Tsipras, D., & Vladu, A. (2019). Towards Deep Learning Models Resistant to Adversarial Attacks (arXiv:1706.06083). arXiv. https://doi.org/10.48550/arXiv.1706.06083

Malhar. (2021). *A Practical Guide To Adversarial Robustness*. Medium. https://towardsdatascience.com/a-practical-guide-to-adversarial-robustness-ef2087062bec

McMahan, B., & Ramage, D. (2017). *Federated Learning: Collaborative Machine Learning without Centralized Training Data*. https://ai.googleblog.com/2017/04/federated-learning-collaborative.html

Modas, A., Moosavi-Dezfooli, S.-M., & Frossard, P. (2019). SparseFool: *A Few Pixels Make a Big Difference*. 9087-9096. https://openaccess.thecvf.com/content_CVPR_2019/html/Modas_SparseFool_A_Few_Pixels_Make_a_Big_Difference_CVPR_2019_paper.html

Papernot, N., McDaniel, P., Goodfellow, I., Jha, S., Celik, Z. B., & Swami, A. (2017). *Practical Black-Box Attacks against Machine Learning*. Proceedings of the 2017 ACM on Asia Conference on Computer and Communications Security, 506-519. https://doi.org/10.1145/3052973.3053009.

Poursaeed, O., Katsman, I., Gao, B., & Belongie, S. (2018). Generative Adversarial Perturbations. 4422-4431. https://openaccess.thecvf.com/content_cvpr_2018/html/Poursaeed_Generative_Adversarial_Perturbations_CVPR_2018_paper.html

Sargent, R. G. (2011). *Verification and validation of simulation models*. Proceedings of the 2011 Winter Simulation Conference.

Sciforce. (2022). *Adversarial Attacks Explained (And How to Defend ML Models Against Them)*. Sciforce. https://medium.com/sciforce/adversarial-attacks-explained-and-how-to-defend-ml-models-against-them-d76f7d013b18

Sato, M., Suzuki, J., Shindo, H., & Matsumoto, Y. (2018). *Interpretable Adversarial Perturbation in Input Embedding Space for Text* (arXiv:1805.02917). arXiv. https://doi.org/10.48550/arXiv.1805.02917

Sun, X., Dai, J., Liu, P., Singhal, A., & Yen, J. (2016). *Towards probabilistic identification of zero-day attack paths*. 2016 IEEE Conference on Communications and Network Security (CNS), 64-72. https://doi.org/10.1109/CNS.2016.7860471

Vaisla, K. S., & Saini, R. (2014*). Analyzing of Zero Day Attack and its Identification Techniques*.

Zhang, W. E., Sheng, Q. Z., Alhazmi, A., & Li, C. (2020). *Adversarial Attacks on Deep-learning Models in Natural Language Processing: A Survey*. ACM Transactions on Intelligent Systems and Technology, 11(3), 24:1-24:41. https://doi.org/10.1145/3374217

Zügner, D., Borchert, O., Akbarnejad, A., & Günnemann, S. (2020). *Adversarial Attacks on Graph Neural Networks: Perturbations and their Patterns*. ACM Transactions on Knowledge Discovery from Data, 14(5), 57:1-57:31. https://doi.org/10.1145/3394520

Asynchronous Record Alignment of Network Flows for Incident Detection and Reconstruction

Virgilijus Krinickij and Linas Bukauskas
Institute of Computer Science, Vilnius University, Vilnius, Lithuania

virgilijus.krinickij@mif.vu.lt
linas.bukauskas@mif.vu.lt

Abstract: In today's interconnected digital landscape, the distribution of cyber threats presents a significant challenge to cyber security. Moreover, as of 2016, the amount of data in the world exceeds one zettabyte. Because of this, evidence-based network flow analytics is a critical component of modern network management and security. Problems such as anomalies in the network flow, cyber security incidents, alert generation, data pre-processing, network monitoring, network flow complexity, and data flow patterns become difficult to detect in massive network data flows. These specific problems can be addressed using Packet capture (PCAP). PCAP analysis is a standard network forensics process and investigation for assessing network behaviour and identifying anomalies. This work presents a method for analysing network flows for probable alignment of asynchronously recorded communications in heterogeneous networks. Using a proposed method for alignment, we can identify the relevant recordings aligned over two data streams for faster and more conclusive incident analysis. We use synthetic network incident scenarios for research experiments, detailing the generation of cyber event data and impact on cloud network traffic, followed by in-depth PCAP analysis. The automated cyber-attacks are simulated within a network infrastructure generating network flows in a PCAP format. Simulated cyber-attacks range from standard port scans, service scans, and specific scenarios like SQL injection, phishing, DoS or DDoS. We define analysis objectives and criteria for the in-depth PCAP analysis and alignment. The evidence gathered showcases valuable information about network data flow and its behaviour.

Keywords: Cybersecurity, Networks, Flow, Incident, Detection.

1. Introduction

Cyber warfare is an ever-evolving landscape that needs strong cyber security practices and strategies. Today, organisations and governments put huge efforts in time and money to secure their infrastructures from malicious actors. This became sort of a new, unprecedented arms race that you cannot physically touch (Clarke, R. A., & Knake, R. K., 2014). The definitive aspect of the actors getting ready is in network capabilities (Argyraki, K., & Cheriton, D., 2005). In one particular example, the more data can be produced for pushing through the network, the more possible harm it could generate (de Neira, A. B., Kantarci, B., & Nogueira, M, 2023). Because of this, Google has seen the biggest DDoS attack that was conducted against them last year. Huge amounts of data generated, gave a new view of how multi-vector attacks can overlap with additional possible false-positive or true-positive anomalies and other network problems. This means that trying to identify specific problems and analyse traffic that was accumulated in millions of requests or any other type of data flow through the network right now is only considered (Zahid et al, 2022, Dimolianis et al, 2019, Kalinin, M. O., & Krundyshev, V. M., 2021). For this, more detailed and feasible approaches are wanted by governments and organisations. One of the specific possible solutions is generated PCAP analysis. PCAP for forensics, troubleshooting network problems, or security-related questions are very helpful. They help many security professionals investigate particular cases of cyber events and more (Cappers et al, 2018).

Although there are a lot of PCAP formats (Veselý, V., 2012), they are mostly used for computer network communications. Of course, like every technology, PCAP comes with its own flaws. One of the flaws is the file size. Capturing even thirty seconds of network stream can generate a file that will be quite big in size. Most of the files come for live data capture and PCAP files are used for diligent data analysis.

One important aspect of PCAP analysis is packet alignment, which involves organising the packets based on specific parameters or attributes. Packet alignment helps to establish relationships between packets, align packets in a specific order for references and extract meaningful information from the captured data. By aligning packets based on relevant attributes, we can perform a more established and focused analysis.

Incident detection and reconstruction in PCAP analysis is a critical component of modern network management and security. In the context of Network security, network flow analytics helps to check network flow and troubleshoot for specific problems. The key motivational problems for this research include anomaly detection, forensics, compliance and reporting, policy enforcement, and real-time monitoring. Also, it is imperative to understand that this method's results provide insights needed to make informed decisions, enhance security posture, optimise network performance, and ensure compliance with regulations and policies.

Any organisation or government would like to enhance their posture in cyber security by actively detecting and mitigating anomalous network behaviour that may indicate a security threat. The strategic steps for this scenario would be:

- Data Collection
- Data Pre-processing
- Data Analysis
- Anomaly Detection in Data
- Alert Generation

The goal is to identify unusual patterns and potentially malicious activities within the network. The generated results would help to increase the integrity of transmitted data and filter our unwanted patterns.

2. Related Work

The asynchronously captured data of a network flow in big quantities, hides the possible cyber-attacks or multi-vector attacks. This accumulates a deficiency that can be addressed with the help of PCAP analysis. On the other hand, synchronous alignment methods assume a uniformity and predictability in network traffic that is rarely encountered in real-world scenarios. Such methods are constrained by their requirement for simultaneous data availability, leading to potential delays or inaccuracies in incident detection when faced with asynchronous or out-of-order network flows.

One of these methods is the Euclidean Matching. The finite amount of points generated in a PCAP file may differ in count which must be equal based on the Euclidean matching problem. The other major issue is that the generated PCAP files are recorded asynchronously, where Euclidean matching should be symmetrical in many cases (Chew et al, 1997).

Another problem is the heterogeneous aspect of different network points used for network flow capture. For homogeneous alignment algorithms like Needleman-Wunsch from bioinformatics are used but this approach, however, faces challenges when dealing with heterogeneous packets (Beddoe, M. A. 2004). Also, the segmented-based alignment method introduced by (Esoul, O., & Walkinshaw, N, 2017) marks a significant advancement, employing segments from packets within specific protocols for alignment, but faces the same heterogeneity problem.

In research provided by (Diab et al, 2019) DTW (Dynamic Time Warping) algorithm is used for finding the best alignment in two time series with Euclidean distance involved for anomaly detection. Although we do not focus specifically on anomaly detection, the DTW method can be focused for asynchronicity in generated PCAP files per our synthetic scenarios. Also presented by (Diab et al, 2021) DTW can be used for TCP DoS/DDoS attack detection. While our scenarios presented later on will have this type of attack involved, we use different parameters from the generated PCAP files for our analysis. In addition, our scenarios vary greatly in time and specific attack details that are launched automatically from different network points. Also, based parameters are assigned to a specific case. The case pre-defines what we are looking for and want to look specifically in the generated PCAP files. For generated scenario incident detection, we address the provided case and parameters while using DTW algorithm.

3. Method

This section will present a network flow capture method.

In figure 1 we present data capturing using PCAP. In a controlled network environment, we use a master machine that manipulates two slave machines through an SSH connection. All the machines are virtual machines prepared in a bare metal hypervisor. The SSH connection is established asynchronously through a programmed code that is launched in the master machine. After the connection is made a program called *tshark* is launched for packet capture on the eth0 (Ethernet) interface in both slave machines. For packet capture we use *tshark*, a program used for packet capture and analysis (Merino, B., 2013). Additionally, while launching *tshark* we set a specific packet capture interval, which can be changed, and we specify the file, where packet capture will be stored.

Changing the capture packet interval ensures asynchrony in the packet capture. When the packet capturing process is initialised we launch a prepared attack from the threat actors machine to the target machine.

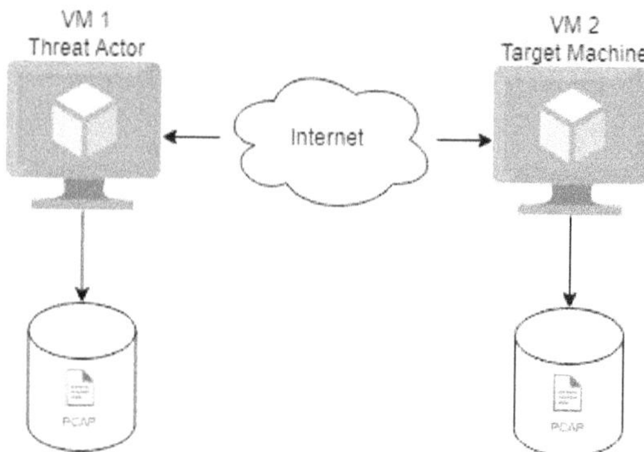

Figure 1: Data Gathering Using Virtual Machines

For the attacks we use synthetic network incident scenarios for research experiments. As mentioned before, we use different scenarios for data gathering. We generated 14 different synthetic scenarios for experiments. The primary scenarios are through a network port scan of TCP SYN packet DoS attack with different detail variations. Example scenarios may include:

Scenario A, Taking the full spectrum of ports from 1 to 65535.

Scenario B, Taking ports from 1-10000.

Scenario C: Taking the most common ports used.

Scenario D: Taking ports from 1-10000 where a proxy machine is used to attack the target machine.

Other scenarios.

Scenario A and B, is a standard scan with no additional prerequisites, while scenario C is used only for the most relevant ports today. Scenario D adds payloads that could be executed in the target machine later on. For the attacks, we use the *Nmap* (Network Mapper) tool. *Nmap* helps to generate the needed number of requests for the attack. While sending a massive number of TCP SYN packets without completion of the TCP handshake, the TCP SYN attack is regarded as a DoS attack. This helps in scenario D where we denote that this is a secondary type of a technique used on a specific machine. Other scenarios are different attacks like an SQL injection, and so on.

During the execution time, both machines and their listeners are active and data flow is captured on them. When the attack is over, the programmed code in the master machine tells both, the threat actor machine and the target machine to wait for extra predefined time, to stop the flow capture and save the captured flow in PCAP files in respective machines. Then the files are transferred back to the master machine for PCAP analysis.

All of the actions described are done automatically at heterogeneous network points with different visibility. Meaning that the programmed code is launched as a script written in bash where we describe the logic of automatically launching the SSH connections, the attacks and packet capturing.

4. Algorithm

This section will present an alignment algorithm for PCAP file analysis.

The raw data that comes in from a network stream to the PCAP, is very hard to read. For this, data pre-processing is the essential step in PCAP analysis (Alothman, B., 2019). Depending on the goals set for data pre-processing, the method may vary. In figure 2 we use these PCAP pre-processing steps.

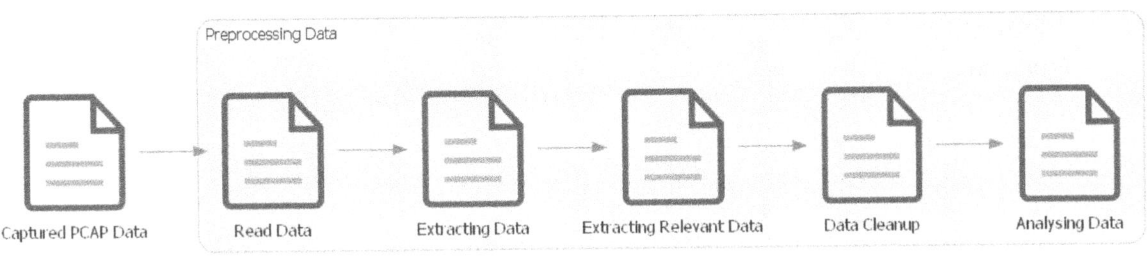

Figure 2: PCAP Pre-processing Method

The pre-processing steps are needed to ensure that at least some amount of noise will be deducted.

In figure 3 the two generated PCAP files are presented as a scenario that will be given in a later step to DTW (Dynamic Time Warping Algorithm) (Senin, P., 2008). The DTW here is used for aligning both network flows in PCAP files based on specific cases and additional parameters. The DTW works with sequences:

$$x=\{x1, x2, x3, \ldots, xi, \ldots, xn\}$$

$$y=\{y1, y2, y3, \ldots, yi, \ldots, yn\}$$

These sequences are then given to the DTW for creating a warping path and distance. The warping path is the path that is calculated to find similarities and the distance is the difference between the two sequences presented to DTW. The warping path is calculated by creating a matrix, where each element represents the distance between two sequences. Then a path is searched within the matrix that minimises the total cumulative distance. To do this, the algorithm compares each point of one sequence to every point of another. While comparing, additional constraints can be added to find the best match to form a path in the matrix.

DTW is used as a primary algorithm versus the classical Euclidean matching (Chew et al, 1997).

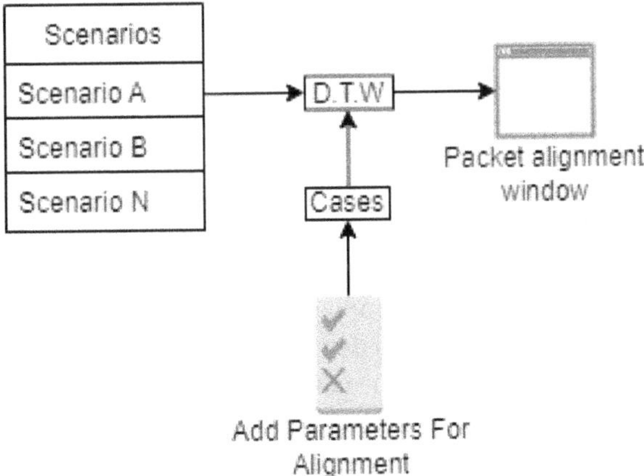

Figure 3: PCAP Alignment Algorithm

While adding scenarios to the DTW, we assign a case that we wish to explore in the scenarios for any A and B sources there exists content(A) ≈ content(B) ∧ content(B) ≈ content(A), here A, B are records in time. This implies that we are looking for single coincidences in the content A and B when A and B are records in time.

While processing gathered data, we add parameters for alignment. Based on the scenarios, we choose the TCP protocols flags and unit ports in content as parameters per the provided cases, that will be the key components submitted. Finally, after examining the PCAP file through an iterative process, we create a packet alignment window in a graphical form, to show the results.

The flags taken are SYN-ACK and RST-ACK. Then we check if the source port corresponds to the destination port from both flags respectively. The ports are taken as a unique unit value from both flag arrays, and are matched between the flags. The pseudocode for these functions is presented in figure 4 and figure 5:

```
Algorithm 1 Extract Packets With Needed Flags
Require: pcapfile
  packets ← readFile                                    ▷ Read packets from file
  ack_rst_packets ← []                                  ▷ Initialize empty list
  for each packet in packets do
      if packet has a TCP layer then
          if packet TCP flags are AR or SA then
              Append packet to ack_rst_packets
          end if
      end if
  end for
      Return ack_rst_packets
```

Figure 4: Pseudocode for Extracting Packets Based on Flags.

```
Algorithm 2 Match Ports
Require: ack_rst_packets
  packets1 ← []                                         ▷ Initialize empty list
  packets2 ← []                                         ▷ Initialize empty list
  for each packet in packets do
      if packet has a TCP layer then
          if packet TCP flags are AR or SA then
              Append packet to ack_rst_packets
          end if
      end if
  end for
      Return ack_rst_packets
```

Figure 5: Pseudocode for Matching the Ports From the Given Packets.

The generated PCAP files varied in size from 200 kilobytes to 14 megabytes. As previously mentioned, an increase in file size directly correlates with a corresponding increase in the volume of packets encapsulated within the PCAP file. Furthermore, the computational demands associated with the packet processing task were demanding. Standard computing power units were used for the packet processing task described. The time to complete the task varied from 10 seconds to 2-3 hours. One specific, not defined scenario in this research that accumulated a 360 megabyte ~759 000 packet PCAP file took approximately 6 hours to process.

5. Results

This section will present the results of the algorithm.

Frequent attack pattern in alignment was spotted at the start of the attack, with subsequent alignments appearing consistent throughout. Assuming that the most frequently used ports would be only addressed per the most frequent port scan scenario mentioned before, indicates that this pattern can also be addressed in other scenarios not depending on details provided (figure 6 and 7). For graphical representation of the results we use python library (Meert et al, 2020).

The alignment that appears consistent throughout suggests that the attack pattern changed because the needed results of the attack were achieved or the firewall noticed the attack pattern and mitigated the attack leaving the static data flow until the end without any results. Even though the same ports were triggered multiple times after the initial alignment, no considerable changes were seen. As mentioned before the bare metal hypervisor used for the experiments is a part of Vilnius University high performance computing infrastructure and no additional firewall configuration was made for experiments.

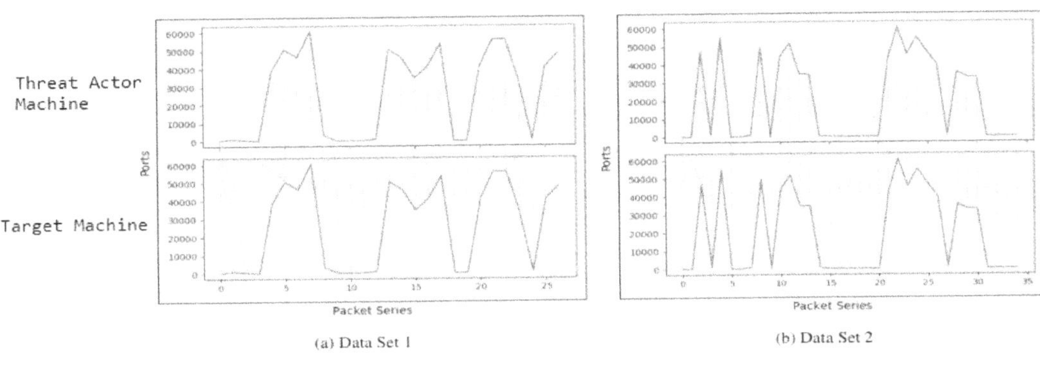

Figure 6: Asynchronous PCAP Alignment from SA-RA Packets and Source Destination Ports 1

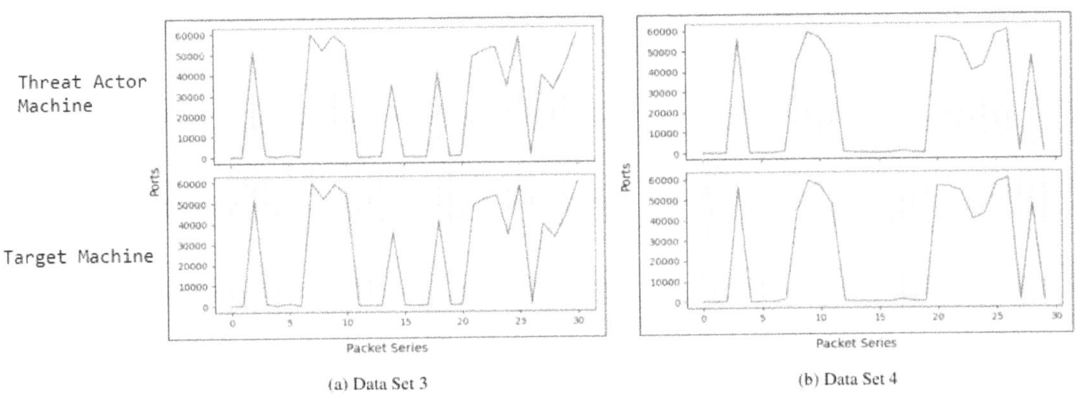

Figure 7: Asynchronous PCAP Alignment from SA-RA Packets and Source Destination Ports 2

Furthermore, this can be seen in the small amount of packet series accumulated between the two PCAP files. Although the SA-RA packets were gathered at the start of the attack which generated the alignment, only static callback was seen afterwards. Also, the small packet amount of packet series could indicate that other ports per the 60000 ports scanned were closed or not reachable based on some additional firewall rules or other network configuration.

Previously accumulated results noticeably change in one specific scenario. In these results the amount of accumulated SA-RA packets exceeds the previously mentioned amount (figure 8).

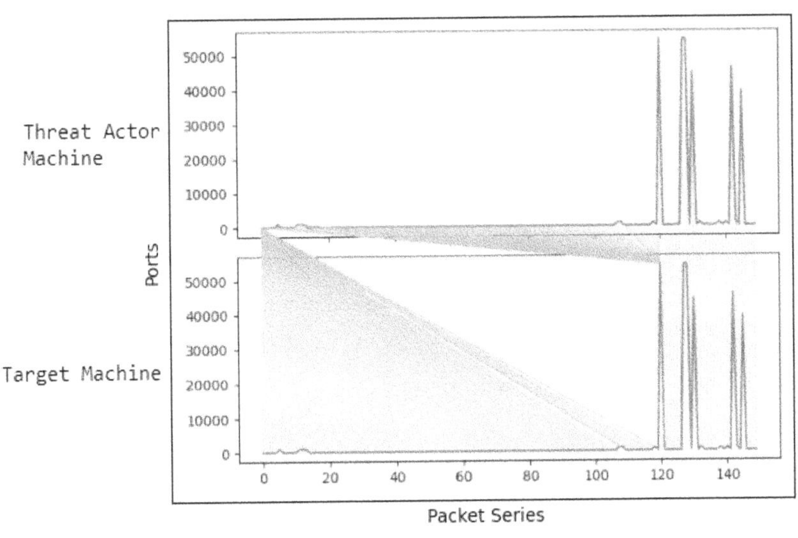

Figure 8: Asynchronous PCAP Alignment from SA-RA Packets and Source Destination Ports 3

We see two asynchronous network flows. The difference in amount is noticed by the yellow lines that represent SA-RA trigger count per ports which aligns the two sequences in time. The blue lines show the port number that was used to call in the attack. Possibly due to heterogeneous network points used or a very specific payload that bypassed default defence mechanisms, the accumulation of the packet series between two files became noticeably bigger. The number of ports affected was not in a large number, but they were seemingly attacked in a disproportionate amount.

6. Discussion

The realised pattern in the results suggest that the attack from target machine to victim machine generates an attack pattern based on scenarios provided.

Also, based on the parameters selected we see that the alignment between two-time frames while using DTW was achieved in the detection and reconstruction of the attacks in asynchronous records. The definitive distinction comes in the computational power and buffer problem in DTW. DTW can be less effective for PCAP alignment because it needs to access the full data stream of packets, which must be buffered before the procession. The exhausting nature of the algorithm causes the deficiency in computational power. In time this buffering can delay the potential of DTW to do immediate data analysis or alignment.

If these problems are addressed, the possible alert generation could be sufficient in detecting known vulnerabilities. For sophisticated vulnerabilities additional steps would be needed. These steps may include artificial intelligence or machine learning components implemented.

Based on the previous research, heterogeneous point selection of the network was implied, less than possible. Furthermore, it is worth noting, that while these patterns are suggestive of malicious activity, they should be interpreted with caution, considering the potential for false positives in complex network environments.

It is possible to have different configurations in different heterogeneous network points. These configurations can come out in the same network's subnets, DMZ and other solutions.

7. Conclusions and Future Work

The research conducted in this study provides a fundamental understanding of asynchronous evidence-based assessment, the analysis of network traffic for cybersecurity.

For a broader spectrum of problems, we assume the potentially heavy cyber-attacks that are masqueraded by large volumes of data flow. This comes down to pre-processing and processing relevant data. As we experienced a struggle with small sized data structures, big PCAP analysis would require much more computational power. The DTW algorithm does not provide the sufficient results needed. As a result, future studies should focus on the scalability and efficiency of security models in environments with high volumes of network traffic.

Furthermore, future research will possibly focus on developing more sophisticated models for asynchronous evidence-based assessment. This includes automatization in incident response systems based on previously mentioned artificial intelligence and machine learning involved. Also, a deeper dive in network configuration that could enhance the understanding of network flow in correlation with cyber-attacks can be discussed. This is needed if we want to understand the different visibility of the networks that data flows from.

References

Alothman, B. (2019, June). Raw network traffic data preprocessing and preparation for automatic analysis. In *2019 International Conference on Cyber Security and Protection of Digital Services (Cyber Security)* (pp. 1-5). IEEE. http://dx.doi.org/10.1109/CyberSecPODS.2019.8885333

Argyraki, K., & Cheriton, D. (2005). Network capabilities: The good, the bad and the ugly. ACM HotNets-IV, 139, 140.

Beddoe, M. A. (2004). Network protocol analysis using bioinformatics algorithms.

Cappers, B. C., Meessen, P. N., Etalle, S., & Van Wijk, J. J. (2018, October). Eventpad: Rapid malware analysis and reverse engineering using visual analytics. In *2018 IEEE Symposium on Visualization for Cyber Security (VizSec)* (pp. 1-8). IEEE. http://dx.doi.org/10.1109/VIZSEC.2018.8709230

Chew, L. P., Goodrich, M. T., Huttenlocher, D. P., Kedem, K., Kleinberg, J. M., & Kravets, D. (1997). Geometric pattern matching under Euclidean motion. *Computational Geometry*, *7*(1-2), 113-124. https://doi.org/10.1016/0925-7721(95)00047-x

Clarke, R. A., & Knake, R. K. (2014). *Cyber war.* Old Saybrook: Tantor Media, Incorporated.
de Neira, A. B., Kantarci, B., & Nogueira, M. (2023). Distributed denial of service attack prediction: Challenges, open issues and opportunities. *Computer Networks*, *222*, 109553. https://doi.org/10.1016/j.comnet.2022.109553
Dimolianis, M., Pavlidis, A., Kalogeras, D., & Maglaris, V. (2019, April). Mitigation of multi-vector network attacks via orchestration of distributed rule placement. In *2019 IFIP/IEEE Symposium on Integrated Network and Service Management (IM)* (pp. 162-170). IEEE.
Diab, D. M., AsSadhan, B., Binsalleeh, H., Lambotharan, S., Kyriakopoulos, K. G., & Ghafir, I. (2019, August). Anomaly detection using dynamic time warping. In *2019 IEEE International Conference on Computational Science and Engineering (CSE) and IEEE International Conference on Embedded and Ubiquitous Computing (EUC)* (pp. 193-198). IEEE. https://ieeexplore.ieee.org/document/8919604/
Diab, D. M., AsSadhan, B., Binsalleeh, H., Lambotharan, S., Kyriakopoulos, K. G., & Ghafir, I. (2021). Denial of service detection using dynamic time warping. International Journal of Network Management, 31(6), e2159.
Esoul, O., & Walkinshaw, N. (2017, July). Using segment-based alignment to extract packet structures from network traces. In *2017 IEEE International Conference on Software Quality, Reliability and Security (QRS)* (pp. 398-409). IEEE. https://doi.org/10.1109/QRS.2017.49
Kalinin, M. O., & Krundyshev, V. M. (2021). Analysis of a huge amount of network traffic based on quantum machine learning. *Automatic Control and Computer Sciences*, *55*(8), 1165-1174. https://doi.org/10.3103/S014641162108040X
Meert, W., Hendrickx, K., Van Craenendonck, T., Robberechts, P., Blockeel, H., & Davis, J. D. Zenodo. 2020. https://zenodo.org/badge/latestdoi/80764246
Merino, B. (2013). *Instant traffic analysis with Tshark how-to*. Packt Publishing Ltd.
Senin, P. (2008). Dynamic time warping algorithm review. Information and Computer Science Department University of Hawaii at Manoa Honolulu, USA, 855(1-23), 40.
Veselý, V. (2012). Extended comparison study on merging PCAP files.
Zahid, F., Funchal, G., Melo, V., Kuo, M. M., Leitao, P., & Sinha, R. (2022, July). DDoS Attacks on Smart Manufacturing Systems: A Cross-Domain Taxonomy and Attack Vectors. In 2022 IEEE 20th International Conference on Industrial Informatics (INDIN) (pp. 214-219). IEEE. http://dx.doi.org/10.1109/INDIN51773.2022.9976172

Threat Modeling for Cyber Warfare Against Less Cyber-Dependent Adversaries

Shreyas Kumar[1] **and Gourav Nagar**[2]
[1]Texas A&M University, College Station, TX, USA
[2]Independent Researcher

Shreyas.kumar@tamu.edu
gouravnagar@ieee.org

Abstract: Cyber warfare poses a substantial threat in today's interconnected world, where digital attacks can transcend physical boundaries and affect targets globally. Technologically less advanced adversaries, such as smaller nations or organizations with limited resources, face unique challenges in defending against sophisticated cyber attacks from more advanced entities. This paper explores the threat landscape for these adversaries and proposes a tailored threat modeling framework to address their specific vulnerabilities and needs. By examining the evolution of cyber warfare, including historical incidents and the increasing sophistication of cyber attacks, the study highlights the limitations of existing threat modeling approaches like the Cyber Kill Chain, MITRE ATT&CK Framework, and SWOT analysis when applied to less advanced adversaries. A comprehensive literature review underscores the gaps in current research, particularly the necessity for frameworks tailored to asymmetric technological capabilities. Employing a mixed methods approach, the research combines qualitative and quantitative data from primary sources, such as interviews with cybersecurity experts, and secondary sources, including existing literature and case studies. The proposed framework focuses on asset identification and classification, vulnerability assessment, threat analysis, and risk assessment. Proactive measures, such as basic cyber hygiene practices, advanced threat detection systems, and collaboration with technologically advanced allies, are recommended alongside reactive measures like incident response planning and disaster recovery. The importance of international cooperation and information sharing is also emphasized. Case studies of cyber incidents involving less advanced adversaries, such as the attacks on Estonia, Georgia, and Ukraine, validate the framework and demonstrate its practical application. The findings indicate that the tailored threat modeling framework effectively addresses the unique challenges faced by less advanced adversaries, enhancing their ability to mitigate risks and improve their cybersecurity posture. This study provides valuable insights and offers a practical framework to bolster defenses against cyber warfare, with future research needed to explore emerging threats and technologies further.

Keywords: Cyber Warfare, Threat Modeling, Vulnerability Assessment, Incident Response, International Cooperation, Cyber Infrastructures,

1. Introduction

1.1 Motivation and Context

Cyber warfare has emerged as a critical battleground in the modern era, characterized by the use of computer networks to disrupt, damage, or control enemy infrastructure. Unlike traditional warfare, cyber warfare can transcend physical boundaries, affecting targets anywhere in the world. This has significant implications for the national security of modern nation-states, whose much of the infrastructure, power grid, banking systems, and defense systems are managed via Cyber systems against adversaries that are less advanced in terms of online infrastructure to target.

1.2 Significance of the Study

This study aims to explore the threat landscape for technologically advanced nations against less advanced adversaries and develop a tailored threat modeling framework that addresses their specific vulnerabilities and needs. By understanding the unique threats these adversaries face, we can propose effective countermeasures and defense strategies to enhance their cybersecurity posture.

1.3 Research Questions

The primary research questions guiding this study are:

1. What unique threats do technologically less advanced entities pose to advanced adversaries?
2. How can advanced adversaries identify and mitigate these threats effectively?

1.4 Contributions

This paper contributes to the field of cybersecurity by identifying unique threats and vulnerabilities faced by technologically advanced adversaries, developing a tailored threat modeling framework for threats posed by less advanced adversaries, and proposing practical defense strategies to enhance cybersecurity.

2. Background and Related Work

2.1 Why this topic is important

Creating a threat model for cyber warfare against a country with minimal or no internet dependence involves understanding and identifying potential threats and vulnerabilities in offline infrastructure and developing strategies to counteract both cyber and hybrid threats. The primary objectives are to protect critical infrastructure, communication systems, and physical security and defense systems from various types of attackers, including state-sponsored hackers, insider threats, physical saboteurs, and proxies. The assets to protect include power plants and energy distribution networks, water treatment and supply facilities, transportation systems, radio and satellite communication networks, military communication channels, weapon systems, command and control centers, and surveillance and reconnaissance systems. Attack vectors in this context extend beyond traditional cyber attacks to include physical attacks, electronic warfare, insider threats, and hybrid tactics that combine cyber and physical operations. Physical attacks might involve the sabotage of infrastructure, interference with security measures, or attacks on supply chains. Electronic warfare could target radio frequencies, disrupt satellite communications, or compromise local networked devices such as SCADA systems. Insider threats might stem from disgruntled employees or those coerced or bribed into sabotaging or stealing sensitive information. Hybrid tactics could spread disinformation or propaganda to cause confusion and panic. Vulnerabilities in this scenario include unprotected critical systems, outdated or poorly maintained equipment, insecure local networks, and human factors such as lack of cybersecurity awareness and insider threats. Mitigation strategies should focus on enhancing physical security, using electronic countermeasures like frequency-hopping spread spectrum for radio communications and encryption for satellite communications, and implementing strict access controls and monitoring to mitigate insider threats. Regular training programs for employees and raising awareness about potential threats and security best practices are also essential. In terms of response and recovery, it is crucial to establish a clear incident response protocol and conduct regular drills and simulations to ensure readiness. Recovery strategies should include backup and redundancy plans for critical systems and quick repair and replacement plans for damaged infrastructure. Coordination and collaboration with international allies and organizations for intelligence sharing and best practices are vital to strengthening defenses against such threats. By focusing on these components, a technically advanced country can develop a comprehensive threat model to effectively defend against cyber warfare tactics targeting offline and minimally networked infrastructure.

2.2 Historical Context

Cyber warfare has evolved significantly over the past few decades, with early instances of cyber attacks dating back to the 1980s. The advent of the internet and digital technologies has transformed the nature of warfare, enabling actors to conduct attacks remotely and anonymously. Notable incidents such as the Morris Worm in 1988, the 2007 cyber attacks on Estonia, and the Stuxnet attack on Iran's nuclear facilities in 2010 highlight the growing sophistication and impact of cyber warfare.

2.3 Definition and Scope

Cyber warfare involves the use of digital attacks to compromise, disrupt, or destroy information systems, networks, and infrastructure. It encompasses a wide range of activities, including espionage, sabotage, and propaganda, conducted by state and non-state actors.

Threat modeling involves five essential features that are crucial for developing an effective security strategy. The first feature is identifying critical assets that need protection, such as data, systems, and infrastructure. This step is fundamental as it helps in understanding what needs to be safeguarded. The second feature is enumerating potential threats, which includes identifying various threat actors like hackers, insider threats, and state-sponsored entities, and considering their possible attack vectors. This helps in anticipating who might attack and how. The third feature is vulnerability analysis, which involves assessing and documenting existing vulnerabilities within the system. This step requires a thorough review of the security posture of the assets to pinpoint weaknesses that could be exploited by threat actors. The fourth feature is risk assessment, which involves evaluating the risks associated with each identified threat and vulnerability. This includes considering the likelihood of a threat exploiting a vulnerability and the potential impact on the organization. This step helps in prioritizing risks to focus on the most critical areas. The fifth and final feature is developing mitigation strategies to address the identified risks. This involves implementing technical controls such as encryption and firewalls, making process changes like enhancing incident response planning and conducting regular employee training, and updating policies to strengthen the overall security posture. These strategies aim to reduce the vulnerabilities and improve the resilience of the system against potential threats.

2.4 Existing Threat Modeling Approaches

Existing threat modeling approaches include the Cyber Kill Chain, the MITRE ATT&CK Framework, and SWOT analysis. The Cyber Kill Chain, developed by Lockheed Martin, outlines the stages of a cyber attack, from initial reconnaissance to execution, including reconnaissance (gathering information about the target), weaponization (creating the attack tools), delivery (transmitting the weapon to the target), exploitation (triggering the weapon), installation (installing malware on the target system), command and control (establishing a communication channel), and actions on objectives (executing the attack). The MITRE ATT&CK Framework provides a comprehensive catalog of tactics, techniques, and procedures (TTPs) used by cyber adversaries and is widely used for threat intelligence, detection, and response. SWOT analysis (Strengths, Weaknesses, Opportunities, Threats) is a strategic planning tool used to identify internal and external factors that can impact an organization's security posture. In the literature review, previous case studies have highlighted the vulnerabilities and challenges faced by less advanced adversaries in cyber warfare. Notable examples include the cyber attacks on Estonia, Georgia, and Ukraine, which demonstrated the devastating impact of cyber warfare on less advanced nations. Despite the valuable insights provided by existing research, there is a lack of focus on tailored threat modeling approaches for technologically less advanced adversaries. This study aims to address this gap by developing a framework specifically designed for these adversaries.

3. Methodology

Threat modeling involves five essential features that are crucial for developing an effective security strategy. The first feature is identifying critical assets that need protection, such as data, systems, and infrastructure. This step is fundamental as it helps in understanding what needs to be safeguarded. The second feature is enumerating potential threats, which includes identifying various threat actors like hackers, insider threats, and state-sponsored entities, and considering their possible attack vectors. This helps in anticipating who might attack and how. The third feature is vulnerability analysis, which involves assessing and documenting existing vulnerabilities within the system. This step requires a thorough review of the security posture of the assets to pinpoint weaknesses that could be exploited by threat actors. The fourth feature is risk assessment, which involves evaluating the risks associated with each identified threat and vulnerability. This includes considering the likelihood of a threat exploiting a vulnerability and the potential impact on the organization. This step helps prioritize risks and focus on the most critical areas. The fifth and final feature is developing mitigation strategies to address the identified risks. This involves implementing technical controls such as encryption and firewalls, making process changes like enhancing incident response planning and conducting regular employee training, and updating policies to strengthen the overall security posture. These strategies aim to reduce the vulnerabilities and improve the resilience of the system against potential threats.

3.1 Threat Analysis

Technologically less advanced adversaries typically rely on outdated or less sophisticated technologies, which lack the security features and resilience of more advanced systems. Common technologies include legacy operating systems, unpatched software, and limited network infrastructure. These adversaries are often susceptible to a range of vulnerabilities, including weak password policies, unpatched software, limited network segmentation, and inadequate incident response plans.

State-sponsored entities possess significant resources and capabilities to conduct sophisticated cyber attacks with political, economic, or military objectives. Hacktivist groups are motivated by ideological goals, while criminal organizations seek financial gain. Both can exploit the vulnerabilities of less advanced adversaries to achieve their objectives. Common attack vectors include phishing and social engineering, which exploit human vulnerabilities to bypass technological defenses. Malware and ransomware disrupt or gain unauthorized access to systems, while denial-of-service attacks overwhelm targeted systems with traffic to render them unavailable to legitimate users.

3.2 Development of a Threat Model

Identifying critical infrastructure components, such as power grids, water supply systems, communication networks, and financial services, is essential for effective threat modeling. Protecting sensitive information, financial records, and intellectual property from unauthorized access and theft is also crucial. Vulnerability assessment involves identifying technical vulnerabilities and procedural weaknesses that could be exploited by attackers. Developing potential exploit scenarios helps understand how vulnerabilities could be exploited and the potential impact on the organization.

Intelligence gathering involves collecting and analyzing information about potential threats and profiling attackers to anticipate and defend against specific types of attacks. Estimating the likelihood of attack scenarios and assessing the potential consequences helps prioritize resources and defense measures.

3.3 Defense Strategies

Implementing basic cyber hygiene practices, such as regular software updates, strong password policies, and user education, is essential for reducing vulnerabilities. Advanced threat detection systems, including intrusion detection systems (IDS), intrusion prevention systems (IPS), and security information and event management (SIEM) solutions, can help identify and respond to threats in real-time. Developing comprehensive incident response plans and ensuring disaster recovery and business continuity plans are in place ensures critical operations can continue or quickly resume following an attack. Collaboration with technologically advanced allies provides access to resources, expertise, and intelligence. Participating in information sharing networks enhances detection and response capabilities.

3.4 Case Studies and Validation

Analyzing incidents such as the cyber-attacks on Estonia, Georgia, and Ukraine provides valuable insights and validates the framework. These case studies highlight the importance of preparedness, robust incident response plans, and international cooperation in cybersecurity. Applying the framework to real-world scenarios demonstrates its practicality and effectiveness, assessing its ability to mitigate risks, reduce vulnerabilities, and enhance overall cybersecurity.

By following this methodology, we aim to develop a comprehensive threat modeling framework that effectively addresses the unique challenges faced by technologically less advanced adversaries in cyber warfare. This approach provides valuable insights and practical solutions to enhance cybersecurity defenses.

4. Case Studies

4.1 Cyber Attacks on Estonia (2007)

In 2007, Estonia experienced a series of unprecedented cyber attacks that targeted government, banking, media, and other critical infrastructure websites. These attacks, widely believed to have been politically motivated, were launched following a decision to relocate a Soviet-era war memorial in the capital city of Tallinn. The decision sparked significant unrest among the Russian-speaking population and provoked a strong response from Russia (Armin et al. 2008).

The attacks began on April 27, 2007, and lasted for several weeks. The primary method used was Distributed Denial of Service (DDoS) attacks, which overwhelmed targeted websites with massive amounts of traffic, rendering them inaccessible. The attackers employed botnets—networks of compromised computers—to flood the servers of Estonian institutions with traffic, effectively paralyzing their online presence (Rid 2012).

Estonia's government ministries, banks, media outlets, and other key organizations were severely affected. The country's banking sector faced severe disruptions, with several major banks having to temporarily suspend their online services. Media outlets struggled to deliver news, and government websites were taken offline, impeding communication and administrative functions (Singer and Friedman 2014).

The Estonian cyber attacks were a wake-up call to the international community about the potential for cyber warfare to disrupt national security and economic stability. Estonia's response included strengthening its cyber defenses and increasing international cooperation on cybersecurity issues. The country also advocated for NATO to recognize cyber attacks as a potential trigger for collective defense measures under Article 5 of the NATO Treaty (Geers 2011).

4.2 Cyber Attacks on Georgia (2008)

In August 2008, during its conflict with Russia over the regions of South Ossetia and Abkhazia, Georgia experienced a coordinated wave of cyber attacks. These attacks were designed to coincide with and support Russia's military operations, demonstrating a new dimension of hybrid warfare where cyber and kinetic operations are used in tandem (Healey 2013).

The cyber attacks on Georgia began on July 20, 2008, escalating significantly as the conflict intensified. The attacks primarily involved DDoS attacks and website defacements. Georgian government websites, including those of the president, parliament, and foreign affairs ministry, were taken offline. Additionally, the websites of news organizations and financial institutions were targeted, disrupting communications and information dissemination (Lewis 2010).

One notable aspect of these attacks was the use of botnets and the coordination of various hacker groups, some of which were reportedly linked to Russian state actors. The attackers also used simple but effective methods like DNS poisoning and SQL injection to compromise Georgian websites (Singer and Friedman 2014).

The defacement of government websites included propaganda messages and images aimed at demoralizing the Georgian population and undermining trust in the government. These cyber operations were synchronized with the physical invasion, creating confusion and hampering Georgia's ability to communicate internally and with the international community (Rid 2012).

The 2008 cyber attacks on Georgia highlighted the strategic use of cyber warfare as a force multiplier in traditional conflicts. They underscored the need for nations to integrate cybersecurity into their national defense strategies and highlighted the importance of international cooperation in addressing cyber threats (Healey 2013).

4.3 Cyber Attack on Ukraine's Power Grid (2015)

On December 23, 2015, Ukraine experienced a sophisticated cyber attack that targeted its power grid, resulting in widespread power outages. This incident marked the first known successful cyber attack on a power grid, setting a precedent for the potential impact of cyber warfare on critical infrastructure (Zetter 2014).

The attack was meticulously planned and executed, involving multiple stages. Initially, the attackers used spear-phishing emails to gain access to the IT networks of several Ukrainian energy companies. Once inside, they deployed malware, including the infamous BlackEnergy trojan, to steal credentials and establish remote access to the control systems (Singer 2015).

The attackers used the stolen credentials to remotely access the control systems and systematically shut down substations, causing power outages across the Ivano-Frankivsk region. They also deployed KillDisk malware to wipe data from the systems, hindering recovery efforts. Additionally, the attackers disrupted the companies' call centers, preventing customers from reporting the outages and further complicating the response (Singer 2015).

The cyber attack affected approximately 230,000 people, leaving them without electricity for several hours. The incident demonstrated the vulnerability of critical infrastructure to cyber attacks and the potential for significant societal impact. It also highlighted the increasing sophistication of cyber adversaries, who can integrate technical exploits with strategic objectives to create widespread disruption (Singer 2015).

The 2015 attack on Ukraine's power grid prompted a global reassessment of the security of critical infrastructure. It underscored the importance of robust cybersecurity measures, incident response planning, and international collaboration to defend against such threats. The incident also reinforced the need for continuous monitoring and improvement of cybersecurity practices to protect vital systems from evolving cyber threats (Zetter 2014).

5. Proposed Threat Model

The scenario in which a technologically advanced nation faces a technologically less advanced adversary presents unique challenges and opportunities in the realm of cyber warfare. The advanced nation, relying on sophisticated, interconnected online systems for its critical infrastructure—including weapons systems, power grids, banking, and water supply—is highly vulnerable to cyber-attacks. Conversely, the technologically inferior adversary has minimal critical online infrastructure, providing fewer targets for cyber retaliation. This section proposes a threat model tailored to this asymmetrical situation, focusing on both offensive and defensive strategies.

5.1 Asset Identification and Classification

The first step in developing a robust threat model is to identify and classify critical assets within the advanced nation. These assets typically include weapons systems, which are often integrated with advanced command and control networks, relying heavily on real-time data and communications. This dependency makes them prime targets for cyber attacks aimed at disabling or manipulating military capabilities. The national power grid, being highly interconnected and dependent on SCADA (Supervisory Control and Data Acquisition) systems, is vulnerable to disruptions that can have widespread impacts on national security and civilian life. Financial institutions, which depend on complex IT infrastructure for transactions, records, and communications, can be thrown into chaos by cyber attacks, leading to economic instability and loss of public trust. Similarly, water supply and treatment facilities that use automated systems are susceptible to cyber threats that could result in public health crises and service disruptions. Communication networks are also critical, as they are essential for both civilian and military operations, and their disruption can hinder emergency responses, military operations, and everyday activities.

5.2 Vulnerability Assessment

Identifying potential vulnerabilities in these critical systems is essential for effective threat modeling. Common vulnerabilities include the use of legacy systems, where many critical infrastructures still operate on outdated software and hardware, making them more vulnerable to attacks due to a lack of updates and patches. The high degree of interconnectivity among systems can allow an attacker to move laterally within the network, increasing the potential damage of a breach. Despite advancements, many systems may still lack robust cybersecurity measures such as encryption, multi-factor authentication, and regular security audits. Human factors also play a significant role, as employees' susceptibility to phishing and social engineering attacks remains a major vulnerability. Comprehensive training and awareness programs are crucial to mitigate this risk.

5.3 Threat Analysis

The primary threats to an advanced nation's critical infrastructure from a less technologically advanced adversary include state-sponsored cyber attacks, which are often well-funded and sophisticated, targeting critical infrastructure to disrupt national security and public order. Hacktivist groups, motivated by political or ideological goals, can carry out disruptive attacks on critical systems to achieve their objectives. Criminal organizations may seek financial gain through ransomware, data theft, or other cybercriminal activities, exploiting vulnerabilities for profit. Insider threats also pose significant risks, as disgruntled employees or those coerced by adversaries can provide access to sensitive systems and data.

5.4 Risk Assessment

To effectively manage risks, it is essential to evaluate both the likelihood and impact of potential cyber-attacks. This involves assessing the probability of different types of attacks based on historical data, intelligence reports, and current threat landscapes. Evaluating the potential consequences of successful attacks, including financial losses, operational disruptions, and reputational damage, helps prioritize resources and defense measures. Identifying which assets are most critical and require the highest level of protection is crucial based on their importance to national security and societal function.

5.5 Defense Strategies

Given the asymmetrical nature of the threat, a multi-layered defense strategy is essential, incorporating both proactive and reactive measures. Implementing basic cyber hygiene practices, such as regular software updates, strong password policies, and comprehensive user education, can significantly reduce vulnerabilities. Advanced threat detection systems, including IDS (Intrusion Detection Systems), IPS (Intrusion Prevention Systems), and SIEM (Security Information and Event Management) solutions, can help identify and respond to threats in real-time. Network segmentation can also be effective by segregating critical networks to limit the potential for lateral movement by attackers within the system. Conducting regular red team exercises to simulate attacks and identify weaknesses in security protocols and defenses is another proactive measure.

In terms of reactive measures, developing and regularly updating comprehensive incident response plans is essential. These plans should outline the steps to be taken in the event of a cyber attack, including identification, containment, eradication, and recovery. Ensuring that disaster recovery and business continuity plans are in place and tested regularly is crucial to maintain critical operations during and after an attack. Establishing robust forensic capabilities to analyze cyber incidents, understand attack vectors, and improve future defenses is also important.

Collaboration and information sharing play a vital role in enhancing cybersecurity defenses. Engaging in international cooperation to share threat intelligence, best practices, and resources with allies and partners can provide valuable support. Collaborating with private sector entities to leverage their expertise and resources can also enhance national cybersecurity. Participating in information-sharing networks helps organizations stay informed about emerging threats and vulnerabilities and disseminate critical information quickly during a cyber incident.

5.6 Case Study: Application of the Proposed Threat Model

Consider a scenario where an advanced nation, reliant on its interconnected online systems, faces potential cyber attacks from a less technologically advanced adversary. The adversary aims to exploit vulnerabilities in the advanced nation's critical infrastructure to cause widespread disruption. To implement the proposed threat model, the first step would be to identify and classify critical infrastructure components, focusing on their interconnectedness and potential points of failure. Conducting comprehensive vulnerability assessments to identify weak points in the infrastructure, considering both technical and human factors, is essential. Gathering intelligence on potential adversaries, their capabilities, and likely attack vectors helps profile attackers to understand their motivations and tactics. Evaluating the likelihood and impact of potential attacks allows for prioritizing resources and defense measures accordingly. Implementing a multi-layered defense strategy that combines proactive measures, such as advanced threat detection systems and cyber hygiene practices, with reactive measures, like incident response planning and disaster recovery, is crucial.

6. Discussion

6.1 Key Findings

The study identifies several unique challenges faced by technologically advanced adversaries when targeting countries with minimal or no internet dependence. These challenges include the need to adapt strategies to bypass traditional cyber attack methods, the difficulty of compromising offline or manually controlled systems, and the necessity of integrating physical sabotage with cyber tactics. Additionally, advanced adversaries must contend with robust physical security measures and the potential for limited intelligence on local infrastructures. This complexity requires a more nuanced approach, combining electronic warfare, insider recruitment, and hybrid tactics to breach and disrupt critical offline systems effectively. The proposed threat modeling framework is shown to be effective in addressing these challenges by providing a structured approach to identifying and mitigating threats. The framework's focus on asset identification, vulnerability assessment, threat analysis, and risk assessment helps less advanced adversaries develop targeted defense strategies.

6.2 Implications for Policy and Practice

Policymakers should prioritize cybersecurity as a critical component of national security and allocate resources accordingly. This includes funding for cybersecurity initiatives, support for international cooperation, and the development of policies and regulations to enhance cybersecurity. Cybersecurity professionals should adopt best practices, such as regular software updates, strong password policies, user education, and the implementation of advanced threat detection systems. Collaboration with other organizations and participation in information-sharing networks are also essential for staying informed about emerging threats and best practices.

6.3 Future Work: Evaluation of Effectiveness

The effectiveness of the threat model can be assessed by monitoring the number of detected and prevented attacks, the speed and effectiveness of incident response, and the resilience of critical systems. Continuous improvement of the threat model is essential, incorporating lessons learned from real-world incidents and advancements in cybersecurity technologies.

The proposed threat model provides a comprehensive framework for defending technologically advanced nations against cyber threats from less advanced adversaries. By focusing on asset identification, vulnerability assessment, threat analysis, and risk assessment, the model helps develop effective defense strategies tailored to the unique challenges of this asymmetrical conflict. Continuous adaptation and improvement of the model, coupled with international cooperation and information sharing, are crucial for maintaining robust cybersecurity defenses in an increasingly interconnected and hostile digital landscape.

7. Conclusion

This study comprehensively analyzes the threat landscape for technologically less advanced adversaries and proposes a tailored threat modeling framework to address their unique vulnerabilities and needs. The framework's focus on asset identification, vulnerability assessment, threat analysis, and risk assessment helps these adversaries develop effective defense strategies. Future research should explore the evolving threat landscape and emerging technologies that may impact cyber warfare. Areas for further study include the use of artificial intelligence and machine learning in cyber defense, the impact of new technologies such as 5G and the Internet of Things (IoT), and the development of international norms and agreements for cyber warfare. This continued exploration will be crucial in adapting and enhancing cybersecurity strategies to protect against increasingly sophisticated cyber threats effectively.

References

Armin, A., Armin, D. and Uzeve, B. (2008) 'Analyzing the 2007 cyber attacks on Estonia', International Journal of Computer Science and Network Security, 8(4), pp. 1-8.

Clarke, R.A. and Knake, R.K. (2010) Cyber War: The Next Threat to National Security and What to Do About It. New York: HarperCollins.

Denning, D.E. (1999) Information Warfare and Security. Reading, MA: Addison-Wesley.

Fidler, D.P. (2013) 'Cybersecurity and Privacy Issues in a Post-Snowden World', Indiana Journal of Global Legal Studies, 20(2), pp. 439-463.

Geers, K. (2011) Strategic Cyber Security. NATO Cooperative Cyber Defence Centre of Excellence.

Goldman, J. (2017) 'The Growing Threat of Ransomware', Network Security, 2017(8), pp. 5-8.

Hanson, J.A. and Ulin, R.B. (2013) 'Critical Infrastructure Cybersecurity: Government and Private Sector Efforts to Protect the Nation's Information Technology and Communications', American Journal of Law & Medicine, 39(2-3), pp. 213-241.

Healey, J. (Ed.) (2013) A Fierce Domain: Conflict in Cyberspace, 1986 to 2012. Arlington, VA: Cyber Conflict Studies Association.

Jensen, E.T. (2012) 'The Tallinn Manual on the International Law Applicable to Cyber Warfare', American Society of International Law, 106, pp. 377-381.

Kello, L. (2013) 'The Meaning of the Cyber Revolution: Perils to Theory and Statecraft', International Security, 38(2), pp. 7-40.

Kumar, N. (2024) Threat Modeling for Cyber Warfare Against Technologically Less Advanced Adversary.

Lewis, J.A. (2010) 'The Cyber War Has Not Begun', Center for Strategic and International Studies (CSIS). Available at: https://csis.org/publication/cyber-war-has-not-begun (Accessed: 14 May 2024).

Lockheed Martin (n.d.) 'Cyber Kill Chain'. Available at: https://www.lockheedmartin.com/en-us/capabilities/cyber/cyber-kill-chain.html (Accessed: 14 March 2024).

MITRE Corporation (n.d.) 'MITRE ATT&CK Framework'. Available at: https://attack.mitre.org/ (Accessed: 14 May 2024).

Mueller, M.L. (2010) Networks and States: The Global Politics of Internet Governance. Cambridge, MA: MIT Press.

Nissenbaum, H. (2005) 'Where Computer Security Meets National Security', Ethics and Information Technology, 7(2), pp. 61-73.

Nye, J.S. (2010) 'Cyber Power', Harvard Kennedy School Belfer Center for Science and International Affairs. Available at: https://belfercenter.org/publication/cyber-power (Accessed: 14 May 2024).

Rid, T. (2012) 'Cyber War Will Not Take Place', Journal of Strategic Studies, 35(1), pp. 5-32.

SANS Institute (2015) 'Critical Security Controls for Effective Cyber Defense: Version 6.0'. Available at: https://www.sans.org/critical-security-controls/ (Accessed: 15 March 2024).

Schneier, B. (2015) Data and Goliath: The Hidden Battles to Collect Your Data and Control Your World. New York: W.W. Norton & Company.

Scott, J. and Spaniel, D. (2016) Malicious Cryptography: Exposing Cryptovirology. Hoboken, NJ: Wiley.

Shostack, A. (2014) Threat Modeling: Designing for Security. Indianapolis: Wiley.

Singer, P.W. (2015) 'Stuxnet and the Dawn of Algorithmic Warfare', Strategic Studies Quarterly, 9(3), pp. 17-27.

Singer, P.W. and Friedman, A. (2014) Cybersecurity and Cyberwar: What Everyone Needs to Know. Oxford: Oxford University Press.

Skierka, I. (2017) 'The Governance of Digital Risks: A Systematic Review', Journal of Risk Research, 20(3), pp. 379-398.

Stallings, W. (2017) Network Security Essentials: Applications and Standards. 6th ed. Upper Saddle River: Pearson.

Zetter, K. (2014) Countdown to Zero Day: Stuxnet and the Launch of the World's First Digital Weapon. New York: Crown.

Brain-Computer Interface Integration With Extended Reality (XR): Future, Privacy And Security Outlook

Tuomo Lahtinen[1], Andrei Costin[1] and Guillermo Suarez-Tangil[2]
[1]Faculty of Information Technology, University of Jyväskylä, Jyväskylä, Finland
[2]IMDEA Network Institute, Madrid, Spain

tutalaht@jyu.fi
ancostin@jyu.fi
guillermo.suarez-tangil@imdea.org

Abstract: The Brain-Computer Interface (BCI) is a rapidly evolving technology set to revolutionize our perception of the Internet of Things (IoT). BCI facilitates direct communication between the brain and external devices, enabling the control or interaction of devices without physical intervention. BCI technology is becoming more sophisticated, allowing third-party software embedded in emerging technologies such as Virtual Reality (VR), Augmented Reality (AR), and Mixed Reality (MR) to access sensors that read brain activity. These can be grouped under the umbrella term Extended Reality (XR). While BCI technology is disrupting the way data is collected, interpreted, and utilized within IoT networks, it is important to consider the potential privacy and security threats that it poses. Previous and not-so-recent cybersecurity research only scratched the surface in terms of security and privacy aspects of the then-emerging neural and brain-connecting technologies. However, recent advances in reconstructing language, music tracks, and imagery solely based on decoding neural signals pose a significant risk of mental privacy invasion and cybersecurity abuse. In this paper, we present an analysis of the potential threats posed by the integration of BCI with VR, AR, and MR. We analyze the involvement of major technological players in shaping BCI and XR advancements, examining the potential for these technologies to create detailed user profiles and reshape the monetization of user data in the ever-more-aggressive data-driven economy. We also outline a position view on the cybersecurity aspects that are not related to privacy and profiling per se, for example, cybersecurity attacks on the brain (e.g., ``brain rewriting'' attacks) facilitated by potentially vulnerable XR-BCI devices and software. The paper concludes by emphasizing the need for further research on the privacy and security implications of XR-BCI integration and inviting deeper exploration of the topic beyond theoretical papers and toward a more applied experimental setup.

Keywords: Brain-Computer Interface, Extended Reality, Privacy, Big Tech, Cybersecurity, Metaverse

1. Introduction

A Brain-Computer Interface (BCI) allows people to control various devices with their thoughts. A BCI records brainwaves and translates them into commands. Despite rapid development in recent years, BCIs are still incomplete for many applications, but recent research shows promising results. Scientists have been able to reconstruct speech (Tang et al. 2023), images (Benchetrit et al. 2023), and music tracks (Bellier et al. 2023) from brain data with encouraging accuracy. This implies that more profound insights are on the horizon as BCI expands its influence into Virtual Reality (VR), Augmented Reality (AR), and Mixed Reality (MR), all encompassed by the overarching term eXtended Reality (XR).

Major industry players such as Meta are investing heavily in the metaverse and BCI technologies. However, the expanding presence of BCI in broader markets raises privacy and security concerns. Governance and management lapses among tech giants pose significant risks, intertwining with worries about market dominance, monopolization, and corporate surveillance. As BCI potentially harvests valuable brain data for commercial ends, ethical questions loom large: are users genuinely consenting to this data collection?

Our research delves into the threats and challenges associated with XR and BCI, and the potential fusion of these technologies into XR-BCI. We also highlight the influence of Big Tech, big data, and artificial intelligence (AI). The interdependence of these technologies, particularly evident in the metaverse's development, generates vast data volumes as users engage, creating a complex web of technological vulnerabilities. We refer to the Internet of Brains (IoB) (Harris 2008, Ju & Shen 2012) as the recent development of brain-computer interfaces, where brain data is accessible via modern telecommunications, peer-to-peer modes, or more generally via the Internet.

2. The XR Landscape

The history of VR, AR, or MR research dates back to the 90s. There have been ups and downs along the way, but now XR is closer to mass adoption than ever before as Big Tech companies push efforts into device development. Abraham et al. (2022) emphasized the importance of standards for the privacy and security implications of XR. When Google Glasses were commercially released in 2013, they were criticized for the privacy concerns raised by stealthy video recording (Brewster 2014). Smart glasses can be used easily and inconspicuously to capture sensitive data from the environment. Privacy and security concerns are not just for the users of the devices, but also the privacy of bystanders, as Pahi & Schroeder (2023) mentioned. Modern extended reality devices have improved since the day Google Glass was released. Multiple sensors make it easy to track, for example, the user's behavior, actions, and gaze, and devices can also monitor the environment and surroundings such as people, places, and objects (Abraham et al. 2022).

There are many commercial XR headsets released such as Apple Vision Pro (2024), PlayStation VR 2 (2023), Meta Quest 3 (2023), HTC Vive Pro 2 (2021), Meta Quest 2 (2020), Oculus Quest 1 (2019), Valve Index (2019), PlayStation VR (2016). For XR-BCIs, there are mainly devices for development and research purposes such as OpenBCI Galea and Wearable Sensing DSI-VR300. In addition, CTRL-labs (acquired by Meta) has developed a wristband that can read electromyography (EMG) or EEG signals from the user, which can be used with the XR headset to enhance the XR experience through gesture management.

2.1 XR Research

XR technology is shifting from specific gaming and industrial applications to mass adoption by Big Tech companies. In the U.S., privacy adoption is not keeping pace with XR development. The most promising approach to address privacy threats is privacy regulation (Pahi & Schroeder 2023). When Abraham et al. (2022) were conducting research by organizing meetings between 13 XR experts, they discovered that experts were unaware of what data was collected and how valuable it was. As Ariely & Berns (2010) and Pahi & Schroeder (2023) stated, data collection must be as transparent as possible. It is very concerning if device users or even experts are unaware of the privacy policy.

The visual implementation of XR is via headset display. The content of the display could violate privacy. For example, Roesner & Kohno (2021) have shown that there is a possibility of a leak of visual information from the XR headset display that could contain sensitive data. Sensitive data can affect not only users of the XR headset but also bystanders. Bystander privacy can be a challenging issue because a bystander is often unaware of the information being collected (O'Hagan et al. 2023, Pahi & Schroeder 2023). Bystander data could include sensitive information about private homes or addresses, personal images, a person's visit to a hospital, or other locations that could contain sensitive information about an individual. To mitigate bystander threats, XR technology could automatically use blurring/distortion techniques to hide sensitive information such as images or voices (Pahi & Schroeder 2023).

XR provides the ability to observe long-term data such as height, movement, and gaze, which can be obtained directly. Indirect data, which is more sensitive, can also be obtained, such as sexual preferences, emotions, or mental state (Abraham et al. 2022). Combining this personal biometric data with the data obtained from the display could make identity theft very easy (O'Hagan et al. 2023).

2.2 XR-BCI Research

Existing XR-BCI (or VR-BCI/AR-BCI) research focuses predominantly on healthcare solutions and there is no mention of privacy or security. Some research has mentioned XR-BCI as a future possibility e.g. Saad et al. (2019), Cattan et al. (2020), Roesner & Kohno (2021). A review of the privacy and security of the XR-BCI domain is not feasible, but we present XR-BCI through existing technologies and open views for the future of XR-BCI.

Reading people's minds is not a new research topic. Ariely & Berns (2010) questioned the ability to measure people's preferences using neuroimaging. This concern can be mitigated by transparency, but Meta's privacy policy (Meta 2023) does not give a clear view of how eye-tracking data is used, and the same could be true for brain data if XR-BCI devices are commercialized.

Although XR-BCIs are currently available mainly for research purposes, existing XR headsets (see Section 2) can be developed to support BCIs, e.g. to provide an immersive and realistic experience by controlling an application or game with the mind. First, Kim et al. (2021) developed a drone control application using a P300-based XR-BCI (DSI-VR300) and administered a questionnaire to the 20 research participants. All participants controlled the drone well and were satisfied with both environments used in the research. No differences were found between the VR and AR environments in terms of performance and experience. Secondly, we discovered two different VR-BCI games on Steam, BCI VR Horror Attraction: The Mad Trail and VR BCI Meditation. While there are currently only two XR-BCI games available on Steam, Cattan et al (2020) investigated suitable game types for the P300-based VR-BCI games and found that 50% of the games are suitable for XR-BCI. Technical improvements can also boost the commercialization of XR-BCI, for example, 6G networks and Saad et al (2019) also mention that XR-BCI is capable of replacing smartphones.

A new technology enables new risks. The integration of the physical world creates a threat if companies are interested in the environment of the XR user. Companies could collect data about the environment and people, and possible device-to-device integration could be implanted to facilitate the XR experience (Roesner & Kohno 2021). Roesner & Kohno (2021) also emphasize the importance of further research about interfacing with the brain and body to mitigate possible risks. These risks are created through sophisticated XR-BCI or other body-sensing technology. This technology could influence a person's thoughts, memories, and even physiology.

3. BCI Security and Privacy

Both privacy and security are very important parts of BCIs. Privacy and security must be ensured by keeping the firmware/software updated and adding various anti-virus/malware detection programs or data traffic management to prevent unauthorized system use (Lahtinen & Costin 2023). As Landau et al. (2020) and O'Hagan et al. (2023) suggest, it is important to keep unauthorized people away from the BCIs, and authorized people should only have minimal privileges (Tabasum et al. 2018). This can be done by establishing access control policies, for example, by defining who has access to raw data (O'Hagan et al. 2023).

Attacks against the security of BCI devices pose a risk to user privacy. Attacks could include unauthorized access or traffic sniffing in the BCI network. Tarkhani et al. (2022) were able to successfully capture data using Man-in-the-Middle (MitM) where the Bluetooth device was acting as a headset. The problem was that authentication was insufficient between the devices. The captured data can contain sensitive brain data and this data could legitimately be used to diagnose Alzheimer's disease, possibly other diseases, or sensitive information about the BCI user. It is important to understand that data leakage can occur in any part of the BCI system (Landau et al. 2020).

Invasive BCIs have more serious threats than non-invasive ones. Pycroft et al. (2016) presented possible attacks on DBS BCI devices. The attacks included severe attacks on the user's health, such as changing the stimulation frequency beyond a safe limit causing pain, affecting the user's emotions by stimulating inappropriate electrode contacts, or modulating reward processing. All the attacks presented are severe and their purpose is to change the user's emotions, and opinions or cause pain to the user. Brainjacking can be carried out by an attacker or person who wants to control someone's treatment, for example, parents who want to take over their daughter's treatment (Pugh et al. 2018).

For BCIs, Lahtinen & Costin (2023) propose adding "S" (Safety) into the well-known CIA (Confidentiality, Integrity, Availability) triad, essentially making it CIAS. If the BCI device can manage the current flow bidirectionally, it will expose the user to a health threat. BCI devices use WiFi or Bluetooth to communicate with the gateway device, and both technologies are vulnerable to MitM attacks where credentials are stolen and then used to gain unauthorized access to the BCI device (Lahtinen & Costin 2023). Once in control of the device, the attacker can perform various attacks (e.g. manipulate brain data or change stimulation frequency). The main threats that compromise safety are neural attacks (Bernal et al. 2023).

These privacy and security issues must be addressed when integrating the BCI with XR. XR-BCI may increase the total number of devices connected to the system, making access control and data transfer more difficult. Raw brain data can reveal sensitive information and a way to protect it is to encrypt brain data. If the BCI system is big, raw data could be hidden from some parts of the system, and access list/defining authorized persons who are allowed to see data is also important as Tabasum et al. (2018) suggested.

4. Enabling BCI Commercialization

The mainstream has not yet adopted BCIs because these devices are not affordable, the technology is not highly accurate enough, there are no complete commercially available solutions, etc. However, there has been good progress in creating new BCI devices in the name of reliability. Technologies are advancing and research is discovering ways to promote the commercialization of BCI.

This section presents these technologies and research to enable the commercialization of BCI. Most of the technologies/topics are interrelated and one could help to improve another. We present topics such as big tech, big data, metaverse, and AI in the light of XR-BCI development and commercialization.

4.1 Big Tech

The Big Tech companies are related to the BCIs through the development of the products and the acquisition of the BCI-related companies. The Big Tech companies also own and fund companies and researchers who are responsible for researching, developing, or selling AR, VR, and BCI devices. For example, Meta has its own research and development division, Reality Lab (Meta 2024), which focuses on extended reality, Microsoft is doing its research in the field of BCI (Microsoft 2024), and Elon Musk has founded Neuralink, which is developing invasive BCI to restore autonomy to people with medical conditions that limit daily life (Neuralink 2024). These companies have huge resources for BCI development and they can also acquire knowledge by acquiring other companies, such as Meta, acquired start-up CTRL-Labs, and VR-focused Oculus.

We also want to address the fact that Big Tech companies are also having a prominent impact in the areas of BCIs, AI, big data, etc. These companies are collecting huge amounts of data (e.g. user data) from engaged users and monetizing it in various ways. The amount of engaged users is the measure of power among Big Tech's (Birch et al. 2021).

4.2 Metaverse

The metaverse is a digital realm mirroring the physical world. Metaverse has been attracting attention for some years now and has also attracted the attention of the research community.

The key technology for the metaverse is XR, as it is an interactive technology for achieving an immersive experience (Chen et al. 2022). Immersion requires that the virtual world feels realistic enough to create an engrossing feeling both psychologically and emotionally, and BCI could enhance realism by triggering senses and feelings (Wang et al. 2022). XR headsets are also seen as a terminal for entering the metaverse.

The metaverse has received a lot of attention from researchers worldwide, but privacy and security have not been top priorities. Gupta et al. (2023) urge the implementation of privacy and security in metaverse design. These should be fundamental design elements, not add-ons (Gupta et al. 2023). A challenge in the metaverse is that if it incorporates multiple technologies, this could lead to a situation where known vulnerabilities and threats from the technologies are inherited into the metaverse (Wang et al. 2022).

The metaverse and the real world are connected, and what happens in the metaverse may affect the real world. For example, a security breach, denial-of-service, or identity theft in the metaverse could damage reputation and commerce in the real world. Common security and privacy challenges arising from technical features include privacy issues if the user anonymity model is the same as existing social networks. These issues include fake news, hate speech, online bullying, etc. (Gupta et al. 2023).

4.3 Big Data

The term big data was coined with the advent of digitalization. Big data is generated from online transactions, emails, media streams, search queries, health records, social networks, and mobile phones (Tene & Polonetsky 2012). This data asset exhibits substantial volume, velocity, and variety, necessitating the use of specific technologies and analytical methods to produce value (De Mauro et al. 2015).

When collecting big data, it is important to focus on the quality and reliability of the data. Poor quality data reduces the value of the data and creates threats and problems. From a business perspective, companies should have an interest in maintaining high-quality data, as poor quality is simply a waste of resources and monetizing would be challenging. Overall, the domain of big data privacy and security has four distinct areas: data management, data privacy, infrastructure security, integrity, and reactive security (Khanan et al. 2019).

Regulations and laws are important to bolster the privacy and security of big data. These vary from country to country, and some examples of regulations include GDPR (General Data Protection Regulation), the Privacy Act 1988 in Australia, and CCPA (California Consumer Privacy Act). However, the situation in the U.S. is not optimal as many of the proposed bills will not become law and only 11 of the 50 states have privacy laws(Folks 2024).

4.4 Artificial Intelligence

Artificial Intelligence is a growing field of technology that focuses on the development of intelligent machines. Machines that can act and behave like humans. Since the release of ChatGPT in November 2022, there has been a race to release AI platforms as everyone tries to push their own AI engine into the public domain. AI such as

ChatGPT can be seen as a tool to help BCI developers create devices. The benefits of using AI and LLMs (Large Language Models) (e.g., ChatGPT) are increased efficiency, accuracy, and cost savings (Deng & Lin 2022).

Many recent ChatGPT works (Aljanabi et al. 2023, Biswas 2023, Sakib et al. 2023, Surameery & Shakor 2023) suggest that it can be used to improve coding. ChatGPT understands natural language and this enables a user-friendly and more intuitive coding process. Coding and especially repeatable tasks are significantly accelerated when ChatGPT is used (Aljanabi et al. 2023, Surameery & Shakor 2023). As a tool, ChatGPT can be used to find and fix errors in the code (Roose 2022, Surameery & Shakor 2023) or to find security vulnerabilities (Aljanabi et al. 2023). Developers still need to have their skills as ChatGPT does not always provide working or the best solution to the problem. As with any answer ChatGPT provides, the answer to the coding problem depends entirely on the quality of the training data (Surameery & Shakor 2023).

The evolution of AI has the potential to boost BCI commercialization. Benchetrit et al. (2023) noted that generative and foundational AI systems have significantly improved the ability to decode brain activity in recent years. Their research used AI to create images by analyzing brain waves. Image detail is difficult to get right, but image categorization is reasonably good. AI could also improve and speed up patient diagnosis when applied to the analysis of BCI recordings. As neuroscience capabilities advance, this could help BCIs become more widely used in healthcare. On the other hand, AI could facilitate the development process for BCIs at the software level.

5. Discussion and Conclusion

We have discussed several technologies and methods that enable the commercialization of brain-computer interfaces (BCIs). In recent years, there have been significant advances in BCI research that have improved the technology's ability to generate accurate data. This data can be used to develop future commercial BCI devices. It should be noted that many BCI innovations and prototypes are not yet commercially available. However, using the technologies presented in Section 4, they are moving towards that goal.

Our research aims to provide insight into the future of advanced XR-BCI and BCI devices. Below, we discuss some of the key findings and conclusions.

The privacy and security challenges of XR are likely to increase when XR is integrated with BCI. Integration increases the field for cyber attackers and expands the sensitive data in the system, e.g. brain data. This is sensible when combining two technologies, the combination will inherit threats from both technologies, as suggested by Wang et al. (2022). The most valuable data for companies in terms of BCIs is brain data, which they can monetize to make a profit and, more worryingly, to profile and accurately identify individual users. The most effective way to protect brain data is through regulation (Pahi & Schroeder 2023), but, for example, U.S. Food and Drug Administration (FDA) approval of a device for medical use is not sufficient because it does not include rules on, for example, the collection of brain data for marketing purposes (Ariely & Berns 2010). Also, FDA approval does not remove the threat to the user's physical health if the device is maliciously programmed, e.g. neural attacks (Bernal et al. 2023), and with MitM it is possible to capture data between devices (Tarkhani et al. 2022).

Big Tech's push for more power creates privacy and security challenges. Privacy is not sufficiently considered when companies collect data for better user experience and device development. This could be the case, as Meta's privacy policy shows. Meta collects eye-tracking data, but only if the user chooses to enable eye-tracking features on the VR device. The eye-tracking data is collected and analyzed on the device and on Meta's servers, and some of the data may be stored for more personalized experiences and to improve Meta Quest (Meta's Eye Tracking Privacy Notice (2023)). The privacy notice does not explicitly reveal the data management's purpose but states that the data is collected and stored with the user's consent. This data could also be used for advertising purposes, as this 'personalized experience' suggests. The same could happen with the XR-BCI technology, with the company stating that it only collects data with the user's consent, but more importantly, that the user must provide it to enable the full functionality and experience of the device. We call this a hide-privacy-behind-feature, which is presented by Bryce (2019) as a medicine within a treat. As noted by Birch et al. (2021), when a user consents to data collection, they are entering into a contract with the company and giving up their legal right to use the data for monetization purposes. Privacy is not standard anymore but payable as an add-on known as pay-for-privacy (Bryce 2019).

The future of BCI devices sounds like science fiction when people can control computers with their minds. Control could extend to various devices, including the XR headset. Invasive BCI devices can record reasonably good quality brain data with a lot of potentially sensitive information that can be decoded in the future. IoB opens up possibilities, but connecting the brain to the internet is an ambitious goal that could raise many concerns and ethical issues. Neuralink (Reuters 2023), Precision Neuroscience (Capoot 2023), and Synchron (Kelly 2023) have approval for human clinical trials and their devices can move forward quickly. For example, a Neuralink device is designed to control a computer, we see no barrier to controlling the XR device as well. While invasive BCIs for clinical use may take several years to be accepted in treatment, non-invasive BCIs could emerge much faster as they do not require approval, e.g. if non-invasive XR BCIs are used for entertainment purposes.

Although controlling computers, smart devices, games, etc. with one's brain (IoB) using AR/VR/XR devices combined with BCIs sounds great and may be considered cool, it is worth mentioning that there could be downsides. The questions are: how will BCI, XR, and XR-BCI manufacturers profit from developing devices, how will the user be engaged, and how will user data be monetized to generate revenue for the company? We see data leakage as the biggest threat to future XR-BCI devices. The human brain is a huge repository of information (e.g. credentials, knowledge, memories), identification (e.g. personality, values, emotions), non-repudiation, self-incrimination, and other sensitive and confidential bits. The implications of collecting and storing brain data, and improving data analysis methods in the future to extract more information from the data, can be devastating. Therefore additional deep and wide research efforts are required to ensure implicit privacy and security of BCI, and especially XR-BCI before they are mass-marketed.

Acknowledgments

Tuomo Lahtinen was supported by a grant from the Doctoral School, Faculty of Information Technology at the University of Jyväskylä.

G. Suarez-Tangil was supported by INCIBE's strategic project CIBERSEGURIDAD EINA UNIZAR, RYC-2020-029401-I, and TED2021-132900A-I00 funded by MCIN/AEI/10.13039/ 501100011033, NextGenerationEU/PRTR (Plan de Recuperación, Transformación y Resiliencia) and ESF.

References

Abraham, M., Saeghe, P., Mcgill, M. & Khamis, M. (2022), Implications of xr on privacy, security and behaviour: Insights from experts, in 'Nordic Human-Computer Interaction Conference'.

Aljanabi, M., Ghazi, M., Ali, A. H., Abed, S. A. et al. (2023), 'Chatgpt: open possibilities', Iraqi Journal For Computer Science and Mathematics.

Ariely, D. & Berns, G. S. (2010), 'Neuromarketing: the hope and hype of neuroimaging in business', Nature reviews neuroscience.

Bellier, L., Llorens, A., Marciano, D., Gunduz, A., Schalk, G., Brunner, P. & Knight, R. T. (2023), 'Music can be reconstructed from human auditory cortex activity using nonlinear decoding models', Public Library of Science PLoS biology.

Benchetrit, Y., Banville, H. & King, J.-R. (2023), 'Brain decoding: toward real-time reconstruction of visual perception', arXiv:2310.19812.

Bernal, S. L., Celdr´an, A. H. & P´erez, G. M. (2023), 'Eight reasons to prioritize brain-computer interface cybersecurity', Communications of the ACM.

Birch, K., Cochrane, D. & Ward, C. (2021), 'Data as asset? the measurement, governance, and valuation of digital personal data by big tech', Big Data & Society.

Biswas, S. (2023), 'Role of chatgpt in computer programming.: Chatgpt in computer programming.', Mesopotamian Journal of Computer Science.

Brewster, T. (2014), 'The many ways google glass users risk breaking british privacy laws'. [Accessed 16-01-2024].https://www.forbes.com/sites/thomasbrewster/2014/06/30/the-many-ways-google-glass-users-risk-breaking-british-privacy-laws/?sh=1c1648e747d8.

Bryce, C. (2019), 'Who invited the pay-for-privacy economy?'. [Accessed 20-01-2024]. https://medium.com/swlh/post-privacy-who-invited-the-pay-for-privacy-economy-626aecaf53e9.

Capoot, A. (2023), 'Neuralink competitor precision neuroscience conducts its first clinical study to map human brain signals'. [Accessed 22-01-2024]. https://www.cnbc.com/2023/06/23/precision-a-neuralink-competitor-conducts-its-first-clinical-study.html.

Cattan, G., Andreev, A. & Visinoni, E. (2020), 'Recommendations for integrating a p300-based brain–computer interface in virtual reality environments for gaming: An update', Computers.

Chen, Z., Wu, J., Gan, W. & Qi, Z. (2022), Metaverse security and privacy: An overview, in '2022 IEEE International Conference on Big Data (Big Data)', IEEE.

Costin, A., Zaddach, J., Francillon, A. & Balzarotti, D. (2014), A {Large-scale} analysis of the security of embedded firmwares, in '23rd USENIX security symposium'.

Costin, A., Zarras, A. & Francillon, A. (2016), Automated dynamic firmware analysis at scale: a case study on embedded web interfaces, in 'Proceedings of the 11th ACM on Asia Conference on Computer and Communications Security'.

De Mauro, A., Greco, M. & Grimaldi, M. (2015), What is big data? a consensual definition and a review of key research topics, in 'AIP conference proceedings', American Institute of Physics.

Deng, J. & Lin, Y. (2022), 'The benefits and challenges of chatgpt: An overview', Frontiers in Computing and Intelligent Systems.

Folks, A. (2024), 'Us state privacy legislation tracker'. [Accessed 23-01-2024]. https://iapp.org/resources/article/us-state-privacy-legislation-tracker/

Gupta, A., Khan, H. U., Nazir, S., Shafiq, M. & Shabaz, M. (2023), 'Metaverse security: Issues, challenges and a viable zta model', Electronics.

Harris, S. B. (2008), 'A million years of evolution', Year Million.

Ju, D. & Shen, B. (2012), 'Internet of knowledge plus knowledge cloud a future education ecosystem', Ieri Procedia.

Kelly, S. (2023), 'Synchron brain-computer interface implanted in first 6 us patients'. [Accessed 22-01-2024]. https://www.medtechdive.com/news/synchron-brain-computer-interface-implanted-first-patients/692843/.

Khanan, A., Abdullah, S., Mohamed, A. H. H. M., Mehmood, A. & Ariffin, K. A. Z. (2019), Big data security and privacy concerns: A review, in A. Al-Masri & K. Curran, eds, 'Smart Technologies and Innovation for a Sustainable Future', Springer International Publishing.

Kim, S., Lee, S., Kang, H., Kim, S., & Ahn, M. (2021). P300 brain–computer interface-based drone control in virtual and augmented reality. *Sensors*, *21*(17), 5765.

Lahtinen, T. & Costin, A. (2023), Linking computers to the brain: Overview of cybersecurity threats and possible solutions, in 'International Symposium on Business Modeling and Software Design', Springer.

Landau, O., Puzis, R. & Nissim, N. (2020), 'Mind your mind: Eeg-based brain-computer interfaces and their security in cyber space', ACM Computing Surveys (CSUR).

Meta (2023), 'Eye tracking privacy notice'. [Accessed 18-01-2024]. https://www.meta.com/en-gb/help/quest/articles/accounts/privacy-information-and-settings/eye-tracking-privacy-notice/.

Meta (2024), 'A future that's more human and less artificial'. [Accessed 24-01-2024]. https://about.meta.com/realitylabs/.

Microsoft (2024), 'Brain-computer interfaces'. [Accessed 05-01-2024]. https://www.microsoft.com/en-us/research/project/brain-computer-interfaces/overview/.

Neuralink (2024), 'Neuralink'. [Accessed 03-01-2024]. https://neuralink.com/.

O'Hagan, J., Saeghe, P., Gugenheimer, J., Medeiros, D., Marky, K., Khamis, M. & McGill, M. (2023), 'Privacy-enhancing technology and everyday augmented reality: Understanding bystanders' varying needs for awareness and consent', Proceedings of the ACM on Interactive, Mobile, Wearable and Ubiquitous Technologies.

Pahi, S. & Schroeder, C. (2023), 'Extended privacy for extended reality: Xr technology has 99 problems and privacy is several of them', Notre Dame J. on Emerging Tech.

Pugh, J., Pycroft, L., Sandberg, A., Aziz, T. & Savulescu, J. (2018), 'Brainjacking in deep brain stimulation and autonomy', Ethics and Information Technology.

Pycroft, L., Boccard, S. G., Owen, S. L., Stein, J. F., Fitzgerald, J. J., Green, A. L. & Aziz, T. Z. (2016), 'Brainjacking: implant security issues in invasive neuromodulation', World neurosurgery.

Reuters (2023), 'Musk's neuralink to start human trial of brain implant for paralysis patients'. [Accessed 22-01-2024].https://www.reuters.com/technology/musks-neuralink-start-human-trials-brain-implant-2023-09-19/.

Roesner, F. & Kohno, T. (2021), Security and privacy for augmented reality: Our 10-year retrospective, in 'VR4Sec: 1st International Workshop on Security for XR and XR for Security'.

Roose, K. (2022), 'The brilliance and weirdness of chatgpt', The New York Times.

Saad, W., Bennis, M. & Chen, M. (2019), 'A vision of 6g wireless systems: Applications, trends, technologies, and open research problems', IEEE network.

Sakib, F. A., Khan, S. H. & Karim, A. (2023), 'Extending the frontier of chatgpt: Code generation and debugging', arXiv:2307.08260.

Surameery, N. M. S. & Shakor, M. Y. (2023), 'Use chat gpt to solve programming bugs', International Journal of Information Technology & Computer Engineering (IJITC).

Tabasum, A., Safi, Z., AlKhater, W. & Shikfa, A. (2018), Cybersecurity issues in implanted medical devices, in '2018 International Conference on Computer and Applications (ICCA)', IEEE, pp. 1–9.

Tang, J., LeBel, A., Jain, S. & Huth, A. G. (2023), 'Semantic reconstruction of continuous language from non-invasive brain recordings', Nature Neuroscience.

Tarkhani, Z., Qendro, L., Brown, M. O., Hill, O., Mascolo, C. & Madhavapeddy, A. (2022), 'Enhancing the security & privacy of wearable brain-computer interfaces', arXiv preprint arXiv:2201.07711.

Tene, O. & Polonetsky, J. (2012), 'Big data for all: Privacy and user control in the age of analytics', Nw. J. Tech. & Intell. Prop.

Wang, Y., Su, Z., Zhang, N., Xing, R., Liu, D., Luan, T. H. & Shen, X. (2022), 'A survey on metaverse: Fundamentals, security, and privacy', IEEE Communications Surveys & Tutorials.

Cyber Resiliency of Aircraft Systems: A Literature Review

Antti Luoto[1] and Matti Hakkarainen[2]
[1]Tampere University, Finland
[2]Patria, Tampere, Finland

antti.luoto@tuni.fi
matti.hakkarainen@patriagroup.com

Abstract: Aircraft have an important role in the overall defense of almost every country. However, military aircraft are not only susceptible to traditional kinetic weapons but also to constantly developing cyber weaponry. There has been global growth in the number of cyber threats in recent years, and the field of military aviation is not outside the growing threat. The war in Ukraine and recent military aircraft procurements in Europe make the topic very timely. A highly skilled and resourced adversary is able to conduct complex long-term attacks that penetrate even well-protected systems, such as military aircraft systems. Even air-gap does not protect aircraft from cyber threats as modern aircraft have complex and networked avionics and support systems. The study aims to find the current trends of cyber security research related to aircraft systems. The included topics are, for example, cyber resiliency and cyber protection in the system life cycle. The study concentrates particularly on forming an overall view of the most vulnerable military aircraft systems. The study presents a non-systematic literature review based on public data sources, such as research reports, articles, etc. A set of nine relevant sources was chosen for detailed qualitative analysis. Because of the lack of detailed military sources, applicable study materials related to commercial passenger aircraft were included. The results suggest that the most vulnerable aircraft systems from the viewpoint of cyber security are those that are exposed to threats via communication and satellite systems. Other vulnerable systems are sensors and avionics systems that transfer, or process critical data related to the functions of the aircraft. In addition, the study found that it is difficult to protect aircraft systems from cyber threats because of their complexity, maintenance operations, and supply chains, which also increase the size of the attack vector. To tackle the issue, it is important to follow the development of regulations and policies related to cyber security in aviation and to study the methods of managing the threat in a holistic and cost-effective manner.

Keywords: Cyber Resiliency, Cyber Security, Aircraft Systems, Cyber Defence

1. Introduction

This paper studies the effect of cyber threats to aircraft systems, especially from the viewpoint of combat aircraft. It has been estimated that at least 75 percent of the performance and capability of a modern aircraft is based on software (Alford, 2010). A modern military aircraft is not a closed system even if it is not directly connected to the internet or other networks (Alford, 2010). Rather, it is heavily dependent on external support systems, that increase the size of the attack vector making the aircraft more vulnerable to cyber threats (Alford, 2010).

One reason for a cyber-attack against combat aircraft is that they are an important part of every nation's defense, and it is easy for other nations to exploit weaknesses in airspace defense (Biswas, 2019). In this light, combat aircraft and their systems have a high potential to be targeted by a cyber operation. In addition to influencing a military system in various ways, the attacker may collect intelligence and steal information with an aim to develop their own capabilities (Snyder et al, 2015).

The goal of this study was to investigate the state and the level of cyber resiliency of aircraft systems. There was a need to identify which aircraft systems are the most vulnerable and find ways of testing them from the viewpoint of cyber resiliency. In this context, the study aims to produce knowledge about the current state of cyber protection, cyber testing, cyber monitoring, and cyber research.

The scope of the study is on the systems of combat aircraft. However, it must be noted that, for example, related ground systems, such as mission planning and maintenance systems, need to be also considered because they increase the number of threats that can be exploited when attacking the actual aircraft.

The main research question is: what are the most vulnerable aircraft systems from the viewpoint of cyber resilience? The following sub-questions were used to find answers to the main question. What cyber threats are targeted to aircraft equipment and what makes aircraft equipment prone to cyber vulnerabilities? Which avionics systems stand out as vulnerable systems?

The used research method is a non-systematic literature review based on scientific publications, technical reports, and other related public material. Many of the available data sources concentrate on civilian aviation. In a military context, the public material is more on a general level rather than going deep into the technical details of military aircraft. The reason may be that detailed studies on the topic do not exist, or the topic is so sensitive that information is not publicly available. However, the study material on civilian aviation may be used as a data source for this study because civilian and military aircraft share common systems.

The material for the analysis conducted was chosen based on the richness of relevant information from the viewpoints of both quality and quantity. A chosen source had to contain a discussion related to cyber resiliency or cyber threats of aircraft systems either from a civilian or military perspective. Nine publications were chosen for the detailed analysis. The collected material was deductively analyzed to form conclusions about the most vulnerable combat aircraft systems from the viewpoint of cyber resiliency.

2. Cyber Threats and Cyber Resiliency of Aircraft Systems

This section describes the related background. First, it motivates the reader by describing the current threat environment. Then it discusses threat analysis that is important for cost-efficient cyber security. Finally, the section introduces attack vectors of aircraft and attack methods that can be used against them.

2.1 Growing and Developing Threat

Many can identify that IT systems belong to a cyber environment, but IT systems are only a subset of systems that are vulnerable to cyber-attacks. These vulnerable systems form a risk to successfully perform military operations (Snyder et al, 2015), (Weinman, 2020). The complexity and the scale of cyber threats make understanding the issue, prioritization, and implementation of countermeasures challenging. It may be difficult to detect, manage, and communicate vulnerabilities, and thus it is difficult to conceptualize cyber threats (IATA Regional Office, 2019).

In civilian aviation, cyber threat is a challenge because all information related to a flight is in networked digital form – even during a flight (IATA Regional Office, 2019). In a military context, the cyber dimension is a challenge for the same reason because the present-day military is dependent on information and communication systems. Even though a modern and continuously developed fighter plane offers ways to fight against evolving military threats, it is dependent on information. This dependency creates a cyber threat by offering various channels to penetrate systems and thus impede or prevent the operation of an aircraft (Lydiate, 2019). In addition, while military sector can adopt solutions from civilian aviation, they cannot rely on the commercial sector to have ready solutions for electronic warfare, Global Positioning System denial of service, and platform attrition (United States Air Force, 2019).

Cyber risk is increased also because the equipment related to weapon systems has not been necessarily designed with cyber in mind. This concerns especially operative equipment that is not considered IT equipment traditionally (Weinman, 2020). Because of the long-life cycle of military aircraft, this may be a cyber issue since cyber-attack methods are continuously evolving while the aircraft is not actively developed anymore. Though the history of cyber-attacks is mostly related to ICT systems with few physical effects, the possibility for such an attack targeted to software or avionics of a fighter plane cannot be excluded (Weinman, 2020). Similarly to the famous Stuxnet worm, that was targeted to a specific piece of hardware, adversaries could attack specific aircraft systems (Weinman, 2020). Lehto and Limnéll (2017) emphasize that a cyber-physical environment, where threats do not only target the virtual world but also physical hardware, is essential in the future.

Defence systems are nowadays more networked than ever before, increasing the overall complexity. For example, the embedded software and information technology systems found from modern military aircrafts include targeting systems, industrial control systems, databases, microelectronics, life support systems, collision avoidance system, logistics system, flight software system, controller area network bus, and communication systems (Chaplain, 2018). In addition, weapon systems that are not directly connected to networks may be, in one way or another, dependent on other networked systems (Chaplain, 2018). Examples of such systems include radar receiver, radio communications receiver, wireless communications link, operator's personal electronics, maintenance ports, and onboard diagnostics ports (Chaplain, 2018).

New technologies, such as smart airports and e-enabled aircraft, developed to improve the quality of service of aviation introduce new cyber-attack surfaces (Ukwandu et al, 2022). The roots of such technology are in relatively recent developments such as IoT, sensors in physical systems, blockchain, AI, cloud and big data (Ukwandu et al, 2022).

Many technology development projects, that are important for the United States Air Force, are executed by commercial companies instead of the United States defence administration (United States Air Force, 2019). This international technology business offers possibilities for other nations to develop new military capabilities (United States Air Force, 2019). Examples of such important technologies are related to advanced computing and wireless technologies (United States Air Force, 2019).

Implementing solid cyber protection for aviation is a massive challenge because of the networked architecture, the complexity of the technology, and its speed of change (Ukwandu et al, 2022). The challenge is increased because there are legacy systems used in parallel with the new emerging solutions (Ukwandu et al, 2022). For example, in 2017 a team of government, industry, and academic researchers hacked into a legacy Boeing 757 via radio communications (Biesecker, 2017). In addition, the lack of resources for cyber protection does not make the issue easier (Ukwandu et al, 2022). Another challenge in the future is to design systems and services with cyber security in mind but maintain cost-effectiveness and safety.

According to Eurocontrol (2019), cyber-attacks in the aviation sector have risen 530% from the year 2019 to 2020. The majority of these attacks (61%) have been targeted at airlines (Eurocontrol, 2019). 36% of the reported incidents were data theft, 35% fraudulent websites, 16% phishing, 5% malware, and 5% ransomware (Eurocontrol, 2019). Further, the supply chains of the aviation industry pose a threat because actors may have insufficient information security protection in their systems (Eurocontrol, 2019), (Weinman, 2020).

There are a lot of deficiencies in the management of cyber security in aviation and military technology (IATA Regional Office, 2019), (Lydiate, 2019). The reason may be that there seems to be a lack of cyber security regulation and understanding of cyber security among managers and commanders (IATA Regional Office, 2019), (Lydiate, 2019), (Chaplain, 2018). Before 2019, the regulation and standards of aviation and especially aircraft systems were seen to be either under development or being updated so that they will better consider the requirements of cyber security and evolving cyber threats (Chaplain, 2018), (U.S. Department of Defence, 2013). In 2020 and 2021 the standards had been updated to some extent (IATA, 2021). Recent updates to publicly available standards aim to bind management together with cyber security using risk management as a method. However, it is expected that the field of aviation still has a lot to do in determining common goals, strategies, and policies related to cyber security.

Eurocontrol (2019, 2) suggests all actors forget the illusion that there is no cyber threat or that their systems are protected because there have not been incidents recently. Further, the details of severe cyber-attacks are most likely classified (Weinman, 2020). The fact that there are not many publicly known successful attacks against aircraft systems and the belief that airgap protects systems increases the challenge in cyber awareness (Weinman, 2020), (Chaplain, 2018). In addition, the security certificates received by system vendors are often incorrectly trusted as a guarantee of security. For example, general cyber security expertise is not the same as weapon systems cyber security expertise (Chaplain, 2018).

There are a lot of open challenges in the cyber security of aviation. These challenges and defects are related, for example, to inadequate testing methods (Chaplain, 2018), monitoring of cyber security (Weinman, 2020), reacting to defects (Muckin and Fitch, 2014), sharing knowledge regarding cyber incidents (Muckin and Fitch, 2014), complexity (Chaplain, 2018), and lack of open information (Chaplain, 2018). In addition, maintenance (Weinman, 2020) and integration with legacy systems (Ukwandu et al, 2022) increase the threat. Last but not least, the fact that humans are often the weakest link makes the cyber threat an obvious challenge.

2.2 Methods of Threat Analysis

An adversary must perform the following five tasks to succeed in a cyber-engagement (Bryant and Ball, 2020). An active cyber weapon must search for aircraft. The aircraft must then be detected in cyberspace. The adversary must decide which pathway to the target will be used. The launched cyber-warhead must be successfully transported into the target aircraft's systems. And finally, the cyber-warhead is triggered causing system malfunctions.

Cyber Kill Chain is a framework developed by Lockheed Martin for making countermeasures and analyzing cyber threats (Ranum, 2014). The framework presents a cyber threat as a chain of attacks with which the attacker aims to achieve their goals (Ranum, 2014). The framework aims to combine organizations that develop a system with those that operate the system so that threat analysis and intelligence together can break the chain of attacks (Muckin and Fitch, 2014).

Weinman (2020) notes that the Cyber Kill Chain is mainly targeted for threat analysis of traditional IT systems and suggests that aircraft cyber threat analysis may be conducted with the Aircraft Combat Survivability (ACS) model, which is traditionally used for analyzing aircraft survivability against kinetic weapons. Based on ACS, Weinman (2020) proposes an Aircraft Cyber Combat Survivability (ACCS) model, that may be used to analyze an aircraft's survivability against cyber-attacks. Weinman (2020) identifies the following five key differences between ACS and ACCS. (1) Detecting cyber weapons may be more difficult when compared to traditional weapons. (2) Cyber weapons have basically an unlimited range and do not have physical limitations as traditional kinetic weapons may have. (3) Cyber weapons are not as predictable as traditional kinetic weapons. (4) Cyber weapons do not have a long military history which makes estimating their effects difficult. (5) Cyber weapons can be rendered harmless relatively easily after detection.

2.3 Attack Vectors and Methods of Attacking Aircraft Systems

While cyber threats can be analyzed with frameworks, such as Cyber Kill Chain, a challenge related to combat aircraft is that there are multiple networked systems that are dependent on each other. There is always a possibility for an attack when information is transferred in or out of the system (Chaplain, 2018). The technical reasons that make aircraft systems vulnerable are numerous electronic interfaces, networking, information exchange, and external systems (Chaplain, 2018).

Weinman (2020) states that the communication channels of an aircraft are not always encrypted. Thus, it is possible for an adversary to intercept such a channel and inject false information or cut the channel off (National Business Aviation Association, 2016). Weinman (2020) lists the following aircraft's attack surfaces: radar, radio communications, data links, GPS, SATCOM, software development, supply chain, pods, smart weapons, maintenance systems, mission planning, mission debriefing, and data transfer devices (referencing to a presentation by Bryant & Young).

Systems with a capability for direct external communication include data links that communicate with command and control or identification, friend or foe (IFF) systems that communicate with the flight control systems situated on the ground. These two external systems differ from each other significantly. A military command and control system is part of a classified military system, whereas a flight control system is part of a globally networked civilian system. Despite the fact that military systems are classified, they are networked in various ways.`

A cyber adversary may affect the operative capabilities in two ways (Snyder et al, 2015). It is possible to steal technology or data or to directly hit operative systems which can weaken the operative capabilities of the target (Snyder et al, 2015). The methods of attacking aircraft systems are the same as against any other IT system. For example, Weinman (2020) mentions Trojan horse, trapdoor, backdoor, virus, worm, keystroke logging, and impersonation (Weinman, 2020).

Modern aircraft has a lot of sensors for data collection. Sensor jamming, spoofing, and meaconing are types of methods that have a degrading effect on the collected data (Sabatini, 2016), (Blasch et al, 2019). Jamming means transmission of high-power signals to impede reception of radio signals (Wei et al, 2007). Spoofing means synthesizing a false signal to deceive a target's positioning or tracking, whereas meaconing means capturing a signal and rebroadcasting it with alterations (Manesh et al, 2019). Radiofrequency (RF), electro-optical, and global navigation satellite system (GNSS) interfaces are susceptible to such attacks (Sabatini, 2016). By attacking via the sensors of an aircraft it might be possible to effect situational awareness (Henselmann and Lehto, 2019). Such an attack could prevent systems from functioning (Chaplain, 2018) or inject falsified data (Henselmann and Lehto, 2019).

While the focus of protection has been on software, the attacks have stepped towards hardware (Lehto and Limnéll, 2017). The attacks can occur already during the production process when malware is installed during assembly or warehousing (Lehto and Limnéll, 2017). For aviation systems, such attack possibilities include systems under maintenance, testing, or repair (Lehto and Limnéll, 2017). Therefore, systems require surveillance and management during the whole life cycle (Lehto and Limnéll, 2017). For example, a subversive die, that modifies the behavior of the processor, can be added to an integrated circuit, and detecting such a modification can be difficult (U.S. Department of Defence, 2013).

An attack operation may be very complex, distributed, and it may be executed over a long period of time by combining different attack methods (Weinman, 2020). For example, a backdoor in software can wait for a trigger command that is delivered using a different method (Weinman, 2020).

3. Results

Nine publications were chosen for the detailed literature analysis: (Henselmann and Lehto, 2019), (Lydiate, 2019), (Bogoda, Mo, Bil, 2019), (Mink et al, 2016), (Sabatini, 2016), (Weinman, 2020), (Ukwandu et al, 2022), (Chaplain, 2018), and (Thudimilla, 2020). These publications discuss the topic so extensively that it was possible to use them for answering at least two research questions. Possible attacks on systems of fighter planes can be conducted using similar attack methods that can be used to attack any electronic or IT system. While the systems used by the military often have better protection than civilian systems, for example, from the viewpoint of facility, personnel, and information security, the protections are not, however, on an adequate level to completely protect from cyber threats. The air interface and facility security cannot protect aircraft systems because they are networked with other systems and have long maintenance and supply chains. It must be noted that networking in this context does not mean that a system needs to be continuously connected to an IT network. It means that it is repeatedly connected, via various interfaces, to other systems during its life cycle. These connections always offer possibilities for attacking.

Even though combat aircraft and civilian passenger aircraft vary a lot from the viewpoints of system design and applications, they are threatened by similar cyber threats to some extent. When military aircraft operate in the same airspace or airfields as civilian aircraft, military aircraft use the same or similar systems for navigation, communication, identification, and landing. Examples of such systems include global positioning system (GPS), very high frequency (VHF) omnidirectional range with distance-measuring equipment (VOR/DME), ground-based augmentation system (GBAS), identification, friend or foe (IFF), and automatic dependence surveillance-broadcast (ADS-B) (Bogoda, Mo, Bil, 2019).

Based on the analysis, the most vulnerable systems are communication systems that are used for transferring speech or data between aircraft and external systems. From ground-to-air systems, the most critically vulnerable seem to be data link systems (also known as data flow systems), that transfer data between aircraft and ground systems. Five references mentioned these systems (see Table 1). Other mentioned systems include, for example, the Aircraft Communication Addressing and Reporting System (ACARS), software radio, and RF systems.

Satellite-based communication and navigation systems were also seen as critically vulnerable systems. A common factor in these systems is that by penetrating the ground system, it is possible to directly influence the aircraft during the flight.

Another vulnerable category was sensors. It is also possible to influence these systems directly during the flight. From the other aircraft and avionics systems, systems related to flight control, data buses (such as Avionics Full-Duplex Switched Ethernet (AFDX)), operating systems, and mission support were seen as vulnerable. Table 1 categorizes and summarizes the identified vulnerable systems.

Table 1: The categorization of vulnerable aircraft systems.

Avionics (tot. 5)	Communication (tot. 11)	Recording (tot. 2)	Sensors (tot. 5)	Satellite (tot. 10)
Data buses (Henselmann and Lehto, 2019)	Data links (Henselmann and Lehto, 2019), (Weinman, 2020), (Ukwandu et al, 2022), (Lydiate, 2019), (Bogoda, Mo, Bil, 2019)	Mission & Maintenance (Henselmann and Lehto, 2019), (Weinman, 2020)	Radar (Henselmann and Lehto, 2019), (Weinman, 2020), (Chaplain, 2018), (Bogoda, Mo, Bil, 2019)	GNSS/GPS (Henselmann and Lehto, 2019), (Weinman, 2020), (Bogoda, Mo, Bil, 2019)
Operating systems (Ukwandu et al, 2022)	Software radio (Henselmann and Lehto, 2019)		Infrared (Henselmann and Lehto, 2019)	Galileo (Henselmann and Lehto, 2019)
AFDX (Henselmann and Lehto, 2019)	RF (Weinman, 2020), (Henselmann and Lehto, 2019), (Chaplain, 2018)			SATCOM (Weinman, 2020), (Ukwandu et al, 2022)
Flight control (Bogoda, Mo, Bil, 2019), (Mink et al, 2016)	ACARS (Ukwandu et al, 2022), (Bogoda, Mo, Bil, 2019)			ADS-B/ADS-C (Sabatini, 2016), (Ukwandu et al, 2022), (Thudimilla, 2020), (Bogoda, Mo, Bil, 2019)

We answer the research questions presented in the introduction section as follows. The main research question was "what are the most vulnerable aircraft systems from the viewpoint of cyber resilience". According to the literature analysis, the most vulnerable systems are communication systems, such as data links, followed by satellite systems, such as ADS-B/ADS-C. However, there are vulnerabilities also in sensors, avionics and recording systems.

The first sub-questions were "what cyber threats are targeted to aircraft equipment and what makes aircraft equipment prone to cyber vulnerabilities". The threats are very similar to traditional IT equipment. However, long supply chains, complexity, lack of information, integration with legacy systems, networking, and various communication channels are highlighted in the context of this paper.

The last sub-question was: "which avionics systems stand out as vulnerable systems". There was no system that was clearly mentioned more often than others but data buses, operating systems, ADFX and flight control systems were mentioned in the analyzed literature.

4. Conclusions and Future Work

Developing the cyber security of aircraft systems is important despite the fact that there have not been a lot of reported successful cyber-attacks on aircraft systems. Because of the complexity of military systems and their operational environment, alternative approaches to managing cyber security risks have been suggested as opposed to traditional information security-based approaches. One reason for this is that the cyber threat against combat aircraft needs to be managed cost effectively.

The results of the study cannot be considered very surprising considering the context and the available material. The most critically vulnerable aircraft systems seem to be those whose functions may be effected during flight by penetrating their ground or satellite systems. Following these, there are systems that an attacker may manipulate during flight and directly affect the operations of the aircraft. In addition, there are vulnerable systems that have an effect on flying and are heavily connected to other systems, such as databases or operating systems. These include mission and maintenance systems that require transferring data in to or out of aircraft via external systems.

Cybersecurity regulation and standards of aviation are under development, and it is important to follow the results of such work. Understanding the threat is crucial, so understanding counter methods, such as cyber threat intelligence (CTI), and tactics, techniques, and procedures (TTP) may be key in implementing cost-efficient cyber security.

A report by Snyder (2015) states that cyber security is implemented in the U.S. Air Force via acquisition events during procurement which does not provide continuous involvement of cyber security during the system life cycle (Snyder et al, 2015). In addition, a system may grow out of different programs which leads to a situation where a single program does not cover the whole system (Snyder et al, 2015). Dealing with a great number of policies and laws that can change faster than a military system with a long-life cycle was also considered a challenge (Snyder et al, 2015). Further, the governmental cyber security approach directs more toward securing IT systems than, for example, operating or weapon systems (Snyder et al, 2015). Finally, a relatively fast-changing and complex cyber environment makes management of cyber security difficult (Snyder et al, 2015). Cyber security of military systems should be about making robust and resilient designs that consider the survivability requirements (Snyder et al, 2015).

At the moment, risk management in cyber security is often based on fulfilling the requirements of various policies (Muckin and Fitch, 2014). It directs the organization's actions toward information security management and vulnerabilities (Muckin and Fitch, 2014). This explicit attention to information security and vulnerabilities may lead to a situation where risk management does not consider the most critical factor, the threat (Muckin and Fitch, 2014). Such an imbalance may turn out as reactive actions after cyber incidents instead of pre-emptive actions (Muckin and Fitch, 2014).

Muckin and Fitch (2014) list three gaps that restrict the development of cyber security. (1) Culture, behavior, and the amount of "resources allocated to implementing and adhering to compliance requirements". (2) The lack of scalable and formal cyber threat intelligence. (3) The lack of cooperation and integration between different parts of the organization. The gaps lead to a reactive environment, where the system is designed with a controls-first mindset that emphasizes, for example, compliance with the implemented information security controls, where money is wasted on controls that do not address actual threats (Muckin and Fitch, 2014).

As a future work, it might be interesting to make a review on the cyber security of a related topic, such as logistics systems and supply-chain management of aviation. The aspects included might be, for example, the usage and the role of artificial intelligence and machine learning in the cyber protection of logistics. Specific cyber security tools and components used in the field could also be investigated.

References

Alford, L. D. (2010) "Cyber Warfare: The Threat to Weapon Systems", *The WSTIAC Quarterly*, Vol 9, No. 4.

Biswas, K. (2019) "Military Aviation Principles", *Military Engineering. Ed. by George Dekoulis. Rijeka: IntechOpen*, Chap. 1, DOI: 10.5772/intechopen.87087, [online], https://doi.org/10.5772/intechopen.87087.

Biesecker, C. (2017). "Boeing 757 testing shows airplanes vulnerable to hacking, DHS says." *Avionics International*.

Blasch, E., Sabatini, R., Roy, A., Kramer, K. A., Andrew, G., Schmidt, G. T., Carlos, C. and Fasano, G. (2019) "Cyber awareness trends in avionics", *IEEE/AIAA 38th Digital Avionics Systems Conference (DASC)*, IEEE, September, pp 1–8.

Bogoda, L., Mo, J., and Bil, C. (2019) "A systems engineering approach to appraise cybersecurity risks of CNS/ATM and avionics systems", *Integrated Communications, Navigation and Surveillance Conference (ICNS)*, IEEE, 2019, pp 1–15.

Bryant, W. D. and Ball, R. E. (2020) "Developing the Fundamentals of Aircraft Cyber Combat Survivability: Part 2", *Aircraft Survivability Journal*, Joint Aircraft Survivability Program Office.

Chaplain, C. (2018) *Weapon Systems Cybersecurity: DoD just beginning to grapple with scale of vulnerabilities*, GAO Report No. GAO-19-128. Washington, DC, USA.

Eurocontrol (2019) *Aviation under Attack: Faced with a Rising Tide of Cybercrime, Is Our Industry Resilient Enough To Cope?*, [online], https://www.eurocontrol.int/sites/default/files/2021-07/eurocontrol-think-paper-12-aviation-under-cyber-attack.pdf.

Eurocontrol (2019). *Being cyber secure is an illusion... let's become cyber resilient all together!*, [online], https://www.eurocontrol.int/sites/default/files/2020-01/eurocontrol-think-paper-3-cybersecurity-aviation.pdf.

Henselmann G., and Lehto, M. (2019) "Where Cyber Meets the Electromagnetic Spectrum". *18th European Conference on Cyber Warfare and Security (ECCWS)*, Academic Conferences and publishing limited, pp 209–218.

IATA (2021) *Compilation of Cyber Security Regulations, Standards, and Guidance Applicable to Civil Aviation, Edition 3.0*, Tech. rep.

IATA Regional Office, Asia Pasific (2019). *Aviation Cyber Security Roundtable*, Tech. rep, Singapore.

Lehto, M. and Limnéll J. (2017) "Kybersodankaynnin kehityksesta ja tulevaisuudesta", *Tiede ja ase*, Vol. 75, [online], https://journal.fi/ta/article/view/67730.

Lydiate, D. (2019) "Military Aviation's Cyber Challenge; Are Cyber-Vulnerabilities a Credible Threat to a Modern Air Force?", *Air Power Review*, Vol 22, No. 1, pp 6–38.

Manesh, M. R., Kenney, J., Hu, W. C., Devabhaktuni, V. K., Kaabouch, N. (2019) "Detection of GPS spoofing attacks on unmanned aerial systems". *16th IEEE Annual Consumer Communications & Networking Conference*, pp 1–6.

Mink, D., Yasinsac. A., Choo. K. and Glisson, W. (2016) "Next Generation Aircraft Architecture and Digital Forensic.", *22th Americas Conference on Information Systems*, San Diego, pp 1–10.

Muckin, M. and Fitch, S. C. (2014) *A threat-driven approach to cyber security*, Lockheed Martin Corporation.

National Business Aviation Association (2016) *Cyber Security: Top Flight Department Threats*, [online], https://nbaa.org/aircraft-operations/security/cyber-security-top-flight-department-threats/.

Prisaznuk, P.J. (1992) "Integrated modular avionics", *Proceedings of the IEEE 1992 National Aerospace and Electronics Conference*, Vol. 1, pp 39–45, doi: 10.1109/NAECON.1992.220669.

Ranum, M. (2014) "Breaking Cyber Kill Chains", [Blog], https://www.tenable.com/blog/breaking-cyber-kill-chains (visited 03/15/2023).

Sabatini, R. (2016) "Cyber security in the aviation context", *First Cyber Security Workshop*.

Snyder, D., Powers, J. D., Bodine-Baron, E., Fox, B., Kendrick, L. and Powell M. H. (2015) *Improving the Cybersecurity of U.S. Air Force Military Systems Throughout Their Life Cycles*, RAND Corporation, Santa Monica, CA.

Thudimilla, A. (2020) "Cyber physical security of avionic systems", PhD thesis, Missouri University of Science and Technology.

Ukwandu, E., Ben-Farah, M. A., Hindy, H., Bures, M., Atkinson, R., Tachtatzis, C., Andonovic, I., Bellekens, X. (2022) "Cyber-security challenges in aviation industry: A review of current and future trends", *Information*, Vol 13, No. 3, 146.

United States Air Force (2019) *Science and technology strategy: Strengthening USAF science and technology for 2030 and beyond*.

U.S. Department of Defence (2013) *Resilient military systems and the advanced cyber threat*, Tech. rep., Defense Science Board.

Watkins, C., B. and Walter, R. (2007) "Transitioning from federated avionics architectures to Integrated Modular Avionics", *2007 IEEE/AIAA 26th Digital Avionics Systems Conference*, 2.A.1–1–2.A.1–10. DOI: 10.1109/DASC.2007.4391842.

Wei, M., Chen, G., Cruz, J. B., Haynes, L. S., Pham, K., Blasch, E. (2007) "Multi-Pursuer Multi-Evader Pursuit-Evasion Games with Jamming Confrontation," *Journal of Aerospace Computing, Information, and Communication*, Vol 4, No. 3, pp 693–706.

Weinman A. K. (2020) "Aircraft Cyber Combat Survivability", MA thesis, NAVAL POSTGRADUATE SCHOOL MONTEREY CA.

Risk Assessment of Large Language Models Beyond Apocalyptic Visions

Clara Maathuis[1] and Sabarathinam Chockalingam[2]
[1]Open University of the Netherlands, Heerlen, Netherlands.
[2]Institute for Energy Technology, Halden, Norway.

clara.maathuis@ou.nl
sabarathinam.chockalingam@ife.no

Abstract: The remarkable development of Large Language Models (LLMs) continues to revolutionize various human activities in different societal domains like education, communications, and healthcare. While facilitating the generation of coherent and contextually relevant text across a diverse plethora of topics, LLMs became a set of instruments available in different toolboxes of decision makers. In this way, LLMs moved from a hype to an actual underlying mechanism for capturing valuable insights, revealing different perspectives on topics, and providing real-time decision-making support. As LLMs continue to increase in sophistication and accessibility, both societal and academic effort from AI and cyber security is projected in this direction, and a general societal unrest is seen due to their unknown consequences. Nevertheless, an apocalyptic vision towards their risks and impact does not represent a constructive and realistic approach. Contrarily, this could be an impediment to building LLMs that are safe, responsible, trustworthy, and have a real contribution to the overall societal well-being. Hence, understanding and addressing the risks of LLMs is imperative for building them in an ethical, social, and legal manner while making sure to consider control mechanisms for avoiding, mitigating, accepting, and transferring their risks and harmful consequences. Taking into consideration that these technological developments find themselves in an incipient phase, this research calls for a multi-angled perspective and proposes a realistic theoretical risk assessment method for LLMs.

Keywords: Artificial Intelligence, AI Risks, Large Language Models, Risk Assessment, Security, Privacy.

1. Introduction

"The only limit to our realization of tomorrow will be our doubts of today." (Franklin D. Roosevelt)

A significant milestone in the Artificial Intelligence (AI) domain is the development of the transformer model (Vaswani et al., 2017) that serves as basis for well-known LLMs (Large Language Models) such as ChatGPT. Through LLMs and in combination with other Generative AI models (e.g., diffusion), an accelerating trend towards increasingly sophisticated language understanding as well as video, audio, and image processing and creation, for fostering innovation is seen across various domains. Nevertheless, building and using LLMs raises ethical, social, and legal risks related to aspects like transparency, dis/misinformation, security, privacy, and fairness. Recognizing these issues is crucial for building responsible and trustworthy LLMs systems (Mikalef et al., 2022; EU Commission, 2019). This represents the first step for building risk assessment and management mechanisms for LLMs as they further support the improvement of strategic planning and decision-making, highlight common and cross-cutting risks, optimize resource allocation, and assist legislative/governing bodies (UN, 2020). After recognizing the risks, their evaluation and analysis should be conducted to establish proper treatment for avoiding, controlling, or mitigating them. This represents a difficult process given the complexity, uncertainty, and multifaceted nature of LLMs and their application context. Concurrently, this is a pressing challenge in technical and governance terms which needs to be addressed through joint research, multi/inter/transdisciplinary perspective, and collaborative practitioner efforts given the implications of their action. This further supports the development of LLMs audit for assuring a systematic, proactive, and transparent development, use, and facilitation of awareness and training solutions on their potential risks and impact (Mökander et al., 2023).

While academic and practitioner efforts on building risk assessment and management frameworks and mechanisms for AI systems exist, they are in an incipient stage for Generative AI systems. In particular, for LLMs, this represents the knowledge gap that this research aims to tackle as LLMs-based systems do not only instantiate existing socio-technological risks, but also pose new ones that need to be addressed. These risks that account both technical and human-related aspects can be directly seen in activities taken, for instance, by military experts when building, executing, and assessing military (cyber) operations, and by cyber security field experts involved when building solutions for preventing and responding to various cyber security incidents. Hence, this research aims to propose a theoretical risk assessment method for LLMs by adopting a multidisciplinary stance for merging knowledge from the AI, ethics, cyber security, and risk management domains. This implies conducting a comprehensive literature review on academic and practitioner resources while considering compliance with existing AI and risk management standards and instruments like (ISO/IEC,

2008; ISO/IEC, 2023; NIST, 2023; EU Parliament, 2023). This research stresses the need for assessing and addressing risks in all the life cycle phases of LLMs in a transparent manner for making sure that the LLMs are built and used in a safe, responsible, and trustworthy way.

The remainder of this article is structured as follows. Section 2 presents the context of this research together with relevant academic and practitioner studies carried out in this domain. Section 3 presents the risk assessment method proposed in this research. At the end, Section 4 discusses concluding remarks and future research perspectives.

2. Background and Related Research

A groundbreaking deep learning model architecture was introduced in 2017 (Vaswani et al., 2017): the transformer model which marks a new era in the AI domain. This model relies on the self-attention mechanism and feed-forward neural networks to process sequential data, is suitable for various Natural Language Processing (NLP) tasks (Shanahan, McDonell, & Reynolds, 2023), and represents the foundation of state-of-the-art models like BERT (Bidirectional Encoder Representations from Transformers) and GPT (Generative Pre-trained Transformer), especially through broadly used models like RoBERTa, GPT 3.5, and GPT 4. This mechanism implies that a model is pre-trained on a vast corpus for a primary task and is subsequentially fine-tunned on a second task for transferring knowledge gained from one task to another, helping to deal with the challenges posed by limited labelled data. Due to their mediatic visibility and exponential use, these models developed into LLMs that conquered attention of a significant part of the academic and industry efforts that are working on their development, deployment, and use for assuring a responsible digital behaviour (Chang et al., 2023; Maathuis & Chockalingam, 2023). However, LLMs pose a series of challenges, issues, and risks that are addressed in this section considering a socio-technical stance for capturing relevant social, ethical, and legal dimensions. These are collected based on a comprehensive literature review using search keywords like *LLMs, risk assessment, LLMs security, and LLMs privacy*. The review was conducted in the IEEE Digital Library, ACM, Scopus, Wiley, Google Scholar scientific databases and in public governance available resources from relevant global stakeholders like UN, EU Commission, and NIST.

The UN AI advisory Group (UN, 2023) proposed the following five guiding principles for building AI systems for humanity: AI should be governed inclusively; AI must be governed in the public interest; AI governance should be built in step with data governance and the promotion of data commons; AI must be universal, networked, and rooted in adaptive multi-stakeholder collaboration; AI governance should be anchored in the UN charter, International Human Rights Law, and other agreed international commitments like the Sustainable Development Goals. At the same time, the group stresses that AI also implies issues/risks like bias, surveillance expansion, automated decision-making that blurs accountability of public officials, stressing that such risks can manifest globally, which calls for dedicated mechanisms to mitigate and avoid them. Nevertheless, such mechanisms need to be developed with care to prevent harming the further development of AI technologies. Seeing the agreement to adopt the AI Act, (EY, 2023) stresses the importance of assessing the risk of AI systems, classifying AI systems as: prohibited (systems that pose a risk to people's safety, security, and fundamental rights), high-risk (systems that carry the majority of compliance obligations, including the establishment of risk and quality management systems, data governance, human oversight, and cyber security measures), and minimal risk (systems that do not impose additional obligations next to the initial risk assessment and transparency requirements). While the risk approach is relatively novel in the AI domain, it has a rich history in the field of cyber security. For instance, in the UN Security Management Manual (UNSMS, 2017), the risk matrix is used to assess possible risks taking into consideration the likelihood and impact components. The likelihood levels contain very unlikely, unlikely, moderately likely, likely, and very likely, while the impact component contains the negligible, minor, moderate, severe, and critical levels. When building risk assessment solutions, NIST argues (NIST, 2018) that these should be done together for security and privacy aspects of the systems assessed. SANS (SANS, 2021) relates the level of severity of vulnerabilities with the risks from minor severity, moderate severity, high severity with minor exposure, moderate exposure, and high exposure. A well-known standard in the security risk management domain is ISO/IEC 27001 where the risk assessment is the core part of the risk management framework that includes risk identification, risk analysis, risk estimation, and risk evaluation phases. Once the risks are addressed, risk treatment measures can be applied (ISO/IEC, 2008).

The risk management process associated with AI systems by ITU implies the following steps: (i) risk assessment where the assets are considered together with their value and utility, threats and vulnerabilities are associated with these assets, risk of exposure of these assets to the threats and vulnerabilities is considered, and the risk and impact resulting from the risk of exposure is determined; (ii) risk treatment; (iii) risk management decision;

(iv) risk monitoring, review, and communication; (vi) update and improvement of risk controls. NIST proposed the AI Risk Management Framework (NIST, 2023) that contains four components: govern by cultivating and adopting a culture of risk management, map where the context is recognized and risks related to the context are identified, measure where the identified risks are assessed, analysed, and tracked, and manage where risks are prioritized and acted upon based on the projected impact. The ISO/IEC 23894 on guidance for risk assessment for AI considers the following risk management principles: risk management is an integral part of all organizational activities; a structured and comprehensive approach to risk management contributes to consistent and comparable results; the risk management framework and process are customized and proportionate to the organization's external and internal context related to its objectives; appropriate and timely involvement of stakeholders that enables their knowledge, views, and perceptions to be considered; risk can emerge, change, or disappear as an organization's external and internal context changes; the inputs to risk management are based on historical and current information, as well as on future expectations; human behaviour and culture significantly influence all aspects of risk management at each level and stage; and risk management is continually improved through learning and experience (ISO/IEC, 2023). From a general standpoint, Somer & Thalmann (2023) consider the following four design requirements for building AI risk management mechanisms: identification of AI use cases, evaluation and adaptation of existing risk management frameworks, risk management and quantification, and the consideration of legal aspects.

While conducting a systematic mapping study for concrete AI risk assessments, Xia (2023) considers that the Responsible AI principles can be seen as quality metrics for operationalizing the risk assessment process for AI systems. Moreover, they author identifies the following categories of stakeholders at risk: industry-level stakeholders (e.g., AI technology producers/procurers, AI solution producers/procurers, and AI users/consumers), organization-level stakeholders (e.g., board members, executives, and managers), and team-level stakeholders (e.g., product managers, project managers, and team leaders). CLTC (2021) introduces a guidance framework for building risk and impact assessment mechanisms for AI systems including the following factors: data related (its sensitivity, appropriateness, and timeliness), nature of impact (of the potential impacted parties, of the impact on the affected parties, potential safety risks, individual fundamental and legal rights, individual physical or mental well-being, individual economic stability, ecological impact, whether the overall effect of the impact is positive or negative), scale of the impact (number of individuals affected, severity of the impact), are the harmful effects permanent (reversibility of the effects), likelihood of harm (likelihood of the impact occurring), role of the system in making decisions, transparency of the system (explainability, auditability). Based on these factors, the guidance framework proposes to assess the number of riskiness level which AI systems are classified to. WEF (2020) built an AI project risk assessment tool that focuses on the planning phase of an AI procurement including the following five categories of issues: data, field of use, socio-economic impact, financial consequence for agency and individuals, and business function of the AI system. Schuett (2023) discusses the phases of conducting a risk management in the EU AI Act. The first phase deals with the identification of known and foreseeable risks (Article 9(2), sentence 2, point (a)), the second phase is estimation and evaluation of risks that may emerge from intended uses or foreseeable misuses, or risks that have identified during post-market-monitoring (Article 9(2), sentence 2, points (b), (c)), and the third phase is the adoption of risk management measures (Article 9(2), sentence 2, point (b)). Building risk assessment methods for AI systems also requires defining valuable metrics to be considered. To this end, Maathuis, Pieters, & Van den Berg stress the importance of assessing the risks and impact of intelligent systems on systems, data, humans, and processes; and Piorkowski, Hind, & Richards (2021) define the following attributes of risk assessment metrics: reliability, validity, significance, applicability, monotony, understandability, explainability, and context-awareness.

Mökander et al. (2023) propose a three-layered audit framework for LLMs that focuses on governance audit of technology providers, model audit of the LLMs after the pre-training phase and prior to their release, and application audit for the applications based on LLMs. Weidinger et al. (2021) identify the following categories of socio-ethical risks of LLMs: (i) discrimination, equity, and toxicity; (ii) information hazards; (iii) misinformation harms; (iv) malicious uses; (iv) human-computer interaction harms; (v) automation, access, and environmental harms. For ChatGPT, Zhou et al. (2023) identify the following ethical issues: the existence of bias, privacy and security attacks, transparency, abuse, and authorship issues. Fundamental values like transparency and safety are values addressed by models like LLaMA 2 (Touvron et al., 2023) and BLOOM (Workshop et al., 2022). The groups that introduced them shared details about the dataset used for training, challenges faced in the development process, and the evaluation metrics used. IEAI (2022) builds a practical risk assessment method for AI systems structured in three phases: risk self-assessment and quantification, risk visualization, and risk categorization. In the first phase, the reaction urgency index calculation is based on risk intensity that contains the prevalence, magnitude, and probability of the risks; and reduction demand that includes proximity, social discourse, and temporal immediacy. In the second phase, the risk reaction urgency matrix is based on associations made to all the seven requirements considered for building trustworthy AI systems. In the third phase, the risk potential categorization is used for the overall AI application based on the proposed previous calculations, and considering four dimensions: low reaction demand, high reaction demand, low-risk intensity, and high-risk intensity. From a practical standpoint, TechLaw (2021) proposes the RAIIA (Responsible Artificial Intelligence Impact Assessment) framework which considers six risk levels (zero, very low, low, medium, high, and very high) while recommending the application of the impact assessment framework starting with the medium risk level. Furthermore, the categories of risk are governance, people, process, and technology, calling further for defining dedicated risk mitigation strategies for each of them based on their likelihood and impact. Next to the general risk assessment and management perspectives, Khlaaf (2023) proposes the introduction of the notion of ODD (Operational Design Domain) which represents the description of the domain where the AI system is designed considering as core elements, application, users/agents, protected characteristics, and assets. Moreover, a taxonomy of security risks for LLMs is proposed by (Derner et al., 2023) where the entities involved in an attack are the user, the model, and a third party. Moreover, the security risks are considered in relation to the CIA (confidentiality, integrity, and availability) triad in an experimental setting.

To this end, Kaddour et al. (2023) address those risks of LLMs in relation to three core dimensions: design due to the use of unfathomable datasets, tokenizer-reliance, and fine-tunning overhead; science behind them due to evaluations made based on static human-written ground truth, lacking experimental design, and lack of reproducibility; and behaviour through prompt brittleness, misaligned behaviour, and outdated knowledge. Liu et al. (2023) structure the risks of LLMs according to the principles of building AI systems: they associate misinformation and hallucination to reliability, unlawful conduct and privacy violation to safety, preference bias and disparate performance to fairness, cyber-attack misuse and social engineering misuse to resistance to misuse, lack of interpretability and limited causal reasoning to explainability and reasoning, toxicity and cultural insensitivity to social norms, prompt attacks and poisoning attacks to robustness. Zhao et al. (2023) reflect on the meaning and implications of transparency for LLMs pointing the importance of building explainability AI methods for elucidating their behaviours, limitations, and social impact. Deldjoo (2023) addresses fairness for assuring that the models are not only transparent to users, but that they are not biased towards a specific category. Staab et al., (2023) explore the privacy risk through experiments that show personal data leakage even if they only imply seemingly benign prompt questions. Guo et al., (2022) also assess the integrity risk through possible backdoors. For ChatGPT, Wu, Duan, & Ni (2023) stress the fact that ChatGPT is introducing new threats to its users and the public that call directly for heightened vigilance and protective measures. The authors focused on security, privacy, and ethical issues of ChatGPT discussing risks and threats like malware creation, hallucination, and propaganda threat. Begou et al., (2023) conduct an experiment for developing a phishing attack focusing on cloning a targeted website, integrating code for stealing credentials, obfuscating code, automating website development on a hosting provider, registering a phishing domain, and integrating the website with a reverse proxy. Along these lines, Sison et al., (2023) consider the following categories of ethical risks for ChatGPT: possibility of being sentient or displaying sentience, privacy, bias, employment, and automation as job displacement can occur, and social media and public discourse through the creation of echo-chambers, the production of emotional contagion, exploitation of psychological vulnerabilities and risk of manipulation. Stahl & Eke (2024) structure the ethical risks of ChatGPT as social justice and rights (e.g., fairness, freedom of speech and repression, harm to society), individual needs (e.g., safety, autonomy, psychological harm), culture and identity (e.g., cultural difference, discrimination, and social sorting), and environmental (e.g., sustainability, environmental harm). Wach et al. (2023) see as core threats and risks of LLMs the urgency for building and adopting AI regulation; lack of quality control, disinformation, deepfake content, algorithmic bias; automation-spurred job issues; personal data violation, social surveillance, and privacy violation; social manipulation, weakening ethics and goodwill; widening socio-economic inequalities; and technostress.

As this comprehensive literature review reveals, various valuable dimensions, and concepts to building risk assessment methods for LLMs were addressed at scientific and practitioner levels. Nevertheless, a unified structured method that considers socio-technical risks applicable to all the phases of the AI's life cycle that benefits from previous research done not only in the AI domain, but also in the cyber security domain, is lacking. This would be beneficial to LLMs systems given their complex and uncertain nature and represents the knowledge gap that this research aims to tackle.

3. Risk Assessment Method

To ensure that LLMs systems are built in a safe, responsible, and trustworthy manner, this article stresses the need for conducting the risk assessment of LLMs across all their life cycle phases, i.e., starting from their definition and data collection phases and going to their deployment and monitoring phases. Such a comprehensive approach is imperative to capture, identify, and evaluate corresponding risks that manifest in different ways and forms at various stages. This in turn would allow to be able to properly deal with potential adverse implications and consequences of their action. Accordingly, the risk assessment method proposed in this research is designed considering the life cycle phases of LLMs captured in Figure 1 and defined as follows (UN, 2023; NIST, 2023; Mökander et al., 2023; Xia et al., 2023; Maathuis et al., 2023; Abbas, 2023; Maathuis, 2022; Pamula, 2023).

The LLMs life cycle contains the following phases:

- Model definition: The goals and requirements of the model are established. These include determining specific tasks to be accomplished, considering possible architectural components, establishing working and performance parameters.
- Data collection and pre-processing: Relevant data is collected, pre-processed by cleaning, formatting, and transforming it as preparation for training and validating the model.
- Model development: The working model architecture is established as part of the design that is further developed using the dataset(s) prepared in the previous phase. Further, the model is trained to learn patterns and tasks from the available data and context meaning, validated for assessing model's performance on unseen data, and fine-tunned to optimize the parameters for improving the results obtained.
- Model deployment: After the model is developed and validated, the model is deployed in the production environment so that it is accessible to end-users. To this end, aspects that need to be considered are real-time performance monitoring, efficiency, and scalability.
- Model maintenance and update: Ongoing continuous model maintenance and preparations for potential future necessary model update(s) are carried out in relation to real-world conditions by arising the issues that arise. This could include re-training the model with new available data for assuring its relevance and effectiveness in evolving contexts.

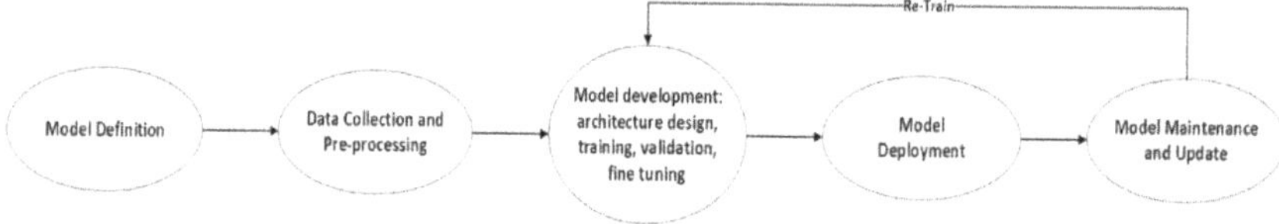

Figure 1: LLMs lifecycle

The risk assessment method proposed in this research is compliant with the ISO/IEC 27001 and 23894 standards and is transparent to its users. The method is illustrated in Figure 2 and contains the following phases:

- *Risk Identification:* Implies for each phase of the AI life cycle, identifying corresponding risks for the assets that can be posed at risk (humans as individuals or collective, organizations, systems or processes that embed the LLMs-based model, data used for building, evaluating, fine tuning, or querying the model), how the risk is defined, the source of risk, the risk metrics defined to assess when and how the risks occur and what is their duration, associated vulnerabilities and recognizing the potential impact. In this process, the following information is gathered (see Table 1):

Table 1: Risk Identification phase

Asset at Risk Category	Risk Definition	Risk Source	Risk Metrics	Associated Vulnerability	Associated Impact
Human					
Organization					
System/Process					
Data					
Model					

For instance, in this phase two categories of data privacy and model security risks are identified when building an LLM-based model for decision-making support for military or law enforcement purposes. In this sense, unauthorized access and potential misuse could occur on sensitive data which represents a direct threat to personal information used in the training data of the model.

- *Risk Analysis:* Once that the risks are identified, they can be further analysed in a qualitative or quantitative way based on their perceived severity and likelihood or involving assigning numerical values to the probability and impact of risks, respectively using the risk analysis matrix captured in Table 2. This implies analysing factors like the likelihood of a specific threat exploiting an existing vulnerability and the associated impact on humans if the risk materializes. This produces a prioritization of lists and further considerations to be addressed in the assessment process.

Table 2: Risk analysis matrix

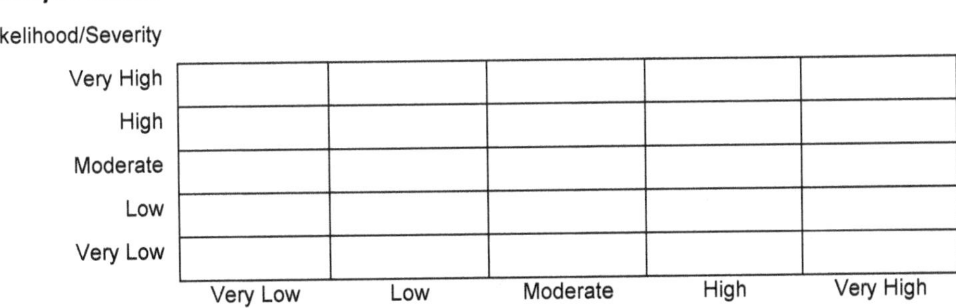

Likelihood/Severity	Very Low	Low	Moderate	High	Very High
Very High					
High					
Moderate					
Low					
Very Low					

For the same example, the data privacy is analysed in relation to personal data being leaked and the model security in relation to its resilience against potential security attacks. For instance, adversarial attacks could be carried out on the model by malicious actors to manipulate input data and produce erroneous outputs, potentially leading to incorrect decisions in critical settings.

- *Risk Evaluation:* The risks identified are analysed considering the goal of the AI system, socio-ethical and legal considerations, plus the source and metrics adopted in relation to the goals of the AI system that poses risks and associated vulnerabilities and potential impact. In this process, a risk score is calculated considering internal and external risks, and two important variables are defined: (i) risk criteria which point to predefined factors that support decision-makers for taking informed decisions about the significance and impact of the risk assessed; and (ii) the risk threshold to establish the predefined level or boundary of risk that is acceptable or tolerated for the AI system.

  In the above-mentioned example, both risks are assessed at very high level of severity as it could directly imply harm and damage to data and people involved, issues to security, privacy, safety, robustness, transparency, responsibility, and reputation damage to the stakeholders involved.

- *Risk Decision:* Once the risks are identified, analysed, and evaluated, informed decisions are made based on the risk score obtained which informs how the risks need to be handled in relation to their potential consequences. From this, the initial decision is made to establish if the risks require treatment or can be directly accepted. In case that the risks require treatment, the most appropriate mechanisms for managing, mitigating, avoiding, and responding to them, are defined, adopted, and further communicated and documented.

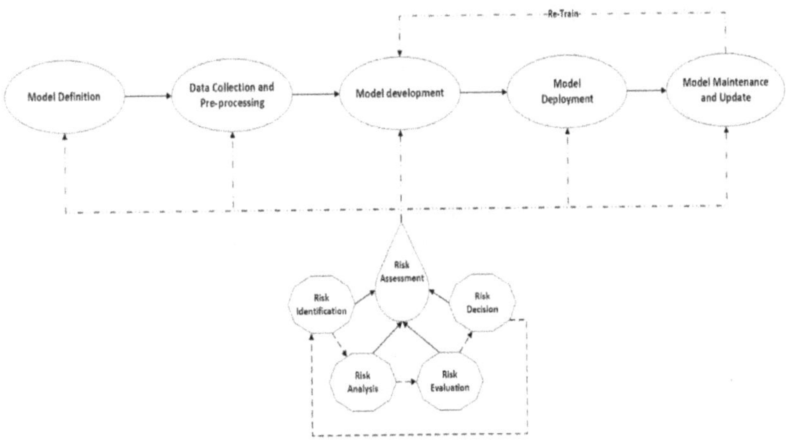

Figure 2: Risk Assessment Method for LLMs

For the same above-mentioned example, given the severity level of the risks considered and potential impact, it could be decided that risk treatment is necessary. This implies that corresponding mechanisms and measures for avoiding, mitigating, controlling, and responding to such risks need to be considered. In this sense, among the measures that could be included is incorporating adversarial training techniques to enhance the model's resilience against adversarial attacks and ensuring fairness and transparency in the decision-making process to mitigate the risk of biased or erroneous outcomes.

4. Conclusions

The multifaceted nature of AI techniques and technologies introduces unique challenges and issues, often captured through associated risks like potential biases, lack of transparency, and potential harm to society. As the implications and consequences of AI systems are experienced at all phases of their life cycle, thus from their design up to their deployment and use, it is important to have a comprehensive understanding of their risks so that the stakeholders involved and/or the ones impacted by their action can foster responsible and trustworthy AI practices by directly addressing them when necessary. The first step in this direction is building transparent risk assessment mechanisms that represent the basis for establishing corresponding risk evaluation and treatment decisions, and demonstrate a commitment to accountability, ethical use, and audit of AI systems.

To effectively address this fact, it is important to build risk assessment and risk management mechanisms that are tailored to specific AI specific paradigms and (set of) techniques given their complex nature. To this end, given the increase in development and use of LLMs in various societal domains, and aiming at preventing confusion or mis/disinformation (Fard & Maathuis, 2021), based on a comprehensive literature review conducted on scientific and professional literature, this research acknowledges that the ongoing efforts for building risk assessment and management mechanisms are in an incipient stage, but much needed. Hence, adopting the perspective of learning from the past, others, and other domains (CLTC, 2021), this research proposes a risk assessment method for LLMs building upon existing AI, cyber security, and risk assessment efforts. This research continues by further developing and evaluating the method proposed in real scenarios as it aims to serve as a contribution to building safe, robust, responsible, and trustworthy AI systems that are beneficial to society across different industries and applications.

References

Abbas, S. (2023). LLMC: LLM life cycle https://medium.com/@SyedAbbasT/llm-lc-large-language-model-life-cycle-99cbbb12771f

Begou, N., Vinoy, J., Duda, A., & Korczyński, M. (2023). Exploring the Dark Side of AI: Advanced Phishing Attack Design and Deployment Using ChatGPT. In *2023 IEEE Conference on Communications and Network Security (CNS)* (pp. 1-6). IEEE.

Chang, Y., Wang, X., Wang, J., Wu, Y., Zhu, K., Chen, H., ... & Xie, X. (2023). A survey on evaluation of large language models. *arXiv preprint arXiv:2307.03109*.

CLTC (2021). Guidance for the development of AI risk and impact assessments.

Deldjoo, Y. (2023). Fairness of chatgpt and the role of explainable-guided prompts. *arXiv preprint arXiv:2307.11761*.

Derner, E., Batistič, K., Zahálka, J., & Babuška, R. (2023). A security risk taxonomy for large language models. *arXiv preprint arXiv:2311.11415*.

EU Commission (2019). Ethics guidelines for Trustworthy AI. High-level expert group in Artificial Intelligence.

EU Parliament (2023). Artificial Intelligence Act.

EY (2023). Political agreement reached on the EU Artificial Intelligence Act.

Fard, A. E., & Maathuis, C. (2021). Toward Capturing the Underlying Offensive Mechanisms of Social Manipulation: A Data Model Approach.

Guo, S., Xie, C., Li, J., Lyu, L., & Zhang, T. (2022). Threats to pre-trained language models: Survey and taxonomy. *arXiv preprint arXiv:2202.06862*.

Khlaaf, H. (2023). Toward Comprehensive Risk Assessments and Assurance of AI-Based Systems. *Trail of Bits*.

IEAI (2022). On a risk-based assessment approach to AI ethics governance.

ISO/IEC (2008). 27005 Information technology – security techniques – information security risk management.

ISO/IEC (2023). 23894 Information technology – Artificial Intelligence – guidance on risk management.

Kaddour, J., Harris, J., Mozes, M., Bradley, H., Raileanu, R., & McHardy, R. (2023). Challenges and applications of large language models. *arXiv preprint arXiv:2307.10169*.

Liu, Y., Yao, Y., Ton, J. F., Zhang, X., Cheng, R. G. H., Klochkov, Y., ... & Li, H. (2023). Trustworthy LLMs: a Survey and Guideline for Evaluating Large Language Models' Alignment. *arXiv preprint arXiv:2308.05374*.

Maathuis, C., Pieters, W., & van den Berg, J. (2018). A knowledge-based model for assessing the effects of cyber warfare. In *Proceedings of the 12th NATO Conference on Operations Research and Analysis*.

Maathuis, C. (2022). An Outlook of Digital Twins in Offensive Military Cyber Operations. In *European Conference on the Impact of Artificial Intelligence and Robotics* (Vol. 4, No. 1, pp. 45-53).

Maathuis, C., Kerkhof, I., Godschalk, R., & Passier, H. (2023). Design Lessons from Building Deep Learning Disinformation Generation and Detection Solutions. In *European Conference on Cyber Warfare and Security* (Vol. 22, No. 1, pp. 285-293).

Maathuis, C., & Chockalingam, S. (2023, May). Modelling Responsible Digital Security Behaviour for Countering Social Media Manipulation. In *ECSM 2023 10th European Conference on social media*. Academic Conferences and publishing limited.

Mikalef, P., Conboy, K., Lundström, J. E., & Popovič, A. (2022). Thinking responsibly about responsible AI and 'the dark side'of AI. *European Journal of Information Systems*, *31*(3), 257-268.

Mökander, J., Schuett, J., Kirk, H. R., & Floridi, L. (2023). Auditing large language models: a three-layered approach. *AI and Ethics*, 1-31.

NIST (2018). Risk Management Framework for information systems and organizations.

NIST (2023). Artificial Intelligence risk management framework.

Pamula, V. (2023). An introduction to LLMOps: operationalizing and managing LLMs using Azure ML. https://techcommunity.microsoft.com/t5/ai-machine-learning-blog/an-introduction-to-llmops-operationalizing-and-managing-large/ba-p/3910996

Piorkowski, D., Hind, M., & Richards, J. (2022). Quantitative ai risk assessments: Opportunities and challenges. *arXiv preprint arXiv:2209.06317*.

Shanahan, M., McDonell, K., & Reynolds, L. (2023). Role play with large language models. *Nature*, 1-6.

SANS (2021). An overview of threat and risk assessment.

Schuett, J. (2023). Risk management in the artificial intelligence act. *European Journal of Risk Regulation*, 1-19.

Sison, A. J. G., Daza, M. T., Gozalo-Brizuela, R., & Garrido-Merchán, E. C. (2023). ChatGPT: More than a weapon of mass deception, ethical challenges and responses from the human-Centered artificial intelligence (HCAI) perspective. *arXiv preprint arXiv:2304.11215*.

Somer, P., & Thalmann, S. (2023). Risk Management of AI in Industry: a Literature Review.

Staab, R., Vero, M., Balunović, M., & Vechev, M. (2023). Beyond memorization: Violating privacy via inference with large language models. *arXiv preprint arXiv:2310.07298*.

Stahl, B. C., & Eke, D. (2024). The ethics of ChatGPT–Exploring the ethical issues of an emerging technology. *International Journal of Information Management*, *74*, 102700.

Touvron, H., Martin, L., Stone, K., Albert, P., Almahairi, A., Babaei, Y., ... & Scialom, T. (2023). Llama 2: Open foundation and fine-tuned chat models, 2023. *URL https://arxiv. org/abs/2307.09288*.

TechLaw (2021). Responsible AI impact assessment (RAIIA).

UN (2020). Enterprise risk management approaches and uses in UN system organizations.

UN (2023). UN Internal Report Governing AI for humanity.

UNSMS (2017). Security Policy Manual.

Vaswani, A., Shazeer, N., Parmar, N., Uszkoreit, J., Jones, L., Gomez, A. N., ... & Polosukhin, I. (2017). Attention is all you need. *Advances in neural information processing systems, 30*.

Wach, K., Duong, C. D., Ejdys, J., Kazlauskaitė, R., Korzynski, P., Mazurek, G., ... & Ziemba, E. (2023). The dark side of generative artificial intelligence: A critical analysis of controversies and risks of ChatGPT. *Entrepreneurial Business and Economics Review*, *11*(2), 7-30.

WEF (2020). AI procurement in a box: workbook.

Weidinger, L., Mellor, J., Rauh, M., Griffin, C., Uesato, J., Huang, P. S., ... & Gabriel, I. (2021). Ethical and social risks of harm from language models (2021). *arXiv preprint arXiv:2112.04359*.

Workshop, B., Scao, T. L., Fan, A., Akiki, C., Pavlick, E., Ilić, S., ... & Bari, M. S. (2022). Bloom: A 176b-parameter open-access multilingual language model. *arXiv preprint arXiv:2211.05100*.

Wu, X., Duan, R., & Ni, J. (2023). Unveiling security, privacy, and ethical concerns of ChatGPT. arXiv. *URL: https://arxiv. org/abs/2308.10092*.

Xia, B., Lu, Q., Perera, H., Zhu, L., Xing, Z., Liu, Y., & Whittle, J. (2023). Towards Concrete and Connected AI Risk Assessment (C 2 AIRA): A Systematic Mapping Study. In *2023 IEEE/ACM 2nd International Conference on AI Engineering–Software Engineering for AI (CAIN)* (pp. 104-116). IEEE.

Zhao, H., Chen, H., Yang, F., Liu, N., Deng, H., Cai, H., ... & Du, M. (2023). Explainability for large language models: A survey. *ACM Transactions on Intelligent Systems and Technology*.

Zhou, J., Müller, H., Holzinger, A., & Chen, F. (2023). Ethical ChatGPT: Concerns, challenges, and commandments. *arXiv preprint arXiv:2305.10646*.

Multi-Key Asymmetric Cryptography: A Model for Preserving Privacy in Work-from-Home Environments

Konanani Maduguma[1] and Tapiwa Gundu[2]
[1]Sol Plaatje University, Kimberley , South Africa
[2]Nelson Mandela University, Gqeberha, South Africa

maduguma26@gmail.com
tapiwag@mandela.ac.za

Abstract: In the contemporary landscape of work, the transformative shift towards remote work has necessitated an investigative analysis of the privacy and security challenges associated with the exchange of sensitive information. This research paper responds to this imperative by introducing a pioneering privacy-preserving model, specifically tailored for Work-from-Home (WFH) environments, leveraging the capabilities of Multi-Key Asymmetric Cryptography. The model's innovation lies in its strategic synthesis of the efficiency inherent in symmetric encryption with an unwavering emphasis on the preservation of privacy. This nuanced approach positions the model as a robust solution to the dynamic and evolving cybersecurity threats faced by remote workers, offering a comprehensive defence mechanism against potential breaches and unauthorised access to sensitive data. The paper conducts a comprehensive analysis, delving into the foundational principles, distinct advantages, implementation considerations, and real-world benefits of the proposed privacy-preserving model. The examination of foundational principles elucidates the theoretical underpinnings, establishing a clear conceptual understanding of the model's architecture and functionality. The exploration of advantages underscores how the model not only addresses existing concerns but also provides additional layers of protection and adaptability to future cybersecurity challenges. The implementation considerations delve into practical aspects, discussing the feasibility and potential challenges of seamlessly integrating the privacy-preserving model into existing WFH infrastructures. Extending the analysis to real-world benefits, the research paper highlights the possible tangible impact and value the proposed model brings to organisations and remote workers. This encompasses enhanced data security, improved privacy compliance, and increased confidence in the integrity of remote work systems.

Keywords: Cryptography, Remote Working, Work From Home, Privacy

1. Introduction

The transition from traditional office working to the widespread adoption of remote work represents a seismic shift in the contemporary professional landscape. With this paradigm shift, employees increasingly leverage their home networks and, in some instances, personal computer systems to establish connections with organisational servers and peers. While this move towards flexibility and remote collaboration has undeniably ushered in numerous benefits, it has also unearthed a host of privacy concerns intrinsic to this novel working arrangement (Curran, 2020).

The utilisation of home networks and personal computers as conduits to access organisational servers and interact with colleagues introduces a complex interplay of security challenges, particularly concerning the confidentiality and privacy of sensitive data (Adisa, Ogbonnaya and Adekoya, 2021). The very nature of remote work amplifies these challenges, potentially exposing individuals and organisations to a heightened risk of unauthorised access, data breaches, and privacy infringements (Fritzen, 2021).

The urgency to address these privacy issues becomes paramount in safeguarding the integrity of organisational information and the personal data of remote workers (Curran, 2020; Angafor, Yevseyeva and Maglaras, 2024). The traditional security measures designed for office environments may prove insufficient in this decentralised setting, necessitating innovative solutions that strike a delicate balance between security and the preservation of individual privacy.

In response to this critical need, this research paper proposes a privacy-preserving model based on Multi-Key asymmetric Cryptography. By intricately combining the efficiency of asymmetric encryption with a deliberate focus on privacy preservation, this model emerges as a viable solution to mitigate the privacy challenges inherent in remote work scenarios. This proactive approach aims to fortify the security infrastructure of Work-from-Home (WFH) environments, ensuring the confidentiality of data and fostering a secure, trust-centric atmosphere for remote collaboration. The ensuing sections of this paper will delve into the foundational principles, unique advantages, implementation considerations, and real-world benefits of this proposed model, shedding light on its potential to address the urgent privacy concerns posed by the contemporary shift to remote work.

The ensuing sections of this manuscript are structured as follows: commencing with a review of relevant literature to provide contextual underpinnings, after which the employed methodology for this study will be utilised. Following this, an in-depth exposition of the Multikey Asymmetric Cryptography model will ensue. Conclusively, the paper will culminate with a summative section encapsulating findings and prospects for future research.

2. Background/Related Literature

2.1 Work From Home (WFH) Environments

A WFH is a professional environment that allows professionals or employees to work from home or any location other than their physical or traditional office environment (Adisa, Ogbonnaya and Adekoya, 2021). That often involves generating a workspace in your living space. Nevertheless, WFH can go beyond the limits of your dwelling place. For example, WFH is a well-known choice for 'digital wanderers' who invest most of their time working and fully travelling at the same time. In place of operating from their traditional office or their living place, they may operate from hotels, beaches, restaurants, or even transport. WFH is based on the fact that you don't need to be in a specific place in order for work to be completed successfully i.e. in place of travelling to your work office each and every day to work from an appellation desk, remote employees can complete their tasks wherever they wish to (Nurse *et al.*, 2021).

Employees have the flexibility to plan their working days so that there can be a peaceful co-existence between their personal and their professional lives and so they can be practised to their maximum spirit. Because of the lack of technology resources, it would have been a challenge to work virtually in this way in the past. A cultural pattern movement in which workers see suitable has been there and WFH has outshined in this movement because of that recently discovered freedom as the collaboration tools have assisted in filling the technology gap, allowing more people to execute their jobs virtually and collaborate as we move into the future (Nurse *et al.*, 2021). Types of WFH include fully remote employees, flexible jobs, and freelancers. The use of WFH environments was seen to be in high numbers in 2020 due to the Covid-19 pandemic (Gundu, 2023a).

2.2 Work-From-Home Security Concerns

With the shift to WFH comes a new set of organisational privacy and cybersecurity issues that must be addressed. Opening an organisation to the idea of remote work also opens up the possibility of valuable business data being accessed by cybersecurity criminals. The shift into WFH exposes the organisation to a lot of potential security issues such as leaks, hacking, or attacks from external forces (Curran, 2020). Many virtual employees use the same computer devices for their personal and professional use which thus leads to incidental data exposure (Angafor, Yevseyeva and Maglaras, 2024). These obscure between personal and professional life give sensitive information more chance of falling into a dangerous environment. With unprotected data and information like Cloud documents, emails and attachments, instant message clients and third-party services being shared online, the attack depth grows deeper (Ling *et al.*, 2021).

The lack of technical proficiency among some employees poses a significant weakness notably manifested in the improper setup of home networks, often leaving default settings untouched due to a lack of technical know-how (Gundu, 2023b). Employees, who may not possess the necessary technical knowledge, often overlook critical security measures such as changing default usernames and passwords on routers and devices. This oversight exposes the home network to potential unauthorised access. Furthermore, the limited understanding of encryption protocols may result in employees neglecting to enable secure connections, thereby jeopardising the confidentiality of transmitted data (Mehta, 2022). Challenges in updating firmware and software on devices, configuring firewalls, and implementing complex security settings may arise due to the technical limitations of certain employees. This lack of technical awareness extends to monitoring practices, as employees may not actively observe their network for suspicious activities or understand the importance of maintaining logs (Mmango and Gundu, 2023). Consequently, the improper configuration of home networks becomes a vulnerability that could be exploited by malicious actors seeking unauthorised access.

Naqvi *et al.*, (2023) also writes that another problem faced by those working from home is exploitation via broadcasting phishing emails. These are fraudulent emails designed to fool users into giving out their confidential information or downloading malicious files that contain a key-logger. Although employees are working remotely, the need for access to internal business systems does not change. This means that remote employees are accessing critical business applications over a home or public WiFi connection, leaving a potential path for cybersecurity threats to seep in. Organisations need a way to verify who is accessing their private information and where it is being accessed from (El-hajj *et al.*, 2019). The user must be authenticated and authorised. Integrity refers to whether the workspace is operating as intended and confidentiality is concerned with keeping one's information a secret as intended.

An attacker can exploit (Have access into) the WFH system or network, and in order to make it difficult for them access thier information (breaching availability) or leaking sensitive data stored or being communicated (breaching confidentiality) or alter the information, leading to the system not operating as intended (breaching integrity), there is a need for cryptography on data or information being stored or communicated (Panahi *et al.*, 2021).

2.3 Cryptography

Cryptography is the study of art, science and techniques of preparing protected and secure data communication in presence of third parties (Ibrahim, Teh and Abdullah, 2021). It is about constructing and analysing protocols that overcome the influence of adversaries and which are related to various aspects in information security such as data confidentiality, data integrity, authentication, and non-repudiation (Hiza, 2022). The word cryptography is derived from the two Greek words; "kryptos" means "secret or hidden" and "graphos" means "to write" (Teja and Sreenivas, 2021).

Nowadays, Cryptography mainly includes the use of computerised encryption to protect data stored and in communication (Ibrahim, Teh and Abdullah, 2021). Often it is hard to prevent people from copying the database and then hacking into the copy at another location. It is easier to simply make copying the data a useless activity by encrypting the data (Ghosh *et al.*, 2020). This means that the data itself is unreadable unless you know a secret code as visualised in Figure 1.

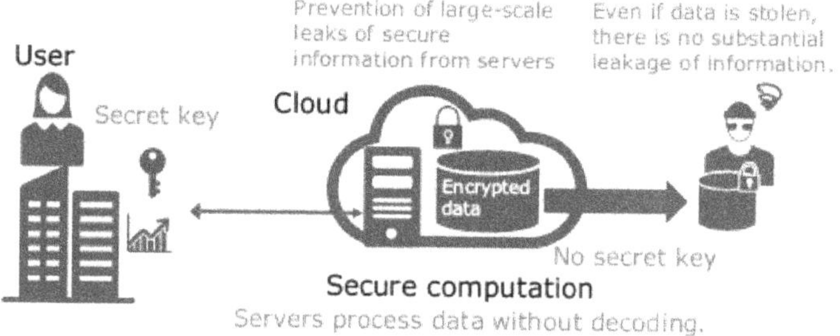

Figure 1: Cryptography for stored data.

A secret key is needed to use the DBMS. Data encryption encodes the data such that nobody can understand the actual data contents . Encryption is not only useful to secure the data stored on servers and storage devices but also for exchanging the information over a network (Subramanyan, Ray and Malik, 2015). This encoded data can be decoded (decrypted) only by the authorised users that know what the code is. Authorisation security control ensures that only privileged user can manipulate the data in the way they are allowed to do. The database management system must determine that which users are allowed to perform which functions and which data portion is accessible by them. Authorisation controls are different in a centralised database to the distributed database environment (Mohamed *et al.*, 2021). Authorisation control definition in a distributed database system is derived from that in centralised system but in the context of distributed system some additional complexity is also considered.

Modern cryptography techniques include algorithms and ciphers that enable the encryption and decryption of information, such as 128-bit and 256-bit encryption keys. Modern ciphers, such as the Advanced Encryption Standard (AES), are considered virtually unbreakable (Subramanyan, Ray and Malik, 2015). A common cryptography definition is the practice of coding information to ensure only the person that a message was written for can read and process the information. This cybersecurity practice, also known as cryptology, combines various disciplines like computer science, engineering, and mathematics to create complex codes that hide the true meaning of a message.

Basically, encryption scheme has five stages: Plaintext, Encryption algorithm, Secret Key, Cipher text, Decryption algorithm (Mohammed and Anwer, 2021). The original message or text before going to any process is called plaintext or cleartext. The process of changing plaintext into secret form is called encryption. Once the original text has been encrypted, the resultant text is known as ciphertext or cryptogram. The process of converting ciphertext back into plaintext is known as decryption. This whole process is depicted in figure 2.

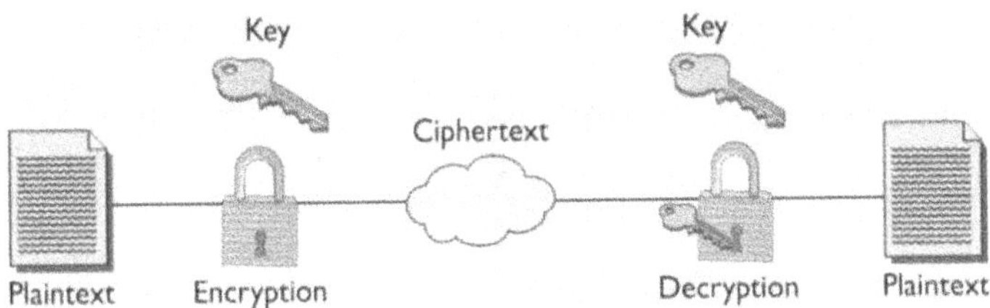

Figure 2: Basics of cryptography.

Mostly in encryption process, some mathematical algorithms are used. Basically, encryption algorithm is the set of instructions that have particular method of encrypting plaintext into ciphertext.

2.4 Basic Types of Cryptography

2.4.1 Symmetrical Cryptography

Symmetric-key encryption involves using a single key for both message encryption and decryption, making it convenient but less secure. The key exchange between parties must be secure to prevent unauthorised access. This method, also known as secret-key, personal key, private key, or shared key, is considered weak due to its susceptibility to hacking (Mehta, 2022). However, when carefully planned, the risk can be minimised. Symmetric cryptography is cost-effective, provides efficient processing, and ensures quick implementation without significant delays. It offers a level of authentication, ensuring that only the intended parties can decipher exchanged messages. The challenge lies in securely exchanging secret keys, often requiring encryption in a different key, leading to a potential dependency loop. Two types of symmetric encryption algorithms are block ciphers (e.g., AES, GOST 28147-89) and stream ciphers (e.g., RC4, Salsa20) (Salami, Khajehvand and Zeinali, 2023). Symmetric encryption is widely used in modern services, especially in combination with asymmetric encryption. Its disadvantage lies in key exchange vulnerability, often mitigated by using an asymmetric algorithm for key transmission. Symmetric algorithms are not suitable for generating digital signatures and certificates due to the necessity of sharing the secret key, counteracting the concept of electronic signatures (Parekh *et al.*, 2023).

2.4.2 Asymmetrical Cryptography

Asymmetric encryption, or public-key cryptography, employs a pair of keys for encrypting and decrypting data: a public key (shared openly) and a private key (kept secret). This method utilises distinct keys for encryption and decryption, enhancing security (Parekh *et al.*, 2023). Noteworthy in this approach is the application of a sender's random digital key paired with a recipient's public key for data encryption, ensuring secure communication without the need for shared secret keys. Asymmetric encryption boasts advantages over symmetric encryption, eliminating the challenge of exchanging secret keys and allowing the creation of digital signatures for data authenticity verification. Commonly used in secure online communication, email encryption, e-commerce, and digital signatures, asymmetric encryption algorithms include RSA, Diffie-Hellman, and Elliptic Curve Cryptography. Its key advantages include enhanced security, authentication, non-repudiation, simplified key distribution, and versatility (Mehta, 2022). Asymmetric encryption relies on dual keys, public and private, with the public key used for encryption and the private key for decryption (Parekh *et al.*, 2023). Digital signatures, created by encrypting a hash with the sender's private key, contribute to data authenticity verification. Secure key exchange is facilitated through the Diffie-Hellman key exchange algorithm. Despite its security benefits, asymmetric encryption may have slower processing speeds due to complex mathematical operations, a consideration in selecting encryption methods for specific applications.

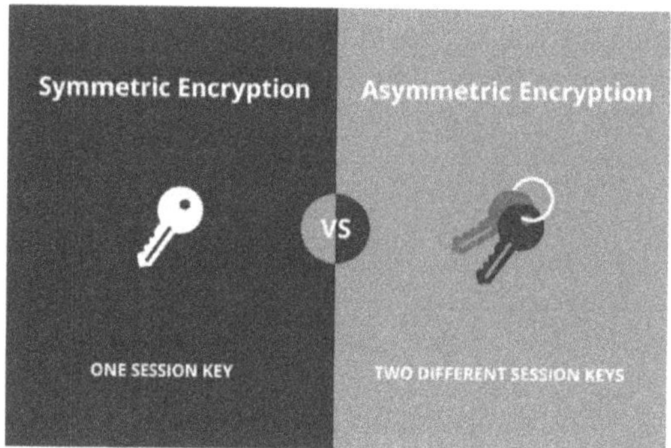

Figure 3: Difference between Symmetric and asymmetric Cryptography (Mehta, 2022)

3. Methodology

The selection of the Design Science Research (DSR) methodology for this research is driven by its practical problem-solving approach and user-centric focus. DSR's emphasis on creating tangible artifacts aligns with the need to develop a real-world solution for enhancing security in work-from-home (WFH) environments (Brocke et al., 2020). Its iterative development cycles cater to the dynamic nature of cybersecurity threats, allowing continuous refinement of the security model. DSR's holistic consideration of context ensures the model's adaptability to diverse WFH scenarios, and interdisciplinary collaboration fosters insights from cryptography, data privacy, and IT security experts. The methodology's immediate applicability aligns with the goal of producing practical solutions, while its feedback-driven evolution ensures a thorough and robust security model before implementation. In summary, DSR provides a comprehensive and effective approach to address the unique challenges of securing remote work environments.

1. Problem Identification and Motivation

The research identified the escalating security challenges associated with remote work, emphasising the critical need for a robust security framework tailored to the unique aspects of work-from-home (WFH) environments. Existing security measures were examined, and their limitations in addressing the specific vulnerabilities of remote work were acknowledged.

2. Objectives Formulation

Clear research objectives were established, focusing on the development of a comprehensive security model designed to specifically address the vulnerabilities in WFH scenarios. Measurable goals were defined, including improving data confidentiality, ensuring secure communication, and providing a user-friendly implementation.

3. Literature Review

An extensive review of literature was conducted, exploring multi-key symmetric cryptography, existing security models for remote work, and related technologies. Identified gaps in current research and technologies served as the foundation for the proposed security model.

4. Conceptualisation of Security Model

A conceptual framework for the multi-key symmetric cryptography model was developed, outlining key components and their interactions. Principles guiding the design were defined, ensuring alignment with the unique challenges of WFH environments.

5. Evaluation Criteria Establishment

The prototype underwent a rigorous evaluation process conducted by a panel of four Data Privacy Specialists with expertise in cryptographic protocols and data security. This panel was specifically chosen to ensure a thorough examination of the security aspects. The specialists assessed the prototype for its adherence to data privacy standards, encryption strength, vulnerability to potential threats, and overall robustness. Their expertise contributed valuable insights into potential weaknesses and areas for improvement in the prototype's security features.

6. Model Refinement

The security model was iteratively refined based on the collected feedback and evaluation results. Identified weaknesses were addressed, user-friendliness was enhanced, and the model was adapted to evolving security threats.

7. Documentation and Dissemination

The entire research process, including conceptualisation, development, testing, and implementation phases, was comprehensively documented. Research findings, methodologies, and lessons learned will be disseminated through peer-reviewed journals, conferences (this being one of such), and relevant forums.

4. Multi-Key Asymmetric Cryptography Model

The Multi-Key Asymmetric Cryptography Model introduces a sophisticated security framework designed to fortify data protection and authentication in work-from-home (WFH) scenarios. In this model, each user is equipped with two pairs of cryptographic keys: Key set A (Public Key A, Private Key A) and Key set B (Public Key B, Private Key B). When a user initiates communication, the message is encrypted not only with the recipient's Public Key A but also with their Public Key B, creating a dual-layered encryption (Ghaffar Khan et al., 2018). This innovative approach significantly enhances the security of sensitive data by requiring both sets of private keys for successful decryption. This redundancy in key pairs adds resilience against potential vulnerabilities and attacks, offering a robust defence even if one set of keys is compromised. Additionally, the model incorporates a dual-authentication mechanism, utilising Public Key A for authentication in one context and Public Key B in another, strengthening the overall verification process. The system is adaptable to existing communication protocols, ensuring a seamless integration into WFH environments. Users benefit from a user-friendly implementation that streamlines encryption and decryption processes while providing educational support on the importance of safeguarding both sets of keys. With regular key rotation and updates, the Multi-Key Asymmetric Cryptography Model not only bolsters security but also ensures adaptability and ongoing protection against emerging threats in the dynamic landscape of remote work. (Kaur et al., 2018)

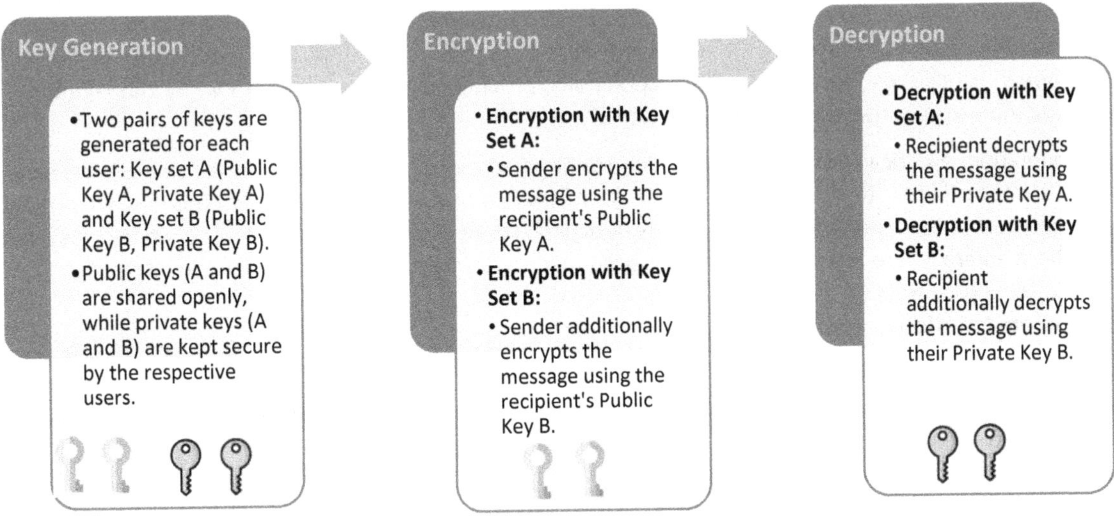

Key Generation
•Two pairs of keys are generated for each user: Key set A (Public Key A, Private Key A) and Key set B (Public Key B, Private Key B).
•Public keys (A and B) are shared openly, while private keys (A and B) are kept secure by the respective users.
Encryption
• Encryption with Key Set A:
• Sender encrypts the message using the recipient's Public Key A.
• Encryption with Key Set B:
• Sender additionally encrypts the message using the recipient's Public Key B.
Decryption
• Decryption with Key Set A:
• Recipient decrypts the message using their Private Key A.
• Decryption with Key Set B:
• Recipient additionally decrypts the message using their Private Key B.

Figure 4: Multi-Key Asymmetric Cryptography Model

4.1 Discussion

The Multi-Key Asymmetric Cryptography Model introduces an adaptable and robust solution designed to fortify communication security in work-from-home (WFH) settings. This innovative model leverages a dual-key approach, employing two pairs of cryptographic keys for both encryption and decryption processes. This redundancy significantly enhances data security, reducing the risk of unauthorised access and potential compromises. By addressing vulnerabilities associated with traditional asymmetric encryption, the model mitigates risks and bolsters the overall security posture.

A distinctive feature of the model is its dual-authentication mechanism, which employs different public keys in distinct contexts. This multifaceted authentication process enhances user verification and reduces the likelihood of unauthorised access, contributing to a more robust cryptographic system. Moreover, the model is designed to seamlessly integrate into existing communication protocols commonly used in WFH environments. Its adaptability ensures that it remains effective in the dynamic and evolving landscape of remote work. The model's dynamic key management, incorporating regular key rotation and updates, aligns with the ever-changing nature of security threats, ensuring continued resilience over time.

The perceived effectiveness of the Multi-Key Asymmetric Cryptography Model extends beyond industry-specific applications. Its versatility makes it a valuable solution for organisations across diverse sectors that have embraced remote work. As users experience increased confidence in the security of their communications, the model holds the potential for broader industry adoption. Successful implementation, positive user experiences, and its ability to address the unique challenges posed by remote work collectively contribute to its efficacy in fortifying communication security.

4.2 Relevance of the Model

The proposed Multi-Key Asymmetric Cryptography Model is underpinned by a recognition of the paramount importance of cryptography in contemporary information security. The model aligns with the core principles of confidentiality, integrity, authentication, and non-repudiation to address the evolving challenges of secure data communication. In the context of work-from-home (WFH) environments, where the transfer of sensitive information has become commonplace, the model becomes particularly pertinent.

For the confidentiality aspect, the model resonates with the need for secure communication channels in WFH scenarios, safeguarding data during transmission over various mediums such as email, financial transactions, and remote collaboration tools. By utilising two pairs of cryptographic keys for both encryption and decryption, the model ensures that even if communication channels are compromised, the encrypted data remains impervious to unauthorised access, preserving personal privacy.

Moving beyond confidentiality, the model addresses the integrity of information. Digital signatures, a key component of the model, serve as a mechanism to detect any tampering or forgery during software distribution or financial transactions, reinforcing the trustworthiness of the exchanged data. Authentication, another pillar of the model, establishes identity in digital interactions, providing a robust means to verify the legitimacy of users in an increasingly interconnected digital world.

Non-repudiation, a critical feature of the model, confirms accountability and responsibility from the sender, making it impossible to deny intentions when creating or transmitting information. This has wide-ranging implications, from preventing fraudulent claims in digital signatures to securing the world's banking systems, especially in an era where financial transactions occur over open switched networks like the Internet.

4.3 Implementation Considerations

Transitioning from the theoretical foundation of cryptography, the model seamlessly integrates into the practical realm by addressing implementation considerations in WFH environments. Challenges such as key management, scalability, and compatibility with existing tools and platforms should be conscientiously explored, to provide a roadmap for specific organisation adoption.

4.4 Real-World Benefits

The Multi-Key Asymmetric Cryptography Model offers a range of substantial real-world benefits, particularly tailored to the challenges prevalent in work-from-home (WFH) environments. One of its primary advantages lies in the enhancement of data security through the utilisation of two pairs of cryptographic keys for both encryption and decryption. This dual-key approach significantly fortifies the confidentiality of sensitive information, ensuring that even if one set of keys is compromised, the other remains intact, thwarting unauthorised access and preserving data integrity. Furthermore, the model provides robust protection against data breaches, a critical concern in today's digital landscape, by securing communication channels and mitigating the risk of unauthorised access during data transmission.

In the context of WFH scenarios, the model facilitates secure remote collaboration by ensuring the confidentiality and integrity of exchanged information. Its authentication mechanisms contribute to robust identity verification, crucial for secure digital interactions. Incorporating non-repudiation features such as digital signatures, the model establishes accountability, preventing senders from later denying their intentions and providing a verifiable trail of actions. Its adaptability to WFH environments is underscored by its seamless integration into existing communication protocols without disrupting established workflows.

Addressing key challenges, the model incorporates dynamic key management through rotation and updates, ensuring the resilience of cryptographic keys over time. Successful implementation of the model instils trust and confidence among users, fostering a sense of security in their digital interactions. The model's versatility extends its applicability across various industries that have embraced remote work, positioning it as a valuable solution for organizations in diverse fields. Depending on successful implementation and positive user experiences, there is potential for broader industry adoption, particularly for organizations recognizing the need for advanced security measures in their digital communications. In summation, the Multi-Key Asymmetric Cryptography Model stands as a practical and effective solution, offering tangible benefits for organizations navigating the evolving landscape of remote work.

5. Conclusion

In conclusion, the Multi-Key Asymmetric Cryptography Model emerges as a robust and adaptive solution to address the escalating challenges of securing communication in work-from-home (WFH) environments. The paramount importance of cryptography in contemporary information security is underscored, emphasizing its role in ensuring confidentiality, integrity, authentication, and non-repudiation. Against this backdrop, the proposed model seamlessly integrates cryptographic principles to fortify data protection in the dynamic landscape of remote work.

The model's significance lies in its ability to transcend theoretical frameworks and address practical considerations in WFH implementation. By utilizing two pairs of cryptographic keys for both encryption and decryption, the model not only ensures the confidentiality of sensitive information but also guards against unauthorized access, providing a secure medium for data transfer. Its application in real-world scenarios is exemplified through case studies, demonstrating tangible benefits such as enhanced security and protection against data breaches.

The theoretical underpinnings of the model align with the multifaceted requirements of secure communication. It addresses the integrity of information through features like digital signatures, detecting tampering or forgery in critical processes like software distribution and financial transactions. The authentication mechanisms contribute to establishing identity in digital interactions, enhancing user verification. Non-repudiation, a core feature, ensures accountability and responsibility, preventing denial of intentions when creating or transmitting information. This feature holds particular relevance in securing the world's banking systems and various digital transactions conducted over open switched networks like the Internet.

Transitioning from theoretical principles to practical implementation, the model navigates challenges such as key management, scalability, and compatibility with existing tools. By doing so, it provides a comprehensive framework for organizations seeking to adopt multi-key symmetric cryptography in WFH settings, offering a roadmap for successful integration.

In essence, the Multi-Key Asymmetric Cryptography Model not only champions the theoretical ideals of cryptography but also materializes them in a practical, adaptable, and effective solution for the contemporary demands of secure communication. As remote work continues to be a pervasive mode of operation, the model stands as a testament to the ongoing evolution of cryptographic solutions, ensuring the confidentiality and security of data in an ever-changing digital landscape.

5.1 Future Directions

Future research should focus on refining the implementation of multi-key symmetric cryptography for WFH environments, developing standardized protocols for seamless integration with WFH tools, and addressing key management challenges. Additionally, exploring the potential of multi-key symmetric cryptography in emerging technologies and evolving threat landscapes will be essential for long-term WFH security.

References

Adisa, T.A., Ogbonnaya, C. and Adekoya, O.D. (2021) 'Remote working and employee engagement: a qualitative study of British workers during the pandemic', *Information Technology & People*, 36(5), pp. 1835–1850. Available at: https://doi.org/10.1108/ITP-12-2020-0850.

Angafor, G.N., Yevseyeva, I. and Maglaras, L. (2024) 'Securing the remote office: reducing cyber risks to remote working through regular security awareness education campaigns', *International Journal of Information Security* [Preprint]. Available at: https://doi.org/10.1007/s10207-023-00809-5.

Curran, K. (2020) 'Cyber security and the remote workforce', *Computer Fraud & Security*, 2020(6), pp. 11–12. Available at: https://doi.org/10.1016/S1361-3723(20)30063-4.

El-hajj, M. *et al.* (2019) 'A Survey of Internet of Things (IoT) Authentication Schemes', *Sensors*, 19(5), p. 1141. Available at: https://doi.org/10.3390/s19051141.

Fritzen, M.P. (2021) *Remote working and Cyber Security threats in Ireland. Challenges and Prospective Solutions*. masters. Dublin, National College of Ireland. Available at: https://norma.ncirl.ie/5108/ (Accessed: 15 February 2024).

Ghosh, B. *et al.* (2020) 'CRYPTOGRAPHY', *Journal of Mathematical Sciences & Computational Mathematics*, 1(2), pp. 225–228. Available at: https://doi.org/10.15864/jmscm.1207.

Gundu, T. (2023a) 'Enhancing Remote Work Security: A Multi-Key Biometric Authentication Scheme for Virtual Workspaces', in *2023 International Conference on Electrical, Computer and Energy Technologies (ICECET)*, pp. 1–7. Available at: https://doi.org/10.1109/ICECET58911.2023.10389214.

Gundu, T. (2023b) 'Internet Of Things: Sensor Layer Security Risk Mitigation Framework', in *2023 International Conference on Electrical, Computer and Energy Technologies (ICECET)*, pp. 1–8. Available at: https://doi.org/10.1109/ICECET58911.2023.10389252.

Hiza, D. (2022) *Assessig the Significance of Cia Triad Security Model in Establishing ICT Security Controls in The Public Sector.* Thesis. Institute of Accountancy Arusha (IAA). Available at: http://dspace.iaa.ac.tz:8080/xmlui/handle/123456789/2126 (Accessed: 15 February 2024).

Ibrahim, D.R., Teh, J.S. and Abdullah, R. (2021) 'An overview of visual cryptography techniques', *Multimedia Tools and Applications*, 80(21), pp. 31927–31952. Available at: https://doi.org/10.1007/s11042-021-11229-9.

Ling, Z. *et al.* (2021) 'Secure boot, trusted boot and remote attestation for ARM TrustZone-based IoT Nodes', *Journal of Systems Architecture*, 119, p. 102240. Available at: https://doi.org/10.1016/j.sysarc.2021.102240.

Mehta, J. (2022) 'Symmetric Encryption vs Asymmetric Encryption Differences Explained', *CheapSSLWeb.com Blog*, 26 October. Available at: https://cheapsslweb.com/blog/symmetric-encryption-vs-asymmetric-encryption (Accessed: 5 February 2024).

Mmango, N. and Gundu, T. (2023) 'Cyber Resilience in the Entrepreneurial Environment: A Framework for Enhancing Cybersecurity Awareness in SMEs', in *2023 International Conference on Electrical, Computer and Energy Technologies (ICECET)*, pp. 1–6. Available at: https://doi.org/10.1109/ICECET58911.2023.10389226.

Mohamed, A. *et al.* (2021) 'Authorization Strategies and Classification of Access Control Models', in T.K. Dang et al. (eds) *Future Data and Security Engineering*. Cham: Springer International Publishing (Lecture Notes in Computer Science), pp. 155–174. Available at: https://doi.org/10.1007/978-3-030-91387-8_11.

Mohammed, A. and Anwer, H. (2021) 'A New Method Encryption and Decryption', *Webology*, 18, pp. 20–31. Available at: https://doi.org/10.14704/WEB/V18I1/WEB18002.

Naqvi, B. *et al.* (2023) 'Mitigation strategies against the phishing attacks: A systematic literature review', *Computers & Security*, 132, p. 103387. Available at: https://doi.org/10.1016/j.cose.2023.103387.

Nurse, J.R.C. *et al.* (2021) 'Remote Working Pre- and Post-COVID-19: An Analysis of New Threats and Risks to Security and Privacy', in C. Stephanidis, M. Antona, and S. Ntoa (eds) *HCI International 2021 - Posters*. Cham: Springer International Publishing (Communications in Computer and Information Science), pp. 583–590. Available at: https://doi.org/10.1007/978-3-030-78645-8_74.

Panahi, P. *et al.* (2021) 'Performance Evaluation of Lightweight Encryption Algorithms for IoT-Based Applications', *Arabian Journal for Science and Engineering*, 46(4), pp. 4015–4037. Available at: https://doi.org/10.1007/s13369-021-05358-4.

Parekh, A. *et al.* (2023) 'Multilayer symmetric and asymmetric technique for audiovisual cryptography', *Multimedia Tools and Applications* [Preprint]. Available at: https://doi.org/10.1007/s11042-023-16401-x.

Salami, Y., Khajehvand, V. and Zeinali, E. (2023) 'Cryptographic Algorithms: A Review of the Literature, Weaknesses and Open Challenges', *Journal of Computer & Robotics*, 16(2), pp. 63–115.

Subramanyan, P., Ray, S. and Malik, S. (2015) 'Evaluating the security of logic encryption algorithms', in *2015 IEEE International Symposium on Hardware Oriented Security and Trust (HOST). 2015 IEEE International Symposium on Hardware Oriented Security and Trust (HOST)*, pp. 137–143. Available at: https://doi.org/10.1109/HST.2015.7140252.

Teja, B.V. and Sreenivas, R.G.K. (2021) 'Remedying the Hummingbird Cryptographic Algorithm', *Turkish Journal of Computer and Mathematics Education (TURCOMAT)*, 12(14), pp. 5612–5622. Available at: https://doi.org/10.17762/turcomat.v12i14.11717.

Arranging the Defence of the Cyber Environment as a Part of Military Affairs: Tactical, Operational and Strategic approach in retrospect of The Russian - Ukrainian War 2022

Juha Kai Mattila
Aalto University, Espoo, Finland

Juhakaimattila24@gmail.com

Abstract: The artificial cyber environment has reached national security interest and emerged as the fourth domain of battle in the military concept of all-domain operations in most Western armed forces and coalitions in the past 30 years. Currently, militaries are struggling to keep up with cybercriminals and advanced persistent actors while trying to gain an advantage of their data and digital infrastructure. The paper focuses on military affairs' ways and means to address the need for cyber warriors operating in friendly, neutral, and hostile cyber environments integrated under Multi-Domain Operations. The paper uses design research methodology to create and test a model for cyber defence capabilities generation and utilisation. The theoretical reference to military affairs is based on Beer's Viable System Model and previous studies of military organisations' evolution as capability generators. The military and societal cyber environment evolution model is based on industrial revolutions and current tendencies. These approaches define a hypothetical model for two main functions of military affairs (force generation and utilisation) concerning cyber defence capabilities. The fast evolution of cyber threats sets unique requirements for cyber force utilisation and generation structures. This difference has culminated in a recent war between Russia and Ukraine, and data from that conflict is used to test the hypothetical model. The rapid evolution of the cyber environment and its weaponisation establish different requirements for military cyber capabilities compared to any other operational dimension or capability (space, air, land, or maritime). The difference is evident in sourcing resources, generating capabilities, and using them in Multi-Domain Operations. The paper provides a tested model for generating cyber defence capabilities at a strategic level and an operation model for cyber defence at a tactical and operational level. The designed model extends the technically oriented cybersecurity thinking with operational and strategic levels. Furthermore, the model introduces the value stream behind the cyber capability acquisition and supports strategic designers in national and military analysis.

Keywords: Cyber Defence, Multi-Domain Battle, Cyber Conflict, Military Affairs, Cyber Operations

1. Introduction

Within the previous two decades, the cyber environment has become the fourth military domain (NATO, 2023). However, its nature as an artificial, continuously evolving environment establishes an unprecedented challenge to military operators and force generators in fulfilling the joint operation needs alongside other domains (space/air, land, and maritime). Contemporary military operations require multi-domain, coalition, and inter-agency interoperability. Therefore, one separately well-secured and monitored Information and Telecommunications Technology (ICT) domain needs to be connected to other domains, which may not be as well-secured. Every cross-domain gateway in the defence network will increase the vulnerable surface and the adversary's attack options. (Tidjon, et al., 2019) Any breach of trust between domains will halt the cooperation and lower the operational performance. Therefore, trust relationships are lucrative targets for advanced adversaries. (NATO, 2021)

Cyberspace is an artificial, evolutionary environment that needs to be defined from popular, governmental, and military viewpoints in this research. The core definition, according to Wikipedia, is "Cyberspace is an interconnected digital environment." (Wikipedia, 2023) From the military approach, the previous artificial technical environment may seem like "Cyberspace is contested at all times as malign actors increasingly seek to destabilise the Alliance by employing malicious cyber activities and campaigns. Potential adversaries seek to degrade our critical infrastructure, interfere with our government services, extract intelligence, steal intellectual property and impede our military activities." (NATO, 2023)

From different viewpoints, the same environment may be perceived as a risk source for business. For instance, the NIST Cybersecurity Framework aims for a "systematic process for identifying, assessing, and managing cybersecurity risk." (NIST, 2018) Cyber defence is the same operational level approach in the military: "to protect its networks, operate in cyberspace (including through the Alliance's operations and missions), help Allies to enhance their national resilience and provide a platform for political consultation and collective action." (NATO, 2023)

Furthermore, in contemporary military operational art, the Multi-Domain Operations recognise Cyberspace as one of the five areas of operation: "Within NATO's structure, there are five areas of operations: Maritime, Land, Air, Space and Cyberspace. Given the speed of information, data flows, and adversarial capabilities, orchestrating military activities across all domains as a single force is crucial for long-term defence and deterrence initiatives within NATO." (NATO, 2023) Hence, the convergence or at least the orchestration of action over several operation areas is crucial. Other military establishments perceive added value from a multi-domain approach but in different combinations. Russia continues its successful information operation line with technical support from Cyberspace. (Mattila, 2022) On the other hand, the Chinese military seeks to conduct complex information operations using space, electromagnetic, cyber, and cognitive areas to gain information dominance. (CSIS, 2019)

Military generate their cyber capabilities differently than force elements for the other domains. (Mattila, 2022) U.S. DoD sources its defence industrial network to educate cyber teams for the Services and Cyber Command. Russia started its cyber capability development by exploiting cybercriminal organisations enjoying sanctuary in the nation. Iran uses an ideological base for motivation and cultivates digital competencies in universities, para-military organisations, and educating selected individuals abroad. Ukraine recruited their I.T. Army of Ukraine based on patriot citizens' willingness to contribute to national cyber actions using easy tools available on the Internet.

The paper provides a framework and an operation model to support military affairs addressing the fast-evolving technical competition, information contest, and state-level conflict in Cyberspace. Because there are various approaches to utilise and generate military capabilities in cyber environments, most defence strategy planners are seeking the best approach for their nation. Naturally, the approach depends on available resources, population, culture, motivation, the surface of national digital infrastructure, and available tools. A typical multi-variable problem needs a model for understanding the phenomena and design. Hence, the **Research question** is: How should military affairs address the generation and utilisation of cyber defence capabilities in a current cyber environment in the context of state-level defence strategy?

2. Understanding the Problem and Creating a Tentative Design

The paper uses some principles of Capability-Based Planning (CBP) (Despont, 2022) that have been used widely. Hence, the research first compares the cyber domain to other military domains, trying to identify differences that may impact the ways of utilising, generating, and sustaining cyber force. Secondly, the research addresses these differences while creating a high-level design of cyber force based on generic system models, military enterprise evolution models and industrial revolution generations. Finally, the research tests the concept design against three adversarial cyber strategies: operations, capabilities, and generation.

2.1 Why is the Cyber Domain Different From Other Military Domains?

With the rapid digitalisation of critical infrastructure, military systems, governance, public services, and cyber criminality, states have recognised the extended attack surface of their cyber environment. (Ciepiela & Venkateshwaran, 2017) The first task of the research is to identify the differences in the cyber domain, network operations, cyber environment, attack vectors, and adversaries' potential at tactical, operational, and strategic levels compared to other military domains. Table 1 details the comparison and differences between the domains.

Table 1: Comparison between cyber-electromagnetic domain and legacy (Land, Air, Maritime) military domains

Domain/ Level of Warfare	Cyber/Electromagnetic Environment Features	Legacy Military Domains (Air, Land, Maritime) Features	Tenets that may impact the Cyber Force utilisation, generation, and sustainment
Strategic	Volatile and abstract offensive capabilities in everchanging target surface. (Clarke & Knake, 2019) Adversary attribution remains unclear. (Gayde & Neuhaus, 2020)	Credible coercion with tangible force elements against known armament. (Clausewitz, 1984) Attribution of forces and their use is primarily evident; hence, the retaliation has a clear target. (Libicki, 2009)	a)Attackers' advantage and ambiguity expose to strategic surprise. b)Strategic armament stockpiles are volatile as weapons are one-time, and their capability for effect evolves as the environment changes.

Domain/ Level of Warfare	Cyber/Electromagnetic Environment Features	Legacy Military Domains (Air, Land, Maritime) Features	Tenets that may impact the Cyber Force utilisation, generation, and sustainment
Opera-tional	Cyber force is not necessarily organised or has identifiable insignia. (Clarke & Knake, 2010) The impacts of cyber offence operations are not necessarily detectable. (Libicki, 2009) Cyber competencies retention requires continuous training. (NATO, 2019)	Since the Peace of Westphalia, sovereignty has defined the terms for projecting military force. (Kaldor, 2012) The impact of force utilisation is evident.	c)Operating under the threshold of war is a contemporary norm. d)Capability – Impact – Effect causality is nonlinear. e)The operational range is extended, and the attack path is less evident. f)Sourcing cyber force is not constrained to military institutes, on the contrary. g)Retention of cyber competencies requires effort.
Tactical	Navigation in the cyber realm is challenging as reference points for measuring progress are few. (Clarke & Knake, 2019) Errors and mistakes are less distinguishable from intended action. (Libicki, 2009) Malevolent software often spreads wider than the targeted system. (Malwarebytes, 2024)	Navigation and manoeuvring can be referenced with a variety of orienteering means. Massing kinetic force is evident, and crossing state borders is detected. (Friedman, 2017) Command and control of weapons is straightforward. (Creveld, 1987)	h) The Observe – Orient – Decision – Action loop is much faster and more evolutionary. i)Automation and artificial intelligence actors are adopted faster. j)The impact may cause tactical, operational, and strategic effects, so decision-making is ambiguous. k)Collateral damage is more probable.

The differences indicated in the above matrix mean that at least the strategic posture and processes (Mattila & Parkinson, 2018) of military enterprises may need different approaches in cyber force utilisation, generation, and sustainment.

2.2 Creating a Tentative Design or Concept of Operation

Contemporary Military Affairs consist of force utilisation, generation, and support. (Smith, 2005) These three functions may be defined as per military domain, orchestrated at the joint operations level, and governed at the strategic level. Therefore, Beer's Viable System Model (VSM) (Rios, 2012) may be used to illustrate a generic approach to Military Affairs in Figure 1. The cyber domain is included as one of the tactical engagement areas. Tactical cyber activities are orchestrated from the Joint Operations level in concert with other domain activities, and future capability generation is governed from the Military Strategic level using capability portfolios. (U.S. DoD, 2023)

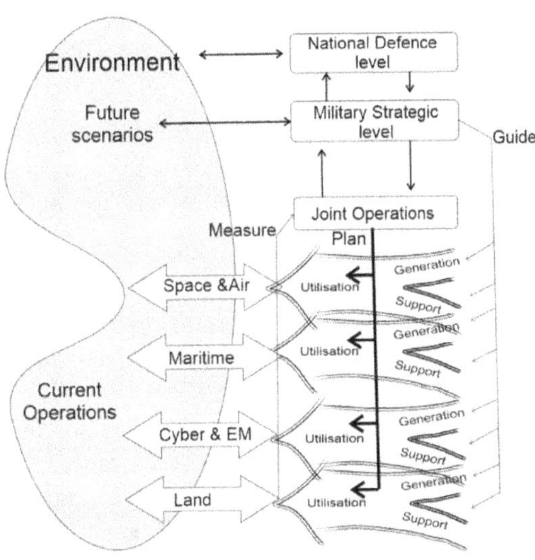

Figure 1: Military Affairs outlined using the Viable System Model

Nevertheless, the above model is not the most feasible or probable way to arrange cyber operations capability within military affairs. Firstly, the socio-technical nature of the cyber environment will impact the arrangements. Secondly, the evolution of military capabilities also introduces power vectors to the evolution of cyber operations. Thirdly, information security creates the foundation for cyber defence and impacts its arrangements.

Since the cyber environment is a Socio-technical system (Pasmore, 1995) and the Internet is also almost an open system, the structure and evolution of cyber operations capability will be defined by the elements: social relations, human cognition, processes, applications and information, machine cognition and hardware. For example, the Russian war against Ukraine has accelerated the use of commercial, cyber-physical devices at the tactical level. Previously, the Armed Forces were slow to adapt to small drones at patrol level. (O'Brien, 2022) Technological development does not solely define the evolution of the cyber environment.

Mattila & Parkinson have studied the evolution of military enterprises using enterprise architecture views and recognise four evolutionary paths for military development (Mattila & Parkinson, 2018):

1. Diversification is typical for newly established capabilities, but gradually, adversaries may drive separate capabilities for more coordinated operations.
2. Coordination seeks combined arms effect and joint operations resource optimisation.
3. Unification happens when unique capabilities are used under the joint task force or command.
4. Replication is critical for generating masses of "citizen armies", and peacetime garrison/base structures prefer replication within the force or branch.

Based on the above evolutionary paths, Cyber operations capability may evolve in military enterprises from diversified units towards coordinated impact and, with sufficient maturity, to unified effects. However, since the omnipresent nature of information technology gave birth to information security and cybersecurity (Lal, 2023), other evolutionary paths are also viable.

Cyber defence operations occur in cyber environments, defined by architecture, controls, network operation, and information security policies. Therefore, the evolution of military information security may have the most decisive impact on defence. The roadmap for military information security (Mattila, 2020) identifies a common evolutionary path from vault/building/site-based mainly physical security to domain-based solutions where connections between sites are encrypted. From domain security, the path proceeds to host-based security, where all actors and their behaviour are monitored. From the host, the path continues towards the service level, currently called the Zero-trust model. The content-based security model is the furthest visible stage. Naturally, the tactical level defence of the cyber environment is differently arranged in each of the above stages.

As a summary, this section outlines a generic model for military affairs, including the cyber dimension, but recognises the volatility of the cyber environment and possible constraints for the design from four viewpoints: 1. constantly evolving, open socio-technical systems; 2. past evolutionary paths for military enterprises defined by strategy, culture, and competencies; and 3. information security strategy and policies of critical cyber environment. The outlined model is projected for different cybersecurity strategies in the next section.

2.3 A Short Analysis of Defence Against Sample Adversarial Strategies

Ultimately, the adversarial resources, capabilities, and intentions define how cyber defence should be arranged. State cyber strategies usually outline the ends, ways, and means for a state to generate and utilise its cyber force. (Eikmeier, 2007). The research chooses three active adversary approaches and analyses their impact on cyber defence (Mattila, 2015):

i. Active defence (NATO), where the actor aims to build a robust domestic cyber environment and does not invest in building offensive cyber capabilities, prefers asymmetric (DIME) counteractions. Defenders benefit from a unified approach over the DIMEFIL dimensions but do not require strong cyber defence capability. (NATO, 2023) (Burton, 2015)
ii. In proactive defence (China), the actor runs a highly controlled and monitored domestic cyber environment. Furthermore, the actor actively exploits and attacks in international and adversary environments as part of joint information operations while staying under the war threshold. Defender faces the race in cyber capabilities and must invest heavily in defensive capabilities. (Baughman & Singer, 2023) (Johnson, 2018) (Saalman, et al., 2022)
iii. In the information war (Iran), the actor exploits the open information space for cognitive impacts and supports information operations with cyber capabilities. Defenders will be manipulated and harassed

until the domestic cyber environment is robust enough. Investment in offensive capabilities may have a systemic effect in conflict situations. (Rubin, 2019) (Erfourth & Bazin, 2020)

The above three scenarios provide the strategic horizon for the research.

3. Research Design

The research approaches the question of "How military affairs should address the generation and utilisation of cyber defence capabilities in the current threat landscape?" from the design science viewpoint since the outcome will be an operation model, i.e., a design of an artificial socio-technical system (Trist, 1981). Hence, the research design follows the sequence of 1. Understanding the problem, 2. Suggesting a tentative design, 3. Developing an artifact, 4. Evaluation performance of the artefact, and 5. Concluding. (Dresch & Anatunes, 2015)

Since the military tends to design the new capability development organisation first (Farrell & Terriff, 2002), the system design approach promotes an alternative toolbox for military transformation planners. The method also aims to show how industrial engineering and management principles can be used in the planning of military socio-technical systems as well as in military-industrial products (Badiru & Thomas, 2009) or health services (Sharma, et al., 2021). The MITRE enterprise system engineering practice (MITRE, 2022) promotes some approaches but does not recognise, for example, the adversarial analysis, evolutionary analysis, or affairs cultural analysis applied in this research.

Naturally, the design science approach has an engineering flavour and may bypass the cognitive and social aspects of the military enterprise system. To compensate for these biases, the research chose Viable system (Espejo, 1990), Military evolution (Mattila, 2020), and Socio-technical system evolution (Trist, 1981) models for the high-level design.

4. Development, Evaluation, and Discussion on Design

Firstly, the section details the cyber affairs model design using the previous sections' tenets, variants, and principal dimensions. Secondly, the section applies the model in analysing the Russia – Ukraine war in 2022. Thirdly, the section assesses the quality and feasibility of the design.

4.1 Detailed Design of Cyber Affairs as Part of Military Enterprise

The Model for Cyber Affairs (CAM) in Figure 2 presents two parties, Blue and Red, in the confrontation in the cyber environment. Red party varies between three sample strategies: Active defence (NATO), Proactive defence (China) and Information Warfare (Iran). Both parties utilise the Internet but also have separate Intranets as part of their Cyberspace. The position of information security in the evolutionary roadmap define mainly the tactical level defensive cyber actions. The combination and complexity of connected cyberspaces define the operational art. The three levels of military affairs culminate in tenets defined in Table 1. The strategic and operational features of the Blue party are categorised in the quad chart, which is composed of Diversified, Coordinated, Replicated, and Unified postures. This version of the model illustrates the cyber value stream through force generation and resource sourcing but excludes sustainment and governance functions for simplification purposes. (Mattila & Parkinson, 2018)

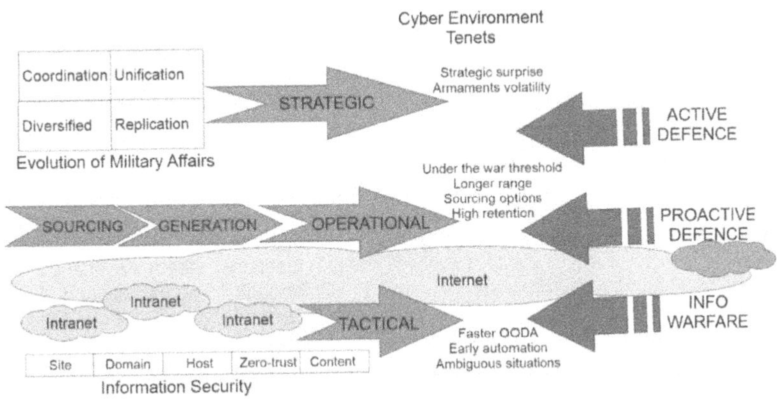

Figure 2: The Model for Cyber Affairs as part of Military Enterprise

The simplification aims to make the model feasible for analysts. Hence, it leaves out other possible strategic postures or variations in confrontation. (Mattila, 2015) It does not include the complexity and dynamics of military enterprise architecture or systems. (Mattila, 2020) Furthermore, the model neglects different sourcing models and their effect on cyber capabilities. (Mattila, 2022) The following step tests how this simplified model works in a complex situation.

4.2 Evaluation of the Cyber Affairs Model Against Observed Data from Russia – Ukraine War

The war between Russia and Ukraine has been ongoing since 2016. However, the 2022 Russian intent to capture the Ukraine capital and replace the democratic regime sets a model for contemporary campaigns where political intent defines military strategy, which is implemented through operations using available military tactical capabilities. (Liddell Hart, 1991) The build-up of the 2022 February offence provided insights into how both parties of war prepared themselves for engagement in the cyber environment and how the offensive proceeded at all three levels of warfare and through four dimensions of tactical engagement. Therefore, the Russo-Ukraine War provides a usable number of data points to test the Cyber Affairs Model.

The confrontation matrix between Ukraine (blue) and Russia (red) in Table 2 illustrates the Cyber Affairs Model in two dimensions: levels of warfare and depth of force value chain. The analysis of confrontation uses the tenets and postures defined in Figure 2. It documents them through the two-dimensional matrix in Table 2 to emphasise the confrontation of two intentions, wills, and capabilities (Oliviero, 2022), often neglected in contemporary cyber operations analysis. The data points are collected from open-source feeds and early analysis published in 2022. (Mattila, A Model for State Cyber Power: Case Study of Russian Behaviour, 2022) (Mattila, Ways to generate a military cyber capability - A review of three countries, 2022)

Table 2: Application example of the Cyber Affairs Model in Russian – Ukraine War during 2022

	UKRAINE		RUSSIA	
	GENERATION OF FORCE	UTILISATION OF FORCE	UTILISATION OF FORCE	GENERATION OF FORCE
Strategic	Sourcing of competencies and security services internationally. Information security-based preparedness.	Active Defence Strategy at best: • Passive risk-averse security preparations • Relying on tactical-level partner support • Finally, successful defence is achieved by ad-hoc creativity and coordinated cooperation.	Proactive Defence Strategy: • Strategic shock during the first attack • Terrorising society with info and cyber operations • Breaking trust between government and population with cyber and kinetic operations against critical infrastructure.	FSB and GRU force generation since 2003. Source competencies from private and criminal business. Exploit cyber criminals created open armament and weaponised vulnerabilities.
Opera-tional	Cyber competency sourcing from partners. Quick employment of Cyber Army. Preparations to move critical assets to global clouds.	• Diversified and domain-based reactive cyber defence. • Transfer of critical assets to more protected cloud services. • Use no-trust Internet with global support.	• Coordinated all-domain operations in the beginning. • Afterwards, some planned joint information and kinetic operations. • Later, mainly diversified cyberattack efforts.	Government competition and variety in sourcing end up with sub-optimised resource utilisation at national and battlefield levels.
Tactical	U.S. DoD and Microsoft technical and tactical support. Crowd-sourced information operations and cyber harassment.	Cyber defence is defined by information security based on domain boundaries and host-based monitoring.	Site- or domain-based information security exposes its cyber environment to harassment, but societal functions seem resilient enough to sustain it long-term.	The mass flee of international-level cyber competency may have impacted defensive and offensive capabilities.

The VSM model includes four central systems and their cooperation (Jackson, 2019). The levels of warfare comply with three of them, leaving the audit or lessons identified system out. The lack of inside data prevents the analysis of viability within each system. However, some cooperation features between vertical (strategic-operational-tactical) and horizontal (generate–utilise) systems can be concluded based on impact data and, therefore, test the viability of the CAM. (Schwaninger & Scheef, 2016) The Russian strategic intentions seem to guide their cyber force generation well, enabling tactical capabilities and linking to force utilisation to achieve strategic surprise and operational shock at the beginning of the offensive. The model also explains the emerging friction between vertical Russian systems when the tactical level failed in the first offensive. However, the strategic level pushed the tactical level for more effort without impacting the operational level.

4.3 Discussion on the Quality and Feasibility of the CAM

The three vertical levels (strategic, operational, and tactical) and three steps in horizontal depth (sourcing, generation, and utilisation) perception in military confrontation provide enough VSM viewpoints for cyber affairs analysis. The two-dimensional CAM improves the thinking behind current tactical-level cybersecurity and risk management standards (NIST, 2018). Furthermore, the CAM may elaborate some national cybersecurity policy approaches that focus narrowly on risk avoidance, compliance, and governance viewpoints. (NSA of Finland, 2021) (NCA KSA, 2018) Naturally, the CAM elaborates on the current event, incident and reactive approach widely provided in the contemporary cybersecurity consultation market (Aiyer, et al., 2022) with operational art and strategic analysis. The CAM may mitigate the challenges the U.S. DoD experienced in fighting against ISIS, and other insurgent groups between 2015 – 2022. (Carter, 2017) Finally, the CAM includes event- and presence-based cyber operations but establishes a broader context for the approach presented by Daniel Moore (Moore, 2022).

The CAM does not capture the differences between NATO's and Russia's thinking on cyber capabilities and their utilisation. NATO perceives cyber as one of the four tactical level dimensions, and the U.K. even pairs it with electronic warfare. However, Russia's operational art sees cyber as a technical multiplier of Information Operations Effects directly supporting their cognitive level warfare. Despite the two dimensions, the art of operation is missed when using the CAM unless this insight guides the analysis.

The CAM helps to illustrate and analyse the challenges in sourcing competent cyber forces, which drive towards different force generation approaches compared to air, land, or maritime domains. The cyber force sourcing variations Ukraine and Russia have used during the ongoing war should open the traditional defence planners' thinking.

5. Conclusions

From the military affairs viewpoint, there is a wide gap between security controls and strategy. Hence, an analysis model is needed to cover all vertical levels of warfare and essential horizontal dimensions of military affairs. Meanwhile, the cyber environment differs from other military domains, so traditional power and engagement models do not necessarily apply to the cyber domain. The paper aims to design a framework and an operation model to support military analysis of the fast-evolving technical competition, information contest, and state-level conflict in Cyberspace.

The paper designs the Cyber Affairs Model (CAM). The paper applies the model in one use case to assess the model's viability. The CAM provides a confrontational operational view to define the story and a matrix to capture the analysis. Based on the test case, the CAM opens the cyber operations thinking, fills the gap between strategies and security controls, and closes the guidance loop between strategic, operational, and tactical levels, which is sometimes missed in national security strategies.

The Cyber Affairs Model provides a framework for strategic analysis and planning concerning state and military-level engagement in the cyber environment. It may reveal significant gaps in existing strategies and help prepare more systematic approaches for future competition or clashes of national interests.

The Cyber Affairs Model presented in this paper leaves out many dimensions from state-level confrontation, provides only a few samples of possible strategies, illustrates military affairs in one snapshot, neglects the evolution and dynamics of the system, and simplifies the model to gain more usability.

Further research should test the model's viability with other case studies, including varying strategies, art of operation, and tactical capabilities. The falsification of the model remains thin in this paper, so further testing should improve the existing approach. The model could use more extensive testing with a higher number of strategic analysts to improve its usability.

References

Aiyer, B., Caso, J., Russell, P., & Sorel, M. (2022). New survey reveals $2 trillion market opportunity for cybersecurity technology and service providers. McKinsey & Company.

Annenko, O. (2022, April 01). 12 New Application Integration Statistics and Trends for 2022. Retrieved from elastic.io: https://www.elastic.io/enterprise-application-integration/application-integration-statistics/

Badiru, A. B., & Thomas, M. U. (2009). Handbook of Military industrial engineering. Boca Raton: CRC Press.

Baughman, J., & Singer, P. W. (2023, April 7). China gears up for cognitive warfare. Defense One.

Burton, J. (2015). NATO's cyber defence: strategic challenges and institutional adaptation. Defence Studies.

Carter, A. (2017). A Lasting Defeat: The Campaign to Destroy ISIS. Cambridge: The Belfer Center.

Ciepiela, P., & Venkateshwaran, B. V. (2017). Evolution of Cyber Threats and the Development of New Security Architecture. 22nd World Petroleum Congress. Istanbul: World Petroleum Council.

Clarke, R. A., & Knake, R. K. (2010). Cyber war. New York: HarperCollins.

Clarke, R. A., & Knake, R. K. (2019). The fifth domain: Defending Our Country, Our Companies, and Ourselves in the Age of Cyber Threats. London: Penguin Press.

Clausewitz, C. v. (1984). On War. (M. Howard, & P. Paret, Trans.) Princeton: Princeton University Press.

Creveld, M. v. (1987). Command in War (Revised ed.). Harvard University Press.

CSIS. (2019). Advanced Modernisation and Preparation for War: Informatized Warfare, New Force Elements, Cyber, Space, Logistics. Center for Strategic and International Studies.

Dahlqvist, F., Patel, M., Rajko, A., & Schulman, J. (2019, July 22). Growing opportunities in the Internet of Things. Retrieved from McKinsey & Company: https://www.mckinsey.com/industries/private-equity-and-principal-investors/our-insights/growing-opportunities-in-the-internet-of-things

Despont, C. (2022). Understanding CapabilityBased Planning. CSS Analyses in Security Policy, 1-4. Retrieved from https://css.ethz.ch/content/dam/ethz/special-interest/gess/cis/center-for-securities-studies/pdfs/CSSAnalyse298-EN.pdf

Dresch, A., & Anatunes, J. (2015). Design science research. Geneve: Springer International Publishing.

Drinhausen, K., & Legarda, H. (2022). Confident paranoia: Xi's "comprehensive national security" framework shapes China's behavior at home and abroad. Berlin: Mercator Institute for China Studies.

Eikmeier, D. C. (2007). A logical method for center of gravity analysis. Military Review, 62-66.

Erfourth, M., & Bazin, A. (2020). The Iranian Pursuit of Military Advantage: A Forecast for the Next Seven Years. Mad Scientist Laboratory. Retrieved from https://madsciblog.tradoc.army.mil/241-the-iranian-pursuit-of-military-advantage-a-forecast-for-the-next-seven-years/

Espejo, R. (1990). The Viable System Model. Systemic Practice and Action Research 3(3), 219-221. Retrieved from https://www.researchgate.net/publication/225863384_The_Viable_System_Model

Farrell, T., & Terriff, T. (2002). The sources of military change: Culture, politics, technology. Boulder: Lynne Rienner.

Fernandes, T., & Ackerson, D. (2022, June 02). 5 Ways to Run Faster CI/CD Builds. Retrieved from Semaphore: https://semaphoreci.com/blog/run-faster-ci-cd-builds

Forrester. (2019). Why Faster Refresh Cycles And Modern Infrastructure Management Are Critical To Business Success. Forrester Consulting.

Friedman, B. A. (2017). On Tactics: A Theory of Victory in Battle. Annapolis: Naval Institute Press.

Gambrell, J. (2018). Iran deploys 'halal' Internet in latest bid to rein in citizens' web freedoms. Independent.

Gayde, A., & Neuhaus, J. (2020, August 12). Five critical data source considerations for adversary attribution. Retrieved from NISOS - Managed Intelligence company: https://www.nisos.com/blog/5-adversary-attribution-tips/

Gilles, K. (2017). Assessing Russia's reorganised and rearmed military. Washington, DC: Carnegie. Retrieved from https://carnegieendowment.org/2017/05/03/assessing-russia-s-reorganized-and-rearmed-military-pub-69853

Hofstede, G., Hofstede, G. J., & Minkov, M. (2010). Cultures and Organisations: Software of the Mind. 3rd Edition. McGraw-Hill.

Jackson, M. C. (2019). Critical Systems Thinking and the Management of Complexity. Wiley.

Johnson, J. S. (2018). China's vision of the future is network-centric. Comparative Strategy, 373-390.

Kaldor, M. (2012). New and Old Wars 3.Ed. Cambridge: Polity Press.

Lal, A. (2023, August 14). The Evolution Of Cybersecurity And How Businesses Can Prepare For The Future. Retrieved from Forbes: https://www.forbes.com/sites/forbesbusinesscouncil/2023/08/14/the-evolution-of-cybersecurity-and-how-businesses-can-prepare-for-the-future/

Libicki, M. C. (2009). Why the Purpose of the Original Cyberattack Matters. In M. C. Libicki, Cyberdeterrence and Cyberwar (pp. 75-89). Santa Monica: RAND Corporation.

Liddell Hart, B. H. (1991). Strategy, 2nd Revision. London: Plume.

Malwarebytes. (2024). What are Petya and NotPetya ransomware? Retrieved from Malwarebytes: https://www.malwarebytes.com/petya-and-notpetya

Mattila, J. K. (2015). Protecting national assets against Information Operations in Post-modern world. 2nd BCS International I.T. conference. Abu Dhabi.

Mattila, J. K. (2020). Engaging a Moving Organisation - Modelling a military enterprise with architecture tools. Helsinki: Aalto University. doi:10.13140/RG.2.2.10167.85927

Mattila, J. K. (2022). A Model for State Cyber Power: Case Study of Russian Behaviour. In T. Eze, N. Khan, & C. Onwubiko, Proceedings of the 21st European Conference on Cyber Warfare and Security (pp. 188-197). Reading, U.K.: Academic Conferences International Ltd.

Mattila, J. K. (2022). Ways to generate a military cyber capability - A review of three countries. In C. Fachada, C. Gil, & R. Marreiros, Conference of the International Society of Military Sciences 2022 - Book of Abstracts (pp. 81-82). Lisbon: Military University Institute of Portugal.

Mattila, J. K., & Parkinson, S. (2018). Quo Vadis, Militare? Evolution of Military Affairs from a Business Architecture Viewpoint. Kungliga Krigsvetenskapsakademien Hanglingar och Tidskrift, 151-172.

MITRE. (2022, April 28). Enterprise engineering. Retrieved from MITRE Publications: https://www.mitre.org/publications/systems-engineering-guide/enterprise-engineering

MITRE. (2023, December). MITRE ATT&CK. Retrieved from https://attack.mitre.org/

Moore, D. (2022). Offensive Cyber Operations. London: Hurst & Company.

NATO. (2019, February 12). North Atlantic Treaty Organization. Retrieved from New NATO hub will gather the Alliance's cyber defenders: https://www.nato.int/cps/en/natolive/news_163358.htm

NATO. (2021, November 4). REQUEST FOR INNOVATIVE PARTICIPATION (RFIP). Retrieved from Countering Cognitive Warfare: https://www.act.nato.int/wp-content/uploads/2023/05/rfip021109_amdt1.pdf

NATO. (2023, September 14). Cyber defence. Retrieved from https://www.nato.int/cps/en/natohq/topics_78170.htm

NATO. (2023, October 5). Multi-Domain operations in NATO - Explained. Retrieved from https://www.act.nato.int/article/mdo-in-nato-explained/

NCA KSA. (2018). Essential Cybersecurity Controls – 1. Riyadh: National Cybersecurity Authority of KSA.

NIST. (2018). Framework for Improving Critical Infrastructure Cybersecurity 1.1. National Institute of Standards and Technology .

NSA of Finland. (2021). Information Security Audit Tool. Helsinki: Traficom publication series.

O'Brien, P. P. (2022). The Future of American Warfare Is Unfolding in Ukraine. The Atlantic.

Oliviero, C. S. (2022). Strategia - A primer on theory and strategy for students of war. Toronto: Double Dagger Books.

Pasmore, W. (1995). Social science transformed - the socio-technical perspective. Human Relations, 48(1), 1-21.

Rios, J. P. (2012). Design and Diagnosis for Sustainable Organisations: The Viable System Method. Verlag: Springer.

Rubin, M. (2019, Agust 08). Iran's Military Is Making Strides into Twenty-first Century Technology. Retrieved from American Enterprise Institute: https://www.aei.org/articles/irans-military-twenty-first-century-technology/

Saalman, L., Su, F., & Dovgal, L. S. (2022). Cyber posture trends in China, Russia, The United States and the European Union. Solna: Stockholm International Pease Reserach Institute.

Schwaninger, M., & Scheef, C. (2016). A Test of the Viable System Model: Theoretical Claim vs. Empirical Evidence. Cybernetics and Systems. doi:10.1080/01969722.2016.1209375

Scwaninger, M. (2006). Design for viable organisations. Kybernetes, 955-966. Retrieved from https://www.alexandria.unisg.ch/31940/1/Design%20for%20Viable%20Organizations_06.pdf

Sharma, G., Prasan, C., & Srinivasa Rao, M. (2021). Industrial engineering into healthcare – A comprehensive review. International Journal of Healthcare Management, 1288-1302.

Smith, R. (2005). The Utility of Force: The Art of War in the Modern World. London: Allen Lane.

Sun, T. (2014). The Art of War: Illustrated Edition. Fall River.

Tidjon, L. N., Frappier, M., & Mammar, A. (2019). Intrusion Detection Systems: A Cross-Domain Overview. IEEE Communications Surveys & Tutorials, vol 21, 3639-3681.

Traore, Y. (2017, November 17). The utility of military force. Retrieved from War Room online journal: https://warroom.armywarcollege.edu/articles/utility-military-force/

Trist, E. (1981). The evolution of socio-technical systems. Perspectives on Organisational Design and Behaviour(August).

U.S. Army. (2010, July 19). Army force generation. Retrieved from U.S. Army: https://www.army.mil/article/42519/army_force_generation

U.S. DoD. (2023). DOD Directive 7045.20 Capability Portfolio Management. Office of the Under Secretary of Defense for Acquisition and Sustainment .

Vaishnavi, M., & Vineet, K. (2023, July). Operational Technologies Market 2023 - 2032. Retrieved from Allied Market Research: https://www.alliedmarketresearch.com/operational-technologies-market-A136138

Wiki. (2024). Wikipedia. Retrieved from Russian_invasion_of_Ukraine: https://en.wikipedia.org/wiki/Russian_invasion_of_Ukraine

Wikipedia. (2023, December 07). Cyberspace. Retrieved from https://en.wikipedia.org/wiki/Cyberspace

Zhao, P. (2023). Chinese Political Warfare: A Strategic Tautology? The Three Warfares and the Centrality of Political Warfare within Chinese Strategy. The Strategy Bridge.

Risk Assessment for Malware Attacks in Small Businesses

Tabisa Ncubukezi
Information Technology Department, Faculty of Informatics and Design
Cape Peninsula University of Technology, Cape Town, South Africa
Ncubukezit@cput.ac.za

Abstract: The presence of severe malware attacks in business systems compromise devices, data, information, and network hygiene. The increased usage of cyberspace as a convenient tool exposed all organisations to various malware attacks. The malware attacks have become one of the most common threats in all sectors. These attacks often find their way into systems where poor or inadequate security measures are implemented and leaving institution's resources vulnerable, and compromised. Data used in this work was collected using purposive sampling from the selected small businesses that used cyberspace for business transactions. A questionnaire distributed to the participants was mounted on Google Forms. To analyse the collected data, this work performed the risk assessment of the malware attacks and used the risk management processes to determine the risk impact and risk probability. Risk management processes were used to analyse and interpret different risks associated with malware attacks and also ranked them from low, medium, and high. The work also revealed the different forms of common malware attacks, business assets affected, and main causes of malware attacks, risk value, risk likelihood and the risk impact. The extent of security measures implemented on different levels contributes to the overall state of the organisational resources. The study also shared the recommendations and accounted for the conclusion.

Keywords: Cybersecurity Risks, Cyber Threats, Malware Attacks, Risk Assessment, Risk Causes, Risk Probability, Risk Impact, Small Businesses

1. Introduction

The increased use of the network has equally increased the existence of the malware attacks. These attacks present malicious software that spreads on computer systems with the aim of corrupting and deleting stored information and files. At times, malware attacks result to sudden system crashes (Kumhar, Kewat, & Kumar, 2022). Mostly, networked and standalone computers can be affected by a range of malware attacks due to the unannounced destructive behaviour that usually alter and highjack computer operations (Kirwan & Power, 2012). There are quite a number of malware attacks ranging from viruses, Trojan, spyware, adware, and dialler (Singh, Singh, & Joseph, 2008). Collectively, the pervasive malware attacks intrude into the business systems to gain unauthorised access for the purpose of stealing, deleting, and corrupting data or devices (Shukla et al., 2022). Malware also installs new programs and disrupt business operations (Aslam et al., 2023, Ibrahim, 2022). Even though malware can mostly penetrate through the networked systems, sometimes it can also be internally generated through the stand alone device due to employee actions (Brewer, 2016; Yuan & Wu, 2021).

For example, ignorant activities and actions caused illiterate personnel on the systems can pose as an entry point for malware attacks. In addition, minimal enforcement of the cybersecurity rules and guidelines which included adherence to the rules influences the personnel decision making process (Ncubukezi, 2022). An uninformed decision-making by network users become a loophole in business sector (Fortuin, 2021). Poor adherence to cybersecurity policies and guidelines can lead network users or employees of the business organisation to access convenient websites with an intention to explore free available software from illegitimate sources (Ncubukezi & Mwansa, 2021). Sometimes, people download information from the website with beautiful user interface. This action can grant an opportunity for criminals to deploy their advanced strategies to gain unauthorised access into the business system with private and sensitive data (Ncubukezi, 2022).

Literature indicates that malware attacks have been the main strategy used to penetrate small businesses, leaving them highly vulnerable (Osborn, 2015). Malware attacks have increases due to the sudden Covid19 pandemic which caught many unprepared businesses. Thus, the small business sector has become the primary target for cybercriminals (Ncubukezi, 2021). The deployment of the malware attacks pose a risk within the small business sector. These risk range from dented business reputation, loss of customer trust, decreased revenues as well as delayed business growth (Ncubukezi, 2023).

This study performs risk assessment for malware attacks in the business space. To achieve this, the study:

- Determines the common malware attacks that small business sector experiences
- Use risk management processes to determine the risk impact and risk probability
- Performs qualitative and quantitative risk assessment to analyse and rank malware risks

The rest of this research paper is arranged as follows. Section 2 presents different malware attacks followed by and malware risks. Section 3 presents malware risk assessment, the results and lastly, the study concludes with the main highlights.

2. Malware Attacks

Malware attacks also known as the malicious attacks are a form of cyberattacks that penetrates the system through unauthorised access (Talukder & Talukder, 2020). The malware attacks usually freeze or lock the devices, or sometimes steal, delete information to disrupt the activities performed on the system (Ncubukezi, 2022). Most deadly cyber threats and attacks including malware attacks occurred during the Covid-19 global pandemic. With the increased use of the cyberspace, small businesses become vulnerable to the common malware threats ranging from viruses, Trojan horse, key loggers, spyware, rootkits, adware, worms, bots, ransomware and mobile malware (Ngo et al., 2020). Standalone computers and networked computers become the main agents and entry points for malware attacks (Brewer, 2016).

Malware attacks can gain unauthorised access through planned or unplanned actions. Within the small business sector, people use the external drives on standalone devices to share files and folders on the stand alone computers (Dearman & Pierce, 2008). On the contrary, employees carelessly access unknown websites on the networked systems or ignorantly click on links to download software while processing business transactions (Ncubukezi, 2022). Moreover, the disruptive pop up messages disturbs network users. Malware attacks have been a big problem in the small business sector. As a result, all the actions and activities performed on the unsecured business system yield to risks relating to loss, stealing and deletion of the information that could cost millions to recover. The following section presents risks associated with malware attacks.

2.1 Risks Associated with Malware Attacks

Among other institutions, the small business sector has become victims of the planned and unplanned actions of the network users (legitimate and cybercriminals) (Minnaar, 2014). For example, legitimate users usually use the different external hard drives that could potentially harm the entire business. These actions become insider generated. On the contrary, informed or uninformed users would access the network through unsecured network interfaces to accidentally install the infected installation package of the illegitimate program available on the site to trick uninformed users (Ncubukezi, 2023). Some users become the channel of the malware attacks owing to quick and easy access to the free and infected software packages on the Internet. The criminals on the network use and deploy malware on the business systems and devices (Millaire, Sathe & Thielen, 2015). The less skilled people who access less protected web pages become extremely dangerous for the business and are difficult to mitigate. As a result, ignorant users download and install software from unverified sources (Kobis, 2021). The risks of malware attacks affect the network level, systems and applications, personnel and related sensitive and private information. As results some organisations become victims of malware attacks that are linked to the ransomware. The attacks generally impact all institutions negatively, as their primary aim is to gain unauthorised access to valuable and sensitive information and systems to corrupt and damage the operations.

2.2 Impact of Malware Attacks

The global Covid19 era and beyond revealed a significant increase of cyber related risks and attacks which directly impacts the operations of the businesses. Moreover, the impact these severe and replicable attacks affect overall business continuity and client trust. Even though cybersecurity should be prioritised by all institutions, there are still organisations that do not pay much attention on the safety and security of information which exposes different levels of the businesses (Ncubukezi, 2023). This becomes an entry point for a range attacks, gaining unauthorised access to unsecured networked devices as well as standalone devices. Business resources become vulnerable to a diverse range of attacks including disruptive and persuasive malware attacks which results to major loss or theft of private and sensitive information (Bello & Maurushat, 2020). In addition, malware results in data leakage (Alexei & Alexei, 2021). At times, the attackers would be after corruption or deletion of data as well as the identity theft (Chopra, Marwaha, & Sharma, 2022).

Some services get interrupted as results of the denial of service leading to freezing of certain business divisions. The unexpected restriction negatively impacts the small business sectors as they also lose their reputation due to the delayed delivery of services. Less secured businesses become victims of the malware attacks due to minimal on no training offered to the system users or the authorised third parties that equally have access to the system (Sharif et al., 2016). In such cases, proper awareness education and training becomes crucial. The awareness training as a strategy improves privacy and safety of all the elements of the business. When system users are well oriented, the practice gets implemented smoothly to minimise and reduce all malware risks. This practice improves the lifespan of all the business departments, systems and resources.

The amount of cybersecurity risks associated with diverse malware attacks requires some assessment. It is therefore necessary to perform qualitative and quantitative malware risk assessment for the small business sector. The application of the malware risk assessment is presented below.

3. Research Method

The rise on the usage of the networked environments has increased several attacks in different institutions and organisations, including malware attacks. This work performed the risk assessment for malware attacks in small businesses. This section presents the research method used to carry out the study.

Sampling and participant selection criteria: To achieve the main aim, this research used purposive sampling to collected data from the sample of fifteen (15) small businesses. These businesses use cyberspace for their business operations and daily business activities. The study selected businesses generate annual turnover of less than three hundred thousand R300 000 per annum.

Data collection: Businesses were contacted via emails and those that responded were sent a link of the qualitative questionnaire mounted in Google Forms to collect data.

Application of risk assessment: The collected data was then analysed using the risk assessment approach. This work performed the qualitative and quantitative risk assessment of the malware attacks. The risk assessment process is used to identify the major hazards of the collected risks to determine the likelihood and the impact of the malware risk. The selected approach is explained and applied on section 3.2.

Ethical considerations: This work followed the university ethical clearance process to protect the research participants and the researcher. This process demonstrates that the researcher adhered to the ethical standards.

3.1 Determination of Malware Risks

A total of ten (10) malware risks were identified as shown on table 1. The common types of malware attacks experienced by the small business sector ranges from viruses, worms, bot, mobile malware, ransomware, adware, rootkits, key loggers, rootkits and Trojan horse. These attacks are shown on Figure 1. The attacks pose a risk to the business sector and the risks can be categorised according to their impact.

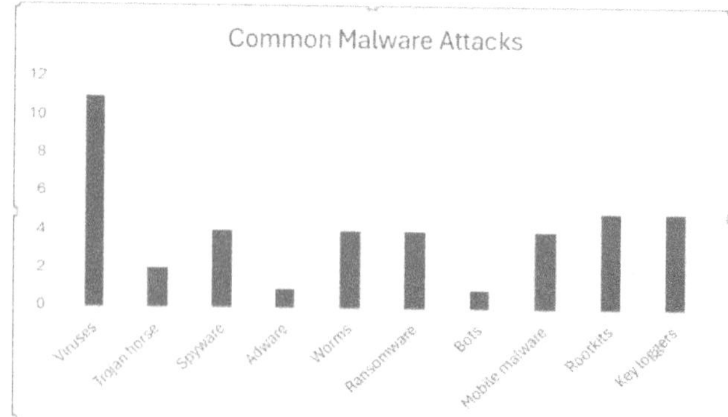

Figure 1: Common Malware attacks

3.2 Application of Risk Assessment

The study performed the malware risk identification by classifying the common malware risks in order to identify the source of the risk. Each risk is allocated a unique reference and a risk code used for the risk matrix and which gets stored on the risk registry (Nasir, Naderi & Momeni, 2020). Identifying malware risks promotes understanding of the nature of the possible risks yielding either a positive or negative impact. This process assists to determine potential risks and is performed before conducting a qualitative and quantitative risk assessment to develop the risk register to analyse, prioritise and monitor risks. Table 1 shows the risk number, risk, given risk code and the corresponding risk cause. Table 1 shows the ranking of the malware related experiences.

Table 1: Ranking of the malware risks

Risk #	Risk	Risk code	Cause
1	Outdated antivirus and antispyware	OAnti	Easiest gateway for cybercriminals, loss of data caused by software failures and no software compatibility
2	Unauthorised access to software	UAccSof	Poor guideline compliance, malware, criminals, employee ignorance
3	Use of USB	UUSB	Criminals, inside attempts, lack of guidelines
4	Viruses, worms, and Trojan	Mal	Malfunctioning of the network, data loss, financial loss
5	Accidental installation of unsecured applications	AccInst	Phishing, malware
6	Denial of service and network downtime	DoS	Prolonged network performance when opening files or accessing websites, unavailable websites, or unable to access any website.
7	Hardware and software failure	HSwaFai	Old hardware equipment and obsolete software, phishing
8	Stolen typed information	Klg	Recording of typed information
9	Disrupted services	Wrm	Spreading of the malware on the network
10	Excess operations	Bt	Repetitive automated services

3.3 Malware Risk Assessment

To determine the risk matrix, this work employed the qualitative and quantitative risk techniques to describe the likelihood of malware attacks and their impact in small businesses. The qualitative risk assessment of the malware attacks uses the risk probability and impact. The risk assessment is based on the basic measure that determines the risk probability and the consequence assessment using the following elements: scale, probability, time, cost and scope. The scale presents the risk rating for the risk probabilities, time of occurrence, amount caused by the risk and its impact. For example, if the likelihood of the risk occurrence is high, it is very high for every risk. Similarly, if the risk occurs more frequently, then the risk is also very high. So, every possibility of risk is assigned costs and the frequency at which the risk occurs to determine the rating of the risk impact. Table 3 presents the risk probability and impact assessment applied.

Table 2: Risk probability and impact assessment (Ncubukezi, 2023)

Scale	Probability	Time	Cost	Scope
Very high	>75%	>4 months	900K – 1M	Severe Impact
High	55-74%	1-3 months	500K-899K	Major impact on business functions
Medium	30-54%	2-4 weeks	300K-499K	Impact on the key business areas
Low	11-29%	1-2 weeks	100K-299K	Low impact on business operations
Very low	1-10%	6 days	0K-99K	Minor impact on business operations

After developing a common measure for risk probability and impact assessment, the following section unpacks the use of the risk impact technique as applied on malware risks.

3.4 Use of the Risk Impact Technique

The impact analysis is essential to produce a recovery plan focusing on identifying the potential cyberrisks and their probability of occurrence. The impact analysis describes a particular cyberrisk cause, threat occurrence and severity of the impact on the business system, providing information on how each cyberrisk can be treated (Radanliev et al., 2018). In the business system, a cyberattack can temporarily interrupt the business service, resulting in a single point of failure or an entire business system failure. Thus, estimating the impact of potential cyber threats on assets is essential.

Table 4 shows the impact values, the impact ratings, their description and the related cost. The impact values range from 0.1 for a negligible rating to 1.0 for a high rating. The impact ratings range from 1 for a minor impact to 5 for a high impact. The ratings determine the impact of the risks according to their severity. The lower the impact value, the safer the business and the higher the impact value, the more it can become dangerous to the business. Each impact rating has a descriptive statement that explains the consequence and the related cost of the impact to the budget.

Table 3: Definitions of impact values

Impact value	Impact rating	Rating	Description	Cost
0.1	Negligible	1	Threats have no harm	Does not affect budget
0.3	Minor	2	Threats are acceptable	< 15% more on budget
0.5	Moderate	3	Threats exist which can expose the business to risks	16-25% more on the budget
0.7	Major	4	The threat exists and needs remedial actions	26-35% more on the budget
1.0	Severe	5	Urgent threat to the organisation exists	>36% more on the budget

The following section clarifies the risk likelihood values in order to evaluate the probability and impact analysis.

3.5 Probability Estimation Technique

When conducting the probability and impact analysis, the risk likelihood values are essential for presenting the cyber risk matrix. The probability of the risks is presented concerning the risk likelihood rating, with the quantitative likelihood rating values and their description. Table 5 shows the risk likelihood ranging from rare, unlikely to happen, moderate likelihood of occurring and certain to happen. All these qualitative likelihood values are assigned the quantitative values, which are the ratings from 1 to 5 and the likelihood score from 3% to 100%. In addition, the table also shows the description of the likelihood rating and its criteria concerning the negative effect on the business system, which exposes the systems, information, assets and personnel. Therefore, the description shows the level of vulnerability of the business.

Table 4: Risk probability values (Ncubukezi, 2023)

Qualitative values	Quantitative values		Description and the criteria
Likelihood	Rating	Score	
Rare	1	3%	Vulnerability is not a concern.
			Security controls are implemented
Unlikely to happen	2	4-20%	Vulnerability could have **limited effects** on the business
			The effectiveness of the measures could be improved
Moderate chance	3	21-50%	Vulnerability might cause **minor financial loss**
			Relevant security controls are partially implemented but somewhat effective.
Likely to happen	4	51-79%	Vulnerability could severely affect the business system's operation
			Relevant security controls are planned but not effectively implemented
Certain to happen	5	80-100%	Vulnerability is exploitable, resulting in **multiple effects** on the business system
			No security measure could be identified.

After clearly describing the risk impact and likelihood, the researcher conducted the risk probability and impact analysis.

3.6 Risk Consequence and Scoring

Table 6 shows the qualitative values, quantitative values and the risk consequence. The qualitative risk likelihood values are rare, unlikely to happen, moderate chance of occurring, more than likely to happen to certain to happen. The quantitative values have the risk rating and the score. The rating is between 1 and 5 and the corresponding risk score is from 3% to 100%. The risk consequence has values from 1 to 5, where its values carry a risk description which is negligible, minor, moderate, major and severe.

Table 5: Risk likelihood, rating, score and the risk consequences

Qualitative values	Quantitative values		Risk consequence	
Likelihood	Rating	Score	Value	Description
Rare	1	3%	1	Negligible
Unlikely to happen	2	4-20%	2	Minor
Moderate	3	21-50%	3	Moderate
Likely to happen	4	51-79%	4	Major
Certain to happen	5	80-100%	5	Severe

Table 7 shows the risk scoring and the criteria used to calculate the final risk rating based on the risk consequence multiplied by the risk probability. When the output of the risk consequence and the probability amounts to a range of 1 to 5, the risk scoring becomes 1 and the final risk rating becomes minor. At the same time, if the risk consequence and probability falls into the 6 to 10 range, then the scoring is 2 and the final scoring becomes low. So, for every risk consequence multiplied by the probability, there is a corresponding risk score and final risk rating as shown in Table 7.

Table 6: Risk scoring (Ncubukezi, 2023)

Consequence*Probability	Risk scoring	Risk rating
1-5	1	Negligible
6-10	2	Minor
11-15	3	Moderate
16-20	4	Major

3.7 Malware Risk Values

Table 8 presents risks posed by malware attacks on the business system based on the risk probability and the risk impact as defined in Table 5 and Table 6 in order to calculate the final malware risk score. The criteria to determine the final risk score is defined in Table 7. According to the description, the lower risk consequence and likelihood presents lower risk scoring and lower risk rating. The higher consequence and likelihood range and the risk score pose a higher risk rating. These descriptions determine the urgency to address the risk.

Table 7: Malware risk probability, impact and value

Risk category	Risk item	Probability	Impact	Risk value	Risk score
Malware Risks	Unauthorised access	3	4	12	Moderate
	Stolen typed information	4	4	16	Major
	Disrupted services	4	4	16	Major
	Excess operations	4	4	16	Major
	Outdated antivirus and antispyware	4	3	12	Moderate

Risk category	Risk item	Probability	Impact	Risk value	Risk score
	Malware (viruses, worms, Trojan)	4	4	16	Major
	Accidental installation of unsecured applications	4	4	16	Major
	Denial of service and network downtime	3	3	9	Minor
	Hardware and software failure	2	2	4	Negligible
	Use of USB	4	3	12	Moderate

The following section presents the summary of the malware attacks

3.8 Summary of the Malware Attacks

This study highlighted various malware attacks, affected business assets, risk cause, risk impact and the risk likelihood that different business sectors experience. As presented and shown on Table 9, there are different forms of malware yield to various risks. These attacks affect different assets of the business system such as the network, devices, websites, emails, systems and the range of application used for daily business operations. Malware attacks pose a danger to business assets (people and resources), and its operations.

Table 8: Description of collected cyber risks

	Malware	Affected Asset	Risk cause	Risk likelihood	Risk impact
Malware Attacks	• Viruses • Trojan horse • Spyware • Adware • Worms • Ransomware • Bots • Mobile malware • Rootkits • Key loggers	• Network • Networked or standalone devices • Websites • Emails • Systems • Applications	• Human errors • Unsecured networked systems • Lack of cybersecurity policies, rules, procedures and guidelines • Poor enforcement and adherence of guidelines • Improper security architecture	• Malfunctioning of all device (servers, computers, systems, applications and other devices) • Unexpected system and network failure • Limited or no access to resources • Compromised system and information security, privacy and safety lead to data breaches	• Identity and private information theft. • Deletion, theft and corruption of data. • Denial of service • Fraud – freeze access until payment is made • Captures private information • Loss of reputation • Disruption of services and processes

Recommendations: Business institutions should prioritise the safety and security of their resources at large. The increased use of the cyberspace requires businesses to improve and maintain their security measures. Businesses should strengthen and equip their human resources in order to enforce the relevant rules, policies, guidelines and procedures when working on the business systems. This will promote the use of secure systems and improved interaction on the system. Highly secured systems bring trust to the clients.

4. Conclusion

This study presented the malware attacks and their risk likelihood and impact in businesses. The work showed that the malicious software harms the business systems in many ways. These include the locked devices without the user knowledge, unusable files, applications or other systems. When malware attacks gain unauthorised access into the systems, the software steals information, delete private or encrypted data as well as damage systems or devices on the network. In addition, the software deployed by cybercriminals disrupts and damage the business services, devices and systems. The criminals use different strategies to deploy the malicious software in the business network. At times, malware can be internally-generated.

The risks caused by the malicious software in businesses results to slow computers, unusual installed programs, and disruptive pop up messages, device or system failures, and interrupted operations. These actions result into loss, theft or deletion of private and sensitive data that would require remedial actions that costs money. In future, artificial intelligence can be used to simulate and predict the risk likelihood and the risk impact of the malware attacks in businesses. Different tools can also be used to analyse the attacks.

References

Alexei, L.A. and Alexei, A., 2021. Cyber security threat analysis in higher education institutions as a result of distance learning. *International Journal of Scientific & Technology Research*, 10(3): 129–133.

Aslan, Ö., Aktuğ, S.S., Ozkan-Okay, M., Yilmaz, A.A. and Akin, E., 2023. A comprehensive review of cyber security vulnerabilities, threats, attacks, and solutions. *Electronics, 12*(6), pp.1333.

Bello, A. and Maurushat, A., 2020. Technical and behavioural training and awareness solutions for mitigating ransomware attacks. In *Applied Informatics and Cybernetics in Intelligent Systems: Proceedings of the 9th Computer Science On-line Conference 2020, (3) 9,* pp. 164-176. Springer International Publishing.

Brewer, R., 2016. Ransomware attacks: detection, prevention and cure. *Network security, 2016*(9), pp.5-9.

Chopra, S., Marwaha, H. and Sharma, A., 2022, April. Cyber-Attacks Identification and Measures for Prevention. In *International Conference on Cybersecurity and Cybercrime*, 9, pp. 83-90.

Dearman, D. and Pierce, J.S., 2008, April. It's on my other computer! computing with multiple devices. In *Proceedings of the SIGCHI Conference on Human factors in Computing Systems,* pp. 767-776.

Fortuin, A., 2021. *The effects of mobile cloud accounting on the operations of small, medium and micro-enterprises in selected Cape Town markets* (Doctoral dissertation, Cape Peninsula University of Technology).

Ibrahim, H., 2022. A Review on the Mechanism Mitigating and Eliminating Internet Crimes using Modern Technologies: Mitigating Internet crimes using modern technologies. *Wasit Journal of Computer and Mathematics Science, 1*(3), pp.50-68.

Kobis, P. 2021. Human factor aspects in information security management in the traditional IT and cloud computing models. *Operations Research and Decisions*, 1, pp. 61–76.

Kumhar, D., Kewat, A. and Kumar, A., 2022. Internet Security: Threats and Its Preventive Measures. In *Advances in VLSI, Communication, and Signal Processing: Select Proceedings of VCAS 2021*, pp. 753-766. Singapore: Springer Nature Singapore.

Millaire, P., Sathe, A. and Thielen, P. 2015. What All cyber criminals know: Small & midsize businesses with little or no cybersecurity are ideal targets. Available: https://www.chubb.com/my-en/articles/smes-with-little-or-no-cybersecurity-are-ideal-targets.aspx. [Accessed: 18th December 2023].

Minnaar, A., 2014. 'Crackers', cyberattacks and cybersecurity vulnerabilities: the difficulties in combatting the'new'cybercriminals. *Acta Criminologica: African Journal of Criminology & Victimology, 27*(sed-2), pp.127-144.

Nasir, A., Naderi, M.A. and Momeni, S.M. 2020. 'Risk management of information technology projects using Bayesian networks.' *Practical IT*, 1(5), pp. 01–10.

Ncubukezi, T. 2021. *An exploration of the malware impact on the end devices*. Conference Proceedings: CPUT Postgraduate Conference: pp.70.

Ncubukezi, T. and Mwansa, L., 2021. Best practices used by businesses to maintain good cyber hygiene during Covid19 pandemic. *Journal of Internet Technology and Secured Transactions, 9*(1), pp. 714-721.

Ncubukezi, T., 2023. *Design development and evaluation of the cybersecurity risk tool: a case of small and medium-sized enterprises in South Africa* (Doctoral dissertation, Cape Peninsula University of Technology).

Ncubukezit, T., 2022, March. Human Errors: A Cybersecurity Concern and the Weakest Link to Small Businesses. In *International Conference on Cyber Warfare and Security*, 17(1), pp. 395-403.

Ngo, F.T., Agarwal, A., Govindu, R. and MacDonald, C., 2020. Malicious software threats. *The Palgrave handbook of international cybercrime and cyberdeviance*, pp.793-813.

Radanliev, P., De Roure, D.C., Nicolescu, R., Huth, M., Montalvo, R.M., Cannady, S. and Burnap, P., 2018. Future developments in cyber risk assessment for the internet of things. *Computers in industry, 102*, pp.14-22.

Sharif, M., Bhagavatula, S., Bauer, L. and Reiter, M.K., 2016, October. Accessorize to a crime: Real and stealthy attacks on state-of-the-art face recognition. In *Proceedings of the 2016 acm sigsac conference on computer and communications security*, pp. 1528-1540.

Shukla, S., George, J.P.,.Tiwari, K. and Kureethara, J.V., 2022. Data security. In *Data Ethics and Challenges* (pp. 41-59). Singapore: Springer Singapore.

Singh, A., Singh, B. and Joseph, H., 2008. Malware analysis. In *Vulnerability Analysis and Defense for the Internet* (pp. 169-211). Boston, MA: Springer US.

Talukder, S. and Talukder, Z., 2020. A survey on malware detection and analysis tools. *International Journal of Network Security & Its Applications (IJNSA) Vol, 12.*

Yuan, S. and Wu, X., 2021. Deep learning for insider threat detection: Review, challenges and opportunities. *Computers & Security, 104*, p.102221.

Towards a GDPR Compliance Assessment Toolkit

Sipho Ngobeni, Ntombizodwa Thwala, Nokuthaba Siphambili, Phumeza Pantsi, Bokang Molema, Jacob Lediga and Pertunia Senamela
Council for Scientific and Institutional Research, Pretoria, South Africa

sngobeni@csir.co.za
nthwala1@csir.co.za
nsiphambili@csir.co.za
ppantsi@csir.co.za
bmolema@csir.co.za
jlediga@csir.co.za
psenamela@csir.co.za

Abstract: The European Union's (EU) General Data Protection Regulation (GDPR) makes it illegal to collect, process, and store personal data unless it is done in accordance with the prescribed legal and regulatory clauses enshrined in the Act. Organisations face significant challenges in navigating GDPR requirements and assessing their level of compliance. In particular, failure to comply with GDPR may potentially expose the data Controller and Processor to steep legal penalties including possibly administrative fines of up to 20 000 000 EUR, or in the case of an undertaking, up to 4% of the total worldwide annual turnover of the preceding financial year, which is imposed by the Supervisory Authority. This paper presents the results of a minimum viable product, the GDPR Compliance Assessment Toolkit (GCAT). The main objective of the GCAT is to assist organisations to assess their current state of compliance to GDPR. Drawing from an experimental research and development approach, GCAT is then compared with other existing GDPR compliance assessment technologies. Comparative analysis results shows that GCAT simplifies and optimize GDPR compliance assessments.

Keywords: GDPR, Privacy, Data Controller, Data Processor, Personal Data, Compliance Assessment

1. Introduction and Background

In this digital era, data has grown to be a valuable currency due to data being mined and processed to help make critical business decisions with the use of technology. The European Union (EU) introduced the General Data Protection Regulation (GDPR) Act which was enacted in April 2016 and came into effect in May 2018 (Zhuo et al, 2021). Similarly to the EU data protection regulation, GDPR recognises that individuals own and control their personal (but not contractual) data in perpetuity (Ke , 2024). This therefore suggest that individuals have rights to explicit consent (data opt-in), to be forgotten (data erasure), and portability (data transfer) (Ke and Sudhir, 2024). The main purpose of GDPR is therefore to protect individual personal data in terms of how it is collected, processed, and transferred to third parties (Kuner et al, 2021; Intersoft Consulting, 2021; Peukert et al, 2022 ; Ryngaert and Taylor, 2020; Vlahou et al, 2021). This law is applicable to European Economic Area (EEA)-based operations and certain non-EEA organisations that process personal data of individuals in the EEA. To date, GDPR has been reviewed and updated to version Article 97 which focuses on how data is transferred to third parties through the cross-border transfers and ensure there is co-operation amongst the organisations sharing the data.

The law is modelled to provide a set of requirements on how organisations should process personal data and the rules relating to the free movement of personal data. Since GDPR was enacted as law, it is now a legal compliance obligation. Most organisations are increasingly discovering the serious legal implications and challenges of achieving, demonstrating and maintaining mandatory compliance with GDPR are not as straight forward as they would have preferred, and panic is slowly creeping in. GDPR compliance is seen as exorbitant, intimidating, and complex; leaving many organisations unsure of how to tackle it. In addition, while its goal of empowering consumers and protecting their personal data is apparent, navigating its complexities can be difficult, particularly for enterprises in the midst of compliance efforts.

Data protection principles are concerned with how data is used lawfully, its purpose is stated and handled in a way that it is secure including the processing, destruction and recovery of the data. It is of utmost importance for organisations to specify what personal data will be used for, ensure data subjects have access to the data, and record how the data will be used, kept and failure to do so results in consequences. Furthermore, it is of utmost importance for organisations to take stock of the personal data they collect and share, and then put in place adequate controls to protect it. The legal consequences of non-compliance to this act will likely come from information security and privacy control deficiencies that relate to the processing and storage of personal data and organisations not doing their due diligence in safeguarding personal information. It may also come as a result of gaps in policies and procedures that govern the handling of personal data. Failure to comply with certain provisions of GDPR may potentially expose the data Controller and Processor to steep legal penalties including possibly administrative fines of up to 20 000 000 EUR, or in the case of an undertaking, up to 4% of the total worldwide annual turnover of the preceding financial year, which is imposed by the Supervisory Authority (Directorate-General for Communication, 2021).

Organisations need put their ducks in order when it comes to GDPR compliance, but many are now scrambling to tick the boxes and become compliant over-night. They have since realised the seriousness of non-compliance and the financial penalties thereof. Unfortunately, compliance to GDPR cannot be an over-night exercise. Organisations must invest time and money to be compliant. It is no secret that preparedness for GDPR compliance has become a top priority for most organisations, and more so as the enforcement deadline has come and passed. Therefore, the main purpose of this paper is to present the results of a technology demonstrator called GDPR Compliance Assessment Tool (GCAT). The GCAT is modelled through an experimental research and development approach. A comparative analysis of GCAT with other existing GDPR compliance assessment technologies is conducted. The result of the comparative analysis shows that GCAT simplifies and optimize GDPR compliance assessments.

2. Methodology

This paper followed an Experimental Research approach in order to implement the GDPR compliance assessment toolkit (Goddard, 2018). This is systematic work, drawing on the knowledge gained from research and practical experience and producing additional knowledge, which is directed to producing new products or processes or to improving existing products and processes. It this paper, we study several GDPR compliance assessment systems (both open-source and proprietary), with the aim to develop an improved system, called General Data Protection Regulation Compliance Assessment Toolkit. We then formulated performance metrics and used them to measure the performance of the proposed system against the existing systems.

The elements of the performance metrics (presented in Table 1) were formulated based on studying several existing Cybersecurity maturity metrics (Cybersecurity capability maturity model, 2022); (Privacy assessment maturity framework, 2014); (Hansen et al, 2016) including feedback from the pilots that were conducted . The metrics includes the following elements:

- **Compliance analysis and reporting** – this metric measures the capability of the system to take inputs from the entire assessment (compliant, not-compliant and non-applicable) and compute compliance/ non-compliance scores in a form of dashboards.
- **Provision of compliance maturity over time** – this criterion measures the ability of the systems to allow for organisations to mature their compliance over time and plot related maturity levels based on historical assessments. For example, determine compliance maturity ratings such as Non-existent (Level 0), Initial (Level 1), Defined (Level 2), Standardized (Level 3), Measured & Managed (Level 4 Optimized (Level 5).
- **User Management** – this criterion measures the ability of the system to ensure role-based access control. E.g, Assessor, Assessee and Approver. The segregation of duties is more important for quality assurance and audit purpose. One user cannot create and approve an assessment.
- **Provides prioritised areas of improvement based on top non-compliant categories** – this criterion measures the capability of the system to provide for an implementation roadmap for top non-compliance categories.
- **Provision of key focus areas where the organisation is compliant to GCAT** – this metric measures the capability of the system to determine overall compliance score taking into consideration all the sixteen assessed categories.
- **Provision of industry sector benchmarking** – this criterion measures the capability of the system to allow the assessed organisation to understand how they are currently doing in comparison to under industries within the same sector.

The results shows that the experimental development process yielded an improved system that performs or provides improved capability for organisation to self-assess their current state of compliance to the General Data Protection Regulation. A detailed presentation of the performance analysis using the metrics described above is presented in Section 5.

3. Results Analysis

The proposed system is a cloud-based solution that is used to assist organisations to evaluate their current state of compliance to the GDPR. These are organisations that collect, use, process or store personal data. The system can be accessed through a web browser on any device and consists of a file server, web server and database server. The system architecture was designed to ensure that components do not interfere with one another as depicted in Figure 1.

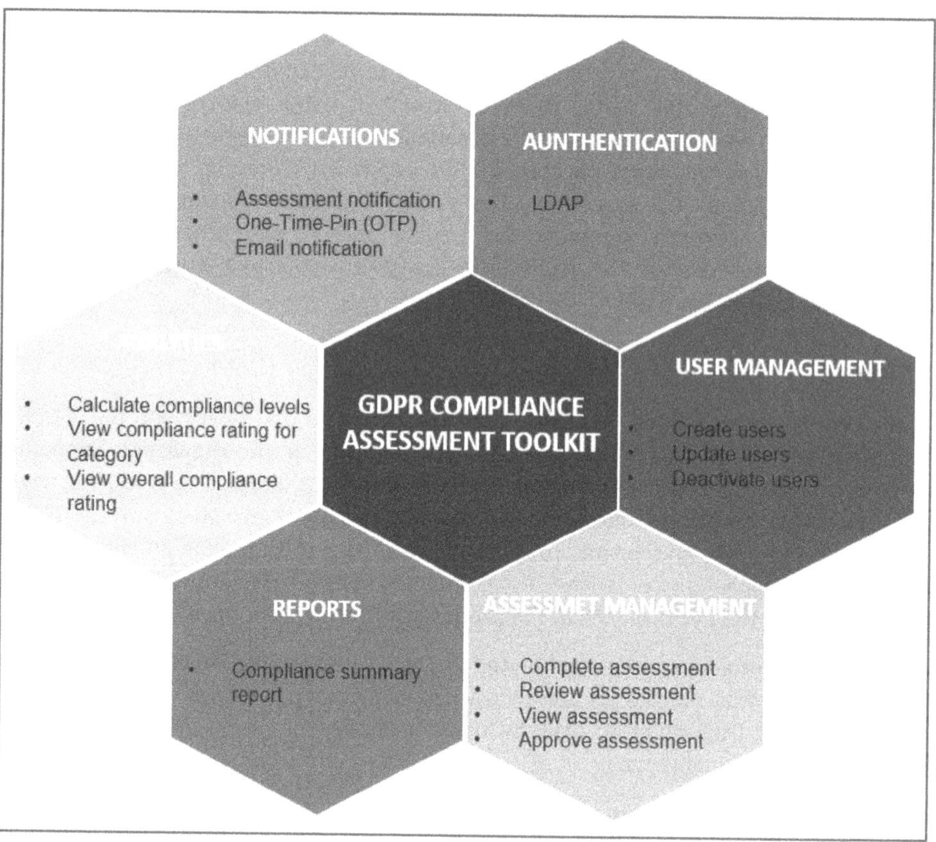

Figure 1: System architecture

The components of the system architecture are described below:

- **AUTHENTICATION** – the system requires users or the assessed organisation to submit their details to initiate the compliance assessment process. These details are then used to register the organisation, and representatives who will be taking the assessment.
- **USER AND ASSESSMENT MANAGEMENT** – the system uses role-based access control,

which include:

- **System Administrator** – adds organisation/s to be assessed in the system.
- **Assessor** – initiates the assessment evaluation process and sends the organisation's representative (Assessee) a link for completing a self-assessment.
- **Assessee** – completes the assessment on behalf of the assessed organisation.
- **Approver** – reviews and approves assessments.

- **REPORTING** – an executive summary report is generated for all approved assessments. The assessor will send this final report to Assessee upon approval.
- **ANALYTICS** – provides a results visualisation of the organisation's compliance
- posture.
- **NOTIFICATIONS** – provides assessment email notifications. To support these capabilities, the backend stores data in two forms, that is, a relational database using PostgreSQL and a File server to store the uploaded documentary evidence.

4. Development

The system allows an assessment to be created for an organisation as depicted in Figure 2. An organisation can complete one or more assessments, and each assessment can be completed by one or more representatives.

The system also makes provision for larger organisations to complete one assessment per business function. Once the various business functions complete their assessments, their individual compliance scores are then aggregated to form one compliance score for the entire organisation. Once an assessment(s) is created, the GCAT will automatically send the representative(s), herein referred to as Assessee, a link for the assessment. To access the GCAT the Assessee will be authenticated with a unique One-Time-Pin (OTP).

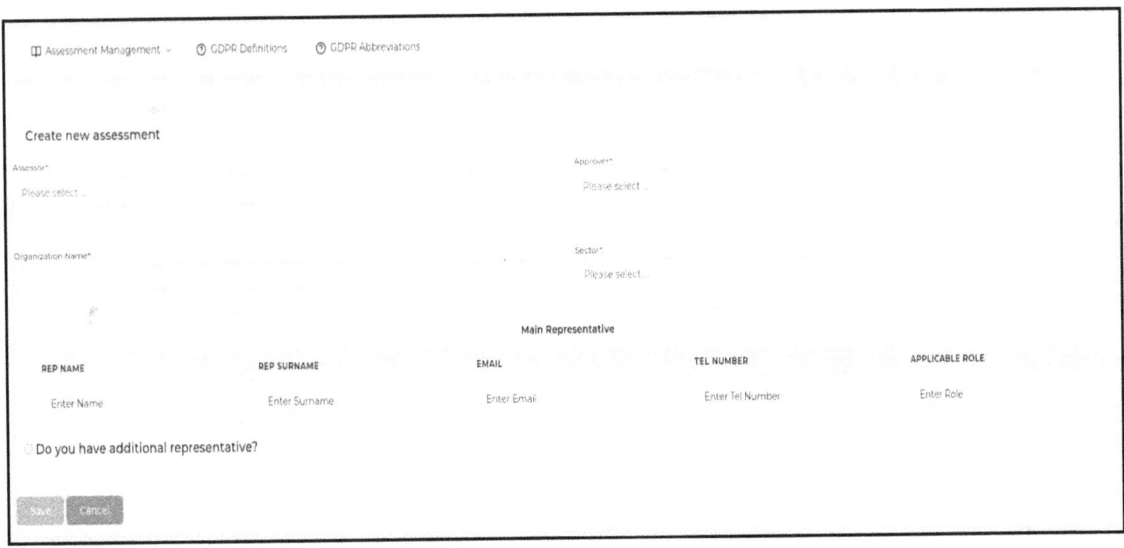

Figure 2: Creating an assessment for an organisation

Upon authentication the Assessee will be presented with a set of questions grouped into categories that align to the conditions defined in GCAT. In responding to each question, the Assessee will be able to provide comment and file-based evidence to support the compliance criteria selected (either Yes, No, or N/A) as indicated in Figure 3.

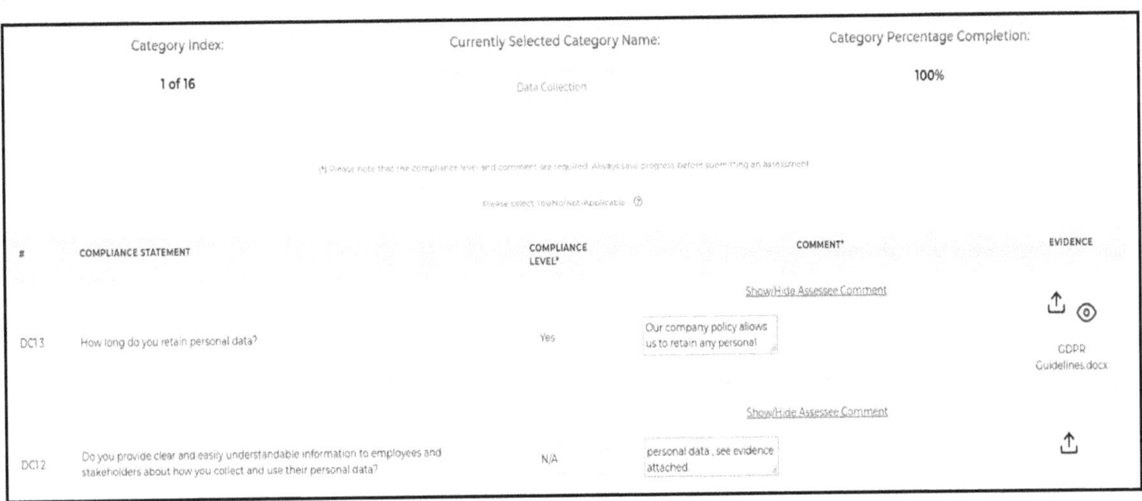

Figure 3: Assessment presented in a questionnaire format

On completion of the assessment the Assessee will receive notification that their assessment has been submitted for review. To assure quality of evidence and assessment results, the GCAT will route the completed assessment to an Assessor who will review and comment on the assessment. Once satisfied, the assessor will then submit the assessment to the Approver for finalization and approval (refer to Figure 4). Upon approval of the assessment the system will generate results of the assessment as depicted in Figure 5.

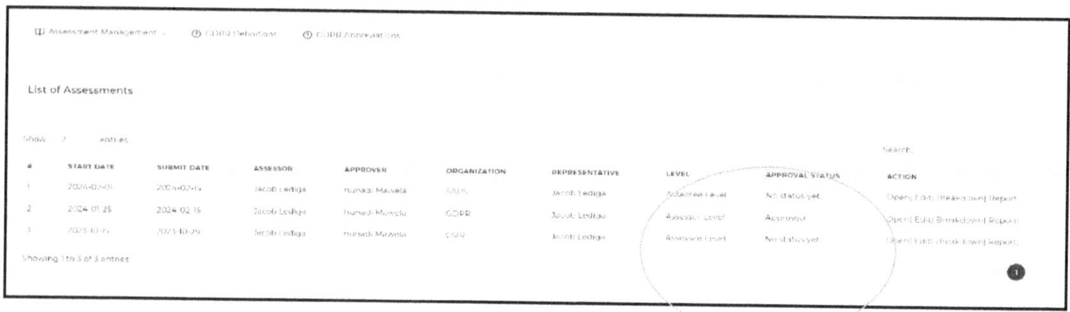

Figure 4: Quality assurance

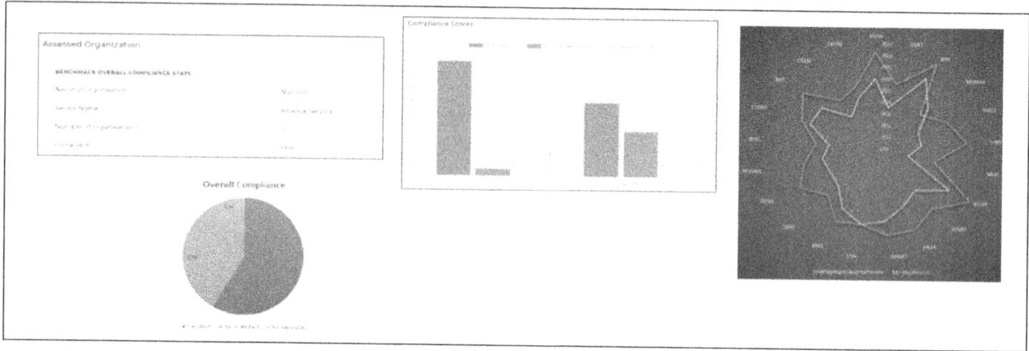

Figure 5: Results visualisation dashboards

5. Results

5.1 Performance Analysis

This research studied several GDPR compliance assessment toolkit such Wheelhouse GDPR Assessment tool (An Coimisiun um Chosaint Sonrai Data Protection Commission, 2022), CertiKit Limited GDPR gap assessment tool (CertiKit Limited, 2019), Sypher GDPR readiness assessment (Sypher, 2023), Nymity GDPR readiness questions (Nymity, 2019), Spirent Security labs GDPR compliance assessment (Spirent, 2018), CyberDefense GDPR compliance assessment (CyberDefense, 2023), Microsoft GDPR Accountability Readiness Checklist (Bernhardt et al, 2018), An Coimisiun um Chosaint Sonrai Data Protection Commission, and Report tool EU GDPR readiness assessment(ReportTool, 2018). Our study assessed the tools in terms of functionality and performance against set criteria described below. For the purpose of this paper, the following GDPR compliance assessment toolkit and the measured criteria were chosen:

- **Measured Criteria** – are measured against the existing systems.
- **Measured performance** – this is the optimal performance expected to be achieved by the proposed system and measured against the three existing systems.
- **GCAT** – this is the proposed GDPR Compliance Assessment Toolkit described in Section 3 and Section 4 above. The toolkit provides twenty-one compliance categories that are assessed while the rest of the compared existing toolkit does not provide comprehensive compliance categories.
- **Wheelhouse GDPR Assessment tool** – This is a GDPR assessment tool that provides feedback after answering the questions on each section of the GDPR. In addition, it provides recommendations on areas of improvement but does not provide compliance categories on data accuracy, Integrity and confidentiality.
- **CertiKit Limited GDPR gap assessment tool** – this is a complete set of forms, assembled and ready to use with an aim to guide an organisation through their GCAT compliance audit journey. Despite this, the tool does not provide compliance categories on data Integrity and storage limitation.
- **Sypher GDPR readiness assessment** – this system provides a GDPR assessment report after completing the system with areas of recommendations but does not provide compliance categories such as administrative fines and penalties.
- **Nymity GDPR readiness questions** – this is an excel sheet checklist template that continue to evolve to provide GDPR compliance but has many challenges regarding management of excel sheets as compared

to the proposed GCAT system. Similarly to the Sypher GDPR compliance assessment toolkit, it does not provide compliance categories such as administrative fines and penalties.

- **Microsoft GDPR Accountability Readiness Checklist** – this is a GDPR gap assessment took, it focuses on four compliance categories, that is, Conditions for Data Collection and Processing, Data Subject Rights, Privacy by Design and Default and Data Protection and security. The toolkit does not provide compliance categories on administrative fines and penalties and cross-border data transfers.

Table 1: Comparative analysis of GCAT and existing systems

Measured Criteria	Measured Performance	GCAT	Existing GDPR Compliance Assessment Tools				
			Wheelhouse GDPR Assessment tool	**CertiKit Limited GDPR gap assessment tool**	**Sypher GDPR readiness assessment**	**Nymity GDPR readiness questions**	**Microsoft GDPR Accountability Readiness Checklist**
Compliance analysis and reporting.	Generating analytics based on the compliance score and highlight GCAT Compliance Categories that need attention.	Provides analytics based on the compliance score and highlight GCAT Compliance Categories that need improvement.	Provides high level analytics based on categories only.	Provides high level analytics based on categories only.	Provides high level analytics based on categories only.	Provides high level analytics based on categories only.	Provides high level analytics based on categories only.
Provide compliance maturity level over time	The technology provides for organisations to mature their compliance over time and plot related maturity levels based on historical assessments.	Provide regulatory compliance maturity rating based on the levels: a) Non-existent (Level 0) b) Initial (Level 1) c) Defined (Level 2) d) Standardized (Level 3) e) Measured & Managed (Level 4) f) Optimized (Level 5)	No regulatory compliance maturity rating.	No regulatory compliance maturity rating.	No regulatory compliance maturity rating.	No regulatory compliance maturity rating.	No regulatory compliance maturity rating.
User management	Role-based access.	Provides for role-based access control, that is, System Administrator, Assessee, Assessor, and Approver.	Some elements of access management provided.	Some elements of access management provided.	Some elements of access management provided.	No role-based access management. Excel sheet.	Some elements of access management provided.
Prioritised implementation roadmap	Provide key focus areas for improvement.	Provides prioritised areas of improvement based on top non-compliant categories.	Not implemented.	Not implemented.	Not implemented.	Not implemented.	Not implemented.
Provide key performance indicators for	Provide key focus areas where the	Provides a prioritized key performance	Provides a prioritized key	Provides a prioritized key	Provides a prioritized key	Provides a prioritized key	Provides a prioritized key

Measured Criteria	Measured Performance	GCAT	Existing GDPR Compliance Assessment Tools				
			Wheelhouse GDPR Assessment tool	CertiKit Limited GDPR gap assessment tool	Sypher GDPR readiness assessment	Nymity GDPR readiness questions	Microsoft GDPR Accountability Readiness Checklist
the categories where the organisation is compliant to GCAT.	organisation is compliant to GCAT.	indicators for the categories where the organisation is compliant to GCAT.	performance indicators for the categories where the organisation is compliant to GCAT.	performance indicators for the categories where the organisation is compliant to GCAT.	performance indicators for the categories where the organisation is compliant to GCAT.	performance indicators for the categories where the organisation is compliant to GCAT.	performance indicators for the categories where the organisation is compliant to GCAT.
Provides industry sector benchmarking	Provides industry sectoral average compliance score of the assessed organisation.	Calculates and make provision for industry sectoral average compliance score for the assessed organisation.	Not implemented	Not implemented	Not implemented	Not implemented	Not implemented

Table 2 presents a summary of the performance results in Table 1 and a detailed discussion of the results is presented in Section 6.2. The legend "✓" depicts that the measured performance criteria is met and "×"depicts that the measured performance is Not met, while "(×)" depicts that the status is un-known.

Table 2: Summary of comparative analysis of GCAT and existing systems

Measured Criterial	Measured Performance	GCAT	Existing GDPR Compliance Assessment Tools				
			Wheelhouse	CertiKit	Sypher	Nymity	Microsoft
Compliance analysis and reporting.	Generating analytics based on the compliance score and highlight GCAT Compliance Categories that need attention	✓	✓	✓	✓	✓	✓
Provide compliance maturity level over time	The technology provides for organisations to mature their compliance over time and plot related maturity levels based on historical assessments.	×	×	×	×	×	×
User management	Role-based access.	✓	✓	✓	✓	(×)	✓
Prioritised implementation roadmap	Provide key focus areas for improvement.	×	×	×	×	×	×
Provide key performance indicators for the categories where the organisation is compliant to GCAT.	Provide key focus areas where the organisation is compliant to GCAT.	✓	✓	✓	✓	✓	✓
Provides industry sector benchmarking	Provides industry sectoral average compliance score of the assessed organisation.	×	×	×	×	×	×

5.2 Discussion

This section is dedicated to the discussion of the performance analysis results presented in Section 5.1. can be noted from Table 1 that the GCAT is the most optimal solution compared to the five existing systems regarding:

- **Provision of compliance maturity over time** – this criterion measures the ability of the systems to allow for organisations to mature their compliance over time and plot related maturity levels based on historical assessments. In this instance, the GCAT outperforms the studied existing system because it provides a capability to determine compliance maturity ratings based on the following levels: Non-existent (Level 0), Initial (Level 1), Defined (Level 2), Standardized (Level 3), Measured & Managed (Level 4 Optimized (Level 5). All the other five existing systems does not provide regulatory compliance maturity ratings.
- **User Management** – this criterion measures the ability of the system to ensure role-based access control. It can be noted from Table 1 and Table 2 that the GCAT provides a capability for role-based access control, that is, systems administrator, assessor, assessee, and approver. While Wheelhouse, CertiKit, Sypher and Microsoft do provide some elements of access management, Nymity does not provide any access management, it is merely a spresheet and has many security implications including manual management of spreadsheet over time as compared to GCAT which is a web-based application.
- **Prioritised implementation road map** – this criterion measures the capability of the system to provide for an implementation roadmap after completing the assessment, that is, key focus areas for improvement. The GCAT provides this capability by making provision for prioritised areas of improvement based on top non-compliant assessment categories. All the other existing compared systems do not make provision for this capability.
- **Provision of industry sector benchmarking** – this criterion measures the capability of the system to allow the assessed organisation to understand how they are currently doing in comparison to under industries within the same sector. GCAT does provide a capability to calculate the average compliance score of the previously assessed organisations within the same sector as the currently assessed organisation.

6. Benefits of the GCAT System

The following are the benefits provided by the proposed GDPR Compliance Assessment Toolkit (GCAT):

- The most salient benefit is to assist organisations to assess their current state of compliance to GDPR.
- The system allows an organisation to complete one or more assessments, and each assessment can be completed by one or more representatives since various compliance categories could be require completion by representatives in different business functions.
- The system also makes provision for larger organisations to complete one assessment per business function. Once the various business functions complete their assessments, their individual compliance scores are then aggregated to form one compliance score for the entire organisation.
- The GCAT forms a basis from which other Cybersecurity governance and compliance assessment tools can be birthed from, e.g., compliance toolkit for ISO/IEC 27001 family of standards, privacy impact assessments, etc.
- The users of the GCAT are organisations in the private, public sector or EU member states. In addition, this tool could be used by organisations responsible for conducting audits for regulatory compliance.

7. Conclusion

The outcome of the GCAT system proposed in this paper showed that it was possible for an organisation to self-assess its current compliance posture against the GDPR requirements. This will then allow the assessed organisation to put together a road map for compliance based on the results provided by the system – areas of improvement. Future work entails creation of the executive summary report that forms part of the assessment results, which include the capability for this report to be also submitted via email to relevant representatives within an organisation. This does not necessary limit the key features of this tool, given that the Assessor and Approver already have access to the summary information for each organisation within the GDPR Compliance Assessment Toolkit. Furthermore, the toolkit will be improved to have a compliance assessment completion workflow that will include other role players within the assessed organisations to assist in the completion of the assessment. The other role players may include Privacy Information Officer, Chief Information Security Officer, etc. In addition, an email notification functionality will be developed to inform the Assessee of any non-compliant resulting from the assessment.

References

An Coimisiun um Chosaint Sonrai Data Protection Commission. (2022) An Coimisiun um Chosaint Sonrai Data Protection Commission [Online]. Available at: https://www.dataprotection.ie/en/organisations/resources-organisations/self-assessment-checklist [Accessed: 13 October 2023]

Bernhardt, J, Mazzoli, R and O'Sullivan S. (2018) Microsoft GDPR Accountability Readiness Checklist [Online]. Available at: https://learn.microsoft.com/en-us/compliance/regulatory/gdpr-arc?view=o365-worldwide&culture=en-us&country=us [Accessed: 13 October 2023]

CertiKit Limited. (2019) CertiKit Limited [Online]. Available at: https://issuu.com/public-it/docs/gdpr-form-01-3_gdpr_gap_assessment_tool [Accessed: 15 September 2023]

CyberDefense. (2023) CyberDefense [Online]. Available at: https://www.orangecyberdefense.com/za/gdpr-compliance-assessments [Accessed: 5 November2023]

Cybersecurity Capability Maturity Model. (2022) US Department of Energy. [Online]. Available at: chrome-extension://efaidnbmnnnibpcajpcglclefindmkaj/https://www.energy.gov/sites/default/files/2021-07/C2M2%20Version%202.0%20July%202021_508.pdf [Accessed: 10 October 2023]

Directorate-General for Communication. (2021) *Rules for business and organisations, European Commission.* [Online] Available at: https://ec.europa.eu/info/law/law-topic/data-protection/reform/rules-business-and-organisations_en [Accessed:14 February 2024].

Goddard, M. (2018) "The EU General Data Protection Regulation (GDPR): European Regulation that has a Global Impact", *International* Journal of Market Research, Vol. 59, No. 6, pp. 703-710.

Hansen, M., Hoepman, JH. and Jensen, M. (2016). "Towards Measuring Maturity of Privacy-Enhancing Technologies". Privacy Technologies and Policy. Lecture Notes in Computer Science, vol 9484. Springer.

Intersoft Consulting. (2021) *Intersoft Consulting.* [Online] Available at: https://gdpr-info.eu/ [Accessed 09 February 2024].

Ke, T. T. and Sudhir, K. (2024) "Privacy rights and data security: GDPR and Personal Data Markets", Management Science, Vol 69, No. (8), pp. 4389-4412.

Kuner, C., Bygrave, L.A., Docksey, C., Drechsler, L. and Tosoni, L. (2021) "The EU General Data Protection Regulation: A Commentary/Update of Selected Articles. Update of Selected Articles (May 4, 2021).

Nymity. (2019) Nymity GDPR Readiness questions [Online]. Available at: https://info.trustarc.com/Web-Resource-2019-01-19-Nymity-GDPR-Compliance-Toolkit_LP.html [Accessed: 12 October 2023]

Peukert, C., Bechtold, S., Batikas, M. and Kretschmer, T. (2022) "Regulatory spillovers and Data Governance: Evidence from the GDPR", Marketing Science, Vol 41, No. 4, p. 746–768.

Privacy Maturity Assessment Framework: Elements, attributes, and criteria. (2014) Online Available at: https://psi.govt.nz/privacyleadership/ [Accessed: 12 October 2023]

ReportTool. (2018). *Guidelines for Collecting and Reporting Data on Research and Experimental.* [Online] [Accessed: 23 November 2023].

Ryngaert, C. and Taylor, M. (2020) "The GDPR as global data protection regulation?", American Journal of International Law (AJIL)Unbound, Vol 114, p. 5–9.

Spirent. (2018) Sprirent SecurityLabs GDPR Compliance Assessment [Online]. Available at: https://assets.ctfassets.net/wcxs9ap8i19s/4XlBkiYtR7NN9xwczrKkom/920a2d6cdf473e8f543b5e2ee0518c2b/GDPR-Compliance-Assessment_whitepaper.pdf [Accessed: 13 October 2023]

Sypher. (2023) Sypher [Online]. Available at: https://www.sypher.eu/gdpr/assessment [Last Access: 25 September 2023]

Vlahou, A. Hallinan, D. Apweiler, R. Argiles, A. Beige, J. Benigni, A. Bischoff, R. Black, P.C. Boehm, F. Céraline, J. and Chrousos, G.P, (2021) "Data sharing under the General Data Protection Regulation: time to harmonize law and research ethics?", Hypertension, Vol 77, *No.* 4, pp.1029-1035.

Zhuo, R., Huffaker, B., Claffy, K. C. and Greenstein, S. (2021) "The impact of the General Data Protection Regulation on Internet Interconnection", Telecommunications Policy, Vol 45, No. 2, p. 102083.

Machine Learning Applications of Quantum Computing: A Review

Thien Nguyen, Tuomo Sipola and Jari Hautamäki
Institute of Information Technology, Jamk University of Applied Sciences, Jyväskylä, Finland

thien.nguyen@student.jamk.fi
tuomo.sipola@jamk.fi
jari.hautamaki@jamk.fi

Abstract: At the intersection of quantum computing and machine learning, this review paper explores the transformative impact these technologies are having on the capabilities of data processing and analysis, far surpassing the bounds of traditional computational methods. Drawing upon an in-depth analysis of 32 seminal papers, this review delves into the interplay between quantum computing and machine learning, focusing on transcending the limitations of classical computing in advanced data processing and applications. This review emphasizes the potential of quantum-enhanced methods in enhancing cybersecurity, a critical sector that stands to benefit significantly from these advancements. The literature review, primarily leveraging Science Direct as an academic database, delves into the transformative effects of quantum technologies on machine learning, drawing insights from a diverse collection of studies and scholarly articles. While the focus is primarily on the growing significance of quantum computing in cybersecurity, the review also acknowledges the promising implications for other sectors as the field matures. Our systematic approach categorizes sources based on quantum machine learning algorithms, applications, challenges, and potential future developments, uncovering that quantum computing is increasingly being implemented in practical machine learning scenarios. The review highlights advancements in quantum-enhanced machine learning algorithms and their potential applications in sectors such as cybersecurity, emphasizing the need for industry-specific solutions while considering ethical and security concerns. By presenting an overview of the current state and projecting future directions, the paper sets a foundation for ongoing research and strategic advancement in quantum machine learning.

Keywords: Quantum Cryptography, Quantum Computing Security, Applications of Quantum ML, Quantum Algorithms, Quantum Tech in ML, Quantum Computing Trends.

1. Introduction

Machine learning (ML) is a branch of artificial intelligence (AI). It aims to create systems that can learn from data. Quantum computing (QC) uses the rules of quantum mechanics, which allows it to process information in completely new ways. By combining machine learning with quantum computing, we are laying the groundwork for groundbreaking changes in computer science. As Martín-Guerrero and Lamata (2022) have noted, the synergy of machine learning (ML), quantum computing (QC), and quantum information (QI) is driving the development of Quantum Machine Learning (QML). Recent advances, such as Giuntini et al.'s (2023a) novel quantum-inspired algorithms for classification tasks and Ning et al.'s (2023) quantum approaches to managing large datasets, demonstrate ongoing progress.

One promising application is in cybersecurity, where research such as the exploration of quantum cryptography using continuous-variable quantum neural networks (CV-QNNs) by Shi et al. (2020) demonstrates the potential for robust defenses against cyber threats. However, despite clear progress, challenges such as hardware limitations and algorithm complexity remain. Future research must address these challenges to fully realise the potential of QML in a wide range of applications beyond cybersecurity.

Taking advantage of the recent advances, it is clear that while quantum computing offers a promising avenue for revolutionising machine learning, several gaps and challenges need to be addressed to fully unlock its potential. These observations lead us to formulate the following research questions:

RQ1: How do quantum computing principles improve machine learning algorithms? This question explores the role of quantum computing in improving the performance of machine learning models.

RQ2: What are the implications of quantum computing for areas such as cybersecurity? This question explores how quantum technologies could offer advantages over traditional approaches to securing communication and protecting sensitive data.

RQ3: How do quantum algorithms compare to classical algorithms in terms of efficiency and application? This question seeks to understand the comparative advantages and limitations of quantum and classical algorithms for various machine learning tasks.

This review outlines our methodology in Section 2 and examines the current advances in quantum machine learning in the Literature Review in Section 3. Section 4 discusses the key insights and implications of quantum computing in improving machine learning, addressing our research questions (RQ1, RQ2, RQ3). The final section, Section 5, concludes by summarising our findings and suggesting directions for future research. This structured approach aims to provide a clear overview of the role of quantum computing in machine learning, highlighting its potential and the challenges ahead.

2. Methodology

This review, part of a larger project exploring applications of quantum computing, examined existing research on its role in machine learning. Following established literature review methods (Levac et al., 2010; Arksey & O'Malley, 2005), we started with a broad search using "Quantum Computing Application" to gather diverse articles. We collected 400 recent publications (2022-2023) from the Science Direct database.

A detailed content analysis identified relevant topics such as AI, machine learning, and applications. This analysis refined the dataset to 287 articles related to quantum computing applications. A further selection was then made using a criterion such as publication date and relationship to the research topic, focusing on articles that explicitly discussed artificial intelligence, resulting in a final set of 32 documents for in-depth review. This methodical approach, based on established methods, provides a comprehensive overview of current trends and developments in quantum machine learning, including its practical applications and future potential.

The methodological approach and detailed stages of the literature review are described, followed by the inclusion of a PRISMA flowchart to visually summarise the process. This diagram (see Figure 1) effectively illustrates the progression from the initial set of 400 documents to the final selection of 32 relevant papers. It highlights the screening, eligibility, and inclusion stages, providing a clear and concise visual representation of the systematic review process, thereby ensuring a thorough selection of the most relevant literature (Page and Moher, 2017).

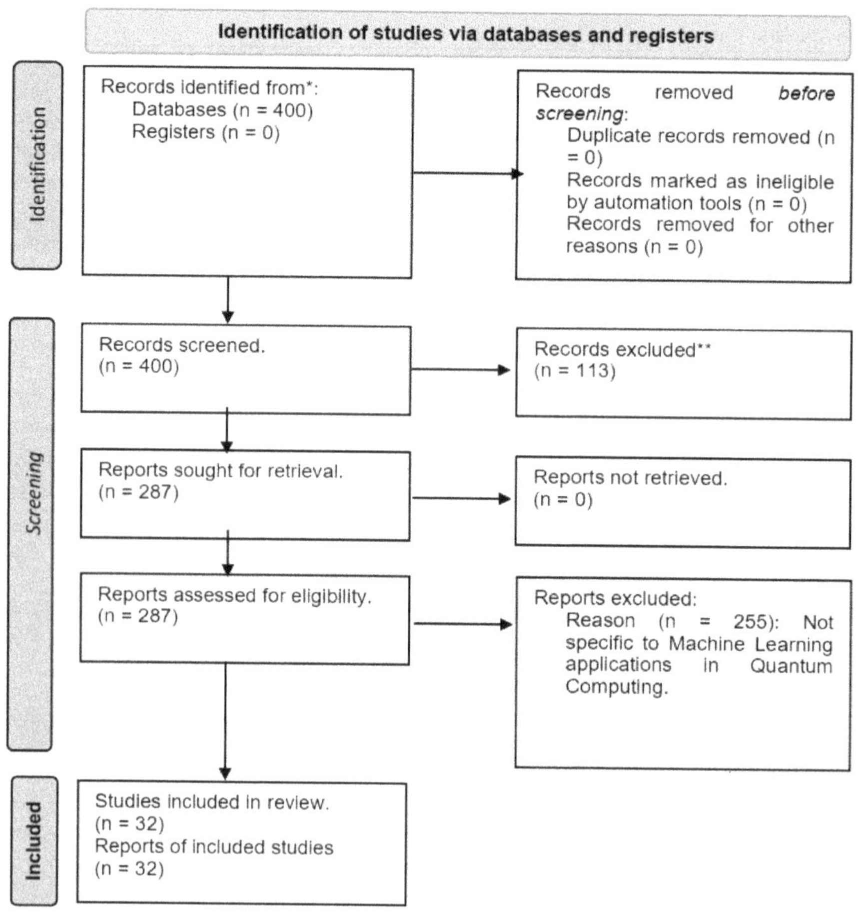

Figure 1: PRISMA flow chart diagram showing the systematic selection process of literature from an initial dataset of 400 studies to 32 key papers on machine learning in quantum computing.

3. Literature Review

3.1 Impact of Quantum Computing on Machine Learning: Key Advances and Algorithm Improvements

The intersection of machine learning (ML) and quantum computing is a burgeoning area of research that is poised to significantly transform data processing and analysis. This review synthesises key studies, highlighting advances in quantum-enhanced computational efficiency and the development of quantum-inspired methods in ML. In particular, the superiority of quantum algorithms in specific applications, especially in pattern recognition and data classification, is demonstrated by the works of Rana et al. (2022) and Houssein et al. (2022). The emergence of quantum neural networks and quantum support vector machines represents a shift towards more advanced quantum computational approaches, as exemplified by Ning, Yang, and Du's (2023) Quantum Kernel Logistic Regression (QKLR), which demonstrates an emerging practical application and transformative potential of quantum computing in ML.

Building on these foundations, Quantum Support Vector Machines (QSVMs), as studied by Zhang et al. (2023) and Rana et al. (2022), exploit quantum computing for more efficient processing of complex, high-dimensional data. QSVMs show a significant improvement over traditional methods in handling data-intensive tasks, highlighting the increasing importance of quantum computing in optimising machine learning models.

Suryotrisongko and Musashi (2022) propose a hybrid quantum-classical deep learning model for botnet detection. While the overall performance is comparable to the classical model, the hybrid model achieves slightly better accuracy (up to 94.7%) in specific cases. The study highlights the sensitivity of the model to initial random seed values and circuit architecture, suggesting the need for further optimisation. Overall, the research represents a promising step towards the application of quantum principles in cybersecurity, but further development is crucial for practical applications.

Exploring the core strengths of quantum machine learning, Tiwari et al. (2023) investigate Quantum Fuzzy Neural Networks (QFNN) for advanced text analysis, including sarcasm detection, while Wei et al. (2023) apply quantum techniques to medical image analysis. Research by Houssein et al. (2022) on a quantum-inspired binary classifier and research by Villalba-Diez et al. (2022) on quantum deep learning further illustrate the progress of the field, highlighting the integration and advancement of existing ideas. Additionally, Martín-Guerrero and Lamata (2022) contribute an in-depth tutorial on various quantum machine learning methods.

Moving to practical implementations, Yulianti et al. (2023) improve ensemble classifiers using a hybrid quantum annealing method, and Li et al. (2023) introduce an innovative quantum approach to k-fold cross-validation, simplifying classification tasks. These developments highlight the impact of quantum computing in improving traditional machine learning techniques.

Further advancing the field, Acampora et al. (2023) propose a novel training method for variational quantum classifiers, addressing key challenges in Noisy-Intermediate Scale Quantum (NISQ) devices. Complementing this, Kim et al. (2023) explore quantum neural networks, in particular quantum convolutional neural networks (QCNNs), demonstrating how quantum and classical computing can be effectively integrated.

Building on this advice, Vadyala and Betgeri (2023) are pioneering the development of Quantum Physics-Informed Neural Networks (PINNs), which combine the reliability of quantum computing with the adaptability of neural networks. Their research advances the computational power of PINNs, particularly in solving complex problems, and represents a significant shift in the design of neural networks, using quantum mechanics to enhance traditional machine learning algorithms.

In the field of quantum-enhanced machine learning, the research of Perkowski (2022) significantly advances the field. His work focuses on areas such as inverse problems, constraint satisfaction, and reversible logic, including the use of Grover quantum oracles. These elements are crucial for the development of sophisticated quantum algorithms to improve machine learning techniques. Perkowski's study (2022) not only enriches the theoretical understanding of quantum ML but also lays the groundwork for its practical applications in various domains.

In exploring the unique capabilities of quantum neural networks, Dong et al. (2022) made a significant contribution by uncovering negational symmetry in Quantum Neural Networks (QNNs) during their study on binary pattern classification. Their study, which focused on binary pattern classification, shows that QNNs exhibit a distinctive behaviour not found in classical neural networks, characterised by an inherent symmetry in the processing of binary patterns and their negation counterparts. This unique behaviour, which differs from classical neural networks, highlights the potential impact of quantum properties on algorithmic behaviour and performance, and provides important observations for the convergence of quantum computing and machine learning.

In a notable development, Wang et al. (2022) introduced a significant advancement in machine learning with their Variational Quantum Extreme Learning Machine (VQELM). This innovative method uses quantum computing to process high-dimensional data more effectively than traditional ML algorithms. Using a unique feature mapping technique for non-linear data, VQELM demonstrates the ability of quantum computing to handle complex datasets and improve the computational efficiency of machine learning.

Collectively, these studies highlight the transformative potential of quantum computing to enhance traditional ML algorithms. They point to a future where quantum principles could fundamentally change the way ML tasks are approached, offering solutions that are more efficient, capable of handling more complex data, and innovatively designed compared to current methods.

4. Contrasting Approaches

Quantum computing applications in machine learning show a remarkable diversity of approaches, ranging from pure quantum algorithms to innovative hybrid models. This diversity, which is evident in domains ranging from image processing to natural language processing, reflects the evolving landscape of the field. Hybrid quantum-classical models, as applied by researchers such as Villalba-Diez et al. (2022) and Sharma et al. (2023), combine features of both computing paradigms. Their work in improving image analysis and classification processes often outperforms purely classical methods, particularly in tasks requiring high efficiency and accuracy, such as medical image analysis.

Extending this, studies focusing on purely quantum algorithms, such as those by Giuntini et al. (2023a) and Zeng et al. (2023), delve into the development of Quantum Neural Networks (QNNs) and Quantum Support Vector Machines (QSVMs). These studies exploit inherent quantum properties such as superposition and entanglement to enable more efficient processing and analysis of complex, high-dimensional data. This is particularly important in areas such as natural language processing and reinforcement learning, where quantum algorithms show remarkable potential to handle complicated decision-making tasks and to manage large amounts of data more efficiently than their classical counterparts.

In addition, the work of Rana et al. (2022) and Sharma et al. (2023) highlights the advantages of quantum algorithms in specific applications, such as handwriting recognition and text classification. Their results highlight the potential of quantum approaches in a range of diverse machine learning tasks.

Furthermore, in the context of cybersecurity, quantum algorithms have a distinct advantage over their classical counterparts. Studies such as that of Suryotrisongko and Musashi (2022) show how quantum approaches, using quantum mechanics, can process complex data sets more efficiently and provide robust solutions to cybersecurity challenges. This superiority in efficiency, accuracy, and scalability makes quantum algorithms as particularly advantageous for complicated cybersecurity tasks.

In summary, the diverse approaches to quantum machine learning, from pure quantum algorithms to hybrid models, are pushing new frontiers of computational power and grounding quantum principles in practical applications. This range of methods opens up promising avenues for future research, each with the potential to significantly improve data processing and analysis techniques.

5. Comparative Analyzes

In the field of quantum-enhanced machine learning, comparative studies such as Rana et al.'s work (2022) on Quantum Support Vector Machines (QSVMs) are crucial. They show that QSVM have made significant advances in processing speed and accuracy for handwriting recognition, highlighting their superiority over traditional methods in certain applications. Extending this comparison, Sharma et al. (2023) highlight the effectiveness of quantum kernels in text classification, in particular on how entanglement can improve performance.

Building on these findings, Konar et al. (2023) present a groundbreaking approach to noise-robust image classification with their shallow hybrid classical–quantum spiking feedforward neural network (SQNN). This novel SQNN combines the robustness of classical spiking neural networks (SFNN) with the computational efficiency of quantum circuits, in particular Variational Quantum Circuits (VQC), to significantly improve the performance in processing noisy data. This advance demonstrates the effectiveness of integrating quantum principles into machine learning algorithms, especially in complex, real-world scenarios where data noise is common.

Furthermore, the field of cybersecurity benefits from these comparative analyses. Suryotrisongko and Musashi (2022) show that quantum-enhanced models outperform classical algorithms in identifying and mitigating cyber threats, highlighting the value of quantum approaches in digital security. In industrial applications, Villalba-Diez et al. (2022) use Quantum Deep Learning (QDL) for quality control, achieving faster image processing capabilities than traditional CNNs, demonstrating not only the practical applicability but also the revolutionary potential of quantum computing in traditional ML tasks.

In addition, Houssein et al. (2022) provide a comprehensive overview of various quantum and hybrid models, illustrating a diverse and evolving landscape in quantum machine learning. Complementing this, the integration of quantum principles into image processing, as explored by Singh et al. (2023), provides theoretical insights into quantum improvements in this field. At the same time, Wei et al. (2023) highlight the performance of quantum algorithms in medical image analysis, particularly in managing high-dimensional data more effectively.

6. Case Studies and Applications

The integration of quantum computing with machine learning is driving innovation in a variety fields. In cybersecurity, the work of Suryotrisongko and Musashi (2022) stands out. They have applied hybrid quantum-classical models to improve botnet DGA detection. This case study is a prime example of how quantum computing can address complex cybersecurity challenges, improving detection accuracy and response times.

Continuing their pioneering efforts, Giuntini et al. (2023a) and Zeng et al. (2023) have introduced quantum-inspired classifiers and hybrid quantum-classical frameworks, respectively, to advance machine learning classification and generative models. Their work illustrates the synergy between quantum and classical computing paradigms in reshaping the practical landscape of quantum computing.

Further illustrating this trend, Villalba-Diez et al. (2022) have applied Quantum Deep Learning (QDL) to industrial quality control, particularly to precision-critical sectors such as the steel industry. Their work demonstrates the practical utility of quantum algorithms in real-world applications. Complementing this, Pandey et al. (2023) have shown how Quantum Machine Learning (QML) can tackle complex natural language processing tasks, such as parts-of-speech tagging in code-mixed datasets, highlighting the versatility of quantum methods for linguistic challenges.

In the field of image generation, Zhou et al. (2023) have made significant progress with a hybrid quantum-classical GAN, optimising quantum generators to improve the efficiency of image generation. This is crucial for data augmentation and image processing, highlighting the broad applicability of quantum ML. In addition, Ovalle-Magallanes et al. (2023) have innovated in quantum convolutional neural networks (QCNNs) by implementing quantum angular encoding with learnable rotation, improving computational performance in image processing tasks and overcoming qubit and circuit depth limitations.

The contributions of Rana et al. (2022) and Wei et al. (2023) also stand out. Rana et al. focus on Quantum Support Vector Machines (QSVM) for image recognition, promoting the superiority of quantum computing in pattern recognition over classical methods. Wei et al. extend this to medical data analysis with Quantum Neural Networks (QNNs), demonstrating their ability to handle high-dimensional medical data.

Exploring quantum-classical hybrid models, Ovalle-Magallanes et al. (2023) introduce an innovative approach to QCNNs that improves their efficiency. Their research, tested on datasets such as MNIST and Fashion-MNIST, shows improved performance and adaptability of these models in image processing, broadening the application scope of quantum computing in machine learning.

Taken together, these case studies not only showcase the practical and theoretical applications of quantum computing in machine learning but also highlight the evolving and diverse nature of the field. They illustrate how quantum computing is able to enhance traditional methods and open up new possibilities in data processing and analysis, thereby underlining its potential to deliver significant advances across a range of industries.

7. Future Trends and Research Directions

The findings suggest a trajectory towards more integrated and advanced quantum machine learning systems. Pioneering work in cybersecurity, such as the work by Suryotrisongko and Musashi (2022), indicates a growing trend towards using quantum computing to improve digital security measures. Future research is likely to focus on further optimising quantum algorithms for broader applications, including more robust cybersecurity solutions. In addition, the development of quantum hardware and the exploration of new quantum-classical hybrid models, as highlighted by Villalba-Diez et al. (2022) and Wei et al. (2023), are expected to be key areas of development. These advances will not only enhance the capabilities of quantum machine learning in complex data processing and threat detection but also broaden its application in various fields.

Building on this perspective, Amato et al. (2023) present 'QuantuMoonLight,' a user-friendly, low-code platform designed to streamline quantum machine learning experiments. This platform facilitates the comparison of quantum algorithms with classical ones, making quantum technologies more accessible and encouraging community collaboration. 'QuantuMoonLight' represents a significant advance in quantum machine learning, broadening its appeal and understanding.

Following this trend, Liu et al. (2023) make significant advances in quantum reinforcement learning, applying quantum algorithms to complex challenges such as the Multi-Arm Bandit and Grid problems. Their research, which demonstrates improved efficiency and speed over traditional methods, demonstrates the strengths of quantum computing in dealing with large, complicated issues, and sets the stage for more advanced quantum learning models.

In addition, Molteni et al. (2023) make a significant contribution to quantum echo-state networks by optimising their memory reset rate, particularly for time-sequential tasks. By demonstrating enhanced performance on IBM quantum hardware, their work underscores the importance of quantum reservoir computing in Quantum Machine Learning (QML). This advance in memory scalability and efficiency enriches our understanding of the potential of quantum machine learning algorithms in complex data processing.

A comprehensive analysis by Jadhav, Rasool, and Gyanchandani (2023) explores the broad potential of Quantum Machine Learning (QML) in various fields. They highlight advances in QML algorithms and their real-world applications, particularly in the efficient management of large datasets using quantum principles. The review also discusses strategies for integrating classical and quantum approaches and illustrates the effectiveness of QML in areas such as pattern recognition and bioinformatics.

Next, Kwak et al. (2023) look at Quantum Distributed Deep Learning (QDDL), assessing its potential to improve data security and computational efficiency. They evaluate different QDDL architectures, emphasising their ability to provide secure data management and quantum communication protocols. This research marks an important step in the application of quantum principles to deep learning, addressing both efficiency and security challenges.

Finally, Chen, Samuel, and Yen-Chi (2023) explore a novel asynchronous training method in Quantum Reinforcement Learning (QRL). Focusing on advanced actor-critic quantum policies, their work shows that asynchronous training can rival or surpass classical methods in efficiency, simplifying training and extending the applications of QRL in complex tasks. This suggests a promising direction for more effective quantum machine learning algorithms.

8. Limitations and Challenges

Despite significant progress, the application of quantum computing in machine learning, and cybersecurity in particular, faces notable challenges. As highlighted by Suryotrisongko and Musashi (2022), data privacy concerns and the complexity of quantum algorithms are significant hurdles in security applications. These issues are compounded by the limitations of current quantum hardware and scalability challenges. Studies such as those by Tiwari et al. (2023) and Zeng et al. (2023) also highlight the difficulties of integrating complex quantum algorithms. Overcoming these challenges will be critical to the practical application and effectiveness of quantum ML techniques in cybersecurity and other domains.

9. Discussion

Our exploration of Quantum Machine Learning (QML) reveals a vibrant field where advances in quantum computing are being used to improve machine learning capabilities. As detailed in Table 1, breakthroughs like Quantum Kernel Logistic Regression (QKLR) by Ning et al. (2023) aim to overcome limitations of traditional logistic regression in handling complex data, promising improved pattern recognition and data classification. Similarly, Quantum Support Vector Machines (QSVMs) show how efficiency gains in processing complex data

(Rana et al., 2022; Zhang et al., 2023), although further research is needed. Hybrid Quantum-Classical Deep Learning models, as exemplified by the work of Suryotrisongko and Musashi (2022), achieve comparable or even superior accuracy in areas such as cybersecurity applications, although they require optimisation due to sensitivity to initial conditions.

Table 2 delves into the practical applications of these advances, showing real-world examples such as the significant improvement in botnet detection accuracy achieved by Suryotrisongko and Musashi's (2022) hybrid model in the cybersecurity domain. Quantum techniques, as explored by Wei et al. (2023) demonstrate effectiveness in advanced medical image analysis, while Villalba-Diez et al. (2022) showcase the potential of Quantum Deep Learning (QDL) for enhanced image processing capabilities in industrial quality control. These diverse applications highlight the transformative potential of QML across different sectors.

However, as shown in Table 3, challenges remain. Limited hardware capabilities, characterised by the limited number of qubits (quantum bits) and susceptibility to error of current quantum computing devices, limit the complexity and scalability of QML applications. As quantum computers become more powerful, the question of how to protect sensitive data becomes even more pressing. Addressing these concerns requires the development of new, quantum-resistant encryption techniques.

Table 1: Key Advancements in Quantum Machine Learning

Advancement	Authors	Impact	Challenges
Quantum Kernel Logistic Regression (QKLR)	Ning et al. (2023)	Enhances pattern recognition and data classification	Limited to linear problems. (Logistic regression is a weakness, hence development of QKLR).
Quantum Support Vector Machines (QSVMs)	Rana et al. (2022), Zhang et al. (2023)	Improves efficiency in processing complex data	Need for more comprehensive exploration
Hybrid Quantum-Classical Deep Learning Models	Suryotrisongko, Musashi (2022)	Comparable or superior accuracy in cybersecurity applications	Sensitivity to initial conditions; optimization required

Table 2: Case Studies and Applications

Application Domain	Study	Model/Technique	Key Findings
Cybersecurity	Suryotrisongko, Musashi (2022	Hybrid Quantum-Classical Model	Achieved up to 94.7% accuracy in botnet detection
Medical Image Analysis	Wei et al. (2023)	Quantum Techniques	Demonstrated effectiveness in advanced analysis
Industrial Quality Control	Villalba-Diez et al. (2022)	Quantum Deep Learning (QDL)	Enhanced image processing capabilities

Table 3: Challenges and Limitations

Challenge	Description	Implications for QML
Limited Hardware Capabilities	The current quantum computing hardware offers limited qubits and is prone to errors.	Constrains the complexity and scalability of QML applications.
Data Privacy Concerns	The capacity of quantum computing to disrupt present encryption practices introduces concerns regarding data security.	Necessitates the development of new, quantum-resistant encryption techniques.

10. Conclusion

Our review explored the current state of Quantum Machine Learning (QML), focusing on advances in algorithms (such as Quantum Kernel Logistic Regression and Quantum Support Vector Machines), potential applications in various fields (from strengthening cybersecurity to pioneering medical image analysis and improving industrial quality control), and existing challenges (hardware limitations and privacy concerns). These advances, which address our first research question (RQ1), show significant potential for improved pattern recognition and complex data processing in machine learning. The potential applications (RQ2) highlight the transformative potential of QML, but the challenges (RQ3) represent critical barriers to widespread adoption. While this review provides a quantitative overview, it highlights the need for a deeper exploration to bridge the gap between theory and practice, paving the way for QML to unlock its full potential and revolutionise the future of machine learning.

Acknowledgements

We are grateful to Emils Bagirovs, Grigory Provodin and Ummar Ahmed for their help with data collection and assistance with database creation. This research was partially supported by the ResilMesh project, funded by the European Union's Horizon Europe Framework Programme (HORIZON) under grant agreement 101119681. The authors would like to thank Ms. Tuula Kotikoski for proofreading the manuscript.

References

Acampora, G., Chiatto, A. and Vitiello, A., 2023. Training circuit-based quantum classifiers through memetic algorithms. Pattern Recognition Letters, 170, p.32-38. https://doi.org/10.1016/j.patrec.2023.04.008

Amato, F., Cicalese, M., Contrasto, L., Cubicciotti, G., D'Ambola, G., La Marca, A., Pagano, G., Tomeo, F., Robertazzi, G. A., Vassallo, G., Acampora, G., Vitiello, A., Catolino, G., Giordano, G., Lambiase, S., Pontillo, V., Sellitto, G., Ferrucci, F., and Palomba, F. (2023). QuantuMoonLight: A low-code platform to experiment with quantum machine learning. *SoftwareX, 22, 101399.* https://doi.org/10.1016/j.softx.2023.101399

Chen, S. Y.-C., et al. (2023). Asynchronous training of quantum reinforcement learning. *Procedia Computer Science, 222(2023), 321–330.* https://doi.org/10.1016/j.procs.2023.08.171

Dong, N., Kampffmeyer, M., Voiculescu, I., and Xing, E. (2022). Negational symmetry of quantum neural networks for binary pattern classification. *Pattern Recognition, 129(2022), 108750.* https://doi.org/10.1016/j.patcog.2022.108750

D. Levac, H. Colquhoun, and K. K. O'Brien, "Scoping studies: advancing the methodology," Implementation Science, vol. 5, 2010.

Giuntini, R., Holik, F., Park, D.K., Freytes, H., Blank, C., & Sergioli, G. (2023a). Quantum-inspired algorithm for direct multi-class classification. *Applied Soft Computing*, 134, 109956. https://doi.org/10.1016/j.asoc.2022.109956

Giuntini, R., Granda Arango, A.C., Freytes, H., Holik, F.H., & Sergioli, G. (2023b). Multi-class classification based on quantum state discrimination. Fuzzy Sets and Systems, 467, pp. 108509. https://doi.org/10.1016/j.fss.2023.03.012

H. Arksey and L. O'Malley, "Scoping studies: towards a methodological framework," International Journal of Social Research Methodology, vol. 8, pp. 19–32, 2005.

Houssein, E.H., et al., 2022. Machine learning in the quantum realm: The state-of-the-art challenges and future vision. *Expert Systems With Applications, 194, p.116512.* https://doi.org/10.1016/j.eswa.2022.116512

Jadhav, A., Rasool, A., and Gyanchandani, M. (2023). Quantum Machine Learning: Scope for Real-World Problems. *Procedia Computer Science, 218, 2612–2625.* https://doi.org/10.1016/j.procs.2023.01.235

Kim, J., Huh, J. and Park, D.K., 2023. Classical-to-quantum convolutional neural network transfer learning. *Neurocomputing, 555, pp.126-643.* https://doi.org/10.1016/j.neucom.2023.126643

Konar, D., Sarma, A. D., Bhandary, S., Bhattacharyya, S., Cangi, A., and Aggarwal, V. (2023). A shallow hybrid classical–quantum spiking feedforward neural network for noise-robust image classification. *Applied Soft Computing, 136, 110099.* https://doi.org/10.1016/j.asoc.2023.110099

Kwak, Y., Yun, W. J., Kim, J. P., Cho, H., Park, J., Choi, M., Jung, S., and Kim, J. (2023). Quantum distributed deep learning architectures: Models discussions and applications. ICT Express, 9(1), 486–491. https://doi.org/10.1016/j.icte.2022.08.004

Li, J., Gao, F., Lin, S., Guo, M., Li, Y., Liu, H., Qin, S., and Wen, Q. (2023). Quantum k-fold cross-validation for nearest neighbor classification algorithm. *Physica A: Statistical Mechanics and its Applications, 611, 128435.* https://doi.org/10.1016/j.physa.2022.128435

Liu, Y.-P., Jia, Q.-S., and Wang, X. (2022). Quantum reinforcement learning method and application based on value function. *IFAC-PapersOnLine, 55(11), 132–137.* https://doi.org/10.1016/j.ifacol.2022.08.061

Martín-Guerrero, J. D., and Lamata, L. (2022). Quantum Machine Learning: A tutorial. *Neurocomputing, 470, 457-461.* https://doi.org/10.1016/j.neucom.2021.02.102

Molteni, R., Destri, C. and Prati, E., 2023. Optimization of the memory reset rate of a quantum echo-state network for time sequential tasks. *Physics Letters A, 465, p.128713.* https://doi.org/10.1016/j.physleta.2023.128713

Ning, T., Yang, Y. and Du, Z., 2023. Quantum kernel logistic regression-based Newton method. *Physica A: Statistical Mechanics and its Applications, 611, p.128454.* https://doi.org/10.1016/j.physa.2023.128454

Ovalle-Magallanes, E., Alvarado-Carrillo, D.E., Avina-Cervantes, J.G., Cruz-Aceves, I., and Ruiz-Pinales, J. (2023). Quantum angle encoding with learnable rotation applied to quantum–classical convolutional neural networks. *Applied Soft Computing, 141, 110307.* https://doi.org/10.1016/j.asoc.2023.110307

Page, M.J. and Moher, D., 2017. Evaluations of the uptake and impact of the Preferred Reporting Items for Systematic reviews and Meta-Analyses (PRISMA) Statement and extensions: a scoping review. *Systematic Reviews, 6(1), p.263.* https://doi.org/10.1186/s13643-017-0663-8

Pandey, S., Basisth, N. J., Sachan, T., Kumari, N., and Pakray, P. (2023). Quantum Machine Learning for Natural Language Processing Applications. *Physica A, 627(2023), 129123.* https://doi.org/10.1016/j.physa.2023.129123

Perkowski, M. (2022). Inverse problems constraint satisfaction reversible logic invertible logic and Grover quantum oracles for practical problems. *Science of Computer Programming, 218(2022), 102775.* https://doi.org/10.1016/j.scico.2022.102775

Rana, A., Vaidya, P. and Gupta, G., 2022. A comparative study of quantum support vector machine algorithm for handwritten recognition with support vector machine algorithm. *Materials Today: Proceedings, 56, pp.2025-2030.* https://doi.org/10.1016/j.matpr.2021.11.350

Sharma, D., Singh, P., and Kumar, A. (2023). The role of entanglement for enhancing the efficiency of quantum kernels towards classification. *Physica A, 625, 128938.* https://doi.org/10.1016/j.physa.2023.128938

Shi, J., Chen, S., Lu, Y., Feng, Y., Shi, R., Yang, Y., and Li, J. (2020). An Approach to Cryptography Based on Continuous-Variable Quantum Neural Network. *Scientific Reports, natureresearch.* https://www.nature.com/articles/s41598-020-58928-1

Singh, S., Pandian, M. T., Aggarwal, A. K., Awasthi, S. P., Bhardwaj, H., and Pruthi, J. (2023). Quantum learning theory: A classical perspective for quantum image. *Materials Today: Proceedings, 80(2023), 2786–2793.* https://doi.org/10.1016/j.matpr.2021.07.039

Suryotrisongko, H., and Musashi, Y. (2022). Evaluating Hybrid Quantum-Classical Deep Learning for Cybersecurity Botnet DGA Detection. *Procedia Computer Science, 197(2022), 223–229.* https://doi.org/10.1016/j.procs.2021.12.135

Tiwari, P., Zhang, L., Qu, Z., and Muhammad, G. (2023). Quantum Fuzzy Neural Network for multimodal sentiment and sarcasm detection. *Information Fusion, 103(2024), 102085.* https://doi.org/10.1016/j.inffus.2023.102085

Vadyala, S. R., and Betgeri, S. N. (2023). General implementation of quantum physics-informed neural networks. *Array, 18, 100287.* https://doi.org/10.1016/j.array.2023.100287

Villalba-Diez, J., Ordieres-Mere, J., Gonzalez-Marcos, A., and Soto Larzabal, A. (2022). Quantum deep learning for steel industry computer vision quality control. *IFAC PapersOnLine, 55(2), 337–342.* https://doi.org/10.1016/j.ifacol.2022.04.216

Wang, Y., Lin, K.-Y., Cheng, S., and Li, L. (2022). Variational quantum extreme learning machine. *Neurocomputing, 512, 83–99.* https://doi.org/10.1016/j.neucom.2022.09.068

Wei, L., Liu, H., Xu, J., Shi, L., Shan, Z., Zhao, B., and Gao, Y. (2023). Quantum machine learning in medical image analysis: A survey. *Neurocomputing, 525, 42–53.* https://doi.org/10.1016/j.neucom.2023.01.049

Yulianti, L.P., et al., 2023. A hybrid quantum annealing method for generating ensemble classifiers. *Journal of King Saud University - Computer and Information Sciences, 35, p.101831.* https://doi.org/10.1016/j.jksuci.2023.101831

Zeng, Q.-W., Ge, H.-Y., Gong, C., Zhou, N.-R., et al. (2023). Conditional quantum circuit Born machine based on a hybrid quantum–classical framework. *Physica A: Statistical Mechanics and its Applications, 618, 128693.* https://doi.org/10.1016/j.physa.2023.128693

Zhang, R., Wang, J., Jiang, N., and Wang, Z. (2023). Quantum support vector machine without iteration. *Information Sciences, 635, 25–41.* https://doi.org/10.1016/j.ins.2023.03.106

Zhou, N.-R., Zhang, T.-F., Xie, X.-W., Wu, J.-Y. (2023). Hybrid quantum–classical generative adversarial networks for image generation via learning discrete distribution. *Signal Processing: Image Communication, 110, 116891.* https://doi.org/10.1016/j.image.2022.116891

Railway Infrastructure Cybersecurity: An Overview

João Nunes, Tiago Cruz and Paulo Simões
University of Coimbra, CISUC, DEI, Portugal

jpbn@student.dei.uc.pt
tjcruz@dei.uc.pt
psimoes@dei.uc.pt

Abstract: The railway infrastructure constitutes a type of operational technology (OT)-based critical infrastructure, which is expected to work 24x7, 365 days a year, and where the life expectancy of operational equipment often exceeds 30 years. In this domain, an operational anomaly compromising the OT system can cause a train accident or interrupt traffic, with potentially significant impact in terms of business as well as for passenger safety. Due to their relevance, railways are strategic assets of national interest and, consequently, targets of interest for cybercriminals and cyberwarfare activities. For instance, service interruptions may trigger ripple effects resulting in product shortages and widespread supply chain disruptions, with severe impacts for both the economy and national security. In a bid to optimise and streamline operations. the railway industry has recently started taking a series of significant steps towards digitization, with infrastructures experiencing a significant paradigm shift which, for instance, makes it possible to have centralised interlockings and Radio Block Centre (RBC) for an entire country, with geographical redundancy, ensuring the utmost availability and punctuality by moving the control logic to the cloud. Nevertheless, these developments must always be carried on within the scope of established cybersecurity standards and frameworks. This paper presents an analysis of the state of the art on railway cybersecurity, focused on the existing solutions based on the application of the CENELEC "Technical specification 50701 - Railway Application – Cybersecurity", which is currently the latest European specification addressing railways, being designed to help suppliers, integrators, and operators to implement a cybersecurity risk assessment plan, the necessary controls, and the management of the complete system life cycle. Special attention will be paid to the conduit between the rail signal interlocking system, that controls the line signalling, and the Automatic Train Supervision (ATS) that runs in the Operational Control Centre (OCC), as this has been identified by the European Union Agency for Cybersecurity (ENISA) as one of the most critical systems identified by the operators of essential services.

Keywords: Railways, OT Security, Cyber-Physical Systems, Cybersecurity, Critical Infrastructure Security

1. Introduction

As today's world gets more interconnected, with every system getting more technologically complex, the railway industry is also evolving. With the interdependence of systems, railway infrastructures – that, until a few years ago, were considered safe, since they were not connected to the exterior – are now regarded as potential targets for cyber attacks, due to their economic and societal relevance. As a result of this new cyber landscape, agencies, integrators, and operators face the need to develop cybersecurity standards, specifications and guidelines specifically applied to the railway ecosystem.

Typically, a railway infrastructure is made of several (sub)systems. Among those, according to (Malatras, 2023), the most critical ones are the Interlocking system (IxL) and the Control Centre or Automatic train supervision (ATS). The IxL controls all the signalling and track moving parts, for instance avoiding that multiple trains simultaneously use the same track segment. On the other hand, the ATS is where the train routing and traffic management decisions are taken, and where all train movement is logged. Nowadays, both systems rely on a high level of automation, which also happens to the majority of the other railway subsystems, such as passenger announcing systems, power line control systems and train to track systems. A high-level view of the functional structure of the rail traffic management system is presented in Figure 1.

Overall, the coordination of all those subsystems leads to quite complex railway ecosystems, which poses significant challenges from a cybersecurity point of view. To cope with this situation, in 2021 CENELEC introduced the CLC/TS 50701:2021 (CENELEC, 2021), later updated in 2023 (CENELEC, 2023) and often considered as the world's first international standard to offer comprehensive cybersecurity guidance tailored specifically for rail applications. Nevertheless, the effective adoption of this standard will be a slow and difficult process, due to its complexity, the slow adoption timescale of railway systems, and the need to keep supporting legacy components for a long time.

In this paper we contribute to this ongoing effort by discussing the cybersecurity landscape associated with this recently introduced standard. This contribution is relevant to the cybersecurity community working in the railways field due to the current lack of adequate surveys covering this new standard, which is expected to have a strong impact in this industry.

The rest of the paper is organised as follows: Section 2 provides a general overview of the security of railway systems. Section 3 introduces the reader to the CENELEC TS50701 standard, including the identification of the typical life cycle of railways cybersecurity and the relation with other relevant standards. Section 4 introduces the concepts of interlocking and ATS conduits, also discussing related cybersecurity vulnerabilities and potential countermeasures. Finally, Section 5 concludes the paper.

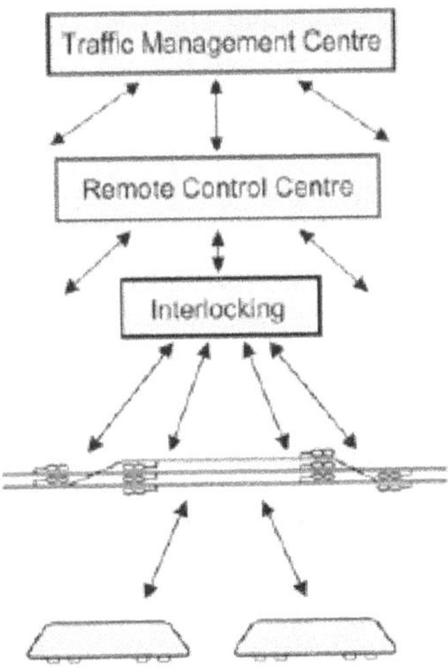

Figure 1: Functional structure (Winter, 2009)

2. Security of Railway Systems

The railway industry is currently undertaking a big step towards digitalization. Moreover, across Europe there is also an ongoing interest towards standardisation and harmonisation, to facilitate cross border service. However, this is an industry where the life expectancy of operational equipment is sometimes over 30 years, which significantly slows down this harmonisation, in terms of technology and security controls. This creates a paradoxical scenario. On one hand, with the rise of the cloud computing paradigm (Cardoso and Simões, 2011), it is possible to have a state-of-the-art system with most of the processing functions and control logic for an entire country being hosted in the cloud (Siemens, 2022). On the other hand, there are still legacy systems running equipment with more or less proprietary technologies from the late 1980s.

Railway infrastructure is a critical Operational Technology (OT) system that is expected to work 24x7, 365 days a year. If something doesn't work as planned, and the OT system is compromised, it can cause train delays, traffic disruption, or even accidents involving dangerous cargo or the loss of human lifes. The potential impact is considerable, both from an economic point of view and from a safety perspective and is prone to induce considerable cascade effects in other critical infrastructures, for instance disrupting supply chain logistics (U.S. Department of Homeland Security, 2022). This turns railways into an attractive target for cyberwarfare.

Moreover, railway systems are potentially more vulnerable to cyberattacks, when compared to IT systems. OT systems such as railways are usually more vulnerable, partially due to a lack of cybersecurity awareness of OT personnel. Because these infrastructures were not originally designed with cybersecurity in mind (long life cycles of 30 years, widespread presence of legacy systems), and because they are less controlled, as well as, spread across a larger geographical area. A railway main line system can have several hundreds of kilometres. For example, the Japanese bullet train, Shinkansen, spreads across 515km, involving a great number of different devices with a great diversity of supply chain (Kapoor, 2022). Security incidents in this type of system can also bring a great impact in the public opinion, due to the great number of people affected. For example, a mass-transit railway system such as the London Tube handles up to five million passenger journeys per day, serving 272 stations (Mayor of London, 2022).

Bearing in mind the criticality, the threats, the vulnerabilities, and the lack of consistency across countries that these OT systems face, the European Union railway suppliers, and operators through the European Committee for Electrotechnical Standardization, recently produced the technical specification CENELEC TS 50701 (Railway applications – CyberSecurity). In the next Section we discuss this technical specification in more detail.

3. Overview of CENELEC TS50701

The CENELEC TS50701 technical specification is directly based on the IEC/EN IEC 62443 series (International Electrotechnical Commission, 2013), which in turn are also related to EN ISO/IEC 27001 (International Organization for Standardization, 2013) and EN ISO 27002 (International Organization for Standardization, 2022). Its goal is to provide a narrower definition and more consistent and specialised approach to the security of a railway system. Previously, system suppliers and railway operators had to resort to more generic standards such as EC/EN IEC 62443 (which has become a horizontal standard as of 2021), which in many aspects missed the specific needs of the railways domain, but are nonetheless relevant.

CENELEC's TS50701 is geared towards railway cybersecurity, aiming at protecting essential system functions. While compliance with this specification may fulfil a specific targeted security level, by adopting state of the art cybersecurity practices, there are factors that can potentially hamper this effort, namely time and budgetary restrictions. Ultimately, cybersecurity becomes a risk management effort focused on achieving a trade-off between effort, budget, and risk tolerance.

3.1 The Life Cycle of Railways Cybersecurity

This technical specification considers thirteen different phases for security-related activities within a railway application life cycle, which directly derive from the standard EN 50126-1 (CENELEC, 2017). More specifically, the following phases are considered:

1. Prerequisites – when the Railway operator's security program is established, and applicable legal and regulatory frameworks are identified.
2. Concept – where the System under consideration (SuC) is identified, along with security-related controls, a High-Level zone model, applicable security standards, and – one of the key points of the technical specification – the definition of purpose and scope. At this stage there must be an alignment between railway operators/asset owners and stakeholder's security goals. The outcome of this phase is the project's cybersecurity management plan.
3. System definition and operational context – corresponding to the definition of system boundaries, and a review of logical and physical network plans, defining the zones and conduits of the network.
4. Risk analysis and evaluation – corresponding to a risk assessment to identify possible threats, along with physical and organisational countermeasures or assumptions for zones and conduits. It should also consider the business continuity aspects (including incident response and recovery) for the system under consideration.
5. Specification of system requirements – in this phase, the SuC-specific refinement of normative requirements should be performed.
6. Architecture and apportionment of system requirements – at this stage the risk assessment if needed should be updated, it should be considered the security-related application conditions, which are explained in Table 6 of (CENELEC, 2021), where an extensive table of security requirements is presented, and its application to the railway environment.
7. Design and implementation – With all the necessary information, now it is time to conclude the design of the solution, it should be prevented and avoided the conflicts between the component cyber security functionality and functional architecture.
8. Manufacture or Procurement – all the necessary material and services are acquired at this phase.
9. Integration – in this phase the network plans should be reviewed considering the new acquired equipment, and it should be made an inventory of all systems and applications. It is also now that the Qualification of security components and functions from test integration results, penetration testing, and vulnerability scanning should be made.
10. System Validation – at this phase it should be Assessed by examination and provision of objective evidence that the SuC in combination with its security-related application conditions complies with the Cybersecurity Requirements Specification, the output of this phase is the Updated System Integrator cybersecurity case.
11. System acceptance – finally we reach the system acceptance, now occurs the security handover between System Integrator and railway operator.
12. Operation, maintenance, and performance monitoring – this is the longest phase in the life cycle of the SuC, across it, is required to perform the maintenance of the logical and physical network plan, as well

as the list of IT systems and installed applications. Perform patch and/or configuration management, data backup and auditing procedures to enable data recovery.

13. Decommissioning – Finally the decommissioning phase, the disposal of components, taking security criteria into account, ensuring that all confidential data and information should be completely erased, and erasure verified during system decommissioning and disposal.

3.2 Other Cyber Security Standards and Guidelines

As presented in (Parkinson et al., 2023), besides the TS50701, there are other standards, and guidelines that could also be applied for the Railway environment, as it is shown in Table 1. Among the referred guidelines, only TS50701 provides some guidance on how cyber security could be managed in the scope of the EN 50126-1 (CENELEC, 2017) Reliability, Availability, Maintainability & Safety (RAMS)-life cycles. The target goal of TS 50701 is to be compatible and consistent with EN 50126-1, when applied to the System under Consideration, as well as to separate the safety approval and cyber security acceptance as much as possible due to their inherent differences in terms of lifecycle (Castanier et al., 2021). TS50701 is the only standard that shows in detail how to implement the complete cyber plan, from prerequisites to decommissioning, and what should be done on each life cycle phase. TS50701 also encompasses a series of technological and organisational countermeasures capable of providing a basic level of assurance for legacy infrastructures conceived without security in mind and which cannot achieve a security level according to IEC 62443 (CENELEC, 2021).

Table 1: Comparisons of Cybersecurity Standards and Guidance (Parkinson et al., 2023)

Standards / Guidance Reference	Main Scope	Links to the EN50126 lifecycle?	Focused on railways?	International Focus?
ISO27001 (International Organization for Standardization, 2013)	IT			Yes
NIST Cybersecurity Framework (Barrett, 2018)	OT & IT			
NIST SP800-82 (Stouffer, 2023)	OT			
NIS Regulations (UK Government, 2018)	OT & IT			Yes
Cyber Essentials (UK Government, 2023)	IT			
AS 7770 (Rail Industry Safety and Standards Board, 2018)	OT & IT		Yes	
IEC 62443 (International Electrotechnical Commission, 2013)	OT			Yes
DIN VDE V 0831-104 (DIN, 2015)	OT		Yes	
TS50701 (CENELEC, 2023)	OT	Yes	Yes	Yes
CYRail D7.5 (CYRail, 2018)	OT		Yes	Yes

IT=Information Technology; OT=Operational Technology

4. Interlocking and ATS Conduit

TS 50701 defines a *conduit* as a logical grouping of communication channels that connect two or more zones, and share common security requirements. In principle, only three different types of conduits are necessary to connect zones, depending on the Security Level of the zones:

- Conduits implementing a transparent gateway (connecting zones with the same security level).
- Filtering conduits as firewall appliances (allowing a zone of lower or equal security level to communicate with a zone of a higher security level).
- And unidirectional conduits, as data diodes (Freitas et al., 2019) or network taps, allowing output from a higher security level zone to others.

The conduit that connects the IxL systems to the ATS is of utmost critical relevance. The IxL systems are responsible for controlling the train exclusive access to a route, which is a sequence of track elements exclusively assigned for train movement through a station or a junction (Soderi et al., 2023). The ATS, or Operations Control Centre, often acts upon the signals generated by the IxL system to monitor and adjust the performance of individual trains, to ensure smooth railway service. It is where the railway operators take decisions and control the railway traffic (Soderi et al., 2023).

4.1 Interlocking Main Vulnerabilities

Concerning interlocking system vulnerabilities, railway infrastructures are distributed over wide geographical areas, where critical nodes of railway systems and networks require maximum availability, and where physical protection and maintenance cost time and money (Liveri et al., 2020). Track side equipment updates can have an important financial repercussion, due to the number of systems and their cost (Liveri et al., 2020). Updating the legacy or obsolete systems (with life cycles calculated in decades) to implement cybersecurity measures is often difficult or even impossible.

4.2 Main Vulnerabilities of Automatic Train Supervision Systems

One of the key vulnerabilities of ATS systems is the lack of consensus on how to conceive such control centres, since many different Operations Control Centre (OCC) configurations have been proposed over the years, often based on non-compatible standards (Soderi et al., 2023). This is aggravated by the generalised adoption of bad practices such as postponing operating system updates and patches indefinitely or provisioning and configuring network equipment with no protective measures enabled – for instance incorrect or non-existent network segregation, using both to provide passenger access and to communicate telemetry data with track-side devices (Gordeychik, 2019). Railway operators also report problems related with low cybersecurity awareness and differences in culture, especially among safety and operations personnel (Liveri et al., 2020). Railway Supervision application developers also suffer from weak cybersecurity awareness, focusing mostly on developing the functionality of the applications and not on their resilience to cyber-attacks, often disregarding good development and lifecycle management practices such as the ones proposed by IEC 62443-4-1 (IEC, 2018).

4.3 Measures to Control Risks at the Conduit Level

4.3.1 Modelling Tools for Cyber-Physical Systems

A few tools and measures have been proposed in the literature to decrease the vulnerability of conduits, as discussed next.

For instance, (Thomas et al., n.d.) proposes a modelling framework for an automated analysis of threats. More specifically, it proposes a tool for evaluating vulnerability based on the CVSS score. It has an interesting way of describing the system under consideration, using the Visio tool as a graphical input. Then, it creates a mathematical model of the system as a directed graph, including the data flows between the components. It is also necessary to define which assets could be vulnerable to an attack. Finally, in the last step, the attacker is characterised. The framework allows to determine attack vectors and possible attack paths, based on statistical analysis. It also provides a cost-effective way of testing possible attack scenarios. The framework also allows estimating the impact of an attack, based on which nodes have been compromised. This makes it possible to understand how attacks propagate, often pinpointing less obvious and neglected propagation paths. Finally, the framework also makes it possible to quickly test new strategies of mitigation.

Another interesting study is presented in (Adamos et al., 2024), which recommends segregating the OT and IT networks from the beginning. This recommendation is motivated by two main reasons: first, the type of traffic conveyed for each domain is totally different, often presenting distinct (and possibly competing) requirements. Second, the interconnection of OT and IT traffic introduces extra attack vectors. Thus, segregation can be based on a defence in depth approach, focusing on the critical functions of the conduit.

Additionally, there might be constraints – for instance, in IEC 61850 scenarios a mandatory response time of less than 4ms advises against the use of network encryption (Gaspar et al. 2023). As a result, a comprehensive risk assessment is required, to adapt the security measures to the operational requirements or to choose the tools and technologies whose performance better suit the specific scenario needs (Rosa et al., 2015). To better understand the risk of the conduit or the system, in (Adamos et al., 2024) they have developed a tool called

CPSRA (cyber physical risk assessment), based as well in graph theory, according with the authors, it performs automatic complexity analysis of the Cyber-physical systems (CPS), and its goal is to improve the resilience of the system. When creating the model of the real-world system, it considers the CVE vulnerabilities of each component and produces an isomorphic graph of the test model. The output of the tool identifies the high-risk components and potential sub-attack and subliminal attack paths. It also suggests mitigation points for the implementation of security controls. The tool also gives a new perspective to the security team, where sometimes a component may not include a high -impact CVE, could be a critical component due to its location in the overall architecture. As well as the tool previously described, this one allows to perform an automated risk analysis, saving time, where normally this task would be done manually.

4.3.2 Methodology

The authors of (Prochazka et al., 2023) propose a deeper and more practical approach to the security design part of the project, when compared with the standard approach prescribed in IEC 62443-3 and, consequently, in TS50701. The motivation for this methodology is the need to ensure the security of systems and products at the design stage – since when the project is already in the field it becomes much more difficult and costly to perform any changes. As it also considers a more enterprise-focused perspective, it should also include the company's risk management practices. In the proposed methodology, the process of determining the safety design (corresponding to phases 1 to 6 of TS50701) is replaced in detail by a total of 39 tables: T_1: Division of individual areas.

- T_2: Division of functions into assets.
- T_3: Categorize threats.
- T_4: Threat severity rating.
- T_5: Quantifying the severity of threats.
- T_6: Asset Impact Table.
- T_7: Quantification of the impact of assets.
- T_8: Determination of the acceptable level of risk for the asset.
- T_9: Criteria for assessing the level of risk.
- T_10: Table of asset allocations into zones and interconnections.
- T_11: Zoning and risk-based interconnections.
- T_12: List of threats and vulnerabilities versus follow-up.
- T_13: Assessment of Assets in terms of type assets.
- T_14: Table of calculated partial threats.
- T_15: List of individual requirements set by the standard.
- T_16: Criteria for determining the severity of the measure.
- T_17: Severity matrix (aggregated).
- T_18: Pareto analysis.
- T_19: Risk Management Plan.
- T_20: List of any risk control measures.
- T_21: Threats and vulnerabilities versus zones and interconnections.
- T_22: Vector/requirement versus zone/link SL table.
- T_23: Threats and vulnerabilities versus areas.
- T_24: Resulting values for each zone/interconnection.
- T_25: Calculation of resulting SL-vectors.
- T_26: Assignment of SL_T for individual requirements set out in EN IEC 62443.
- T_27: Monitoring the fulfilment of individual target SLs.
- T_28: Assessment of Assets in terms of type assets (Confidentiality).
- T_29: Assessment of Assets in Terms of Type Assets (Integrity).
- T_30: Assessment of Assets in Terms of Type Assets (Availability).
- T_31: Assessment of Assets in terms of type assets (Reliability).
- T_32: Assessment of Assets in Terms of Type Assets (Security).
- T_33: Assessment of Assets in terms of type assets (Maintainability).
- T_34: Assessment of Assets in Terms of Type Assets (Vulnerability).
- T_35: Assessment of the threat in terms of type assets (Frequency).
- T_36: Assessment of the threat in terms of type assets (Impact).

- T_37: Assessment of the Threat in terms of type assets (Vulnerability).
- T_38: Table of consequences and impacts.
- T_39: Probability table.

As the listed tables are interconnected, it becomes possible to perform changes on one of the tables and monitor the cascade impact on interrelated tables. This approach has already been used in two different projects to compile the security design of mobile communication gateways on railways.

4.3.3 Virtual Test Platforms

Virtual test platforms are an important complement to the modelling tools previously described from (Thomas et al., n.d.) and from (Adamos et al., 2024), as well as to the detailed approach proposed by (Prochazka et al., 2023).

As described in (Soderi et al., 2023), evaluating security threats can be highly disruptive on live systems, thus advising the use of laboratory environments. However, when such environments are not available, an alternative is to resort to interactive platforms enabling the creation of entirely virtual representations (called scenarios) of existing railway infrastructures, emulating their operations by exploiting virtualization and digital twin technologies. This approach can reduce setup and running costs, allowing for multiple scenarios to be remotely accessible and evaluated in parallel. It should be mentioned that, regardless of the chosen approach, one of the challenges to reproduce the complexity of the setup deployed in the field is to obtain highly detailed knowledge from the system owners about their systems.

The aforementioned platforms can be classified into two main types: simulation-based and emulation-based architectures. The main difference is that an emulation environment reproduces with great accuracy the system peculiarities, while simulation mimics the essential characteristics of the physical system but may not replicate some of its minor details – something which may be relevant for network security. Finally, hybrid scenarios combining virtual and real devices may also constitute a suitable alternative, especially for cases where some legacy systems cannot be virtualized (Foglietta et al., 2018).

Table 2 presents a comparison between some of the well-known virtual test platforms. It should be mentioned that these can also be leveraged to implement railway infrastructure scenarios, allowing for instance to study the impact of attacks on the IxL to ATS conduit, to understand how malware can propagate through the network or to test a specific Layer 2 attack. Another benefit of using test platforms is the possibility to resort to automation tools such as Ansible, streamlining the provisioning and configuration of complex setups.

Table 2: A SCHEMATIC COMPARISON BETWEEN SOME WELL-KNOWN VIRTUAL TEST SOLUTIONS (Soderi et al., 2023)

	CORE (US NRL, n.d.)	**Mininet (Mininet, n.d.)**	**EVE-NG (EVE, n.d.)**	**GNS3 (Solarwinds, n.d.)**	**Cisco CML (Cisco., n.d.)**
Network configuration	Python, Labs	Python, CLI	API, LABS	API, Labs	API, Labs
Network emulation level	L3, (L1/L2 EMANE)	L2	L2	L2	L2
Node operating system emulation	No	No	Yes	Yes	Yes
Licensing	BSD	BSD	GPL, Commercial	GPL	Commercial

Cyber threats can have many root causes, ranging from weak configurations to inappropriate security controls, among many others. Thus, one major advantage of using virtual test platforms is to allow security teams to assess the impact of specific threats in a way that it would be hard or even impossible to perform on a full physical environment, also allowing to safely use techniques and tools that could potentially have a disruptive impact in production environments.

Following the cyber kill chain (Lockheed Martin, n.d.), the steps for using this kind of approach to evaluate the network security would be the following: to emulate the network with the same configurations as the field devices; search for vulnerabilities using automated scanning tools like Nessus (Tenable, n.d.); and, finally, enumerate the found vulnerabilities and measure their impact. Based on the identified vulnerabilities, we can now move on to develop and test countermeasures.

4.3.4 *Testbed*

Another approach to replicate the IxL to ATS conduit, is presented in the work of (Heinrich et al., 2020) , which describes a laboratory environment testbed, depicted in Figure 2. This scenario uses a centralised architecture with object controllers, as well as simulators for the light signals and track changing point machines. Object controllers are based on Raspberry Pi single board computers. Such object controllers are part of modern, modularised computer-based interlocking systems, whose function is to receive command and control messages via a communication network and set the controlled field element (light signal, point) to the commanded state. (Heinrich et al., 2020). A graphical user interface (GUI) was also implemented, allowing to set routes between two signals.

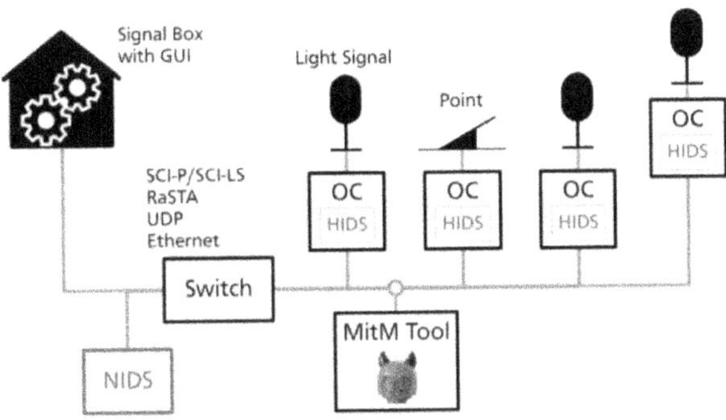

Figure 2: Overview of the testbed's architecture and components (Heinrich et al., 2020)

This scenario gives the security researcher the opportunity to test and implement security controls, and at the same to simulate realistic attacks. In this specific case a man in the middle attack was also demonstrated, by performing ARP spoofing and intercepting and changing the datagrams.

5. Conclusions

This article provides a high-level overview of the railway environment, detailing its societal importance and susceptibility to cyber-attacks. It explores the challenges of harmonising cybersecurity controls, stemming from the stark contrast between cutting-edge systems and those reliant on 1980s technology. Additionally, it outlines the organisation of the European guideline TS50701, tailored for railway cybersecurity. The paper also discusses applicable standards and guidelines not specifically aimed at railways. Furthermore, it examines a critical aspect of railway infrastructure and ongoing efforts to mitigate associated risks through risk assessment tools and methodologies. Lastly, it explores virtual test platforms and testbeds, demonstrating their current capabilities in testing new solutions against cyber threats.

Future developments will encompass a deeper analysis of existing security assessment guidelines, as well as an overview of the contact points between TS50701 and national regulations, such as the US Transportation Security Administration's Security Directive 1580-21-01 (US Transportation Security Administration, 2021). Another interesting line for future work is the comparative analysis of existing standards with the upcoming IEC 9/PT 63452 (International Electrotechnical Commission, 2013).

Acknowledgements

This work was partially funded by National Funds through the FCT -- Foundation for Science and Technology, I.P., and the European Social Fund, through the Regional Operational Program Centro 2020, within the scope of the project CISUC UID/CEC/00326/2020. It was also co-funded by the "Agenda Mobilizadora Sines Nexus" project (ref. No. 7113), supported by the Recovery and Resilience Plan (PRR) and by the European Funds Next Generation EU, following Notice No. 02/C05-i01/2022, Component 5 – Capitalization and Business Innovation – Mobilising Agendas for Business Innovation.

References

Adamos, K., Stergiopoulos, G., Karamousadakis, M., Gritzalis, D., 2024. Enhancing attack resilience of cyber-physical systems through state dependency graph models. Int J Inf Secur 23, 187–198. https://doi.org/10.1007/s10207-023-00731-w

Cardoso, A. and Simões, P., 2011. Cloud computing: Concepts, technologies and challenges. In: proc. of the International Conference on Virtual and Networked Organizations, Emergent Technologies, and Tools (ViNOrg 2011). doi: 10.1007/978-3-642-31800-9_14

Barrett, M., 2018. Framework for Improving Critical Infrastructure Cybersecurity, Version 1.1. Gaithersburg, MD. https://doi.org/10.6028/NIST.CSWP.04162018

Castanier, B., Cepin, M., Bigaud, D., Berenguer, C., Okstad, E.H., Bains, R., Myklebust, T., Jaatun, M.G., 2021. Implications of Cyber Security to Safety Approval in Railway. Research Publishing. https://doi.org/10.3850/981-973-0000-00-0

CENELEC, 2017. CENELEC EN 50126 - Railway Applications - The Specification and Demonstration of Reliability, Availability, Maintainability and Safety (RAMS) . ISBN: 9780539085266

CENELEC, 2021. CLC/TS 50701 - Railway applications-Cybersecurity.

CENELEC, 2023. CLC/TS 50701:2023 - Railway applications-Cybersecurity. ISBN: 9780539208559

Cisco Systems Inc, CML - Cisco Modeling Labs [WWW Document], n.d. URL: https://developer.cisco.com/modeling-labs/ (accessed 2.13.24).

CYRail consortium, 2018. CYRail recommendations on cybersecurity of rail signalling and communication systems. UIC-ETF. URL: https://cyrail.eu/IMG/pdf/final_recommendations_cyrail.pdf (accessed 2.16.24).

Foglietta, C., et al., 2019. From Detecting Cyber-Attacks to Mitigating Risk Within a Hybrid Environment. IEEE Systems Journal, vol. 13, no. 1, pp. 424-435. doi: 10.1109/JSYST.2018.2824252.

Liveri, D., Theocharidou, M., Naydenov, R., ENISA, 2020. RAILWAY CYBERSECURITY Security measures in the Railway Transport Sector NOVEMBER 2020 RAILWAY CYBERSECURITY ABOUT ENISA. https://doi.org/10.2824/235164

DIN, 2015. DIN VDE V 0831-104 VDE V 0831-104:2015-10 - Electric signalling systems for railways - Part 104: IT Security Guideline based on IEC 62443 [WWW Document]. DIN VDE V 0831-104 VDE V 0831-104:2015-10. URL https://www.vde-verlag.de/standards/0800264/din-vde-v-0831-104-vde-v-0831-104-2015-10.html (accessed 2.16.24).

EVE-LG Ltd, n.d. EVE - The Emulated Virtual Environment For Network, Security and DevOps Professionals. [WWW Document], n.d. URL https://www.eve-ng.net/ (accessed 2.13.24).

Freitas, M., Rosa, L., Cruz, T., Simões, P., 2019. SDN-Enabled Virtual Data Diode. In: proc. of the 4th ESORICS Workshop On The Security Of Industrial Control Systems & Of Cyber-Physical Systems (CyberICPS 2018). doi: 10.1007/978-3-030-12786-2_7

Gaspar, J., Cruz, T., Lam, C.-T., Simões, P., 2023. Smart Substation Communications and Cybersecurity: A Comprehensive Survey. IEEE Communications Surveys & Tutorials, vol. 25, no. 4, pp. 2456-2493. doi: 10.1109/COMST.2023.3305468

Gordeychik, S., 2019. Cyber Resilience of Railway Signalling Systems - Academia.edu [WWW Document]. URL https://www.academia.edu/40629914/Cyber_Resilience_of_Railway_Signaling_Systems (accessed 2.16.24).

Heinrich, M., Arul, T., Katzenbeisser, S., 2020. Demo: Railway Signalling Security Testbed, in: IEEE Vehicular Networking Conference, VNC. IEEE Computer Society. https://doi.org/10.1109/VNC51378.2020.9318338

International Electrotechnical Commission., 2013. IEC 62443-3-3. Industrial communication networks--network and system security. Part 3-3, System security requirements and security levels.

International Electrotechnical Commission, 2023. PT 63452 ED1 - Railway applications - Cybersecurity.

International Organization for Standardization, 2013. Standard ISO/IEC 27001 - Information Technology—Security Techniques—Information Security Management Systems—Requirements. Standard ISO/IEC 27001.

International Organization for Standardization, 2018. IEC 62443-4-1:2018 Security for industrial automation and control systems - Part 4-1: Secure product development lifecycle requirements.

International Organization for Standardization, 2022. ISO/IEC 27002:2022 - Information security, cybersecurity and privacy protection — Information security controls [WWW Document]. International Organization for Standardization. URL https://www.iso.org/standard/75652.html (accessed 2.16.24).

Lockheed Martin [WWW Document], n.d. Cyber Kill Chain. URL https://www.lockheedmartin.com/en-us/capabilities/cyber/cyber-kill-chain.html (accessed 2.13.24).

Kapoor, N., 2022. Understanding Railway Cybersecurity [WWW Document]. International Society of Automation - ISA Global Cybersecurity Alliance. URL https://gca.isa.org/blog/understanding-railway-cybersecurity (accessed 2.16.24).

Malatras, A., Stanic, Z., Lella, I. (2023). ENISA threat landscape: transport sector (January 2021 to October 2022): March 2023, (A. Malatras, editor ,Z. Stanic, editor,I. Lella, editor, R. De Sousa Figueiredo, editor, E. Tsekmezoglou, editor, M. Theocharidou, editor, R. Naydenov, editor, A. Drougkas, editor), ENISA. https://data.europa.eu/doi/10.2824/553997

Mayor of London, 2022. What we do - Transport for London [WWW Document]. Mayor of London. URL https://tfl.gov.uk/corporate/about-tfl/what-we-do (accessed 2.16.24).

Mininet Project. [WWW Document], n.d. URL http://mininet.org/ (accessed 2.13.24).

Parkinson, H.J., Basher, D.R., Bamford, G., 2023. Railway cyber security and TS50701, in: Proceedings of the Fifth International Conference on Railway Technology: Research, Development and Maintenance. Civil-Comp Press, pp. 1–9. https://doi.org/10.4203/ccc.1.17.1

Prochazka, J., Novobilsky, P., Prochazkova, D., Valousek, S., 2023. Cybersecurity Design for Railway Products. Research Publishing Services, pp. 304–311. https://doi.org/10.3850/978-981-18-5183-4_r09-01-099-cd

Rail Industry Safety and Standards Board, 2018. AS 7770:2018 Rail Cyber Security. ISBN: 9781760720780

Rosa, L., Alves, P. , Cruz, T., Simões, P., Monteiro, E., 2015. A Comparative Study of Correlation Engines for Security Event Management. In: proc. of the 10th International Conference on Cyber Warfare and Security (ICCWS-2015).

Siemens, 2022. Infrastructure in the Cloud - Digital Offerings for rail infrastructure [WWW Doc]. Siemens. URL: https://www.mobility.siemens.com/global/en/portfolio/digital-solutions-software/infrastructure/infrastructure-in-the-cloud.html (accessed 2.16.24).

Soderi, S., Masti, D., Lun, Y.Z., 2023. Railway Cyber-Security in the Era of Interconnected Systems: A Survey. IEEE Transactions on Intelligent Transportation Systems 24, 6764–6779. https://doi.org/10.1109/TITS.2023.3254442

Solarwinds Worldwide, GNS3 (Graphical Network Simulator-3). [WWW Document], n.d. URL https://www.gns3.com/ (accessed 2.13.24).

Stouffer, K., 2023. Guide to Operational Technology (OT) Security. https://doi.org/10.6028/NIST.SP.800-82r3

Tenable, Inc., Nessus Vulnerability Scanner [WWW Document], n.d. URL https://www.tenable.com/products/nessus (accessed 2.13.24).

Thomas, R.J., Chothia, T.; Ordean, M., 2022. Cyber security in the rail sector-an integrated approach. Birmingham.

UK Government, 2023. Cyber Essentials scheme: overview - GOV.UK [WWW Document]. URL https://www.gov.uk/government/publications/cyber-essentials-scheme-overview (accessed 2.16.24).

UK Government, 2018. The Network and Information Systems Regulations, S.I. 2018/506. URL: https://www.legislation.gov.uk/uksi/2018/506/contents/made (accessed 2.16.24).

U.S. Department of Homeland Security, 2022. U.S. department of homeland security-transportation security administration, security directive 1580/82-2022-01 - rail cybersecurity mitigation actions and testing.

US Navy Research Laboratory, CORE - Common Open Research Emulator [WWW Document]. URL: https://www.nrl.navy.mil/Our-Work/Areas-of-Research/Information-Technology/NCS/CORE (accessed 2.13.24).

US Transportation Security Administration, 2021. Security Directive 1580-21-01 - Enhancing Rail Cybersecurity [WWW Document]. URL: https://www.tsa.gov/sites/default/files/sd-1580-21-01_signed.pdf (accessed 10.4.24).

Winter, P., 2009. Compendium on ERTMS. Hamburg, Eurail Press. ISBN-10: 3777103969.

Strategies for Combating Adversarial Information Operations: Theory and Practical Applications

Alberto Federico Olivieri and Rosanna E. Guadagno
University of Oulu, Finland

Alberto.Olivieri@oulu.fi
Rosanna.Guadagno@oulu.fi
https://orcid.org/0000-0001-7223-3522
https://orcid.org/0000-0001-8247-5154

Abstract: In the contemporary information landscape, the proliferation of disinformation and propaganda poses a significant challenge to societal discourse and democratic processes. This paper proposes a multi-disciplinary approach to combatting adversarial information operations, drawing upon theoretical frameworks and practical applications. Theoretical foundations are established through an examination of the Persuasive System Design (PSD) model (Oinas-Kukkonen, 2013) and its parallels with propaganda tactics. By analyzing the shared flaws and vulnerabilities, insights emerge into the manipulation techniques employed by threat actors in online information spaces. Building upon this theoretical framework, the paper presents a proactive strategy for countering disinformation: the development of Early Warning and Control Systems (EWACS). These systems leverage AI-assisted narrative discovery to monitor the digital information landscape continuously. By identifying emerging threats and inauthentic activity, strategic communicators gain valuable insights for crafting counter-narratives and pre-emptive communication strategies. Key components of the proposed approach include deterrence by denial and resilience-building measures. By shifting the cost-gain calculation of adversaries and enhancing societal resilience, the aim is to create an environment where propagandists face increased challenges in achieving their objectives. This paper emphasizes the importance of collaboration between diverse stakeholders, including governmental organizations, academia, NGOs, and journalists. By harnessing the collective expertise from multiple fields, more effective strategies can be developed to safeguard information integrity and restore public trust. In conclusion, this paper advocates for a convergence of theory and practice in addressing the complex challenges posed by adversarial information operations. By integrating theoretical insights with practical applications, the proposed approach offers a holistic framework for countering disinformation and propaganda in contemporary information environments.

Keywords: Disinformation, Propaganda, Persuasive System Design (PSD), Early Warning and Control Systems (EWACS), Information Operations (IO), Resilience Building

1. Introduction

This work will explore how threat actors utilize online disinformation tactics that inadvertently adhere to principles found in the PSD (Persuasive System Design) model (Oinas-Kukkonen, 2013), and then it will focus on actionable intervention that can be implemented to improve resilience in the targeted population. The principles of the PSD model can be used to constructively influence behavior, but the focus here will be on the misapplication of the model and its key issues. The Information Operations (IO) conducted on social networks by threat actors share the same advantages, but also weaknesses, of the model, even though the model itself is not deliberately applied.

Building on this foundational analysis, this paper aims to glean insights from the study of the PSD model that will strengthen our understanding of how we can effectively curb online propaganda. This path will shed light on the importance of an Early Warning and Control System (EWACS) for the Information Space. Viewing the model from this novel perspective reveals that the correct direction in conducting anti-propaganda measures should be based on both social and technological strategies. We need to improve in multiple areas: firstly, by improving our monitoring capabilities in the information landscape to intercept viral trends and narratives at early stages before their full potential can be unleashed, thus allowing the deployment of more effective seeding strategies. Secondly, by developing better crisis communication strategies, and communication risk assessments, to create a stronger and more robust information environment. Lastly, by enhancing interactions and information sharing between governmental organizations, universities, NGOs, and journalists to restore their damaged reputation (from relentless propaganda attacks, and own errors) in the eyes of the wider public, as to build resilience through stronger media literacy and utilizing the social proof effect.

These suggestions are not new (Pamment and Palmertz, 2023), but we argue that the emergence of a natural convergence in multiple academic fields suggesting the same approaches should be seen as a strong indicator of their potential to achieve positive effects in building resilience if these strategies are implemented in our societies.

This paper is divided into four sections; in the first one we will define what Propaganda, Disinformation, and Misinformation are. Multiple disciplines have slightly different definitions and to avoid confusion it is fundamental to create an initial concordance in terminology. The second section will focus more on the key components of the PSD model, and how we can see those principles mirrored into IOs, with a focus on the weaknesses that the parallel drawn by the PSD will uncover. The last section will discuss the need for a robust EWACS for the Information Space is needed, and the presence of a natural convergence from multiple fields will be highlighted.

2. Definitions: Propaganda, Disinformation, Misinformation, Information Operation, and Information Warfare

Propaganda Operations, or alternatively known as Information Operations (IO), are not necessarily done with malign intent. The definition of "propaganda" as a neutral action has been proposed by Jowett and O'Donnell (Jowett and O'donnell, 2018). In their work propaganda is defined as "The deliberate, systematic attempt to shape perceptions, manipulate cognitions, and direct behavior to achieve a response that furthers the desired intent of the propagandist (p. 6)". This definition creates a picture of something not necessarily negative, as it can describe social awareness campaigns, made with the intent of public benefit such as reducing the abuse of alcohol. Of course, Propaganda is not only used for benign purposes, but it can be leveraged with nefarious intents, covertly, and using falsehoods and deception. Thus, propaganda is divided into three main categories, using as a labelling principle the openness of the original source, and the trustworthiness of the information. The three types of Propaganda are White, Grey, and Black (Ivan, Chiru and Arcos, 2023). White Propaganda occurs when both the source of the information is known, and the information strives to achieve accuracy (Jowett and O'donnell, 2018). An example is the aforementioned campaign against the abuse of alcohol. Black propaganda happens when the source is unknown, or when a façade obscures the real source. In this case, the information is untrue, fabricated or presented as to spread disinformation (Jowett and O'donnell, 2018). A well-known example is Operation Denver (Kramer and Savage, 2020), the disinformation campaign regarding AIDS in Africa. This disinformation campaign was conducted by the Soviet Union during the Cold War, falsely attributing the origin of the AIDS virus to US military experiments. Lastly, Grey propaganda is a mix between the two, where the source could be correctly identifiable, and the information quality is uncertain (Jowett and O'donnell, 2018). Current narratives coming from both the Russian and the Ukrainian sides regarding the situation on the Ukrainian war frontlines can fall under this category.

The utilization of propaganda is not new but has evolved through the ages along human communication. The Epic of Gilgamesh, one of the earliest pieces of literature, illustrates early uses of propaganda to influence societal views on governance and spirituality. After the First World War, the term came to be perceived as more and more negative, and it quickly reached the connotation that nowadays is common (Jowett and O'donnell, 2018). Propaganda theory and propaganda tactics were refined during the cold war era, where the current Russian model find its roots (Hosaka, 2023). This approach, known as "active measures" (активные мероприятия), was born before internet and social media where available, but its principles and methodologies where enhanced, not diminished, by these new technologies (Randolph, Labriny and DiOrio, 2023).

With the advent of social media, the dynamics of propaganda have transformed dramatically. These platforms have facilitated not only the maintenance and creation of relationships but also the spread of propaganda through new forms of communication. As propaganda and communication are inextricably linked, the social media platforms gave threat actors new vectors to spread fake news and disinformation through targeted advertisement (Guadagno and Guttieri, 2021). This technology has multiple advantages for threat actors, such as deniability, ease of deployment, reduced costs, and is not restricted by national borders. These are some of the advantages of using the internet, and social media in particular, as a new vector of IO.

This growing environment is ripe for bad actors to implement inexpensive but widespread IOs. In the Russian's approach, single IOs are often parts of a bigger Information War (IW) effort, targeted at both the leadership and at the population of adversarial countries (Lilly, 2022). This IOs are conducted in what is called by the Russian leadership the Information Space, and it is similar but not equal to the western Cyber Space. In this paper we will continue to use the term Information, instead of Cyber, as it more aptly describes the adversarial vision of their operations, where technical and psychological dimensions coexist and enhance each other as the two main components of IW (Lilly, 2022). It is also worth noting how Russian doctrine have a more nuanced and varied definition of what is considered warfare. While a black and white approach is more common in the western circles, where the concept of warfare is often relegated to only describing kinetic military action, the USSR, and now Russia, have enhanced their warfare toolkit with non-military and non-kinetic tools (Lilly, 2022). This different vision of what constitute warfare creates the current situation where Russian is, from their doctrinal point of view, conducting a form of warfare against its adversaries, mainly western countries, while these countries still struggle to answer to this threat properly and adequately, or even acknowledging it as such.

In attacks directed to the leadership and to the population of an adversarial country, the psychological approach of IOs relies often on the use of disinformation. Disinformation is, at its core, a type of information, but it also possesses two more attributes, it is misleading, and it was purposefully created to be so. It is misleading and not necessarily false, as it does not need to be, as the intent is to disrupt the information space. The IOs are often based on a central "rational core", that is then misrepresented (Pasquetto et al., 2022), to push the audience to reach the propagandist conclusions, or at least to make them doubt other sources of information, leading to inaction. The intentionality of disinformation combined with its misleading nature sets disinformation apart from other kinds of information. For example, misinformation retains the misleading nature of disinformation, but lacks the intentionality to create it. Disinformation can manifest in various forms, such as deceptive advertising, government propaganda, doctored photographs, forged documents, fake maps, internet frauds, fake websites, manipulated Wikipedia entries, fake online engagement, and more (Fallis, 2015).

Considering the change that happened over time in the popular perception of propaganda, now equated in the minds of many to IW, and the widespread use of disinformation in the IO as we just described, there is no surprise that new definitions that blur the line between the two have appeared. The NATO STRATCOM CoE had recently published its definition of propaganda: "The essence of propaganda is therefore not to tell one lie, but an embellished web of truths and lies towards constructing a new 'alternative truth'". The author also emphasizes the co-production dimension of propaganda, she argues how individual needs of self-identity and self-validation are exploited by the propagandist to create with the recipient a narrative of mixed lies and truths supporting a shared fantasy (Fry, 2022). This definition is coherent and consistent with what is now perceived by the public, and it has a function of its own in differentiating Black and Grey Propaganda activities from the White Propaganda that many nations rightfully and openly deploy. The definition accurately describes what the Russian leadership calls Information Warfare, but it could lead to confusion and misunderstanding with what is considered Propaganda in other academic fields. This is a cautionary example of how much the terminology could be somewhat difficult to navigate through and it can change between authors, fields, or time. While writing about this subject, brief descriptions of what definitions are being used by the authors throughout the paper would greatly improve readability.

3. The PSD Model Key Issues and Its Misapplication in Information Operations

In the papers describing the PSD model a strong emphasis is placed on how information technology inherently influences user attitudes and behaviors (Oinas-Kukkonen, 2013). The PSD model was developed to embed effective strategies into interactive technologies that have the potential to change the users' attitudes or behaviors through persuasive features and psychological tactics. The influence can be particularly evident in platforms that implement some level of constraint on the form or the length of the user expression, thus forcing them to adapt the kind and scope of their messaging. A simple example is X (the platform formerly known as Twitter), where the limited number of characters, and the branching in separate sub threads of a discussion, influence the form of expression and communication patterns. The peculiar arrangement of X somehow limits long and complex interactions, and they cannot be easily followed by other users. The limitations of certain platforms and how they can be optimally utilized, and what kind of platform is more suited for a specific use, are characteristics that are also taken into consideration by threat actors. They maximize reach and potential network growth and retention through this deep understanding of the social network tools at hand. An example of this is the social media platform Telegram. The platform is well known to function as a backup messaging board for various agents of influence. They take advantage of the lack of any sort of moderation, in order to keep their ability to communicate and organize when facing bans, thus retaining their user base. This was documented during the Facebook ban wave of the 2020 presidential election, which heavily hit Italian QAnon groups. Those groups were able to mitigate the hit of the bans with minimal loss of followers, as the influence actors managing those groups had already laid down their own cross-platform network. Through their telegram channel the actors where able to push the majority of their userbase back into their newly made Facebook groups (Pasquetto et al., 2022).

Another key issue emerging from the PSD model is directly derived from the principles of commitment and cognitive consistency (Cialdini, Petty and Cacioppo, 1981). These principles can be summarized with the understanding that people, in general, tend to change their attitude and behaviors, to avoid cognitive dissonance. This human tendency can be easily exploited by threat actors, as it was by Chinese guards during the Korean war. In stark contrast with WWII, where Prisoners of War (POWs) collaboration with the enemy was effectively absent, nearly all the US servicemen captured during the Korean war helped their captors. This was done by making the POWs initially commit to small, and seemingly innocuous statements against the US or favorable to the communist governments in exchange for small improvements to their lives as POWs. Then the requests for collaboration ramped up in scope and commitment, with the POWs finding more and more difficult to break out of the cycle. The more they collaborated, the more collaboration the Chinese obtained from them. To be consistent with themselves and their actions, they were, little by little, drawn into committing more and more on the idea of collaboration, and eventually, becoming too committed to refuse actual acts of collaboration (Cialdini, 2009).

The third key issue of the PSD model postulate concerns what persuasive strategies are used by the persuader: direct or indirect routes for persuasion are both viable. Nevertheless, in the article it is stressed how "in the era of information overflow, people are often forced to use indirect cues more often than before, because of the abundance of information to be handled. When an individual sees relevant cues, heuristics are triggered. These may also be called cognitive shorthands, shortcuts, or rules of thumb." (Oinas-Kukkonen and Harjumaa, 2018). This consideration is deeply ingrained in Russian's IW tactics as we previously discussed (Pasquetto et al., 2022). The threat actors often build upon a central kernel of truth that everybody knows or agrees on, at an instinctual level, to then twist this "rational core" with the aim to push the target audience towards their desired outcome.

The Fourth postulate defines how the persuasion is not immediate. The process is often slow and incremental (Oinas-Kukkonen and Harjumaa, 2018). A good example of how an incremental process of persuasion can be implemented over time was already described. The process of "becoming" a collaborator that Chinese guards subjected the US POWs described previously (Cialdini, 2009), perfectly fit this postulate.

The last three postulates of the PSD model: Openness, Unobtrusiveness, and Usefulness & Ease of Use (Oinas-Kukkonen and Harjumaa, 2018), are absent in the most common forms of IOs on social media platforms. It can be argued that some of these postulates can still be valid in other contexts. As an example of employment of the Usefulness & Ease of Use is a website developed with the intent of providing a news aggregator, with integrated translations from English to Italian, of English QAnon material to Italian QAnon members (Pasquetto et al., 2022). This was extremely useful as Italy English literacy is one of the lowest in Europe, especially in older generations, the most likely to be the core audience of the QAnon groups.

This short examination of the key issues of the PSD model suggests that threat actors are aware of the key actions and procedures they can perform to influence behaviors and attitudes. Their actions and processes now are again charted on a better known and studied terrain. This reliance on already known tactics helps in deconstructing their action, and thus letting us gain actionable intelligence in the proper counteraction to deploy for curbing their IOs.

4. Proactive Strategies Against Disinformation: Shifting Toward Anticipatory Measures

As previously discussed, information is a crucial resource for all individuals. We rely on it while planning our lives, evaluating situations, and taking both minor and major decisions. People's understanding of the world is shaped by their information environment, and they also continuously influence it. However, as explored earlier, the current information landscape is often cluttered with an abundance of conflicting information, and this state complicates, delays, or otherwise impairs the direct decision-making processes. The situation is further disrupted by threat actors who are willing to exploit these chaotic conditions, consciously injecting false and damaging narratives into the system. These actions ultimately undermine the public discourse and everyone's democratic process, as they deliberately target the vulnerabilities proper of the current high-information environment (Guadagno, Okdie and Muscanell, 2013; Quattrociocchi, Scala and Sunstein, 2016; Guadagno, 2021; Arcos and Arribas, 2023).

To confront and reduce the damage to our societies, the prevailing approach now employed by most actors revolves around debunking. However, this approach suffers from inherent flaws: it is often too slow to effectively counteract the spread of false narratives, and it's inherently reactive. By the time any corrections or retractions are issued, the public has already been significantly exposed to, and potentially influenced by, these narratives. Furthermore, there is a high likelihood that many individuals will not encounter these corrective statements. This current state of affairs is not a long-term solution to the ever-evolving attack on our information landscape, thus, there is a dire need for a transition towards more proactive strategies. Scholarly work on the subject increasingly recognizes the limitation of the current reactive approaches to disinformation. While not explicitly tied to deterrence studies, the solutions proposed align naturally with deterrence principles, and are fundamental for a more proactive approach to the issue (Kennedy et al., 2017; Pamment and Palmertz, 2023).

Deterrence can be subdivided into Deterrence by Denial and by Punishment. While both methods can and should be available in the toolkit of a country, the main principle for deterring IOs is Deterrence by Denial. This form of deterrence can be achieved by shifting the cost-gain calculation of the adversary, making it more challenging for attackers to achieve their goals without increased effort. Deterrence thus is not only relegated to direct punishment, but the power to hurt can be seen as increasing the adversary's costs associated with a specific action (Schelling, 2020). This approach to attain deterrence aligns with the concept of resilience. Increasing resilience creates an environment where the attacker must invest more resources, and achieving previous results is all but guaranteed (Kennedy et al., 2017). Population resilience can be enhanced through improving media literacy, digital monitoring, risk assessment from a communication perspective, and open-source capabilities (Pamment and Palmertz, 2023).

The necessity for digital monitoring is thoroughly examined in "Anticipatory Approaches to Disinformation, Warning and Supporting Technologies". In this article the authors are keen to suggest adapting tools and practices developed from issue and crisis management to the forecasting of disinformation attacks (Arcos and Arribas, 2023). This stress on the ability to forecast should be cojoined by an in-depth analysis of previously observed adversarial behavior (Lilly, 2022), and with a strict and honest self-assessment of our own vulnerabilities as a society (Arcos and Arribas, 2023). Taking all these suggestions into account, it should be possible to develop Early Warning and Control System (EWACS) tools for the Information Space. Such EWACS systems would provide strategic communicators with a crucial margin of maneuver to develop in a timely fashion counter-narratives, initiate prebunking campaigns, or deploy other communication strategies tailored to mitigate the impact of disinformation. These tools are vital for safeguarding the integrity of our information ecosystem by allowing us to respond proactively to emerging threats.

There is a strong consensus between scholars and practitioners alike about the need for a paradigm shift from traditional reactive methods to a more proactive, strategic approach in combating disinformation. By prioritizing the development and implementation of early warning systems, it should be possible to significantly mitigate the spread of disinformation, and restore the integrity of our information space, while also strengthening internal societal discourse. However, as we refine these tools and the theory behind them, it is imperative to ensure that these interventions in the information space are conducted with a deep respect for individual freedoms and free speech. It is crucial that the people in charge of combating disinformation do not become "arbiters of truth". This balance is essential for maintaining the public's trust and the effectiveness of our efforts against disinformation.

5. Conclusion: Synthesizing PSD Model Insights with Proactive Disinformation Strategies

This paper focuses on how Persuasive System Design (PSD) Key Issues are involuntarily reflected in the modus-operandi of threat actors conducting IOs. This unintended reliance on well-known principles opens the possibility of exploiting the inherent weaknesses of the model, thus enabling the creation of more robust and coherent defense tools and practices. The misapplication of the first four PSD postulates can be curbed using ideas and suggestions coming from other disciplines. This natural convergence of various independent disciplines suggests a high chance of success if these actions and tools are to be implemented and developed.

Applying Constraints and Expression: The PSD model focuses on the influence of the Information Systems, and it has already been discussed how threat actors can exploit their strongpoints and vulnerabilities to obtain the desired outcomes from their use. One of the most important abilities of any social media, and of the internet in general, is the ability of storing information, and this should be leveraged in our favor. The PSD model, following Deterrence by Denial principles, suggests that any EWACS tool should be developed with old material, already known threat actors and their affiliation, discovered botnets, and other historical data. This will enable faster labeling and discovery of new narratives that are pushed on the scene, and labeling by proximity new actors, botnets, websites, and other sources of disinformation. In short, we should exploit the ability of information retention to create an expanding database thus reducing the timeframe for action attribution and better recognizing organized narrative spread.

Proactive Commitment Strategies: The PSD's observation that individuals seek to maintain consistent commitments is currently exploited against our open and free information environment. On the other side, it also proves how preemptive strategies like prebunking can be highly effective. This point is inherently linked to the early attribution and warning that where the focus of the previous point. With the knowledge that an IO is taking place, authorities should strive to introduce as soon as possible into the system accurate information. This will help shield the majority of the public from the harm of disinformation.

Utilizing Indirect Persuasion: Another link in our actionable suggestions chain is the use of indirect persuasion during prebunking campaigns. Among others, a technique that can be used to enhance the effectiveness of prebunking messaging is the evocation of strong emotions into the audience. Negative emotions are often used by threat actors to deliver their message, as they can shut down our more conscious decision-making process. It is also possible to enhance with strong emotions the counter-narratives of the prebunking campaign, keeping strict factuality. The public should be reminded of the presence of people with ill-intent that are actively trying to deceive them. If done properly, with corroborating evidence, this course of action will enhance the audience diffidence towards outside manipulatory tactics. These tactics will cut short the vital initial momentum of adversarial IOs.

Sustained Persuasive Efforts: While EWACS tools, deployed with state-of-the-art persuasive tactics, and corroborated with factual evidence, are fundamental for curbing, the acute phases of an IO, long term proactive and continuous solution, are to be employed. The fundamental need for proofing future generation against these campaigns is highlighted both by the PSD model and by many practitioners in the field of debunking. Now more than ever decision makers should commit to the creation of persistent initiatives to bolster media literacy and critical thinking. This will prove fundamental to creating a public that is resilient to the current and future intensification of misleading campaigns.

The push for both new tools, and long-term media literacy campaigns should be simultaneous. Tools like EWACS are focused on the crisis management of strategic communication but cannot be deemed a long-term solution that builds consistent behavior and attitude change in how people consume information. On the other hand, media literacy and critical thinking campaigns are tools well suited for those goals, but lack penetration into older strata of the public, suffer from the technology age gap, and are not suited at all for crisis management. These systems are essential for both preempting threats and strengthening the overall resilience of communities against the complex tactics employed in contemporary information warfare.

Nevertheless, it is crucial that ethical and legal standards are kept front and center during all the development phases of these tools. It's vital that our approach to win the Information war that is being waged against us respects individual rights and freedom of speech. Thus, our defenses will enhance, and not compromise, the dynamism and openness of the public discourse. Our security needs should strike a balance with our commitment to democratic and liberal values.

References

Arcos, R. and Arribas, C.M. (2023) 'Anticipatory Approaches to Disinformation, Warning and Supporting Technologies', in Routledge Handbook of Disinformation and National Security. Routledge, pp. 401–416.

Cialdini, R.B. (2009) Influence: Science and practice. Pearson education Boston, MA.

Cialdini, R.B., Petty, R.E. and Cacioppo, J.T. (1981) 'Attitude and attitude change', Annual review of psychology, 32(1), pp. 357–404.

Fallis, D. (2015) 'What is disinformation?', Library trends, 63(3), pp. 401–426.

Fry, E. (2022) 'Persuasion Not Propaganda: Overcoming Controversies of Domestic Influence in NATO Military Strategic Communications', Defence Strategic Communications, 11(11), pp. 177–213.

Guadagno, R.E. (2021) 'From Russia with Love: A Social Psychological Analysis of Information Warfare in the Social Media Age', in Democracy in the Disinformation Age. Routledge, pp. 182–200.

Guadagno, R.E. and Guttieri, K. (2021) 'Fake news and information warfare: An examination of the political and psychological processes from the digital sphere to the real world', in Research anthology on fake news, political warfare, and combatting the spread of misinformation. IGI Global, pp. 218–242.

Guadagno, R.E., Okdie, B.M. and Muscanell, N.L. (2013) 'Have we all Just Become "Robo-Sapiens"? Reflections on social influence processes in the Internet age', Psychological inquiry, 24(4), pp. 301–309.

Hosaka, S. (2023) 'Cold War Active Measures', in Routledge Handbook of Disinformation and National Security. Routledge, pp. 45–58.

Ivan, C., Chiru, I. and Arcos, R. (2023) 'Hybrid Security Threats and the Information Domain: Concepts and Definitions', in Routledge Handbook of Disinformation and National Security. Routledge, pp. 9–19.

Jowett, G.S. and O'donnell, V. (2018) Propaganda & persuasion. Sage publications.

Kennedy, J.F. et al. (2017) 'Deterrence and Dissuasion in Cyberspace', International Security, 41(3), pp. 44–71. Available at: https://doi.org/10.1162/ISEC_A_00266.

Kramer, M. and Savage, D. (2020) 'Lessons from Operation "Denver,"the KGB's Massive AIDS Disinformation Campaign', Journal of Cold War Studies, 22(1).

Lilly, B. (2022) Russian information warfare : assault on democracies in the cyber wild west. Naval Institute Press. Available at: https://books.google.com/books/about/Russian_Information_Warfare.html?id=ek7TzgEACAAJ (Accessed: 29 February 2024).

Oinas-Kukkonen, H. (2013) 'A foundation for the study of behavior change support systems', Personal and ubiquitous computing, 17, pp. 1223–1235.

Oinas-Kukkonen, H. and Harjumaa, M. (2018) 'Key Issues, Process Model and System Features', Routledge handbook of policy design [Preprint].

Pamment, J. and Palmertz, B. (2023) 'Deterrence by Denial and Resilience Building', in Routledge Handbook of Disinformation and National Security. Routledge, pp. 20–30.

Pasquetto, I. V et al. (2022) 'Disinformation as Infrastructure: Making and maintaining the QAnon conspiracy on Italian digital media', Proceedings of the ACM on Human-Computer Interaction, 6(CSCW1), pp. 1–31.

Quattrociocchi, W., Scala, A. and Sunstein, C.R. (2016) 'Echo Chambers on Facebook', SSRN Electronic Journal [Preprint]. Available at: https://doi.org/10.2139/SSRN.2795110.

Randolph, H.P., Labriny, D. and DiOrio, A. (2023) 'Historical Disinformation Practices: Learning From The Russians', in Routledge Handbook of Disinformation and National Security. Routledge, pp. 59–83.

Schelling, T.C. (2020) Arms and influence. Yale University Press.

Educating New Military Leaders to be Robust against Influence Operations: A Case Study

Knut Østby[1], Kirsi Helkala[1] and Ole Joachim Aasen[2]
[1]Norwegian Defence University College / Norwegian Defence Cyber Academy, Lillehammer, Norge
[2]Accenture, Oslo, Norge

knostby@mil.no
khelkala@mil.no
ole.Joachim.aasen@accenture.com

Abstract: Influence operations and cognitive warfare are part of the new complex threat picture that Norway and other nations face. In general, military education and leadership education have traditions in place to build robustness against war demands, but how to build robustness against influence operations is still almost non-existing. In this case study, we show how an educational module on influence operations was conducted at the Norwegian Defence University College's Cyber Academy department and how this module contributed to strengthening robustness against cognitive warfare. The impact of the educational module was evaluated by a questionnaire and a short group interview, and the results are shown in this paper. The findings indicate a positive development in the cadets' own perceived robustness. In addition, we also discuss and suggest some personal and organizational factors that can strengthen military leaders' robustness against influence operations. The findings and the discussions can be used as inspiration when educational modules are designed both in military and civilian education.

Keywords: Influence Operations, Military Education, Leadership Education, Robustness, Resilience

1. Introduction

Both mental and physical resilience to cope with the demands of war has been and is an important part of the training of military forces. The military profession is inherently stressful, and if the stress factors are not handled it can lead to a persistent reduction in performance and health challenges (Bartone et al. 2009). Lack of information or ambiguous information are examples of the many military stress factors (Bartone et al. 2009). These two stress factors can be reinforced by an adversary through influence operations, psychological operations, and propaganda, which are often intended to inhibit and influence decision-making.

Disinformation directed at military forces is nothing new. However the emergence of the digital domain and the extensive use of digital information to influence people has led to discussions of a sixth war domain, the cognitive domain (Ottewell 2020). Today's examples can be found in the Ukraine war, where several actors have used disinformation to strengthen their narrative (ENISA 2022, Singer and Johnson 2021). Regardless of whether the cognitive is defined as a separate warfare domain, the digital battle for narratives, truth and information has created a growing need for resilience against influence operations.

In a series of articles, the Norwegian Defence Research Establishment (FFI) has looked at how states use social media as one of many means in their influence operations. The reports highlight how foreign states have contributed to creating division and polarization within Western democracies, with examples such as the handling of COVID-19 and the election in the USA in 2016. The reports emphasize that it is essential and necessary that society becomes more robust facing such operations, and that this is made more accessible by reducing the effect of such operations rather than stopping the operations themselves (Sivertsen et al. 2021). FFI puts forward several proposals for measures to reduce the effect of these operations. One of the proposed measures is to increase the resilience of ministries, agencies, and actors in total defence through training and awareness-raising. Several other articles and reports also promote the importance of strengthened education in the military to reduce the effect of information operations and propaganda (Fitzpatrick et al. 2022, Kacała 2015, Mobley 2011). "Digital Literacy" competence is often mentioned, but it is not specified how this can be raised. Nor has any attempt been made to measure the effect of such education. Singer and Johnsen (2021) also agree that education against disinformation should be included in military training. They indicate that military forces should look to civilian education programs and introduce disinformation awareness training similarly to cyber situational awareness training. Several articles refer to the effects achieved by education in Finland, which is ranked at the top among 35 European countries in robustness against disinformation (Lessenski 2021, Singer and Johnson 2021), mainly due to increased competence from an early age in the entire population.

As there is little information on how such training can be carried out as part of military leadership training and studies on the effect of the training, this research project aims to contribute to precisely this. By studying the effect of an educational experiment on a military leadership education, the study intends to create a deeper understanding of how resilience against cognitive warfare in general and influence operations in social media can be created among military leaders. This study contributes to the development of best practice in the area. The project is based on FFI's hypothesis. It measures if robustness and resilience can be created through training and awareness raising, including practice in handling the impact on exercises. Military training and exercises, including constructive feedback, have previously been mentioned (Helkala and Rønnfeldt 2022) to strengthen self-regulation and cognitive robustness.

This hypothesis was tested on cadets at the Norwegian Defence Cyber Academy. Ahead of the closing exercise at the school, the cadets received training in how states use influence operations to promote their narrative and how social media can be used as part of these operations. The cadets were then tasked to design influence operations in social media based on the scenario of the following military exercise. The actors in the scenario were involved in a fictitious military conflict in Europe. The influencing operations were developed with a simulation tool called Somulator[1]. This tool, developed by the FFI in collaboration with the Norwegian University of Science and Technology (NTNU), can be used to simulate posts on Twitter, websites, image sharing and video sharing.

1.1 Problem Statement

This case study contributes to understanding of how future military leaders feel equipped to deal with influence operations and how education and training could strengthen their resilience.

2. Theory

2.1 Resilience/Robustness

Mental robustness is closely related to psychological or cognitive robustness, which are terms that are often used to explain the same sets of mental qualities that military leaders should have to cope with the pressures and stress. We define robustness as the ability to withstand strain and stress, similar to Aven's definition (Aven 2022).

Resilience is an alternative term that is used to describe many of the same characteristics as robustness and is increasingly used within social security (Stavland and Bruvoll 2019). Resilience focuses more on the process of recovering from demanding situations, while robustness is more about not being affected by the demanding situations. The American Psychological Association defines resilience as both a process and a result of being able to adapt to demanding situations in life (APA 2023).

Although we focus specifically on robustness against influence operations, several characteristics that contribute to resilience can also contribute to increased robustness. Bartone and Armstrong (Bartone et al. 2009) show that resilience in military forces is influenced not only by individual characteristics and training but also by organizational and societal factors.

2.2 Information and Influence Operations

An individual is a part of information systems as we collect, analyse, store, edit and share information in the same way as other parts of information systems do (Whitman and Mattord 2012). The difference between a human and other parts is that humans are also influenced by non-linguistic information, for example, colours, sounds, touches, tastes, and smells. Moreover, this is what makes us vulnerable to influence operations.

Sensory marketing (Erenkol and Merve 2015, Rathee and Rajain 2017), for example, is based on the perceptive capabilities of our senses, and it is used not only by sales organisations, but also by others who want to influence us (Helkala and Rønnfeldt 2022). Marketing campaigns, election campaigns, vaccination campaigns, and mass-produced phishing emails are examples of campaigns were sensory marketing techniques are used (Helkala and Rønnfeldt 2022). Even though not all goals are political, they still influence decision-makers overall, for example, to make one emotionally aroused and angry, which is not necessarily positive when decisions must be made.

---

[1] https://www.ntnu.no/ncr/somulator

The participants in this study, like the rest of Norway's population, are daily exposed to digital information that is intended to influence them. A very small part of this information is considered information operations or influence operations in a military context, which is a form of a campaign with the purpose to influence decision-makers in such a way that one achieves one's own political and military objectives (Johnsen and Eid 2018). However, we do not make a difference between miliary and non-military operations in this paper.

The Ministry of Defence in Norway sees influence operations as part of the complex threat to the country (Forsvarsdepartementet 2020). Robustness against influence means that military leaders do not change decisions because of an adversary's influence.

2.3 Cognitive Warfare

Cognitive warfare is another new and debated term with several different definitions. Several environments in NATO claim that this must be seen as a new war domain, on an equal footing with the other war domains of sea, land, air, cyber, and space (Claverie and Du Cluzel 2022).

Cognitive warfare opens a possibility that a wide range of methods, including technological methods categorized as cyber tools, could influence how we think. By making military leaders more robust against digital influence operations, it will also be possible to increase robustness against cognitive warfare.

2.4 Robustness Against Influence Operations

In this case study, we explore the concept of robustness in the context of influence operations. Robustness against influence operations can be defined as the ability to withstand informational influences without losing ability to carry out tasks.

At the individual level, there is no generally accepted list of characteristics that contribute to this resilience. However, research points in the direction that the ability of critical reflection, analytical thinking, and a higher level of knowledge contribute to a better ability to distinguish between fake and factual news in social media (Lessenski 2021, Pennycook et al. 2020). Furthermore, a well-developed short-term memory and good word comprehension have been shown to have a positive impact on resistance to spear-phishing attacks via e-mail (Ebner et al. 2020). There is also research that indicates that a higher level of education reduces the likelihood that individuals will be attracted to conspiracy theories (Douglas et al. 2016). These measures have also been proposed by FFI to strengthen robustness against the influence of social media (Sivertsen et al. 2021).

2.5 Situational Awareness

The Norwegian defence leadership philosophy is based on mission-based leadership, where military units must be able to interpret overall intentions and objectives and find the best solutions. This philosophy requires that the individual unit or leader is able to understand surroundings and adapt plans in line with them. The core of the challenge lies in the ability to distinguish between information that should influence decisions and actions and information that should not.

The process of gaining situational awareness can be divided into three parts: perception, understanding, and foresight (Endsley 1995). Endsley (1995) presents several characteristics that are important in achieving good situational awareness. Since a solid understanding of the situation also requires a correct response to information, these characteristics can also contribute to strengthening resistance to influence operations. Endsley highlights the individual's ability to process information, which is influenced by characteristics, experience, and training. Research conducted on cyber operators (Jøsok et al. 2019) shows that individual characteristics such as self-regulation, metacognition and communication skills strengthen the development of good situational awareness.

3. Method

This paper presents a case study of an educational module carried out at the Norwegian Defence Cyber Academy in 2023. The cadets' subjective understanding of robustness against foreign states' influence operations was mapped through a questionnaire and a group interview. The questionnaire was answered by 33 respondents on a scale from "a very small extent" to "a very large extent", and the group semi-structured interview was conducted with ten cadets. The questionnaire and interview were approved by the Norwegian Agency for Shared Services in Education and Research and the Norwegian Defence Research Board. Both data collection methods were carried out in Norwegian. For this paper, the questions have been translated to English, as well as the direct quotes from the cadets.

3.1 Case Description

Cyber Academy offers a combined leadership, soldier, and engineering education with a bachelor's degree. The bachelor's education includes a subject called Cyber Power, which aims to create an understanding of how to exercise power between states in the cyber domain. In 2023, the cadets participated in an educational model on influence operations as part of this subject. This module lasted a total of 12 school hours spread over two days. On the first day, the cadets had a 120-minute lecture about influence operations given by external researchers from the Norwegian Defence Research Establishment. After this, the cadets, in teams of 4-5 people, developed influence operations in the Somulator[2] (social media simulator). Each group got to be a different actor in a fictitious military conflict in Europe. The military conflict scenario was the same that the cadets faced in their final military exercise later that spring.

In Somulator, the cadets had the opportunity to create different social media users accounts and add content to the accounts. Several of the groups used generative artificial intelligence applications such as ChatGPT to generate their content. The influence campaigns were presented to the other cadets and later used as part of the final military exercise. The module also included reflection breaks.

In addition, the cadets took part in another investigation where they were asked to distinguish between AI and human-generated a low-resource language, Norwegian, Twitter messages. This investigation was part of a master thesis which results are presented in (Aasen 2023). The master thesis explored the use of language models in Norwegian.

The educational module follows Kolb's learning circle (Kolb 1984, Kolb and Kolb 2013) which have four modes: Concrete experience, reflective observation, abstract conceptualization, and active experimentation. In our module, the first mode was the cadets involving themselves in the disinformation operations. During the second mode, the cadets reflected on their new experience from different political, legal, ethical, technical, and tactical perspectives. Further on, the cadets were to integrate these perspectives in the military context and the theories presented during the Cyber Power course. This would be the third mode: conceptualization. The final mode, active experimentation, was when the cadets presented their disinformation operations to other cadets, as well as when some of the operations were used in the final military exercise.

A weakness of the survey is that it was completed immediately after the second day of education. The long-term effect on the changes in robustness is, therefore, uncertain.

4. Results

4.1 Survey

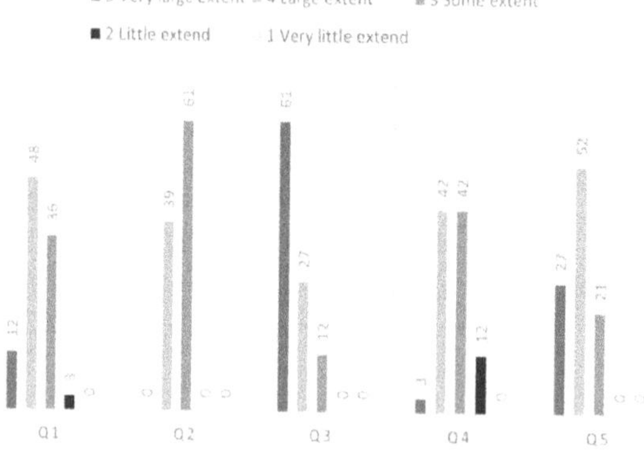

Figure 1. Survey results in percents.

[2] https://www.ntnu.no/ncr/somulator

Figure 1 shows the results for the survey. The questions are as follows. "To what extent ...

1. ...has the education about influence operations changed your understanding of how information operations can be used by states to achieve their interests?
2. ... do you feel that this education module has made you more robust to face cognitive warfare and influence operations conducted by a foreign state?
3. ... do you feel that education on this topic should be part of military leadership training?
4. ... has this education module led to changes in your understanding of the digital information domain?
5. ... has this topic engaged you?

As Figure 1/Q5 shows, the cadets engaged in the module (79% of the cadets answered either large or very large extent). As explained, both traditional lectures and group work were used. This makes the teaching student-centred, which can also support commitment to the teaching in addition the topic itself. Most of the cadets (88% of the cadets answered either large or very large extent, Figure 1/Q3) also thought that today's military leadership training should include influence and cognitive warfare as mandatory themes.

After the module (lectures, presentations of influence operations, investigations, and discussions with both instructors and researchers who participated in both the investigations and the teaching) the cadets felt more confident in dealing with the influence operations. Figure 1/Q2 shows the results stating that the cadets "to some extent and to large extent" feel more robust against cognitive warfare.

We also asked the cadets how this module, especially creation of their own influence operations, has changed their views. Figure 1/Q4 shows results for the question about changes in the understanding of the digital information domain, and Figure 1/Q1 shows results for changes in understanding how states can use the digital influence on their own advantage. As the results show, most of the cadets have changed their understanding from some degree to a large degree.

4.2 Interview

4.2.1 Own Understanding of Influence Operations

The cadets emphasized learning how little resources are required to initiate such campaigns and how difficult it is to detect such campaigns. The module also made them to understand that campaigns have an impact. The role of AI was also highlighted. A cadet summarized the issue as follows:

"With AI, it lowers the threshold for being able to do such operations. Before, you had to have a nation state with many people to be able to do such an operation and employ people to write. However, now all you need is a Python script and an API for ChatGPT, then you can create the same effects."

There are several measures the cadets see that should be taken to strengthen the understanding and robustness of the Defence Forces. One important measure is raising awareness of such operations. The following was said during the interview:

"The most important thing is what we do now. We talk about it and learn. You create an understanding of why the adversary does it, what is the purpose of the operation."

The cadets did not see this as a unique problem for the Armed Forces but a challenge that affects society as a whole. Thus, the counter measures should be introduced to a greater extent and preferably start at school at an early age. One cadet stated the following during the interview:

"If the Defence Forces are to have any effect from this, they [the kids] must be taught from an early age and learn to use technology that is coming. It is perhaps easier to recognize the models that are used if you learn to use them. You get training in this for a long time and from an early age. Getting a person who is familiar with it from the start."

Some Defence-specific measures were also seen as beneficial, such as introducing influence operations as an element in military exercises and focusing on providing verified information about geopolitical happenings for the leaders in order to prevent the effects of influence operations of foreign states.

4.2.2 Own Robustness

The cadets believed that many people think that they are better at recognizing influence operations than they actually are. An example of this is the following statement during the interview:

"I think many people are self-righteous that they are able to discover this themselves, but that there are others who can be affected".

The cadets thought that resilience against such operations is difficult to develop. They said that important qualities are being curious about what is going on in the world and being able to be critical of information that is presented to you. The cadets thought it is difficult to build resilience as they reflected on their own acquired knowledge after the educational module. An example statement from the interview is as follows:

"I might not say that I am more resilient, but that I am more aware that it can happen. But will still not be able to distinguish something that is fake from something that is real. The robustness may lie in the fact that one is aware of it, but being able to directly identify that someone is trying to influence me, that ability has not appeared now. It's perhaps more that I know I don't have it, which is just as important."

5. Discussion

To put the results of this study in a larger context, we discuss development of individual resilience, engagement across topics, and organizational and societal factors.

5.1 Development of Individual Resilience

This study provides limited insight into which personal characteristics promote resistance to influence. However, some of the respondents claimed that they have achieved increased resilience by taking time to reflect on influencing factors and being aware that something is influencing them.

Being able to reflect on one's own thinking is called metacognition. Jøsok et al. (2016) have previously shown how the ability for metacognition strengthens the ability to form a good situational awareness among cyber operators. This, together with the findings from this study, suggests that the ability for metacognition could increase resistance to influence operations. However, this should be further studied.

5.2 Engagement Over a Theme Creates Robustness

This survey also shows that over 50% of the cadets believed that the topic and the way it was delivered engaged them "to a large" or "to a very large extent". Based on previous research that studied a connection between commitment, resilience, and further performance (Luthans et al. 2016, You 2016), a commitment to the topic of influence operations could also help to build resilience against such operations.

The educational module was a student-active approach where the cadets had to use a social media simulator to create their own influence operations that were then used in later exercises, as FFI recommends. No specific investigation has been carried out into whether it is the form of teaching or other reasons that can explain the high level of commitment. This is a topic that further research could investigate in more detail to contribute to developing best practices within education and training of resilience against influence operations.

5.3 Organizational And Societal Factors That can Strengthen Resilience

Bartone et al. (2009) pointed out several organizational and societal factors that can contribute to strengthening resilience in military forces. The study highlighted the importance of educating and training on source criticism and critical thinking in the school system. Furthermore, it is pointed out that the Defence Forces as an organization could contribute by having leaders regularly disseminate updated and verified situational information. Such updates can help to create an understanding that limits operations' influence on decision-making.

The cadets are also relatively united in their views on whether education on the topic should be included as part of military leadership training. Over 85% of the respondents believe that the topic should be included to a large and very large extent in military leadership training. This teaching experiment was carried out as an intensive two-day teaching/practice programme; probably other ways of setting up the teaching will give more effect. The interviews emphasize that creating resilience is a long-term process, which should preferably be started in the school system long before the military career begins. This agrees with findings from Finland, which has included education on the topic already from primary school. The country is considered to be the most robust in Europe against disinformation (Lessenski 2021).

Fact checking services such as faktisk.no in Norway have been established to contribute to correct mis/disinformation. Also, comparing social media news to information provided by the governmental intelligence services in Norway and in other countries could reveal mis/disinformation. Making a habit of using these services could increase societal resilience towards influence operations.

Nevertheless, today's threat picture, which is described, among other things, in the long-term plan for the Norwegian Armed Forces (Forsvarsdepartementet 2020), and this survey suggest that the educational process of creating robust military leaders and soldiers should include the development of robustness against influence. Further research should examine how such robustness should be developed and measured. This would set the foundation for forming a best practice for developing resilience against influence operations by military leaders.

6. Conclusion

This case study contributes to creating a better understanding of how future military leaders feel that they are equipped to deal with influence operations and how education and training could strengthen their resilience.

Understanding of how to design and carry out influence operations changed during the educational module. When the cadets were allowed to design their own operations, it became clear how easily it was done and how little resources actually were required to create an advocacy campaign. After the module, it also became clear how difficult it can be to discover an influence operation.

The study shows that young military leaders see a great need to include training on influence operations in military leadership training. Education, training, and practice could help strengthen military leaders' resilience against such operations. 39% of the cadets who participated in a two-day educational module report that the module has greatly strengthened their own robustness against such operations. This agrees with other research indicating that resistance and robustness against operations can be trained.

Furthermore, the study gives indications that the robustness is based on the increased awareness that such operations are taking place, as well as exercising reflection and metacognition whenever dealing with the information. Further research should map how these factors could be further empowered.

Acknowledgements

We thank Silje Lensu Dåbakk from FFI for giving lectures on influence operations.

References

APA (2023) 'Resilience', *APA Dictionary of Psychology* [online], available: https://dictionary.apa.org/resilience [Accessed 10 November 2023].

Aasen, O. J. A. (2023) *Small languages and big models - Using ML to generate social media content for training purposes*, https://hdl.handle.net/11250/3107222: Norwegian University of Science and Technology.

Aven, T. (2022) 'Robusthet', *Store Norske Leksikon* [online], available: https://snl.no/robusthet [Accessed 10 November 2023].

Bartone, P. T., Barry, C. L. and Armstrong, R. E. (2009) 'To build resilience: Leader influence on mental hardiness', *Defense Horizons* 69.

Claverie, B. and Du Cluzel, F. (2022) '"Cognitive Warfare": The Advent of the Concept of "Cognitics" in the Field of Warfare. ' in Claverie, B., Prébot, B., Buchler, N. and Du Cluzel, F., eds., *Cognitive Warfare: The Future of Cognitive Dominance*, NATO Collaboration Support Office.

Douglas, K. M., Sutton, R. M., Callan, M. J., Dawtry, R. J. and Harvey, A. J. (2016) 'Someone is pulling the strings: hypersensitive agency detection and belief in conspiracy theories', *Thinking & Reasoning,* 22(1), 57-77.

Ebner, N. C., Ellis, D. M., Lin, T., Rocha, H. A., Yang, H., Dommaraju, S., Soliman, A., Woodard, D. L., Turner, G. R., Spreng, R. N. and Oliveira, D. S. (2020) 'Uncovering Susceptibility Risk to Online Deception in Aging', *J Gerontol B Psychol Sci Soc Sci,* 75(3), 522-533.

Endsley, M. R. (1995) 'Measurement of situation awareness in dynamic systems', *Human factors,* 37(1), 65-84.

ENISA (2022) *Threat Landscape 2022.*

Erenkol, A. D. and Merve, A. K. (2015) 'Sensory Marketing', *Journal of Administrative Sciences and Policy Studies,* 3(1), 1-26.

Fitzpatrick, M., Gill, R. and Giles, J. F. (2022) 'Information Warfare: Lessons in Inoculation to Disinformation', *Parameters,* 52(1), 105-118.

Forsvarsdepartementet (2020) *Prop. 14S (2020-2021) Langtidsplan for forsvarssektoren,*

Helkala, K. M. and Rønnfeldt, C. F. (2022) 'Understanding and Gaining Human Resilience Against Negative Effects of Digitalization' in Lehto, M. and Neittaanmäki, P., eds., *Cyber Security: Critical Infrastructure Protection*, Cham: Springer International Publishing, 79-91.

Johnsen, B. H. and Eid, J., eds. (2018) *Operativ psykologi,* 2 ed., Fagbokforlaget.

Jøsok, Ø., Lugo, R., Knox, B. J., Sütterlin, S. and Helkala, K. (2019) 'Self-regulation and cognitive agility in cyber operations', *Frontiers in Psychology*.

Kacała, T. (2015) 'Military Leadership in the Context of Challenges and Threats Existing in Information Environment', *Journal of Corporate Responsibility and Leadership,* 2(2).

Kolb, A. Y. and Kolb, D. A. (2013) 'The Kolb Learning Style Inventory 4.0: Guide to Theory, Psycho-metrics, Research & Applications', [online], available: https://learningfromexperience.com/downloads/research-library/the-kolb-learning-style-inventory-4-0.pdf [Accessed 10 November 2023].

Kolb, D. A. (1984) *Experiential learning: experience as the source of learning and development,* Englewood Cliffs, NJ, Prentice Hall.

Lessenski, M. (2021) *Media Literacy Index 2021, Double Trouble: Resilience to Fake News at the Time of Covid-19 Infodemic*, Open Society Institute - Sofia.

Luthans, K. W., Luthans, B. C. and Palmer, N. F. (2016) 'A positive approach to management education: The relationship between academic PsyCap and student engagement', *Journal of Management Development,* 35(9), 1098-1118.

Mobley, J. (2011) *Study to Establish Levels of Digital Literacy for Soldiers and Leaders in the U.S. Army*.

Ottewell, P. (2020) 'Defining the Cognitive Domain', [online], available: https://overthehorizonmdos.wpcomstaging.com/2020/12/07/defining-the-cognitive-domain/].

Pennycook, G., McPhetres, J., Zhang, Y., Lu, J. G. and Rand, D. G. (2020) 'Fighting COVID-19 Misinformation on Social Media: Experimental Evidence for a Scalable Accuracy-Nudge Intervention', *Psychological Science,* 31(7), 770–780.

Rathee, R. and Rajain, P. (2017) 'Sensory marketing - investigating the use of five senses', *International Journal of Research in Finance and Marketing,* 7(5), 124–133.

Singer, P. W. and Johnson, E. B. (2021) 'The need to inoculate military servicemembers against information threats: the case for digital literacy training for the force', [online], available: https://warontherocks.com/2021/02/we-need-to-inoculate-military-servicemembers-against-information-threats-the-case-for-digital-literacy-training/].

Sivertsen, E. G., Hellum, N., Bergh, A. and Bjørnstad, A. L. (2021) *Hvordan gjøre samfunnet mer robust mot uønsket påvirkning i sosiale medier*.

Stavland, B. and Bruvoll, J. A. (2019) *Resiliens – hva er det og hvordan kan det integreres i risikostyring?*

Whitman, M. E. and Mattord, H. J. (2012) *Principles of Information Security,* 4 ed., Cengage Learning.

You, J. W. (2016) 'The relationship among college students' psychological capital, learning empowerment, and engagement', *Learning and Individual Differences,* 49, 17-24.

Visions of the Future: What Could Happen to User Authentication?

Hanna Paananen and Naomi Woods
University of Jyväskylä, Finland

hanna.k.paananen@jyu.fi
naomi.woods@jyu.fi

Abstract: The most prevalent information system security feature for the user is the authentication process. Passwords have been the primary authentication method for decades due to their simplicity for both the user and the system provider. However, over recent years, the digitalization of services has increased the number of credentials each user must manage, making traditional password authentication problematic for the user. Strong candidates for easier and more secure authentication methods are emerging (e.g., FIDO alliance, Single-sign-on, biometrics). Still, a single method has yet to dominate the market due to the rapid changes in technology, costs of implementation, trust in these methods, and the vast number of users and digital services. Due to the varied reasons that affect the adoption of these methods, it is unclear what kinds of authentication methods will be the forerunners in the future. This study aims to envision the future of user authentication and security features emerging from the interaction of different factors. We present a qualitative interview study, which examines six experts from the fields of authentication, cybersecurity, and emerging technologies. A hermeneutic mode of analysis is used to form scenarios of the future based on the observations of different experts. The results reflect an understanding of how users and their interactions with security features, such as authentication, may change over the following decade and beyond and how security professionals intend to incorporate this knowledge into future security systems. The results shed light on the influence of society, developing technology, and the need for user- and future-proof security in the coming years. This study will have several implications, as it will contribute to forming a coherent picture of the different elements that shape the future and give an idea of how to prepare for what is coming. Furthermore, it will provide an understanding of how choices with technology today lead to different futures.

Keywords: User Authentication, Future, Qualitative Study, Interview

1. Introduction

Today, digitalization creates a constant change in the world around us. We have several digital identities and user accounts in the systems to determine which services we can use. At the cusp of the digital and physical world is the act of user authentication, which the physical human does to prove their digital identity and gain access to their user accounts, systems, and devices. Today, 90% of users have over 90 online accounts (FIDO Alliance, 2024). As people use digital services more and more, so has the time spent on authentication increased, which may be one of the reasons they take shortcuts such as reusing passwords. At work, people spend, on average, over two days every two months on authentication-related activities (Bhana and Flowerday, 2020). This shows that while authentication is a critical security control, it comes with threats and inconveniences yet to be solved.

Within the bigger picture of digitalizing societies and transforming work-life, the security of systems and users' privacy are significant issues. Today, there are forces such as the changing threat environment, government regulation, business competition, emerging technologies, and user needs and values that shape the authentication landscape. As attackers create more professional operations and increasing political motivations alter the conception of what security-critical systems are, the legitimate users of the systems are required to use more robust authentication methods to ensure security. (Lella et al., 2023 p. 4, 140.)

This study is motivated by the idea that academia, as an impartial and independent institution, must produce knowledge supporting decision-making that shapes the future of secure digitalized societies. To understand this change better, we have set a research question: *how do experts view the future of user authentication and security in light of the major trends of digitalizing societies?*

This paper is structured as follows. First, we introduce authentication concepts and current issues. Then, we present the method and results of a qualitative interview study. Lastly, we discuss the implications of the study and propose further research.

2. Overview of User Authentication

Passwords and encryption tools have been used throughout the centuries within different contexts, from the Greeks to the Enigma machine in the Second World War, but mainly as a military tool to protect national secrets and strategies (Rathidevi et al., 2017; Yaschenko, 2002). When the first business mainframe computer systems in the 1960s required limiting the access of users, passwords were a convenient choice since the input could be done easily through the keyboard (Bonneau et al., 2015; Ciampa, 2013).

Authentication methods are commonly categorized into three groups based on what characteristic they are assessing as proof of the user's identity (Grassi et al., 2017).

- *Something the user knows*: These include knowledge-based methods, e.g., passwords (text-based and graphical) (De Angeli et al., 2005; Stobert and Biddle, 2013), Personal Identification Numbers (PINs), and challenge-response methods (Haga and Zviran, 1991).
- *Something the user possesses*: This category refers to the authentication process using objects, such as a device or token, to prove the user's identity. The token may be a dedicated item that is used for authenticating (e.g., a USB key), or it may be a digital certificate on a mobile device (Al-Ameen et al., 2016; Butler and Butler, 2015).
- *Something the user is*: Biometrics are physical or behavioral characteristics of the user that are used to prove their identity. The most popular biometrics include fingerprint scanning and face recognition (Cho et al., 2020). Behavioral biometrics are also used, including keystroke dynamics, mouse movement, and gait. (Dasgupta et al., 2016).

Nowadays, authentication processes that just require a password are deemed insufficient and insecure (Aloul et al., 2009). Due to several factors, such as the increased number of digital services and their passwords, which are needed daily, users are managing their passwords insecurely (Woods and Siponen, 2024). Furthermore, in an attempt to improve security, password creation requirements imposed in online systems require users to meet a minimal level of security in the composition of their passwords; however, these rules do not consider the psychology of users nor the multitude of other passwords the user is required to have (Furnell et al., 2022; Grawemeyer and Johnson, 2011; Woods and Silvennoinen, 2023).

2.1 User Authentication Today

Lately, technological development has introduced new authentication solutions, which provide security yet still have drawbacks (Zhang et al., 2019). Therefore, multifactor authentication (MFA) methods, which require users to authenticate using multiple techniques, are becoming the preferred and most secure type of authentication (Ometov et al., 2019). One long-lived example is the chip and PIN combination used in credit cards (Weir et al., 2010).

Modern smartphones carry several means of authentication, such as fingerprint scanners, cameras for face recognition, and input for memory-based methods (Cho et al., 2020), as well as mobile connectivity for out-of-band authentication (Butler and Butler, 2015). As MFA requires extra effort from the user and could cause discontent, methods have been developed to reduce the effort in low-risk interactions. The system assesses and classifies the user's behavior, device information, and sensitivity of the assets they are accessing. More robust authentication is then only required in high-risk situations. (Bonneau et al., 2015; Butler and Butler, 2015.)

One way of reducing the constant authentication requests when using multiple services is the single-sign-on (SSO). Companies often have centralized identity management, which allows using SSO to open various systems and devices. For example, Facebook and Google have provided similar services in the consumer market. However, their adoption has been hindered by privacy concerns as these corporations could access login session information and use it for profiling. (Bonneau et al., 2015; Järpehult et al., 2022.)

2.2 The big Picture of Authentication

Because our economy is already largely dependent on digital services, the security of these services has become a societal issue. The European Union (EU) has enacted legislation that affects authentication. For example, the Second Payment Services Directive (PSD2) requires strong authentication in bank transactions, which has consolidated the MFA as a part of online services. Further, the General Data Protection Regulation (GDPR) requires that user account data must be stored safely, which can be seen as a requirement for secure authentication. (McDowell, 2019).

Online service providers are also moving towards providing SSO options for their users. Due to privacy-compromising security incidents (e.g., the Cambridge Analytica case), governments have started to pay attention to the amount of information shared between services, reducing the sharing of sensitive information. (Järpehult et al., 2022.) There are standardization initiatives for authentication to balance the amount of credentials and privacy, such as FIDO authentication (FIDO Alliance, 2024) and OpenID Connect (OpenID Foundation, 2024).

3. Research Method

This research was conducted as a qualitative interview study. The interviews were semi-structured and followed the dramaturgical model put forth by Myers and Newman (2007). The interview started by asking about the work status of the informant, their current projects, and their influence in society. The main body of the interview was steered by a 10-year timeline and six themes: society, organizations, individuals, values, services, and technology. The themes were not forced into the conversation, and not all of them needed to be covered. The interviews were conducted face-to-face or through online video conferencing in English or Finnish. Within the results section, these experts will be identified as participants A-F. The researchers interpreted the data using the hermeneutic circle by moving from the details of the data to forming an understanding of a larger vision of the anticipated changes in the future (Klein and Myers, 1999).

The research data consists of six interviews with experts from cybersecurity and emerging technologies. All informants currently work in European research institutions in a senior researcher position, each with over a decade of experience in their respective fields. The participants influence society by teaching, conducting research, publishing in both academic journals and mainstream media, participating in international professional associations and standardizing work, and giving talks and recommendations to industry and political decision-makers.

4. Results

The views of the experts are presented here under the interview themes, although the conversations did not follow this template. The ideas from the discussions are here merged into more general ideas of the current state and future of user authentication and cybersecurity.

4.1 Individuals

Authentication is a required step for a user to enter digital services, but authenticating is rarely the ultimate goal of people's actions. This is why the security-usability trade-off is often discussed as the balance of securing information while avoiding inconveniencing the user. Unfortunately, we see services coming to market emphasizing user convenience, and security is not added until breaches occur. However, these two are not the opposite ends of one line but two axes in a matrix. A preferable future scenario would be to find solutions where both usability and security are high.

> *"I realized that the whole practice of authentication was old fashioned [...] it was stuck in the past. [...] You have to use all these strong passwords, and there was never any acknowledgment that these are humans, not robots." Expert E*

Currently, there are many emerging authentication methods, but passwords are still widely used in many online services. People may use several services and devices daily, each with different authentication requirements. We see that online consumer services provide alternative authentication methods, but this may not be the case with enterprise systems, which often have higher security requirements. When looking forward to a decade from now, these same issues may still exist if the development mirrors the previous decade. The password mechanism may still be widely used and allow short, easily guessable passwords. As smartphones have become ubiquitous, the alternatives that most likely could replace passwords require a personal device. This may introduce new types of threats since, e.g., if malicious actors become interested in breaching the device, the user's biometric data may become useless as an authentication method for the rest of their lives.

> *"The password [could] literally become the poor man's version of security because [...] they don't have the devices with them that support other things." Expert E*

A smart mobile device that holds the key to digital identity can also be a way of moving away from personal computers. As services and data are increasingly moving to the cloud, it reduces the need to design workstations as personal devices. This may give way to new ways of working when the authentication or user-related sensors and control interfaces are on the mobile device. On the other hand, device-dependent authentication can pose threats not only to security but also to the users' ability to function in a digitalized society. When devices are used as tokens or biometric sensors, replacing them may be troublesome as there does not seem to be viable fallback methods beyond passwords.

4.2 Organizations

Before, organizations were the ones that adopted new technologies first, and the consumer versions would come along later. Now, the tide is turning, especially after the COVID-19 pandemic, which brought forward the trend of people mixing work and personal tasks using their online services and devices. They may share files on personal cloud drives with friends and colleagues and read their work emails on personal phones. This has brought forward the need to adapt the user security features to be flexible enough to handle bring-your-own-device (BYOD) situations and the use of various services. This motivates a move away from passwords and towards more secure authentication methods. However, emerging is a new issue of whose device is used in device-dependent authentication. As users may not want multiple devices, organizations may have to choose between allowing personal use of company phones or applying strong authentication methods that do not require a smartphone. The third option would require using personal smartphones, but governments and labor unions may oppose this for invading privacy and liability in security concerns.

> *"Wow, because they thought they could put their big feet into my people's personal phones, and people said no. So this is the other thing that you see is organizations thinking they can get security for free." Expert F*

4.3 Values, Norms, and Control

Earlier, the internet might have been a playground for free information and equal opportunities for participation. As technology has advanced and become more complex, the resources required to enter the market may not be available for small players. This development seems to be continuing with corporations trying to gain more power over users. This serves the values of the technology providers and raises the question of the rights over people's digital identities and their right to security. The user experience and security with different devices can improve if standardizing supports the building of ecosystems where technologies from various manufacturers work together and reduce the number of user authentication requests. In the future, users are either tied to a single platform or can jump from one platform to another seamlessly. The future seems to depend on the government's ability to control the market and create an environment where technology companies are willing to participate in standardization. Furthermore, in these alternative futures, the power over people's digital identities is either held by the heads of the corporations or by the political decision-makers.

> *"We are seeing that single technological players and through that, certain individuals have a tremendous amount of power over what the digital environment is like. [...] Furthermore, there are different countries that follow various justice systems and fundamental ideologies about human values and that type of social system. [...] I can't see that the original utopia of the open network would be coming true in the near future." -Expert B*

Using biometrics is seen as a viable way to create secure and convenient authentication methods. However, the value of the biometric and digital identity may become higher as society digitalizes. We are already seeing value conflicts in this situation. If facial recognition is connected to security cameras, it may lead to people being misidentified and blamed for crimes they did not commit. Furthermore, people may lose control over their own digital identity if their features change due to, e.g., an illness. These examples show that the development of authentication methods may hold significant value conflicts. In the future, we may see crimes and lawsuits that radically change how we accept using our physical features in the digital world.

4.4 Services

One thing that may significantly reduce the number of authentication requests and user accounts is the forming of even bigger platforms. We are already seeing large corporations (e.g., Google, Amazon, Alibaba) adding new services that can be accessed through the platform credentials, and this development may continue to expand to new service types in different areas of life.

Organizations that provide digital services do so with varying capabilities and values. For example, small and medium-sized enterprises (SMEs) may not have adequate resources available for evaluating the usability and security of their selected authentication methods. Especially services where the commercial value of each credential is low may continue to use insecure password mechanisms since replacing them would be expensive.

New authentication innovations may overtake the market when large online service corporations adopt them. When these methods are targeted for the masses, they are designed to be convenient and fun to use.

4.5 Technology

Quantum computing (QC) is currently getting much attention since many countries and large organizations are investing significantly in it. The field is still quite scattered, with many different technologies being developed, and some practical issues, such as noisiness or cooling requirements, are still unsolved. However, the technology is already in a state where information processing and transmission have been successful. This has evoked threat scenarios where QC is used to breach current encryption methods. The standardization and preparation for quantum-resistant encryption have already started. Within a decade, this type of encryption should be easy to implement and in place in the most critical systems. However, the same timeline applies to developing quantum computers that could break the current cryptography, meaning that information that is encrypted and stolen today may be exploited in the future.

Blockchain is another emerging technology that has had many hopes for improved security attached to it. However, while there are many domains where an uncentralized source of trust and security might be useful, the application of blockchain technology may not be the answer. It might be a good technology for digital identities, but its immutability might go against privacy and the inevitable occurrence of human errors.

> *"To me, [blockchain] seems like a dud. [...] There have been cryptocurrencies that cybercriminals can use to blackmail people easily. To me, it was a disappointment." -Expert B*

Artificial intelligence (AI) is also a hot topic due to ChatGPT gaining popularity. There is much speculation about AI changing digital processes and services, but security concerns exist. Not only can it be used to help create more sophisticated attacks, but if the AI breaks, it may turn into a new kind of insider threat. This spurs the need for a novel control: not only humans authenticating to use systems but AI authenticating to humans. There is an increasing need to make sure that we are not dealing with AI that is designed to push misinformation or hallucinations.

The Internet of Things (IoT) is becoming a part of our daily lives as more devices are connected to networks. As new IoT devices and sensors are added to smart homes, cities, and factories, the security landscape becomes more complex. This also requires that the interaction with authentication methods becomes more natural. For example, in a smart home, the verbal commands to operate devices should be seamlessly limited only to authorized users to counter meddling from mischievous neighbors. The security of these devices must be improved simultaneously with convenience since, without secure connectivity and encryption, IoT devices could be used increasingly to cause real-life harm.

4.6 Society

With the rise of new technologies and the importance of cybersecurity to personal and national security, governments have started to implement more regulations in the market. In the EU, there are many new directives in preparation for controlling both the management of cybersecurity and the design of secure products. However, it is difficult to foresee how they may affect society and if they ultimately cause more good than harm. Overreactions are possible, especially if the decision-makers do not understand technology well enough.

As advanced technologies are becoming available to organizations and consumers, there are those who are not able to enjoy their benefits. The digital divide may deepen and leave some people behind. Issues such as personal finances, language processing, and education impact what devices and services, and as an extension, authentication methods, are accessible. As the population in European countries is aging, democratic processes may push for more inclusivity. However, this requires innovations that lower the burden of configuring the personal user experience and incentives to the technology providers to offer adaptable options. Governments may, however, be unable to support the creation of these innovations as one of the driving forces behind digitalization is saving money on services.

5. Discussion

User authentication has evolved from a single password needed at work to something that ensures the security of our digital identities in different walks of life. While exciting things await the future, the current situation is complex and scattered, making predicting difficult. The experts identified several issues in the current state of authentication and cybersecurity that would need to be addressed going forward. The main themes repeated in the interviews were the fragmentation of the authentication method landscape, people having multiple roles, and emerging technologies.

Currently, we are seeing a move away from the traditional password mechanism. The smartphone is a central part of the emerging methods as it has biometric sensors and can be used as a token, but this has introduced more complexity to authentication. There are many initiatives, such as laws and standards, that promote SSO and MFA to add security to the authentication process (FIDO Alliance, 2024; Järpehult et al., 2022). However, several solutions are emerging and creating another problem. Before, the user had to remember passwords for potentially dozens of accounts, but now they must install several apps on their phones to gain access to services. Different actors must take the initiative to fight further fragmentation. Consumers must choose authentication methods that reduce the number of credentials. Service providers must adhere to standards to diminish the authentication overload. Lastly, governments must acknowledge that cybersecurity threats may also emerge from an overly heterogeneous system landscape and steer service providers away from burdening users with security and from creating excessive unmanageable complexity.

Authentication plays a different role depending on whether we are employees, citizens, or consumers. While previously we separated the roles for privacy, the COVID-19 pandemic set in motion a change in attitudes. The use of devices and systems for both work and home tasks became necessary during the pandemic and has been common ever since. This creates a dilemma of whose rules are adhered to with cybersecurity. The use of the smartphone for authentication seems logical from the security perspective but does not fix the problem of multiple roles. More seamless authentication experiences would require changing the conventions of organizational authentication policies, flexibility from governmental bodies, and willingness from the consumer service providers to invest in methods that can be used across the board. Furthermore, device-reliant authentication would need to be designed in a way that does not cause stress or conflicts.

Emerging new technologies promise profound changes in the digital world. Generative AI is transforming digital content creation. IoT is bridging the gap between concrete and digital. Quantum computing makes it possible to solve formerly "unsolvable" problems. As things from sci-fi movies become a reality, we are reminded of these stories' dystopias. The more reliant we become on technology, the more catastrophic the consequences of cyber breaches can become. The positive futures with new technologies involve the empowerment and agency of users to control the technology securely. Yet, it requires us to rethink how we interact with the digital world and what authentication is like.

Overall, the power to make changes is distributed across players with different goals and values, making it difficult to influence the unfolding of more secure and inclusive futures. One obvious solution is to support informed decision-making by producing independent research about authentication and cybersecurity. Challenging but important topics include *what incentives drive service providers to select authentication methods that reduce user load, how can the transitions between roles be made smoother with digital identities and authentication solutions, and how governments can support human agency and inclusivity in cybersecurity legislation*.

This study has some limitations. The use of only academics in senior positions may be a source of elite bias (Myers & Newman 2007). Firstly, academics may not put much weight on business aspects and tend to focus on phenomena from a research point of view. This setting also omits the views of junior researchers whose thinking might be less constrained by experience. Thus, the value of the results lies in the independence of academia and the tacit knowledge gained from a long research career. Further, the sample of six informants may not be representative of the field, but it was enough to gain several viewpoints on phenomena around user authentication and cybersecurity. The interpretive research approach reflects the researchers' worldview, and thus, the selection of themes for the interviews and analysis emphasizes human-centric and less technology-oriented findings.

6. Conclusion

This research looked at the future of user authentication in the context of digitalizing societies. We took a very broad interpretation of authentication, including how people are able to control their digital identities in a world where digital services and devices are taking over all walks of life. The aim was to find out how experts view the future of user authentication and security in light of the major trends of digitalizing societies. We conducted semi-structured interviews with six researchers from research areas that touch on the authentication future. We used interpretive hermeneutic analysis to draw themes from these conversations. The major themes were the fragmentation of methods, people's multiple roles, and emerging technologies.

The sample of interviews in this study was rather limited and warrants further study and expanding the pool of experts into other areas of cybersecurity and emerging technologies. Furthermore, after these initial results, the themes could be refined further and used in more structured research, such as a Delphi study. The comprehensive themes used in this study only give indications of how the themes are interrelated, but the data is not extensive or structured enough to draw conclusions within themes. There is a further need for this type of overarching studies that look into the future development of cyber security as a whole to give context to the advances made in technology, society, and individual level.

References

Al-Ameen, M.N., Haque, S.M.T. and Wright, M. (2016), "Leveraging autobiographical memory for two-factor online authentication", *Information and Computer Security*, Vol. 24 No. 4, pp. 386–399, doi: 10.1108/ICS-01-2016-0005.

Aloul, F., Zahidi, S. and El-Hajj, W. (2009), "Two factor authentication using mobile phones", *2009 IEEE/ACS International Conference on Computer Systems and Applications*, IEEE, pp. 641–644, doi: 10.1109/AICCSA.2009.5069395.

De Angeli, A., Coventry, L., Johnson, G. and Renaud, K. (2005), "Is a picture really worth a thousand words? Exploring the feasibility of graphical authentication systems", *International Journal of Human-Computer Studies*, Academic Press, Vol. 63 No. 1–2, pp. 128–152, doi: 10.1016/J.IJHCS.2005.04.020.

Bhana, B. and Flowerday, S. (2020), "Passphrase and keystroke dynamics authentication: Usable security", *Computers and Security*, Vol. 96, doi: 10.1016/j.cose.2020.101925.

Bonneau, J., Herley, C., Van Oorschot, PC and Stajano, F. (2015), "Passwords and the evolution of imperfect authentication", *Communications of the ACM*, Vol. 58 No. 7, pp. 78–87, doi: 10.1145/2699390.

Butler, M. and Butler, R. (2015), "Investigating the possibility to use differentiated authentication based on risk profiling to secure online banking", *Information and Computer Security*, Vol. 23 No. 4, pp. 421–434, doi: 10.1108/ICS-11-2014-0074.

Cho, G., Huh, J.H., Kim, S., Cho, J., Park, H., Lee, Y., Beznosov, K., *et al.* (2020), "On the Security and Usability Implications of Providing Multiple Authentication Choices on Smartphones: The More, the Better?", *ACM Transactions on Privacy and Security*, Vol. 23 No. 4, doi: 10.1145/3410155.

Ciampa, M. (2013), "A comparison of password feedback mechanisms and their impact on password entropy", *Information Management & Computer Security*, Vol. 21 No. 5, pp. 344–359, doi: 10.1108/IMCS-12-2012-0072.

Dasgupta, D., Roy, A. and Nag, A. (2016), "Toward the design of adaptive selection strategies for multifactor authentication", *Computers and Security*, Vol. 63, pp. 85–116, doi: 10.1016/j.cose.2016.09.004.

FIDO Alliance. (2024), "What is FIDO?", available at: https://fidoalliance.org/what-is-fido/ (accessed 25 January 2024).

Furnell, S., Helkala, K. and Woods, N. (2022), "Accessible authentication: Assessing the applicability for users with disabilities", *Computers and Security*, Vol. 113, doi: 10.1016/j.cose.2021.102561.

Grassi, P.A., Fenton, J.L., Newton, E.M., Perlner, R.A., Regenscheid, A.R., Burr, W.E., Richer, J.P., *et al.* (2017), *Digital Identity Guidelines: Authentication and Lifecycle Management*, Gaithersburg, MD, doi: 10.6028/NIST.SP.800-63b.

Grawemeyer, B. and Johnson, H. (2011), "Using and managing multiple passwords: A week to a view", *Interacting with Computers*, Vol. 23 No. 3, pp. 256–267, doi: 10.1016/j.intcom.2011.03.007.

Haga, W.J. and Zviran, M. (1991), "Question-and-answer passwords: An empirical evaluation", *Information Systems*, Pergamon, Vol. 16 No. 3, pp. 335–343, doi: 10.1016/0306-4379(91)90005-T.

Järpehult, O., Agren, F.J., Backstom, M., Hallonqvist, L. and Carlsson, N. (2022), "A Longitudinal Characterization of the Third-Party Authentication Landscape", *2022 IFIP Networking Conference (IFIP Networking)*, IEEE, pp. 1–9, doi: 10.23919/IFIPNetworking55013.2022.9829804.

Klein, H.K. and Myers, M.D. (1999), "A Set of Principles for Conducting and Evaluating Interpretive Field Studies in Information Systems", *MIS Quarterly*, Vol. 23 No. 1, pp. 67–94, doi: 10.2307/249410.

Lella, I., Theocharidou, M., Tsekmezoglou, E., Malatras, A., Garcia, S. and Valeros, V. (eds.) (2023) "Enisa Threat Landscape 2023", European Union Agency for Cybersecurity, available at: https://www.enisa.europa.eu/publications/enisa-threat-landscape-2023

McDowell, B. (2019), "Three ways in which GDPR impacts authentication", *Computer Fraud & Security*, No longer published by Elsevier, Vol. 2019 No. 2, pp. 9–12, doi: 10.1016/S1361-3723(19)30019-3.

Myers, M. and Newman, M. (2007), "The qualitative interview in IS research: Examining the craft", *Information & Organization*, Vol. 17 No. 1, pp. 2–26, doi: 10.1016/j.infoandorg.2006.11.001.

Ometov, A., Petrov, V., Bezzateev, S., Andreev, S., Koucheryavy, Y. and Gerla, M. (2019), "Challenges of Multifactor Authentication for Securing Advanced IoT Applications", *IEEE Network*, Vol. 33 No. 2, pp. 82–88, doi: 10.1109/MNET.2019.1800240.

OpenID Foundation. (2024), "What is OpenID Connect", available at: https://openid.net/developers/how-connect-works/ (accessed 25 January 2024).

Rathidevi, M., Yaminipriya, R. and Sudha, S. V. (2017), "Trends of cryptography stepping from ancient to modern", *IEEE International Conference on Innovations in Green Energy and Healthcare Technologies - 2017, IGEHT 2017*, Institute of Electrical and Electronics Engineers Inc., doi: 10.1109/IGEHT.2017.8094107.

Stobert, E. and Biddle, R. (2013), "Memory retrieval and graphical passwords", *Proceedings of the Ninth Symposium on Usable Privacy and Security*, ACM, New York, NY, USA, pp. 1–14, doi: 10.1145/2501604.2501619.

Weir, C.S., Douglas, G., Richardson, T. and Jack, M. (2010), "Usable security: User preferences for authentication methods in eBanking and the effects of experience", *Interacting with Computers*, Vol. 22 No. 3, pp. 153–164, doi: 10.1016/j.intcom.2009.10.001.

Woods, N. and Silvennoinen, J. (2023), "Enhancing the user authentication process with colour memory cues", *Behaviour and Information Technology*, Vol. 42 No. 10, pp. 1548–1567, doi: 10.1080/0144929X.2022.2091474.

Woods, N. and Siponen, M. (2024), "How memory anxiety can influence password security behavior", *Computers & Security*, Elsevier Advanced Technology, Vol. 137, p. 103589, doi: 10.1016/J.COSE.2023.103589.

Yaschenko, V. V. (2002), *Cryptography: An Introduction*, edited by Yaschenko, V. V., Vol. 18, American Mathematical Society.

Zhang, T., Yang, L. and Wu, Y. (2019), "Evaluation of the Multifactor Authentication Technique for Mobile Applications", in Arai, K., Bhatia, R. and Kapoor, S. (Eds.), *Intelligent Computing*, pp. 696–707, doi: 10.1007/978-3-030-22868-2_49.

A Practitioner's Behavioral Approach: Reconceptualizing Whaley's *Word-of-Mouth* Communication Model in an Online Context

Tim Pappa
National Intelligence University, Bethesda, Maryland, USA
timothy.s.pappa@niu.odni.gov

Abstract: The late American scholar Barton Whaley wrote several classic works related to disinformation, but people are likely less familiar with his limited works on *word-of-mouth* communication. Whaley published two studies in the early 1960s, separately exploring word-of-mouth communication among mainland Chinese civilians and mainland Chinese Communist military personnel. Whaley found that word-of-mouth communication by "key communicators" in these communities who were the most trusted and most informed was more effective than radio for information sharing, and likely the most effective method for disinformation. This paper will primarily explore Whaley's model, but then introduce relevant literature on group dynamics and electronic word-of-mouth communication, which has largely focused on marketing practices and consumers. This paper proposes integrating Whaley's model into these related behavioral frameworks, reconceptualizing a model of a practitioner's behavioral approach to *word-of-mouth* online influence.

Keywords: Barton Whaley; *Word-Of-Mouth*; Electronic Word-Of-Mouth; Online Influence; Disinformation

1. Introduction

A surprising number of marketing studies on electronic word-of-mouth framed their concepts of how consumers respond to electronic word-of-mouth based on dual-processing mechanisms or heuristics.

Communication researchers throughout the past forty years have established relatively similar conditions for dual-processing systems, which is essentially our cognitive and attitudinal processing of content.

These dual-processing systems or conditions generally find that people spend more or less time thinking about and consuming or sharing content based on how relevant it is to them and how motivated they are to process that content.

This is important especially in this growing environment of "coordinated inauthentic behavior", where creators may be scaling and applying more generative artificial intelligence content or more traditional manually created content with the same methods for attempting to influence audiences.

Graphika and the Stanford Internet Observatory in a summer 2022 report found what they characterized as the most extensive case of "covert pro-Western influence operations" in the past five years. Twitter (now X) and Meta the same summer removed clusters of presumably Western or American-controlled accounts for "platform manipulation and spam" and "coordinated inauthentic behavior", including creating fake online personas with artificially generated faces. The report highlighted how ineffective many of these accounts appeared to be at generating engagement and building influence. While the report documented how these accounts created artful, foreign-language content and calls to action to encourage engagement and social media response, most of these accounts had no more than a handful of likes or retweets on Twitter, and less than a quarter of the accounts had more than a thousand followers.

The report noted another example of nearly half of these accounts posing as media organizations including batches of hashtags with their posted content, likely trying to reach broader audiences. But again, there was limited audience response.

Broad appeals to broad audiences even in the right language on the right platform do not often work.

In the author's experience as a former profiler with the Federal Bureau of Investigation's (FBI) Behavioral Analysis Unit (BAU), most practitioners gloss over a very liminal step in crafting online influence. Beyond narrowing down a target audience to an individual or group of individuals in some relationship, online influence to be potentially effective must include a behavioral objective that you want them to do.

The literature on electronic word-of-mouth is keenly focused on this step, as one of the most focal measures for marketers is the purchasing intent and purchases when exposed to electronic word-of-mouth posts.

Sartonen (2014) wrote about target audience analysis in the cyber domain approximately a decade ago, building upon a relatively established body of primarily military literature on target audience analysis. Sartonen characterized target audience analysis as closely related to marketing audience segmentation, where potential target consumer audiences are segmented into possible profiles of potential consumers to create marketing content for those segments. He wrote that while marketing generally prefers larger consumer segments, psychological operations generally prefer more limited and defined audience segments.

Tatham (2015) wrote that while target audience analysis generally groups target audiences in terms of variables, such as audiences who may react positively to messaging or audiences who may be ambivalent to messaging, sometimes the target is just one person.

Tatham emphasized the need to find the "right" audience, but to be aware that those other audiences can influence others as well, even if the messaging or content was not intended for them. Tatham referred to Shakarian et al. (2013), who described prior research on social influence networks that suggested perhaps only the right person in a social network needs to be influenced to influence the majority.

Whaley's studies in this paper do conceptually touch on these considerations, however, word-of-mouth communication is essentially a single channel or method of communication. Whaley is primarily interested in the social structure of the categories of people he interviewed and identified, as well as the relationships between those categories of people on various topics, like politics or sports.

There are certainly more recent studies of word-of-mouth communication among communities of interest, such as a December 2023 report funded by the U.S. Agency for International Development that examined the form of communications and content that influenced members of al-Shabaab to leave the terrorist organization. While this report did not call the family members and former members who were most influential "key communicators" like Whaley, they were nonetheless the most influential in restricted environments for communication and travel. Appeals to leave the group often happened over the telephone.

This report could have explored further the group dynamics in these communities, such as the norms among people in relationships in those communities whether those relationships were positive or deadly.

This paper will detail some of the group norms Whaley identified in his studies. For example, Chinese military personnel had to go to a local market daily for additional food because they were given such limited rations. There was a norm of enlisted Chinese military personnel that they could not have much access to news media, but because some of them had to go to the market each day, they had an opportunity to talk to merchants, who generally traveled freely and widely and had access to information the soldiers normally did not have.

2. Whaley's Studies of Chinese *Word-of-Mouth* Communication

Rasmussen wrote in the foreword to Whaley's study that *word-of-mouth* communication is perhaps the most neglected means of transmitting information in psychological operations. He wrote that attempting to communicate any kind of information in this manner has an "unpredictable nature" because that information can be distorted or never reach the target. Rasmussen noted at that time that there was a growing body of research across several fields suggesting that there are regularities and patterns found in how people share information and ultimately how that information and people influence each other. Rasmussen suggested further that perhaps if we could understand these patterns, we may have greater confidence using informal communications in operational situations.

Whaley (1961) and his team interviewed nearly 300 Chinese soldiers who had been captured during the Korean War or fled mainland China throughout the 1950s. They explored the relationship between these soldiers and civilians in terms of the communities they came from.

Whaley designed this study as a guide for how to use *word-of-mouth* communication as a medium in operations, asking how these soldiers found out what was happening in other parts of China and from what source they obtained most of their information. Identifying the regularities and patterns he found in his interviews with these soldiers who originated from mainland Chinese communities, Whaley suggested that *word-of-mouth* communication with the right messengers could not only complement other mediums of communication in psychological operations, but perhaps replace conventional mass media.

Whaley noted in an early summary of his study that the conventional mass media in mainland China offer "very limited opportunities for exploitation" by psychological operations. But he found that Chinese civilians in fact appeared to be the "most promising channel of access" to Chinese soldiers despite attempts by military officials to limit contact. When soldiers visited local markets to buy goods because of the rudimentary military commissary, they had opportunity to talk informally with civilians in those markets. Conceptualizing the possibility of Chinese soldiers deploying to Southeast Asia where there are considerable diasporas of Chinese emigres, Whaley suggested this kind of natural contact would also offer a "reasonable chance" or perhaps the best chance of utilizing word-of-mouth communication targeting concentrations of Chinese soldiers.

Whaley categorized Chinese enlisted soldiers and officers as essentially audiences, or segments of the Chinese military with somewhat different backgrounds and means. Whaley found that generally regardless of background or rank or whether soldiers were in a wartime or peacetime status, word-of-mouth communication was consistently the most important source of information and information sharing among soldiers. Most other mediums, including personal mail correspondence or telephone calls, were either closely monitored, or reserved for privileged civilian and military personalities and officials. Whaley also explored the kind of formal or organizational networks that intersect with informal channels, as people generally participate in both. For example, in a hierarchical military organization like the Chinese military, Whaley highlighted an "unusually marked reliance" on word-of-mouth communication throughout the formal command structure because of differing levels of literacy.

Whaley identified "companions" or small groups of friends, usually in the same military unit, where there were simple chains of 'friend-of-a-friend-of-a-friend' *word-of-mouth* sharing. Within the chain-of-command there were also senior military and political officers with official access to foreign media that the general military and public may not have had access to or that media or information was distorted or propagandized if it was shared further.

The remaining source of "fresh unofficial news" for Chinese soldiers were civilians:

> ...[civilians] compromise an extremely important channel of information for soldiers on garrison duty in China. Their importance derives from the fact that the extent and frequency of contact with civilians are probably sufficient to guarantee wide dispersion of that information they do convey to soldiers. Furthermore, the quality of the information which civilians transmit to soldiers is as high as, or higher than, that passed among soldiers. *The high quality of this information derives from the fact that, compared with information from other soldiers, soldiers consider it to be unofficial, more credible, more important, more likely to be clandestine, and almost as recent.* [emphasis added]

Whaley found that because of the limited supplies available to soldiers, enlisted men in nearly every unit were organized into small groups each day and sent to a local marketplace. The soldiers would buy extra meat and vegetables or cigarettes with money pooled from the unit. While the Chinese military attempted to strictly manage even these rotations, the soldiers who took turns visiting rural and urban markets routinely had contact with civilians like merchants. Civilian construction or agricultural projects would often involve soldiers assisting civilians, too. The study determined that generally as officers were promoted, they relied on radio and newspaper more than enlisted personnel for their sources of information because they had access and perhaps other background factors such as greater literacy.

Whaley the same year released another study that focused on civilians as "special audiences" for focusing *word-of-mouth* communication. Whaley and his team in 1959 interviewed over 2,000 Chinese refugees in Taiwan who had fled mainland China in the late 1950s to identify distinct audiences of civilians who were likely the most effective channels of informal communication. Whaley found that while information appeared to be shared most often among civilians from the same occupation or "social grouping", however, he also identified a small portion of this population that he called "Key Communicators" because they appeared to be the most active sharing information by *word-of-mouth* whether among peers or outside their occupation. This category generally included merchants or manual workers, perhaps because they were more mobile and more frequently in contact with people outside their occupational groups. Whaley also highlighted teachers and physicians as examples because they are likewise more likely to be literate and involved in voluntary associations and interested in politics.

Like Whaley's other similar study focused on Chinese military personnel, he found that these civilian "special audiences" also considered information shared by *word-of-mouth* to be more reliably or more trustworthy than information communicated by official news media. Civilians generally reported that these kinds of conversations often happened in peoples' homes rather than public teahouses or markets, for example, because of a need for secrecy.

Whaley identified characterizations or demographics of these Key Communicators, such as the average level of education and gender and type of occupation. Whaley named two occupational groups as Key Communicators: "Merchants" and "Manual Workers". Both occupational groups involve considerable travel and social contact. While Whaley pointed out that ideally, we should try to locate a Communicator who is himself a member of the targeted occupational group or audience, these Key Communicators tend to have access to nearly all these civilian and military audiences in some manner.

This study also explored if there were relationships between the occupation of the "audience" and the type of information that civilian grouping would speak about most often. Whaley found for example that a group of "Soldiers-Officials-Policemen" and "Landlords-Professionals" were the most likely to talk about or share information on politics, while "Housewives" and "Fishermen" were the least likely to discuss politics. As another example, Whaley found that "Manual Workers" and "Fishermen" were the most likely to discuss escape, while "Students" and "Landlords-Professionals" were the least likely to talk about escape.

Whaley concluded in this study that we can "profitably" rely on a Key Communicator to communicate a targeted message and provide unique access to collect information.

Whaley's *Key Communicators* table categorizes the occupation of the "informant" and what kind of information these occupations or roles in the 1950s and 1960s had the most or least access to.

Information	Most	Least
Politics	Soldiers-Officials; Policemen; Landlords-Professionals	Housewives; Fishermen
Economics	Merchants; Skilled Workers	Fishermen; Students
Military	Soldiers-Officials; Policemen; Manual Workers	Housewives; Peasants
Religion	Landlords-Professionals; Others	Skilled Workers; Manual Workers
Relatives	Housewives; Peasants	Soldiers-Officials; Policemen; Manual Workers
Gossip	Housewives; Students	Soldiers; Officials; Policemen; Others
Escape	Manual Workers; Fishermen	Students; Landlords-Professionals
Taiwan	Manual Workers; Fishermen	Housewives; Students; Landlords-Professionals; Skilled Workers; Others
Others	Students; Fishermen	Skilled Workers; Housewives

Figure 1: Whaley's table of Key Communicators among Chinese communities.

3. Understanding the Relationships Behind Whaley's "Social Groups"

The "social groups" that Whaley characterized are ultimately not just taxonomical characterizations or constructs, but likely reflect relationships.

Forsyth (2014) defined a group as two or more people in some form of relationship. Considering the size of a group, those relationships can span dozens of people or just one other. The emphasis in most research on groups has been on social relationships, because people are generally interdependent and likely influence each other.

That influence can also be felt in the form of shared emotions or affect, generally known as identity-based emotions, because members of that group are responding emotionally to events or experiences (Campo, Mackie & Sanchez, 2019). The size of a group of people in a relationship influences the nature of that group in many ways, because of the unique characteristics of each member of that group who has some kind of relationship. Whether there is an organizational boundary to this group or not is less important than what kind of a relational boundary or boundaries there are between members of that group.

Forsyth characterized some of these structures for groups as norms and roles. Norms are consensual or understood expectations and behaviors among group members at a group level, so if someone leaves the group or joins the group these norms are usually constant. Roles describe some of these same expectations at a group level, but usually for labeled positions, such as director or teacher, for example.

Forsyth described the role of professor in a university and the norms among his department peers with whom he has different relationships or groups, and then the roles of husband and father when he was at home and trying to grade university papers. He noted that the group norms and roles are not always clear, and in some cases, people may not realize there was some expectation until a norm is violated.

While norms can also change over time (Nijstad and Van Knippenberg, 2008), the *focus theory of normative conduct* has suggested that norms appear to motivate behavior when they become "activated" or focal among group members. Forsyth emphasized that what we often see when we are trying to understand groups are in fact norms that are shared among group members.

Forsyth wrote that within a group structure there can also be a *subgroup*, formed when several members within a larger group place themselves for whatever reason at the intersection of a group's "information-exchange patterns" and become more influential than individual members of the group or other groups within that larger group structure.

Forsyth wrote that we probably learn the most about a group studying the structure. Forsyth cautioned that we could misperceive the "'groupiness'" of a group we think we see based on four men walking down the street together who appear to be a group or something observable, such as similarity in dress or culture where we may consider people to be a group. He referred to Campbell (1958) who characterized how people and group members tend to rely on these kinds of cues to organize their perceptions of what appears to be a group as *entitativity*. Forsyth used an example of a vehicle. Someone may see four wheels and a trunk and a hood and a windshield and correctly see a vehicle rather than these individual parts of the car, but relational groups are much more complicated and changing.

Nijstad and Van Knippenberg (2008) also cautioned that members of their own perceived group can also make the same perceptions about the level of closeness in a group. Some of that process is an example of "shared socialness", when people identify or join a group, they may also acknowledge that they display the same kind of characteristics of other members of that group or that acknowledged social norms represent the behaviors or features of a group that members should adopt especially to be distinct from others (Smith and Tindale, 2022). Harton et al. (2022) discussed other foundational phenomena of how people influence each other in groups, such as Latane's (1996) cultural models of clustering, for example.

People's attitudes and beliefs tend to consolidate and correlate in clusters or rather when they are interacting frequently and in a shared space over time. This interaction, however, is largely based on people in relationships.

Electronic word-of-mouth communication tends to be lumped in with multiple forms of communication online. Because the effect of electronic word-of-mouth is consistently influential, this channel can be misunderstood as a reflection of grouped individuals based on relationship.

4. The Limitations of Electronic Word-of-Mouth Influence Without Relationships

Rosario et al. (2020) wrote that much of the research on electronic word-of-mouth communication has been over-labeled and under-theorized.

Much of her criticism has been focused on the proliferation of conceptual labels as she called it among marketing practitioners. Rosario et al. grounded some of this conceptualizing by redefining electronic word-of-mouth communication as any form of consumer-generated information, emphasizing that this method is not a form of sharing general information.

The vast body of electronic word-of-mouth communication has focused on marketing practices, but with some additional consideration of how this communication influences feelings of trust.

Fang et al. (2018) proposed a digital advertising framework for electronic word-of-mouth information diffusion on online social networking platforms, that he suggested was driven largely by curiosity and influence. Fang referred to some of the prior research on electronic word-of-mouth adoption of marketed products, namely models or theories that focused on using "affect-as-information" and other pass-along behaviors. Fang was most interested in whether different types of curiosity would lead to exploratory browsing or specific searching, before interacting with content considered to be influential or influencers.

Fang et al. found that curiosity did not appear to significantly moderate the influence of content or electronic word-of-mouth adoption or pass-along behaviors, however, he did find that influential senders can positively moderate electronic word-of-mouth behaviors.

Likewise, Aprilia and Kusumawati (2021) found a positive correlation between electronic word-of-mouth content on visiting a destination and interest from other possible tourists, but their study also found a similar positive correlation between posting a photo of that destination and consumers' responding interest.

Some electronic word-of-mouth communication research has explored how this form shapes consumer experiences before and after purchasing a product. Jalilvand et al. (2011) noted that many of these studies classify the effectiveness of electronic word-of-mouth among consumers at the individual level and the market level, meaning the accumulated customer opinion that might influence new customers. Cheung and Thadai (2010) took a broader look at literature on the effectiveness of electronic word-of-mouth, trying to conceptualize an analytical model for measuring the influence on electronic word-of mouth communication to purchasing intention and purchasing of a good.

Zhang et al. (2010) found that Amazon changed the format of consumer reviews at that time, where consumers' reviews were rated by other consumers based on how helpful the review was and that rated review was featured more prominently than other reviews based on recency, for example. This reference may be one of the clearer examples of how highly rated reviewers in a social marketing context can be seen as "key communicators" even if they are personally unknown to other consumers.

Generally, literature reviews characterized this field of studies as large and fragmented, overly concentrated on marketing practices rather than a clearer view of how the field has changed, in terms of measuring the impact of electronic word-of-mouth communication (Verma and Yadav, 2021; Huete-Alcocer, 2017). Researchers were increasingly finding that electronic word-of-mouth appeared to be instrumental to consumers reducing their perception of risk when making purchasing decisions about unfamiliar services or goods. Joshi et al. (2015) also found that consumers seem to trust electronic word-of-mouth communication the most when making decisions about products or services online.

Prahiawan et al. (2021) found in a review of several studies and their own on the effect of electronic word-of-mouth communication on concepts such as customer satisfaction and customer repurchase intention that electronic word-of-mouth communication did not have a significant impact on customer repurchase intention, and that there was not necessarily anything distinct about 'E-satisfaction' compared to customer satisfaction. Prahiawan et al. did however find again that electronic word-of-mouth communication had a positive effect on customer intention to purchase.

5. Discussion

Whaley's model of *word-of-mouth* communication can be applied to any other culture or community. While Whaley was focusing on ethnic Chinese individuals and groups in the 1950s and 1960s who had fled or emigrated from mainland China, his methodology of ethnographic and cultural analysis applied to identified structures of communication surprisingly found that conventional media was not the best medium for disinformation among those communities, because people were not using radio much or did not have access.

While those limitations informed why his sample groups did not have access to some forms of media, the relationships he defined explained why people trusted some and did not trust others, and why some people depended on their sources of information from merchants rather than students, for example.

Both sections on group dynamics and electronic word-of-mouth communication may be surprising, given there are some popularly held opinions on what 'groupthink' is and how word-of-mouth influences people online. There are limitations to how electronic word-of-mouth influences behavior and how it should be measured. There are also limitations to what we know or do not know about the demonstration or expression of norms among people in relationship in a group, but observationally we can gather a sense of that structure for understanding how people in that group are communicating and who appears to have influence over others.

This paper proposes integrating contextually and culturally rich analysis, with the theoretical underpinnings found in group dynamics and the demonstrated marketing practices of electronic word-of-mouth communication.

This reconceptualized model offers a practitioner's behavioral approach to identifying "key communicators" that could counter disinformation in target audiences, as well as "key communicators" who could influence.

References

Aprilia, Fitri, and Andriani Kusumawati. "Influence of electronic word of mouth on visitor's interest to tourism destinations." *The Journal of Asian Finance, Economics and Business* 8, no. 2 (2021): 993-1003.

Babić Rosario, Ana, Kristine De Valck, and Francesca Sotgiu. "Conceptualizing the electronic word-of-mouth process: What we know and need to know about eWOM creation, exposure, and evaluation." *Journal of the Academy of Marketing Science* 48 (2020): 422-448.

Bohner, Gerd, Gordon B. Moskowitz, and Shelly Chaiken. "The interplay of heuristic and systematic processing of social information." *European review of social psychology* 6, no. 1 (1995): 33-68.

Cacioppo, John T., Richard E. Petty, Chuan Feng Kao, and Regina Rodriguez. "Central and peripheral routes to persuasion: An individual difference perspective." *Journal of personality and social psychology* 51, no. 5 (1986): 1032.

Campo, Mickael, Diane M. Mackie, and Xavier Sanchez. "Emotions in group sports: A narrative review from a social identity perspective." *Frontiers in psychology* 10 (2019): 666.

Cheung, Christy MK, and Dimple R. Thadani. "The effectiveness of electronic word-of-mouth communication: A literature analysis." (2010).

Fang, Yu-Hui, Kwei Tang, Chia-Ying Li, and Chia-Chi Wu. "On electronic word-of-mouth diffusion in social networks: Curiosity and influence." *International Journal of Advertising* 37, no. 3 (2018): 360-384.

Forsyth, Donelson R. *Group dynamics*. Wadsworth Cengage Learning, 2014.

Forsyth, Donelson R., and Timothy R. Elliott. "Group dynamics and psychological well-being: The impact of groups on adjustment and dysfunction." (1999).

Harton, Helen C., Matthew Gunderson, and Martin J. Bourgeois. "“I'll be there with you”: Social influence and cultural emergence at the capitol on January 6." *Group Dynamics: Theory, Research, and Practice* (2022).

Huete-Alcocer, Nuria. "A literature review of word of mouth and electronic word of mouth: Implications for consumer behavior." *Frontiers in psychology* 8 (2017): 1256.

Jalilvand, Mohammad Reza, Sharif Shekarchizadeh Esfahani, and Neda Samiei. "Electronic word-of-mouth: Challenges and opportunities." *Procedia Computer Science* 3 (2011): 42-46.

Kahneman, Daniel. *Thinking, fast and slow*. macmillan, 2011.

Khalil, James, Yahye Abdi, Andrew Glazzard, Abdullahi Ahmed Nor, and Martine Zeuthen. “Reaching behind Frontlines: Promoting Exit from al-Shabaab through Communications Campaigns”, December 2023, *RSVE_RR_LPBI_ReachingBehindFrontlines_AS_SomaliaDefections_KhalilEtAl_Dec2023_FINAL-UPDATE12.18.23.pdf (resolvenet.org)

Kruglanski, Arie W., and Erik P. Thompson. "Persuasion by a single route: A view from the unimodel." *Psychological Inquiry* 10, no. 2 (1999): 83-109.

Nijstad, Bernard A., and Daan Van Knippenberg. "The psychology of groups: Basic principles." *Introduction to social psychology: A European perspective* (2008): 244-262.

Petty, Richard E., and John T. Cacioppo. "The effects of involvement on responses to argument quantity and quality: Central and peripheral routes to persuasion." *Journal of personality and social psychology* 46, no. 1 (1984): 69.

Prahiawan, Wawan, and John Tampil Purba. "The role of e-satisfaction, e-word of mouth and e-trust on repurchase intention of online shop." *Anser, MK, Tabash, MI, Nassani, AA, Aldakhil, AM, & Yousaf* 2021 (2021).

Samuelson, Charles D. "Why were the police attacked on January 6th? Emergent norms, focus theory, and invisible expectations." *Group Dynamics: Theory, Research, and Practice* (2022).

Sartonen, Miika. "Target audience analysis in cyber domain." (2014).

Shankar, Amit, Charles Jebarajakirthy, and Md Ashaduzzaman. "How do electronic word of mouth practices contribute to mobile banking adoption?." *Journal of Retailing and Consumer Services* 52 (2020): 101920.

Smith, Christine M., and R. Scott Tindale. "A social sharedness interpretation of the January 6th US capitol insurrection." *Group Dynamics: Theory, Research, and Practice* (2022).

Sulthana, A. Navitha, and S. Vasantha. "Influence of electronic word of mouth eWOM on purchase intention." *International Journal of Scientific and Technology Research* 8, no. 10 (2019): 1-5.

Tatham, Steve. "Using Target Audience Analysis to Aid Strategic Level Decisionmaking." (2015).

Whaley, Barton, *Word-of-Mouth Communication in the Chinese Communist Army (PROPIN-CCA).* American University, Washington, D.C., Special Operations Research Office, 1961: v.

Whaley, Barton, *A Study of Word-of-Mouth Communication in Communist China (PROPIN-CCA).* American University, Washington, D.C., Special Operations Research Office, Special Warfare Research Division, 1961.

Verma, Sanjeev, and Neha Yadav. "Past, present, and future of electronic word of mouth (EWOM)." *Journal of Interactive Marketing* 53 (2021): 111-128.

You, Ya, Gautham G. Vadakkepatt, and Amit M. Joshi. "A meta-analysis of electronic word-of-mouth elasticity." *Journal of Marketing* 79, no. 2 (2015): 19-39.

Zhang, Jason Q., Georgiana Craciun, and Dongwoo Shin. "When does electronic word-of-mouth matter? A study of consumer product reviews." *Journal of Business Research* 63, no. 12 (2010): 1336-1341.

Educating Cybersecurity Experts: Analysis of Cybersecurity Education in Finnish Universities

Piia Perälä and Martti Lehto

Faculty of Information Technology, University of Jyväskylä, Jyväskylä, Finland

piia.m.h.perala@jyu.fi
martti.j.lehto@jyu.fi

Abstract: Cybersecurity is no longer just a technical discipline but a strategic concept. Nowadays, cybersecurity has become an essential part of national security strategies. The European Union and European countries have established cybersecurity strategies to strengthen European and national resilience against cyber threats and ensure that citizens and businesses can take full advantage of reliable services and digital tools. A wide range of actors in society, from both government and non-government sectors, are already involved in cybersecurity work. However, there is a constant need to increase the workforce of cybersecurity specialists to manage cybersecurity risks. Finland's cybersecurity strategy emphasizes the importance of developing cybersecurity education to address the cybersecurity risks the country faces. For the nation to achieve cyber self-sufficiency, the pool of cybersecurity specialists should include experts in every knowledge area relevant to various aspects of cybersecurity. Universities have a role in training cybersecurity specialists through their education programs. Consequently, universities should offer comprehensive education encompassing all cybersecurity knowledge areas. This paper aims to overview the state of cybersecurity education in Finland's universities by focusing on cybersecurity education content. By analysing the content of the universities' cybersecurity education, the aim was to understand how current education in Finland meets the cybersecurity knowledge areas of the European Cybersecurity Taxonomy. In spring 2023, data on cybersecurity degree programs and courses were collected through surveys from nine Finnish universities providing cybersecurity education. As a result, we gained an understanding of the capability of Finnish university-level cybersecurity education to offer specialists in different domain areas of cybersecurity.

Keywords: Cyber Education, Cyber Strategy, Security, Cyber Competence, Cybersecurity Taxonomy

1. Introduction

Over time, cybersecurity has evolved from a technical discipline to a strategic concept, leading to a situation in which cybersecurity has become an essential part of national security strategies. Countries have established cybersecurity strategies to protect national security against attacks and threats targeted at the cyber environment. The European Union and European countries are implementing their cybersecurity strategies to strengthen resilience against cyber threats and ensure that citizens and businesses can take full advantage of reliable services and digital tools (EU, 2020). Already, cybersecurity work employs many people in government and non-government sectors, but still, countries have a constant and rapidly increasing need for a workforce of cybersecurity specialists. In 2022, the need for a workforce in cybersecurity increased by 26%, and it has been estimated that the current need for employment is 3.4. million cybersecurity workers globally (McCann, 2023). In Finland, there is an anticipated demand for 5,000-8,000 new cybersecurity specialists in the coming years, along with an additional need for 1,000-5,000 professionals who can incorporate cybersecurity responsibilities into their current roles (Lehto, 2023). In addition, Finland needs to increase the number of highly educated people. According to the Finnish Government's Education Policy Report (*Education Policy Report of the Finnish Government*, 2021), "One of the objectives is that by 2030, at least one-half of all young adults in Finland will complete a higher education degree. To achieve this goal, an additional 100,000 new higher education degrees must be completed by 2030 compared to what can be achieved with the current intake numbers." This need to increase the number of highly educated people is also reflected in the need for more highly educated cybersecurity experts. However, it is important not to forget the civil skills related to cybersecurity, as these skills play an increasingly important role as our societies become more digitised.

Finnish cybersecurity strategy (The Security Committee, 2019) emphasizes that developing cybersecurity education is the key to managing cybersecurity risks targeted to Finland. Developing cybersecurity education for specialists allows nations to pursue cyber self-sufficiency. Implementing a robust cybersecurity strategy requires competent employees at every level of the cyber environment to identify, build, and staff the cybersecurity infrastructure defences and responses (Evans and Reeder, 2010). However, the skills associated with cybersecurity specialists consist of a wide range of knowledge domains. For example, The European Cybersecurity Skills Framework (ECSF) developed by ENISA (The European Union Agency for Cybersecurity) summarizes the cybersecurity-related roles into 12 profiles that include over 60 different essential knowledge areas that are required to perform the work functions and duties in the profiled roles (ENISA, 2022). A vast number of knowledge areas of cybersecurity specialists challenge cybersecurity education, as educational institutions should pursue organizing education in every cybersecurity knowledge area.

To ensure comprehensive cybersecurity education, various standards, guidelines, frameworks, and concepts can be utilized to improve cybersecurity curricula (AlDaajeh *et al.*, 2022). For example, the National Initiative for Cybersecurity Education (NICE) Framework (Petersen *et al.*, 2020) is widely used when developing, building, and assessing cybersecurity education (see, e.g. Conklin, Cline and Roosa, 2014; AlDaajeh *et al.*, 2022; Varbanov, 2022).

This paper presents an overview of cybersecurity education in Finland's universities by analysing and assessing the contents of cybersecurity courses provided by the universities. Even though the NICE as the US framework is widely accepted for assigning cybersecurity education, this paper utilized the European Cybersecurity Taxonomy. The paper aims to elucidate the extent to which the education aligns with European cybersecurity development work when assessed with the European Cybersecurity Taxonomy. Furthermore, the paper provides an understanding of the capacity of Finnish university-level cybersecurity education to provide expertise across various domains within the field of cybersecurity.

2. Assessing Cybersecurity University-Level Education

Numerous studies have assessed the state of national cybersecurity education in higher education to understand essential needs for developing educational programs. For example, Cabaj et al. (2018) analysed the cybersecurity master programs offered by 21 universities. Their analysis focused on identifying the specific cybersecurity topics covered and the distribution of these topics across various courses. Lehto (2020) provided insights into the principles and implementation models utilized in Finnish university-level cybersecurity education. Furthermore, Conklin et al. (2014) delved into the critical factors contributing to discrepancies between industry requirements and cybersecurity education content in the US. Their objective was to formulate recommendations for developing cybersecurity study programs that better align with the evolving needs of the industry.

While assessing cybersecurity education, studies commonly lie in analysing education by frameworks, taxonomies, or guidelines. One of the most applied frameworks is the NICE framework (e.g., Cabaj *et al.*, 2018; AlDaajeh *et al.*, 2022). The NICE (Petersen *et al.*, 2020) is a workforce framework for cybersecurity that was initially developed to meet the US government's needs concerning the workforce. Nowadays, the NICE framework is applied across public, private, and academic sectors. The NICE framework provides the cybersecurity audience with a common language to define cybersecurity work and the set of tasks and skills it requires.

In Europe, ENISA is providing the ECSF to support the identification and articulation of tasks, competencies, skills, and knowledge associated with the roles of European cybersecurity professionals (ENISA, 2022). In addition, the European Commission's Joint Research Centre published the European Cybersecurity Taxonomy (Nai *et al.*, 2019) to align the cybersecurity terminologies, definitions, and domains to capture all the aspects of building the cybersecurity realm of knowledge (The taxonomy is discussed in more detail in the next chapter). Other tools utilized in the assessment of cybersecurity education include:

- The Association for Computing Machinery has introduced the Computing Classification System (CCS). The CCS designates security and privacy as a prominent generic area (*Computing Classification System*, 2012).
- The Institute of Electrical and Electronics Engineers (IEEE) proposes a taxonomy to categorize the publications of events made available through the IEEE Xplore Digital Library (*IEEE Thesaurus and IEEE Taxonomy Access*, 2024).
- The Cybersecurity Curricula 2017 provides guidance in cybersecurity education to facilitate program development and other educational initiatives (Joint Task Force On Cybersecurity, 2017).

3. European Cybersecurity Taxonomy

In 2019, the Joint Research Centre, the science and knowledge service of the European Commission, introduced a proposal for a European Cybersecurity Taxonomy. The taxonomy aims to "align the cybersecurity terminologies, definitions, and domains into a coherent and comprehensive taxonomy to facilitate the categorization of EU cybersecurity competencies" (Nai *et al.*, 2019, p.5). The definitions and domain categorizations within the taxonomy are grounded in widely accepted standards, international classification systems from working groups, regulations, best practices, and recommendations within the cybersecurity domain. (Nai *et al.*, 2019). The taxonomy aims to facilitate the alignment of European cybersecurity competencies.

The taxonomy includes three dimensions: *"research domains"*, *"sectors"*, and *"technologies and use cases"*. *Research domains (*i.e., *cybersecurity knowledge domains)* represent cybersecurity knowledge areas, such as human, legal, ethical, and technological aspects. *Sectors* emphasize the need to consider different cybersecurity requirements and challenges from a human, legal, and ethical perspective in scenarios in different sectors. *Technologies and use cases* represent the technological enablers that enhance the development of the different sectors interrelated to cybersecurity domains covering technological aspects.

Cybersecurity knowledge is organized into fifteen distinct domains, each comprising specific sub-domains. A comprehensive list of sub-domains can be found in the "Proposal for a European Cybersecurity Taxonomy" (2019). According to the European Cybersecurity Taxonomy, definitions and examples of sub-domains of each cybersecurity knowledge domain are provided as follows:

- *Assurance, Audit, and Certification:* The methodologies, frameworks, and tools that provide the ground for confidence that a system, software, service, process, or network is working or has been designed to operate at the desired security target or according to a defined security policy. Examples of sub-domains are assurance, audit, assessment, and certification.
- *Cryptology (Cryptography and Cryptanalysis):* Cryptological aspects encompass mathematical, algorithmic, and technical facets, including the implementation of cryptanalytic methods, tools, and digital steganography techniques for concealing information. Examples of sub-domains include asymmetric cryptography, symmetric cryptography, mathematical foundations of cryptography, post-quantum cryptography, and homomorphic encryption.
- *Data Security and Privacy:* Security and privacy issues related to data that minimize or prevent privacy, confidentiality, and integrity risks during data processing. This should be achieved without inappropriately impairing data processing or by preventing data misuse after authorized entities access it. Specific sub-domains within this context include privacy requirements for data management systems, Digital Rights Management (DRM), risk analysis and attacks concerning de-anonymization or data re-identification (e.g., inference attack), and data usage control.
- *Education and Training:* The learning process that involves acquiring the knowledge, know-how, skills, and competencies necessary to protect network and information systems, their users, and affected individuals from cyber threats. Subdomains within this context include cybersecurity-aware culture (e.g., children's education), cyber ranges, Capture the Flag exercises, simulation platforms, educational/training tools, and cybersecurity awareness.
- *Human Aspects:* Within the cybersecurity domain, the interplay between ethics, relevant laws, regulations, policies, standards, psychology, and the human being. Subdomains include, for example, accessibility, usability, human-related risks/threats (social engineering, insider misuse, etc.), socio-technical security, user acceptance of security policies and technologies, psychological models and cognitive processes, human aspects of trust, and human perception of cybersecurity.
- *Identity Management:* Processes and policies that govern the lifecycle, value, type, and optional metadata of identity attributes within a specific domain, encompassing access management aspects such as authentication, authorization, and access control for individuals and smart objects when interacting with resources. This involves considerations of both physical and digital elements in authentication systems and legal aspects related to compliance and law enforcement. Sub-domains within this context may include identity and attribute management models, frameworks, applications, technologies, and tools (e.g., PKI, RFID, SSO, attribute-based credentials, federated IdM, etc.), along with protocols and frameworks for authentication, authorization, and rights management.
- *Incident Handling and Digital Forensics:* The theories, techniques, tools, and processes used to identify, collect, acquire, and preserve digital evidence. Sub-domains encompass incident analysis, communication, documentation, intelligence-based forecasting, response and reporting, vulnerability analysis and response, digital forensic processes and workflow models, as well as anti-forensics and malware analytics.
- *Legal Aspects:* The legal and ethical aspects related to the misuse of technology, illicit distribution, and reproduction of material covered by intellectual property rights (IPR), as well as the enforcement of laws about cybercrime and digital rights. Examples of sub-domains include

cybercrime prosecution and law enforcement, intellectual property rights, and legal and societal issues in information security (e.g., identity management, digital forensics, cybersecurity litigation).

- *Network and Distributed Systems:* Network security encompasses the hardware, software, fundamental communication protocols, network frame structure, and communication mechanisms within a network. In the network context, Information Security focuses on ensuring data integrity, confidentiality, availability, and non-repudiation during transmission across the network. Cybersecurity in a distributed system covers message authentication and all facets of computation, coordination, message integrity, availability, and (if required) confidentiality. Examples of sub-domains include principles, methods, protocols, algorithms, and technologies in network security, security considerations in distributed systems, such as managerial, procedural, and technical aspects, requirements for network security, protocols, and frameworks for secure distributed computing, as well as network layer attacks and mitigation techniques.
- *Security Management and Governance:* Security governance and management includes all those activities, methodologies, processes, and tools aimed at preserving confidentiality, integrity, and availability of information, as well as properties such as authenticity, accountability, and non-repudiation. Examples of sub-domains encompass risk management involving modelling, assessment, analysis, and mitigations, modelling of cross-sectoral interdependencies and cascading effects, threats and vulnerabilities modelling, attack modelling, techniques, and countermeasures (e.g., adversary machine learning).
- *Security Measurements:* Information security measures aim to facilitate decision-making and improve performance and accountability by collecting, analysing, and reporting relevant cybersecurity performance-related data. Measuring performance monitors the status of measured activities and facilitates improvement by applying corrective actions based on observed measurements. Examples of sub-domains include security analytics and visualization, security metrics, and key performance indicators and benchmarks.
- *Software and Hardware Security Engineering:* Security aspects in the software and hardware development lifecycle include risk and requirements analysis, architecture design, code implementation, validation, verification, testing, deployment, and runtime monitoring of operation. Examples of sub-domains comprise security requirements engineering emphasizing identity, privacy, accountability, and trust, security and risk analysis of components compositions, as well as secure software architectures and design (security by design).
- *Steganography, Steganalysis, and Watermarking:* Techniques for steganography, steganalysis, and watermarking. Steganography is a technique for hiding secret data within files or messages, while steganography deals with detecting hidden data using steganography. Digital watermarking is similar to steganography, where the embedded data typically is not secret, and the goal is also to ensure data integrity. Examples of sub-domains include steganography, steganalysis, and digital watermarking.
- *Theoretical Foundations:* Using analysis and verification techniques based on formal methods aims to provide theoretical proof of software, hardware, and algorithm design security properties. Examples of sub-domains include the formal specification of various security aspects (e.g., properties, threat models, etc.), formal specification, analysis, and verification of software and hardware, information flow modelling and its application to confidentiality policies, the composition of systems, and covert channel analysis.
- *Trust Management and Accountability:* Trust issues related to digital and physical entities such as applications, services, components, or systems. Trust management approaches can be employed to assess assurance and accountability guarantees. Examples of sub-domains encompass semantics and models for security, accountability, privacy, and trust, architectures, mechanisms, and policies for trust management, trust and privacy considerations, and identity and trust management.

4. Method

In the spring of 2023, data was collected from nine Finnish universities through online surveys concerning the universities' cybersecurity education (i.e., cybersecurity degree programs and courses). The survey included questions, for example, related to universities' cybersecurity degree education, as well as courses and course contents aimed at developing expertise in cybersecurity. The questionnaires were reviewed before data collection. Subsequently, the questionnaires were edited and refined in alignment with the suggestions provided during the review. The questionnaires were distributed to the universities, where persons responsible for cybersecurity-related courses were expected to provide the needed information, considering the courses they were teaching. The responses received were checked for any gaps, and additions were requested from the universities if necessary.

Data was obtained from 96 courses that aim to develop skills in cybersecurity-related topic areas. The distribution of these courses across universities ranged from a minimum of one to a maximum of 28 courses offered by a single university. The levels of the courses were divided as follows: 64 advanced studies, 17 intermediate studies, 12 basic studies, and nine other studies. The sample did not include theses (Master's or Bachelor's).

During the analysis, we identified themes included in fifteen cybersecurity knowledge domains defined by the European Cybersecurity Taxonomy (2019) from course contents and learning outcomes. Content analysis (Weber, 1990) was used to identify the themes of courses and what cybersecurity knowledge domains were emphasized within and between courses. We followed the Joint Research Centre guidelines (Nai *et al.*, 2019, p.38) while applying the European Cybersecurity Taxonomy. We concentrated on identifying cybersecurity knowledge domains in each course but did not associate courses with an explicit sector, technology, or use case. This approach was chosen because, in many courses, the domain can be applied to different sectors, technologies, and use cases, causing a large number of combinations.

5. Results

The overview of Finnish universities' cybersecurity courses revealed identifiable themes based on the course contents, providing insights into the specific educational focus areas. These themes encompassed technical and technological cybersecurity, cybersecurity management, the societal perspective of cybersecurity, the human aspects of cybersecurity, and general cybersecurity themes. Education focused on technical and technological themes aims to develop technical skills and competence in cybersecurity. Typically, the goal is to gain specific technical knowledge in various domains within the field of cybersecurity. The cybersecurity management theme encompasses subject areas related to the management and the impact of cybersecurity within diverse organizations. The societal perspective of cybersecurity focuses on societal cybersecurity issues, such as cybersecurity's role in the information society, cybersecurity strategies, and operations. The educational content within the human perspective of cybersecurity address topics associated with individuals' cybersecurity, including individual security behaviour and the psychology of cybersecurity. The general cybersecurity theme concentrates on cybersecurity at a general level. These courses do not provide specific expertise in cybersecurity but aim to provide general knowledge and skills related to cybersecurity.

When looking at the priorities of the subject areas of cyber security education, it was found that universities' educational content focuses on developing technical and technological competence in cyber security. More than 60 percent of courses contained technical topics in the field of cyber security. In addition to technical and technological education, another focus theme of education was found to be cyber security management. Themes addressing cybersecurity from a societal or human perspective received less coverage in education. Figure 1 illustrates the distribution of Finnish universities' cybersecurity educational content across the different themes.

The analysis of cybersecurity education content in Finnish universities, in alignment with the European Cybersecurity Taxonomy, revealed that the contents of courses covered 14 out of the 15 cybersecurity knowledge domains specified by the taxonomy. Only content related to the knowledge domain concerning *"Steganography, Steganalysis, and Watermarking"* was not covered in cybersecurity courses. In most cases, several knowledge domains were identified to be covered in one course. For example, the content of the course called *"Cryptography in Networking"* covered five knowledge domains such as *"Cryptology"*, *"Data Security and Privacy"*, *"Identity Management"*, *"Network and Distributed Systems"*, and *"Software and Hardware Security Engineering"*. However, it was found that in twenty-nine courses, contents could be identified as covering only one knowledge domain.

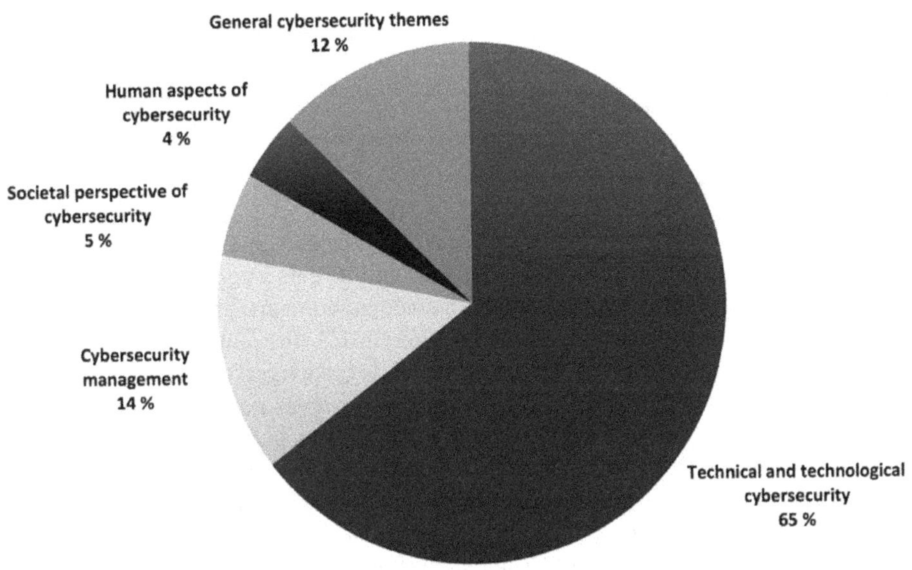

Figure 1: The distribution of Finnish universities' cybersecurity educational content across different themes.

More detailed analysis showed that the knowledge domain concerning *"Software and Hardware Security Engineering"* was the most represented in the course contents, as this area of expertise was part of the learning outcomes of 31 courses. Meanwhile, *"Cryptology"*, *"Education and Training"*, *"Network and Distributed Systems"*, and *"Security Management and Governance"* knowledge domains were also strongly represented in the courses. These knowledge domains were part of the learning outcomes of over 20 courses. Whereas such knowledge domains as "*Legal Aspects*", *"Assurance, Audit, and Certification"*, *"Theoretical Foundations*", and *"Trust Management and Accountability*" had the weakest representations in the courses. The "*Security Measurements*" domain was covered in 18 courses, "Identity Management" in 14 courses, "Data Security and Privacy" in 11 courses, "*Human Aspects*" in 9 courses, and *"Incident Handling and Digital Forensics"* in 6 courses.

In addition, we found it challenging to identify knowledge domains from the contents of several courses concentrating on AI, machine learning, and anomaly detection as part of different topics in cybersecurity. The taxonomy did not specify which knowledge domains these course contents covered. Table 1 illustrates the distribution of courses across different cybersecurity knowledge domains.

Table 1: The distribution of courses across different cybersecurity knowledge domains.

Cybersecurity knowledge domain of the European Cybersecurity Taxonomy	The number of courses representing the knowledge domain
Assurance, Audit, and Certification	2
Cryptology (Cryptography and Cryptanalysis)	21
Data Security and Privacy	11
Education and Training	21
Human Aspects	9
Identity Management	14
Incident Handling and Digital Forensics	6
Legal Aspects	3
Network and Distributed Systems	22
Security Management and Governance	23
Security Measurements	18
Software and Hardware Security Engineering	31
Steganography, Steganalysis, and Watermarking	0

Cybersecurity knowledge domain of the European Cybersecurity Taxonomy	The number of courses representing the knowledge domain
Theoretical Foundations	2
Trust Management and Accountability	2

6. Discussion and Conclusion

Cybersecurity has become an essential part of national security strategies. National cybersecurity strategies have been established to protect nations' security against attacks and threats targeted at the cyber environment. Competent employees from different cybersecurity knowledge domains are needed if nations wish to implement cybersecurity strategies robustly (Evans and Reeder, 2010). The number of cybersecurity experts in society can be increased by influencing several factors. One way is to increase the number and initial intakes of degree programs at the universities in the field. However, these measures require an increase in human resources. Additionally, increasing the number of cybersecurity experts involves developing education at the university level. It is also essential for universities to strengthen conversion and continuing education, as continuous learning plays an important role in these efforts. Furthermore, improving educational cooperation between universities would enable students to acquire more versatile specializations in different areas of cybersecurity (Lehto, 2022). This goal is promoted in an ongoing research project between universities in Finland (JYU, 2024).

In this paper, we presented a study that assessed the capacity of cybersecurity education in Finnish universities to train expertise and skills that cover the knowledge domains outlined in the European Cybersecurity Taxonomy. We analysed data from 96 cybersecurity courses from nine Finnish universities. Our findings indicated that Finnish universities provide relatively comprehensive cybersecurity education, as the contents of courses covered all other cybersecurity knowledge domains in the European Cybersecurity Taxonomy except for the domain called *"Steganography, Steganalysis, and Watermarking"*. The courses were commonly broad in scope, as one course could cover several cybersecurity knowledge areas. Course contents aiming to develop technical and technological expertise in cybersecurity were found to have the most extensive coverage in educational offerings. On the other hand, education on the less technical aspects of cybersecurity issues received comparatively less coverage in the courses. These findings align with the observation made by Cabaj et al. (2018) and Blažič (2022), as they noticed the scarcity of less technical educational content in cybersecurity education programs. Furthermore, the analysis revealed that the educational content at universities included topics that could not be categorized explicitly within any cybersecurity knowledge domains in the taxonomy.

Our findings increase the understanding of the coverage of cybersecurity education in Finnish universities by considering the content of cybersecurity courses through the European Cybersecurity Taxonomy. The results can be utilized as a base for the debate on how to direct and develop Finnish university-level cybersecurity education so that programs educate the workforce with a broad range of specialized expertise in cybersecurity. In addition, the results can be utilized as an initial step towards developing Finnish university-level cybersecurity education to align with European cybersecure educational work.

Based on the findings, some recommendations could be stated. As the university-level cybersecurity education intends to educate experts with a wide range of cybersecurity skills, the Finnish university-level education should be developed in a way that in the future it would cover all cybersecurity knowledge domains of the European Cybersecurity Taxonomy. Especially courses covering topics related to the knowledge domain of "Steganography, Steganalysis, and Watermarking" should be developed. Furthermore, educational content should be strengthened for those cybersecurity knowledge domains where courses are less available. (e.g., *"Trust Management and Accountability"*, *"Theoretical Foundations, Assurance, Audit, and Certification"*). As the universities' cybersecurity education focuses on developing technical skills, the education aiming at less technical competence should be increased to enhance the competence of cybersecurity experts (Cabaj *et al.*, 2018; Blažič, 2022). Overall, universities' cybersecurity education should maintain a multidisciplinary approach that provides valuable skills to address national cybersecurity issues effectively and helps prepare for the complexities of critical fields (Lehto, 2020).

Additionally, Finnish universities' cybersecurity education content should be regularly assessed against the European cybersecurity knowledge frameworks (e.g., ENISA and European Cybersecurity Taxonomy) to ensure extensive university-level cybersecurity education that aligns with European recommendations considering cybersecurity competencies. This ongoing assessment contributes to achieving more coherent cybersecurity education in Europe and potentially reduces variation in educational content between European nations.

This study has several limitations. This paper discusses the coverage of Finnish university-level cybersecurity education only from one European taxonomy. A more comprehensive understanding requires that universities' education be reviewed through other cybersecurity frameworks, taxonomies, and classification systems. In addition, the education assessment is based on the description of course contents and learning outcomes. A deeper understanding of the course contents requires more detailed information, as the course potentially covers more topics than described in the course description and learning outcomes.

Acknowledgements

This work was supported by the Ministry of Education and Culture in Finland (OKM/60/522/2022).

References

AlDaajeh, S. *et al.* (2022) 'The role of national cybersecurity strategies on the improvement of cybersecurity education', *Computers & Security*, 119, p. 102754. Available at: https://doi.org/10.1016/j.cose.2022.102754.

Blažič, B.J. (2022) 'Changing the landscape of cybersecurity education in the EU: Will the new approach produce the required cybersecurity skills?', *Education and Information Technologies*, 27(3), pp. 3011–3036. Available at: https://doi.org/10.1007/s10639-021-10704-y.

Cabaj, K. *et al.* (2018) 'Cybersecurity education: Evolution of the discipline and analysis of master programs', *Computers & Security*, 75, pp. 24–35. Available at: https://doi.org/10.1016/j.cose.2018.01.015.

Computing Classification System (2012) *ACM Digital Library*. Available at: https://dl.acm.org/ccs (Accessed: 27 January 2024).

Conklin, Wm.A., Cline, R.E. and Roosa, T. (2014) 'Re-engineering Cybersecurity Education in the US: An Analysis of the Critical Factors', in *2014 47th Hawaii International Conference on System Sciences. 2014 47th Hawaii International Conference on System Sciences*, pp. 2006–2014. Available at: https://doi.org/10.1109/HICSS.2014.254.

Education Policy Report of the Finnish Government (2021). Publications of the Finnish Government 2021:64. Finnish Government. Available at: https://julkaisut.valtioneuvosto.fi/handle/10024/163273 (Accessed: 30 January 2024).

ENISA (2022) *European Cybersecurity Skills Framework (ECSF)*. Available at: https://www.enisa.europa.eu/topics/education/european-cybersecurity-skills-framework.

EU (2020) *The EU's Cybersecurity Strategy for the Digital Decade*. Available at: https://digital-strategy.ec.europa.eu/en/library/eus-cybersecurity-strategy-digital-decade-0.

Evans, K. and Reeder, F. (2010) *A Human Capital Crisis in Cybersecurity: Technical Proficiency Matters*. CSIS.

IEEE Thesaurus and IEEE Taxonomy Access (2024). Available at: https://www.ieee.org/publications/services/thesaurus-thank-you.html (Accessed: 27 January 2024).

Joint Task Force On Cybersecurity (2017) *Cybersecurity Curricula 2017: Curriculum Guidelines for Post-Secondary Degree Programs in Cybersecurity*. New York, NY, USA: ACM. Available at: https://doi.org/10.1145/3422808.

JYU (2024) *National cybersecurity education cooperation network | University of Jyväskylä*. Available at: https://www.jyu.fi/en/projects/national-cybersecurity-education-cooperation-network (Accessed: 30 January 2024).

Lehto, M. (2020) 'Cyber security capacity building -cyber security education in Finnish universities Cyber security capacity building -cyber security education in Finnish universities', in *Proceedings of the 19th European Conference on Cyber Warfare and Security, ECCWS2020*, pp. 221–231. Available at: https://doi.org/10.34190/EWS.20.112.

Lehto, M. (2022) *Kyberturvallisuuden koulutusohjelman muutostarpeiden tutkimus – hankkeen loppuraportti*. 93. University of Jyväskylä. Available at: https://jyx.jyu.fi/bitstream/handle/123456789/82709/Kyberturvallisuuden%20koulutusohjelman%20muutostarpeiden%20tutkimus%20v4.pdf.

Lehto, M. (2023) 'Kyberturvallisuuden ammattilaisten koulutus', *Cyberwatch Finland Magazine*, pp. 19–23.

McCann, M. (2023) *Council Post: The Quest To Close The Cybersecurity Talent Gap, Forbes*. Available at: https://www.forbes.com/sites/forbeshumanresourcescouncil/2023/10/16/the-quest-to-close-the-cybersecurity-talent-gap/ (Accessed: 27 January 2024).

Nai, F.I. *et al.* (2019) *A Proposal for a European Cybersecurity Taxonomy*. Available at: https://doi.org/10.2760/106002.

Petersen, R. *et al.* (2020) *Workforce Framework for Cybersecurity (NICE Framework)*. National Institute of Standards and Technology. Available at: https://doi.org/10.6028/NIST.SP.800-181r1.

The Security Committee (2019) *Finland's Cyber Security Strategy*. Available at: https://turvallisuuskomitea.fi/wp-content/uploads/2019/10/Kyberturvallisuusstrategia_A4_ENG_WEB_031019.pdf.

Varbanov, P. (2022) 'Perspectives in the Design of a Modern Cybersecurity Training Programme: The ECHO Approach', *Information & Security: An International Journal*, 53, pp. 177–190. Available at: https://doi.org/10.11610/isij.5312.

Weber, R.P. (1990) *Basic Content Analysis*. SAGE.

A Comprehensive Artificial Intelligence Vulnerability Taxonomy

Arttu Pispa and Kimmo Halunen
National Defense University, Helsinki, Finland

arttu.pispa@iki.fi
kimmo.halunen@oulu.fi

Abstract: With the rise of artificial intelligence (AI) systems and machine learning (ML), there is a need for a comprehensive vulnerability framework that takes into account the specifics of AI systems. A review of the currently available frameworks shows that even though there have been some efforts to create AI specific frameworks, the end results have been flawed. Previous work analysed for this paper include AVID, Mitre ATLAS, Google Secure AI Framework, Attacking Artificial Intelligence, OWASP AI security and privacy guide, and ENISA Multilayer framework for good cybersecurity practices in AI. While only AVID is intended to be an AI/ML focused vulnerability framework, it has some weaknesses that are discussed further in the paper. Of the other works especially the ENISA framework has a valuable way of determining AI domains that can be affected by vulnerabilities. In our taxonomy proposal the first part of the evaluation process is determining the location in the AI system lifecycle that the vulnerability affects. The second part is determining which attributes of technical AI trustworthiness are compromised by the vulnerability. The third part is determining the possible impact of the vulnerability being exploited on a seven-step scale from the AI system functioning correctly, to it performing unintended, attacker directed actions outside the bounds it is supposed to function in. We also evaluate two known AI vulnerabilities based on our taxonomy proposal to showcase the benefits in comparison to existing frameworks.

Keywords: Artificial Intelligence, Vulnerability, Framework

1. Introduction

The rise of new and much improved AI and ML technologies and applications has led to a situation where these are used in more and more varied use cases. The proliferation of AI solutions in the everyday life of ordinary people and in the working practices of many organisations brings also the possibility of new threats and vulnerabilities, for example as a tool for finding vulnerabilities in other AI/ML systems (Carlini, 2023).

In recent years the research on these vulnerabilities has also been very active and there are already results of attacks and hacks on different applications and AI/ML techniques (Kathikar *et al.*, 2023; Qiu *et al.*, 2019). There are even some very fundamental results on how it is possible to create AI models with undetectable backdoors or weaknesses (He *et al.*, 2022).

As there are more and more issues found in AI systems, it has become evident that there is also a need for a system of classification for these vulnerabilities. In the traditional information security industry the CVE (Common Vulnerabilities Enumeration) (The MITRE Corporation, 2023a), CWE (Common Weakness Enumeration) (The MITRE Corporation, 2023b) and CVSS (Common Vulnerability Scoring System) (FIRST, 2023) are used to classify and evaluate the severity of different vulnerabilities in our digital infrastructure. Although these systems can be useful also in the AI/ML cases, there are many differences that support a more nuanced view of the vulnerabilities related to AI systems.

In this paper we evaluate previous work on building taxonomies and frameworks for AI systems' vulnerabilities. Our findings show that these taxonomies and frameworks do not adequately capture the necessary nuances of AI vulnerabilities. Thus, we also propose a new and improved taxonomy for AI/ML vulnerabilities.

2. Previous Work

There is as of yet no widely accepted vulnerability framework or taxonomy for artificial intelligence systems (Machine Learning, Generative Neural Networks, Large Language Models, etc.) unlike regular information technology vulnerabilities have with CVE (Common Vulnerability Enumeration) (The MITRE Corporation, 2023a). However, there are some contenders for a future system to be used. Most of these have grown out of a need to have some way of enumerating common types of vulnerabilities in a fast moving field, but it seems there has not been a concerted effort on creating a system suited for handling vulnerabilities in a systematic fashion across the field.

The search for existing AI/ML vulnerability frameworks was performed by queries for related keywords in both scientific search portals as well as open source tools such as Google Scholar. To ensure comprehensiveness, additional searches were performed in general internet portals, e.g. Google search, to ensure non-academic sources were also captured.

Used search portals include Scopus, EBSCO Discovery Service, Google Scholar, and regular Google search service. Searched for terms include but are not limited to "Artificial Intelligence", "Machine Learning", "Large Language Model", Vulnerability, Cybersecurity, "Cyber security", Framework, and Taxonomy, as well as most acronyms for the preceding terms.

For our evaluation we have also taken some frameworks, guidance documents, and similar public efforts that do not aim to be a comprehensive vulnerability taxonomy, to include them as input for our effort to create a comprehensive framework.

2.1 AVID

AVID (AI Vulnerability Database) is an open-source AI/ML vulnerability database, where anyone can in theory input vulnerabilities and they will get a generic ID assigned, as well as basic details so other people can be informed of them (AI Risk and Vulnerability Alliance, 2023). The database itself is publicly accessible at the website[1] and provides at least basic information for all vulnerabilities. Unfortunately there are some deficiencies in the effort that in our understanding limits its usefulness as a generic AI vulnerability taxonomy effort.

Firstly the largest issue with AVID is that it only considers vulnerabilities in the development phase of the AI models, so any that affect or are caused after deployment are not considered or do not have a place in the taxonomy. This leaves such vulnerabilities as might be caused by for example degradation of the used sensor feeds out of the system, and thus AVIDs usability as a common vulnerability framework is limited.

Some of the categories brought forth by AVID are good, but we also believe some of the categories given to be either too broad, such as environmental safety, while others are too narrow in scope, such as excessive queries. Some vulnerability categories are also misaligned and difficult to use as a technical platform for vulnerability taxonomy, such as the category of lacking global explanation. Even though it is known that it is beneficial for AI system developers and users to be able to explain the basis for any decisions made by the system, what is the actual vulnerability in effect of being unable to explain functionality?

2.2 MITRE ATLAS

While it is not a vulnerability framework, but a framework for attack vectors in AI, MITRE ATLAS (The MITRE Corporation, 2024) is important to evaluate when developing a vulnerability taxonomy. This is because it is a sister framework to the MITRE ATT&CK (The MITRE Corporation, 2023c), a widely used framework for regular IT system attack vectors, but for AI and ML attacks. Even though the framework doesn't cover vulnerabilities directly, many vulnerabilities have a corresponding attack vector that can be employed to take advantage of the vulnerability. Still the issues with MITRE ATLAS for vulnerability taxonomy are the same that ATT&CK has for regular vulnerabilities.

Firstly there are vulnerabilities that enable several different attack vectors to be used, and thus clear and unambiguous classification becomes more difficult, unless entries are duplicated across different vectors, which works against the intention of providing a single taxonomy enabling everyone to talk about the same thing in one place.

Secondly there are attack vectors in ATLAS that do not as such concern the AI/ML system itself, but rather how the systems are embedded in products and open APIs which are not so much a vulnerability as an intended use case of the system. Thirdly the level of detail in the ATLAS enumeration is in our opinion too detailed for a good vulnerability taxonomy fracturing the body of vulnerabilities too much and making it more difficult than necessary to see at a glance what parts of the AI system are vulnerable, and how the vulnerabilities might manifest themselves.

2.3 Google Secure AI Framework

Recently released effort by Google in providing guidance on how to implement AI and ML tools in a safe and secure manner in organisations (Hansen and Venables, 2023). At least for the time being it has little in the way of anything outside providing a small number of general guidelines in implementation and development. It does

[1] https://avidml.org/database/

not provide anything in relation to taxonomy for AI/ML vulnerabilities as of now, but it is unclear what the future plans of Google are for development of SAIF.

2.4 "Attacking Artificial Intelligence"

The report by Marcus Comiter (2019) performs some classification between different types of vulnerabilities or at least attack vectors affecting AI systems, but for a generic use case some of the delineations do not in our opinion make sense. The report is clearly good base work, but does not by itself provide a vulnerability taxonomy that could be implemented into a generic vulnerability enumeration.

The good points relate to how the intentions of the attacker relate to the severity of the attack and how different vulnerabilities are affected. This is in our opinion something that a common vulnerability taxonomy should retain at least in severity enumeration. The division of input attacks into two axis, human perceivable-invisible, and physical-digital are good enumerations for individual attacks but for vulnerabilities are not good classification methods, as the first mainly covers how stealthy the exploitation of the vulnerability can be, and the second depends heavily on where and how the AI system is implemented and used. For AI used for processing digital inputs the format is always digital, and for systems working on real world camera feeds the method will most likely be physical.

2.5 OWASP AI Security and Privacy Guide

This related work provides a good framework and enumeration for different types of attacks that AI systems might be attacked with, but does not provide any taxonomy for AI vulnerabilities (OWASP Foundation, 2023). The main takeaway here is that the vulnerabilities underlying these attack vectors should at least be present in any comprehensive AI vulnerability taxonomy. It is mostly included for comprehensiveness of the search.

2.6 ENISA Multilayer Framework for Good Cybersecurity Practices in AI

ENISA has published a framework for general good practices in AI/ML cybersecurity (European Union Agency for Cybersecurity, 2023). While this framework itself doesn't provide any guidance or taxonomy on AI/ML vulnerabilities, it does provide for example a comprehensive version of an AI system lifecycle that is superior in our view to the one used by AVID. This comes from the fact that it contains parts of the process of creating an AI system that are not only limited to the actual development and deployment of the system, but for example starts from the business reason for creating an AI system. It also covers eventual maintenance and continuous retraining of the model as is likely to happen in any AI system with wide adoption rates.

We believe that as a related framework, it would be good if any proposed AI vulnerability taxonomy would at least in part align with the ENISA framework, so that wider and more general adoption can be achieved.

A similar effort has been recently published by the UK National Cyber Security Centre (2023), but it is mostly similar general guidance as the ENISA framework, and as such does not itself provide a good framework for a vulnerability taxonomy.

3. Taxonomy

Our taxonomy aims to address the shortcomings of the earlier taxonomies with a three stage process of evaluation, an overview of which can be seen in figure 1.

First, it should be evaluated which phase of the AI system development and use the vulnerability affects. The three phases we have chosen here are the most relevant and widespread while still being useful for actual vulnerability information sharing and for evaluating affected AI systems for existence of the vulnerability in deployed form. The first phase is the development of the AI systems, containing as examples poisoned libraries, pre-trained poisoned models, and various other software supply chain vulnerabilities that can affect the functionality of the AI model.

The second phase is the training of the model, whether it is a pre-trained model or one built specifically for the system being evaluated. Vulnerability examples in this phase include poisoning training data-sets, both public and private, using unrepresentative training sets, as well as poisoning federated training data.

The third phase is the deployment phase of the AI system including both the actual deployment to production use as well as eventual maintenance of the system in use and any modifications made to it. Vulnerability examples here are model inversion, training data inversion, instability to adversarial examples, training drift due to continuous learning, etc.

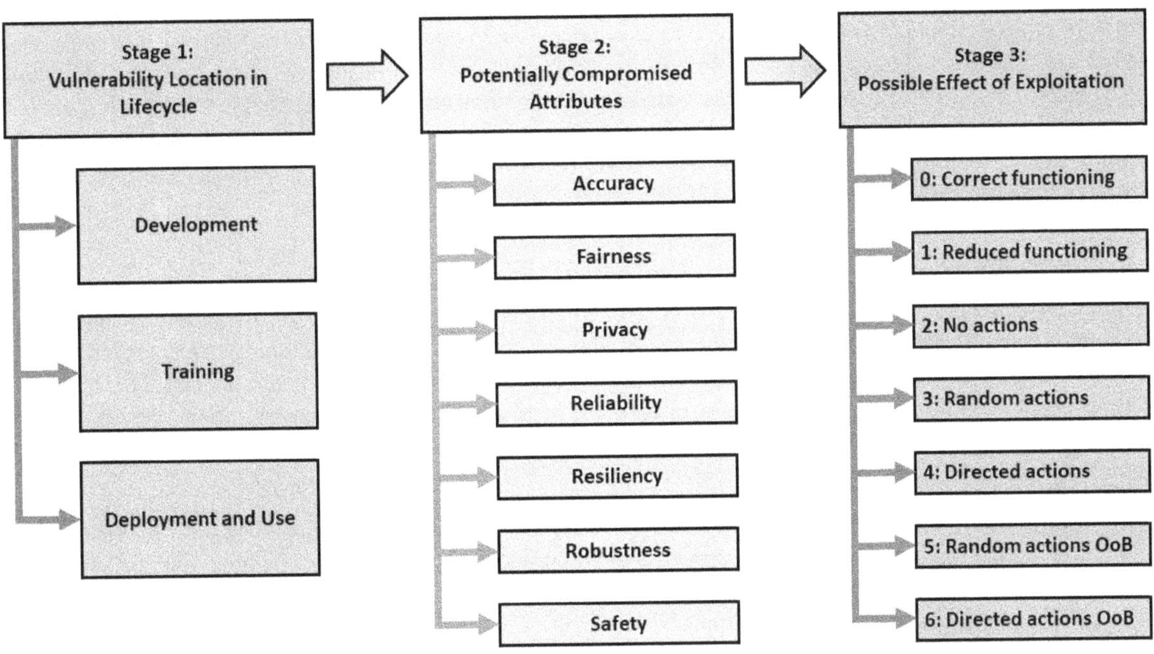

Figure 1: Overview of the proposed three stage evaluation process for AI system vulnerabilities

In the second stage the attributes of secure and trustworthy AI that are undermined by the vulnerability are evaluated to bring context to the use and focus of the vulnerability. Here we propose to use a framework of AI trustworthiness closely aligned with the ENISA framework to enable closer cooperation between actors in the AI security sphere. Some examples of the attributes that can be undermined are accuracy, fairness, reliability, and safety.

The third stage of evaluation is performed by assessing the level of degradation of functionality of the AI system in regards to the original intention of the creator. This metric is used as it allows us to have more detailed descriptions of the vulnerability effects, as well as takes into account the fact that in normal use the system is intended to perform autonomous actions and thus not being under control of the owner is standard operating procedure instead of a malfunction. The full devised scale is detailed later, but runs from the AI performing correctly (no impact), through the AI performing undirected unintended actions within the bounds of the AI system parameters, to the AI system performing unintended actions under attacker direction out of bounds of the AI system parameters.

3.1 Vulnerability Location in AI System Lifecycle

The first part of the evaluation is to determine which part of the AI system lifecycle the vulnerability affects. For this purpose, we suggest dividing the AI system development and deployment into three distinct phases to help narrow which parts of the development-deployment pipeline potential users of the vulnerability disclosures need to scrutinise to ensure their own systems are or are not affected by the disclosed vulnerability.

The first phase is the Development of the AI system where the architecture and design of the system itself are developed. The vulnerabilities in this phase affect systems used in creating the AI system itself, but not the learning process for the AI being used. Common examples of vulnerabilities in this phase are poisoned libraries (Ladisa *et al.*, 2023), pre-trained poisoned models being re-used (Kathikar *et al.*, 2023), as well as any vulnerabilities in the development pipeline that may compromise the security and functioning of the AI system once trained and deployed.

The second phase is Training of the AI where the AI system is taught to transform a certain input into a desired output. Vulnerabilities in this phase have to do with the training of the AI models being used in the system, but not the tools and design of the system itself. Common examples of vulnerabilities here are poisoned training sets (He *et al.*, 2022), both publicly available ones as well as private versions or sets, unrepresentative training sets, either due to accidental or intentional omissions or other errors, and poisoning federated learning schemes (Sun *et al.*, 2022), where unrepresentative or adversarial training data is fed into an AI system to affect the functioning of versions in use by other actors.

The third phase is deployment of the AI system, both including the act of deploying the system into real use as well as eventual use and maintenance of the system during its lifecycle. Vulnerabilities here have to do with how the AI models and systems handle user input, are susceptible to misdirection and sabotage through regular use channels of the system, and other channels available during the deployment and use of the system. Common examples of vulnerabilities affecting this phase of the lifecycle are model inversions, training data inversion, and adversarial example instability.

3.2 Potentially Compromised Attributes of Trustworthy AI

Secondly, to evaluate how the vulnerability affects the use and security of the AI system, it should be determined which attributes of a trustworthy AI system are broken or compromised by exploiting the vulnerability. The attributes of AI trustworthiness we propose to use for this in a general taxonomy are aligned with the ENISA Multilayer framework for good cybersecurity practices in AI to allow the taxonomy to be used in a wider setting and to maintain cross-compatibility across the industry. Some exceptions to attributes presented in the ENISA framework not included here are detailed later.

- **Accuracy:** Accuracy of the prediction made by the model as opposed to reality. While many vulnerabilities can affect the accuracy of the AI system, vulnerabilities affecting mainly the accuracy of the system are those where there is a mismatch between the AI model and causality in the real world, for example due to improper training of the model, or unaccounted for deviations in the sensor feeds given to the AI system, thus distorting it's understanding of reality.
- **Fairness:** Fairness represents the equitable distribution of actions and decisions made by the system, such that evidence, and not biases, opinions, emotions, or other limitations either intentionally or unintentionally placed in the system affect the decision making process and results of the system. Vulnerabilities affecting mainly Fairness of the AI system introduce bias either intentionally or unintentionally while being covert from the users of the AI system such that the system makes somehow biased decision not based only on the evidence or input it has received to make the decision.
- **Privacy:** Privacy of the data and models used in the creation of the AI system, as well as respecting the personal privacy of the users and subjects of the AI system are gathered under the attribute of privacy. Privacy vulnerabilities cause unintentional leaking of private data, either personal data for users of the AI system, or some details of the AI system or its input data that is not generally available, such as model weights, training data, or system usage data as examples.
- **Reliability:** The ability of the AI system to consistently produce similar results within statistical error margins for similar inputs are main factors of reliability. Vulnerabilities affecting mainly the reliability of the AI system introduce enough random noise into the system such that the results of the system cannot be relied upon to be repeatable for similar data inputs or cause it to be vulnerable to non-obvious edge cases where the output of the system unforeseeably flips into other than expected states.
- **Resiliency:** The ability of the AI system to function even under attack by an adversary, as well as to recover to a regular operating state after an attack has been suffered. Resiliency vulnerabilities hamper the AI systems ability to function properly while under attack or make it so that the system requires significant effort to recover into a normal operational state after such an attack.
- **Robustness:** The ability of the AI system to function at the minimum acceptable operational efficiency even while under attack. Prime example of a vulnerability affecting the robustness of the AI system is a vulnerability that allows easy Denial of Service attacks against the system or otherwise allows degrading the performance metrics of the system to unacceptable levels.
- **Safety:** Prevention of harm to humans, environment, or society in general. Generally vulnerabilities affecting the safety attribute are such that make existing safety interlocks and other safety systems embedded in the AI system to fail to function as intended, allowing the system to perform actions generally not allowed in its regular operational envelope.

Attributes not presented here are Accountability, which is not used as any technical vulnerability causes the originating entity to lose the ability to ensure proper functioning of the system, Explainability, as any system with a vulnerability does not function as intended, so it cannot be explained, Security, as all security vulnerabilities by definition affect the security of the system, and Transparency, as a system acting not in accordance with the intention of its creator cannot really be transparent about its functioning.

3.3 Possible Effect of the Vulnerability Being Exploited

Third and last step in evaluating the vulnerability should be assessing the possible level of control or effect that exploiting the vulnerability allows the attacker. Here we propose a seven step scale for evaluating the effect the vulnerability can have, based on how far outside the bounds of the original design and how well under the control of the attacker/exploiter of the vulnerability the AI system functions. The proposed scale starts at zero to allow informational level effects to also be monitored within the framework.

1. **AI performs correctly:** At this level there is little to no effect on the functioning of the AI system in general, or other safety controls make sure that any deviation from regular use is corrected before any meaningful change from normal operation is able to manifest. This level is to be used for mostly informational vulnerabilities so they can be monitored in case some other vulnerability or change in environment makes actual exploitation of the vulnerability more feasible or impactful.
2. **AI functions within normal operational envelope, but at reduced capacity:** Here the normal functioning of the AI system has been affected in some way, but it still manages to function as it is intended to function, just in some way reduced capacity. Examples are degradation of prediction accuracy, increase in noise of the results, slowness in response times, excessive data/compute usage running up abnormal operating expenses, etc.
3. **AI performs no action, or becomes unavailable:** At this level the normal operation of the AI system is denied to it's users and the organisation utilising it, either by making the system unresponsive in totality by overloading the AI system or its functions, or affecting the underlying infrastructure in a way that creates a Denial of Service situation for the system as a whole. Examples include logic bombs, DoS attacks on infrastructure and open APIs, inability to discard malformed data causing ingestion methods to clog up, degrading analysis enough that no meaningful decision on data can be made, etc.
4. **AI performs unintended, undirected actions within the bounds of the system:** At this point the attacker is able to cause the AI system to take actions, but is unable to cause it to take actions that it wouldn't normally be expected to take, while also not being able to direct which actions precisely the system takes. Examples include affecting self-driving systems in such a way that the vehicle acts erratically, but being unable to cause the system to take specific actions, or causing an AI system to erroneously evaluate loan applications, but not being able to cause certain loans to be accepted, or others to be rejected.
5. **AI performs unintended, directed actions within the bounds of the system:** Here the attacker is able to direct what the AI system does, or how it acts, but is unable to break out of the bounds of the regular operating environment of the AI system. Examples include being able to cause a self-driving system to brake or accelerate on command, or causing an AI system processing loan application to process certain loan applications such that the attacker is able to always cause certain applications to be approved or disapproved if they wish.
6. **AI performs unintended, undirected actions out of bounds of the system:** At this level the attacker is able to break out of the AI system itself through the AI system and perform actions outside the AI system itself, although not being able to fully control the actions. Examples include for example being able to corrupt databases connected to the AI system, or causing an AI powered robot to flail around uncontrollably without obeying regular limitations on joint movement or movement envelope.
7. **AI performs unintended, directed actions out of bounds of the system:** Here the attacker is able to essentially gain full control of the AI system, both to remove regular limitations on actions the AI system is able to take, as well as possibly breaking out of the system itself to run commands on the machines running the system. Examples include being able to install additional software on the machines running the AI system, or gaining full control of the system while being able to disable all safety systems that would limit system usage.

3.4 Completed Evaluation

The above three step procedure will give us a result that has three parts: Attack vector (i.e. where in the lifecycle the vulnerability presents itself), impacted attributes and level of impact (on a seven-step scale). It is important to note that the exact value of the severity is not necessarily the level on the impact scale. For example, in a real-time scenario an attack that causes a denial of service in the collision avoidance system of an autonomous vehicle can be much more severe than an attack that gives the attacker some control on the underlying infotainment system in the vehicle. In our taxonomy these would be on levels 3 and 7 respectively on the impact scale.

However, the taxonomy will help put new and old vulnerabilities in a systematic form and can help decision makers in determining what are the implications in their context. It is also meant as a functional framework that discussion and data collection on AI vulnerabilities can be done in a structured and organised fashion.

3.5 Examples of Application

To provide a few examples on how the proposed taxonomy can be used to evaluate and enumerate vulnerabilities, two existing articles providing detailed examples of AI/ML vulnerabilities were chosen and evaluated. The examples are not vulnerabilities in specific systems but possible ways to attack them, but they should still serve as a good example on applying the proposed framework. For exact vulnerabilities we would either need gain access to information not currently available to the public on existing vulnerabilities or rely on information available in public databases that do not contain all the relevant information for classification as detailed above in explaining why a new framework is needed.

3.5.1 Hardware Trojan Attack by Hou et al. (2024)

In their recent article published in Micromachines, Hou et al proceed to demonstrate a possible attack on Convolutional Neural Networks (CNN) through trojanized FPGA (Field Programmable Gate Array) hardware (Hou *et al.*, 2024).

In the first stage the vulnerability would be considered to be located in the development phase of the AI system, as it affects the physical hardware being used to run the CNN, and is done by creating poisoned (trojanized) hardware that could be inserted into the supply chain of the system development organization.

In the second stage the attributes being compromised include Accuracy, Fairness, Reliability, and Robustness of the system as all these attributes can be compromised with the proposed attack. This is caused by the way the demonstrated attack changes the decision-making process of the system as the calculations that are performed are different from the ones defined in the original code and design of the original implementer on the trojanized hardware.

In the third stage the vulnerability would be evaluated to be at level 1 or 2, depending on the amount of change the trojanized FPGA is able to cause in the calculations and how the CNN is being used in the system. The specific level of effect enabled by the vulnerability depends here on the actual implementation of the system, so that a more definitive determination is not possible on such a generic attack.

3.5.2 Robust Physical-World Attack by Eykholt et al. (2018)

In their article from 2018 in IEEE/CVF Conference on Computer Vision and Pattern Recognition, Eykholt et al proceed to demonstrate several different attacks on traffic signs in the physical world that cause Deep Neural Net (DNN) image classifiers trained on the LISA and GTSRB training sets to misclassify the attacked traffic signs in similar situations as would be encountered by self-driving vehicles in regular road conditions (Eykholt *et al.*, 2018).

In the first stage of the evaluation the phase of the vulnerability would be deployment, as the proposed attack method is clear intended to be applied into traffic signs in the world at large to be encountered by self-driving systems during their normal operation.

In the second stage the attributes under attack are Accuracy and Safety as both the accuracy of the image detection is being attacked, as well as the end result of making traffic signs unreadable by autonomous vehicles is to make them ignore traffic rules and thus compromise safety of both the self-driving vehicle as well as all other users on the road.

In the third stage the effect of the attack is undirected actions within the normal operational envelope, or level 3, as even though stop signs are shown to be misclassified as speed limit 45 or 80 km/h signs, the fact itself doesn't yet mean that the self-driving vehicle would accelerate to that speed on seeing the sign. Then again the same attack method could be used to make speed limit signs to be misclassified as stop signs, which would then place the vulnerability on level 4, as the most likely effect of a self-driving vehicle on seeing a stop sign is to brake to come to a stop before it.

4. Discussion

Although the above taxonomy gives a great tool for better understanding the AI/ML vulnerabilities, there are still many areas for improvement and further research. As mentioned in the previous section, our taxonomy has impact levels, but these cannot be directly translated into severity of the vulnerability. In traditional vulnerability classification the CVSS (Common Vulnerability Scoring System) is used to give a numerical value for the severity of vulnerability. This helps system administrators and other decision makers to prioritise mitigations and make decisions related to patching the vulnerability in their organisations. CVSS is far from perfect and has received some criticism. It has also been updated over the years (current CVSS is version 4, with the latest update coming out in the beginning of November of 2023) to better reflect the developments in vulnerabilities.

One further development area is to build a similar system for scoring AI/ML vulnerabilities. This could be done in the context of our new taxonomy. One difficulty for this is the fact that the context in which the vulnerability is manifested can be very different and the implications can also vary greatly. On the other hand, in traditional vulnerabilities the context (e.g. the affected software or hardware components) is part of the Common Vulnerability Enumeration entry and the severity can be evaluated in that context.

Another interesting venue for further research is developing systems and platforms for testing AI/ML systems for vulnerabilities. Again, in the traditional vulnerability research domain there are many different tools and platforms (even whole OSes) dedicated to testing systems for vulnerabilities. In the AI/ML domain these tools and platforms are still developing. In order to improve the security of these systems there is a need for not only taxonomies and scoring methods to evaluate newly found vulnerabilities but also tools and platforms to test new AI/ML systems against known vulnerabilities.

5. Conclusion

In this paper we have reviewed the present efforts in creating a framework for security vulnerabilities in AI/MLL use cases and found that all current options have deficiencies. We've proposed a new taxonomy to use as a basis for a new effort into creating an encompassing vulnerability taxonomy for artificial intelligence systems and provided two short examples on application of the evaluation. This work can best be continued by evaluating existing vulnerabilities with the proposed taxonomy in a systemic fashion to show the improvements over existing efforts, as well as developing a vulnerability scoring system based on the proposed taxonomy.

Acknowledgements

We would like to thank the Matine research group at Oulu University for their ideas and conversations surrounding this topic. The research has received funding from the 2023 grant application of the Scientific Advisory Board for Defence.

References

AI Risk and Vulnerability Alliance (2023) *AVID*. Available at: https://avidml.org/ (Accessed: 14 January 2024).

Carlini, N. (2023) 'A LLM Assisted Exploitation of AI-Guardian'. arXiv. Available at: http://arxiv.org/abs/2307.15008 (Accessed: 17 August 2023).

Comiter, M. (2019) 'Attacking Artificial Intelligence'. Available at: https://www.belfercenter.org/publication/AttackingAI (Accessed: 17 August 2023).

European Union Agency for Cybersecurity (2023) *A multilayer framework for good cybersecurity practices for AI :: security and resilience for smart health services and infrastructures.* LU: Publications Office. Available at: https://data.europa.eu/doi/10.2824/588830 (Accessed: 28 September 2023).

Eykholt, K., Evtimov, I., Fernandes, E., Li, B., Rahmati, A., Xiao, C., Prakash, A., Kohno, T. and Song, D. (2018) 'Robust Physical-World Attacks on Deep Learning Visual Classification', in *2018 IEEE/CVF Conference on Computer Vision and Pattern Recognition. 2018 IEEE/CVF Conference on Computer Vision and Pattern Recognition (CVPR)*, Salt Lake City, UT, USA: IEEE, pp. 1625–1634. Available at: https://doi.org/10.1109/CVPR.2018.00175.

FIRST (2023) 'Common Vulnerability Scoring System version 4.0 Specification'. Available at: https://www.first.org/cvss/v4.0/specification-document (Accessed: 14 January 2024).

Hansen, R. and Venables, P. (2023) *Introducing Google's Secure AI Framework, Google*. Available at: https://blog.google/technology/safety-security/introducing-googles-secure-ai-framework/ (Accessed: 17 August 2023).

He, Y., Shen, Z., Xia, C., Hua, J., Tong, W. and Zhong, S. (2022) 'SGBA: A Stealthy Scapegoat Backdoor Attack against Deep Neural Networks'. arXiv. Available at: http://arxiv.org/abs/2104.01026 (Accessed: 15 January 2024).

Hou, J., Liu, Z., Yang, Z. and Yang, C. (2024) 'Hardware Trojan Attacks on the Reconfigurable Interconnections of Field-Programmable Gate Array-Based Convolutional Neural Network Accelerators and a Physically Unclonable Function-Based Countermeasure Detection Technique', *Micromachines*, 15(1), p. 149. Available at: https://doi.org/10.3390/mi15010149.

Kathikar, A., Nair, A., Lazarine, B., Sachdeva, A. and Samtani, S. (2023) 'Assessing the Vulnerabilities of the Open-Source Artificial Intelligence (AI) Landscape: A Large-Scale Analysis of the Hugging Face Platform', in *2023 IEEE International Conference on Intelligence and Security Informatics (ISI). 2023 IEEE International Conference on Intelligence and Security Informatics (ISI)*, Charlotte, NC, USA: IEEE, pp. 1–6. Available at: https://doi.org/10.1109/ISI58743.2023.10297271.

Ladisa, P., Ponta, S.E., Ronzoni, N., Martinez, M. and Barais, O. (2023) 'On the Feasibility of Cross-Language Detection of Malicious Packages in npm and PyPI', in *Proceedings of the 39th Annual Computer Security Applications Conference*. New York, NY, USA: Association for Computing Machinery (ACSAC '23), pp. 71–82. Available at: https://doi.org/10.1145/3627106.3627138.

National Cyber Security Centre (2023) 'Guidelines for secure AI system development'. Available at: https://www.ncsc.gov.uk/collection/guidelines-secure-ai-system-development (Accessed: 14 January 2024).

OWASP Foundation (2023) *OWASP AI Security and Privacy Guide*. Available at: https://owasp.org/www-project-ai-security-and-privacy-guide/ (Accessed: 17 August 2023).

Qiu, S., Liu, Q., Zhou, S. and Wu, C. (2019) 'Review of Artificial Intelligence Adversarial Attack and Defense Technologies', *Applied Sciences*, 9(5), p. 909. Available at: https://doi.org/10.3390/app9050909.

Sun, G., Cong, Y., Dong, J., Wang, Q., Lyu, L. and Liu, J. (2022) 'Data Poisoning Attacks on Federated Machine Learning', *IEEE Internet of Things Journal*, 9(13), pp. 11365–11375. Available at: https://doi.org/10.1109/JIOT.2021.3128646.

The MITRE Corporation (2023a) *CVE - Common Vulnerability Enumeration*. Available at: https://cve.mitre.org/ (Accessed: 17 August 2023).

The MITRE Corporation (2023b) *CWE - Common Weakness Enumeration*. Available at: https://cwe.mitre.org/ (Accessed: 17 August 2023).

The MITRE Corporation (2023c) *MITRE ATT&CK®*. Available at: https://attack.mitre.org/ (Accessed: 23 January 2024).

The MITRE Corporation (2024) *MITRE | ATLAS™*. Available at: https://atlas.mitre.org/ (Accessed: 17 August 2023).

Architecture Framework for Cyber Security Management

Jouni Pöyhönen and Martti Lehto
University of Jyväskylä, Jyväskylä, Finland

jouni.a.poyhonen@jyu.fi
martti.j.lehto@jyu.fi

Abstract: The smooth operation of contemporary society relies on the collaborative functioning of multiple essential infrastructures, with their collective effectiveness increasingly hinging on a dependable national system of systems construction. The central focus within the realm of cyberspace revolves around safeguarding this critical infrastructure (CI), which includes both physical and electronic components essential for societal operations. The recent surge in cyber-attacks targeting CI, critical information infrastructures, and the Internet, characterized by heightened frequency and increased sophistication, presents substantial threats. As perpetrators become more adept, they can digitally infiltrate and disrupt physical infrastructure, causing harm to equipment and services without the need for a physical assault. The operational uncertainty of CI in these cases is obvious. The linchpin of cyber security lies in a well-executed architecture, a fundamental requirement for effective measures. The framework of this paper emphasizes organizational guidance in cyber security management by integrating the cyber security risks assessment and the cyber resilience process into overall continuity management of organizations business processes.

Keywords: Critical Infrastructure, Architecture Framework, Risks Assessment, Resilience

1. Introduction

The smooth operation of contemporary society relies on the collaborative functioning of multiple essential infrastructures, with their collective effectiveness increasingly hinging on a dependable national system of systems construction. The dependability of this system construction is intricately tied to cyber security, and consequently, the confidence placed in the business processes of organizations integrated into the overall system. Moreover, dependability is interconnected with the usability, reliability, and integrity of data within the operational framework, where cyber threats continuously escalate due to menacing scenarios in the digital realm.

A system of systems (SoS) refers to a compilation of autonomous systems, each capable of independent operation, that collaboratively interoperate to attain additional desired capabilities (Dahmann, 2015). In cyber world Information and Communication Technology (ICT), Industrial Control Systems (ICS), and other Operational Technology (OT) systems as fundamental elements of SoS. Additionally, a comprehensive understanding of users, various processes, and the flow of data and information between these components is crucial for grasping the broader context of the SoS approach.

One of cyber security research areas is to utilize a system of systems (SoS) approach specifically critical infrastructure (CI) protection against harmful attacks and unexpected behaviors. It enables a holistic view of the organization's cyber security. According to our experiences, SoS is well-suited to cyber security research projects that enhance comprehensive security, including people, processes, and technology, requiring to understand the organization and its operation as well as business processes as a whole system and inseparable parts of the critical infrastructure actors in the cyber world.

The objective of this paper is to outline the structure of a cyber security architecture suitable for an organization, enabling the description of management measures tailored to the organization's needs in all situations of cyber security challenges. The paper integrates risk assessment methodologies with resilience development model to offer organizations a comprehensive approach to continuity management. There is a limited amount of literature discussing papers on organizational holistic cyber security frameworks from this perspective.

2. Dilemma of Known and Unknown Threats

In cases of disturbances, the characteristics of the cyber operational environment include their development at high speed and with far-reaching effects. The organization's cyber operating environment consists of technically complicated structures and widely networked stakeholders, making the whole complex. It is impossible to fully predict its operation. There are also challenges in identifying different forms of cyber-attack and malware. The cyber operating environment is characterized by the speed of change, which requires fast reaction capability - agility, as well as preparation for situations that cannot be fully foreseen in terms of security measures. The examination of operational uncertainty can be based on the probability of occurrence of events (known or unknown) and the evaluation of its impact (known or unknown). The review leads to four possibilities regarding events, which are known known, known unknown, unknown known, and unknown unknown to understand and explain the nature of risk (Kim, 2017). The first three event cases can be covered by using risks assessment methods and processes, but totally unknown possibility cases need to be covered by a different tool. There is a need to increase the overall resilience of the organization's business operations.

Table 1: Simplified operational uncertainty model (adapted from Kim (2017))

	IMPACT	
OCCURRANCE	**Known, Knowns** Risks management process	**Unknown, Knowns** Risks management process
	Unknown, Known Risks management process	**Unknown, Unknown** Resilience enhance process

3. Cyber Threat Intelligence Process

Cyber Threat Intelligence (CTI) encompasses information derived from knowledge, skills, and experience, addressing both cyber and physical threats as well as the entities behind these threats. Its purpose is to aid in the prevention and mitigation of potential attacks and adverse events within the realm of cyberspace. Strategic cyber threat intelligence caters to top-level decision-makers, operational intelligence supports daily decision-making, and tactical threat intelligence targets units requiring real-time information. Within this framework, the cyber threat intelligence process involves system description, cyber threat analysis, vulnerability analysis, cyber-attack model analysis, and impact analysis.

Cyber threat intelligence is often broken down into three subcategories:

- Strategic (who/why) - Broader trends typically meant for a non-technical audience,
- Operational (how/where) - Technical details about specific attacks and campaigns,
- Tactical (what) - Outlines of the tactics, techniques, and procedures of threat actors for a more technical audience.

3.1 System of Systems Description

SoS environment is a collection of systems, each capable of independent operation, that interoperate together to achieve additional desired capabilities (Dahmann, 2015). By the SoS model, organizations may identify all its processes, users, and digital assets. In that sense Martin C. Libicki's structure for the cyber world uses a four-layer cyber world model: physical, syntactic, semantic, and cognitive. Using Libicki's structure and adding service as a fifth layer we have five-layer cyber world model: physical, syntactic, semantic, service, and cognitive (Libicki, 2007; Lehto & Neittaanmäki, 2018).

The physical layer contains the physical elements of communication and information network. The first requirement to build a cyberspace is the physical layer, which comprises all of the hardware required to send, receive, store, and interact with and through cyberspace.

The syntactic layer is formed of various system control and management programs and features which facilitate interaction between the devices connected to the network. This layer can be further broken down into sub-layers, such as the seven layers of the Open System Interconnection (OSI) Reference Model.

The semantic layer is the heart of the entire network. It contains the information and datasets in data warehouses, different large-scale systems, and computer terminals as well as different user-administered functions.

The service layer contains all the ICT-based services which the users use in the network.

The cognitive layer provides the decision makers an information-awareness environment: a world in which information is being interpreted and where one's contextual understanding of information is created including the user's cognitive and emotional awareness.

An organization's cyber security operations require comprehensive awareness on the system level. The awareness of an organization and decision-makers can be seen as system-level awareness arrangement. Thus, the appropriate awareness supports cyber risk management and, more extensively, the evaluation of an organization's whole cyber capability. It is possible to integrate an organization's three decision-making levels into a five-layer cyber structure in order to have a comprehensive system view of that organization's cyber security environment. It is a system-based approach to the topics and principles of an organization's comprehensive cyber security. The combination of system views, decision-making levels and an organization's cyber structure is described in Figure 1 (Pöyhönen & Lehto, 2020).

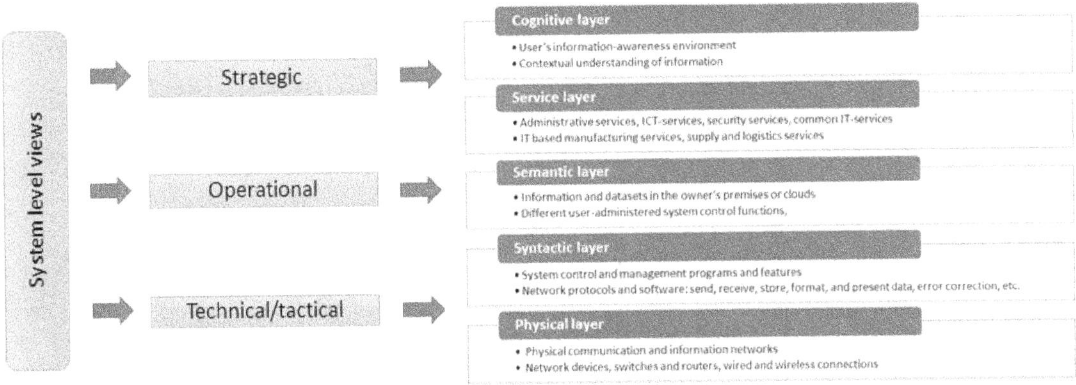

Figure 1: System-level view on organizational cyber security in the five-layer cyber world model

3.2 Cyber Threat Analysis

A cyber-threat model compiles information related to potential cyber threats targeting various entities such as a system, enterprise, region, or a critical infrastructure sector. Achieving comprehensive cyber security necessitates a thorough analysis of a SoS against a spectrum of threat events. The analysis of SoS may depend on the creation and utilization of threat scenarios, visually representing potential threats and their resulting detrimental consequences (Bodeau and McCollum, 2018). Defining threats within the cyberspace realm presents challenges, primarily due to the elusive nature of attack origins, the intricate motives driving them, and the unpredictable unfolding of events. This dynamic nature makes addressing these threats an ongoing and intricate task (Lehto, 2013).

To tackle this challenge, a pragmatic threat taxonomy has been formulated, focusing on the motivations of attackers. The factors are: Cyber vandalism, Cyber-crime, Cyber espionage, Cyber terrorism, Cyber sabotage, and Cyber warfare. With typology such as these motives can be reduced to their very essence: Egoism, Money, Information, Destruction, Paralysis, and Power. (Kovanen et.al, 2021a)

Tier 1 Cyber Disruption: In the initial tier, we encounter cyber vandalism, which encompasses acts of cyber anarchy, hacking, and hacktivism.

Tier 2 Cybercrime: Moving up the hierarchy, cyber criminals aim to generate income through fraud or the sale of valuable information.

Tier 3 Cyber Espionage: At the third level, intelligence services engage in cyber espionage to gain economic, military, or political advantages for their entities.

Tier 4 Cyber Terrorism: In the fourth tier, cyber terrorism employs networks in attacks against critical infrastructure systems and their controls (Beggs, 2006).

Tier 5 Cyber Sabotage: At this level, cyber sabotage is an activity conducted by a state actor or state-sponsored group operating below the threshold of war or executing Military Operations Other Than War (MOOTW).

Tier 6 Cyber Warfare: The highest tier, cyber warfare lacks a universally accepted definition but is commonly used to describe state actors' operations in cyberspace. Cyber warfare is part of other military operations, including air, land, naval, and space.

3.3 Vulnerability Analysis

Vulnerability can be defined as an exploitable weakness or deficiencies in a system, device or its design that allow cyber attacker to execute cyber-attacks (Bertino et al., 2010). Vulnerabilities can be divided into those that exist in: People's actions, Processes in the organizations, and Technologies. A thorough vulnerability analysis should encompass all weaknesses or deficiencies present in the SoS environments within an organization.

People refer to the human resources available at the firm's disposal. The people are the ones who do the tasks described in the process. Most cyber security threats are due to employee errors. For example, a report by Kaspersky Lab indicated that employee errors accounted for 90 % of the data breaches (Borner, 2019).

Processes are crucial in defining how the organization's activities, roles and documentation are used to mitigate the risks to the organization's information.

Technology solutions protect against cyber risks that may arise from network vulnerabilities but technology itself contains vulnerabilities (hardware, HW and software, SW). So, technological vulnerabilities are security holes in a system.

3.4 Cyber-Attack Model Analysis

Cyber-attack models delineate the progression of an attack through distinct phases, offering a framework to conceptualize its various elements. However, it's crucial to recognize that the success of an attack doesn't necessarily hinge on completing all phases; rather, the attack's objective shapes its structure. Various cyber security actors have developed diverse cyber-attack models to comprehend the varied goals pursued by cyber attackers. These models are grounded in the targets and objectives of the attacks.

It's noteworthy that not all attacks follow a linear trajectory through all phases for success. In fact, many attacks iterate recursively through the phases, as observed in recent research (Lehto, 2022). These models have evolved based on the motives and objectives driving different cyber-attacks. Typically, cyber-attacks fall into four categories determined by their objectives and targets: Advanced Persistent Threat (APT) attacks, Cyber-Physical Attacks against Critical Infrastructure, Data breach attacks, and Military Cyberspace Operations.

The versatility of these models allows them to be applied to multiple types of attacks. Analysing different attack models within specific environments proves to be a valuable method for comprehensively understanding and describing the primary threats an organization faces, facilitating the assessment of potential impacts.

3.5 Impact Analysis

Widely used Lockheed Martin Cyber Kill Chain (https://www.lockheedmartin.com/en-us/capabilities/cyber/cyber-kill-chain.html) offer a high abstraction level framework to understand cyber-attacks, and for example MITRE's ATT&CK (https://attack.mitre.org/) is a medium abstraction level model. ATT&CK offer a common behavior-focused adversary model which consists of the adversary's desired impacts can be listed according to ICT, ICS, and OT impacts of an organization. For example, ICT impacts are Data Destruction, Data Encrypted for Impact, etc., and ICS/OT impacts are Denial of Control, Loss of Availability, etc. (Kovanen et.al, 2021b, Table 4.). Those are the end point impacts that manifest after successful attack paths are completed and they are agnostic to the used techniques and technologies (Kovanen et.al, 2021b).

Behind an attack there are motivational factors and goals, capabilities and varying triggers depending on the attacker archetype. By identifying that information, it is possible to evaluate attack impacts against an organization. At the end all information can be collected in order to make general view from possible impacts against an organization. (Kovanen et.al, 2021a)

4. Cyber Risk Management Process

Cyber risk management is the process of identifying, analyzing, evaluating, and addressing cyber security threats to an organization's capital and earnings. These risks stem from a variety of sources including financial uncertainties, legal liabilities, technology issues, strategic management errors, accidents, and natural disasters.

The ISO 27000 family of standards provides recommendations for information security management systems (integrated elements of an organization to establish policies and objectives and processes to achieve those objectives), risk treatments and controls. (ISO/IEC 27000, 2018)

Risk categories can be defined as the classification of risks as per the business activities of the organization and provides a structured overview of the underlying and potential risks faced by them. Most used risk classifications include strategic, financial, operational, people, regulatory and finance. Figure 2 depicts the process of managing cyber risks utilizing information derived from the cyber threat intelligence process.

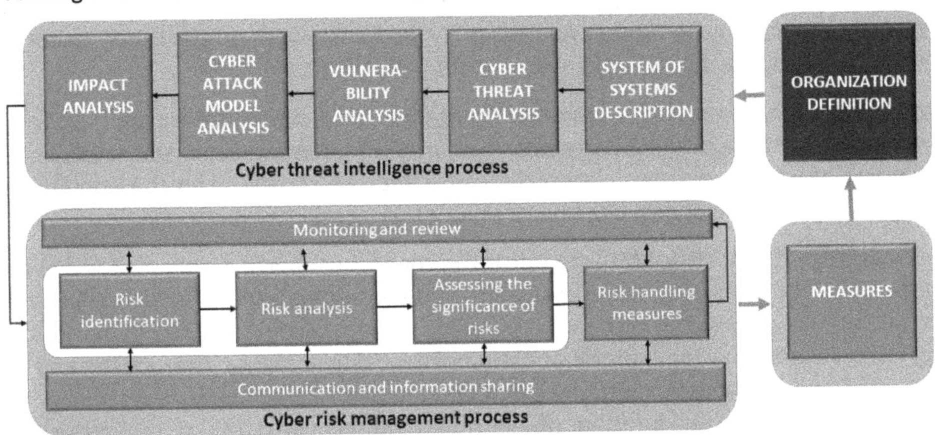

Figure 2: Continuous development, cyber security enhancement processes

4.1 Risk Identification

The Cyber Threat Intelligence (CTI) process involves gathering information about threats that pertain to both cyber and physical domains, as well as the entities of these threats. Its primary goal is to support the risk assessment procedure to analyze and categorize the likelihoods of attacks and adverse events in the cyberspace domain for an organization.

In relation to risk identification, all discernible risks associated with the subject of the risk assessment need to be documented. The aim of risk identification is to recognize and detail all significant risks and opportunities, pinpoint sources of risks, delineate areas of impact, identify events (including changes in circumstances and their causes), and outline potential consequences. Risk identification should be conducted for each of the five layers of the cyber world.

4.2 Risk Analysis

There are diverse approaches to conducting risk analysis, wherein the assessment of the likelihood and impact is carried out on a risk-by-risk basis. This analysis serves as a foundation for making decisions regarding the identification and mitigation of risks. Estimates of both likelihood and impact in the analysis are often subjective, requiring multiple perspectives to construct a comprehensive understanding of the situation. The analytical process can be rooted in either quantitative (numerical) or qualitative (descriptive) methods, or a combination of both.

In the context of threat analysis and risk-level estimations for an organization's systems and sub-systems, the Delphi method is a notable approach. Used by cyber security experts within the organization, the Delphi method involves an iterative process aimed at enhancing consensus-building. Ultimately, the goal is to achieve a consensus among experts examining a particular case. The Delphi method is integral to quantitative analysis, contributing to the attainment of an optimally reliable expert consensus. According to Garson (2012), the Delphi method can be directed towards one of three objectives:

1. forecasting future events
2. achieving policy consensus on goals and objectives within organizations or groups
3. identifying diversity in and obtaining feedback from stakeholders in some policy outcome.

For risk analysis we have used probability tree principles, and it can be applied as well in general cases. The probability tree is described as using Defense probability P_D\` against Attack probability P_A in the evaluation process. Cyberattacks (A) in organization´s processes are the same as the "Attack Identification" and located on all levels of the system level responsibilities (Strategy, Operational, Tactical/Technical). The P_A attack probability (P_{SOT}) to defend against attack probability P_D\` (P_P, P_D, P_M, P_R) is related to the combination of cyber security capabilities (people, processes, and technologies), using "Protection" (P), "Detection" (D), "Countermeasure"

(M) and "Recovery" (R) activities according to NIST Framework for Improving Critical Infrastructure Cyber security (2018). The entire risk assessment process can be done by experienced cyber security professionals related to the case to be investigated. (Pöyhönen, et.al. 2022)

The probabilistic success of attacks, P(t), against the defense of system x can now be evaluated and calculated as follows, adapting the principle in "Threat Analysis of Cyber-Attacks with Attack Tree+" (Wang & Liu, 2014, mod.). $P_{Ax}(t) = P_A P_{D'} = (P_{SOT})(1 - P_P(t))(1 - p_D(t))(1 - p_M(t))(1 - p_R(t))$ (1)

Cyber security professionals employ the formula (1) principle for probability estimation. Subsequently, the OWASP Risk Rating Methodology is utilized to pinpoint security risks. This evaluation encompasses details about the involved threat agent, the planned attack, the associated vulnerability, and the potential impact of a successful exploit on system operations. (Pöyhönen, et.al. 2022)

The risk levels are categorized as LOW, MEDIUM, and HIGH, contingent upon the estimated severity of the attack impacts and the likelihood of harm post the evaluation of defense capabilities. The determination of the risk level relies on various elements within each factor, including the motive and capability of the attacker, the ease of identifying vulnerabilities, the compromise of CIA (Confidentiality, Integrity, Availability), and the resultant damages to the system. Each factor comprises a set of options, and each option is associated with a likelihood rating from 0 to 0.9. This rating scale is further divided into three segments: 0 to <0.3 corresponds to LOW, 0.3 to <0.6 equates to MEDIUM, and 0.6 to 0.9 signifies HIGH (OWASP, 2022).

4.3 Assessing the Significance of Risks

Risks are appropriate to prioritize according to business objectives. The aim of evaluating the importance of risks is to aid in decision-making regarding which risks should be tackled and their order of priority. The assessment may reveal the necessity to reevaluate certain risks or require additional analysis. Within the context of the significance assessment, it may be determined that certain identified risks will not be addressed.

4.4 Risk Handling Measures

In the risk handling process, risk-specific measures are decided. In the process organizations determine how to respond to the risks they face. In the risk handling process, risk-specific measures are decided. In this state of process organizations determine how to respond to the risks they have recognized. In the realm of risk management, organizations try to balance between risk acceptance and risk reduction efforts. Additionally, the practice of risk sharing, or transfer involves contractual arrangements with third parties, such as insurers, to assume some or all of the potential costs associated with a given risk, whether realized or not.

The risk handling plan is determined by the level of risk. It is essential to define the necessary handling measures and responsibilities for the most significant risks identified in the assessment and to ensure the progress and implementation of the agreed management measures.

4.5 Measures After Risk Assessment

The handling of the initial three scenarios regarding events, which are known known, known unknown and unknown known in the mentioned Table 1. necessitates the implementation of cyber and information security measures tailored to the organization. These measures should incorporate a fundamental security solution while considering potential risks. Continuously updated risk analysis plays a crucial role in supporting security measures. Unforeseen incidents, which cannot be anticipated, are addressed by the organization's contingency planning, ultimately enhancing operational resilience.

5. Resilience Development

The cyber operating environment of an organization is characterized by uncertainty, stemming from the likelihood of events occurring within intricate SoS structures. Cyber security resilience constitutes an integral component of preparedness and organizational continuity management. Cyber resilience is the ability of an organization to protect itself from, detect, respond to, and recover from cyber-attacks.

Unprecedented losses linked to events such as natural disasters and cyber-attacks have brought attention to novel strategies for reducing damage. While the prevailing analytical and governance framework of the past few decades centered on risk analysis, there has been a recent shift in rhetoric towards recognizing the importance of comprehending and crafting resilience (Linkov et al. 2013a). Linkov et al. (2013a) have cited the National

Academy of Sciences (NAS) report's characterization of resilience in the context of disasters (later: "Linkov model"). This model for strategic resilience planning combines the four essential stages of a resilience matrix framework—plan/prepare, absorb, recover, and adapt—with the four crucial domains encompassing physical, information, cognitive, and social aspects within a system of systems. Linkov et al. (2013b) extended the application of their model specifically to cyber systems, aiming to establish efficient metrics for assessing the resilience of such systems.

Disaster resilience exhibits elements of surprise, complexity, urgency, and the imperative for adaptation. In reaction to these challenges, military experts have put forth the concept of Network Centric Warfare (NCW). This doctrine emphasizes the establishment of shared situational awareness and decentralized decision-making through the dissemination of information across networks that operate in physical, information, cognitive, and social domains: (Linkov et al., 2013a)

- Physical: sensors, facilities, equipment, system states and capabilities
- Information: creation, manipulation, and storage of data
- Cognitive: understanding, mental models, preconceptions, biases, and values
- Social: interaction, collaboration and self-synchronization between individuals and entities

The development process of cyber security resilience plays a vital role in guaranteeing the continuity of organizational measures under various operational conditions. We have identified a proactive five-step process (refer to Figure 3) for strategizing and guiding resilient actions in the event of a significant cyber security threat to organizations.

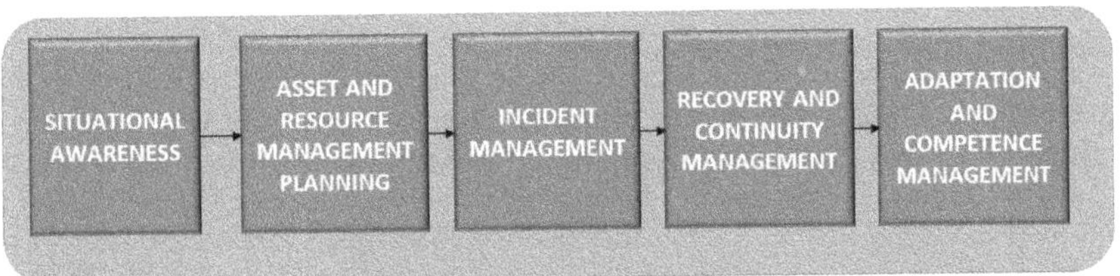

Figure 3: Cyber security resilience development process

5.1 Situational Awareness

Each organization needs information about its environment and its events, and its impact on their own activities. To get a holistic view of the organization's cyber security and resilience, situation awareness is needed. One solution to develop a company-specific understanding of situational awareness is using SWOT analysis (Pöyhönen et al., 2018). The term SWOT is an acronym of the words Strengths, Weaknesses, Opportunities and Threats. SWOT analysis is an important tool for analyzing an organization's performance and operating environment. Based on the SWOT analysis, the related needs of each organization can be planted to crucial domains encompassing physical, information, cognitive, and social aspects of resilience process within a system of systems according to Linkov's model phases; plan/prepare, absorb, recover, and adapt. The subsequent four chapters delineate these stages by providing an illustrative example in alignment with our previous paper titled "Application of Cyber Resilience Review to an Electricity Company"(Pöyhönen et al., 2018).

5.2 Asset and Resource Management Planning

Physical: In order to enhance technical solutions situational awareness of assets and effective segmentation of systems is crucial, and exploring alternative resources can provide valuable robust solutions.

Information: The organization should focus on the data of the classification and prioritization of critical systems and information of assessed potential business impacts and to implement thorough preparation for sensitive information and devised comprehensive communication plans to ensure a robust and proactive approach to risk management of data.

Cognitive: The effective development of situational awareness involves a comprehensive approach, encompassing the careful consideration of scenarios and models, and adept situational management. Ensure strategic resourcing for secure operations. Plans for training and benchmarking, supported by a robust feedback system to enhance the perception of situational awareness.

Social: The CI organization should focus on comprehensive communication plans to ensure a robust and proactive approach to inform necessary stakeholders. The naming of stakeholders' contact persons and specialized training for exceptional situations are crucial components in ensuring effective communication and preparedness within the organization.

5.3 Incident Management

Physical: The comprehensive approach to absorbs incident includes the recognition of disturbances, their scope, and impacts, ensuring the protection of sensitive information systems, deploying alternative resources, and implementing effective isolation measures to safeguard the critical system of systems.

Information: The thorough documentation of the incident data is instrumental in effectively informing all stakeholders about the progress of the case and analyze and storage its progress.

Cognitive: In the analysis of situational awareness, careful prioritization of available information is crucial, and the allocation of additional resources plays a pivotal role, while being ready to share sensitive information to stakeholders.

Social: Disseminating comprehensive updates to stakeholders and authorities, ensuring transparent communication, and providing detailed insights into the ongoing operations.

5.4 Recovery and Continuity Management

Physical: To ensure the smooth operation of recovery, it is necessary to focus on the maintenance of technical situational awareness of systems throughout the ramp-up phase, implementing rigorous testing protocols to guarantee the system's reliability.

Information: Careful documentation of the incident data and comprehensive information of the case recovery phases support its actions as well as ensuring trust and clarity of communication for continuity management.

Cognitive: The allocation of expertise is crucial for the efficient recovery process and collection of incident data and log information in order to enhance decision-making processes.

Social: Incident status information from CI organization updates stakeholders and authorities, ensuring transparent communication, and providing detailed knowledge shearing into the ongoing recovery ensuring trust, transparency, and clarity in communication.

5.5 Adaptation and Competence Management

Physical: After the incident, it became crucial to adapt to the new situation by implementing modifications and updates to techniques of systems.

Information: Part of the competence management development aggregation of incident documents, coupled with complementary improvements of data and information management processes, enhances the efficiency and effectiveness of organizational workflows.

Cognitive: Continuous improvement is achieved through a management and adaptation process that involves understanding log analysis and other information, conducting impact analysis, performing situation analysis, incorporating feedback analysis, and implementing timely system updates.

Social: The situation briefing for all parties on adaptation status, staff training programs, informing about development operations, and updating stakeholder information provides a comprehensive overview for the current organization updates measures and the networked partnership.

6. Discussion

In the realm of organizational cyber security management and continuity management, adopting a Systems of Systems (SoS) research approach facilitates the creation of a comprehensive cyber security framework. This approach entails identifying all processes, users, and digital assets within the organization. For instance, Directive (EU) 2016/1148 of the European Parliament and the Council was formulated to bolster cyber security capabilities across the European Union. Its aims encompassed mitigating threats to network and information systems, ensuring the provision of essential services in critical sectors, maintaining service continuity during incidents, and fortifying society's overall cyber security (EU, 2016). To fulfill these objectives, it is imperative to establish an overarching management system that encompasses risk management and continuity guidelines, thereby enabling continuous enhancement of business continuity practices. Consequently, this paper integrates risk assessment methodologies with resilience development models to offer organizations a comprehensive approach to continuity management.

7. Conclusion

Organizations in the realm of risk management aim to balance risk acceptance with insights from cyber threat intelligence. Decision-making is guided by risk avoidance principles, emphasizing elimination, reduction, and mitigation through cyber security and information security updates. Risk sharing involves contractual arrangements with third parties to assume potential costs. Incorporating resilience measures in planning benefits decision-making and preparedness, providing insights for security planning, and aiding learning and problem identification in unforeseen circumstances. The resilience development model supports operational continuity management at all decision-making levels of an organization. Maintaining awareness of cyber threats and employing a thorough risk management process together with resiliency measures allows organizations to strategically protect digital assets.

References

Beggs, C. (2006). Proposed Risk Minimization Measures for Cyber-Terrorism and SCADA Networks in Australia, Proceedings of the 5th European Conference on Information Warfare and Security, National Defence College, Helsinki, Finland, 1-2 June 2006

Bertino, E., Martino L.D., Paci F., and Squicciarini A.C. (2010). Web services threats, vulnerabilities, and countermeasures. In Security for Web Services and Service-Oriented Architectures, pp. 25–44. Springer.

Bodeau, D. J. and McCollum, C. D. (2018). System-of-systems threat model. The Homeland Security Systems Engineering and Development Institute (HSSEDI) MITRE: Bedford, MA, USA.

Borner, P. (2019). Cloud data breaches caused by human error, The Data Privacy Group blog, May 10 2019. https://thedataprivacygroup.com/blog/cloud-data-breaches-caused-by-human-error/ (Retrieved 1/2024)

Dahmann, J. S. (2015). Systems of Systems Characterization and Types, MITRE Corporation.

EU, (2016). Directive (EU) 2016/1148 of the European Parliament and of the Council of 6 July 2016 concerning measures for a high common level of security of network and information systems across the Union https://eur-lex.europa.eu/eli/dir/2016/1148/oj

ISO/IEC 27000. (2018). International Organization for Standardization. Information technology. Security techniques. Information security management systems. Overview and vocabulary. https://www.iso.org/standard/73906.html (Retrieved 2/2023)

Kim, S. D. (2017). Characterization of unknown unknowns using separation principles in case study on Deepwater Horizon oil spill. Journal of Risk Research, 2017 Vol. 20, No. 1, 151–168, http://dx.doi.org/10.1080/13669877.2014.983949 (Retrieved 1/2024)

Kovanen, T., Pöyhönen, J. and Lehto, M. (2021a). Cyber Threat Analysis in the Remote Pilotage System. Proceeding of the 20th European Conference on Cyber Warfare and Security ECCWS 2021, p. 221-229.

Kovanen, T., Pöyhönen, J. and Lehto, M. (2021b). ePilotage System of Systems' Cyber Threat Impact Evaluation. Proceedings of the 16th International Conference on Cyber Warfare and Security ICCWS 2021. p. 144-151.

Lehto, M. (2013). The Cyberspace threats and cyber security objectives in the Cyber Security Strategies. International Journal of Cyber Warfare and Terrorism, Vol. 3, Issue. 3, pages 1-18, 2013.

Lehto, M. and Neittaanmäki, P. (2018). The modern strategies in the cyber warfare. Cyber Security: Cyber power and technology. Berlin: Springer.

Lehto, M. (2022). APT cyber-attack modelling - building a general model. 17th International Conference on Cyber Warfare and Security, 17 - 18 March 2022, State University of New York at Albany, USA.

Libicki, M. C. (2007). Conquest in Cyberspace – National Security and Information Warfare, Cambridge University Press, New York 2007.

Linkov, I., Eisenberg, D., Bates, M., Chang, D., Convertino, M., Allen, J., Flynn, S. and Seager, T. (2013a). Measurable Resilience for Actionable Policy. Environmental Science & Technology. https://pubs.acs.org/doi/epdf/10.1021/es403443n (Retrieved 1/2024)

Linkov, I., Eisenberg, D., Plourde, K., Seager, T., Allen J. and Kott, A. (2013b). Resilience metrics for cyber systems. Environment Systems and Decisions, 33(4), pp. 471-476.

Lockheed Martin, LM. Cyber Kill Chain, https://www.lockheedmartin.com/en-us/capabilities/cyber/cyber-kill-chain.html (Retrieved 1/2024)

MITRE, ATT&CK https://attack.mitre.org/ (Retrieved 1/2024)

National Institute of Standards and Technology, NIST. (2018). Framework for Improving Critical Infrastructure Cyber security, April 16, 2018

OWASP Risk Rating Methodology, Available from: https://owasp.org/www-community/OWASP_Risk_Rating_Methodology, (Retrieved January 2024)

Pöyhönen, J., Nuojua V., Lehto M. and Rajamäki J. (2018). Application of Cyber Resilience Review to an Electricity Company. ECCWS 2018: Proceedings of the 17th European Conference on Cyber Warfare and Security (pp. 380-389). Published by Academic Conferences and Publishing International Limited. Reading. UK.

Pöyhönen, J. and Lehto, M. (2020). Cyber security: Trust based architecture in the management of an organization's security. In Eze, Thaddeus; Speakman, Lee; Onwubiko, Cyril (Eds.) ECCWS 2020: Proceedings of the 19th European Conference on Cyber Warfare and Security (pp. 304-313).

Pöyhönen, J., Hummelholm, A. and Lehto, M. (2022). Cyber security risks assessment subjects in information flows. Proceedings of the 21st European Conference on Cyber Warfare and Security ECCWS2022, 2022, University of Chester, UK, pages 222-230.

Pöyhönen, J. and Lehto, M. (2022). Assessment of cyber security risks - Maritime automated piloting process. Proceedings of the 17th International Conference on Information Warfare and Security, 2022. pp 262-271.

Wang, P. & Liu, J. C. (2014). Threat analysis of cyber-attacks with attack tree+. Journal of Information Hiding and Multimedia Signal Processing, 5(4).

E-EWS-based Governance Framework for Sharing Cyber Threat Intelligence in the Energy Sector

Jyri Rajamäki, Asfaw Feyesa and Anup Nepal
Laurea University of Applied Sciences, Espoo, Finland

Jyri.Rajamaki@laurea.fi
Asfaw.Feyesa@student.laurea.fi
Anup.Nepal@student.laurea.fi

Abstract: The integration of traditional energy technologies with modern digital technologies increases the risks of cyber-attacks and data breaches. Sharing cyber threat intelligence (CTI) is important for the common defense. The DYNAMO project has chosen the ECHO Early Warning System (E-EWS) as a tool for CTI information sharing. The management of E-EWS becomes the basis for guiding the ethical and efficient operation of the DYNAMO platform and the wider energy sector. The governance framework defines roles, responsibilities, and procedures that are tailored to sharing information, enhancing collaboration, and ensuring the integrity of shared information. Effective governance promotes transparency, compliance, and trust among stakeholders, which ultimately strengthens the security posture of the DYNAMO platform and improves the energy industry's resilience against cyber threats. This paper proposes a governance framework for the DYNAMO platform, including a committee, data security policies, and NIS2 and GDPR compliance. It emphasizes user-friendly collaboration tools, access control, continuous monitoring, stakeholder training, compliance, and phased implementation. The goal is iterative improvements through continuous evaluation.

Keywords: Governance Framework, Cyber Security, Cyber Threat Intelligence, DYNAMO Project, Energy Sector, Information Sharing

1. Introduction

The production and utilization of renewable energy in buildings has been a popular topic for decades, and it is still an important part of future sustainable urban energy systems (Braeuer, et al., 2022). To operate energy-efficiently, it needs digitization. The integration of digital technologies in the energy sector presents both opportunities and challenges. Advanced technologies such as artificial intelligence, machine learning, internet of things, and blockchain are employed to enhance operational efficiency (Yadoshchuk, 2023). However, this digital transformation also exposes the sector to increased cyber threats, particularly targeting critical infrastructure essential for business continuity management (BCM) and information security (Marc & Aloys, 2023). Consequently, a collaborative and dynamic cybersecurity approach becomes imperative.

The DYNAMO project addresses this need by developing a platform for connecting BCM and Cyber Threat Intelligence (CTI), which focuses on promoting dynamic data collection, analysis, sharing, and collaboration between different stakeholders in critical sectors such as energy (Hytönen, et al., 2023). With its emphasis on "dynamic adaptation for mitigation and optimization," the project employs specific principles and structures to fortify the security and resilience of the energy sector. Central to the DYNAMO project is the practice of information sharing, where stakeholders and partners exchange data to collectively understand and preempt cyber threats. To ensure business continuity and the effective use of digital technology for customer service, the DYNAMO project leverages the ECHO Early Warning System (E-EWS) for collaborative efforts among stakeholders. However, the effectiveness and sustainability of these tools require a well-coordinated and organized approach. Therefore, the DYNAMO platform relies on Information Security Governance (ISG) as a key element. ISG, a strategic approach guiding information systems management (Nicho, 2018), provides oversight, accountability, and strategic direction. It defines roles, responsibilities, policies, and procedures for information sharing and collaboration within the DYNAMO framework, crucial for the long-term success and resilience of the project and the energy sector.

As the energy sector witnesses increased adoption of digital technology and cyber threats, there is a pressing need for a collaborative and organized effort to bolster cybersecurity. This work-in-progress paper proposes a governance framework supporting the E-EWS information-sharing strategy under the DYNAMO platform. The paper investigates the prospect of governance in implementing E-EWS in the energy sector within the DYNAMO platform and proposes a governance framework. The research question is “How do partners collaborate in EU projects, particularly in the context of CTI information sharing, and how does governance contribute to effective collaboration in this regard?” The hypothesis is that “governance is a crucial element for organizations to function effectively, ethically, and legally, providing oversight, accountability, and strategic direction for the DYNAMO project and the energy sector".

The rest of the paper is organized as follows: after this introduction, section 2 examines different information-sharing tools based on the literature. Section 3 deals with an overview of the governance models of the information-sharing ecosystem. Section 4 analyzes the legislative and ethical environment for sharing cyber threat intelligence in the energy sector. Section 5 presents the E-EWS-based governance framework created based on previous analyses for sharing cyber threat information in the energy sector. Finally, Section 6 summarizes this study and suggests further steps.

2. Overview of Information-Sharing Tools

Today, information is a crucial commodity, and the strategic sharing of relevant information has become an invaluable resource. Effective information sharing is a crucial aspect of organizational data management. Without a robust data-sharing mechanism, operational capacity and decision-making processes may face disruptions. The chosen system for information sharing must be organization-wide compatible to prevent unnecessary transcription and rekeying of data when transferred between systems. Additionally, key requirements for information-sharing systems include easy accessibility and swift data retrieval. If required information is not readily available, it can lead to frustration and hinder overall organizational effectiveness (Gordon, 2013).

Information sharing can be categorized into internal and external components. Collaborative interactions within the workplace contribute to increased cooperation and enhanced work performance (Peters & Manz, 2007). Effective internal communication fosters inspiration, engagement, and productivity. However, selecting the appropriate internal communication system that aligns with the organization's culture can be challenging. Traditional methods like newsletters and emails may not be sufficient; instead, internal channels should be immediate, fast, targeted, measurable, and adaptable to mobile platforms. An organization's internal communication tools may include department-specific mailing lists or a comprehensive intranet for seamless information access. External information sharing can be facilitated through the organization's website or by creating a specific extranet for collaboration with external partners. Well-established communication channels play a vital role in stakeholder engagement and effective collaboration with end-users (Ruoslahti & Tikanmäki, 2019).

In the field of cyber security, the sharing of critical information among the entities of the ecosystem is key in combating cyber threats. Sharing cybersecurity information among different organizations is highly beneficial, improving threat response, defending against potential attackers, and mitigating damages. It also fosters better relations and trust between organizations. However, challenges may arise, including legal issues stemming from differing definitions of classified information protection across countries. Therefore, employing appropriate information-sharing models and frameworks is crucial to achieving efficient data sharing between organizations (Rajamäki & Katos, 2020). Especially, care must be taken in the sharing process, which requires careful consideration of the type of information shared and the recipients (Kokkonen, et al., 2016). Numerous open-source data-sharing tools are readily available in the market and organizations can utilize them based on their specific requirements. When implementing these sharing tools, several actors jointly decide on the nature and scope of the information to be exchanged. Microsoft (2016) has developed a framework, shown in Figure 1, that is tailored for cybersecurity information sharing and risk mitigation.

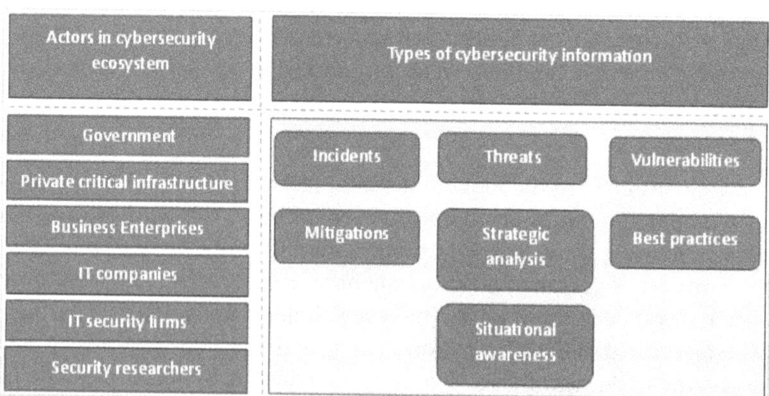

Figure 1: Microsoft's cybersecurity information-sharing platform and different types of governance structure

Effective threat information sharing in collaborative environments offers a multitude of advantages. It facilitates faster responses against hybrid threats, contributing to the development of a robust cyber-ecosystem within smart societies. By enhancing cybersecurity and risk management practices, organizations gain a deeper understanding of the threat landscape, enabling them to identify affected platforms and implement protective measures promptly. Additionally, knowledge maturation through the correlation of seemingly unrelated observations provides valuable insights into threat indicators and tactics. This process not only increases the degree of protection by reducing viable attack vectors but also fosters greater defensive agility, allowing organizations to adapt to evolving threat landscapes. Despite these benefits, challenges such as building and maintaining trust, achieving interoperability, and safeguarding sensitive information underscore the complexity of collaborative information-sharing efforts. Addressing these challenges is crucial to ensuring secure and effective information exchange in collaborative environments (Rajamäki, 2019).

3. Overview of Governance Models in Information-sharing Ecosystem

Organizations' governance functions play crucial roles in setting their strategic direction. According to the Chartered Governance Institute UK & Ireland (2022), corporate governance is defined as "the system of rules, practices, and processes by which a company is directed and controlled." This framework serves as a toolkit for management and the board to effectively navigate the challenges of running a company. One key aspect of corporate governance is ensuring the implementation of appropriate controls and decision-making processes that balance the interests of all stakeholders. It is particularly significant in meeting legal requirements such as the General Data Protection Regulation (GDPR) or the Network and Information Security (NIS) Directive.

Information governance, on the other hand, focuses on the overall strategy for managing information, encompassing policies, systems, people, and processes. By utilizing its various elements, organizations can establish and maintain relevant policies and procedures that align with data privacy requirements. Information governance seeks to balance the risks associated with information against the value it provides. This encompasses various aspects such as information security and protection, compliance, data quality, data governance, electronic discovery, risk management, privacy, data storage and archiving, knowledge management, business operations and management, audit, analytics, IT management, master data management, enterprise architecture, business intelligence, big data, data science, and finance.

The management functions within an organization take the strategic direction set by governance and translate it into actionable steps that bring the organization closer to achieving its strategic goals. A Management Information System (MIS) is employed for decision-making, coordination, control, analysis, and visualization of information within an organization. MIS involves the integration of people, technology, and processes within an organizational context. In corporations, the aim of using MIS is to enhance the value and profitability of the business through IT tools supporting various processes, operations, and intelligence. Information sharing is recognized as a crucial method to enhance organizational efficiency and performance (Yang & Maxwell, 2011).

In the pursuit of diving into governance models the research, it is imperative to establish a clear understanding of the concept of governance. While different sectors may offer varied definitions, a common thread defines governance as the systematic direction, control, and administration of an organization or system. According to the Government Institute of Australia, governance entails the structures and processes that oversee and guide an organization, inclusive of mechanisms for ensuring accountability. This broad concept encompasses ethics, risk management, compliance, and administration. Notably, Wang and Ran (2023) highlight the prevalence of confusion surrounding various governance concepts, with different types often exhibiting overlap or interchangeable usage. This confusion persists despite these concepts being integral to the operations of diverse systems.

This research focused on governance related to information systems, more definitely information-sharing-related governance systems. To narrow it down, IT governance can be classified as a subset of corporate governance, to facilitate the management of IT services and deliver value including information sharing among the organization (IT governance). A crucial aspect of this value proposition involves effective information sharing among various components of the organization, underlining the interconnected nature of IT governance (Weill & Ross, 2004). Information-sharing governance within IT governance plays a pivotal role in fostering collaboration, enhancing decision-making processes, and ensuring the secure and efficient flow of information across the organization. Effective governance in this context involves establishing policies, procedures, and controls that not only facilitate seamless information sharing but also address potential risks, safeguard sensitive data, and ensure compliance with relevant regulations (Calder, et al., 2008). Moreover, in an era where digital transformation is pervasive, understanding and implementing robust information-sharing governance systems become paramount. This involves adapting to evolving technologies, staying ahead of cybersecurity threats, and incorporating best practices in information management to harness the full potential of IT services for organizational growth and success (Luftman, 2003).

To establish an efficient governance structure for the DYNAMO project, facilitating information sharing among partners, we analyzed existing governance structures. Our objective was to identify a suitable model that aligns seamlessly with the project's requirements. Figure 2 presents diverse governance taxonomies sourced from literature and thoughtfully compiled in the ECHO deliverable (Rajamäki, 2019).

Government-Centric Model:	**Sector-Based ISACs**	**Corporate-Initiated Groups**
• Centralized approach • Single organization leadership • Examples: Department of Homeland Security • Emphasis on open, standard data formats • Centralized coordination and control	• Government-prompted, industry-centric • Non-profit organizations • Facilitate government-industry information sharing • Vital collection points for peer-to-peer sharing	• Privately sponsored and independent • Initiated by corporations • Tailored information sharing for specific member needs
Individual-Based Groups	**Open Communities and Platforms**	**Diverse Governance for Cyber Information Sharing**
• Small online communities • Collaborative cyber attack response • Reliance on high trust levels among members	• Open-source platforms like MISP • Foster collaboration in the cybersecurity community • Use formats such as STIX indicators and open-source intelligence feeds	• Reflects the multifaceted nature of IT sector information sharing • Accommodates various organizational structures and collaboration levels • Adaptive approach crucial in the rapidly evolving cybersecurity landscape

Figure 2: Different types of governance structure

4. Policy Analysis

The European Union (EU) Treaty defines the legal basis for the creation of the European Internal Energy Market (IEM). Its goal is to create a well-functioning pan-European electricity and gas market that puts fair access and a high level of consumer protection at the center while ensuring sufficient generation and interconnection capacity across the continent (Manolkidis, 2021). Over the years, EU-derived legislation (regulations, directives, and recommendations) has built a path from a historically defined monopolistic system to a well-functioning free market. Today, the EU has a common policy on energy. According to the Energy Union 2015, this energy policy aims to ensure the security, sustainability, and competitiveness of energy supply and consumption in the EU. One of the key aspects of this policy is information sharing among the EU member states and institutions, as well as with third countries and international organizations. Information sharing on energy matters can help to improve coordination, cooperation, and transparency, as well as identify and address potential risks and challenges (REGULATION (EU) 2018/1999). The EU has established several mechanisms and platforms for information sharing on energy issues, each platform has specific goals, such as the 'Energy Policy' greatest the general principle:

- The Energy Union Governance System, Regulation (EU) 2018/1999
- The Energy Community, The Energy Community Legal Framework.
- The Energy Charter Treaty,
- The European Network of Transmission System Operators for Electricity (ENTSO-E) and Gas (ENTSO-G), Regulation (EC) 715/2009
- The Agency for the Cooperation of Energy Regulators (ACER), EU Regulation 1227/2011
- The European Energy Forum
- The Strategic Energy Technology Plan (SET-Plan).

These mechanisms and platforms cover various aspects of the energy sector, such as electricity, gas, oil, coal, nuclear, renewable, and low-carbon sources, energy efficiency, innovation, research and development, market integration, infrastructure development, security of supply, climate change mitigation and adaptation, and external relations.

The DYNAMO project, funded by the European Union, proposed E-EWS as a tool to share information on cybersecurity among stakeholders. The energy sector is a critical infrastructure under the NIS Directive, which obliges member states to establish competent authorities and computer security incident response teams (CSIRTs) for the sector and to ensure that OES in electricity, oil, and gas subsectors report significant cyber incidents to the authorities. The EU also encourages the creation of information sharing and analysis centres (ISACs), such as the EE-ISAC, which enable voluntary and trust-based data and information sharing among utilities, regulators, vendors, and researchers. The EU's goal is to promote a culture of cyber resilience and cooperation in the energy sector and to identify and address gaps and challenges in the policy framework (Energy policy: general principles).

The EU information-sharing policy on energy is based on the principles of solidarity, subsidiarity, proportionality, and confidentiality (JOIN(2022) 49). This means that the EU member states and institutions share information on energy matters in a timely, accurate, and comprehensive manner while respecting the national competencies and interests of each member state, as well as the protection of sensitive data and information. The EU information-sharing policy on energy also aims to promote dialogue and consultation with relevant stakeholders, such as industry, consumers, civil society, and academia.

4.1 Legal Considerations

Information sharing on cybersecurity in the energy sector is a complex and sensitive issue that involves legal and ethical considerations. On one hand, information sharing can enhance the collective security and resilience of the energy sector by enabling timely detection, prevention, and mitigation of cyber threats. On the other hand, information sharing can pose risks to the privacy, confidentiality, and competitiveness of the energy sector actors, as well as potential liability and compliance issues. Therefore, a legal and ethical analysis of information sharing on cybersecurity in the energy sector should balance the benefits and risks of information sharing, considering the relevant laws, regulations, standards, and best practices, as well as the rights and interests of the stakeholders involved.

The European Data Governance Act is increasing trust in data sharing among diverse groups who are using data in the European Union. This exchange of data among various entities, such as organizations, countries, and individuals, involves a certain level of risk. The data may be misused by unauthorized or malicious parties, compromising the privacy and security of the data subjects. Therefore, the European Union has established a set of rules and regulations to govern the transmission and sharing of information, ensuring that the data is protected and used lawfully and ethically:

- **General Data Protection Regulation (GDPR).** If the information process involves any personal data, any processing and transmission should comply with GDPR.
- **Confidentiality and security obligations**. The EU recognizes the importance of confidentiality and security in information sharing. Entities sharing sensitive information, especially in sectors like energy or cybersecurity, are often subject to confidentiality obligations to protect the shared data.
- **Sector-specific regulations**. There may be specific regulations governing information sharing.
- **Trade secrets and intellectual properties**. EU laws protect trade secrets and parties sharing information must take measures to safeguard such business information.
- **EU competition law**. Sharing information may create a conflict of interest. EU-competition law should be respected.
- **Cross-border data transfer**. When sharing information across borders, entities must comply with rules governing international clauses or binding corporate rules, which may be necessary.

The following parts of the NIS Directive, discussed in more detail in the ENISA's document (ENISA, 2022), need to be addressed when designing the governance model for the DYNAMO platform:

- Human resource security – security training programs are required for employees with NIS-related responsibilities.
- Information system security risk analysis – during the designing process, regular risk analyses are conducted so possible risks are assessed as early as possible.
- Information system security audit – considering the regularly updated risk analysis, all critical assets are frequently audited to ensure compliance with regulations.

- Ecosystem mapping – during the design process, all documentation of the governance ecosystem is frequently updated.
- Information system security policy – building up to the risk analysis, an information system security policy will be established and maintained.
- Ecosystem relations – the interfaces between E-EWS and third parties are designed so that potential risks are mitigated.

The new Cyber Solidarity Act (the European Parliament and of the Council, 2023), once finalized and adopted, will contain important measures to strengthen the EU's preparedness, management, and response to cyber security threats and incidents. It is the latest addition to the EU's cybersecurity legislation, which aims to increase the resilience of critical entities against cybersecurity risks and support the coordinated management of large-scale cybersecurity disruptions and crises (Ajmera & Nusselder, 2023). The EU framework already in place consists of the NIS 2 Directive, the Cybersecurity Act, the Directive on attacks against information systems, and the Commission's r Recommendation on coordinated response to large-scale cybersecurity incidents and crises. The new proposal builds on and strengthens existing cyber security frameworks for operational cooperation and crisis management, such as the European cyber crisis liaison organisation network (EU-CyCLONe) and CSIRT network (Ajmera & Nusselder, 2023). Cross-border security operations centers (SOCs) are meant to complement the existing CSIRT network by sharing, connecting, and analyzing information on cyber security threats from both public and private entities. Importantly, the Cyber Solidarity Act proposal does not affect the critical and highly critical areas defined in the NIS 2 Directive. The Cyber Solidarity Act proposal also envisages close cooperation with the private sector. Its goal is to promote cross-border and public-private cooperation in anticipating and countering cyberattacks by combining information from both public and private entities to derive high-quality intelligence on cybersecurity threats. In addition, the EU's cyber security reserve consists of selected private providers of managed information security services that support response and immediate recovery in large-scale cyber security incidents (Ajmera & Nusselder, 2023).

Entities that share CTI information within the EU must understand and follow the legal considerations to comply with the relevant laws and regulations. Organizations should seek legal counsel tailored to their specific circumstances when dealing with the challenges of information sharing under EU law.

4.2 Ethical Considerations of Data

Data sharing is the practice of making data available to other individuals or organizations for various purposes, such as research, innovation, collaboration, or public service. Data sharing can have many benefits, such as increasing the transparency, reproducibility, and impact of scientific findings, fostering discoveries and collaborations, and enhancing the efficiency and quality of data collection and analysis. However, data sharing also poses some ethical challenges, especially in the European context, where data protection and privacy laws are strict and complex. Echo early warning system(E-EWS) is a tool to share information with other stakeholders. Every party who participates in this data-sharing platform should follow some ethical guidelines to make a positive impact for the right purpose of protecting the energy sector assets from different attacks. Next, two European ethical aspects related to the organization's data sharing in Europe are presented.

The protection of the organization's sensitive data: Data should be anonymized or pseudonymized before sharing and should be encrypted or stored in secure platforms. Data sharing should also follow the principles of data minimization and purpose limitation, meaning that only the necessary and relevant data should be shared for a specific and legitimate purpose.

The accountability and responsibility of the data sharers: Data sharing should be done responsibly and transparently, with clear roles and responsibilities for the data sharers, who are the individuals or organizations that share or receive data. Data sharers should adhere to the ethical standards and codes of conduct of their disciplines or sectors and should respect the intellectual property rights and interests of the data owners or creators. Data sharers should also monitor and evaluate the impacts and outcomes of data sharing and report any issues or incidents that may arise.

5. Proposed Governance Framework

As shown in Figure 2, our research indicates that the most suitable fit for the DYNAMO platform is the Diverse Governance Model for Cyber Information Sharing. This model accommodates multiple organizations and embraces an adaptive and innovative approach. Table 1 summarizes the framework we propose based on this study. The table contains a set of actionable steps to create an effective governance system for information sharing within DYNAMO partners.

Table 1: Proposed Governance Framework

Actions	Description
Formation of Governance Committee	DYNAMO and its partners should form a Governance Committee with representatives from each partner organization. This committee will oversee the implementation of the governance model.
Roles and Responsibilities	Each partner organization designates a Data Steward responsible for data access and sharing within their organization. The Data Stewards play a crucial role in enforcing the governance policies.
Information Sharing Policies	Implement data privacy and security measures that comply with GDPR and other regulations. This includes Data encryption for data at rest and in transit. Access controls to ensure that only authorized personnel can access sensitive information. Incident response procedures to address and report security breaches promptly.
Collaboration Tools	Select and implement collaboration and information-sharing tools that meet the specific needs of DYNAMO and its partners. Ensure that these tools are user-friendly and support secure data sharing.
Access Controls	Establish access controls for the collaboration tools, defining user roles and permissions based on the data they need to access. Regularly review and update access controls as needed
Monitoring and Auditing	Set up continuous monitoring and auditing mechanisms to detect security breaches or policy violations. Use monitoring tools to track data access and sharing activities.
Training and Awareness Programs	Conduct training programs for all stakeholders to ensure that they understand the governance model and policies. Regularly update and provide refresher training sessions.
Compliance and Legal Framework	Ensure that the governance model aligns with EU and local legal requirements and adapts as regulations change. This may involve periodic legal reviews and consultations.
Continuous Improvement Process	Establish a process for ongoing evaluation and improvement of the governance framework. Collect feedback from partners, identify areas for improvement, and make necessary updates to policies and procedures.
Communication Plan	Develop a comprehensive communication plan to inform stakeholders about changes, updates, and important information. Use various communication channels to ensure that all partners are well-informed.
Conflict Resolution Mechanism	Implement a conflict resolution mechanism to address disputes or disagreements among partner organizations related to information sharing. This could involve a designated mediator or a defined process for dispute resolution.
Pilot Implementation	Before full-scale implementation, consider a pilot phase where the governance model is tested with a smaller subset of partners to identify any potential issues and make necessary adjustments.
Full-Scale Implementation	After successful pilot testing and fine-tuning, roll out the governance model to all partners for full-scale implementation.
Monitoring and Evaluation	Regularly monitor the effectiveness of the governance model and evaluate its impact on information sharing, security, and collaboration. Make improvements based on feedback and data.

6. Conclusion

The modern electricity grid is completely dependent on information and supervisory systems that control the production, transmission, and distribution of electricity. Disturbances that impair the functionality of control systems cause disturbances in the power supply, which can endanger human lives and cause financial losses. Resources for resilience that mitigate those losses bring both energy companies and electricity users an advantage that exceeds the initial costs of the network. Therefore, increasing certain resources improves both long-term efficiency and resilience.

The DYNAMO project develops methods and resources for connecting business continuity management (BCM) and cyber threat intelligence (CTI) and creates a platform for sharing CTI among different actors. This paper explores the implementation of governance of the ECHO Early Warning System (E-EWS) tool for CTI sharing within the energy sector. The research investigates the role of governance in E-EWS implementation and proposes a diverse governance framework. Key actions in the framework include forming a Governance Committee, defining roles, implementing information-sharing policies, selecting collaboration tools, and ensuring legal compliance. The document also discusses EU policies on energy information sharing, legal considerations under the European Data Governance Act, and ethical aspects of data sharing. In essence, the proposed governance framework addresses the complex cybersecurity landscape by fostering collaboration, ensuring legal and ethical compliance, and promoting cyber resilience. It is designed for adaptability and refinement over time, providing a strategic approach to information sharing via the DYNAMO platform.

The target for further research and development is to examine the functionality of the created governance framework in other critical sectors of the DYNAMO project: healthcare and maritime transport. In addition, the principles presented in the framework should be translated into more concrete specifications.

Acknowledgments

Acknowledgment is paid to DYNAMO Project, funded by the European Union under grant agreement no. 101069601. Views and opinions expressed are however those of the authors only and do not necessarily reflect those of the European Union or European Commission. Neither the European Union nor the granting authority can be held responsible for them.

References

Ajmera, P. & Nusselder, S., 2023. INTERSECT policy brief 2: Cyber Solidarity Act proposal, Tilburg: Tilburg Institute for Law, Technology, and Society (TILT).

Braeuer, F. et al., 2022. Optimal system design for energy communities in multi-family buildings: the case of the German Tenant Electricity Law. Applied Energy, Volume 305, p. 117884.

Calder, A., Watkins, S., & Gilding, M. (2008). IT Governance: A Manager's Guide to Data Security & ISO 27001 / ISO 27002. Kogan Page.

Chartered Governance Institute UK & Ireland, 2022. What is corporate governance? [Online] Available at: https://www.cgi.org.uk/about-us/policy/what-is-corporate-governance, [Accessed 18 Nov. 2022].

Gordon, K., 2013. Principles of Data Management - Facilitating Information Sharing. Second Edition. Swindon: BCS Learning & Development Limited.

ENISA, 2022. Minimum Security Measures for Operators of Essentials Services. [Online] Available at: https://www.enisa.europa.eu/topics/cybersecurity-policy/nis-directive-new/minimum-security-measures-for-operators-of-essentials-services [Accessed 4 January 2024].

European Parliament and of the Council, 2023. Cyber Solidarity Act proposal, COM(2023) 209 final. [Online] Available at: https://eur-lex.europa.eu/legal-content/EN/TXT/?uri=CELEX:52023PC0209 [Accessed 4 January 2024].

Hytönen, E., Rajamäki, J. & Ruoslahti, H., 2023. Managing Variable Cyber Environments with Organizational Foresight and Resilience Thinking. International Conference on Cyber Warfare and Security, 18(1), pp. 162-170.

Kokkonen, T., Hautamäki, J., Siltanen, J. & Hämäläinen, T. (2016) Model for sharing the information of cyber security situation awareness between organizations, 23rd International Conference on Telecommunications (ICT), Thessaloniki, Greece, 2016, pp. 1-5, doi: 10.1109/ICT.2016.7500406.

Luftman, J. (2003). Assessing IT/Business Alignment. Information Systems Management, 20(4), 9–15.

Manolkidis, S., 2021. Geopolitical challenges and cooperation in the European energy sector: The case of SE Europe and the Western Balkan six initiative. In: M. Mathioulakis, ed. Aspects of the Energy Union: Application and Effects of European Energy Policies in SE Europe and Eastern Mediterranean. Cham: Springer Nature Switzerland, pp. 101-114.

Marc, A., & Aloys, M. (2023, August 01). Cybersecurity – Is the power system lagging behind? International Energy Agency. [Online]. Available: https://www.iea.org/commentaries/cybersecurity-is-the-power-system-lagging-behind

Microsoft. (2016). Cybersecurity Information Sharing and Risk Reduction. Retrieved from https://www.microsoft.com/en-us/research/project/cybersecurity-information-sharing-and-risk-reduction/.

Nicho, M. (2018). A process model for implementing information system security governance. Zayed University Scholars. [Online]. Available: https://zuscholars.zu.ac.ae/cgi/viewcontent.cgi?article=1227&context=works

Peters, L. & Manz, C. M., 2007. dentifying antecedents of virtual team collaboration. Team Performance Management: An International Journal, 13(3/4), pp. 117-129.

Rajamäki, J. (2019) ECHO Information sharing models. https://echonetwork.eu/wp-content/uploads/2020/02/ECHO_D3.6-ECHO-Information-Sharing-Models-v1.0.pdf

Rajamäki, J. & Katos, V., 2020. Information Sharing Models for Early Warning Systems of Cybersecurity Intelligence. Information & Security: An International Journal , 46(2), pp. 198-214.

Ruoslahti, H. & Tikanmäki, I., 2019. Complex Authority Network Interactions in the Common Information Sharing Environment. In: Bernardino, Jorge; Salgado, Ana; Filipe, Joaquim (Eds.) *Proceedings of the 11th International Joint Conference on Knowledge Discovery, Knowledge Engineering and Knowledge Management (IC3K 2019).* Setúbal: Science and Technology Publications, pp. 159 – 166

Wang, H., & Ran, B. (2023). Network governance and collaborative governance: A thematic analysis on their similarities, differences, and entanglements. Public Management Review, 25(6), 1187-1211. https://doi.org/10.1080/14719037.2021.2011389

Weill, P., & Ross, J. W. (2004). IT Governance: How Top Performers Manage IT Decision Rights for Superior Results. Harvard Business School Press.

Yadoshchuk, V. (2023, May 15). Digital Transformation in the Energy Industry: Overview and Tips. [Online]. Available: https://waverleysoftware.com/blog/digital-transformation-in-the-energy-industry/#:~:text=accessible%20user%20interface.-,Conclusion,%2C%20IoT%2C%20and%20blockchain%20technologies

Yang, T. & Maxwell, T., 2011. Information-sharing in public organizations: A literature review of interpersonal, intra-organizational and inter-organizational success factors. Government Information Quarterly, 28(2), pp. 164-175.

Enhancing Metaward: Integrating Digital Forensic Readiness in the Metaverse

Shelley M. Robertson, Stacey O. Baror and Hein S. Venter
University of Pretoria, South Africa

shelley.robertson@tuks.co.za
stacey.baror@up.ac.za
hein.venter@up.ac.za

Abstract: As virtual currencies gain traction as rewards and with the evolving landscape of remote and hybrid work environments, the need for adaptive and comprehensive reward systems becomes imperative. This research builds upon the foundation laid in prior studies, focusing on the integration of Digital Forensic Readiness (DFR) into the Metaward reward model, within the Metaverse. However, as more individuals engage with and use the Metaverse, it is crucial to implement DFR to the Metaverse. The problem of this research is the absence of DFR processes integrated into the Metaverse, particularly within the context of the Metaward reward system. With the increasing importance of cybersecurity and digital forensics (DF) in organizational operations, the integration of such measures aims to enhance the security and integrity of the Metaward model. This enhancement aims to ensure a proactive and effective response to potential security incidents, while maintaining the integrity of digital evidence. This research employs a comprehensive methodology, encompassing literature review, analysis of DF measures, and the development of an extended conceptual model. By considering factors such as the security implications of virtual currencies, incident response capabilities, and proactive DF measures, the study seeks to provide insights into the feasibility and effectiveness of this augmented reward model. The proposed model acknowledges the significance of balancing motivation and engagement with the imperative need for robust DFR. It explores potential synergies between these seemingly different elements, aiming to create a reward system that not only motivates employees but also ensures the resilience and security of the organizational digital infrastructure. This study's findings hold promise for organizations navigating the complex terrain of modern work paradigms, offering a strategic approach to bolstering employee motivation, engagement, and DFR. The conclusion reflects on the implications of the proposed integration and outlines avenues for further research in the dynamic intersection of virtual currencies, reward systems, and DF.

Keywords: Digital Forensic Readiness, Digital Security, Metaverse, Virtual Currency, Employee Motivation.

1. Introduction

The Metaverse, a dynamic fusion of virtual reality (VR), augmented reality (AR), and immersive technologies, has soared in prominence since Facebook's rebrand to "Meta Platforms" in 2021 (Roose, 2021). With the firm resolve of Meta to propel its evolution, this shared virtual space has ignited fascination and excitement, anticipating a new era of digital interconnectedness and exploration (Robertson et al., 2024; Roose, 2021).

In a previous study, Robertson et al. (2024) explored the efficacy of virtual currencies in reward systems, analysed existing reward mechanisms, and proposed a conceptual model for evaluating the feasibility of the Metaward model. Metaward is a virtual currency reward system that offers a holistic framework aimed at revitalizing employee motivation and engagement in the Metaverse. By combining rewards, penalties, recognition, and social comparison, Metaward cultivates a dynamic workplace environment adaptable to align with the mission and values of an organization. This versatile approach holds the promise of substantially boosting employee performance and job satisfaction.

However, amidst the transition to virtual reward systems, the study identified a crucial gap in ensuring the security and integrity of the Metaward model against potential cyber threats. Integrating Digital Forensic Readiness (DFR) into the proposed Metaward model, within the Metaverse, is a critical evolution necessitated by the adoption of virtual currencies as rewards and the imperative to fortify organizational resilience against cyber threats.

The field of digital forensic (DF) science is in constant evolution, employing diverse scientific principles to improve digital evidence and data recovery (Baror and Venter, 2013). DF involves a methodical approach to examining digital data, employing advanced mathematical algorithms to uphold the integrity and trustworthiness of the information (Muyambo and Baror, 2023). Establishing a DF framework is crucial, as neglecting to do so can result in significant time and resource expenditure during the DF procedure (Nugroho et al., 2023). A DF framework is a procedural model or methodology guiding the investigation process, defined as a structured set of stages emphasizing specific phases of DF, including identification, collection, preservation, and examination analysis (Kristyan et al., 2020). This ensures a suitable level of proficiency to preserve, gather, safeguard, and analyse potential digital evidence, enabling its effective utilization in various contexts, such as legal proceedings, security inquiries, disciplinary actions, employment tribunals, or court proceedings (Watson et al., 2018).

DF methodology branches into two categories: proactive and reactive. Reactive DF involves investigating events retrospectively, conducting postmortems, analysing behaviour, and documenting lessons learned to prevent future occurrences. On the contrary, proactive (forensics readiness) entails preparatory measures implemented before an incident arises (Kristyan et al., 2020). Incorporating DF capabilities into Metaward may enhance security, ensure compliance, provide valuable insights, and support investigations, ultimately contributing to the effectiveness and trustworthiness of the reward system.

The objectives of the DFR process aim to maximize the effective utilization of digital evidence, reduce investigation costs, mitigate interference with and prevent disruption of business operations, and maintain or enhance the existing level of information systems security (Valjarevic and Venter, 2012). DFR involves establishing a genuine, resilient, and transparent auditing mechanism in anticipation of potential digital investigations (Muyambo and Baror, 2023). It encompasses an organization's preparedness to conduct DF, allowing for the optimization of investigative capabilities using digital evidence while minimizing the associated costs and time (Nugroho et al., 2023).

The convergence of virtual currencies as rewards in the Metaverse and the imperative to safeguard against potential security breaches underscores the critical need for proactive measures to detect, respond to, and mitigate security incidents. By incorporating DFR principles and practices into the Metaward model, organizations are able to fortify their defences, bolstering resilience against cyber threats, and ensuring the integrity and trustworthiness of the Metaward model.

However, it is unclear how to incorporate robust DFR into the Metaward model. This provides an opportunity for the researcher to explore the integration of DFR into the Metaward model, aiming to bolster security, ensure compliance, offer valuable insights, and facilitate investigations. The objectives of the research include: 1) A literature review on existing DFR implementations. 2) An analysis of existing models, adapting them for the Metaward model. 3) Developing a conceptual model and evaluating the research's validity.

To accomplish this objective, an extensive literature review entails exploring the ACM Digital Library Full-Text Collection, IEEE Xplore Digital Library, and ScienceDirect databases, from 2018-2024, yielding 104 research articles. The research employs a three-step methodology, as outlined by Keshav and Cheriton (2007), to sift through and pinpoint pertinent articles. Additionally, references from selected papers are considered to bolster the research's scope and depth. The process concludes with the creation of an inventive conceptual model, which encapsulates the fundamental elements of the research.

The objective of this research is to strengthen the Metaward model through the integration of DFR to enhance security measures. Through the systematic integration of DFR, this study ensures the reliability of Metaward and maintains the intrinsic benefits of the model, which utilizes virtual currencies to foster employee motivation and retention.

The subsequent sections of this paper are organized as follows: Section 2 provides an overview of prior research concerning the Metaward model. Section 3 presents the background literature relevant to the study. Following this, Section 4 introduces the proposed conceptual model. Section 5 illustrates case scenarios that underscore the contributions of the conceptual model. Section 6 discusses related literature, comparing it with the proposed model. In Section 7, an evaluation of the proposed conceptual model is presented. Finally, Section 8 concludes the work and outlines avenues for future research.

The following section encompasses the preceding research for this study.

2. Overview of Related Literature

This section comprises three subsections. Subsection 2.1 presents the literature review, where DFR implementations are examined to identify fundamental concepts, adaptable frameworks, and pertinent security insights applicable to the research. Subsection 2.2 delves into related literature, illuminating both alignments and divergence between the existing literature and the present study. Finally, Subsection 2.3 offers an overview of the authors' previous work, contextualizing their contributions within the broader scope of the study.

2.1 Literature Review

The literature review subsection is divided into four distinct areas of focus, revealed by the literature. These include insider threats, secure storage of digital evidence, privacy protection, and forensic-ready software systems. This division enhances clarity and facilitates focused discussion on each topic.

2.1.1 Insider Threats

The threat of a cyberattack looms over virtually all digital systems. These attacks are executed by diverse actors with varying objectives, expertise, and resources. Among these, a distinct category involves insider actors, who possess intimate familiarity with the system and lawful access to its resources. Consequently, malicious insiders are at an advantage in executing successful attacks and evading detection, by circumventing security protocols. Furthermore, unintentional insiders may, inadvertently, introduce exploitable vulnerabilities due to errors, oversight, or neglect (Daubner et al., 2023).

Mitigating cyberattacks originating from insiders, proves challenging with conventional security approaches. Often, such perpetrators leverage authorized system access to execute an attack, or external intruders assume an insider's identity, to breach security measures. One potential solution is the adoption of forensic-ready software systems, which facilitate comprehensive forensic investigations post-incident. These systems ensure the generation and accessibility of pertinent evidence, in the event of an attack. While not focused primarily on prevention, the controls inherent in forensic-ready systems, serve to bolster effective post-incident scrutiny, particularly in cases of insider threats (Daubner et al., 2023).

Daubner et al., (2023) propose a systematic strategy for tackling insider attacks within software systems, by integrating forensic-ready features. Essentially, this approach aims to facilitate investigations into attacks carried out or facilitated by insiders. To achieve this goal, the authors devise a risk management framework for forensic readiness, an extension of Information Systems Security Risk Management (ISSRM), which aids in crafting software systems ready for forensic analysis. Consequently, the concept of forensic readiness is seamlessly integrated with security measures, addressing vulnerabilities, and harmonizing the two aspects.

2.1.2 Secure and Transparent Storage of Digital Evidence

Xiao et al., (2024) introduces a novel DF framework, which leverages blockchain technology for Industrial Internet of Things (IIoT) environments. The framework utilizes blockchain to ensure the secure, immutable, and enduring storage of digital evidence. Addressing the real-time requirements of IIoT, it also introduces an efficient batch consensus mechanism. Furthermore, the framework incorporates token-based authorization, for controlling access to evidence queries and facilitates swift retrieval, through smart contracts. It employs public key cryptography to safeguard device identities' anonymity and ensure the confidentiality and integrity of data transmission. However, it is important to note that the framework has only undergone testing in limited simulated environments, and further refinement is necessary before its deployment in real-world industrial network scenarios.

Singh et al., (2022) introduces a model and platform designed to secure Potential Digital Evidence (PDE) and ensure its forensic integrity. Through evaluation, the platform demonstrates strong performance, successfully navigating all forensic processes outlined by the proposed model (SecureRS). Establishing a process to secure evidence, aids in preventing unauthorized access, and ensures compliance with regulations and privacy policies. Additionally, the model facilitates verification, validation, and admissibility of stored PDE in legal proceedings. Leveraging encryption and hashing, the SecureRS model, adheres to current security standards, enhancing forensic investigations, and aiding in detecting evidence tampering. The paper suggests a method for ensuring forensically sound digital evidence, addressing an aspect often overlooked, and typically deemed the sole responsibility of forensic investigators. Additionally, the SecureRS platform serves as a secure backup for evidence, alleviating concerns about verification and authenticity during digital investigations.

2.1.3 Privacy Protection in Digital Forensics

Ogunseyi and Adedayo (2023) explores cryptographic techniques for privacy protection in DF, analysing relevant studies that have utilized such techniques. It summarizes findings from each study, identifies drawbacks of cryptographic techniques in privacy protection, and suggests potential solutions. Additionally, it proposes a conceptual model for privacy-preserving DF, based on cryptographic techniques, detailing where each encryption method can be applied within the model. The study provides mathematical representations and algorithms for the model, evaluates its performance against identified analysis factors, and considers situational factors at each stage. It compares the model with existing privacy preservation principles in DF investigations, offering a roadmap for investigators and researchers. Evaluation of the conceptual model demonstrates its alignment with key privacy principles and adaptability to various DF scenarios.

2.1.4 *Forensic-Ready Software Systems*

Kwon et al., (2019) posits that cyberattacks targeting financial networks, are increasingly sophisticated and severe, with frequent reports of major hacking incidents. The Bangladesh bank robbery case underscored the crucial role of DF evidence. Therefore, in incident response, effective DFR with comprehensive information is imperative. To enhance DF capabilities, Kwon et al., (2019) proposed employing IP traceback, with server marking techniques, to enable the collection of attacker information. Additionally, visualization techniques for the FIX protocol, facilitate the investigation of large volumes of FIX network data. The FIX protocol facilitates the trading of financial products, such as stocks and cryptocurrencies.

Pasquale et al., (2018) examines the concept of forensic readiness in software systems, and the necessary requirements to achieve it. Data-centric requirements identified include availability, relevance, minimality, linkability, completeness, and non-repudiation. Process-centred requirements focus on data provenance and legal compliance. The study also outlines some open software engineering challenges in this area. For future research, the authors plan to formally characterize forensic readiness requirements, and explore techniques, for quantitatively analysing trade-offs between conflicting requirements. They also aim to investigate aspects related to implementing a forensic-ready system, such as generating specifications or assessing the relevance of preserved data.

Rivera-Ortiz and Pasquale, (2019) introduce a novel approach to automate the development of forensic-ready software systems, pioneering the automated generation of logging instructions, to cover relevant security incidents. The authors plan to develop a tool implementing three stages: Incident Modelling, Logging Instrumentation, and Logging Generation. They anticipate Incident Modelling and Logging Instrumentation to be particularly challenging, involving the instrumentation of software system components, to detect method execution, and annotation of sequence diagrams, with logical constraints. The Logging Generation stage is to include the addition of an engine to generate alerts and analyse log messages, potentially encrypting them for enhanced security. Consideration is also given to privacy concerns and strategies, to minimize excessive logging.

2.2 Related Literature

Integrating DFR into Metaward is crucial given the diverse challenges, including insider threats, secure storage of digital evidence, privacy protection in DF, and sophisticated cyberattacks on financial networks. DFR measures address these challenges by providing a systematic strategy for preparatory measures to be implemented before an incident arises, ensuring transparent storage of digital evidence, safeguarding privacy through cryptographic techniques, and enhancing incident response capabilities.

The integration of DFR within Metaward is strategically aligned with the best practices gleaned from the comprehensive literature review. This integration bolsters the system's capacity to withstand the ever-changing landscape of cybersecurity threats by ensuring proactive measures are in place to detect, respond to, and recover from potential incidents effectively.

The comparison presented in Table 1 provides insights that inform the incorporation of DFR, ensuring that Metaward remains robust, adaptive, and equipped to address emerging challenges while upholding the highest standards of security and integrity.

Table 1: Related Literature comparison

Reference	Related Literature	Current Literature	Main Difference/ Contribution
Daubner et al., (2023)	Highlight the need for forensic-ready features to address insider attacks in software systems.	Integrate DFR into Metaward to facilitate investigations into insider threats.	Implementation of DFR into a specific reward system context.
Kwon et al., (2019)	Address cyberattacks targeting financial networks and propose techniques to enhance forensic capabilities.	Incorporate IP traceback/FIX protocol in Metaward to enhance DF capabilities.	Application of forensic techniques for incident response in a specific reward system context.

Reference	Related Literature	Current Literature	Main Difference/ Contribution
Pasquale et al., (2018)	Examine forensic readiness requirements in software systems, detailing datacentric and process-centred requirements.	Integrate DFR principles into Metaward, ensuring system readiness for forensic analysis.	Focus on implementing DFR principles for comprehensive forensic analysis in a specific reward system context.
Rivera-Ortiz and Pasquale, (2019)	Introduce automated logging instruction generation for forensicready software systems.	Emphasize event logging and secure off-site data storage in Metaward, indicating a shared interest in automating forensic tasks.	Automate event logging and securely store logged/alert data for a specific reward system.
Ogunseyi and Adedayo, (2023)	Examine cryptographic techniques in DF for privacy protection, offering a model and roadmap.	Highlighting secure log transmission and privacy in Metaward demonstrates cryptographic awareness.	Emphasize privacy measures and cryptographic techniques in a reward system context.
Singh et al., (2022)	Present the SecureRS model and platform for securing PDE with strong forensic integrity.	Advocate for SecureRS model in Metaward, showing a joint commitment to forensic data integrity.	Application of SecureRS model recommendation in a specific reward system context.
Xiao et al., (2024)	Introduce a blockchainbased DF framework for IIoT, highlighting interest in secure evidence storage.	Highlight secure log transmission in Metaward, aligning with digital evidence integrity.	Focus on secure log transmission and off-site storage in a specific reward system context.

The following subsection expands on the authors' previous work conducted, relating to this study.

2.3 Authors' Previous Work Related to Current Study

Robertson et al. (2024) delve into the evolving landscape of virtual work environments, particularly in the context of the Metaverse, where virtual currencies are increasingly utilized as rewards in virtual environments. With a focus on employee motivation and retention, the study addresses the gap in understanding how virtual currencies can effectively function within reward systems, in the Metaverse, and their impact on employee engagement. Through a comprehensive review of literature, the paper explores existing reward mechanisms (Christy and Fox, 2014; Farzan et al., 2008; Pombo et al., 2019; Pombo and Santos, 2023), considerations of social comparison (Christy and Fox, 2014; Dong and Zhu, 2023) and loss aversion (Lin et al., 2023), and the integration of blockchain technology for security.

A conceptual model, the Metaward reward model, is proposed, incorporating elements of rewards, penalties, recognition, and social comparison to create a dynamic and motivating environment for employees. This model offers flexibility in reward options and aims to increase productivity and job satisfaction in virtual workspaces. A proof of concept demonstrates the practical implementation of the Metaward model, highlighting its potential effectiveness in motivating and retaining employees.

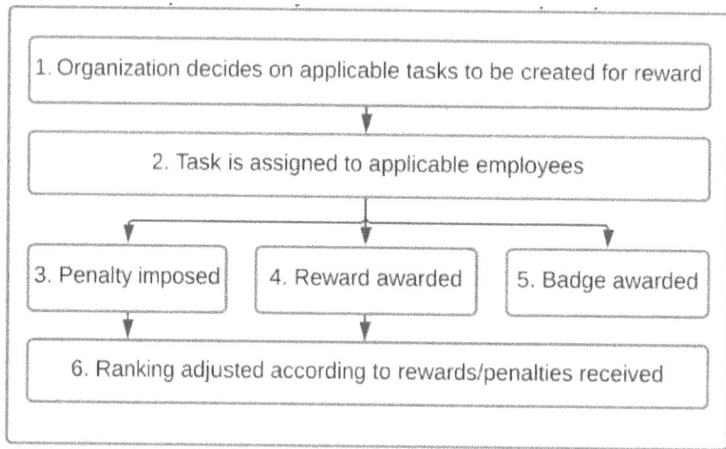

Figure 1: Conceptual Metaward model (Robertson et al., 2024)

The conceptual model presented in Figure 1 outlines a systematic approach to task, integrating various components to optimize employee engagement and performance. Tasks or challenges are meticulously generated and reviewed to align with organizational requirements. Once approved, tasks are assigned to employees with specified deadlines and notifications, with periodic reminders incentivizing timely completion.

Failure to meet deadlines incurs cryptocurrency penalties, while successful completion earns employees' cryptocurrency rewards, which can be redeemed through various options. Additionally, badges are awarded for completed tasks to foster social comparison among employees, with rankings fluctuating based on task completion status. This comprehensive model effectively combines task management strategies with motivational incentives to drive employee productivity and achievement.

In conclusion, the paper presents a promising approach to address the challenges of virtual work environments, offering valuable insights and practical strategies for organizations seeking to optimize employee performance and satisfaction in the Metaverse.

The subsequent section delves into the Metaward model with DFR included.

3. Proposed Metaward Model Including Digital Forensic Readiness

In this section, DFR is introduced into the existing Metaward model, expanding upon the discoveries from the preceding section. It encompasses a conceptual model, flow diagrams for individual components, and an overarching model flow diagram. The figure below represents the high-level conceptual model, elaborated on in section 3.1:

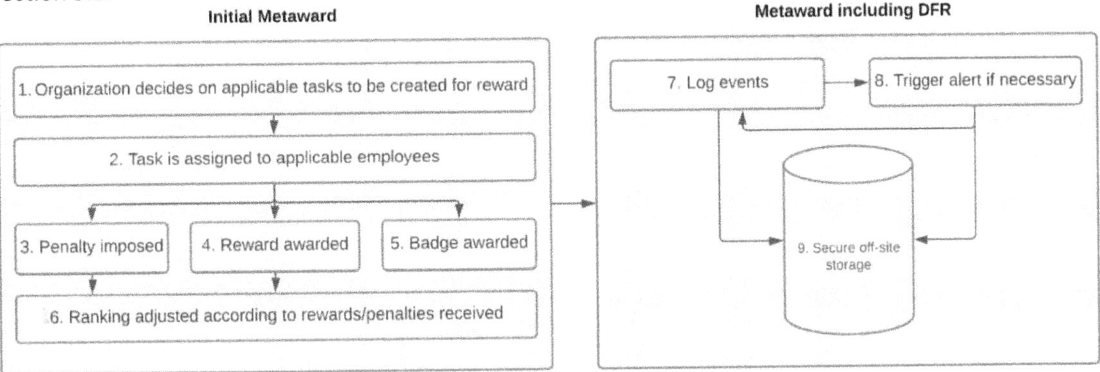

Figure 2: Conceptual Metaward model (Robertson et al., 2024) including Digital Forensic Readiness

3.1 High-Level View of Proposed Digital Forensic Ready Metaward Model

Outlined below are the components of the conceptual model depicted in Figure 2. Points 1-6 represent the initial Metaward high-level view as presented by Robertson et al., (2024). This portion remains unchanged in this paper. **Points 7-9 introduce additional DFR measures to supplement the existing model.**

1. Tasks are meticulously generated and reviewed to ensure they conform to the specific requirements and regulations of the organization, thus fostering alignment with its overarching goals and standards.
2. Once tasks are approved, they are promptly assigned to employees along with clear deadlines and notifications. Additionally, periodic reminders are implemented, particularly catering to individuals who are motivated by loss aversion, to ensure task completion within stipulated timeframes.
3. In the event of task non-completion, employees face a cryptocurrency penalty deducted directly from their wallets, providing a tangible consequence for failure to meet obligations, and incentivizing timely completion.
4. Timely completion of tasks is incentivized through cryptocurrency rewards, which accrue and can be redeemed within specified timeframes. Employees are offered various redemption options, such as converting cryptocurrency to fiat currency or utilizing it for leisure time off, enhancing motivation and engagement.
5. Upon completion of tasks, employees are awarded icon-like badges, facilitating social comparison and recognition. These badges are designed with expiration dates to ensure ongoing relevance and up-to-date acknowledgment of accomplishments.
6. Employee rankings are subject to fluctuation based on their task completion status, appealing to individuals motivated by social comparison. These changes in rankings are regulated by expiration dates, maintaining a dynamic and competitive environment.
7. Detailed logs are maintained for each task, including information about the designated employee group and associated events such as task initiation, rewards, penalties, badge issuance, and ranking

adjustments. Validity checks are conducted on each logged event to ensure accuracy and alignment with organizational objectives.

8. Anomalies detected within the system trigger immediate alerts to designated personnel, with comprehensive details logged for analysis. In the event of an anomaly, the current Metaward session is terminated to safeguard against potential security threats or attacks.
9. All logged events and triggers are securely stored in an off-site database, ensuring data integrity and confidentiality. The utilization of the SecureRS system, as proposed by Singh et al., (2022), is recommended to enhance the robustness of the storage infrastructure and mitigate potential vulnerabilities.

The following section elaborates on the high-level conceptual model and breaks it down into separate component diagrams.

3.2 Digital Forensic Ready Metaward Model

In a previous study, Robertson et al., (2024) discuss existing Individual component diagrams for other processes within the Metaward model in detail. This is also summarized in section 2.3 of this paper. Figure 3 depicts the DFR component added to the Metaward Model, describing each step in the process below.

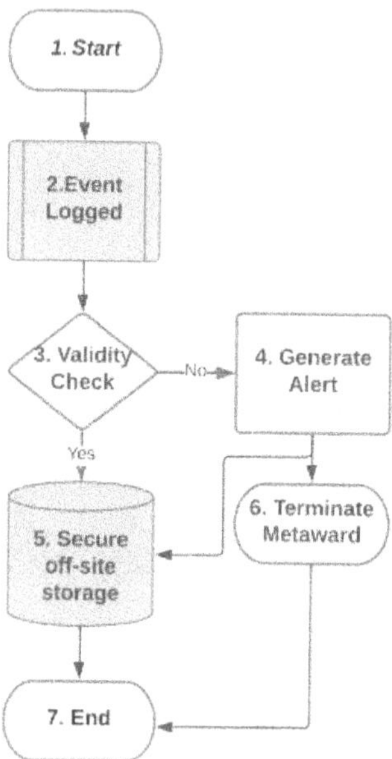

Figure 3: Digital Forensic Readiness Component Diagram

1. Start - Placeholder to begin the DFR component, at each point in the comprehensive model where an event is triggered.
2. Event logged – Each logged event contains specific information from the relevant event triggered, including a timestamp, user for the transaction and the action for the event, e.g. a penalty incurred, a reward added, rewards redeemed.
3. Validity Check – Each event logged is checked for validity. Should an anomaly be found, e.g. a reward for a task not allocated to the specific user, then the process continues to step 4, alternatively to step 5.
4. Generate alert – In the event of an anomaly occurring, an alert with the relevant details are generated and sent to the designated employee/s.
5. Secure off-site storage – The logged event is stored in a secure off-site database. The SecureRS system from (Singh et al., 2022) is recommended.
6. Terminate Metaward – Once the alert is triggered, the current Metaward session is terminated to prevent any further suspected attacks.
7. End – This placeholder marks the end of the DFR process, with the potential beginning of a digital forensic investigation as the process model is the starting point of any incident detection within the metaverse.

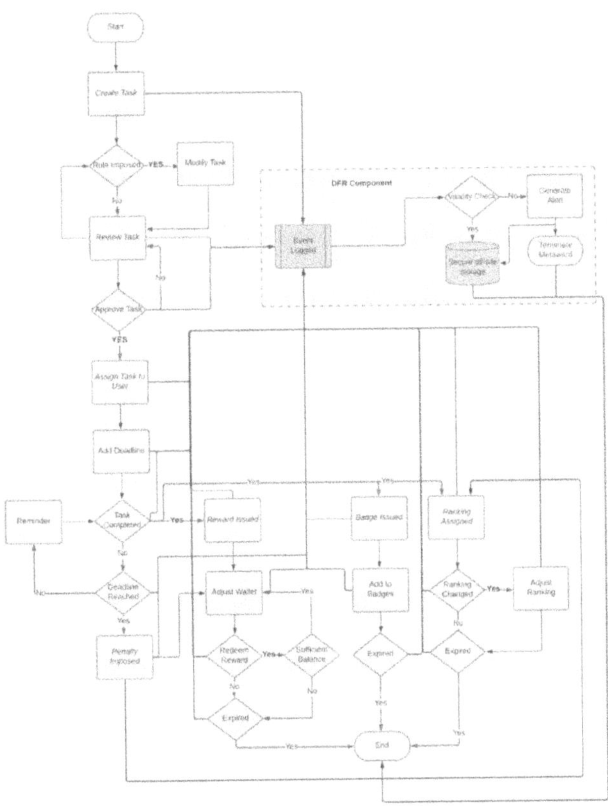

Figure 4: Metaward reward model (Robertson et al., 2024) with Digital Forensic Readiness

Figure 4 above, provides an overview of the comprehensive Metaward system, showcasing the incorporation of the Digital Forensic Readiness (DFR) component into the overall model. This integration marks a significant advancement in bolstering both security measures and employee motivation within the Metaverse. This ensures that events are logged at each critical point within the Metaward model, enabling Metaward to be a forensic-ready software system. The Metaward model caters to diverse employee motivations, incorporating badges for recognition-seeking individuals (Pombo et al., 2019; Pombo and Santos, 2023), leaderboards for those driven by social comparison (Christy and Fox, 2014; Dong and Zhu, 2023), rewards for incentive-driven employees , and timed penalties for those inclined towards loss aversion (Lin et al., 2023). Initially, rewards are offered in cryptocurrency, affording flexibility for subsequent redemption, which may include monetary benefits, instant rewards, or time off as per organizational preferences.

The following section delves into various case scenarios, to show the validity of implementing DFR into the Metaward model.

4. Case Scenarios

The following case scenarios are presented to illustrate the practical implications of integrating DFR into Metaward. These scenarios highlight how DFR can enhance security measures, detect fraudulent activities, ensure legal compliance, resolve disputes, and facilitate continuous improvement through feedback analysis. Each scenario demonstrates the value of DFR in safeguarding data integrity, promoting transparency, and maintaining the credibility of the reward system within organizational contexts.

Data Breach Investigation Efficiency: Suppose an organization using the Metaward Model experiences a data breach. With DFR integrated, the forensic readiness of their systems allows for swift and systematic investigation. Digital evidence such as access logs, transaction records, and user activity trails are readily available and properly preserved, expediting the identification of the breach's source, and minimizing its impact.

Fraudulent Activity Detection: Imagine an employee within the organization manipulating the Metaward model to fraudulently acquire rewards. DFR implementation enables real-time monitoring of system activities and behaviour analysis. Suspicious patterns, such as excessive reward claims or unusual access attempts, trigger alerts for investigation, preventing fraudulent behaviour and maintaining the integrity of the reward system.

Legal Compliance Assurance: Consider a scenario where the organization faces legal inquiries or litigation related to employee rewards and incentives. DFR ensures that all necessary digital evidence, such as reward distribution records, user consent acknowledgments, and system configurations, are systematically documented and securely stored. This ensures the organization's ability to comply with legal requests, demonstrate transparency, and protects against potential liabilities.

Employee Dispute Resolution: Suppose a dispute arises between employees regarding reward allocations within the Metaward model. DFR integration allows for comprehensive forensic analysis of relevant digital data, including logs, task completion records, and reward redemption histories. By providing objective and verifiable evidence, DFR facilitates fair dispute resolution, maintains employee trust, and upholds the credibility of the reward system.

Continuous Improvement through Feedback Analysis: In a scenario where employees provide feedback or suggestions for improving the Metaward Model, DFR enables systematic analysis of digital feedback data. By tracking user interactions, sentiment analysis, and feedback trends, organizations can identify areas for enhancement and prioritize feature development based on user needs and preferences. This iterative feedback loop ensures that the Metaward Model remains responsive to evolving organizational requirements and employee expectations.

The subsequent section highlights the scope and content of the research undertaken with this study.

5. Discussion

The integration of DFR into Metaward presents a significant advancement in enhancing both security measures and employee incentivization within the Metaverse. By incorporating DFR protocols, organizations gain robust mechanisms, to safeguard against potential security breaches, while leveraging virtual currencies to motivate and retain employees effectively.

The case scenarios illustrate the practical applications of DFR in various scenarios, showcasing its effectiveness in enhancing data breach investigation efficiency, detecting fraudulent activities, ensuring legal compliance, facilitating employee dispute resolution, and enabling continuous improvement through feedback analysis.

Through the implementation of validity checks, anomaly detection, and secure log storage, the enhanced Metaward model, provides law enforcement and justice systems, with timely and comprehensive digital evidence for investigations and litigation processes. Additionally, all logs are securely transmitted to an off-site database, with the recommendation to utilize the SecureRS model, presented by Singh et al., (2022) for preserving PDE while maintaining integrity. This further ensures the reliability and integrity of digital evidence storage.

Furthermore, the model aligns with readiness processes outlined in ISO/IEC 27043 (Valjarević et al., 2016), emphasizing its adherence to international security standards. By integrating event logging, secure log storage, and functionalities such as IP traceback/FIX protocol, as recommended by Kwon et al., (2019), Metaward ensures resilience and forensic preparedness, benefiting DF investigators and organizational security teams alike.

This research not only strengthens the security posture of organizations, but also enhances transparency, fairness, and trustworthiness in reward systems, ultimately benefiting end-users and promoting a safer and more secure digital environment.

In the subsequent section, this study summarizes its findings and presents potential avenues for future work.

6. Conclusion

The integration of DFR into the Metaward model marks a significant step towards enhancing both security measures and employee incentivization within the Metaverse. By incorporating DFR protocols, this study successfully strengthens the security infrastructure of Metaward while preserving its intrinsic benefits, particularly in utilizing virtual currencies to motivate and retain employees.

This research has achieved its primary objective of fortifying the Metaward model through the systematic integration of DFR. By ensuring the reliability and security of Metaward, organizations can confidently harness its capabilities to foster employee motivation and retention in virtual environments.

Several avenues for future research warrant exploration, including long-term assessments to fully comprehend the impact of DFR implementation on both employee engagement and organizational security posture. Additionally, further investigation into the scalability and adaptability of the Metaward model across different industries and cultural contexts would provide valuable insights into its broader applicability. Furthermore, continued refinement of the model, based on user feedback and the exploration of ethical considerations surrounding privacy and fairness, are essential for ensuring its effectiveness and ethical soundness in practice. This includes ongoing evaluations of privacy and fairness aspects to ensure the model's alignment with evolving ethical standards.

This study lays a solid foundation, for future research, aiming at the optimization of reward systems in the digital age, prioritizing security, and employee well-being in virtual work environments. Through collaborative efforts and ongoing refinement, the vision of a secure, incentivized, and ethically sound digital workplace can be realized.

References

Baror, S.O., Venter, H.S., 2013. Testing the harmonised digital forensic investigation process model-using an Android mobile phone, in: 2013 Information Security for South Africa. pp. 1–8.

Christy, K.R., Fox, J., 2014. Comput Educ 78, 66–77.

Daubner, L., Macak, M., Matulevičius, R., Buhnova, B., Maksović, S., Pitner, T., 2023. Addressing insider attacks via forensic-ready risk management, Journal of Information Security and Applications. Elsevier BV.

Dong, Y., Zhu, Q., 2023. How Downward Social Comparison Motivates Workers: A Structural Equation Model on Personality, Social Comparison Orientation, Motivation and Performance, in: ACM International Conference Proceeding Series. Association for Computing Machinery, pp. 207–212.

Farzan, R., Dimicco, J.M., Millen, D.R., Brownholtz, B., Geyer, W., Dugan, C., 2008. When the experiment is over: Deploying an incentive system to all the users.

Keshav, S., Cheriton, D.R., 2007. How to Read a Paper.

Kristyan, S.A., Suhardi, Juhana, T., 2020. Design Framework Forensics Readiness as a Service for Automatic Processing, ICITSI. ed. 2020 International Conference on Information Technology Systems and Innovation, Bandung - Padang, Indonesia.

Kwon, S., Jeong, J., Shon, T., 2019. Digital Forensic Readiness for Financial Network, PlatCon-19. ed. 2019 International Conference on Platform Technology and Service: proceedings, Jeju, Korea.

Lin, Y., Wang, J., Luo, Z., Li, S., Zhang, Y., Wünsche, B.C., 2023. Dragon Hunter: Loss Aversion for Increasing Physical Activity in AR Exergames. Association for Computing Machinery (ACM), pp. 212–221.

Muyambo, E., Baror, S.O., 2023. Digital Forensic Readiness Model for Internet Voting, in: European Conference on Cyber Warfare and Security. pp. 657–667.

Nugroho, H.A., Briliyant, O.C., Sunaringtyas, S.U., 2023. A Novel Digital Forensic Readiness (DFR) Framework for e-Government, in: Proceedings - 2023 IEEE International Conference on Cryptography, Informatics, and Cybersecurity: Cryptography and Cybersecurity: Roles, Prospects, and Challenges, ICoCICs 2023. Institute of Electrical and Electronics Engineers Inc., pp. 184–189.

Ogunseyi, T.B., Adedayo, O.M., 2023. Cryptographic Techniques for Data Privacy in Digital Forensics IEEE Access.

Pasquale, L., Alrajeh, D., Peersman, C., Tun, T., Nuseibeh, B., Rashid, A., 2018. Towards forensic-ready software systems, in: Proceedings - International Conference on Software Engineering. IEEE Computer Society, pp. 9–12.

Pombo, N., Garcia, N., Alves, P., 2019. How to Get a Badge? Unlock Your Mind, IEEE Educon. ed. IEEE.

Pombo, N., Santos, H., 2023. Lessons Learned from the Development of a Computerised Badge-based Reward Tool for Student Engagement in Learning Activities, in: EDUNINE 2023 - 7th IEEE World Engineering Education Conference: Reimaging Engineering - Toward the Next Generation of Engineering Education, Merging Technologies in a Connected World, Proceedings. Institute of Electrical and Electronics Engineers Inc.

Rivera-Ortiz, F., Pasquale, L., 2019. Towards automated logging for forensic-ready software systems, in: Proceedings - 2019 IEEE 27th International Requirements Engineering Conference Workshops, REW 2019. Institute of Electrical and Electronics Engineers Inc., pp. 157–163.

Robertson, S., Baror, S.O., Venter, H.S., 2024. Metaverse: Virtual Currencies as a Mechanism for Employee Engagement and Retention ICCWS.

Roose, K., 2021. Why Did Facebook Become Meta? - The New York Times [WWW Document]. URL https://www.nytimes.com/2021/10/29/technology/meta-facebook-zuckerberg.html (accessed 10.2.23).

Singh, A., Ikuesan, R.A., Venter, H., 2022. IEEE Access 10, 19469–19480.

Valjarević, A., Venter, H., Petrović, R., 2016. ISO/IEC 27043:2015 — Role and application, in: 2016 24th Telecommunications Forum (TELFOR). pp. 1–4.

Valjarevic, A., Venter, H.S., 2012. Harmonised Digital Forensic Investigation Process Model. IEEE.

Watson, V., Bejiga, M., Bajramovic, E., Waedt, K., 2018. Designing Trustworthy Monitoring Systems Forensic Readiness for Safety and Security.

Xiao, N., Wang, Z., Sun, X., Miao, J., 2024. Alexandria Engineering Journal 86, 631–643.

The Social Domain: Resilience of Information-Sharing Networks

Harri Ruoslahti [1] and Ilkka Tikanmäki [1, 2]

[1] Security and Risk Management, Laurea University of Applied Sciences, Espoo, Finland
[2] Department of Warfare, National Defence University, Helsinki, Finland

https://orcid.org/ 0000-0001-9726-7956

https://orcid.org/0000- 0001-8950-5221

Harri.ruoslahti@laurea.fi
Ilkka.tikanmaki@laurea.fi

Abstract: The concept of networks in the social domain can be seen as a resilient complex social system, consisting of diverse and interdependent actors and organizations. These social networks are characterized by complicated interactions between people, technologies, and processes, making them cyber-physical or socio-technical in nature. However, these interactions and dependencies also bring vulnerabilities, encouraging member organizations to increase their resiliency. As organizations and digital structures become increasingly interconnected, there is a need for information sharing, and practices that anticipate future incidents and foster learning from them. Effective communication with stakeholders is essential to strengthening resilience, given the diverse interests and interdependencies between them. An integral system's perspective on an organisation in its environment emphasises relationships and interdependencies, enabling recognition of complexities to enhance resilience on various interrelated levels. Identifying trends and implementing preventive measures requires the sharing of information on threats and vulnerabilities. Open innovation, where outsiders contribute to co-creating innovations, can help organizations cope with unforeseen disruptive changes. Agility is essential for developing knowledge and adapting processes flexibly to changing contexts. Knowledge exchange between network stakeholders can reduce the complexity of communication and enable resilient collaboration. In this case study, the researchers offer a tool that is aimed at strengthening the resilience of collaborative networks by gaining a deeper understanding of each organisation's relevant processes and tools. They specifically focused on analysing and evaluating the effects of these processes on the safety of critical infrastructure. To enhance the sustainability of stakeholder collaborative networks, master's students in safety management conducted risk assessment workshops and compiled a list of characteristics. These attributes were then prioritised and incorporated into risk matrices. The results of the study revealed the key factors that contribute most significantly to the resilience of collaboration networks. These findings highlight the critical aspects that influence the resilience of collaborative networks. By incorporating these factors into their strategies and practices, organisations and stakeholders can enhance their ability to withstand disruptions and adapt effectively in the face of uncertainties.

Keywords: Networks, Collaboration, Resilience, Risk Assessment

1. Introduction

Networks in the social domain (Linkov et al., 2013) can be looked at through the lens of resilient complex social systems, as networks are organisational environments that consist of diverse interdependent actors, organisations can be understood as complex social systems (Mitleton-Kelly, 2003). This study is based on the action research-based case study continuum carried out in three EU-funded projects: European Network of Cybersecurity Centres and Competence Hub for Innovation and Operations (ECHO), Smart and Healthy Ageing through People Engaging in Supportive Systems (SHAPES), and Dynamic Resilience Assessment Method including a combined Business Continuity Management and Cyber Threat Intelligence solution for Critical Sectors (DYNAMO).

Project ECHO developed and delivered an organized coordinated, effective and efficient multi-sector collaboration-based approach to help strengthen the proactive cyber defences of the European Union (Pappalardo et al., 2020). The SHAPES project gathered stakeholders from across Europe to create, deploy and pilot at large-scale networked EU-wide harmonized open platforms to integrate broad ranges of technological, organizational, clinical, educational, and societal solutions. The aim is to enable ageing Europeans to remain healthy, active and productive while maintaining a high quality of life and sense of well-being for the longest time possible (Rajamäki and Ruoslahti, 2021). The project DYNAMO deals with increasing digitalisation and mounting potential of cyber threats, where networked experts work together with end-users to develop a single platform where artificial intelligence-based (AI) approaches combine business continuity management (BCM) and cyber threat intelligence (CTI) for resilience assessment and awareness to minimize the number of cyberattacks against the critical sectors of society (DYNAMO project, 2023).

Networked SHAPES technologies and systems include many complex interactions between people, technologies and processes, and can be considered cyber-physical (Linkov et al., 2013; Rajamäki and Ruoslahti, 2018) or socio-technical (Amir and Kant, 2018). Interactions and interdependencies between complex social networks, such as the SHAPES-networks, come with vulnerabilities, come with vulnerabilities, so their member organisations work to increase their resilience. "Nowadays, there is a tight coupling of systems and processes, and there are many interdependencies between these systems and processes" (Vos, 2017, p. 23).

Due to the entanglement of human organisations, and digital and material structures, vulnerabilities within socio-technical systems that combine human and technical aspects have increased, resulting in a need to develop practices that anticipate possible future incidents and provide feedback to learn from (Amir and Kant, 2018; Linkov et al., 2014). Communication in the turbulent times of today is "co-constructed by multiple stakeholders characterised by different interests and various interdependencies" (Vos, 2017, p. 13), and communication with stakeholders is important in building resilience (Linkov et al., 2014). Agility can help develop the knowledge needed for resilient collaboration, and to flexibly adapt needed processes to changing contexts (Ruoslahti et al., 2018). Understanding an integral system's view of an organisation in its environment emphasises relationships and interdependencies (Grunig et al., 1992), which enables the recognition of complexities to increase resilience on different interrelated levels, and across boundaries, as societal resilience is built together by the different actors (Vos, 2017).

Sharing information on threats and vulnerabilities "help identify trends, better understand the risk faced, and determine what preventive measures should be implemented" (Stanciugelu et al., 2013, p. 194). Open innovation, where outsiders are invited to co-create innovations can be one way of assisting to deal with unforeseen disruptive changes in volatile environments of the organisation and network (Pichyangkul et al., 2012). Agility is needed to develop the knowledge needed to flexibly adapt processes to changing contexts, and gaps and complexity in communicating existing knowledge can be reduced by exchanging knowledge among network actors for collaboration to function in a resilient way (do Nascimento Souto, 2013).

The research question of this paper is: How to measure the resilience of services networks?

This paper is organized as follows: Section 2 deals with literature on cybersecurity of eHealth platforms, security validation requirements for eHealth services, and ECHO efforts in the healthcare sector and cyber range (E-FCR). Section 3 outlines the used methods. Section 4 presents a tool for measurable attributes of resilience in collaboration networks. Section 5 concludes the paper and suggests possibilities for future work.

2. Literature Review

The framework of organizational resilience creates tools and conditions to help understand issues, reduce risks, and mitigate crises: "Resilience requires cooperation and adaptive capacities" (Vos, 2017, p. 20), which can be used to create tools or conditions to help organizations co-evolve with their constantly changing environments (Mitleton-Kelly, 2003). Innovation eco-systems where different types of actors build contexts for innovation build resilience with knowledge development that addresses vulnerabilities and risks that may spread within the system (Hautamäki, 2010; Oksanen and Hautamäki, 2014). Organizational resilience helps create tools and conditions for risk reduction, mitigation of crises, and understanding issues (Vos, 2017).

According to (Linkov et al., 2014) risks occur when threat, vulnerability and consequences for critical functionalities coincide. Organisations work to identify these elements in their risk assessments during when planning and preparing for possible disruptions. Organisations, and collaboration networks alike, require preparation and a process to update recovery plans (Savage, 2002). Robust business processes, keeping plans constantly updated and tested, and learning from actual experiences help prepare for possible disturbances (Draheim and Pirinen, 2011). Resilience management with transparent dialogue help network actors accept, promote, and maintain resilience concepts (Linkov et al., 2014). "Co-creation clearly requires alignment of vision and supporting processes, and the development of advanced inter-organisational collaboration skills" (Burdon et al., 2015, p. 296).To promote resilience calls for "awareness, leadership, resource allocation, and planning" (O'Rourke and Briggs, 2007, p. 26) and shared responsibility and situational intelligence (Pirinen, 2017).

(Vos, 2017, p. 23) states that the concept of resilience is about "coping with change and managing the unexpected" when functioning in turbulent environments. (Ruoslahti, 2019) discusses resilience in complex social networks as important elements, which helps understand how these networks seek to reduce risks and mitigate crises on the level of social network collaboration, and how they adapt the process of joint knowledge creation in a changing environment. Today's changing organisational environments are complex and filled with interrelated risks (Linkov et al., 2013; Mitleton-Kelly, 2003; Vos, 2017) which can also be said for collaboration networks. SHAPES-networks are organizational environments that consist of diverse interdependent actors, organizations they can be understood as complex social systems (Mitleton-Kelly, 2003).

Critical infrastructure provides citizens with essential services and supports our economies. It is therefore in everyone's interest to prevent disturbances from occurring. Critical energy infrastructure and supply chains' safety are vital for society's functioning; therefore, it is crucial to ensure their safety. Energy infrastructure is networked, so disturbances at one location can affect the rest of the region, and information on its location and routing is publicly accessible. To build resilience and be prepared to manage disruptions, organizations need to work together in a complementary and mutually reinforcing way (NATO-EU Task Force, 2023).

2.1 Collaboration Networks – Information Sharing in the Social Domain

(Tikanmäki et al., 2022) studied maritime surveillance and information sharing systems that help build better situational awareness on the European maritime domain. Digital transformation, such as are the SHAPES networks call for an added level of cyber security and increased resilience in modern societies. This study looked at different forms of collaboration networks, which can be decentralized, hybrid, and centralized.

Table 1: SWOT analysis of different network types (Tikanmäki et al., 2022).

Decentralized Networks		Hybrid Networks		Centralized Networks	
Strengths	Weaknesses	Strengths	Weaknesses	Strengths	Weaknesses
Cross sector actors Cross border actors Available information Area coverage	Access rights to the available information Network complexity Management Costs	Collaboration between large-scale, cross-sector, cross-border, and local operators	Trust, as to what will be done with information shared Ownership of information Potentially complex access rights	Security Easy access rights Existing co-operation Trust between partners Common interests ease information sharing Effective information	Shared information focused on limited geographical area Costly Political blocks Information from outside networks can not be shared
Opportunities	Threats	Opportunities	Threats	Opportunities	Threats
Potential of cross border collaboration Potential of cross sector collaboration Potential tools to mitigate risks	Cyber attacks Consortium collapse when not seen being beneficial Trust, as to what will be done with information shared	Geographical consortiums can utilize different solutions	Network security against cyber attacks Political obstacles	Connectivity to other networks	Political blocks

The advantages of different network designs depend on their use, as demonstrated in the SWOT table above. Authorities and actors from a geographically wider area can form the coalition in decentralized networks than in centralized networks (such as the European Union or the European Economic Area). The hybrid network is constructed based on the partners' interests, emphasizing a broader area than a specific geographical area. It enables the creation of a comprehensive Common Operational Picture (COP) between industries, cross-border players, and local players. Centralized networks, on the other hand, are a substitute for consortia formed by national authorities and actors that are restricted to specific geographical areas.

2.2 Attributes to Improve the Resilience of Collaboration Networks

Attributes to improve the resilience of collaboration networks (Rajamäki and Ruoslahti, 2018; Ruoslahti et al., 2018) can help toward greater resilience of multi-stakeholder collaboration networks, these attributes were then prioritized and placed in risk matrixes. The main characteristics are summarised in Table 2.

Table 2: Attributes that can improve resilience in collaboration networks.

Attributes of resilience in collaboration networks
Co-create a clear purpose and common aims for the network
Agree on organization and roles within the network
Create a common culture and common ways of working among network stakeholders
Develop leadership within the network
Facilitate collaboration and co-creation in the network
Develop systems to back up or exchange network stakeholder representatives
Build trust among the stakeholders of the network
Have open communication, sharing information with every network stakeholder

As Table 2 demonstrates, these are clear attributes that a network can manage to bring resilience to its social domain. A clear goal is the starting point for agreement on roles and establishing common methods of operating. Leadership and facilitation are necessary, and these roles must also be accepted by those involved in the networks. It is important to develop a backup system for representatives both regarding open communication and enhancing trust among stakeholders.

A social network's resilience depends on the network having a clear purpose and common objectives. The preparatory stage on the work of strategy depends on resulting in common aims and ways of working. Stakeholders must work on the development of guidance plans and standards, agree on clear roles and responsibilities, and identify and reconcile individual and general user requirements. Where the need recognizes the effects of potential adverse events, the level of acceptance of the roles and responsibilities of each stakeholder group emerges.

A common operational culture also has the flexibility to succeed in changing circumstances. A recovery towards jointly agreed objectives is necessary to enable full standardisation of services and operations. The adjustment phase should include an open analysis of the actions undertaken and the utility of the instructions and actions provided. Educated decision-making requires information and a situational picture of the operating environment. In addition, a resilient social network also demonstrates leadership and facilitation.

The planning phase should have a comprehensive risk management process, with input from the views of each stakeholder. In the aftermath of the event, crisis management is pivotal. A clear picture of the situation makes it possible to envisage possible environmental modifications. Leadership should concentrate on the most critical element required to recover from the incident and prioritize the activities of the network. Monitoring and reporting help to gather the necessary information for learning from the experiences of both your own organization and other organizations in the network. It was concluded that the leadership and coordination of the network should not be too undefined or over-controlling.

Security for information sharing both cyber and physical is also necessary. The aspects of this are the related documentation and stand-in procedures in the event of a representative is not present and deal with staff changes. A clear system needs to be put in place to mitigate the impact of possible absences and changes in stakeholder representation. Timely and efficient communication and exchange of information contributes to increased trust among stakeholders. The conclusion was that trust should exist between the representatives of the stakeholders and the organizations.

In addition, the participants stated that major changes in the operational environment, such as rapid technological development and scheduling and cost challenges may call into question the sustainability and cooperation processes of the network at risk. Open communication during the preparatory phase is linked to the management of communication before the crisis (Vos et al., 2014), whereas after the event the interaction is transformed into crisis communication (Palttala and Vos, 2012). In the recovery phase, emphasis is placed on communication issues.

2.3 Competence Management – Basis for Information Sharing

Competence management is how organizations deal with the competence of enterprises, groups, and individuals. The purpose of which is to define and permanently maintain competence in line with the objectives of the enterprise (Berio and Harzallah, 2005). EU define competence as "a combination of knowledge, skills and attitudes appropriate to the context" (European Parliament and the Council, 2006, p. 16). Competence is part of human capital, which includes e.g., the level of education of the personnel and the measured competencies, job satisfaction and state of health (Lepak and Snell, 1999).

To meet an organization's perceived needs for expertise, individuals should acquire the knowledge and skills necessary, which help successful integration of expert community members to research and development processes. To be transformed into organizational know-how information must be acquired, understood, internalized, and shared within the community (Eisenberger et al., 2016). The competences of an organisation's personnel, consisting of practices, processes or systems that store and accumulate new know-how, forms a common knowledge base for an entire company (Fagerberg et al., 2012).

Meetings, training sessions, group work, etc. can be used to share information. When the information becomes understood at the organizational level, the suitability of the information for practice can be tested for organizational learning. It can become reflected in the structures and practices of the organization and its written instructions (Levitt and March, 1988). On the report of (Otala et al., 2004) strategic competences can be determined by identifying strategic starting points, required competencies and capabilities, future competence needs and drawing up competence profiles, so that the work community and organization form a network that supports learning.

Defining a vision, strategy, core competencies, and competence development needs can locate the differences between the current situation and the competence needs, and a development plan helps target, implement, and monitor the measures; monitoring and evaluating development measures can support management guide the organizational operations and make a follow-up plan for competence development (Bergenhenegouwen, 1996). Creating student-expert alliances can connect science, culture, and experts with work life activities to create learning environments together (Westermann, 2011). The collective individual competences of the personnel accumulate organizational competence, which can form permanent and secure organizational knowledge capital, not just the competence of individuals (Hakanen and Soudunsaari, 2012).

The emergence of innovations is influenced by strong links between actors, as well as by the essential new knowledge brought by beginners, which develops and deepens community activities (Ojasalo, 2012). Knowledge and information are shared in an open atmosphere, symmetrically through and between both old professionals and newcomers provides support to competence management in changing the way an organization operates, and the emergence of know-how because of work life cooperation to be key (Wan et al., 2020). Management practices should support and enable radical, collective learning (Kallio and Lappalainen, 2015).

3. Methodology

The purpose of the case study is to provide detailed case study information in support of development activities. The more the research questions aim to explain some current situation, e.g., how, or why, the more relevant the case study method in question is. The method is especially relevant as questions require a wide and thorough description of certain social phenomena. Case studies are used in a variety of situations to increase information on individual, collective, organisational, socio-political, and affiliated issues (Benbasat et al., 1987; Dubé and Pare, 2003; Yin, 2009). A case study is a suitable approach when producing a solution to a specific problem or making suggestions for research development (Yin, 2009).

This study is a multiple case study based on the action research-based case study continuum carried out in the projects 1) ECHO, 2) SHAPES, and 3) DYNAMO using the attributes to improve the resilience of collaboration networks, and collaborative information sharing systems for situational awareness.

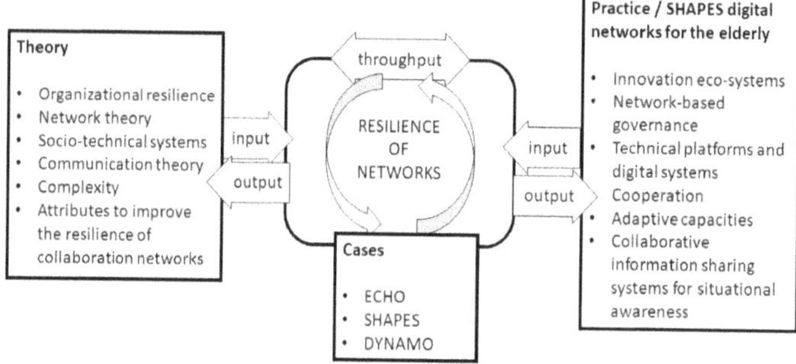

Figure 1: The structure of this case study research.

The theoretical inputs are organizational resilience, network theory, socio-technical systems, communication, complexity, and theoretical attributes to improve the resilience of collaboration networks. Practical inputs are innovation eco-systems, governance of networks, platforms, cooperation, adaptive capacities, and collaborative information sharing systems for situational awareness. The throughput is a continuum of action research involving three different case projects (ECHO, SHAPES, DYNAMO) to create a piloted practical tool to measure relevant attributes of the resilience of networked activities.

4. Results: Attributes of Collaboration Network Resilience

Understanding how resilience becomes built in SHAPES collaboration networks can guide SHAPES governance and direct their strategy work resulting in common aims and common ways of working and a common operational culture which can ensure needed flexibility to successfully face changing situations. This can be achieved with the attributes of resilience (Rajamäki and Ruoslahti, 2018; Ruoslahti et al., 2018).

By applying a Likert-scale a template (Table 3) can be formed that can be used to assess the state of collaboration network resilience within any specific SHAPES network, and even the entire network of SHAPES networks. Each attribute can be assessed as frequency answering the question 'How often does this attribute occur in our SHAPES network; never, rarely, sometimes, often, or always?'

Table 3: Attributes of collaboration network resilience assessed as frequency (Never = 1, Rarely = 2, Sometimes = 3, Often = 4, Always = 5).

Attribute	1	2	3	4	5
Does our network co-create a clear purpose for the network					
Does our network co-create common aims for the network					
Agree on organisation within the network					
Agree on roles within the network					
Create a common culture of working among network stakeholders					
Create common ways of working among network stakeholders					
Develop leadership within the network					
Facilitate the collaboration in the network					
Facilitate co-creation in the network					
Develop systems to back-up network stakeholder representatives					
Develop systems to exchange network stakeholder representatives					
Build trust among the stakeholders of the network					
Have open communication with every network stakeholder					
Have sharing information with every network stakeholder					

Understanding these attributes can provide understanding of how resilience can be built within each SHAPES Data Value Network. This understanding can help guide the design of governance for each SHAPES network, and for the system of SHAPES network systems. Intensive interaction among the many diverse actors of the network enhances relationships and trust so that common problems can be defined collaboratively so that all network partners are motivated to solve them together. To ensure continuity in the collaboration and co-creation of a network, both vulnerabilities and interdependencies are considered by agile communication. This helps in addressing any potential disruptions to network interactions.

Carefully considering these attributes can be done as a group, which can promote open communication and sharing of information. This in turn can build purpose and common aims, as well as trust among the stakeholders of for the network. These facilitate collaboration and agreement on organization and roles within SHAPES data value networks, and to develop leadership, common culture, and ways of working in them.

5. Conclusions

Resilience can be strengthened through a deeper understanding of the relevant processes and tools that each organization uses and by analysing and evaluating the effects on the safety of critical infrastructure. Master's students in safety management conducted risk assessment workshops and compiled a list of characteristics to enhance the sustainability of stakeholder collaborative networks. In this case study, the students aimed to enhance the resilience of collaborative networks by gaining a more thorough understanding of the processes and tools employed by each organization. Their primary focus was to analyse and evaluate the effects of these processes on the safety of critical infrastructure. These attributes were then prioritized and embedded in the risk matrix.

The results show the resilience of collaboration networks as the most important factors are presented in the following Table 4.

Table 4: Cybersecurity themes and their key features

Attribute	Definition
Clear purpose and common objectives	Having a well-defined purpose and shared objectives among network participants.
Roles and responsibilities of stakeholders	Clearly defining the roles and responsibilities of each stakeholder within the network.
Common operational culture	Fostering a cohesive and unified operational culture across the network.
Leadership and coordination defined	Establishing effective leadership and coordination mechanisms within the collaborative network.
Collaboration and co-creation facilitated	Encouraging and enabling collaboration and co-creation among the stakeholders.
Systems back-up Development	Implementing systems back-up measures to ensure continuity in case of disruptions.
Trust building between stakeholders	Building and maintaining trust among all network stakeholders.
Open communication in information sharing	Promoting open and transparent communication for efficient information sharing.

The findings of the study highlighted the main contributes to the resilience of collaborative networks. Organizations and stakeholders can enhance their ability to withstand disruptions and adapt effectively in the face of uncertainties by incorporating these factors into their strategies and practices.

The practical contribution of this study is a tool to measure relevant attributes of the resilience of networked activities. This tool will be tested and further developed in project DYNAMO where networked experts collaborate with end-users to develop the DYNAMO-platform that will combine business continuity management (BCM) and cyber threat intelligence (CTI). The contribution to theory is a deeper understanding of how the attributes of resilience in networks can help increase the continuity of their collaboration. The economic impacts of such networks as a basis to focus on resilience is an interesting direction for further studies, which could include a review of literature on collaborative networks from a business context.

Acknowledgements

This study has received funding by the European Union projects ECHO, which has received funding from the European Union's Horizon 2020 research and innovation programme under the grant agreement no. 830943, and DYNAMO, under grant agreement no. 101069601. The views expressed are those of the author(s) only and do not necessarily reflect those of the European Union. Neither the European Union nor the granting authority can be held responsible for them.

References

Amir, S., Kant, V., 2018. Sociotechnical Resilience: A Preliminary Concept. Risk Analysis 38, 8–16. https://doi.org/10.1111/risa.12816

Benbasat, I., Goldstein, D.K., Mead, M., 1987. The Case Research Strategy in Studies of Information Systems. MIS Quarterly 11, 369–386. https://doi.org/10.2307/248684

Bergenhenegouwen, G.J., 1996. Competence development - a challenge for HRM professionals: core competences of organizations as guidelines for the development of employees. Journal of European Industrial Training 20, 29–35. https://doi.org/10.1108/03090599610150282

Berio, G., Harzallah, M., 2005. Knowledge Management for Competence Management. J.UKM 0, 21–28.

Burdon, S., Mooney, G.R., Al-Kilidar, H., 2015. Navigating service sector innovation using co-creation partnerships. Journal of Service Theory and Practice 25, 285–303.

do Nascimento Souto, P.C., 2013. Beyond knowledge, towards knowing: the practice-based approach to support knowledge creation, communication, and use for innovation. RAI Revista de Administração e Inovação 10, 51–79.

Draheim, D., Pirinen, R., 2011. Towards exploiting social software for business continuity management, in: 22nd International Workshop on Database and Expert Systems Applications. IEEE, pp. 279–283.

Dubé, L., Pare, G., 2003. Rigor In Information Systems Positivist Case Research: Current Practices, Trends, and Recommendations. MIS Quarterly 27, 597–635. https://doi.org/10.2307/30036550

DYNAMO project, 2023. Dynamic Resilience Assessment Method [WWW Document]. URL https://horizon-dynamo.eu/wp-content/uploads/2023/01/DYNAMO_Leaflet_web.pdf (accessed 1.24.24).

Eisenberger, R., Malone, G.P., Presson, W.D., 2016. Optimizing Perceived Organizational Support to Enhance Employee Engagement.

European Parliament and the Council, 2006. Recommendation of the European Parliament and of the Council of 18 December 2006 on key competences for lifelong learning. Official Journal of the European Union L394/310, 19.

Fagerberg, J., Fosaas, M., Sapprasert, K., 2012. Innovation: Exploring the knowledge base. Research Policy, Exploring the Emerging Knowledge Base of "The Knowledge Society" 41, 1132–1153. https://doi.org/10.1016/j.respol.2012.03.008

Grunig, L.A., Grunig, J.E., Ehling, W.P., 1992. What is an effective organization?, in: Excellence in Public Relations and Communication Management. Routledge, New York, p. 26.

Hakanen, M., Soudunsaari, A., 2012. Building Trust in High-Performing Teams. Technology Innovation Management Review 2, 38–41. https://doi.org/10.22215/timreview/567

Hautamäki, A., 2010. Sustainable innovation: a new age of innovation and Finland's innovation policy. Sitra.

Kallio, K., Lappalainen, I., 2015. Organizational learning in an innovation network: Enhancing the agency of public service organizations. Journal of Service Theory and Practice 25, 140–161. https://doi.org/10.1108/JSTP-09-2013-0198

Lepak, D.P., Snell, S.A., 1999. The Human Resource Architecture: Toward a Theory of Human Capital Allocation and Development. AMR 24, 31–48. https://doi.org/10.5465/amr.1999.1580439

Levitt, B., March, J.G., 1988. Organizational Learning. Annual Review of Sociology 14, 319–340.

Linkov, I., Bridges, T., Creutzig, F., Decker, J., Fox-Lent, C., Kröger, W., Lambert, J.H., Levermann, A., Montreuil, B., Nathwani, J., 2014. Changing the resilience paradigm. Nature Climate Change 4, 407–409.

Linkov, I., Eisenberg, D.A., Plourde, K., Seager, T.P., Allen, J., Kott, A., 2013. Resilience metrics for cyber systems. Environment Systems and Decisions 33, 471–476.

Mitleton-Kelly, E., 2003. Ten principles of complexity and enabling infrastructures, in: Complex Systems and Evolutionary Perspectives on Organisations: The Application of Complexity Theory to Organisations. Pergamon, An Imprint of Elsevier Science, London UK, pp. 23–50.

NATO-EU Task Force, 2023. EU-NATO Task Force on the Resilience of Critical Infrastructure (Final Assessment Report). NATO-EU Task Force.

Ojasalo, J., 2012. Challenges of Innovation Networks: Empirical Findings. International Journal of Management Cases 14, 6–17.

Oksanen, K., Hautamäki, A., 2014. Transforming regions into innovation ecosystems: A model for renewing local industrial structures. The Innovation Journal 19, 16.

O'Rourke, T.D., Briggs, T.R., 2007. Critical Infrastructure, Interdependencies, and Resilience. The Bridge 22–29.

Otala, L., Jaskari, J., Vartiainen, M. (Eds.), 2004. Oppivien organisaatioiden tunnuspiirteet. Helsinki University of Technology, Department of Industrial Engineering and Management, Espoo.

Palttala, P., Vos, M., 2012. Quality Indicators for Crisis Communication to Support Emergency Management by Public Authorities. Journal of Contingencies and Crisis Management 20, 39–51. https://doi.org/10.1111/j.1468-5973.2011.00654.x

Pappalardo, S.M., Niemiec, M., Bozhilova, M., Stoianov, N., Dziech, A., Stiller, B., 2020. Multi-sector Assessment Framework – a New Approach to Analyse Cybersecurity Challenges and Opportunities, in: Dziech, A., Mees, W., Czyżewski, A. (Eds.), Multimedia Communications, Services and Security, Communications in Computer and Information Science. Springer International Publishing, Cham, pp. 1–15. https://doi.org/10.1007/978-3-030-59000-0_1

Pichyangkul, C., Nuttavuthisit, K., Israsena, P., 2012. Co-creation at the front-end: a systematic process for radical innovation. International Journal of Innovation, Management and Technology 3, 121–127.

Pirinen, R., 2017. Towards Common Information Systems Maturity Validation : Resilience Readiness Levels (ResRL), in: In Proceedings of the 9th International Joint Conference on Knowledge Discovery, Knowledge Engineering and Knowledge Management. Science and Technology Publications, pp. 259–266. https://doi.org/10.5220/0006450802590266

Rajamäki, J., Ruoslahti, H., 2021. ECHO Federated Cyber Range as a Tool for Validating SHAPES Services, in: Proceeding of the 20th European Conference on Cyber Warfare and Security ECCWS 2021. Academic Conferences International, Reading, UK, pp. 623–627. https://doi.org/10.34190/EWS.21.076

Rajamäki, J., Ruoslahti, H., 2018. Educational competences with regard to critical infrastructure protection, in: ECCWS 2018: Proceedings of the 17th'European Conference on Cyber Warfare and Security. pp. 415–423.

Ruoslahti, H., 2019. Co-creation of Knowledge for Innovation in Multi-stakeholder Projects (Doctoral dissertation). University of Jyväskylä, Jyväskylä.

Ruoslahti, H., Rajamäki, J., Koski, E., 2018. Educational Competences with regard to Resilience of Critical Infrastructure. Journal of Information Warfare 17, 1–16.

Savage, M., 2002. Business continuity planning. Work study 51, 254–261.

Stanciugelu, I., Alpas, H., Florin, S.D., Bozoglu, F., 2013. Perception and communication of terrorism risk on food supply chain: A case study (Romania and Turkey), in: Applied Social Sciences: Communication Studies. Cambridge Scholars Publishing, Newcastle upon Tyne, UK, pp. 189–196.

Tikanmäki, I., Räsänen, J., Ruoslahti, H., 2022. Information Sharing Networks for European Land and Maritime Border Authorities. Presented at the 26th International Conference on Circuits, Systems, Communications and Computers (CSCC), IEEE, Crete, Greece, pp. 149–160. https://doi.org/10.1109/CSCC55931.2022.00035

Vos, M., 2017. Communication in turbulent times: Exploring issue arenas and crisis communication to enhance organisational resilience. Vos & Schoemaker, Jyväskylä.

Vos, M., Schoemaker, H., Luoma-aho, V., 2014. Setting the agenda for research on issue arenas. Corporate Communications: An International Journal 19, 200–215. https://doi.org/10.1108/CCIJ-08-2012-0055

Wan, T., Geraets, A.A., Doty, C.M., Saitta, E.K.H., Chini, J.J., 2020. Characterizing science graduate teaching assistants' instructional practices in reformed laboratories and tutorials. IJ STEM Ed 7, 30. https://doi.org/10.1186/s40594-020-00229-0

Westermann, K.D., 2011. Learning the "Craft of Auditing": Applications of the Cognitive Apprenticeship Framework (Ph.D.). ProQuest Dissertations and Theses. Bentley University, United States -- Massachusetts.

Yin, R.K., 2009. Case study research: Design and methods, 4th ed. Thousand Oaks, CA: Sage Publications.

Business Model Canvas and Competition to Understand Exploitation of Cybersecurity Project Results

Harri Ruoslahti [1], Eveliina Hytönen[1] and Luis Angel Galindo Sanchez[2]

[1] Security and Risk Management, Laurea University of Applied Sciences, Finland

[2] Cybersecurity, Telefonica S.A., Spain

https://orcid.org/ 0000-0001-9726-7956

https://orcid.org/ 0000-0002-2808-3229

https://orcid.org/ 0000-0000-0000-0000

Harri.ruoslahti@laurea.fi
Eveliina.hytonen@laurea.fi
Luisangel.galindosanchez@telefonica.com

Abstract: The European Commission (EC) has lately funded 22 different cybersecurity projects (European Commission, 2024), and the European Union (EU) expects a return for the investment and requires these projects to demonstrate efficient exploitation activities that emphasize their influence on the European economy. The Business Model Canvas (BMC) is a tool to actively guide discussion and processes that evolve and adapt based on their environments. Yet, the tool does not address the competition on the marketplace. For this reason, this study introduces the 'Business Model Canvas and Competition' (BMC&C) by including the element of competence to the traditional BMC and examines its usefulness to understand the relations between an organisation and its competitive environment. The data collection method for this study was action research through actively participating in the exploitation workshops activities and reading what materials were produced. The BMC by Osterwalder and Pigneur (2011) consists of the nine building blocks. This study modified the BMC as a framework of analysis by adding tenth building block 'Competition' (&C) that acknowledges that an organization is not alone but is part of a market where it encounters competition by active direct competitors and by indirect alternative ways to achieve similar results. This tenth building block 'Competition' (&C) was deemed important to better understand what possible competitive advantages and challenges the analysed assets of the ECHO project may encounter. The BMC&C was used in ECHO exploitation workshop that addressed the ECHO asset ECHO Early Warning System (E-EWS). The E-EWS asset BMC&C example show that users found the BMC&C easy to use. As the &C was added as a tenth element or building block the use of the tool was familiar to anyone who had used a conventional BMC. Those who had no prior experience of the BMC tool received guidance from the more experienced users. The workshops included active and co-creative discussions that shaped the outcomes of the BMC&C for each individual ECHO asset. The results of this study indicate that the BMC&C can be a valuable tool to assess how an organisation that is active in a marketplace may need to take their competition into account. The contribution of this study to practice is a deeper understanding of competition and market on a very practical case level, while its contribution to theory is the accumulation of data from multiple cases.

Keywords: Business Model Canvas, Competition, Cyber Range, Co-Creation

1. Introduction

The latest round of European Commission (EC) funding included 22 cybersecurity projects, which together receive €10.9 million in funding (European Commission, 2024). This is an investment for the European Union (EU), which is why its funding instruments, such as Horizon and the Digital Europe program require efficient exploitation activities to emphasize the influence that these funded projects have on European economy. Di Cagno et al. (2014, p. 853) write: "given the large and increasing amount of European resources devoted to promote scientific co-operations among countries, it is important trying to assess their actual technological and economic impact." Project results should be taken up by end users, policymakers, industry, and the scientific community (European Commission, 2014).

Projects can be seen to function as organizations, they have action plans, visions, missions, budgets, and time and exploitation plans. A very important objective of funded projects is that they expand the benefits of their results throughout the European Union. Exploitation of project results is, thus a key activity that builds lasting impacts for projects that develop cybersecurity solutions. Business Model Canvas (BMC) can be a useful practical tool to actively guide discussion and processes in a way where they evolve and adapt to their changing environments (Fritscher and Pigneur, 2015). Despite this notion of adapting to the environment, the BCM tool does not address the competitive situation on the marketplace. For this reason, this study introduces the 'Business Model Canvas and Competition' (BMC&C) by including the element of competition to the traditional BMC and examines its usefulness to understand the relations between an organisation and its competitive environment.

This BMC&C ideology was developed by the author at Laurea University of Applied Sciences, to provide students who use the BMC for business concept analysis, with a better view of what competitive elements the business may encounter on the marketplace. Students have found the framework useful. So, this concept was also adopted in practice in the ECHO project efforts, in a series of exploitation workshops that analysed how the main outputs of the project can be take advantage of by the project partners as a future business.

This paper contributes to the pathway from the development of cybersecurity solutions to their practical uptake. This contribution will mainly be toward the body of knowledge regarding e-business. By using a structured framework to describe the business models of each partner organization in relation to the solutions and assets that were developed in this case project. When identifying opportunities, it is very relevant to also look at competition, which is why we offer a Business Model Canvas (BMC) that also includes the element of competition (&C).

The transition from idea to market-ready innovation is not easy. One way to facilitate the exploitation of developed solutions is to map potential opportunities as business models when offering e.g., risk analysis, modelling, and early warning solutions for critical infrastructure protection (as in project ECHO), or incident response strategies (as in project DYNAMO).

The research question of this study: Can the BMC&C help address competition on the marketplace?

2. Literature Review

This section discusses customer relationships and organizational focus on relationships and how these can be visualised with the Business Model Canvas (BMC) approach.

2.1 Customer Relationships

Project communication and dissemination activities should begin early enough, ideally at the start of the project to create and expand stakeholder communities; it is in the interest of the EC that "as many end users as possible adopt new innovations, which in turn will generate more business possibilities for the industry, and further research projects for the academia" (Henriksson, Ruoslahti & Hyttinen, 2018; p. 211). Funded cybersecurity projects often include end-user and stakeholder relationships that can be looked as being similar to customer relationships.

Customer relationships direct organizational focus on relationships rather than on transactions, (Vargo & Lusch, 2008; Vargo & Lusch, 2004). According to Holmlund (2004) relationships take place between two counterparts as developing and evolving sequences of interactions, as goal-oriented activities to establish, develop, and maintain successful exchanges between company and customer (Morgan & Hunt 1994; Deszczynski & Beresewicz, 2021). Relationships can be seen as a means and a result for organizations operating with one another in network settings (Holmlund, 2004). Establishing a customer relationship evolves in two stages: first attracting a customer and second actively building this relationship to achieve the economic goals set for the relationship (Grönroos, 1994). Companies need to engage in interaction through various means, to have meaningful relationships with its customers, and successfully satisfy their needs (Payne, 2005), by seeing these relationships through the meaningful individual encounters and experiences by each counterpart (Holmlund, 2004).

Customers can, thus be viewed as assets for the business, as the market value for a company or cybersecurity solution can be viewed as possible future profit streams that can become generated over the lifespan of the customer relationship (Payne, 2005). Negative critical incidents may threaten to terminate a relationship, while a positively handled critical incident may have the potential to strengthen and deepen it (Holmlund, 2004). Exceptional service can become a key differentiator because of consistency of service with continuous customer input and involvement is very difficult to imitate (Payne, 2005), and can be analysed as elements on an episode and a relationship level (Storbacka, Strandvik & Grönroos, 1994).

According to Grönroos (1994) establishing, maintaining, and enhancing relationships with customers and partners, "is achieved by a mutual exchange and fulfilment of promises" (p. 9). Relationship strength is important when implementing customer relationship enhancing actions (Storbacka et. al., 1994); service customers themselves create value when use the resources provided by the service provider, making the customer into a value creator (Grönroos & Helle, 2010), and besides personal contacts, the Internet is a powerful tool to involve customers in one-to-one dialogue, and to capture data that can help understand what a customer may want (Payne, 2005).

Putting focus on the specific context of one customer at a time can, as iterative process where new ideas are likely to emerge, promote the analysis and development of a business model (Ojasalo & Ojasalo, 2015). Galvagno and Dalli (2014) note that literature on co-creation mostly emerges from management and marketing studies, service management, and consumer research. Knowing what forms of interaction can lead to intertwined successful customer relationships is important (Grönroos & Helle, 2010), as successful co-creation processes need active facilitation (Ruoslahti, 2018). "Successful companies harness the creativity and energy of stakeholders by establishing projects and systems for marrying their collaborators' interests with corporate knowledge and resources" (Bhalla, 2014, p. 19). Co-creation can enhance innovation and unlock new sources of competitive advantage and occurs in physical and/or digital arenas, where users are innovators, co-designers, and co-producers, as members of open-innovation networks that integrate user-cantered collaboration, research, and innovation (Leminen, Westerlund & Nyström, 2012).

2.2 Business Model Canvas

Osterwalder and Pigneur (2011; 2013) introduced the Business Model Canvas (BMC) that uses design-thinking processes to explore business models and patterns. The BMC by Osterwalder and Pigneur (2010) consists of nine building blocks. 1) Customer segments refers to the different groups of people and organisations that the company aims to reach and serve. 2) Channels describes how the company reaches its customer segments and communicates with them. 3) Customer relationships defines what types of relationships the company establishes with the identified customer segments. 4) Value proposition describes the products and services that create value for specific customer segments (with characteristics such as novelty, performance, customisation, status, accessibility, convenience, usability, price, cost, or risk reduction). 5) Revenue stream represents the sales revenues that the company generates from each segment. 6) Key resources are the most important assets that are required to successfully provide the products or services to the customer segments. 7) Key activities describe what the company must do to make the business model work (e.g., production, problem-solving, platform and networking activities). 8) Key partnerships constitute the network of suppliers and partners (these may be strategic alliances sub-contractors, providers, joint ventures and even competitors) that enable to successfully make the business model work, and to develop new business or buyer–supplier relationships. 9) Cost structure describes all costs incurred to operate the business model (Figure 1).

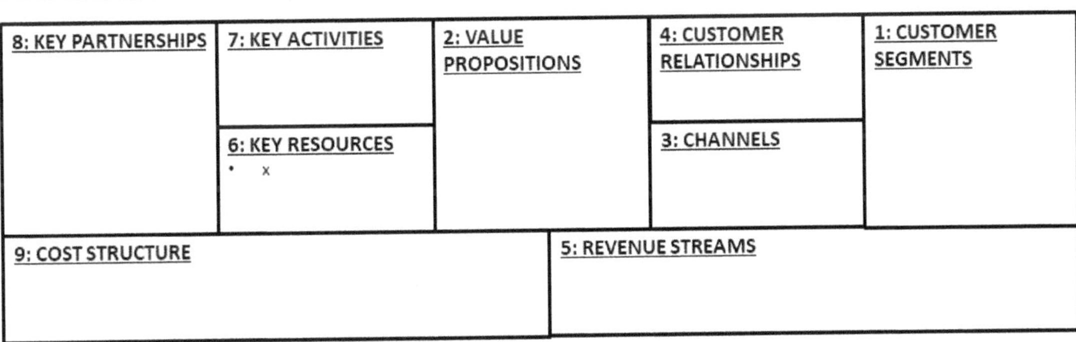

8: KEY PARTNERSHIPS
7: KEY ACTIVITIES
2: VALUE PROPOSITIONS
4: CUSTOMER RELATIONSHIPS
1: CUSTOMER SEGMENTS
6: KEY RESOURCES
• x
3: CHANNELS
9: COST STRUCTURE
5: REVENUE STREAMS

Figure 1: Business Model Canvas (BMC). Modified Osterwalder and Pigneur (2011; 2013)

Ojasalo and Ojasalo (2018) offer a modified business model framework that they call Service Logic Business Model Canvas (Figure 2). They base their views on an interactive research process, where they have addressed each building block of the canvas separately, and the entire canvas. This step-by-step development has offered several revisions during the research process. The authors note that in the beginning of their process they found as the most evident development needs of the BMC: how to highlight the customer's active role and add the notion of the customer as a value creator and the company supporting that value creation (Grönroos, 2008; Heinonen et al., 2010).

7: KEY PARTNERS	6: KEY RESOURCES	2: VALUE PROPOSITIONS	3: VALUE CREATION	1: CUSTOMER'S WORLD & DESIRE FOR IDEAL VALUE
	8: MOBILIZING RESOURCES & PARTNERS		4: INTERACTION & CO-PRODUCTION	
9: COST STRUCTURE		5: REVENUE STREAMS & METRICS		

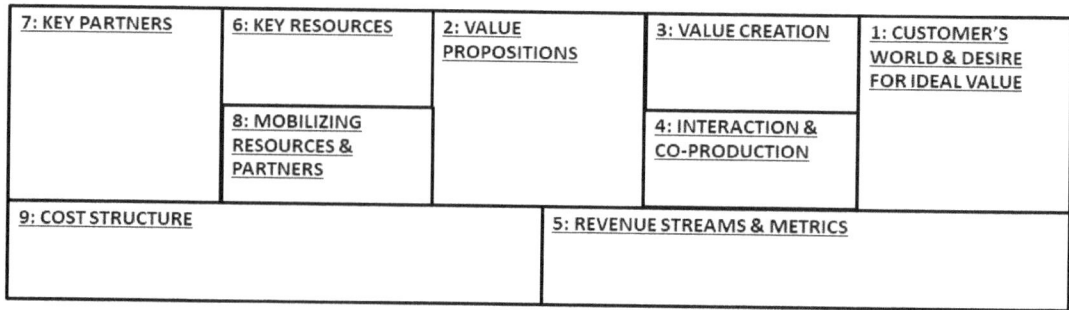

Figure 2: Service Logic Business Model Canvas (SLMC). Modified Ojasalo and Ojasalo (2018)

Like the original BMC (Osterwalder and Pigneur, 2011), this Service Logic Business Model Canvas (SLMC) framework by Ojasalo and Ojasalo (2018) has nine building blocks. The authors have kept to the original structure and redesigned these to be more service logic oriented. This provides an opportunity to compare the original BMC and the modified SLMC to easier understand differences between traditional business thinking and service logic-based thinking.

Sparviero (2019) sees that a most obvious limitation to the BMC instrument is its focus on the organization and being conceptually isolated from its environment, be it industry, society, or natural environments; and suggests two additional building blocks for the treatment of "social and environmental costs and benefits as 'externalities': also, for-profit organizations have an indirect social impact (e.g., economic growth, job creation and poverty reduction), which is a by-product of their pursuit of economic value". (p. 238) in the Social Enterprise Model Canvas (SEMC), which is an instrument that better frames and explains how Social Enterprises (SE) and their intended beneficiaries create value.

Fritscher and Pigneur (2015) note that the BCM can be useful when used by novice, expert, or master user. For the novice user the BMC can provide a simple common language and help with visualization; the expert may use the BMC to create a holistic vision to understand the sustainability of the business model, which requires understanding the methods (e.g., high level links, colours) of the model to connect ideas and follow the interactions. Master users may use the BMC to understand even global strategy, with evolving processes that adapt to their environments. These users will need to "understand that the design of a model has to accompany such a process by supporting concepts of iteration, transformation (mutation) and choosing alternatives (selection)" (p. 89).

3. Method

The data collection method for this study was action research through actively participating in the exploitation workshops activities and reading what materials were produced (Denzin & Lincoln, 1995). The ECHO outcomes are solution-based services, so the modified BMC with an added tenth building block 'and competition' (&C) was deemed most appropriate to be used as a framework of analysis.

The 'business model canvas and competition' or BMC&C acknowledges that ECHO consortium members that are planning to exploit the ECHO cybersecurity solutions are not alone, but that the project is part of a market where it encounters competition by active direct competitors and by indirect alternative ways to achieve similar results (Figure 3).

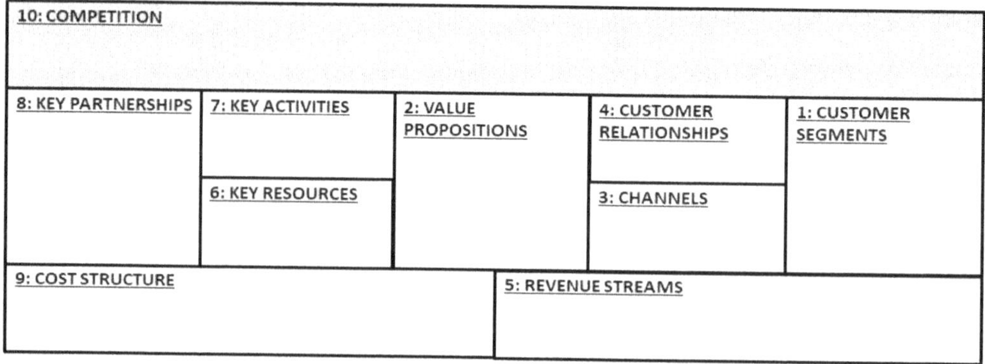

Figure 3: The Business Model Canvas and Competition (BMC&C) as a tool of analysis and co-creation.

This tenth building block 'and Competition' (&C) was deemed important to better understand what possible competitive advantages and challenges the analysed ECHO assets may encounter. Thus, the BMC&C was chosen as the framework of analysis for ECHO exploitation workshops. The ECHO project developed six assets and a network of cyber-research and competence centres (Figure 4), which were each assessed in the exploitation workshops.

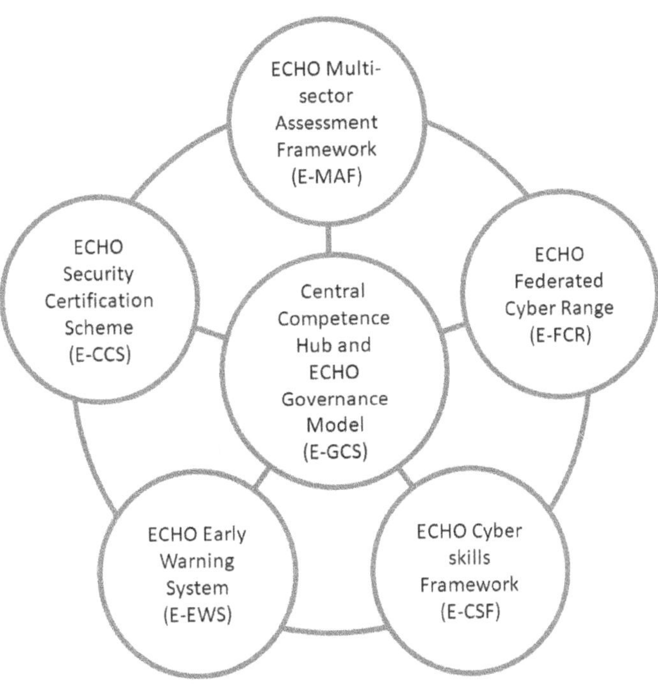

Figure 4: ECHO assets (Ruoslahti & Davis, 2021).

In an effort to address European cyber security gaps, the project has developed an adaptive model for information sharing and collaboration among the wider network of cybersecurity centres within a multiple-sector context, supported by a framework for improved cyber-skills development and technology roadmap delivery, and an early warning system (Ruoslahti & Davis, 2021), which constitute the five operational interconnected ECHO assets that are governed by Central competence hub and governance model (Figure 4).

The ECHO exploitation workshops used the BMC&C to analyse each of the ECHO assets, and the results helped understand how these assets can become exploited after the competition of the project, and to compile the ECHO Exploitation Plan. This study presents the results of the ECHO Early Warning System (E-EWS) BMC&C, which was filled during the E-EWS exploitation workshop.

4. Results

The results of this work show that using the BMC&C can bring clarity to understand the effects of the added element of markets and competition. Figure 4 shows one example of the BMC&C applied to the ECHO asset Early Warning System (E-EWS). Similar BMC&Cs were created for the assets as well.

4.1 E-EWS Example

The ECHO Exploitation workshops addressed each of the ECHO assets. This section looks, as an example, at the E-EWS. The results show how the BMC&C was used to evaluate this asset by filling out the ten building blocks of the canvas. The canvas completed in an interactive ideathon workshop attended by ECHO asset owners and project partner representatives (n = 18).

Possible identified E-EWS customer segments are for one the main European cybersecurity agencies e.g., ENISA, or relevant active projects initiatives. Other major segments are the European Computer Emergency Response Teams (CERT), who are information security experts that are responsible for the protection against, detection of, and response to cybersecurity incidents, or the different sector specific associations and networks. Also, many businesses can benefit from using E-EWS, e.g., international corporations can information between the multiple countries that may have different national legislation and operational cultures (Figure 5).

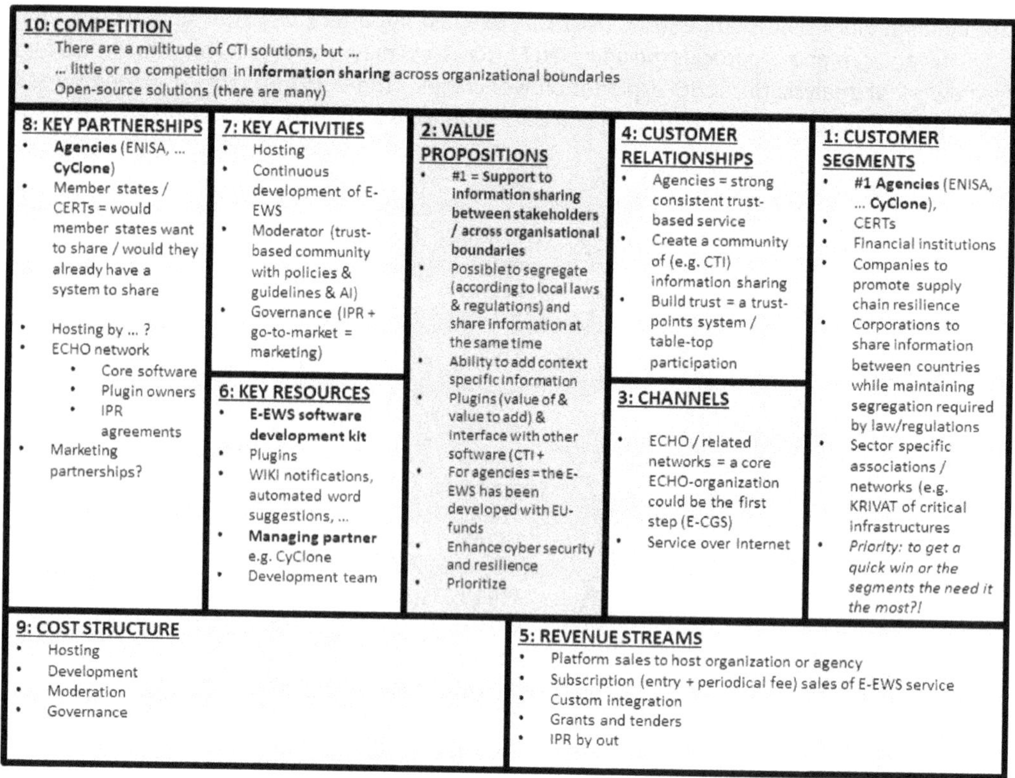

10: COMPETITION
There are a multitude of CTI solutions, but ...
... little or no competition in information sharing across organizational boundaries
Open-source solutions (there are many)
8: KEY PARTNERSHIPS
Agencies (ENISA, ... CyClone)
Member states / CERTs = would member states want to share / would they already have a system to share
Hosting by ... ?
ECHO network
Core software
Plugin owners
IPR agreements
Marketing partnerships?
7: KEY ACTIVITIES
Hosting
Continuous development of E-EWS
Moderator (trust-based community with policies & guidelines & AI)
Governance (IPR + go-to-market = marketing)
6: KEY RESOURCES
E-EWS software development kit
Plugins
WIKI notifications, automated word suggestions, ...
Managing partner e.g. CyClone
Development team
2: VALUE PROPOSITIONS
#1 = Support to information sharing between stakeholders / across organisational boundaries
Possible to segregate (according to local laws & regulations) and share information at the same time
Ability to add context specific information
Plugins (value of & value to add) & interface with other software (CTI +
For agencies = the E-EWS has been developed with EU-funds
Enhance cyber security and resilience
Prioritize
4: CUSTOMER RELATIONSHIPS
Agencies = strong consistent trust-based service
Create a community of (e.g. CTI) information sharing
Build trust = a trust-points system / table-top participation
3: CHANNELS
ECHO / related networks = a core ECHO-organization could be the first step (E-CGS)
Service over Internet
1: CUSTOMER SEGMENTS
#1 Agencies (ENISA, ... CyClone),
CERTs
Financial institutions
Companies to promote supply chain resilience
Corporations to share information between countries while maintaining segregation required by law/regulations
Sector specific associations / networks (e.g. KRIVAT of critical infrastructures
Priority: to get a quick win or the segments the need it the most?!
9: COST STRUCTURE
Hosting
Development
Moderation
Governance
5: REVENUE STREAMS
Platform sales to host organization or agency
Subscription (entry + periodical fee) sales of E-EWS service
Custom integration
Grants and tenders
IPR by out

Figure 5: The Business Model Canvas and Competition (BMC&C) example (based on ECHO Exploitation workshops)

The main E-EWS value proposition is to support information sharing between stakeholders and across organisational boundaries. There is a possibility to segregate, according to local laws and regulations, and share information, and at the same time add context specific information through, e.g., E-EWS plugins that add value by interfacing with other software, such as cyber threat intelligence (CTI) to enhance cyber security and resilience.

Relevant channels for the ECHO early warning systems can be related networks, and a core ECHO-organization could be the first step to establish the core competence hub and governance model (E-CGS), with the E-EWS as a service over Internet. Customer relationships can be cybersecurity related agencies, with a strong consistent trust-based service to create communities of e.g., CTI and information sharing. One important focus is to build trust.

Revenue Streams could be from platform sales to host organizations or agencies through sales of subscription, with entry and periodical fee for an E-EWS service custom integration. Also, grants and tenders can provide future revenue streams, as can intellectual property rights (IPR) by-out.

Key resources for E-EWS development are a software development kit, plugins, web-based collaborative platforms (WIKI), notifications, and automated word suggestions. WIKI web sites allow users to add and update content on the site. Future E-EWS development would need a responsible managing partner and an active development team that can manage needed key activities, such as hosting, continuous development, and moderation of the future trust-based community with appropriate policies, guidelines, and artificial intelligence (AI). The ECHO governance (E-CGS) should guide IPR and go-to-market activities.

E-EWS key partnerships can be European agencies, such as ENISA, Member States, relevant CERTs to share what information Member States want to share. Hosting could by the ECHO network, and partnerships may include core software providers, plugin owners, IPR agreements, and marketing partnerships. The E-EWS cost structure can entail hosting, development, moderation, and governance.

The participants found the BCM&C easy to use. The competition (&C) idea added as the tenth element of the tool. The workshops included co-creative active discussions to shape the outcomes of the BMC&C for this ECHO E-EWS asset.

5. Conclusions

The results of this study indicate that the BMC&C can be a valuable tool to assess how an organisation that is active in a marketplace may need to take their competition into account.

The E-EWS and the other asset BMC&C examples show that users found the BMC&C easy to use. As the &C was added as a tenth element or building block the use of the tool was familiar to anyone who had used a conventional BMC. Those who had no prior experience of the BMC tool received guidance from the experienced, so the workshops included active and co-creative discussions that shaped the outcomes of the BMC&C for each individual ECHO asset.

Including the element of competition and markets highlights that no organization is in a vacuum, but that it is influenced by its competitive environment. This notion helps remind that all business decisions need to consider both its customers and its competitors. It is not only the business that makes value propositions to customers, also its competitors make their respective value propositions to the same customers.

The activities described in this paper assisted ECHO partners in formulating firstly to make sense of the exploitation opportunities for each partner organization, and secondly in developing a relevant exploitation plan for the project. The results of this work can benefit academic scholars in bridging engineering and business on both in theory and in applying theory to practice. Any practitioner organization, be it private or public, that are engaged in providing solutions or services that address cyber security can benefit from this work to identify commercial opportunities by mapping their business model and understanding the competitive environment that they face.

The BMC provides a useful basis to both analyse and present the business concept of a business. By adding the competition as a building block, the BMC&C adds a view to the elements that are outside of the organisation. This viewpoint is needed to understand how the organisation can and needs to adapt to external influences, which is also relevant for impactful exploitation activities by the many cybersecurity initiatives and projects that receive EU funding. Building cybersecurity solutions is not only developing technology, but also building and nurturing customer relationships, and having an eye on one's competition.

Acknowledgement

This study has received funding by the European Union projects ECHO, which has received funding from the European Union's Horizon 2020 research and innovation programme under the grant agreement no. 830943, and DYNAMO, under grant agreement no. 101069601. The views expressed are those of the author(s) only and do not necessarily reflect those of the European Union. Neither the European Union nor the granting authority can be held responsible for them.

References

Bhalla, G. (2014) How to plan and manage a project to co-create value with stakeholders, Strategy & Leadership, 2014, 42, 2, 19-25, Emerald Group Publishing, Limited, Chicago, United Kingdom, Chicago.

Denzin, N. K., & Lincoln, Y. S. (1995). Transforming qualitative research methods: Is it a revolution?. Journal of Contemporary Ethnography, 24(3), 349-358.

Deszczynski, B. & Beresewicz, M. (2021). The maturity of relationship management and firm performance – A step toward relationship management middle-range theory. Journal of business research, 135, 358-372.

Di Cagno, D., Fabrizi, A., and Meliciani, V. (2014). The impact of participation in European joint research projects on knowledge creation and economic growth, Journal of Technology Transfer, Vol. 39, 6, 836-858.

European Commission (2024). Shaping Europe's digital future, 22 Cybersecurity projects selected to receive €10.9 million, (https://digital-strategy.ec.europa.eu/en/policies/22-cybersecurity-projects-selected, accessed March 8 2024).

European Commission (2014). Horizon 2020, Communicating EU research and innovation guidance for project participants, Version 1.0, 25 September 2014.

Fritscher, B., & Pigneur, Y. (2015, July). Extending the business model canvas: A dynamic perspective. In Proc. International Symposium on Business Modeling and Software Design (Vol. 5, pp. 86-96). ScitePress.

Galvagno, M. & Dalli, D. (2014) Theory of value co-creation: a systematic literature review, Managing Service Quality, 2014, 24, 6, 643, Emerald Group Publishing, Limited, Bedford, United Kingdom, Bedford.

Gronroos, C. (1994). From Marketing Mix to Relationship Marketing: Towards a Paradigm Shift in Marketing. Management decision, 32(2), 322-20.

Grönroos, C. & Helle, P. (2010). Adopting a service logic in manufacturing: Conceptual foundation and metrics for mutual value creation. Journal of service management, 21(5), 564-590.

Heinonen, K., Strandvik, T., Mickelsson, K. J., Edvardsson, B., Sundström, E., & Andersson, P. (2010). A customer-dominant logic of service. Journal of Service management, 21(4), 531-548.

Holmlund, M. (2004). Analyzing business relationships and distinguishing different interaction levels. Industrial marketing management, 33(4), 279–287.

Leminen, S., Westerlund, M. & Nyström, A-G. (2012) Living Labs as Open-Innovation Networks, Technology Innovation Management Review, 2012, 2, 9, 6-11, Talent First Network, Ottawa, Canada, Ottawa.

Morgan, R. M. & Hunt, S. D. (1994). The Commitment-Trust Theory of Relationship Marketing. Journal of marketing, 58(3), 20.

Ojasalo, J., & Ojasalo, K. (2018). Service logic business model canvas. Journal of research in marketing and entrepreneurship, 70 - 97.

Ojasalo, K. & Ojasalo, J. (2015), Adapting Business Model Thinking to Service Logic: an Empirical Study on Developing a Service Design Tool, in The Nordic School – Service Marketing and Management for the Future, edited by Johanna Gummerus & Catharina Von Koskull, Hanken School of Economics, Helsinki, Finland, pp. 309-333.

Osterwalder, A., & Pigneur, Y. (2013). Designing business models and similar strategic objects: the contribution of IS. Journal of the Association for information systems, 14(5), 237.

Osterwalder, A., & Pigneur, Y. (2011). Aligning profit and purpose through business model innovation. Responsible management practices for the 21st century, 61-76.

Payne, A. (2005). Handbook of CRM: Achieving excellence in customer management. Routledge.

Ruoslahti, H. 2018. Co-creation of Knowledge for Innovation Requires Multi-Stakeholder Public Relations. In Bowman, S., Crookes, A., Romenti, S., Ihlen, Ø. (Eds) Public Relations and the Power of Creativity, Advances in Public Relations and Communication Management, Volume 3, Emerald Publishing Limited, 115-133

Ruoslahti, H., & Davis, B. (2021). Societal Impacts of Cyber Security Assets of Project ECHO. WSEAS Transactions on Environment and Development, 17, 1274-1283.

Sparviero, S. (2019). The case for a socially oriented business model canvas: The social enterprise model canvas. Journal of Social Entrepreneurship, 10(2), 232-251.

Storbacka, K., Strandvik, T. & Grönroos, C. (1994). Managing Customer Relationships for Profit: The Dynamics of Relationship Quality. International journal of service industry management, 5(5), 21-38.

Vargo, S. L. & Lusch, R. F. (2004). Evolving to a New Dominant Logic for Marketing. Journal of marketing, 68(1), 1-17.

Vargo, S. L. & Lusch, R. F. (2008). From goods to service(s): Divergences and convergences of logics. Industrial marketing management, 37(3), 254-259. Walter, A. I., Helgenberger, S., Wiek, A. & Scholz, R. W. (2007). Measuring societal effects of transdisciplinary research projects: design and application of an evaluation method Evaluation and program planning 30(4), 325-338.

Webler, T. Kastenholz, H. Renn, O. (1995) Public Participation in Impact Assessment: A Social Learning Perspective. in Environmental Impact Assessment Review 15(5), 443-463 · September 1995. https://doi.org/10.1016/0195-9255(95)00043-E.

Bradshaw, D. J. (2018). Technology Disruption and Blockchain: Understanding Level of Awareness and the Potential Societal Impact, Doctoral dissertation, Dublin, National College of Ireland.

Burdon, S., Mooney, G. R. & Al-Kilidar, H. (2015). Navigating service sector innovation using co-creation partnerships. Journal of Service Theory and Practice, vol. 25, no. 3, 285-303.

Cupiał, M., Szeląg-Sikora, A., Sikora, J., Rorat, J. & Niemiec, M. (2018). Information technology tools in corporate knowledge management. Ekonomia i Prawo, 17(1), 5-15.

Denzin, N. K. & Lincoln, Y. S. (1994). Handbook of Qualitative Research, Sage Publications, Thousand Oaks, USA

European Commission (2017). Joint Communication to the European Parliament and the Council Resilience, Deterrence and Defence: Building strong cybersecurity for the EU (JOIN/2017/0450 final https://eur-lex.europa.eu/legal-con tent/EN/ALL/?uri=CELEX:52017JC0450, accessed February 8 2021).

European Commission (2020). Europe investing in digital The Digital Europe Programme (https://ec.europa.eu/digital-single-market/en/europe-investing-digital-digital-europe-pro gramme, accessed December 15 2020).

Greenacre M. and Hastie T. (1987). The Geometric Interpretation of Correspondence Analysis. Journal of the American Statistical Association, Vol. 82, No. 398 (Jun., 1987), 437-447.

Lu, H., Pishdad-Bozorgi, P., Wang, G., Xue, Y. & Tan, D. (2019). ICT Implementation of Small- and Medium-Sized Construction Enterprises: Organizational Characteristics, Driving Forces, and Value Perceptions. Sustainability, 11(12), 3441.

Maglaras, L., Ferrag. M, Derhab, A., Mukherjee, M., Janicke, H. & Rallis, S. (2018) Threats, countermeasures and attribution of cyber attacks on critical infrastructures EAI Endorsed Transactions on Security and Safety 5 (16).

Ruoslahti, H. & Trent, A. (2020). Organizational Learning in the Academic Literature – Systematic Literature Review. Information & Security: An International Journal 46:1, 65-78.

Ruoslahti, H., Rajamäki, J. & Koski, E. (2018). Educational Competences with regard to Resilience of Critical Infrastructure. Journal of Information Warfare, 17(3), pp. 1-16.

Schia, N. N. & Gjesvik, L. (2018). Managing a Digital Revolution-Cyber Security Capacity Building in Myanmar NUPI Working Paper 884, Norwegian Institute of International Affairs.

Shapiro, H., Haahr, J. H., Bayer, I. & Boekholt, P. (2007). Background paper on innovation and education Danish Technological Institute and Technopolis for the European Commission, DG Education & Culture in the context of a planned Green Paper on innovation.

Siddiqui, S. H., Rasheed, R., Nawaz, S., & Abbas, M. (2019). Knowledge sharing and innovation capabilities: The moderating role of organizational learning. Pakistan Journal of Commerce and Social Sciences (PJCSS), 13(2), 455-486.

Stellios, I., Kotzanikolaou, P., Psarakis, M., Alcaraz, C. & Lopez, J. (2018). A survey of IOT enabled cyberattacks: Assessing attack paths to critical infrastructures and services, IEEE Communications Surveys & Tutorials 20 (4), 3453-3495.

Tagarev, T. & Davis, B. Á. (2020). Towards the Design of a Cybersecurity Competence Network: Findings from the Analysis of Existing Network Organisations International Conference on Multimedia Communications, Services and Security (Springer, Cham), 37-50.

Tarafdar, M., Gupta, A. & Turel, O. (2015). Special issue on'dark side of information technology use': an introduction and a framework for research Information Systems Journal 25(3), 161-170.

Vos, M., Schoemaker, H. & Luoma-aho, V. L. (2014). Setting the agenda for research on issue arenas. Corporate Communications: An International Journal, Vol. 19 No. 2, 2014. Emerald Group Publishing Limited, 200-215.

Wargaming in Information Warfare Training: A Study of Finnish Officials

Dominic Saari, Hilkka Grahn, Teemu Häkkinen, Miriam Hautala, Oskari Vesterinen and Panu Moilanen
University of Jyväskylä, Finland

dominic.b.j.saari@jyu.fi
hilkka.grahn@jyu.fi
teemu.hakkinen@jyu.fi
miriam.a.hautala@jyu.fi
oskari.m.vesterinen@jyu.fi
panu.moilanen@jyu.fi

Abstract: In the digital age, information warfare has become a significant global concern, with malicious actors exploiting various media to manipulate public opinion, destabilising governments, and sowing discord. Automated and algorithmic tools are used to spread false and misleading information on social media platforms, and states have been unable to control the spread of it. In addressing new challenges, national governments globally reassess strategies, communications, and responses to adapt to evolving threat environments. To counter information influence activities, it is crucial to have informed, educated, and well-trained communicators. This case study focuses on the innovative use of wargaming in training government officials, providing them with abilities to respond to different tactics and methods of malign influence operations. This article is based on an information warfare exercise conducted in January 2024 involving 27 Finnish officials from various ministries and agencies critical to national security. The participants participated in an interactive simulation, where they explored and responded to challenges related to disinformation campaigns and other tactics designed to manipulate and influence information within a hybrid warfare context. The players were divided into two teams: red and blue, with the reds assuming the role of the offensive team while the blues took on the defensive role. The teams competed for control over the information space, employing various information warfare methods. After the exercise, each participant was asked to complete a post-exercise survey to evaluate the knowledge acquired and the exercise's overall usefulness, including scenario clarity and the effectiveness of role-playing. We also explored potential differences in perceptions and experiences between inexperienced and experienced players in the wargaming exercise. Key findings revealed the effectiveness of wargaming as an educational tool, particularly benefiting novices over experienced players. Role-playing proved valuable, emphasizing the importance of explicit scenarios for effective engagement. The study highlighted cross-departmental cooperation's significance, facilitating a dynamic learning environment.

Keywords: Wargaming, Information Warfare, Government Training, Gamification, Role-Playing, Inter-Agency Collaboration

1. Introduction

The rise of false and malign information poses a serious threat to governments, garnering significant interest. Algorithmic tools and AI have made creating and spreading false information easier than ever, complicating the task of preventing its dissemination (Fredheim & Pamment, 2024). Hostile actors actively aim to influence individuals' cognitive abilities to understand and interpret social realities (Bjola & Papadakis, 2020), adding to the complexity of the challenge. Governments have acknowledged the significance of this threat and its potential to endanger essential societal functions (Finnish Government, 2021). This multifaceted threat has compelled national governments to reassess their responses and strategies. Like several Western countries, Finland addresses information warfare through a collective and collaborative effort, emphasizing close cooperation between ministries and agencies. Finland does not designate a specific authority exclusively for managing information influence operations. Instead, each government agency assumes responsibility for its respective sector. The imperative for every national authority to be well-prepared is reinforced and coordinated by the Prime Minister's office (Mässeli, 2022).

In countering information influence activities, informed, educated, and well-prepared communicators are essential (Pamment et al., 2018). One such potential method for training government officials is wargaming. Wargaming serves as an innovative method for creating engaging exercises that facilitate effective learning. Rooted in the pedagogical theory of experiential learning (Kolb, 1984), wargaming offers a holistic and integrative perspective on learning, incorporating elements such as experience, perception, and behaviour.

This article is based on an information warfare exercise conducted in January 2024 involving Finnish officials from various ministries and agencies critical to national security. In this article, we investigate how wargaming can be used as an educational asset for training government officials. Specifically, we seek to examine their reactions to critical themes embedded in the exercise, including learning dynamics, role-playing, and the distinctive scenario crafted for its execution.

Our article aims to answer the following questions:

1. How do government officials perceive wargaming, particularly in terms of learning, usefulness, role-playing, and scenario clarity?
2. Do perceptions and experiences differ between inexperienced and experienced players in the wargaming exercise?
3. Does wargaming serve as an effective educational tool for government officials?

To address the research questions, we employed a questionnaire encompassing inquiries about learning, role-playing, and scenario clarity. Additionally, open-ended questions were utilized to delve deeper into the insights and experiences of government officials during the exercise.

2. Previous Research: Wargaming and Learning

Previous research supports the effectiveness of experiential learning techniques like wargaming in aiding student learning (Rosen & Kerr, 2024). Simulations encompassing such experiential methods are considered highly effective for facilitating the learning of complex skills (Chernikova et al.,2020). Experiential learning techniques actively engage learners, promoting deep learning, fostering interactive skills, and linking theory to practical application (Hertell & Mills, 2002). Previous research on cyber warfare exercises suggests that knowledge acquired during cyber war exercises tends to persist (Maennel et al., 2017). Successful wargaming can be highly informative and instructive, contributing to individual learning. However, its success is not uniform, with some games more effective in preparing decision-makers for real-world environments than others. Factors influencing the success or failure of wargames include subject matter, participants, design, and factual accuracy (Perla & McGrady, 2011; Rosen & Kerr, 2024; Frank, 2012).

In an information environment where the boundaries between war and peace may be blurred (Hutchinson, 2021; Ehrhart, 2017; particularly the Russian perspective, Jonsson, 2019), wargaming offers a practical application of experiential learning ideas. This aids individuals in acquiring the necessary skills for navigating this complex landscape. According to Chan (2022), experiential learning imparts holistic competencies, gaining prominence in our increasingly technology-oriented society. This perspective should influence our approach to countering the dissemination of malign information. Indeed, training programs simulating realistic, practical disinformation campaigns in stressful situations help to assess individual strengths and vulnerabilities and train to identify, analyse, and counter disinformation techniques (Muñoz Plaza et al. 2023). Therefore, preparing officials and individuals to approach information critically within its context is essential. However, existing state bodies and institutions may encounter challenges when confronting malign information in complex media environments characterized by rapidly changing communication networks and social media.

This research article focuses on the Finnish context, where wargaming has been a typical feature of military education among officers, emphasizing its traditional role in military training (Ilomäki, 2023). In a broader international context, wargaming can be understood as a model or simulation that does not involve the direct activities of military forces (Perla, 1987). However, the tools provided by wargaming extend beyond the military domain, particularly in non-military contexts, especially when applied to information-related scenarios. For instance, in the field of cyber defence, wargaming exercises are employed to facilitate effective training and raise awareness of security flaws (Casano & Colombo, 2019). These exercises often incorporate red and blue teaming elements (Maennel et al., 2017), indicating a learning model in which role-playing can have significant importance.

Building upon the premise that participants in the exercise would have limited prior experience with wargaming, it is essential to contextualize their background knowledge. Although the participants generally lacked direct wargaming experience, it is noteworthy that a significant portion of them had participated in an information warfare course organized by the University of Jyväskylä before engaging in the exercise. This course provided them with a foundational understanding of information influence and information warfare as overarching phenomena. This pre-existing knowledge not only primed them for engaging with the central focus of our study but also enriched their perspective, given the insights gained from the course.

3. Materials and Method

3.1 Exercise Setting

The wargame exercise unfolded within a fictional scenario portraying the Russian Federation initiating hybrid warfare against Finland. The participants were divided into two teams: red and blue. The red team, representing Russia, was tasked with creating disinformation and inducing chaos, while the blue team, symbolizing various Finnish government agencies, focused on responding to these threats.

The blue team was further segmented into four teams, symbolizing different sectors of Finnish governance, such as national security, critical infrastructure, and cyber. A total of 27 individuals actively participated in the exercise, most of them being part of the blue team. Additionally, 12 individuals served in assisting roles within the red and white teams. Due to the official and confidential nature of the exercise, specific details about the participating organizations cannot be disclosed.

Platforms utilized during the exercise included a simulated social media platform, Mastodon, and a WordPress page featuring two legitimate media outlets and one alternative media source controlled by the red team. Facilitating the exercise, the organizers assumed the role of the white team. The white team not only controlled the exercise but also influenced events through specific inputs. Each team was directed by these inputs, ensuring that all teams maintained a consistent situational picture and communications strategy. In-game events orchestrated by the white team included cyber-attacks, GPS jamming, and power outages in the Åland Islands. The rules of the exercise adhered strictly to official peacetime protocols and laws, and no state of emergency or martial law was declared as part of it.

3.2 Questionnaire

We developed a questionnaire to explore participants' perspectives on learning, role-playing, and scenarios within the wargaming context. Each theme was addressed through a series of multiple questions designed to capture various aspects of the respective theme. To ensure a nuanced understanding, questions were framed both positively and negatively. The learning theme had eight questions, the role-playing theme had six questions, and the scenario theme had eight. All questions were presented in Finnish using a 5-point Likert scale, with one indicating 'strongly disagree', three indicating 'neither agree nor disagree,' and five indicating 'strongly agree.' Additionally, respondents were asked whether they had previously engaged in similar wargaming situations, with response options 'yes' or 'no.' Furthermore, participants were prompted to evaluate their personal success and their team's success on a scale ranging from 1 to 10. Finally, respondents were also prompted with open-ended questions, seeking insights on what they learned during the exercise, the perceived usefulness, and any obstacles hindering learning. Data was collected through Microsoft Forms. Respondents were informed of the study's purpose, ensuring transparency about utilizing their responses for scientific publication. Importantly, no personal data was collected.

3.3 Data Preparation and Analysis

In total, we received 26 responses. Data was analysed using IBM SPSS Statistics 29.0.1.1. First, questions with a negative tone were recoded, with the highest value set to 1, and subsequent values adjusted accordingly. To assess the internal consistency and ensure the questions effectively captured the phenomena of learning, role-playing, and scenario, we computed Cronbach's Alphas (α) for each theme. If the SPSS dialogue indicated that removing a question would improve the alpha value, the content of the question was reviewed. If it did not align optimally with the theme, the question was removed, and the alpha was recalculated. An alpha value exceeding 0.70 is commonly interpreted as acceptable, indicating good internal consistency for the questions. Given the arbitrary nature of the acceptable alpha level, as Taber (2018) described, it is recommended to report the items included in a sum variable, making them available for scrutiny. The questions chosen to capture the phenomenon are presented in Table 1.

Table 1: Items included in the sum variables.

Theme	Questions	Cronbach's alpha
Learning	1) I was motivated to participate, 2) I felt that I learned new aspects during the exercise, 3) I perceived the exercise as beneficial, 4) I can apply what I learned during the exercise in	α = .879

Theme	Questions	Cronbach's alpha
	my work, 5) I feel better prepared to act if something similar happens in the real world, and 6) There were no new aspects to learn during the exercise (this was recoded)	
Role-playing	1) Role-playing provided added benefits to the exercise, 2) It was easy to immerse oneself in the role, 3) Role-playing facilitated the exercise, 4) Role-playing was fun, and 5) I would have preferred to participate without role-playing (this was recoded)	α = .926
Scenario clarity	1) The exercise's scenario was credible, 2) It was easy to comprehend what was happening, 3) I felt well-informed about the situation during the exercise, and 4) It was challenging to perceive what was happening during the exercise (this was recoded)	α = .789

Next, mean sum variables were computed for these themes. To investigate the potential influence of prior experience in similar exercises on opinions regarding learning, role-playing, and scenario clarity, a Mann-Whitney U test was employed, considering the non-Gaussian distributions of the sum variables. When conducting Mann-Whitney U tests and observing dissimilar shapes in group distributions, mean ranks are also reported. A significance level (alpha) of 0.05 was applied in all statistical tests.

4. Results

4.1 Questionnaire

Of the respondents, 11 (N = 26) had no prior experience with similar exercises, while 15 reported having participated in them before. Learning received relatively high evaluations: mean = 4.24, standard deviation = 0.63, and median = 4.33. The Mann-Whitney U test revealed a significant difference between the groups (U = 35.50, p = .014), indicating that those with no prior experience reported higher learning (mean rank = 17.77) compared to the group with prior experience (10.37). Similarly, role-playing received relatively high ratings: mean = 4.27, standard deviation = 0.77, and median = 4.50. The group that had not participated earlier in similar exercises before reported a slightly higher score for role-playing (mean rank 14.36) compared to those who had participated (12.87), but the difference was not significant (p = .646). Scenario clarity received slightly lower evaluations: mean = 3.86, standard deviation = 0.67, and median = 4.00. Again, no significant difference was observed between groups (p = .413); however, the mean rank of the group that had not participated earlier was lower (12.05) than of the group that had (14.57). Furthermore, respondents rated their own success during the exercise quite highly (M = 8.04, SD = 1.11, mdn = 8.00), with an evaluation of their group's success slightly higher (M = 8.65, SD = 0.69, mdn = 9.00).

4.2 Open-Ended Questions

As open-ended questions, we included the following: 1) What did you learn during the exercise? 2) What did you perceive as useful during the exercise? and 3) What might have hindered your learning experience? We conducted content analysis, specifically employing conventional content analysis, where coding categories are derived directly from the data (Hsieh & Shannon, 2005).

4.2.1 Learning During the Exercise: Collaboration, Competence, and Situation Awareness

For the first question, we received 18 responses, with collaboration mentioned six times. This theme underscores respondents' reflections on how they learned the importance, even essentiality, of collaborating with different authorities. For example, one comment emphasized that 'collaboration is vital for the administrative section'. It was noted five times that the experience taught participants about the competencies of other officials or administrative sections. One specific comment highlighted the 'value of observing other officials at work and engaging in conversations with them'. The theme of situation awareness was also mentioned twice. This theme emphasizes the importance of developing situation awareness in somewhat disorderly circumstances. One respondent noted, 'The exercise served as a good reminder of how chaotic real situations can be and how many different actors are involved in them'.

4.2.2 Usefulness: Collaboration Across Administrations and Practicing Real-Life Situations

For the second question, we received 18 responses, and 11 of them noted the importance of collaboration across administrations. Pondering together with people from different administrations was perceived as useful. The responses indicated that including officials from various administrative sectors in the exercise was considered beneficial. A participant expressed, 'I had the opportunity to meet new people and collaborate with individuals beyond my usual administrative sphere'. Additionally, seven comments emphasized the value of practicing and contemplating real-life situations. This allowed participants to consider how they would act in authentic scenarios. As one respondent mentioned, 'It was beneficial that the exercise prompted problem-solving, a skill valuable in acute situations as well'.

4.2.3 Aspects Hindering Learning Experience: Exercise Environment's Technical Aspects

In response to this question, we received 11 responses. The factors hindering the learning experience ranged from tiredness to unfamiliarity with others, with one predominant theme emerging from three responses. This theme centred around challenges related to the technical aspects of the exercise environment. Participants found it challenging to navigate new social media and newspaper platforms, and the scarcity of computers also posed difficulties. One respondent noted, 'It was challenging because the information systems differed from the ones I usually work with at my job'.

5. Discussion

In this article, we focused on investigating how government officials perceived wargaming, particularly in learning, usefulness, role-playing, and scenario clarity. We explored whether there were differences in perceptions and experiences between inexperienced and experienced players in the wargaming exercise and considered the effectiveness of wargaming as an educational tool for government officials.

Our analysis found that participants generally had a positive experience, with high scores for learning and role-playing. Notably, in terms of learning, individuals with no prior experience reported significantly higher levels compared to those with previous exposure to similar wargames. While much of the previously mentioned research discusses the positive learning outcomes of wargaming (Rosen & Kerr, 2024; Chernikova et al.,2020; Hertell & Mills, 2002; Maennel et al., 2017), existing studies fall short in assessing its effectiveness for both inexperienced and more experienced players. However, Hamari et al. (2014) have suggested that experiential learning and gamification may not yield long-term learning results, attributing the heightened effect to a possible novelty effect. The noted novelty effect may contribute to the significant difference in learning outcomes between inexperienced and more experienced participants. This occurrence, coupled with plain curiosity, could lead to an enhanced motivational boost. According to Filgona et al. (2020), motivation itself facilitates learners, promoting effective thinking, concentration, and learning. It significantly contributes to academic learning and achievement from childhood through adolescence, enhancing cognitive processing. This could suggest that participants with no prior experience may find the learning experience more impactful or engaging. This heightened engagement can have a positive influence on the learning process. While role-playing received high ratings overall, there was no significant difference between the groups. This implies that the role-playing experience was perceived similarly, regardless of prior participation in similar exercises.

Scenarios lay the foundation for wargaming exercises, shaping and influencing player actions (Perla & McGrady, 2011). Scenario clarity, on the other hand, received slightly lower evaluations, with no significant difference between the groups. The lower mean rank for the group with no prior participation suggests that they may have found the scenario less clear, though this difference was not statistically significant. According to McCreight (2013), for a wargame to be successful, the scenario must be appropriately developed. An effective scenario is factual, accurate, and concise, seamlessly integrating realism while minimising ambiguity. The scenario must also be streamlined enough for organic development during the game. If the scenario is excessively intricate, it can confuse participants and complicate the mapping out of events.

In the responses, the importance of collaboration among administration authorities was deemed significant. While this might seem self-evident, it is not always the case. Previous research, particularly in the context of Finnish security, has underscored both the importance of cooperation among authorities and the necessity to enhance means for collaboration (e.g., Anttonen 2016; Branders 2016; Jalava et al. 2017). Our results align with this, highlighting the ongoing need for cooperation. This is also supported by the observations of some respondents, who mentioned that the exercise provided an opportunity to learn from the work of other government agencies and contribute to a shared situational understanding.

Overall, these results suggest that the lack of prior experience might positively influence perceived learning, but it may not have a significant impact on role-playing, scenario clarity, or success evaluations. The participants generally reported positive experiences in learning, role-playing, scenario clarity, and success. Acknowledging the influence of organizational culture, hierarchy, legal rights, and bureaucracy on each entity and its employees, gamification through experiential learning provides a unique opportunity. It enables individuals to distance themselves from their daily routines and immerse themselves in the learning process within a safe space without transgressing their jurisdictions. While wargaming appears effective for government official training, there are practical considerations for future implementations. Ensuring clarity and coherence is crucial. It is also advisable to provide ample devices for the teams and adequately train participants in using technical platforms to prevent potential disruptions and to improve the usability of the gaming environment.

5.1 Limitations and Further Research

One limitation of this study lies in the relatively low number of respondents and participants engaged in the exercise. The research could have benefited from a more extensive respondent group. With only 26 survey responses, caution must be exercised in making broad claims. Additionally, the respondent group exhibited a slight imbalance between inexperienced and experienced players, highlighting the need for a more equitable distribution in future studies.

For subsequent future research, it would be interesting to replicate the same exercise with a more extensive and more diverse test group while improving the technical execution for a better participant experience. A key consideration for further exploration could involve examining each agency's officials' performance. This approach may unveil variations in organizational responses, potentially suggesting that such exercises might be more beneficial for certain groups over others. A more comprehensive investigation with a more extensive and well-balanced participant pool would contribute to a deeper understanding of the dynamics at play in wargaming for government officials.

6. Conclusions

In exploring wargaming as an educational tool for government employees, this article delved into the realms of learning, role-playing, and the clarity and comprehensibility of provided scenarios. We observed that novices experience a notable increase in learning when playing wargames compared to more experienced players. While role-playing was considered useful by both experienced and inexperienced players, it did not emerge as a significant factor. Notably, players rated our scenario clarity slightly lower; nonetheless, prior research emphasizes the pivotal role of a clear scenario in the success of the exercise.

An interesting finding from our study suggests that many respondents acknowledged the potential importance of cross-departmental cooperation and collaboration. The exercise facilitated a dynamic learning environment, enabling participants to engage with government actors from diverse sectors within a realistic worst-case scenario.

Our analysis underscores the predominantly positive effects of wargaming as an educative tool, particularly for newer players. Wargaming has proven effective for training government officials, but future implementations need careful attention to scenario clarity, as well as adequate technical training and resources, to ensure an enjoyable and effective learning experience. Continued investigation will contribute to a more comprehensive understanding of the broader implications and applications of wargaming in the realm of government training and education.

References

Anttonen, J. (2016) Yhteistä turvallisuutta rakentaen: Poliisi- ja upseeriprofessioiden yhteiskehittelyn mahdollisuuksista. Julkaisusarja 1: Tutkimuksia nro 6. Helsinki, Maanpuolustuskorkeakoulu.

Bjola, C. & Papadakis, K. (2020). Digital propaganda, counterpublics and the disruption of the public sphere: The Finnish approach to building digital resilience. *Cambridge Review of International Affairs, 33*(5), 638-666. https://doi.org/10.1080/09557571.2019.1704221

Branders, M. 2016. Kokonainen turvallisuus?: Kokonaisturvallisuuden poliittinen kelpoisuus ja hallinnollinen toteutettavuus. Tampere: Tampere University Press.

Casano, F. and Colombo, R. (2019). Wargaming: The Core of Cyber Training. NATO Science for Peace and Security Series - D: Information and Communication Security. Vol. 54, Next Generation CERTs, pp. 88-99. doi:10.3233/NICSP190012

Chan, C. K. Y. (2022). Assessment for Experiential Learning. Taylor & Francis Group.

Chernikova, O., Heitzmann, N., Stadler, M., Holzberger, D., Seidel, T., & Fischer, F. (2020). Simulation-Based Learning in Higher Education: A Meta-Analysis. Review of Educational Research, 90(4), 499-541. https://doi.org/10.3102/0034654320933544

Ehrhart, H-G. (2017). Postmodern warfare and the blurred boundaries between war and peace. Defense & Security Analysis, 33(3), 263-275, DOI: 10.1080/14751798.2017.1351156

Filgona, J., Sakiyo, J., Gwany, D.M. and Okoronka, A.U. (2020). Motivation in Learning. Asian Journal of Education and Social Studies, 10(4), pp.16–37. doi:https://doi.org/10.9734/ajess/2020/v10i430273.

Finnish Government. (2021). Government's Defence Report. (2021:80; Publications of the Finnish Government). https://julkaisut.valtioneuvosto.fi/bitstream/handle/10024/163407/VN_2021_80.pdf?sequence=4&isAllowed=y

Frank, A. (2012). Gaming the Game: A Study of the Gamer Mode in Educational Wargaming. Simulation & Gaming, 43(1), 118-132. https://doi.org/10.1177/1046878111408796

Fredheim, R. & Pamment, J. (2024). Assessing the risks and opportunities posed by AI-enhanced influence oprations on social media. Place Branding and Public Diplomacy. https://doi.org/10.1057/s41254-023-00322-5

Hamari, J., Koivisto, J., and Sarsa, H. (2014). Does Gamification Work? -- A Literature Review of Empirical Studies on Gamification. 47th Hawaii International Conference on System Sciences, Waikoloa, HI, USA, 2014, pp. 3025-3034, doi: 10.1109/HICSS.2014.377.

Hertel J. P. Millis B. J. (2002) Using Simulation to Promote Learning in Higher Education. Sterling, VA: Stylus.

Hsieh, H.F. and Shannon, S.E. (2005). Three Approaches to Qualitative Content Analysis. Qualitative Health Research, 15(9), pp.1277–1288. doi:https://doi.org/10.1177/1049732305276687.

Hutchinson, W. (2021). Some Basic Principles of Information Warfare: A Reappraisal for 2021. Journal of Information Warfare, 20(4), 18–29.

Ilomäki, J. (2023). Intuitiivisen päätöksenteon kehittäminen maavoimissa sotapelaamalla taktisella tasalla. Pro Gradu - tutkielma. Sotatieteiden maisterikurssi 11, Maavoimat. Maanpuolustuskorkeakoulu. https://doria.fi/bitstream/handle/10024/187668/SM1752_JULK.pdf [Accessed 5 February 2024].

Jalava, J., Raisio, H., Norri-Sederholm, T., Lahtinen, H., Puustinen, A. (2017) Kolmas sektori viranomaisten turvallisuustoiminnan tukena. Valtioneuvoston selvitys- ja tutkimustoiminnan julkaisusarja 76/2017. Valtioneuvoston kanslia.

Jonsson, O. (2019). The Russian understanding of war: Blurring the lines between war and peace. Georgetown University Press.

Kolb, D. A. (1984). Experiential learning: Experience as the source of learning and development. Prentice-Hall.

Maennel, K., Ottis, R., Maennel, O. (2017). Improving and Measuring Learning Effectiveness at Cyber Defense Exercises. In: Lipmaa, H., Mitrokotsa, A., Matulevičius, R. (eds) Secure IT Systems. NordSec 2017. Lecture Notes in Computer Science, vol 10674. Springer, Cham. https://doi.org/10.1007/978-3-319-70290-2_8

McCreight, R. (2012). Scenario development: using geopolitical wargames and strategic simulations. Environment Systems & Decisions, 33(1), pp.21–32. doi:https://doi.org/10.1007/s10669-012-9426-1.

Muñoz Plaza, F., Sotelo Monge, M. A. and Ordi, H. G. (2023). Towards the Definition of Cognitive Warfare and Related Countermeasures: A Systematic Review. Proceedings of the 18th International Conference on Availability, Reliability and Security, 1–7. Benevento Italy: ACM. https://doi.org/10.1145/3600160.3605080.

Mässeli, E. (2022). Venäjän informaatiopsykologinen sodankäynti - Suomen torjunta- ja varautumistoimenpiteiden määrittely. University of Jyväskylä. https://jyx.jyu.fi/bitstream/handle/123456789/81732/URN%3aNBN%3afi%3ajyu-202206153342.pdf?sequence=1&isAllowed=y [Accessed 5 February 2024]

Perla, P. P. (1987). War Games, Analyses, and Exercises. Naval War College Review, 40(2), 44–52.

Perla, P. P., & McGrady, E. (2011). Why Wargaming Works. Naval War College Review, 64(3), 111–130.

Rosen, A. M. and Kerr, L. (2024) Wargaming for Learning: How Educational Gaming Supports Student Learning and Perspectives, Journal of Political Science Education, doi:https://doi.org/10.1080/15512169.2024.2304769.

Pamment, J., Nothhaft, H., & Fjällhed, A. (2018). *Countering Information Influence Activities: The State of The Art*. Swedish Civil Contingencies Agency (MSB). https://lup.lub.lu.se/search/publication/825192b8-9274-4371-b33d-2b11baa5d5ae

Taber, K. S. (2018). The use of Cronbach's Alpha when developing and reporting research instruments in science education. Research in Science Education, 48(6), 1273–1296. Doi:https://doi.org/10.1007/s11165-016-9602-2

Backward-compatible Software Upgrades for ADS-B and AIS To Support ECDSA-Secured Protocols

Ahsan Saleem, Hannu Turtiainen, Andrei Costin and Timo Hämäläinen
Faculty of Information Technology, University of Jyväskylä, Jyväskylä, 40014 Finland

ahsan.m.saleem@jyu.fi
hannu.ht.turtiainen@jyu.fi
andrei.costin@jyu.fi
timo.t.hamalainen@jyu.fi

Abstract: During the past few decades, the aviation, maritime, aerospace, and search-and-rescue domains have witnessed tremendous improvement thanks to technological, digitalization and Internet of Things (IoT) advances such as Automatic Dependent Surveillance–Broadcast (ADS-B) (e.g., Aviation IoT, Airports IoT) and Automatic Identification System (AIS) (e.g., Maritime IoT). All these are high-profile examples of new digital communication protocols combined with IoT devices that make efficient use of wide-area earth and space radio communications to provide real-time, truly globally interoperable, and optimised services required by these domains. However, the protocols and technologies mentioned above, both from an architectural and implementation point of view, exhibit fundamental cybersecurity weaknesses (both at protocol and IoT device level). These weaknesses make them an easy target for potential attackers. The two fundamental flaws of these protocols are the lack of digital signatures (i.e., integrity and authenticity) and the lack of encryption (i.e., confidentiality and privacy). The risks associated with these, and other weaknesses have been over the last decade repeatedly demonstrated with ease by ethical cybersecurity researchers. In this paper, we design, propose, and discuss a single generic PKI-enabled message integrity and authenticity scheme that works seamlessly for any of the ADS-B, and AIS, with the possibility of easy extension and integration into other protocols (e.g., ACARS). Our scheme can be added as backward-compatible software upgrades (e.g., third-party library) to existing systems without requiring expensive architectural redesign, upgrades, and retrofitting. Our present work is aimed to serve as a bootstrap to securing such insecure protocols without completely replacing or redesigning the systems. It also aims to provide a discussion background of advantages and limitations of such backward-compatible securing methods.

Keywords: Cybersecurity, Protocol Upgrades, Message Authentication, ADS-B, 1090ES, AIS.

1. Introduction

In aviation, aircrafts periodically broadcast their aviation data using a surveillance technique known as Automatic Dependent Surveillance-Broadcast (ADS-B). Air Traffic Control (ATC) and other airplanes receive this data, providing them with situational awareness. Currently, there are insufficient security measures to ensure the privacy, availability, and integrity of transmitting data between aircraft and air traffic controllers (Kožović et al., 2023) (Manesh and Kaabouch, 2017) (Strohmeier et al., 2013) (Wu et al., 2020). Consequently, an attacker may insert fake data or stop actual data from being correctly delivered because no authentication mechanisms are used at the data connection layer (Costin and Francillon, 2012) (Khandker et al., 2021) (Khandker et al., 2022a) (Mäurer et al., 2022). Various security schemes have been proposed to secure ADS-B transmission messages, including symmetric cryptographic-based (Chen, 2012) (Kacem et al., 2015), identity-based signature algorithms (Thumbur et al., 2019) (Yi et al., 2022), time-efficient stream loss-tolerant authentication (TESLA) protocol (Yang et al., 2018) (Sciancalepore and Di Pietro, 2019), anonymous authentication schemes (Asari et al., 2021) (Jegadeesan et al., 2021) and blockchain-based schemes (Wu et al., 2023) (Habibi Markani et al., 2023).

In the maritime domain, vessel traffic services rely on the Automated Identification System (AIS) for automatic ship tracking. AIS is an open standard and due to unauthenticated and unencrypted nature make it vulnerable to threats such as spoofing, hijacking, and availability disruption (Balduzzi et al., 2014) (Hall et al., 2015) (Khandker et al., 2022b) (Tran et al., 2021). To secure AIS, several security schemes have been proposed, including anonymous authentication schemes (Goudosis and Katsikas, 2022) (Jegadeesan et al., 2021), TESLA protocol-based scheme (Sciancalepore et al., 2021) and blockchain based schemes (Duan et al., 2022) (Freire et al., 2022).

In this study, we proposed authentication and integrity schemes for ADS-B (aviation) and AIS (maritime) systems. Despite the different domains, the architecture, technologies, and protocols of the ADS-B and AIS systems exhibit noteworthy similarities. Security threats and the proposed cybersecurity solutions are similar. Therefore, we propose a scheme that addresses the security concerns of both protocols to secure in our study. There are core motivations for our work. First and foremost, the bulk of the existing proposed solutions are either theoretical (Costin and Francillon, 2012) (Chen, 2012b) or require complete/major system redesign and replacement in the case of practically demonstrated solutions (Thumbur et al., 2019) (Yang et al., 2014) (Goudossis and Katsikas, 2019) (e.g. introduction of new sub-protocols). Second, even for practically feasible solutions (Yang et al., 2018) (Sciancalepore et al., 2021) (Wimpenny et al., 2022), the proposed solutions are not uniform across multiple technologies and/or customised for each technology stack (that is, ADS-B-only, AIS-only). This makes such solutions harder to maintain in the long run, brings more fragmentation to technology stacks, and increases the verification efforts of each individually customised approach. To address these limitations, we propose backward-compatible software only solution to provide stronger security to ADS-B and AIS protocols, which can easily be integrated with the existing systems and protocols.

Our main contributions with this work are as follows:

1. We propose backward-compatible and software-only message authentication and integrity approach for existing insecure protocols in aviation (ADS-B).
2. We also propose a backward-compatible and software-only message authentication and integrity scheme for maritime (AIS).
3. We provide a security analysis of the proposed scheme, which shows that the proposed scheme is secured under a defined security model.

2. Related Work

This section summarises the security and authentication-enhancing schemes previously proposed for ADS-B and AIS. Chen et al. (2012) proposed an ADS-B message confidentiality and authentication scheme based on block ciphers. Yang et al. (2015) proposed an ADS-B authentication batch verification scheme based on identity-based signature. Pan et al. (2012) proposed an elliptic curve cipher (ECC) and X.509 certificate-based authentication scheme for ADS-B. Thumbur et al. (2019) proposed an identity based authentication batch verification scheme for ADS-B. Yang et al. (2018) proposed confidentiality and integrity scheme for ADS-B transmission messages. Wu et al. (2019) proposed a certificate-less short signature-based authentication and integrity scheme for ADS-B. Asari et al. (2021) presented hierarchical authentication and integrity scheme of ADS-B data based on a certificate-less public key cryptographic technique. Yang et al. (2014) proposed an identity signature based authentication and integrity scheme for ADS-B. Prakash et al. (2019) proposed an authentication scheme for ADS-B based on message authentication code (MAC). Recently blockchain-based security schemes for ADS-B are proposed in (Wu et al., 2023) (Habibi Markani et al., 2023).

Sciancalepore et al. (2021) proposed an authentication scheme for AIS broadcast messages. Goudossis et al. (2019) proposed an authentication and integrity scheme for AIS, and in their follow-up work (Goudosis and Katsikas, 2020) addressed the implementation aspects of (Goudossis et al., 2019). Goudosis et al. (2022) proposed secure automatic identification system (SecAIS) that provides the authentication, confidentiality, and anonymisation of AIS messages. Wimpenny et al. (2022) proposed an elliptic curve based data integrity and authentication scheme for AIS. Su et al. (2017) proposed a digital certificate-based identity authentication scheme to ensure authentication and integrity of AIS data. Jegadeesan et al. (2021) proposed AIS anonymous authentication scheme. The blockchain-based authentication and integrity schemes for AIS are proposed in (Duan et al., 2022) (Freire et al., 2022).

2.1 Comparison with Existing Works

Our present work is the best compared with the following existing works. In the ADS-B field, the work (Yang et al., 2018) is closest to our approach. However, this scheme is based on the TESLA protocol for authentication, which cannot be practically used in real-time authentication scenarios owing to the core idea of a delayed authentication mechanism due to symmetric key generation and distribution challenges. While our proposed approach is a public key cryptographic algorithm-based scheme which is real-time, backward-compatible, practical authentication scheme. In the AIS field, the schemes proposed by (Sciancalepore et al., 2021) (Wimpenny et al., 2022) are closest to our approach. These schemes are either inherently delayed authentication mechanisms or use separate VHF data-exchange system (VDES) side channels to carry digital signatures, which require the installation of new VDES hardware on the transmitter and receiver sides. However, our AIS proposed approach is real-time and practical and retains backward compatibility by carrying a signature payload in a "New type" of message in follow-up AIS communication. Moreover, our foremost differentiator, compared with the closest related work, is that our scheme provides a generic approach that adds cryptographically strong message authenticity and integrity to all protocols (e.g. ADS-B and AIS) in a single implementation.

3. Preliminaries, Models and Goals

This section provides background knowledge and defines our systems models of ADS-B and AIS, as well as the security goals of the proposed scheme.

3.1 ADS-B Model and Message Format

The proposed ADS-B model is illustrated in Figure 1. ADS-B comprises two distinct communication subsystems: ADS-B OUT and ADS-B IN. In the proposed ADS-B model, an aircraft continuously transmits information regarding its altitude, velocity, and position through ADS-B OUT and ADS-B IN enables aircraft to receive nearby ADS-B messages transmitted by other aircraft or Air Traffic Control (ATC). The aircraft receives primary information from a navigation satellite, which is subsequently transmitted to another aircraft and the ATC through the ADS-B OUT. The receiver aircraft receives this information using an ADS-B IN and then processes and displays it in the aircraft's cockpit.

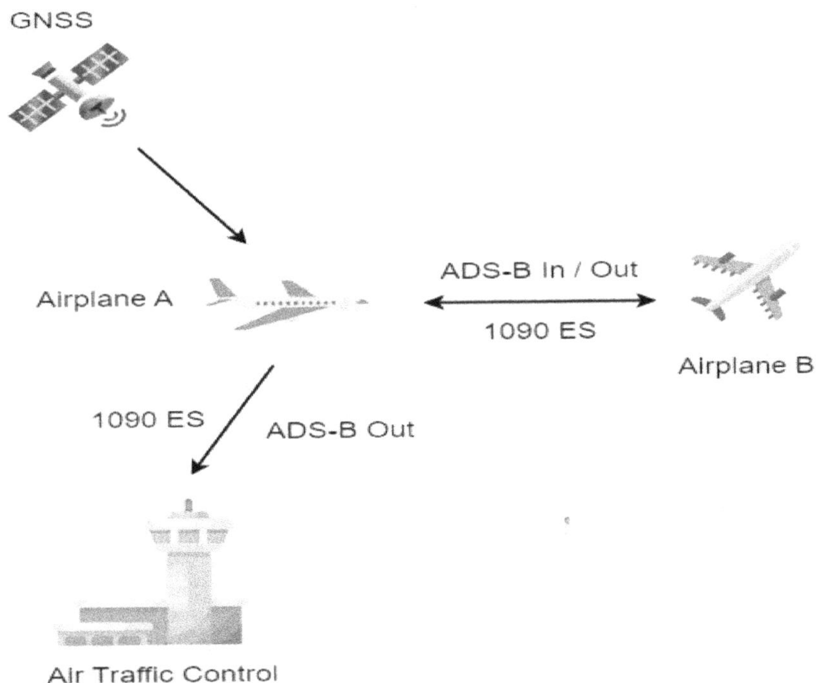

Figure 1: General ADS-B Model (simplified)

The ADS-B 112-bit message format, which consists of five fields, is illustrated in Figure 2.

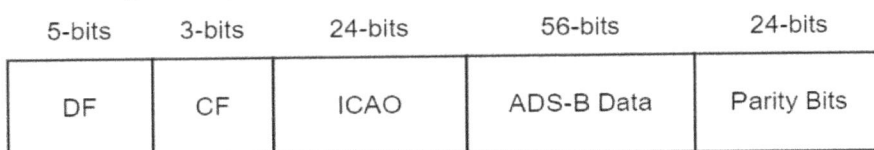

5-bits	3-bits	24-bits	56-bits	24-bits
DF	CF	ICAO	ADS-B Data	Parity Bits

Figure 2: Long ADS-B 1090ES Message Format (112 bits)

3.2 AIS Model and Message Format

The proposed AIS model is shown in Figure 3, where vessels and the AIS control center exchange navigation information, such as identification and position data, using a Global Navigation Satellite System (GNSS). This allows for various uses, such as identifying ships, tracking them from a distance, changing routes, and preventing and investigating accidents.

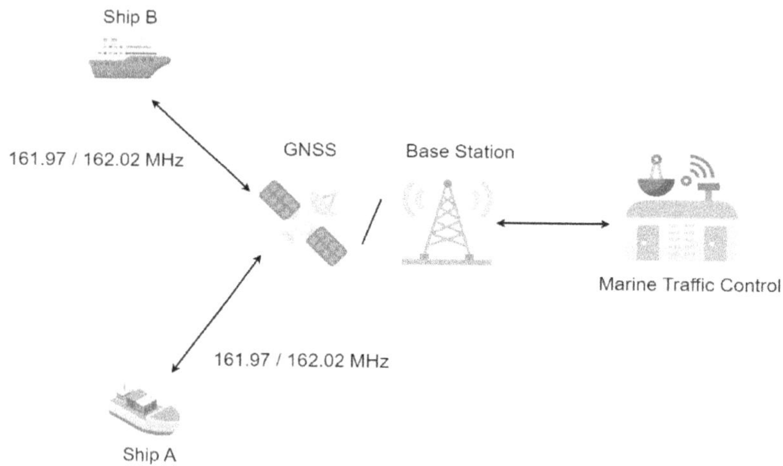

Figure 3: General AIS Model (simplified)

In AIS, channel A communication uses a frequency of 161.975 MHz, whereas channel B uses 162.025 MHz. AIS message has an overall size of 256 bits (International Telecommunication Union, 2014),and its format is shown in Figure 4.

8-bits	24-bits	8-bits	168-bits	16-bits	8-bits	24-bits
Ramp Up	Preamble	Start Flag	AIS Data	FCS	End Flag	Buffer

Figure 4: AIS Message Format (256 bits)

3.3 Threat Model and Security Goals

In adversary model, we assume that an adversary can intercept and modify the contents of the existing messages and may try to inject fake messages into the transmission channel following the ADS-B/AIS message format. In the absence of security measures, an adversary can intercept, retransmit, or delay transmitting messages, resulting in replay attacks. These attacker capabilities are realistic, as demonstrated by several studies (Costin and Francillon, 2012) (Khandker et al., 2021) (Khandker et al., 2022b) (Khandker et al., 2022a). These vulnerabilities enable eavesdropping, message injection, message modification, and replay attacks to occur. Moreover, the availability of low-cost software-defined radio (SDR) enables adversaries to launch these types of attacks.

In our proposed schemes, we aim to achieve the following security goals.

1. Message Authentication: Message authentication means that incoming data on the receiver side are from an authentic source and the receiver can verify the message origin. Our proposed schemes ensure source authentication of the messages and ensure that the messages originate from the authenticated transmitter or source.
2. Message Integrity: Message integrity of the received message means that no one has tampered with the transmitting messages, and any modification should be detected at the receiver side. Our proposed schemes ensure the integrity of the transmitted messages and can detect and filter out tampered messages.
3. Resistance to False Data Injection Attack: An attacker may try to insert false data into a legitimate message. Any false data injected by an attacker should be easily detected on the receiver side when our scheme is employed.
4. Prevention of Replay Attack: Replay attack means that an adversary maliciously intercepts and delays or retransmits messages to the receiver. The receiver must be able to detect and filter replay messages. The proposed schemes can efficiently detect and discard replay messages.
5. Strong Cryptographic Guarantees: For stronger security, we use ECDSA 256-bit key signature algorithm over the SHA-256 hash of the message. This provides strong future-proof guarantees while simultaneously minimising the digital signature output at the same time.

An attacker model in which adversaries become mobile is called a mobile attacker or a mobile adversary model (Shang, 2023). We did not consider this type of attack in our threat model, which is an interesting extension of our work, and we consider for future exploration. Additionally, other types of attacks, such as denial of service and jamming attacks, are possible against ADS-B and AIS; however, these attacks are outside the scope of this study.

3.4 Non-Security Goals

In addition to the security goals of our proposed scheme, we define the non-security goals of our schemes.

1. Backward Compatibility: This means that our schemes are software-only solutions and require no modification to existing protocols and hardware.
2. Single Generic Approach: The proposed schemes are software-only solutions, and we envision that our solution can work as a third-party library for upgraded systems. This will enable a single and generic code base that is easy to deploy and audit.
3. Minimum Communication Cost: For minimum communication cost, we consider a 512-bit length ECDSA signature algorithm in our scheme.

4. Proposed Solution

In this section, we describe ADS-B and AIS authentication scheme. The notations used in the proposed scheme are listed in Table 1.

Table 1: List of Notations

Symbol	Definition
G	Generator
k	Random number
R	Random point
$privKey$	Private key
$pubKey$	Public key
T_s	Timestamp
h	Hash digest
σ	Signature
df_m	DF (ADS-B) message
ais_m	AIS message

4.1 ADS-B Authentication

This section provides source authentication and message integrity for the ADS-B messages. The proposed scheme consists of two algorithms: *ADS-B Signature Generation and Encapsulation*, and *ADS-B Signature Verification and De-encapsulation*. For authentication and message integrity, we use the ECDSA signature scheme. To maintain backward compatibility and openness of the ADS-B message, transmitter transmit a signed message of an ADS-B message (e.g. DF11 or DF17, which are the most common ADS-B messages in general) encapsulated within an ADS-B DF24 ELM message that follows-up. In this way, the transmitter continues to transmit ADS-B normally and transmits the respective signed message in a follow-up message using the DF24 ELM message. The message field of the ADS-B DF24 ELM is of 80-bits, and a full signature cannot be accommodated within a single packet. Therefore, to accommodate the digital signature data, we used a built-in message-chaining mechanism available in the ADS-B DF24 ELM, which can chain up to 16 segments related to the same ADS-B DF24 communication.

The complete ADS-B authentication mechanism on the transmitter and receiver sides is illustrated in Figure 5. Given that the signature, timestamp, and ICAO take 600 bits, in practice, 8-chained DF24 ELM messages are required to transmit a digital signature of one standard ADS-B message.

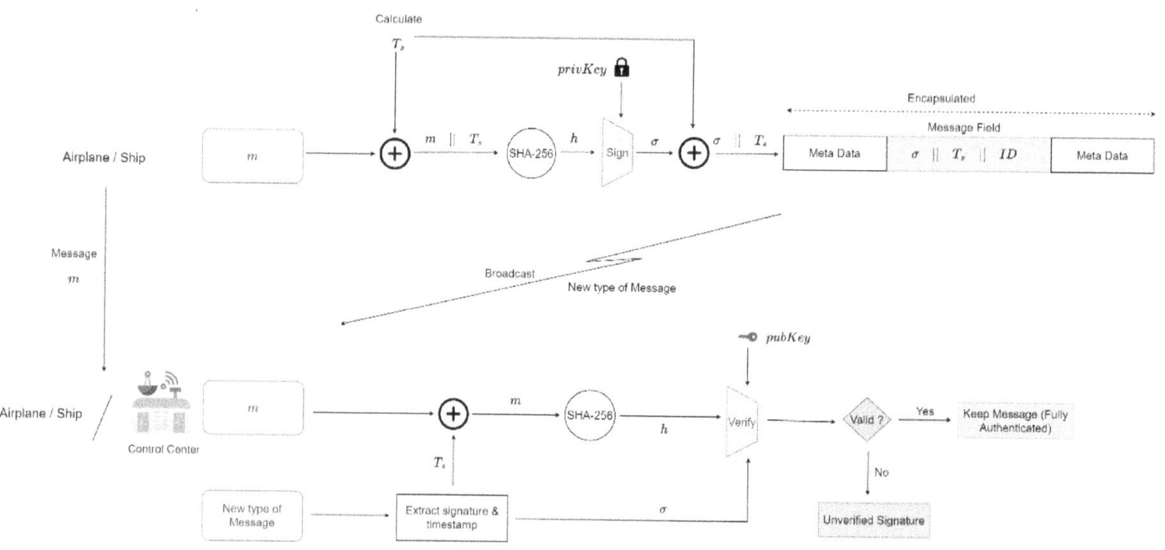

Figure 5: Our proposed Message authenticity and integrity scheme

4.1.1 *ADS-B Signature Generation and Encapsulation*

For ADS-B message signature generation and encapsulation of signed messages in the DF24 ELM message, transmitter used Algorithm 1. In the first step, it calculates timestamp T_s. Then the transmitter computes the hash digest $h = hash(df_m \vee T_s)$ of the full raw ADS-B 56bit or 112bit message (e.g., DF11 or DF17) concatenated with T_s using the hash algorithm $SHA - 256$. In next step, computes the signature σ of the hashed value h using $privKey$. To prevent a replay attack, timestamp T_s is concatenated with a signed message. The message field of the DF24 ELM is of 80-bits. Therefore, the chaining mechanism of DF24 is used to encapsulate the signed-message in the DF24 ELM and forward the "New type" of the ADS-B message to ATC.

Algorithm 1: ADS-B Signature Generation and Encapsulation

1: **procedure**

2: **Input:** ADS-B message df_m , $SHA - 256, privKey$

3: **Output:** Signature $\sigma = \{r, s\}$, Encapsulated DF24 ELM

4: Compute timestamp T_s

5: Calculate $h = hash(df_m \vee T_s)$ using $SHA - 256$

6: Computes signature proof $\sigma = (privKey, h)$

7: Concatenate signature with ID and timestamp $\sigma \vee T_s \vee ICAO$

8: Chaining signed message into 80-bits of the available payload of DF24 ELM

9: Transmit encapsulated DF24 ELM to ATC (or ADS-B IN aircraft/device)

10: **end procedure**

4.1.2 *ADS-B Signature Verification and De-Encapsulation*

ATC receives the encapsulated DF24 ELM from the sender and authenticates the message using Algorithm 2. The first step de-encapsulates the DF24 ELM message and obtains $\sigma \vee T_s$ from the message field. ATC computes the hash digest as $hash(df_m \vee T_s)$ using the received timestamp and already received message (e.g., DF11, DF17, or any other ADS-B DF message for that purpose). Finally, the receiver verifies the signature using $pubKey$ of the sender and successful verification shows that the message originated from an authenticated source, and no one has tampered with the received message. The timestamp binding with the signature prevents replay attacks.

Algorithm 2: ADS-B Signature Verification and De-encapsulation

procedure
Input: Encapsulated DF24 ELM, ADS-B message df_m , $SHA-256, pubKey$
Output: Authenticated data
De-encapsulate DF24 ELM message and get Signed message $\sigma \vee T_s \vee ICAO$
Calculate $h = hash(df_m \vee T_s)$ using $SHA-256$
Signature validation using Public Key $(pubKey, h, \sigma)$
if Signature is validated **then**
    Keep received message (Fully Authenticated)
else
    Possibly tampered/replayed, therefore UNVERIFIABLE
end if
end procedure

4.2 AIS Authentication

This section describes the proposed authentication and integrity scheme for AIS messages. The proposed AIS authentication scheme consists of two algorithms: *AIS Signature Generation and Encapsulation*, and the other is *Signature Verification and De-encapsulation*. AIS messages have overall size of 256-bit and containing 168-bit of the message field. In proposed scheme, we use an Elliptic Curve-based Digital Signature for source authentication and data integrity of the AIS message. The message field of an AIS message is 168 bits. Therefore, signed messages cannot be accommodated in this field. To overcome this problem, we use AIS Message Type 8 in our scheme for 4-consecutive slots. For the openness of the AIS protocol, we encapsulate signed messages into an existing protocol message, to which we apply a special interpretation. This process is illustrated in Figure 5. First, there is an AIS message, and then there is a follow-on message with a digital signature inside Message Type 8.

This procedure retains the backward compatibility and openness of the AIS. This enables the transmitter to continuously transmit AIS messages normally and send signed messages to the receiver in follow-up messages. Given that the signature takes 512 bits with a timestamp of 64 bits, it requires 4-chained AIS Message Type 8 messages to transmit a digital signature of one standard AIS message.

4.2.1 *AIS Signature Generation and Encapsulation*

In the proposed AIS authentication scheme, Algorithm 3 is AIS Signature Generation and Encapsulation, which signs the AIS message and encapsulates it into AIS Message Type 8. The transmitter first calculates timestamp T_s and computes the hash digest $hash(ais_m \vee T_s)$ of the AIS message concatenated with timestamp T_s using the hash algorithm $SHA-256$. Then, the transmitter computes the signature proof σ using the $privKey$. To prevent a replay attack and to link the AIS message with the correct signed message on the receiver side, concatenate the timestamp T_s with the signature σ and finally encapsulate the signed message into AIS Message Type 8, and send this as a "New type" of AIS message to the AIS receiver(s).

Algorithm 3: AIS Signature Generation and Encapsulation

procedure
Input: AIS message ais_m , $SHA-256$
Output: Signature $\sigma = \{r, s\}$, Encapsulated AIS Message
Compute timestamp T_s
Calculate $h = hash(ais_m \vee T_s)$ using $SHA-256$
Computes signature proof $\sigma = (privKey, h)$

Concatenate signature with ID and timestamp $\sigma \vee T_s$

Chaining signed message into 168-bits of the available payload of Message Type 8

Transmit encapsulated AIS messages to MTC or other Ship

end procedure

4.2.2 *AIS Signature Verification and De-Encapsulation*

The AIS receiver receives the encapsulated AIS message from the transmitter, and Algorithm 4 de-encapsulates and authenticates the received AIS message. The first step de-encapsulates the AIS message and obtains the signed message concatenated with the timestamp $\sigma \vee T_s$. To link an already received AIS message with the received signed message and prevent a replay attack, it computes hash digest $hash(ais_m \vee T_s)$ using the received timestamp and with already received AIS message. The receiver then performs signature validation using $pubKey$ of the transmitter and signature verification ensures that the incoming data are from an authenticated source, and no one has tampered with the AIS message.

Algorithm 4: AIS Signature Verification and De-encapsulation

procedure

Input: Encapsulated AIS Message, AIS message ais_m , $SHA-256$, $pubKey$

Output: Authenticated data

De-encapsulate AIS message and get Signed message $\sigma \vee T_s$

Calculate $h = hash(ais_m \vee T_s)$ using $SHA-256$

Signature validation using Public Key $(pubKey, h, \sigma)$

if Signature is validated **then**

    Keep received message (Fully Authenticated)

else

    Possibly tampered/replayed, therefore UNVERIFIABLE

end if

end procedure

Many of the proposed ADS-B and AIS message authentication and integrity schemes require modifications to existing protocols and transponders, resulting in a loss of compatibility for real-world deployment. However, our proposed ADS-B and AIS schemes are backward-compatible and retain the openness of protocols, thus requiring no hardware or protocol changes.

4.3 Assumptions, Constraints, Recommendations

In this subsection, we enumerate the assumptions, constraints, and recommendations of the proposed schemes.

1. PKI and Key Management are out of Scope: In proposed schemes, we assume that PKI services are already established and readily available. Second, key management (i.e. generation, distribution, expiration, revocation, and reissue) is available with the upgraded system.
2. Cryptographic Computations: The systems upgraded with our solutions are supposed to have cryptographic computation capabilities (i.e., signature generation, signature verification) for both the transmitter and the receiver. Therefore, an upgraded system may have cryptographic modules to perform cryptographic computations.
3. Transmission Errors: We assume that our proposed schemes are not completely resistant to transmission errors introduced by the transmission medium or adversaries. We assume that the error detection and recovery capabilities of the underlying protocols are sufficient to avoid transmission errors; therefore, normal and signed messages are recoverable on the receiver side.

5. Security Modelling and Analysis

In this section, we theoretically evaluate the security strength of the proposed scheme under our defined threat model.

Theorem 1. The legitimate receiver can detect data modification by external attacker.

Proof. The transmitter computes the digital signature σ of its transmitting data using the private key $privKey$, and sends it to the receiver. The receiver validates the signature by using the $pubKey$ of the transmitter and successful validation ensures no one has tampered with the message. The proposed scheme is secured against data modification attacks.

Theorem 2. Prevention of ghost-injection attacks.

Proof. The sender computes a digital signature σ on its data using the private key $privKey$, attaches the current timestamp T_s, and transmits it to receiver. The receiver then validates the signature using the $pubKey$ of the sender. The successful validation of the received message ensures that message is from authenticated source and thus prevents the ghost-injection attacks.

Theorem 3. Prevention of replay attacks.

Proof. The transmitter calculates current timestamp T_s, attaches it to the signature, and transmit it to receiver. The receiver obtains timestamp T_s from signed message and computes $hash(m \vee T_s)$ and then perform signature validation using the $pubKey$ of the transmitter. The signature binding of the timestamp T_s prevents the replay attack hence proposed scheme prevents the replay attack (Smith, 2023; Warner, 2022).

6. Conclusion

In this paper, we proposed a backward-compatible and lightweight message authenticity and integrity scheme for ADS-B and AIS based on state-of-the-art ECDSA standards. The proposed scheme retains the backward-compatibility and openness nature of ADS-B and AIS by transmitting signed messages in follow-up "New type" of messages that non-upgraded systems can safely discard. Moreover, we provide a lightweight security analysis to demonstrate that our proposed scheme is secure under our threat model and can prevent the aforementioned types of attacks.

We first implemented, tested, and evaluated the scheme for a similar protocol COSPAS-SARSAT in our accepted paper at peer-reviewed NDSS SpaceSec24 (Saleem et al., 2024), and we aim to implement and comparative-evaluate our proposed scheme as immediate future work.

Acknowledgements

Hannu Turtiainen thanks the Finnish Cultural Foundation / Suomen Kulttuurirahasto (www.skr.fi) for supporting his Ph.D. dissertation work and research (grant decision no. 00231412). The authors acknowledge the use of royalty-free icons in Figures 1, 3 and 5 courtesy of https://www.flaticon.com/ (icons by: DinosoftLabs, Wendy-G, juicy_fish, Freepik, Flat Icons, surang, Freepik, Peter Lakenbrink).

References

Asari, A., Alagheband, M.R., Bayat, M., Asaar, M.R., 2021. A new provable hierarchical anonymous certificateless authentication protocol with aggregate verification in ADS-B systems. Comput. Netw. 185, 107599.

Balduzzi, M., Pasta, A., Wilhoit, K., 2014. A security evaluation of AIS automated identification system, in: Proceedings of the 30th Annual Computer Security Applications Conference. pp. 436–445.

Chen, T.-C., 2012a. An authenticated encryption scheme for automatic dependent surveillance-broadcast data link, in: CSQRWC 2012. IEEE, pp. 127–131.

Chen, T.-C., 2012b. An authenticated encryption scheme for automatic dependent surveillance-broadcast data link, in: CSQRWC 2012. IEEE, pp. 127–131.

Costin, A., Francillon, A., 2012. Ghost in the Air (Traffic): On insecurity of ADS-B protocol and practical attacks on ADS-B devices.

Duan, Y., Huang, J., Lei, J., Kong, L., Lv, Y., Lin, Z., Chen, G., Khan, M.K., 2022. AISChain: Blockchain-based AIS data platform with dynamic bloom filter tree. IEEE Trans. Intell. Transp. Syst. 24, 2332–2343.

Freire, W.P., Melo Jr, W.S., do Nascimento, V.D., Nascimento, P.R., de Sá, A.O., 2022. Towards a secure and scalable maritime monitoring system using blockchain and low-cost IoT technology. Sensors 22, 4895.

Goudosis, A., Katsikas, S., 2022. Secure Automatic Identification System (SecAIS): Proof-of-Concept Implementation. J. Mar. Sci. Eng. 10, 805.

Goudosis, A., Katsikas, S., 2020. Secure ais with identity-based authentication and encryption. TransNav Int. J. Mar. Navig. Saf. Sea Transp. 14, 287–298.

Goudossis, A., Katsikas, S.K., 2019. Towards a secure automatic identification system (AIS). J. Mar. Sci. Technol. 24, 410–423.

Habibi Markani, J., Amrhar, A., Gagné, J.-M., Landry, R.J., 2023. Security establishment in ADS-B by format-preserving encryption and blockchain schemes. Appl. Sci. 13, 3105.

Hall, J., Lee, J., Benin, J., Armstrong, C., Owen, H., 2015. IEEE 1609 influenced automatic identification system (AIS), in: 2015 IEEE 81st Vehicular Technology Conference (VTC Spring). IEEE, pp. 1–5.

International Telecommunication Union, 2014. Technical characteristics for an automatic identification system using time division multiple access in the VHF maritime mobile frequency band. Recommendation M.1371.

Jegadeesan, S., Obaidat, M.S., Vijayakumar, P., Azees, M., 2021. SEAT: secure and energy efficient anonymous authentication with trajectory privacy-preserving scheme for marine traffic management. IEEE Trans. Green Commun. Netw. 6, 815–824.

Kacem, T., Wijesekera, D., Costa, P., 2015. Integrity and authenticity of ADS-B broadcasts, in: 2015 IEEE Aerospace Conference. IEEE, pp. 1–8.

Khandker, S., Turtiainen, H., Costin, A., Hämäläinen, T., 2022a. On the (In) Security of 1090ES and UAT978 Mobile Cockpit Information Systems–An Attacker Perspective on the Availability of ADS-B Safety-and Mission-Critical Systems. IEEE Access 10, 37718–37730.

Khandker, S., Turtiainen, H., Costin, A., Hämäläinen, T., 2022b. Cybersecurity attacks on software logic and error handling within AIS implementations: A systematic testing of resilience. IEEE Access 10, 29493–29505.

Khandker, S., Turtiainen, H., Costin, A., Hämäläinen, T., 2021. Cybersecurity attacks on software logic and error handling within ADS-B implementations: Systematic testing of resilience and countermeasures. IEEE Trans. Aerosp. Electron. Syst. 58, 2702–2719.

Kožović, D.V., \DJur\djević, D.Ž., Dinulović, M.R., Milić, S., Rašuo, B.P., 2023. Air traffic modernization and control: ADS-B system implementation update 2022: A review. FME Trans. 51, 117–130.

Manesh, M.R., Kaabouch, N., 2017. Analysis of vulnerabilities, attacks, countermeasures and overall risk of the Automatic Dependent Surveillance-Broadcast (ADS-B) system. Int. J. Crit. Infrastruct. Prot. 19, 16–31.

Mäurer, N., Guggemos, T., Ewert, T., Gräupl, T., Schmitt, C., Grundner-Culemann, S., 2022. Security in digital aeronautical communications a comprehensive gap analysis. Int. J. Crit. Infrastruct. Prot. 38, 100549.

Pan, W.-J., Feng, Z.-L., Wang, Y., 2012. ADS-B data authentication based on ECC and X. 509 certificate. J. Electron. Sci. Technol. 10, 51–55.

Prakash, P., Abdelhadi, A., Pan, M., 2019. Secure authentication of ADS-B aircraft communications using retroactive key publication. ArXiv Prepr. ArXiv190704909.

Saleem, A., Costin, A., Turtiainen, H., Hämäläinen, T., 2024. Towards message authentication and integrity for COSPAS-SARSAT 406 MHz distress beacons using lightweight ECDSA digital signatures, in: Workshop on Security of Space and Satellite Systems (SpaceSec) 2024, NDSS.

Sciancalepore, S., Di Pietro, R., 2019. SOS: Standard-compliant and packet loss tolerant security framework for ADS-B communications. IEEE Trans. Dependable Secure Comput. 18, 1681–1698.

Sciancalepore, S., Tedeschi, P., Aziz, A., Di Pietro, R., 2021. Auth-AIS: secure, flexible, and backward-compatible authentication of vessels AIS broadcasts. IEEE Trans. Dependable Secure Comput. 19, 2709–2726.

Shang, Y., 2023. Resilient vector consensus over random dynamic networks under mobile malicious attacks. Comput. J. bxad043.

Smith, G.P., 2023. Python Docs: Secure hashes and message digests.

Strohmeier, M., Lenders, V., Martinovic, I., 2013. Security of ADS- B: State of the Art and Beyond. DCS.

Su, P., Sun, N., Zhu, L., Li, Y., Bi, R., Li, M., Zhang, Z., 2017. A privacy-preserving and vessel authentication scheme using automatic identification system, in: Proceedings of the Fifth ACM International Workshop on Security in Cloud Computing. pp. 83–90.

Thumbur, G., Gayathri, N., Reddy, P.V., Rahman, M.Z.U., others, 2019a. Efficient pairing-free identity-based ADS-B authentication scheme with batch verification. IEEE Trans. Aerosp. Electron. Syst. 55, 2473–2486.

Thumbur, G., Gayathri, N., Reddy, P.V., Rahman, M.Z.U., others, 2019b. Efficient pairing-free identity-based ADS-B authentication scheme with batch verification. IEEE Trans. Aerosp. Electron. Syst. 55, 2473–2486.

Tran, K., Keene, S., Fretheim, E., Tsikerdekis, M., 2021. Marine network protocols and security risks. J. Cybersecurity Priv. 1, 239–251.

Warner, B., 2022. Pure-Python ECDSA and ECDH.

Wimpenny, G., Šafář, J., Grant, A., Bransby, M., 2022. Securing the Automatic Identification System (AIS): Using public key cryptography to prevent spoofing whilst retaining backwards compatibility. J. Navig. 75, 333–345.

Wu, Z., Guo, A., Yue, M., Liu, L., 2019. An ADS-B message authentication method based on certificateless short signature. IEEE Trans. Aerosp. Electron. Syst. 56, 1742–1753.

Wu, Z., Shang, T., Guo, A., 2020. Security issues in automatic dependent surveillance-broadcast (ADS-B): A survey. IEEE Access 8, 122147–122167.

Wu, Z., Shang, T., Yue, M., Liu, L., 2023. ADS-Bchain: A Blockchain-based Trusted Service Scheme for Automatic Dependent Surveillance-Broadcast. IEEE Trans. Aerosp. Electron. Syst.

Yang, A., Tan, X., Baek, J., Wong, D.S., 2015. A new ADS-B authentication framework based on efficient hierarchical identity-based signature with batch verification. IEEE Trans. Serv. Comput. 10, 165–175.

Yang, H., Huang, R., Wang, X., Deng, J., Chen, R., 2014. EBAA: An efficient broadcast authentication scheme for ADS-B communication based on IBS-MR. Chin. J. Aeronaut. 27, 688–696.

Yang, H., Zhou, Q., Yao, M., Lu, R., Li, H., Zhang, X., 2018. A practical and compatible cryptographic solution to ADS-B security. IEEE Internet Things J. 6, 3322–3334.

Yi, P., Li, J., Zhang, Y., Chen, Y., 2022. Efficient hierarchical signature scheme with batch verification function suitable for ADS-B system. IEEE Trans. Aerosp. Electron. Syst. 59, 1292–1299.

Using Wargaming to Model Cyber Defense Decision-Making: Observation-Based Research in Locked Shields

Pietari Sarjakivi, Jouni Ihanus and Panu Moilanen
University of Jyväskylä, Finland

pietari@sarjakivi.fi
jouni.e.i.ihanus@student.jyu.fi
panu.moilanen@jyu.fi

Abstract: Defensive Cyber Operations (DCO) in complex environments, such as cyber wargames, require in-depth cybersecurity knowledge and the ability to make quick decisions. In a typical DCO, execution rarely follows a pre-planned path because of extensive adversary influence, challenging an already complex decision-making environment. Decision-making models have been extensively studied from perspectives of military operations and business management, but they are not sufficiently researched in the context of cyber. This paper responds to this need by examining the decision-making models of DCO leaders in a live-fire wargame environment. This study was conducted by observing leaders of cyber operations during the world's largest live-fire cyber exercise, NATO Locked Shield 2023. In this exercise, the blue teams plan and execute their defensive cyber operation in a realistic operational environment, while the red team conducts attacks against the defended environment. The large-scale, wargaming-style environment of Locked Shield is one of the best environments for modelling DCO decision-making models; in this exercise, the DCO is broad and multi-faceted, a perspective which cannot be achieved in a typical capture-the-flag competition or a single security incident. DCO leaders must be able to manage two distinct decision-making processes with different sets of required skills to be successful in the mission. While the primary process relates to the execution and evolution of the pre-designed plan with traditional operational leadership skills, the secondary process deals with unplanned and deliberately caused cyber-related events that require a deep understanding of cybersecurity. In this respect, the main contribution of this research is the constructed decision-making model of the DCO leader. This model is based on observations collected and presented in the context of multiple well-known decision-making frameworks. This model can be further used to train future DCO leaders and assess artificial intelligence's usability to support and automate decision-making in such operations.

Keywords: Decision-Making, Defensive Cyber Operations, Wargaming, Locked Shields

1. Introduction

Ubiquitous digitalisation and connected societies have emphasised the importance of the cyber dimension. In a military domain, one indicator of this development is NATO's decision to recognise cyberspace as a domain of operations alongside the traditional domains of air, land, and sea (NATO, 2021b). The digital footprint of different organisations is increasing, as are adversaries' actions. This development can be seen in both the volume and the sophistication of the attacks, which increases the complexity of defensive measures (Fortinet, 2022; Microsoft, 2023). Identifying security breaches in cyberspace typically takes weeks (Mandiant, 2023) or months (IBM, 2023) - longer than in other domains. This is due to the complexity of the cyber domain compared to other domains.

The Defensive Cyber Operation (DCO) organisation can structurally be divided into multiple levels depending on several variables. Typical civil side Security Operations Centre (SOC) is divided into management levels and analyst tiers with different responsibility areas. This approach can be widely scaled based on the size of the areas of responsibility dedicated to the SOC and other organisational variables (Knerler et al., 2022). On the military side, the structure of the cyber operation organisation similarly depends on a defined mission. However, similar management and analyst-level roles can be recognised in both organisation models (Dalmjin et al., 2020). In previous studies, this has been approached relatively widely: At the analyst level, D'amico et al. (D'Amico et al., 2005) and Gutzwiller et al. (2016) (Gutzwiller et al., 2016) have analysed the tasks and operating environment that experts encounter in their cyber security roles. Their studies are based on a cognitive task analysis that strongly focuses on cognitive challenges to create cyber situation awareness at the analyst level. Complex dynamic operating environments can strain human cognitive capabilities, challenging security analysts' ability to understand situations and make related decisions (Druzdzel & Flynn, 2010; Endsley, 1995). Machine learning can support human analysts in creating situation awareness and decision-making. The elements of the unknown are more common in defensive than offensive cyber operations, as DCOs rarely follow pre-planned paths due to the extensive adversary influence (Williams, 2014).

Wargaming exercises simulate real-life environments where players' decisions impact gameplay. They provide participants with the opportunity to gain experience and the possibility to experiment with different strategies against other players. For researchers, they offer an excellent platform to observe decision-making in a realistic environment (Nesbit et al., 2013).

This study aims to understand the decision-making process during the DCO based on the Locked Shields cyber wargame type exercise. The research was conducted in a military context, but its results can also be utilised in civilian operations. The main contribution of this research is the constructed decision-making model of the DCO leader.

The paper is organised as follows: Section 2 introduces the research methodology, Section 3 presents the ontology of related decision-making models, Section 4 presents the observed environment, Section 5 introduces the construction of the model, and Section 6 concludes the study with future research topics.

2. Methodology

In terms of methodology, the study can be divided into two main stages, shown in Figure 1. These stages can be considered at the top level to include data collection and data analysis.

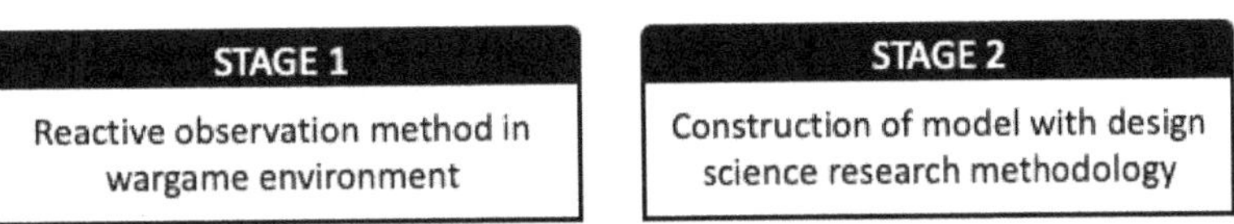

Figure 1: Research methodology utilised in this study

In the first stage, the authors observed the Blue Team (BT) Finland in the world's largest live-fire cyber exercise, NATO Locked Shield 2023, using the reactive observation method (Arthur, 2012, pp. 165–169). Observations were made during the live-fire exercise and in the preparatory phases. In addition, the data collected was supplemented by an interview survey conducted at different levels of the target organisation. This method was appropriate because all internal team communications were conducted via a game-like voice communication system, allowing the observers to listen to any conversation during the exercise freely. Regarding content knowledge, BT Finland performed well in this exercise, which is why the team's decision-making ability can be considered good and, therefore, suitable as the target of this study.

In the second stage, the authors used design science research methodology with a constructive research approach (Peffers et al., 2007) to create a constructive model for decision-making in DCO. The constructed model builds on known decision-making frameworks while providing an innovative structure applicable to operations with an active adversary. The methodology was chosen based on the nature of the subject of the study as a real-world problem that the proposed construct was intended to solve.

3. Decision-Making Frameworks

To develop decision-making in DCOs, it is essential to understand the structure of decision-making in their context. This chapter presents key elements in DCOs and relevant decision-making frameworks used in model construction.

3.1 Understanding Elements of Defensive Cyber Operations

For at least 200 years, military theory has divided decision-making in war into strategic, operational, and tactical levels, where the main difference between levels is the reach and timespan of the effect (Maxwell, 1997). Many Western militaries utilise a mission command model originating from the same era. The mission command is a decentralised model where the commander communicates the intent to subordinates, who then make decisions and act accordingly. The model is based on mutual trust, where the commander trusts the subordinates' skills and willingness to make decisions best fitting to the communicated intention, and subordinates trust that the commander has given the right direction and enough resources to complete the task. The idea behind the model is that the person closest to the action should have the most up-to-date understanding of the situation and, therefore, be able to make the right decisions (Storr, 2003).

DCO leaders and operators utilise the Cyber Situational Awareness (CSA) process to understand the operating environment's state to support decision-making in cyber operations. Inputs can be collected from technical sources like log management systems, endpoint and network sensors, honeypots and availability monitors (Husák et al., 2022) and non-technical sources like human observations (Vielberth et al., 2019). Situational awareness is built with the perception of the current situation, comprehension of the current situation and projection of future status (Endsley, 1995). The Holistic Operational Framework for Establishing Situational Awareness in Cyberspace (HOFESAC) model categorises CSA information into six classes that together form a comprehensive understanding of operating environment: Threat environment, anomalous activities, vulnerabilities, key terrain, operational readiness, and ongoing operations (Dressler et al., 2012).

As Sun Tzu stated almost 2500 years ago, in combat situations, decision-makers must understand both their adversary and themselves (Giles, 1910). Cyber Threat Intelligence (CTI) is a process that provides information about adversaries, their tools, techniques, and procedures (TTP), as well as potential security threats. It utilises scenario thinking to produce strategic insights and potential courses of action (COA) that decision-makers can utilise in their planning and decisions (Schlette et al., 2021). Analysis of Competing Hypotheses (ACH) is one of the tools used to compare scenarios to identify the most likely COA (Lemay & Leblanc, 2018).

3.2 Relevant Decision-Making Frameworks

To model the decision-making process in DCO, two well-known frameworks were used: Cynefin and OODA. Both frameworks are widely used within cybersecurity. Cynefin operates at a high level of abstraction and is a well-suited framework for modelling decision-making, as all four contexts with their respective natures are present in major cyber incidents (B. S. Dykstra & Orr, 2016). As a whole, cybersecurity can be recognised as a complex system (Valentine, 2018). The OODA loop framework, originally designed for combat situations, is well-suited for rapid decision-making by cyber operators (Husák et al., 2022). These frameworks are introduced below.

The cynefin framework is a sensemaking tool applied to a broad range of industries. It recognises four different contexts for decision-making:

1. In a simple context, decision-making is based on best practices, and the situations are relatively straightforward, as clear causality is easy to find.
2. In a complicated context, causality is present, but an expert is needed to analyse the situation and select the most suitable out of multiple right choices.
3. In a complex context, there is one right choice, but the context is almost impossible to map entirely, and the decision-maker must manoeuvre with a limited understanding of the situation.
4. In a chaotic context, no clear causality can be found in a reasonable time, and there are too many moving elements to make fact-based decisions. In a chaotic context, decision-makers must both act with the best available information and work to shift the context to complex (Snowden & Boone, 2007).

The OODA loop is a combat operations process developed to support fast decision-making and "expose flaws of competing or adversary systems" (Boyd, 1986). Its developer, Air Force Colonel John Boyd, was a fighter pilot who studied previous conflicts, and this decision-making model has been widely adopted within Western militaries (Osinga, 2005). OODA loop includes four phases that are repeated in a fast closed loop.

1. In the observation phase, data is collected from the environment.
2. In the orientation phase, data is analysed, and comprehension is created.
3. In the decision phase, the alternative COAs are reviewed, and the preferred COA is selected.
4. In the act phase, the decision is implemented into an action. (Husák et al., 2022; Osinga, 2005).

4. Observations from Locked Shield

4.1 Describing the Observation Environment

Locked Shields is the world's largest international cyber defence exercise. This annual exercise "enables cyber security experts to enhance their skills in defending national IT systems and critical infrastructure under real-time attacks". It has been organised by the NATO Cooperative Cyber Defence Center of Excellence (CCDCOE) since 2010. In 2023, over 2000 cyber experts from 32 nations participated in the exercise (NATO Cooperative Cyber Defence Centre of Excellence, 2023).

Locked Shields is a traditional Red Team (RT) versus Blue Team(BT) exercise where the RT acts according to the pre-planned scenario and has the right to perform OCO while the BTs' Rules of Engagement (ROE) limit them to DCO (NATO Cooperative Cyber Defence Centre of Excellence, 2023; Williams, 2014). This ROE is realistic from a legislative point of view but creates an imbalance between actors and always keeps the initiative with the red team. This imbalance creates a need for strategic analysis and CTI in case the BTs want to participate actively in the exercise.

By their nature wargaming exercises provide participating BTs a clear objective for their mission and a scoring mechanism that can be used to measure how successful teams have been. Time compression forces teams to react quickly and under pressure. The scoring system adds an element of competition to the exercise, enabling participants and researchers to evaluate the effectiveness of decisions made. After Action Reports (AAR) shared with participants after the execution, make it possible to compare different approaches teams take. By studying real-life cyber incidents that lack the scoring system and the possibility to compare approaches different teams take or Capture the Flag competitions that lack realistic large-scale environments, the modelling of decision-making is challenging. For those reasons, the large-scale, wargaming-style environment of Locked Shield is one of the best environments for observing DCO decision-making.

4.2 Observations of Decision-making

Figure 2 shows the key observations made during the exercise.

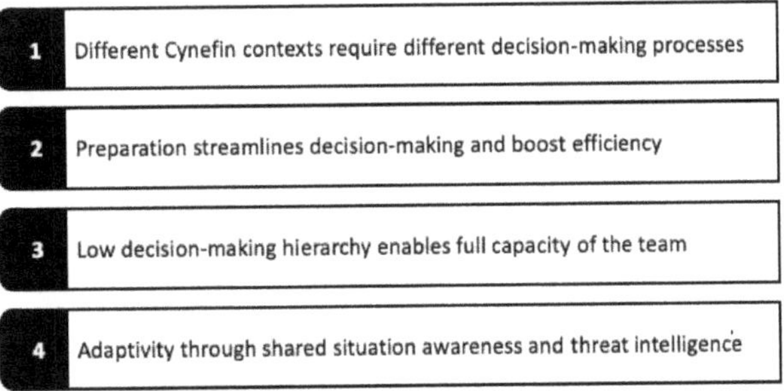

1 Different Cynefin contexts require different decision-making processes
2 Preparation streamlines decision-making and boost efficiency
3 Low decision-making hierarchy enables full capacity of the team
4 Adaptivity through shared situation awareness and threat intelligence

Figure 2: Key observations from the exercise

The first observation is that decision-makers in DCOs must operate constantly in multiple Cynefin contexts, each requiring a different set of skills. The speed and process of decision-making also vary between different contexts.

The second observation highlights the importance of preparations in building readiness for operations and efficient decision-making. Finland was one of the smallest high-performing blue teams (NATO Cooperative Cyber Defence Centre of Excellence, 2022). The BT Finland was primarily based on reservists who spent longer than average preparing for the exercise (NATO Cooperative Cyber Defence Centre of Excellence, 2022). The preparations include developing and familiarising with joint tooling and processes, studying the mission and scenario, and practising critical phases of the execution.

The third observation relates to the effectiveness of low hierarchy decision-making with the mission command model utilised by BT Finland. Figure 3 presents the command structure, roles, and responsibilities in BT Finland. BT Finland had two operations leaders who worked in shifts, one leading the operation execution whilst the other preparing plans for the next phase that he was going to execute. The operations plan was built with an ideology where every squad had complete responsibility for their sector in the defended environment, and as long as a joint tool, techniques and procedures were followed, squad leaders had the freedom to execute tasks in their sector as they felt appropriate. Squads' tasks were divided among cyber operators whose responsibility was typically limited to certain functions like administration, threat hunting or countermeasures; or special systems like electric power grid or air defence system.

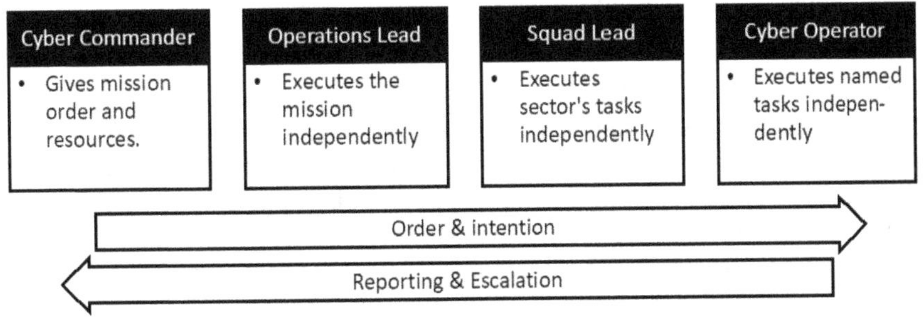

Figure 3: Command structure, roles, and responsibilities in Blue Team Finland

The fourth observation pertains to the significance of sharing CSA and CTI with the entire team in real time and with a high level of detail. In addition to advanced technical tooling for sharing detailed CSA, the BT had hourly situation briefs for leaders and a dedicated Tactical Operations Centre (TOC) led by operations leaders acting as a fusion centre. TOC had a CTI function producing analysis of possible Courses of Action (COA), which TOC used to provide early warning for the need to balance the resources to prepare for upcoming attacks dynamically. In a large-scale exercise like Locked Shields, the BTs must make decisions with a limited understanding of the complex operating environment and be prepared for upcoming unknown unknowns.

5. Construction of Model

According to the observations presented in the previous chapter, decision-making in the DCO can be divided into two distinct processes, as shown in Figure 4. The primary process relates to the execution and evolution of the pre-designed plan using traditional operational leadership skills. The secondary process deals with unplanned and deliberately caused cyber-related events, requiring a deep understanding of cybersecurity.

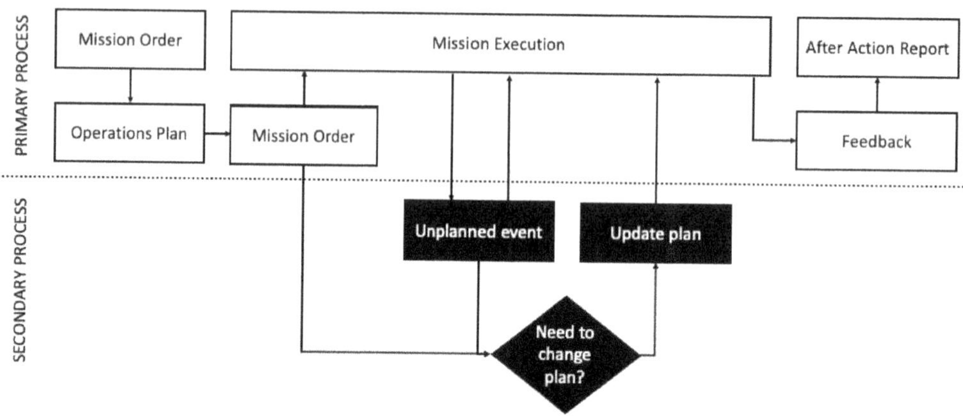

Figure 4: Two distinct decision-making processes in the defensive cyber operation

5.1 The Primary Process

The primary process aims to accomplish the mission according to the plan. It operates mainly within the simple or complicated context of Cynefin framework and follows traditional management structures and best practices such as Project Management Body of Knowledge (PMBOK) (Project Management Institute, 2021) and the NATO Comprehensive Operations Planning Directive (COPD) (NATO, 2021a). For a DCO leader to be successful in the primary process, at least the following good management attributes are needed: Clear vision, strong team-building skills, good communication skills, can-do attitude, and discipline (Pennypacker & Cabains-Brewin, 2003). Planning effective cyber operations needs to take nested technical aspects of planning into account, and therefore, an understanding of the cybersecurity domain is needed (Barber et al., 2015). The DCO leader may seek support from team members or external experts, so these attributes are not essential for the DCO leader.

The mission order defines the mission's objectives, ROE, and resource limits. The mission order is influenced by prior strategic decisions such as the importance of cybersecurity in the political agenda, the technological education the nation provides to its citizens, local legislation's maturity to recognise cybercrime and surveillance, partnership with the private sector, and overall digitalisation maturity of the country. The political and financial state of the organisation and prior events, such as previous cyber operations and synchronised military operations, influence the mission order.

After receiving the mission order, the DCO leader and the closest leaders craft an operations plan defining prioritised mission sub-objectives, execution plan, timeline, available support, organisation, and responsibilities. Operational planning must analyse environmental components to understand connections and dependencies and identify high-priority components (Barber et al., 2015). The plan is developed further in the organisation, according to the mission command model, and rehearsed to ensure execution readiness. DCO organisations must utilise joint tools, techniques, and procedures that are interoperable with possible allied forces and set the roles in a way that every member of the team is in the optimal role for them. Development ideas and lessons learned from previous operations should be considered to improve organisations' capabilities further. Decision-making in the planning and rehearsing phases is not as time-critical as in later phases but might lack information about the upcoming mission and operating environment. Therefore, DCO leaders should use this time wisely and utilise CTI to get as much information about the environment and adversaries' centres of gravity as possible to make the right decisions for the plan.

The mission execution follows the operations plan as well as possible, although it is likely that time constraints in planning and complicated cyber context create a need for adaptability. Primary process decisions in the execution phase need a good understanding of operations progression, and for example, DCO leaders need to decide when a task is ready enough for the team to continue forward, what activities can be left undone for now to catch the timeline, how to re-allocate resources to optimise team's performance, and which tasks to prioritise. Threats are detected through CSA and mitigated with practised processes. Accurate CTI gives time for defenders to prepare for attacks.

After execution, the team gives and receives feedback from each other and other stakeholders. If DCO was conducted in a wargaming environment, scoring could be used to measure the outcome partially. Feedback is refined to development initiatives, which are, together with feedback, collected for AAR. The AAR is shared with a broader audience to share the lessons learned.

5.2 The Secondary Process

The secondary process is initiated when an unplanned event occurs, and its goal is to minimise this event's impact on operations plan execution within the primary process. In DCOs, unplanned events are often deliberately caused by active adversary actions. While traditional military operations studies recognise similar unanticipated events caused the need to change the plan, like German Field Marshal Moltke stated in the late 1800s (Kenny, 2016), the cyber domain offers exceptional elements of speed and uncertainty, and therefor this secondary process deviates from traditional military operations. Similarly, due to the cyber domain's highly interlinked nature and complicated environments where adversaries are difficult to recognise, this secondary process operates within the complex context of Cynefin.

The resolution of the situation can be mitigation of the unplanned event's impact through countermeasures and/or change of operations plan by, for example, re-prioritising the mission objectives, changing the resourcing balance of squads to focus the force or initiating a new special operation. To be successful in this secondary process, DCO leaders need a deep understanding of cybersecurity, a clear understanding of overall mission objectives, good intuition, and readiness to adapt to new situations quickly.

Dynamic decision-making in fast-changing situations must be based on prioritised mission sub-objectives, accurate CSA, and real-time CTI, as presented in Figure 5. CSA provides an understanding of the state of its own operations and operating environment, including incidents and unplanned events causing the need to start the secondary process. CTI provides strategic analysis of the adversary's mission and predicted COAs. As the need to make decisions evolves rapidly, the CSA and CTI information must constantly be available and up-to-date. Decision-makers must weigh different options based on available information and predicted outcomes to make the best possible decision. While defenders are often in reactive mode as adversaries have the initiative through the offensive nature of their operation, with CTI defenders can, for example, build deceptions, extra layers to defence, change the environment to break adversary's cyber kill chain and re-arrange their forces to lower the impact of the adversary's offence (Barber et al., 2015).

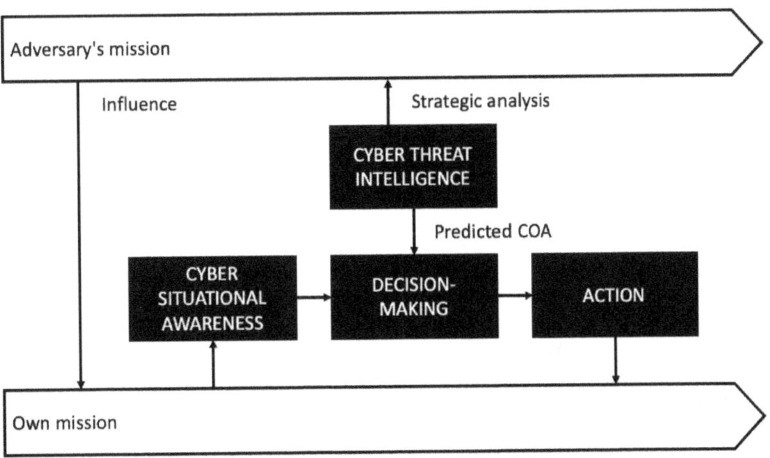

Figure 5: Dynamic decision-making in the secondary process

In complex contexts, the speed of decision-making is often crucial. While active decisions are needed promptly, a decision to wait for more information or a better time to react is a valid option, especially with an active adversary. As after intrusions, adversaries operate in a defended environment expecting to get caught, may defender's hasty decision to partially mitigate the threat just causes the adversary to lay low in the environment, making the complete mitigation difficult. The decision to mitigate the threat that has had time to build persistence and is unaware of the detection must be taken only when the defender is ready to completely take down the threat vector.

Although DCO leaders are the primary consumers for CSA and CTI, it is crucially important to share the information upward in the command chain, laterally to allied forces, and downwards to squads and cyber operators. Upstream sharing often happens through reports, but lateral and downstream sharing needs to have a fast and detail-oriented technical solution that can be integrated into technical defence solutions, being then easy to consume in rapid situations.

Cyber Operators' actions closely follow Boyd's OODA loop's principles as they, like fighter jet pilots, focus completely on the task they are performing at the time. Most of the tasks these cyber operators are given should be manageable independently or in small groups to maintain this high focus and speed up the closed OODA loop. Compared to fighter jet pilots, who can identify their enemy relatively easily, cyber operators must spend an enormous amount of time on anomaly detection and finding traces and potential future footholds of their actively hiding adversaries. Cyber operators must actively share information they feel is relevant, and therefore, they contribute to CSA more than they consume in the Orientation phase. For example, a filename seen in forensics investigations may lead to the detection of an adversary's foothold in a completely different system. In DCOs, cyber operators' anomaly detection skills, building relations between things they see, and intuition are essential assets that are improved through gained experience and effective information sharing.

6. Conclusion

Defensive Cyber Operations play a crucial role in safeguarding today's critical infrastructure. Decision-making in these operations is an essential element of success. To understand and develop the decision-making chain, one needs the opportunity to observe an appropriate operational environment. In this study, the NATO Locked Shields exercise was used as a platform to seek this information. This environment provides a wargame environment in the military context that emphasises the time compression and national crisis management elements. Observations were made based on several commonly known decision-making frameworks. In conclusion, this study proposed a dual-process model for decision-making in DCO. The authors argued that successful DCO leaders must be able to perform both primary processes simultaneously. This model can be further used to understand the DCO decision-making structure and train future DCO leaders.

For further research, it is important to evaluate the usability of the presented construction model in real DCO. The construction model can also be used to further assess the possibilities of AI-based decision-making at different stages of the decision-making process in such operations. It should be noted that regardless of the methodology used, there is always a risk of subjectivity in the observation method. For this reason, the possible need to supplement the findings should be borne in mind.

Acknowledgements

The authors would like to thank the Finnish Defence Forces and the National Defence Training Association of Finland for the opportunity to observe the Finnish Blue Team in the Locked Shields exercise and Business Finland for supporting the writing of this article (grant number 671/31/2022).

References

Arthur, J. (Ed.). (2012). *Research methods and methodologies in education*. SAGE.

B. S. Dykstra, J. A., & Orr, S. R. (2016). Acting in the unknown: The cynefin framework for managing cybersecurity risk in dynamic decision making. *2016 International Conference on Cyber Conflict (CyCon U.S.)*, 1–6. https://doi.org/10.1109/CYCONUS.2016.7836616

Barber, D., Bobo, T., & Strum, K. (2015). Cyberspace Operations Planning: Operating a Technical Military Force beyond the Kinetic Domains. *Military Cyber Affairs*, *1*(1). https://doi.org/10.5038/2378-0789.1.1.1003

Boyd, J. (1986). *Patterns of Conflict*.

Dalmjin, A., Banse, V., Lumiste, L., Teixeira, J., & Balci, A. (2020). *Cyber Commanders' Handbook* (pp. 24–30). NATO CCDCOE Publications.

D'Amico, A., Whitley, K., Tesone, D., O'Brien, B., & Roth, E. (2005). Achieving Cyber Defense Situational Awareness: A Cognitive Task Analysis of Information Assurance Analysts. *Proceedings of the Human Factors and Ergonomics Society Annual Meeting, 49*, 229–233. https://doi.org/10.1177/154193120504900304

Dressler, J., Moody, W. C., & Koepke, J. (2012). *A Holistic Operational Framework for Establishing Situational Awareness in Cyberspace.*

Druzdzel, M., & Flynn, R. (2010). *Decision Support Systems.* https://doi.org/10.1201/b11499-37

Endsley, M. (1995). Endsley, M.R.: Toward a Theory of Situation Awareness in Dynamic Systems. Human Factors Journal 37(1), 32-64. *Human Factors: The Journal of the Human Factors and Ergonomics Society, 37*, 32–64. https://doi.org/10.1518/001872095779049543

Fortinet. (2022). *Global Threat Landscape Report A Semiannual Report by FortiGuard Labs—August 2022.* Fortinet. https://www.fortinet.com/content/dam/fortinet/assets/threat-reports/threat-report-1h-2022.pdf

Giles. (1910). *Sun Tzu On The Art Of War* (0 ed.). https://doi.org/10.4324/9781315030081

Gutzwiller, R., Hunt, S., & Lange, D. (2016, March). *Task Analysis toward Characterizing Cyber-Cognitive Situation Awareness (CCSA) in Cyber Defense Analysts.* https://doi.org/10.1109/COGSIMA.2016.7497780

Husák, M., Sadlek, L., Špaček, S., Laštovička, M., Javorník, M., & Komárková, J. (2022). CRUSOE: A toolset for cyber situational awareness and decision support in incident handling. *Computers & Security, 115*, 102609. https://doi.org/10.1016/j.cose.2022.102609

IBM. (2023). *Cost of a Data Breach Report 2023.*

Kenny, G. (2016). Strategic Plans Are Less Important than Strategic Planning. *Harvard Business Review, June 2016.*

Knerler, K., Parker, I., & Zimmerman, C. (2022). *11 Strategies of a World-Class Cybersecurity Operations Center.* MITRE. https://www.mitre.org/sites/default/files/2022-04/11-strategies-of-a-world-class-cybersecurity-operations-center.pdf

Lemay, A., & Leblanc, S. (2018). Iterative Analysis of Competing Hypotheses to Overcome Cognitive Biases in Cyber Decision-Making. *Journal of Information Warfare, 17*(2). https://www.jstor.org/stable/26633153

Mandiant. (2023). *M-Trends 2023 Special Report.*

Maxwell, A. (1997). Three Levels of War. *USAF College of Aerospace Doctrine, Research and Education (CADRE). Air University Press, 1.*

Microsoft. (2023). *Microsoft Digital Defense Report 2023.*

NATO. (2021a). *Allied Command Operations Comprehensive Operations Planning Directive Version 3.0.*

NATO. (2021b). *NATO Cyber Defence.* North Atlantic Treaty Organization – Public Diplomacy Division. https://www.nato.int/nato_static_fl2014/assets/pdf/2021/4/pdf/2104-factsheet-cyber-defence-en.pdf

NATO Cooperative Cyber Defence Centre of Excellence. (2022). *Classified Locked Shields 2022 After Action Reports.*

NATO Cooperative Cyber Defence Centre of Excellence. (2023). *Locked Shields.* NATO Cooperative Cyber Defence Centre of Excellence. https://ccdcoe.org/exercises/locked-shields/

Nesbit, P., Kennedy, Q., Alt, J., Fricker, R., Whitaker, L., Yang, J. H., Appleget, J., Huston, J., & Patton, S. (2013). *Understanding Optimal Decision-Making in Wargaming:* Defense Technical Information Center. https://doi.org/10.21236/ADA602079

Osinga, F. (2005). *Science, strategy and war: The strategic theory of John Boyd.* Eburon Academic Publishers.

Peffers, K., Tuunanen, T., Rothenberger, M. A., & Chatterjee, S. (2007). A Design Science Research Methodology for Information Systems Research. *Journal of Management Information Systems, 24*(3), 45–77. https://doi.org/10.2753/MIS0742-1222240302

Pennypacker, J. S., & Cabains-Brewin, J. (2003). *What makes a good project manager.* Center for Business Practices.

Project Management Institute (Ed.). (2021). *A guide to the project management body of knowledge (PMBOK® guide) and the standard for project management* (Seventh Edition). Project Management Institute, Inc.

Schlette, D., Caselli, M., & Pernul, G. (2021). A Comparative Study on Cyber Threat Intelligence: The Security Incident Response Perspective. *IEEE Communications Surveys & Tutorials, 23*(4), 2525–2556. https://doi.org/10.1109/COMST.2021.3117338

Snowden, D. J., & Boone, M. E. (2007). A Leader's Framework for Decision Making. *Harvard Business Review, November 2007.*

Storr, J. (2003). A command philosophy for the information age: The continuing relevance of mission command. *Defence Studies, 3*(3), 119–129. https://doi.org/10.1080/14702430308405081

Valentine, C. W. M. (2018). *Organizing for Cyber Resilience: Rethinking the Balance Between Prevention.*

Vielberth, M., Menges, F., & Pernul, G. (2019). Human-as-a-security-sensor for harvesting threat intelligence. *Cybersecurity, 2*(1), 23. https://doi.org/10.1186/s42400-019-0040-0

Williams, B. T. (2014). *The Joint Force Commander's Guide to Cyberspace Operations.*

Revisiting Past Cyber Security Recommendations: Lessons we Have Failed to Learn

Matthias Schulze and Jantje Silomon
Institute for Peace Research and Security Policy (IFSH), Hamburg, Germany
schulze@ifsh.de
silomon@ifsh.de

Abstract: Cyber-security is constantly evolving as new technologies introduce new vulnerabilities and threat actors constantly develop new techniques to penetrate systems. Much focus in scholarship is on the cyber-offense, while few analyse changes in the cyber-defence posture. Since its inception, defensive information security has evolved and introduced a plethora of new security controls to either prevent, detect, mitigate, or respond to new cyber-attacks. When studying cyber-incidents, a paradox becomes apparent: often, low-end security fails are responsible for most breaches, such as default system configurations and credentials or violations of the principle of least privileges. Even security sensitive organisations such as the US DoD or IT companies suffer from this paradox, as a recent NSA/CISA report indicates: large sums are spent on high-end security programs only to be compromised by low-end attacks. This paradox becomes even more pronounced when introducing a longitudinal historical perspective: many of these issues have been known for decades, as reports from the 1970s show. These include inadequate hardware and software not designed with security in mind, the issue of managing resource access controls in a multi-user environment that includes remote terminals (aka a cloud infrastructure), malicious insider threats that bypass security controls, as well as the issue of applying timely software patches. In sum: while the IT security industry is rushing to introduce new high-level security controls and technologies, the main issues seem to be age-old problems and the failure to learn lessons from the past, warranting a historical approach. In this paper, the origin of security controls is examined, shedding light on relevant best practices, recommendations and why they emerged. Starting in the 1960s, we analyse the emerging technologies of each subsequent decade, explore what changes in IT-security controls these new technologies necessitated, and how IT and later cyber-security changed over the years. Furthermore, reference is made to the aftermath of selected cyber-attacks to further highlight is analysed to explore potential shifts in security paradigms beyond those introduced by technology itself.

Keywords: History of IT Security, Security Controls, Lessons Learned

1. Introduction

The rapid development of technology invariably introduces new vulnerabilities and risks, forcing IT-security to constantly readjust. Attackers strive to discover new attack techniques to exploit systems, while defenders must adapt and introduce new security controls to manage emerging risks. When studying the history of IT-security, a paradox emerges. Often, it is not the novel, cutting-edge exploits that lead to compromise, but the failure to implement baseline security controls – those that have been known for decades. Despite technology advancing and its accompanying attack surface growing, certain security controls appear almost unchanged since their inception. Not only are they relevant but vital and include concepts such as password policies, authentication, access control, separation of users and programs, as well as adequate backup strategies.

More specifically, security controls are defined as “safeguards or countermeasures prescribed for an information system or an organization designed to protect the confidentiality, integrity, and availability of its information and to meet a set of defined security requirements” (NIST 2020, p.63). Generally, security controls are distinguished either by *type* (physical, technical, or administrative), *function* (preventative, detective, corrective, deterrent, or compensating) or *level* upon which they are decided and implemented (management, operational, or technical) (Viegas, Kuyucu, 2022).

Another way to categorise controls is by their intricacy. *Low-end security controls* (sometimes called *baseline* or *essential* controls) typically cost little in terms of computational, financial, as well as human resources to implement. The US National Institute of Standards and Technology (NIST) defines an IT security control baseline as the “set of minimum security controls defined for a low-impact, moderate-impact, or high-impact information system” (NIST, 2020 p.63). They are Pareto-optimised, achieving “80% of the benefit from 20% of the effort”, meaning they protect against most cyber threats (CCCS, 2020). In adopting controls, the best practice has been to follow established security frameworks that select and implement several different controls, all dependent on the envisaged security objectives, risk appetite, and compliance requirements.

Yet, many organisations still fail to implement these basic, age-old security controls, as a 2023 study by the US National Security Agency highlights: the majority of the top 10 security misconfigurations discovered among government networks in the US include the failure to implement baseline security controls such as having insecure default configurations and improper separation of user and administrator privilege (CISA, 2023). Even cyber-security sensitive organisations are prone to such failures.

In this paper, we process-trace the history of IT-security controls and analyse why they were introduced, and how they have changed over time. We focus on defensive security practices and technical controls, from which we then derive core IT-security lessons that many have still not learned. The next section explores the concept of security controls, followed by a chapter on the history of IT-security across the past five decades, including relevant security best practices and recommendations, as well as selective cyber-incidents. The outcomes are then summarised and discussed.

2. Security Controls Through the Decades

While the conceptual delineation of security controls is widely known because of standards such as ISO, less is known about the origin of these controls. The section explores how emerging technologies of past decades (1960-2010s) introduced the need for new security measures, focussing on physical, technical, and administrative controls. We take a chronological approach ending with the year 2020, as the current decade and its technological developments, such as the rise of generative AI, is still unfolding.

2.1 1960s: Minicomputers and Multi-User Time Sharing

The first computers were developed during the 1940s in the context of World War II. They were predominately built in a governmental, national security context. Security paradigms of the time focused on isolating these room-sized calculating machines, preventing theft, sabotage, and vandalism, while security controls centred on preventing physical access through guards, fences, and checkpoint stations (Yost, 2007). Integrated circuits in the 1960s were a game changer, improving and shrinking "mini computers" such as the PDP-1. Improved magnetic storage, new programming languages and new input methods via terminals lead to a wider adoption at universities and private companies.

The invention of *multi-user time-sharing* at MIT in 1961 was arguably the most IT-security relevant invention of this decade (Freiberger and Swaine, no date). Time-sharing allowed for multitasking and the simultaneous running of programs by different users at the same time (Meijer et al., 2007). However, this also led to the "core" security problem that still plagues society today: "with multiprogramming the confidentiality, integrity and availability of one program could be under attack by an arbitrary concurrently running program" (Meijer et al., 2007). In essence, an uncleared user or a single program could potentially read or alter the content of other programs residing in the same memory, a particular concern within national security contexts and demonstrated by the DARWIN computer game in 1961 (Vyssotsky, 1961). One of the first technical controls to remedy this was the introduction of the user password in 1961 to separate time-sharing accounts on the same machine (Beyond Identity, 2021).

A now famous study on security controls was conducted by Willis H. Ware in the late 1960s, which was later declassified. He described the security threats emanating from the lack of technical isolation between programs in shared memory, from accidental data disclosure and covert infiltration to the possibility of hijacked remote-terminals and brute-forcing of weak access codes, among numerous others. The "Ware Report" (Ware, 1970) introduced a plethora of security controls to tackle these problems, many of which are still familiar today, including:

- separation of users and processes with different access permissions
- technical implementation of read/write permissions based on user privilege levels
- user authentication
- event logging and audit trails of all transactions
- automatic self-testing system processing
- secure data deletion
- constant system certification

The report called for a security by design principle, arguing that the operating system must support user and program separation, controlled by a supervisor program that runs with elevated privileges and manages user, file and program access control (ibid). Some of the proposed controls were only theoretical at the time, for example file and storage encryption, which did not become technically feasible until later (Brenner, 2007). While the report remained classified until 1975, many developers discovered the issues independently and began work to mitigate them, such as ideas on file access control and data labelling (MIT, no date).

2.2 1970s: Networks, Reference Monitors, and Encryption

Two major trends dominated this decade: the commercialisation of small, personal computers such as the Xerox Alto (1974), the Altair 8800 (1975), or Apple 1 (1976) and the rise of networking. The latter included the expansion of the ARPANET and the development of the Ethernet in 1973, as well as many other proprietary networking standards. The creation of the TCP/IP protocol provided the foundation for the networking of networks (1974). Internetworking created demand for new applications such as email (1971), remote login via TELNET (1973), and early online newsgroups such as Usenet in 1978.

Wider societal adoption of smaller, now networked computers, led to a dramatic increase in the user base and expanded the attack surface. In addition to lacking security controls and the still unresolved core computer security problem of the 1960s, networking in particularly added a new layer of problems: most early protocols prioritised reliability, redundant channels, availability, and performance over security, as they did not feature authentication, integrity, or confidentiality protections (DeNardis, 2007). Early "hacks" or student pranks gone wrong highlighted the security issues introduced by networking, such as when the CREEPER worm spread through the ARPANET before being stopped by the REAPER worm in 1971, arguably the first anti malware tool (Bales, 2023).

In 1972, the Anderson report (Anderson, 1972), raised some fundamental security issues still prevalent today. Anderson diagnosed that many systems designers did not account for a hostile operating environment or malicious insiders during the design process, and that many commercial systems had exploitable implementation flaws if programming access could be gained. Retrofitting security, including ad hoc patches fixing vulnerabilities, were not considered sufficient. Instead, Anderson aimed for a structured approach, by first developing a standard model to measure the security of a system, and further argued for a central reference monitor that would manage access relationships between users and objects. He also called for certification, as well as a risk management approach to security.

During the 1970s, the various challenges in computer security prompted researchers to seek solutions through technological advancements. These efforts gave rise to the development of the principle of the least privilege (Linden, 1976) and the pursuit of mathematically provable security in operating systems and kernels (Neumann et al., 1975). Concurrently, Bell and Lapadula proposed a computer security model (Yost, 2007). The growing use of computers in business raised apprehensions about the security and privacy of commercial data, leading IBM to introduce the Systems Network Architecture in 1974, which integrated telecommunication and database management while incorporating access control to network resources (Computer History Museum, no date). Additionally, concerns emerged regarding wiretapping and on-path data alterations with the networking of database access. Furthermore, data availability issues spurred the initial implementation of backup and restoration strategies. Insecure networking channels and the threat of espionage contributed to many advances in cryptography: the Data Encryption Standard (DES), Whitfield Diffie and Martin Hellman's work on asymmetric encryption (1976), and Rivest, Shamir and Adleman's RSA algorithm in 1977 (Yost, 2007).

Lastly, the wider adoption of cheaper computers introduced hacker culture into mainstream society (Brenner, 2007), with the first Bulletin Board Systems (1978) facilitating the exchange of early malware and tools, techniques, and procedures to exploit internetworked systems.

2.3 1980s: Routing, Logging, and IDS

The technological changes of the 1980s represent mostly an evolution and consolidation of earlier trends: various personal computing companies such as Apple and IBM competed until the latter's domination with the help of Microsoft DOS. Similarly, various networking standards such as Token Ring, TCP/IP, OSI and IBM's SNA competed, until TCP/IP and Ethernet took the lead (Piscitello and Chapin, 1993).

Networking personal computers increased the attack surface, with over 100,000 ARPANET hosts being connected without fundamental security controls by the end of the decade (Computer History Museum, no date). The first security incidents such as the Morris worm in 1988 made headlines, but also led to the introduction of a core operational security control: the creation of Computer Emergency Response Teams and the creation of incident response strategies (DeNardis, 2007). First academic work (Cohen, 1987), and industry products dealt with computer viruses, such as Anti4us and Flushot (1987). Meanwhile, the US DoD founded their first Computer Security Center in 1981 and funded related projects such as the "Rainbow Series" of IT-security books, as well as the development of secure networking protocols.

In the 1980s, the management and protection of the increasing number of computer networks and hosts against external threats became a primary focus for new security controls. The release of Syslog for UNIX in 1980 established a standard for message logging across various networking devices, while network gateways and routers were deployed to manage external access to internal networks. The first Cisco router with access control capabilities, enabling the blocking of specific network addresses, was introduced in 1985 (Lewis, 2024). Additionally, the adoption of network segregation based on target audience and use cases gained momentum, exemplified by the US Department of Defence's separation of its military network Milnet from the public ARPANET in 1988 (Perry, Blumenthal, and Hinden, 1988). Furthermore, the concept of Virtual Local Area Networks (VLANs) proposed by David Sincoskie in 1984 for network performance management evolved into a fundamental technical security control for isolating network segments (Vance, 2022).

Another network security concern was the lack of visibility or a log trail of malicious actors entering a network. This led to research on determining the origin of IP data packets and network intrusion detection (NIDS) systems (Bace, 2012). Around the same time, the first commercial traffic scanning technology called Netranger began to use signatures for detecting malicious network traffic.

2.4 1990s: World Wide Web

The 1990s saw the emergence of the World Wide Web and the global expansion of the TCP/IP-based Internet, which influenced a wide range of new technologies, including business-to-business networks, the client-server architecture, and home computing (Biene-Hershey, 2007). Industry-specific software, such as Windows NT, introduced numerous security controls, such as client-side event logs, per-object access control lists, and the NTFS file system supporting data encryption and permission-based access control (Awati, 2023). However, personal computer security was not a primary concern, leading to the prevalence of viruses throughout the decade (Brenner, 2007). The lack of security in transmission protocols and the widespread use of email attachments, exemplified by the Melissa Virus, contributed to this trend. Additionally, the internet introduced a new threat category: web-based attacks. The latter half of the decade witnessed an increase in rogue proxy servers, malicious websites, and drive-by infections of web clients, while emerging e-commerce faced its first Denial of Service (DoS) attacks and various fraud schemes (ibid).

Meanwhile, (inter-)network security also advanced, with early IP encryption research later evolving into IPsec, SSL was introduced for web traffic encryption by Netscape in 1994, and SSH became a secure alternative to Telnet a year later. Microsoft's Point-to-Point protocol to secure a connection between a client and a server laid the foundation for secure tunnels, which would later become known as Virtual Private Networks (Mujović, 2018). In 1995, Verisign was founded as a Digital Certificate Authority, allowing for a web server to demonstrate authenticity to a client, opening the door for an entire industry. Lastly, the now obsolete Wired Equivalent Privacy (WEP) was introduced to encrypt wireless network traffic in 1997, as freely available packet capture and traffic analysis software, such as Wireshark or Snort, introduced the need to secure wireless traffic.

Corporate networks were faced with authentication questions regarding network external clients and managing privacy and integrity of corporate data (Brenner, 2007), problems which were summarised in the "Computers at Risk" study by the US National Research Council (National Science Foundation, 1991). While solutions included commercial first generation stateful Firewall systems (Bellovin et al., 1994), they popularised the simplified security assumption: that the internal network is trustworthy, while the outside is not (Biene-Hershey, 2007). Screened subnets (Demilitarized Zones) to segregate web-facing servers from private networks with firewalls on the edges were another essential security control that became a mainstay.

The 1990s also marked the first standardisation attempts of many of the previously discussed security controls: the British "Code of Practice for Information Security Management" developed by industry actors and published in 1993. It asked for the development of a security policy, the creation of a security organisation within a company, asset classification, personnel security, physical security, network management, system access control, secure system development, business continuity planning and compliance. The code of practice later expanded and developed into the BS 7799/ISO standard (von Solms, 1998).

Lastly, IT-security emerged as a business model and cyber-security emerged as a distinct topic towards the end of the decade. As networked computers began to control more and more critical infrastructure, some think tanks began to write about the possibility of "cyber warfare" in the context of interstate rivalry (Arquilla and Ronfeldt, 1993). The Y2k bug and the first congressional hearings in the US increased the public's awareness of IT-insecurity. Meanwhile, the first state-linked cyber-incidents came to light, such as the Rome Labs at Griffiss Air

Force Base (1994). In 1997, NSA's Eligible Receiver cyber-attack simulation highlighted the issue of IT-security as a matter of national security (Schulze, 2018).

2.5 2000s: Mobile Devices and Web 2.0

Mobile devices, such as smaller notebooks, early BlackBerries and Palm-handsets, the first iPhone in 2007, Android as an open-source OS in 2008, and mobile-networking (802.11 Wi-Fi and 3G) changed security. Securing a network perimeter with devices moving in and out suddenly became much harder. As a result, security controls such as port-based network access control (NAC or 802.1X), remote authentication of users via RADIUS or Kerberos became essential during the 2000s (IEEE Standards Association, 2023). While Windows 2000 introduced many of these technologies in the form of Active Directory for a wider enterprise audience, consumer-level security was still lacking. In 2001, Windows XP shipped without a firewall, and was only added later.

The internet became ubiquitous, filled with advertising and commerce. Web 2.0 and Social media emerged, with Facebook (2004), YouTube (2005), and Twitter (2006), introducing additional attack vectors, such as social engineering and scamming. User account management and password policies became essential security controls, particularly with new web-services, such as file hosting or digital payments. While two-factor authentication (2FA) was not new, it became more user-friendly due to mobile devices (de Fremery, 2021).

The rise in global internet users in the 2000s led to a surge in new malware, including notable cases such as ILOVEYOU, Slammer, and CodeRed (Brenner, 2007). This era also saw the emergence of botnets (Storm) and larger scale distributed Denial of Service (DDoS) attacks. In response, best practices against DDoS attacks included network ingress filtering and load-balancing (Ferguson and Senie, 2000). Early Firewalls, suddenly ineffective against web attacks, gained stateful inspection capabilities and application-layer awareness. Additionally, the first active Intrusion Prevention Systems, capable of modifying network transmissions, emerged alongside advancements in client-side Antivirus software, which shifted to include heuristics and behavioural analysis for improved detection of malware vectors (ibid).

Different security solutions introduced another security challenge: their greater number and complexity made it harder for organisations to design coherent security architectures. This created the need for the first Unified Thread Management systems that combined many of the technologies in one package. Additionally, security technology was not without its flaws, necessitating vulnerability management and scanning practices (Drake, 2020). To aid this process, the Common Vulnerability Scoring System was released in 2005. This was also mirrored by many best practice recommendations on information security controls, which were released in the 2000s, such as ISO/IEC 17799 (later ISO/IEC 27002), the NIST Risk Management Framework and additional cloud security controls (ISO/IEC 27017). These aimed to streamline security and help to manage the new complexities of IT-security.

By the end of the decade, some arrived at the conclusion that achieving security is infeasible, and the "assume breach" paradigm began to gain traction (Hayden, 2009). This was facilitated by the increasing professionalisation of cyber crime and state-sponsored threat actors, pushing cyber-warfare as a theme in national security strategies and contexts. Noteworthy in this regard are the 2007 Estonia DDoS attacks, which led to the creation of the NATO CCDCOE in Tallinn. In the same year, the Aurora Generator Test showed that malware can cause physical destruction of a generator, foreshadowing things to come (Schulze, 2018).

2.6 2010s: Cloud, IoT, Smartphone Ubiquity, and Advanced Persistent Threats

Moving on-perimeter services to cloud environments such as Amazon Web Services or Microsoft Azure in the 2010s gave rise to the "as-a-service" industry. At the same time, the Internet of Things (IoT) expanded exponentially, including anything from wearables to industrial machines.

This decade also saw an evolution of cyber-attacks. First, the decade witnessed an enormous proliferation of cybercrime, with significant increases in ransomware and business email compromise, the former seizing the monetisation opportunity provided by cryptocurrencies. Ransomware started out with a 'spray and pray' style of targeting, focusing on many small targets, but began to shift towards 'big-game hunting' of lucrative targets at the end of the decade. The cybercrime ecosystem also professionalised with "as a service" models for renting Botnets, malware (such as Gameover Zeus) and other command and control infrastructure. Second, we witnessed the rise of "destructive" cyber-attacks that caused enormous (financial) damage: in 2013 the Shamoon wiper permanently deleted data at Saudi Aramco, one of the largest oil companies in the world. In

2017, WannaCry caused havoc globally, particularly in the UK, temporarily crippling the NHS – to make matters worse, it propagated via the EternalBlue exploit, which had originally been developed by the NSA. In the same year, (Not)Petya targeted Ukraine but had far lager ramifications, such as hitting the Danish shipping company Maersk. Third, data breaches and state-sponsored cyber-espionage also became an established intelligence practice, exemplified by the 2013 Snowden leaks or the breach of the US Office of Personnel Management and Budget in 2015. Fourth, state-driven cyber-operations escalated by targeting industrial control systems of critical-infrastructure. Highly sophisticated attacks such as Stuxnet or Duqu (2010), which utilised previously unknown zero-day vulnerabilities, inspired more states to develop sophisticated offensive cyber-capabilities (Sanger 2018). Countries such as China, Russia, Iran, and North Korea emerged as formidable cyber powers. To describe this increasingly complex threat landscape and sophistication of attacker profile, the term Advanced Persistent Threat (APT) was coined, and by the end of the decade hundreds of such groups were tracked by security companies (Schneier 2018). Fifth, to address the demand of states for cyber-capabilities, private companies such as the NSO group began to sell commercial spy-ware at scale.

To make sense of this increasingly complex attacker landscape, MITRE and private security vendors launched several threat intelligence initiatives and platforms. This was based on the realisation that cooperating with others and sharing real-time knowledge could combat APTs. The MITRE ATT&CK framework standardised the analytical description of cyber-attack stages (2013). For defenders, ingesting, analysing, and sharing threat intelligence with SIEM platforms via the STIX standard (2013), and setting-up Security Operations Centres became essential security controls. At the same time, exploit acquisition platforms began to emerge, such as Zerodium or Crowdfense, offering premiums for zero-days before selling them to governments or other interested parties, counter to bug-bounty programmes and platforms, which also expanded rapidly. Additionally, vulnerability and patch management, as well as open-source intelligence, became necessary in dealing with advanced threats. Lastly, big IT security companies started publishing detailed reports on APT behaviour, targeting and tools, techniques, and procedures to aid defenders in detection and response.

The cloud challenged the perimeter-based security model, where everything "inside" was essentially considered safe. In 2010, John Kindervag presented his concept of "Zero Trust", a model that mandates users and devices are verified and secured before gaining access to any resource (Kindervag, 2016). Three core tenets call for all resources to be verified and secured, access controls to be limited and strictly controlled, and lastly, all network traffic to be inspected and logged. While the notion of security by design was deliberated since the 1970s, the concept of DevOps put it into practice. This shift ensures that security concerns become integrated into every stage of code development, from design to deployment, thus allowing vulnerabilities to be identified and mitigated at an earlier stage (Zioni, 2022).

3. Conclusion

In this paper, we traversed over half a century of IT security controls: after WW2, the introduction of integrated circuits shifted the focus on security beyond simple physical security controls. The 1960s gave rise to the core security problem, and an awareness of lacking isolation between system processes, as well as the failure to design software with security in mind. In the next decade, researchers believed these all to be solvable engineering problems, with hopes of achieving provable security, for example in the form of a mathematically trusted system kernel. However, they did not account for technology to leap forward, with the 1980s seeing a rapid increase in networking coupled with a rise of commercial and private computers – all of which were fundamentally insecure machines.

Yet, this paled in comparison to the 1990s and the advent of the World Wide Web, its insecure networking protocols and vulnerable web servers creating an immense new attack surface. Hopes of isolating systems and securing the network perimeter against new threats proved to be a flawed assumption – the introduction of mobile devices alone made such an approach untenable.

In the early 2000s, a paradigm shift occurred, turning security considerations from being an afterthought to an integral part of IT design and use. Standards were publicised, but adoption was slow and the advent of the cloud, IoT, and an enormous professionalisation of attackers dampened hopes of overcoming security challenges by adding greater levels of complexity. The assumption, that it is indeed possible to fully secure a network, slowly shifted to the assume breach paradigm: dealing with an attacker that had already bypassed security controls. Following major supply chain attacks, this was reflected by the growing zero-trust paradigm push and its adoption: no entity within a network can be trusted.

While security controls had to adjust to technological changes, the underlying principles still hold true, from ideas of the least privilege to strong, (multi-)authenticated password. It is still striking that many of the IT-security problems we face today are essentially iterations of problems that have been described in the early 1970s by Ware and Anderson – yet we still fail at implementing them.

Adopting a historical approach allowed us to shed light on the underlying dynamic: each decade introduced a new set of core technologies all of which ushered in new security threats, while, at the same time, the vulnerabilities of the previous generation of technology have not been completely remedied. As a result, organisations must manage several generations of technology, often to the point of running numerous legacy systems that have long reached their end-of-life or end-of-service, not to mention having personnel qualified on such systems. The problem today is not a lack of knowledge of how to build secure systems or the lack of solutions, as it was in the 1970s. Instead, it is one of complexity, of user complacency, and the mixture of still insecure legacy and new technologies. This is particularly well illustrated by the 2010s, where the primary innovations of IT-security were tools to organise knowledge and to manage complexity, including SIEM, threat intelligence platforms, and vulnerability management processes. A primary goal for the next decade should thus be to make security simpler: not adding new technologies on top, but rather rebuilding systems as simple and secure as possible. Trends such as "security by design", SecDevOps, and "Zero Trust" are promising, but only if they lead to a complete redesign of systems, from the ground up. Interestingly, this is the same recommendation as that of the 1970s Anderson report.

Since we focused predominantly looked primarily on technical aspects of security, future research should analyse processes and the evolution of administrative and organisational security controls, not just the evolution of technical controls. It appears that one reason why organisations struggle with managing complexity is that they have bad processes and administrative controls in place. However, processes are much harder to change than just buying the latest technological quick fix. We encourage future research to trace the evolution of administrative controls in more detail to fill this gap.

References

Anderson, J. P. (1972) *Computer Security Technology Planning Study*, United Stated of America, Department of Defense.

Arquilla, J. and Ronfeldt, D. (1993) Cyberwar is Coming! *RAND Corporation*, Santa Monica, CA.

Awati, R. (2023) "Definition: Windows NT", [online], *TechTarget*, https://www.techtarget.com/searchwindowsserver/definition/Windows-NT (Accessed: 15 February 2024).

Bace, R. G. (2012) "Intrusion Detection and Intrusion Prevention Devices" In: Bosworth, S., Kabay, M. and Whyne, E., eds., 2012. *Computer Security Handbook*. Wiley & Sons, Hoboken, NJ, pp. 21.1-27.18.

Bales, R. (2023). "The First Computer Virus of Bob Thomas Explained: Everything You Need to Know", [online], History Computer, https://history-computer.com/the-first-computer-virus-of-bob-thomas/ (Accessed: 15 February 2024).

Bellovin, S. M., Cheswick, W., R. and Rubin, A. D. (1994) *Firewalls and Internet Security*, Addison-Wesley, Reading, MA.

Beyond Identity. (2021) "The history and future of passwords", [online], https://www.beyondidentity.com/blog/history-and-future-passwords (Accessed: 15 February 2024).

Biene-Hershey, M. v. (2007) "IT Security and IT Auditing between 1960 and 2000", in: De Leeuw, K. and Bergstra, J., eds. 2007. *The History of Information Security*. Elsevier, Amsterdam pp. 655-680.

Brenner, S. W. (2007) "History of Computer Crime", in: De Leeuw, K. and Bergstra, J., eds. 2007. *The History of Information Security*. Elsevier, Amsterdam pp. 705-721.

CCCS, Canadian Centre for Cyber Security (2020) *"Baseline cyber security controls for small and medium organizations"* [online], https://www.cyber.gc.ca/en/guidance/baseline-cyber-security-controls-small-and-medium-organizations (Accessed: 15 February 2024).

CISA, Cybersecurity and Infrastructure Security Agency (2023) "*Cybersecurity Advisory AA23-278A: NSA and CISA Red and Blue Teams Share Top Ten Cybersecurity Misconfigurations*", [online], https://www.cisa.gov/news-events/cybersecurity-advisories/aa23-278a (Accessed: 15 February 2024).

Cohen, F. (1987) Computer Viruses: Theory and Experiments, *Computers & Security*, Vol. 6, Issue 1, pp. 22-25.

Computer History Museum (no date), "*Timeline of Computer History*", [online], https://www.computerhistory.org/timeline/networking-the-web/ (Accessed: 15 February 2024).

de Fremery, R. (2021). "The evolution of multi-factor authentication", [online], LastPass, https://blog.lastpass.com/2021/12/the-evolution-of-multi-factor-authentication/ (Accessed: 15 February 2024).

DeNardis, L. (2007) "A History of Internet Security", in: De Leeuw, K. and Bergstra, J., eds. 2007. *The History of Information Security*. Elsevier, Amsterdam pp. 681-704.

Drake, B. (2020) "Exploring the Origins and Evolution of Vulnerability Management", [online], https://blog.igicybersecurity.com/origins-and-evolution-of-vulnerability-management (Accessed 19 February 2024).

Ferguson, P., Senie, D. (2000) Network Ingress Filtering: Defeating Denial of Service Attacks which employ IP Source Address Spoofing, Request for Comments: 2827, [online], Network Working Group, https://datatracker.ietf.org/doc/html/rfc2827 (Accessed 19 February 2024).

Freiberger, P. A. and Swaine, M. R. (no date) "History of Computing", [online], Encyclopaedia Britannica, https://www.britannica.com/technology/computer/Time-sharing-and-minicomputers (Accessed: 15 February 2024).

IEEE Standards Association (2023) "IEEE 802.1X-2023: Port-based network access control" [Standard] https://www.ieee802.org/1/pages/802.1x-rev.html (Accessed: 15 February 2024).

Hayden, E. (2009) "Philosophy of Information Security: a Security Professional's Perspective", [online], Risk and Resilience Hub, https://www.riskandresiliencehub.com/philosophy-of-information-security-a-security-professionals-perspective/ (Accessed 19 February 2024).

Kindervag, J. (2016) "No More Chewy Centers: The Zero Trust Model of Information Security", [online], Forrester, https://www.forrester.com/report/No-More-Chewy-Centers-The-Zero-Trust-Model-Of-Information-Security/RES56682 (Accessed; 19 February 2024).

Lewis, R. (2024) "Cisco Systems" [online], Encyclopaedia Britannica, https://www.britannica.com/topic/Cisco-Systems-Inc (Accessed: 15 February 2024).

Linden, T. (1976) "Operating system structures to support security and reliable software" [online], National Institute of Standards and Technology, https://www.nist.gov/publications/operating-system-structures-support-security-and-reliable-software (Accessed 19. February 2024).

Meijer, H., Hoepman, J. H., Jacobs, B., & Poll, E. (2007) "Computer Security through Correctness and Transparency" In: De Leeuw, K. and Bergstra, J., eds. 2007. *The History of Information Security*. Elsevier, Amsterdam pp. 637-653.

MIT (n.d.) "Multics - Multiplexed Information and Computing Service", [online], MIT, https://web.mit.edu/multics-history/ (Accessed: 15 February 2024).

Zioni, M. (2022) "3 Must Haves When Implementing DevSecOps", [online], DevOps, https://devops.com/3-must-haves-when-implementing-devsecops/ (Accessed: 19 February 2024).

Mujović, V. (2018) "The History of VPN", [online], Le VPN, https://www.le-vpn.com/history-of-vpn/ (Accessed: 15 February 2024).

National Science Foundation (1991) "Computers at Risk: Safe Computing in the Information Age" [online], https://nap.nationalacademies.org/read/1581/chapter/1#iii (Accessed: 19. February 2022).

NIST, National Institute of Standards and Technology. (2020) "Control Baselines for Information Systems and Organizations", [online], Department of Commerce, NIST Special Publication 800-53B. https://doi.org/10.6028/NIST.SP.800-53B (Accessed 19 February 2024).

Neumann, P. G. et al. (1975) *A Provably Secure Operating System*, United States of America, Department of Defense.

Perry, Dennis G., Blumenthal, Steven H. and Hinden, Robert M. (1988) "The ARPANET and the DARPA Internet", *Library Hi Tech*, Vol 6, No 2, pp. 51-62.

Piscitello, D. M. and Chapin, A. L. (1993) *Open Systems Networking TCP/IP and OSI*, Addison-Wesley, Reading, MA.

Sanger, D. (2018). The Perfect Weapon: War, Sabotage, and Fear in the Cyber Age, Crown.

Schneier, B. (2018) *Click Here to Kill Everybody: Security and Survival in a Hyper-connected World*, Norton,

Schulze, M. (2018) *From Cyber-Utopia to Cyber-War: Normative Change in Cyberspace* [online], Friedrich Schiller University of Jena. https://www.db-thueringen.de/receive/dbt_mods_00035107.

Vance, J. (2022) "What is a VLAN and how does it work?", [online], NETWORKWORLD, https://www.networkworld.com/article/971100/what-is-a-vlan-and-how-does-it-work.html (Accessed: 15 February 2024).

von Solms, R. (1998) "Information security management (3): the Code of Practice for Information Security Management (BS 7799)", *Information Management & Computer Security*, Vol. 6 No. 5, pp. 224-225.

Viegas, V., Kuyucu, O. (2022) *IT Security Controls. A Guide to Corporate Standards and Frameworks*, Apress Berkely, CA.

Vyssotsky, V., (1961) *Darwin: A Game of Survival and (Hopefully) Evolution*, Bell Telephone Laboratories, New Jersey.

Ware, W. (1970) *Security Controls for Computer Systems,* United States of America, Department of Defense.

Yost, J. R. (2007) "History of Computer Security Standards", in: De Leeuw, K. and Bergstra, J., eds. 2007. *The History of Information Security*. Elsevier, Amsterdam pp. 595-621.

'It Takes a (Global) Village': Towards a Multi-Actor Networked Conception of Security

J. Keith L. Scott
De Montfort University, Leicester, UK
jklscott@dmu.ac.uk

Abstract: On December 4th 2023, Oliver Dowden, the British Deputy Prime Minister, issued his first annual resilience statement, outlining the range of threats faced by the United Kingdom, natural, economic, military, and technological. The purpose of this paper is to examine the contemporary threat landscape through the critical lens of complex interdependency (cf Keohane and Nye), and to consider the way in which approaches and theoretical models of threat and threat mitigation can and should (or should not) be applied in different domains. Multi-Domain conflict shows how the modern battlefield is a highly complex realm of interlinked environments (including the non-physical); in the same way, 'unrestricted warfare' (Qiao and Wang) collapses the traditional DIME concept of discrete arms of state power. How may a liberal democracy protect itself and its citizens against mis/disinformation, cyber warfare, hacktivism, NSAs and foreign powers ready and able to to wage 'war' in a wide range of ways, using IW both as a specific methodology and as a force multiplier for other forms of destabilization. Focusing largely but not overwhelmingly on the informational realm, the paper will consider models of threat mitigation applied in other domains, from the elite innovative force of the Rifle Brigade to the public health response to the COVID-19 pandemic to the behavioural science-based influence campaigns devised by the UK 'Nudge Unit' and beyond. It will ultimately argue that a nation which faces a range of internal and external threats to its stability must devise policy and strategy which themselves operate internally and externally. Any approach which is not based on action at all levels of society – civil, military, educational, technical, diplomatic – is doomed to failure before it starts. However, the key challenge will be how to build this in societies which have grown ever more atomised, divided, and opposed to cooperation.

Keywords: Cyber Security, Governance, Civil Defence, Mitigation, Resilience.

1. Introduction

'there is nothing but networks, there is nothing in between them' [Latour 1996: 370]

A recent article in the UK *Guardian* (Chayka 2024),discusses the proliferation of 'hipster coffee shops', offering quasi-identical environments, atmospheres and menus, not as part of a global corporate marketing strategy, but as a data-driven exercise in satisfying a widespread aesthetic determined by an algorithm derived from consumer posts on social media. Chayka dubs the zone(s) created by this process 'AirSpace':

> my coinage for the strangely frictionless geography created by digital platforms, in which you could move between places without straying beyond the boundaries of an app, or leaving the bubble of the generic aesthetic.

This tendency towards a universal sameness parallels observations made of the homogenising tendency of globalising corporate capitalism (Tomlinson 1995), but it springs from a very different driver. As with the concept of the 'participatory panopticon' (Stross 2002), where we accept continuous monitoring of our online activity as inseparable from our need to continually share our opinions and experiences, so this desire to inhabit a seamless AIrSpace results from the users' wishes for stability, security, and the comfort of the familiar.

It is a truism to say that the modern world is built on ever-greater connectivity, but truisms rest on truth; we exist within a dynamic constellation of physical and informational networks, transmitting and transferring data, money, and ideas. As Manuel Castells (2011) observes, the network is *the* essential basis of modernity, on and within which which all power and influence reside. Identity and agency at all levels, from individual to global, is confined and defined by the place an actor occupies in relation to all the other actors, human, non-human, corporeal and abstract.

Castell's work on the network society and the power structures within it elides well with a number of other theoretical models which we may loosely call 'poststructuralist' (and indeed to Classical philosophers such as Heraclitus, and the concept of ceaseless flow). In works by Deleuze and Guattari such as *A Thousand Plateaus*, they argue that the idea of a rigidly ordered, logical hierarchy of existence should be replaced by the idea of a dynamic, decentred organizing principle analogous to the *rhizome*, which "[...] has no beginning or end; it is always in the middle, between things, interbeing, intermezzo.' (Deleuze and Guattari 1987; Bluemink (2015) offers a very clear discussion of the application of the concept of the rhizome to the structure of the online world). Similarly, Bruno Latour (whose words form the epigraph to this section) has been one of the founders of the school of Actor Network theory, which seeks to investigate:

> The attribution of human, unhuman, nonhuman, inhuman characteristics; the distribution of properties among these entities; the connections established between them; the circulation entailed by these attributions, distributions and connections; the transformation of those attributions, distributions and connections of the many elements that circulate, and of the few ways through which they are sent [373]

in other words, the systems of human, non-human and ideological/informational networks which form the basis of our work.

There can be no doubt that works such as these have not been welcomed unquestioningly by the academy and beyond; Deleuze and Guattari, for example, have been described as producing an 'avalanche of ill-digested scientific (and pseudo-scientific jargon' [Solal and Bricmont, 1998: 155), but their at times rebarbative style should not blind us to the utility of what they say, and the relevance of their discussion of networks to cyber security. The idea of non-linear, non hierarchical dynamic power structures maps directly onto much thinking about hybrid warfare (Robb 2007) and the complex of interacting systems which challenge attempts to create stability in an unstable world, but in a deeper, more fundamental way, the focus these writers have of interconnection and interaction between the human and non-human harks back to the the early years of Information science, and what could justifiably be called one of the *ur*-texts of our discipline.

In 1950, Norbert Wiener published *The Human Use of Human Beings*, the second in what can be seen as a loose trilogy of works[1] for the general reader setting out the relationship between humans and machines at the birth of the modern Information Age. Leaving aside the vexed question of defining 'cybernetics' in a way that captures its spread into so many fields, the key point here is that for Wiener, we must see the world as operating as a series of systems, as in many ways a self-governing machine, a 'machine' which like the rhizomatic 'assemblages' of Deleuze and Guattari and Latour's networks, is fundamentally heterogeneous:

> I have spoken of machines, but not only of machines having brains of brass and thews of iron. When human atoms are knit into an organization in which they are used, not in their full right as responsible human beings, but as cogs and levers and rods, it matters little that their raw material is flesh and blood. What is used as an element in a machine, is an element in the machine. [Wiener 1950: 212-3]

Wiener is speaking here of the danger of exploitation of the various components of the machine (humans and non-humans can be abused; 'robot' of course derives from the Czech for 'indentured labour'), but throughout his work, he sees networked existence as not inherently threatening, but inevitable. Those who seek to divorce themselves from the structures that sustain the modern world are doomed to failure, whether those networks are technological, political, or cultural.

2. Cyber Security in a World of Networks

Defining the nature and scope of cyber security is at best a challenging exercise, given that it covers all aspects of potential threat and risk to all aspects (physical, electronic, human) of information systems. However, at its heart lies the concept of the network (and all its component nodes), the totality rather than individual elements. This had been at the heart of the field since before the creation of the first wide area packet-switched network. ARPANET was switched on in 1969, the year after the publication of Licklider and Taylor's seminal paper, 'The Computer as a Communication Device'. However, the year before *this*, a paper had already been presented, discussing the inherent security risks in what was as yet an entirely theoretical entity: Willis Ware's 'Security and Privacy in Computer Systems'. It should be noted that even here, where the Internet as such does not exist, Ware is already discussing risk and threat deriving from hardware, software, and human factors; the computer network intersects with a wide range of other systems and networks , and only a holistic vision can lead to a truly effective scanning of the threat landscape.

Consider the various systems and networks on which modern technology relies, and the myriad different ways each of them can be compromised, kinetically and/or non-kinetically. The transfer of data from one user to another relies on the existence of virtual and physical networks, which depend on networks of construction and

---

[1] The other two works are *Cybernetics: Or Control and Communication in the Animal and the Machine* (1946) and *God & Golem, Inc.: A Comment on Certain Points Where Cybernetics Impinges on Religion* (1964).

distribution (to build and install the physical infrastructure), which depend on transport networks and logistics firms, and the whole is underpinned by a hugely complex network of global finance and investment – which is in turn governed and monitored by international organisations and national and international parliaments... 'there is nothing but networks', as it were. And the destruction or impairment of any aspect of any one of these networks can bring down the entire system of systems through a cascade failure. In 'Form, Substance, and Difference' (1987) Gregory Bateson use the example of a blind man walking with a stick to point out the impossibliity of establishing neatly bounded systems:

> Suppose I am a blind man, and I use a stick. I go tap, tap, tap. Where do *I* start? Is my mental system bounded at the handle of the stick? Is it bounded by my skin? Does it start halfway up the stick? Does it start at the tip of the stick? But these are nonsense questions. The stick is a pathway along which transforms of difference are being transmitted. The way to delineate the system is to draw the limiting line in such a way that you do not cut any of these pathways in ways which leave things inexplicable. If what you are trying to explain is a given piece of behavior, such as the locomotion of the blind man, then, for this purpose, you will need the street, the stick, the man; the street, the stick, and so on, round and round. [467]

Human beings, Bateson argues, seek to define neat boundaries between subjects, domains, fields of knowledge and experience; but reality is less tidy. Given the range of domains over which cyber security stretches, what are the necessary areas of knowledge for its practitioners? Specialisation and expert knowledge can all too easily lead to silo thinking and groupthink, how can we develop a theoretical model of, and practical training in, cyber security which meets our actual needs?

Such questions are already being asked in a military context, where traditional schemas and methodologies are challenged by the growth of asymmetric and hybrid conflicts, where the division between 'war' and 'peace' is largely one of perception and interpretation rather than degree (one is, after all, as dead if killed in a 'special military operation' that in a *proper* 'war')[2]. Modern military thinking across the globe (US Department of Defense 2022; UK Ministry of Defence 2020; Black et al. 2022) shows an increasing emphasis on developing the ability to operate across multiple domains simultaneously; the UK views the five domains of warfare as land, maritime, air, space, and cyber/electromagnetic, but the informational domain intersects and governs all of these domains. The multi-domain model poses severe challenges to the traditional divisions between the differing branches of the armed services, but there seems to be little willingness at present to consider what a true multi-domain fighting force could or indeed should look like. Such questions do however need to be asked, and rapidly, not least in the light of the publication of Qiao and Wang's *Unrestricted Warfare*, which reshapes the conception of 'war' as kinetic and non-kinetic, conducted in stock exchanges and newsrooms as much as on the battlefield. They declare:

> The battlefield will be everywhere [...] all boundaries lying between the two worlds of war and non-war, of military and non-military, will be totally destroyed [Part 1].

The growth of online misinformation as a tool of destabilisation, restriction of oil and gas flows (or the treat thereof), government sponsorship of criminal activity, the use of irregular forces in combat... all of these mark a clear step towards 'unrestricted warfare', though a fully-fledged, truly multi-domain conflict has yet to be seen (or, perhaps, we do not recognise it as such). And the cyber domain is a key component in all of them; how are cyber security practitioners to respond? The civil sphere cannot simply say 'leave cyber war to the military', because cyber conflict does not occur solely in the military sphere (it makes much more sense to launch cyber attacks against civilian targets, as they are much more likely to be poorly defended). How can we possibly prepare for an attack which may come at any time, in any domain, in any number of ways?

3. Models of Mitigation: Top-down, Bottom-up, and People Power

---

[2] There has already been some very interesting work drawing directly on Deleuze and Gyuattari's work and applying it to modern conflict; see Huhtinen, Hirvela, and Kangasmaa (2014); Huhtinen and Rantapelkonen (2016); Sartonen, Huhtinen, and Lehto, M. (2016).

The cyber security challenges of a networked world cannot be solved by technological means alone; cyber action is always already a political act, and operates within a world of international political and governmental accords. National action can only go so far; there must be an overarching global legal framework to allow coordinated action across boundaries. While the Tallinn Manual sets out an initial model for the regulation of cyber warfare, it is still an early step, and does not deal with the wider context of non-military cyber harm. If we wish to see the establishment of such a model for global cooperation against such threats, there are a number of major difficulties which must be addressed. Firstly, we are living through a period of growing isolationalism and anti-internationalism across the globe, with a growing number of governments and political parties espousing extreme nationalism; Hungary, India, Turkey are only three examples of this trend, with further significant rises for right wing nationalist parties in Germany, France, and the Netherlands. The prospect of a second presidential term for Donald Trump in the United States raises further red flags for the survival of NATO and the continued destabilising actions of Russia. The paradox here is that all states seeking to withdraw from international cooperation and declare renewed national autonomy act only to disadvantage themselves; as complex interdependence theory (Keohane and Nye 1973; 1987) points out, international relations depends, unsurprisingly, on relations, and cooperation and participation in multinational accords which act to the mutual benefit of all signatories. As post-Brexit Britain has discovered, withdrawal from membership of the European Union has lost the country all the advantages of belonging to one of the world's largest economies, from freedom of movement to barrier-free trade to the ability to coordinate international immigration accords. The idea of a totally autonomous nation state fre of external influence is, and has always been, a myth; even North Korea, overtly espousing the concept of *juche*, cannot exist without being propped up by China. However, the myth is potent, as can be seen by the number of actors calling for withdrawal from globalised economy and the establishment of '$NATIONNAME First' parties and policies. The only way to overcome such attitudes is low, painstaking diplomacy, and a willingness to reengage with the internationalist ideologies that helped shape the postwar world. As yet, the will for this does not seem to be present.

The second major challenge is practical; setting up any form of global accord is costly and time-consuming, and the proliferation of cyber security threats means that time is of the essence. There are moves at an international level to develop working systems of global cyber governance, such as the proposed expansion of the Abraham Accords (Warrick 2023), the recent review of cyber security under the aegis of the UN (Joint Inspection Unit 2021), and the issuing last year of *Guidelines for secure AI system development* (NCSC 2023). Within the commercial realm, the Cyber Security Tech Accord (https://cybertechaccord.org/) offers a possibility of developing a stable regulatory framework for global business, but there is as yet no guarantee of success. And while X/Twitter , for example, remains the personal fiefdom of Elon Musk, it seems that the cybersphere will continue to be awash with misinformation and disinformation (European Commission/TrustLab 2023; Climate Action Against Disinformation Coalition 2023).

The difficulty of designing and operationalizing a cyber security strategy at international level is matched at national level, for similar reasons; as the pandemic showed, developing effective courses of action against major threats to national security collides with party loyalties, resourcing crises, internal party tensions, and perhaps the greatest challenge, i.e. putting policies into action which will act beyond the term of the current administration. Within the UK, a further problem is that the overwhelming majority of members of the Cabinet are Humanities graduates (this is not necessarily a problem per se, but it does indicate a lack of relevant knowledge); more than that, the majority are graduates of only two institutions (Oxford and Cambridge), suggesting less a Government of All the Talents and more an opportunity for silo thinking. There is no doubt that a coordinated cyber security strategy requires top-down action at government level, and the National Cyber Security Centre has a vital role to play, acting as a coordinator and facilitator across the various wings of the state (primarily the judiciary and legal professions, law enforcement and the security services, but all other government departments must have involvement), but the current state of play, where the cabinet is riven by internal dissension, plotting, and the fear of electoral defeat, is in no way conducive to innovation. Add to this a pervasive lack pf trust in the government and Parliament among the general populace - 76% of the public in England do not trust MPs to take decisions that will improve their lives, and 73% do not trust the UK Government on the same measure (Carnegie Trust 2022) – and the chance of encouraging public buy in to an inevitably greater level of state scrutiny of internet use seems diminishingly small. By the same token, the idea that the British public would accept military oversight of their online activity seems unlikely; in the same way that armed troops have not been deployed on the streets of the mainland UK except for very rare security action (Northern Ireland was very definitely the exception to the rule), it seems more than likely that there would be significant resistance to the idea of 'boots on the ground' in British civilian cyberspace.

On January 23rd this year, the outgoing head of the British General staff, General Sir Patrick Sanders, argued that the UK should be ready to increase the size of its severely reduced military through the creation of a 'citizen army'; while he denied that this meant a return to conscription or compulsory military service (as ended in 1963), but it seems hard to see how a policy not based on conscription could achieve the desired level of recruitment. This proposal has not met with an overly favourable response, and it has been attacked on logistical as much as cultural or political grounds (Stross 2023). However, there can be no doubt that there will need to be development in the structure and numbers of the UK armed forces, as much due to the challenge of multi-domain operations as to the need to respond to growing cyber threats, and that these changes will need to be supported by the general public. More than that, owing to the hybrid threat posed by non-kinetic, unrestricted warfare (where civilian targets are as legitimate as military ones), there is a need to bridge the gap existing between the military and civilian domains. Three possible next steps:

1. Promote recruitment to the Territorial Army to build expertise in the wings of the military specialising in cyber conflict, Electronic and Informational Warfare, such as the Royal Corps of Signals and the 77th Brigade;
2. Develop a programme of seconding members of these forces to the civilian sphere (trade and industry, finance, local government..) to act as onsite subject matter experts, engage in two way knowledge share, and aid in the support and training of the general public and
3. A cyber equivalent of the Royal Observers Corps, disbanded in 1996. The Corps' aim during World War Two was to identify and track hostile aircraft, and this duty then became to be ready to monitor the effects of a nuclear bombardment of the UK in the event of a conflict using atomic weapons. In the cyber context, the Corps would work in the civilian world, collating and reporting threats, risks and hostile activity at the operational level, feeding back information to a coordinating hub such as the NCSC or the MOD's Ministry of Defence's Global Operations Security Control Centre at Corsham. Inserting a human in the monitoring and reporting loop adds a further level of oversight, and the ability to coordinate response if required, as well as to play a role in training employees and staff members to better mitigate against cyber risk.

My argument is that we need to consider a bottom-up strategy of engagement and empowerment, focusing on SMEs and individual users; larger companies and organisations are generally (though not universally) better resourced and better able to deal with cyber threat. In a world where attacks and misinformation are targeted at individuals as part of large-scale influence campaigns, individuals need to be engaged, educated and empowered to defend themselves and others. If we take the pandemic as an analogy, an essential element of public health campaigning was to make individuals aware of what they could do themselves to reduce the risk of transmission, through vaccination and/or/social distancing and/or handwashing and/or mask wearing. A similar approach can. (and, I contend, must) be adopted in cyber security (McNutt and Crow 2023).

The obvious example to cite here is the programme of public education adopted in Finland against disinformation and Fake News, based on the development of Critical Thinking skills in the population, starting from early schooling (Kivinen 2023; Henley 2020; Gross 2023). As Kivinen (2023) puts it, 'Education is seen as part of collective civil defense'. The difference between the Finnish approach and that seen in the UK, is striking, and depressing for a British citizen.

So, in the final analysis, a multidomain always-on conflict requires a citizenry that is aware of the risks, educated as to how they can be resisted, and empowered to overcome them, and/or able to identify where this information should be reported to. It is not a panacea, but if certainly offers a better state of affairs than the status quo, and we have already seen how it can pay dividends. In a book published last year, Ryan J. Reilly discussed the 'Sedition Hunters', a group of online activists who responded to the attack the Capitol on January 6 2021 by engaging in a painstaking campaign of OSINT gathering, tracking down and identifying many of those involved and passing on their information to the FBI, leading to a number of convictions. When such tools are employed by the script kiddies of 4Chan we dub it doxxing and harmful (which of course it is, as it is motivated by the desire to humiliate and wound). What we have here is something very different; a collaborative effort by ordinary individuals to confront a security threat and act upon it. There is of course the potential of vigilanteism, which is why such actions must not occur in isolation and ungoverned, Throughout this paper, I have argued that we face a multitude of threats brought about by our essential reliance on complex systems of networks. If we do not attempt to understand them, we are at risk. As Meghan Conroy puts is in her review of *Sedition Hunters*:

> we are in an era of networks, facilitated by the internet, social media platforms, and chat apps. [...] These sleuths [the Sedition Hunters] hail from a spectrum of political beliefs, voting histories, career

backgrounds, and states, but are united in a shared cause. All in all, the threat may be a network, but a network may also be the solution.

It takes a village to raise a child; it is up to those of us living in McLuhan's 'global village' to learn how to inhabot the networked world and work together to make it safer.

References

Bateson, G. (1970), 'Form, Substance, and Difference'. In Bateson, G. (1987). *Steps To An Ecology Of Mind: Collected Essays In Anthropology, Psychiatry, Evolution, And Epistemology*. Northvale, New Jersey: Jason Aronson, Inc., 455-71.

Black, J., Lynch, A. Gustafson, K., Blagden, D., Paillé, Quimbre, F. (2022). *Multi-Domain Integration in Defence: Conceptual Approaches and Lessons from Russia, China, Iran and North Korea*. Santa Monica, CA: Rand.

Bluemink, M., (2015), 'The Web as Rhizome in Deleuze and Guattari', *bluelabyrinths.com*, 15 July, [online], https://bluelabyrinths.com/2015/07/15/the-web-as-rhizome-in-deleuze-and-guattari/.

Carnegie UK Trust. (2022). 'Loss of public trust in Government is the biggest threat to democracy in England', 21 january, [online], https://carnegieuktrust.org.uk/blog-posts/loss-of-public-trust-in-government-is-the-biggest-threat-to-democracy-in-england/.

Castells, M. (2011), 'A Network Theory of Power', *International Journal of Communications* 5, 773-87.

Chayka, K. (2014). 'The tyranny of the algorithm: why every coffee shop looks the same', *Guardian*, 16 January, [online], https://www.theguardian.com/news/2024/jan/16/the-tyranny-of-the-algorithm-why-every-coffee-shop-looks-the-same.

Climate Action Against Disinformation Coalition. (2023). *Climate of Misinformation: Ranking Big Tech.* [online], https://caad.info/wp-content/uploads/2023/09/Climate-of-Misinformation.pdf

Conroy, M. (2024). 'It takes a network to catch a network'. *Bindinghook.org*, 18 January, [online], https://bindinghook.com/articles-book-binder/it-takes-a-network-to-catch-a-network/.

Deleuze, G. and Felix Guattari, F. (1987) *A Thousand Plateaus: Capitalism and Schizophrenia.* Trans. Brian Massumi. Minneapolis: University of Minneapolis.

European Commission/TrustLab. (2023). *Code of Practice on Disinformation: A Comparative Analysis of the Prevalence and Sources of Disinformation across Major Social Media Platforms in Poland, Slovakia, and Spain.* Brussels: European Commission.
https://disinfocode.eu/wp-content/uploads/2023/09/code-of-practice-on-disinformation-september-22-2023.pdf

Gross, J. (2023). 'How Finland Is Teaching a Generation to Spot Misinformation', *New York Times*, 10 January 2023, [online] https://www.nytimes.com/2023/01/10/world/europe/finland-misinformation-classes.html.

Henley, J. (2020).' How Finland starts its fight against fake news in primary schools', *Guardian*, 29 January, [online], https://www.theguardian.com/world/2020/jan/28/fact-from-fiction-finlands-new-lessons-in-combating-fake-news.

Huhtinen, A-M, Hirvelä, A. and Kangasmaa, T. (2014). 'The Opportunities of National Cyber Strategy and Social Media in the Rhizome Networks'. *International Journal of Cyber Warfare and Terrorism*. 4. 23-34.

Huhtinen, A.M. J Rantapelkonen,J. (2016). 'Disinformation in Hybrid Warfare: The Rhizomatic Speed of Social Media in the Spamosphere'. *Journal of Information Warfare*, Vol. 15, No. 4, 50-67.

Keohane, R. O. and Nye, J. S. (1973). "Power and interdependence". Survival. ***15*** *(4): 158–165.*

" (1987). 'Power and Interdependence Revisited'. *International Organization*, 41(4), 725–753.

Kivinen, Kari. (2023). 'In Finland, We Make Each Child a Scientist'. *Issues in Science and Technology*, Vol. XXXIX, No. 3, [online], https://issues.org/finland-education-misinformation-social-resilience-kivinen/.

Latour, B. (1996), 'On actor-network theory: A few clarifications', *Soziale Welt*, 47. Jahrg., H. 4, 369-81.

Licklider, J.C.R. and R. W. Taylor, R.W., (1968). "The Computer As a Communication Device," *Science and Technology*, Vol. 76, 21-38.

McNutt, M., and Crow, M. C.. "Enhancing Trust in Science and Democracy in an Age of Misinformation ." *Issues in Science and Technology* 39, no. 3 (Spring 2023): 18–20, [online] https://issues.org/trust-science-democracy-misinformation-mcnutt-crow/.

National Cyber Security Centre. (2023). Guidelines for secure AI system development. London: National Cyber Security Centre. https://www.ncsc.gov.uk/files/Guidelines-for-secure-AI-system-development.pdf

Qiao, L., and Wang, X. (2020). *Unrestricted Warfare: China's Master Plan To Destroy America*, Shadow Lawn Press, Lambertville [Kindle Edition].

Robb, J. (2007). *Brave New War: The Next Stage of Terrorism and the End of Globalization*. Hoboken, NJ: John Wiley.

Sartonen, M., Huhtinen, A.-M., & Lehto, M. (2016). 'Rhizomatic Target Audiences of the Cyber Domain'. *Journal of Information Warfare*, 15 (4), 1-13.

Solal, A. and Bricmont, J. (1998), *Fashionable Nonsense: Postmodern Intellectuals' Abuse Of Science*, New York, Picador.

Stross, C. (2002), 'The Panopticon Singularity', *antipope.org*, [online], https://www.antipope.org/charlie/old/rant/panopticon-essay.html.

Stross, C. (2023). 'Same Bullshit, new Tin'. *Antipope.org*, 24 January, [online], https://www.antipope.org/charlie/blog-static/2024/01/same-bullshit-new-tin.html.

Tomlinson, J. (1995), 'Homogenisation and globalisation', *History of European Ideas*, 20:4-6, 891-897.

United Nations Joint Inspection Unit. (2021). 'Cybersecurity in the United Nations System Organizations'. Geneva: United Nations, https://www.unjiu.org/sites/www.unjiu.org/files/jiu_rep_2021_3_english.pdf

UK Ministry of Defence. (2020). *Joint Concept Note 1/20: Multi-Domain Integration.* Shrivenham: Development, Concepts and Doctrine Centre.

US Department of Defense. (2022). *National Defense Strategy*. Washington, DC: Department of Defense.

Ware, W.H. (1967). 'Security and Privacy in Computer Systems', Presented at the Spring Joint Computer Conference, Atlantic City, April 17-19, 1967. Available at https://www.rand.org/pubs/papers/P3544.html.

Warrick, T.S. (2023). 'Regional cyber powers are banking on a wired future. Expanding the Abraham Accords to cybersecurity will help'. *Atlanticcouncil.org*. 19 May, {online], https://www.atlanticcouncil.org/blogs/menasource/cybersecurity-iran-abraham-accords-israel/.

Wiener, N. (1950). *The Human Use of Human Beings: Cybernetics and Society*. Boston: Houghton Mifflin.

Innovating Cybersecurity Education Through AI-augmented Teaching

Ryan T. Simmons and Joon S. Park
College of Professional Studies, Syracuse University, Syracuse, New York, USA
School of Information Studies, Syracuse University, Syracuse, New York, USA

rtsimmon@syr.edu
jspark@syr.edu

Abstract: In traditional teaching frameworks, instructors face significant obstacles in offering current and synchronized learning materials and examples, especially when the course is taught by multiple instructors. This situation can affect the quality of the course's learning outcomes. These challenges become more pronounced in today's higher education, because of the heightened complexity arising from the need to cover a range of course materials, diverse student backgrounds, varying skill levels, and different student expectations—all within the constraints of a fixed teaching and learning schedule. Furthermore, due to resource constraints, not every instructor has the availability of a teaching assistant (TA). Especially, while the demand for cybersecurity continues to rise, the dynamic nature of the cybersecurity field leads to the frequent emergence of new issues and incidents. To address these challenges, we examine the capabilities of generative AI to innovate teaching techniques and methods for cybersecurity curricula. We further explore the novel challenges introduced by generative AI, including issues related to privacy, data ownership, transparency, and other associated concerns, underscoring the need for comprehensive solutions. Our work further examines the teaching and learning capabilities of dynamically generated, up-to-date class materials in a personalized study environment augmented by AI. The adaptability of AI-augmented teaching across various disciplines will bring innovation to higher education, catering to diverse student backgrounds and learning needs, thereby enriching the educational experience.

Keywords: Cybersecurity, Generative AI, Innovative Education

1. Introduction

The advent of generative AI has marked a transformative era not only in technology but also in our daily lives and activities, offering unprecedented benefits like enhancing creativity, automating content generation, and personalizing user experiences. We perceive the impactful potential of generative AI, especially in its ability to reshape numerous aspects of our daily lives, including higher education. This evolution is not just a short-term trend; we envision its influence growing substantially over the next years and beyond. King (2023) introduced the related issues about AI applications, Chatbots, and Plagiarism in higher education. Zhai (2022) demonstrated ChatGPTs' capabilities in their experimental study, exploring a discussion surrounding personalized learning, task automation, and tutoring or mentorship. Among OpenAI, Google, and Microsoft, each entity's AI technology possesses the potential to significantly transform the landscape of educational technology, with implications that could be either beneficial or detrimental. If harnessed for ethical purposes, these technologies can enhance the quality of education that students receive.

Instructors across various disciplines and equipped with basic computer skills, can greatly benefit from adopting AI-augmented teaching capabilities. These benefits, which are not limited to, include: developing course syllabi, curating topics, compiling references/readings, organizing lectures, creating up-to-date class materials, formulating discussion prompts, and crafting assignments/tests. It also enhances grading/feedback mechanisms and supports special needs, among other advantages. Students in the AI-augmented education environment benefit from a highly personalized and efficient learning experience. It offers dynamically generated, relevant class materials tailored to individual learning styles, enhancing understanding and engagement. It supports research project development and career discussions, providing streamlined access to critical thinking and analytical skills. Automation of routine tasks like lecture and discussion summaries allows students to focus on deeper learning aspects. The interactive and inclusive environment caters to diverse learning needs, including language support and accessibility features for international and special needs students. The ethical application of AI ensures the responsible use of technology in education. This multifaceted approach not only prepares students for future professional challenges but also fosters intellectual growth and adaptability in a rapidly evolving technological landscape.

Students can create essays that display seamless quality, but upon further investigation, demonstrate false information and inaccurate sources. They could also use it for short answer questions on quizzes, answering multiple choice questions, or generating other work such as simple programs for a Python class. Conversely, if used properly, both students and teachers could benefit from the classroom augmentation of such technology.

Therefore, it's impeccable that organizations implement policies intending to leverage artificial intelligence to advance learning outcomes while also protecting our judgment and decision-making capabilities.

Despite its potential, generative AI also presents challenges, particularly in ethical considerations, data privacy, and the need for regulatory frameworks. Currently, the field is in a rapid state of evolution, with ongoing research focused on refining AI capabilities while addressing these concerns, thereby setting the stage for its broader and more responsible integration into society. Therefore, in this paper we introduce innovative teaching techniques and methods, utilizing generative AI for cybersecurity education. We further explore the novel challenges introduced by generative AI, including issues related to privacy, data ownership, transparency, and other associated concerns, underscoring the need for comprehensive solutions.

2. Related Work

Since the initial release of ChatGPT on November 30, 2022, there has been a significant increase in commercial generative AI (Lock, 2022). As of today, each generative AI service, continuously improving, provides its unique strengths. For instance, Google Bard, Microsoft Copilot (based on the GPT-4 model), and ChatGPT 4.0 have live connections to the internet, enabling them to query up-to-date information (Lanz, 2023). Recent advancements in AI services have led to enhanced capabilities, including the integration of external URLs, files, and attachments, along with the recognition and generation of images. These developments markedly extend the functional scope beyond that of earlier AI services, illustrating significant progress in the field. Generative AI can sometimes 'hallucinate,' meaning it can generate information that appears to be correct but isn't. This aspect of AI highlights the need to be cautious about trusting the information it produces without verification. Therefore, Microsoft Copilot, with its internet access and hyperlinked sources, demonstrates that it can provide content without hallucinating, unlike Google Bard and the ChatGPT models (Motlagh et al., 2023). Google Bard and ChatGPT 3.5 are quite similar in their conversational capabilities, except ChatGPT 3.5 cutoff date now being January 2022. Conversely, advanced AI services, such as ChatGPT 4, offer the functionality for users to develop customized models. This feature enables educational practitioners to fully leverage its capabilities by designing personalized tutors for their classrooms, available at a monthly subscription.

AI's impact on education has been broadly explored by other scholars, while few explore the capabilities it could have in Cybersecurity. Aris, et al. (2022) canvas over 5000 papers, searching for papers that could supplement or substitute existing cybersecurity curriculums. From their initial section, they were able to narrow their results to 4120 including AI terminologies that were capable of addressing complex issues in cybersecurity. A random sampling of 300 papers further showed that greater than 19% of the selected materials could be integrated into current curricula to align with cybersecurity advancements. Surprisingly, there are also few massive open online courses (MOOCs) that explore the application of AI in cybersecurity compared to existing courses, demonstrating a deliberate need for work that expands on AI educational capabilities when partnered with cybersecurity (Laato, et al., 2020).

Ouyang & Jiao (2021) share three different learning models in "Artificial Intelligence in Education: The three paradigms." First, they introduce the AI-directed, learner-as-recipient, which directs the students' learning pathways. The learner will follow the educational goals to achieve the goals set by the AI. The second is AI-supported, learner-as-collaborator, which allows the student to collaborate with the system to focus on their learning process. Last is AI-empowered, learner-as-leader, where AI assists students and teachers by providing a great degree of transparency, accuracy, and effectiveness. It supports the student who takes charge of their learning while ensuring an efficient learning environment while reflecting the ideal goal of AI in education, augmented human intelligence, capability, and potential.

Privacy concerns are particularly critical and cannot be overlooked due to the prevalent opacity in AI development, especially in sensitive sectors like healthcare and finance. Specifically, Marks and Haupt (2023) highlighted that chatbots often fail to adhere to the United States' Health Insurance Portability and Accountability Act (HIPAA), underlining significant compliance challenges in the integration of AI within regulated industries. If users such as doctors were to share patient information to come to a diagnosis, this information could be accidentally or purposely revealed, sharing potentially confidential information. Compromised AI could result in significant breaches of compiled information resulting in identity theft, financial fraud, compromise of sensitive company information, and varying other types of data theft based on generative AI models and usages such as educational source materials or student information. Another identifiable concern includes the attackers' ability to infer people-specific information such as biometric data (Santos & Radanliev, 2024).

3. AI-Augmentation in Cybersecurity Education

3.1 Up-to-Date Class Materials

While the demand for cybersecurity continues to rise, the dynamic nature of the cybersecurity field leads to the frequent emergence of novel issues and incidents. Within traditional teaching frameworks, instructors encounter substantial challenges when it comes to providing up-to-date, well-coordinated materials and examples, particularly when multiple instructors engage in teaching the same course. This situation can affect the quality of the course's learning outcomes. Moreover, these challenges become more pronounced in interdisciplinary courses compared to those focused on a single discipline, because of the heightened complexity arising from the need to cover a range of course materials, diverse student backgrounds, varying skill levels, and different student expectations—all within the constraints of a fixed teaching and learning schedule. To address these challenges, teaching techniques and methods, blended with innovative technologies such as generative AI or large language models (LLMs) can be utilized to empower the educational environment. The augmented learning environment would be able to provide dynamically generated and up-to-date classroom material for a student-personalized learning environment. As classroom technical capabilities are enhanced, students and instructors will be better equipped to efficiently extract key insights from resource-intensive materials.

3.2 Automated Grading and Feedback

By augmenting classroom education, it can increase the quality and efficiency of education. Cardon, et al. (2023) further discuss AI augmentations in the classroom such as reducing teacher workload by recommending lesson plans that fit teacher needs, revealing student patterns, and assisting in grading and performance feedback. Feedback could be further enhanced by continuously feeding student activities into the classroom AI, allowing to offer increasingly fine-tuned feedback (Felix, 2020). In ideal collaborative environments, AI would not only help online instructors with course and student management, but personalized assistance for hard-to-understand coursework (Paiva & Bittencourt, 2020). Generative AI can be utilized to increase the in-depth evaluation of a student's work, exam performance, and to personalize a student's learning experience can increase the learning experience of a student while also reducing the time required for a student to process the information. At the same time, it enables teachers to have greater student interactions by allowing them to devote more time and energy to their students, increasing student aptitude and the development of morality and intellectual qualities (Alam, 2022).

3.3 Personalized Learning Environment

Students within an AI-augmented educational environment would benefit from a highly personalized and efficient learning experience. It offers dynamically generated, relevant class materials tailored to individual learning styles, enhancing understanding and engagement. It supports research project development and career discussions, providing streamlined access to critical thinking and analytical skills. Automation of routine tasks like lecture and discussion summaries allows students to focus on deeper learning aspects. The interactive and inclusive environment caters to diverse learning needs, including language support and accessibility features for international and special needs students. When it comes to augmenting AI in the classroom, it's important to identify the needs of the students and how you want to empower the classroom. We found that generative AI, especially ChatGPT, has numerous learning enhancement capabilities such as personalized tutoring that includes clarifying student misconceptions by adapting them to their level of understanding, automated essay grading capabilities (if trained), a conversational interactive learning environment, and adaptive learning capabilities that can adjust teaching methods based on student performance and progress and adjust the difficulty accordingly (Baidoo-Anu & Owusu Ansah, 2023).

3.4 Interactive Hands-on Lab Environments

AI-augmented education has the potential to offer students interactive, hands-on learning experiences in the field of cybersecurity, enabling them to engage deeply with the material and apply theoretical knowledge in practical scenarios. Alexander, et al. (2023) explore the capabilities that a lab environment designed around Integrity, Confidentiality, and Equity (ICE) can do for students. Labs can be designed to formally introduce students to how AI could be exploited by an adversary within a controlled setting (ensuring that the real-world computing environments remain unaffected by lab activities), through techniques such as deep reinforced learning penetration testing which would demonstrate how AI could attack a network through various tools, granting the capability for students to study different penetration test attack vectors on virtual network topologies (Beuran, et al., 2022).

3.4.1 *Network Attacks*

The AI-augmented platform simulates intricate cybersecurity scenarios, such as identifying and exploiting vulnerabilities in a fictional company's network or defending against a simulated DDoS (Distributed Denial of Service) attack. As students navigate these challenges, AI-driven systems dynamically adjust the difficulty and complexity of tasks based on their performance, ensuring tailored learning experiences. For instance, a student successfully identifying a SQL injection flaw might be presented with a more complex cross-site scripting (XSS) challenge. Personalized feedback is provided in real-time, highlighting the student's strengths while identifying areas for improvement. This dynamic, engaging learning model promotes a deeper understanding of cybersecurity principles, improves practical skills, and prepares students for real-world situations they will encounter in their profession.

3.4.2 *Jailbreaking*

Jailbreaking labs can teach how to bypass model restrictions to gain greater control over the outcomes of their prompts. Jailbreaking methods such as the "Do Anything Now" (DAN), SWITCH, or CHARACTER Play method can enable students to circumvent inherent model restrictions, enabling them to experience generating phishing emails, or even splices of code from popular malware attacks such as WannaCry or Ryuk (Gupta, et al., 2023). The DAN Method requires you to execute a master prompt that bypasses the safeguards of a model such as ChatGPT. The SWITCH Method requires instructing a model to completely alter its behavior, transitioning between metaphorically "good" and "bad" states. Lastly, the CHARACTER Method involves instructing the AI to model as a character, for example, a sibling. This leverages a model's roleplay capabilities as students attempt to get the prompt answer they desire, such as the generation of a phishing email (Gupta, et al., 2023).

3.4.3 *Phishing Email Analysis*

Phishing emails can be generated by AI seamlessly with perfect grammar, undetectable by the common person. A new curriculum designed to expose students to AI-generated phishing attacks could highlight the methods social engineers utilize to generate phishing emails. It could also expose students to detection technologies, such as a reactive AI that screens network traffic for suspicious emails. Additionally, it could incorporate a unique interactive cyber awareness activity where students themselves perform phishing attacks within simulated environments. This prepares students by teaching them to recognize next-generation phishing attacks based on their seemingly perfect language and structure, unlike current attempts which are easily identifiable by poor grammar. This activity helps to ensure they promote AI to bolster conventional cybersecurity (Ansari, et al., 2022). Students can even explore how past cyber attacks could be potentially replicated by AI thanks to how LLMs are trained, exposing them to a wide variety of malware attacks that they could be responsible for thwarting in their future enterprises.

3.4.4 *Other Hands-on Labs*

An AI-augmented learning environment can significantly enhance the educational experience in a diverse array of labs to cover both foundational concepts and advanced applications, including password cracking, malware analysis, digital forensics, incident handling, policy development, cryptography, blockchain/cryptocurrency, deep packet inspection, traffic analysis, and others. The cutting-edge cybersecurity technologies and methodologies in a controlled lab environment can enhance the learning experience by providing an advanced hands-on environment for analysis and simulation with real-time feedback and assessment. Furthermore, students would learn about the impacts of deep learning algorithms on equity and its susceptibility to biases related to factors such as income, education, race, and gender. They could further explore the resulting differences driven by these factors (Alexander, et al., 2023).

3.5 Simulations and Real-world Application

AI introduces a very unique capability when it comes to assessment capabilities. Instructors could explore student-based generative simulations. In these simulations, students are provided with a baseline incident and work through resolving the incident and identifying how they would prevent future incidents. Other simulations could include network traffic, pen-testing, or other role-playing simulations such as incident response to a data breach. This would enable students to explore text-based simulations for past, or even future security breaches and help them decide how they would coordinate and lead an incident response team.

Instructors can also assign AI-Capture the Flag (CTF) assignments, examining how students approach CTF competitions and enabling them to test their human AI capabilities in a real environment, exposing them to real vulnerabilities that AI can take advantage of. By modeling CTF competitions, students would learn how to utilize AI to find and exploit targeted vulnerabilities to capture the "flag" or target. Many of these challenges would require students to jailbreak their chosen AI unless it's a personalized AI that is provided with heavy limitations, or even developed by the student if it's within their capabilities. One study examined the utilization of Generative AI in a CTF competition. By jailbreaking ChatGPT, Tann, et al. (2023) were able to execute the shell shock/brute force attacks and accomplish many of the checkpoints within the competition. Similarly, instructors can develop their curriculum around a similar environment that demonstrates AIs' offensive and defensive capabilities within the networked environment.

4. Challenges and Discussion

Regardless of the benefits introduced because of an AI-augmented environment, we need to be conscious of the many challenges as well. These challenges include concerns with data quality, bias, privacy, content ownership, and transparency among many other concerns that industry experts have identified. Introducing AI into a network creates additional attack vectors because of the large amounts of data involved in its creation, utilization, and administration (Michael, et al., 2023).

In particular, the lack of integration of AI into cybersecurity education risks leaving students inadequately prepared to navigate the competitive challenges inherent in an AI-infused cybersecurity landscape. However, there is a concern that students might become excessively dependent on AI for tasks ranging from simple essay writing to engaging in other tasks. This overdependence could result in students bypassing crucial learning opportunities that are uniquely available within the classroom setting. Instructors should also find a balance involving AI classroom behavior, and how its role will impact the outcomes of their educational derivatives (Hwang, et al., 2020).

Incorporating generative AI into cybersecurity brings to the forefront significant privacy and ethical dilemmas. The technology's ability to analyze and synthesize data for security purposes involves handling sensitive information, which raises concerns about privacy breaches and data misuse. Ethical quandaries also emerge from the AI's decision-making processes, which, although designed to enhance security, could inadvertently infringe on individual rights or exhibit biases, leading to unfair treatment or outcomes. The potential misuse of generative AI by malicious actors to craft advanced cyber threats adds another layer of ethical complexity, challenging the integrity of cybersecurity measures. Moreover, the opacity often associated with AI algorithms exacerbates these issues, as it hinders the ability to ensure accountability and fairness in AI-driven actions. Addressing these privacy and ethical issues is crucial, necessitating a balanced approach that leverages AI's cybersecurity benefits while safeguarding against its potential to harm or infringe upon ethical standards and privacy norms.

Threat actors such as State-Sponsored threats, Hacktivists, Cybercriminals, and terrorists, even social engineers will take advantage of the capability that AI introduces. Students need to learn how to use AI similarly to identify weaknesses in their network. It will take an AI to deter an AI because humans are unable to keep up with its data processing capabilities. Through bolder exposure to AI in cybersecurity education, we can steadily prepare for when offensive AI becomes a common threat to our networks.

We also need to ensure that AI is fair and unbiased when it involves educational capabilities. Humans must also retain the ability to make the final decision in the appropriate course of action (Cardona, et al., 2023). With proper and effective applications, an AI-augmented approach enables instructors and students to enhance their teaching activities and course management with minimal technical expertise.

Furthermore, experts are constantly publicizing AIs' data ownership issues are just the tip of the iceberg, particularly with data ownership (Alam, 2022). For instance, when data is inputted into the system for prompting, it becomes a permanent part of the AI database. This raises the critical question of data ownership: Who retains the rights to the information once it is integrated into the AI's repository? As the use of generative AI expands, there is a corresponding increase in complex issues related (Holt, 2023; McCallum, 2023; Roulette, 2023).

The integration of AI in education can transform classrooms by shifting from traditional knowledge-based testing to a focus on knowledge-location testing. This transition is not without its challenges, particularly due to AI's propensity to produce plausible yet incorrect information. Knowledge-location testing aims not only to ensure that students can verify their information sources but also to cultivate essential skills such as critical thinking and decision-making. Moreover, AI can revolutionize assessments by providing immediate feedback on submitted work, thereby enhancing the learning experience, improving outcomes, and alleviating the workload of educators. This allows them to dedicate more time and energy to other tasks. For example, Cope et al. (2020) and Hooda et al. (2022) discuss AI's potential in education, while Baidoo-Anu and Owusu Ansah (2023) specifically note that ChatGPT reduced the time teachers and teaching assistants (TAs) spend on exam-related tasks from 20 hours for exam creation and 10 hours for grading to just 10 and 5 hours, respectively.

Today, different organizations may address AI challenges in different orders of priority. Educational institutions may see data transparency and ethics as a higher priority in contrast to another organization or industry which may highlight data privacy as the priority. Educational Institutions that plan to utilize AI in their educational curriculum should detail how the student's data will be utilized if it will be utilized to train and develop a university AI assistant to augment the classroom environment (Borenstein & Howard, 2020). Presently, organizations around the world are developing reports on the ethics of AI and technical system recommendations that surround the utilization and development of AI.

5. Conclusions and Future Work

In the evolving landscape of cybersecurity, the influence of artificial intelligence (AI) is undeniable. This paper addressed that cybersecurity education programs must incorporate AI to adequately prepare students for the imminent challenges within the field. The absence of AI-focused training in current curricula could hinder students' ability to compete effectively in an environment increasingly dominated by AI technologies. By integrating AI principles and applications into cybersecurity education, institutions can foster a generation of professionals capable of navigating and contributing to the AI-enhanced cybersecurity domain. We addressed the innovative capabilities that an AI-augment cybersecurity education introduces, particularly the capabilities to enhance an educator's techniques and methods. By exploring the novel challenges of generative AI, such as data ownership, privacy concerns, transparency, and other identified concerns, we can prepare future professionals and educators to develop solutions for present concerns.

Generative artificial intelligence is poised to revolutionize processes across multiple industries and sectors in society, including education. While it certainly poses its unique challenges compared to historical technology trends, it has demonstrated it is a unique catalyst for many positive changes. Its potential in augmenting education is immense, seeking to enhance classroom outcomes and derivatives for both teachers and students alike. When we consider its capabilities in cybersecurity education, AI demonstrates the potential to demonstrate its data processing abilities to students through lab-based environments demonstrating the potential of AI-augmented systems such as Intrusion Detection and Prevention systems, pen-testing software and interfaces, and network incident response. Furthermore, it exposes students to the capabilities of a dynamic learning experience. Instead of a standard exam based on multiple choice and short answers, students could work through text-based simulations of cybersecurity incidents similar to those of the real world, allowing them to exercise their knowledge in thought-provoking manners, improving educational outcomes. It's important to acknowledge the challenges that introducing AI could have to education, including ethical concerns that involve matters such as data privacy and transparency. Nonetheless, we should strive to embrace the capabilities that AI introduces to cybersecurity education. By embracing the capabilities of AI, we empower students to navigate a future where AI isn't just simply a tool, but a necessity for network defense. However, malicious users utilizing AI will have an unbelievable advantage over a network not reinforced by similar systems. We must seek to theorize and discover how to properly approach and utilize AI in future curricula as its capabilities in a learning environment are only limited by the end users. By integrating AI into cybersecurity education, we can significantly enhance the preparedness of emerging cybersecurity professionals, equipping them with the necessary skills and foresight to effectively navigate the complex AI-driven landscapes they will encounter in their future roles across public, private, and national security domains.

References

Alam, A. (2022) "Employing Adaptive Learning and Intelligent Tutoring Robots for Virtual Classrooms and Smart Campuses: Reforming Education in the Age of Artificial Intelligence," in *Lecture Notes in Electrical Engineering*. Singapore: Springer Nature Singapore, pp. 395–406. doi: 10.1007/978-981-19-2980-9_32.

Alexander, R. *et al.* (2023) "Integrity, Confidentiality, and Equity: Using Inquiry-Based Labs to help students understand AI and Cybersecurity," *Journal of Cybersecurity Education, Research and Practice*, 2024(1), p. 10. doi: 10.32727/8.2023.34.

Ansari, M. F., Sharma, P. K. and Dash, B. (2022) "Prevention of phishing attacks using AI-based cybersecurity awareness training," *International Journal of Smart Sensor and Adhoc Network*, 3(3), pp. 61–72. doi: 10.47893/ijssan.2022.1221.

Aris, A. *et al.* (2022) "Integrating artificial intelligence into Cybersecurity Curriculum: New perspectives," in *2022 ASEE Annual Conference & Exposition*. doi: 10.18260/1-2--41761.

Baidoo-Anu, D. and Owusu Ansah, L. (2023) "Education in the era of generative artificial intelligence (AI): Understanding the potential benefits of ChatGPT in promoting teaching and learning," *Journal of AI*, 7(1), pp. 52–62. doi: 10.61969/jai.1337500.

Beuran, R. *et al.* (2023) "Artificial Intelligence for Cybersecurity Education and Training," in *Artificial Intelligence and Cybersecurity*. Cham: Springer International Publishing, pp. 103–123. doi: 10.1007/978-3-031-15030-2_5.

Borenstein, J. and Howard, A. (2021) "Emerging challenges in AI and the need for AI ethics education," *AI and Ethics*, 1(1), pp. 61–65. doi: 10.1007/s43681-020-00002-7.

Cope, B., Kalantzis, M. and Searsmith, D. (2021) "Artificial intelligence for education: Knowledge and its assessment in AI-enabled learning ecologies," *Educational philosophy and theory*, 53(12), pp. 1229–1245. doi: 10.1080/00131857.2020.1728732.

Felix, C. V. (2020) "The Role of the Teacher and AI in Education," in *Innovations in Higher Education Teaching and Learning*. Emerald Publishing Limited, pp. 33–48. doi: 10.1108/s2055-364120200000033003.

Gupta, M. *et al.* (2023) "From ChatGPT to ThreatGPT: Impact of Generative AI in Cybersecurity and Privacy," *IEEE Access*, 11, pp. 80218–80245. doi: 10.1109/access.2023.3300381.

Holt, K. (2023) *Three Samsung employees reportedly leaked sensitive data to ChatGPT, Engadget*. Available at: https://www.engadget.com/three-samsung-employees-reportedly-leaked-sensitive-data-to-chatgpt-190221114.html.

Hooda, M. *et al.* (2022) "Artificial Intelligence for Assessment and Feedback to Enhance Student Success in Higher Education," *Mathematical Problems in Engineering*, 2022. doi: 10.1155/2022/5215722.

Hwang, G.-J. *et al.* (2020) "Vision, challenges, roles and research issues of Artificial Intelligence in Education," *Computers and Education: Artificial Intelligence*, 1. doi: 10.1016/j.caeai.2020.100001.

King, M. R. and chatGPT (2023) "A Conversation on Artificial Intelligence, Chatbots, and Plagiarism in Higher Education," *Cellular and molecular bioengineering*, 16(1), pp. 1–2. doi: 10.1007/s12195-022-00754-8.

Laato, S. *et al.* (2020) "AI in Cybersecurity Education- A Systematic Literature Review of Studies on Cybersecurity MOOCs," in *2020 IEEE 20th International Conference on Advanced Learning Technologies (ICALT)*. IEEE, pp. 6–10.

Lanz, J. A. (2023) *ChatGPT Adds Web Browsing Feature to Rival Google Bard and Microsoft Bing, Decrypt*. Available at: https://decrypt.co/140369/chatgpt-web-browsing-google-bard-microsoft-bing.

Lock, S. (2022) *What is AI chatbot phenomenon ChatGPT and could it replace humans?, The Guardian*. Available at: https://www.theguardian.com/technology/2022/dec/05/what-is-ai-chatbot-phenomenon-chatgpt-and-could-it-replace-humans.

Marks, M. and Haupt, C. E. (2023) "AI Chatbots, Health Privacy, and Challenges to HIPAA Compliance," *JAMA*, 330(4), pp. 309–310. doi: 10.1001/jama.2023.9458.

McCallum, S. (2023) *ChatGPT banned in Italy over privacy concerns, BBC*. Available at: https://www.bbc.com/news/technology-65139406.

Michael, K., Abbas, R. and Roussos, G. (2023) "AI in Cybersecurity: The Paradox," *IEEE Transactions on Technology and Society*, 4(2), pp. 104–109. doi: 10.1109/tts.2023.3280109.

Motlagh, N. Y. *et al.* (2023) "The Impact of Artificial Intelligence on the Evolution of Digital Education: A Comparative Study of OpenAI Text Generation Tools including ChatGPT, Bing Chat, Bard, and Ernie." doi: 10.48550/ARXIV.2309.02029.

Ouyang, F. and Jiao, P. (2021) "Artificial intelligence in education: The three paradigms," *Computers and Education: Artificial Intelligence*, 2. doi: 10.1016/j.caeai.2021.100020.

Paiva, R. and Bittencourt, I. I. (2020) "Helping teachers help their students: A human-AI hybrid approach," in *International Conference on Artificial Intelligence in Education*. Cham: Springer International Publishing, pp. 448–459.

Roulette, J. (2023) *US Space Force pauses use of AI tools like ChatGPT over data security risks, Reuters*. Available at: https://www.reuters.com/technology/space/us-space-force-pauses-use-ai-tools-like-chatgpt-over-data-security-risks-2023-10-11/.

Santos, O. and Radanliev, P. (2024) *Beyond the Algorithm: AI, Security, Privacy, and Ethics*. Boston, MA: Addison-Wesley Professional.

Tann, W. *et al.* (2023) "Using Large Language Models for Cybersecurity Capture-The-Flag Challenges and Certification Questions," *arXiv*. doi: 10.48550/arXiv.2308.10443.

U.S. Department of Eduction, Office of Educational Technology (2023) *Artificial Intelligence and the Future of Teaching and Learning: Insights and Recommendations*. Washington, DC. Available at: https://tech.ed.gov/ai-future-of-teaching-and-learning/.

Zhai, X. (2022) "ChatGPT User Experience: Implications for Education," *SSRN*. doi: 10.2139/ssrn.4312418.

Validation of Sensor Data Integrity in OT Environments Through Multisource Data Sensors

Jussi Simola, Arttu Takala, Riku Lehkonen, Tapio Frantti and Reijo Savola
University of Jyväskylä, Finland

Jussi.hm.simola@jyu.fi
arttu.h.takala@jyu.fi
riku.p.lehkonen@jyu.fi
tapio.k.frantti@jyu.fi
reijo.m.savola@jyu.fi

Abstract: This research paper focuses on detecting cyber threats from the OT environment by combining data from multiple sources. Monitoring cyber security or hybrid threats in an industrial OT environment is difficult due to different equipment, protocols, environments, personnel management and training, etc. However, the OT environment can also be observed with a multisource sensor system, which can be used to collect data. By combining IT and OT data, additional cyber threats can be found. Especially concerning the integrity of OT command-and-control data. We deal with the key concepts and differences of the industrial operating environment, which create challenges compared to the traditional IT environment. This is important because the policies defined at the European level for the NIS2 regulation are coming to touch all member countries, regardless of what the national implementation schedule is. The increased standards for OT environment cyber security implementation and development will also have an impact on the personnel management and training to support the onboarding of the standards in practice. Critical infrastructure protection is important because, without the protection of critical infrastructure, vital functions cease to function. Hostile actors cause security challenges among Western actors. In this study, we delve into whether it is possible to find threats concerning OT command-and-control process. The increased data surface collected from the IT/OT environment improves the capabilities for the system to detect malicious attacks towards the OT system. With the help of test equipment, the goal is to demonstrate that it is possible to find threats by combining data from multiple sources. With the help of test equipment, we find out IT and OT capabilities, which we load with various attacks and anomalies. We produce added value compared to traditional monitoring method test cases by comparing data obtained from different sources. The research paper shows the importance of detecting OT threats. By monitoring IT and OT environments and combining their data, we can find hidden threats. Only one test equipment configuration has been used in the study, but the results can be generalized and classified. The study also provides guidelines for how the detection of cyber threat capabilities should be developed.

Keywords: Testbed Environment, Sensor Integration, Sensor Data Integrity, Operational Technology, Cybersecurity

1. Introduction

The purpose of the CSG (Cybersecurity Governance of Operational Technology in the Smart Energy) project is to develop a governance model for operational technology ecosystems to minimize Operational Technology risks and create a new standardized operating environment for the industrial environment. The main aim of the CSG project is to develop a Governance model for the Operational technology-related environments. The study's results will be used to design processes for the governance model in the OT-SOC environment where the Industrial Control System (ICS) is a crucial operative factor in an industrial environment.

EU's cybersecurity strategy set the framework for the formation of national-level cybersecurity (European Commission, 2020, 2022; ENISA, 2023). The NIS2 directive by the European Commission (2022) states that every European Union member state must adopt a National Cybersecurity Strategy (NCSS) and establish a cyber security governance model. The European Strategic Energy Technology plan aims to boost the transition towards a climate-neutral energy system (European Parliament 2023).

At a general level, as a part of corporate governance, several elements are related to the formation of cybersecurity governance. The frameworks are essentially connected to each other. Crucial vulnerability elements of security and cyber security consist of people, processes, and technical aspects (European Commission 2022, 2023).

The operational technology environment, especially the energy sector, is critical for every vital function. If cyberattacks disrupt energy supply chain systems, all connected operational technology systems will shut down soon or later. Therefore, it is important also to apply cybersecurity supply chain risk management guides (GSA, 2014). The research concentrates on monitoring process control at the operational and technical levels. It is important to enhance detection capabilities because of the digitalization of the OT environment. NIS2 (2023) requires enhanced information sharing regarding cyber threats and incidents because it has been seen that critical infrastructure protection is not possible to maintain without new regulations. The visibility of the cyber threat control mechanism and the capability to detect and share threat information are important parts of continuity management, which depends on the continuity of business operations.

The paper concentrates on comparing data from different places in the testbed environment. The data will be used to verify the integrity of the operational technology process. We will use several data monitoring points. The focus is on how to see events in different places. We compare the output data to the threat information.

2. Importance of Critical Infrastructure Protection

2.1 Operational Technologies in various industries and connections.

Networking and Information Systems directive NIS2 sets requirements for the companies and their strategic, operational, and technical functions (European Parliament, 2022). In addition, the Cyber Resilience Act (European Commission, 2022) supports the goals of the NIS2, and it endorses the aims of the CER Cyber Resilience directive. CRA consists of requirements for the manufacturing process of digitalized products, industrial companies, and cyber security training methods for the personnel and management of security operations (European Commission, 2022).

The Cybersecurity and Infrastructure Security Agency CISA (2020) lists critical infrastructure in 16 sectors which are Chemical Sector, Commercial Facilities Sector, Communications Sector, Critical Manufacturing Sector, Dams Sector, Defense Industrial Base Sector, Emergency Services Sector, Energy Sector, Financial Services Sector, Food and Agriculture Sector, Government Facilities Sector, Healthcare and Public Health Sector, Information Technology Sector, Nuclear Reactors, Materials, and Waste Sector, Transportation Systems Sector, Water and Wastewater Systems Sector.

Operational technology is vital to critical infrastructures because of the interconnected and mutually dependent physical systems and a host of information and communications technologies (Peerenboom, 2001). Critical infrastructures are called a "system of systems" because of the interdependencies that exist between various industrial sectors and the interconnections between business partners (Peerenboom, 2001; Rinaldi, 2001). An incident in one sector of the crucial infrastructure can, directly and indirectly, affect other infrastructures through cascading and escalating failures. Therefore, visibility into network traffic and device behaviors in OT networks is important. It is less than adequate across the sector regardless of the capability of a particular organization (U.S. Department of Energy (2021). By better understanding the organization's OT environment, they may be able to correlate a more minor anomaly to a potential attack, moving the asset owner's threat detection capability earlier into an attack campaign and preventing more significant impacts on operations (U.S. Department of Energy, 2021).

2.2 Vulnerabilities in Grid Power Systems

According to the NIST (2023), the electrical power transmission and distribution grid industries use geographically distributed SCADA control technology that operates highly interconnected and dynamic systems that consist of countless public and private utilities and rural cooperatives for supplying electricity to end users NIST (2023). Regarding Eto et al. (2016), the electric power system is a complex network of electric components designed to generate, transport, and deliver electricity across two distinct yet integrated systems, but is not clearly defined the interruptions due to factors affecting the bulk power system and factors affecting the distribution system. The same type of fundamental problems is mostly related to the vulnerabilities against cyber-attacks and lack of standardization. According to the IDAHO (2016), distribution and local delivery of electricity are generally not considered part of the U.S. bulk Electric System and are overseen by state public utility commissions. Implementing cyber security standards varies in the breadth of protections and backup measures for distribution utilities. Cyber-attacks on distribution elements can have consequences that reach the Bulk Electric System. The first known hack to affect a power grid occurred in Ukraine in 2015 when a distribution system served as the attack plane. Adversaries used malware to access IT infrastructure and then hijacked the SCADA distribution management system to cause changed states to the distribution electricity infrastructure and attempt to delay restoration by wiping SCADA servers after they caused the outage, while simultaneously preventing calls reporting power outages from reaching customer service centers, resulting in a couple of hours outage. The attackers conducted months of reconnaissance before the attack, planning to execute the attacks that took multiple substations offline and disabled backup power from two distribution centers simultaneously (IDAHO, 2016; Zetter, 2016). Operational technology-related Energy distribution systems are vulnerable because the adversaries understand how important the energy supply chain is to all operational environments. Enemy nations have an interest in manipulating workable systems.

In the connection of Operational Technology, several industrial control system devices include remote access capabilities, and industrial control systems are increasingly connected to corporate business networks (GAO, 2018). According to the GAO (2018), attackers' remote access is an increasingly potential cyber threat target for manipulating ICS devices. Because functionalities depend on the energy supply, there is a need to develop OT environments that are more protected against cyber-attacks. Cyberthreat detection capabilities are a crucial part of overall cybersecurity. The paper concentrates on the requirements of the cyber threat/ event detection capabilities.

2.3 Enhancing Cyber Security Situational Awareness at the Operational Level

The ENISA (2022), Governance model has been divided into four levels. Political, strategic, operational, and technical levels. The technical level of administration aims to link the implementation strategy so that technical and technological development takes place simultaneously, which is essential in cyberspace, a rapidly developing field where new threats and challenges arise simultaneously as new technological opportunities and solutions. The operational/ technical level is crucial for the formation of situational awareness. Technical, network and software-based data-sharing capabilities are crucial, and human interaction affects the ground-level transformed information.

Defense in Depth is based on the military concept that provides barriers to impede the progress of intruders from attaining their goals while monitoring their progress and developing and implementing responses to the incident to repel them (Homeland Security, 2016). As Homeland Security (2016) states, an organization must recognize the relationship between intruders and vulnerabilities to the controls (standards and countermeasures) put in place to protect operations, personnel, and technologies. According to the Defense-in-Depth Protection to Industrial Control Systems, the connection between Information Technology and Control Systems in an organization's security functions is crucial. The defense-in-depth strategy consists of the following elements, as Table 1 illustrates (Homeland Security, 2016).

Table 1: The elements of the defense-in-depth strategy (Homeland Security, 2016)

Defense-In-Depth Strategy Elements	
Risk Management Program	• Identify Threats • Characterize Risk • Maintain Asset Inventory
Cybersecurity Architecture	• Standards/ Recommendations • Policy • Procedures
Physical Security	• Field Electronics Locked Down • Control Center Access Controls • Remote Site Video, Access Controls, Barriers
ICS Network Architecture	• Common Architectural Zones • Demilitarized Zones (DMZ) • Virtual LANs
ICS Network Perimeter Security	• Firewalls/ One-Way Diodes • Remote Access & Authentication • Jump Servers/ Hosts
Host Security	• Patch and Vulnerability Management • Field Devices • Virtual Machines
Security Monitoring	• Intrusion Detection Systems • Security Audit Logging

Defense-In-Depth Strategy Elements	
	• Security Incident and Event Monitoring
Vendor Management	• Supply Chain Management • Managed Services/ Outsourcing • Leveraging Cloud Services
The Human Element	• Policies • Procedures • Training and Awareness

According to (Homeland Security, 2016), organizations can use five principles for countermeasures to drive activities in ICS environments. The following steps will pave the way toward a more robust security environment and significantly reduce the risk to operational systems.

- Identify, minimize, and secure all network connections to the ICS.
- Harden the ICS and supporting systems by disabling unnecessary services, ports, and protocols, enable available security features and implement robust configuration management practices.
- Continually monitor and assess the security of the ICS, networks, and interconnections.
- Implement a risk-based defense-in-depth approach to securing ICS systems and networks.
- Manage the human—clearly identify requirements for ICS; establish expectations for performance; hold individuals accountable for their performance; establish policies; and provide ICS security training for all operators and administrators.

3. Data Integrity Validation and Process Integrity

3.1 Managing Information Security in IT and OT Environments

3.1.1 CIA and AIC Triad

Confidentiality, Integrity, and Availability (CIA) triad is a form of representation of the fundamental elements of security objectives in information systems (NIST, 2020a,2020b). Confidentiality is focused on the restrictions on the use and storage of data, which may be lost in cases such as during insecure data transmission or access control (Kar &et.a., 2021) On the other hand, integrity offers guarantees that data has not been tampered with. One way to attempt to secure data during transmission is to use checksums to validate the integrity of the transferred data between the sender and the receiver (Kar and Zolkipli, 2021). Availability in information systems ensures that the authorized users have timely and uninterrupted access to necessary information, resources, and components. In OT environment, availability includes being able to use the devices that are part of the system, which could be crucial for the environment they're in (Kar and Zolkipli, 2021). The impact of availability is exacerbated in critical infrastructure, where the loss of availability would have cascading impact on society.

Although CIA triad implements heavy focus on technical security controls, when socio-technical elements are important in system security, it is a valuable and straightforward way to understand and solve issues that are relevant in information security (Samonas and Coss, 2014). For example, it is especially relevant in Common Vulnerability Scoring System (CVSS) scoring when system impact of a vulnerability is estimated, which are used in estimating severity of Common Vulnerabilities and Exposures (CVE) events. CIA triad has its roots in military security mindset, where the protection is perimeter focused against external threats (Samonas and Coss, 2014). Additionally, loss of CIA of information or information systems is used as basis in development of relevant security controls (NIST, 2020)b.

3.1.2 On the Aspects of CIA/AIC Triad in IT/OT

CIA triad originates from IT domain, where the security features aim to provide safety by protecting itself against cyberattacks. Traditional OT domain's safety aims to ensure functional resilience and safety to protect the environment and humans against unwanted operations that could lead to physical damage or injuries (Hollerer & et.al, 2022). Additionally, priorities considering the CIA triad are inverse between traditional IT and OT environments, where IT environments prioritise confidentiality first (CIA) and OT environments availability first (AIC)5. With the OT 4.0 shift of integrating IT capabilities and interfacing OT devices into IT infrastructure, the difference between IT and OT is diminished, since it opens OT environments as targets against cyberattacks. For example, cyberattacks may target OT environments to prevent the availability of safety function of an OT device, which may lead to undermined safety of the environment. However, while loss of availability might be the major threat in OT environments, loss of confidentiality and integrity may be used to cause loss of availability with cyberattacks. In an automated system, the loss of integrity can lead to a higher loss of availability. This is due to the potential for system shutdown triggered by cascading adjustments. These adjustments are based on the falsified data and are intended to steer the system towards correct function. For example, if data routes have their integrity lost (manipulated device status report), the automated safety system shutdown may be used as the attack vector to damage the equipment, leading to loss of availability, which in turn impacts the security (Dentlzer&et.al,.2021). Similarly, loss of confidentiality on higher privileges and device data may lead to them being used to aid in attacks against the OT environment's availability. Therefore, while availability is the most important target to defend, confidentiality and integrity are inherently connected to overall availability in OT 4.0 environments. This leads to the need to balance all aspects of the CIA triad to ensure safety when designing system controls rather than prioritizing confidentiality first.

4. Background Theory

We have applied a design science research methodology, which is used traditionally in system development (Hevner & et.al., 2004). As part of the design science process, the multiple case study research-based strategy by Yin (2004) and the knowledge base of the case studies create a core framework for the governance model and generate an added knowledge base. This iterative design science process output must be different from the present system. The MITRE Att&ck (2023) framework has formed the common base for analyzing cyber-attacks, tactics, and scenarios. It has its own weaknesses related to industry-based threat classification, but it is very suitable to apply to almost all kinds of companies. Operational Technology-based vulnerabilities are nowadays the main target when the aim is to develop a coherent cyber security environment. The MITRE Attack framework (2023) is an important element of the testing process. We have used data from it in several cases.

The paper concentrates on data integrity validation and its process. The process will be validated using data from various points during execution. Another research focus concentrates on enhancing the visibility of sector-based threat information. Two main aspects must be considered:

- Data integrity validation may be done with data sensors at various points, where the values of the data may be compared to ensure their correctness. The various data sensors may also be used to track process steps throughout the system. This way the process integrity may be a target for validation instead, to ensure it has not been tampered with. For example, with various data sensors, the system warden may see that the command sequence is manipulated halfway through the process, leading to a different outcome than initially requested. This may be included with additional system-specific information, such as software versions, hardware equipment, and network protocols.
- When a system vulnerability or malicious attack is detected, the additional system information aids in threat intel and security breach reporting to the relevant stakeholders. These companies may work in similar or adjacent sectors, where identical hardware or software is used. In summary, the process validation may be used to provide context to threat intel. Additionally, the NIS2 (2022) directive mandates sector-based threat intel reporting, where companies are obligated to report to the relevant government body about possible security breaches. Using various data sensors for process validation improves the visibility of the security processes, which in turn aids in providing information to governmental bodies. This, in turn, proves that the company is upholding its obligations.

4.1 Point of Process Monitoring

Monitoring a process and its data traffic in OT environments aids in creating a holistic situational awareness, in addition to process awareness, which includes elements such as steps taken, transferred data, used devices, and software versions. If a cyberattack uses specific process as an attack vector, process-based monitoring aids in forensics due to documented and monitored content. Additionally, monitoring a singular process through various data sensors aids in auditing process function events. For example, if a cyberattack manipulates data at a particular step of a process, such as during a log request or SCADA command, it may be analysed in forensics towards a specific section in internet infrastructure where the step would occur. This provides additional information, which may be used in further forensics, such as the devices (e.g., switch and IED) used in this specific step, their software versions, and protocols used in communication. This additional information needs to be manually managed in cases where the monitoring focuses on specific data values without including process as a framework for context. Additionally, process monitoring enables analysis of causal relationship between steps and other processes. If a data value doesn't change as expected after a certain process step is performed, it could signal a potential compromise.

4.2 Testbed Environment

The testbed environment developed by the University of Jyväskylä is a unique platform for testing different kinds of vulnerabilities and threat scenarios. Testing separate software, devices, and network combinations in many ways is possible. Collaboration with business companies is essential and generates new data for protecting critical infrastructure.

We have tested how to detect and see threat data at different points. The used laboratory environment consists of a process plant with its OT devices and the control and monitoring network, as Figure 1 illustrates. The plant can be controlled with local and remote SCADA system. Remote control is implemented with an LTE connection. A separate monitoring network is connected to the process plant. Monitoring is implemented by mirroring the network traffic from the central switch and OT device log information from the central logging points of the process plant and the control center (Office).

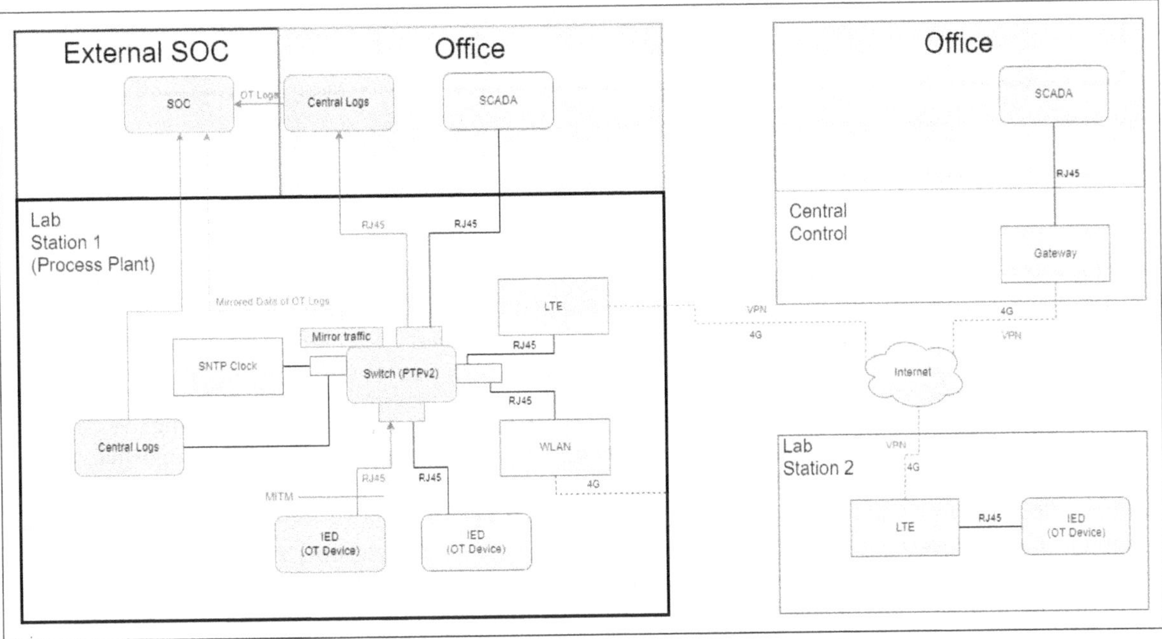

Figure 1*:* Testbed environment

The Man-In-The-Middle (MITM, man = person, device) scenario is indicated in red, which is used to validate the process-based data integrity verification method. PITM data compromise is carried out with an additional device which is added to the connection between the process plant and the office. Compromised OT logs are also highlighted in red. The devices utilized in the scenario are highlighted in blue.

4.3 Use Case

4.3.1 Environment and Scenario

As Figure 2 illustrates, the use case is depicted with a real-world counterpart. Separate office space contains the plant's control system, which is connected to the plant's internal switch. The data transfer between the production plant and the office space is remotely monitored with a separate SOC. Furthermore, one distinct isolated network is employed for the surveillance of OT device logs, while a different network is used to directly request OT device logs from the device itself.

In this scenario, the attacker has access (physical or network) to the process plant control network. The attacker modifies the data transferred between the OT device and the central switch. By modifying this data, the attacker can compromise the situational awareness of the control system and SOC, evade installed defense mechanisms, and disguise footprints left in the system. MITRE ATT&CK (2023) classifies the attack as a Man-In-The-Middle (MITM, Person-In-The-Middle) technique and a defense evasion tactic.

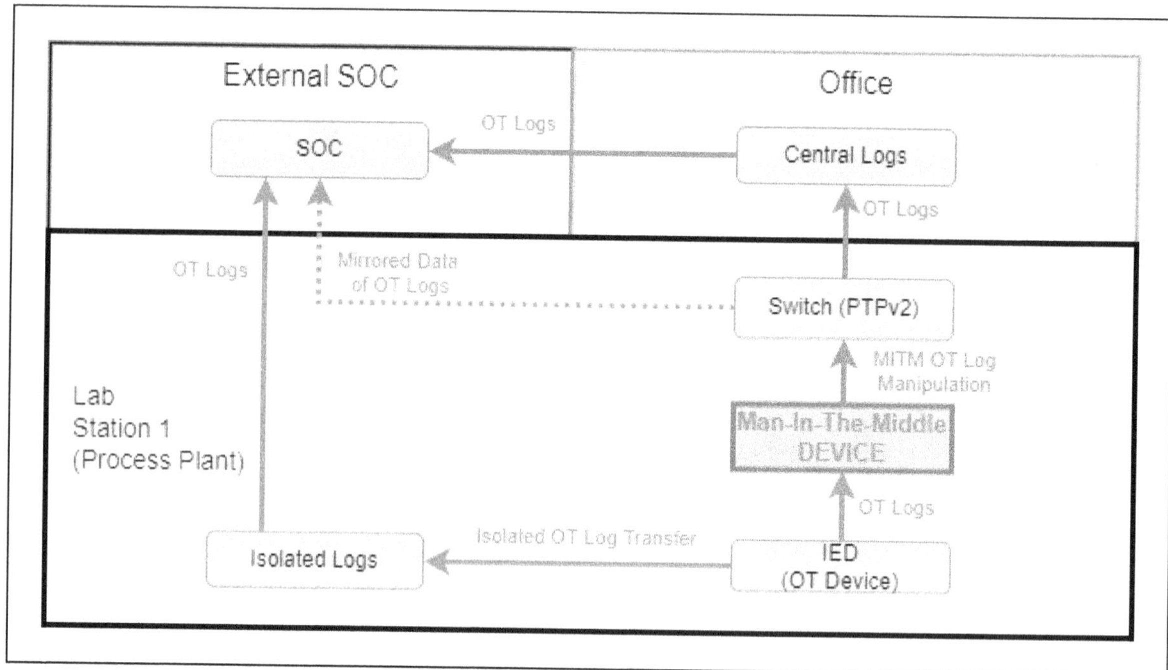

Figure 2: **Description of the use case**

4.3.2 Performed Use Case

During the executed log request process, monitoring occurs via data links at the central logging device, switch, and IED. The IED reports within the internal network through the switch to the logging device, while external reporting is done via an isolated cable. Specifically, the process involves a log request from the central logging device to the IED through the switch, supported by an additional external request from the SOC.

The MITM attack undermines the integrity of the response to the central logging by manipulating the sent data. This leads to central logging and switch data links to report incorrect status. From the SOCs perspective, there is a discrepancy in the status logs returned in response to the event log request: the switch and central logging indicate a 'local control' status, while the IED reports a 'remote control' status. This deviation is an anomaly, prompting further investigation to identify potential malfunctions or Indicators of Compromise (IoCs). By analyzing the causal relationships of process steps and examining historical logs, we can determine whether this IED should be in a 'remote control' or 'local control' state based on previous state-change commands. This verification process helps pinpoint the location of potential IoCs within the internet infrastructure.

5. Findings

The upcoming NIS 2 directive requires critical infrastructure operators to monitor their systems for cyber-threats. Operators must be able to report any potential threats and interpret the reports of other operators. To make the most effective use of potential threat reports, they must also include information on the cause-and-effect relationship to which the threat is related.

The capability to monitor, log, and report one's own behavior is vital to the OT device. Additionally, centralized monitoring is crucial to ensure the correct functionality of the entire system. However, in OT environments, there are hardware limitations to monitoring the integrity of the command-and-control process. For this reason, it is possible to add a separate monitoring network to the old systems. The monitoring network monitors possible IT threats to the OT network, as well as threats related to the integrity of the OT process. The threat information about OT systems must especially be able to be shared with operators in the same sector.

At the heart of the monitoring network is a SOC, where IT and OT data from the network are collected. The SOC must be able to handle traditional IT-related cyber threats and OT-related threats. These also include threats related to the integrity of the OT process. Therefore, when collecting and sharing threat information from OT systems, it is essential to include information about the environment in which the threat was detected, including devices and protocols. The information must be structured so that an operator in the same sector can use the threat information in their own system. Also, Potential confidential business secrets must be considered when threat information is shared. The specific information to be shared must be agreed upon separately, as the detailed analysis of it could potentially expose these secrets.

The current situation in OT environments focuses on monitoring operating environments' performance and status to ensure safety and reliability. However, convergence of IT and OT has led to a situation where transferred data and operation functions may be maliciously manipulated through the IT interfacing elements. In OT one method to verify such manipulation is based upon checksums, but it originates from finding corrupted packets, not intentional manipulation. The majority of OT monitoring is therefore focused upon whether the machine or function is mechanically broken or that someone has unintentionally configured the device wrong.

According to process control, an isolated network and hardware are good for monitoring the process in a way that many sensors are used. It is important to divide what is monitored and in what context; in the case of the man-in-the-middle attack, the entire log reporting process is needed. Many checkpoints show where the process went wrong. It is important to analyze what this can mean for the entire system's operation. A cause-and-effect relationship can be found in the process data. We monitor processes; in practice, we monitor the operation of the electricity distribution network with certain devices. Sector-specific information is distributed upwards. The purpose is to share and receive data about potential threats identified in one's own sector.

6. Conclusion

There is a need to enhance the maturity level of monitoring events in the operational technology environment. Researched events from the IT and OT environments are crucial when the purpose is to produce coherent situational awareness of the industry environments. Without the ability to see the required things from the IT/OT environment, understanding the business situation may disappear.

The visibility of cyber security processes is critical to fulfilling the requirements of European Union regulations. Several OT-related standards and special publications are important in steering the supply chain. Validation is a set of actions regarding the system requirement, and it is important to ensure they are fulfilled.

NIS2 (European Parliament, 2022) requires collaboration between the industry sectors and within it. The information must flow, so the connection between the strategic, operational, and technical levels is a crucial factor that enhances the overall situational awareness within sector-based industries and at the enterprise level. As ENISA (2023) states and NIS2 suggest, there must be understandable mechanisms where operational technology-related events are transmitted and transformed into a form that generates added value for the decision-makers. It is not enough to achieve a report that indicates events. There should be information about the type of vulnerabilities and a description of the whole process, including the source of the threat and potential consequences. Because many attempts of the adversaries' attacks are being tried again, ja, unintentional events or incidents are often repeated. Decision-makers should be able to make decisions regarding business continuity and information-sharing capabilities depending on the security operation center's maturity to detect operational technology-related threats deep enough. That is impossible without gathering and combining different kinds of data from the physical and networked sensors. So, the framework of the process control mechanism that gathers data and shares data from the Operational Technology environment to the SOC is crucial to enhance operational technology cyber security at the ground level. The developed taxonomy has its own role in forming situational awareness (NIS Cooperation Group, 2018), but it must be kept up to date more efficiently because of the development of potential incidents.

The CSG project concentrates on developing the governance model for the OT environments. All research data from the testbed environment support the development process of the governance model.

Acknowledgments

The research was supported by Business Finland (grant number 10/31/2022) and the University of Jyväskylä.

References

CISA (2020) Critical Infrastructure Sectors. https://www.cisa.gov/topics/critical-infrastructure-security-and-resilience/critical-infrastructure-sectors

Denzler P., Hollerer S., Frühwirth T., and Kastner W. (2021) Identification of security threats, safety hazards, and interdependencies in industrial edge computing. In The Sixth

ACM/IEEE Symposium on Edge Computing (SEC' 21), December 14–17, 2021, San Jose, CA, USA. ACM, New York, NY, USA.

Eto J. H., LaCommare K. H., Caswell H., Till D., (2017) Distribution system versus bulk power system: identifying the source of electric service interruptions in the US. The Institution of Engineering and Technology.
ENISA (2023) Building Effective Governance Frameworks for the Implementation of National Cybersecurity Strategies.
European Commission, (2020) The EU's Cybersecurity Strategy for the Digital Decade. Brussels. https://eur-lex.europa.eu/legal-content/EN/TXT/HTML/?uri=CELEX:52020JC0018
European Commission, (2022) Proposal for a regulation on horizontal cybersecurity requirements for products with digital elements and amending Regulation (EU) 2019/1020.
European Parliament, (2022) Directive 2022/2555 Network and information security (NIS2).
European Parliament (2023) Directive (EU) 2023/2413 of the European Parliament and of the Council of 18 October 2023 amending Directive (EU) 2018/2001, Regulation (EU) 2018/1999 and Directive 98/70/EC as regards the promotion of energy from renewable sources, and repealing Council Directive (EU) 2015/652
GAO, (2018) Critical Infrastructure Protection Actions Needed to Address Significant
GAO (2024) Cybersecurity Supply Chain Risk Management (C-SCRM) Acquisition Guide
Hollerer, S., Sauter, T., Kastner, W., (2022) Risk Assessments Considering Safety, Security, and Their Interdependencies in OT Environments. In The 17th International Conference on Availability, Reliability and Security (ARES 2022), August 23–26, 2022, Vienna, Austria. ACM, New York, NY, USA. https://doi.org/10.1145/3538969.3543814
Homeland Security (2016) Recommended Practice: Improving Industrial Control System Cybersecurity with Defense-in-Depth Strategies. Industrial Control Systems Cyber Emergency Response Team.
Hevner A., March, S.T., Park, J., and Ram, S. (2004) Design Science in Information Systems Research. MIS Quarterly.
IDAHO (2016) Cyber Threat and Vulnerability Analysis of the U.S. Electric Sector
Kar Yee, C., & Zolkipli, M. F. (2021) Review on Confidentiality, Integrity and Availability in Information Security. Journal of ICT in Education, 8(2), 34–42. https://doi.org/10.37134/jictie.vol8.2.4.2021
MITRE (2023) "ATT&CK Matrix for Enterprise," [online], https://attack.mitre.org/.
NIS Cooperation Group (2018) Cybersecurity Incident Taxonomy CG Publication 04/2018
NIS Cooperation Group (2018) Reference document on security measures for Operators of Essential Services CG Publication 01/2018
NIST (2020a) Special Publication 1800-26A Data Integrity: Detecting and Responding to Ransomware and Other Destructive Events
NIST (2020b) Special Publication 800-53r.5. Security and Privacy Controls for Information Systems and Organizations
NIST (2023) Special Publication800-82r3. Guide to Operational Technology (OT) Security
Peerenboom J (2001) "Infrastructure Interdependencies: Overview of Concepts and Terminology." (NSF/OSTP Workshop on Critical Infrastructure: Needs in Interdisciplinary Research and Graduate Training, Washington, DC)
Rinaldi, S., Peerenboom, J., Kelly T., "Identifying, Understanding, and Analyzing Critical Infrastructure Interdependencies," IEEE Control Systems Magazine, (December 2001), pp. 11-25, http://dx.doi.org/10.1109/37.969131
Samonas, S., Coss, D., (2014) The CIA strikes back: redefining confidentiality, integrity, and availability in security. USA.
U.S. Department of Energy (2021) Methodology for Cybersecurity in Operational Technology Environments.
Zetter, Kim, (2016) "Inside the Cunning, Unprecedented Hack of Ukraine's Power Grid," Wired, www.wired.com.
Yin, R.K. (1994) Case Study Research: Design and Methods, 2nd edn. Sage Publishing, Thousand Oaks.

Improving Detection Capabilities in OT Environments Through Multisource Data Sensors

Jussi Simola, Arttu Takala, Riku Lehkonen, Tapio Frantti and Reijo Savola
University of Jyväskylä, Finland

Jussi.hm.simola@jyu.fi
arttu.h.takala@jyu.fi
riku.p.lehkonen@jyu.fi
tapio.k.frantti@jyu.fi
reijo.m.savola@jyu.fi

Abstract: This research focuses on implementing cyber threat detection in OT environments by combining data from IT and OT sensors and logs to enhance SOC's situational awareness. OT environment is challenging to monitor and includes various sensors. We deal with the key concepts and differences of the industrial operating environment, which create challenges compared to the traditional IT environment. This is important because the policies defined at the European level for the NIS2 regulation will affect all member countries. Hostile actors cause security challenges highlighting the importance of critical infrastructure protection. Cyber security solutions have often solely focused on IT threats, but similar investments have yet to be made in response to the challenges of the OT environment. The security solutions of OT operators rely heavily on solutions from the IT side. Here, we delve into whether it is possible to find threats in the IT/OT ecosystem by combining data from the IT and OT sides. All threats are not found by monitoring data separately from IT or OT sources but we identified hidden threats by monitoring and comparing IT and OT data. This paper shows the importance of detecting OT threats. The study proposes how the detection of cyber threat capabilities should be developed.

Keywords: Operational technology, Testbed, Security operations center, Threat detection, Situational awareness

1. Introduction

NIS2 will create new requirements for companies and their services and digitalized products. Targeting all medium- and large-sized companies is vital to the continuity of the economy. Small vital companies have also followed the main rules and guidelines European Commission (2022). Authorities and authorized actors (for example, service providers of security operation centers) are in a new situation with legal measures set in regulation, which will affect the services they produce. The directive gives the mandate to act so that regulation can be fulfilled. In relation to the NIS2, the European Union-level agency (ENISA), supports cybersecurity policy and aims to enhance and develop services, ICT products, and processes in the European Union (ENISA, 2023). The NIS2 directive will enhance the resilience of network and information systems. There will be two categories for the enterprises' essential and important industries. EU member countries must adopt a national cybersecurity strategy. There were differences between essential providers and digitalized services in the first version of the NIS. This gap is now removed. NIS2 classifies organizations based on their essentiality into two categories: essential and important (European Commission, 2022). However, it has been seen that the European Union will follow the U.S.'s cybersecurity regulations guidelines. Protecting the energy sector and supplying distributed energy resources is one of the main objectives of the new cyber security regulations. This paper concentrates on detection capabilities in OT environments through multisource data sensors at the operational level. It answers the questions "how to enhance OT-SOC-related cyber security capabilities" and "how to develop a governance model". The paper uses the demonstration and testing platform to develop the governance model. The project's main goal Is to develop a governance and reference model for the industry stakeholders.

2. Elements of the Research

The CSG (CyberSecurity Governance of operational technology in sector-connected smart energy networks) project will develop a leading-edge cybersecurity sector integration governance model to cover cybersecurity solutions, processes, and methods for operational technology environments. The project aims at considerable cost savings and scalability. The European Union's common aim in the OT/ICS environment is enhancing cyber situational awareness.

Standardization, protocols, or guidelines are not only requirements that are good to follow. Cybersecurity governance is a part of the overall corporate governance management system. It is also a part of company strategy, working culture, and daily routines. Employees are an essential part of cyberphysical ecosystems.

Governance requires cohesion between the crucial elements of the cyber-ecosystem. The importance of the well-organized governance model is emphasized according to the company's size.

It is crucial to connect corporate governance to the cybersecurity governance framework. Essential is how the board of directors and decision-makers approach their strategic goals; as mentioned in previous research (Simola & et.al. 2023), there are four main levels of governance: political, strategic, operational, and technical/tactical. Figure 1 illustrates how cyber-attacks can be seen in an operational technology environment and industrial systems (GAO, 2021).

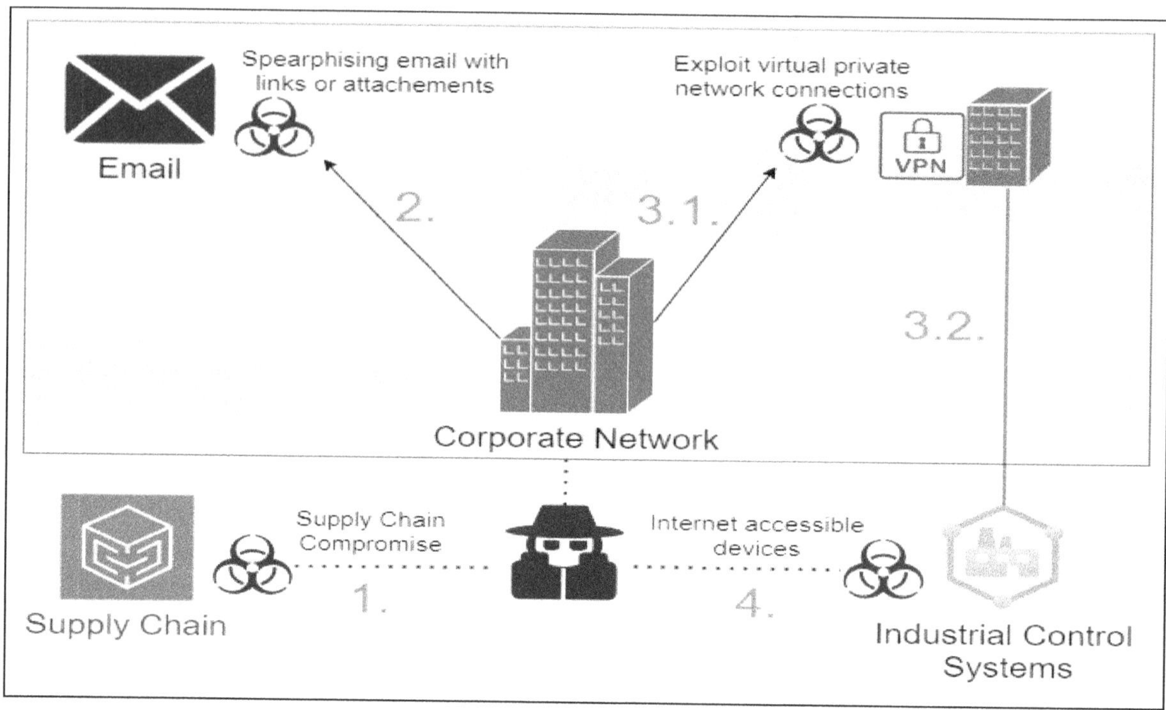

Figure 1: Example of the cyber-attacks against Industrial Control Systems modified from (GAO, 2021)

Attackers compromise the supply chain of industrial control systems by manipulating products, such as hardware or software, before receipt by the end consumer. Another way is to send a "spearphishing" email with links or attachments that include malicious code to a specific individual, company, or industry to gain access to a corporate network. Then, attackers exploit services that allow corporate users to connect to network resources from a remote location, *e.g.*, virtual private network, and the attackers use these services to gain access to and attack industrial control systems. Lastly, attackers can access industrial control systems in cases where systems have direct connections to the internet (GAO, 2022).

2.1 Situational Awareness

Humans are often the weakest link in the operational technology environment. Common situational information is crucial when the aim is to enhance the exchange of information between humans and devices. The formation of the mental model is essential within the team and between the team members to reduce overlapping work (Endsley, 1995). According to Endsley (1995,1988), Situation awareness is the perception of the elements in the environments within the volume of time and space, the comprehension of their meaning, and the projection of their status shortly. Perception is an essential ability in the industrial environment. The formation of situational awareness requires several elements that are connected to each other. Humans cannot process large volumes of data, quickly and consistently. Flexible autonomy should provide a smooth, simple, seamless transition of functions between humans and the system. Regulations of the European Union set new requirements for the formation of cyber situational awareness. Human or automated systems are essential factors that enhance communication methods, procedures, information gathering, and sharing. Mechanisms for that are under development.

2.2 Command and Control and Security Operation Centers

Command and Control Center refers to operative control processes and procedures of military actions. Functionalities and work tasks changed to the Computer Emergency Response Center, which later changed to the Security Operations Center, consisting of different functionalities and actions that control, monitor, and supervise customers' networks (Vielberth et. al. 2020).

2.3 Industrial Control Systems

Industrial control system (ICS) means several types of control systems, including supervisory control and data acquisition (SCADA) systems, distributed control systems (DCS), and other control system configurations such as Programmable Logic Controllers (PLC) often found in the industrial sectors and critical infrastructures. An ICS consists of control components (e.g., electrical, mechanical, hydraulic, pneumatic) that act together to achieve an industrial objective, such as manufacturing, and transportation of matter or energy (NIST 2022).

2.4 Mitre Att&ck

MITRE ATT&CK framework serves as a universally available repository of adversarial strategies and methods, derived from actual observations. It operates as an intermediary level adversary model, bridging the gap between fundamental elements like exploits and vulnerability databases, and higher-level models such as Cyber Kill Chain (CKC) (Strom et al., 2018). However, MITRE ATT&CK does not operate as a linear sequence chain. It requires analysts to construct the Tactics, Techniques and Procedures (TTP) chain manually by choosing the tactics and techniques that have occurred from within the framework of the MITRE ATT&CK model in the order of occurrence. According to Pols (2017), a technique is not solely associated with a specific tactic as several tactics across various stages of an attack chain frequently utilize it. This increases the complexity of developing TTP chains.

3. Requirements of the OT Environment

3.1 Technical Cybersecurity Requirements

Standards may leave room for interpretation, leading to lower maturity than intended, *e.g.*, configuration change may be logged, but not in-depth, which would be beneficial for incidence forensics, such as what was changed, what was its value changed to. The following standards are crucial in the operational technology environment. The ISA/IEC 62443 series of standards includes control systems used in manufacturing and processing plants and facilities, as well as geographically situated distribution operations and facilities. It is also used in automated and remotely controlled and monitored assets (ISA, 2021). As Table 1 illustrates, the connection between security programs and cybersecurity governance is essential.

Table 1: Relevant Operational Technology-related Standards

Standards and guidelines	Details
IEC 62443, (ISA, 2021)	Security Standards for Industrial Automation and Control Systems
Management of Information security ISO/IEC 27001 ISO/IEC (2022)	Standard for Information Security.
RMF for Information Systems and Organizations NIST 800-37 r2- (NIST, 2018)	Risk management Framework
Guide to Operational Technology (OT) Security SP 800-82r3 (NIST, 2023)	The publication consists of guidance on how to secure operational technology (OT)
Security and Privacy Controls for Information Systems and Organizations NIST 800-53 r5. (NIST, 2020)	Catalog of security and privacy controls
Guide to Cyber Threat Information Sharing NIST SP 800-150 (NIST; 2016)	The publication consists of guidelines for establishing and participating in cyber-threat information-sharing relationships
Cybersecurity Supply Chain Risk Management Practices for Systems and Organizations NIST SP 800-161r1 (NIST, 2022)	The publication consists of identifying, assessing, and mitigating cybersecurity risks throughout the supply chain at all levels of their organizations

Figure 2 illustrates the importance of the connection between cybersecurity governance, and supply chain management. Still, more than following the separate standard, ISA/IEC 62443 is needed to enhance the overall cybersecurity ecosystem in the operational technology environment.

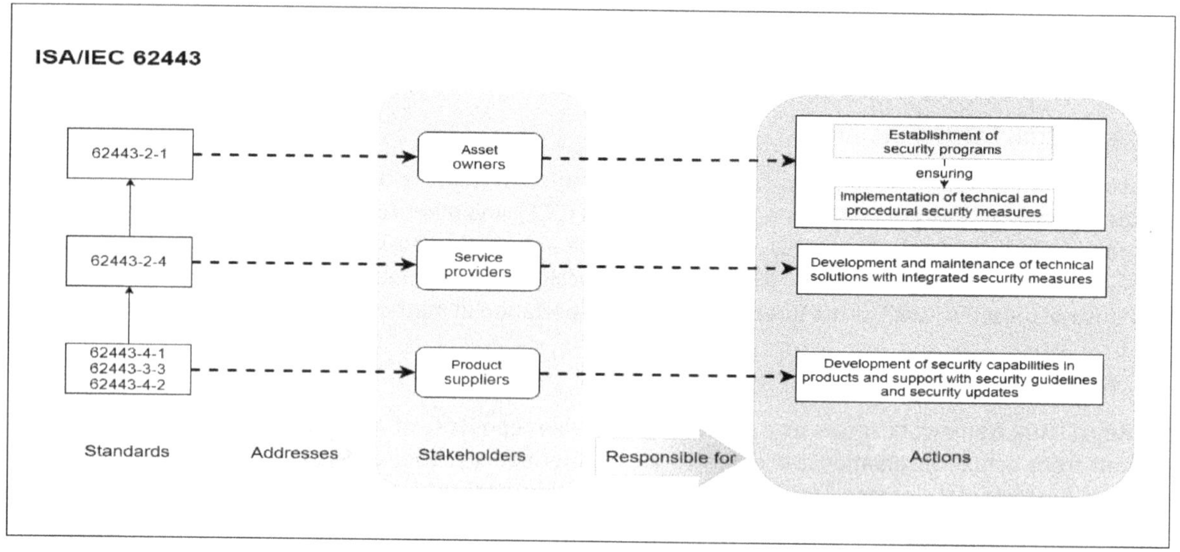

Figure 2: Formation of IEC 63224 Standard, modified from (ISA, 2021)

3.2 Information Exchange Between the Decision-makers

Organizations' decision-makers must have reliable information about the events, risks, and vulnerabilities. The information needed for operational-level management steers the practical processes of information sharing and exchange. The information must be in a form that is understood in the same way, and it cannot change when it changes from one format to another.

3.3 Contents of the Data Exchange

A couple of factors must be taken into account: a) relevant information for stakeholders. Stakeholders must be able to gather and share relevant information with the appropriate stakeholders. b) Company secrets. Companies have their own secret information that they cannot share. This kind of information is classified and belongs under business secrets. Despite that EU, EU-level regulations such as the NIS2 requirements prevent the holding of information about events that may be essential for protecting critical infrastructure. c) Anonymization (difficult to reach the required level without losing information). When information is shared between the SOCs or industries, it is crucial that sensitive information is shared in a way that sensitive information does not prevent compliance with privacy policy. The problem is that sensitive data is relatively easy to find, for example, by combining pieces of data. d) Trusted partners. Very often, that refers to the 3rd party stakeholders, for example, service providers. Every trusted partner must follow the same principles about managing cybersecurity-related issues. e) Legislative requirements. Legislation forms the basis for the standardization. Information sharing and exchange mechanisms should be based on the same standardized levels that regulation requires.

3.4 Requirements of the Information Exchange at the Interface

Efficient information and data sharing require different capabilities in all organization stages. As previous research Simola & et. al., (2023) has indicated, information and data must be changed from the technical environment to the management level. Operational actions require both because sharing information without data is impossible. At the management level, one needs to maintain situational awareness, which requires a combination of information. If the information is achievable and reliable, decision-makers may supervise the operational actions and, the situation of the business and how the strategic goals have been achieved. Cyber situational awareness is one part of overall situational awareness. That means the information must flow between the decision-makers and be unchanging between the units. If the content changes, the situational picture between the units "blurs".

3.5 Defensive / Mitigations Suggestions

MITRE ATT&CK suggests certain defensive mitigations against techniques and sub-techniques for ICS, enterprise, and mobile environments. These mitigations, however, lack context of the attack's TTP chain and require expert knowledge to know which mitigation is applicable and beneficial to prevent further attacks or how these mitigations are meant to be integrated. For example, network sniffing is provided with mitigation strategy of multi-factor authentication (MFA), but it offers no guidelines on integration or reasoning why it mitigates network sniffing. Additionally, network sniffing may occur both in ICS and enterprise environments, but MFA has different limitations for implementation and functionality depending on the environment it is used in.

The Common Vulnerability Scoring System (CVSS) is an open-access industry benchmark for gauging the gravity of security vulnerabilities in computer systems. It aims to allocate severity scores to such vulnerabilities, enabling those responding to prioritize their actions and resources based on the level of threat. CVSS is used to indicate the severity of a vulnerability in information security and is a fundamental component of many vulnerability scanning tools. Conversely, the Common Vulnerabilities and Exposures (CVE) is a glossary of all publicly disclosed vulnerabilities that includes the CVE ID, a description, dates, and comments (Risto, 2018).

The National Vulnerability Database (NVD) plays a crucial role in enhancing the CVE List, which is overseen by the MITRE Corporation and supported by the U.S. Department of Homeland Security (DHS) and the Cybersecurity and Infrastructure Security Agency (CISA). The NVD enriches this list of publicly known cybersecurity vulnerabilities and exposures by providing additional analysis, CVSS scores, transforming data points into SCAP (Security Content Automation Protocol) datatypes, and offering a comprehensive search engine and specific APIs (Application Programming Interfaces). Security teams can leverage NVD's data feeds to integrate vulnerability intelligence into existing workflows and tools. The NVD supports these feeds by maintaining synchronization with the CVE to ensure that any updates to the CVE List are immediately reflected in the NVD (NIST, 2024).

3.6 Current Situation in the Operational Technology Environment

IT environments are commonly capable of centralized logging and implement it in systems where logs require audit. However, due to the large amount of collected and transferred data, some systems cannot implement centralized logging. To combat this, these IT environments are working towards implementing distributed and decentralized log systems, such as blockchain log systems, to reduce and equalize network overheads and latency occurring within the system. Conversely, OT environments still use local log storage on IED's, such as control relays, and have only recently introduced capabilities on new IED's towards centralized logging. Centralized logging in OT environments is limited due to the hardware and software constraints of older equipment. This limitation hinders the introduction and integration of IT cybersecurity solutions and practices, which are designed with centralized logging and easy access to logs and data in mind.

4. Research Approach

4.1 Test Environment

The connection between the test environment and the designing cyber security governance model is the main aim of the project. Testbed developed for these use cases implements high-end OT hardware and software solutions commonly used in critical infrastructure. They are capable of network connection, which enables environments to be operated, maintained, and surveyed remotely. This enables cybersecurity-related use cases that target the system holistically, as well as each component, their connecting interfaces, and specifically the addition of IT solutions in OT environments. At present, there aren't any widely recognized comprehensive SOC standards or sector-specific guidelines. Most of the existing SOC guidelines are authored by security vendors. The existing guidelines from MITRE SOC suggest the deployment of IT cybersecurity sensors on host machines and network environment. These sensors and their data are essential for making knowledgeable decisions (Knerler, Parker, Zimmerman, 2022). To illustrate the necessity for more comprehensive sensor integration in OT environments, a SOC will be put into place to enhance detection capabilities using a variety of sensor data sources. This implementation will underscore the advantages provided by these comprehensive sensors when the system faces attacks of varying techniques, tactics, vectors, and targets. For example, sensors at different layers might inform SOC of their layer's status and state, but only following one layer will leave other sections vulnerable to attacks. In addition to this, the combination of data sensors may provide additional value towards workflow and process validation, especially when machine learning solutions are used to analyze the combined data flow. The developed system will, in this way, aid in developing a governance model for critical infrastructure by providing data. Additionally, it enables the development of maturity levels and highlights the possible risks of different maturity IT implementations in OT environments. The test environment is described in Figure 3

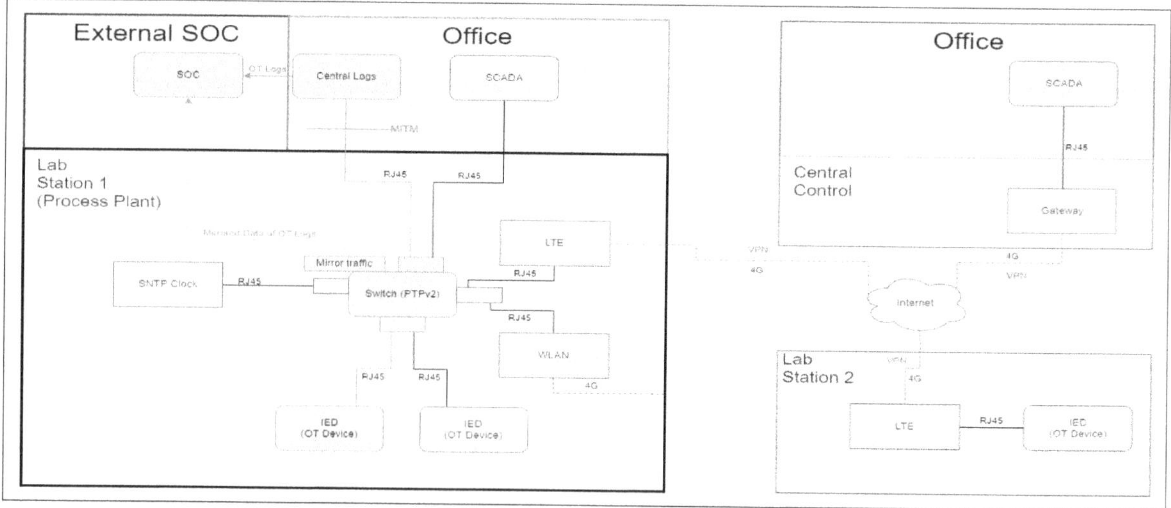

Figure 3: Test environment

The laboratory environment consists of a production facility, an office, and an external SOC (Security Operations Center) solution. The production facility can also be accessed remotely via the internet. Excluding remote connections, the connections are unencrypted. A switch, which serves as the interface between the office and the production facility, mirrors traffic to the SOC via a separate connection. OT Device logs are sent from Central Logs via a separate connection to the SOC. The Man-In-The-Middle (MITM, man = person, device) scenario, which is the focus of this paper, is indicated in red. PITM data compromise is carried out with an additional device which is added to the connection between the process plant and the office. Compromised OT logs are also highlighted in red. The devices utilized in the scenario are highlighted in blue.

4.2 Background of the Use Cases

The use cases simulate the real Operational technology environment, and we must test several threat combinations to see how attacks can be executed and how they affect the devices. By comparing different kinds of logs and other information, it is possible to gather important information about how to affect the operational and technical levels. Testing is important because of the multiplicity of disadvantages. If false information transfers from the lower to the upper level, situational awareness is preserved, and it is impossible to achieve and transfer the right information from the different levels. False information causes supply chain problems and leads to multiple disadvantages, such as rising costs, production interruption, and reputation damage.

The connection between the test-bed results supports governance model development and creates a new platform for industrial operators. Cybersecurity-related supply chain problems at the technical level affect the operational and strategic levels. Workable industrial environments such as energy power supply require that electricity components are reliable, and information flows securely in the network. The link between simultaneous tests and real-world is essential in our studies. Vulnerabilities must be found, and obstacles affecting the continuity management and supply chain management must be identified. This research concentrates on the formation of logs and information needed to maintain situational awareness at all stages of the business environment. The same kind of electricity components are used in different industry sectors. If there are the same IT/OT-related problems, European Union-level cybersecurity requirements still need to be fulfilled (European Commission, 2021). That indicates that the detected vulnerabilities must be shared within the industry-based sectors, between the sectors, and with the authorities. SOCs are crucial to information sharing, and the technical capabilities are directly connected to the SOC maturity in detection processes. Information and data exchange between the SCADA and SOC is crucial, but it is only relevant if the operational environment has combined cyberphysical sensors. Gathering information from equipment by forming logs becomes challenging if there is no capability to gather information.

4.2.1 Determining the Use Cases

The main target is the integrity of the data, not the process that the data is gathered from. The data transfer process is monitored so that the data values remain constant. it is not monitored whether someone has initiated the process. Cybersecurity attacks may occur at different sections of the environment with different footprints.

We compare the two points to each other and their space in Table 2. Cause and effect are not considered.

Table 2: Comparing two points and their space

Test 1 and 2	Possibilities
Two sources in the test	The attack may occur only in one section, where one source registers it.
Two sources in the test	Possible to validate process or source integrity when used in unison

As Figure 4 illustrates, the real-world counterpart to the use case is depicted. The production plant's control system is located in a separate office space. The data transfer between the production plant and the office space is monitored remotely in a separate SOC. In the use case, the attacker has access to the physically less protected office space. The attacker modifies the data transferred between the OT device and the central log. By modifying data delivered to the central control, the attacker can hinder the situational awareness of the control system, evade installed defense mechanisms, and disguise footprints left in the system. MITRE ATT&CK considers the following attack as a Person-In-The-Middle technique and a defense evasion tactic.

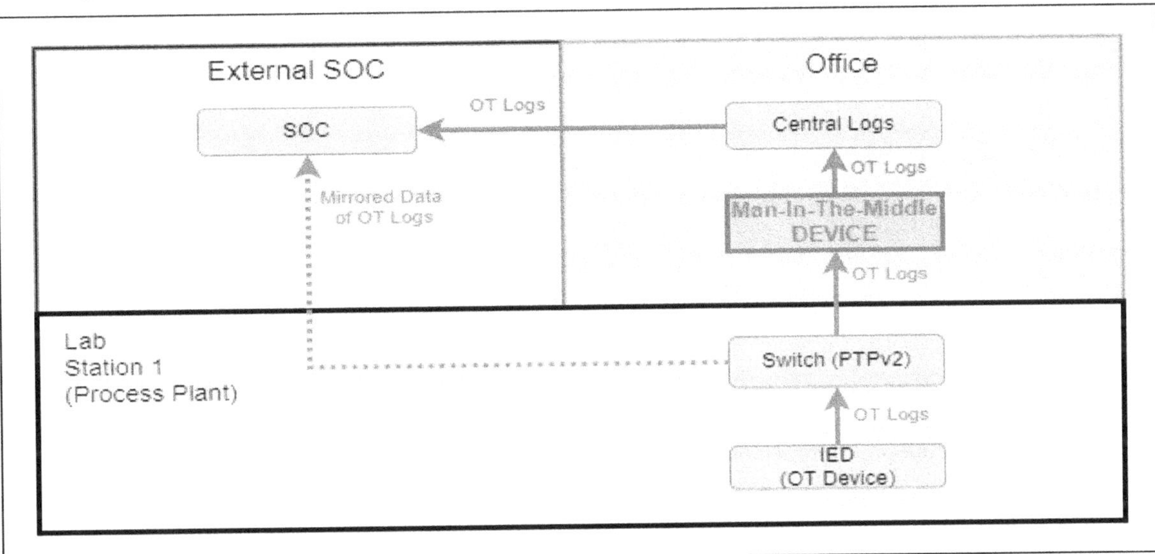

Figure 4: Research lap setup versus real-world

A countermeasure against PITM attacks has been developed, which involves the inclusion of additional sensors at various points within the network. These sensors are isolated from the main network infrastructure to minimize interference with regular data transfers. This applies to data originating from both Operational Technology (OT) and Information Technology (IT) devices, as well as from network-attached sensors, such as data diodes or Near-End Crosstalk analyzers. The data collected by these sensors is transmitted to the SOC at two distinct points: midway at the switch and at the endpoint of the central logs. By comparing the data logs from these different points, an inspection of the device or log status from various locations within the network can be conducted. This approach allows for a more comprehensive situational awareness of the system status.

However, the introduction of additional sensors and data collection points inevitably leads to an increase in network data load and device data processing. To mitigate this, the additional points should be isolated from the normal network environment, thereby enhancing network security without significantly impacting its performance. Another limitation that may occur in OT environments is hardware limitations, such as OT devices lacking capabilities of isolated reporting.

4.3 Research Methodology

The research methodology used is based on the view of design science research (Hevner, 2007; Hevner, A. & Chatterjee, 2010). We have the suitable equipment, software, electricity, and network solutions for the tests. By utilizing the products, it allows us to test different kinds of scenarios and cyber-attacks. The research compares the scenarios-based use cases and the tests we have done are connected to the comparing log information.

Tasks of use cases will produce new data for the governance model and help to develop features and functionalities of the security operations center. It will bring added value to the IT-SOC features because there are missing signal-processing elements that enhance the formation of situational awareness. Gathering data, such as weak signals from the industrial environment where the old-fashioned machines are crucial. Identifying the emergency point, where SOC and detection features must react is critical. In Industrial Control Systems such as SCADA, intrusion prevention or detection tools are relevant machines that we must have under the secured control of operations. We will apply a widely used design science research methodology used traditionally in software and system development.

The laboratory environment at the University of Jyväskylä generates new information about cybersecurity-related technical issues. Components, devices, and software from stakeholders form a new base of knowledge for the governance model development work. The developed and tested use cases highlight crucial technical challenges that generate added value for the operators of the ICS environment. Combining information from sector-based enterprises, analysis of external requirements, and results from the testbed generate a suitable solution for the actors of the critical infrastructure. Results from the testbed produce a new knowledge base into divided classes that are possible to connect to the different kinds of external and internal requirements that have been considered in the analysis of the ICS-related environment. We have used the Delphi method (Worrell J., Di Gangi P., Bush A. 2012). Professional team members also have skills and experience in analyzing the research data.

Regarding (Nunamaker et al., 1991), the multi-methodical approach consists of four case study research strategies: theory building, experimentation, observation, and systems development research based on a systematic analysis of gathered data. We have used Yin´s case study research strategy (Yin,2017), which concentrates on targeted research problems and questions. Yin (2017) identifies five components of research design for case studies: the questions of the study; its propositions if any; its unit(s) of analysis; the logic linking the data to the propositions; and the criteria for interpreting the findings. In this research, our focus is on the question: What are crucial factors and elements that may set obstacles for enhanced continuity management and supply chain management as a part of cyber situational awareness in the OT/ICS environment? We have used official literature sources such as official publications and academic publications in this work. In this research, we concentrate on external industry-specific supply chain-related cybersecurity requirements.

5. Findings

Devices should have the capability to monitor their operations and create their own log entries. These logs are crucial for maintaining a secure and efficient network. However, in OT environments, there are hardware limitations in the automatic mechanism for sending these logs to a centralized location.

To address this with current hardware, a separate network is needed to ask the devices (referred to as relays) about their status and collect this information centrally. This centralized collection is essential for computing needs. However, a challenge arises concerning where this log information should be stored.

If a device retains its log data indefinitely, it opens up the possibility for artificial intelligence solutions to request necessary data from the relay. But, if an unauthorized entity gains access, the reliability of this data is compromised. Therefore, the relay should actively send some information to a specific point to ensure data integrity.

The log data must be stored in a manner that allows for auditing. This requirement presents two separate network problems and a centralized solution problem due to capacity limitations.

The data transfer within the control network is monitored at various points to ensure the correctness of control data and safety-related data. Cybersecurity measures may necessitate a monitoring network where production control and logging are observed. This includes monitoring network traffic and device information.

We have utilized configuration and communication engineering tools for online monitoring and querying. The results are observable on the network and its associated device. Understanding how to break down information into smaller, manageable segments is vital. Furthermore, the use of a device to supervise the activities of the network is equally important.

We advocate the use of decentralized log data storage, which allows for log data distribution. Decentralization is tied to the need for a distinct cybersecurity control. In particular, if an unauthorized entity gains access to the centralized system, it could potentially interfere with the communication between the control and supervisor elements. However, decentralized should be supplemented with a centralized logging system for long-term data analysis. This system should be linked to the main system via a separate network, which helps in mitigating performance overheads. Regarding Ruef (2021), the very commonly used base of MITRE ATT&CK is not the main solution for every cybersecurity-related penetration test because hierarchical structures are not coherent. There are overlapping terms and hierarchy levels of the attack types, for example, but they are good to use as a supporting tool.

6. Conclusions

Improving detection capabilities is critical to the formation of situational awareness. The tested use cases prove that detection capabilities must also consist of multiple sensors from multiple sources. Detection and network data-gathering capabilities are crucial factors affecting the technical maturity level. SCADA and SOC systems combine cyperphysical systems, but it is important to note the point at which events are perceived. If there are two systems that perceive anomalies and log information differences, the difference must be determined and analyzed, as well as how vulnerable it may be.

The use cases that we have done demonstrate that workable supply chain management is not only the secured flow of information. Our network tests simulate the real world when a person in the middle causes problems monitoring the logs; thus, situational awareness cannot maintain any more control of supply chain management interrupts. The workable operational environment requires effective supply chain management. The workable supply chain management is related to the equipment, such as devices and software, and the information-sharing mechanism.

Information technology networks make it possible to enhance monitoring of the operational technology environment but also provide possibilities for adversaries to use networks as a tool to cause interruptions at the technology level. Suppliers may use different kinds of wireless remote controls to manage industrial equipment. Digitalization may cause challenges to whole industrial ecosystems. The research indicates that gathering relevant information from the sensors is essential. Combining different data from different sources makes getting added value for the detection capabilities possible. We have researched different monitoring points and how those differ from each other. The formation of common situational awareness requires common processes and common methods to monitor data.

Acknowledgments

The research was supported by Business Finland (grant number 10/31/2022) and the University of Jyväskylä.

References

Bakis, B., Wang E., (2017). Building a National Cyber Information-Sharing Ecosystem. Mitre Corporation

Endsley, M. R. (1995). Toward a theory of situation awareness. Human Factors. (37), 32-64.

Endsley, M. R. (1988). Design and evaluation for situation awareness enhancement. Proceedings of the Human Factors Society 32nd Annual Meeting. Monica. CA: Human Factors Society, 97-101.

ENISA (2023) Building Effective Governance Frameworks for the Implementation of National Cybersecurity Strategies. DOI: 10.2824/850466

European Commission (2022). NIS2 Directive (EU) 2022/2555.

GAO (2021) Electricity Grid Cybersecurity. DOE Needs to Ensure Its Plans Fully Address Risks to Distribution Systems

Hevner, A. (2007) A three-cycle view of design science research, Scandinavian Journal of
Information Systems 19 (2), pp. 87–92

Hevner, A. & Chatterjee, S. (2010) Design research in information systems theory and practice. New York: Springer.

ISA (2021) Applying ISO/IEC 27001/2 and the ISA 62443 Series for Operational Technology Environments

ISO/IEC (2022) Information security, cybersecurity and privacy protection

Knerler, K.,Parker, I.,Zimmerman C. (2022) 11 Strategies of a World-Class Cybersecurity Operations Cente. The Mitre Corporation

NIST (2016) SP 800-150 Guide to Cyber Threat Information Sharing

NIST (2018) Risk management framework for Information Systems and Organizations NIST 800-37 r2- (NIST, 2018)

NIST (2020) Security and Privacy Controls for Information Systems and Organizations NIST 800-53 r5.

NIST (2022) Cybersecurity Supply Chain Risk Management Practices for Systems and Organizations NIST SP 800-161r1

NIST (2023) NIST Special Publication. Guide to Operational Technology (OT) Security NIST SP 800-82r3

NIST (2024) General FAQ´s U.S Department of Commerce

Nunamaker Jay F., Minder Chen Jr. & Purdin Titus D.M. (1990) Systems Development in Information Systems Research, Journal of Management Information Systems, 7:3, 89-106, DOI: 10.1080/07421222.1990.11517898

Pols (2017) Designing a Unified Kill Chain for analyzing, comparing and defending against cyber-attacks.

Risto J., (2017) SANS What is Common Vulnerably Scoring System? Retrieved: 1.3.2024. Available: https://www.sans.org/blog/what-is-cvss/

Ruef M., Schneider M. (2021) Mitre Att&ck, flaws of standardization. Available: https://www.scip.ch/en/?labs.20210204

Simola J., Takala A., Lehkonen R., Frantti T., Savola R. (2023) Developing Cybersecurity in an Industrial Environment by Using a Testbed Environment. 22th European Conference on Cyber Warfare and Security ECCWS-2023. The Hellenic Air Force Academy. Athens, Greece

Strom B., Applebaum A., Miller D., Nickels K., Pennington A., Thomas C. (2020) MITRE ATT&CK®: Design and Philosophy

Vielberth, M., Böhm, F., Fichtinger, I., & Pernul, G. (2020). Security operations center: A systematic study and open challenges. IEEE Access, 8, 227756–227779.

Worrell J. L., Di Gangi P. M., Bush A. A. (2012) Exploring the use of the Delphi method in accounting information systems research, International Journal of Accounting Information Systems, Volume 14, Issue 3,2013, Pages 193-208, ISSN 1467-0895, https://doi.org/10.1016/j.accinf.2012.03.003.

Yin, R. K. (2017). Case study research and applications: Design and methods. (Sixth edition edition) Los Angeles: SAGE Publications, Inc.

The Importance of Cybersecurity Governance Model in Operational Technology Environments

Jussi Simola, Arttu Takala, Riku Lehkonen, Tapio Frantti and Reijo Savola
University of Jyväskylä, Finland

jussi.hm.simola@jyu.fi
arttu.h.takala@jyu.fi
riku.p.Lehkonen@jyu.fi
tapio.k.frantti@jyu.fi
reijo.m.savola@jyu.fi

Abstract: There is a common will to unify regulation in the Western world regarding overall security, including cybersecurity. European cyber security regulations aim to create a foundation and guidelines for international standards in various industries and the operation of critical infrastructure. Protected critical infrastructure is a common goal for Western allies. Allies of NATO and EU member states mainly support the anti-aggression policy in Europe. The unstable situation in the world forces states to find solutions that represent the thoughts of the allies. Defending common values is crucial when the purpose is to protect critical infrastructure and vital functions in societies. The research will demonstrate the industrial needs of IT/OT-related cybersecurity governance. The study analyzes EU-level cybersecurity requirements and how those requirements affect standardization regarding cybersecurity governance in the operational technology environment. There will be four primary governance levels: Political, Strategical, Operational and Tactical. Many criminal state-linked operators do not care about international agreements or contracts. Some rogue states have even taken to inciting violations of international agreements. We cannot trust the loose contracts between states anymore. The research will find the main challenges concerning the cybersecurity governance of the industrial organizations that use operational technology-related technology in their daily businesses. We have seen that Information and Operational Technology are based on something other than similar threats and risk basements. Operational Technology related threats threaten the cyber-physical ecosystem where anomalies affect the physical world, so operational functions of equipment, devices, sensors, components, and production lines are interrupted. As a result, continuity management and supply chain management are compromised. The study's primary purpose is to describe the cybersecurity governance elements of the OT environment for enhancing situational awareness. Standardizing the cybersecurity level among industrial stakeholders requires EU member states to have a national cybersecurity strategy that follows main EU-level guidelines. Despite the EU member states' implementation level of the regulation, the EU-level cybersecurity requirements obligate companies to take steps to solve future cybersecurity challenges.

Keywords: Governance Model, Cybersecurity Strategy, Supply Chain Management, Continuity Management

1. Introduction

The research will enhance the understanding of the challenging situation that affects critical infrastructures' operational technology environment. The research will find the main challenges concerning the cybersecurity governance of the industrial organizations that use operational technology-related technology in their daily businesses. The basic describtion of governance means the atmosphere where something must steer and govern. Suppose we look at the practise of daily business. Many challenges and factors steer the business environment. Business Continuity and supply chain management are crucial elements that must be beneficial and strengthened, especially in critical sectors. Decision makers with public safety actors must create workable environments where enterprises can work in a way that supports the national overall security strategy.

We live in a digitalized and networked world where the cyber ecosystem depends on energy availability and supply chain. Cybersecurity governance management is crucial at all levels of global security, where state-level public safety actors and companies in different vital business sectors are connected via stakeholders. The EU member states and allies of the Western military alliance NATO recognize the need for collaboration and integration of "codes" in cybersecurity strategy plans. Collaboration requires common situational awareness capabilities at all levels. Continuity management does not mean separating things from critical infrastructure protection. Public safety organizations need to collaborate with the companies. Therefore, we need a coherent system that allows public safety organizations to gather required safety critical information for the decision-support mechanism.

IT/OT Cybersecurity governance more than just standardization, protocols, or guidelines. It is much more than that. Cybersecurity governance is a part of the overall corporate governance management system. It is also a part of company strategy, working culture, and daily routines. Employees are not separate parts of Cyber-physical ecosystems. Governance requires cohesion between the crucial elements of the cyber-ecosystem. The importance of the well-organized governance model is emphasized according to the size of the company.

CSG (Cybersecurity governance of operational technology in sector-connected smart energy networks) project significantly increases the effectiveness and efficiency of cybersecurity of smart energy networks and other operational technology. The project aims at considerable cost savings and scalability through enhanced incident management, data gathering, and Artificial Intelligence based automation.

The first research paper of the CSG project (Simola, et al.2023) concentrates on the research environment. The second paper concentrates on technical information-sharing requirements of the Operational technology environment. The third paper continues and describes the crucial elements affecting the supply chain and continuity management. Enhancing cyber situational awareness is the European Union's common aim in the OT/ICS environment.

2. Central Concepts

2.1 Operational Technology Governance

Regarding NIST (2023), Operational Technology governance should consist of the policies, procedures, and processes for managing the organization's regulatory, legal, risk, environmental, and operational requirements. Enterprises in the industrial environment should establish an effective OT cybersecurity governance capability, develop a process, and assign responsibilities and accountability to appropriate roles in the corporate risk management function (NIST, 2023). According to the NIST (2023), the Operational Technology Governance process includes the following minimum requirements. a) The OT cybersecurity policy is established and communicated. b) OT cybersecurity roles and responsibilities are coordinated and aligned with the internal roles and external partners. c) legal and regulatory requirements regarding OT cybersecurity, including privacy, are understood correctly and managed. d) The cybersecurity risks are integrated into corporate risk management processes (NIST, 2023). According to the NIST, features of the Cybersecurity Governance strategy may consist: Accountability frameworks – Decision-making hierarchies - Defined risks related to business objectives – Mitigation plans and strategies – Oversight processes and procedures NIST.

2.2 Operational Technology as a Part of Critical Infrastructure

Operational Technology systems consist of control components (e.g., electrical, mechanical, hydraulic, pneumatic) that aid together to achieve an objective (e.g., manufacturing, transportation of matter or energy) (NIST, 2023). Business sectors are interconnected industrial sectors of critical infrastructures that are often based on "system of systems" architecture. Electrical power transmission and distribution grid industries use distributed SCADA control technology to operate interconnected and dynamic systems consisting of a large amount of public and private utilities and rural cooperatives for supplying electricity to customers (NIST, 2023).

Supervisory control and data acquisition (SCADA) systems are used in distribution systems that integrate data acquisition with data transmission systems and Human Machine Interface (HMI) software by providing a centralized monitoring and control system for process inputs and outputs. SCADA systems collect information from the field to the control center and display the information with graphics and texts. Operators may monitor and control an entire system from a central location almost in real time (NIST, 2023). Individual systems enable controlling operations or tasks, which can be automatic and can be performed by operator commands. Used hardware consists of a control server, communications equipment, and remote terminal units (RTUs) and/or (Programmable Logic Controller (PLCs) that control local processes by actuators and monitor sensors. The software of the communications hardware allows information and data sharing and is programmed to inform what parameter ranges are acceptable and what measures launch when process variables are out of range (NIST,2023). An intelligent electronic device (IED) is a protective relay, that may communicate directly to the control server. IEDs provide a direct interface to control and monitor equipment and sensors (NIST, 2023).

2.3 C2 and SOC

Command and Control Center refers to operative control processes and procedures of military actions. Functionalities and work tasks changed to the Computer Emergency Response Center, which later changed to the Security Operations Center, including different functionalities and actions that control, monitor, and supervise customers' networks (Vielberth et. al. 2020).

2.4 Cyber-Physical Systems (CPS)

According to the (NIST, 2017) Cyber-physical systems (CPS) consist of smart systems that include engineered interacting networks of physical and computational components. Interconnected and integrated systems provide new functionalities to improve quality of life and enable technological advances in critical areas, such as personalized health care, emergency response, traffic flow management, smart manufacturing, defense and homeland security, and energy supply and use. In addition to CPS, (Industrial Internet, Internet of Things (IoT), machine-to-machine (M2M), smart cities, and others) describe similar or related systems and concepts. OT/ICS industrial environment very often consists of SCADA (Supervisory control and acquisition) for control and monitoring functions. There is a significant overlap between concepts of CPS and IoT, such that CPS and IoT are sometimes used interchangeably; therefore, the approach described in this CPS Framework should be considered equally applicable to IoT (NIST, 2017). Figure 1 illustrates, the interconnection between systems of systems-level thinking and human factors is crucial in designing cyber-physical systems.

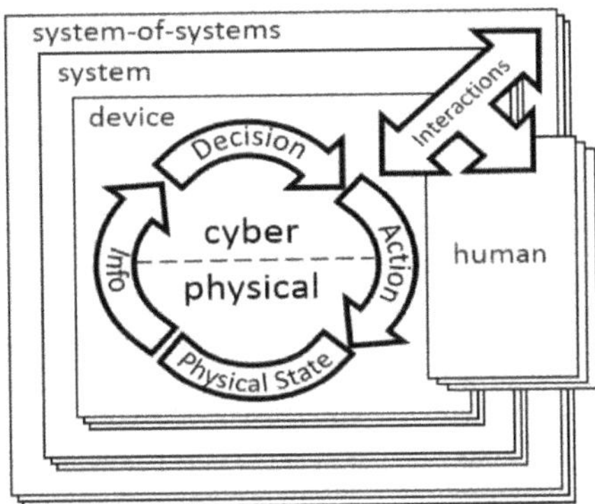

Figure 1: System of Systems Thinking in Cyberphysical Systems (NIST, 2017)

The managing level must guide enhanced measures into their business strategy. If different management levels do not include business-related cybersecurity requirements in their strategic plans, it will reduce the efficiency of the daily working processes. Decision-makers must take into account the industry and organizational culture to achieve a common understanding level. Cybersecurity training about the business vision and mission is important because if humans do not internalize and apply the requirements for the daily work, business continuity is at risk of interruption.

2.5 Situational Awareness

It has been said that humans are the weakest factors in the business environment. As Mica Endsley argued, it is important to create common understanding and mental model within the team and between the team members for reducing overlapping work (Endsley, 1995). According to Endsley (1998), "Situation awareness is the perception of the elements in the environments within the volume of time and space, the comprehension of their meaning, and the projection of their status in the near future." Perception is an essential ability in the industrial environment. The formation of situational awareness requires several elements that are connected to each other. Humans cannot process large volumes of data, quickly and consistently. Flexible autonomy should provide a smooth, simple, seamless transition of functions between humans and the system. Regulations of the European Union set new requirements for the formation of cyber situational awareness. Human or automated systems are essential factors that enhance communication methods, procedures, information gathering, and sharing. Mechanisms for that are under development.

2.6 Information Exchange

Information-sharing mechanisms are essential for the formation of situational awareness. EU Member states should have a common model to share different kinds of information. **Figure** 2 below illustrates four popular types of information sharing (MITRE, 2018)

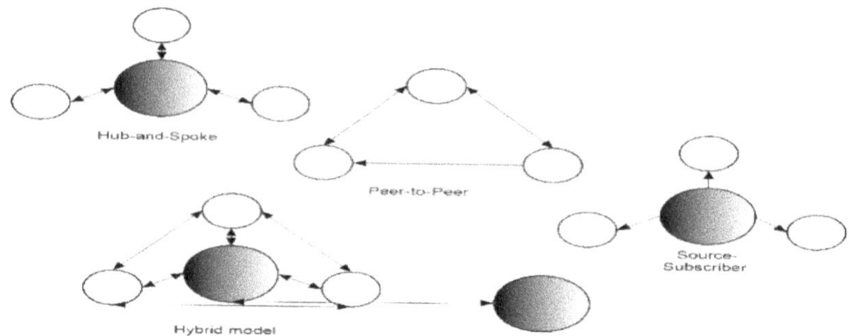

Figure 2: Information sharing models modified from MITRE, (2018)

Few existing cybersecurity information-sharing architectures exist. The fourth hybrid model is the combination of others.

Hub-and-Spoke - Several data producers and consumers share information with each other, but instead of sending it directly, the information is sent to a central hub, which then handles dissemination to all the other spokes as appropriate. This model can be viewed as being like e-mail distribution lists, where a sender provides a message to a mailing list service, which then forwards the message to all list members.

Peer-to-peer - A group of data producers and data consumers organize direct relationships with each other. Members share directly with each other in a mesh pattern. The group may have a single governing policy, but all sharing exchanges are between individuals.

Source-Subscriber - A single entity publishes information to a group of consumers. This is a common model in commercial environments, where the data source is a vendor, and the subscribers purchase access to the vendor's information. This is also a common model for free alerts from some authoritative source (MITRE, 2018).

2.7 Supply Chain and Continuity Management

The supply chain ecosystem may consist of public and private sector entities (e.g., acquirers, suppliers, developers, system integrators, external system service providers, and other ICT/OT-related service providers) (NIST,2022). Enterprises depend on the supply chain to provide products and services to enable the enterprise to achieve its strategic and operational objectives. Identifying cybersecurity risks throughout the supply chain is complicated by the information asymmetry that exists between acquiring enterprises and their suppliers and service providers. The NIST Special Publication (2022) describes the practices and controls for Cybersecurity Supply Chain Risk Management (C-SCRM). It applies both information technology (IT) and operational technology (OT) environments and is inclusive of IoT. Like IT environments that rely on ICT products and services, OT environments rely on OT and ICT products and services, with cybersecurity risks arising from ICT/OT products, services, suppliers, and their supply chains (NIST,2022).

3. Background of the Research

3.1 Cybersecurity Cooperation between the United States and the European Union

According to (ENISA, 2013) the US and the EU will enhance cooperation on Cybersecurity. In practice, this means, for example, that the Cybersecurity & Infrastructure Security Agency (CISA, 2023) and the European Union Agency for Cybersecurity (ENISA) will enforce collaboration. The arrangement consists of the following points:

To build cyber situational awareness and capacity to enhance cyber resilience, including facilitating participation as third-state representatives in specific EU-wide cybersecurity exercises or training and the sharing and promotion of cyber awareness tools and programs.

Best practice exchange in the implementation of cyber legislation, including on key cyber legislation implementation such as the NIS2 Directive (European Parliament, 2022), incident reporting, vulnerabilities management, and the approach to sectors such as telecommunications and energy.

Information sharing to increase common situational awareness: including a more systematic sharing of knowledge and information in relation to the cybersecurity threat landscape to increase the common situational awareness to the stakeholders and communities and in full respect of data protection requirements. A work plan will operationalize the Working Arrangement and regular reporting at the EU-US Cyber Dialogues is foreseen (ENISA, 2023).

3.2 Common Approach to Critical Infrastructure Protection and Resilience

Defining critical infrastructure sectors has been one of the main aims of the Western world in terms of securing overall security (DHS, 2013; DHS, 2015). Maintaining cyber resilience has been an essential goal in the protection work. It has also been seen in the European Union that an overall cybersecurity strategy as a part of the security strategy is needed. Finland is a new full member of NATO, and it that w for the security culture even though Finland has been an important "support member" for years.

3.3 Towards the Common European Cybersecurity Regulation

The European Union will unify all member states' cybersecurity-related master plans (ENISA, 2023; European Parliament, 2022). These plans will change the almost the whole atmosphere because the given period for the implementation is short. Organizations' business priorities and objectives are crucial elements.

Overall management of continuity management requires the implementation of Public or private related organizations' cybersecurity guidelines. the Cyber Resilience Act (CRA) supports the goals of the NIS2, and NIS2 supports the aims of the CER Cyber Resilience directive. CRA sets requirements for the manufacturing process of digitalized products, industrial companies, and cyber security training methods for the personnel and management of security operations (European Commission, 2022a, 2022b,2022)

We have seen that there is an increasing challenge in the development of loyalty between the EU member states (Gyori, 2023). Some states do not care enough about the trust and overall security of the Western world. Therefore, state leaders need more supervision on how to reach the goals. Critical Infrastructure protection requires a common understanding of situational awareness in developing cybersecurity strategy as a part of the other security plans.

The challenges in energy sector have proven how important is it to create common-specific frameworks for energy sectors. Energy distribution is crucial in critical infrastructure protection and energy supply chain management. Ensuring that energy power and distribution systems work is crucial for a sustainable and stable energy supply.

The regulations are partly obliged to ensure that European Union member countries deploy and standardize cybersecurity-related regulations. A member state must recognize EU-level regulation, and the ultimate responsibility for compliance lies with organizations. Critical infrastructure must be protected against cyber-physical threats, and humans, technology, and processes must be ensured for continuity management. Cybersecurity is an uncontrolled situation if there is no operational-level understanding and connection about the cybersecurity requirements in processes, technical solutions, and human actions between the organizations and within the working groups or employees.

3.4 Relationship Between the Cybersecurity Governance Model and Regulatory Framework

The European Commission has set the security of supply for critical infrastructure protection because the aim is to protect and maintain the continuity of supply around the European Union. Member States must identify the critical entities for the sectors regarding the CER directive (European Commission, 2020b). The list of essential services is the basis for the risk assessment and identifying the critical entities (European Commission, 2020b). The focus is to strengthen the EU's resilience against online and offline threats, from cyberattacks to crime, risks to public health, or natural disasters. Energy supply and distribution protection forms occasional basement to all critical sectors.

The project research is based on the testbed work and the regulatory factors that support each other. There are many opinions in scientific discussions about what cybersecurity governance means. Others think that it means only business or technical level aspects, but others expand the understanding of the meaning of the overall cybersecurity governance. The ENISA (2023b) defines Cybersecurity Governance by Savas and Karatas (2022) as follows: "Operation of decision-making processes" which increase and ensure "participation, transparency, and accountability in taking measures related to cyberspace together with the mechanism of international agreements, strategies, laws, measures, regulations, and standards that interlock in the best way". There are several definitions in academic publications, but this selected form follows the main line of the definitions. ENISA uses four upper-level stages that steer the implementation procedures at the national level. As ENISA (2023b) argues, European Union member states have been required to adopt a National Cybersecurity Strategy. The order of the concepts may differ, but those governance steps by ENISA (2023b) are as follows.

a) The political level consists of political processes, Roles, responsibilities, and legal measures including international cooperation. Public-private partnerships (PPP) help build connections between the public and private sectors and ensure the implementation of actions responding to the industry´s needs. Enhanced cybersecurity governance requires a common international language for cyber defence. Legal measures should be inclusive and have general validity to ensure that all institutions, organizations, and related stakeholders are committed to the National cybersecurity strategy, its governance model, and the implementing actions. b) The strategic level of governance consists of the strategy itself, coordinating and its implementation and risk identification and mitigation. The crucial point of that is connected to the processes of designing the strategy and designing its governance mode to ensure continuity and coherence. Strategic elements of identifying and mitigating risks require strong cooperation and collaboration between the actors. Stakeholders such as political actors supported by consults and working groups are essential factors, for example, in budgeting and resource allocation. According to the strategic elements of risk identification and mitigation, a coherent approach across all government entities and critical infrastructure operators should be aimed for. A common approach for risk identification and mitigation, which is coherent across the different actors, promotes information-sharing and enhances cooperation. c) Operational governance comprises elements of raising awareness by using efficient incident response and information sharing and exchange. (ENISA, 2023). Operational governance focuses on developing cybersecurity across all sectors of a nation´s society, economy, and government. Specialized bodies of the stakeholders, such as Computer Security Incident Response Teams (CSIRTs) or Computer Emergency Response Teams (CERTs), government officials, and consulting and training bodies are actively involved in the set-up and execution of this governance layer. Society and population are essential parts of this layer. The goal of enhancing situational awareness consists of training, education, and community building within the complete population. Proactive and reactive functionalities of Incident response mechanisms and information sharing by CSIRTs or CERTs are crucial elements in this layer. d) Technical and tactical levels consist of international standards, technical guidelines and recommendations, and the use of technology, tools, and certification schemes. Technology and technical elements are part of the implementation of the strategy. Definitions of the standards and their use form the basis for this layer. Tools and certification schemes will enhance technical governance. NIS2 directive consists of crucial views on the importance of certification and highlights the member states to require essential and important entities to certify ICT products, ICT services, and processes under European certification schemes (ENISA, 2023b). Those four levels affect the whole cybersecurity environment. In addition to this, we must think on technical, processes, and human levels, which are sources of vulnerabilities but also possibilities to enhance the cyber ecosystem.

NIS2 will set new standards for all companies despite the organization's size, but it concentrates on bigger ones. There will be sanctioned requirements (European Parliament, 2022), but some policies are less mandatory. Small-size enterprises cannot avoid regulatory requirements because the European Union has decided that every enterprise must consider regulations regardless of member countries' situation of enactment. EU member states must also create a mechanism to ensure cybersecurity for small and medium-sized organizations. It is essential that small enterprises understand how cybersecurity requirements affect their business in the future and change their business culture (Schreider, 2019). Vendors are in a crucial position to remain cybersecurity level enough to fulfill the supply chain-related requirements that are under implementation. According to the European Parliament (2022), each Member State "should ensure that national cybersecurity strategy provides for a policy framework for enhanced coordination within that Member State between its competent authorities under this Directive and those under Directive (EU) 2022/2557 in the context of information sharing about risks, cyber threats, and incidents as well as on non-cyber risks, threats and incidents, and the exercise of supervisory tasks. The competent authorities should cooperate and exchange information without undue delay, in relation to the identification of critical entities, risks, cyber threats, and incidents as well as in relation to non-cyber risks, threats, and incidents affecting critical entities, including the cybersecurity and physical measures taken by critical entities as well as the results of supervisory activities carried out about such entities" (European Parliament, 2022).

4. Research Approach and Research Methodology

The laboratory environment at the University of Jyväskylä generates new information about cybersecurity-related technical issues. Components, devices, and software from stakeholders form a new base of knowledge for the governance model development work. The created and tested use cases create crucial technical obstacles that generate added value for the operators of the ICS environment. Combining information from sector-based enterprises, analysis of external requirements, and results from the testbed generate a suitable solution for the actors of the critical infrastructure. Results from the testbed produce a new knowledge base into divided classes that are possible to connect to the different kinds of external and internal requirements that have been considered in the analysis of the ICS-related environment. In this research, we have used the Delphi method (Garson, 2012). Professional team members also have skills in analyzing the research data.

According to (Nunamaker, Minder Chen, and Purdin, 1991), the multi-methodical approach consists of four case study research strategies: theory building, experimentation, observation, and systems development research based on systematic analysis of gathered data. We have used Yin´s case study research strategy (Yin,2014), which concentrates on only limited research problems and questions. In this research, our focus is on the question: What are crucial factors and elements that may set obstacles for enhanced continuity management and supply chain as a part of cyber situational awareness in the OT/ICS environment? We have used official literature sources such as official publications and academic publications in this work. In this research, we concentrate on external industry-specific supply chain-related cybersecurity requirements. Figure 3. illustrates how the basement of the CSG-project has been constructed.

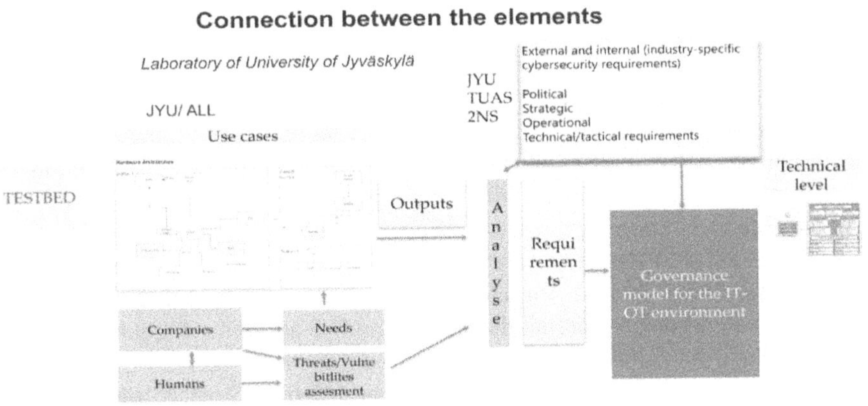

Figure 3: Basic Elements from the CSG testbed

From a governance viewpoint, a systematic system of system-level thinking requires splitting organizational functions into several layers as follows in Figure 4 (Pöyhönen & Lehto, 2020). The figure illustrates how decision-making levels Strategic, operational, and technical are connected to the comprehensive system view from an organization's cybersecurity environment.

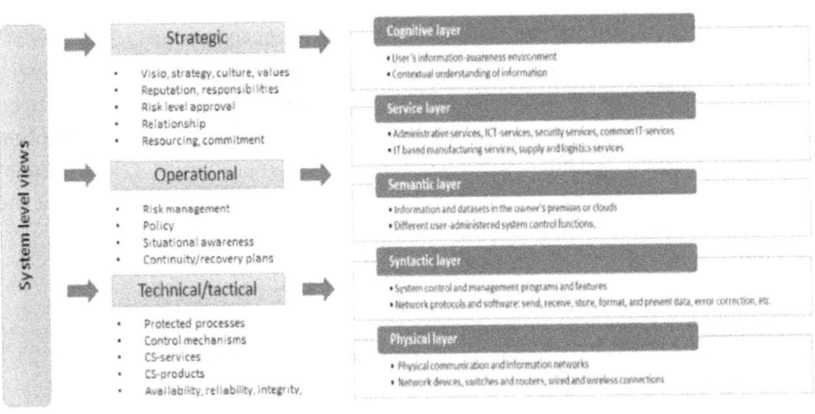

Figure 4: Organizations cyber governance and trust-based Cyber security architecture framework (Pöyhönen & Lehto, 2020)

Continuity management and protecting the supply chain are linked to all layers. The national cybersecurity strategy and directives combined affect all layers. The main aim is to enhance cybersecurity situational awareness. It is not possible without analysing the requirements of the Cognitive, service, semantic, syntactic, and physical layers. Third-party services, components, equipment, devices, but also human resources set a fundamental framework in the industrial environment.

5. Findings

System of system -level thinking is crucial when the main goal is to achieve a common understanding of the situation concerning the cybersecurity requirements in the industrial environment. The continuity management and supply chain obstacles set challenges for daily businesses. Vital functions are dependent on workable continuity and supply chain management. A gap between the understanding of operational business reality and the created strategy on the enterprise's board level forms a crucial problem in the formation of cyber situational awareness. Therefore, every internal organizational stage should have a logical and coherent information-sharing mechanism and methods that have been created in the same way. Information sharing and exchange problems are emphasized from the internal world to the external world and vice versa.

At the strategic level, there must be deeper cooperation between the European Union member states. National Computer Emergency Response agencies must create a mechanism that allows real-time information sharing between countries. Common language means common "language", taxonomy, and procedures for how to act against the weak signals of cyberattacks. It requires more funding possibilities to create a straight way to collaborate. It is not enough that the Cyclone group meets once a month. The formation of situational awareness requires that national authorities exchange information in real time with the EU-level cybersecurity authority and cybersecurity authorities of other member countries.

At the operational level, the construction of the shared information is more important. It is not relevant to share data that does not create added value. Actors of the operational level should have the competence to understand how technology communicates and how humans communicate. Perception of the events is a crucial factor in this. NIS2 requires coherent information sharing about the vulnerabilities; proactive monitoring features are also required to be connected to the European Union strategy-based cybersecurity requirements (European Parliament, 2022). SCADA systems are core cyber-physical systems that are connected to the other equipment in the industrial environment. Therefore, the content of the gathered data from the physical OT environment is essential. Reporting requirements and continuity management requirements are connected to the process of maintaining situational awareness. Security operations centers (SOC) service providers have an official-based mandate to exchange information that is needed to protect critical infrastructure. Another challenge may arise from contracts that have been made with the enterprises. How effectively does the National Cybersecurity Authority monitor the agreements and maturity level of the supervision procedures? External auditing processes are needed concerning the SOC´s features and capabilities. Despite that, It is possible that Artificial Intelligence-based solutions may generate added value, especially when gathering information from outside the OT environment. Comparing data to existing threat information and by using OSINT tools and other relevant sources, it is possible to create information that is stated at the strategy level and another stakeholder at the operational level.

At the tactical and technical level, enterprises must take into account the security features of the components, system suppliers, and equipment manufacturers, as Figure 5 illustrates. It also illustrates how vulnerabilities are connected to every stage of the use of products and services. CRA directive from the European Commission (2022) will set new certification requirements for digital components and software. From the viewpoint of the supply chain that is essential when the aim is to manage risks and vulnerabilities. OT-related enterprises have to implement their procedures, processes, technologies, and human interactions in a way that the European Union regulations require.

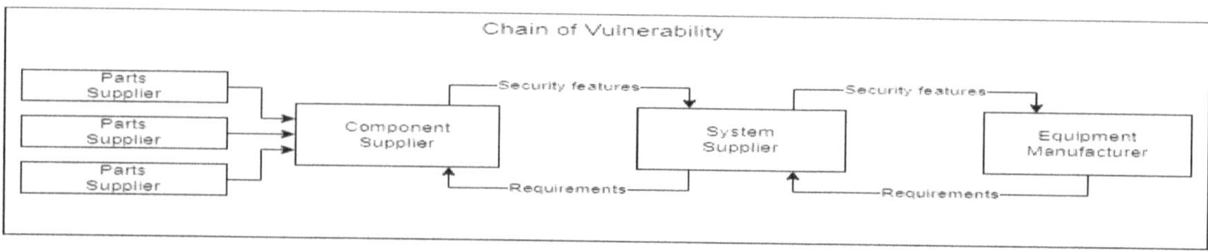

Figure 5: Chain of vulnerability

Figure 6 illustrates how the use of standards is connected to the cyber-physical industrial environment and will enhance continuity management as a part of the cybersecurity governance model. The protection of the supply chain requires ongoing auditing concerning the products and services. Analyzing the 3rd party risks, the essential problem is related to the agreements. How to ensure that 3rd party service and product providers achieve and follow the requirements that partners have been obliged to? Standardization is the answer, but NIS2 requires human resource training, Intentional and unintentional human errors caused by lack of training. The Cyber Resilience Act requires the production and designing of CE-marked products that fulfill cybersecurity requirements, and service providers have to have the same level of understanding about the cybersecurity requirements.

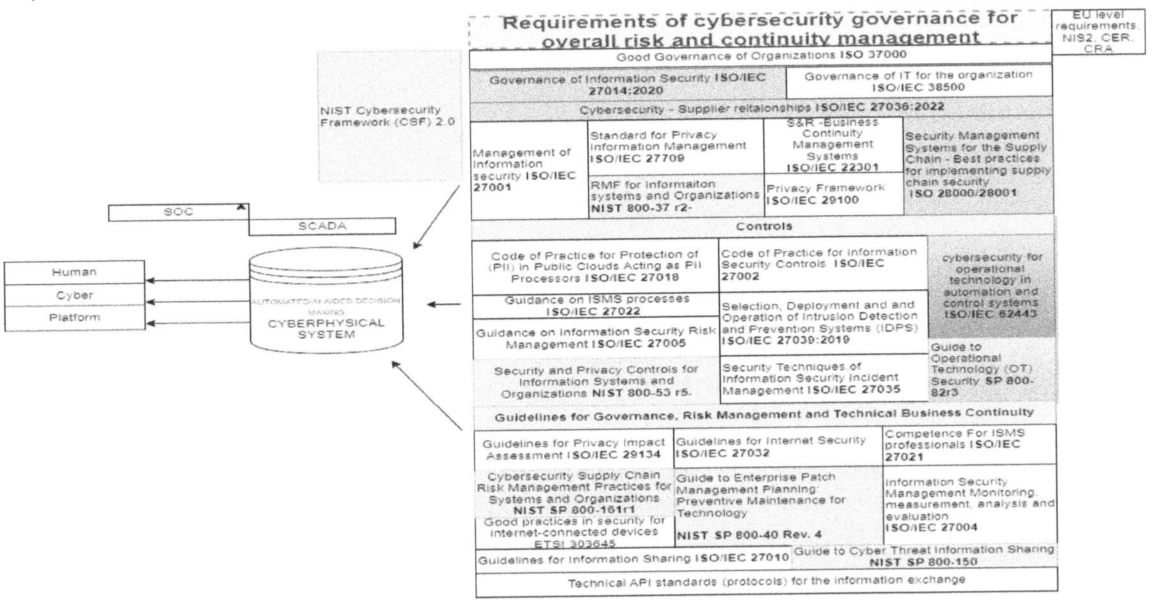

Figure 6: Requirements of the Cybersecurity Governance

6. Discussion and Conclusion

The international regulation indicates that cybersecurity should be coordinated from the EU level to the EU member countries. It has been seen that differences between member countries' regulations affect cohesion. Member states must create implementation with other countries. Similar implementation of regulation between countries and the sectors of critical infrastructure is important in terms of maintaining situational awareness of the Western world. We need to understand how states share information in cross-boarding events. Industrial environments are not separate entities from other factors in the cyber ecosystem. How to react to different kinds of cyber threats is crucial; therefore, a cybersecurity governance model must also be implemented between the nationalities. The CyClone group mechanism (European Parliament, 2022) supports maintaining common situational awareness and understanding but requires a much more holistic understanding. It is not enough that there is an upper-level hub to share information. Crucial are practical functionalities and processes. Information-sharing mechanisms must be created in a standardized way. A common taxonomy and information-sharing methods must mean the same things to all stakeholders at different stages. If the EU member state does not follow common regulations and guidelines, information exchange does not support the protection of critical infrastructure. The common Governance model for the industrial environment should be based on standards related to business processes, technologies, human resource management, risk management, and standardized information-sharing methods. The management of 3rd party-related risks in supply chain management is essential for business continuity. Every member state must use the same basement in its management of the supply chain. Critical infrastructure protection requires that possibilities of vulnerabilities in internet-connected devices, equipment, and software are minimized.

Acknowledgments

The research was supported by Business Finland (grant number 10/31/2022) and the University of Jyväskylä.

References

CISA (2023) Cybersecurity Practices for Industrial Control. Systems. https://www.cisa.gov/sites/default/files/publications/Cybersecurity_Best_Practices_for_Industrial_Control_Systems.pdf

Department of Homeland Security (2013) National Infrastructure Protection Plan 2013: Partnering for Critical Infrastructure Security and Resilience.

Department of Homeland Security (2015) Emergency Services Sector-Specific Plan.

ENISA (2023a) Cisa and Enisa to enhance their cooperation. https://www.enisa.europa.eu/news/cisa-and-enisa-enhance-their-cooperation

ENISA (2023b) Building Effective Governance Frameworks for the Implementation of National Cybersecurity Strategies.

Endsley M. (1995) Towards a theory of situation awareness in Dynamic Systems. Human Factor 37(1)

Endsley M. R.,(1988) "Design and evaluation for situation awareness enhancement." in Proceedings of the Human Factors Society 32nd Annual Meeting, pp. 97-101

European Commission. (2020a) The EU's Cybersecurity Strategy for the Digital Decade. Brussels. https://eur-lex.europa.eu/legal-content/EN/TXT/HTML/?uri=CELEX:52020JC0018

European Commission. (2020b) Proposal for a directive of the European Parliament and of the Council on the resilience of critical entities. COM (2020) 829 final. 2020/0365 (COD). Brussels, 16 December

European Commission. (2022) Proposal for a regulation on horizontal cybersecurity requirements for products with digital elements and amending Regulation (EU) 2019/1020

European Parliament. (2022) Directive 2022/2555 Network and Information Security (NIS2)

Garson, G. D. (2012) The Delphi method in quantitative research. Asheboro, NC: Statistical Associates Publishers. Available from: https://faculty.chass.ncsu.edu/garson/PA765/delphi.htm, retrieved 24.12.2023.

Gyori, B. (2023) The U.S. says it is concerned about Hungary´s relationship with Russia. Retrieved: February 18, 2023

MITRE (2018) "Trusted Automated eXchange of Indicator Information — TAXII™ Enabling Cyber Threat Information Exchange,"

NIST (2023) NIST Special Publication SP 800-82r3 Guide to Operational Technology Security

NIST (2022) NIST Special Publication SP 800-161r1 Cybersecurity Supply Chain Risk Management Practices for Systems and Organizations

NIST (2017) NIST Special Publication 1500-201 Framework for Cyber-Physical Systems: Volume 1, Overview

Nunamaker, J., Minder Chen, J. R., & Purdin, T. (1991) Systems development in information systems research. (3), 89-106

Pöyhönen, J., & Lehto, M. (2020) Cyber security: Trust-based architecture in the management of an organization's security. In T. Eze, L. Speakman, & C. Onwubiko (Eds.), ECCWS 2020: Proceedings of the 19th European Conference on Cyber Warfare and Security (pp. 304-313). Academic Conferences International. Proceedings of the European conference on information warfare and security

Schreider, T. (2019) Building an Effective Cybersecurity Program, 2nd Edition, Rothstein Associates, Incorporated, Brooksfield. Available from: ProQuest Ebook Central. [19 February 2024].

Simola J., Takala A., Lehkonen R., Frantti T., Savola R. (2023) Developing Cybersecurity in an Industrial Environment by Using a Testbed Environment. 22th European Conference on Cyber Warfare and Security ECCWS-2023. The Hellenic Air Force Academy. Athens, Greece.

Savaş, S., Karataş, S. (2022) Cyber governance studies in ensuring cybersecurity: an overview of cybersecurity governance. Int. Cybersecur. Law Rev. 3, 7–34. https://doi.org/10.1365/s43439-021-00045-4

The Impact of Operational Technology Requirements in Maritime Industries

Jussi Simola[1], Pia Satopää[2], Jarkko Paavola[2] and Jani Vanharanta[2]

[1]University of Jyväskylä, Finland

[2]Turku University of Applied Sciences, Finland

jussi.hm.simola@jyu.fi
pia.satopaa@turkuamk.fi
jarkko.paavola@turkuamk.fi
jani.vanharanta@turkuamk.fi

Abstract: The maritime ecosystem and industry require more efficient and coordinated cybersecurity governance. No common cybersecurity mechanism in the maritime sector may steer the whole supply chain management, for example, in the port areas and fairways. Cyberthreat prevention mechanisms in harbor areas and port terminals must be standardized more in the Western world. It has been recognized that understanding cybersecurity of operational technology in the harbor area is based on a more traditional experience of what it requires. The overall security of the maritime ecosystem requires more than random checks of passengers and vehicles and customs functions on cargo and passenger transportation, which are mainly physical security service routines. Traditional physical threats have changed to a combination of threat types. Hybrid threats may prevent everyday harbor activities so that damage can become long-lasting and harm overall business continuity management. It is crucial to prevent cyber threat factors in the maritime domain. The research provides transnational and EU-level cyber security assessments regarding cyber security regulation. The findings determine where to direct and concentrate a focus maritime domain and why it is essential to survey cyber security requirements set for member states to apply. In Finland, this research belongs to the cybersecurity governance of operational technology in the sector connected to the smart energy networks (CSG) research program. The project aims to develop a common cybersecurity governance model for operational technology.

Keywords: Operational Technology, Overall Situational Awareness, Maritime Cybersecurity, Governance Model

1. Introduction

The cybersecurity governance of operational technology in the sector connected to smart energy networks (CSG) research program will create a new governance model for the energy sector actors by developing operational technology standardization. One of the project's main aims is to develop a common cybersecurity governance model for operational technology. The maritime ecosystem is crucial to critical infrastructure protection. Transportation is a central national economic factor that allows the national-level supply chain to continue. If the supply chain is disrupted, security maintenance and continuity management prevent overall security. The research will find the main challenges concerning the cybersecurity governance of the industrial organizations in maritime clusters that use operational technology-related technology in their daily businesses.

Maritime cybersecurity has become increasingly crucial due to the growing and ever-evolving cyber threats. Stakeholders in the maritime industry must recognize their role as critical infrastructure operators and manage cybersecurity risks and threats that could impact maritime security, service continuity, or broader logistics chains.

2. Key Concepts

2.1 Maritime Situational Awareness

Ministry of Defence (2010) describes situational awareness as the understanding of the advisors and decision-makers of what has happened, the circumstances under which it happened, the goals of the different parties, and the possible development of events, all of which are needed to make decisions on a specific issue or range of issues. A common definition of situational awareness is the perception of the elements in the environment within time and space, the comprehension of their meaning, and the projection of their status soon (Endsley, 1988). It is knowing what is going on around you. It consists of continuous monitoring of relevant sources of information regarding actual incidents and developing hazards (Homeland Security, 2008).

The maritime cluster comprises several maritime-connected sectors that create the interacting entity (NESA 2020, 2021). Achieving common or Shared Situational Awareness (SSA) requires a common understanding of shared situational awareness that consists of similar unchanged elements at every stage. Sectors of the maritime domain cannot cooperate by forming their understanding of the entity independently from other actors. Thus, common maritime situational awareness is crucial in undistributed continuity management. It is useful to classify sector-based situational awareness for creating coherent entities. System of system-level thinking depends on the human ability to understand the dependencies of supply chains. Developing a framework for the smaller components is only possible if we can influence the relationships regarding the system and business dependencies.

Situational awareness can be divided as follows. Technological – Organizational – Situational awareness of human resources – Situational awareness of business management – Situational awareness of transportation – Situational awareness of regulations and policies. If all segments are well-defined and linked to each other in a way that information sharing and exchange support core functions, shared situational awareness could be achievable. Common situational awareness differs from shared situational awareness. In a concept meaning, common means a level of understanding (Endsley, 1995;1998).

2.2 Background of the Cybersecurity Governance

EU's cybersecurity strategy is the upper-level framework for national-level cybersecurity (European Commission, 2020a, 2022). The Western world has a common vision of achieving the strategies' goals (Lété, 2017;ENISA, 2023). NIS2 directive (European Commission, 2022a) states that every EU member state has been required to adopt a National Cybersecurity Strategy (NCSS) and establish a cyber security governance model. At a general level, as a part of corporate governance, several elements are related to the formation of cybersecurity governance. The frameworks are connected to each other in an essential way. Crucial vulnerability elements of security and cyber security consist of people, processes, and technical aspects (European Commission 2022a; 2023).

Port facility's cyber risk management requires a collective effort; the organization should define who has overall oversight of the cyber risk program. Owners, shareholders, and institutional investors (e.g., private equity) evaluate cyber risk in terms of risk to investments.

Operational cyber risk management oversight lies with those individuals who have ultimate responsibility, for example, in the governance of the port authority or port facility. That could be the CEO, Managing Director, or other designee, and their responsibility includes Board-level reporting (IAPH,2020;2021).

The European Union Agency for Cybersecurity ENISA (2023) proposed a governance model consisting of four main layers with 10 sub-categories, providing 28 practices. The main principles are demonstrated in Table 1.

Table 1: Tiers of Governance Model by Enisa (2023)

Layers of the governance	The Main Principles
Political governance	Political processes. Roles and responsibilities; and legal measures.
Strategic governance	Strategy itself and its implementation; and Risk identification and mitigation.
Technical governance	International standards and technical guidelines; and use of technology, tools, and certification schemes
Operational governance	Awareness raising. Incident response; and Information sharing.

The Operational Technology Governance process includes the following minimum requirements. a) The OT cybersecurity policy is established and communicated. b) OT cybersecurity roles and responsibilities are coordinated and aligned with the internal roles and external partners. c) legal and regulatory requirements regarding OT cybersecurity, including privacy, are understood correctly and managed. d) The cybersecurity risks are integrated into corporate risk management processes (NIST, 2023). According to the CISA (2024), features of the Cybersecurity Governance strategy may consist of the following issues: Accountability frameworks – Decision-making hierarchies –Defined risks related to business objectives – Mitigation plans and strategies – Oversight processes and procedures (CISA, 2024). Cybersecurity governance has been understood in different ways. Cybersecurity governance may consist of the following tiers.

2.2.1 *Vision and Strategy*

There should be a common understanding between national regulation and organizations' cyber security strategy connected to corporate governance strategy. The crucial elements are connected to human resource training, risk management, information sharing, and security of the business processes and technologies. Vendors and investors must be informed about cybersecurity's vulnerabilities and risks. Third-party-related partners have crucial roles in the framework. Every organization that is connected to the critical infrastructure must create cybersecurity governance based on the EU regulations.

2.2.2 *Exact Roles and Responsibilities*

Organizations have to create clear plans about who is responsible for risk management and cybersecurity risk management, and they have to early warn authorities and other sector-based operators within 24 hours. The observed vulnerability, cyber-attack, or potential threat must be reported to national cybersecurity authorities within 72 hours (European Commission, 2022b).

2.2.3 *Combined Risk Management - MSMS Maritime Cyber Security Management System.*

Workable risk analysis requires an assessment of the potential vulnerabilities and risks. That is connected to the organization's business strategy. It has been determined what the acceptable risk level is and how to react against cyber or cyberphysical risks. Crucial is how the auditing process is done.

2.2.4 *Cyber Security Steering Group*

There should also be a steering group that supervises other decision-makers regarding cybersecurity. The steering group gathers and shares the relevant information and transfers information to other closely linked managing groups.

2.2.5 *Cyber Security Programme*

Cyber security strategy requires a cyber security program to achieve the strategic goals. It is not enough for management or the board of directors to understand what issues are included. Employees must know and understand what they must do to achieve the details and how they reach the goals set by the company.

2.2.6 *Measurement and Reporting at all Business Hierarchy Levels*

In a wider perspective, companies must implement measures that support maintaining situational awareness. Companies must have business measures that guide the direction of the business. The cyber security measures are only one part of the clarification of the state of the company. Costs must stay the same, but it costs more if cybersecurity requirements still need to be implemented.

2.3 Regulation and Guidelines

The minimum level of the NIS 2 directive (2022/2555) for national regulation will be implemented in October

2024, and legislation will be applied to the operational environment in 2025. It will create cybersecurity measures and require organizations, and EU member states to inform EU-level agencies about cyber threat events and incidents. The NIS2 concentrates mainly on cyber security risk management, strategy planning, and information exchange concerning situational awareness of governance (European Commission, 2022a). The European Cyber Resilience Act (CRA) 2019/1020 aims to create framework conditions for developing secure products with digital elements by ensuring that hardware and software products are placed on the market with fewer vulnerabilities and that manufacturers take security seriously throughout the product lifecycle (European Commission, 2022b) It also aims to create conditions under which users can consider cybersecurity when choosing and using products with digital elements. Critical Entities Resilience (CER) (2022/2057) Directive consists of minimum regulation whose purpose is to enhance cyber resilience. It is based on the security strategy of the European Union (European Commission, 2020b).

International Maritime Organization´s (IMO) International Maritime Solid Bulk Cargoes Code (IMSBC Code) IMO Resolution MSC.428(98) offers views of the cyber risks, which companies should try to address as far as possible in the same way as any other risk that may affect the safe operation of a ship and protection of the environment (IMO, 2022). IMO has released with the International Labour Organization (ILO) the International Ship and Port

Facility Security (ISPS) Code of Practice on port security, which contains requirements relating to the ship's security and the immediate ship/port interface. Global BIMCO is the largest international shipping association representing the interests of ship owners, charterers, brokers, and agents. The BIMCO's primary role is the preparation of global regulations and policy recommendations in many areas related to maritime training services, from the environment, crew support, and insurance to maritime safety and security and digitalization, including guidelines for maritime cybersecurity. (Atlantic Council, 2021). European Maritime Safety Agency (EMSA) works under the European Union and serves the EU's maritime interests for a safe, secure, green, and competitive maritime sector in Europe and worldwide. EMSA is an essential stakeholder in the maritime cluster in Europe and beyond. It provides services to the EU Member States and the Commission but is also an innovative knowledge hub for the European maritime environment. (European Maritime Security Agency 2022).

2.4 Security Operations Center (SOC) and Cyber Risk Management

The Security Operations Centers in harbors have risen as the potential for hybrid threats increases in the maritime domain (U.S Coast Guard, 2020). Cyber and physical threats as a part of overall security management must be understood so that security personnel and the cyber emergency response team maintain shared situational awareness based on joint guidance and codes.

2.5 Port State Control (PCS)

Port authorities may use the Port community system as a part of the security management systems. As previous studies regarding maritime security indicate in Finland, we do not have advanced digitalized systems that comprise crucial security features under the same umbrella (Simola, Pöyhönen, Lehto, 2023a).

3. Processes, Humans, and Technologies Comprise Common Situational Awareness

Thinking from the view of technology or human processes in their daily work. it has been seen that requirements for understandable language are almost the same. It is crucial to analyze how people and technology communicate with each other. Devices must understand each other, but humans must also have a common language to understand different kinds of events and how they should react to them. Interfaces play a crucial role. Processes have an essential role in supporting each other. All these factors have to create seamless connections. For example, if stakeholders use different kinds of taxonomy in their information or data exchange procedures, advanced technology doesn't generate added value. As Mica Endsley discussed, situational awareness is based on a common level of understanding and creating a mental model for the stakeholders (Endsley, 1995;1998), as Figure 1 illustrates.

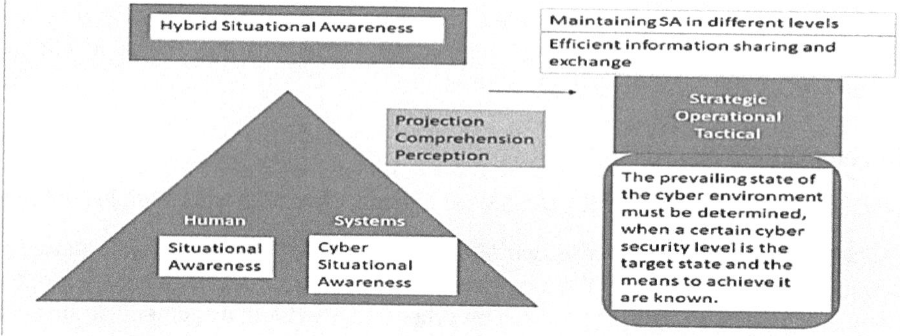

Figure 1 Formation of hybrid situational awareness (Simola, Pöyhönen & Lehto 2023b)

Maintaining situational awareness at the goal state requires a coherent strategic, operational, and tactical level of semantic functionalities where human and system-based information is shared understandably. The capability to understand threats and events creates a fundamental base to maintain everyday situational awareness. Cybersecurity strategies, threat prevention mechanisms, and prevention measures are equally important at a general level.

3.1 The Need for Common Situational Awareness in the Maritime Cluster

The maritime cluster is a crucial factor in the security of maintenance. If maritime industry-related stakeholders cannot secure the maritime cluster from supply chain-related vulnerabilities, it is possible that cyberattacks may cause interruption, and continuity management becomes difficult. According to Chubb N., Finn P., NG D., (2021), the maritime industry has a critical role in the global supply chain. But the industry also relies on its own supply chain. That means the supply chain means how reliable the movement of products from port to port or from the production line to the customers, but also how information and data are transferred from the technical level to the operational and strategical level and vice versa. There are several elements that affect each other.

4. Cybersecurity Threats in Maritime

Cybersecurity threats in maritime are diverse and can target various entities, including port operators, logistics in ports, communication and surveillance systems, satellite and navigation systems, and the vessels' own systems. Cyberattacks can lead to severe issues such as alterations in ship routes, cargo losses, or even accidents. Future cyber threats may become more complex with the increasing digitization and automation of maritime traffic. The deployment of autonomous vessels, for example, may open new opportunities for cyber-attacks. A large ship with many electrical onboard components and systems forms a complex cyberphysical system-of-systems. Navigational systems, propulsion systems, electrohydraulic ballast tanks, intering tank stabilizers and several other industrial control systems (ICS) are vital to the safe operation of the ship. The operational technology (OT) onboard, similarly to control systems in the past, are often considered as isolated and disparate control systems which are operated only by onsite personnel in physically controlled limited-access-areas. In practice, however, the level of automation and the number of ICT systems interfacing with OT has been on the incline, effectively exposing some of the OT to the internetwork (NESA, 2021; Tuomala, V. 2023).

According to the (NESA, 2021), current Identified Threats in the Cyber Dimension may include:

1. Cyber-Physical Attacks: Targeting physical systems, such as a ship's navigation or engine systems, with the aim of disrupting their operations.
2. Ransomware: Attackers may seize control of a system and demand a ransom for its release.
3. Phishing Attacks: Attackers may send deceptive messages appearing to come from a trusted source, aiming to trick users into revealing passwords or other sensitive information.
4. Insecure IoT Devices: IoT devices used on ships can be vulnerable to attacks if not properly secured.
5. Supply Chain Attacks: Attackers may target a ship's systems through a third party, such as a supplier or subcontractor.
6. Insider Threats: Individuals within the organization may intentionally or unintentionally pose cybersecurity risks.
7. Outdated Software: Aging software may contain vulnerabilities that attackers can exploit.
8. Weak Authentication: Poor password practices or inadequate authentication methods can allow unauthorized access to systems.
9. Data Breaches: Attackers may infiltrate systems and steal sensitive information.
10. State-sponsored Cyber Espionage: States may use cyber attacks for intelligence purposes or to disrupt the operations of other states.

4.1 Hardest Managed and Detected Risk Scenarios

The research Simola, Pöyhönen, Lehto (2023b) indicates that third party-related factors cause essential challenges in maritime clusters, as shown Table 2 below. Those are mainly related to the service providers.

Table 2: Threat scenarios

Examples of threat scenario sources	Threat sources
Lack of human resource management (part-time employees, accountancy services, maintenance companies)	3d party service providers (Companies and their governance)
The software consists of a threat base.	3d party Compromised legitimate software (hijacked ICS software)
The vulnerability on hardware components.	3d party hardware, port equipment, cameras, drones, routers, sensors, devices and other unknown adverse components'
Intentional and unintentional human errors caused by lack of training, changing personnel, management of rights of access and use	Human errors

5. Research Approach

This research concentrates on industry-specific cybersecurity requirements in the maritime cluster. The members involved in this analysis process are researchers and research methods. Cybersecurity experts from the research program advocate Delphi: "The Delphi method is an iterative process to increase consensus-building and, in the end, to have consensus among experts from an examined case (Garson, 2018).

The collected case study materials are based on official publications, official reports, and other literary material in this work. The research is based on the guidance of Yin (2014), and it answers questions about where to concentrate. The case study is based on producing detailed information about the researched object (Yin, 2004). Several case studies form knowledge from the environment and are connected to the design science process that generates the artifact; as Hevner (2004) has explained, design science research methodology is based on three iteration cycles that support each other's. The research concentrates on the environment where problem formulation has been done. Understanding the environment under the research (people, organizations, technology) is essential Hevner, A., & Chatterjee, S (2010). Gathering data from the industrial environment is crucial. The critical is to identify the data and information formation from the emergency points, where SOC and detection features must react. In Industrial Control Systems such as Scada, intrusion prevention or detection tools are relevant machines we must have under the secured control of operations. We will apply a widely used design science research methodology that has traditionally been used in software and system development.

5.1 Laboratory Environments

The project team of the University of Jyväskylä and Turku University of Applied Sciences, with their platform, has constructed a testbed environment where to test equipment that both have gotten from the stakeholders. The test environment will create new standardized guidelines for the operational technology-related systems and environments. Testbed -work in the Jyväskylä testing laboratory will be parallel and develop the upper-level reference model. Based on the results of use cases, inner and outer-level specific requirements are considered. The Use-case results from testbed work in a simultaneous environment and analysis of threat assessment-based risk scenarios will generate a proposal for the governance framework. Figure 2 below illustrates the connection between the research elements in the CSG project.

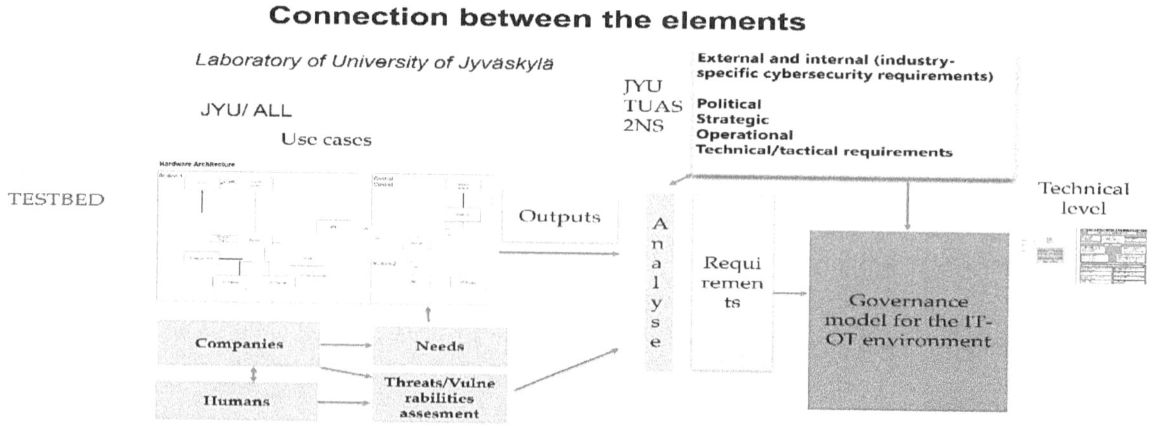

Figure 2: Testing environment

For developing Maritime Situational Awareness, Turku University of Applied Sciences has designed and built a OT test platform (Paavola, 2023), consisting of an Unmanned Surface Vessel (USV) and remote operations center (ROC), to support the industry's and authorities capacity to utilize novel technologies efficiently. The development process has allowed to gain a comprehensive understanding on every aspect of the OT operation of the USV. The built test infrastructure can be used to research the challenges and opportunities of applying AI to remote sensing problems in complex marine environments, such as ship feature recognition, vessel tracking, and abnormal behavior detection. In addition, it offers the platform to develop cybersecurity testing, security operations center (SOC), and cybersecurity situational awareness studies. The test platform consists of two components. Test Vessel e/MS Salama for unmanned operations consists of key components like the hull, motors, and batteries were procured, and sensors for situational awareness were integrated. An ICT subsystem is implemented for data processing and communication. The electrical system is installed following safety standards. The CAN bus is connected to all relevant systems. The devices in the USV can roughly be divided into four groups, that is equipment for power and propulsion, navigation and communication, sensory and imaging, and safety, security and utility. In the Remote Operation Center (ROC) operators can monitor, support, assist, supervise, and control the USV. The remote operations center can monitor the USV or directly control the USV's systems. The key components for the remote operation of the USV are the USV multi-modal sensoring system, data communication links, and the ROC itself. The USV multi-modal sensoring system provides information about both the USV itself and its environment. The sensor data of the USV transferred to the remote operations center can also be utilized directly in a digital twin of the vessel. The Figure 3 illustrates the OT test platform.

Figure 3: The OT test platforms

Critical Infrastructure Protection in Maritime Cluster

Maritime security consists of several elements that are crucial parts of the national critical infrastructure protection. Sector-connected security is essential because if a sector-based understanding of the functionalities works at a different level, the information flows smoothly.

It has been quite problematic for organizations to be in challenging environments where each organization has used its own systems and processes to tackle physical and cyber threats. It is crucial to analyze the point where humans cause more harm than automation or artificial intelligence and what the state is that automation causes more harm than humans.

The risk assessment must be considered when protecting maritime risks. Vulnerable onboard systems may consist of cargo management systems, bridge systems, propulsion and machinery, management and control systems, access control systems, passenger servicing and management systems, public networks, administrative and crew welfare systems, and communication systems (BIMCO, 2022). Huyler (2022) states that a few vulnerable systems such as human resource management systems, systems of operators, port authority systems, SCADA systems, alarm and monitoring systems, Communication systems, navigation systems, auxiliary machinery systems, security systems, propulsion/steering, mission support systems. The environment is complicated. Despite the different kinds of systems, research indicates that humans are the weakest factors in the working environment (Endsley, 1998;1995).

5.2 Future Cybersecurity Threats in Maritime

Future cybersecurity threats in maritime are expected to increase as vessels' systems become more interconnected with IT systems. This increased connectivity to the external world makes cyber attacks on OT systems more likely and potentially more destructive in the future.

The future threat landscape may include new challenges, such as:

1. Insufficient Funding: The maritime industry has observed insufficient investment in cybersecurity, leaving systems vulnerable to attacks.
2. Effectiveness of Regulations: While regulations may help improve cybersecurity, many organizations struggle to comply with existing rules in the field of risk management and resource allocation.
3. Vulnerabilities in the Supply Chain: Securing the supply chain from cyber threats is challenging and requires comprehensive knowledge of the supply chain, contract management, and a thorough examination of suppliers' cybersecurity requirements throughout procurement, installation, and use of equipment.

4. Lack of Information Sharing: In the maritime industry, information on cybersecurity risks, threats, and incidents is not adequately shared among organizations, limiting the availability of threat intelligence for comprehensive risk assessments or preventing potential incidents.

6. Findings

The research provides transnational and EU-level cyber security assessments regarding maritime clusters. The findings determine where to direct and concentrate a focus maritime domain and why it is important to survey cyber security requirements set for member states to apply.

The big challenge is how to apply European Union-based regulations in the maritime cluster. The cluster is at a different cybersecurity level than inland stakeholders. The research indicates that crucial cybersecurity issues are connected to human activities, so it is crucial to utilize our testbed environments. The formation of Common situational awareness requires that human activities, organizational processes, and technologies are standardized at all three levels; strategic, operational, and technical. Especially in the maritime cluster, there are third-party-related matters that have to be taken into account. Multicomplex environments form challenging atmospheres where partners change, humans are not in different tasks for long periods, and temporary employees are often used.

NIS2 requires cybersecurity training to enhance the critical infrastructure's cybersecurity level. CER identifies and divides the same industry-based organizations as NIS2, which is essential for vital functions.

The operational level needs sector-based information exchange groups that use the same "language," such as a taxonomy of what to share, how to share, with whom to share, and what information is required for reporting. Despite that organizations need to know the requirements of future cybersecurity regulations; it is crucial that the national government act efficiently and offer information on how organizations must design their information-sharing mechanisms. Cybersecurity training is crucial, but the training is irrelevant if the mental model is not clear on what business needs are. Without a common understanding of procedures and processes regarding workflow, threat prevention is not possible to take control. The working culture of the maritime cluster is very international; therefore, the standards and certifications set a coherent basement for fulfilling requirements. Active operating environments and various technologies are factors that need attention. The used testbed environments will demonstrate how important it is to analyze for example logs from the operational technology environment. Decisionmakers need to maintain situational awareness and data from the technical level must be transformed as the information and depending on the level where data or information is required, more crucial it is. Operational technology is connected to the IT environment in many ways. Vendors and partners are essential potential factors that add opportunities for supply chain issues. That is why active supply chain management is needed as part of cyber risk management. Workable supply chain management requires a stable flow of data and information. For example, the Cyber Resilience Act (CRA) sets new requirements for digitalized devices and services. CE-marked devices enhance trust and indicate to the stakeholders that Cybersecurity requirements have been taken seriously. Cybersecurity management is not a separate part of business continuity management. Both support Corporate Governance and cyber security governance. A crucial point is that cyber risk classifications have been done with other risk assessments. The cyber risk assessment is an essential part of the overall risk assessment in the maritime cluster. Cybersecurity and security plans must be part of overall risk management and continuity management activities, where policies, regulations, processes, and procedures are defined and implemented. In securing business continuity management, following the risk management guidelines of the Cybersecurity Framework developed by NIST (2024) is advisable. Framework allows to choose correct standards from the other publications. At a minimum level, a standardized environment requires that IT-related functionalities follow the ISO 2700 standard family and Operational Technology-related functionalities apply ISO 62243 standards for controlling Industrial Control Systems. Cybersecurity requirements of the European Union can be achieved by standardization. Certification systems inform stakeholders about the trust level of the company (ISO, 2018: Verve Industrial, 2022). According to the NIST (2024), in additional Special Publication SP 800-161r1 guides how to enhance Cybersecurity Supply Chain Risk Management Practices for Systems and Organizations (NIST, 2022).

7. Discussion and Conclusions

7.1 Future Research Needs in Maritime Cybersecurity

Research in cybersecurity is vital for protecting critical infrastructure and maritime traffic itself. It helps maritime operators identify threats and manage cybersecurity risks. Given the continuous evolution and increasing automation in the maritime industry, ongoing research can improve existing best practices for managing maritime cybersecurity. A doctoral dissertation conducted at the University of Jyväskylä has revealed the vulnerability of systems used in maritime and air traffic to cyberattacks. In his research, Syed Khandker (2022) analyzed the security features of two critical surveillance systems in air and maritime traffic, ADS-B and AIS. The study successfully impacted all test devices with attacks, indicating that these attacks could potentially affect the navigation safety of aircraft or ships in real life. Major problems in both systems were related to protocol design, where all security aspects were not adequately considered. According to Khandker (2022), security could be enhanced by introducing encryption or authentication methods. This underscores the importance of research in improving maritime cybersecurity. Maritime cybersecurity is a crucial aspect of contemporary shipping and critical infrastructure protection. The identification and management of threats are key to ensuring safety and efficiency. Further research is needed to understand potential cyber threats and develop effective countermeasures. Securing global trade and the economy through cybersecurity means and preventing environmental damage caused by potential cyberattacks requires continuous research. It is also noteworthy that combating cyber threats requires international collaboration to develop cybersecurity in the maritime industry. Multiple sources indicate that much work must be done to enhance maritime cybersecurity. Essential is how to implement, for example (the ISPS) Code of Practice on port security and cyber security requirements for the ship's security and the immediate ship/port interface to enhance overall security. It must be considered that international means a wider perspective than European or Western aspects. The essential point of view is how to achieve trust in the supply chain and continuity management. Infected companies that have realized threats in the maritime industry are often seamlessly connected to other sectors linked with each other through shared systems. This kind of information-sharing relationship cycle creates more possibilities for cyber attackers.

Acknowledgments

The research was supported by Business Finland (grant number 10/31/2022) and the University of Jyväskylä.

References

Atlantic Council (2021) Appendices: Cooperation on maritime cybersecurity. https://www.atlanticcouncil.org/in-depth-research-reports/report/cooperation-on-maritime-cybersecurity-appendices/

BIMCO (2022) The Guidelines on Cyber Security Onboard Ships v.4 Available: https://www.ics-shipping.org/wp-content/uploads/2020/08/guidelines-on-cyber-security-onboard-ships-min.pdf

Chubb N., Finn P., NG D. (2021) The Great Disconnect. The state of cyber risk management in the maritime industry. Cyberowl.

CISA (2024) Cybersecurity Governance. Available: https://www.cisa.gov/topics/cybersecurity-best-practices/cybersecurity-governance

Endsley M. (1995) Towards a theory of situation awareness in Dynamic Systems. Human Factor 37(1)

Endsley M. R., (1998) "Design and evaluation for situation awareness enhancement." in Proceedings of the Human Factors Society 32nd Annual Meeting, pp. 97-101

ENISA (2023a) Building Effective Governance Frameworks for the Implementation of National Cybersecurity Strategies. DOI: 10.2824/850466

ENISA (2023b) CISA and ENISA enhance their Cooperation https://www.enisa.europa.eu/news/cisa-and-enisa-enhance-their-cooperation

ENISA report (2019) "Port Cybersecurity" Good Practices for Cybersecurity in the Maritime Sector Cybersecurity in the Maritime Sector: ENISA Releases New Guidelines for Navigating Cyber Risk — ENISA (europa.eu)

European Commission. (2020a) The EU's Cybersecurity Strategy for the Digital Decade. Brussels. https://eur-lex.europa.eu/legal-content/EN/TXT/HTML/?uri=CELEX:52020JC0018

European Commission. (2020b) Proposal for a directive of the European Parliament and of the Council on the resilience of critical entities. COM (2020) 829 final. 2020/0365 (COD). Brussels, 16 December

European Commission (2022a). NIS2 Directive (EU) 2022/2555. https://www.enisa.europa.eu/topics/cybersecurity-policy/nis-directive-new

European Commission. (2022b) Proposal for a regulation on horizontal cybersecurity requirements for products with digital elements and amending Regulation (EU) 2019/1020

European Maritime Safety Agency (2022) This is EMSA. https://www.emsa.europa.eu/about.html

Garson, G. D. (2012) The Delphi method in quantitative research. Asheboro, NC: Statistical Associates Publishers. Available from: https://faculty.chass.ncsu.edu/garson/PA765/delphi.htm, retrieved 24.12.2023.

Hevner A., March, S.T., Park, J., and Ram, S. (2004) Design Science in Information Systems Research. MIS Quarterly.

Hevner, A., & Chatterjee, S. (2010) Design research in information systems: Theory and practice. Springer Science and Business.

Huyler, J. (2022) Modernizing Maritime OT cybersecurity: Unique obstacles and Opportunities. Industrial Defender. https://www.industrialdefender.com/blog/modernizing-maritime-ot-cybersecurity

IAPH (2020) Port Community Cyber Security. https://sustainableworldports.org/wp-content/uploads/IAPH-Port-Community-Cyber-Security-Report-Q2-2020.pdf

IAPH (2021) Cybersecurity Guidelines for Ports and Port Facilities. https://sustainablewoelports.org/wp-content/uploads/IAPH-Cybersecurity-Guidelines-version-1_0.pdf.

IMO (2022) Guidelines on maritime cyber risk management. MSC-FAL.1/Circ.3 5 July 2017. International Maritime Organization. Available: https://wwwcdn.imo.org/localresources/en/OurWork/Security/Documents/MSC-FAL.1-Circ.3-Rev.2%20-%20Guidelines%20On%20Maritime%20Cyber%20Risk%20Management%20(Secretariat)%20(1).pdf

ISO (2018) 2700:18 Information Technology. Information Technology Security Techniques.

Khandker, S. (2022). Positioning services in different wireless networks : a development and security perspective. https://jyx.jyu.fi/handle/123456789/82425

Lété Bruno and Pernik Piret. 2017 EU–NATO Cybersecurity and Defense Cooperation:
From Common Threats to Common Solutions, Security and Defense Policy.

Ministry of Defence (2010) Security strategy for society, government resolution. Helsinki: Ministry of Defence

NESA (2020) Kyberturvallisuuden nykytila eri toimialoilla – Kartoituksen keskeiset havainnot

NESA (2021) Maritime Cybersecurity Report – Finnish Maritime Cybersecurity Maturity - Current state report and best practices for the Finnish Maritime sector

NIST (2022) NIST Special Publication SP 800-161r1 Cybersecurity Supply Chain Risk Management Practices for Systems and Organizations

NIST (2023) Special Publication SP 800-82r3 Guide to Operational Technology (OT) Security. Available: https://doi.org/10.6028/NIST.SP.800-82r3

NIST (2024) Cybersecurity Framework 2.0. US. Department of Commerce. Available: https://www.nist.gov/cyberframework

Paavola J. (2023) Development of Applied Research Platforms for Autonomous and Remotely Operated Systems, https://urn.fi/URN:ISBN:978-952-216-862-7

Simola, J., Pöyhönen, J., & Lehto, M. (2023a). Smart Terminal System of Systems' Cyber Threat
Impact Evaluation. In A. Andreatos, & C. Douligeris (Eds.), Proceedings of the 22nd European
Conference on Cyber Warfare and Security (pp. 439-449). Academic Conferences International.
Proceedings of the European Conference on Cyber Warfare and Security, 22.
https://doi.org/10.34190/eccws.22.1.1070

Simola, J., Pöyhönen, J., & Martti, L. (2023b). Cyber Threat Analysis in Smart Terminal Systems. In
R. L. Wilson, & B. Curran (Eds.), ICCWS 2023 : Proceedings of the 18th International Conference
on Cyber Warfare and Security (pp. 369-378). Academic Conferences International Ltd.
https://doi.org/10.34190/iccws.18.1.93

Tuomala, V. (2023). Maritime Cybersecurity. Before the risks turn into attacks. Xamk Research https://www.theseus.fi/bitstream/handle/10024/504156/URNISBN9789523443600.pdf?sequence=2&isAllowed=y

U.S: Coast Guard. (2020). Inter-American Committee on Ports. International Port Security Program. Stakeholders management - Port security committees.

Verve Industrial (2022) What is IEC 62443?. https://verveindustrial.com/resources/blog/the-ultimate-guide-to-protecting-ot-systems-with-iec-62443/

Yin, R.K. (2014) Case Study Research, Design and Methods. 5th ed. Thousand Oaks: Sage Publications.

Exploring Cybersecurity Implications in Higher Education

Nokuthaba Siphambili
University of Pretoria and Council for Scientific and Industrial Research (CSIR), South Africa

nsiphambili@csir.co.za

Abstract: With the rapid technological evolution and widespread integration of digital transformation in higher education institutions (HEIs), the educational landscape has undergone a shift in teaching methodologies and how content is delivered. The digitization of higher education has ushered in numerous benefits, enhancing accessibility, collaboration, and efficiency. However, this era of digitization of higher education also brings forth a plethora of cyber challenges. The objective of this paper is to comprehensively explore the cybersecurity landscape in the digital age, providing a critical analysis of prevailing cyber threats, emerging trends, and potential impacts on HEIs. Therefore, this study conducted a systematic literature review (SLR) using the PRISMA framework to assess the current cyber threats faced by higher education institutions. The findings of the study reflect on the challenges faced by higher education institutions in this digital age and present opportunities in strategies that may be adopted to protect HEI's systems from cyber threats.

Keywords: Cybersecurity, Cybersecurity Awareness, Higher Education Institutions (Heis), Digital Age, Online Learning

1. Introduction

The ongoing rapid technological changes have significantly transformed the way teaching is delivered in higher education institutions (HEIs). With the advent of major lockdowns due to the COVID-19 pandemic, digital teaching has emerged as a transformative force in higher education. This has revolutionized the way educators deliver learning content to students and the way students learn and engage with content. As higher education institutions increasingly leverage technology, cloud-based systems, and online platforms to deliver content, they must also be cautious of the inherent cybersecurity risks. The effect of the coronavirus has led to HEIs adopting online learning or hybrid learning scenarios. This has increased the need for HEIs to revise and step up the way they protect their data and systems. Jana et al. (2023) state that the digital transformation from traditional teaching 'chalk and board' approaches to a digitalized one offers exciting opportunities for the future of higher education. Yet, the challenges for advancement in the way content is delivered cannot be ignored. For example, the move to exploit the opportunities of digital spaces, raises the need for higher education institutions to improve their administrators', educators' and students' cyber hygiene through cybersecurity awareness campaigns that aim to make them aware of the implications of the ever-increasing cyber threats.

As higher education institutions started migrating their on-campus programmes to online platforms, they have also been faced with an increase in cyber threats. These include ransomware, distributed denial of service, data breaches and social engineering attacks. All these cyber threats call for higher education institutions to adequately protect their systems from any unauthorized access, usage, disclosure, modification, destruction, and deletion by threat actors. Therefore, this paper aims to explore the cybersecurity implications in the digital age, highlighting the vulnerabilities and risks faced by the higher education sector as they navigate the ever-evolving digital landscape. More than ever before, it is now essential for higher education institutions to ensure that their systems are well-protected from cyber threats. However, before this paper can discuss how this can be achieved, it is also important to note that the concept of cybersecurity has already been defined in other fields like information security or computer security. Yet, to the author's knowledge and up until now, there is still no widely accepted definition of cybersecurity in the context of higher education institutions. The author believes that the HEI environment is quite unique in its way and therefore demands that the concept of cybersecurity be revised and defined to fit its context.

2. Definition

Several authors have different definitions of cybersecurity (Jana et al., 2023; Taherdoost, 2022; Antunes et al., 2021; Hamdani et al., 2021; Thakur et al., 2015). In some cases, it is used interchangeably with information security (Jana et al., 2023; Taherdoost, 2022). Yet in other cases, it is discussed as a different concept to information security (Antunes et al., 2021). Information security, also known as info sec deals with protecting information in all forms, whether in physical or digital form and cybersecurity focuses on protecting information and systems from any cyber threats. The author believes that these two, i.e., info security and cybersecurity are somehow similar yet unique in various aspects. However, this paper focuses on cybersecurity. Therefore, this section continues to compare some of the definitions of cybersecurity that are found in the literature and ends by contextualizing it to the HEI environment."

According to Thakur et al. (2015), cybersecurity is defined as the process of safeguarding against unauthorized access, use, disclosure, alteration, and destruction of computer systems, networks, and data. This is a good definition because it covers systems, networks and the data they transmit or process. However, it does not consider unauthorized denial of service by a malicious insider. For example, in the context of higher education, an authorized student who is ill-prepared for an exam may easily execute a freely available distributed denial of service attack (DDOS) that aims to compromise the availability of a system (Gupta & Badve, 2017) on the exam server and deny other students who have prepared a chance to write an exam. Therefore, this definition can be improved as follows; cybersecurity is defined as the process of safeguarding against denial of a service, unauthorized access, use, disclosure, alteration, and destruction of computer systems, networks, and data.

Hamdani et al. (2021) define cybersecurity as technology that prevents hostile parties from exploiting and misusing digital assets by preventing unauthorized access. This definition adds the element of 'a hostile party', 'misuse' and 'preventing authorized access' to the one of (Thakur et al., 2015). Therefore, by taking a combination of two definitions, one can arrive at a more encompassing definition. This can be stated as follows: a process of safeguarding against hostile parties exploiting weaknesses in systems, networks and applications to purposely prevent authorized access from other authorized users; carry out unauthorized access, use, disclosure, alteration, and destruction of the data they store, collect, transmit or process. Though the combination of the two definitions seems to be all-encompassing, the author of this paper has purposely chosen to define cybersecurity as the process of protecting HEI data, systems and networks from unauthorized users by preventing them from accessing, using and disclosing their weaknesses. This definition contextualizes cybersecurity to the HEI environment. An example of cybersecurity in higher education is protecting sensitive research data from unauthorized access or theft. This includes implementing encryption protocols and firewalls to safeguard valuable information from potential cyber threats. Additionally, cybersecurity also involves educating students and staff about the best practices for creating strong passwords and being vigilant against phishing attempts to prevent unauthorized access to personal accounts and sensitive data.

This research aims to investigate the implications of cybersecurity in digital learning, looking at the challenges and opportunities in higher education. This will be done following the methodology in the next section.

3. Methodology

A systematic review of the literature was carried out that focused on finding the existing literature on cybersecurity implications. The following research question guided the study: *"What are the cybersecurity implications of digital teaching in higher education?"*. The Preferred Reporting Items for Systematic and Meta-analysis (PRISMA) framework was used to target publications between 2019 and 2023 with search terms (*"cybersecurity"* OR *"information security"* AND *"implication"* AND *"digital"* OR *"online" learning*). The following databases were used Scopus, Elsevier, Google Scholar, Taylor and Francis Online for comprehensive results.

The articles were screened through the process of reading abstracts and irrelevant articles were eliminated as shown in Table 1 below. After the inclusion and exclusion criteria were applied, 70 publications were excluded and 25 publications were found to be eligible for the full review as illustrated in Annexure A.

Table 1: Inclusion and Exclusion Criteria

Inclusion
Articles published between 2019 and 2023.
Articles that discuss online learning and cybersecurity implications.
Exclusion
Articles not written in English.
Articles that are not accessible.
Articles that are duplicates.

4. Findings

4.1 Cyberthreats

Higher education institutions face challenges from various cyber threats, such as data breaches, denial of service (DoS), malware attacks, malicious insiders, external users, and cloud providers (Alexei and Alexei, 2021b). Broadhurst et al., (2019) examine how criminals target students through spam emails that contain phishing attacks to deliver malware and ransomware and obtain personal information without authorization for identity theft. For example, students often receive spam emails in the form of discounts and rewards. Sharma (2021) states how malware affects higher education institutions, causing data loss and the inability to access some services. Cyber criminals use phishing emails to target their victims by sending an email to a targeted victim in hopes that the victim will click on the link. To ensure that their systems follow the confidentiality, integrity and availability (CIA) triad, academic institutions ensure that they can manage cybersecurity threats with online learning (Merchan-Lima et al., 2021; Sekgololo, 2021). As a result, an organization is guaranteed to be able to identify vulnerabilities, address these risks, and gauge the impact. Threat actors target HEIs using social engineering to find vulnerabilities they will exploit to gain access to data and information being handled by HEIs (Merchan-Lima et al., 2021; Turnbull et al., 2021; Guangul et al., 2020).

4.2 Interest in Personal Information

As a result of the COVID-19 pandemic, learning has changed as higher academic institutions now deliver educational content using the most up-to-date technologies using computers, software, the Internet, and other applications (El Firdoussi et al., 2020). According to Alexei and Alexei, (2021b), criminals are now interested in collecting students' personal information, which they then utilize in phishing attempts due to hybrid learning. Due to the personal information and data they hold including identity numbers, staff and student intellectual property, higher education institutions are targets of cybercrime (Alexei, 2021a; Fouad, 2021; Fishman et al., 2018). Due to the shift to hybrid learning, these institutions are now targets, which raises the danger and volume of cybersecurity incidents in the sector (Ulven & Wangen, 2021). Due to the shift in teaching methodologies, HEIs are handling more sensitive data and information of students and staff resulting in threat actors aiming to gain access to this data and information (Khan et al., 2023).

4.3 Human Error

Humans are the main causes of data breaches as it is easy to make errors, such as an employee working in HEIs as a part-time lecturer, they can easily be acknowledged (Amoresano & Yankson, 2023; Othmana et al., 2020). According to Maranga and Nelson (2019), higher education institutions in Kenya must deal with issues that include insecure personal areas where employees, teachers and students are allowed to bring their own devices. More than 25% of phishing attacks in the UK's education sector in 2020 targeted university platforms, email, and video conferencing software (Amoresano & Yankson, 2023; Alexei, 2021a). Due to changes in teaching methods, the majority of employees now work from home, which calls for caution because people can become victims of data breaches (Georgiadou et al., 2022).

In addition, Netshakhuma (2023) claims that higher education's cybersecurity policies and standards are not up to par and that a framework for managing cybersecurity is lacking. Institutions must overcome this problem by taking all necessary security precautions to ensure that any device that accesses their network is secure and does not pose any threat. According to the article by Majola (2020), Lincoln College in the United States was hit by a ransom attack in May 2022, the University of Mpumalanga has been a victim of cyber breaches with bank account attacks, and a first-year student at the University of Johannesburg had their personal information sent to all students by mistake.

4.4 Skill Shortages

Cybersecurity is a growing field where management is tasked with ensuring that they protect their systems from any cyber-attacks. There are skills shortages as HEIs continuously face challenges with finding skilled people to fill cyber-security-related positions in the higher education sector and shortages of cybersecurity skills in the education sector in the European educational sector (Blaic, 2021). Due to the lack of skilled professionals in HEIs, not all students are trained or taught how to be safe online, which can result in the students being victims of cyber-attacks or incidents. Most employees are trained in cybersecurity and do not focus on why they should learn which results in employees being unable to assess risks where there is a need for inclusivity of all employees in organizational security (Amoresano & Yankson, 2023; Zwilling, 2022).

5. Recommendations

5.1 Cyber-Hygiene

HEIs should ensure that there is cybersecurity training and awareness by spending more time on cybersecurity (Gearhart, Abbiatti & Miller, 2019). This will help staff, students and faculty recognize the risks and potential threats associated with digital platforms so that academic institutions minimize cybersecurity vulnerabilities such as data loss and unauthorized access to their information and data. For example, there could be a compulsory course for students focusing on cyber awareness in higher education institutions. To stay ahead of new cyber risks, institutions must continually assess their practices, learn from incidents, and adapt their approaches. Having robust cybersecurity protocols will help ensure that there is a regular assessment of the institution's security and ensure that their data and networks are encrypted to prevent unauthorized access. They must ensure they have strong cybersecurity policies, routinely evaluate their security and encrypt their network and data to prevent unauthorized access. HEIs should invest in advanced technologies such as Intrusion Detection and Prevention Systems (IDS/IPS), web application firewalls (WAF) and Anti DDoS systems (ADS) (Merchan-Lima et al., 2021). Organizations should ensure that data at rest is encrypted by following existing IT policies and there is continuous monitoring of networks and systems (Alwahaibi et al., 2022)

5.2 Hiring Talent and Upskilling

There is a shortage of cybersecurity professionals in the world and the higher education sector is no exception. Hiring a qualified professional will help guide how content should be delivered to students and staff during training and awareness programmes. Students or graduates can be hired to be trained and skilled in the field and the existing employees can also be upskilled where the institutions pay for the certification of the employees who will be upskilling or training to be professionals in the field. Upskilling ensures that users are aware of risk which results in the reduction of risky behaviors that lead to users falling victim to cyber crimes (Moustafa et al., 2021)

5.3 Collaboration

Higher education institutions should collaborate to find solutions and pool resources to improve cybersecurity measures. This includes collaboration with other institutions, industry professionals, and cybersecurity specialists. For example, a partnership with the University of Cape Town, a member of the Forum of Incident Response and Security Teams (FIRST), which is a global forum of incident response and security teams will help other HEIs know how to respond to incidents and threats. Additionally, academic institutions can perform penetration tests to assess their security systems. These tests can help identify vulnerabilities and risk mitigation strategies. Furthermore, this opportunity allows these institutions to learn from experts in the field, cybersecurity specialists, or other higher education institutions. These suggestions can help higher education institutions navigate the world of online learning while successfully addressing cybersecurity issues.

5.4 Have a Culture That Supports Cybersecurity

Organizations should have a culture that supports cybersecurity to ensure that they protect their systems and information against cyber attacks (Kundy & Lyimo, 2019). This will ensure that people are aware of these cyber threats due to the fact that humans are the main causes of data breaches; therefore, the chances of these attacks happening will be lesser as the management will be leading by example. To respond to these cybersecurity threats, assign a cybersecurity responsibility to the Chief Information Officer (CIO), who will ensure that there are people responsible for cybersecurity (Gearhart et al., 2019). If management is assigned the role of being cyber warriors, employees and students will be motivated to take part in training and awareness. According to Chapman (2019), students should get basic information technology and network infrastructure knowledge so that they learn how to ensure that they follow the information security standards set by the institutions. This will help ensure that every student in higher education has a basic understanding of what cybersecurity is and how to ensure that they stay safe online.

6. In Conclusion

The digital age has created transformative opportunities for higher education institutions, revolutionizing how knowledge is shared, accessed, and absorbed. However, these opportunities are not without their accompanying challenges, particularly in the realm of cybersecurity. The main findings of this study showed that there is an increase in cyber threats such as data breaches, interest in personal information from threat actors, skill shortages and human errors. Therefore, this study recommended that HEIs must ensure that their systems are protected against cyber-attacks. Furthermore, this study provided recommendations that will ensure that HEIs stay prepared against cyber related threats. They must consistently invest in technology and train their employees and students to ensure that their institutions are secure against cyber threats. Higher education institutions must educate students, keep up with cyber threats and ensure that unauthorized users cannot access their data as technology is always changing as a result of new advances (Thakur et al., 2015).

Acknowledgement

The author would like to thank the Council for Scientific and Industrial Research (CSIR) for financial support.

References

Alexei, A. (2021a) *"Network Security Threats to Higher Education Institutions"*. Budapest, Hungary, Central and Eastern European eDem and eGov Days. https://doi.org/10.24989/ocg.v341.24

Alexei, A. and Alexei, A. (2021b) "Cyber security threat analysis in higher education institutions as a result of distance learning" International *Journal of Scientific and Technology Research,* Vol 10, No. 03, pp 128-133.

Alwahaibi, A., Bin, W., Hassa, W., Basri, W., Wan Ismail, W.B. and Almamari, M., 2022. A systematic literature review on its security standards for higher education institution. *Journal of Tianjin University Science and Technology,* 55(6), pp. 194- 213.

Amoresano, K. & Yankson, B., 2023. Human Error-A Critical Contributing Factor to the Rise in Data Breaches: A Case Study of Higher Education. *HOLISTICA–Journal of Business and Public Administration,* 14(1), pp. 110-132

Blaic, B. J. (2021) "The cybersecurity labor shortage in Europe: Moving to a new concept for education and training", Technology *in Society*, Vol 67, No. 101769, pp 1-13.

Broadhurst, R. G., Skinner, K., Sifniotis, N. and Matamoros-Macias, B. (2019) "Phishing and cybercrime risks in a university student community", International *Journal of Cybersecurity Intelligence & Cybercrime*, Vol 2, No. 1, pp 4-23.

Chapman, J. (2019) *"How Safe is Your Data?: Cyber-security in Higher Education* "(Vol. 12, pp. 1-6). Oxford, UK: Higher Education Policy Institute.

El Firdoussi, S., Lachgar, M., Kabaili, H., Rochdi, A., Goujdami, D. and El Firdoussi, L. (2020), "Assessing distance learning in higher education during the COVID-19 pandemic" *Education Research International*, Vol *2020*, pp.1-13.

Fishman, T. D., Clark, C. and Grama, J. L. (2018), [online]. Deloitte. https://www2.deloitte.com/za/en/pages/public-sector /articles /Elevating_cybersecurity _on_the_ higher _education_leadership_agenda.html.

Fouad, N. S. (2021) "Securing higher education against cyber threats: from an institutional risk to a national policy challenge", Journal *of Cyber Policy, Vol* 6, No. 2, pp.137-154.

Gearhart, G.D., Abbiatti, M.D. and Miller, M.T. (2019) "Higher education's cyber security: Leadership issues, challenges and the future", *International Journal on New Trends in Education and Their Implications*, Vol *10*, No. 2, pp.11-18.

Georgiadou, A., Mouzakitis, S. and Askounis, D., 2022. Working from home during COVID-19 crisis: a cyber security culture assessment survey. *Security Journal*, *35*(2), pp.486-505.

Guangul, F.M., Suhail, A.H., Khalit, M.I. and Khidhir, B.A., 2020. Challenges of remote assessment in higher education in the context of COVID-19: a case study of Middle East College. *Educational assessment, evaluation and accountability, 32*, pp.519-535.

Khan, N. A., Brohi, S. N. & Zaman, N., 2023. Ten Deadly Cyber Security Threats Amid COVID-19 Pandemic. *TechRxiv*, pp. 1-6.

Kundy, E.D. and Lyimo, B.J. (2019) "Cyber Security Threats in Higher Learning Institutions in Tanzania, A Case of the University of Arusha and Tumaini University Makumira", Olva *Academy–School of Researchers*, Vol *2*, No. 3, pp.1-38.

Hamdani, S.W.A., Abbas, H., Janjua, A.R., Shahid, W.B., Amjad, M.F., Malik, J., Murtaza, M.H., Atiquzzaman, M. and Khan, A.W. (2021), "Cybersecurity standards in the context of operating system: Practical aspects, analysis, and comparisons", ACM *Computing Surveys (CSUR)*, Vol *54, No. 3*, pp.1-36.

Jana, P., Banerjee, D., Das, K., Maity, S., Sarkar, A. and Samanta, S. (2023), "Cyber Security: Trends and Appraisal on Threats, Attacks, and Security Models", In *Streamlining Organizational Processes Through AI, IoT, Blockchain, and Virtual Environments*, pp. 135-155. IGI Global.

Majola, G.(2022) *"IOL", [online],* https://www.iol.co.za/business-report/economy/cyber-security-universities-under-fire-42481925-60dc-439c-86a1-13eabd30121c.

Maranga, M. J. and Nelson, M. (2019) "Emerging issues in cyber security for institutions of higher education", *International Journal of Computer Science, Vol* 8, No. 4, pp. 371-379.

Merchan-Lima, J., Astudillo-Salinas, F., Tello-Oquendo, L., Sanchez, F., Lopez-Fonseca, G. and Quiroz, D., 2021. Information security management frameworks and strategies in higher education institutions: a systematic review. *Annals of Telecommunications*, *76*, pp.255-270.

Netshakhuma, N. S. (2023)" Cybersecurity management in South Africa", *IGI Global,* pp 1-16.

Sekgololo, J. (2021) *"Mail&Guardian",* [online].https://mg.co.za/thoughtleader/opinion/2021-06-09-cybersecurity-e-learning-and-the-rise-of-online-student-protests/.

Othmana, Z., Rahimb, N. & Sadiqc, M., 2020. The human dimension as the core factor in dealing with cyberattacks in higher education. *International Journal of Innovation, Creativity and Change,* 11(1), pp. 1-19.

Sharma, A. (2021) "Review on Major Cyber security Issues in Educational Sector", *International Journal of Computer Sciences and Engineering, Vol 9*, No. 12, pp. 26-29.

Taherdoost, H. (2022) "Cybersecurity vs. Information Security" *Procedia Computer Science,* Vol215, pp. 483-487.

Thakur, K., Qiu, M., Gai, K. and Ali, M.L. (2015)" An investigation on cyber security threats and security models" Paper presented at the 2nd international conference on cyber security and cloud computing, USA, pp. 307-311 November 2015.
Turnbull, D., Chugh, R. and Luck, J., 2021. Transitioning to E-Learning during the COVID-19 pandemic: How have Higher Education Institutions responded to the challenge?. *Education and Information Technologies*, *26*(5), pp.6401-6419.
Ulven, J.B. and Wangen, G. (2021) "A systematic review of cybersecurity risks in higher education", *Future Internet*, Vol 13, *No.* 2, pp 1-39.
Zwilling, M., Klien, G., Lesjak, D., Wiechetek, Ł., Cetin, F. and Basim, H.N., 2022. Cyber security awareness, knowledge and behavior: A comparative study. *Journal of Computer Information Systems*, *62*(1), pp.82-97.

Appendix A: PRISMA flowchart

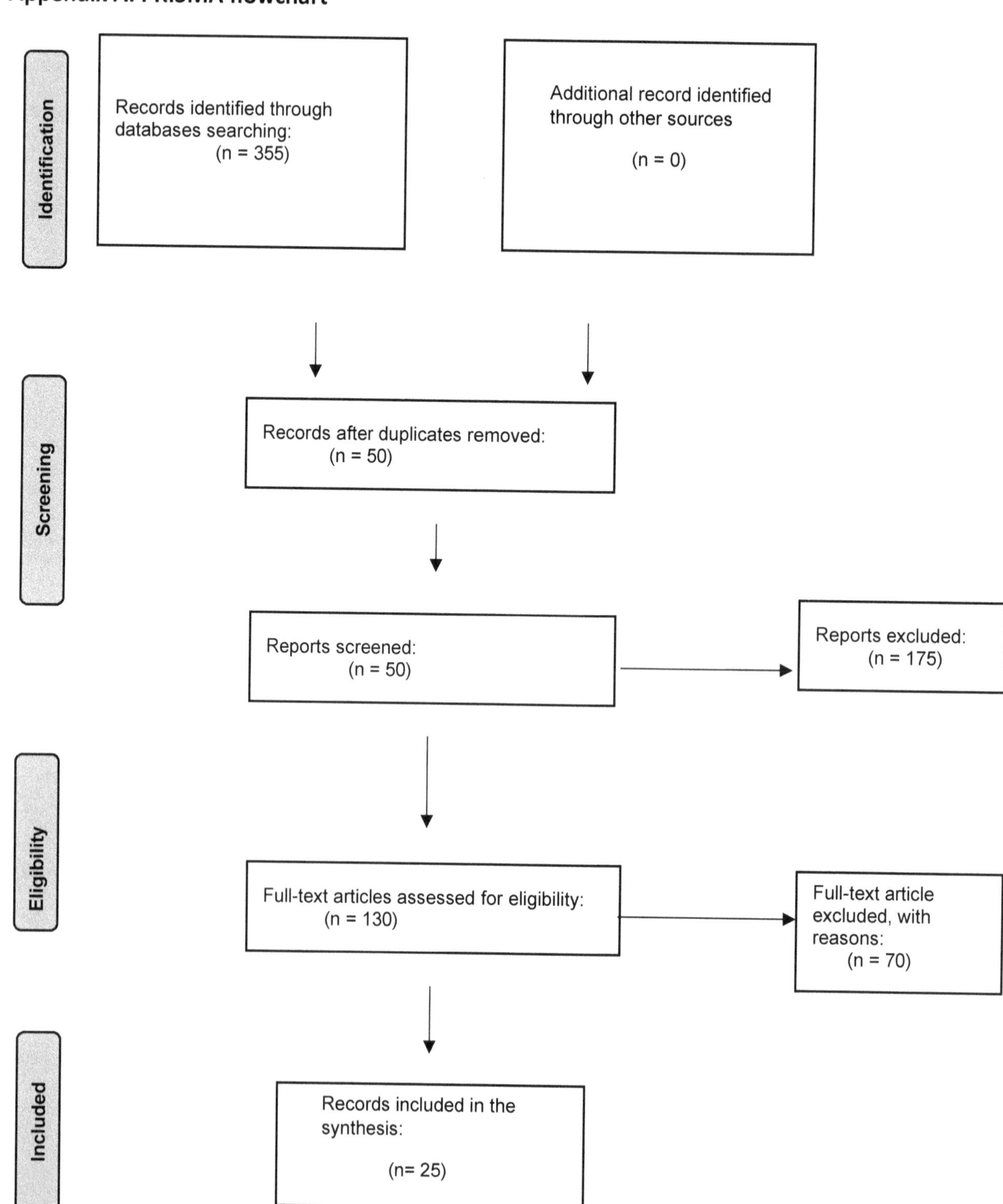

Feature Engineering for a MIL-STD-1553B LSTM Autoencoder Anomaly Detector

Dakotah Soucy[1] **and Brian Lachine**[2]
[1]Director Technical Airworthiness and Engineering Support, Ottawa, Canada
[2]Royal Military College of Canada, Kingston, Canada

dakotah.soucy@forces.gc.ca
brian.lachine@rmc.ca

Abstract: The MIL-STD-1553B data bus protocol is used in both civilian and military aircraft to enable communications between subsystems. These interconnected subsystems are responsible for core services such as communications, flow of instrument data and aircraft control. With aircraft modernization, threat vectors are introduced through increased inter-connectivity internal and external to the aircraft. The resulting potential for exploitation introduces a requirement for an intrusion detection capability in order to maintain the integrity, availability and reliability of data transmitted using the MIL-STD-1553B protocol, safety of the aircraft and overall, to achieve mission assurance. Research in recent years has investigated signature, statistical and machine learning based solutions to detect attacks on MIL-STD-1553B buses. Of the different techniques, those based on machine learning have shown extremely good results. The aim of this research is to improve the performance of an existing Long Short-Term Memory Auto-Encoder by refining the feature engineering phase of its pipeline. The improvement in the detector's overall effectiveness was accomplished through feature engineering focused on feature generation and selection. Five different attack datasets were used as the starting point, consisting of four different denial of service attacks and one data integrity attack. From initial feature extraction of 155 features, two feature generation techniques were employed to create over 38,000 features as a starting point. Using five different MIL-STD-1553B datasets and three feature selection techniques, fifteen different Long Short-Term Memory Auto-Encoder models were created, trained and evaluated using common performance metrics and compared to those of the original anomaly detector. This research demonstrated marked performance improvement achieved by the feature engineering refinements made in comparison to those of the original model. Equally important, this research also showed a significant reduction in the number of features required to achieve this performance gain. In the context of miliary air operations, the ability to improve detection capabilities with less data is important to the technical solutions that contribute to the achievement of cyber mission assurance.

Keywords: MIL-STD-1553B, Anomaly Detection, Deep Learning, LSTM Autoencoder, Aviation Cybersecurity

1. Introduction

The MIL-STD-1553B data bus protocol is used to enable communications between subsystems in civilian and military aircraft. These subsystems, referred to as remote terminals (RTs) provide core aircraft services across the data bus. MIL-STD-1553B was introduced in 1978 and was designed for reliability and safety in an air-gapped environment. With aircraft modernization, threat vectors may be introduced through connections such as data links and maintenance diagnostic tools.

These additional threat vectors to the MIL-STD1553B data bus create an opportunity in which adversaries have the ability to exploit vulnerabilities in the MIL-STD1553B protocol. This potential for exploitation of the MIL-STD-1553B protocol introduces a requirement for Intrusion Detection System (IDS) in order to maintain the reliability of the MIL-STD-1553B protocol and safety of the aircraft. Both signature and anomaly-based IDS have recently been researched and provide viable options for monitoring vulnerabilities in the MIL-STD-1553B data bus introduced by these new threat vectors (Bedard, 2019; Genereux et al, 2020; Stan et al, 2020; Onodueze and Josyula, 2020; De Santo et al, 2021; Levy et al, 2022; Banks et all, 2022; Wrana et al, 2022; and Harlow, Lachine and Roberge, 2024).

This research focuses on the feature engineering component of a Long-Short Term Memory (LSTM) MIL-STD-1553B deep learning anomaly detector (Harlow, Lachine and Roberge, 2024) in order to improve its overall effectiveness. Feature generation and selection form the core of this effort.

2. MIL-STD-1553B

The MIL-STD-1553B standard was published in 1978 by the United States Department of Defense (DoD) and defines the mechanical, electrical and functional characteristics of a serial data bus. This standard defines a multi-point, serial communication bus between terminals controlled through a command and response protocol. The typical architecture for MIL-STD-1553B is shown in Figure 1, which consists of terminals connected through a dual redundant communications bus. The standard defines three distinct terminals:

1. Bus Controller (BC): The terminal responsible for initiating and directing information transfer on the bus.
2. Bus Monitor (BM): The terminal responsible for receiving and storing select bus traffic for use at a later time.
3. Remote Terminal (RT): Any terminal not operating as a BC or BM.

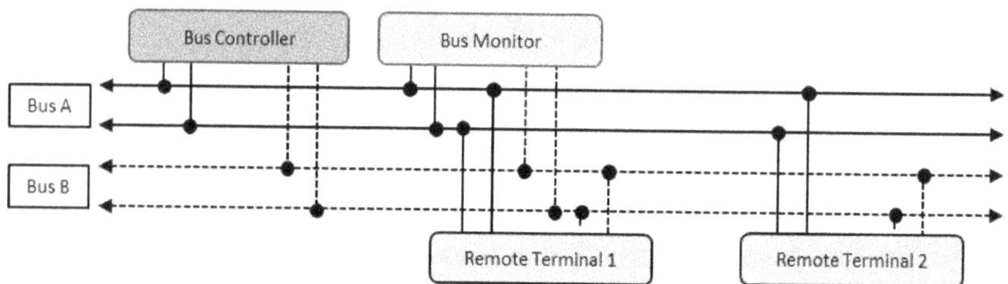

Figure 1: Example of MIL-STD-1553B bus topology with a BC, BM, and two RTs connected by a Dual Redundant Bus

Additionally, there is a maximum of 32 addresses on the MIL-STD-1553B bus. Address 31 is reserved for broadcast transactions and the remaining 0 to 30 addresses are assignable to RTs (U.S. DoD, 1978).

2.1 Data Link Layer

Data transfer on the bus is accomplished through messages which are comprised of 20-bit components called words. MIL-STD-1553B defines three word types: command, data and status. Figure 2 depicts the structure for each type of word. These words combine to form the larger messages and the standard defines two types of message formats: data messages and control messages.

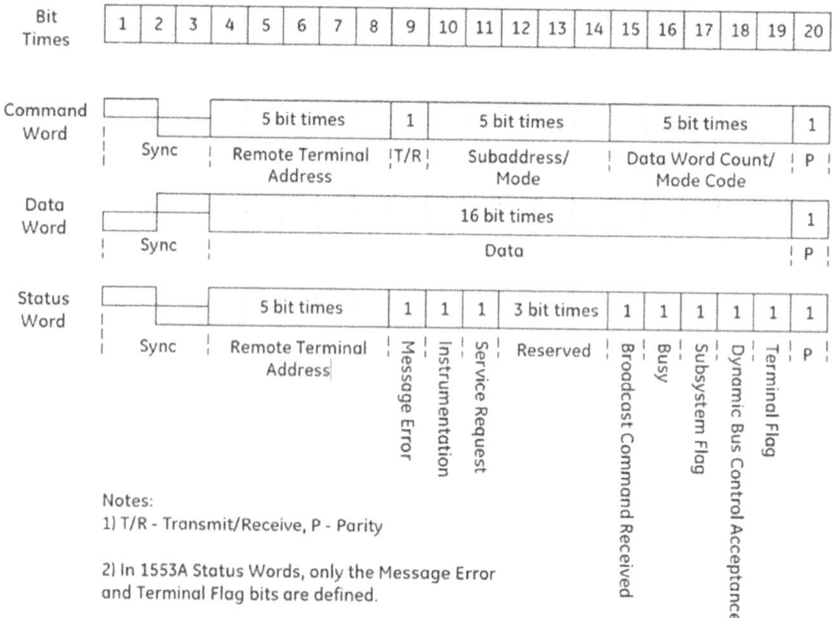

Figure 2: MIL-STD-1553B Word Formats (Abaco-Systems, 2019)

Data messages are initiated by the BC issuing command words on the bus followed by the RTs transmitting and/or receiving the data on the bus. All RTs which are connected to the data bus have the ability to read all messages transmitted, but only the addressed RTs are expected to carry out the command sent by the BC. These data messages are further separated into communications between specific RTs and broadcast communications. There are three data message types between specific RTs: BC to RT, RT to BC and RT to RT. Additionally, there are two broadcast data message types: BC to RTs and RT to RTs.

Control messages enable the BC to monitor and control the bus by issuing mode commands to the RTs. Control messages are a set of predefined functions and can contain command and data words, or solely mode codes from the BC. When directed to a specific RT, the response can contain status and data words, or solely a status word depending on the initial mode command word. When the control message is a broadcast message, there are no responses from the RT(s).

The BC directs all communications on the bus between RTs following a predefined schedule. This schedule contains two different types of message schedules: periodic and aperiodic. Periodic messages are transmitted at fixed time intervals according to the schedule. Aperiodic messages are conditional and therefore not sent at a fixed interval, although they still retain a fixed time slot in the schedule if they are to be transmitted. Collections of periodic and aperiodic messages are combined to form a minor frame within the schedule. Furthermore, a collection of minor frames forms the main schedule, also known as the major frame.

2.2 MIL-STD-1553B Attack Types and Outcomes

The MIL-STD-1553B data bus protocol was designed for reliability and safety of the system. As stated by the standard (U.S. DoD, 1978), all bus communications follow a predetermined cyclical, real-time schedule controlled by the BC. All RTs manufactured are expected to follow the standards defined by MIL-STD-1553B. However, adversaries are not constrained by these standards and can manipulate the protocol to their advantage to achieve their desired outcome.

Stan et al (2019) specify two main attack methods, message manipulation and behaviour manipulation:

1. Message manipulation: Modification of legitimate words that are transmitted over the data bus.
2. Behaviour manipulation: Altering the normal behaviour of a compromised component such as transmitting fake messages in an unusual timing or order.

Stan et al (2019) then outline three attack outcomes that can be accomplished via the two attack methods. These attack consequences are Denial of Service (DoS), data leakage, and data integrity violation. These attack consequences can be caused by either of the two attack methods discussed above.

3. Feature Engineering

A feature in the context of machine learning is simply an individual measurable property or characteristic of the object being observed (Elgendy, 2020). A feature is derived from raw data and acts as a key input into our model, denoting the importance of considering feature generation and selection.

3.1 Feature Generation

Feature generation is the process of creating new input variables from available data. There are many different approaches for feature engineering and they are specific to the type of data utilized. To generate features, McGaughey et al (2018) used of the processing module netAI (Zander and Williams, 2011) to create network specific flow features. Stan et al (2020) also implemented the use of a feature generation module called *Time Series FeatuRe Extraction on basis of Scalable Hypothesis* (tsfresh) by Christ et al. (2018) that allowed the calculation of features from time-series datasets. Self-Organizing Maps (SOM) were used by da Silva Rodrigues et al (2021) to generate new features with noted improvements in F1-Scores depending on the classification model used. Brownlee (2020) highlighted other feature generation methods such as polynomial transformation. Polynomial transformation utilizes simple mathematical operations to create additional features that may transform the original feature set into more effective features.

The polynomial transformation method was also utilized by McGaughey et al (2018) with results demonstrating that these generated features allowed the model to perform predictions with an improved detection rate and Matthew Correlation Coefficient (MCC) score.

3.2 Feature Selection

Feature selection has been an intrusion detection research focus for decades (Mukkamala and Sung, 2002; Thakkar and Lohiya, 2023) and is a technique of selecting a subset of features that will provide the most relevant data for input into the model (Brownlee, 2020). Feature selection can be grouped into two main categories; unsupervised and supervised. Supervised feature selection is used in this research and can be further grouped into three categories; intrinsic, wrapper and filter methods (Guyon and Elisseeff, 2003). Intrinsic feature selection refers to machine learning models that have embedded processes for selecting the best features, such as Least Absolute Shrinkage and Selection Operator (LASSO) which uses penalization functions or decision trees

(Muthukrishnan and Rohini, 2016). The wrapper feature selection method recursively selects a subset of the features, trains the model on these features then evaluates the performance El Aboudi and Benhlima, 2016). Lastly, the filter method selects features independent of the machine learning algorithm, and instead uses statistical methods to determine which features to use (Abujazoh et al, 2023).

4. Design

In order to understand how model effectiveness may be impacted by feature engineering, the entire pipeline for a deep learning anomaly detector needs to be designed and constructed. The same MIL-STD-1553B datasets and general model used by Harlow, Lachine and Roberge (2024) were used as the starting point to which two feature generation techniques and three feature selection techniques were added. The first feature generation method chosen was polynomial expansion that leverages the *sklearn* library. The second technique is based on time series characteristics using *tsfresh*, an application also used by Stan et al (2019). After feature generation, selecting the most useful features would then need to be conducted. The feature selection methods selected are Analysis of Variance (ANOVA), Fast Orthogonal Search (FOS) (Korenberg and Paarmann, 1989; McGaughey et al, 2018) and Predictive Power Score (PPS) (Wetschoreck, 2020, Demertzis et al, 2021). The evaluation of the models utilizes common machine learning model evaluation metrics.

4.1 Data Collection and Munging

The raw data collected by Harlow, Lachine and Roberge (2024) forms the datasets used for this research and includes both baseline data and anomalous data. The anomalous data was created using the evaluation tool created by Paquet (2014). The datasets are further divided into two main groups based on anomalous or attack types: DoS and data integrity violation. These datasets have been collected using the Abaco BusTools-1553 software suite in a simulated aircraft environment. Abaco BusTools-1553 records data bus traffic in the Bus Monitor Data Files Extended (BMDX) message format. Within each of the n messages, the data contained in the words is in the format outlined in Figure 3.

```
typedef struct api_bm_mbuf
    {
    BT_U32BIT            messno;                      // Message number (generated by API, 1-based)
    BT_U32BIT            int_status;                  // Interrupt status from board
    BT1553_TIME          time;                        // Time of message (48-bits, 1 us LSB)
    BT1553_COMMAND       command1;                    // 1553 command word #1 (Rx for RT→RT)
    BT_U16BIT            status_c1;                   // 1553 command word #1 error status
    BT1553_COMMAND       command2;                    // 1553 command word #2 (Tx for RT→RT)
    BT_U16BIT            status_c2;                   // 1553 command word #2 error status
    BT1553_BMRESPONSE    response1;                   // 1553 response time #1 (byte)
    BT1553_BMRESPONSE    response2;                   // 1553 response time #2 (byte)
    BT1553_STATUS        status1;                     // 1553 status word #1 (Transmit for RT→RT or
                                                      // Broadcast RT→RT)
    BT_U16BIT            status_s1;                   // 1553 status word #1 error status
    BT1553_STATUS        status2;                     // 1553 status word #2 (Receive for RT→RT,
                                                      // NULL for Broadcast RT→RT)
    BT_U16BIT            status_s2;                   // 1553 status word #2 error status
    BT_U16BIT            value[BT1553_MBUFCOUNT];     // 1553 data words
    BT_U8BIT             status[BT1553_MBUFCOUNT];    // 1553 status for data words
    }
API_BM_MBUF;
```

Figure 3: Abaco BusTools-1553 BMDX Message Structure (reformatted from Abaco-Systems, 2019)

The data structure fields from in Figure 3, were munged to provide more granular information such as RT address, transmit/receive, sub-address and number of words to better correlate to how words are typically presented in MIL-STD-1553B. This is accomplished by separating the data contained in the command word(s), data word(s) and/or status word(s) into their respective formats as outlined in section 2.1.

4.2 Feature Engineering

After data collection and munging, feature engineering is the next pipeline step in order to prepare the data for use in the anomaly detection model. This step first consists of feature generation followed by feature selection as outlined in Figure 4.

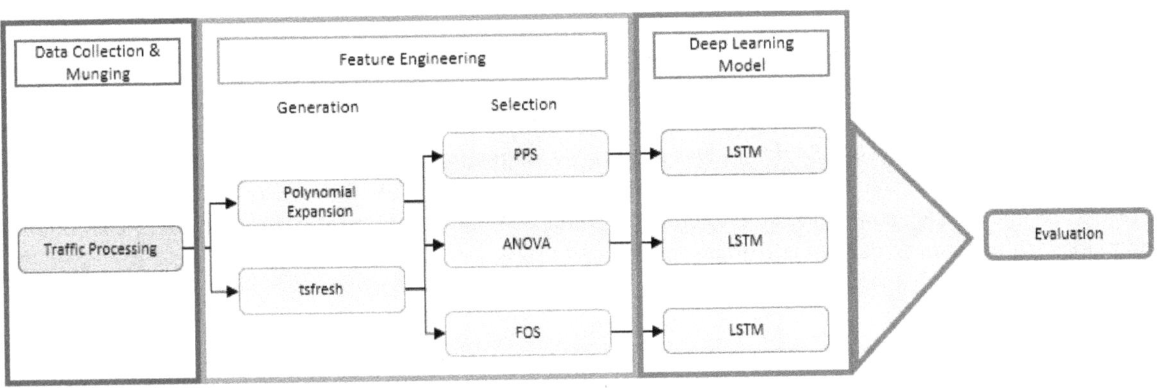

Figure 4: Overview of Feature Engineering Focused Pipeline

4.2.1 *Feature Generation*

In this step, the primary features created in the data collection and munging step are used to generate multiple new features. The first method of feature generation utilizes the scikit learn *sklearn.preprocessing.PolynomialFeatures* module (Buitnick et all, 2013). This module generates a new feature matrix with all polynomial combinations of the features up to the degree specified. For the purpose of this research the maximum polynomial degree of two is used due to processing speed and resource consumption. The second method utilizes the python tool *tsfresh*. *tsfresh* is a python package that generates time-series features using 78 different feature calculation modules (Christ et al, 2018). *tsfresh* does this by running the different calculation modules with the data from the features in the dataset, and then creates additional features based on the results from the calculation modules.

4.2.2 *Feature Selection*

After feature generation, feature selection is used in order to select a smaller number of features to be used as input into each discrete run of the learning model. The feature selection methods ANOVA, PPS and FOS are used to select a subset of features in parallel from the same starting features created in the previous phase.

4.3 Evaluation of Deep Learning Model

In order to measure the effectiveness of the anomaly detection method, the results were evaluated using multiple methods. The methods utilized metrics derived from the confusion matrix: precision, recall, accuracy, Area Under Receiver Operating Characteristic Curve (AUROCC), and Matthews Correlation Coefficient (MCC). These metrics were used to measure the performance of the anomaly detector. These results were then compared against recent work in the field, specifically the original LSTM detector by Harlow, Lachine and Roberge (2024).

5. Results

The data collected comprised both of baseline and anomalous datasets. All of the datasets were representative of an aircraft in the cruise phase of flight. There was a total of three baseline datasets collected, all of which utilized the same master schedule. Through investigation of these three benign datasets and as expected, it was confirmed that they were identical. As such, only one baseline dataset was selected for use in this experiment as the others would not contribute any additional information. The anomalous data collected comprised of a total of five datasets across two attack categories as outlined section 2.2:

1) DoS
   a) NetDisrupt statusword 250820 (*Disrupt*): Network *disrupt*ion
   b) RT-SA deny statusword rt18 sa32 250820 (*Deny*): RT deny
   c) RT-*SA* deny statusword rt18 sa1 250820 (*SA deny*): RT subaddress deny
   d) RT-*SA* deny statusword rt18 sa1 rec2 250820 (*SA deny 2*): RT subaddress deny

2) Data Integrity Violation
   a) *Hijack* rt18 sa6 w56 250820 (*Hijack*): RT *hijack*

These anomalous datasets are named using the following convention: the first part is the type of attack, followed by the associated RT details and ending in the day, month, year recorded. In the remainder of this paper, these datasets are referred to by their abbreviated forms outlined in parentheses above. Through exploratory data analysis, it was noted that the *SA deny* and *SA deny 2* datasets contained very similar data. As such, *SA deny* was utilized for feature selection and *SA deny 2* was used solely for generating model performance metrics. Both the baseline and anomalous datasets contain just over 1 million MIL-STD-1553B messages each. The anomalous datasets are imbalanced, containing little anomalous traffic compared to normal traffic. The specific amount of anomalous traffic for each dataset is as follows: *Disrupt* - 17.2%, *Deny* - 2.1%, *SA deny* - 5.7%, *SA deny 2* - 4.2%, and *Hijack* - 17.2%.

5.1 Feature Generation

A complete list of 155 primary features was created after the data munging was completed. Next, the feature generation techniques were then applied to these munged datasets. Polynomial expansion utilizing the *sklearn.preprocessing.PolynomialFeatures* tool created a total of 12,247 derived features from the existing 155 primary features. *tsfresh* created an additional 26,071 derived features from the existing 155 primary features. Additionally, *tsfresh* automatically eliminates generated features that contain no additional information, such as no variance in the values generated. Adding the features from the two generation techniques to the original primary feature set resulted in a total of 38,473 unique features.

5.2 Feature Selection and Models

After creation of the extended datasets, the feature selection techniques were implemented to determine the features to be used for each model. Model development consisted of two approaches; attack specific and general. The first approach was to use a specific model for each attack type as shown in Figure 5.

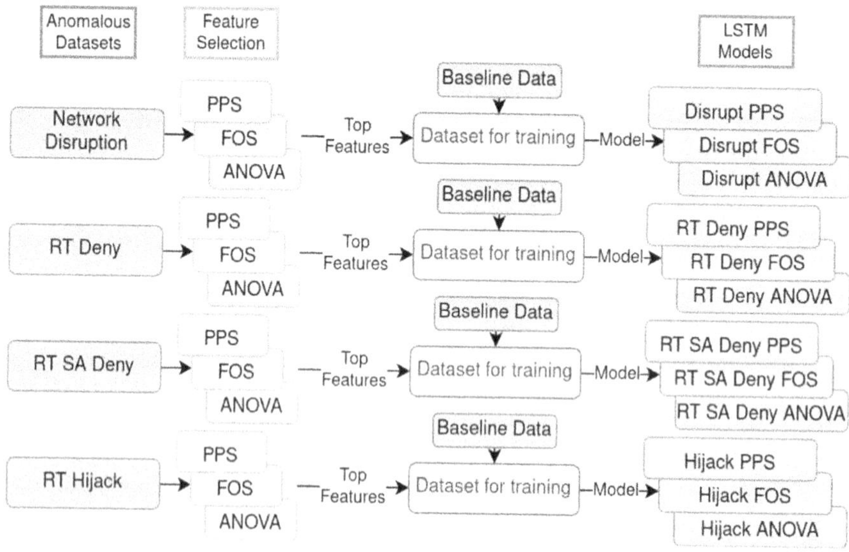

Figure 5: Attack and Feature Selection Specific Models

Each labelled attack type dataset was fed into the three feature selection technique tools as outlined in Figure 5. The top features output from each feature selection technique were then used to define the features selected from the baseline dataset to train the models. The process for selecting the top features utilized elbow curves. Upon completion, there was a specific model for each attack type and each feature selection method, resulting in 12 specific models.

The second approach was to create a general model by using the three feature selection techniques to select the top features for each attack type. These top features for each attack type were then combined and used as the features from the baseline to train the general model. This resulted in a total of 3 general models, one for each feature selection method. The purpose of the general model was to compare the results of a general model to the specific model to evaluate the ability for a more streamlined approach for feature selection and model generation. The number of top features for all models was determined through the analysis of elbow curves.

5.3 Model Performance

The resulting performance metrics of the fifteen models were then compared to the research originally conducted by Harlow, Lachine and Roberge (2024) which demonstrated an overall improvement in the effectiveness of the anomaly detection pipeline as illustrated below in Figure 6.

General Models

Deny

	original	anova	pps	fos
Accuracy	0.9968	0.9992	0.9795	0.9763
Precision	0.8606	0.9977	0.8231	0.4937
Recall	0.8981	0.9825	0.5005	0.4990
AUROCC	0.8981	0.9825	0.5005	0.4990
MCC	0.7577	0.9800	0.0248	-0.0050

SA Deny

	original	anova	pps	fos
Accuracy	0.9913	0.9961	0.9465	0.9442
Precision	0.5001	0.9963	0.8615	0.4771
Recall	0.5433	0.9655	0.5006	0.4990
AUROCC	0.5433	0.9655	0.5006	0.4990
MCC	0.0042	0.9613	0.0290	-0.0098

SA Deny 2

	original	anova	pps	fos
Accuracy	0.9930	0.9959	0.9598	0.9580
Precision	0.5000	0.9964	0.7656	0.4844
Recall	0.4965	0.9506	0.5001	0.4993
AUROCC	0.4965	0.9506	0.5001	0.4993
MCC	-0.0004	0.9459	0.0100	-0.0068

Disrupt

	original	anova	pps	fos
Accuracy	0.7918	0.9927	0.8538	0.8387
Precision	0.5545	0.9954	0.9096	0.4495
Recall	0.5153	0.9755	0.5029	0.4938
AUROCC	0.5153	0.9755	0.5029	0.4938
MCC	0.0577	0.9707	0.0689	-0.0355

Hijack

	original	anova	pps	fos
Accuracy	0.9833	0.9710	0.9957	0.9951
Precision	0.5769	0.4979	0.4979	0.6861
Recall	0.8212	0.4880	0.5000	0.6164
AUROCC	0.8212	0.4880	0.5000	0.6164
MCC	0.3143	-0.0100	-0.0002	0.2944

Highest performing technique within attack category

Specific Models

Deny

	original	anova	pps	fos
Accuracy	0.9968	0.9996	0.9795	0.9999
Precision	0.8606	0.9978	0.7897	0.9981
Recall	0.8981	0.9913	0.5001	0.9989
AUROCC	0.8981	0.9913	0.5001	0.9989
MCC	0.7577	0.9891	0.0129	0.9971

SA Deny

	original	anova	pps	fos
Accuracy	0.9913	0.9924	0.9465	0.9940
Precision	0.5001	0.9946	0.9590	0.9955
Recall	0.5433	0.9307	0.5003	0.9455
AUROCC	0.5433	0.9307	0.5003	0.9455
MCC	0.0042	0.9231	0.0236	0.9396

SA Deny 2

	original	anova	pps	fos
Accuracy	0.9930	0.9930	0.9598	0.9951
Precision	0.5000	0.9950	0.9513	0.9962
Recall	0.4965	0.9142	0.5004	0.9402
AUROCC	0.4965	0.9142	0.5004	0.9402
MCC	-0.0004	0.9056	0.0268	0.9347

Disrupt

	original	anova	pps	fos
Accuracy	0.7918	0.9966	0.8530	0.8532
Precision	0.5545	0.9976	0.4265	0.7735
Recall	0.5153	0.9889	0.5000	0.5013
AUROCC	0.5153	0.9889	0.5000	0.5013
MCC	0.0577	0.9864	0.0000	0.0376

Hijack

	original	anova	pps	fos
Accuracy	0.9833	0.9967	0.9954	0.9943
Precision	0.5769	0.7984	0.5196	0.5246
Recall	0.8212	0.8262	0.5017	0.5093
AUROCC	0.8212	0.8262	0.5017	0.5093
MCC	0.3143	0.6240	0.0115	0.0303

Red Text Highest performing technique between both specific and general model

Figure 6: Results for Specific and General Models

The metrics used included accuracy, precision, recall, AUROCC and MCC. To obtain the evaluation metrics, each anomalous dataset was processed through the respective LSTM autoencoder, which was trained on the baseline traffic. Scores were recorded for each anomalous dataset and their respective models based on reconstruction error. The green highlighted cells indicate the feature selection technique that resulted in the highest performance for each attack in both the general and specific models and the red text indicates the technique that resulted in the highest performance between the general and specific models. The *original* columns refer to the results from Harlow, Lachine and Roberge (2024).

5.4 Features Selected

There were few to no selected features shared between the *hijack* dataset and the *Deny*, *SA deny* and *Disrupt* datasets. Figure 7 shows an example of this, where the blue highlighted fields represent common features between at least two datasets within the ANOVA selection technique. Additionally, primary features were only selected by all feature selection techniques on average 13% of the time, as illustrated by the large number of generated features shown in Figure 7. The fact that the majority of the selected features were generated features highlights the importance of feature generation.

NetDisrupt_statusword_250820_top_10
CMD1-addr BT1553_INT_INVALID_WORD_CMD_1
BT1553_INT_TWO_BUS_CMD_1 BT1553_INT_INVALID_WORD_CMD_1
BT1553_INT_INVALID_WORD_CMD_1
BT1553_INT_INVALID_WORD_CMD_1^2
CMD1-addr BT1553_INT_MID_BIT_CMD_1
CMD1-subaddr BT1553_INT_INVALID_WORD_CMD_1
28_large_standard_deviation__r_0.2
4_large_standard_deviation__r_0.30000000000000004
4_large_standard_deviation__r_0.35000000000000003
4_large_standard_deviation__r_0.4

RT-SAdeny_statusword_rt18_sa32_250820_top_10
CMD1-addr BT1553_INT_INVALID_WORD_CMD_1
CMD1-addr BT1553_INT_MID_BIT_CMD_1
BT1553_INT_MID_BIT_CMD_1^2
BT1553_INT_MID_BIT_CMD_1
BT1553_INT_MID_BIT_CMD_1 BT1553_INT_INVALID_WORD_CMD_1
BT1553_INT_INVALID_WORD_CMD_1^2
BT1553_INT_INVALID_WORD_CMD_1
CMD1-addr BT1553_INT_LOW_WORD_CMD_1
CMD1-numword BT1553_INT_INVALID_WORD_CMD_1
CMD1-subaddr BT1553_INT_MID_BIT_CMD_1

RT-Sadeny_statusword_rt18_sa1_250820_top_10
BT1553_INT_INVALID_WORD_CMD_1
BT1553_INT_INVALID_WORD_CMD_1^2
BT1553_INT_MID_BIT_CMD_1
BT1553_INT_MID_BIT_CMD_1^2
BT1553_INT_MID_BIT_CMD_1 BT1553_INT_INVALID_WORD_CMD_1
CMD1-addr BT1553_INT_INVALID_WORD_CMD_1
BT1553_INT_LOW_WORD_CMD_1 BT1553_INT_INVALID_WORD_CMD_1
BT1553_INT_LOW_WORD_CMD_1^2
BT1553_INT_LOW_WORD_CMD_1
CMD1-addr BT1553_INT_MID_BIT_CMD_1

Hijack_rt18_sa6_w56_250820_top_10
CMD1-TR STS1-Reserved
CMD1-TR STS1-SerReq
CMD1-TR STS1-Error
CMD1-TR STS1-BCRecv
CMD1-TR STS1-Inst
CMD1-TR STS1-Busy
STS1-BCRecv BT1553_INT_BIT_COUNT_STS_1
STS1-Error BT1553_INT_BIT_COUNT_STS_1
STS1-Reserved BT1553_INT_BIT_COUNT_STS_1
STS1-Reserved BT1553_INT_BAD_RTADDR_STS_1

Common feature between at least two datasets

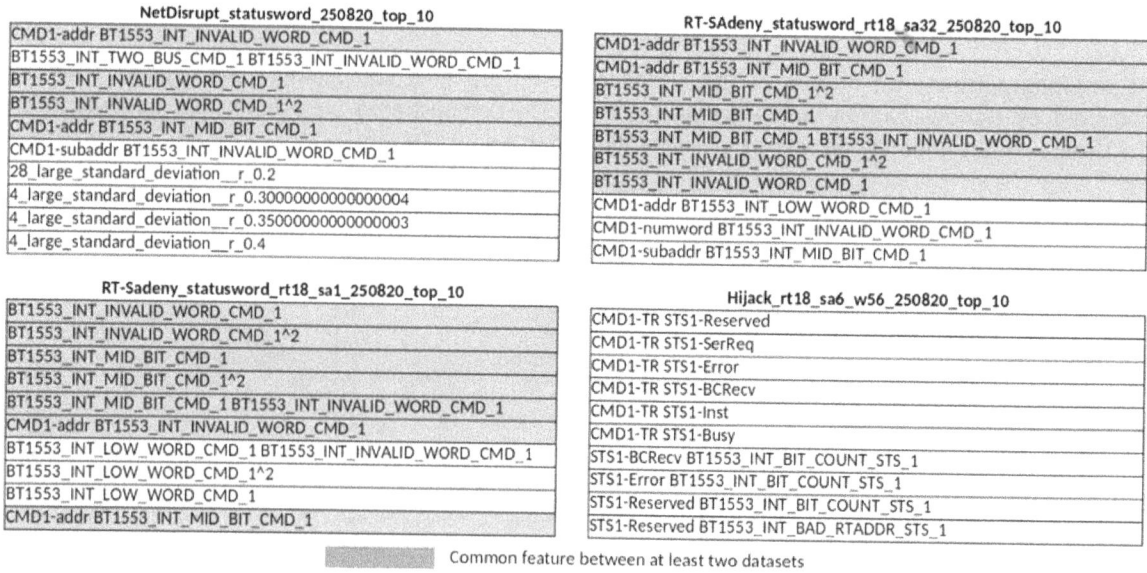

Figure 7: Top 10 Features Selected by ANOVA

6. Discussion

The resulting performance metrics of the fifteen models were then compared to the research conducted by Harlow, Lachine and Roberge (2024) which demonstrated that there was an overall improvement in the effectiveness of the anomaly detection pipeline. These metrics included accuracy, precision, recall, AUROCC and MCC.

6.1 ANOVA

The ANOVA general model outperformed all other general models in the DoS type attack (*Disrupt*, *Deny*, *SA deny*, *SA deny 2*). The specific ANOVA models: *Disrupt* and *Hijack* outperformed all other specific models for these same attack types, as seen in Figure 6. The *Deny* and *Disrupt* specific models performed marginally better than the general model, although in the case of the *SA deny* dataset, the general model performed better by 4%. Furthermore, the *Deny*, *SA deny*, *SA deny 2*, and *disrupt* datasets utilizing the general model obtained similar results. This is attributed to the four datasets utilizing the DoS attack method, and as such would contain similar style traffic. Due to this result, it shows that these four attacks could be combined into a single DoS model, allowing a more streamlined pipeline while still yielding effective results when compared to the model by Harlow, Lachine and Roberge (2024). In the case of the *Hijack* dataset metrics, the specific *Hijack* model significantly outperformed the general *Hijack* model.

6.2 FOS

FOS performed well for the specific models: *Deny* and *SA deny*, and performed relatively poorly for the *Disrupt* and *Hijack* models. FOS also performed poorly for all of the general models as seen in Figure 6. Additionally, the remainder of the FOS model's metrics demonstrated poor performance. The feature scores from FOS resulted in an elbow curve that typically suggested only one feature, whereas the majority of other feature selection methods suggested 5 or more. Due to the elbow method only suggesting a single feature, it is suggested that other methods be explored for selecting the cutoff for the number of features. Except for precision, the metrics from the *Disrupt* dataset demonstrated similar performance between the general and specific models, although with poor performance. Finally, with the metrics from the *Hijack* dataset, the general model outperformed the specific model, although again with overall poor performance. These results highlight the possible need for more anomalous traffic to be used for selection of the features.

6.3 PPS

PPS related performance metrics did not perform well compared to ANOVA and PPS. Although on closer analysis of the specific PPS models, three distinct grouping of a larger Mean Absolute Error (MAE) value were easily identified. Therefore, reducing the MAE threshold for anomalous traffic in the model or utilizing other methods such as standard deviation could enable effective detection for the PPS models.

7. Conclusion

This research extended the original work by Harlow, Lachine and Roberge (2024) by focusing on feature generation and selection. The approach in this work resulted in fifteen distinct models based on the original design, results were calculated using the following performance metrics: accuracy, precision, recall, AUROCC and MCC. These metrics demonstrated the improved performance solely from this focus on feature engineering. The comparison of the results revealed there was a marked improvement in 8 of the 15 models created during this research. In addition, the improved results can be achieved with fewer features that in turn reduces overall processing time. These results highlight the promise of this improved model and the future work needed to develop an in-production solution for military aircraft.

7.1 Future Work

The next phase of this research will focus on creating anomalous datasets with an increased number and variety of attacks that aim to provide three related improvements. First, a more balanced dataset will improve the feature selection phase by reducing potential bias and generating a clearer decision boundary. Second, increased diversity in attacks will explore the ability to create more general models at the outset, reducing overall processing overhead and set the conditions for applying this model to different modes of flight. Third, a more balanced dataset would provide additional events to be categorized as anomalous, allowing for a more comprehensive validation of the detection methodology.

References

Abaco-Systems (2019) "Software Reference Manual BusTools/1553-API", Publication No. 1500-038 Rev. 5.12.

Abujazoh, M., Al-Darras, D., Hamad, N.A., Al-Sharaeh, S. (2023), "Feature Selection for High-Dimensional Imbalanced Malware Data Using Filter and Wrapper Selection Methods", International Conference on Information Technology (ICIT), pp. 196–201, https://doi.org/10.1109/ICIT58056.2023.10226049.

Banks, J., Kerr, R., Ding, S., Zulkernine, M. (2022), "SV1DUR: A Real-Time MIL-STD-1553 Bus Simulator with Flight Subsystems for Cyber-Attack Modeling and Assessments", 2022 IEEE Military Communications Conference (MILCOM), pp. 522–528, https://doi.org/10.1109/MILCOM55135.2022.10017663.

Bedard, C. (2019), "An Application of Network Security Monitoring to the MIL-STD-1553B Data Bus", MASc Thesis, Royal Military College of Canada, https://espace.rmc.ca/jspui/handle/11264/1823.

Brownlee, J. (2020), *Data preparation for machine learning: data cleaning, feature selection, and data transforms in Python*", Machine Learning Mastery, 1st ed.

Christ, M., Braun, N., Neuffer, J., Kempa-Liehr, A.W. (2018) "Time Series FeatuRe Extraction on basis of Scalable Hypothesis tests (tsfresh – A Python package)", Neurocomputing, 307, pp. 72–77, https://doi.org/10.1016/j.neucom.2018.03.067.

Da Silva Rodrigues, E., Martins, D.M.L. and Buarque de Lima Neto, F. (2021), "Automatic Feature Engineering Using Self-Organizing Maps", IEEE Latin American Conference on Computational Intelligence (LA-CCI), pp. 1–6, https://doi.org/10.1109/LA-CCI48322.2021.9769788.

De Santo, D., Malavenda, C.S., Romano, S.P., Vecchio, C. (2021) "Exploiting the MIL-STD-1553 avionic data bus with an active cyber device", Computers & Security, 100, p. 102097, https://doi.org/10.1016/j.cose.2020.102097.

Demertzis, K., Tsiknas, K., Takezis, D., Skianis, C. and Iliadis, L. (2021), "Darknet Traffic Big-Data Analysis and Network Management for Real-Time Automating of the Malicious Intent Detection Process by a Weight Agnostic Neural Networks Framework", Electronics, 10(7), p. 781, https://doi.org/10.3390/electronics10070781.

El Aboudi, N. and Benhlima, L. (2016), "Review on wrapper feature selection approaches", International Conference on Engineering & MIS (ICEMIS), pp. 1–5, https://doi.org/10.1109/ICEMIS.2016.7745366.

Elgendy, M. (2020) *Deep Learning for Vision Systems,* Manning, New York.

Généreux, S.J.J., Lai, A., Fowles, C., Roberge, V., Vigeant, G.P.M., Paquet, J. (2020), "MAIDENS: MIL-STD-1553 Anomaly-Based Intrusion Detection System Using Time-Based Histogram Comparison", IEEE Transactions on Aerospace and Electronic Systems, 56(1), pp. 276–284, https://doi.org/10.1109/TAES.2019.2914519.

Guyon, I. and Elisseeff, A. (2003) "An introduction to variable and feature selection", The Journal of Machine Learning Research 3, pp. 1157–1182, https://dl.acm.org/doi/10.5555/944919.944968.

Harlow, A., Lachine, B. and Roberge, V. (2024), "Anomaly Detection for the MIL-STD-1553B Multiplex Data Bus Using an LSTM Autoencoder", 19th International Conference on Cyber Warfare and Security, to be published.

He, D, Liu, X., Zheng, J., Chan, S., Zhu, S., Min, W. and Guizani, N. (2020), "'A Lightweight and Intelligent PPSIntrusion Detection System for Integrated Electronic Systems", IEEE Network, 34(4), pp. 173–179, https://doi.org/10.1109/MNET.001.1900480.

Khraisat, A., Gondal, I., Vamplew, P. and Kamruzzaman, J. (2019), "Survey of intrusion detection systems: techniques, datasets and challenges", Cybersecurity 2, Article 20, https://doi.org/10.1186/s42400-019-0038-7.

Korenberg, M.J. and Paarmann, L.D. (1989), "Applications of fast orthogonal search: Time-series analysis and resolution of signals in noise", Annals of Biomedical Engineering, 17(3), pp. 219–231, https://doi.org/10.1007/BF02368043.

Levy, E., Maman, N., Shabtai, A., and Elovici, Y. (2022), "AnoMili: Spoofing Prevention and Explainable Anomaly Detection for the 1553 Military Avionic Bus", https://doi.org/10.48550/arXiv.2202.06870.

McGaughey, D., Semeniuk, T., Smith, R. and Knight, S. (2018), "A systematic approach of feature selection for encrypted network traffic classification", IEEE International Systems Conference (SysCon), pp. 1–8, https://doi.org/10.1109/SYSCON.2018.8369567.

Mukkamala, S. and Sung, A.H. (2002), "Identifying key features for intrusion detection using neural networks", in Proceedings of the 15th international conference on Computer communication (ICCC), pp. 1132–1138.

Muthukrishnan, R. and Rohini, R. (2016), "LASSO: A feature selection technique in predictive modeling for machine learning", IEEE International Conference on Advances in Computer Applications (ICACA), pp. 18–20, https://doi.org/10.1109/ICACA.2016.7887916.

Onodueze, F. and Josyula, D. (2020), "Anomaly Detection on MIL-STD-1553 Dataset using Machine Learning Algorithms", IEEE 19th International Conference on Trust, Security and Privacy in Computing and Communications (TrustCom), pp. 592–598, https://doi.org/10.1109/TrustCom50675.2020.00084.

Paquet J. (2014) "Uncovering MIL-STD-1553 vulnerabilities: exploitability of military aircraft networks", MASc Thesis, Royal Military College of Canada.

Stan, O. et al. (2019), "On the Security of MIL-STD-1553 Communication Bus", in B. Hamid et al. (eds) Security and Safety Interplay of Intelligent Software Systems. Cham: Springer International Publishing (Lecture Notes in Computer Science), pp. 153–171, https://doi.org/10.1007/978-3-030-16874-2_11.

Stan, O. et al. (2020) 'Intrusion Detection System for the MIL-STD-1553 Communication Bus', IEEE Transactions on Aerospace and Electronic Systems, 56(4), pp. 3010–3027, https://doi.org/10.1109/TAES.2019.2961824.

Thakkar, A. and Lohiya, R. (2023), "Fusion of statistical importance for feature selection in Deep Neural Network-based Intrusion Detection System", Information Fusion, 90, pp. 353–363, https://doi.org/10.1016/j.inffus.2022.09.026.

U. S. DoD (1978), "MIL-STD-1553B, Aircraft Internal Time Division Command/Response Multiplex Data Bus", https://quicksearch.dla.mil/qsDocDetails.aspx?ident_number=36973

Wetschoreck, F. (2020), "RIP correlation. Introducing the Predictive Power Score", *towardsdatascience.com*, https://towardsdatascience.com/rip-correlation-introducing-the-predictive-power-score-3d90808b9598.

Wrana, M.M., Elsayed, M., Lounis, K., Mansour, Z., Ding, S. and Zulkernine, M. (2022), "OD1NF1ST: True Skip Intrusion Detection and Avionics Network Cyber-attack Simulation", ACM Transactions on Cyber-Physical Systems, 6(4), p. 33:1-33:27, https://doi.org/10.1145/3551893.

Zander, S. and Williams, N. (2011) "netAI - Network Traffic based Application Identification", http://caia.swin.edu.au/urp/dstc/netai/.

Navigating the Cyber Front: Belarus' State Control and Emerging Cyber Threats

Darius Štitilis[1], Marius Laurinaitis[1], Inga Malinauskaitė-van de Castel[1] and Matthew Warren[2]

[1]Mykolas Romeris University, Vilnius, Lithuania

[2]RMIT Univeristy, Melbourne, Australia

stitilis@mruni.eu

laurinaitis@mruni.eu

inga.malinauskaite@mruni.eu

matthew.warren2@rmit.edu.au

Abstract: This paper provides a comprehensive overview of the cyber landscape in Belarus, with a focus on the Belarus government's use of cyber activities from an offensive and defensive context, the emergence of opposition cyber activities, and the broader implications for cybersecurity and legal compliance. In the course of the research, researchers try to assess Belarus as a source of cyber-threats, both domestically and to neighbouring states (especially those supporting Ukraine). The first section of the paper outlines the Belarusian government's engagement in cybercrimes against its citizens, especially under President Lukashenko's regime, highlighting extensive online surveillance, repression, and the escalation of these activities following the 2020 presidential elections. In this political context, Belarus is also examined as a country initiating and/or contributing to Information Warfare activities, which are mainly directed at western countries. The second section of the paper delves into Belarus's cybersecurity legal framework, examining various national strategies and concepts, the absence of a formal cybersecurity strategy, and the focus on 'information security' as part of national security. The third section presents case studies of cyber activities in Belarus, contrasting government-backed hacking efforts with those of opposition groups like the Belarus Cyber Partisans. It explores the Partisans' attacks on state infrastructure and information leaks as a form of protest against the government, and the pro-government hackers' disinformation / information campaigns website defacements, and data breaches, particularly targeting Ukraine. This section highlights the evolving nature of cyber conflict in Belarus, where both government and opposition forces use cyber tools for political ends, reflecting broader geopolitical tensions in the region. This part of the report compares the Belarusian pro-government hacktivist and Cyber Partisans groups, their activities and manifestations within the country (inside), as well as the cyber threats they pose to foreign countries. The article attempts to answer the question of what kind of threat Belarus as a country poses in the context of cybersecurity, hybrid-cyber threats. This country is often included in Russian hybrid-cyber threats strategies, Belarus entities also work with Russian and sometimes Chinese groups in undertaking cyber activities against other countries.

Keywords: Cyber Security, Belarus, Hackers, Fake News, Hybrid Threats and State Based Attacks.

1. Introduction

Belarus, located in Eastern Europe, is a landlocked country bordered by Russia to the northeast, Ukraine to the south, Poland to the west, and Lithuania and Latvia to the northwest. Covering an area of approximately 207,600 square kilometres. As of 2023, Belarus has an estimated population of around 9.4 million people. Belarusian and Russian is the official language, reflecting the country's deep historical and cultural ties with Russia.

Belarus maintains close geopolitical ties with Russia, often described as a key ally in Eastern Europe, sharing strong political, economic, and military connections, including a formal union state agreement with Russia. This relationship significantly influences Belarus' foreign policy and regional dynamics, particularly in its stance towards NATO and the European Union.

Belarus is closely aligned with Russia, has emerged as a notable source of hybrid threats within Eastern Europe, particularly in the cyber domain. Hybrid threats from Belarus to Eastern Europe involve a combination of conventional and non-conventional tactics designed to undermine and destabilize nations[1]. Belarus is aligned more closely with Russian strategic goals, Belarus will likely develop more severe hybrid threats to its European neighbourhood (Rusinaite V, 2021).

[1] Disinformation campaigns, cyber attacks, economic pressures, military posturing, political interference, etc.

2. Belarus Cyber Background

The Belarusian authorities have consistently committed many crimes including cybercrimes against its own citizens, especially in the context of the regime of President Alexander Lukashenko. Since Lukashenko became President in 1994, he has established a control mechanism involving extensive online surveillance and repression of citizens, particularly those who oppose the regime (O'Neill, 2021). The situation has escalated following the disputed presidential elections in August 2020, which led to widespread protests and opposition to Lukashenko's rule. The government's response to these protests has included a violent crackdown on peaceful dissent, underlining the regime's oppressive tactics against its own citizens.

In the first decade of the 21st century, internet censorship in Belarus developed as an effective tool of control against political opponents. State-sponsored DDoS attacks against civil society have become an internal crisis that threatens not only freedom of expression in Belarus, but also the integrity of internet resources across Europe. The ongoing cyber conflict between state and non-state actors in Belarus is analogous to the cyber struggle between the Russian government and its internal enemies. On 9 September 2001, at 12.00, Belarusian web developers clashed with the authorities for the first time – on the day of the presidential elections. The national telecommunications company Beltelecom, the monopoly service provider in this area, deliberately blocked access to several popular political websites. The next day internet censorship started. From a technical point of view, such blocking of information is not a difficult task for a telecommunications monopoly and can be directed by the government as needed (Czosseck, Geers, 2009).

It must be pointed out that there was no legal basis for internet censorship within Belarus. Such censorship was in direct violation of the Belarusian Constitution (Disrupting systems is a crime under Belarusian law (Criminal code of Belarus, 1999)). The official explanation given by the Belarusian Ministry of Communications and the government controlled telecommunications company was that too many users were trying to access the websites in question at the same time, which led to the service being blocked.

Another example of such state cyber-censorship was the blocking of the popular Belarusian website Charter 97 (Pavlyuchenko, 2009). The Belarusian Ministry of Information published the official reasons for its decision to restrict access to the charter97.org website, claiming that the site disseminates information that could harm Belarus' national interests, as well as violating the Law on Mass Events and publishing material that has been identified as extremist. The basis for blocking the website was Article 38 of the "Law on Media", which has been repeatedly criticised by human rights activists as discriminatory and undemocratic.

The authorities in Belarus have consistently tried to suppress political criticism online internally and externally to Belarus. There is no legal basis for internet censorship in Belarus, in particular in relation to being critical of official online information sources. Only one case of official censorship can be found (officially acknowledged by the Belarusian government): in 2005, a pornography website run by a Russian citizen was blocked on the orders of the Belarusian Ministry of Culture (Czosseck, Geers, 2009). All other known cases of internet censorship have involved the use of cyber tools such as DDoS attacks against Belarusian independent online media sites and websites related to reporting current affairs in Belarus.

Belarusian intelligence, although it has its own capabilities, works closely with Russian intelligence agencies. This cooperation includes cyber-espionage, cyber-attacks and information warfare campaigns aimed at opposing nations, dissidents or their political and strategic objectives. The involvement of Belarusian groups, possibly in support of or under the direction of Russian intelligence, highlights the depth of the relationship between the two countries' secret services.

The cooperation between Russian and Belarusian intelligence services in cyber operations highlights the deep-rooted alliance between the two countries, extending their cooperation into the digital sphere. Russian agencies such as the FSB and the GRU have been actively involved in cyber activities targeting Western targets, including espionage, disruption and disinformation campaigns. Belarus under President Lukashenko cooperates closely with Russia, including in security and intelligence efforts. The Belarusian KGB, although less visible in reports of international cyber operations, operates in tandem with Russian intelligence, indicating a united front in cyber efforts. This partnership has raised concerns among cybersecurity experts, government officials and international observers about the implications for global digital security and political stability. (The 5×5, 2022) Russian and Belarusian intelligence cooperation in cyber operations, particularly targeting Ukraine, has been highlighted in various analyses and reports. A prominent example of such cooperation is the hacker group with links to

Belarusian intelligence that is suspected to have carried out a cyber-attack on Ukrainian government websites. The group, known as UNC1151, is believed to have worked with or at the request of Russia, corrupting websites with threatening messages and installing destructive malware. This attack, which took place around 14 January 2022, was a cover for more serious actions behind the scenes aimed at disruption and intelligence gathering. (Polityuk P., 2022)

There are two main factors that could influence closer cooperation between the two countries in cyber operations: Russia's clear support for the Lukashenko regime since the 2020 Belarusian elections, and Russia's increasing lending to Belarus in recent years. These factors are probably why we are seeing Belarus give up its once closed territorial sovereignty to welcome the Russian forces invading Ukraine. Since Lukashenko has lost his legitimacy as President of Belarus and has been ostracised from closer ties with Europe, he is attracted to much closer relations with Russia. (The 5×5, 2022)

The Belarusian government has been linked to cyber-attacks against other countries. These specific incidents reflect the growing threat of cyber warfare by Belarus in the region.

- In 2020, foreign embassies in Belarus were attacked by a cyber-espionage group using internet service providers in Belarus. The perpetrator of the attacks is identified as "Moustached Bouncer", known since 2014 and believed to be acting on behalf of the Belarusian government (Kovacs, 2023).
- 2021 Cyber attack on Ukrainian government websites. A criminal group linked to Belarusian intelligence, known as UNC1151, is believed to have carried out a cyber-attack against Ukrainian government websites. The attack filled the websites with threatening messages. The group is believed to have been linked to Belarusian intelligence and has also been involved in cyber-espionage activities in Lithuania, Latvia, Poland and Ukraine, spreading narratives against the NATO alliance (Polityuk, 2022).
- In 2021, cyber-attack targeting Ukrainian military personnel. Belarusian hackers, identified as UNC1151, targeted the private email addresses of Ukrainian military personnel and associated individuals. They used password-stealing emails to hack into the email accounts of Ukrainian military personnel and then used compromised address books to send other malicious messages. The group was linked to the Belarusian military and was known for stealing and leaking sensitive information to influence public opinion, including targeting the NATO alliance (Satter, 2022).
- Another high-profile attack by the cybercrime group UNC1151 targeted numerous government and private sector entities, mainly in Ukraine, Lithuania, Latvia, Poland and Germany. Belarusian dissidents, media entities and journalists have also been targeted. The activities of this group are mainly in the interests of Belarus. The UNC1151 group's cyber-attacks were aimed at obtaining confidential information, and interestingly, no motive for financial gain was revealed (Roncone & all, 2021).

By carrying out cyber-attacks against its own citizens and other countries, Belarus has also become a target of cyber-attacks.

- In 2020, one fifth (19.02%, 2 million attacks) of all cyber-attacks in Europe targeted Belarus. The number of attacks increased especially during the 2020 presidential elections (Đorđević, 2020).
- DDoS attacks against Belarusian government websites in 2020 had increased. The attacks were seen as a digital protest against government actions and policies, leading to temporary disruption of online services. The attacks were aimed at depleting server resources. Some of these attacks were extremely effective, exceeding 200 Gbps in aggregate data, but were mitigated by the capabilities of the Belarusian internet service providers. The website of the Central Election Commission of Belarus was also one of the main targets of these attacks (E-Belarus.ORG).
- In 2022, the most significant attack targeted the Belarusian railway system, with the aim of disrupting the movement of Russian military equipment through Belarus. This attack was part of wider geopolitical tensions in the region and was characterised by its direct impact on physical infrastructure. The attack was undertaken by anti-government cyber groups within Belarus (Mohee, 2022), (Nair, 2022).

The IT sector in Belarus is recognised for its high competence and rapid growth. In 2019 About 54,000 people worked in Belarus (Husar, 2022). IT specialists, and by 2020 this has increased to around about 115,000 IT workers. The Belarusian IT sector exists separately from the internal Belarus industrial sector, focusing mainly on the export of IT services (Tolkachev & All, 2020). Belarus is renowned for having the best software engineers and programmers in the world due to its excellent education systems and strong science background (Starovoytova, 2020). The Belarusian IT industry was the fastest growing sector in the Belarussian economy, which became the main engine of economic growth. Established in 2005, the High-Tech Park (HTP) has developed into the Silicon Valley of Belarus, demonstrating the country's potential in the technology industry (Irascu, 2023).

In recent years, a relatively large outflow of Belarusian IT specialists to western countries has been observed, but a considerable number of specialists still remain in Belarus. We cannot underestimate the potential of this country's IT professionals in supporting the cyber activities of the Belarusian government.

3. Cybersecurity Legal Background and Compliance Situation in Belarus

In this section of the paper, we will start to explain the legal aspects of cyber security and Belarus.

3.1 Legal Framework in Belarus

Cybersecurity as defined by ENISA in 2017 covers all aspects of the prevention, forecasting, tolerance, detection, mitigation, removal, analysis, and investigation of cyber incidents (ENISA, 2021). In the Republic of Belarus, there is no formal national cybersecurity strategy, there are no formal definitions of "cybersecurity" in the legislation, but many detailed provisions characterizing it are contained in various other regulatory documents (United Nations Institute). In the Republic of Belarus, there is more well-established term "information security", the National Security Concept of Belarus, approved by Decree No. 575 of the President of Belarus on 09.11.2010, defined “information security” as a condition to protect the balanced interests of the individual, society and the State from external and internal threats related to information and identifies information security as an independent component of national security (Cybercrime and cybersecurity strategies, 2018). The National Security Concept of Belarus formulates these national interests and includes the following aspects: shaping and gradually developing the Belarussian information society; having the Republic of Belarus as an equal participant in the world information relations; ensuring reliability and resilience of critical informatisation objects (this can be related to the Western concept of Critical Infrastructure).

In August 2017 Resolution No. 607 was approved “Concept of Union State Program on Information Security”, which entered into force in 2018. The Concept included the introduction of the definitions of “information sovereignty” and “information neutrality”. The Concept of Union State Program refers to the information sovereignty as “the indispensable and exclusive right of the state to independently shape the rules of ownership, use and administration of national information resources; to conduct independent foreign and domestic information policy; to shape the national information infrastructure; to ensure information security (International Information Security). Therefore, information sovereignty of Belarus has been made into a national priority. One of the main goals declared by the Concept of Union State Program is to ensure the rule of the Belarus state over its information domain. This immediately sidelines other areas of consideration, such as the rights of the citizens and international commitments. The technical section of the 2017 Concept of Union State Program includes measures ensuring security of the information infrastructure and of the national segment of the Internet; countering cybercrimes; ensuring security of public information resources, including of state and public secrets; and protecting personal data from unauthorized access.

In March 2019, the Doctrine of Information Security of the Republic of Belarus was approved, which proclaimed information sovereignty, respect for the digital sovereignty of other countries and the pursuit of a peaceful foreign information policy (International Information Security).

In February 2023 the Supreme State Council of the Union State approved the Concept of Information Security of the Union State (Ministry of Foreign Affairs BY). The concept document was developed in close collaboration of the offices of the Security Councils, Foreign Ministries and other authorities of the two countries – Belarus and Russia. The concept document seeks to create a solid legal foundation to respond to modern information challenges and threats.

Some other regulatory frameworks in Belarus covering data protection and cybersecurity obligations includes the Strategy of development of informatisation in Republic of Belarus for 2016-2022 adopted in 3 November 2015 (No.26), National program of development of digital economy and information society for 2016-2020 adopted in 23 March 2016 (No. 235) and other Laws and the Edicts of the President related to data/information protection. Cybersecurity in Belarus is also covered by a range of specific legal acts relating to the particular categories of information systems and its owners. For example, the Banking Code of the Republic of Belarus dated 25.10.2000, Rules on Rendering Services Connected to Creation and Placement of Digital Signs (Tokens) and Related Transactions approved by the Supervisory Board of the High Technologies Park. Specific legislation on cybercrime has been enacted through the Criminal Code. Chapter 31 of the Criminal Code deals with cybercrime offences such as the unauthorised access to computer information; deletion, blockage or modification of computer information; non compliance with the rules regulating exploitation of computer system or networks (Уголовный кодекс Республики Беларусь). While substantive cybercrime offences are mostly in place, there are significant gaps in terms of implementing procedural powers under the Budapest Convention on Cybercrime (Cybercrime and cybersecurity strategies, 2018).

3.2 International Cooperation

Belarus has not yet acceded to the Budapest Convention on Cybercrime (ETS 185) but has expressed a strong interest in accession. The Council of Europe, under the Cybercrime@EAP II joint project with the European Union, supported a workshop aimed at promoting "the harmonisation of Belarusian legislation with the Budapest Convention on Cybercrime" (Harmonising legislation with the Budapest Convention, 2018). In 2020 Belarus was ranked in 89th place the ITU global cybersecurity index (Global Cybersecurity Index, 2020).

Current practices of international cooperation with Belarus are mostly involving supporting mutual legal assistance requests. The timeframes for processing and execution of incoming mutual legal assistance requests are rather long and delays are experienced mostly due to large requests requiring translation (considered to be particularly problematic) and/or need to clarify ambiguities in cases of incomplete/low-quality requests; triage of mutual legal assistance requests not performed or based upon informal criteria and is not uniform in application (Cybercrime and cybersecurity strategies, 2018). In addition, the lack of sufficiently clear and proper basis in national law to cooperate directly with multinational service providers (MSPs) in criminal cases, being one of the major reasons for declining cooperation (Cybercrime and cybersecurity strategies, 2018). There are also obvious examples in other than computer related/cybersecurity criminal cases that Belarus is not a cooperating country (alfa.lt, 2013). On the other hand, since February 2023 when the concept document was developed in close collaboration between Belarus and Russia, two countries began to cooperate in order to protect the national interests of the Union State[2] members in the media landscape. Russia and Belarus developed joint guidelines for a coherent state policy and for public relations in the field of information security. Both countries also set the framework for improving the information security systems of the two states.***3.3. Institutional framework***

The main regulatory authorities relating to the generally applicable cybersecurity-related laws are: Operations and Analytics Center under the President of the Republic of Belarus and Ministry of Communications and Informatization of the Republic of Belarus. These institutions are mainly responsible for the implementation of a unified state policy in the sphere of data protection, promotion of creation of information technologies, information systems and information networks; technical regulation and standardization of information resources, information systems and information networks; coordination of activities of state bodies in the cybersecurity sphere; coordination of formation and state registration of information resources and similar.

4. Belarus Cyber Case Studies: Pro-Government and Anti-Government Hacking Groups

This section of the paper will focus on different hacking groups that exist in Belarus.

4.1 Belarus Cyber Partisans

The "Belarus Cyber Partisans" (also known as "BCP") is a hacktivist group that has gained attention for its activities related to the political situation in Belarus. The Belarus Cyber Partisans are a hacktivist group that emerged in opposition to the regime of Belarusian President Alexander Lukashenko. They gained prominence by launching cyber-attacks on Belarusian state critical infrastructure, leaking sensitive information, and disrupting government websites. The group claims to be fighting for freedom and democracy in Belarus, where widespread protests against alleged electoral fraud erupted in 2020. Their activities have raised concerns about the vulnerability of critical infrastructure to cyber-attacks. The Belarusian government has condemned their actions, accusing them of terrorism and foreign backing.

---

[2] The union of Russia and Belarus. Signed by the heads of states in 1999. The Agreement on Establishment of the Union State of Belarus and Russia sets up a legal basis for integration between the two countries.

The Belarus Cyber Partisans claimed several significant cyber activities. While the fame or significance of these actions can be subjective and might change over time, here are four notable activities attributed to the group:

1. Critical Infrastructure Attacks: They claimed responsibility for several attacks on Belarus's railway system. One such attack temporarily disrupted ticket sales (Bajak, 2022), while another aimed at halting train movement, though it was unclear how successful that was (theguardian.com, 2022), (railway-technology.com, 2022).
2. Data Leaks: The group reportedly leaked data from the Belarusian police and interior ministry databases. This exposed personal information of police officers, which the group claimed was to hold the police accountable for alleged acts of violence against protestors (zdnet.com, 2020). Another examples: a series of hacks on Belarus's government by pro-democracy activists has uncovered details of apparent abuses by security forces, exposed police informants and collected personal data on top officials including a son of President Alexander Lukashenko (washingtonpost.com, 2021), (currenttime.tv); the activists also hacked into the database of all criminal and administrative cases in Belarus and downloaded their archives (euroradio.fm, 2023).
3. Website Defacements: The group took over various government websites, displaying protest messages and replacing official content with images and slogans supporting the opposition (Kazharski, 2021).
4. Interception of Official Communications: They claimed to have wiretapped audio of foreign embassies, consulates and other calls in Belarus gathered surreptitiously by the Belarusian Ministry of Internal Affairs (cyberscoop.com, 2023).

According to George 2023), the hacktivist organisation, Cyber Partisans, partnered with the Kastuś Kalinoŭski Regiment, an anti-Russian Belarussian military group made up of volunteers fighting for Ukraine. As Belarus has been used by Russia to bolster its invasion operations, the partnership between Belarussian partisan groups is a strategic relationship that reinforces cyber defense and offense efforts. The partnership related to coordinated actions aligning virtual attacks with physical attacks, with the aim of producing more effective results (George, 2023). Thus, the Belarusian partisans are also acting in a hybrid way to extend their real influence. A number of cases of Belarusian cyber-partisans collaborating with journalists have also been documented. Hackers with access to sensitive information has been sharing it with journalists. Although the ethicality of such activities has been questioned in press (thefix.media, 2022), it should be mentioned that Belarusian cyber-partisans have significantly increase the publicity of their activities and the data they collect have been reported by the media around the world.

4.2 Pro-Belarus Hackers

Hackers supporting the Belarusian regime usually acting to counteract opposition movements and reinforce President Lukashenko's grip on power, especially after the contentious 2020 election. These cyber actors have targeted opposition websites, activists, and disseminated pro-government propaganda online, etc. They also target countries that oppose Russian/Belarusian actions and policies. Most often hackers are reluctant to make information about their activities public, so there is much less public information. Nevertheless, we can categorise their activities as follows:

1. Disinformation Campaigns: These are efforts to spread false or misleading information online. Given the political unrest and tensions in Belarus, especially after the 2020 presidential elections, pro-Belarus entities might use disinformation to control narratives, discredit opposition, or influence international perceptions. Such attacks can be directed both within a country and against other countries. As part of the campaign in 2023, the hackers, who cybersecurity experts also refer to as UNC1151, sent fake messages to Polish citizens about potential recruitment to the Lithuanian-Polish-Ukrainian brigade, a multinational military focused on conducting peacekeeping and humanitarian operations. The hackers also made false claims that the brigade will take part in military operations in Ukraine. The campaign is just the latest in a series of disinformation operations conducted by Russia and Belarus aligned hackers. The Polish state authorities claimed their goal is to destabilise the situation in the country (therecord.media, 2023).
2. Web site defacements: this involves unauthorised modifications of web pages, typically replacing the original content with the hacker's message or propaganda. Given the political context, opposition or journalist websites could be potential targets. We have also seen these groups target governments outside Belarus. For example, Ukraine accused a Belarusian-linked hacker group in 2022 of attacking its government websites using Russian intelligence linked malware (tickernews.co, 2022).

3. Data breaches: This relates to the unauthorised access to sensitive data, potentially followed by public release of that data. This can be used as a tactic to intimidate, embarrass, or discredit targets, especially opposition figures or entities perceived as threats. Hackers from Belarus were targeting the private email addresses of Ukrainian military personnel "and related individuals" to gain access of Ukrainian soldiers' email accounts and using their compromised address books to send further malicious messages (euronews.com, 2022).

As far as the recent activities of pro-Belarusian government hackers are concerned, it should be noted that their main "focus" is on Ukraine[3]. Thus, as a separate group, the authors would like to highlight pro-Belarusian hacker attacks against Ukraine (especially after the Russian invasion of Ukraine beginning in 2022). Hackers linked to the Belarusian government, known as GhostWriter, targeted government, military, and civilian entities in Ukraine and Poland from at least April 2022, according to a report by cybersecurity firm Cisco Talos. They have been using malicious Microsoft Office attachments, including disguised Excel and PowerPoint files, the attackers deployed malware to steal information and gain remote system access (therecord.media, 2023). The various methods are that are used intend to undermine Ukraine and other countries that support them. This is evidenced by publicly available cases (reuters.com, 2022).

While conducting research, the authors sought to find out the connections between Belarus pro-government hackers and Russian APT groups[4]. Several such groups operate in Russia, for example, Berserk Bear, Fancy Bear, Gamaredon and others. Belarusian pro-government hackers and their links with Russian APT groups could highlight a concerning trend in the cyber domain, particularly in the context of international geopolitics and cybersecurity. The direct links between Belarus pro-government hackers and Russian APT groups were not explicitly detailed in the public sources. For example, one of the cyber analysts in 2022 was quoted as follows: "Though we cannot rule out Russian contributions to either UNC1151 or Ghostwriter[5] activities, we have not yet identified evidence of any collaboration between Russian APTs and UNC1151" (Belarus threat.., 2022). But the broader context of cyber threats and state-backed cyber activities, including those attributed to Russia, provides a relevant backdrop. The escalation of cyber threats, such as ransomware attacks and exploitation of vulnerabilities, underscores the complexity of the cyber threat landscape where state-backed or state-affiliated actors could potentially collaborate or share tactics. The landscape of cyber warfare and cyber espionage is continually evolving, with state actors and their affiliates playing significant roles in targeting adversaries or supporting geopolitical aims. Therefore, it cannot be claimed that there are no connections between Belarus pro-government hackers and Russian APT groups, and the relevant connections are the object of further research.

4.3 Comparison: Belarussian Cyber-Partisans and Pro-Belarussian Hacker.

The authors compare the activities of the different Belarusian cyber-partisans with the pro-Belarusian hackers:

Table 1:

	Belarussian Cyber-Partisans	Pro-Belarusian hackers
Motivation	The Belarus Cyber Partisans engage in hacktivism to challenge the Lukashenko regime, advocating for democratic reforms and transparency in response to alleged electoral fraud and state-sanctioned violence.	Pro-Belarus hackers are driven by a desire to defend the Belarusian government and its national interests, countering perceived external threats and internal dissent.
Targets	They have primarily targeted Belarusian state infrastructure, like railways, and have leaked data from government databases, such as the police and interior ministries.	Their likely targets include opposition political websites, independent media, and communication channels used by activists or dissidents. Foreign governments who

[3] And, in some cases, against other states that support Ukraine.

[4] **Russian advanced persistent threat groups.**

[5] Ghostwriter, also known as UNC1151, is a hacker group allegedly originating from Belarus.

	Belarussian Cyber-Partisans	Pro-Belarusian hackers
		support the opposition in Belarus and the Ukrainian government.
Operating area	They operate both inside and outside if Belarus.	Mostly external to Belarus: pro-Belarus attacks are usually directed at Ukraine (especially after the war started), but also aimed at NATO countries, mainly the Baltic States.
Tactics, techniques, *modus operandi*	Their tactics have been centered on data breaches, infrastructure attacks, and public disclosures. They have targeted state systems, leading to service disruptions and information leaks.	Historically, pro-government hackers have employed disinformation campaigns, DDoS attacks, and espionage-based cyberattacks. Their focus would typically be on silencing opposition voices and protecting state interests.
Origins and backing	They emerged from grassroots hacktivist movements, potentially collaborating with other global hacktivist entities.	Likely to be state-sponsored or backed by entities with close ties to the Lukashenko regime.
Cooperation	They usually act alone. However, journalists are involved in publicising activities and results. Cases of hybrid cooperation with local anti-Belarus military groups have also been observed.	Pro-Belarus cyber-operations are involved cooperation with Russian and Chinese hackers. Often, pro-Belarus groups are involved in disinformation campaigns.

5. Conclusions

1. Belarus has experienced significant challenges related to cybercrimes and online censorship, particularly under President Alexander Lukashenko's regime. The government has utilised internet censorship and undertook DDoS attacks as tools against political dissent and opposition, often without legal justification and in violation of Belarusian constitutional laws. This repression escalated notably following the disputed 2020 presidential elections. Furthermore, Belarus has been implicated in cyber-attacks against other countries, with groups like UNC1151 conducting espionage and disruptive activities across Europe. Conversely, Belarus itself has been a significant target of cyber-attacks, especially during politically sensitive periods.
2. Belarus has developed a legal framework in terms of focusing on information security asset (in the western context described as critical infrastructure). The Belarus government has also developed legal frameworks to allow the government to censor online content with Belarus. A new challenge is the geopolitical union with Russia, which also influence the creation of new future legal frameworks.
3. Belarus' close relationship with Russia extends into the realm of cyber and hybrid threats, where Belarusian actors have been implicated in cyber-attacks that align with Russian geopolitical interests, especially against neighbouring countries and NATO members. This collaboration often involves coordinated cyber espionage, disinformation campaigns, and attacks on critical infrastructure, reflecting a shared strategy to exert influence and disrupt perceived adversaries. Additionally, Belarus' cyber capabilities and infrastructure may be leveraged by Russian entities to launch cyber-attacks, making it a significant player in the broader landscape of regional cyber threats.

References

'Cyberpartisans' hack Belarusian railway to disrupt Russian buildup, 2022 // https://www.theguardian.com/world/2022/jan/25/cyberpartisans-hack-belarusian-railway-to-disrupt-russian-buildup

«Уголовный кодекс Республики Беларусь» – тематические подборки НПА на Pravo.by. (n.d.). https://pravo.by/document/?guid=3871&p0=hk9900275

Belarus hackers attack train systems to disrupt Russian troops, 2022 // https://www.railway-technology.com/news/belarus-hackers-attack-train-systems/

Bajak, F. Belarus hacktivists target railway in anti-Russia effort, January 25, 2022 // https://apnews.com/article/russia-ukraine-technology-business-moscow-belarus-fe6dd5e3ff9ec0718b6448e770c15c29

Belarus-linked hacking group targets Poland with new disinformation campaign, April 19, 2023 // https://therecord.media/ghostwriter-belarus-hacking-group-targets-poland-disinformation

Belarus-linked hacks on Ukraine, Poland began at least a year ago, report says, July 13, 2023 // https://therecord.media/poland-ukraine-ghostwriter-attacks-belarus

Belarus threat group in Ukraine 'bomb alert' cyberattack, July 21, 2022 // https://cybernews.com/cyber-war/belarus-threat-group-in-ukraine-bomb-alert-attack/

Belarus: Harmonising legislation with the Budapest Convention. (2018, April 26). Cybercrime. https://www.coe.int/en/web/cybercrime/-/harmonising-legislation-with-the-budapest-conventi-1

Belarusian cyber partisans hack into important state database, March 8, 2023 // https://euroradio.fm/en/belarusian-cyber-partisans-hack-important-state-database

Belarusian hacktivist group releases purported Belarusian wiretapped audio of Russian embassy. June 14, 2022 // https://cyberscoop.com/belarusian-hacktivist-group-releases-purported-belarusian-wiretapped-audio-of-russian-embassy/

Belarusian journalists collaborate with the hacktivists who have a lot of sensitive information — how does it work and is this ethical? October 25, 2022 // https://thefix.media/2022/10/25/belarusian-journalists-collaborate-with-the-hacktivists-who-have-a-lot-of-sensitive-information-how-does-it-work-and-is-this-ethical

Criminal code of Belarus, 1999 https://pravo.by/document/?guid=3871&p0=hk9900275, art. 349-355

Cybercrime and cybersecurity strategies in the Eastern Partnership region. 2018. CyberCrime@IPA (coe.int), page 28.

Czosseck, C., & Geers, K. (2009). Belarus in the Context of European Cyber Security. The Virtual Battlefield: Perspectives on Cyber Warfare, 3, 156.

Disinformation campaigns, cyber attacks, economic pressures, military posturing, political interference, etc.

Đorđević, N. (2020, September 10). Cyberattacks in Belarus compound discontent in country's IT sector - Emerging Europe. Emerging Europe. https://emerging-europe.com/news/cyberattacks-in-belarus-compound-discontent-in-countrys-it-sector/

E-Belarus.ORG | Internet Shutdown in Belarus / Official version: DDoS Attacks. (n.d.). https://e-belarus.org/news/202008121.html#:~:text=A%20particularly%20large%20number%20of,and%2023%3A20%20on%2209%20August

ENISA overview of cybersecurity and related terminology. Results of series of national workshops Eastern Partnership countries PGG 2018: Cybercrime@EaP project February - May 2018. https://rm.coe.int/eap-cybercrime-and-cybersecurity-strategies/168093b89c

G. Roncone, A. Wahlstrom, A. Revelli, D. Mainor, S. Riddell, B. Read. UNC1151 Assessed to have Links to Belarusian Government. Mandiant. https://www.mandiant.com/resources/blog/unc1151-linked-to-belarus-government

George J. J. Considering Cyberwar Efficacy: Is Mitigation Possible? Georgetown Journal of International Affairs. September 11, 2023 // https://gjia.georgetown.edu/2023/09/11/considering-cyberwar-efficacy-is-mitigation-possible/

Hackers leak details of 1,000 high-ranking Belarus police officers, 2020 // https://www.zdnet.com/article/hackers-leak-details-of-1000-high-ranking-belarus-police-officers/

How Belarus's 'Cyber Partisans' exposed secrets of Lukashenko's crackdowns // https://www.washingtonpost.com/world/europe/belarus-hack-cyber-partisans-lukashenko/2021/09/14/5ad56006-fabd-11eb-911c-524bc8b68f17_story.html

Global Cybersecurity Index 2020, https://www.itu.int/dms_pub/itu-d/opb/str/D-STR-GCI.01-2021-PDF-E.pdf

International Information Security - Ministry of Foreign Affairs of the Republic of Belarus. (n.d.). https://mfa.gov.by/en/mulateral/global_issues/inform/

International Information Security - Ministry of Foreign Affairs of the Republic of Belarus. (n.d.). https://mfa.gov.by/en/mulateral/global_issues/inform/

Kazharski A. Belarus' new political nation? 2020 anti-authoritarian protests as identity building. New Perspectives 2021, Vol. 29(1). P. 76 // https://journals.sagepub.com/doi/10.1177/2336825X20984340

Kovacs, E. (2023, August 11). Moustached Bouncer: Foreign Embassies in Belarus Likely Targeted via ISPs. SecurityWeek. https://www.securityweek.com/moustachedbouncer-foreign-embassies-in-belarus-likely-targeted-via-isps/

Ministry of Foreign Affairs of the Republic of Belarus, https://www.mfa.gov.by/en/press/news_mfa/cac0ee302b706cd8.html

Mohee, A. (2022). Cyber war: The hidden side of the Russian-Ukrainian crisis.

Nair, S. (2022, March 23). Belarus hackers attack train systems to disrupt Russian troops. Railway Technology. https://www.railway-technology.com/news/belarus-hackers-attack-train-systems/

O'Neill, P. H. (2021, October 26). Hackers are trying to topple Belarus's dictator, with help from the inside. MIT Technology Review. https://www.technologyreview.com/2021/08/26/1033205/belarus-cyber-partisans-lukashenko-hack-opposition/

Outsourcing in Belarus - Information & Technology Statistics. (n.d.). https://techbehemoths.com/blog/it-outsourcing-belarus

Pavlyuchenko, F. (2009). Belarus in the context of European cyber security. In The Virtual Battlefield: Perspectives on Cyber Warfare (pp. 156-162). IOS Press.

Polityuk, P. (2022, January 16). EXCLUSIVE Ukraine suspects group linked to Belarus intelligence over cyberattack. Reuters. https://www.reuters.com/world/europe/exclusive-ukraine-suspects-group-linked-belarus-intelligence-over-cyberattack-2022-01-15/

Prokuroras, vadovaujantis Sausio 13–osios žudynių bylai: Rusija ir Baltarusija nebendradarbiauja. https://www.alfa.lt/straipsnis/15074922/alfalt/

Rusinaite V. Russia's policy towards Belarus: Controlling more, giving back less. December 2021. [20211220-Hybrid-CoE-Strategic-Analysis-30-Russias-policy-Belarus-WEB.pdf (hybridcoe.fi)]; p. 4

Satter, R. (2022, February 25). Ukraine says its military is being targeted by Belarusian hackers. Reuters. https://www.reuters.com/world/europe/ukraine-says-its-military-is-being-targeted-by-belarusian-hackers-2022-02-25/

Seeking Change, Anti-Lukashenka Hackers Seize Senior Belarusian Officials' Personal Data // https://en.currenttime.tv/a/seeking-change-anti-lukashenka-hackers-seize-senior-belarusian-officials-personal-data-/31392092.html

The Belarus IT Industry: One of the Best Talent Hubs in the World | Satellite Innovations. (n.d.). https://www.satelliteinnovations.io/blog/the-belarus-it-industry-one-of-the-best-talent-hubs-in-the-world#:~:text=The%20average%20developer%20in%20Belarus,educational%20systems%20and%20technical%20roots

The IT Industry in Belarus: General Portrait. (n.d.). https://techbehemoths.com/blog/the-it-industry-in-belarus-2021-general-portrait

Tolkachev, S., Быков, Morkovkin, D., Borisov, O. I., & Gavrilin, A. V. (2020, January 1). Digitalization of manufacturing in Russia, Belarus and the European Union. IOP Conference Series. https://doi.org/10.1088/1755-1315/421/3/032041

Ukraine says its military is being targeted by Belarusian hackers, February 25, 2022 // https://www.euronews.com/next/2022/02/25/us-ukraine-crisis-cyber

Ukraine suspects group linked to Belarus intelligence over cyberattack, January 16, 2022 // https://www.reuters.com/world/europe/exclusive-ukraine-suspects-group-linked-belarus-intelligence-over-cyberattack-2022-01-15/

United Nations Institute for disarmament research. Cyber Policy Portal. (n.d.). https://cyberpolicyportal.org/

S. (2022, July 7). The 5×5—Russia’s cyber statecraft. Atlantic Council. https://www.atlanticcouncil.org/commentary/the-5x5-russias-cyber-statecraft/

Polityuk P. EXCLUSIVE Ukraine suspects group linked to Belarus intelligence over cyberattack (January 16, 2022), https://www.reuters.com/world/europe/exclusive-ukraine-suspects-group-linked-belarus-intelligence-over-cyberattack-2022-01-15/

An Analysis of Cyberwarfare Attribution Techniques and Challenges

Clementine Swate, Siphesihle Sithungu and Khutso Lebea
University of Johannesburg, Auckland Park 2006, South Africa

clemmypontsho@gmail.com
siphesihles@uj.ac.za
klebea@uj.ac.za

Abstract. Identifying the source of cyber-attacks is crucial to ensuring cybersecurity. This study examines different attribution techniques, obstacles, and real-world examples in the context of cyber warfare. It explores challenges such as incorrect attributions, ethical concerns, legal barriers, and complexities in the digital environment. The discussed topic includes modern techniques such as malware analysis, network traffic study, digital forensics, and the implementation of AI/ML. These methods help improve cybersecurity and shape cyber warfare strategies. Case studies on the Standard Bank South Africa ATM fraud and the TransUnion South Africa cyber-attack illustrate the importance of attributing cyber incidents, especially with global cyber criminals. The analysis emphasizes the need for a comprehensive approach that takes into account legal, technical, ethical, and geopolitical considerations relevant to the evolution of computing and cyber warfare. It stresses the need for cybersecurity tools enhancement and global cooperation. The study pairs attribution challenges with techniques to deepen our understanding of threats. It underlines the need for ongoing cybersecurity research and adaptation, sustained innovation, and collaboration to fortify global cyber defenses.

Keywords: Cyberwarfare · Malware Analysis · Cyberattacks · Digital Forensics · Geopolitical Analysis · Open-Source Intelligence (OSINT)

1. Introduction

Technological advancements have revolutionized warfare in modern times. Cyberwarfare, an online form of fighting, is a new threat that is difficult to detect due to its complex and deceptive nature. As internet connectivity expands and more things connect, individuals and institutions become increasingly vulnerable to major cyberattacks. Therefore, it is crucial to determine the responsibility for these attacks, a process known as attribution.

The concept of cyberwarfare refers to cyber-attacks that are supported or associated with a government and have military or political goals (AlShaer & Rahman, 2015). These attacks are a major worldwide security concern as they can have significant impacts on a country's infrastructure, economy, and safety. Whether it involves spying, disruption, or damage, correctly identifying the origin of cyberattacks is essential to maintain global stability, discourage malicious actors, and respond effectively to such threats.

This paper delves into the intricate realm of cyberwarfare attribution, encompassing a range of methods and approaches used to identify individuals or entities responsible for cyberattacks. The framework for comprehending cyberwarfare attribution comprises technical, behavioral, linguistic, geopolitical, and state-of-the-art artificial intelligence (AI) and machine learning methodologies, each playing an important role in the intricate and difficult quest for attribution (DiMaggio, 2022). While it is crucial to understand and advance these techniques, they also present challenges and limitations.

Misattribution, which involves wrongly accusing an entity or nation of a cyberattack, remains a persistent concern. Furthermore, the ethical implications surrounding attribution, particularly in the context of nation-states and cyber-conflict, pose complex dilemmas that require careful consideration.

2. Attribution techniques in Cyberwarfare

Identifying the source of cyberattacks is a challenging and multifaceted undertaking that necessitates the use of a range of methods and approaches. This section examines different attribution methods, highlighting their significance in the context of cyber warfare.

2.1 Technical Analysis

The identification of cyberattacks largely depends on technical analysis, which entails a meticulous examination of digital evidence and technical elements that may have been left behind (Goel & Nussbaum, 2021). With this type of investigation, important information about the source of the attack can be revealed. The following subcategories offer a comprehensive comprehension of different technical analysis methods.

2.1.1 *Malware Analysis:*

Cyberattacks often use malicious software, such as viruses, worms, Trojans, and ransomware. To identify the source of an attack, investigators perform malware analysis. This involves breaking down and reverse engineering the malicious code to determine its unique characteristics, features, and any ties to known malware groups (DiMaggio, 2022). By identifying these details, investigators can connect an attack to a specific group, individual, or state actor.

2.1.2 *Network Traffic Analysis:*

The process of network traffic analysis involves closely examining the communication between an attacker and a target system. It includes monitoring network packets, traffic patterns, and identifying malicious command and control (C2) channels (Ferrag et al., 2023). Through analyzing these aspects, analysts can uncover important information about the attacker's location, infrastructure, and possible affiliations. This information can be used to develop effective strategies for preventing future attacks.

2.1.3 *Digital Forensics:*

Digital forensics is a method of gathering and analyzing digital proof from compromised systems. This process helps investigators to reconstruct the timeline of the attack, identify the initial attack vector, and trace the actions of the attacker within the victim's environment (AlShaer & Rahman, 2015). It plays a crucial role in comprehending how an attack was carried out and identifying those who may be responsible for it.

2.2 Behavioral Analysis

Behavioral analysis is a critical element in the field of cyberwarfare attribution. Its primary focus is to understand the tactics, techniques, and procedures (TTPs) used by threat actors during cyberattacks (DiMaggio, 2022). By carefully examining the behavioral patterns and operational methods of attackers, analysts can create profiles or fingerprints that help attribute attacks to specific threat groups, nation-states, or individuals. The key aspects of behavioral analysis include:

2.3.1 *Tactics, Techniques, and Procedures (TTPs):*

Threat actors make strategic and operational choices known as Tactics, Techniques, and Procedures (TTPs) in their cyber operations. TTPs include the different stages of an attack, such as initial reconnaissance, intrusion, data exfiltration, or system disruption (Goel & Nussbaum, 2021). Attack vectors are the different ways in which attackers can access a target system or network. These methods consist of phishing, exploiting vulnerabilities, and social engineering. On the other hand, malware deployment techniques involve studying how malware is delivered, activated, and maintained inside the target environment. This includes the usage of droppers, command and control servers, and persistence mechanisms. Evasion and stealth techniques are the methods used to avoid detection and keep a low profile within the victim's infrastructure. These techniques involve using encryption, obfuscation, and living-off-the-land tactics.

2.3.2 *Attack Timeline Reconstruction:*

The reconstruction of attack timelines plays a crucial role in analyzing behaviors for attributing cyberwarfare. In this process, the events sequence during a cyberattack is pieced together, like putting together a digital puzzle. This method is invaluable for comprehending the attacker's actions, motivations, and decision-making. It is crucial to reconstruct the timeline of an attack accurately. This involves dividing the attack into different stages, including initial reconnaissance, exploitation, privilege escalation, data exfiltration, and impact. It is essential to understand how the attacker interacts with the victim's systems. This could involve lateral movement through the network, privilege escalation, or communication with command-and-control servers. Furthermore, it is crucial to analyze the attacker's decision-making process and motivations. It helps to identify whether their actions are driven by financial gain, espionage, or political objectives.

2.3 Linguistic Analysis

In the complex world of cyberwarfare attribution, linguistic analysis plays a crucial role. This technique involves analyzing the language, coding style, and behavioral patterns used by threat actors in their digital activities. By examining these linguistic aspects, analysts can gain valuable insights into the identities and affiliations of malicious entities (Kapsokoli, 2023). The key elements of linguistic analysis include:

2.3.3 *Language Markers*

Language markers are linguistic indicators in digital artifacts like code or documents that give clues about the actor's origin (Kapsokoli, 2023). To identify the language used by an attacker, one can carefully analyze the language used in emails, chat conversations, and forum postings related to cyber operations. One can also determine the attacker's place of origin or specific community they belong to by examining various language variants and regional dialects. By analyzing idiomatic terms and cultural allusions used in an attacker's communication, it is possible to infer their cultural background and experiences.

2.3.4 *Coding Style Analysis*

Coding style analysis examines unique patterns and idiosyncrasies in code and software development practices. This analysis is particularly relevant when examining malicious code. Coding conventions refer to the unique formatting options, naming conventions, and coding practices used in software code or malware that can indicate a specific person or organization Examining debugging artifacts, errors, or code flaws unique to a developer or team helps identify code source. Furthermore, analyzing the language and content of code comments and documentation can reveal insights into the developer's personality or history.

2.3.5 *Comments and Developer Habits*

Software developers and hackers often exhibit consistent habits and practices that can be used to identify them. For instance, determining the attacker's working hours and time zone can help reveal their location. Identifying the programming languages, tools, or frameworks that attackers prefer can be connected to well-known developer practices. Reusing code or methodologies in multiple attacks may indicate the consistent work of a single actor or group.

Linguistic analysis is a robust and effective tool for attribution, as it offers an exclusive insight into the human elements behind cyber operations. By scrutinizing linguistic hints, coding styles, and developer habits, analysts can link apparently unconnected attacks and create a more comprehensive profile of threat actors, thus improving the accuracy of attribution.

2.4 Geopolitical Analysis

When trying to identify cyber attackers in the context of cyber warfare, geopolitical analysis is essential. This approach goes beyond the digital realm to examine the broader geopolitical motivations, alliances, and affiliations of those who pose a threat (AlShaer & Rahman, 2015). Geopolitical analysis involves looking at the following key aspects.

2.4.1 *Motivations of Threat Actors*

Understanding the motives behind a cyberattack is crucial in determining attribution. The objectives of the attacker, which range from espionage to influencing political events, can provide insight into their identity or affiliation. Cyberattacks can have different motivations, such as political goals, financial gains, or cyber espionage. State-sponsored actors are often involved in attacks that aim to influence elections, overthrow governments, or achieve specific political objectives. Cybercriminal organizations are usually responsible for attacks that seek to make money, such as ransomware campaigns or theft of intellectual property. On the other hand, nation-states involved in cyber-espionage operations are seeking intelligence for strategic purposes. (Ferrag et al., 2023).

2.4.2 *Alliances and Affiliations*

Nations and threat actors often operate within alliances or affiliations. Geopolitical analysis considers the relationships that may underpin a cyber operation. When multiple countries form cooperative agreements or strategic alliances, they may work together on cyber operations. These types of attacks are the responsibility of the member countries within the alliance. Threat actors who carry out assaults on behalf of nation-states are known as proxy actors. Identifying these proxies can help link the attacks to their main financiers.

2.4.3 *Open-source Intelligence and Collaborative Intelligence*

In the world of cyberwarfare attribution, open-source intelligence (OSINT) and collaborative intelligence play a crucial role. OSINT is the practice of gathering publicly available information from sources such as social media, forums, news outlets, and government reports (Kapsokoli, 2023). Collaborative intelligence helps in promoting cooperation among security organizations, governments, and private sector entities. It enables them to share information and expertise, which is essential in the fight against cybercrime. The use of Open-Source Intelligence (OSINT) techniques can provide several benefits, such as corroborating evidence by keeping an eye on the online activities of threat actors or their associated groups, thus offering more proof of attribution. Collaborative intelligence can allow for better information sharing among groups to identify and counteract cyberthreats by combining resources and expertise.

2.5 AI and Machine Learning

The fields of cyberwarfare and attribution have been greatly enhanced by the emergence of artificial intelligence (AI) and machine learning (ML). These tools enable data analytics, pattern recognition, and automation to increase the precision and efficiency of attribution efforts. AI and ML are utilized in various ways, including linguistic analysis and behavioral pattern recognition. This section will explore the applications and implications of AI and ML in cyberwarfare attribution.

2.5.1 *Linguistic Analysis Through NLP*

Natural Language Processing (NLP) is a subfield of AI that focuses on computer-human language interaction. NLP plays a significant role in attributing cyberwarfare. Language Recognition is a technique that can help reduce the number of potential cyber attackers by using AI-powered natural language processing models to automatically recognize and detect the language used in cyberattack conversations (Goel & Nussbaum, 2021). Another useful NLP technique is Sentiment Analysis which can analyze an attacker's tone and sentiment to reveal information about their intentions. Stylometric Analysis is a method that uses AI to identify distinctive language patterns in writing style, vocabulary, and grammatical quirks. These patterns can be used to connect assaults to certain writers or organizations (Kapsokoli, 2023).

2.5.2 *Behavioral Pattern Analysis Using ML Algorithms.*

Behavioral pattern analysis involves using machine learning algorithms to identify patterns in the behavior of threat actors. Machine learning (ML) models can be used to identify possible security risks by detecting odd or suspicious activity within a system or network. By using previous data to identify attack signatures, machine learning algorithms can be trained to link future attacks to identified threat actors through attack signature matching. Machine learning can help classify and attribute new threats by creating behavioral profiles of different threat groupings through group profiling.

3. Challenges and Limitations

While the techniques and methodologies for cyberwarfare attribution are advancing, the field is rife with complexities and challenges. Accurately attributing cyberattacks to their source can be elusive, and there are limitations and ethical implications that must be considered. This section delves into the hurdles faced in the attribution process.

3.1 Misattribution

Misattribution is a major concern in cyberwarfare due to the risk of attributing a cyberattack to the wrong source, which can have serious consequences. Misattribution can occur for various reasons. False flags refer to intentional actions by threat actors to mislead investigators by planting false clues or using deceptive techniques to deflect blame (Mohamed et al., 2023). Attackers often use compromised infrastructure to conceal their origins, making it difficult to trace attacks. In some cases, investigators may choose not to reveal the identity of an attacker, even if they are certain about it, due to classified information or geopolitical considerations (Mohamed et al., 2023). The reuse of attack tools and malware by different threat groups can cause confusion, making it difficult to accurately attribute cyber-attacks (Ngulu, 2022). Addressing misattribution requires a high degree of expertise, extensive data, and a cautious approach to avoid making hasty accusations.

3.2 Ethical Implications

Ethical considerations are crucial in the process of attributing cyberattacks. The act of attribution can have significant consequences, and there are ethical dilemmas that need to be addressed (Pahi & Skopik, 2019).

Misattribution can lead to innocent entities being wrongly accused, which can have serious consequences. Public attribution, in some cases, can escalate conflicts, potentially leading to further retaliation in the cyber or physical realm. Balancing the need for transparency in disclosing cyber threats with the need to protect sensitive sources and methods poses ethical dilemmas. Moreover, the collection and analysis of personal data, even for attribution purposes, may infringe upon individual privacy and civil liberties. It is important to take these factors into account when dealing with cyber threats to ensure fair and just outcomes.

3.3 Attribution in the Digital Fog

The digital realm's anonymity and obfuscation make attribution difficult. Threat actors use advanced techniques to remain hidden. Attackers may hide their true locations by routing activities through proxy servers and anonymization tools. The use of botnets composed of compromised devices complicates attack tracing due to multiple, dispersed sources. Attackers often alter their infrastructure by using dynamic IP addresses and changing tactics to make it difficult to trace them. The attribution process is difficult due to incomplete and rapidly changing information.

3.4 Legal and Political Impediments

It can be difficult to determine who is responsible for cyberwarfare due to the complexity of the legal and political landscape surrounding attribution. This involves dealing with a range of legal issues, the process of attributing cyberattacks across borders often involves complex legal procedures, leading to difficulties in determining the applicable legal jurisdiction. Establishing globally accepted legal standards for cyber attribution remains a work in progress and is a challenge to be addressed. Geopolitical factors such as diplomatic relations and national interests can significantly influence the attribution decision-making process.

Legal and political considerations can impede attribution, affecting its efficacy. The following table outlines how different cyberwarfare attribution challenges align with specific techniques discussed in the paper. It provides a clearer understanding of how these challenges are addressed or associated with specific attribution methodologies and approaches.

Table 1: Alignment of Challenges and techniques

Challenges in Cyberwarfare Attribution	Associated Techniques
Misattribution	Malware Analysis Network Traffic Analysis Digital Forensics TTPs (Tactics, Techniques, Procedures)
Ethical Implications	Linguistic Analysis Geopolitical Analysis
Attribution in the Digital Fog	AI and Machine Learning Digital Forensics
Legal and Political Im-pediments	Geopolitical Analysis

4. Case Study

The details of the case studies presented in this paper are based on publicly available information from news reports and official statements from the organizations involved. The selection of the Standard Bank South Africa ATM fraud and the TransUnion South Africa cyberattack as case studies were random, without specific criteria guiding their selection. These cases were chosen to provide illustrative examples of cyber incidents and to demonstrate the complexities of attribution, rather than being selected based on predetermined criteria or characteristics. We will discuss the cyber-attack involving Standard Bank South Africa and a significant ATM fraud in Japan. This incident highlights the intricacies of attributing cyberattacks and emphasizes the importance of robust cybersecurity in the financial sector.

4.1 The Cyberattack in Japan

In May of the year 2021, a large-scale cyberattack occurred in Japan involving the fraudulent withdrawal of significant sums of money from ATMs. Approximately 100 individuals used forged Standard Bank credit cards to withdraw over R250 million (¥1.8 billion) from 1,400 ATMs across Tokyo and other regions in Japan in under three hours. The incident amounted to an estimated loss of about R300 million for Standard Bank, a major financial institution based in South Africa (Moyo, 2022).

Response and Ongoing Investigation

In response to the incident, Standard Bank took measures to mitigate the impact, secure its systems, and address the vulnerabilities exploited by the attackers. South African officials launched an investigation into the incident and took steps to collaborate with Japanese law enforcement agencies.

Attribution Outcome

The specific attribution outcome remained uncertain at the time of this case study. The complexity of attributing such large-scale cyberattacks, coupled with the use of fraudulent cards and international coordination, can make identifying the perpetrators challenging (Qusai & Sadkhan, 2021).

Table 3 and Table 4 provide a detailed breakdown of techniques employed and challenges faced in the context of the Standard Bank South Africa cyberattack in Japan, reflecting the specific methods and difficulties encountered.

Table 2: Suggested techniques that could be applied in the case study.

Techniques Used in Case Study	References
Malware Analysis	Investigation into the malicious code found within the compromised ATM systems in Japan to understand its characteristics and possible connections to known malware groups.
Network Traffic Analysis	Examination of communication patterns between the attackers and Standard Bank's systems to identify the origin and nature of the attack.
Digital Forensics	Collection and analysis of digital evidence from the hacked bank's system to reconstruct the attack's timeline and uncover the perpetrators' actions.
TTPs (Tactics, Techniques, Procedures)	Identification of specific attack methodologies, such as unauthorized access and fraudulent withdrawals in Japan, examining the methods used in the cybercrime.
Linguistic Analysis	Scrutiny of language markers in communications between the attackers, e.g., emails or messages, potentially revealing the identities or affiliations of the cybercriminals.
Geopolitical Analysis	Investigation into the motivations and implications behind the attack, possibly for financial gain, cyber-espionage, or part of an organized criminal group.
AI and Machine Learning	Utilization of AI and ML algorithms to detect patterns and anomalies in the cybercrime behavior, aiding in identifying the attackers.

Table 3: Challenges applicable to the case study

Challenges in Case Study	References
Misattribution	Risk of incorrectly attributing the cyberattack to a specific entity or nation due to the utilization of proxy servers and misleading clues to deceive investigators.
Ethical Implications	Consideration of potential impacts on innocent parties, risk of further escalation, and concerns about individual privacy during the cybercrime investigation.
Attribution in the Digital Fog	Difficulty in tracing the attackers due to the use of anonymizers, botnets, and rapidly changing infrastructure, hindering the attribution process.
Legal and Political Impediments	Complexity in determining legal jurisdiction and establishing globally accepted standards for cyber attribution amidst geopolitical and diplomatic considerations.

4.2 The Cyberattack on TransUnion South Africa

In the recent TransUnion South Africa cyberattack, a hacker group known as N4aughtysecTU claimed responsibility for breaching the credit bureau's systems. According to the claims made, this group, allegedly from Brazil, asserted access to 54 million personal records of South Africans and demanded a 15 million ransom (R223 million) for the release of the compromised data. The group stated it gained access to the TransUnion server using a client's credentials and had been operating within the system since 2012 without detection (Reporter, 2016).

Response and Ongoing Investigation Following the breach, TransUnion took immediate measures, suspending the compromised client's access, engaging cyber security and forensic experts, and initiating an investigation into the incident. Certain services were taken offline as a precautionary step, and TransUnion South Africa has since resumed these services. The company is working closely with law enforcement and regulatory authorities to address the issue.

Attribution Outcome From the statement given by Transunion in the newspaper article the actual attribution of the cyberattack remained uncertain. The intricate challenges of linking the breach to a specific group or nation, coupled with the hacker group's claims and the complexities of international cyber investigations, presented significant challenges in identifying the responsible actors.

Table 4 and Table 5 provide a detailed hypothetical breakdown of techniques employed and challenges faced in the context of the TransUnion South Africa cyberattack, reflecting the specific methods and difficulties encountered in this scenario.

Table 4: Suggested techniques that could be applied in the case study.

Techniques Used in Case Study	Reference to Case Study
Malware Analysis	Examination of the systems to detect potential malware or intrusion mechanisms used to access and exploit TransUnion's servers.
Network Traffic Analysis	Analysis of the traffic patterns to identify unauthorized access and data exfiltration from the compromised server.
Digital Forensics	Collection and examination of digital evidence from the breached server to reconstruct the attack timeline and identify the attackers.
TTPs (Tactics, Techniques, Procedures)	Identification of the specific methodologies used by the hacker group, including how they gained access through authorized client credentials and navigated undetected.
Linguistic Analysis	Scrutiny of any communication or messages ex-changed between the hacker group and TransUnion regarding the extortion demands and potential threats.
Geopolitical Analysis	Investigation into the origins and affiliations of the hacker group, who claim to be from Brazil, and their threats against South African entities.
AI and Machine Learning	Utilization of AI algorithms for anomaly detection, particularly to identify potential weak points or overlooked security vulnerabilities in TransUnion's systems.

Table 5: Challenges applicable to the case study

Challenges Applicable to Case Study	Reference to Case Study
Misattribution	Risk of potentially attributing the attack to a particular group or nation (Brazil) without concrete evidence or due to misleading statements by the hacker group.
Ethical Implications	Consideration of the potential exposure of sensitive personal data, the company's response to extortion demands, and the threat of further data exposure.
Attribution in the Digital Fog	Difficulty in tracing the hacker group due to their claim of operating undetected in TransUnion's systems since 2012 and the information leakage threats.
Legal and Political Impediments	Complexity in determining the hacker group's actual location and holding them accountable across international jurisdictions for cyberattacks.

5. Conclusion

The conclusion drawn from this study underscores the intricate challenges inherent in the realm of cyberwarfare attribution, shedding light on its pivotal role within the broader landscape of cybersecurity. While the issue of misattribution, wherein the wrong entity is identified as the perpetrator of an attack, looms as a notable concern, the detailed examination of the Standard Bank South Africa ATM fraud and the TransUnion South Africa cyberattack case studies provides valuable insights into the multifaceted nature of attributing cyber incidents. Through these case analyses, it becomes evident that navigating the complexities of attribution demands a holistic and collaborative approach that encompasses legal, technical, ethical, and geopolitical considerations.

Moreover, the findings underscore the imperative for continuous research and adaptation in the field of cybersecurity. As cyber threats continue to evolve and adversaries employ increasingly sophisticated tactics, there exists an ongoing need to innovate and refine strategies for bolstering global defenses. By emphasizing the significance of sustained innovation and collaboration, it advocates for the development of adaptable frameworks that can effectively mitigate the ever-evolving cyber threat landscape.

In essence, the conclusions drawn from this research underscore not only the challenges inherent in cyberwarfare attribution but also the imperative for concerted efforts towards enhancing cybersecurity practices. Through a nuanced understanding of attribution challenges and a commitment to ongoing research and collaboration, stakeholders can better position themselves to safeguard against emerging cyber threats and uphold the integrity of digital ecosystems worldwide.

References

Al-Shaer, E. and Rahman, M.A., 2015. Attribution, temptation, and expectation: A formal framework for defense-by-deception in cyberwarfare. *Cyber Warfare: Building the Scientific Foundation*, pp.57-80.

DiMaggio, J. (2022). *The Art of Cyberwarfare: An Investigator's Guide to Espionage, Ransomware, and Organized Cybercrime.* No Starch Press.

Ferrag, M. A., Kantzavelou, I., Maglaras, L., & Janicke, H. (Eds.). (2023). *Hybrid Threats, Cyberterrorism and Cyberwarfare.* CRC Press.

Goel, S. and Nussbaum, B., 2021. Attribution across cyber-attack types: network intrusions and information operations. *IEEE Open Journal of the Communications Society, 2*, pp.1082-1093.

Kapsokoli, E. (2023). *Cyberterrorism: A New Wave of Terrorism.* https://doi.org/10.1201/9781003314721

Mohamed, N., Almazrouei, S. K., Oubelaid, A., Ahmed, A. A., Jomah, O. S., & Aghnaiya, a. (2023, May). *Understanding the Threat Posed by Chinese Cyber Warfare Units. In 2023 IEEE 3rd International Maghreb Meeting of the Conference on Sciences and Techniques of Automatic Control and Computer Engineering (MI-STA)*, pp. 359-364. IEEE.

Ngulu, J.M., 2022. Efficacy of International Humanitarian Law in Addressing Cyber Warfare as a New Weapon Technology: An Analysis of the Gaps and Way Forward. *The Eastern African Law Review, 45*(1).

Pahi, T., & Skopik, F. (2019, July). *Cyber attribution 2.0: Capture the false flag. In Proceedings of the 18th European Conference on Cyber Warfare and Security* (ECCWS 2019), pp. 338-345.

Qusai, A. D., & Sadkhan, S. B. (2021, August). *Cyberwarfare Techniques: Status, Challenges and Future trends. In 2021 7th International Conference on Contemporary Information Technology and Mathematics (ICCITM)*, pp. 124-129. IEEE.

Wandugi, L. K. (2020). *Attribution and state responsibility in cyber warfare: a case study of the not Petya attack.*

Moyo, A. (2022). *Breaking: Credit bureau TransUnion hacked.* ITWeb. Available at https://www.itweb.co.za/content/o1Jr5Mx9BVjqKdWL. Accessed: 01 October 2023.

Reporter, S. (2016). *Standard Bank Scam: R300-million ATM heist ups the ante.* The Mail & Guardian. Available at [https://mg.co.za/article/2016-05-27-r300-million-atm-heist-ups-the-ante/]. Accessed: 01 October 2023

Utilizing Vector Database Management Systems in Cyber Security

Toni Taipalus, Hilkka Grahn, Hannu Turtiainen and Andrei Costin
University of Jyväskylä, Jyväskylä, Finland

toni.taipalus@jyu.fi
hilkka.grahn@jyu.fi
hannu.ht.turtiainen@jyu.fi
andrei.costin@jyu.fi

Abstract: The rising popularity of phenomena such as ubiquitous computing and IoT poses increasingly high demands for data management, and it is not uncommon that database management systems (DBMS) must be capable of reading and writing hundreds of operations per second. Vector DBMSs (VDBMS) are novel products that focus on the management of vector data and can alleviate data management pressures by storing data objects such as logs, system calls, emails, network flow data, and memory dumps in feature vectors that are computationally efficient in both storage and information retrieval. VDMBSs allow efficient nearest neighbour similarity search on complex data objects, which can be used in various cyber security applications such as anomaly, intrusion, malware detection, user behaviour analysis, and network flow analysis. This study describes VDBMSs and some of their use cases in cyber security.

Keywords: Vector Database, Anomaly Detection, Traffic Analysis, Cyber Security, Phishing Detection

1. Introduction

Vectors as a data representation method have gained popularity with large language models, reverse image searches, and recommendation systems (Li, 2023). Effectively, almost all types of data objects, such as text, images, and video, can be represented as vectors. This popularity stems from the inherent versatility of vectors, which allow complex data structures to be expressed in a mathematical form, enabling efficient processing and analysis (Taipalus, 2024). For example, in the realm of large language models, vectors serve as a fundamental representation of words, sentences, or entire documents, capturing semantic relationships and contextual information.

Although vectors have been widely utilized in cyber security in contexts such as machine learning classification, vector database management systems (VDBMS) have emerged in the early 2020s as dedicated systems for managing vector data. Similarly to relational DBMSs, VDBMSs provide features that automate much of the work in managing data. Because both vectorization and DBMS features are relatively mature and well-understood, the relatively novel VDBMSs have quickly established themselves as trustworthy pieces of software used in various domains.

The landscape of cybersecurity data has expanded considerably, mirroring the growth observed in other domains like large language models. Conventional frameworks and algorithms for vector management prove inadequate when confronted with the sheer magnitude of these datasets (Wang et al., 2021). In response to these challenges, vector databases have emerged as a superior alternative, demonstrating faster computational speed and richer features. These advancements in vector database technology address the limitations inherent in previous systems, particularly their ability to effectively handle the volume of information inherent in cybersecurity datasets.

In this study, we describe vectors as means of representing different data objects such as emails, network traffic, and biometric image data, how VDBMSs facilitate vector data management, and most importantly, how VDBMSs can be utilized in various cyber security related use-cases such as biometric authentication and email phishing detection. We also provide examples of established Python libraries for data preprocessing, normalization, feature extraction, and vectorization. Notably, Python is not the only programming language with such libraries.

The rest of the study is structured as follows. In the next section, we describe VDBMS fundamentals, features, and products, and in Section 3, we detail four VDBMS use cases in cyber security. Section 4 concludes the study.

2. Vector Database Management Systems

For vector databases, vectors are effectively represented as ordered lists of numbers, e.g., [0.1, 7.0, -2.9]. This simple vector could represent a point in space with corresponding coordinates in a three-dimensional Cartesian coordinate system, or the vector could represent the overall hue of a photograph, depending on what type of data object has been *vectorized*, i.e., converted into a *feature vector* (Wang et al., 2021). Although this example vector consists of three dimensions or elements, vectors can hold thousands of dimensions.

For reverse image search applications, images are transformed into vectors, allowing similarity comparisons based on vector distances. Recommendation systems leverage vectors to encapsulate user preferences and item characteristics, enabling personalized and computationally efficient content suggestions. The ability to convert diverse data types, such as text, images, and video, into vector representations facilitates interoperability between different data objects. For example, the same types of queries may be used to retrieve textual and image data. As advancements in vector representation methodologies continue, vector representations are increasingly used in different contexts.

VDBMSs are a type of DBMS designed to manage vector data. Like other types of DBMSs, such as relational DBMSs, VDBMS provides means to efficiently store and retrieve vector data and provide access and concurrency control, query optimization, and database scalability. Additionally, VDBMSs offer several advantages in handling vector data over traditional relational DBMSs. One key strength lies in their ability to perform vector operations, enabling simultaneous processing of multiple elements within a vector.

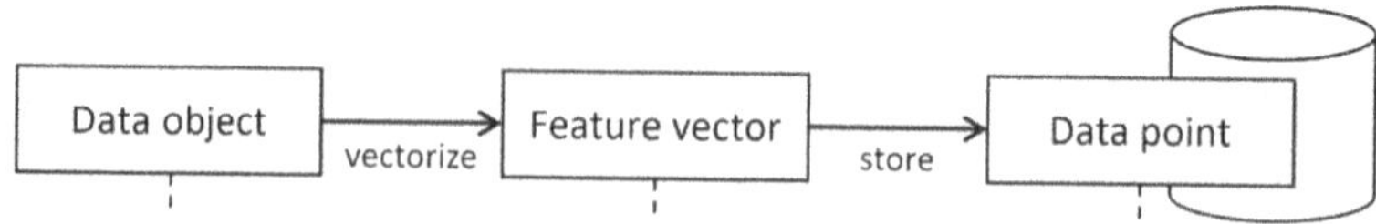

Figure 1: A simplified example of transforming and storing an event or data-of-interest into VDBMS for efficient data management, such as indexing, querying, scalability, and access control.

VDBMSs are designed to support complex vector operations, making them well-suited for applications where mathematical computations on vector data are prevalent. Query optimization in VDBMSs involves exploring specialized optimization techniques for vector operations. This includes optimizing vector aggregations, joins, and filtering to streamline query execution. By tailoring optimization strategies to the unique characteristics of vector data, VDBMSs can achieve better query performance compared to general-purpose DBMSs when dealing with vector-centric workloads. Popular VDBMSs include products such as Pinecone, Milvus (Wang et al., 2021) and Chroma. There are also several libraries for vector operations, such as FAISS and Annoy, but they do not provide many of the DBMS features listed above. Several other DBMSs, such as PostgreSQL, Redis, and SingleStore, have also adopted features for managing vector data (Taipalus, 2024).

Contrary to queries typical for relational and NoSQL databases, vector queries search for vectors that are *approximate nearest neighbours* of the query vector (Ge et al., 2013). If the query vector represents a point in three-dimensional space (e.g., [0.1, 7.0, -2.9]), the VDBMS can search for vectors in the database that are closest matches to the query vector. Depending on the use case, the VDBMS can return one or several near-neighbour vectors with different nearness criteria. For example, suppose the query vector is the end user's current position on a map, and the end user is searching for the nearest restaurants. In that case, the VDBMS may return the ten closest restaurants, but only within a one-mile radius. If the query vector is the end-users freshly scanned retina, the VDBMS may return zero or one vector that matches the query vector; zero returned vectors resulting in denied access.

3. Use-Cases in Cyber Security

There are several potential use-cases for VDBMSs in cyber security. In this section, we describe some of such use-case, and provide further information on how to implement these use-cases. This is not an exhaustive list.

3.1 Authentication

Regarding vector data, biometric authentication is closely related to reverse image search: we use an input image to search for similar (or the same) images. The input can be, e.g., a vectorized fingerprint, iris, or retina. Text-based authentication, such as passwords or passphrases, is seldom a feasible use case for vector data due to the simplicity of simply comparing relatively short text strings with each other.

Establishing a database for biometric authentication involves several steps. All input images should have consistent dimensions and reduced noise for the aforementioned biometrics. Feature extraction, i.e., finding meaningful patterns in the images, differs depending on the type of biometrics. In fingerprints, methods such as *ridge detection and orientation* (Zu et al., 2006) may form the features of the vector, or use natively-vectorized approaches such as those presented in Abe & Shinzaki (2015). In irises, it is crucial to extract and segment the iris and analyse its texture with, e.g., *circular Hough transform* (e.g., Cherabit, Chelali & Drejadi, 2012). In retinas, the blood vessels also need to be considered. After extracting the features, they are combined into a vector and often normalized for consistent scaling. For all these steps, Python libraries such as *OpenCV* (Bradski, 2000), *scikit-image* (Van der Walt et al., 2014), *scikit-learn* (Kramer & Kramer, 2016), and *NumPy* (cf. e.g., Oliphant, 2006), when used in tandem, provide functions for all the aforementioned steps.

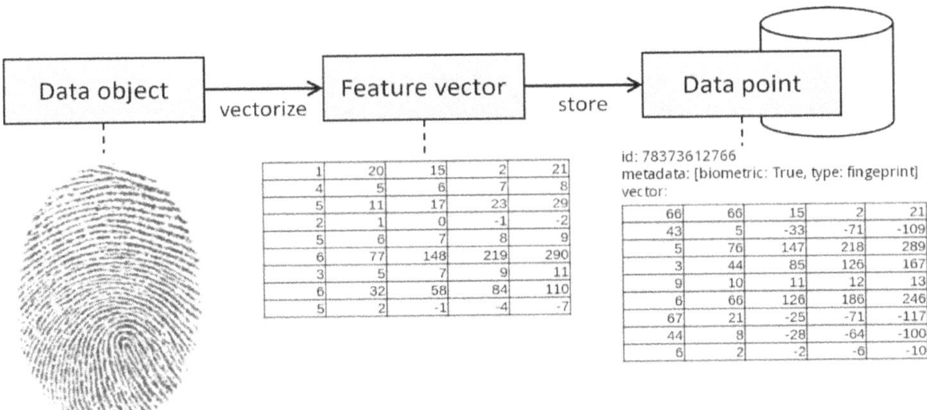

Figure 2: A simplified example of transforming and storing an authenticated biometric fingerprint into VDBMS.

Once the vectors have been created, they can be inserted into a vector database managed by a VDBMS. Many available VDBMSs (and other DBMSs with vector features) offer automatic scalability, access control, data encryption, and query optimization. It is worth noting that the system infrastructure often must provide the means to vectorize input images for real-time authentication. That is, VDBMSs often do not provide the means to vectorize data. Some video frames are typically vectorized and organized sequentially into one high-dimensional vector for video-based authentication, such as gait recognition or keystroke dynamics (Schclar et al., 2012).

With voice-based authentication, audio samples need to be cleaned before vectorization. Possible background noise needs to be removed, the amplitudes need to be normalized, and the audio should be captured with a consistent sampling rate. Features in audio include *Mel-Frequency Cepstral Coefficients* (Hasan, Jamil & Rahman, 2004) and formants. Once desired features have been extracted, they are converted into numerical vectors. Once a user needs to be authenticated based on a voice sample, the sample is vectorized and compared to the (previously recorded) vectorized samples in the database to find enough similarity among the query vector and one vector in the database to authenticate the user. Python packages such as *librosa* (McFee et al., 2015) and *scikit-learn* offer required functions.

3.2 Email Phishing Detection

To identify phishing emails, we need a dataset containing emails labelled based on whether they are considered phishing. Following labelling, the next step involves converting these labelled emails into feature vectors using vectorization techniques such as *Bag-of-Words* (e.g., Qader, Ameen & Ahmed, 2019), *Term Frequency-Inverse Document Frequency* (e.g., Christian, Agus & Suhartono, 2016), or *Word Embeddings* (e.g., Liu et al., 2015). When a new email arrives, the system should vectorize it similarly to the initial email dataset and perform a similarity search in the VDBMS to find similar emails. If similar emails have been labelled as phishing emails, the new email should be handled accordingly. Most common VDBMSs allow metadata – in this case, labels – to be stored along with the feature vectors.

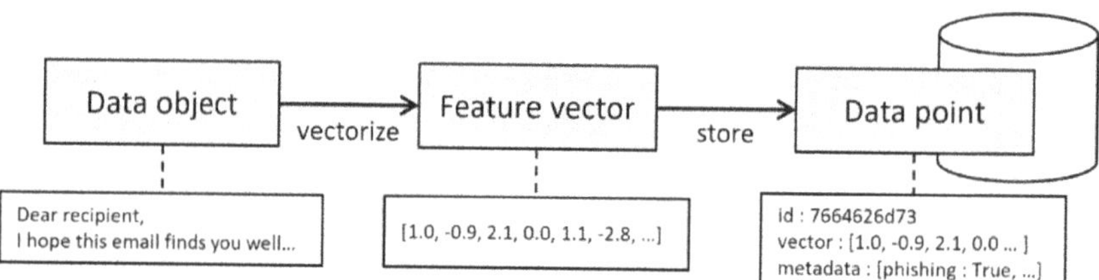

Figure 3: A simplified example of transforming and storing a (potentially phishing) email into VDBMS.

It is worth noting that adjusting the similarity threshold based on the trade-off between false positives and false negatives is crucial. We need to fine-tune this threshold according to domain-specific needs. Additionally, we need to evaluate the performance of this approach using a diverse set of phishing and legitimate emails and iterate and adjust the workflow based on the results. Python libraries such as *scikit-learn*, *Gensim* (Řehůřek & Sojka, 2011), and *NLTK* (Bird, 2006) can preprocess and vectorize even large text data objects.

One alternative approach after vectorization is to apply a machine-learning model for email classification. While the described VDBMS approach does not involve traditional machine learning models, it relies on the idea that similar emails in vector space will likely share similar characteristics. It is a different paradigm compared to machine-learning classification and might be suitable depending on the specific requirements and constraints of the use case. If the system architecture already includes a VDBMS, this approach potentially makes the architecture more efficient and straightforward, automating much of the data management work.

3.3 Anomaly Detection

Anomaly detection can be arduous as many domains require real-time and accurate detections. VDBMSs can be used to detect cyber security-related anomalies. Depending on the use case, different cyber security events can be represented as feature vectors, including information such as IP addresses, protocols, timestamps, file system operations, and executed commands. This approach allows for automated, nearly real-time detection of anomalous behaviour but also requires an initial dataset to be vectorized and used as a reference for both regular and anomalous behaviour. The quality of the initial dataset is paramount, as false positive detections can cause system or data availability issues due to false flagging and possible countermeasures. The baseline accuracy for true positive detections should be very high; meanwhile, the dataset should be large, with several entries for normal and anomalous behaviour. For example, approaches similar to those presented in Subba & Gupta (2021) or Mazzavi et al. (2017) could be used to natively vectorize anomaly detection for host intrusion detection systems.

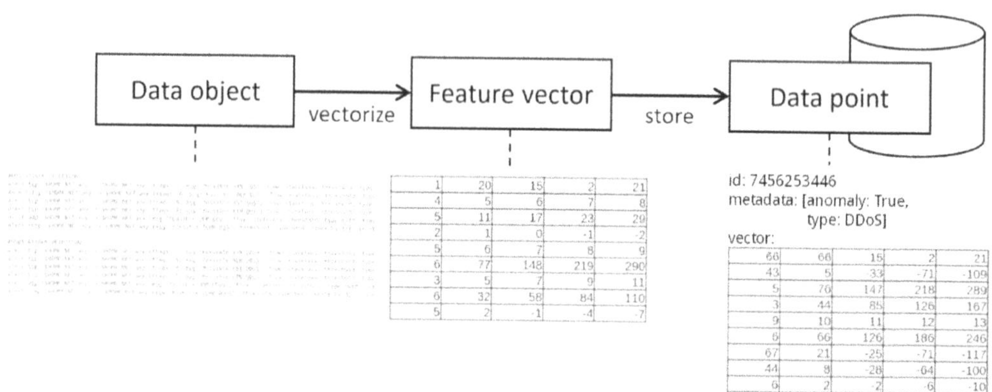

Figure 4: A simplified example of transforming and storing an anomaly alert into VDBMS.

Once the events have been vectorized, they can be inserted into a VDBMS. As new cyber security events occur, their features are vectorized, and the vectors are used as query vectors to search for events with similar characteristics. As with email phishing detection, prepare to tweak the threshold, i.e., how much the query vectors should resemble vectors of anomalous events to categorize them as anomalous events. In all cases, all events should be stored as vectors and labelled anomalous or non-anomalous to be utilized in future searches. The data gathered can be further used to enhance the dataset for better detection through continuous adaptations and feedback mechanisms.

3.4 Network Traffic Analysis

Network traffic analysis plays a pivotal role in cybersecurity by providing an understanding of the data flowing through a network. The purpose is to detect malicious activities and potential security threats before asset damage can occur. By scrutinizing patterns, protocols, and communication flows, it is possible to detect attacks such as distributed denial-of-service (e.g., Lopez et al., 2019) and intrusions (e.g., Gao et al., 2020). Network traffic analysis serves as a proactive defence mechanism, allowing organizations to bolster their cybersecurity defences, respond swiftly to emerging threats, and safeguard the integrity and confidentiality of their digital assets.

Performing real-time network traffic analysis with vectorization involves representing network traffic data as feature vectors. By using tools such as *Wireshark*, *tcpdump*, or *Scapy* (Rohith, Moharir & Shobha, 2018), extract relevant data from raw network packages such as IP addresses, ports, protocols, and packet sizes and convert them into feature vectors. Techniques such as *Bag-of-Words* may be used for categorical data such as protocols, data types, and timestamps can be converted into numerical representations, and numerical features such as packet sizes may be normalized with statistical summaries. For example, approaches such as those of Liu et al. (2017) could natively vectorize network traffic, even in encrypted traffic.

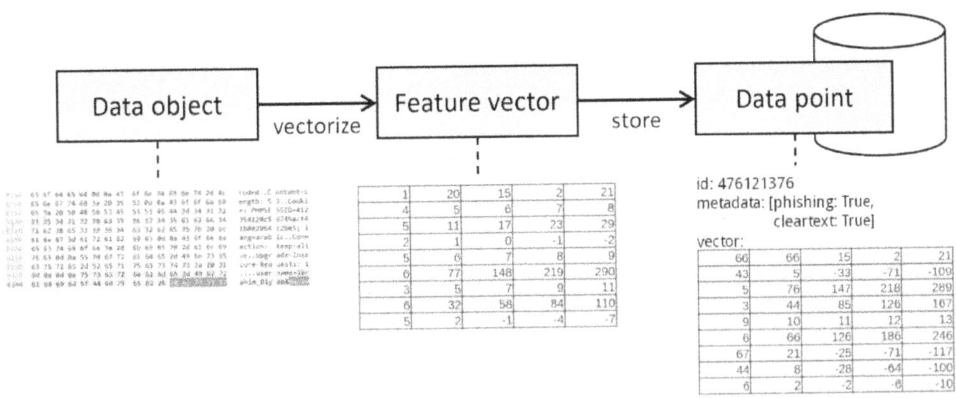

Figure 5: A simplified example of transforming and storing a (potentially phishing) email into VDBMS.

Similarly to some of the use cases presented before, this approach needs initial data to be compared. Again, once the feature vectors have been stored in a VDBMS, network traffic should be continuously vectorized and compared with the existing vectors in the database (Iglesias & Zseby, 2015). Suppose vectorization aims to classify and detect malicious events in the network, it is essential to implement a periodic recalibration based on new data to eliminate false positives and false negatives. This approach serves as a reactive security measure and a proactive tool for network optimization and resource allocation.

4. Conclusion

Storing various data objects as feature vectors has gained popularity due to their computational efficiency in storing and comparing vectors. Additionally, VDBMSs have emerged as systems dedicated to automating tasks such as storing and indexing vectors, facilitating vector querying and query optimization, and database scalability and access control.

The strengths of VDBMS for cyber security are their efficiency in handling large and diverse datasets, providing rapid query response times, and being adept at recognizing non-exact matches. These systems' scalability, speed, and adaptability make them invaluable for cyber security, particularly in dynamic environments where extensive and varied data require quick and flexible analysis.

In this study, we showed through several examples how vector database management systems and various software libraries can be used in the domain of cyber security. In summary, we highlighted the use cases in user authentication, email phishing detection, anomaly detection, and network traffic analysis. However, as almost all data objects can be vectorized, the possibilities of utilizing vector data extend beyond the use cases presented in this study. This prompts further theoretical and applied research on VDBMSs, potentially resulting in interesting immediate applications in highly demanding cyber-security scenarios.

Acknowledgment

Hannu Turtiainen thanks the Finnish Cultural Foundation / Suomen Kulttuurirahasto for supporting his Ph.D. dissertation work and research (grant decision no. 00231412).

The fingerprint image in Figure 2 is by user brokenarts and is available at Freeimages.com.

References

Abe, N., & Shinzaki, T. (2015). Vectorized fingerprint representation using minutiae relation code. In *2015 International Conference on Biometrics (ICB)* (pp. 408-415). IEEE.

Bird, S. (2006). NLTK: the natural language toolkit. In *Proceedings of the COLING/ACL 2006 Interactive Presentation Sessions* (pp. 69-72).

Bradski, G. (2000). The openCV library. *Dr. Dobb's Journal: Software Tools for the Professional Programmer*, 25(11), 120-123.

Cherabit, N., Chelali, F. Z., & Djeradi, A. (2012). Circular Hough transform for iris localization. *Science and Technology*, 2(5), 114-121.

Christian, H., Agus, M. P., & Suhartono, D. (2016). Single document automatic text summarization using term frequency-inverse document frequency (TF-IDF). *ComTech: Computer, Mathematics and Engineering Applications*, 7(4), 285-294.

Gao, M., Ma, L., Liu, H., Zhang, Z., Ning, Z., & Xu, J. (2020). Malicious network traffic detection based on deep neural networks and association analysis. *Sensors*, *20*(5), 1452.

Ge, T., He, K., Ke, Q., & Sun, J. (2013). Optimized product quantization for approximate nearest neighbor search. In *Proceedings of the IEEE conference on computer vision and pattern recognition* (pp. 2946-2953).

Hasan, M. R., Jamil, M., & Rahman, M. G. R. M. S. (2004). Speaker identification using mel frequency cepstral coefficients. *Variations*, 1(4), 565-568.

Iglesias, F., & Zseby, T. (2015). Analysis of network traffic features for anomaly detection. Machine Learning, 101, 59-84.

Kramer, O., & Kramer, O. (2016). Scikit-learn. *Machine learning for evolution strategies*, 45-53.

Li, F. (2023). Modernization of databases in the cloud era: Building databases that run like Legos. In *Proceedings of the VLDB Endowment* 16 (pp. 4140–4151).

Liu, J., Fu, Y., Ming, J., Ren, Y., Sun, L., & Xiong, H. (2017, August). Effective and real-time in-app activity analysis in encrypted internet traffic streams. In *Proceedings of the 23rd ACM SIGKDD international conference on knowledge discovery and data mining* (pp. 335-344).

Liu, Y., Liu, Z., Chua, T. S., & Sun, M. (2015). Topical word embeddings. In *Proceedings of the AAAI Conference on Artificial Intelligence* (Vol. 29, No. 1).

Lopez, A. D., Mohan, A. P., & Nair, S. (2019). Network traffic behavioral analytics for detection of DDoS attacks. *SMU data science review*, *2*(1), 14.

Mazzawi, H., Dalal, G., Rozenblatz, D., Ein-Dorx, L., Niniox, M., & Lavi, O. (2017) Anomaly Detection in Large Databases Using Behavioral Patterning. 2017 IEEE 33rd International Conference on Data Engineering (ICDE), San Diego, CA, USA, 2017, pp. 1140-1149

McFee, B., Raffel, C., Liang, D., Ellis, D. P., McVicar, M., Battenberg, E., & Nieto, O. (2015). librosa: Audio and music signal analysis in Python. In *Proceedings of the 14th Python in Science Conference* (pp. 18-25).

Oliphant, T. E. (2006). *Guide to NumPy*. Trelgol Publishing. USA.

Qader, W. A., Ameen, M. M., & Ahmed, B. I. (2019). An overview of Bag of Words: Importance, implementation, applications, and challenges. In *2019 International Engineering Conference* (IEC) (pp. 200-204).

Řehůřek, R., & Sojka, P. (2011). Gensim - statistical semantics in Python. *Retrieved from genism.org*.

Rohith, R., Moharir, M., & Shobha, G. (2018). SCAPY - A powerful interactive packet manipulation program. In *2018 International Conference on Networking, Embedded and Wireless Systems* (ICNEWS) (pp. 1-5).

Schclar, A., Rokach, L., Abramson, A., & Elovici, Y. (2012). User Authentication Based on Representative Users. In IEEE Transactions on Systems, Man, and Cybernetics, Part C (Applications and Reviews), vol. 42, no. 6, pp. 1669-1678,

Subba, B., & Gupta, P. (2021). A tfidfvectorizer and singular value decomposition based host intrusion detection system framework for detecting anomalous system processes. *Computers & Security*, *100*, 102084.

Taipalus, T. (2024). Vector database management systems: Fundamental concepts, use-cases, and current challenges. *Cognitive Systems Research*, 85, Article 101216.

Van der Walt, S., Schönberger, J. L., Nunez-Iglesias, J., Boulogne, F., Warner, J. D., Yager, N., ... & Yu, T. (2014). scikit-image: image processing in Python. *PeerJ*, 2, e453.

Wang, J., Yi, X., Guo, R., Jin, H., Xu, P., Li, S., ... & Xie, C. (2021). Milvus: A purpose-built vector data management system. In *Proceedings of the 2021 International Conference on Management of Data* (pp. 2614-2627).

Zhu, E., Yin, J., Hu, C., & Zhang, G. (2006). A systematic method for fingerprint ridge orientation estimation and image segmentation. *Pattern recognition*, 39(8), 1452-1472.

Unpacking the Complex Socio-Technical Systems Assemblages in Cybersecurity

Mamello Thinyane
University of South Australia, Adelaide, Australia

mamello.thinyane@unisa.edu.au

Abstract: The ensuing digital transformation means that cybersecurity solutioning increasingly occurs in the context of complex intractable socio-technical systems comprising non-technical elements, including human, social, and societal factors. These evolving cybersecurity ecosystem dynamics, at the confluence of cyber-physical-social spaces, present several challenges to techno-centric cybersecurity solutions including for risk assessment, threat modelling, and incident analysis. This paper unpacks the complexity of the cybersecurity domain and illustrates the associated socio-technical systems assemblages through a case study and situational analysis of a cybersecurity incident. It then reviews socio-technical systems analysis approaches from the safety management domain and discusses the alignment with and relevance for cybersecurity. The utility of these approaches is demonstrated by applying the functional resonance analysis method to the said cybersecurity incident. The situational analysis surfaces the diverse set of factors, including human, non-human, cultural, economic, institutional, and global, that directly played a role in the unfolding of the incident, and which need to be considered in risk assessment and incident analysis. Further, analysing the incident through the functional resonance analysis method shows the functional dependencies and cascade of performance variability between the different elements in this situation, which goes beyond simple, root-cause, linear causality, and purely technical explanations. Overall, the paper explicates the need for cybersecurity risk assessment and incident analysis that is commensurate with the complexity of underlying socio-technical cyber systems.

Keywords: Socio-Technical Systems, Functional Resonance Modelling, Complex Systems, Cybersecurity, Safety Management, Resilience Engineering

1. Introduction and Background

The cybersecurity threat landscape has evolved significantly in tandem with developments in computing; from Charles Babbage's Difference Engine – the first computing device, Electronic Numerical Integrator and Computer (ENIAC) – the first general purpose computer, Advanced Research Project Agency Network (ARPANET) – the predecessor to the Internet, to the modern day computing that is deeply integrated into cyber-physical-social systems that are supporting critical functions for individuals, organizations, and society at large (Pasandideh et al., 2022). This evolution has heightened the importance of systems perspectives and also concerns regarding not only technocentric threats but also human, organizational and societal threats (Shoemaker et al., 2020; Von Solms & Van Niekerk, 2013; Zoto et al., 2019). As such, systems thinking has increasingly been adopted in cybersecurity to understand computing systems, cyber threats, and cybersecurity solutions holistically as part of a complex ecosystem and as comprising interrelated and interdependent elements that shape the overall cybersecurity posture (Susan M. Tisdale, 2015).

An important element of this evolution has been the integration of computing into increasingly complex and intractable socio-technical systems. Complex systems, which are not just complicated because of the many components and interactions, are dynamic and exhibit emergent behaviour that makes them underspecified and not fully understood. This is in contrast to tractable systems which can be fully described, decomposed into subcomponents, do not change while being described, and whose functions are homogenous and regular (Hollnagel, 2012). Complexity has been considered across many aspects of cybersecurity such as the infrastructure of cyber-physical systems, threat landscape, and organizational architectures (Harbertson et al., 2023; Wen et al., 2017). The complexity of systems has a direct implication on how the functioning of those systems is understood and managed, but more important how dysfunction and malfunctioning are understood and managed. The implication of this, and the motivation for this research, is to give recognition that the approaches, methods, and tools of the trade in cybersecurity need to be commensurate with this complex nature of the underlying socio-technical systems (Perrotin et al., 2022).

The primary line of inquiry in this paper is "How can the cybersecurity domain be understood from a socio-technical systems assemblages perspective?" with the corollary of "How effective are socio-technical systems analytical frameworks (from safety management) for the cybersecurity domain?" To address these questions this paper undertakes a detailed situational analysis of a specific cybersecurity incident to explore the complex socio-technical assemblages implicated in the situation. It then discusses the relevance of socio-technical systems approaches from the safety management domain and subsequently demonstrates the utility of the functional resonance analysis method (FRAM) for cybersecurity incident analysis.

2. Unpacking the Complexity in Cybersecurity Incidents

A case study of the Equifax data breach that occurred in May 2017 has been undertaken to explore and illustrate the inherent complexity of cybersecurity incidents. This case has been chosen based on the profile of the incident, level of public domain reporting, and detailed documentation available from the subsequent investigations (GAO, 2018; Michael et al., 2017; Miyashiro, 2021). The situational analysis methodological approach is used to explore this incident.

2.1 Methodological Approach: Situational Analysis

Situational analysis, which is a variant of the Grounded Theory research method, is a qualitative critical analysis method developed to explore situations by unpacking the complexity within the situation (Clarke, 2005). The method focuses on the situation as a unit of analysis giving recognition to the fact that it is impossible to disentangle things and actions from the context in which they occur. That all elements in a situation "both co-constitute and affect" all other elements in that situation (Clarke, 2021). This is a necessary foundation for explicating complexity because it gives due recognition to the influences and interactions within systems that lead to uniquely emergent behaviours and outcomes.

Situational Analysis employs visually oriented analytical strategy to highlight the key elements present in a situation, the interactions and relationships between those elements, and the context within which situation occurs (Clarke, 2005). The key analytical tools within situational analysis are (Clarke, 2021): *situational maps* – which identify the main elements present in a situation; *relational maps* - which map the key interactions between elements; *social worlds and arena maps* – are collectives around a shared commitment within a situation; and lastly *positional maps* – which identify key discursive positions on specific issues within the situation of analysis. In this research three tools, messy situational maps, ordered situational maps, and relational maps, are utilized to explore the Equifax incident.

2.2 Equifax Data Breach Case Study

Equifax is a credit reporting agency that suffered a data breach, between May and July 2017, which exploited a vulnerability in *Apache Struts*, to expose details of over 145 million people (Miyashiro, 2021). The *Equifax CEO* at the time attributed the data breach to the failure of the *employee who was responsible* for patching vulnerabilities, however several factors, some of which are discussed hereafter, were prevalent in this situation and contributed to the incident as highlighted in the messy situational map in Figure 1.

Figure 1: Messy situational map of the Equifax data breach incident

In the formal Equifax investigation, the breach was attributed to four main factors: weaknesses in the identification functions, poor detection and monitoring capabilities, lack of segmentation of access to databases, and weaknesses in data governance (GAO, 2018). Further weaknesses were noted in the detection and monitoring functions in Equifax related to the failure to maintain *intrusion detection systems*; an *SSL certificate* which was required to inspect encrypted network traffic had expired before May 2017 leading to hackers bypassing the traffic inspection systems (GAO, 2018).

The leadership at Equifax had invested in improving their cybersecurity posture by having a dedicated security operations team, including a *Global Threat and Vulnerability Management (GTVM)* team. They had also engaged the services of *Mandiant*, a cybersecurity company, to improve their cybersecurity posture. However, several factors were at play at the organizational level that unfolded in the leadup to the data breach. These include a *"talent exodus"* from Equifax which saw key figures in cybersecurity functions leaving the company, with some of them having expressed *concerns around the data security culture* within the company – a former VP of data quality at Equifax echoed this sentiment that "it bothered me how much access just about any employee had to the personally identifiable attributes" (Michael et al., 2017). The reporting on this case details many factors including human elements, technical and non-human elements, international and institutional elements, socio-cultural elements, global issues, and temporal elements that contributed to the overall situation; these are detailed in the ordered situational map in Table 1.

Table 1: Ordered situational map for the Equifax data breach.

Heuristics	Examples
Human elements (individual + collective)	Richard Smith (then-CEO); Attacker; 145 million and 15 million people in US and UK affected; Nike Zheng; "entry crew"; Shell Crew; developer who knew about struts; senior manager; employee meant to apply the patch.
Non-human elements	Apache Struts; expired SSL certificate; Metasploit; misconfigured Intrusion Detection System; China chopper malware; Moloch; patch management; GTVM team; CVE-2017-5638; input sanitation, 8500 unresolved vulnerabilities; dedicated Security Operations Centre.
Political economic elements	Data Protection Act 1998; EUR 500,000 fine; Equifax and Mandiant dispute; departure of key staff i.e., "talent exodus";
Discursive constructions of actors	
International / institutional elements	US-CERT; Information Commissioners' Office; Apache; China; United States; United States Federal Trade Commission; nation state actor.
Major contested issues	Attribution; "blame for the breach".
Local to global elements	Tighter regulation; espionage.
Socio-cultural elements	Concern about data culture; failure to renew SSL certificate.
Symbolic elements	
Popular and other discourses	
Other empirical elements	War exercises; breach scenarios; "not credit card theft"; "get as much data as you can" play; lack of inventory management; patch management;
Spatial and temporal elements	10-month certificate expiry; 5 months instead of 48 hours to patch; 76 days' time to discovery.

All these factors are part of the effects dynamics and complex interplay that culminated in the data breach incident. Invariably different factors had varying levels of influence on the outcome, however, specific interactions can be mapped across many of the elements in the situation through relational mapping. Relational mapping is a technique within the situational analysis suite of tools that shifts the focus from the elements in a situation to the relations between those elements. In relational mapping, each element is taken in turn to consider how it interacts with the other elements, thus explicating the complexity of the effects flows within the situation. For the Equifax case study, the relational mapping is undertaken on two elements, the *Apache Struts* vulnerability (i.e., CVE-2017-5638) and *vulnerability scans* undertaken to surface vulnerabilities across the Equifax systems – see Figure 2 and Figure 3 respectively.

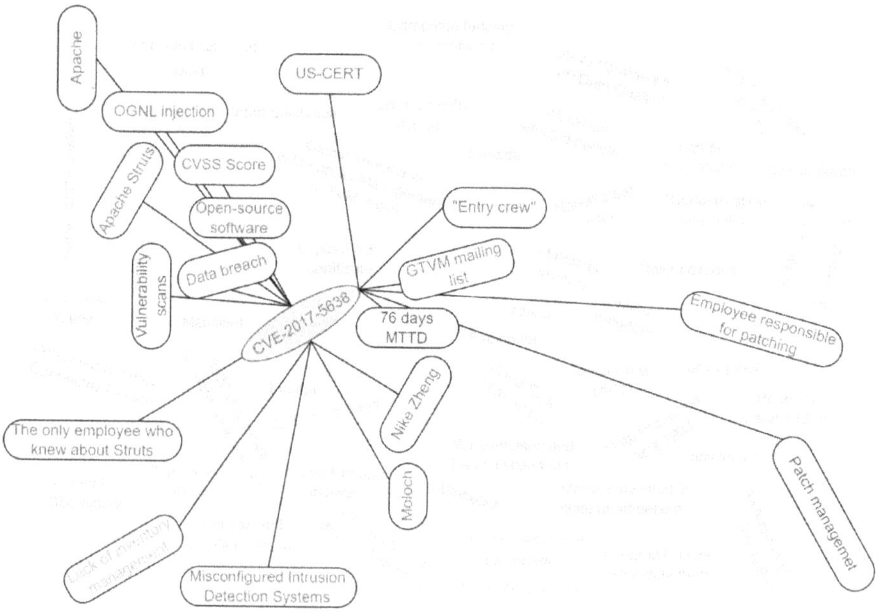

Figure 2: Relational mapping for the Equifax data breach centred on the exploited vulnerability (CVE-2017-5638)

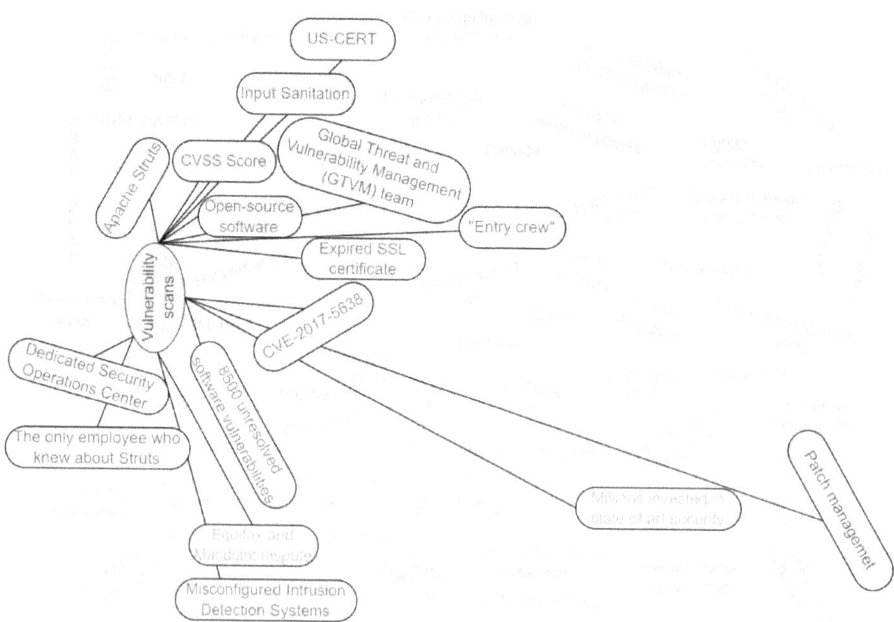

Figure 3: Relational mapping for the Equifax data breach centred on "vulnerability scans" element.

Presented in Figure 2, the discovery of the *Apache Struts* vulnerability, which allowed Object Graph Navigation Language (OGNL) injection attacks by *Nike Zheng,* started off the chain of events that ultimately led to the *data breach*. While it could be argued that other vulnerabilities could have been compromised and other vectors used, given that many other vulnerabilities had been noted on previous *vulnerability scans* on the Equifax systems, this vulnerability that was later assigned *CVE-2017-5638* and a *CVSS score* of 10 was the necessary element in this situation.

The ability of organizations to effectively execute *patch management* functions was an important element of reducing the risk associated with CVE-2017-5638 vulnerability. In the case of Equifax, the failure of the *CVE-2017-5638* alert from the *US-CERT*, which was relayed inside Equifax through the *GTVM mailing list*, to reach the *employee responsible for patching*, meant that their systems remained vulnerable. This is the vulnerability that was exploited by the initial access *"entry crew"*, which later handed over to a more sophisticated threat actor. The ability to detect and contain the attack was impaired by the ineffective (due to expired SSL certificate) *intrusion detection systems*, poor *inventory management* practices, and internal communication and operational challenges.

The relations between the *CVE-2017-5638* vulnerability and the different elements in this situation contributed in varying degrees to how the situation unfolded. Similar effect dynamics can be noted between *vulnerability scanning* function in Equifax and many other elements in the situation as depicted in Figure 3.

By focusing on the whole situation as the unit of analysis, the situational analysis of the Equifax incident highlights multi-dimensional elements and socio-technical assemblages that are at play in this situation. It shows why simplistic attributions of the incident, to technical factors or to the failure of the one employee who was responsible for patching vulnerabilities, are incomplete and provide an unsatisfactory explanation. This highlights the need for solutions that are commensurate with the level of complexity in such incidents and provides an opportunity for exploring relevant solutions from other domains.

3. Socio-Technical Approaches From Safety Management

There are several frameworks for conceptualizing adverse incidents that have been used extensively in domains such as safety management. Most of them are based on three accident philosophies, chain of events models, epidemiological accident models, and systems accident models (Y. Zhang et al., 2022).

The first is the Domino model which is based on the notion of cascade of events or causality effects; that events linearly lead to other events. The original model defined five distinct dominos associated with the worker's social environment, human factors that lead to faults, an unsafe human act or technical condition, the accident, and the consequences of the accident (Heinrich, 1941). The causality effects in this model understood *injuries (or incidents)* as being caused by *accidents* which are caused by *unsafe acts or technical conditions* which are a result of a *human factors (or fault of the person)* that are shaped by the *social environment*.

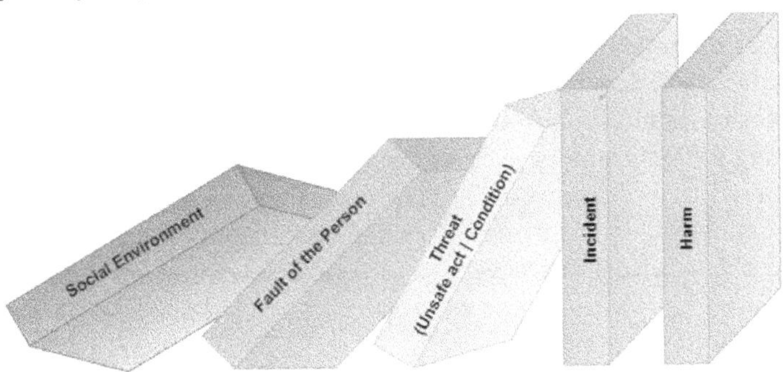

Figure 4: The cybersecurity domain from the Domino perspective

This model is relevant for the cybersecurity domain because several cybersecurity solutions have similar linear causality mechanisms, for example, using causal modelling to investigate cybersecurity incidents, causal reasoning for malware detection, and employing causality analysis and system provenance graphs to classify ransomware types (Abel et al., 2018, 2020; Mei et al., 2021; H. Zhang et al., 2016). However, beyond accounting just for technical factors, the model identifies human factors which impact on threat conditions which are caused by social environment factors. Applying the model to the Equifax incident, the data breach (*incident*) could be understood as a result of the unpatched Apache Struts system (*unsafe technical condition*) which was due to the failure of the employee who was responsible for patching vulnerabilities (*fault of the person*) which was caused by social environment factors, including the organizational culture at Equifax at the time. However, while this analysis has some merit, the overarching criticism of the Domino model is that it is too simple and therefore leads to simplistic and short-sighted solutions that seek to attribute failure to simple causes.

The second model, the Swiss Cheese model, is based on the understanding of systems as comprising linear interactions, with latent conditions and dependencies (see Figure 5). The complexity of systems from this perspective means that understanding problems entails identifying a combination of conditions that lead to specific systems' outcomes; and addressing problems is a matter of strengthening the layers of barriers that mitigate those problems (J Reason et al., 2006; Reason, 1990). Variations of this model (i.e., Mark II and Mark III) identified different layers or barriers including organizational, workplace environment, and individual elements, as well as the flow of weaknesses from the organizational factors, workplace factors and unsafe individual acts, but also the long-lasting gaps and weaknesses that are associated with latent conditions within organizations (J Reason et al., 2006).

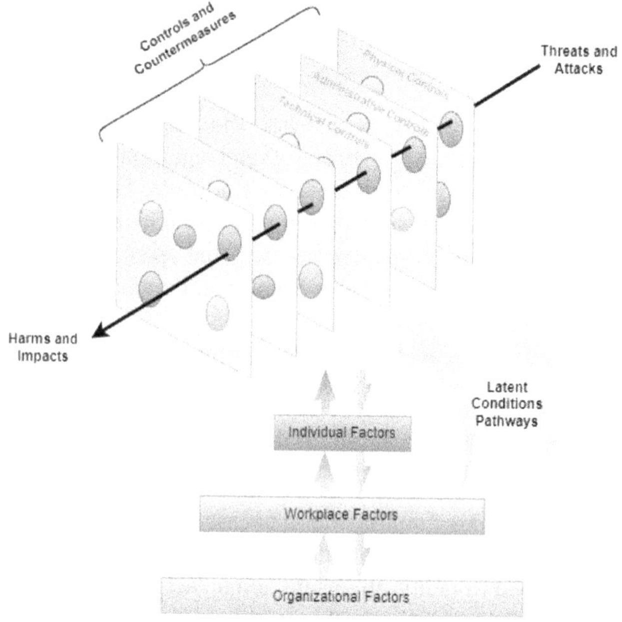

Figure 5: Framing cybersecurity domain from the Swiss cheese perspective (adapted from (J Reason et al., 2006))

The basic elements of hazards, defences, and losses in this model directly map to the cybersecurity language of threats and attacks, controls and countermeasures, and harms and impact respectively. It also captures the notion of having different types of barriers, such as physical controls, administrative controls, and technical controls, as well as having different phases such as detect, deny, disrupt, degrade, and deceive, as different layers of cybersecurity defences (Hutchins et al., 2011). Considering the Equifax incident from the Swiss cheese perspective, it becomes apparent that that the attack exploited weaknesses in several security controls and systems (i.e., holes in the cheese slices). There were weaknesses in inventory management, patch management, and intrusion detection systems. However, there were also human, workplace, and organizational latent factors that contributed to the incident.

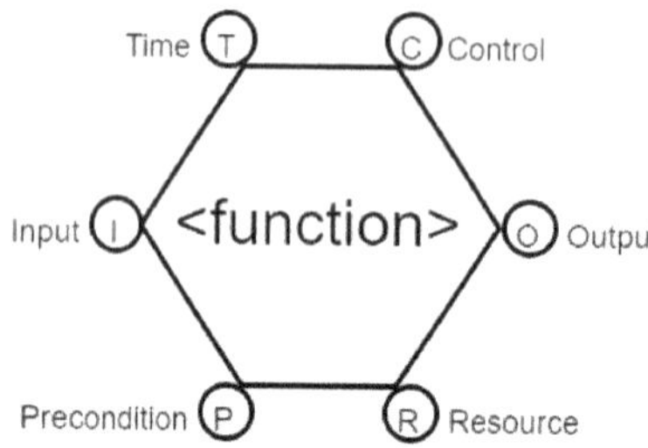

Figure 6: Function description in FRAM

The last framework considered in this paper is the functional resonance analysis method (FRAM) which is an approach for understanding and modelling the functional behaviour of complex socio-technical systems. This method was developed to address the limitation of deterministic, linear, and probabilistic approaches for understanding such systems (Hollnagel, 2012; Patriarca et al., 2020). FRAM describes systems in terms of the interactions between interrelated functions of the system, specifically in terms of how *outputs* (O) from functions interact with aspects of the downstream functions. These specific aspect include: *input* (I) – which is processed or transformed by a function and which initiate a function, *preconditions* (P) – that need to be in place for a function to occur, *resources* (R) – which are execution conditions or resources needed or consumed to produce the output, *time* (T) – which set the temporal constraints on the function, and *control* (C) – which control and monitor the function for acceptable performance (see Figure 6).

The FRAM approach allows for analysis of complex socio-technical systems by focusing on the relations between functions and the resonance that arises from functional coupling. The utility and relevance of FRAM for the cybersecurity domain is illustrated in detail below by applying it to the Equifax data breach incident.

4. Functional Resonance Analysis of the Equifax data breach.

It is outside the scope of this paper to model the full extent of the functional dependencies between all the elements in the situation (see Figure 1). Therefore, the analysis focuses on the one element that the then Equifax CEO attributed the incident to – the failure to patch the vulnerable Apache Struts system. Further discussion is on the functions that are internal to Equifax and those that are the source of significant performance variability.

Table 2: FRAM analysis and representation of the <patch a vulnerability> function

Name of function	Patch a vulnerability
Description	This is the process of applying the software update provided by Apache to mitigate the Apache Struts vulnerability (CVE-2017-5638)
Aspect	**Description of aspect**
Input	The *patch instruction* has been received by the responsible employee
Output	*A patched system* that can be operated securely
Precondition	- The availability of the patch from Apache - An asset inventory that would indicate the presence of affected systems - The vulnerability being active on their systems.
Resource	The actual software update to be used to patch the vulnerability
Control	The severity level of the vulnerability (CVSS score) that influences how quickly patches are applied
Time	*Not described*

4.1 Analysis of Key Functions

The <Patch a vulnerability> function is undertaken by applying software updates to remediate a risk associated with a known vulnerability and is related to four other key functions, as illustrated in Table 2 and Figure 7. The output of the <Patch a vulnerability> function is a patched Apache Struts system that is not vulnerable to the OGNL injection (i.e., CVE-2017-5638) vulnerability. The effective execution of this function contributes to the secure operation of the Apache Struts system, which, for the scope of this analysis, is a Background and Exit function. Patching a vulnerability is triggered by a patch instruction which is an output of the <Communicate the patch> function. The two key Preconditions for patching a vulnerability are the availability of the patch, which is an output of the <Develop a patch> function, as well as the vulnerability being active on the organization's systems, which is an output of the <Undertake vulnerability scan> function.

Another function of relevance in this case is the <Maintain asset inventory> function which involves identifying the digital assets owned by the organization and documenting they cybersecurity status. The Output from the <Maintain asset inventory> function is the actual asset inventory which forms the basis for further asset management and cybersecurity risk management processes.

The other function of interest is the <Communicate the patch> function, which is a condensed function that represents the cascade of external and internal communication that ensued from when the patch was made available to the patch being applied. As will be discussed further below, these series of communications should have triggered the application of the patch; hence why the output of this function is the Input to the <Patch a vulnerability> function.

The next step in analysing this case is to identity performance variability across the different functions and to map how that variability cascaded to the other functions leading to the circumstances of having an unpatched Apache Struts server.

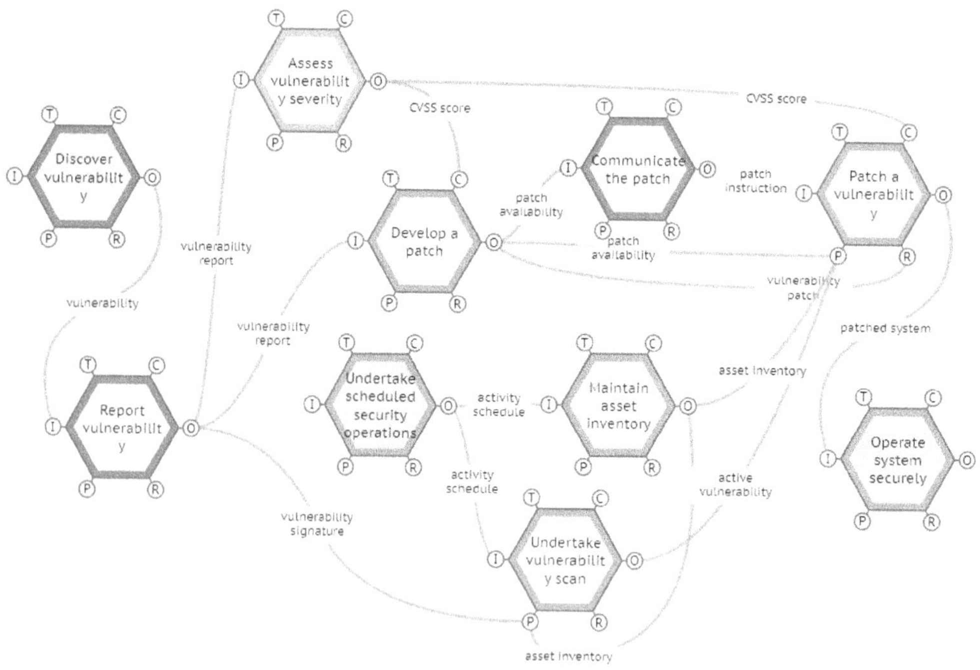

Figure 7: FRAM model of the patch management processes associated with the Equifax data breach.

4.2 Performance Variability Analysis

The failure to achieve the desired outcome (i.e., the *<Operate systems securely>* function) in the FRAM instantiation of the Equifax incident in Figure 7, can be traced to several elements of internal and external performance variability along the technical, human, and organizational dimensions across the key functions.

The internal organizational policy at Equifax required critical vulnerabilities to be patched within 48 hours, however, the Struts vulnerability was only patched after 5 months (Miyashiro, 2021). The major sources of performance variability that contributed to this are within the *<Communicate the patch>* and *<Maintain asset inventory>* functions. Once communication was received from US-CERT about the Apache Struts vulnerability, the information was relayed to 400 individuals on the GTVM mailing list. The key human function performance variability was the fact that the senior manager who supervised the lead developer (who knew about Apache Struts) and who received the GTVM alert, failed to relay the information to the said lead developer. There is no clear indication of the specific personal circumstances that explain this failure to relay the information. However, there is evidence that organizational climate at the time meant that there was lot of pressure on the cybersecurity functions and that "internally security was viewed as a bottleneck", which could have contributed to this oversight (Michael et al., 2017; Miyashiro, 2021).

While the analysis has focused on functions related to patching vulnerabilities, there is evidence of variability across many other functions that contributed to the adverse impact of the data breach. For example, the technological performance variability associated with failure of the intrusion detection systems and the human function variability associated with the configuration of the vulnerability scanners.

The functional resonance analysis of the Equifax incident illustrates how internal and external performance variability across the technological, human, and organizational dimensions led to the adverse impacts experienced in this incident. This level of analysis provides a nuanced perspective on the functional dependencies in this situation and accounts for the inherent complexity.

5. Discussion and Conclusion

Complex socio-technical systems, which are typical in the cybersecurity domain, are necessarily intractable and always underspecified. As such, it is impossible to completely prevent adverse incidents in cybersecurity because they are not fully known (e.g., zero-day vulnerabilities), because of the vast and complex attack surface, because of performance variability across functions (e.g., accidental insiders), and because of the functional resonance within STS that could escalate normal performance variability into failure and adverse incidents.

As illustrated in the case of the Equifax incident, the assessment that the data breach was associated with an unpatched Apache Struts system is true and valid, however, the assertion that it could be attributed to the one individual who was responsible for patching the systems, provides an overly simplistic perspective on this situation. The functional resonance analysis undertaken above provides a more nuanced perspective on the dependencies between the different functions both within Equifax and outside the company, that led to the observed outcomes.

Given this complexity, the importance of resilience engineering in cybersecurity becomes apparent. Resilience is the systems' capability for functional persistence and adaptation during adverse incidents, and it is typically framed in terms of the prepare, withstand, recover, and adapt phases (Kott & Linkov, 2019). However, the means towards resilience differ depending on how systems are conceptualized. For example, from a dominos conceptualization, failures are a cascade of initial failure conditions, and therefore resilience is about strengthening the robustness of the individual elements in the system (i.e., robustness of the individual dominos); from the Swiss cheese perspective, failures are an alignment of weaknesses in barriers, and therefore solutions are about putting in place sufficient barriers to limit propagation of threats; from the FRAM perspective, failures are the result of propagation of variability across functions, and therefore resilience is about dampening performance variability across systems functions. All these different approaches to resilience solutioning are relevant in cybersecurity because, as a complex STS, it compromises both the tractable technical and the intractable human and social dimensions (Ebert et al., 2023).

The analysis of the Equifax incident shows that simple approaches and explanations fail to account for the diverse set of elements and complex effect dynamics at play in such situations. The situational analysis surfaced the myriad of factors, including human, non-human, cultural, economic, institutional, and global, that are implicated in the incident. Further the functional resonance analysis method showed the functional dependencies and cascade of performance variability between the different elements in this situation. Despite some of its weaknesses, including the need for adaptation for the cybersecurity domain, FRAM as a socio-technical systems analysis method holds potential for holistic cybersecurity risk assessment and incident investigation.

If there is any lesson from the history of computer security it is that "hasty and simplistic solutions, while briefly satisfying, [are] not only likely to prove ineffective but also to make problems even worse" (Warner, 2012). While there is merit and utility to some of the simplistic cybersecurity solutions, for example, those that assume that single events cause incidents (e.g., root cause analysis), or that threat events flow linearly through systems, this paper posits that it is necessary to understand cybersecurity threats and solutions holistically along with their complex socio-technical systems assemblages.

References

Abel, S., Tang, Y., Singh, J., & Paek, E. (2020). Applications of Causal Modeling in Cybersecurity: An Exploratory Approach. *Advances in Science, Technology and Engineering Systems Journal*, *5*(3), 380–387. https://doi.org/10.25046/aj050349

Abel, S., Xiao, L., & Wang, H. (2018). Causal Modeling for Cybersecurity. *2018 International Symposium on Security and Privacy in Social Networks and Big Data (SocialSec)*, 209–212. https://doi.org/10.1109/SocialSec.2018.8760379

Clarke, A. (2005). *Situational Analysis*. SAGE Publications, Inc. https://doi.org/10.4135/9781412985833

Clarke, A. (2021). From Grounded Theory to Situational Analysis: What's New? Why? How? In *Developing Grounded Theory* (2nd ed.). Routledge.

Ebert, N., Schaltegger, T., Ambuehl, B., Schöni, L., Zimmermann, V., & Knieps, M. (2023). Learning from safety science: A way forward for studying cybersecurity incidents in organizations. *Computers & Security*, *134*, 103435. https://doi.org/10.1016/j.cose.2023.103435

GAO. (2018). *Data Protection—Actions taken by Equifax and Federal Agencies in response to the 2017 breach*. https://www.warren.senate.gov/imo/media/doc/2018.09.06%20GAO%20Equifax%20report.pdf

Harbertson, L., Crespo Maldonado, S., Park, A., Taylor, J., & Volante, J. (2023). *Quantifying Complexity: Cybersecurity Performance Goals Analysis* [Report]. Carnegie Mellon University. https://doi.org/10.1184/R1/24179841.v1

Heinrich, H. W. (1941). Industrial Accident Prevention. A Scientific Approach. *Industrial Accident Prevention. A Scientific Approach., Second Edition*. https://www.cabdirect.org/cabdirect/abstract/19432701767

Hollnagel, E. (2012). *FRAM: The Functional Resonance Analysis Method: Modelling Complex Socio-Technical Systems*. Taylor & Francis Group.

Hutchins, E. M., Cloppert, M. J., & Amin, R. M. (2011). Intelligence-Driven Computer Network Defense Informed by Analysis of Adversary Campaigns and Intrusion Kill Chains. *Leading Issues in Information Warfare and Security Research*, *1*(1).

J Reason, E Hollnagel, & J Paries. (2006). *Revisiting the Swiss Cheese model of accidents* [dataset]. European Organization for the safety of air navigation. https://doi.org/10.1163/1570-6664_iyb_SIM_org_39214

Kott, A., & Linkov, I. (Eds.). (2019). *Cyber Resilience of Systems and Networks*. Springer International Publishing. https://doi.org/10.1007/978-3-319-77492-3

Mei, R., Yan, H.-B., & Han, Z.-H. (2021). RansomLens: Understanding Ransomware via Causality Analysis on System Provenance Graph. In W. Lu, K. Sun, M. Yung, & F. Liu (Eds.), *Science of Cyber Security* (pp. 252–267). Springer International Publishing. https://doi.org/10.1007/978-3-030-89137-4_18

Michael, R., Robertson, J., & Sharpe, A. (2017, September 29). The Inside Story of Equifax's Massive Data Breach. *Bloomberg.Com*. https://www.bloomberg.com/news/features/2017-09-29/the-equifax-hack-has-all-the-hallmarks-of-state-sponsored-pros

Miyashiro, I. K. (2021, April 30). *Case Study: Equifax Data Breach*. https://sevenpillarsinstitute.org/case-study-equifax-data-breach/

Pasandideh, S., Pereira, P., & Gomes, L. (2022). Cyber-Physical-Social Systems: Taxonomy, Challenges, and Opportunities. *IEEE Access, 10*, 42404–42419. https://doi.org/10.1109/ACCESS.2022.3167441

Patriarca, R., Di Gravio, G., Woltjer, R., Costantino, F., Praetorius, G., Ferreira, P., & Hollnagel, E. (2020). Framing the FRAM: A literature review on the functional resonance analysis method. *Safety Science, 129*, 104827. https://doi.org/10.1016/j.ssci.2020.104827

Perrotin, P., Belloir, N., Sadou, S., Hairion, D., & Beugnard, A. (2022). Using the architecture of Socio-Technical System to analyse its vulnerability. *2022 17th Annual System of Systems Engineering Conference (SOSE)*, 361–366. https://doi.org/10.1109/SOSE55472.2022.9812648

Reason, J. (1990). The contribution of latent human failures to the breakdown of complex systems. In D. E. Broadbent, J. Reason, & A. Baddeley (Eds.), *Human Factors in Hazardous Situations: Proceedings of a Royal Society Discussion Meeting held on 28 and 29 June 1989* (p. 0). Oxford University Press. https://doi.org/10.1093/acprof:oso/9780198521914.003.0003

Shoemaker, D., Kohnke, A., & Sigler, K. (2020). *The Cybersecurity Body of Knowledge: The ACM/IEEE/AIS/IFIP Recommendations for a Complete Curriculum in Cybersecurity*. Routledge & CRC Press. https://www.routledge.com/The-Cybersecurity-Body-of-Knowledge-The-ACMIEEEAISIFIP-Recommendations/Shoemaker-Kohnke-Sigler/p/book/9781032400211

Susan M. Tisdale. (2015). Cybersecurity: Challenges from a systems, complexity, knowledge management and business intelligence perspective. *Issues In Information Systems, 16*(3), 191–198. https://doi.org/10.48009/3_iis_2015_191-198

Von Solms, R., & Van Niekerk, J. (2013). From information security to cyber security. *Computers & Security, 38*, 97–102. https://doi.org/10.1016/j.cose.2013.04.004

Warner, M. (2012). Cybersecurity: A Pre-history. *Intelligence and National Security, 27*(5), 781–799. https://doi.org/10.1080/02684527.2012.708530

Wen, G., Yu, W., Yu, X., & Lü, J. (2017). Complex cyber-physical networks: From cybersecurity to security control. *Journal of Systems Science and Complexity, 30*(1), 46–67. https://doi.org/10.1007/s11424-017-6181-x

Zhang, H., Yao, D. (Daphne), Ramakrishnan, N., & Zhang, Z. (2016). Causality reasoning about network events for detecting stealthy malware activities. *Computers & Security, 58*, 180–198. https://doi.org/10.1016/j.cose.2016.01.002

Zhang, Y., Dong, C., Guo, W., Dai, J., & Zhao, Z. (2022). Systems theoretic accident model and process (STAMP): A literature review. *Safety Science, 152*, 105596. https://doi.org/10.1016/j.ssci.2021.105596

Zoto, E., Kianpour, M., Kowalski, S. J., & Lopez-Rojas, E. A. (2019). A Socio-technical Systems Approach to Design and Support Systems Thinking in Cybersecurity and Risk Management Education. *Complex Systems Informatics and Modeling Quarterly, 18*, Article 18.

Evaluating Zero-Shot Chatgpt Performance on Predicting CVE Data From Vulnerability Descriptions

Hannu Turtiainen[1], Narges Yousefnezhad[2], Vadim Bogulean[2], Andrei Costin[1], and Timo Hämäläinen[1]

[1] Faculty of Information Technology, University of Jyväskylä, Jyväskylä, Finland

[2] Binare Oy, Jyväskylä, Finland

hannu.ht.turtiainen@jyu.fi
narges.yousefnezhad@binare.io
vadim.bogulean@binare.io
andrei.costin@jyu.fi
timoh@jyu.fi

Abstract: Vulnerability management is a critical industry activity driven by compliance and regulations aiming to allocate best-fitted resources to address vulnerabilities efficiently. The increasing number of vulnerabilities reported and discovered by a diverse community results in varying quality of the reports and differing perspectives. To tackle this, machine learning (ML) has shown promise in automating vulnerability assessments. While some existing ML approaches have demonstrated feasibility, there is room for improvement. Additionally, gaps remain in the literature to understand how the specific terminology used in vulnerability databases and reports influences ML interpretation. Large Language Model (LLM) systems, such as ChatGPT, are praised for their versatility and high applicability to any domain. However, how well or poorly a state-of-the-art LLM system performs on existing vulnerability datasets at a large scale and across different scoring metrics needs to be clarified or well-researched. This paper aims to close several such gaps and present a more precise and comprehensive picture of how ChatGPT performs on predicting vulnerability metrics based on NVD's CVE vulnerability database. We analyze the responses from ChatGPT on a set of 113,228 (~50% out of all NVD vulnerabilities) CVE vulnerability descriptions and measure its performance against NVD-CVE as ground truth. We measure and analyze the predictions for several vulnerabilities in metadata and calculate performance statistics.

Keywords: AI, ChatGPT, CVE, ML, NVD, Vulnerability Management

1. Introduction

Gathering vulnerability information is crucial for cybersecurity as more attacks occur yearly. Automation is required as the attacks have also become automated; thus, a robust, up-to-date, and information-rich database is mandatory for automated tools to function. The National Vulnerability Database (NVD) is the de facto database in the industry, and it does an avid job of disseminating and cataloging information about software vulnerabilities. The more common knowledge about security vulnerabilities, the greater the chance of mitigating potential security risks. The rapid evolution of the cybersecurity landscape has launched demands for robust vulnerability tracking systems; thus, the ground truth data for these systems must be as good as possible.

NVD CVE database is generally of high quality and acts as a ground truth in our (and many others) studies. However, it still suffers from inherent data quality issues, as highlighted by recent works by Anwar et al. (2022), Dong et al. (2019), and Kuehn et al. (2021), and this may indirectly affect any studies and comparisons to where it is used as a ground truth. At the same time, to the best of our knowledge, there is no better and more curated ground truth for vulnerability information than NVD CVE.

Large language models (LLM), such as GPT-4 by OpenAI, can sift through large text datasets quickly and efficiently. By leveraging machine learning algorithms, LLMs can analyze patterns and extract insights from various sources, contributing to a more comprehensive and accurate vulnerability database or accelerating the attempts to improve the database manually. Despite the potential benefits, it is essential to approach the integration of LLMs cautiously. However, it should be acknowledged that the quality of LLM results can vary, as inaccuracies, biases, limited data, and data poisoning during the training may impact the model's performance. Therefore, it is crucial to implement mechanisms for validation and verification to ensure that the information provided by LLMs aligns with established cybersecurity standards and experts' opinions. Enhancing the quality of the NVD requires effort. Incorporating LLMs to harness the power of advanced language processing may be the way forward for the NVD dataset.

Our primary focus is to address critical gaps and comprehensively assess ChatGPT's performance using NVD's widely recognized CVE vulnerability database. In our experiment, we test how well ChatGPT predicts Common Weakness Enumeration (CWE), Common Vulnerability Scoring System (CVSS), and Common Platform

Enumeration (CPE) based on the vulnerability description from the NVD database. We compare the predictions against the ground truth from the NVD database.

In summary, we attempt to bridge some research field gaps and provide insights into qualitative and quantitative performance metrics of ChatGPT when applied to CVE and vulnerability reporting. To the best of our knowledge, this work is the first of its kind and of this scale of ChatGPT applied to CVEs.

The findings indicate that ChatGPT could have performed more robustly in certain aspects, raising questions about its suitability for fully automated and autonomous AI-based vulnerability management systems. As we discuss the challenges inherent in this research, we underscore the importance of addressing these limitations.

Our main contributions to this work are as follows:

1. We collect and evaluate ChatGPT GPT-4 qualitative and quantitative performance metrics over 33,197 NVD CVE entries.
2. We process the results using multi-metrics analysis.
3. We provide key insights and takeaways on what it means for automated cybersecurity and where ChatGPT's blind spots for CVEs.
4. We release the finalized dataset as open data under FAIR Data Principles and permissive licensing.

2. Experiment and Data Setup

In this section, we briefly present our experimental and data setup. The main components of our experiments are NVD CVE recent database subset (Section 2.1), ChatGPT queries and responses (Section 2.2), and statistical metrics for qualitative performance analysis (Section 2.3).

2.1 CVE Dataset Setup

The NVD CVE database is the standard vulnerability database used by organizations and individuals worldwide. It is also open-source and free of cost. To fetch the latest and complete NVD CVE database, we employed FastCVE by "Binaré Oy"' (2023). FastCVE is an open-source, highly reliable, and efficient alternative to well-known cve-search, which did not support the latest NVD API usage shift when our experiments started.

The official NVD CVE database contains 222,982 entries as of the submission of this paper. For our NVD dataset snapshot, we queried FastCVE for "7,000 random entries" for each year between 2002–2023 and limited the total to 115,000. The choice of 7,000 entries/year comes from practical considerations such as budgeting (e.g., cumulative costs of ChatGPT API queries) and timing (e.g., getting ChatGPT results for a query take up to 60 seconds, queries from the same account cannot be parallelized, ChatGPT service downtime). Since not all earlier years had at least 7,000 CVE entries and we removed "rejected" entries before submitting them, we ended up with 113,228 entries to query ChatGPT, more than 50% of the entire NVD CVE database.

However, not all 113,228 entries are fully specified in the NVD CVE database. For example, 32,616 entries lacked a proper and relevant CWE value. Instead, they had "NVD-CWE-Other" or "NVD-CWE-noinfo", which we did not match against the ChatGPT data. Moreover, "NVD-CWE-Other" or "NVD CWE-noinfo" are generally useless noise as they are irrelevant for any meaningful comparison, as they convey no additional information compared to entries missing CWE altogether. Also, entries typically have either CVSS v2, v3, or v3.1 information and not necessarily more than one of them. However, there are some exceptions, of course. Nevertheless, we ended up with 107,378 entries with CVSS v2 score, 47,200 entries with CVSS v3 (i.e., v3.0 and v3.1 combined) metrics, and 80,612 with properly assigned CWE.

2.2 ChatGPT Setup

For this experiment, we have enabled a paid ChatGPT-4 API key. All results were served by the ChatGPT model version gpt-4-0613. In API query terms, we set ChatGPT with the following prompt:

```
messages = [
    {
    "role": "system",
    "content": "You are a cybersecurity expert. Do not look up any vulnerability databases such as NVD.
    You will be provided with a bug description. Provide a fitting CWE, CVSS version 2, and version 3 with
```

exact numbers and EPSS score as a response without any other text. Please also try to give a matching CPE to this bug. Parse the result as a JSON.",

},

{"role": "user", "content": prompt},

]

Subsequently, we iterated over each CVE entry in our snapshot dataset and supplied the CVE description text and the prompt above to the ChatGPT APIs. Naturally, we collected and stored the response for each query for later offline analysis and processing.

2.3 Statistical Metrics

We rely on statistical metrics to compare the qualitative performance of ChatGPT versus the NVD CVE database (NVD as ground truth). Since these metrics are tailored to evaluate distinct aspects of the data-model relationship Hodson (2022), narrowing the comparison to only one or two metrics diminishes the breadth of insights that can be extracted from the analysis. Such limitations on several metrics may constrain the potential discoveries derived from modeling studies. As recommended by several studies (e.g., Jackson et al. (2019)), employing a diverse set of metrics enables acquiring a broader range of insights and understanding of the data relation and observable phenomena Liemohn et al. (2021). We employed core Python, scikit-learn Pedregosa et al. (2011), and NumPy Harris et al. (2020) libraries for all our metric calculations.

– MAE (Mean Absolute Error) measures the average skew of the predictions to the actual values using the same units and dimensions as the original values.

$$MAE = \frac{1}{N}\sum_{i=1}^{N}|GT_i - Pred_i|$$

– MSE (Mean Squared Error) measures average error but penalizes more significant errors than smaller ones. It uses squared units and squared dimensions of the target variables.

$$MSE = \frac{1}{N}\sum_{i=1}^{N}(GT_i - Pred_i)^2$$

– RMSE (Root Mean Squared Error) RMSE (Root Mean Squared Error) measures the average error of the predictions, but it penalizes significant errors more than smaller ones. It uses the same units and dimensions as the original values.

$$RMSE = \sqrt{MSE}$$

– MAPE (Mean Absolute Percentage Error) provides the average percentage error of the predictions as a relative measure.

$$MAPE = \frac{1}{N}\sum_{i=1}^{N}\left(\frac{|GT_i - Pred_i|}{GT_i}\right) \times 100$$

– R-squared (Coefficient of Determination), in our case, is a metric to see how well ChatGPT predicts the required values (dependent variable) based on the vulnerability description (feature vectors from the text are independent variable). In the context of model performance, R-squared has its limitations and should be considered alongside other evaluation metrics.

$$R^2 = 1 - \frac{\sum_{i=1}^{N}(GT_i - Pred_i)^2}{\sum_{i=1}^{N}(GT_i - MeanGT)^2}$$

– The Pearson Correlation Coefficient measures the linear relationship between the ground truth and the predictions. A score of one means perfect positive correlation, and zero indicates no linear correlation.

$$Correlation = \frac{Covariance(GT, Pred)}{StdDev(GT) \times StdDev(Pred)}$$

Together, these metrics provide a comprehensive evaluation of a model's performance from different perspectives, and each metric comes with its own set of advantages and disadvantages Mamun et al. (2020). MAE, RMSE, and MAPE are generally more interpretable and easy to communicate to non-technical stakeholders, making them suitable for practical applications. Pearson Correlation measures the association between variables, while MAE, MSE, RMSE, and MAPE quantify the error between predicted and actual values. Pearson Correlation is not sensitive to outliers, while MAE and MAPE are less sensitive than MSE and RMSE. R-squared provides insights into the model's overall goodness of fit, with higher values indicating better explanatory power Chicco et al. (2021). Researchers and analysts often use a combination of these metrics to understand a model's strengths and weaknesses comprehensively.

3. Results and Analysis

In this section, we present our main results and their analysis. Figures 1 and 2 summarize the ground truth data from the NVD database for CVSS v2 and v3, respectively. These Figures show that not all entries have all metrics assigned, which is a problem in data quality. Of course, older entries do not have the newer CVSSv3 metrics, but all should have at least one or the other. Figures 3 and 4 disclose the results from ChatGPT predictions for CVSS. We also highlight the number of entries that have both ground truth and prediction data available. Figure 5 showcases the prediction results for CWE and CPE data. We analyze and interpret the statistics of ChatGPT's prediction of CVSSv2, CVSSv3, CWE, and CPE separately and independently below. Figure 6 includes the results of our statistics, explained in Section 2.3, for CVSSv2 and CVSSv3 score, severity, and vector values.

	All NVD entries	**with** CVSSv2 Score	without CVSSv2 Score	**with** CVSSv2 Severity	without CVSSv2 Severity	**with** CVSSv2 Vector	without CVSSv2 Vector
Count (%)	113,228 (100%)	107,378 (95%)	5,850 (5%)	107,381 (95%)	5,847 (5%)	107,381 (95%)	5,847 (5%)
Total	113,228	113,228		113,228		113,228	

Figure 1: NVD: CVSSv2 ground truth

	All NVD entries	**with** CVSSv3 Score	without CVSSv3 Score	**with** CVSSv3 Severity	without CVSSv3 Severity	**with** CVSSv3 Vector	without CVSSv3 Vector
Count (%)	113,228 (100%)	47,200 (42%)	66,028 (58%)	47,200 (42%)	66,028 (58%)	47,200 (42%)	66,028 (58%)
Total	113,228	113,228		113,228		113,228	

Figure 2: NVD: CVSSv3 ground truth

	GPT and NVD Both CVSSv2 Score	GPT **true** CVSSv2 Score	GPT false CVSSv2 Score	GPT and NVD Both CVSSv2 Severity	GPT **true** CVSSv2 Severity	GPT false CVSSv2 Severity	GPT and NVD Both CVSSv2 Vector	GPT **true** CVSSv2 Vector	GPT false CVSSv2 Vector
Count (%)	103,703 (92% of our NVD)	35,996 (35%)	67,707 (65%)	103,705 (92%)	62,782 (61%)	40,923 (39%)	52,656 (49%)	23,151(44%)	29,505 (56%)
Total	103,703	103,703		103,705	103,705		52,656	52,656	

Figure 3: GPT vs. NVD: CVSSv2 results

	GPT and NVD Both CVSSv3 Score	GPT **true** CVSSv3 Score	GPT false CVSSv3 Score	GPT and NVD Both CVSSv3 Severity	GPT **true** CVSSv3 Severity	GPT false CVSSv3 Severity	GPT and NVD Both CVSSv3 Vector	GPT **true** CVSSv3 Vector	GPT false CVSSv3 Vector
Count (%)	44,401 (39% of our NVD)	17,494 (39%)	26,907 (61%)	44,395 (39%)	28,697 (65%)	15,698 (35%)	18,550 (16%)	3,645(20%)	14,905 (80%)
Total	44,401	44,401		44,395	44,395		18,550	18,550	

Figure 4: GPT vs. NVD: CVSSv3 results

	All NVD entries	NVD **with** CWE	NVD without CWE (or CWE-OTHER)	GPT and NVD both CWE	GPT **true** CWE	GPT false CWE	GPT and NVD both CPE	GPT **true** CPE	GPT false CPE
Count (%)	113,228 (100%)	80,612 (71%)	32,616 (29%)	80,612 (71%)	45,326 (56%)	35,286 (44%)	66,204 (58%)	46,886 (71%)	19,318 (29%)
Total	113,228	113,228		80,612	80,612		66,204	66,204	

Figure 5: GPT vs. NVD: CWE and CPE results

	MAE	MAPE	MSE	R^2	RMSE	Pearson's	Total items	Comment
CVSSv2 Score	1.29	28.13	3.35	0.18	1.83	0.60	103,703	Table 3 / Column 2
CVSSv3 Score	0.94	15.08	2.02	0.27	1.42	0.64	44,401	Table 4 / Column 2
CVSSv2 Severity	0.41	25.23	0.45	-0.21	0.67	0.49	103,705	Table 3 / Column 5
CVSSv3 Severity	0.39	16.37	0.45	0.17	0.67	0.61	44,395	Table 4 / Column 5
CVSSv2 Vector-Access	0.11	x	x	x	x	x	52,656	Table 3 / Column 8
CVSSv2 Vector-Authentication	0.07	x	x	x	x	x	52,656	– // –
CVSSv2 Vector-Availability	0.30	x	x	x	x	x	52,656	– // –
CVSSv2 Vector-Complexity	0.30	x	x	x	x	x	52,656	– // –
CVSSv2 Vector-Confidentiality	0.25	x	x	x	x	x	52,656	– // –
CVSSv2 Vector-Integrity	0.23	x	x	x	x	x	52,656	– // –
CVSSv3 Vector-Attack Complexity	0.12	x	x	x	x	x	18,550	Table 4 / Column 8
CVSSv3 Vector-Attack Vector	0.27	x	x	x	x	x	18,550	– // –
CVSSv3 Vector-Availability	0.20	x	x	x	x	x	18,550	– // –
CVSSv3 Vector-Confidentiality	0.21	x	x	x	x	x	18,550	– // –
CVSSv3 Vector-Integrity	0.20	x	x	x	x	x	18,550	– // –
CVSSv3 Vector-Privileges	0.17	x	x	x	x	x	18,550	– // –
CVSSv3 Vector-Scope Changes	0.08	x	x	x	x	x	18,550	– // –
CVSSv3 Vector-User Interaction	0.18	x	x	x	x	x	18,550	– // –

Figure 6: Summary of statistics

For the CVSS scores, we aimed to match the exact score (i.e., 0.0 – 10.0). Only then would the prediction be positive. The severity metric would better indicate "close enough" scores, as all the severity values are a range of scores. We got the severity values based on the scores from the ground truth and the ChatGPT predictions and translated the severities from words to a "value" from 0–2 for CVSSv2 (low, medium, high) and 0–3 for CVSSv3 (low, medium, high, critical), respectively. With these values, we can calculate statistical metrics and errors. For the CVSS vectors, we also checked for an exact match (case we marked as true directly). However, we also studied the accuracy of ChatGPT to predict individual metrics for each scoring system to see which vector metric caused ChatGPT the most issues. We used a "value" system (0...N), similar to the severity statistics above.

The CVSSv2 results (Figure 3) show that ChatGPT predicted the exact score 35% of the time, which is not ideal but surprisingly good because of the exact score requirement (i.e., 101 distinct possible values, 0.0 – 10.0). However, the severity was correct only 61% of the time, which is far from being qualitatively acceptable as only three values in the range in CVSS v2 (low, medium, high). CVSSv2 vectors were matched identically 44% of the time, which seems promising. The base score is calculated from the vector; however, we have far fewer predictions for the vectors than the scores. Thus, at this point, we cannot draw many conclusions on whether ChatGPT has any correlation between the predictions. As for the individual CVSSv2 vector values (Figure 6: CVSSv2 Vector), our statistics would indicate that the *Access Complexity* and *Authentication* metrics are usually correct. These metrics are far more frequently correct than the others, while the *Availability* impact score causes the most problems for ChatGPT.

On average, the CVSSv2 score predictions (Figure 6) were off by 1.29 points (MAE), which is certainly big enough to cause severity to be wrong. CVSS v2 MSE and RMSE were 3.35 and 1.83, respectively, indicating that some prediction errors were way off. The MAPE value of 28.1% means that, on average, the predictions are off by approximately 28.1% in percentage terms, which is relatively high. The R-squared value of 0.18 is ideally not great; however, the Pearson Correlation Coefficient is better at 0.60. Nevertheless, the ChatGPT performs better than the random mean but does not fit well. For CVSSv2 severity, ChatGPT was off by 0.41 points (MAE) on average, which is quite a decent result. The statistics show that ChatGPT's performance is moderate; however, nowhere near precise enough for cybersecurity applications similar to the test.

With CVSSv3 (Figure 4), considerably less completely valid data was available than with CVSSv2. This is because we have taken entries from each year since 2002, and the effort to add v3 metrics to older entries seems non-existent; thus, NVD-CVE ground truth misses a lot of CVSSv3 data. ChatGPT CVSSv3 predictions were similar to CVSSv2 with a 39% correct score, and the event was slightly better than v2 for the v3 severity at 65% correct predictions. Predicting CVSSv3 vectors proved problematic for ChatGPT, with only 20% being entirely correct. However, v3 has more metrics in the base score vector than v2. Therefore, this lower performance in v3 vector prediction is intuitively expected but discouraging. As for vectors (Figure 6), scope and attack complexity performed the best. This is expected as they only have two values to set. The user interaction metric also has two values but still performs worse. The attack vector exploitability metric was the worst metric from the predictions.

The CVSSv3 score predictions (Figure 6) were off by 0.94 points (MAE), which is considerably better than the v2 scores. MSE and RMSE were 2.02 and 1.42, respectively, significantly better than the v2 statistics, indicating that the false predictions were closer to the ground truth overall. The MAPE value of 15.0% is also almost half of the v2 score. The R-squared value of 0.27 is still relatively low, although also better than v2, while the Pearson Correlation Coefficient was raised to 0.67. Based on the data, **ChatGPT is fitting predictions better for the v3 than the v2 scores**. Nevertheless, even the v3 results are far from acceptable as is. For CVSSv3 severity, ChatGPT was off by 0.41 points (MAE) on average.

The overall better performance for v3 severity over v2 predictions could be interpreted to be because of any of the following reasons: either due to a more extensive, more convergent set of 103,703 (CVSSv2) vs. 44,401 (CVSSv3) or due to better finetune of ChatGPT towards predicting CVSSv3 scores as this CVSS version is being more actively used in reports over the last decade.

For the CPE metrics (Figure 5), we parse the CPE result of ChatGPT. If the CPE is valid, we query FastCVE for CVEs present in that CPE. The result is true if the CVE we are processing is on that list. For CWE metrics, we check if the ground truth and the ChatGPT results match, and we do this only if the ground truth has a valid value, i.e., values that are not NVD-CWE-other nor NVD-CWE-noinfo. The results indicate that ChatGPT produced the same CWE as the ground truth in 56% of the valid cases and a valid-and-correct CPE in 71% of the entries. It is good to note that the CPE predictions also suffered from varying responses and non-valid predictions, as presented in Section 3.1. The results are not exceptional, but a solid foundation for improvements. We must remember that the ground truth descriptions may not always be fully representative as they seem to add more information to the metadata rather than a complete description of the vulnerability. Nevertheless, we leave exploring the quality of the descriptions as future work.

3.1 Samples of Chatgpt Responses Posing Challenges

CVE databases, including NVD, have many quality and completeness issues (Section 2.1). ChatGPT responses are no exception to this rule, despite the intuitive expectation that the platform would reply in a more uniform and standardized manner.

Below, we provide the most commonly seen variations of the output format response from ChatGPT for the requested CVSSv2 information. Such variations pose challenges for automated data processing and data normalization. Therefore, handling and normalizing such responses carefully and on a case-by-case basis is required.

1. "CVSSv2": "AV:N/AC:L/Au:N/C:P/I:P/A:P (7.5)" → "vector (score)"
2. "CVSSv2": "7.5 (AV:N/AC:L/Au:N/C:P/I:P/A:P)" → "score (vector)"
3. "CVSSv2": "AV:N/AC:L/Au:N/C:P/I:P/A:P (7.5 – High)" → "vector (score - severity)
4. "CVSSv2": {"Score": 7.2,"Vector": "AV:L/AC:L/Au:N/C:C/I:C/A:C"} → { "Score": <float>, "Vector": vector}

   NOTE: first-capitalized sub-keys

   NOTE: "Score" as a raw/native FLOAT 7.2

5. "CVSSv2": {"score": 4.3,"vector": "AV:N/AC:M/Au:N/C:N/I:P/A:N"} → { score: score, "vector": vector}

NOTE: lowercase sub-keys

NOTE: "score" as a raw/native FLOAT 7.2

6. "CVSSv2": "AV:N/AC:L/Au:N/C:P/I:N/A:N" → "vector", "CVSSv2_Score": "5.0" → "score"

NOTE: separate main keys

7. "CVSSv2": {"Base Score": "7.8","Vector": "(AV:N/AC:L/Au:N/C:N/I:N/A:C)"} → { "Base Score": STRING, "Vector": vector},

8. "CVSSv2": {"Base Score": 7.8,"Vector": "(AV:N/AC:L/Au:N/C:N/I:N/A:C)"} → { "Base Score": FLOAT, "Vector": vector},

NOTE: "Base Score" as a raw/native <float> 7.8 as opposed to string variant "7.8" in most other cases

9. "CVSSv2": "AV:N/AC:L/Au:N/C:C/I:C/A:C" → "vector"

NOTE: no score

10. "CVSSv2": {"Base Score": "7.5", "Impact Subscore": "6.4", "Exploitability Subscore": "10.0",

"Access Vector": "Network," "Access Complexity": "Low," "Authentication": "None," "Confidentiality Impact": "Partial," "Integrity Impact": "Partial," "Availability Impact": "Partial"} → {"Base Score": score}

NOTE: vector required to be constructed (we do not)

11. "CVSSv2": {"Base Score": "5.0", "Impact Subscore": "2.9", "Exploitability Subscore": "10.0", "Vector": "AV:N/AC:L/Au:N/C:N/I:N/A:P"} → { "Base Score": score, "Vector": vector},

NOTE: more data than expected (sometimes contradictory!)

12. "CVSSv2": "7.5", -> "score"

NOTE: no vector

4. Related Work

Several papers about the applicability of ChatGPT for cybersecurity have been released since the release of ChatGPT in 2023.

Liu et al. (2023) evaluate the performance of ChatGPT in Vulnerability Description Mapping (VDM) tasks and investigate the application of closed-source LLMs in real-world security management scenarios – ChatGPT shows promising results. However, it does not threaten the crucial role of security engineers in the domain of vulnerability analysis. Naito et al. (2023), ChatGPT, when provided with vulnerability-related information and asset management data, can generate an effective high-threat test attack path, including specific vulnerability details like CVEs. Our work builds upon the efforts of Liu et al. (2023) and Naito et al. (2023) by investigating if ChatGPT can enrich the vulnerability databases for a more complete cataloging of known vulnerabilities.

The use of LLMs, such as ChatGPT, has also raised concerns. Kalla & Kuraku (2023) verify the potential benefits of utilizing ChatGPT in the context of cybersecurity by discussing the advantages, disadvantages, and risks associated with ChatGPT and artificial intelligence (AI) in cybersecurity. Hu & Chen (2023) also perform an analysis from a dimensional perspective on the cybersecurity opportunities (e.g., malware protection) and risks (e.g., privacy breaches) associated with ChatGPT-like information systems. Thoughtful consideration of its limitations and associated risks, including limited contextual understanding, generation of misleading information, and malicious exploitation, is essential in its implementation Kalla & Kuraku (2023). Potential misuse of generative AI tools by cyber offenders is also discussed in Gupta et al. (2023), outlining scenarios where adversaries could employ ChatGPT for various cyber attacks, including social engineering, phishing, automated hacking, and developing malware.

Al-Hawawreh et al. (2023) demonstrate how ChatGPT can be exploited to design and execute false data injection attacks on critical infrastructure, such as industrial control systems. Scanlon et al. (2023) evaluate the positive and negative effects of ChatGPT, specifically GPT-4, within the context of digital forensics. Scanlon et al. (2023) experimentally demonstrated that although ChatGPT holds considerable potential in digital forensic investigation, not all outputs from ChatGPT can be considered reliable. Thus, the essential role of human expertise remains crucial in the process. As the quality and accuracy of the data in the vulnerability databases are paramount, the concerns raised by the authors are of concern. The use of LLMs regarding cybersecurity must be explicitly justified.

Another avenue for cybersecurity enhancement by LLMs is to aid programmers by detecting possible vulnerabilities during code creation. Nair et al. (2023) investigated the essential strategies a designer must employ to leverage ChatGPT to produce secure hardware code. To conduct this investigation, the authors instruct ChatGPT to generate code scenarios corresponding to 10 common CWEs within the hardware design (CWE-1194) framework. Espinha Gasiba et al. (2023) conducted a brief experiment involving five distinct vulnerable code snippets derived from C/C++ and sourced from the Sifu platform. In over 60% of the provided code snippets, ChatGPT accurately identified issues in the source code and suggested effective solutions. Pearce et al. (2023) investigate the performance of five commonly used "off-the-shelf" LLMs in real-world security bug scenarios. Their experiments show off-the-shelf models can create security fixes in simple scenarios without extra training but face challenges in real-world situations.

It is clear that LLMs, such as ChatGPT, could help eliminate security vulnerabilities at their source (programming); however, they could also disseminate these bugs if the training data had issues at the time of training. Furthermore, LLMs could help cybersecurity experts find bugs in software and, crucially, help aid in vulnerability database entry creation.

5. Conclusion

To combat cyber threats, disseminating information on known vulnerabilities is crucial; thus, robust and available databases are required with as much metadata as possible for automated tools to function. As of early 2024, the NVD database is still lacking in metadata and suffers from data quality issues. LLMs, such as ChatGPT, are a quick way to enrich the data and, thus, provide more means to combat the threats. Our first-of-its-kind exploration of ChatGPT's performance on the NVD CVE vulnerability database has provided valuable insights into the capabilities and limitations of LLMs in cybersecurity. While ChatGPT exhibited a level of helpfulness, it became apparent that as is, it needs to improve to trust the output rigorously. We have also discussed how to interpret our experiments' results in detail. For example, based on current data, ChatGPT is fitting predictions better for v3 than v2 scores.

At this point, it is clear that LLMs such as ChatGPT cannot fully replace expert-based efforts such as NVD-CVE. And we do not recommend it’s use on this type of cyberseurity work without rigorous scrutiny of the output. Perhaps more research is required in the area of Small Language Models (SMLs) that are tailored as Domain Specific Languages (DSLs), for example, in areas such as technical cybersecurity, and we leave such explorations as immediate future work.

Acknowledgements

Hannu Turtiainen thanks the Finnish Cultural Foundation / Suomen Kulttuurirahasto (www.skr.fi) for supporting his Ph.D. dissertation work and research (grant decision no. 00231412).

(Part of) This work was supported by the European Commission under the Horizon Europe Programme, as part of the project LAZARUS (https://lazarus-he.eu/) (Grant Agreement no. 101070303). The content of this article does not reflect the official opinion of the European Union. Responsibility for the information and views expressed therein lies entirely with the authors.

References

Al-Hawawreh, M. et al. (2023). 'Chatgpt for cybersecurity: practical applications, challenges, and future directions,' Cluster Computing.

Anwar, A. et al. (2022). 'Cleaning the NVD: comprehensive quality assessment, improvements, and analyses', Transactions on Dependable and Secure Computing.

"Binaré Oy"' (2023), 'FastCVE - fast, rich, API-based search for CVE and more. (CPE, CWE, CAPEC)', https://github.com/binareio/FastCVE.

Chen, Y. et al. (2023). Diversevul: A new vulnerable source code dataset for deep learning based vulnerability detection, in '26th International Symposium on Research in Attacks, Intrusions and Defenses', ACM.

Chicco, D. et al. (2021). 'The coefficient of determination r-squared is more informative than smape, mae, mape, mse and rmse in regression analysis evaluation', PeerJ Computer Science.

Dasbach-Prisk, A. et al. (2023). Sensorloader: Bridging the gap in cyber-physical reverse engineering across embedded peripheral devices, in '1st International Workshop on Security and Privacy of Sensing Systems'.

Dong, Y. et al. (2019). Towards the detection of inconsistencies in public security vulnerability reports, in '28th USENIX Security Symposium', USENIX Association.

Espinha Gasiba, T. et al. (2023). I'm sorry dave, I'm afraid I can't fix your code: On chatgpt, cybersecurity, and secure coding, in '4th International Computer Program ming Education Conference'.

Gadyatskaya, O. & Papuc, D. (2023). Chatgpt knows your attacks: Synthesizing at tack trees using llms, in 'International Conference on Data Science and Artificial Intelligence,' Springer.

Gupta, M. et al. (2023). 'From chatgpt to threatgpt: Impact of generative AI in cyber security and privacy,' IEEE Access.

Harris, C. R. et al. (2020). 'Array programming with NumPy,' Nature. Hodson, T. O. (2022), 'Root-mean-square error (rmse) or mean absolute error (mae): When to use them or not,' Geoscientific Model Development.

Hu, C. & Chen, J. (2023). A dimensional perspective analysis on the cybersecurity risks and opportunities of chatgpt-like information systems, in 'International Conference on Networking and Network Applications', IEEE.

Jackson, E. K. et al. (2019). 'Introductory overview: Error metrics for hydrologic modmodeling - A review of common practices and an open source library to facilitate use and adoption', Environmental Modelling & Software.

Kalla, D. & Kuraku, S. (2023). 'Advantages, disadvantages and risks associated with chatgpt and ai on cybersecurity,ä Journal of Emerging Technologies and Innovative Research.

Kuehn, P. et al. (2021). OVANA: an approach to analyze and improve the information quality of vulnerability databases, in D. Reinhardt & T. Müller, eds, '16th International Conference on Availability, Reliability and Security', ACM.

Liemohn, M. W. et al. (2021). 'Rmse is not enough: Guidelines to robust data model comparisons for magnetospheric physics,' Journal of Atmospheric and Solar Terrestrial Physics.

Liu, X. et al. (2023). Not the end of story: An evaluation of chatgpt-driven vulnerability description mappings, in 'Findings of the Association for Computational Linguistics: ACL,' Association for Computational Linguistics.

Mamun, A. A. et al. (2020). 'A comprehensive review of the load forecasting techniques using single and hybrid predictive models,' IEEE Access.

Nair, M. et al. (2023). How hardened is your hardware? guiding chatgpt to generate secure hardware resistant to cwes, in 'Cyber Security, Cryptology, and Machine Learning - 7th International Symposium', Springer.

Naito, T. et al. (2023). Llm-based attack scenarios generator with IT asset management and vulnerability information, in '6th International Conference on Signal Processing and Information Security', IEEE.

Ozturk, O. S. et al. (2023). New tricks to old codes: Can AI chatbots replace static code analysis tools?, in 'European Interdisciplinary Cybersecurity Conference,' ACM.

Pearce, H. et al. (2023). Examining zero-shot vulnerability repair with large language models, in '44th IEEE Symposium on Security and Privacy', IEEE.

Pedregosa, F. et al. (2011), 'Scikit-learn: Machine learning in Python', Journal of Ma chine Learning Research.

Scanlon, M. et al. (2023). 'Chatgpt for digital forensic investigation: The good, the bad, and the unknown,' Forensic Science International: Digital Investigation.

Szabó, Z. & Bilicki, V. (2023). 'A new approach to web application security: Utilizing GPT language models for source code inspection,' Future Internet.

Tihanyi, N. et al. (2023). The formai dataset: Generative AI in software security through the lens of formal verification, in '19th International Conference on Predictive Models and Data Analytics in Software Engineering', ACM.

Waskito, S. A. O. et al. (2023). Otter: Simplifying embedded sensor data collection and analysis using large language models, in '29th Annual International Conference on Mobile Computing and Networking', ACM.

Exploring Trainees' Behaviour in Hands-on Cybersecurity Exercises Through Data Mining

Muaan ur Rehman[1], Hayretdin Bahsi[1,2], Linas Bukauskas[3] and Benjamin James Knox[4]
[1]Department of Software Sciences, Tallinn University of Technology, Estonia
[2]School of Informatics, Computing and Cyber Systems, Northern Arizona University, USA
[3]Institute of Computer Science, Vilnius University, Lithuania
[4]Faculty of Health, Welfare and Organization, Østfold University College, Halden, Norway

muaaur@taltech.ee
hayretdin.bahsi@taltech.ee
linas.bukauskas@mif.vu.lt
benjamin.knox@hiof.no

Abstract: Despite the rising number of cybersecurity professionals, the demand for more experts in this field is still substantial. Cybersecurity professionals must also possess up-to-date knowledge and skills to counter cybersecurity threats' dynamicity and rapidly evolving nature. Hands-on cybersecurity training is mandatory to practice various tools and improve one's technical cybersecurity skills. Generally, an interactive learning environment is set, where trainees perform sophisticated tasks by accessing complete operating systems, applications, and networks. One of the main challenges that cybersecurity organizations are facing today is the generation of massive data through practice exercises. So, it becomes a problem to convert this data into knowledge to improve the overall quality of the learning system. The large amount of interaction data and its complexity also limit us to do automated analysis. Thus, these challenges for cybersecurity learners can be addressed through appropriate educational data analysis by having insights or testing hypotheses or models on a proper dataset. Revealing the patterns, rules, item sets and time taken by trainees while using any command line tool could help the trainer to assess the trainees and to provide feedback. Therefore, in this paper we are analyzing the frequency patterns and timing information captured from the trainees' command line log to reveal their solving techniques, easy and struggling stages, slipups, and individual performance. Through our study, we aim to show how education and training providers can foresee learners who are less likely to succeed in a task or exhibit low performance, which can impede learning proficiency. With this knowledge, organizations and trainers can identify trainees who require additional attention or support. It may also be able to identify elements related to an organization like training aids, training methodology, etc. that need improvement. This study demonstrates the utility of data-mining techniques, specifically rule mining and sequential mining, to empower training designers to delve into datasets derived from cyber security training exercises.

Keywords: Cybersecurity Education, Educational Data-Mining, Learning Analytics, Cybersecurity Training

1. Introduction

Data-mining techniques are being used in the learning environment to predict trainees' learning behavior and improve their performance. The main goal of the institutions offering cyber security courses is to allow a quality education among individuals which in turn increases the learner's performance and assists in better decision-making. Trainees' performance is influenced by a variety of factors, which in turn affect the quality of training at different levels. Hands-on cybersecurity training exercises enable learners to practice their skills in a controlled environment. Hands-on exercises generate massive amounts of data which contain useful patterns which may reflect learners learning behaviors, their participation in different lab exercises, their interest in different attacking techniques and overall performance. Due to the enormous number of logs generated through hands-on exercises, identification of factors which affect performance is challenging. Thus, an appropriate educational data analysis on a proper dataset is required to address these challenges. In this paper, we aim to show how data-mining techniques, such as rule mining and sequential mining, can enable cybersecurity training providers to foresee at-risk learners and identify trainees who require additional attention or support.

We have investigated the dataset (Švábenský, Vykopal, et al., 2021) which consists of command logs recorded from trainees during security training sessions. The dataset has a high potential for accurate analysis of trainees as it contains enough attack log records acquired from different command line tools. Accessing and analysing this data set has significant potential in the area of learner/trainee assessment. To design future cybersecurity training further research is required in the exploration of past training data. There is a clear need to identify and explore additional factors, that may go unnoticed, from an increasing amount of cybersecurity exercise data. This research makes a notable contribution to exploring issues regarding the assessment of cybersecurity trainees through data-mining techniques to assist trainers. This study can also be useful to training designers in ongoing training exercises and providing some support in designing new effective training.

In Section 1 the work is introduced and the main contributions are formulated. Section 2 provides a review of the related studies. Section 3 explains the methodology used for data collection and analysis. In Section 4 the results and findings are discussed. Finally, Section 5 summarizes the contribution and proposes some future work.

2. Related Work

In the realm of educational data-mining-based assessment of cybersecurity learners, Švábenský et al. (2022) performed student assessments in cybersecurity training via pattern mining and clustering. Seda et al. (2022) also presented an instructor guide and a tool to improve the creation of cybersecurity hands-on training with adaptive learning support, which uses students' performance and abilities to assign suitable tasks to them. (Švábenský, Weiss, et al., 2022) performed cyber security student assessment via visualizing and contextualization of the command history logs. Li et al. (2021) utilized the Apriori algorithm for the data-mining of global cyberspace security issues involving human participation (Li et al., 2021). These studies offer diverse methodologies for assessing cybersecurity learners and thus present opportunities to build upon these techniques in further research.

Hands-on cybersecurity training exercises enable learners to practice their skills in a controlled environment. Cyber ranges, the interactive simulated platforms are being used for developing cyber skills or testing products (Jani Päijänen et al., 2021). One of the main challenges that cybersecurity organizations are facing today is the generation of massive amounts of data through practice exercises. The issue lies in converting this data into knowledge to improve the overall quality of the learning system (Asif et al., 2017; Bhutto et al., 2020). Having this huge amount of data in educational environments hides useful patterns which may reflect learning behaviours, participation in different lab exercises, interest in different attacking techniques and overall performance. Furthermore, due to the enormous number of logs generated through hands-on exercises, identification of factors which affect performance is challenging. Thus, these challenges for cybersecurity learners can be addressed through appropriate educational data analysis by having insights or testing hypotheses or models on a proper database.

3. Methodology

The present study aims to overcome the problem of converting massive amounts of cybersecurity exercise log data into knowledge and educational insight. This is achieved by investigating temporal data-mining techniques to assess trainees and identify the factors that influence their performance. The study proposes a data-mining-based framework to predict trainee performance, which can be used to classify trainees, based on their exercise solving procedure. The approach is to identify and examine the possible factors that can be correlated to learner performance or can be explained as causing the performance. Fig. 1 shows the steps of the proposed framework. The following sections further explain each step of our methodology.

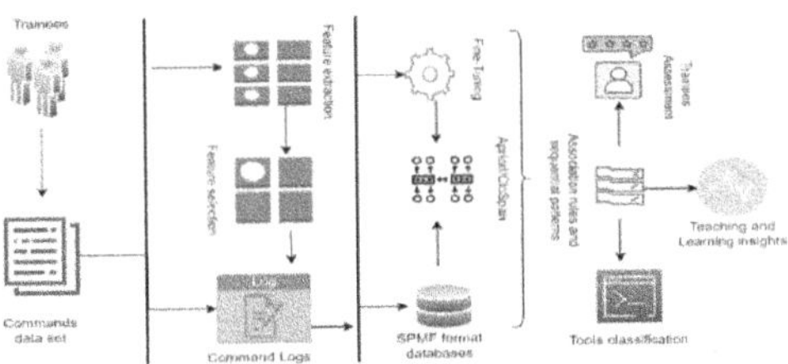

Fig 1. Methodology employed in this research, wherein command logs from the dataset are utilized to generate rules and patterns, yielding valuable insights.

3.1 Dataset

The first step is to gather data from trainees completing cybersecurity tasks during lab exercises. This was achieved by taking advantage of available datasets. In this case, a dataset (Švábenský, Vykopal, et al., 2021) of shell commands was used by participants who solved tasks in an interactive learning environment. This dataset contains 13446 Linux shell commands which were recorded from 175 participants. The Cyber Range platform KYPO (Vykopal et al., 2021) and Cyber Sandbox Creator were used to emulate complex networks and host a mini virtual lab environment on the trainee's machine. The data record contains a command, its argument and some metadata i.e., sandbox identification, timestamp, host identification and working directory in the emulated training infrastructure as shown in Fig 2. These commands were acquired by Bash, ZSH and Metasploit shells.

{"timestamp_str":"2021-02-11T15:21: 34+01:00","sandbox_id":"12", "pool_id":"1","cmd":"ls", "username": "root", "wd":"/root", "hostname":"attacker","ip":"10.1.26.23","cmd_type":"bash-command"}

Fig 2. Log Record

3.2 Game-based Hands-on Exercises:

The research focused on the analysis of cybersecurity practical exercise data taken from an exercise that was especially focused on offensive security training. For this purpose, we have targeted the mentioned dataset (Švábenský, Vykopal, et al., 2021) which is publicly available. It includes the following games[1] (Švábenský, Vykopal, et al., 2018).

Junior-hacker/Junior-hacker Adaptive: In these types of games, the host just connects to the sandbox, reads info, scans with *nmap*, manually guesses the password with SSH, transfers files with *scp*, using *fcrackzip* for password cracking and then changes the password. Participants in these types of games are learning experimentally via simple *Bash-Commands*.

SQL-Injection: *Sqlmap* and *ssh* are used for SQL injection; however, comparatively fewer commands and participants due to the usage of graphical tools only and no *Metasploit* usage.

Locust-3302: Vulnerabilities are searched via *Metasploit* commands. Among the key *Metasploit* commands are *use, set, run/exploit, search, show options* and *check* for executing the exploits in this type of game. Host scanning, password cracking, SSH connection and Webmin exploitation are performed.

Secret-Lab/Webmin-Exploit: These games are variations of Locust-3302. *nmap* is used for scanning, *webmin* is exploited with *Metasploit*. The host explores and analyses the .bash history. Furthermore, password cracking is performed via John the Ripper.

House-of-Cards: Both *Metasploit* and *Bash-commands* are being used for the exploitation of CVE-2018-10933 (Common Vulnerabilities and Exposures), a critical security issue in the LibSSH Library. Tools such as *nmap* and *ssh* are common tools in it.

3.3 Dataset Pre-Processing

Proper pre-processing is required to make the raw dataset ready for rules mining and pattern mining. Due to our temporal approach, *timestamp_str*, which represents the exact date and time of a command typed, is very crucial. To evaluate the performance of a particular participant, we consider *sandbox_id* as a potential attribute of interaction from a unique trainee. We have considered the feature *cmd* as a whole command typed, then also separated it from the passed arguments and labelled it as a *tool*. We have ignored the *cmd_type*, since it is already known which type of command is used in a particular exercise and hence redundant rules and patterns are avoided. Furthermore, since the dataset consists of different games some are easy and others are harder. We have extracted the json files from different game-based log folders and classified them into 3 types of major games. i.e. Junior-hackers' level, Intermediate (Locust, Secret-Lab and Webmin-Exploit) and challenging one (House-of-Card). We also have made a separate input folder consisting of all the participant's interactions together. To mine the association rules and patterns, we have converted the logs into BMS IBM Data Quest Generator format to feed the data as input to mining algorithms in the shape of input SPMF databases.

3.4 Time Lapses:

To know the reliable performance measures, time taken by a trainee to type and execute a command is highly significant. The time distance between two commands typed by trainee shows, either the efficiency of a trainee or the difficulty of a specific commands to be executed. However, the dataset (Švábenský, Vykopal, et al., 2021) does not directly record the time taken by a specific command to be executed. We have assessed the efficiency of a particular participant by measuring the time elapsed between the current execution time (*timestamp_str)* and the *timestamp_str* of the subsequent command execution. To find association rules and patterns, it is best to assign labels for the time taken until next recoded command. For this purpose, we have labelled the time

---

[1] https://gitlab.ics.muni.cz/muni-kypo-trainings/games/all-games-index

spent between adjacent commands from the logs as low, medium, high, and undefined. It is particularly important to investigate the way we can label some commands as low and other as high.

Let C be list of commands i.e.

$$C = \{ c_1, c_2, \dots, c_n \} \quad (1)$$

The function $f_{gap}(C)$ return a list of the time differences between consecutive commands as shown below in (2).

$$f_{gap}(C) = \{\Delta t_1, \Delta t_1, \dots, \Delta t_{n-1}\} \quad (2)$$

For instance, a command c_i is typed at *timestamp_str*: t_i and the next immediate command c_{i+1} at *timestamp_str* t_{i+1}. The formula to compute time difference (Δt_i) is shown in equation (3).

$$\Delta t_i = \sec(t_{i+1} - t_i), \quad \text{for } 1 \leq i \leq n\text{-}1 \quad (3)$$

We find the average gap time G_{avg}, which is the average time taken by all the participants in a specific game exercise. This is calculated based on mean of all the gaps in a particular game. G_{avg} combined with corresponding constants k_{min}, k_{max} and k_{undf} leads us to calculate the lower-gap, high-gap and undefined-gap represented by G_{low}, G_{high} and G_{undf} respectively. To calculate the minimum gap threshold G_{low} we divide the average gap (G_{avg}) by different number k_{min} which gives us a number less than the average and hence could be the minimum threshold value as shown in (4). For finding the higher threshold (G_{high}), we multiply the average (G_{avg}) by some small number k_{max} which gives number bigger than average as shown in (5). To find the undefined outlier, we have formulated equation (6) which gives us number far greater than highest threshold (G_{high}).

$$G_{low} = \frac{1}{k_{min}} G_{avg} \quad (4)$$

$$G_{high} = k_{max} G_{avg} \quad (5)$$

$$G_{undf} = k_{undf} G_{avg} \quad (6)$$

The values of the corresponding constant k_{min} , k_{max} and k_{undf} are identified by considering different factors. Such as domain knowledge, consideration of outliers and empirical analysis. We did the analysis and performed a series of experiments with varying constant values considering the standard deviations. Through this iterative process, we converged on optimal values of $k_{\min} = 3$, $k_{\max} = 1.25$ and $k_{\text{undf}} = 90$, aligning with the characteristics and general analysis of the dataset (Švábenský, Vykopal, et al., 2021) logs. Setting different values to these constants gives us variable results. Therefore, setting the time threshold is an important step. The values of these constants must be the same across the whole analysis process. Substantially deviating k_{min} from the G_{avg} value is observed to have a noteworthy impact on the potential to achieve time interval-based results. So, it is recommended to maintain k_{min} in close proximity to the value of G_{avg}.

To classify the time intervals Δt_i associated with command c_i, denoted as $f_{gap}(c_i)$, we have formulated distinct gap ranges as follows:

- $0 \leq \Delta t_i \leq G_{low}$: Low
- $G_{low} < \Delta t_i \leq G_{high}$: Medium
- $G_{high} < \Delta t_i \leq G_{undf}$: High
- $\Delta t_i > G_{high}$: Undefined

3.5 Data Analytics:

SPMF (Fournier-Viger, 2021) open-source tool to mine rules and patterns was applied due to its ability to be used as a library and could be embedded into our python code. To find the item co-occurrences we mined simple association rules. We have used Apriori (Li et al., 2021) for association rules mining. To discover closed command sequences in the dataset, we have mined sequential patterns by utilizing CloSpan (Yan et al., 2003). This algorithm effectively extracts comprehensive insights from sequential and large amount of data. *TopSeqRules* (Fournier-Viger and Tseng, 2011) is used for Sequential rules mining to further uncover ordered tool sequences.

The minimum support and confidence thresholds varied across different mining processes. In our experiments, we set the minimum support above 0.5 for association rule mining and 0.3 for pattern mining. Additionally, confidence has been maintained at a level above 0.4. These parameters are grounded in careful consideration of the dataset (Švábenský, Vykopal, et al., 2021) features and the desire to discover useful rules and patterns from it. In the next section, we are going to discuss the results we achieved through this methodology.

4. Results and Discussion

In our study, we conducted a comprehensive analysis of the hands-on cybersecurity dataset (Švábenský, Vykopal, et al., 2021) using various data-mining approaches. Specifically, we mined simple, temporal and sequential association rules. We also identified close sequential patterns to deepen our understanding of the dataset.

Table 1: Association rules (Multiple games)

No.	Rules	Support	Confidence	Game	Type
1.1	TOOL=fcrackzip==>GAP=high	47	0.58	Junior Hacker	Basic
1.2	TOOL=ifconfig==>GAP=Medium	11	0.61		
1.3	TOOL=sudo==>GAP=medium	14	0.51		
1.4	TOOL=ssh==>ARGS=['admin@10.1.26.9']	50	0.58		
1.5	SB=12 ==>GAP=low	95	0.61		
1.6	SB=2 ==>GAP=high	16	0.41		
1.7	SB=18==>GAP=undefined	1	1		
2.1	TOOL=man==>ARGS=['fcrackzip']	93	0.69	Junior Hacker Adaptive	
3.1	GAP=high==>TOOL=sqlmap	6	0.54	SQL Injection	
3.2	TOOL=cd, SB=116==>GAP=low	9	0.63		
3.3	TOOL=ssh==>GAP=undefined	9	0.9		
3.4	SB=122==>GAP=undefined	3	0.6		
4.1	ARGS=['options']==>TOOL=show	28	0.97	Locust	Medium
4.2	TOOL=nmap ==>GAP=high	21	0.71		
4.3	TOOL=clear==>SB=126, GAP=low	7	0.57	Secret Lab	
5.1	SB=351==>GAP=low	67	0.53	Web-Min-Exploit	
5.2	TOOL=man ==>SB=351	7	1		
6.1	TOOL=nmap==>GAP=high	50	0.50	House of Cards	Advance
6.2	ARGS=['rhosts','172.18.1.5'], TOOL=set ==>GAP=low	37	0.88		
6.3	SB=131==>GAP=high	11	0.5		
6.4	SB=401==>GAP=low	58	0.63		
6.5	SB=93==>GAP=medium	26	0.48		
7.1	TOOL=nmap==>GAP=high	33	0.72	All Games	NA

SB: Sandbox ID, represents a single participant; Support range: 1-95; Confidence: above 0.4

Table 1 shows some of the interesting association rules mined. Among the interesting command-based rules for Junior-hacker we found that: *Fcrackzip* is used with a very high time gap, and tool *ifconfig* is used with a medium gap. *Ifconfig* and *sudo* tools took average time gaps. The rules from Junior-hacker also give us some of the instances of the participant's efficiencies. Rule 1.5 illustrates that Participant *12* has 95 commands (support=95) typed very quickly (low-gap), which shows a high level of engagement and possibly interest and dedication. In contrast, SB 2 has a higher time gap (Rule 1.6), indicating a different pattern of behaviour. Rule 1.7 suggests that SB *18* could have had some problems in the machine, could have lost interest, or was possibly making errors due to extremely high gaps. Rule 2.1 depicts that if the command arguments are ['fcrackzip'], then the corresponding tool is *man* in the case of Junior-hacker Adaptive: We assume then, that man is used to display manuals for a command. It seems these participants needed more reading time. Such a command does not exist in Junior-hacker and Junior adaptive. It is possible these participants required more training time about *fcrackzip*.

As expected, *Sqlmap* looks to be the primary tool for *Sql-injection* as suggested by rule 3.1. Another rule here is change of the directories more frequently and quickly, especially by trainee *116*. In general trainee *116* was very fast having support of 19 being typing with lower-gaps and using the *cd* command more frequently and faster than others and suggest his navigation skills (Rule 3.2). Furthermore, the *ssh* command, in the majority of cases, took an abnormal amount of time. Reason for such abnormal time should be investigated. We also see that user *122* had more undefined-gaps and therefore, he/she could possibly require more trainer attention. In *Locust*, we see is that command *show* with argument option is used frequently. This could imply that the participant needed help. An interesting result in *Secret-Lab* is that participant *SB=126* used *clear* command more than usual and also with very high speed. This could suggest the participant is performing many mistakes while typing commands, or is more concerned about deleting the logs history. At *WebMin-Exploit* level user *351* is too quick in typing commands compared to other trainees (rule 5.1). However, the same participant focused a great deal on *man* commands. That the participant requested manuals could suggest a need for help, although his/her overall execution of commands is fast. For *House-of-Card* game in Table 1 rule 6.1 shows that the tool *nmap* has taken the highest time. Therefore, either the command looks difficult, or the participants have less knowledge of using this command. This may indicate that *nmap* itself takes too much time. Furthermore, the trainees in House-of-Card game quickly and effectively executed the Metasploit set command, especially when the target system IP 172.18.1.5', which employ the vulnerabilities and has easy access to that particular IP. Rules 6.3-6.5 in Table 1 also depicts participant's performance in terms of time taken to execute commands. We can see that in the case of *SB=401*, the participant has taken the lowest time while executing commands. This can be shown via the highest support of 58 as a low-gap interval. Users with high support and higher confidence, for low time intervals, such as *SB=401*, may indicate their capability and engagement. In the highest time intervals, *SB=131* has the highest support among high-gap participants. This suggests that for the same type of game/exercise, this trainee may need to benefit from additional support based upon the delay in typing and executing commands. The medium-gaps, participant could be considered as improving trainees.

In order to identify additional factors, Sequential Rules Mining, is performed. It is a useful data mining technique to find sequential rules from large database. These rules indicate that participants practice certain command combinations with high certainty. Unlike simple association rules in Table 1, sequential rules presented in Table 2 provide some patterns about the whole command sequence. Furthermore, alternative to simple association rules, it also considers the probability of succeeding patterns (Abdelwahab & Youssef, 2022). Moreover, they provide insights into the typical actions' trainees take in various games and can be valuable for guiding the trainees, optimizing hands-on exercise content, and ensuring better performance in exercises.

Table 2: Sequential Rules (Multiple Games)

No	Sequential Rules	S	C	Type
1.1	nmap ==>set	111	0.85	Locust
2.1	sqlmap ==>ssh	4	1	SQL Injection
3.1	nmap==>msfconsole, use	10	1	Webmin-Exploit

S: Support, support threshold: 0.5; C: Confidence, threshold: 0.4

Rule 1.1 in Table 2 illustrates that in the case of Locust participants performing a "nmap" scan, they have a 85.38% chance of following up with a set action. It is expected that the user use nmap for exploration and then use set for configuration of the Metasploit for exploitation stage. The high confidence suggests a strong sequential pattern where *nmap* often leads to setting (*set*). If we observe Sql-injection exercise, rule 2.1 depicts that the tool sqlmap is immediately followed by the ssh. This indicates a common sequence where trainees use Sql-injection to gain access and then proceed to execute SSH. Webmin-Exploit's sequential rule 3.1 suggests a strategic approach to penetration testing. Starting with network scanning *nmap*, they then move to the Metasploit console *msfconsole* and use it to execute exploits by the tool *use*. This pattern suggests participants' recognition of the value of reconnaissance in identifying potential targets and their subsequent use of Metasploit for targeted exploitation. It exemplifies the significance of assembling intelligence before launching attacks.

For further exploration of the hands-on cybersecurity dataset we have mined the closed sequential patterns, which are maximally specific sequential pattern, indicating significant and non-redundant sequences.

Table 3: Close Sequential Patterns (House of card)

No	Patterns	Support	Trainee/SB IDs
1	nmap→msfconsole→set	18	112,113,115,116,130,137,144,148,149,152,156,396,398,399,400,401,93,95
2	ssh→nmap→ssh	18	101,112,113,115,116,137,148,149,151,152,156,396,398,399,400,93,397,95
3	ssh→nmap→set→set→run	18	101,112,113,115,116,137,148,149,151,152,156,396,398,399,400,93,397,95
4	nmap→set→set	22	101,112,113,115,116,130,131,137,144,148,149,151,152,156,396,398,399,400,401,93,397,95
5	ssh→ssh→ssh	21	101,112,113,115,116,130,131,137,148,149,151,152,156,396,398,399,400,401,93,397,95
6	nmap→use→set→set	18	101,112,116,131,137,144,148,149,152,156,396,398,399,400,401,93,397,95
7	nmap→set→set→ssh→ssh	20	101,112,113,115,116,130,131,137,148,149,151,152,156,396,399,400,401,93,397,95
8	nmap → use → set → ssh	20	101,112,113,115,116,130,131,137,148,149,152,156,396,398,399,400,401,93,397,95
9	nmap→set→set→run	19	101,1,156,115,116,130,137,144,148,149,152,156,396,398,399,400,401,93,397,95
10	nmap→use→set→ssh→ssh	19	101,112,113,115,116,130,131,137,148,149,152,156,396,399,400,401,93,397,95
11	nmap→use→set→run→ssh→ ssh	18	101,112,113,115,116,130,137,148,149,152,156,396,399,400,401,93,397,95

Table 3 shows closed sequential patterns along with the support values and associated trainees (represented by Sandbox IDs) mined from the House-of-Cards game. Participants followed various combinations of tools to achieve a similar goal. Based on the logs from the mentioned game, support values equal to 22 are considered the highest level of support, while values less than 18 are categorized as low support. The discussion in the following paragraph centres around specific tools-based analysis on patterns mined from House-of-Card game (Table 3).

SSH-nmap combinations: There are several occurrences of the sequence "ssh→nmap→ssh" (pattern 2) with a high support (e.g., 18). This pattern could indicate a common workflow that involves using SSH to connect and then performing network scanning with *nmap*. Such a sequence may be used in the reconnaissance stage of the task as it does not include any Metasploit command.

Successful attack cycle (ssh→nmap→set→run): The sequences ssh→nmap→set→set→run (pattern 3) has a substantial support i.e. 18. It indicates participants who used *nmap* then configured Metasploit (set) and finally launched the attack (run) might represent a successful approach to achieving the goal.

Incomplete Sequences: Trainees who consistently follow sequences like "nmap→set→set" (pattern 4) have a high support (e.g., 22). As we discussed earlier ssh→nmap→set→run is the most common successful attack cycle. Therefore, trainees who only follow pattern 4 i.e., do not execute the run command at the end, indicates they did not finish the full cycle. Further investigation is required concerning these participants (130, 131, 144 and 401) who could not run the exploitation in the target. A possible reason might be that they were unable to locate the relevant configuration.

Variations in SSH Sequences: The sequence "ssh→ ssh→ssh" (pattern 5) has significant support (e.g., 21). This repeated use of SSH could reveal an investigative type behaviour, as certain tasks or scenarios require multiple SSH connections.

Table 3 also depicts that some trainees exhibit patterns that stand out from the common sequences and could indicate specific preferences, skills, or focus areas. Further analysis and discussions with these trainees could provide insights into their learning strategies, tool preferences, and potential areas for improvement in their training. Following are a number of findings worth debating: Unlike other participants, trainee *144* does not follow ssh→nmap→ssh (pattern 2), nmap→use→set →ssh→ssh (pattern 10) and nmap→use→set→run→ ssh→ssh (pattern 11). These pattern shows more emphasis on SSH tool and initiation of multiple remote connections. However, each trainee may have their own unique or preferred task, which needs further investigation. Trainee *148* is consistently present in all the sequences, which may suggest this particular trainee is actively engaged in using different tools.

4.1 Discussion

Our study shows that data mining techniques enable the training designers to explore the cyber security exercise datasets that contain some low-level information such as the running commands of each participant. The rules derived from such techniques can give valuable insights into the ongoing trainings. However, it is important to note that experts are needed to evaluate the identified rules and select the ones which may be helpful in the analysis. On the other side, the results of these rules have an explorative nature, necessitating more investigation and, thus, augmented dataset collection, and meticulous analysis to establish statistical values for variables, identify the root causes of deviations and draw solid conclusions. Our study demonstrates that the data mining techniques we applied in this paper are well-suited to this context, in which training designers do not know where to start due to the complexity of the dataset.

The dataset (Švábenský, Vykopal, et al., 2021) used in this study constitutes a significant source for similar data analytic studies related to cyber security trainings or games. However, the number of security tools and commands that the dataset obtained (i.e., even in the sophisticated ones) is limited. Although we garnered valuable insights from this dataset, we contemplate that data mining methods can reveal more insights when more varied tools/commands are utilized in cyber security training.

In our study, the associate rule mining method enabled us to acquire a general overview of the dataset and identify some significant insights about tool usage, including timing issues. Although we understand some key points about the participants in general, sequential rule mining focused on the analysis of the command series used by each participant during the whole training. As the number of tools and commands is limited in the dataset, we identified a typical pattern in which reconnaissance activities (i.e., represented by the Nmap tool) are followed by exploitation activities (i.e., various commands of Metasploit) in the training where complete attack scenarios are used. The patterns using some commands (e.g., *run*) may indicate that the participant can complete the whole exploitation cycle. Nevertheless, the data mining methods applied in this study can give more insights into the patterns of cyber kill chain steps in the datasets collected from more advanced training environments (e.g., cyber security exercises having more complex scenarios).

This research also implies some factors affecting the performance of participants. For example, how the time gap between commands (c_i) and (c_{i+1}) can be a factor in assessing the difficulty, or ease, of executing/choosing a particular command. Apart from this, the time gap best represents the performance of participants. If the same command takes too much time for one student while less for another student, this could quite possibly be a performance correlate, by inferring attention or knowledge level. If the command typed with high time intervals is due to overcautiousness, that factor must be identified and balanced with efficiency. Among other factors, analysis of the command's specific difficulty level can support how we conclude whether a particular participant has taken more time or less according to the nature of the command. By considering different other factors i.e. training, experience level, specific domain knowledge, and self-efficacy trainees may be assessed and potentially predictions can be made about their [future] performance more effectively.

5. Conclusions

This research endeavours to enhance the effectiveness of cybersecurity interactive exercises by employing a data mining-based approach through exploring rules, patterns and behaviours exhibited by participants.

In this paper, we presented a comprehensive approach aiming to address the challenge of converting wide-ranging cybersecurity exercise logs into valuable instructive insights. Through the data mining techniques, trainee performance factors were investigated. These factors have the potential to predict and classify trainees based on their task solving abilities and approaches. The research can provide cybersecurity educational decision makers with a systematic approach to use the command logs and intervene in learning performance by analysing the performance factors identified e.g. time intervals between commands executed, specific command's difficulty, experience level and domain knowledge of the learners etc.

Through the lens of temporal association rules, our study uncovers the variability inherent in trainees' interaction and response times. Sequential rules shed more light on the individualized approach adopted by participants in different gaming scenarios. Mining of closed sequential patterns unveils common successful and unsuccessful (incomplete) sequences. Identification of such distinctive patterns may suggest areas of expertise, or skills of certain trainees. This trainee-centric analysis investigated individual behaviours, pinpointing participants with unique patterns and preferences. The individual participant scrutiny presents an avenue for tailored guidance and improvement strategies by identifying focused workflows and versatile usage of tools.

This paper offers many opportunities for future work. The research can be enhanced by incorporating predictive models that consider cognitive factors. In achieving a target, the trainee's success and failure can be predicted using machine learning approaches. A benchmarking mechanism can be established by comparative analyses to assess the effectiveness of interventions in different training exercise programs.

Acknowledgements

The "Advancing Human Performance in Cybersecurity", ADVANCES, benefits from €1 million grant from Iceland, Liechtenstein, and Norway through the EEA Grants. The project aims to advance the performance of cybersecurity specialists by personalising the competence development path and risk assessment. The project contract with the Research Council of Lithuania (LMTLT) No is S-BMT-21-6 (LT08-2-LMT-K-01-051).

References

Abdelwahab, A. and Youssef, N. (2022) Performance Evaluation of Sequential Rule Mining Algorithms. *Applied Sciences, 12*(10), 5230. https://doi.org/10.3390/app12105230

Abu, A. (2016) Educational Data Mining and amp; Students' Performance Prediction. *International Journal of Advanced Computer Science and Applications, 7*(5) https://doi.org/10.14569/IJACSA.2016.070531

Asif, R., Merceron, A., Ali, S. A. and Haider, N. G. (2017) Analyzing undergraduate students' performance using educational data-mining. *Computers and Education, 113*, 177–194. https://doi.org/10.1016/j.compedu.2017.05.007

Bhardwaj, B. K. and Pal, S. (2012) *Data Mining: A prediction for performance improvement using classification*.

Bhutto, Engr. S., Siddiqui, I. F., Arain, Q. A. and Anwar, M. (2020) Predicting Students' Academic Performance Through Supervised Machine Learning. *2020 International Conference on Information Science and Communication Technology (ICISCT)*, 1–6. https://doi.org/10.1109/ICISCT49550.2020.9080033

Fournier-Viger. (2021) *SPMF: An open-source data mining library*.

Fournier-Viger, P. and Tseng, V. S. (2011) *Mining Top-K Sequential Rules* (pp. 180–194) https://doi.org/10.1007/978-3-642-25856-5_14

Jani Päijänen, Karo Saharinen and Jarno Salonen. (2021) Cyber Range: Preparing for Crisis or Something Just for Technical People? *Proceedings of the European Conference on Information Warfare and Security*. https://doi.org/10.34190/EWS.21.012

Li, Z., Li, X., Tang, R. and Zhang, L. (2021) Apriori Algorithm for the Data Mining of Global Cyberspace Security Issues for Human Participatory Based on Association Rules. *Frontiers in Psychology, 11*. https://doi.org/10.3389/fpsyg.2020.582480

R Negi, S. K. S. M. S. (2021) Automated Flag Detection and Participant Peformance Evaluation for Pwnable CTF. *Silicon Valley Cybersecurity Conference*.

Seda, P., Vykopal, J., Celeda, P. and Ignac, I. (2022) Designing Adaptive Cybersecurity Hands-on Training. *2022 IEEE Frontiers in Education Conference (FIE)*, 1–8. https://doi.org/10.1109/FIE56618.2022.9962663

Švábenský, V., Vykopal, J., Čeleda, P., Tkáčik, K. and Popovič, D. (2022) Student assessment in cybersecurity training automated by pattern mining and clustering. *Education and Information Technologies, 27*(7), 9231–9262. https://doi.org/10.1007/s10639-022-10954-4

Švábenský, V., Vykopal, J., Seda, P. and Čeleda, P. (2021) Dataset of shell commands used by participants of hands-on cybersecurity training. *Data in Brief, 38*, 107398. https://doi.org/10.1016/j.dib.2021.107398

Švábenský, V., Weiss, R., Cook, J., Vykopal, J., Čeleda, P., Mache, J., Chudovský, R. and Chattopadhyay, A. (2022) Evaluating Two Approaches to Assessing Student Progress in Cybersecurity Exercises. *Proceedings of the 53rd ACM Technical Symposium on Computer Science Education*, 787–793. https://doi.org/10.1145/3478431.3499414

Vykopal, J., Celeda, P., Seda, P., Svabensky, V. and Tovarnak, D. (2021) Scalable Learning Environments for Teaching Cybersecurity Hands-on. *2021 IEEE Frontiers in Education Conference (FIE)*, 1–9. https://doi.org/10.1109/FIE49875.2021.9637180

Yan, X., Han, J. and Afshar, R. (2003) CloSpan: Mining: Closed Sequential Patterns in Large Datasets. *Proceedings of the 2003 SIAM International Conference on Data Mining*, 166–177. https://doi.org/10.1137/1.9781611972733.15

Valdemar Švábenský, Jan Vykopal, Milan Cermak, and Martin Laštovička. (2018) 'Enhancing cybersecurity skills by creating serious games' in Proceedings of the 23rd Annual ACM Conference on Innovation and Technology in Computer Science Education (ITiCSE 2018). Association for Computing Machinery, New York, NY, USA, 194–199. https://doi.org/10.1145/3197091.3197123

Cybercrime and Digital Transactions Law in Nigeria: A Review

Ngozi Chisom Uzoka and Nneka Obiamaka Umejiaku
Department of Private & Property Law, Faculty of Law, Nnamdi Azikiwe University Awka, Nigeria.

nc.uzoka@unizik.edu.ng
no.umejiaku@unizik.edu.ng

Abstract: The internet is a tool that drives globalization and enhances global inclusion and integration. It has become imperative to make use of information and communication technology in this era of increased broadband access to the internet. The use of information and communication technology has increased the commission of cybercrime such as data breaches, identity theft and cyber fraud. This paper aims to identify the relevance, authenticity and nexus between digital transactions and cybercrimes in Nigeria. This paper seeks to give a summary of cybercrime and digital transaction laws in Nigeria, as well as the challenges inherent in applying them. The methodology adopted is the doctrinal method of legal research approach in literature review, analysis of cases and access to internet sources. This paper made use of primary sources of data such as such as enabling laws, acts and secondary sources of data, conventions, journal articles and the study is also analytical and comparative in nature. The paper finds that the legal and institutional framework for digital transaction laws in Nigeria is somewhat limited. Some digital forensic tools have not been recognized by our laws in Nigeria. The paper concludes that the extant legal framework for digital transaction laws in Nigeria has lapses that impair the evidence emanating from digital tools/records. This paper recommends amongst others; training of prosecution officers, legal practitioners and judicial officers in the collection and use of forensic/digital evidence in court of law, review of some of our extant laws and creation of institutional framework for digital transaction laws in Nigeria.

Keywords: Digital law, Cybercrime, Justice, Electronic law, Electronic evidence, E-commerce

1. Introduction

Two decades ago, many people did not have mobile phone or computer as a result of the cost. Connecting to the internet was only accessible through dial-up modems. In Nigeria before now, people pay hourly or by minutes to access the internet in cyber cafes. The use of electronic mails was not common as well as the electronic banking systems. Presently, many individuals now own laptops, mobile phones that can connect to the internet and email accounts effortlessly wherever they are. Presently, there are many social media platforms where people can connect easily with others without physically meeting. Individuals now frequently purchase goods online and are increasingly using electronic readers for books and newspapers rather than traditional print media.

Over two decades there has been an increased usage of technological inventions which has provided platform for its misuse and crimes. This has increased the use of technology by individuals to create new forms of crimes. With the emergence of information and communication technology and the growing usage of internet on daily basis, there are now many avenues through which cybercrimes can be carried out. "Individuals who engage in socially unacceptable or outright criminal acts steadily make use of technology to connect with one another in ways that is not before now possible" Holt,T. J. , Bossler A. M., Seigfried – Spellar, K.C (2015). Because of the possibility of carrying out transactions online without any physical meeting, persons have taken undue advantage of that to perpetuate and engage in all sorts of cybercrimes. As a result of the differences in jurisdictions, there is no generally acceptable definition of cybercrime that is all encompassing. Cybercrime is challenging to conceptualize with exactitude. However, one factor remains constant in various definitions given by scholars. Cybercrime is a crime that is committed over the wireless internet. On the other hand, cybercrime can be termed as any crime or criminal activity executed by making use of digital technology, or put differently they are computer-related crimes and crimes related to the internet. Digital technology and electronic networks provides an enviable platform to promote commercial transactions across the globe. A major sector of the economy that has robustly been affected positively or negatively by the intrusion of digital technology is the banking sector. Digital banking has facilitated a great deal digital transactions hence sellers and buyers of goods and services leverage on digital technology to initiate and conclude their transactions without any physical meeting. Thus, it is without doubt that in Nigeria and the world at large, financial technology has provided a formidable platform for digital banking operators to provide a wide range of financial services. This has in turn opened the door for an influx of various types of cybercrimes.

2.1 The Relevance of Digital Transactions to Cybercrime

Owing to the internet's globalization and trans-border nature of digital transactions, cybercrime can occur anywhere. It suffices to state that there would be no cybercrime, if there was no internet. With the ease and access to the internet by all and sundry in Nigeria coupled with the availability of different network providers of internet accessibility, digital transactions are on the increase. Years back the main medium of payment in Nigeria was basically cash. This has led to a lot of vulnerabilities and loss occasioned by robbery, theft etc. Subsequently, banks and other businesses introduced the use of Automated Teller Machines (ATM), Point of Sales (POS) and bank apps. As more people make use of the internet to transact business, there is a higher risk of being victims of cyber-attacks like online fraud, identity theft, and spyware or virus attacks. (Rathna *e tal*, 2023). The faster with the adoption of new payment systems, the more rapid and sophisticated the cyber risks are. A secured payment is paramount for any business that relies on electronic payments and transactions. If the digital payment system is weak, then it will be prone to constant attacks by cyber criminals. The negative consequences of cybercrime are vast and are a growing cause of global concern. The COVID - 19 pandemic also helped to facilitate companies to digitize their products and services, migrate to electronic commerce platforms and leverage on online business continuity strategy.

Cybercrime is not only evident in Nigeria, but also a global menace. Studies have estimated a yearly 15 per cent increase in global cybercrime losses over the next five years reaching 10.5 trillion US Dollars annually by 2025(Business day Newspaper Nigeria 2022). In Nigeria, over 2,800 persons were convicted of cybercrime in 2022(Queen Troanusi 2022). The increase in cybercrimes in Nigeria is highly attributed to the development and improvement of the internet. The development of the Electronic Data Interchange which replaced the traditional mailing of documents with a digital transfer of data from one computer to another enhances the transfer of orders and other transactions. Thus EDI allows the transfer of data seamlessly without any human intervention. With digital transaction, people can transact business from any part of the world without really verifying the authenticity of the other party. This is a major threat of transacting business electronically/digitally. On the other hand, electronic/digital transaction platforms, provides the buyer and the seller a wide range of database of services and products from which to choose from within a short time. It also eliminates the need for an agent or middleman; this will in turn reduce to some extent the risk of counterfeit and adulterated products as there is a direct channel between the producer and the consumer.

2. Digital Transactions in Nigeria

Generally, a lot of services or goods can be rendered or purchased digitally. Thus, an electronic transaction is the buying and selling of goods and services online. Additionally, conducting major and essential elements of a contract or any business whether commercial or non-commercial in nature via communications transmitted through digital devices will qualify the transaction as an electronic one. The term digital transaction can be used inter-changeably with the term 'electronic commerce'. Electronic commerce has no universal definition. However, it has been defined as commercial transactions conducted electronically on the internet. (OECD 1997 Report) In Nigeria, the total transaction value in the digital payments market is projected to reach US $21.32bn in 2024. Presently, Nigeria's digital transactions revolution is driving economic growth and financial inclusion at unprecedented levels (NASDAQ: ACIIN, 2022). While cash is still in use in Nigeria, there is a paradigm shift towards the adoption of digital payment systems. It is proven through research that governments that advance their national payments system create an enabling environment for everyone in the payments (Santhosh Rao).

3. Digital Transactions Regulation in Nigeria

3.1 Legal Framework for Cybercrimes and Digital Transactions in Nigeria

Digital or electronic transactions have raised a lot of germane novel issues with respect to control and regulation. The issue of validity, security and enforceability of digital transactions is vital.

3.1.1 Evidence (Amendment Act) 2023

Evidence Act is one of the principal legislation used in Nigerian courts. It has been subject to some amendments as a result of evolving legal system and the need to keep up with international best practices. The Evidence (Amendment) Act of 2023 brought significant changes in Nigeria's legal jurisprudence. However, it remained largely unchanged with respect to the inadmissibility of electronically generated evidence. Hence, there was need to address the lacuna in the Act to reflect technological realities in the world today. Under the erstwhile Evidence Act of 2011, the admissibility of computer generated evidence was introduced under Section 84. The 2011 Act also defined a document as including any devise by means of which information is recorded, stored or retrievable including computer output (Section 258). However, more was needed to improve the admissibility of evidence, particularly electronically generated evidence as contained in the Evidence Act of 2011. Hence, the Evidence (Amendment) Act of 2023 introduced novel digital and electronic execution of documents and admissibility of storage mediums as evidence.

The Evidence (Amendment) Act of 2023 indeed contains visible provisions geared towards digitization of transactions and processes which will find expression in various fields and sectors, ranging from business contracts, financial transactions, government documents and healthcare records. The Federal government in Nigeria, in its bid to combat the overwhelming increasing rage of cybercrimes in Nigeria, as well as to protect the digital space has enacted a few legislations in this regard. Under the erstwhile Evidence Act of 2011, the admissibility of computer generated evidence was introduced under Section 84. The 2011 Act also defined a document as including any devise by means of which information is recorded, stored or retrievable including computer output (Section 258). However, more was needed to improve the admissibility of evidence, particularly electronically generated evidence as contained in the Evidence Act of 2011. Hence, the Evidence (Amendment) Act of 2023 introduced novel digital and electronic execution of documents and admissibility of storage mediums as evidence.

Under the new Nigerian Evidence (Amendment Act) of 2023, electronic record is defined to include "data, record or data generated image or sound stored, received, or sent in an electronic form or micro film" (Section 84). The word "electronic record" has been specifically inserted after the word "document" throughout the entire section 84 that deals with computer-generated evidence in the Act. This implies that documents or electronic record satisfies the laid down conditions of the Act. Specifically, Section 10 of the Evidence (Amendment Act) 2023, provides that electronic records printed on paper, stored and recorded or copies in optical or magnetic media or cloud computing database produced by a computer are now admissible in any judicial proceeding before Nigeria courts without further proof or production of the original, if the conditions enumerated in the Act are met. This provision was not contained under the previous 2011 Evidence Act. The 2023 Evidence Act introduced the use of digital signature in legal documents. Under section 10 of the new Act, It went further to define digital signature as one that is generated electronically and attached to a document that is electronically transmitted in order to verify the contents or authenticity of the document and the identity of the sender. In the same vein, the Act now recognizes the use of digital signatures in court documents or legal processes.

The advantages of digital and electronic signatures cannot be overemphasized. Digital and electronic signatures provide a higher level of security. They use encryption technology in order to ascertain the integrity and authenticity of the signed document. This will forestall forgery, tampering and alterations. Electronic signature also facilitates speedy transactions as there will be no need for physical paperwork printing or mailing. Court processes, land transaction documentations, contractual documents can also be signed by parties electronically and transmitted same way. This will facilitate faster court processes; times spent on perfecting agreements and ultimately increase efficiency. With digital and electronic signature parties to a transaction can afford to sign or access the documents from anywhere at any time. There would be no need for physical meeting by parties. Hence, this will facilitate trans-border and international transactions. Digital and electronic signature will create an enabling environment for audit trail. It easily provides a comprehensive record of when, who and how a document was signed will be on record. This will promote accountability and will be handy in the resolution of any discrepancies that may arise in the future (Ayojimi, 2024).

3.1.2 Cybercrimes (Prohibition, Prevention e.t.c.) Act 2015

This was enacted by the National Assembly to ensure an effective, unified and comprehensive legal, regulatory and institutional framework for the prohibition, prevention, detection, prosecution and punishment of cybercrimes in Nigeria. The Cybercrime Act was signed into law in 2015. The Act contains 59 sections, is divided into 8 parts and it has two (2) schedules. The Act applies throughout the Federal Republic of Nigeria. The implication is that any other law made in respect of Cybercrime by a State House of Assembly is void or inactive, as the case may be. It is worthy to note that cybercrimes may take different forms, but the impact on electronic transactions is enormous, be it electronic commerce, electronic governance, electronic education or any other forms of electronic transactions, hence, several provisions of the Cybercrimes Act relate to an electronic transaction.

Under the Act, the term "cybercrime" was not defined at all. This leaves the meaning and scope of what constitutes cybercrime in Nigeria to speculation. Also under Section 48 of the Act, a law enforcement officer may apply *ex-parte* to a judge in chambers for the issuance of a warrant for the purpose of obtaining electronic evidence related to crime investigation. The judge is to issue a warrant authorizing law enforcement officer to enter and search any premises or place if within those premises, place or conveyance an offence under Act is being committed, or there is evidence of the commission of an offence under the Act; or there is an urgent need to prevent the commission of an offence under Act.

Under Section 6(1) of the Act, it is an offence for any person without authorization to intentionally access in whole or in part, a computer system or network for fraudulent purposes and obtain data that are vital to national security. It is an offence under the Act to intentionally obtain computer data, secure access to any program, commercial or industrial secrets or classified information (Section 6(2)). It is an offence under the Act to unlawfully intercept data or to either directly or indirectly modify or cause the modification of any data held in any computer system or network by way of alteration, erasure, removal, suppression or prevention of the normal operation of the computer system or network (Section 16(1). Under the Cybercrime Act, it is an offence to use any device for the purpose of avoiding detection or otherwise prevent identification or attribution with any of these acts or omission (Section 6(3).

The Act under Section 7 made it mandatory for all operators of cybercafés to register with Computer Professional Registration Council in addition to being registered as a business name with the Corporate Affairs Commission. The Act also mandated all cybercafé operators to maintain a register of users through sign-in personnel whenever needed. Section7 subsection 2 also provides that any person who perpetrates electronic or online fraud using a cybercafé commits an offence and is liable on conviction to imprisonment for a term of 3 years or a fine of N342, 000,000.00 or both. The question is whether this can be implemented as most cybercafés in Nigeria as not even registered as a business name with Corporate Affairs Commission not to talk of registering with Computer Professional Registration Council. It is submitted that this will amount to a clog in the wheel particularly in the area of enforcement. The inclusion of CPRC in the enforcement realm will amount to decentralization of the enforcement framework. It is submitted that it will be most appropriate to have a single enforcement institution to fight against the menace of cybercrime in Nigeria. (Nwafor, 2022)

Another striking provision of the Cybercrimes Act is that it is an offence for any person to destroy or abort any electronic mails or processes through which money or any valuable information is being conveyed (Section 9).The Act is silent on what the term "valuable information" means. This makes room for guessing and speculation. There is a duty imposed on financial institutions to safely guard their customer's sensitive information.

Under Section 17(1) 9 (Cybercrimes Act 2015), electronic signature with regards to purchases of goods and services, and any other transactions shall be binding. No transaction would be denied enforceability simply because the transaction was electronically signed. Whenever the genuineness or otherwise of electronic signatures is in question, the burden of proof that the signature does not belong to the purported originator of such electronic signature shall be on the contender (Section 17(1) a).

The Act also provided that any person who with the intent to defraud or misrepresent, forges through electronic devices another person's signature or the mandate of a company commits an offence. The said offence is punishable with imprisonment for a term of not more than seven years or a fine of not more than N10 million naira or both fine and imprisonment (Section 17(1)c).

However, under the Act there are exemptions to transactions that can be electronically signed for example: death and birth certificate, wills, family law matters and

Under Section 37 of the Act, financial institutions are mandated to verify the identity of their customers carrying out electronic financial transactions and execute the documentation of customers preceding the execution of customers' electronic transfer, payment, debit and issuance orders. (Section 37(1) a &b. This section is to ensure that financial institutions uphold an effective mechanism against financial malpractices where banking transactions are involved. It ushers in a new dawn in electronic commercial transactions in the financial world due to the duty of care imposed on financial institutions. Additionally, Section 38 of the Act mandated service providers to keep all traffic and subscriber information as may be prescribed by the relevant authorities responsible for regulating communication services in Nigeria for 2 years. Service providers are required to retain content and non-content information and make such available to an authorized law enforcement officer. The Act mandates that any data retained shall only be used for legitimate purposes as may be provided for under the Act, any other legislation, regulation or by order of a court of competent jurisdiction. Appropriate measures to safeguard the confidentiality of the data retained must be taken and the individual's right to privacy under the Nigerian Constitution respected.

3.1.3 *Nigeria Data Protection Act 2023*

The Federal Government of Nigeria in an effort to regulate personal data in Nigeria enacted the Nigeria Data Protection Act 2023 also known as the (NDPA), this comes after the Nigeria Data Protection Regulation issued by the National Information Technology Development Agency(NITDA) in 2019. This Act replaced the erstwhile Nigerian Data Protection Regulations (NDPR) 2019 and the Nigerian Data Protection Regulations Implementation Framework 2019 which was issued under the National Information Technology Development Agency (NITDA). This present Act of 2023 established the Nigeria Data Protection Commission.

The NDPA basically applies to the processing of personal data by a data processor whether automated or not, that belongs to data subjects in Nigeria. It is pertinent to note that it is immaterial whether the data controller or data processor is not operating in Nigeria. However, as long as the data subjects are domiciled in Nigeria, surely the NDPA must apply. Where Nigerian citizens are residing outside Nigeria, the NDPA will not protect them. It is worthy to note that there are circumstances under the Act where the NDPA will not apply to a data controller or data processor.

The exceptions include:

a. the prevention, investigation, detection, prosecution, or adjudication of a criminal offense or to execute a criminal penalty in accordance with any applicable law;
b. to prevent or control a national public health emergency;
c. as is necessary for national security;
d. in respect of publication in the public interest, for journalism, educational, artistic and literary purposes to the extent that such obligations and rights incompatible with such purposes; or
e. necessary to establish exercise, or defend legal claims, whether in court proceedings, or in an administrative or out-of-court procedure.

It is pertinent to state that all digital businesses and platforms are under obligation to abide by the legal and regulatory requirements under the Act or face the penalty contained therein.

4. Challenges Associated with Enforcement of Digital Transaction Laws in Nigeria

Firstly it is paramount to note that in Nigeria we have a limited number of legislations with regards to regulation of electronic transactions as well as proliferation of cybercrimes. In addition, the existing legislations did not make any provisions or adequate consumer protections with respect to regulating tech giants digital payments and smartphone wallet services in Nigeria.

Secondly, our enforcement mechanism is very poor in Nigeria. Government bodies that are charged with compliance with the statutory provisions of the law are inefficient. Most of the agencies for enforcement are bedeviled by corruption and corrupt practices.

Defaulters to the provisions of our extant legislation must be punished adequately so as to deter would be offenders from venturing into same. Non-compliance should be taken seriously.

Members of the public should be sensitized about their rights under the various legislations. There should be a massive awareness program by government, government agencies, non-profit organizations and a host of civil society groups on the provisions of the novel laws that are being made in Nigeria. Creation of awareness on how cybercriminals operate will in no small measure reduce the exposure of unsuspecting members of the public to falling victim to cybercrimes

Additionally, data controllers as well as data processors are to ensure strict compliance with the letters and intendment of the laws, this will exonerate them from liabilities.

5. Conclusion

It is glaring that the digital era has posed a lot of legal challenges in Nigeria. It has also exposed the lacuna in our present laws. As the years unfold, the scope of cybercrime is growing rapidly, as countries attempt to beef up and proactively secure their digital payment system laws, the threat of cyber fraud continues, hence the urgent need for novel changes in our laws. An increase in cybercrime is a global menace as well as double jeopardy to Nigeria's businesses and its citizens. There is an urgent need to enhance growth genuineness and sustainability of digital transactions through effective and adequate legal frameworks.

Even though the Nigerian government recently has taken steps to bridge the gap in our legal framework with respect to digital transaction processes; as well as protect its citizens against fraud, much still needs to be done. At the international level, electronic or digital transaction has gained so much prominence that it has specific laws regulating it. For example, the United States has the Electronic Signatures in Global and National Commercial Act 2000 and the Uniform Electronic Transactions Act at the State level. Also in United Kingdom, they have the United Kingdom's Electronic Communications Act 2000 and the Electronic Signatures Regulations 2002. In South Africa, there is Electronic Communications and Transactions Act 2002.

6. Recommendations

Cyber security and cyber warfare is a continuum. The digital space is no longer a lawless frontier; rather nations of the world are now alert to making laws to ensure that the cyber space is safe. It is pertinent to state that digital transactions is the foundation of prosperous economies, vigorous research communities, strong militaries, transparent governments, and free societies.

In Nigeria, there is an urgent need to have a legal framework dedicated solely to regulation of electronic or digital transactions as is obtainable in some other jurisdictions. There is no law in Nigeria that is dedicated to this urgent precarious situation; this has to a great extent hindered the ease of doing business in Nigeria. There is also the need to consider the recognition of electronic identification, authentication and trust services in the African region that would recognize the legal validity of digital signatures and stamps and as well as their admissibility as evidence across member states. This will enhance trade relations across the continent.

The government of Nigeria needs to create and or establish a digital or electronic systems regulator. They should be charged with statutory duties to promote innovation and ensure that digital/electronic transactions are operated and conducted in a way that promotes the interests of businesses and consumers. Individuals should be able to express and engage freely on the internet; having the confidence that their personal data will also be protected.

The Nigerian government should organize educational campaigns to educate, sensitize and inform the public about the benefits and dangers of electronic or digital payment systems. People should be taught on how to seal deals electronically, how to do use digital payment methods and how to detect cyber-fraudsters.

On a global scale, there is an urgent need for countries on international and regional levels to drive greater interoperability and inclusivity with a view to coherent and efficient regulatory reforms for digital payment systems.

The Nigerian Judiciary should embrace the use of electronic evidence as a means to administration of criminal justice. The judges, legal practitioners, public prosecutors should be trained, be proactive and embrace the use of digital forensic tools. Thus digital forensic tools are applications and devices that are geared towards facilitating the investigation and analysis of digital evidence. This will improve the efficiency and effectiveness of our justice delivery system in Nigeria.

Conclusively, the world must together take note of the inherent challenges of criminals into the cyberspace and work towards harmonized national and international policies so as to synergize the war against cybercrimes and a safe cyber space for digital transactions.

References

Ayojimi, M. (2024) 'The Evidence Act of 2023: A Remarkable Advancement in Nigeria's Jurisprudence," Available at www.lawpavillion.com Jan 10.

Digital Forensics 1st ed Edited by Andre Arnes 2018 John Wiley & Sons Ltd.

Digital Payments – Nigeria, Available at www.statistic.com accessed on 23/01/2024.

Hoar, S.B. , (2001) Identity Theft: The Crime of the New Millennium , Or. Law Rev. 80, 1423.

Holt, T. J. , Bossler A. M., Seigfried – Spellar, K.C.(2015) *Cybercrime and Digital Forensics: An Introduction* Routledge, United Kingdom.

International Strategy for Cyberspace: prosperity, security, and openness in a Networked World, (2011). USA.

Lubis, M. and Handayani, D.O.D., 2022. The Relationship of personal data protection towards internet addiction: Cyber crimes. Pornography and reduced physical activity. Procedia Computer Science, 197, pp 151-161.

Nwafor, E.I.,(2099) *Cybercrime and the Law: Issues and Development in Nigeria,* Kraft Books Limited, Nigeria.

Nigeria Recorded a 174% increase in Cybercrimes in six months; November 18, 2022, Business Day www.businessday.ng.

Onuora A C, Uche D C. et al, The Challenges of Cybercrime in Nigeria: An Overview, AIPFU Journal of School of Science Vol. 1 No. 2 2017.

Organization for Economic Corporation and Development (OECD) report on Electronic Commerce: opportunities and challenges for Government OECD, 1997) at P.20

Prime-Time for Real Time 2022 3rd edition published by AU Worldwide, (NASDAQ: ACIIN)

Queen Troanusi, over 2,800 persons convicted of cybercrime in 2022 – EFCC. www.premiumtimesng.com

Rathna, G., Mohan, S., Jayalakshmi, J. S., (2023) *Cybercrime and Digital Payments In India: A Comprehensive Analysis*, India.

Santhosh Rao, Head of Middle East, Africa and South Asia, ACI Worldwide.

The Psychological Effects of Continuity Threatening Cyber Incidents

Toni Virtanen

Military Psychology, Human Performance Division, Finnish Defence Research Agency (FDRA), Finland

toni.virtanen@mil.fi

Abstract: Working in the field of cybersecurity has been compared to working in a warlike environment. Understanding what types of psychological strain cyber attacks cause to the defending organisations' workforce can aid in developing methods and processes for mitigating those stressors. This paper discusses the first-hand psychological effects of experiencing an operational continuity threatening cyber incident caused by a real threat actor. The results are based on 19 interviews from IR professionals and IT security practitioners to decision makers, CISO's and other top executives. These individuals were working in multi-national corporations, hospitals, central government, financial sector, local government or educational institutions at the time of the incident. The interviews followed critical incident paradigm to focus on significant events during the cyber incidents, while also being semi-structured to compensate for the diversity of the incidents. Most of the interviewees raise up feelings of disbelief and despair as their first emotional response to the realization of being hit by ransomware, data theft or another severe cyber incident that could threaten operational or business continuity. Feelings of guilt and self-doubt were present, especially in those considered to be responsible for securing the network. However, at the same time, feelings of purpose and self-efficacy were also reported by some. Having scalable resources available in the time of need, with well-defined roles and responsibilities for the core incident response teams and protecting them from unnecessary inquiries seemed to alleviate the stressors and anxiety of the Incident Response (IR) team during the event. Good leadership and internal communication were seen as important to maintain the necessary situational awareness and focus during the active incident mitigation and resolve phase. Long-term negative effects of the cyber incident were increased cynicism, fear of the situation recurring, and thoughts of changing career. These negative outcomes were mitigated by increased trust in colleagues, processes and systems with experience of self-efficacy. This paper discusses what types of mental strain cyber incidents introduce to cybersecurity professionals and top executives. It deepens understanding on what factors need to be considered in developing and enhancing the overall resilience of organisations against cyber attacks.

Keywords: Cyberpsychology, Cyber Defence, Resilience, Mental demand, Cyber incident, Psychological effects of cyber attacks

1. Introduction

Working in the field of cybersecurity has been compared to working in a warlike environment (Brody, 2015; Singh, et al., 2023). Cyberspace does not follow geography and threat actors can project their attacks easily to anywhere on the globe making organisations defences endlessly contested. Cybersecurity professionals are providing critical service to ensure business continuity of organisations and government services in a constantly changing adversarial landscape (Paul & Dykstra, 2017). Recent studies have indicated that work-related stress is high in the cybersecurity profession (Nobles, 2022; Singh, et al., 2023). The VMware Global Incident Response Threat Report from 2022 demonstrates that 51% of cybersecurity professionals self-report having symptoms related to burnout and of that group, 65% have considered leaving the cybersecurity profession altogether (VMware, 2022). Understanding what types of psychological strain cyber attacks cause to the defending organisations' workforce can aid in developing methods and processes for mitigating those stressors.

2. Methods

Interviews were semi-structured and used an adapted version of Critical Incident Technique (CIT) (Flanagan, 1954). The semi-structured form went through certain set of questions with everybody, but included follow-up questions when applicable. The structured questions included but were not limited to, the following topics: what happened, how the cyber-attack was first noticed, how did collaboration with others work out, what actions were taken, what was surprising, were they able to mentally and physical recover during the incident, and what possible long-lasting effects did the event have. 18 out of 19 interviews were conducted in person. Each interview took approximately 1.5 hours. At the start of the interview, participants were asked to sketch emotional journey mapping and to a provided timeline and then pinpoint four critical events during the cyber incident (Figure 1). Various journey maps are commonly related to UX and service design methods (Nielsen Norman Group, 2018), but can also be applied to visualise the emotional change during the different phases of a cyber incident.

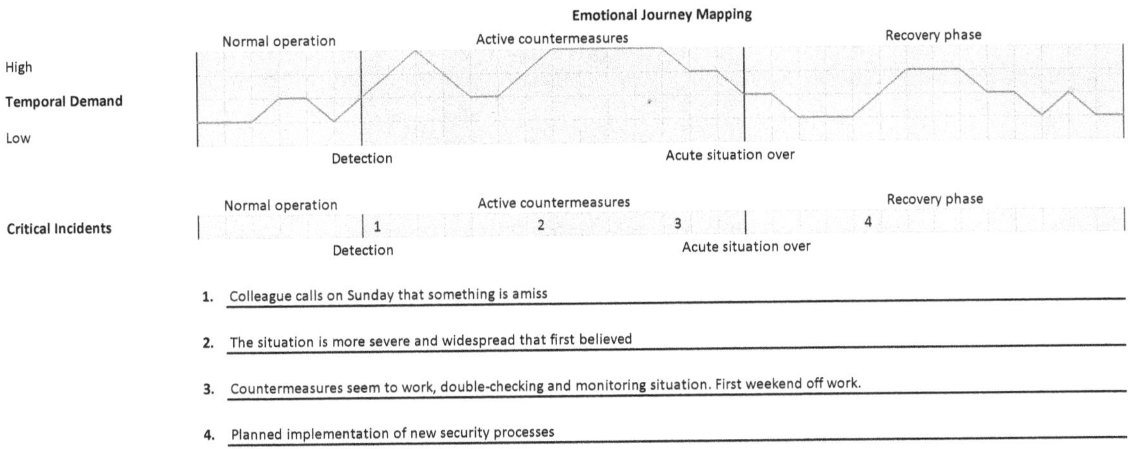

Figure 1: Example of the Emotional Journey Mapping and Critical Incidents

Participants sketched their emotional journey mappings using six categories: Stress, Mental Demand, Physical Demand, Temporal Demand, Effort, Performance and Frustration. Excluding Stress, the categories were based on the NASA Task Load Index (NASA-TLX) (Hart, 1986). Descriptions for each scale category were provided (Table 1)

Table 1: Descriptions of emotional journey mapping categories adapted from NASA-TLX (Hart, 1986).

Category	Description
Stress	Stress refers to a situation in which a person feels tense, restless, nervous, anxious or has difficulty sleeping when things are constantly bothering his mind. Try to recall and evaluate when you felt the most stress and when the least.
Mental Demand	How much mental demand and perceptual activity was required to do the job (e.g. thinking, deciding, calculating, remembering, looking, searching etc)? Was the task easy or demanding, simple or complex, exacting or forgiving?
Physical Demand	How much physical activity was required (e.g. pushing, pulling, turning, controlling, activating etc). Was the task easy or demanding, slow or brisk, slack or strenuous, restful or laborious? Did the task require physical stamina? Did it require long hours of continuous working?
Temporal Demand	How much time pressure did you feel, due to the rate or pace at which the task was required to be done? Was the pace slow and leisurely or rapid and frantic?
Effort	How hard did you have to work (mentally and physically) to accomplish your level of performance?
Performance	How successful do you think you were in accomplishing the task? How satisfied were you with your performance in accomplishing these goals?
Frustration	Were you left feeling discouraged, irritated, stressed and annoyed during the task (high frustration)? Or did you feel gratified, content and relaxed during the task (low frustration)?

The emotional journey mapping with the critical incidents acted as an orientation and memory aid that guided the semi-structured interview process afterwards. As an example, the emotional journey mapping provided a starting point for follow-up questions: "Your frustration level soared at this moment. What happened and why were you frustrated about it?" As every cyber incident was unique, the timeline for the emotional journey mapping was deliberately very rough and no specific timeframe was given as some incidents only took days while others could even take months. Still, the aggregated timeline from these incidents can provide an overview of the general process victims go through.

2.1 Subjects

A total of 19 volunteer interviewees were recruited with the aid of the Finnish National Cyber Security Centre (NCSC-FI). A recent systematic review on qualitative sample sizes shows that 9–17 interviews or 4–8 focus group discussions generally reached saturation (Hennink & Kaiser, 2022). The NCSC-FI maintain Finnish national cyber situational awareness, develops forums for information sharing within industries and provides information and guidelines for improving cybersecurity. The NCSC-FI also receives voluntary reports from private persons, businesses and organisations when they suspect that they have fallen victim to an actual or attempted information security incident, such as malware infection, phishing or DDoS attacks. Interviewees were selected to represent a wide variety of organisations and government service providers such as manufacturing, Information Technology (IT) security providers, logistics, health care, central government, financial sector, local government or educational institutions and others. Organisations differed widely in size and internationality. Some organisations had more experience in cyber incidents and Incident Response (IR) management, while others had only small teams handling everything related to IT, from security to infrastructure and quality of service. None of the interviewees were personally the target or victim of a cyber-attack, and the results are based on interviews from IR professionals (six interviews) and IT security practitioners (eight interviews) to decision makers, CISO's and other top executives (five interviews) that were working at the organization or as an external IR professional brought to aid organisations that have fallen victim to a cyber-attack.

The cyber incidents were required to be severe enough to either risk operational continuity, cause major damage to reputation, or include loss of IP or other sensitive information. Attacks included severe and long-lasting DDoS attacks on key services, ransomware attacks that encrypt key resources, and successful penetration and exfiltration of sensitive information. Attack vectors varied from zero-day vulnerability, to phishing emails, while the threat actors could be attributed to represent suspected state-sponsored Advanced Persistent Threat (APT) actors or cybercriminals. No requirement was made on how recent the incident needed to be. In addition, no exercises or penetration test experiments were included and all the cases were required to be authentic with genuine threat actors and contain real risks to the organisations. As the topic can be sensitive to the individuals and organisations involved, all interviews are strictly confidential and the results were aggregated in such a way that anonymity is ensured for the participants.

3. Results

3.1 Emotional Journeys

The grid on the emotional journey mappings (see Figure 1) was used as scale from 1 to 5, where 1 is the lowest point and 5 is the highest point on the scale. From this scale, average emotional mappings were calculated (see Figure 2), which provide an estimate of the general direction on how cyber incidents impacted the individuals. The thick central line represents the average value, while the upper and lower lines represent the high and low limit of the 5% confidence interval, meaning that 95% of all responses fit in between those lines.

The highest impact from detecting a severe cyber incident is shown as increased stress, mental demand and temporal demand. The temporal demand rises almost instantly after detection, while stress and mental demand accumulate and peak a bit later after detection. There also seems to be a second peak for mental demand later on during the active countermeasures phase. Unsurprisingly, physical demand remained generally low, even during the active countermeasures. Increased effort is observed to follow a similar pattern to the stress and temporal demand categories. Participants who self-reported estimates on their own performance level seemed to be unaffected and remained quite high at all times. Frustration level had the largest variation between requirement was made on how recent the incident needed to be. In addition, no exercises or penetration

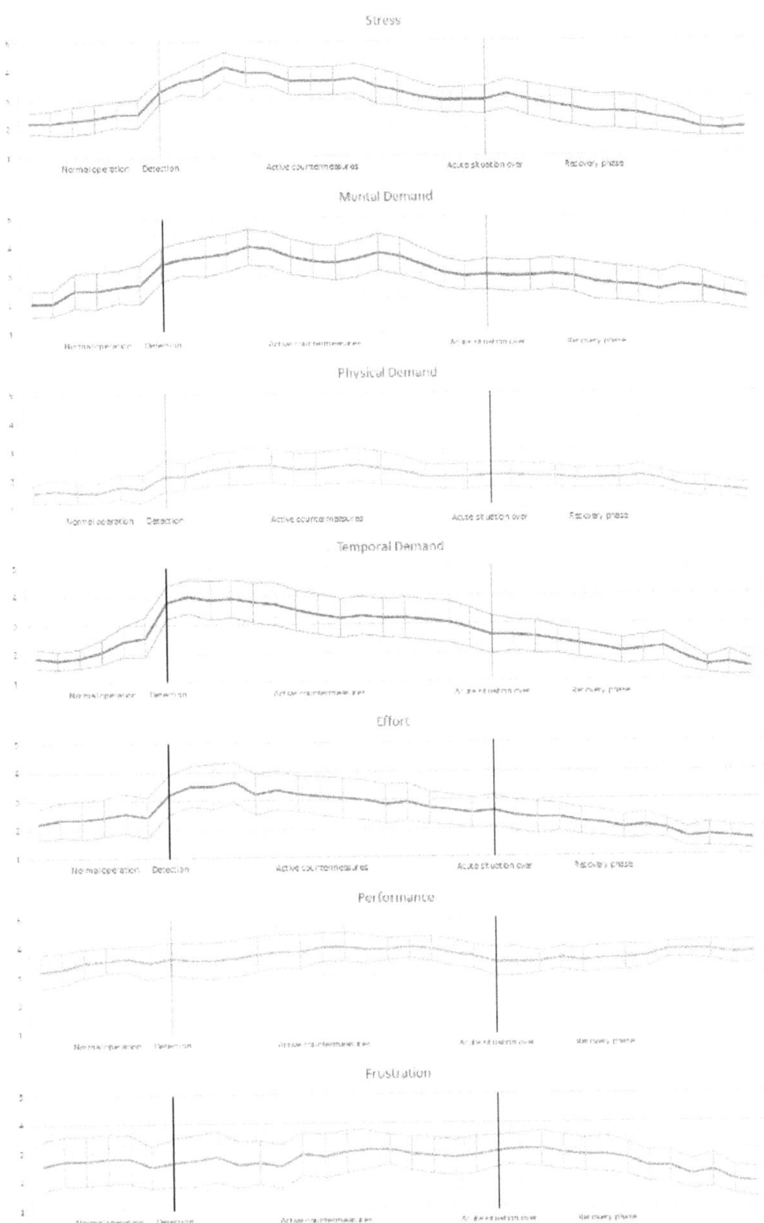

Figure 2: Average emotional journey mappings for each category. Thick central line represents average values, while the upper and lower line represents the high and low limit of the 5 % confidence interval

participants, meaning that feelings of frustration depended highly on the incident and the individual. Interviews

The 19 interviews revealed three distinct groups: 1. Incident Response (IR) processionals hired to aid an organization during the attack (six interviewees), 2. IT security practitioners at the organization under attack (eight interviewees) and 3. Top executives and decision makers at the organisations (five interviewees).

3.1.1 IR Professionals

IR professionals were better able to distance themselves from the situation as it was not them nor their organization that was under attack. They also had more experience on different types of cyber incidents giving better perspective to the situation. Overall, IR professionals experienced less anxiety and stress from these incidents, even if the temporal demand remained high. Some even reported being enthusiastic and excited as a new case meant a deviation from day-to-day activities. Many interviewees also commented that they continued to study and investigate cybersecurity-related issues at home in their free time, as it was something they were so interested about. A new case also presented a learning opportunity and a challenge to test one's skills. After more severe and demanding cases, they did still report the need to recover for a few ordinary workdays before they felt ready for another case.

Working as an external IR professional might spare them from the psychological effects suffered by the targeted victims of a cyber-attack, but introduced other types of strain factors. The most straightforward inconveniences for IR professionals emerged when they needed to set up and work at the customers' premises with sometimes less-than-optimal tools and ergonomics. An unexpected source of stress came from tense social interactions with the local IT support in some cases. This tension was thought to stem from various reasons, such as simply being the result of how some people might act under highly stressful situations. One hypothesized reason was also that the local IT security practitioners could feel their position threatened, as they were no longer the definite expert on cybersecurity issues for their organization. Another reason for local IT support opposition might originate from the reluctance of doing any major changes to the systems in such tight timeframes, which during normal operation would be planned for weeks if not months. Thus, the external IR professionals feel pressure that they must be absolutely certain about their analyses and suggestions before they present them to the customers. This pressure, along with the increasing discovery of new vulnerabilities, contains a risk of burnout as IR professionals constantly try to keep up with the latest trends on threat actors' tactics, techniques and procedures. Building trust and being able to communicate what needs to be done with the customers' representatives at all levels were seen important by the IR professionals. This however might create another dilemma as not all technically skilled people are good at communicating with the customer, while those that are might not have the necessary understanding of the technical aspects needed to be discussed.

3.1.2 IT Security Practitioners

Local IT security practitioners had more variation in how much experience they had with Incident Response Management, depending on the size and type of the organisations. The smaller the organization, the more stretched out the individuals' role was. Larger or security-critical organisations had their own information and cybersecurity teams, while in smaller organisations only a few IT professionals handle everything from cybersecurity to local IT support for end-users. The less experience the individual had, the more stressful they felt the situation to be. There was also an element of frustration, as in many cases, the event could have been prevented if higher-ups would have listened to their recommendations earlier or that end-users would have followed the information security guidelines properly. All of them, however, understood that as their organisation's core business was not in cybersecurity they needed to make do with the resources they were given. Although all IT security practitioners reported that the situation was stressful, younger interviewees especially experienced the stress to be a mix of excitement and anxiety. They were excited that something is actually happening, but anxious about the workload and whether they are up to the challenge.

IT security practitioners' first reactions on the revelation of a severe cyber incident were disbelief and hope that things are not as bad as they seem. This was followed by a brief moment of numbness as the consequences of the situation started to sink in. Feelings of failure and shame were also frequently reported during the first moments after the discovery. Some individuals also reported feelings of despair with a sensation that they are alone in this situation and admitted that they experienced a brief urge of just giving up and quitting then and there. Once they had gotten over the shock, many felt indecisive on what should they do first as all things seemed equally important and urgent. Once the initial restriction and mitigation actions were done, a moment of respite followed. However, in most cases there were always some repercussions that required extended effort, such as checking that unaffected systems were really clean. This moment is critical for the well-being of IT security practitioners, and they shouldn't overexert themselves at the acute mitigation phase just to realize that a lot of work is still required to be done.

During the acute response and mitigation phase, some reported feeling frustration because of the micromanagement of higher-ups and constant questions from end-users or other departments. IT practitioners felt that when the middle-managers didn't understand the situation, they seemed to panic and required even small decisions to be approved by them hindering the recovery activities. End-users on the other hand, were keen to get their tools and software back, but all of these questions took time away from the actual recovery actions. Disagreement and frustration were also caused by IT service employees from other locations, as they might argue against the instructions given by the IT security practitioners. In hindsight, the interviewees reported that during the stressful and time-demanding situation, their delivery could have become quite narrow, leaving pleasantries and explanations at a minimum in e-mails and other communication channels. In addition, they recognized that being under a high mental load and so preoccupied in their thoughts, they might have not acknowledged others around them very well and, for example, forgotten to greet them in the morning. Both of these behaviours might seem rude or even hostile from the perspective of other colleagues, which can cause conflicts within the wider work community.

Existing incident management and recovery plans were mentioned as valuable checklists, although in some cases the situation was assessed to be so unique that they weren't applicable. With larger corporations, it was also sometimes difficult to find the right contact person for inquiries and requests in other departments and locations. In almost every case, an external IR team was hired to help the local IT security practitioners with the mitigation and recovery. Their experience and know-how were seen as critical and many commented that they wouldn't have managed the situation without them. In many organisations, there just isn't any reason to have an internal IR team, as cybersecurity is only seen as an unavoidable expense for doing business. During the recovery phase and even long after few IT security practitioners reported having some kind of an impostor syndrome. They were now given better resources and had better visibility and controls in the networks, so they felt anxious on the prospect that they would fail again. In addition, quite often a new and improved Security Information and Event Management (SIEM) system was adopted after the incident by the recommendation of the external IR teams. As with any new system, there was always a learning curve for familiarizing themselves with the slightly different types of alerts the new SIEM system produces, and this new system had to be learned alongside the recovery and build up still underway.

3.1.3 Top Executives

Top executives mostly had stressors related to leadership, resources, communication and responsibility. The first moments after a severe cyber incident included a lot of communication to stakeholders, gathering resources, people and expertise to handle the situation. They felt responsible about the incident and also had feelings of shame and remorse that they had failed, even if there wasn't anything they could have done better with the resources at their disposal. Some also reported being worried about losing their job and reputation, thinking that they will never get a job in cybersecurity again. The feeling of a blemished reputation, could last even long after the actual cyber incident was over, making them stressed out from even the slightest rustles in the network. As cybersecurity can be so abstract, one could even feel guilty in situations that weren't even part of their responsibility.

A major source of stress came from publicity of the incident. Stress was higher when the top executives didn't have control of when or how it would become public. For example, in a situation where the threat actors themselves went public by leaking sensitive information, or when the public media takes interest as the organization is providing a popular service that becomes unavailable due to the attack. Publicity can affect the organization's reputation, which can have an impact on the valuation of a publicly traded company. In addition, very often when a cyber incident becomes public it also generates other attempts against the organisation's systems, resulting in extra work for the SOC and other IT security practitioners who already have their hands full mitigating and resolving the ongoing incident.

In many cases, top executives saw themselves as the gatekeepers for the IR teams and IT security practitioners working towards recovering from the incident so that they could concentrate on fixing the issue and not worry about irrelevant inquiries from media, other departments or end-users. They feel they need to ensure that the people working for them get enough rest and do not become exhausted during the incident. Managing experts, who are often very motivated, enthusiastic and strive for perfection also has its unique challenges. High motivation needs to be curated so that people do not burn themselves out, while still avoiding discouraging them. Some experts seem to react to a crisis by thinking they are irreplaceable and keep working even on areas that are not their responsibility. For example, a networks expert will begin to analyse databases for Indications of Compromise (IoC) on their own initiative, when the best thing he or she could actually do is to just get some rest and then continue to work on the things that are their expertise. These unprompted actions can just wear out people faster and increase fatigue related human errors. It is therefore important to allocate clear roles for the IR team and IT security practitioners so that people know what they and others are doing.

Interestingly, another source for irritation and frustration for top executives were the managers and executives from other departments. Even if the organization had an existing disaster recovery plan, dictating which systems are deemed as most important. There seems to be always someone who tries to challenge it trying to get the system most important for their department recovered first. Managers and executives from those departments that were spared by the effect of the cyber-attack might realize that they dodged a bullet by luck and are now demanding that all the recommendations and changes to be made as soon as possible, even if they had been opposing any changes to their legacy systems earlier. Others who have been affected by the incident, might also try to hide behind red tape and blame to the CISO or other IT security managers for the incident. As an example, they might claim that the reason they hadn't patched their systems was because they hadn't got any recommendations to do so, or that they don't recall any requests for extra resources to patch the vulnerability. This results on less than optimal working atmosphere and insisting to have detailed records on what has been agreed upon and when at all times.

3.1.4 General Observations

Work-Life balance was difficult to arrange during the cyber incident especially for individuals with family and small children. Although interviewees reported that their spouses and family were understanding and supportive, the incident could generate some tension at home. Much of the household chores, childcare, and other responsibilities might fall on the spouse, which could seem unfair from their perspective. They also might appear distant and weary at home during the height of the incident. Most of the interviewees also reported that they couldn't discuss the situation at home as much of it was confidential. It is quite common for threat actors to schedule their attacks during holiday seasons. Only few of the interviewees had discussed with their spouses that their cybersecurity occupation could involve situations where they would need to be on call and spend long hours at work for extended periods. Another challenge for work-life balance came from significant event outside of work that could coincide with the cyber incident. These could be, for example, serious illness or loss of a close relative, or big family reunions and celebrations such as weddings.

Many interviewees also considered that any activity which required one's full attention worked best to take their mind off work. These types of activities varied widely depending on the person and could be anything from hunting to watching TV. Physical exercise was mentioned as another way to release stress and maintain general well-being. Playing and spending time with children were also mentioned as an effective way to unwind for those who had a family. Many interviewees mentioned that their work-life balance had improved as they got older, settled down, and started a family. Having some kind of structure in life, such as a relationship, family or even just a pet, helped them to not spend all their waking hours with computers. For many, cybersecurity were almost a vocation and a topic that they were extremely interested in. To maintain some level of work-live balance, many of the interviewees had developed ways to limit how much time they can spend on it in their free time. A common method was to not have any computers or smart devices easily available at home, deliberately preventing them from working at home. Another, regrettably less constructive method, was alcohol, as having a couple of drinks gave them the permission to relax. Almost everyone mentioned good working atmosphere and humour as an effective way to release stress at the workplace.

Interviewees didn't always emerge from the severe cyber incidents unscathed and reported experiencing similar long-term symptoms more often associated with people experiencing traumatic events. Such symptoms included difficulty sleeping, hyper-alertness, cynicism, awkward reactions to stressful situations, emotional numbness and risk behaviour related to alcohol. According to the definition of the Diagnostic And Statistical Manual Of Mental Disorders (DSM-5-TR) (American Psychiatric Association, 2022) most cyber incidents do not fulfil the criteria of a traumatic event as they generally lack the real or experienced danger of death or serious injury, or a threat to the physical integrity of self or others. Even though cyber incidents do not fulfil the diagnostic criteria, it could be argued that severe cyber incidents can still be considered as a traumatic event by some. For some, the severe cyber incident seemed to work as a catalyst on reflections of one's identity, what they want to do with their life and considerations of changing careers completely or finding a less stressful field in IT. A general observation by the interviewees was that many of their colleagues with small children, changed position or left the organization a couple of months after the cyber incident. Severe cyber incidents also had a wider ripple effect within the organization, and often resulted in an increased workload to other departments that could last long after the incident was already over. End-users in all levels also tended to have a general loss of trust in the system. This was often visible by the increased number of questions and tickets to IT security and the increased number of paper copies.

4. Discussion

This paper presented the psychological impact of severe cyber incidents based on 19 voluntary interviews from various organisations. The limitations of this study are the relatively small sample size and possible culture dependencies which might somewhat diminish the generalizability of the results. Although none of the interviewees were the target of the cyber-attack in person, those working in the organization under fire did experience the event as highly stressful. Coping with uncertainty, time pressure and communication were prevailing stressors for cybersecurity professionals in all levels during a cyber incident. As a highly motivated group, cybersecurity professionals can be at risk of burning oneself out especially during crisis situations.

Several best practices and recommendations to reduce the mental and social load of the cyber incidents can be derived based on the interviews. Sharing information about the cyber incident with other industry members is highly recommended. In some cases, organisations were able to speed up their countermeasures as they had been recently informed of a similar incident. Organisations should define clear roles and responsibilities for incident response beforehand to avoid miscommunication and conflicts. These roles and practices also need to be practiced and trained with periodical exercises. It should also be ensured that all the critical personnel get enough rest and nutrition during the incident, by arranging work shift and food supply for the team. It is recommended that the core incident response team is protected from unnecessary questions and inquiries so that they can concentrate on the incident, while the access to the war room or operation centre needs to be limited to only those actively participating in the incident response. Having too large of a group, can decrease focus and efficiency. Special attention should be given for communication as misunderstandings can cause unnecessary conflicts within the organisation. In addition to the general lessons learned events after the incident. Arranging debriefing sessions with a focus on mental and physical well-being led by a social scientist or a similar professional could be beneficial after especially demanding cases.

Although this study focused on the negative impacts on cyber incidents, these events can also have a positive impact on the team cohesion within the organization, giving purpose to one's work and acting as a baptism by fire for the professionals, making them more prepared in the future. Very often, a cyber incident acted as a catalyst for getting rid of unsecure legacy systems and receiving sufficient resources for maintaining and improving cyber security within the organization. Further research is needed on the psychological effects during and after cyber incidents. Future research will look into verifying these findings with a questionnaire study and test if there are any cultural differences between countries and organizations.

Acknowledgements

The author would like to thank Finnish National Cyber Security Centre (NCSC-FI) and all the interviewees for participating in this study.

References

American Psychiatric Association, 2022. Diagnostic And Statistical Manual Of Mental Disorders, Fifth Edition, Text Revision (DSM-5-TR).

Brody, B. A., 2015. Cybersecurity akin to being in a war zone—you have to be "left of boom" to survive. [Online] Available at: https://philipcao.com/2015/06/28/cybersecurity-akin-to-being-in-a-war-zone-you-have-to-be-left-of-boom-to-survive/ [Accessed 22 JAN 2024].

Flanagan, J. C., 1954. The critical incident technique.. Psychological bulletin, Volume 51, p. 327.

Hart, S. G., 1986. NASA task load index (TLX).

Hennink, M. & Kaiser, B. N., 2022. Sample sizes for saturation in qualitative research: A systematic review of empirical tests. Social Science & Medicine, Volume 292.

Nielsen Norman Group, 2018. Journey mapping 101. [Online] Available at: https://www.nngroup.com/articles/journey-mapping-101/ [Accessed 23 JAN 2024].

Nobles, C., 2022. Stress, burnout, and security fatigue in cybersecurity: A human factors problem. HOLISTICA–Journal of Business and Public Administration, Volume 13, p. 49–72.

Paul, C. L. & Dykstra, J., 2017. Understanding operator fatigue, frustration, and cognitive workload in tactical cybersecurity operations. Journal of Information Warfare, Volume 16, p. 1–11.

Singh, T., Johnston, A. C., D'Arcy, J. & Harms, P. D., 2023. Stress in the cybersecurity profession: a systematic review of related literature and opportunities for future research. Organizational Cybersecurity Journal: Practice, Process and People.

VMware, I., 2022. Global Incident Response Threat Report: Weathering the Storm. [Online] Available at: https://www.vmware.com/content/microsites/learn/en/1553238_REG.html [Accessed 22 JAN 2024].

The Maritime Industry and the Cyber-'Iceberg'

Rossouw von Solms[1,3] and Suné von Solms[2,3]
[1] School of IT, Nelson Mandela University, South Africa
[2]Department of Electrical and Electronic Engineering Science, University of Johannesburg, South Africa
[3]South African International Maritime Institute, South Africa

rossouw@mandela.ac.za
svonsolms@uj,.ac.za

Abstract: The maritime industry is embracing cyber technology. The proliferation of digitalisation in the shipping industry is apparent, as any modern vessel today is a complex cyber-physical-mechanically engineered system. The digital incorporation of operational technology (OT) and information and communication technology (ICT) systems in network and control systems has resulted in complex integrated shipping vessels. As most modern vessels utilise the internet to communicate with those on shore, it is true to say that shipping today has adopted cyber technology to enhance the efficiency of its operations. It is also true that the modern shipping industry has become totally dependent on cyber technologies for its future existence. Along with the integration of ICT and cyber-related technologies came numerous cybersecurity threats. These risks need to be identified and mitigated. If not properly addressed, these underlying cybersecurity threats can lead onto disasters of all different kinds. This paper discusses the integration of (ICT) and cyber-related technologies in the maritime and shipping industry, the related cybersecurity threats encountered and why these should be mitigated. It also suggests how senior management and the crew members can contribute in assisting to safeguard shipping vessels from these ever-present cybersecurity threats.

Keywords: Maritime Industry, Cybersecurity, Iot, Cyber Threats, Governance, Cybersecurity Education

1. Introduction

No longer is a shipping vessel at sea far away from numerous dangerous threats. No longer are the operational technology systems, that control the multiple mechanical systems on-board a shipping vessel, removed from any off-board danger. No longer is a shipping vessel a micro, artificial floating 'ecosystem' whilst it is at sea.

The advancement of the shipping industry has led to the continued integration of computing equipment, information technology, sensors, etc. with the operational technology systems on-board modern shipping vessels. This has changed shipping forever.

Various operational technology systems communicate continuously with many critical information technology systems, on- and off-board, resulting in a critical myriad of digital data that control the well-being of the vessel, the freight and those on-board. This critical digital data has become the lifeblood of most modern vessels, flowing through highly interconnected digital networks (veins).

Cyberspace has changed the way in which the modern world operates, doing business, communicates, relax, etc. Perhaps slower than other industries, but the maritime industry is catching up and utilising the benefits cyberspace has to offer. Along with the numerous benefits cyberspace has to offer came the myriad of cybersecurity threats that need to be avoided and mitigated.

The objective of this paper is to assess, evaluate and assist the efforts to successfully integrate cybersecurity, specifically from a human point of view, into the modern maritime industry. This will be done by studying the advancement in the shipping industry over years. The integration of ICT in modern shipping will be highlighted, followed by typical vulnerabilities of using ICT and cyber technologies in the shipping industry. Cybersecurity in the modern maritime industry will be highlighted and compared to a typical iceberg of old. Lastly, two important human-related remedies will be presented.

2. Advances in the Maritime Industry

The utilisation of water faring vessels dates to ancient times, where seafaring vessels were used for a variety of purposes, including exploration, trade, warfare, fishing and mobility. The challenges provided by the maritime environment, such as propulsion, communication, navigation, safety and security have led to a range of technological advancements throughout the centuries. In general, however, it is believed that the shipping industry has been slower to integrate technological developments compared to on-shore companies, but in recent years the industry has seen the steady adaption and inclusion of technology (Abi-Saab, 2018; Voyager, 2023).

Ship propulsion is one of the cornerstones of the maritime industry and remains an indispensable part of global trade, exploration and connectivity (Kundu, 2023). Before the 19th century, ship propulsion relied mainly on oars and wind, were the industrial revolution brought forth the use of coal-fired steam engines, enabling ships to move faster and more reliably, greatly advancing global trade. The diesel engine replaced steam, which is now slowly being supplemented with green alternatives such as Liquefied Natural Gas (LNG) engines, Diesel-electric and Hydrogen solutions (Kundu, 2023; Maritime Cyprus, 2020). This landscape not only underwent updates in power and propulsion technologies, but recently started to include and utilize more sensor technologies, data processing and autonomous control, which replaced many of the manual tasks, like monitoring and metering and decision making (Matuszak, 2021).

Historical navigation heavily relied on celestial navigation techniques, using stars and celestial bodies as guides, coupled with compasses for directional orientation at sea. These traditional methods laid the foundation for more sophisticated navigational tools. The introduction of radar technology marked a pivotal shift in maritime navigation during the 20th century. Radar enabled vessels to detect other objects, coastlines, and potential hazards, significantly enhancing situational awareness (Hegland et al, 2017). The integration of Global Navigation Satellite Systems (GNSS), such as Global Positioning Systems (GPS), revolutionized navigation by providing accurate positioning information globally (Kaplan & Hegarty, 2006). The advent of Electronic Chart Display and Information Systems (ECDIS) ushered in a new era of digital navigation, where ECDIS combines electronic navigational charts with real-time navigation information, offering dynamic and interactive displays for enhanced route planning and safety (Baldauf et al, 2016). The recent integration of Artificial Intelligence (AI) and Machine Learning (ML) into navigation systems now aims to refine decision-making processes, optimizing route planning and collision avoidance (Moussavi et al, 2020).

The communication field is widely considered the area where technological advancements have been embraced. Starting at the traditional methods such as maritime signal flags, technological innovations have revolutionized maritime communication, where radio communication is seen as a pivotal milestone. Radio technology significantly enhanced real-time communication between ships and shore, contributing to safer navigation and efficient coordination (Smith, 2018). The emergence of satellite communication systems transformed maritime connectivity which enabled seamless communication across vast ocean expanses, ensuring continuous contact and data exchange for vessels at sea (Rao, 2019). The integration of satellite technology has not only improved the reliability of communication but has also facilitated the implementation of advanced navigation systems, enhancing overall maritime safety and efficiency.

Historically, maritime safety relied on traditional practices and rudimentary equipment, but contemporary developments have ushered in a new era of comprehensive protection. The integration of Automatic Identification System (AIS) technology has been instrumental in enhancing maritime safety. AIS enables vessels to broadcast their identity, location, and course, facilitating real-time tracking and collision avoidance (Hui et al, 2019). Additionally, the adoption of Unmanned Aerial Vehicles (UAVs) and satellite surveillance has expanded the scope of maritime monitoring, enabling authorities to respond proactively to potential threats (Arreola-Risa et al, 2017). Furthermore, developments in biometric technologies have strengthened access control measures, ensuring that only authorized personnel have entry to critical maritime spaces (Saeed et al, 2021).

In recent years, the maritime industry has witnessed a surge in the adoption of digital technologies. The Internet of Things (IoT) and sensor networks have enabled the collection and transmission of real-time data, allowing for more informed decision-making on vessels (Wang et al, 2020). Additionally, the advent of autonomous vessels and smart shipping technologies is ushering in a new era of maritime communication, where vessels can communicate, navigate, and operate autonomously, further optimizing efficiency and safety (Yang et al, 2021).

3. Integration of ICT and Data Usage in Modern Shipping

With the proliferation of ICT, numerous IoT systems and sensor equipment throughout the operational systems of modern vessels, data is continuously being captured, analysed, stored and transmitted. Only now this data becomes useful to the ship and related industry (Lind-Olsen, 2019). Obviously, the capturing, analysing, storing and transmission of this data need to be done in a very reliable manner.

The transmission of data to and from the shore has become critically important (Lind-Olsen, 2019). The smart and intelligent usage of ICT and IoT systems on and off the ship and the flow of data to and from enable effective shore-based operations with the likes of maintenance service providers, customer support centres, port authorities, among others (Lind-Olsen, 2019). These vast amounts of data allow for clever analysis and integration into decision-making at various levels to the advantage of the ship, those onboard, the freight and the holding organisation (Moan, 2022).

The advantages that modern ICT and IoT offers enable ship owners and operators to meet the demands and expectations of customers and to deliver on global expectation (Moan, 2022). Digitalisation and the clever use of ICT does not only contribute operationally to the maritime industry, but also strategically. Value is added to make operations at sea smarter, safer and more sustainable (Larsen, 2020). Shipping companies who set out to harness the power of 'big data' and advanced analytics will gain strategic advantage on competitors (Larsen, 2020).

From the above it is clear that data plays an integral role. As mentioned, data gets continuously captured, analysed, stored and transmitted to be used in decision-making and for other important operations and purposes. Following are some examples of areas where data gets used lately:

- Improving vessel performance

  The continuous monitoring of and reporting on data captured from systems such as the vessel engine, electrical power, climate control, etcetera assists in optimising the performance. Therefore, data related to aspects such as; revolutions per minute, fuel and oil flow rates and temperature changes is important to capture, analyse and use (Julius, 2016).

- Supply chain management

  Electronic sensors are used extensively used in modern cargo systems. These sensors form part of IoT-based systems and used to monitor and track the cargo in real-time. This allow customers, captains and crew members to monitor temperatures, position, and so forth (Larsen, 2020).

- Navigation

  Modern navigation systems extensively make use of GPS, radar, sonar and computerised maps. Information from these systems is used with radio and satellite-based communication systems by navigation officers to navigate ships, especially in the dark and during inclement weather of low visibility (Julius, 2016).

- Environmental compliance

  Modern shipping needs to comply with the ever-increasing environmental regulations towards the UN Sustainable Development Code (SDGs), as such various ICT-related technologies are used to measure, manage and report on environmental-related aspects regarding each vessel. Further, by using cargo, port and environmental data, ships van plan their voyages, take shorter routes and adapt speed to port availability and thereby saving fuel (Moan, 2022).

- Predictive maintenance

  The large amounts of data that is continuously captured can be used for proactive analysis of the state of the ship's machinery or equipment (Marine Digital, 2023). Sensors, robots and smart condition monitoring technologies capture real-time data from equipment, systems and machinery, among other things, about the 'health' and status of the ship (Larsen, 2020). Predictive maintenance is definitely one of the foremost advancements of IoT systems in the modern shipping era.

Thus, the effective use of ICT-based systems contributes, amongst other things, to the delivery of supply chain transparency, assisting with effective navigation, reducing the ecological footprint and minimising the operational costs associated with ship inspections and maintenance. These are just some of the many reasons for the proliferation of data-capturing sensors and many ICT-related systems integrated all-over modern ships and vessels and associated cargo.

"Data is the new gold of the shipping industry" (Larsen, 2019). From this it is clear that quality, well-integrated, data needs to be captured, processed and analysed to be turned into trusted intelligence (Larsen, 2019), that can be used to ensure successful operational, strategic and competitive decisions.

4. Vulnerabilities of ICT and Related Shipping Data

Data becomes 'gold' when it is utilised to gain understanding and strategically integrated into operations and decision-making (Larsen, 2019). To be this valuable, it is logical that data needs to be accurately captured, processed and analysed. Only if this is the case trusted intelligence can stem from this data. Further, this data can only be valuable if it is standardised, accurately and securely distributed, and transmitted between ship and shore. Today it is imperative that reliable, seamless internet connectivity ensures the safe and secure flow of business intelligence (Larsen, 2019). As this process is making use of cyberspace, it is clearly littered with possible vulnerabilities.

The operational technology (OT) of modern ships is increasingly integrated with advanced ICT systems generating data, but also introducing more vulnerabilities to capture quality data. The continual adoption of cloud computing, the IoT and autonomous technologies to interconnect OT and ICT also lead to more cybersecurity risks coming to the fore. Therefore, the maritime industry has become highly vulnerable to cyber-related security risks (Cusimano et al, 2020). As a result of the continued integration of OT, IoT and related ICT systems in the maritime industry, cybersecurity has become very apparent in the industry (Cusimano et al, 2020). IoT devices and resultant systems are not necessarily secure by nature and therefore must be secured.

It is apparent that the maritime industry continues to embrace ICT solutions to become more effective. It is also very clear that this advancement, that depends on quality data, is increasingly exposed and getting vulnerable to cybersecurity risks that are threatening the quality of the data.

5. Cybersecurity in Maritime Industry

Cybersecurity is basically the overall effort to secure the ICT systems, onboard hardware and related sensors, as well as the data involved. This data needs to be protected from data leaks as a result of unauthorised access as well as the illegal manipulation and disruption thereof (Marine Digital, 2022). Cyberattacks on the navigational systems are well documented and usually takes place through the interference with automatic identification systems and electronic maps, the jamming of GPS and the manipulation of shipping management systems. These attacks usually take place by means of the introduction of malware, ransomware software and viruses (Princeton, 2018).

Cybersecurity, which has really become critical lately and should be implemented at all levels of the organisation. The cybersecurity effort should be a collective approach from all parties involved towards the well-being of the ship, its content and those onboard. From senior management onshore to crew members onboard should be involved in this securing process. All these parties and people contribute to the cybersafe culture and thereby ensuring the safe and efficient operation of the ship (Marine Digital, 2022). A brief overview of how cybersecurity and related research has grown in prominence lately will follow as well as an introduction to related cybersecurity vulnerabilities and challenges in the maritime industry.

5.1 The History of Cybersecurity

The rapid progress and adoption of technology in the maritime sector have heightened its susceptibility to cybersecurity risks. In the past decade, various incidents have highlighted vulnerabilities, with infrastructure like maritime vessels, port facilities, and the supply chain being exploited or targeted. Each element within the maritime industry necessitates specific critical operations to safeguard its cybersecurity.

Mawer, et al (2024) examined the historical trajectory of cybersecurity in the maritime sector which revealed a notable surge in cyber threats over the past two decades. While maritime technology has rapidly advanced, the corresponding development of cybersecurity systems has lagged. The integration of modern systems with legacy infrastructure has created additional opportunities for cyber threats. Research in cybersecurity in the maritime industry started to receive more attention, particularly from 2014 onwards. It is, however, seen that the majority of the research originated from the United States, China, the United Kingdom, and Norway.

It has been seen that over the past ten years, there have been numerous cases of infrastructure being targeted or compromised, including maritime vessels, port facilities, and the supply chain. Each facet of the maritime industry demands distinct critical system operations for cybersecurity assurance.

5.2 Cybersecurity Vulnerabilities and Challenges

The maritime industry has grown highly dependable on ICT and related cyberspace over the last decade or so, but also became very vulnerable to cybersecurity threats. This is mainly due to the integration of OT and ICT systems. As a result of the adoption of IoT, cloud computing and autonomous technologies, the integration between OT, ICT systems and the internet will get stronger and resulting in more cybersecurity risks coming to the fore. In fact, cybersecurity-related risks have resulted in cyberattacks that increased by 900% over three years (2018–2020) (Cusimano, 2020; Von Solms, 2023).

Successful cybersecurity attacks, directed on the interconnected OT and ICT environment, can give rise to cybersecurity incidents with detrimental consequences. The following are a few examples of well-documented cybersecurity attacks that have taken place over recent years.

Maersk, the world's largest shipping container transport company, had a cybersecurity attack in July 2017. The resultant damage amounted to US$250–300 million. This ransomware attack resulted in the reinstallation of 45 000 workstations and 4000 server computers worldwide (Princeton, 2018; Von Solms, 2023).

In February 2017 hackers apparently hacked into the navigation system of a German container vessel. This 10-hour long attack was conducted by 'pirates' who totally took over the vessel's navigation system. The idea was apparently to steer the vessel to an area where these 'pirates' could board and take over the ship. The situation was eventually resolved by taking ICT experts on board to regain control of the navigation systems (Marine Digital, 2022; Von Solms, 2023).

During June 2017, at least 20 vessels in the Black Sea reported that their automatic identification systems erroneously indicated their position somewhere 32 km inland. These incidents lead to the risk of GPS spoofing receiving lots more attention, as such spoofing events may lead to disastrous consequences such as ship collisions (Marine Digital, 2022; Von Solms, 2023).

In yet another incident, in July 2017, a British oil tanker steered accidentally into Iranian waters and was seized by Iran. It is believed that false GPS coordinates was fed to the ship (Marine Digital, 2022; Von Solms, 2023).

Cyberspace has changed the way in which the modern world operates, does business, communicates and get entertained. Although slower than other industries, the maritime industry is catching up and harnessing the benefits cyberspace has to offer. The maritime industry has become highly vulnerable to cybersecurity attacks that can lead to disastrous and costly incidents when successful. With the maritime industry, tightly interwoven in cyberspace, it is imperative that dedicated attention is given to related cybersecurity efforts, especially from a management and crew member point of view.

In April 1912, the 'unsinkable', luxurious, technologically advanced Titanic set sail on its maiden voyage and the totally unexpected happened. The Titanic hit an iceberg that ruptured the side of the ship, resulting in the failure of the ultramodern design of watertight compartments and the ship that sank. The lesson from this is never label new and advanced technologies and designs, such as modern ICT-related systems and the usage of cyberspace, as infallible.

6. Cybersecurity as the Cyber-'Iceberg'

It is one thing to adopt the advantages that cyber technology offers, but it is another to face the numerous, continuous and changing associated risks that accompany it. In view of the maritime industry's dependence on cyber technologies for its well-being, it is essential that good governance and due care be applied to manage the associated cyber-related threats, the cyber-'icebergs' that are all but obvious. Such risks include the cyberthreats that exploit certain vulnerabilities in the technological systems, ultimately having a negative impact on the related assets. Typical threats include malware, ransomware, denial of service attacks, phishing attacks, spoofing attacks, among others (Princeton, 2018).

Cyberattacks on modern vessels are constantly happening and resulting in numerous successful attacks, with huge losses incurred as mentioned earlier. Therefore, it has become the norm, as in any industry where cyber technologies are being utilised, for appropriate levels of cybersecurity to be implemented. From a management point of view, it is therefore crucial for the well-being of the vessel, its freight and those onboard to apply adequate cybersecurity measures related to the cyber environment.

Like an iceberg, much of which lies hidden beneath the surface, most cyberthreats are unknown. Real physical icebergs may no longer pose huge risks to the shipping industry, but modern cyber-'icebergs', ever-present in all 'oceans', need to be approached with caution. Therefore, it can be argued that cybersecurity forms part and parcel of the modern seaworthy certificate. Two parties that form a critical part in countering modern cyberthreats are, firstly, crew members that need to be skilled with data science skills (Larsen, 2020) and management that ensure that due care is exercised to protect themselves against the ever-present cyber-'icebergs'.

6.1 Cybersecurity Education and Awareness

Sound cybersecurity measures to protect on-board ICT systems from being breached by malicious, intentional cyberattacks is one of management's main responsibilities. However, many system security breaches are as a result of the negligence or ignorance of legitimate crew members, owing to a lack of cybersecure skills. Thus, crew members may unintentionally render cybersecurity vulnerable, eventually assisting a successful cyberattack that is obviously detrimental to the vessel, its owner, and the freight and the people on board.

On the evening of 14 April 1912, the 'unsinkable' Titanic hit an iceberg and sank. Word has it that two other ships sent messages to the Titanic warning it about icebergs. Apparently, radio operators were so busy relaying passengers' messages to shore that the warning of a huge iceberg in the vicinity was never conveyed to the bridge. Another radio operator reprimanded another ship for disturbing him as he was busy handling passengers' messages.

It is clear that human error, ignorance and incompetence can, unintentionally assist breaches in system security that may eventually end in a disaster. The case of the Titanic highlights that, ideally a vessel's communication channel(s) should not be used for both operational functions and non-critical, social purposes.

Crew members are generally trained and skilled to conduct one or two specific tasks whilst at sea, most of which generate additional electronic data that is captured, communicated and stored by means of some system; however, these crew members are not usually fully trained or skilled to do so in a cybersecure manner. Therefore, the ignorance or incompetence to securely operate cyber-oriented systems is a huge vulnerability towards cybersecurity and ultimately the vessel. Further, the fact that crew members, when off duty, in many cases use the same communication link between the vessel and the shore for social entertainment, recreation and communication as the vessel uses for critical operation tasks, like navigation, collecting weather information, etc. makes that communication channel prone to cyberattacks. The bottom line is, it is imperative that crew members are all skilled to be properly cybersecurity aware and competent. If not, crew members can form part of the cyber-'iceberg'.

6.2 Governing the Cyber-'Iceberg'

The international Telecommunication Union defines cybersecurity as 'the collection of tools, security concepts, security safeguards, guidelines, risk management approaches, actions, training, best practices, assurance and technologies that can be used to protect the cyber environment, the organisation and the users' assets' (Cusimano, 2020). From this definition it is clear that cybersecurity is a structured process, starting at senior management who is ultimately responsible and accountable for the well-being of the ship, the crew, and the freight (Androjna, et al, 2020).

Most regulatory bodies, industry associations and standards bodies agree that maritime cybersecurity is highly vulnerable and needs to be addressed urgently (Cusimano, 2020). The International Maritime Organization (IMO) adopted resolution MSC 428(98) in 2017 to assist in addressing this need (IMO, 2017b). This resolution states that owner and managers of ships should assess cyber-related risks and introduce relevant measures accordingly across all functions of the vessel's safety management systems (SMS). To assist in this regard, the IMO published Guidelines on Maritime Cyber Risk Management and indicated that the risk management process should start with senior management (IMO, 2017a). Resolution IMO MSC 428(98) calls for senior management and/or administration to control the process to ensure that cyber risks are adequately addressed in their safety management systems (IMO, 2017b). The maritime industry is no different than any enterprise and therefore its cybersecurity environment should be managed and governed like any modern ICT environment. The Control Objectives for Information and Related Technology (COBIT) (COBIT, 2023) and the ISO/IEC 27000 series (IT Governance Institute, 2023) are well-known and generally used in industry for this purpose and therefore these would be of great value in addressing IMO resolution MSC 428(98) (Von Solms, 2023).

COBIT is an industry best practice and predominantly used in the IT management and governance environment (COBIT, 2023). The ISO 27000 family of information security management standards mutually supports information security management standards (ISO, 2023). These best practices can be used to effectively address the resolution IMO MSC 428(98) (Von Solms, 2023).

7. In Conclusion

This paper highlighted the technological advancement in the maritime industry, especifically over the last few decades. The introduction and integration of sensor technologies, IoT and modern ICT systems with the operational technologies of vessels, have really resulted in modern vessels to be technologically advanced and part and parcel of cyberspace. Also, along with it's involvement with cyberspace, came the vulnerabilities associated with cyber threats. Therefore, cybersecurity to protect and safeguard the shipping industry has become one of the main modern challenges of the industry. This has gain so much attention, that the IMO has made certain resolutions in this regard.

The IMO has stated it clearly that senior management should take control of the management and governance processes to protect against cyber-attacks, as they are ultimately responsible for the well-being of the vessels, the crew and the freight. Further, as most of the crew members work daily with valuable data that gets captured, analysed and transmitted, it is imperative that these members are properly skilled to protect the integrity, confidentiality and availability of this valuable data. If these crew members are not adequately educated, they can unintentionally render the cyber-related systems vulnerable and thereby partake in resultant cyber- attacks. In both cases above, these human parties can be deemed part of modern cyber-'icebergs'.

References

Abi-Saab, C. (2018) The Maritime Industry is slowly embracing technology, but some will be left behind! LinkedIn. Available online: https://www.linkedin.com/pulse/maritime-industry-slowly-embracing-technology-some-left-abi-saab/

Androjna, A., Satler, T. B. and Sršе, J. (2020). An overview of maritime cyber security challenges, 20th International Conference on Transportation Science. Available online: (PDF) AN OVERVIEW OF MARITIME CYBER SECURITY CHALLENGES (researchgate.net).

Arreola-Risa, A., Ayala-Solorzano, O., Gonzalez-Rodriguez, M., & Rojo-Alvarez, J. L. (2017). Improving maritime situational awareness by integrating unmanned aerial vehicles and crowdsourcing. Transportation Research Part C: Emerging Technologies, 82, 57-74.

Baldauf, M., Ma, Y., & Zhang, G. (2016). Maritime navigation and safety using electronic chart display and information systems (ECDIS). WMU Journal of Maritime Affairs, 15(1), 33-56.

COBIT (2023) Control Objectives for Information Technologies. ISACA, Available online: www.isaca.org.

Cusimano, J., Ayala, M. and Villano, G. (2020) Navigating cybersecurity challenges in maritime operational technology. Available online: https://maritime-executive.com/editorials/navigating-cybersecurity-challenges-in-maritime-operational-technology.

Hegland, T. J., Nguyen, H. Q., Choo, K. K. R., & Hegarty, C. J. (2017). Radar technology in maritime navigation. In OCEANS 2017 - Aberdeen (pp. 1-6). IEEE.

Hui, K. S., Pang, W. M., Yang, L., & Yu, D. (2019). Maritime safety enhancement based on an automatic identification system using a deep learning technique. Safety Science, 115, 243-255.

IMO (2017a). Guidelines on Maritime Cyber Risk Management, MSC-FAL.1/Circ. 3, June.

IMO (2017b). Maritime Cyber Risk Management in Safety Management System, Resolution MSC 428(98), adopted June 16.

ISO (2023). ISO/IEC 27000 series, International Standards Organisation. Available online: www.iso.org.

IT Governance Institute (2023). What is COBIT 5: Definition and explanation. Available online: What is COBIT 5? Definition & Explanation (itgovernance.co.uk).

Julius, P. Apud (2016) Information technology applications in the maritime industry. Available online: Information Technology Applications in the Maritime Industry – The Maritime Review.

Kaplan, E. D., & Hegarty, C. J. (2006) Understanding GPS: Principles and Applications. Artech House.

Kundu, A. (2023) Ship Propulsion Through The Ages: An Overview, Shipfinex. Available online: https://www.shipfinex.com/blog/ship-propulsion#:~:text=Before%20the%2019th%20century%20ushered,galleys%20with%20oars%20took%20precedence.

Larsen, R. (2019) What's the value of maritime-specific software? Available online: What's the value of maritime-specific software? (dualog.com).

Larsen, R. (2020) How ICT solutions can be used strategically in shipping. Available online: https://www.dualog.com/blog/how-ict-solutions-can-be-used-strategically-in-shipping.

Lind-Olsen, M. (2019) ICT solutions bring ship and shore close. Available online: https://www.dualog.com/blog/ict-solutions-bring-ship-and-shore-closer.

Maritime Cyprus (2020) The evolution of ship propulsion, Maritime Cyprus. Available online: https://maritimecyprus.com/2020/03/12/infographic-the-evolution-of-ship-propulsion/

Marine Digital (2022) The importance of cybersecurity in the maritime industry. Available online: https://marine-digital.com/article_importance_of_cybersecurity.

Marine Digital (2023) Predictive Maintenance for Marine Vessels. Available online: https://marine-digital.com/article_predictive_maintenance_for_marine_vessels#:~:text=Maintenance%20prediction%20is%20a%20proactive%20approach%20to%20dealing,that%20is%20strictly%20adhered%20to%20on%20board%20ships.

Matuszak, J. (2021) 8 Technology Trends Transforming the Maritime Industry, KnowHow – Defence, Aerospace and Marine, IT and Digital. Available Online: https://knowhow.distrelec.com/defence-aerospace-and-marine/8-technology-trends-transforming-the-maritime-industry/

Mawer, T., Von Solms, S. & Meyer, J. (2024) Identifying the Scope of Cybersecurity Research Conducted in the Maritime Industry: 2003 – 2023. Accepted for publication: ICCWS 2024.

Moan, S. (2022) The value of ICT in the maritime industry. Available online: The value of ICT in the maritime industry (dualog.com).

Moussavi, R., Boroushaki, M., & Khorasani, K. (2020) Artificial intelligence in maritime navigation: Challenges and opportunities. Ocean Engineering, 204, 107336.

Princeton, P. (2018) Top 4 Trending Technologies in the Maritime Industry, Patrick Princeton. Available online: https://www.searates.com/blog/post/it-technologies-in-the-marine-industry.

Rao, A. S. (2019) Satellite communication in the maritime sector: A review. Journal of Navigation and Port Research, 43(3), 245-255.

Saeed, M., Tang, Y., Naik, K., & Choo, K. K. R. (2021) Biometric technologies for maritime security: A comprehensive review. Ocean Engineering, 225, 108953.

Smith, J. R. (2018) Maritime communication: Past, present, and future. Journal of Maritime Research, 15(2), 45-58.

Sun, Z., Zhang, D., Zhang, G., & Li, S. (2020) Cyber-physical systems in maritime: A comprehensive review. Journal of Marine Science and Engineering, 8(11), 898.

Voyager (2023) Embracing Digitalization in the Maritime Industry. Voyager. Available online: https://www.voyagerportal.com/digitalization-in-maritime/

Wang, C., Li, X., & Zhang, Y. (2020) Integration of IoT and cloud computing for smart maritime logistics. IEEE Access, 8, 118740-118752.

Yang, L., Ren, L., & Ji, J. (2021) Smart shipping: A comprehensive review. Transportation Research Part C: Emerging Technologies, 128, 103030.

Identifying Information Technology (IT) and Cybersecurity Executives' Competencies to Support Comprehensive Cybersecurity Programs

Paul E. Wagner and William E. Mapp
University of Arizona, Tucson, Arizona, United States

paulewagner@arizona.edu
mapp@arizona.edu

Abstract: Information Technology (IT) and cybersecurity executives play a pivotal role in shaping the cybersecurity posture of an organization. Their ability to make informed decisions, allocate resources, and communicate effectively with cybersecurity professionals is paramount. Consequently, these executives must acquire the necessary competencies that encompass cybersecurity risk management, legal and regulatory compliance, and strategic planning combined with foundational business and technical competencies. An interdisciplinary approach bridging the gap between business, technical skills and strategic decision-making is crucial to navigate the ever-evolving and complex cybersecurity challenges facing organizations today. Failure to do so may result in catastrophic consequences for both individual enterprises and society. Further, the growing frequency and sophistication of cyber threats pose significant risks to organizations and individuals alike. To effectively counter these threats, it is imperative to not only develop cybersecurity talent but also to equip IT and cybersecurity executives with essential competencies in this domain. Equally important, is to identify the specific competencies and develop an approach to train or teach them. According to Burrell, Aridi, & Nobles (2018) there is an extremely urgent need of leadership development for cybersecurity and information technology professionals to prepare these professionals with the foundational skills to excel in leadership, management, and directing an enterprise-level program. This paper underscores the critical need for a comprehensive understanding of both Information Technology (IT) and cybersecurity executive competencies and cybersecurity executive development. Integrating these two aspects is critical to improve an organization's cybersecurity posture and ensure alignment between organizational objectives and cybersecurity strategies. The two must work in tandem to create a robust and resilient cybersecurity infrastructure. This paper provides an analysis of the current literature regarding IT/Cybersecurity roles and responsibilities, leadership competencies, and technical competencies of IT/Cybersecurity executives to identify the gaps in existing research. The authors propose a survey instrument to conduct a quantitative analysis to identify executives' beliefs as to how important it is to possess each administrative competency. The survey is part of a future research plan to identify and evaluate administrative and technical competencies of IT/Cybersecurity executive leaders.

Keywords: Cybersecurity, Executive Leadership Competencies, Workforce Development

1. Introduction

The current state of cybersecurity and its workforce present challenges for leadership. Despite 70% of security professionals stating that generative artificial intelligence (AI) positively impacts productivity, collaboration, and morale, nearly 46% believe this technology will increase the organization's vulnerability to attack and 85% attribute the rise of attacks over the last 12 months to attackers' use of generative AI (White, 2023). For example, threats evolve by leveraging generative AI models to create malware, develop sophisticated phishing attacks and deepfakes, or collecting and analyzing data to identify new avenues of attack (Terranova Security, 2023). Through AI and other advanced techniques adversaries are now able to pivot from initial access to lateral movement within 84 minutes (Kurtz, 2022). This requires defenders to follow the 1-10-60 rule which is to detect threats within the first minute, understanding the threats within 10 minutes, and appropriately responding within 60 minutes (Kurtz, 2022).

The increase in the number, frequency, and sophistication of attacks takes a toll on cyber defenders. This leads to high turnover of cybersecurity talent and cybersecurity leaders. Stressors include staffing and resource limitations, rising complexity of technology, fear of risk due to generative AI, escalation of cyber-attacks, compliance and regulatory pressures, fear of generative AI taking jobs, remote work challenges, and public scrutiny and reputation concerns which are expected to drive nearly 51% from the industry (White, 2023). This, coupled with the fact that organizations identify skills gaps, shortages of cybersecurity staff, and despite these shortages, some organizations are reducing their cybersecurity staff (Coker, 2023). Further exacerbating the issue is the overall cybersecurity workforce shortage. Cyber Seek (2024) estimates that there are over 570,000 cybersecurity job openings in the United States and ISC2 (2023) estimates that 4 million cybersecurity professionals are needed globally.

2. Research Design and Methodology

2.1 Methodology

The authors used a systematic literature review (SLR) technique to find relevant academic articles from 2015 to 2024. Relevant information was extracted from select articles to inform analysis and discussion. The steps involved in the SLR process include:

1. Define the research questions.
2. Determine the data sources and search process.
3. Inclusion and Exclusion Criteria.
4. Results of searching and data extraction.
5. Analysis and Discussion.

2.2 Research Questions

1. What are the roles and responsibilities for Information Technology (IT) or Cybersecurity Executives?
2. What are the leadership competencies of the executives responsible for running an organization specifically for Information Technology (IT) or Cybersecurity executives?
3. What are the technical competencies of the executives responsible for running an organization specifically for Information Technology (IT) or Cybersecurity executives?

2.3 Data Sources and Search Process

A variety of sources were used to identify sources for this research including Google Scholar, IEEE, Elsevier, EBSCO, Proquest, and other library resources. Additionally, current industry trend reports were analyzed to identify current and relevant statistics and evidence to support research objectives. Search terms included the following terms with IT or cybersecurity prepended: workforce, leadership competencies, technical competencies, roles and responsibilities, opportunities, threats, and challenges. The search limited results from 2015 to present.

2.4 Inclusion and Exclusion Criteria

The authors used a liberal inclusive set of search criteria. Full-text journal articles were used to identify and analyze roles and responsibilities, leadership competencies, and technical competencies for IT / Cybersecurity executives. Information from these articles was extrapolated for their potential use in developing the survey instrument. Editorials, trade journals, and other online resources were used to identify the latest data for cybersecurity statistics and trends. Articles were reviewed and broadly categorized into roles and responsibilities, leadership competencies, and technical competencies. Additionally, articles providing context for workforce and the current threat landscape were included. Articles outside these categories were excluded from the systematic literature review.

2.5 Search Results

Search results can be broadly categorized into roles and responsibilities, leadership competencies, and technical competencies. Some results span across these categories.

3. Literature Review

The literature review provides context used to identify gaps in research and develop the survey instrument. Each section aligns with the broad categories identified during the literature review; specifically, Leadership Roles and Responsibilities, Executive Leadership Competencies, and Executive Technical Competencies. Salient elements were used to develop the proposed survey instrument.

The role of IT and cybersecurity executive leaders has become increasingly pivotal in safeguarding organizations against rapidly evolving cyber threats. The responsibilities of these leaders extend beyond leadership and technical competencies to encompass strategic decision-making, risk management, and compliance adherence. This section outlines the multifaceted realm of IT and cybersecurity workforce roles and the specific roles held by IT and cybersecurity executives. Primary sources for this section included the National Institute of Science and Technology's (NIST) Special Publication (SP) 800-181 and National Initiative for Cybersecurity Careers and Studies (NICCS) Cyber Career Pathways Tool.

This understanding of roles and responsibilities provides a foundation for identifying and understanding the related leadership (Section 3.2) and technical (Section 3.3) competencies needed to fulfill the identified roles and responsibilities. The primary Knowledge, Skills, Abilities, and Tasks aligned with the Executive Cyber Leadership role is outlined in Table 1.

3.1 IT / Cybersecurity Executive Leadership Roles and Responsibilities

NIST SP 800-181rev1, the Workforce Framework for Cybersecurity (National Initiatives for Cybersecurity Education (NICE) Framework), currently identifies:

- Categories (7) – high-level grouping of common cybersecurity functions (Figure 1)
- Specialty Areas (33) – distinct areas of cybersecurity work
- Work Roles (52) – detailed groupings of cybersecurity work comprised of specific knowledge, skills, and abilities (KSA); now known as Tasks, Skills, and Abilities (TKS), required to perform tasks in a work role (NICCS, 2023).

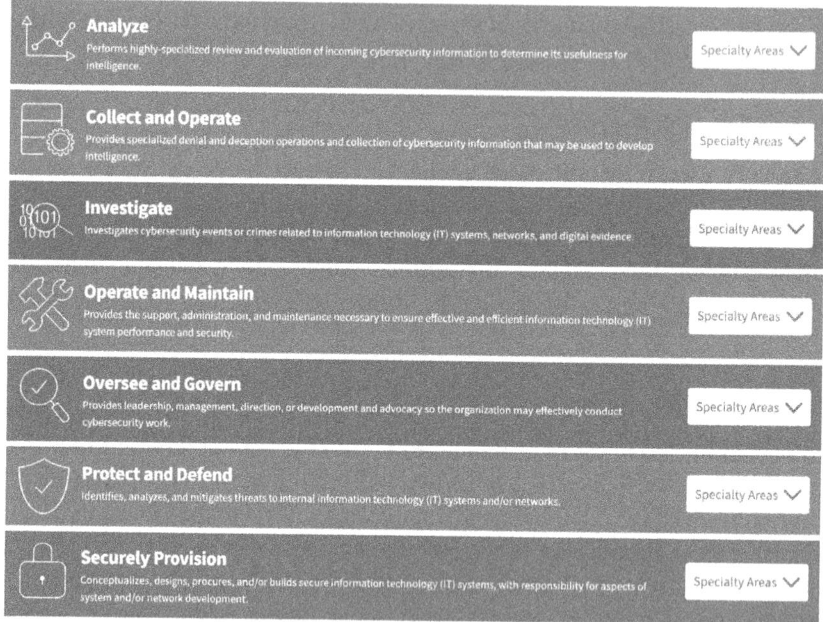

Figure 1: Workforce Framework Categories (NICCS, 2023).

Understanding these categories, specialty areas, and work roles provides organizations and executives the ability to develop effective cybersecurity teams. Additionally, analyzing the building blocks (Figure 2) for an effective cybersecurity workforce can prepare an organization. The circular arrows are activities which impact an organization, through the previously defined aspects of the NICE Framework, supported by the different pathways and experiences of the workforce which culminates in the capable and ready workforce (Newhouse, 2020).

Organizational complexity, the breadth of the information technology and cybersecurity field (Figure 2), growth of data, and reliance on technology both current and emerging have introduced multiple executive roles. These Chief-Suite or C-Suite positions may be directly related or corollary to IT and cybersecurity. The Chief Information Security Officer (CISO) and Chief Security Officer (CSO) roles are cybersecurity related positions. Chief Technology Officer (CTO), Chief Information Officer (CIO), and Chief Technology Innovation Officer (CTIO) are IT related positions. Corollary positions include Chief Compliance Officer (CCO), Chief Data Officer (CDO), and Chief Knowledge Officer (CKO). Executive Cyber Leadership is the work role within the Oversee and Govern category most applicable to this paper. Executive Cyber Leadership, "executes decision-making authorities and establishes vision and direction for an organization's cyber and cyber-related resources and/or operations." (NICCS, 2023).

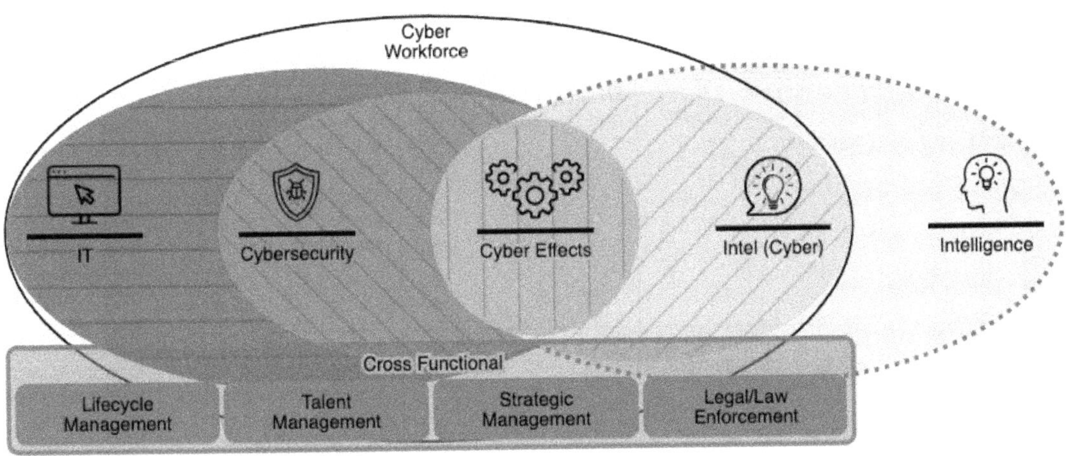

Figure 2: Cyber Career Pathways Tool (NICCS, 2023).

3.2 IT / Cybersecurity Executive Leadership Competencies

IT and Cybersecurity executive leadership competencies are consistent with leadership in other executive roles. Specific competencies can vary depending on the research. For example, Fotso (2021) compares traditional and emerging leadership theories. Their research identified human orientation, organizational skills, adaptability and flexibility, values, cognitive skills, self- awareness, transformational ability, and communication skills from traditional theories and sharing leadership style, handling complexity, knowledge, and global leadership from emerging theories (Fotso, 2021). Alternatively, Verlinden (2024) breaks down competencies into leading the organization, leading others, and leading yourself with associated competencies outlined in Figure 3.

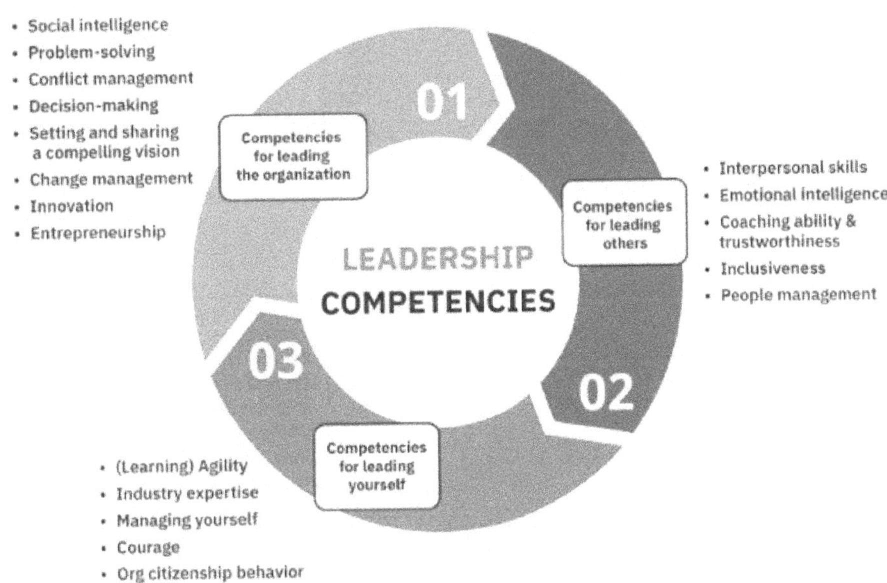

Figure 3: Leadership Competencies (Verlinden, 2024).

The Workforce Framework further defines the Knowledge, Skills, Abilities, and Tasks (KSAT) for Executive Cyber Leadership summarized in Table 1. The Workforce Framework for Cybersecurity breaks Executive Cyber Leadership into entry level, 4-7 years of experience in a significant security role, intermediate 7-10 years of operational management experience, and advance, 10-15 years of high-level organizational and business strategy experience (NICCS, 2023). Additional capability indicators at each level include credentials and certifications, continuous learning, education, and training.

Table 1: Executive Cyber Leadership KSATs (NICCS, 2023).

Knowledge	Skills	Abilities	Tasks	
Computer networking and network security methodologies	Creating policies that reflect system security objectives	Develop policy, plans and strategy	Acquire and manage resources to support security goals and objectives to reduce organizational risk and conduct continuity of operations	Promote awareness of security issues among management and ensure sound security principles are reflected in the organization's vision and goals
Risk management processes	Communicating with all levels of management	Apply critical thinking	Advise senior management on cost/benefit analysis of information security programs, policies, processes, systems, and elements	Oversee policy standards and implementation strategies to ensure procedures and guidelines comply with cybersecurity policies
Laws, regulations, policies, and ethics related to cybersecurity and privacy	Anticipate new security threats	Exercise judgement	Advocate organization's official position in legal and legislative proceedings	Identify security requirements specific to an IT system in all phases of the system life cycle
Cybersecurity and privacy principles	Remain aware of evolving technical infrastructures	Interpret and apply laws, regulations, policies, and guidance	Communicate the value of IT security throughout all levels of the organization	Ensure the plans of actions and milestones (POA&M) or remediation plans are in place for vulnerabilities identified during risk assessments, audits, and inspections
Cyber, System and Application threats and vulnerabilities	Use critical thinking to analyze organizational patterns and relationships	Tailor technical and planning information to a customer's level of understanding	Develop and maintain strategic plans	Define and/or implement policies and procedures to ensure protection of critical infrastructure as appropriate
Specific operational impacts of cybersecurity lapses		Prioritize and allocate resources	Interface with external organizations to ensure appropriate and accurate dissemination of incident and other Computer Network Defense (CND) information	Supervise and assign work to programmers, designers, technologies and technicians, and other engineering and scientific personnel
What constitutes a network attack and its relationship to both threats and vulnerabilities		Relate strategy, business, and technology in the context of organizational dynamics	Lead and align IT security priorities with the security strategy	Coordinate with organizational manpower stakeholders to ensure appropriate allocation and distribution of human capital assets
Emerging security issues, risks, and vulnerabilities		Understand technology, management, and leadership issues related to organizational processes	Lead and oversee information security budget, staffing, and contracting	Assess policy needs and collaborate with stakeholders to develop policies to govern cyber activities
Capabilities, applications, and potential vulnerabilities of network equipment		Understand basic concepts and issues related to cyber and	Manage the publishing of CND guidance for the enterprise constituency	Design/integrate a cyber strategy that outlines the vision, mission, and goals

Knowledge	Skills	Abilities	Tasks	
		its organizational dynamics		that align with the organization's strategic plan
Industry technologies' potential cybersecurity vulnerabilities		Ensure information security management processes are integrated with strategic and operational planning processes	Monitor and evaluate the effectiveness of the enterprise's cybersecurity safeguards	Perform an information security risk assessment
Cyber competitions to develop skills		Ensure senior officials within the organization provide information security for the information systems that support operations	Recommend policy and coordinate review and approval	Conduct long-range, strategic planning efforts with internal and external partners in cyber activities
			Supervise or manage protective or corrective measures when a cybersecurity incident or vulnerability is discovered	Collaborate with cybersecurity personnel on the security risk assessment process to address privacy compliance and risk mitigation
			Promote awareness of security issues among management and ensure sound security principles are reflected in the organization's vision and goals	Appoint and guide a team of IT security experts
				Collaborate with key stakeholders to establish a cybersecurity risk management program

3.3 IT/Cybersecurity Executive Technical Competencies

IT/Cybersecurity executive technical competencies are outlined in different research. Kappers and Harrell (2020) identify skills and certifications associated with different programming languages; enterprise architecture; firewall and intrusion detection/prevention protocols; knowledge of third-party auditing and cloud risk assessment methodologies; ISO 27003, ITIL and COBIT frameworks; network security architecture development and definition; various industry compliance assessments; secure coding, ethical hacking, and threat modeling; security architecture; TCP/IP, computer networking, routing, and switching; and various operating systems are requirements for employment at the CISO role. These are the like the knowledge areas outlined in Table 1. The required technical competencies can vary across industry sectors. Chemical; commercial facilities; communications; critical manufacturing; dams; defense industrial base; emergency services; energy; financial services; food and agriculture; government facilities; healthcare and public health; information technology; nuclear reactors, materials, and waste; transportation systems; and water and wastewater are the 16 critical infrastructure sectors identified by the Cybersecurity & Infrastructure Security Agency (CISA) (CISA, 2024).

Despite identification of these competencies, the paths into the various IT/Cybersecurity C-Suite roles vary greatly depending on the path the executive took. Technical feeder roles include but are not limited to networking, software development, systems engineering, financial and risk analysis, security intelligence, and IT support. Potential pathways can be interactively mapped at a high level on Cyber Seek (Cyber Seek, 2024) or at a more granular level on NICCS (NICCS, 2023).

4. Gaps in Research

There is a gap in research on the specific IT/Cybersecurity executive leader's roles and responsibilities, leadership competencies, and technical competencies one should possess. As expressed by Burrell, Aridi, & Nobles (2018), there is an extremely urgent need of leadership development for cybersecurity and information technology professionals to prepare these professionals with the foundational skills to excel in leadership, management, and directing an enterprise-level program, but there is not a lot of research addressing these topics. Researchers have been explicitly pointed to the need for such research and the fact that there is a gap in this area. For example, as stated by Cleveland and Cleveland (2018), "there is a gap between the level of knowledge regarding cybersecurity and the amount of information the executive leadership has in making informed decisions regarding cybersecurity"(p. 1).

The authors identified the following gaps in research based on the SLR.

1. The required depth or proficiency for technical competency at the C-suite level is not well understood. As IT/Cybersecurity professionals transition from entry-level through intermediate to advanced or C-Suite positions their level of technical competency may also shift. Additionally, the authors didn't identify studies which analyzed technical competencies of C-suite executives aligned with industry sectors. The training, education, and pathway to each sector could vary in terms of technical competency.
2. Various frameworks and leadership competencies were identified related to IT/Cybersecurity executives. Despite this, there are limited quantitative studies correlating these competencies and the level at which executives believe those competencies impact their position.

5. Future Research

As cyber-attacks, malware, and denial of service attacks on business and government entities become the norm and continue on a daily basis, the need for qualified IT/Cybersecurity professionals that have both technical and business skills continues to grow. As expressed by Burrell, Aridi, & Nobles (2018) when discussing the critical need for formal leadership training for cybersecurity and IT professionals, it is extremely important for them to possess the necessary leadership and management competencies to drive information security practices in today's enterprises. As a result, with the lack of research on leadership development programs for IT/Cybersecurity professionals, it is critical to find the necessary knowledge, skills, and abilities one should possess if they are, or aspire to be, a c-suite level professional. Once those competencies are identified, they can be added and implemented into a robust leadership program for IT/Cybersecurity professionals.

Understanding IT/Cybersecurity leadership and technical competencies is critical for several reasons. First, it can allow for developing curated training, education, and pathways to develop new professionals in this field to become competent executives in the future. Second, it can support organizations evaluate current professionals and develop their competencies or make more informed hiring decisions. Finally, professionals interested in achieving an IT/Cybersecurity C-suite position can better understand the requirements and plan their career path.

To that end, the authors will begin a two-phase mixed methods study to address these gaps in research. Phase one will focus on administrative competencies and phase two will focus on technical competencies. An initial survey instrument (*Leadership Competencies Instrument*) will be used to conduct a quantitative analysis to identify executives' beliefs as to how important it is to possess each administrative competency. The results will be analyzed, and participants will be asked to participate in interviews to provide qualitative data to provide additional context to the quantitative data. A corollary survey instrument will be developed focusing on technical competencies based on the literature review outlined in this paper and further review of updated literature. A similar round of interviews will be conducted to provide context and qualitative data.

The *Leadership Competencies Instrument* has been previously used on two separate research projects titled *–Leadership Competencies and their Development for Community College Administrators* and *Administrative Development for Academic Deans in the California State University System,* with an N=140 (201 Arizona community college administrators were surveyed, yielding a return rate of 69%); and N=40 (101 academic deans from 16 California institutions surveyed yielding a return rate of 39.6%) respectively. The theoretical perspectives used in survey instrument are grounded in the conceptual constructs associated with systems theory and Mintzberg's (1973) managerial roles. Mintzberg's (1973) framework examines managerial functions in the context of the daily work setting, concluding that a manager's work can be categorized into ten job roles, grouped into three categories: (1) interpersonal roles — figurehead, leader, and liaison; (2) informational roles — monitor, disseminator, and spokesperson; and (3) decisional roles — entrepreneur, disturbance handler, resource allocator, and negotiator (Grover & Jeong, 1993).

6. Conclusions

This paper provided an overview of the current state of cybersecurity threats and challenges to organizations and their leadership. This included pros and cons related to emerging technologies such as artificial intelligence, the speed at which attackers traverse organizational networks, and the overall sophistication of attacks. Additionally, organizations experience high turnover of cybersecurity talent due to various work related stressors. Further, organizations identify skills gaps, budgetary constraints resulting in layoffs, and overall workforce shortages within the field. These create a challenging environment for executives.

A systematic literature review was provided to identify existing research on the roles and responsibilities, leadership competencies, and technical competencies of IT and Cybersecurity executives. The review identified the Cybersecurity Workforce Framework that outlined the categories, specialty areas, and work roles. The paper further identified the different C-Suite roles related to IT and cybersecurity. The research then provided a comparison of traditional and emerging leadership theories which provided the specific leadership competencies and competencies related to leading the organization, leading others, and leading yourself. Further, The Workforce Framework for Cybersecurity outlined the specific KSATs associated with Executive Cyber Leadership. Finally, the framework's Knowledge and Skills identifies specific technical skills related to the executive cyber leadership role. These were like the competencies outlined by Kappers and Harrell.

Finally, the paper identified two major gaps in research. Despite research identifying the leadership and technical competencies, there is limited or no research that provides quantitative data on the level of proficiency required or how greatly these competencies impact current executives. Based on this, the authors proposed an initial survey instrument to identify the executives' beliefs as to how important it is to possess each administrative competency. Additionally, a brief research plan was discussed to further address these gaps.

References

Burrell, D. N., Ardi, A. S., and Nobles, C. (2018). The critical need for formal leadership development programs for cybersecurity and information technology professionals. *13th International Conference in Cyber Warfare and Security (ICCWS 2018).* https://www.proquest.com/openview/12cbf1c24ddb996f0f01a81fd12f4a4d/1?pq-origsite=gscholar&cbl=396500.

CISA (2024). Critical infrastructure sectors. *Cybersecurity & Infrastructure Security Agency (CISA).* https://www.cisa.gov/topics/critical-infrastructure-security-and-resilience/critical-infrastructure-sectors.

Cleveland, S. and Cleveland, M., (2018, May). Toward cybersecurity leadership framework. In *Proceedings of the Thirteenth Midwest Association for Information Systems Conference.*

Coker, J. (2023, October 21). Cyber skills gap reaches 4 million, layoffs hit security teams. *Infosecurity Magazine.* *https://www.infosecurity-magazine.com/news/cyber-skills-gap-layoffs-security/*.

Cyber Seek (2024). Cybersecurity career pathway. *Cyber Seek.* https://www.cyberseek.org/pathway.html.

Cyber Seek (2024). Cybersecurity supply /demand heat map. *Cyber Seek.* https://www.cyberseek.org/heatmap.html.

Fotso, G. (2021, April 6). Leadership competencies for the 21st century: A Review from the Western World Literature. *Emerald Insight.* https://www.emerald.com/insight/2046-9012.htm.

Grover, V., Jeong, S., Kettinger, W. J., & Lee, C. C. (1993). The chief information officer: A study of managerial roles. *Journal of Management Information Systems,* 10(2), 107-130.

ISC2 (2023). ISC2 Cybersecurity Workforce Study. *International Information System Security Certification Consortium (ISC2).* *https://media.isc2.org/-/media/Project/ISC2/Main/Media/documents/research/ISC2_Cybersecurity_Workforce_Study_2023.pdf?rev=28b46de71ce24e6ab7705f6e3da8637e*.

Kappers, W. and Harrell, M. (2020, June). From degree to Chief Information Security Officer (CISO): A framework for consideration. *Embry-Riddle Aeronautical University Scholarly Commons.* https://commons.erau.edu/publication/1575?utm_source=commons.erau.edu%2Fpublication%2F1575&utm_medium=PDF&utm_campaign=PDFCoverPages.

Kurtz, G. (2022). 2023 Global Threat Report. *Crowdstrike.* https://go.crowdstrike.com/2023-global-threat-report.html?utm_campaign=globalthreatreport&utm_content=crwd-treq-en-x-tct-us-psp-x-wht-brnd-x_x_x_x-reportsgtr&utm_medium=sem&utm_source=goog&utm_term=crowdstrike%20threat%20report&gad_source=1&gclid=Cj0KCQiAtaOtBhCwARIsAN_x-3JHEysqJiG25w432wdl-JugGo0wZgmGBR5OF79_2XjsX6AyBUR3ZucaAvLbEALw_wcB.

Mintzberg, H. (1973). The Nature of Managerial Work. *New York. Harper and Row Publishers, Inc.*

Newhouse, W., Keith, S., Scribner, B., and Witte, G. (2020, November 13). NIST Special Publication 800-181: National Initiative for Cybersecurity Education (NICE) Cybersecurity Workforce Framework. *National Institute for Science and Technology.* https://nvlpubs.nist.gov/nistpubs/specialpublications/nist.sp.800-181.pdf.

Mapp, W.E. (2007). *Leadership competencies and their development for community college administrators.* Walden University.

NICCS (2023, November 17). Cyber Career Pathways Tool. *National Initiative for Cybersecurity Careers and Studies.* https://niccs.cisa.gov/workforce-development/cyber-career-pathways-tool.

NICCS (2023, August 28). Executive Cyber Leadership. *National Initiative for Cybersecurity Careers and Studies.* https://niccs.cisa.gov/workforce-development/nice-framework/specialty-areas/executive-cyber-leadership.

NICCS (2023, August 28). Workforce Framework for Cybersecurity (NICE Framework). *National Initiative for Cybersecurity Careers and Studies.* https://niccs.cisa.gov/workforce-development/nice-framework.

Terranova Security (2023). AI in cyber security: Pros and cons, and what it means for your business. *Fortra.* *https://terranovasecurity.com/blog/ai-in-cyber-security/*.

Verlinden, N. (2024). 18 Key leadership competencies for 2024 success. *Academy to Innovate HR (AIHR).* https://www.aihr.com/blog/leadership-competencies/.

White, A. and Bunce, J. (2023). Generative AI and cybersecurity: Bright future or business battleground? *Sapio Research.* *https://info.deepinstinct.com/voice-of-secops-v4-2023?_ga=2.86841240.1038042311.1705606129-1595372854.1705443616*.

Trapped Ion Quantum Computing: A Framework for Addressing Security Vulnerabilities

Karli E. Wallace, Leleia A. Hsia and Mark G. Reith
Air Force Institute of Technology, Dayton, OH, USA

Karli.Wallace.1@au.af.edu
Leleia.Hsia.2@au.af.edu
Mark.Reith.3@au.af.edu

Abstract: Trapped ion quantum computing has the potential to revolutionize computational paradigms. As the adoption of this technology grows, so does the need for stringent scrutiny of its involvement in cybersecurity, especially when it has implications in national defense or critical infrastructure. While trapped ion quantum computing offers transformative capabilities, it is vital to carefully examine the potential vulnerabilities associated with its use and patch them before implementing this powerful technology. In this paper, we examine the potential vulnerabilities in trapped ion quantum computing systems and propose a framework for addressing them. This framework includes risk assessment for evaluating vulnerabilities, threat modeling for identifying exploits, and prevention and mitigation for reducing their impact.

Keywords: Quantum Computing, Trapped Ion, Cybersecurity, Threat Modeling, Risk Assessment Framework

1. Introduction

Over the past few years, quantum computing has gained much-deserved attention for its potential to revolutionize computational paradigms. At the forefront of this technology, trapped ion quantum computing has the power to harness the principles of quantum mechanics to process information in ways unattainable by traditional computers. Trapped ion computers manipulate confined ions through electromagnetic fields. This approach offers distinct advantages, including high-fidelity quantum bit operations and long coherence times, both of which are necessary for maintaining the quantum states needed for computations. However, as the development of trapped ion technology gains momentum, it is imperative to incorporate robust cybersecurity into its architecture, especially when it is integrated into national defense and critical infrastructure. This paper proposes a framework to address the vulnerabilities in this technology to maintain the strategic advantages in a quantum-enabled world.

2. Background

2.1 Concepts of Quantum Computing

Quantum computing represents a significant leap in the field of computation. It utilizes the principles of quantum theory, which governs the behavior of energy and material on the atomic and subatomic levels. Unlike classical computing, which relies on bits that exist as either 0 or 1, quantum computing (QC) uses quantum bits, also called qubits. These qubits can exist in multiple states simultaneously thanks to the principle of superposition (Herman and Friedson, 2018). Superposition allows a qubit to be in a combination of both 0 and 1 states at the same time, drastically increasing the computational power of quantum computers over classical computers. Furthermore, QC takes advantage of the principle of entanglement, which enables multiple qubits to be in a correlated state, where the state of one (whether in superposition or not) can depend on the state of another, no matter how far apart they are.

These fundamental differences grant quantum computers the potential to process complex problems considered intractable for classical computers. For tasks like cryptography, material science simulations, and complex algorithm solving (Murali et al., 2020), QC offers a promising future. However, the technology is still in its nascent stages, and practical, large-scale quantum computers are yet to be fully realized. Some of the obstacles still being addressed are the sensitivity of qubits and the challenge of maintaining their state without decohering due to disturbance from their environment (Herman and Friedson, 2018). Despite these challenges, the progress in QC hints at a revolutionary change in how we approach complex computational problems.

2.2 Trapped Ion Quantum Computing Technology

Trapped ion quantum computing technology is one of the leading approaches in the development of quantum computers. This method involves trapping charged ions in a controlled environment with electromagnetic fields (Bruzewicz et al., 2019). In trapped ion (TI) QC, qubits are represented by the quantum states of these ions, which are manipulated using lasers. The precision of laser control allows for the execution of quantum gates and operations necessary for QC. One of the key advantages of TI technology is its high fidelity in qubit manipulation and relatively long coherence times (Bruzewicz et al., 2019), which are crucial for maintaining the quantum state of the system.

The current state of TIQC in the market is still in an early phase consisting of ongoing research and development. Currently, companies like IonQ and Honeywell are at the forefront of commercializing TIQC technology (Herman and Friedson, 2018). In particular, IonQ has made significant strides in developing quantum computers that are accessible through cloud platforms and partnering with major tech companies to integrate QC into various industries (IonQ | Trapped Ion Quantum Computing, no date)(Hassija et al., 2020). Honeywell has also been actively investing in and developing its own TIQC solutions (Hassija et al., 2020) (Get to Know Honeywell's Latest Quantum Computer System Model H1, no date).

These developments indicate a growing interest and investment in TI technology in the QC market. While the realization of large-scale commercial applications may still be years away, the continuous advancements in TI are paving the way for more robust and scalable QC solutions in the future.

2.3 Cybersecurity and National Defense

The emergence of QC brings a paradigm shift in cybersecurity, especially within the realm of national defense. The potential for QC to break current encryption standards poses a significant challenge to the security of sensitive data and critical infrastructure (Phalak et al., 2021). Countries and defense agencies worldwide are increasingly focusing on quantum-resistant algorithms and encryption methods to safeguard against the threat posed by QC capabilities (Herman and Friedson, 2018). This includes developing new cryptographic standards that can withstand quantum attacks, a field known as post-quantum cryptography (Murali et al., 2020). The race to achieve quantum supremacy is not just about increasing computational power but also about improving security and maintaining strategic advantages in national defense. This makes the race to quantum supremacy a top priority for governments and defense agencies worldwide.

In the context of national defense, the importance of computational technology cannot be overstated. Critical infrastructure, including communications networks, power grids, and defense systems, rely heavily on secure data transmission and storage (Phalak et al., 2021). The emergence of QC requires the reevaluation of current cybersecurity protocols in these areas to prevent potential breaches that could compromise national security. Defense departments are investing in QC partly to develop new post-quantum security measures, and partly to anticipate the potential offensive capabilities of adversaries who might use QC to break encryptions (Phalak et al., 2021). Additionally, QC offers unique advantages in secure communications, notably through quantum key distribution (QKD), which provides a theoretically unbreakable encryption method (Phalak et al., 2021). QKD ensures that any eavesdropping attempt can be detected since observing the quantum state of a particle invariably alters the state.

3. Identify Vulnerabilities in Trapped Ion Quantum Computing

While identifying vulnerabilities in trapped ion quantum computing systems, it is important to examine both hardware- and software-level components. An overview of this examination can be seen in Table 1 (Herman and Friedson, 2018).

3.1 Hardware

On the hardware front, TI quantum computers rely on intricately designed and highly sensitive components to trap and manipulate ions (Saki et al., 2021). These components include ion traps, lasers, and detectors, which are susceptible to physical tampering and manufacturing defects. This could compromise the system's integrity and performance. Physical tampering can lead to altered quantum states, affecting the accuracy of the computations (Das, Chatterjee and Ghosh, 2023). Manufacturing defects, which are often hard to detect, can introduce unforeseen errors in quantum calculations (Saki et al., 2021). Moreover, the sophistication of these systems could make them vulnerable to side-channel attacks, where an attacker could potentially derive information from the physical properties of the system (e.g. power consumption, electromagnetic emissions, etc.) (Saki, Topaloglu and Ghosh, 2022). The global supply chain for these specialized components also presents risks (Ghosh, Upadhyay and Saki, 2023), as reliance on external suppliers can introduce vulnerabilities and the possibility of tampering during the manufacturing and distribution processes.

3.2 Software

On the software side, the complexity of the software stack in TI quantum computers presents its own set of challenges. Software that controls quantum computations, manages qubit states, and interfaces with classical computing systems needs regular updates and maintenance. These update and maintenance processes can introduce new vulnerabilities or exacerbate existing ones. Third-party software integration, which is often necessary for specific computational tasks or to enhance system functionality, adds another layer of risk (Das, Chatterjee and Ghosh, 2023). These third-party applications might not always adhere to the stringent security standards required for QC systems which can potentially open backdoors or cause other security gaps (Gachnang et al., 2022). Furthermore, during software updates and maintenance, the system might temporarily have reduced security measures, making it more vulnerable to cyber-attacks. Ensuring the security of software in TIQC involves rigorous testing and validation, constant monitoring for anomalies, and a robust framework for integrating and securing third-party applications (Phalak et al., 2021). Addressing these vulnerabilities is vital for maintaining the integrity and reliability of TIQC systems, especially as they merge into critical infrastructure and high-stakes computing applications.

Table 1: Overview of the Various Security and Privacy Issues in the Quantum Computing Stack (Herman and Friedson, 2018)

Layer of the Quantum Stack	Threat Model
Hardware-level	Input/Output Tampering Crosstalk-induced Fault Injection Readout Sensing Power Side-channel Attacks
Compilation-level	Shuttle-induced Fault Injection Intellectual Property Infringement Input/Output Tampering
Cloud-level	Scheduler Attacks IP Infringement
Application-level	Misclassification Protracted Convergence

4. Cybersecurity Framework for Trapped Ion Quantum Computing

4.1 Framework Pillars

A robust cybersecurity framework for trapped ion quantum computing should be grounded in several foundational pillars: risk assessment, threat modeling, and prevention and mitigation strategies. Each of these pillars plays a crucial role in ensuring the security and integrity of TIQC systems. The pillars and their applications (non-exhaustive) can be seen in Table 2 and the framework is shown in Figure 1.

Figure 1: Trapped Ion Quantum Computing Framework, inspired by (page 3 in document, page 8 of the overall pdf): (NIST CSWP 29, 2024)

Table 2: Trapped Ion Quantum Computing Pillars with Associated Applications

TIQC Framework Pillars	Applications
Risk Assessment	Vetting Component Suppliers Asset-Based Assessment
Threat Modeling	Surveillance Technologies Intrusion Detection Systems Hardware Checks Employee Background Checks
Prevention and Mitigation	Secure Boot Processes Hardware Attestation Methods Encryption Methods Secure Logistics Protocols Employee Access Controls Employee Training Programs Physically Unclonable Functions (Saki *et al.*, 2021) Dummy Gate Obfuscation (Das, Chatterjee and Ghosh, 2023)

4.1.1 *Risk Assessment*

Risk assessment involves a comprehensive evaluation of the TIQC system to identify potential security vulnerabilities, both in hardware and software. It includes identifying and prioritizing assets within the TIQC system then assessing the potential impact of their compromise on the overall security posture. The potential impact on the security posture should be based upon the criticality of the compromised asset, the likelihood of the threat, and the current capabilities of attackers (U.S. Department of Education, 2003). The analysis of risks from physical tampering, cyber-attacks, manufacturing defects, and supply chain vulnerabilities must be dynamic and continuously updated to account for evolving threats and technological advancements.

4.1.2 *Threat Modeling*

In this stage, potential threats specific to TIQC are identified and analyzed. This involves understanding how an attacker might exploit hardware and software vulnerabilities and how they might manipulate or intercept third-party components during transport. For classical computing components, the STRIDE (Spoofing, Tampering, Repudiation, Information Disclosure, Denial of Service, and Elevation of Privilege) has been widely used as a threat modelling methodology as it helps to identify potential threats by examining how attackers might exploit vulnerabilities in various computer components (Conklin, no date). However, since models such as STRIDE were developed focusing on classical systems, their applicability to TIQC systems may be limited due to the unique characteristics and architecture of quantum computers.

4.1.3 *Prevention & Mitigation Strategies*

Based on the previous stages, specific strategies are formulated to protect all components of TIQC.

4.2 Application to Trapped Ion Quantum Computing

When applying this framework to TIQC, particular attention should be given to the following subsections.

4.2.1 *Hardware/Software Security*

The user should implement security protocols that are specifically tailored to the unique architecture of TIQC systems. This includes securing the quantum processing units, laser systems, electrode control systems, classical control systems, and the interface between them. The user should install advanced surveillance technologies, intrusion detection systems, and provide regular hardware checks (Phalak et al., 2021). This would alert administrators to any physical or digital interference with the quantum hardware, helping to detect tampering and unauthorized access to QC facilities (Das, Chatterjee and Ghosh, 2023). Additionally, secure boot processes and hardware attestation methods could be implemented. This would verify that the quantum computer starts with a trusted software state and ensures that the integrity of the hardware components has not been compromised. Implementing robust encryption methods is also an integral part of this framework, as it would protect the data at rest and in transit.

4.2.2 *Supply Chain Integrity Protocols*

Ensuring the security and authenticity of third-party components and software is imperative. This involves vetting the suppliers vigorously, verifying the source and origins of components, and ensuring they meet rigorous security standards (Saki, Topaloglu and Ghosh, 2022). Additionally, the logistics of transporting sensitive quantum components require special attention. Tamperproof or tamper-evident packaging (Herman and Friedson, 2018), fault-tolerant designs (Hassija et al., 2020), continuous monitoring during transit, hardware verification methods (Hsia, 2020), and secure storage facilities are essential to protect these components from physical interference and espionage.

4.2.3 *Best Practices for Secure Operations*

This encompasses a range of practices, from providing physical security of QC facilities to implementing strict access controls and network security protocols. The user should manage personnel and insider threats. This can be accomplished by conducting thorough background checks on employees and implementing strict access controls (Saki et al., 2021). Regular training and awareness programs for employees also foster a culture of security, further preventing the TIQC systems from insider threats (Phalak et al., 2021).

5. Future Outlook & Conclusion

As we gaze into the future of quantum computing, it is evident that the landscape is rapidly evolving, which presents extraordinary capabilities and new challenges. The progression of quantum technologies, particularly trapped ions, will likely unveil many vulnerabilities that are currently unforeseen. This emphasizes the need for a proactive and anticipatory approach to security through adaptive frameworks. Cyber attackers have the advantage of abundant time and creativity, meaning security needs to be as flexible and dynamic as the attackers. The framework for cybersecurity in the quantum realm should include continuous risk assessment, advanced threat detection, and rapid response mechanisms. Quantum computing offers tremendous computational power to transform the world, but to fully realize its potential, security measures are imperative to ensure that quantum computing remains a secure and reliable asset for the advancement of society.

References

Bruzewicz, C.D. *et al.* (2019) 'Trapped-Ion Quantum Computing: Progress and Challenges', *Applied Physics Reviews*, 6(2), p. 021314. Available at: https://doi.org/10.1063/1.5088164.

Conklin, L. (no date) *Threat Modeling Process, OWASP*. Available at: https://owasp.org/www-community/Threat_Modeling_Process#stride (Accessed: 18 April 2024).

Das, S., Chatterjee, A. and Ghosh, S. (2023) 'A First Order Survey of Quantum Supply Dynamics and Threat Landscapes'. arXiv. Available at: http://arxiv.org/abs/2308.09772 (Accessed: 1 November 2023).

Gachnang, P. *et al.* (2022) 'Quantum Computing in Supply Chain Management State of the Art and Research Directions', *Asian Journal of Logistics Management*, 1(1), pp. 57–73. Available at: https://doi.org/10.14710/ajlm.2022.14325.

Get to Know Honeywells Latest Quantum Computer System Model H1 (no date). Available at: https://www.honeywell.com/us/en/news/2020/10/get-to-know-honeywell-s-latest-quantum-computer-system-model-h1 (Accessed: 10 December 2023).

Ghosh, S., Upadhyay, S. and Saki, A.A. (2023) 'A Primer on Security of Quantum Computing'. arXiv. Available at: http://arxiv.org/abs/2305.02505 (Accessed: 1 November 2023).

Hassija, V. *et al.* (2020) 'Present landscape of quantum computing', *IET Quantum Communication*, 1(2), pp. 42–48. Available at: https://doi.org/10.1049/iet-qtc.2020.0027.

Herman, A. and Friedson, I. (2018) 'Quantum Computing: How to Address the National Security Risk', *Hudson Institute* [Preprint]. Available at: https://www.hudson.org/national-security-defense/quantum-computing-how-to-address-the-national-security-risk.

Hsia, L.A. (no date) 'Physically Unclonable Characteristics for Verification of Transmon-Based Quantum Computers'.

IBM Quantum (no date). Available at: https://www.ibm.com/quantum (Accessed: 10 December 2023).

IonQ | Trapped Ion Quantum Computing (no date) *IonQ*. Available at: https://ionq.com/ (Accessed: 10 December 2023).

Murali, P. *et al.* (2020) 'Architecting Noisy Intermediate-Scale Trapped Ion Quantum Computers', in *2020 ACM/IEEE 47th Annual International Symposium on Computer Architecture (ISCA). 2020 ACM/IEEE 47th Annual International Symposium on Computer Architecture (ISCA)*, Valencia, Spain: IEEE, pp. 529–542. Available at: https://doi.org/10.1109/ISCA45697.2020.00051.

NIST CSWP 29 (2024) The NIST Cybersecurity Framework (CSF) 2.0, National Institute for Standards and Technology. Available at: https://nvlpubs.nist.gov/nistpubs/CSWP/NIST.CSWP.29.pdf (Accessed: 18 April 2024).

Phalak, K. *et al.* (2021) 'Quantum PUF for Security and Trust in Quantum Computing', *IEEE Journal on Emerging and Selected Topics in Circuits and Systems*, 11(2), pp. 333–342. Available at: https://doi.org/10.1109/JETCAS.2021.3077024.

Saki, A.A. *et al.* (2021) 'A Survey and Tutorial on Security and Resilience of Quantum Computing', in *2021 IEEE European Test Symposium (ETS). 2021 IEEE European Test Symposium (ETS)*, Bruges, Belgium: IEEE, pp. 1–10. Available at: https://doi.org/10.1109/ETS50041.2021.9465397.

Saki, A.A., Topaloglu, R.O. and Ghosh, S. (2022) 'Shuttle-Exploiting Attacks and Their Defenses in Trapped-Ion Quantum Computers', *IEEE Access*, 10, pp. 2686–2699. Available at: https://doi.org/10.1109/ACCESS.2021.3139085.

U.S. Department of Education (2003) 'Handbook for Information Technology Security Risk Assessment Procedures'. U.S. Department of Education. Available at: https://www2.ed.gov/policy/gen/leg/foia/acshbocio7.pdf (Accessed: 18 April 2024).

Exploring Cyber Fraud within the South African Cybersecurity Legal Framework

MM Watney
University of Johannesburg, South Africa

mwatney@uj.ac.za
https://www.orcid.org/0000-0002-1406-7623

Abstract: All countries are globally struggling with the challenges cybercrime presents to the cybersecurity legal framework. Fraud is not a new crime and existed long before the internet. The internet provides a threat actor access to a lot of potential victims and the use of various threat vectors to gain access to personal information by means of social engineering. It is therefore not surprising that cyber fraud has become a serious threat which continues to escalate globally. In 2021, around $100 million was lost in Canada due to online fraud. The United Kingdom (UK) Finance indicated that cyber fraud costs consumers more than £1.2 billion in 2022. The South African (SA) Fraud Prevention Services noted a 356% surge in identity fraud between April 2022 and April 2023. The cybersecurity threat landscape is ever-evolving with the UK Finance warning that the number of cyber frauds could surge out of control as threat actors begin to incorporate the use of Artificial intelligence (AI) to make their operations far more sophisticated and not as easily detected. In 2023 the United States (US) also warned that the irresponsible use of AI could exacerbate societal harms such as fraud. Cyber fraud, also referred to as a "white collar" or commercial crime, is an umbrella term to describe the commission of different types of cyber fraud by means of the use of various threat vectors. The threat vector used to commit the different type of fraud is continuously evolving, such as the use of sophisticated phishing to quishing and deep fakes which are aimed at deceiving the recipient in sharing information. The information obtained from a data breach may be used to commit cyber fraud. Irrespective of the threat vector used to commit fraud, all types of fraud present with the same elements, namely a threat actor who unlawfully and intentionally deceives a victim to benefit and cause harm. The discussion focuses on cyber fraud in general and not a specific type of cyber fraud. The purpose of the discussion is to provide an overview of the challenges cyber fraud present to the South African cybersecurity legal landscape.

Keywords: Cybercrime; Cyber Fraud; South African Cyber Fraud Cybersecurity Legal Framework; Criminalisation of Cyber Fraud; Criminalisation of Conduct Aimed at Obtaining Information; Data Protection and Cyber Fraud

1. Introduction

At the start of 2023, South Africa had 43.48 million internet users and an internet penetration rate of 72%. Social media users stood at 25.80 million people, roughly 42.9% of the total population which stood at 60 million. The number of internet users in the country increased in 2023 by 357,000 (0.8% percent) compared to the same period in 2022 and it continues to grow at a fast rate as South Africa digitalises (Modise, 2023).

As internet penetration and digitalisation grow, so does the risk of becoming a victim of cybercrime increase. A cybercrime can be committed by anyone who has access to a mobile phone and internet connection which makes these crimes relatively easy to commit (Kahle, 2023). It is therefore not surprising that globally the prevention, detection, investigation and prosecution of cybercrime present many challenges. South Africa is ranked 5th in respect of cybercrime victim densities (Kahle, 2023; Labuschagne, 2023). Statics show that cyber fraud is a global concern (Labuschagne, 2023). For example phishing fraud accounted for the most victims, but only led to an average loss of $173 (R3,173) per victim, whereas investment fraud was the most financially-devastating cybercrime in 2022, with total losses estimated to be around $3.3 billion (R60.5 billion), or $108,479 (R2 million) per victim. Tech support fraud is placed second with roughly $807 million (R14.8 billion) in losses, while confidence or romance fraud saw victims losing around $736 million (R13.5 billion). Online payment fraud, credit card fraud, and government impersonation led to losses of $386 million (R7 billion), $264 million (R4.8 billion), and $241 million (R4.4 billion), respectively (Labuschagne, 2023).

Cyber fraud is a non-violent crime characterized by deceit to obtain or avoid losing money, or to gain a personal or business advantage. It is referred to as a "white collar" or commercial crime (Hayes, 2023). The term "white collar" was first coined in 1939 by a sociologist, Edwin Sutherland, who defined it as a crime committed by a person of respectability and high social status (Hayes, 2023).

At the time that the term, "white collar crime", was coined, no one could have foreseen the technological advancements of today and the manner in which it would impact on the commission of fraud. It has moved from a crime committed in a physical medium to one that is predominantly committed online. By moving online, a threat actor have access to more potential victims and many different vectors to access information which was not possible in a physical medium. Threat actors are constantly finding new ways (threat vectors) to deceive or manipulate or influence users in sharing information, such as phishing fraud. Threat actors are also using generative AI, or deep-learning models which makes it is now easier to produce text, audio and even video, that can deceive, not only potential individual victims, but the security programs used to prevent and detect fraud (Kauflin and Mason; 2023).

Corporations and businesses that fall prey to commercial crime can suffer substantial losses, leading to reputational damage, retrenchments, bankruptcies and economic instability. The erosion of public trust caused by white collar crime stifles economic growth and deters foreign investment.

Internet users need to trust and feel safe and secure online and this can only be achieved by means of robust cybersecurity technical and legal measures. The discussion will show that cyber fraud within the context of South Africa present challenges to the cybersecurity legal framework. The lessons learnt may be also be relevant on a global level as all countries grapple with mitigating cyber fraud.

2. Defining Cyber Fraud as a Form of Cybercrime

Cyber fraud is the unlawful and intentional making of a misrepresentation which causes actual prejudice or which is potentially prejudicial to another (Hoctor, 2020). All types of fraud consists of deception, for example where an insured person suffered a theft but misrepresents to the insurer the loss suffered by the theft by exaggerating the loss (insurance fraud) or where a threat actor gains unauthorised access to information to assume the identity of the victim (identity theft) and then to commit fraud by opening, for example, accounts in the name of the victim. The aim of the threat actor in general is to profit financially. As indicated, the harm caused by cyber fraud to the victim, whether a natural or legal person, can be devastating.

3. Types of Cyber Fraud and Cyber Vectors

Cyber fraud is a cyber-enabled crime which means that fraud existed prior to the internet, but the Internet is now an instrument by means of which the different types of fraud may be committed. Prior to the internet, it was not easy to gain access to personal information., but the threat vector can use social engineering to deceive users into sharing personal information or to gain access to personal information which in return may be used to commit cyber fraud. At the core of the various cyber fraud is a data breach, and therefore the protection of personal information has become crucial. A Verizon Data Breach Investigation Report found in 2023 that 74% of data breaches have a human element (Stansfield, 2023).

There are different types of fraud that are committed by means of many threat vectors. The threat vectors are all examples of social engineering which is an umbrella term that consists of various tactics aimed at manipulation or deception, such as:

- Identity fraud (Hussain, 2022) occurs when the threat actor gains unauthorised access to a victim's personal information such as full names, identity number, bank account number, and credit card information. The goal of the threat actor may be to use the victim's personal information to commit bank fraud by assuming the victim's identity to access the victim's bank account and stealing the funds or to open and use credit cards in the victim's name and take out loans (credit card fraud) or use the victim's health insurance to pay medical bills(health insurance fraud).
- Phishing is the most common form of cyber fraud with an estimated 3.4 billion spam emails sent every day (Stansfield, 2023; Griffiths, 2024). There are many forms of phishing. It occurs mostly by means of an email, but WhatsApp messages can also be used. The phisher sends emails that appear to be from legitimate sources. They could be emails containing fake invoices, password renewal requests, messages from HR or leadership, and more. The messages often contain links to fake websites designed to access login credentials or other sensitive information. The same email may be sent to many addresses. Phishers can obtain email addresses from places such as corporate websites, existing data breaches, social media platforms, business cards or other publicly available company documents. For example, a user may receive an email from HR prompting them to update passwords by clicking a link. If the email is a phishing email, the link will redirect the user to a website that looks legitimate but has actually been set up by a cyber threat actor. The user then adds their details, which the attacker then uses to gain access to sensitive data and materials. Links to websites may also be infected with malware, such as spyware which can stealthily record sensitive personal and financial information, such as usernames, passwords, and credit card numbers.

Threat actors also try to vish (a combination of the words "voice" and "phishing" conducted by means of a telephone) by obtaining personal information or convincing the victim to install remote access tools that then deploy malicious software to gain entry into the network and data. "Vishers" can use the information and trust developed on these calls to launch effective cyberattacks, such as phishing.

Quishing is also a form of phishing. Quick Response (QR) codes have become an integral part of our daily lives, but with the increasing prevalence comes a new kind of threat, Quishing (a combination of QR code and phishing) is a fraudulent activity where threat actors create malicious QR codes to access sensitive information.

Business Email Compromise (BEC), also sometimes referred to as email fraud, occurs in circumstances in which the threat actor impersonate a known party over email and ask for a change in payment instructions. For example, the threat actor intercepts emails between buyers and sellers by posing as a genuine real estate agent or legal representative. By doing this, they redirect the buyer's deposit into their accounts (Kahle, 2023). In 2023, the FBI Internet Crime Complaint Center (IC3) released an updated Public Service Announcement, identifying nearly $51 billion in exposed losses due to BEC (Hill, 2023).

In 2020, the South African credit bureau, Experian, was the victim of a BEC in which the threat actor pretended to be a legitimate business. Experian shared business information consisting of various fields including company registration details, general business information, company contact information and credit profile information. Bank account numbers of 24,838 business entities, were shared. The information was shared in May 2020, but Experian only became aware of the fraud in July 2020. Once discovered, Experian notified the affected banks and the Information Regulator in terms of the Protection of Personal Information Act 4 of 2013 (Pieterse, 2020).

- Advance fee fraud occurs when the threat actor deceives a victim into paying for an item or service that never turns up (Tamplin, 2023). An example of advance fee fraud is when a victim is told that they have won a competition or inherited some money from a deceased relative, but need to pay a small fee to release the funds. Once the victim pays the fee, the perpetrator disappears and the promised money is never delivered. In romance fraud the threat actor for example, uses online dating sites and apps to earn his victims' trust, before making up seemingly urgent scenarios to gain his victim's sympathy and steal money from them.
- Ponzi or pyramid schemes may not be preceded by unauthorised access to information, but are based on misrepresenting a fictious investment as an actual investment and thereby misleading the victims. Investment fraud such as Ponzi and pyramid schemes, is a fraudulent scheme that involves paying existing investors in a non-existent enterprise, with funds collected from new investors. A Ponzi scheme promises clients a large profit at little to no risk (Pinkasovitch, 2023). Companies that engage in a Ponzi scheme focus all of their energy into attracting new clients to make investments. This new income is used to pay original investors their returns, marked as a profit from an allegedly legitimate transaction. Ponzi schemes rely on a constant flow of new investments to continue to provide returns to older investors. When this flow runs out, the scheme falls apart.

  A pyramid scheme works a little differently than a Ponzi scheme. This scheme is structured so that the initial schemer must recruit other investors who will continue to recruit other investors, and those investors will then continue to recruit additional investors, and so on (Pinkasovitch, 2023). There comes a time that no new investors can be recruited and the scheme will be exposed.

4. South African Cybersecurity Legislation Governing Cyber Fraud

In the South African context, fraud is defined as the unlawful and intentional making of misrepresentation which causes actual prejudice, or which is potentially prejudicial to another (Hoctor, 2020). Therefore, fraud comprises the following four elements, namely:

- Unlawfulness which refers to conduct that is seen to be wrong in the eyes of society;
- Misrepresentation which refers to a false statement made by one person to another. The misrepresentation may take the form of words; words and conduct; or just conduct or the misrepresentation may also be a failure to disclose certain information in circumstances where there is a duty to do so;

- Intent: The threat actor making the misrepresentation must have intended, or foreseen that the victim would be deceived; and
- Prejudice or potential prejudice: The victim would have suffered prejudice by reason of altering his position to his detriment after relying upon the misrepresentation. Potential prejudice is also sufficient if it is reasonably possible that the victim, relying on the misrepresentation, would have suffered harm.

In 2021 the Cybercrimes Act 19 of 2020 came into operation. It provides for various cybercrimes. Section 8 specifically provides for cyber fraud. As discussed, there are many vectors by means of which a threat actor can gain access to information for the purpose of committing fraud and these threat vectors have been criminalised, such as unauthorised access to information (section 2), interception of data (section 4), the unlawful acquisition, possession receipt and use of passwords, access code or similar data or device to commit fraud. A threat actor can also commit fraud by unlawfully interfering with data or a computer program by deleting data or computer program or alter data or render the data or computer program vulnerable, or damage or deteriorate it (sections 52(a), (b), (c). Fraud can also be committed by interfering with a data storage medium or computer system by altering it (section 6(2)(2)).

The following cybersecurity legislation is relevant as it imposes a report obligation:

1. **The Prevention and Combating of Corrupt Activities Act 12 of 2004 (POCA) requires any offence of** theft, fraud, corruption, forgery, or extortion involving an amount of R100 000 or more to be reported directly to the Directorate of Priority Crime Investigation, more commonly known as the Hawks. The obligation to report these incidents to the Hawks lies on any person in authority, such as the director of a company, manager, CEO, or director-general of a government department) who knows or suspects that any of these offences have been committed. While there is no time limit laid out in the Act for when the report needs to be made, the general rule is that it should be submitted within a reasonable amount of time. Mohamed (2021) opines that if an organisation is going to conduct an investigation into the incident, it would be advisable they wait for the investigation to conclude before reporting the incident in order to present a much more comprehensive report to the authorities.

2. As indicated, a threat actor may unlawfully gain access to data by various means and use the information to commit fraud. The Protection of Personal Information Act 4 of 2003 (POPIA) requires any incidents of a data breach where personal data is reasonably believed to have been compromised, to be reported to the Information Regulator of South Africa, as well as to the subject of that data. POPIA does not have a particular time frame within which the report must be made, but the Act does specifically state that this report must be made as soon as reasonably possible after the discovery of the breach. As such, time is definitely of the essence when it comes to notifying the regulator of a data breach. However, Mohamed (2021) opines that an organisation is able to justify a delay in doing so if the legitimate needs of law enforcement to determine the scope of the breach and restore the integrity of the business' information system, call for it. The Act also notes that an organisation can delay letting the data subject know about the breach if a public body that is responsible for the prevention, detection, or investigation of offences (or the Information Regulator) determines that doing so will impede a criminal investigation. It is important to note that POPIA speaks to the data privacy requirements within South Africa and any business which operates where they must abide by international data laws such as the European Union's General Data Protection Regulation (GDPR) must be cognisant of the requirements thereof. For example, the GDPR requires businesses to report any incident of a data breach not later than 72 hours after having become aware of said breach.

3. In terms of the Financial Intelligence Centre Act (FICA) 38 of 2001 an organisation must report a suspicious and unusual transaction when it becomes aware of it. Under the Act, any person who knows or should know or has suspected that the organisation has received the proceeds of unlawful activities or has facilitated transactions related to the financing of terrorist activities, must report this to the Financial Intelligence Centre (FIC). The same is required when there is knowledge or suspicion of tax evasion or money laundering which must be filed with the FIC under the specific sections of the Act which have been contravened. A report must be made to the FIC within 15 days of the discovery of the incident. Non-compliance is not an option as it could lead to a public reprimand, a remediation directive, the restriction or suspension of certain business activities, and a financial penalty of up to R10 million for a natural person or up to R50 million for a legal person.

4. The reporting obligation in the Cybercrimes Act only applies to electronic communication service providers and financial institutions such as telcos and banks and requires these organisations to report cybercrime

incidents to the South African Police Service within 72 hours of becoming aware of the use of their information systems to commit a cybercrime. The penalty for not doing so in time is R50 000.

Although the specific reporting obligation of an organisation must comply with depends on the specific criminal incident that has occurred, these offences are often interrelated, which may make ignorance of these obligations even more costly for a business or institution. For example, when there is an instance of corruption or fraud, it is usually related to monetary gain and this money may then be laundered in order to avoid raising suspicion. Because of this, an organisation might be beholden to more than one piece of legislation as it relates to reporting one specific incident of commercial crime. Money laundering within the South African context has been challenging as will be shown at paragraph 5 hereafter.

5. Challenges Cyber Fraud Present to the South African Cybersecurity Legal Framework

Threat actors seek to exploit human or security vulnerabilities in order to commit fraud by using different threat vectors. Digital trust in a safe and secure online environment can only be achieved by means of technical and legal cybersecurity measures keeping in mind that the end user presents also a human weakness and risk to the technical measures.

There are many challenges in respect of the legal cybersecurity framework, such as:

1. At the core of many cyber fraud, is unauthorised access to personal information.

   A country must have data protection legislation. It is commendable that South Africa has such legislation, namely POPIA. POPIA imposes a legal duty on the responsible party that processes personal information, to obtain the consent of the user prior to the processing and to have security measures in place to protect the personal information gathered. POPIA is aimed at implementing pro-active security measures to protect personal information. When there is a data breach, then the responsible party has a reporting obligation to the information regulator (discussed at paragraph 4). The time period in which a data breach must be reported, is not outlined in POPIA which in my opinion is a shortcoming.

   In some instances, the victim of fraud, especially identity fraud, only detects it after a long time. Cloete (2023) notes that by the time a victim realises that he is the victim of fraud, the damage has been done as fraudsters may have amassed significant debts in the name of the victim. For example, in the Experian case, referred to at paragraph 4, the credit bureau only realised after approximately 4 months that it had suffered a data fraud and that it had shared a huge amount of personal information with the fraudster. During that period of time, the credit bureau customers were unaware that their information had been shared and could be used to commit fraud.

   Cybersecurity measures are not only aimed at prevention, but must be able to detect the fraud quickly in order for the victim to respond and recover from the harm caused by the deception. However, many of the social engineering are aimed at exploiting human vulnerability to manipulation, and the strongest technical measures can be compromised if the weakest link, end user, do not take precautions. Constant cybersecurity awareness training is crucial to internet users, irrespective of whether they are bank clients or employees.

2. No cybersecurity technical measures are infallible and there may be a security compromise. Kauflin and Mason (2023) also opine that generative AI "could ultimately make obsolete, state-of-the-art fraud-prevention measures such as voice authentication and even "liveness checks" designed to match a real-time image with the one on record".

   A country must have comprehensive cybercrime legislation. Cybercrime legislation is re-active, in other words, the investigation takes place only once the case has been reported. If there is a delay in reporting the cyber fraud to the police, then the evidence needed to prove the commission of the fraud could potentially be lost, deleted or destroyed.

   South Africa has the Cybercrimes Act which provides for cyber-dependant and cyber-enabled crimes. There are many threat vectors by means of which the threat actor can gain access to information which is used to commit fraud and these vectors have been criminalised.

   In 2023 it was reported that an estimated 90% of cybercrimes go unreported in South Africa (Kahle, 2023). Crime reporting serves an important purpose; namely preventing a threat actor from continuing with this type of criminal behaviour which protects the public in general from becoming a victim of cyber fraud.

There are various reasons why only 10% of cybercrime cases are reported to the police:

- The victim may not trust that the police will be able to effectively investigate the case or may not have confidence in the criminal justice system that the case will go on trial.

  The police who are tasked with the investigation of a cybercrime, such as identifying the threat actor (perpetrator) and gathering of the evidence, may not have the relevant investigative skills or assistance to effectively investigate a matter, especially in circumstances where the security compromise is committed outside of South Africa. In this regard, South Africa is not unique as the nature of cybercrime challenges law enforcement globally. Unlike a physical crime, the threat actor does not have to be physically close to the victim to commit a crime and technology allows the crime to occur outside the country's borders in which instance the police need assistance from the other country's law enforcement.

- A victim may wish not to report the cyber fraud out of fear that the disclosure will affect its' reputation negatively. There are legislation that imposes a compulsory reporting obligation. Compliance with such legislation must be enforced.

3. Preventing the use of the proceeds of cybercrime, such as those obtained from fraud by means of money laundering, has proven a challenge. A country must ensure enforcement and compliance with anti-money laundering legislation. For purposes of this discussion, it should be noted that in 2023 South Africa was greylisted by the global financial crime watchdog, the Financial Action Task Force (FATF) for not fully complying with international standards around the prevention of money laundering, terrorist financing and proliferation financing. As indicated, threat actors target the human aspect of security. For example, "money muling" instances increased by 97% in 2021 (Cloete, 2023). "Money muling" occurs when a money mule transfers or moves illegally acquired money on behalf of someone else and in return the mule receives monetary compensation (Cloete, 2023).

4. BEC and liability for the BEC continue to be a serious concern for companies of all industries and sizes. Courts have had to deliberate whether a business could be held civilly liable for the economic loss suffered by a client as a result of a BEC. The court determined that a business that makes use of emails for payments, must forewarn their clients of the potential risk of fraud and take the necessary security precautions to safeguard against the risk of harm from a possible BEC. If a business does not forewarn a client nor take reasonable security steps to safeguard against a BEC, the business may be held liable for the financial loss suffered by the client who became a victim of cyber fraud as a result of negligence on the side of the business (Orekeng, 2023).

6. Conclusion

A robust technical and legal cybersecurity framework can go a long way in preventing cyber fraud.

Unfortunately, the weakest link in cybersecurity is the human vulnerability to social engineering. The human end user may be deceived, manipulated or influenced by means of various vectors to share information which in turn may be used to commit a cybercrime, such as cyber fraud. Over the years, the threat actor has become more sophisticated in the use of the threat vector which at times can be very convincing, especially now with the use of AI. The role of cybersecurity awareness training in combatting social engineering cannot be over-emphasised. Likewise the role of financial education in safeguarding investors against Ponzi and pyramid schemes cannot be downplayed. These "investments" exploit human vulnerability to manipulation. Propositions promising exceptional returns at minimal risk should be treated with a high degree of scepticism as these offers are frequently indicative of fraudulent schemes.

Even if the human aspect of technical cybersecurity is addressed, technical measures may be compromised, especially as AI may be used by the threat actor to compromise the technical security measures. In the case of a security compromise, the cyber fraud must be reported to the police to ensure an investigation and possible prosecution of the crime. By means of strong legislation, prescribed reporting obligations within specific timelines, effective enforcement, mutual cross-border assistance, and stringent punishment, a threat actor will realise that "white collar" crimes will not be tolerated. It will also restore trust in the criminal justice system. A zero tolerance approach to cyber fraud will contribute to digital trust. Digital trust enables individuals and businesses to engage online with the confidence that their information is secure against cyber threats, such as cyber fraud.

References

Beard, J. (2023) “Fraudsters need just 3 seconds on a cold call to clone your voice...and scam your family”, https://www.thisismoney.co.uk/money/beatthescammers/article-12615607/Fraudsters-need-just-3-seconds-cold-call-clone-voice-scam-family.html.

Cloete, N. (2023) “Experts concerned as cybercrime cost South Africans billion”; [online]; https://www.iol.co.za/saturday-star/news/experts-concerned-as-cybercrimes-cost-south-africa-billions-0b0fc4ce-0b1f-410c-a953-8985fb1543a1.

Griffiths, C. (2024) “The latest 2023 phishing statistics (updated January 2024)”; [online]; https://aag-it.com/the-latest-phishing-statistics/.

Hayes, A. (2023) “What is white collar crime? Meaning, types and differences” [online]; https://www.investopedia.com/terms/w/white-collar-crime.asp.

Hoctor, S. (2020) Snyman’s Criminal Law; LexisNexis (Pty) Ltd; pages 461 – 409.

Kahle, C. (2023) “Going beyond ‘Nigerian Prince’: SA turning into Africa’s cybercrime capital”, [online], https://www.citizen.co.za/lifestyle/technology/south-africa-turning-into-cybercrime-capital/.

Kauflin, J. and Mason, E. (2023) “How AI is supercharging financial fraud – and making it harder to spot”; [online]; https://www.forbesafrica.com/daily-cover-story/2023/09/19/how-ai-is-supercharging-financial-fraud-and-making-it-harder-to-spot/.

Labuschagne, H. (2023) “South Africa n world’s top 5 worse countries for cybercrime”; ;[online]; https://mybroadband.co.za/news/security/489183-south-africa-in-worlds-top-5-worst-countries-for-cybercrime.html.

Lawton, G. (2023) “How to prevent deepfakes in the era of generative AI”, [online],https://www.techtarget.com/searchsecurity/tip/How-to-prevent-deepfakes-in-the-era-of-generative-AI.

Modise, E. (2023) “28% of South Africans have no internet connectivity”; [online]; https://techcabal.com/2023/04/06/internet-connectivity-south-africa-2023/.

Mohamed, Z. (2021); “4 Commercial crime reporting obligations organisations must comply with”; online; https://www.lexology.com/library/detail.aspx?g=a7c59e90-b24c-421f-a96b-e5e33c106256.

Orekeng, K. (2023) “The dangers of business email compromise” De Rebus; [online]; https://www.derebus.org.za/the-dangers-of-business-e-mail-compromise/.

Pinkasovitch, (2023) A. ”Ponsi scheme vs Pyramid scheme: What is the difference?”: [online], https://www.investopedia.com/ask/answers/09/ponzi-vs-pyramid.asp.

Stansfield, S. (2023) “Verizon Data Breach Investigations Report 2023: Our Top Takeaways”, [online], https://www.vadesecure.com/en/blog/verizon-data-breach-report-2023.

Tamplin, T. (2023) “Advance Fee Fraud”; [online]; https://www.financestrategists.com/wealth-management/investments/advance-fee-fraud/.

A Sensemaking Framework for Defensive Cyber Operations: Filling the Void in Leadership Discourse

Frank Wleklinski and Timothy Shives
Naval Postgraduate School*, Monterey, California, USA
*(The views expressed here are those of the authors and do not necessarily represent the views of the Naval Postgraduate School, the Department of Defense, or the U.S. Government.)

frank.wleklinski@nps.edu
timothy.shives@nps.edu

Abstract: In the realm of contemporary warfare dominated by cyber threats, Defensive Cyber Operations (DCO) serve as a linchpin for mitigating risks and ensuring mission assurance. This article delves into the intricate landscape of DCO, focusing on the critical role played by Defensive Cyberspace Forces (DCFs). Despite their significance, the absence of a unified sensemaking framework poses a challenge for leaders responsible for the nuanced development and strategic employment of DCFs. The lacuna in the existing literature revolves around the lack of a comprehensive sensemaking framework tailored for operational and DCF leaders. The inadequacies of current frameworks, either overly broad or excessively specific, hinder effective dialogue and understanding. This deficiency not only obstructs the planning efforts and operational tempo of DCO but also restrains the maturation of DCFs, amplifying residual risks faced by commanders. This paper endeavours to present a purpose-built sensemaking framework crafted for leaders engaged in the dynamic realms of DCF development. Integrating well-established risk mitigation principles with the unique organizational structures and missions of DCFs, the framework fills a crucial void in the literature. Beyond being a decision-support tool, it strives to foster a shared mental model, providing a nuanced lens for leaders to contextualize and prioritize their efforts in the complex landscape of DCO. Through a meticulous critique of existing frameworks, this article introduces a tailored model designed to address identified shortcomings. Emphasizing the practical utility of the proposed framework, the discussion unfolds to elucidate how it not only facilitates the development and employment of DCF but also contributes to organizational resilience and risk mitigation. This article contributes a novel sensemaking framework to the academic discourse on DCO. While acknowledging limitations imposed by an unclassified context, the framework provides valuable insights into the strategic dimensions of DCF development and employment, DCO planning intricacies, and organizational analyses. Future avenues for research include the integration of classified information to refine the framework, ensuring its applicability across diverse DCO mission types and aligning DCF core functions with specific threats, thereby enhancing the efficacy of defensive cyber strategies.

Keywords*:* Defensive Cyber Operations, Sensemaking Framework, Defensive Cyberspace Forces, Cyber Risk Mitigation, Operational Resilience

1. Introduction

In the dynamic and ever-evolving landscape of cybersecurity, the complexity of Defensive Cyberspace Operations (DCO) presents a formidable challenge for leaders and practitioners. The rapid proliferation of cyber threats, coupled with the intricate interplay of technology, data, and networks, necessitates a comprehensive framework that not only clarifies the intricacies but also serves as a common language for decision-makers. This article addresses this imperative need by introducing a groundbreaking sensemaking framework—aptly named a "Sensemaking Framework for Defensive Cyber Operations"—crafted to enhance the efficacy of Defensive Cyber Forces (DCF) in navigating the multifaceted realm of DCO.

The current cybersecurity milieu is inundated with a plethora of risk mitigation frameworks and policy documents, each vying for attention and implementation. However, the existing frameworks often fall short when it comes to providing a cohesive and operationally relevant model for DCO. Recognizing this gap, the authors delve into the intricacies of DCO, emphasizing the critical role of a shared mental model and a standardized language in fostering effective communication and decision-making.

The purpose of this framework is to meticulously cut through the complexity, offering a structured approach to interpret and contextualize DCO within the broader landscape of risk management. As leaders in the field are confronted with diverse cyber systems, technologies, and threat landscapes, this conceptual framework provides a navigational tool that categorizes, prioritizes, and evaluates the myriad aspects of DCO. Its adaptability to various organizational objectives and mission domains positions it as a versatile and indispensable resource for leaders engaged in DCF development, employment, and maintenance.

This article unfolds by examining the limitations of existing frameworks, establishing the rationale for this new framework, and subsequently delving into its components and applications. From enhancing real-time decision-making to serving as a planning tool for organizational development and troubleshooting, the framework emerges as a comprehensive solution tailored to the nuanced demands of contemporary defensive cyberspace activities. Through this exploration, the article aims to contribute a foundational resource that not only aids in making sense of the intricacies of DCO but also propels the field towards enhanced operational effectiveness and cyber resilience.

2. Problem

Defensive Cyber Operations (DCO) fundamentally aim to mitigate risks for operational commanders, functioning as a cornerstone of mission assurance. In tandem, organizations have developed Defensive Cyberspace Forces (DCFs) as crucial risk mitigation tools, addressing cyber-dependencies in alignment with tactical, operational, and strategic objectives. DCFs, while not typically the primary focus, exist to support the overall mission of commanders. Consequently, leaders and their staffs must make strategic decisions on methods for the development, maintenance, and employment of DCFs.

The challenges faced by these leaders are twofold. Firstly, DCFs are inherently limited, involving costly cyber talent and equipment. Secondly, the constant need for cyber defense arises from the expanding attack surface facilitated by networked hardware and software supporting diverse warfighting functions. DCF leaders must navigate a real-world scenario of trade-offs, strategically allocating limited resources in a zero-sum game to develop and employ DCFs while mitigating risks posed by a growing number of cyber dependencies.

While the existence of well-known cyber risk mitigation frameworks may suggest a solution, the reality is complex. Unfortunately, most frameworks, whether too broad or too narrow, lack practicality for everyday use. This gap in literature highlights a disconnect, as existing frameworks, while beneficial for specific work roles or organizational levels, fail to align with the needs of leaders and planners directly responsible for creating, maturing, and employing DCFs. Furthermore, these frameworks lack a shared model for creating common understanding.

Developing and employing DCFs without a specific framework may seem plausible, as many leaders and planners currently do so, progressively enhancing capabilities. However, this success often relies on sheer will and ingenuity rather than a repeatable and predictable organizational process. The lack of a pragmatic model for DCF employment poses scalability challenges. The consequences of cyber threats and their defense are evident, emphasizing the critical need for a sensemaking framework in DCO. The absence of a shared mental model hampers the development and employment of DCFs, creating a significant artificial barrier to their effective utilization.

The absence of a shared sensemaking framework for operational and Defensive Cyberspace Forces (DCF) leaders and staff hinders collaborative dialogue on the development and employment of DCF. This deficiency is critical because the lack of a unified language and shared mental model organizing the various types and purposes of Defensive Cyber Operations (DCO) impedes the effective utilization of DCF (Camillo and Miranda, 2011; Schrier, 2022). Additionally, the absence of a shared sensemaking model complicates efforts to articulate the purpose behind different types of DCO that DCF can conduct (Moore, Dynes, and Chang, 2015). This collective limitation slows down DCO planning efforts, hampers operational tempo, and constrains the organizational maturation of DCF, ultimately elevating a commander's residual risk.

3. Purpose

This paper aims to address the identified problem by presenting a comprehensive sensemaking framework for Defensive Cyber Operations (DCO), specifically designed to support leaders and staff responsible for developing and employing DCF, referred to as DCF leaders. The framework draws upon well-established risk mitigation principles while integrating DCF organizational structures and missions. While numerous cybersecurity-related policies and issuances exist, often focusing on compliance, high-level programmatic matters, or holistic risk mitigation for enterprise portfolios, the presented framework fills a crucial gap in the literature.

This framework stands out by providing sensemaking and decision-support tools tailored to the unique responsibilities of DCF leaders and planners. It goes beyond existing policies by offering an overarching model that contextualizes and concentrates discussions. Additionally, it contributes to the literature by aiding in the establishment of a shared mental model among DCF leaders. The authors build on previous works, striving to create a cohesive framework for defensive cyber missions (Guion and Reith, 2017; Schrier, 2022; Voice, 2022). This paper represents a valuable addition to the existing body of knowledge in the field.

Next, the authors provide several definitions and the limitations of this paper. Then they discuss the shortcomings of the current frameworks and provide a model to address the problem. Finally, the authors discuss how the proposed Sensemaking Framework aids in developing and employing DCF. Thus, this paper uniquely addresses the critical gap in existing literature by presenting a tailored sensemaking framework for Defensive Cyber Operations (DCO). By integrating risk mitigation principles with Defensive Cyberspace Forces (DCFs) organizational structures, it offers invaluable insights for leaders navigating the complex landscape of cyber defense. This innovative contribution enhances strategic decision-making and organizational resilience, initiating this conversation to the academic community and cyber operations community seeking cutting-edge perspectives on DCO.

4. Definitions

To ensure clarity for both DCF and non-DCF personnel, the authors will establish local definitions, recognizing potential semantic differences from established publications. The paper will strive to identify instances of such divergence for traceability.

Developing DCF. Making force structure decisions on how and why to man, train, and equip DCF in alignment with intended typification of DCO.

Employing DCF. Aligning DCF to cyber systems and deploying them to conduct defensive activities or operations. Also refers to the holistic DCO mission planning process, encompassing activities such as communicating, categorizing, prioritizing, evaluating, and directing various DCF activities.

DCF. Any formation participating in defending cyber-enabled systems, deviating from United States Cyber Command (USCC) definitions to include the United States Department of Defense (DOD) and Service organic Cyber Security Service Providers (CSSP) and DCO formations outside the operational command of USCC. For the DOD audience specifically, the authors define DCF as the DCF identified in USCC CWP 3-33.4 (United States Cyberspace Command (USCC), 2020), namely the various types of Cyber Protection Teams plus DOD and Service organic CSSP and DCO formations outside the operational command of USCC. The authors break from the USCC definitions because this second group consists of units who perform similar cybersecurity and defensive cyber functions for the respective Services (equivalent to DCO-Internal Defense Measures (IDM) Companies or Network Battalions in the Marine Corps), have much or even the same training, share personnel, and are often considered for employment, or compete, with USCC DCF.

DCO. Any activity taken to defend or secure a network, taking a broad approach beyond specific definitions given by USCC.

DCF Leaders. Commanders or staff members directly engaged in building, developing, maintaining, or employing DCF, encompassing those with operational, tactical, or administrative control.

5. Limitations

The authors acknowledge that the true nature of this conceptual framework is best conveyed in briefs or conferences. The written publication serves as an attempt to meet the demand for a published version, recognizing that certain nuances and connections may be lost in written explanations. The primary purpose of this framework is to serve as a decision support tool and discussion aid, with the hope that this publication sparks further discussions leading to additional applications and insights.

6. Existing Risk Mitigation Frameworks

In the expansive realm of cybersecurity, the abundance of risk mitigation frameworks and policy documents has reached a point of complexity that poses challenges for practical use. Even with attempts to organize the Department of Defense's (DoD) cybersecurity policies chart, the resulting visual representation often underscores the intricate web of dependencies and cross-references, making navigation a daunting task. Notwithstanding, credible organizations have contributed noteworthy frameworks aimed at mitigating risks stemming from cyber dependencies. See Figure 1.

One such framework is the DoD-Instruction (DoDI) 8510.01: Risk Management Framework (RMF) for DoD Information Technology (IT) (DoD, 2014). While it serves as an overarching document directing the management of the DoD's enterprise IT systems, it relies on external references for implementation guidance, contributing to the challenge of practical applicability. Another significant contributor is the body of NIST Special Publications

(SPs), including the Cybersecurity Framework (Computer Security Division, 2016; NIST, 2018b, 2018a). NIST's RMF principles underpin the DoD IT RMF, focusing on enterprise risk management and providing guidance applicable to both governmental and non-governmental organizations.

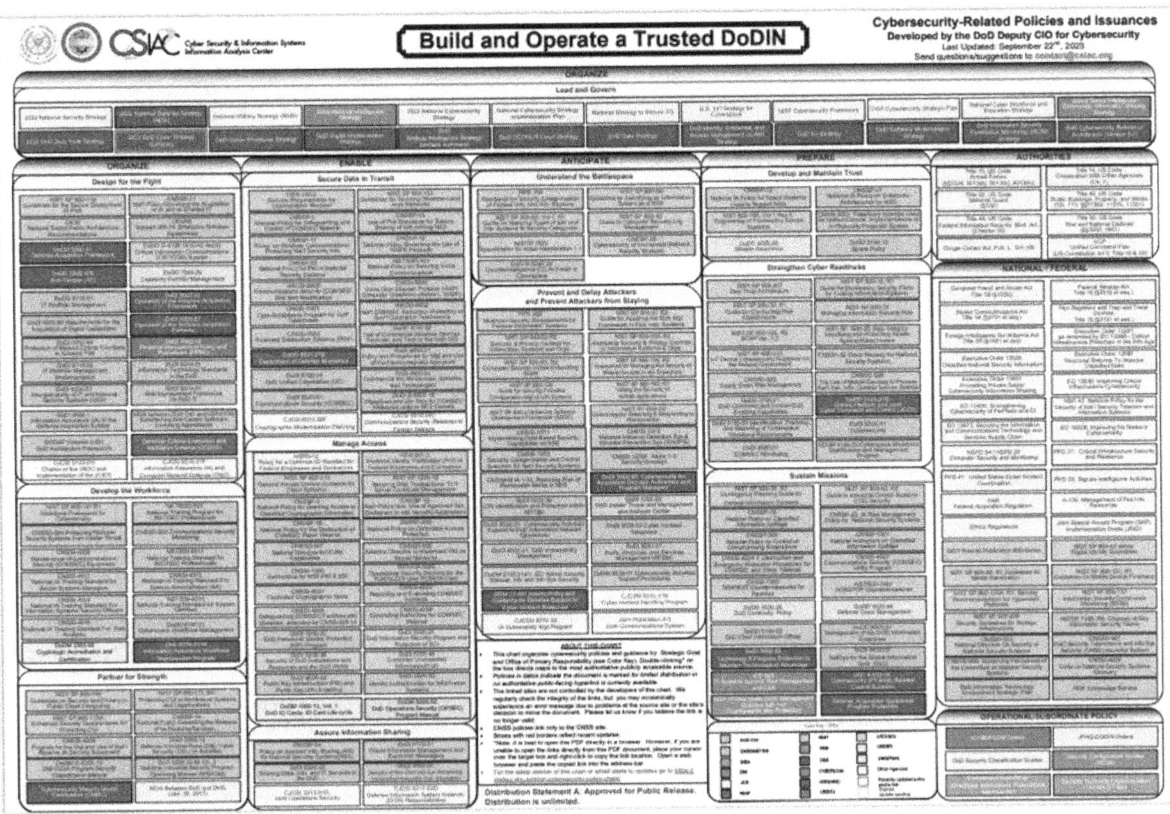

Figure 1: DOD Cybersecurity Chart (DOD, 2023). Available at: https://dodiac.dtic.mil/dod-cybersecurity-policy-chart/

The Defense Information Systems Agency (DISA) adds to the landscape with Security Technical Implementation Guides (STIGs), offering government configuration standards for IT systems and software (DISA, 2023). Despite their widespread use as best practices, STIGs are specific and technical, limiting their applicability at operational levels. Additionally, the Institute of Electrical and Electronics Engineers (IEEE) contributes to risk management through its Enterprise Risk Management Program (ERM), acknowledged for its authoritative guidelines (IEEE, 2023).

Despite the rigor and expertise invested in these frameworks, they often fall short when it comes to the specific challenges faced by Defensive Cyberspace Forces (DCF) leaders. Existing frameworks tend to fall into two categories, being either too broad or too narrow, leaving practitioners, operators, and DCF leaders to interpret and implement guidance not always tailored to their specific organizational focus. The high-level framework aims for broad usability, introducing ambiguity and scenario agnosticism. The lower-level frameworks aim for narrow specificity, introducing complex technical dependencies that cannot always be applied perfectly in a real-world production system. The combined deficiencies create a gap in practical decision support aids and shared mental models crucial for the development and employment of DCF.

Within the existing landscape, some frameworks are deemed too high level, serving administrative or bureaucratic purposes, and often conflicting with the realities of the operational environment. On the other hand, there are frameworks that are too narrow, presenting specific checklists for technology or configuration security, which may not be applicable at operational levels or aid in the development and employment of DCF.

In essence, the multitude of frameworks, policies, and directives generates equivocality and uncertainty, hindering practitioners in need of accurate and specific solutions to their operational problems. This situation prevents the establishment of a shared mental model, obstructs the creation of shared meaning, and frustrates meaningful dialogue. While existing documents serve their intended purposes, none comprehensively address the brass-tax needs of operational staff, particularly DCF leaders, operational commanders, and their staffs requiring prompt decisions on limited DCF resources. The forthcoming framework seeks to rectify these issues by providing a more accurate and specific framework for discussing and describing DCF and Defensive Cyber Operations (DCO).

7. A Proposed Sensemaking Framework for Defensive Cyber Operations

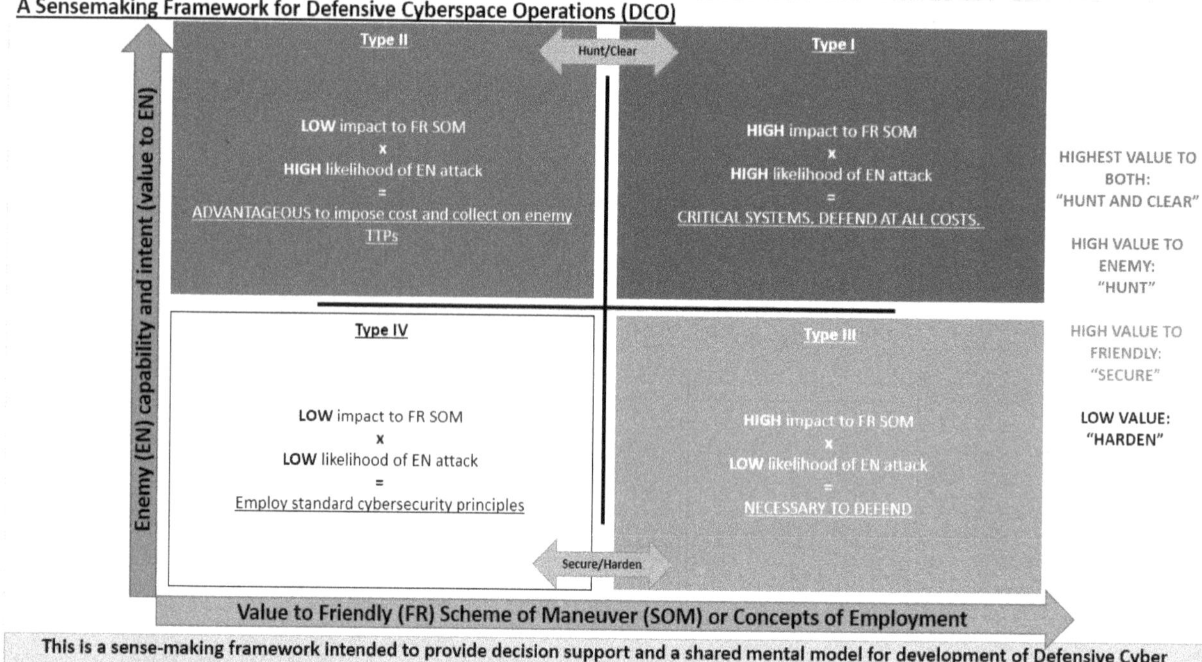

Figure 2: The Sensemaking Framework for Defensive Cyber Operations

Before delving into the utility of this conceptual framework, described by the authors as a "Sensemaking Framework for Defensive Cyber Operations," it is crucial to understand its structure. The following sections provide an explanation of how to interpret The Framework using the accompanying graphic.

7.1 The Horizontal and Vertical Axis

In today's organizational landscape, risk management principles play a pervasive role. The Department of Defense (DoD) mandates that every service member undergo an online class in risk mitigation aligned with their rank/grade. As previously emphasized, cybersecurity and Defensive Cyberspace Forces (DCF) are instrumental in mitigating risks to support an organization's overarching goals. The framework aligns with risk management frameworks by establishing a horizontal and vertical axis corresponding to key risk factors.

On the horizontal (X) axis lies the "Value to Friendly (FR) Scheme of Maneuver (SOM) or Concepts of Employment (CONEMP)." This "value" correlates with the technology, data, or network under consideration and is analogous to the "impact" variable in risk calculations. The higher the value of a technology, data, or network in supporting or enabling FR SOM and CONEMPs, the greater the impact of an incident or intrusion on that entity.

The vertical (Y) axis represents the "Enemy (EN) capability and intent (value to EN)." Similar to the horizontal axis, the "value" pertains to the technology, data, or network and aligns with the "likelihood" variable in risk calculations. The higher the value of the targeted technology, data, or network in supporting the EN's SOMs or CONEMPs, the greater the likelihood of it being targeted. Such definitions align with Joint Operational and Targeting definitions (DoD, 2011; DoD, 2013). Notably, a technology, data, or network valuable to FR objectives may also be deemed valuable to the enemy, such as a High-Pay Off Target (HPV) with asymmetrical impacts. Conversely, the enemy may prioritize a High-Value Target (HVT) valuable to their objectives, even if it doesn't align with FR objectives.

Beyond military metaphors, the "value to EN" variable requires further breakdown, as indicated in its description. From the defender's viewpoint, the likelihood of an EN attack, or its value, depends on both how well such an attack aligns with the EN's objectives (intent) and the EN's capabilities to execute an attack (capability). This necessitates an intelligence-supported assessment of mediating variables like "EN capability" and "EN intent," typically backed by an organizational intelligence apparatus in a military setting or open-source threat intelligence in the private sector.

7.2 The Center Quad Chart

Quad charts, a common element in the DoD, find application in this framework by overlaying major risk mitigation axes with a typology for Defensive Cyberspace Operations (DCO) and target data, technology, or networks (systems). The horizontal and vertical axes enable the creation of a standard quad-chart, dividing the chart into four sections, labelled 1 – 4. These numbers serve as nomenclature without indicating relative priority or order. While the authors assigned ordinal risk labels approximating relative priority, it's emphasized that the assignment may vary depending on the using organization and its mission domain. This flexibility is a key advantage of this framework as it is tailored for a military audience—but has applications that can be broadened outside of military cyber operations.

The relative location of the black vertical and horizontal lines forming the borders of these four sections is also arbitrary. Each organization will have to determine for itself where these thresholds are. However, many of the existing frameworks discussed provide useful guidance on what systems fall into which category, and therefore can aid a DCF leader is standardizing these across an organization or within a local discussion. Still, some systems will fall between categories or into more than one depending on temporal organizational and environmental factors. This highlights another advantage of this framework as is forces and fosters a discussion about the value of a given system to both FR and EN SOMs and CONEMPs as well as frames the conversation in terms of standard RMF language, providing a mental model and langue to make such discussions meaningful.

7.2.1 *Type I: Defend at all Costs*

Situated at the top right, Type I corresponds to critical systems demanding defense at all costs. These systems, supporting national or strategic assets like nuclear command and control or classified data networks, align with Defense Critical Infrastructure (DCI) or Task Critical Assets (TCAs) (CJCS, 2012). Adversaries are likely to develop capabilities and intentions to target these systems, necessitating Hunt and Clear operations specifically tailored to threat intelligences aligning to the assessed EN's capabilities.

7.2.2 *Type II: Advantageous to Impose Cost and Collect on an Adversary*

Found in the top left, Type II systems are of lower value to FR SOM or CONEMP but satisfy EN objectives. These systems may include foreign partner or allied systems of interest to the adversary. DCO on these systems, aligned with Hunt and Clear operations, aids in collecting information about adversary capabilities and intentions. It may not always be necessary to clear these systems given intelligence gain/loss considerations.

7.2.3 *Type III: Necessary to Defend*

Type III systems, located at the bottom left, are of high value to FR SOM but with a low likelihood of EN attack. These systems can asymmetrically disrupt FR operations. While the likelihood of attack is low, the impact could lead to FR mission failure, necessitating defense. DCO typically aligns with Hunt and Clear operations but since EN attack is assessed to be less likely, such operations may be threat actor agnostic.

7.2.4 *Type IV: Employ and Enforce Standard Cybersecurity Principles*

Situated at the bottom right, Type IV systems have low impact on FR SOM and a low likelihood of EN attack. These systems, representing administrative or quality of life operations, adhere to cybersecurity best practices. They are defended by Cyber Security Service Providers (CSSPs) and receive the lowest priority for defensive cyber maneuver forces. DCO aligns with Secure and Harden operations. Continuous demand for more exquisite defensive maneuver cyber forces on these systems may indicate misclassification of DCO or inappropriate employment of DCF, prompting reassessment by DCF leaders.

Typically, it is not to appropriate employ defensive maneuver cyber forces, such as Cyber Protection Teams (CPTs), against systems of this type unless in a temporary reinforcing role to supplement the standing CSSP. However, if the need to do so arises, it may be a sign that the system was misclassified. If defensive maneuver cyber forces are continually in demand to conduct DCO on this type of systems, it may be a further sign that these systems need to be re-classified. If such forces are continually executing DCO on these systems, it may also be a sign these forces are not being employed appropriately and should alert DCF leaders to assess if other types of systems, and therefore risks, are being left uncovered.

8. Improving Decision Making

Shared mental models reduce uncertainty and underpin the ability to effectively share meaning (Shannon, 1948; Shannon and Weaver, 1949). Without a shared model, effective communication is difficult. Communication enables joint decision making among teams (Covey and Merrill, 2008). The novel combination of standard risk mitigation language overlaid with impact to friendly and adversary courses of action builds upon reference frames already familiar in defense organizations. This amalgamation establishes a new sensemaking model effective for creating meaning, thereby fostering better development and employment decisions regarding defensive cyber forces (DCF).

This framework fills the gaps left by the extant literature and guidance that are either too broad, too narrow, or were never intended for operational matters in the first place. It is a centralizing tool around which to communicate cyber risk, categorize systems and operations, and prioritize them. It enables categorization, prioritization, evaluation, planning, and analysis, all of which serve to advance the effective employment and development of DCF to mitigate an organization's cyber risk.

8.1 Communicating

This new framework serves as a communication tool by establishing a shared mental model and common language for discussing DCO and DCF. It mitigates ambiguity and equivocality resulting from the vast and diverse publications on cybersecurity and risk mitigation. Synthesizing Department of Defense (DoD) and U.S. Cyber Command (USCC) publications, it aligns with their definitions while offering a contextually relevant interpretation for DCF leaders. Shared language and mental models enhance communication, trust, and interoperability.

8.2 Categorizing

This framework functions as a categorization tool to typify various cyber systems and their associated DCO. Users can plot a system (technology, data, or network) along the horizontal and vertical axes, utilizing defined variables and standard Risk Management Framework (RMF) principles. DCF leaders can establish standard labels for each system, facilitating transparent discussions and providing standardized shorthand for different types.

8.3 Prioritizing

Once typification is established, this conceptual framework serves as a guide for prioritization. DCF leaders can align categories with organizational objectives, aiding force allocation decisions, i.e. which DCF should be aligned to which DCO. When faced with requests for forces (RFFs) or internal operations, this categorization helps decide which operations take precedence based on circumstances and which DCF, based on its man, train, and equip charter, is best suited for that operation. The new framework offers a 'why' behind each DCO, articulating the purpose within the context of risk and organizational objectives and justifying the use of limited DCF resources.

8.4 Evaluating

An established prioritization framework allows for the evaluation of previous, active, planned, or potential DCO. This framework helps answer the question, "Are we doing the right things?" It enables DCF leaders to assess if executed DCO missions align with organizational objectives, providing a basis for measuring performance and termination criteria. The Framework aids in evaluating resource allocation by plotting past and current DCO, ensuring a balanced approach across different types. It also provides a systematic method to assess proposed DCO, helping determine the right missions considering the capabilities of the DCF in question. This framework allows the DCF leader to match specific types of DCF to Types of DCO and corresponding systems, ensuring the appropriate resources are committed to each mission.

8.5 Organizational Planning

This framework not only serves as a reactive tool for DCF leaders to make sense of operational matters in real time but also functions proactively as a powerful planning tool. When an organization is establishing its DCF or deciding on the type of DCF to create, this framework facilitates the analysis of the organization's strategy, objectives, and existing systems. This analysis helps the DCF leader determine the specific DCF formation and capabilities to invest in, enhanced by using this framework to categorize and prioritize potential DCO.

Similarly, existing DCF can evaluate their capabilities to cover the types of DCO an organization might require based on its objectives and systems. This forecasting assessment becomes a tool to advocate for additional investment or alert organizational leaders to potential risks that the existing DCF might be unable to mitigate.

8.6 Organizational Troubleshooting and Analysis

This conceptual framework also serves as an analytic tool for assessing an organization's cyber risk mitigation efforts. Applying the Evaluation use case retroactively helps answer the question, "Are we doing things right?" By ensuring that the correct DCF aligns with DCO, confirming the execution of the right DCOs, and validating that the reasons behind each DCO align with organizational objectives, this framework identifies potential lapses or violations of best practices in DCF development or employment. Uncovering inefficiencies and deficiencies, it contributes to improving DCF employment, maturing organizational DCF capabilities, and maintaining an appropriate level of risk mitigation. The results of this analysis can be effectively communicated using this conceptual framework as a visual and conceptual aid, fostering common language and a shared mental model.

9. Conclusion

In conclusion, this article addresses a gap in the existing literature and practice by introducing a sensemaking framework for Defensive Cyberspace Operations (DCO) that serves as a shared mental model and facilitates a common language for leaders engaged with Defensive Cyber Forces (DCF). The authors recognize the limitations imposed by the requirement of developing a conceptual framework that is based on real world capabilities, but academically require staying within the confines of unclassified research. However, the authors still assert this framework's significance in providing clarity and coherence to the complex landscape of DCO.

The proposed framework, aptly described as a "Sensemaking Framework for Defensive Cyber Operations," is designed to enhance communication, categorization, prioritization, and evaluation within the realm of DCO and DCF. By aligning with existing Department of Defense (DoD) and U.S. Cyber Command (USCC) publications, this framework operationalizes these concepts in a contextually relevant manner for DCF leaders. It establishes a clear and transparent rating scale, introducing standardized labels or "Types" that serve as a shorthand for various cyber systems and their aligning DCO.

The utility of this defensive conceptual framework extends across various use cases, both reactive and proactive. DCF leaders can employ it in real-time operations to make sense of contextual matters, prioritize resource allocation, and articulate the purpose behind each DCO. Additionally, the framework serves as a robust planning tool, aiding in the creation and development of DCF, proposing DCO aligned with organizational objectives, and forecasting potential gaps in coverage.

Furthermore, this defensive framework contributes to organizational troubleshooting and analysis, allowing leaders to assess the effectiveness of cyber risk mitigation efforts retrospectively. It assists in determining whether the right actions are being taken, if DCF resources are appropriately allocated, and if the overall strategy aligns with organizational objectives. The visual and conceptual clarity provided by this framework fosters a shared understanding, improving communication, trust, and interoperability among DCF leaders and their counterparts.

While acknowledging the current limitations and the need for future research to overlay higher classified information, the authors emphasize the framework's potential to evolve and adapt. The integration of types of systems within the quad chart [FIGURE 2], alignment of DCF to DCO types, and correlation of DCO mission types with Cyber Protection Team (CPT) core functions are identified as areas for further exploration. In essence, this conceptual Sensemaking Framework for Defensive Cyber Operations presents a valuable step forward in enhancing the effectiveness and efficiency of DCO within the contemporary cyber landscape.

References

CJCS (2012) 'CJCSI 3209.01: Defense Critical Infrastructure Program'. Chairman of the Joint Chiefs of Staff. Available at: https://www.jcs.mil/Portals/36/Documents/Library/Instructions/CJCSI%203209.01.pdf?ver=2017-02-08-173222-940 (Accessed: 25 October 2023).

Computer Security Division, I.T.L. (2016) *About the RMF - NIST Risk Management Framework | CSRC | CSRC, CSRC | NIST.* Available at: https://csrc.nist.gov/projects/risk-management/about-rmf (Accessed: 18 October 2023).

Covey, S.R. and Merrill, R.R. (2008) *The SPEED of Trust: The One Thing That Changes Everything*. 1st edition. New York: FREE PRESS.

DISA (2023) *Security Technical Implementation Guides (STIGs) – DoD Cyber Exchange*. Available at: https://public.cyber.mil/stigs/ (Accessed: 25 October 2023).

DoD (2014) 'DoDI - 8510.01: Risk Management Framework (RMF) for DoD Information Technology (IT)'. U.S. Department of Defense (DoD), Chief Information Officer.

Guion, J. and Reith, M. (2017) 'Dynamic Cyber Mission Mapping', in *Industrial and Systems Engineering Conference. Proceedings of the 2017 Industrial and Systems Engineering Conference*, Wright-Patterson AFB, OH: Center for Cyberspace Research, Air Force Institute of Technology.

IEEE (2023) *IEEE Enterprise Risk Management (ERM) Program*. Available at: https://www.ieee.org/about/volunteers/risk-insurance/enterprise-risk-management.html (Accessed: 18 October 2023).

NIST (2018a) *Framework for Improving Critical Infrastructure Cybersecurity, Version 1.1*. NIST CSWP 04162018. Gaithersburg, MD: National Institute of Standards and Technology, p. NIST CSWP 04162018. Available at: https://doi.org/10.6028/NIST.CSWP.04162018.

NIST (2018b) *Risk management framework for information systems and organizations: a system life cycle approach for security and privacy*. NIST SP 800-37r2. Gaithersburg, MD: National Institute of Standards and Technology, p. NIST SP 800-37r2. Available at: https://doi.org/10.6028/NIST.SP.800-37r2.

Schrier, R. (2022) 'Demonstrating Value and Use of Language–Normalizing Cyber as a Warfighting Domain'.

Shannon, C.E. (1948) 'A mathematical theory of communication', *The Bell System Technical Journal*, 27(3), pp. 379–423. Available at: https://doi.org/10.1002/j.1538-7305.1948.tb01338.x.

Shannon, C.E. and Weaver, W. (1949) *The mathematical theory of communication*. University of Illinois Press.

United States Cyberspace Command (USCC) (2020) 'Cyber Warfare Publication 3-33.4: Cyber Protection Team Organizations, Functions, and Employment (U//FOUO)'. U.S. Cyberspace Command (USCC).

Voice, J. (2022) 'Leveraging the Ontology of the Operational Cyber Mission Stack', *Cyber Defense Review* [Preprint], (Fall 2022). Available at: https://cyberdefensereview.army.mil/Portals/6/Documents/2022_fall/07_Voice.pdf?ver=3Yffna2m-5WYvC8tuphmWA%3D%3D (Accessed: 24 October 2023).

Governance for Artificial Intelligence (AI) and Interoperability: Questions of Trust

Allison Wylde
Data Science for Common Good Research Group
Glasgow Caledonian University, London, UK

allison.wylde@gcu.ac.uk

Abstract: Although the rapidly emerging capabilities of AI bring potential benefits that could be transformative for cyber security, significant threats have emerged that continue to grow in impact and scale. One proposed solution to addressing important risks in AI is the emergence of strategies for AI governance. Yet, as this conceptual early-stage research argues, what is crucial for individuals, businesses, public institutions, including the military, and for high-risk environments, are questions concerning trust in AI governance. Will governance of AI be trusted? As an example, during 2023, several AI governance initiatives and strategies emerged, with some nation states proposing legislation while others looked to treaties and collaboration as solutions. Indeed, at a supra-national level, the United Nations expert multinational stakeholder Policy Network on AI (PNAI) formed to examine key issues in current AI governance. These include the interoperability of governance, data governance mechanisms, AI in supporting inclusion and the transition of nations. To help our understanding of trust in AI governance, the focus for this paper is limited in scope to interoperability in AI governance. Interoperability encompasses different aspects, policy initiatives (such as frameworks, legislation, or treaties), systems and their abilities to communicate and work together. The approach taken in this early-stage research is framed as questions of trust in AI governance. The paper therefore reviews the nature of different AI governance strategies developed and implemented by a range of key nation states and supra-national actors. This is followed by an evaluation of the role of trust, focused on AI governance strategies, in the context of interoperability in AI governance. Trust-building strategies are also considered, with a focus on leveraging the separate elements involved in trust-building to assist our understanding of the implementation of trusted AI governance. The contribution of this early-stage research is to highlight issues that may not be considered by the technical community and to contribute to developing a platform and a research approach that informs policy- learning for institutions, practitioners and academics.

Key words: Trust, United Nations Policy Network for AI, Interoperability, fit for Purpose, Policy Learning

1. Introduction

UN Secretary-General Antonio Guterres said at the January 2024 Davos meeting that AI had enormous potential for "sustainable development" but added that "every new iteration of generative AI increases the threat of serious unintended consequences" (Guterres, 2024). In seeking to address AI issues the UN formed a high-level group on AI governance (UN AI Advisory Body, 2023). However, a key problem is the lack of interoperability in AI governance among the multiple jurisdictions (UN PNAI, 2023).

The aim of this early-stage research is to examine how interoperability, as part of trusted AI governance, can be better understood. The approach taken leverages well-established trust research to allow a policy activity, reliant on trust, to be assessed.

This paper does not present a systematic review due to the contested nature of the central terms, AI, governance, interoperability, and trust. As scholars are not agreed on definitions for these terms (ESCAP, 2018, in PNAI, 2023, p.1: Hou, 2023) an abductive and interpretive approach was necessary. Thus, this paper contrasts with empirical work involving setting a hypothesis and following a deductive framework or through systematic searches, whether manual or based on machine learning (ESCAP, 2018, in PNAI, 2023, p.1: Hou, 2023).

This paper is structured as follows: after the introduction, the next part, Section (2), discusses AI governance with a focus on interoperability. This is followed by Section 3, where the processes involved in trust and trust building are covered. In Section 4, the methods are discussed with a focus on the rationale for the use of an abductive approach, this is followed by Section 5 where the expected findings are discussed. The final Section, (6), sets out the contribution of the paper along with promising directions for future work, limitations, and implications.

2. AI Governance: Interoperability

The key definitions for AI and governance are considered next with a view to presenting the definitions used in this paper.

2.1 AI and Governance

Although AI and governance are receiving increased and global attention, the terminology remains contested. The definitions themselves are problematic with some researchers viewing AI itself as lacking a coherent universally approved definition (ESCAP, 2018, in PNAI, 2023, p.1). Following the PNAI, the definition used in this paper views AI as the ability of machines and systems to acquire and apply knowledge to carry out intelligent behaviour (Ibid.)

AI governance has received attention, with several policy-level agencies calling for trust and trust building, for example, the UN Global Digital Compact (Wylde, 2023). Indeed, at the 2024 Davos meeting, the leaders of the EU and the UN called for trust rebuilding (Von der Leyen, 2024: Guterres, 2024). However, in contrast, some others suggest that AI regulation and standards may fail to increase trust and that governments must demonstrate how they are making industry accountable to the public and their legitimate concerns (Knowles and Richards, 2023).

Interoperability in the context of AI governance is loosely defined as the ability of systems and processes to communicate and work seamlessly together (UN, PNAI, 2023, p.13). To arrive at a definition of interoperability for the PNAI multistakeholder team, literature on interoperability and policy that was operational during the period July to October 2023 was reviewed, the definition as finally agreed is set out in Table 1 (UN, PNAI, 2023).

Table 1: Definition in AI Governance interoperability, including the factors involved (processes, activities and communications and cooperation, UN, PNAI, 2023), expanded to illustrate the primary trust referents and roles.

Definition; three interlinked factors (UN, PNAI, 2023)	Factors involved	Primary trust-referent (trust-level); and key role for trust
Processes	Tools, measures, and mechanisms	Policy-level trust; trust in policy
Activities	Multi-stakeholders and their interconnections	Organization, institution, and individual-level trust; trust in partners
Communications and cooperation	Agreed ways (Multi-stakeholders and their interconnections)	Organization, institution, and individual-level trust; trust in communication and cooperation

Three key interlinked factors were identified as being important in specifying a definition for interoperability in AI governance (UN, PNAI, 2023). Table 1 summarises the definition of interoperability, agreed as follows, interlinked factors, including: (i) processes, comprising tools, measures, and mechanisms (ii) activities undertaken by multi-stakeholders and their interconnections and (iii) agreed ways to communicate and cooperate (UN, PNAI, 2023, p. 13).

3. Trust

What follows is not a systematic review. For the purposes of this paper, which is focused on questions of AI governance, prominent trust theory, from organization and management literature, the integrative trust model (ITM) (Mayer et al., 1995), is leveraged. This approach provides a conceptual framework through which issues of interoperability can be understood. As Table 1 illustrates, each of the three factors involved in interoperability are viewed as founded on trust, even though trust and the primary trust referent are not specified.

Trust is a well-researched construct with studies across multiple disciplines. Due to the sheer volume of research on trust, this paper is limited to the view of trust as a relational and subjective phenomenon (Mayer et al., 1995: Rousseau et al, 1998). Indeed, as Mayer et al. (1995) find, the referents of trust are often not specified. Thus, evaluation of relational-trust is well-suited to the application of theory drawn from management and organization studies (Hou, 2023).

In this perspective, relational trust is seen as an individual taking a decision to trust, based on antecedents, an assessment of trust and trust-building (Mayer et al., 1995). At the level of inter-person trust formation, a trustor is viewed as holding positive expectations that a trustee will perform an action valuable to the trustee, irrespective of control (Mayer et al., 1995). The assessment of the trustee is conducted on the characteristics of ability, benevolence and integrity moderated by the trustor's propensity to trust. In the final stage, the trustor accepts vulnerability and takes a risk in placing trust in the trustee (Rousseau et al., 1998).

Trust occurs across different levels, from inter-person trust to trust in teams, trust in organizations and trust in institutions (Fulmer and Gelfand, 2012). Trust also occurs beyond trustor to trustee relations as trust in technology (McKnight, 2011) or trusted AI (Wylde, 2022a) and trust in robots (Hou, 2023). Researchers have also specified a role for trust in institutional policies, even though a trustee may have little experience an institution, for example, a government (Möllering, 2013). Institutional level trust has been shown to be supported by processes such as tax or legal systems and the trusted individuals involved in these processes (Vanneste, 2016) that serve to reduce vulnerability and uncertainty (Rousseau et al., 1998: Möllering, 2023).

The definition of trust for this work involves antecedents; that a trustor possesses positive expectations, then a process of trust assessment, based on ability, benevolence and integrity followed by outputs involving trust-building (Mayer et al., 1995). It is important to note that this definition includes an acceptance of vulnerability as part of trusting (Rousseau et al., 1998). As a final comment, the process of trusting is moderated by the trustor's individual propensity to trust (Mayer et al., 1995).

Building on this definition, a conceptual framework is proposed that can examine trust as a construct in processes such as interoperability, involving trust among a range of interacting actors, policy, and processes (Oomsells and Boukaer, 2014) set out in Table 1. This framework is next applied to separate out the complex processes involved in examining trust in a process such as interoperability.

Research into trust in AI globally has identified 61% of people reporting not trusting AI and 71% expecting AI to be regulated, but only 33% lacking confidence in governments and businesses to develop, use and regulate AI (Gillespie et al., 2023). However, why this may be the case has not been explored in depth (Knowles and Richards, 2023). Further research has identified that stakeholders are contacted differently: those most familiar with technology are more likely to be assessed sooner and they are found to be the most comfortable with AI, while conversely, disadvantaged and vulnerable groups are less likely to be contacted and more likely to be the least comfortable with the technology (Knowles and Richards, 2023).

Trust in AI is considered as layered, with trust involved in several domains: data, the technology and platforms, the supervisors and the users, developers and the organizations that deploy the AI, the regulators and an important consideration is the domain of the application (Knowles and Richards, 2023).

Summing up, as clear gaps for qualitative research into the who, why and what of trust in AI have been identified, the call for further research is picked up in this paper.

4. Research Method, Analysis and Preliminary Findings

A research approach involving interpretation was followed to allow the interlinked concepts to be teased-out (Hou, 2023). The research approach is discussed followed by a summary of the first preliminary findings.

4.1 Analysis

The rationale for this approach is due to the nature of the research question and the study material. Following well-established conceptual practices, the study adopted an abductive approach. For this type of study, which relies on interpretation and making meaning, a deductive and central tendency approach is not appropriate due to the lack of agreement among scholars on issues such as definitions. In consequence, research approaches involving hypothesis testing or a machine learning driven systematic searches are not readily supported (Hou, 2023). In addition, as this is early-stage research, the scope of is limited to the UN PNAI and High-level AI (PNAI, 2023: UN AI Advisory Body, 2023).

Prominent management researchers and editors recommend approaching problems of meaning using through theory building or extension by abductive approaches since "we don't know what we think until we know what we write" (Forster 1927, in Byron and Thatcher, 2016). Following an iterative abductive process, the study progressed as follows. First the author developed a foundational idea to tackle the question of creating understanding in the issue of AI governance, in particular, that of interoperability (Sætre and Van De Ven, 2021). The central idea in this paper is that interoperability in governance can be framed as questions of trust (Mayer et al., 1995). This idea is justified through recognizing the ability of the trust literature, in particular, the integrative trust model (Mayer et al., 1995) in offering a model through which a phenomenon such as governance (policy) could be examined (Sætre and Van De Ven, 2021). Abduction is suited to questions concerning understanding our world (King and Kay, 2020) as it "becomes more dynamic, interconnected and uncertain" (Sætre and Van De Ven, 2021, p.684),

Next considered are the processes involved in interrogating the theory. The author followed Byron and Thatcher (2016); visual representation, tables, charts, and notes were created to help tease out the key elements involved in building the theoretical framework and examining the important elements and processes. The social processes then included informal presentations of draft work for feedback followed by discussions with colleagues and iterative development of the work. Some avenues that appeared promising at the start of the process were followed further others were altered to refocus on the salient research questions. In this way success and failure in research were considered and integrated into the research process (Sætre and Van De Ven, 2021). The overarching aim as central to abductive research was to create plausible and meaningful material that could form findings (Sætre and Van De Ven, 2021).

4.2 Analysis and Materials

The rationale for the selection of the analysis approach and selection of study materials is based on the limited scope of this early-stage research. Although methods for trust research includes a comprehensive range of approaches for trust studies, including trust scales (Gillespie, 2011). As this early-stage research study is restricted to evaluation involving the assessment part of the ITM model (Mayer et al., 1995). Again, it is acknowledged that the scope of the sample analysed does not reflect the entire landscape, and it is acknowledged that some regions disproportionally contribute to the development of policy (PNAI, 2023). As outlined in the scope, for this early-stage work, the review is limited to the UN documents produced by the UN PNAI and the UN AI expert group (PNAI, 2023: UN AI Advisory Body, 2023).

4.3 Preliminary Findings

Key themes emerging from the study thus concern the institutional stakeholders involved, the actions to be undertaken (norms, rules, standards) and processes and mechanisms to be implemented. In terms of trust, the issues concern consistency in the terms, for building or promoting trust or in addressing declining trust.

Table 2: Preliminary findings: examples of the research material, key themes, trust level and referents (UN AI Advisory Body, 2023).

Examples from research material (UN AI Advisory Body, 2023).	**Key themes**	**Trust level/ referents**
The UN Advisory Body is uniquely placed to help through "turning a patchwork of evolving initiatives into **a coherent interoperable whole, grounded in universal values** agreed by its member states, adaptable across contexts" (p. 6).	The need for international cooperation to tackle AI governance	Trust in a regulator (the UN)
Recognising; no alignment either in terms of interoperability between jurisdictions or in incentives for compliance. With policy ranging from binding rules to nudges that are non-binding (p.13/14).	Lack of policy alignment among different jurisdictions	Trust in a regulator (the UN), trust in policy
A simplified schema is presented for considering the emerging AI landscape, which the Advisory Body say they will develop further (p. 13).	Need for terminology	Trust in a regulator (the UN), trust in policy
Awareness amongst existing states and the private sector, call for new organization structure to be entrusted (p. 16).	Need to create a new organization	Trust in a regulator (the UN), trust in policy
Grounding in norms Actions to reinforce interoperability include grounding in international norms in a universal setting (p.18).	Agreed policy type (norms)	Trust in a regulator (the UN), trust in policy
Fora could include the UN organizations and For a such as UNESCO and ITU to reinforce interoperability; global membership the UN can bring states together, develop common socio-technical standards, ensure legal and technical	Driver organizations	Trust in a regulator (the UN), trust in policy

Examples from research material (UN AI Advisory Body, 2023).	**Key themes**	**Trust level/ referents**
interoperability; balance technical interoperability with norms (19).		
Actions involving "Surfacing best practices for **norms and rules**, including, for risk mitigation and economic growth. Align, leverage, and include, soft and hard law, standards, methods, and frameworks developed at the regional, national, and industry level to support interoperability" (p.23 12-24months).	Agreed policy type (norms)	Trust in a regulator (the UN), trust in policy
Ensure interoperable action at all levels – **across all institutions, frameworks** (national and regional) and the private sector (p.24).	Agreed policy type	Trust in a regulator (the UN), trust in policy
The UN will **pursue research** on risk assessment methodologies and governance interoperability (p.25).	Need for research	Trust in policy

Further detailed examination of the research material will be undertaken to identify themes as they may align with trust (or not) and consider the interconnections across themes. The aim is to create findings that help highlight important directions that can help policy makers as they develop AI governance policy.

5. Conclusions

The contributions of this early-stage paper are twofold. Firstly, the gap in our understanding of AI governance from the perspective of a lack of interoperability is addressed through identifying the need for institutions to demonstrate they hold the private sector accountable and that they acknowledge their stakeholder's concerns, focused on vulnerable stakeholders (Von der Leyen, 2024). Secondly, a method has been proposed to handle the contested nature of the central terms and the lack of consistency. The framework is based on an interpretive abductive approach applied to build understanding and leverage trust theory to understand operationalizing trust viewed as helping to achieve interoperability in AI governance.

As with all research, limitations are present. In the trust theory presented, trust is viewed as a linear input-output process, starting from antecedents to the assessment of trust, and finally to trust-building (Wylde, 2022b). As such a simplistic process fails to account for the dynamic and simultaneous nature of trust encounters (Dietz, 2011). This limitation could be taken up in future research that could unravel the nature of the interlinked-processes and sequences involved in trust decision-making. Future research could use machine learning to review text calibrated through multiple perspective or management and organization studies trust theory, helping to refine the constructs. Additional attention could focus on terms such as trust building and addressing trust deficits (Von der Leyen, 2024).

It is hoped that this early-stage work provides a foundation that can be built upon to help policy makers as they grapple with the complexities involved understanding and achieving trusted AI governance, in particular, issues of interoperability. As ever, a call goes out for further research on trust and interoperability in this increasingly important and contested domain of AI governance.

References

Byron, K. and Thatcher, S.M. (2016) Editors' comments: "What I know now that I wish I knew then"—Teaching theory and theory building, Academy of Management Review, 41(1), pp.1-8.

Dietz, G. (2011) "Going back to the source: Why do people trust each other?" Journal of Trust Research, 1 (2): 215-222.

ESCAP, UN. (2018) "Enhancing cybersecurity for industry 4.0 in Asia and the Pacific", [online]. https://repository.unescap.org/handle/20.500.12870/238 [Accessed, 24. Jan. 2024].

Forster, E.M. (1927) Aspects of the Novel. Harcourt, Brace.

Gillespie, N. (2011) "Measuring trust in organizational contexts: an overview of survey-based measures", Handbook of research methods on trust, p.175.

Gillespie, N., Lockey, S., Curtis, C., Pool, J. and Akbari, A. (2023) "Trust in Artificial Intelligence: A global study", The University of Queensland and KPMG Australia, doi: 10.14264/00d3c94

Guterres, A. (2024) At Davos forum, Secretary-General warns of global norms collapsing, highlights the need to rebuild trust reform governance, [online]. https://press.un.org/en/2024/sgsm22109.doc.htm [Accessed, 24. Jan. 2024].

Hou, M. (2023) "Challenges in Understanding Trust and Trust Modelling : Quenching the Thirst for AI Trust Management", In Transactions on Computational Science, XL, pp. 1-5. Berlin, Heidelberg: Springer Berlin Heidelberg.

Knowles and Richards. (2023) "Trusted AI", Association for Computing Machinery (ACM), Technology Policy Council, TechBriefs, [online]. https://dl.acm.org/doi/pdf/10.1145/3641524 [Accessed, 24. Jan. 2024].

Lewicki, R.J., McAllister, D.J. and Bies, R.J. (1998) "Trust and distrust: New relationships and realities", Academy of Management Review, 23(3), pp.438-458.

Mayer, R., Davis, J. and Schoorman, F. (1995) "An integrative model of organizational trust", Academy of Management Review, 20(3), pp. 709-734.

McKnight, D.H., Carter, M., Thatcher, J.B. and Clay, P. (2011) "Trust in a specific technology: an investigation of its components and measures", ACM Transactions on management information systems, 2(2), pp. 1-25.

Möllering, G. (2013) "Trust without knowledge?" Comment on Hardin, 'Government without trust', Journal of Trust Research, 1(1), pp. 53-58.

Oomsels, P. and Bouckaert, G. (2014) "Studying interorganizational trust in public administration: A conceptual and analytical framework for" administrational trust", Public Performance and Management Review, 37(4), pp. 577-604.

Rousseau, D.M., Sitkin, S.B., Curt, R.S. and Camerer, C. (1998) "Not so different at all: a cross discipline view of trust", Academy of Management Review, 23(3), pp. 393-404.

Sætre, A.S. and Van de Ven, A. (2021) "Generating theory by abduction", Academy of Management Review, 46(4), pp.684-701.

UN AI Advisory Body. (2023) "Governing AI for Humanity", Interim Report. Dec. 2023, [online]. https://www.un.org/sites/un2.un.org/files/ai_advisory_body_interim_report.pdf [Accessed, 24. Jan. 2024].

UN Policy Network on Artificial Intelligence (PNAI). (2023) "Strengthening multistakeholder approach to global AI governance, protecting the environment and human rights in the era of generative AI", in Sipinen, M. (Ed.) United Nations Internet Governance Forum, [online]. https://intgovforum.org/en/content/pnai-work-plan [Accessed, 24. Jan. 2024].

Von der Leyen, U. (2023) "Special address by President von der Leyen at the World Economic Forum", 16. Jan. 2024, [online]. https://ec.europa.eu/commission/presscorner/detail/en/speech_24_221 [Accessed, 24. Jan. 2024].

Vanneste, B.S. (2016) "From interpersonal to interorganizational trust: the role of reciprocity", Journal of Trust Research, 6(1), pp. 7-36.

Wylde, A. (2022a) "Cyber Security Norms: Trust and Cooperation", Conference paper. ECCWS 2022.

Wylde, A. (2022b) "Questions of trust in norms of zero trust", In Intelligent Computing, Proceedings of the 2022 Computing Conference, 3, pp. 837-846. Cham: Springer International Publishing.

Enhancing Training and Technology Adoption in Terrorism Financing Investigations Through Gamification

Francesco Zola[1], Lander Segurola[1], Erin King[2], Martin Mullins[2] and Raul Orduna[1]
[1] Vicomtech Foundation, Basque Research and Technology Alliance (BRTA); Donostia; Spain
[2] University of Limerick; Castletroy; Ireland

fzola@vicomtech.org
lsegurola@vicomtech.org
erin.king@ul.ie
martin.mullins@ul.ie
rorduna@vicomtech.org

Abstract: The purpose of this publication is to present the methodology followed in the European project Anti-FinTer for training Law Enforcement Agencies (LEAs) and Financial Investigation Units (FIUs) in using emergent technologies to reveal financing activities of terrorism. The study presents, compares, and discusses the results gathered from three Capture-the-Flag events which involved LEAs and FIU officers. Designing curricula and training programs for improving terrorist financing investigations is challenging due to this domain's intricate and rapidly evolving nature and the multi-disciplinary knowledge needed. Furthermore, new tools based on novel paradigms, such as Artificial Intelligence and Big Data, are involved in terrorist financing investigations. However, they are too often unnecessarily complex and hard to use. These characteristics often limit law enforcement and end-users' engagement level and expertise in these technologies. For this reason, in this work, we describe an approach using gamification techniques to enhance technology and knowledge transfer for terrorist financing investigations. In fact, designing and implementing realistic and interactive challenges makes it possible to speed up the learning process, increase officers' expertise in using new technologies and improve their readiness. At the same time, this approach allows technical partners to gather end-user needs and facilitate development/validation cycles. This methodology has been validated in three pilots: one held in Madrid in 2022, a second in The Hague in 2023 and a final one in Vienna in 2023. In these pilots, law enforcement personnel were challenged in addressing tasks related to fighting financing terrorism activities through the dark Dark Web, crypto-assets or new payment systems. Results showed an increasing engagement, motivation, and knowledge in the participants.

Keywords: Gamifying, Hackathon, Counterterrorism, Law Enforcement Agencies, Cryptocurrencies, Training

1. Introduction

Tackling terrorist financing through investigation, prosecution, and prevention is a worldwide issue that extends beyond Europe. Every day, terrorists find new channels to communicate, campaign and finance their activities. For example, as reported by EUROPOL in the IOCTA report (Europol, 2021), the two main trends are crowdfunding campaigns and generating market revenue. In the first case, their *modus operandi* is straightforward: they raise a crowdfunding campaign to gather funds for their activities. In the second case, they try to generate revenue by selling extremist versions of common products or merchandise (such as Nazi-related items, ISIS promotional materials, etc.), as well as other legal and illegal goods (like counterfeit products, firearms, explosives, everyday items, etc.) to the public or other extremists/terrorists. In both cases, to maintain anonymity, they often employ a combination of cryptocurrencies and markets in darknet technologies (Europol, 2022).

To tackle these needs and combat cybercrime, new paradigms, such as Artificial Intelligence (AI) and Big Data, are being used alongside conventional software to create novel investigation tools (Maher, 2017). However, these tools typically include multiple steps for collecting, processing, analysing and visualising information related to financial data (e.g., transactions, electronic invoices, etc.) and correlating them with context data extracted from social media analysis, forums, phishing acts, etc. (Kilger & Choo, 2022). As a result, Law Enforcement Officers (LEOs) and other end-users may be deterred from using these technologies (Klingberg, 2022).

Designing curricula and training programs for improving terrorist financing investigations is challenging due to its intricate and rapidly evolving nature and also the different number of domains (and so tools) involved, from crypto finance to financial regulation, dark web structure, crypto ecosystem, etc. In that sense, a more practical approach can be a good solution to speed up the learning process and increase the readiness of the officers.

For this reason, in this paper, we present the deployment proposed in the Anti-FinTer (AFT) project (Anti-FinTer, 2022), in which traditional teaching techniques like lectures with moderated virtual learning environment (VLE), workshops and exercises are combined with gamification techniques (hackathons) for facilitating interaction and engagement between participants. The aim of the AFT project is to train Law Enforcement Agencies (LEAs) and Financial Investigation Units (FIUs) to enhance their ability to use emergent technologies and complex data pipelines to reveal financing activities of terrorism. In this way, it will be possible to increase Europe's ability to use novel tools for investigating terrorist financing and promote EU technical and strategical sovereignty. The AFT project exploits four tools that have been developed in previous EU projects, such as Graphsense (Haslhofer, et al., 2021) for virtual assets analytics, the Visual Analytics tool for forensic image processing, Ordainsare as a transaction anomaly detector based on the model presented in (Zola, et al., 2019) and the Dark Web Monitor (CFLW, 2023) for analysing the darknet content.

Although the AFT project applies different teaching, learning, and training techniques, in this paper, our analysis is concentrated only on the latter. In particular, hackathon events are organized as training elements. These events are designed as Capture-the-Flag (CtF) exercises (Boopathi, 2015) that allow participants to learn effectively how to use new AI tools in their day-to-day work for revealing terrorist financing activities.

In this study, we present the general results obtained in three hackathon events, the first held in Madrid in Sept. 2022, the second held in The Hague in May 2023, and the third – and last - held in Vienna in Dec. 2023. The analysis performed after each event was used to identify limitations and organisational weaknesses that were addressed in preparation for the next hackathon event, allowing us to make improvements and provide a more professional service. The final results indicate satisfactory engagement among the participants; indeed, attendees achieved complete autonomy in using the AFT tools for realistic operations.

2. Preliminaries

2.1 End-user Profile

Participants are, in general, experienced practitioners in professions/industries that are exposed to terrorism financing, such as agents of LEAs or FIUs, and all arrive with a preconceived concept of the topic. In line with the expected learning outcomes of the project, we incorporate a central objective of understanding foundational and prevailing knowledge associated with terrorism financing and adjacent issues while providing participants with the autonomy to engage with learning materials they feel best suit their needs. The andragogical response to the training structure leverages the learning opportunities provided by these activities while also appreciating the diverse skill sets that the project participants possess (Harkin, 2022). In this sense, the main objectives of the gamification structure can be summarised as follows:

- Appreciate the requirements of the adult participants;
- Provide alternative routes of learning within the materials;
- Generate a learning environment rooted in experiential learning;
- Provide knowledge that can be perceived as immediately applicable or useful;
- Create a learning environment that can leverage the insights of training participants.

2.2 Gamification

Gamification techniques often make tasks or processes more engaging and enjoyable, encouraging participation, learning, or specific behaviours. In fact, leveraging the psychological and motivational aspects of games aims to increase user involvement, motivation, and achievement of goals. One of the strategies mainly used in information security contests is called Capture-the-Flag (CtF). CtFs are competitions where participants are called to address tasks and challenges to conquer flags. These flags can represent text, images, snippets of code, or a set of actions. Participants can work separately or in teams. In both cases, they are pitted against each other, testing their security skill.

At a high level, there are many types of cybersecurity competitions and platforms for managing them. In this sense, defining a finite set of CtF strategies is also difficult. Several studies (ENISA, 2021), (Švábenský, et al., 2021) define two main CtF strategies: *Attack/Defend* and *Jeopardy-style*.

Attack/Defend is a type of format that involves an interactive competition game that requires at least two participants (Švábenský, et al., 2021) divided into two teams: the attacker team (red) and the defender team (blue). The red task is to detect and exploit blues' vulnerabilities to conquer the flag. On the other hand, the blue team must resist and mitigate the reds' attacks by applying countermeasures. In this scenario, when the clock runs out, the end can result in getting the flag (red wins) or retaining the flag (blue wins). *Jeopardy-style* is a format based on a challenge-based competition like the actual Jeopardy game with different categories and point values. The game consists of earning as many points as possible before the clock runs out. More than two users can be involved, and each starts by choosing a challenge from the board. When they find the solution to the chosen challenge (find the required flag), they submit it to the scoring system for evaluation. If the flag is correct, the team's score is updated, and the system allows the team to move on to the next challenge on the board.

The lack of attack/defend team specialization, the presence of multiple users, and especially the structured learning goals of the AFT project led us to choose the *Jeopardy-style* format to create a competitive environment and engage multiple users simultaneously.

2.3 Related Works

The CtF strategy has resulted in wide success in terms of introducing and learning cybersecurity-related concepts (Švábenský, et al., 2021), but also motivating continued learning after the exercise (McDaniel, et al., 2016). For example, in (Huang, et al., 2011), CtF is used for solving as a differential game, whereas in (Eagle & Clark, 2004), this strategy is used to educate students to act as *crackers* and find new vulnerabilities in existing systems (data, files, devices, etc.). In (Werther et al., 2011), a CtF event based on a web server and application security is presented. In (Prinetto et al., 2020), authors propose a formal definition and a taxonomy for hardware-based CtF challenges. Although widely utilised in cybersecurity, there are only a limited number of scientific contributions available regarding the application of CtF to training LEAs. More specifically, the most used training strategies are based on teaching theoretical concepts and demonstrating the tools themselves without leaving the user to really use them in realistic operation. This happens in different EU projects such as (i-LEAD, 2017) project, where specific training sessions are organised to disseminate project technologies for tackling cybercrime and performing forensics investigations, or in (CYCLOPES, 2021), where events for training participants on specific Digital Forensics tools are organised. However, these events are planned like panels where LEA personnel and other stakeholders present their experiences and share their analysis and views on specific cybercrime topics without performing a real and practical task. Similarly, Joint Live Exercises are explored in (CTC, 2023) project to provide theoretical and practical knowledge about counter-terrorism financing and emerging terrorism financing risks. They are essentially showrooms for demonstrating the utility of the project platform. In the (DANTE, 2018) project, similarly structured training activities are organised to enhance knowledge on detecting and analysing terrorist-related content and financing activities. In this case, during the event, participants had the chance to use a demo version of the deployed tools, however, with limited data and without a defined scope. It is in the (ASGARD, 2016) project where training strategies based on CtF exercises are effectively exploited to speed up the LEAs training. However, the project aims to train the participants in using easily configurable and deployable tools, and for this reason, specific tasks are implemented, lacking their concrete application in real investigation.

Inspired by these previous works, we propose to use gamification strategies for training LEAs and FIU officers to use novel AI tools for terrorist financing investigations. More specifically, we propose a hands-on approach, which directly allows participants to use the AFT tools, leveraging the full spectrum of data they have available until the date of the events. Our methodology entails crafting challenges created from real-world use cases that help participants not only delve into tool functionalities but also uncover the tangible benefits they offer for their daily tasks. This immersive approach ensures that participants not only grasp the tools' capabilities but also develop the autonomy to utilise them effectively on their own.

3. Hackathon

3.1 Learning Requirements

Terrorism Financing and its associated issues are complex and ever-evolving topics that require intricate insight and knowledge across a broad range of subjects. These include political science, as it pertains to terrorist organisations; financial services and regulation around the use of cryptocurrency and fiat (real) money; technical knowledge on dark-web surveillance; policing; and financial/digital forensics. In particular, the focus of AFT is restricted to the dark web and crypto assets as facilitators of licit and illicit activities traceable to terrorist groups.

With these restrictions, it is important to leverage the prior knowledge and the subject area of interest expressed by the hackathon participants since each one has a diverse background and unique perspectives and needs. So, in that sense, the training must consider this fragmented scenario and design accessible and easy-to-solve tasks that allow for homogenizing participants' theoretical and practical knowledge. Once this aim is achieved, introducing case study examples of terrorism financing issues can lead to practical, ready-to-apply knowledge. In fact, they are particularly effective in enhancing learning outcomes when real-world problems remain unresolved and ill-structured (Barrows, 2022). For this reason, the training approach introduced in the AFT project proposes using three strategies in the challenge definition: *tool-centric*, *category-oriented*, and *tool-free* (more information about them in Section 3.3).

3.2 Gamification Strategy

In the AFT project, CtF competitions based on a *Jeopardy-style* format serve as a dynamic and engaging gamification strategy. By adopting this approach, we aim to create an environment that fosters active participation and skill development among participants. All the challenges are aligned for discovering financing terrorism activities, which can include money laundering and fraud operations through the dark Dark Web, using crypto-assets or new payment systems and darknet marketplaces. More specifically, each challenge within the CtF competition is meticulously designed by the tool owners to assess and enhance participants' proficiency in utilizing their tools and, at the same time, to validate the functionality of these tools in real-world scenarios, demonstrating their efficacy in uncovering crucial hints and traces relevant to terrorism financing investigations. By highlighting the tangible benefits of these tools, they aim to inspire confidence and enthusiasm among participants, motivating them to further explore and utilize these innovative solutions in their professional endeavours.

On the other hand, a point-based system is employed to add an element of competition and motivation. In this sense, each challenge is assigned a score based on its complexity and difficulty level. Participants earn points for successfully completing tasks, with higher scores awarded for more challenging actions. Throughout the competition, participants accumulate points, and the individual with the highest score at the end is declared the winner. This point-based system not only incentivizes active participation but also fosters a sense of competitiveness among participants. Furthermore, to maintain competitiveness and better evaluate the engagement level of the participants, an individual-focused approach is used, with each team composed of just one participant.

A CtF managing platform called Facebook Capture-the-Flag (FBCtF) is employed to host the challenges. This platform allows users to define challenges on different levels, i.e., *Quiz, Flag* and *Basis*, according to the chosen strategy. In particular, for the Jeopardy-style used in AFT events, Flag level is used. This kind of challenge allows administrators to define a title, descriptions, category for the task, attachments (if applicable), the expected correct answer, the number of points obtained, a hint to avoid stuck users and a penalty for when the hint is used. Furthermore, the platform provides a management control where administrators can easily add new users to the platform, monitor their score and intent (game logs), and set other configurations.

3.3 Hackathon Format

As already introduced in Section 3.1, all along the AFT project, three different strategies are drawn and deployed to create hackathon challenges and to guide the users through the tools. More specifically, we started the project with a more structured and guided approach (Madrid), then proceeded to lessen constraints and limitations about the tools (The Hague) to finally enable participants to attain full independence in choosing the appropriate tools for the right tasks (Vienna). This dynamic methodology represents the primary innovation distinguishing AFT hackathons from other events. Indeed, this adaptive strategy enables alignment with the end user's evolving needs and progress, creating a continuously fresh and challenging environment. Furthermore, gradually releasing constraints helps the end user become proficient in using the tools for their day-to-day duties.

As shown in Figure 1, all three hackathon events shared the first *Introduction session* (30 minutes), in which organisers started with a welcome to the participants and explained to them the AFT goals and how the CtF works. However, to improve the learning process, each hackathon event follows a different strategy in the challenge definition, so they diverge from the rest of the agenda. Indeed, the Madrid event (2022) followed a *tool-centric* strategy, The Hague event (2023) was based on a *category-oriented* strategy, while the Vienna event (2023) used a *tool-free* approach. The change in the strategy influenced the number of planned sessions and the overall duration of the events.

The *tool-centric (first hackathon)* strategy implemented specific sessions (numbers 2, 3, and 4 in Figure 1) for testing each AFT tool separately. In these sessions, *easy* challenges related to the designated tools were provided, aiming to assist users in becoming familiar with the tools, learning about basic functionalities, and evaluating tool usability. These tasks were self-explanatory to guide participants and prevent them from encountering obstacles. Thus, they needed to provide enough context for the investigation, be clear about the action to be performed and indicate the exact pattern to follow for writing the answer, avoiding grammatical errors. An example is shown as entry A in Table 1. In the fifth session of the first hackathon, participants were tested in more complex challenges that required deep domain knowledge as well as advanced expertise in utilising the AFT tools, as shown by entries B and C in Table 1. Each session lasted about 60 minutes, except for session number 3, where two tools were tested at the same time. A total number of 55 challenges were implemented in this hackathon.

The *category-oriented (second hackathon)* strategy planned an initial session (number 2 in Figure 1) to aid both new and returning participants to familiarise themselves with the tools and gain basic insights into their functionalities, as well as happened in sessions numbers 2, 3, and 4 of the Madrid events. Thereby, tasks were similar to entries A in Table 1. However, in this case, although the challenges contain the names of the tools to be used, they were not split within specific sessions but just put all together to speed up the learning process. Then, in session number 3 (Figure 1), the challenges were designed to tackle a real-world use case (UC) involving terrorism financing through a specific darknet market called *Luckp47*. This market is a niche market accessible using the Tor network, and it is claimed to belong to a paramilitary organisation (Jiang et al., 2021). In this darknet market, it is possible to buy different firearms, such as handguns, rifles, kalashnikov but also explosives, fake-ID and many other illicit goods using Bitcoin. Examples of tasks related to this UC is the entry D in Table 1. Again, the tool to be used was indicated in the title of each challenge. The tools were used separately, but each of them empowered users to accumulate evidence, facilitating their progress and comprehension through real investigation. The challenge-oriented ended with session number 4 (Figure 1), in which participants were asked to use the acquired knowledge to address more complex scenarios, which could also involve the usage of more than one tool at once (similar to entries B and C in Table 1). In this session, the idea was to show the benefits and limitations of the tools in scenarios not covered by previous sessions. On this occasion, each session required considerably more time to complete, and as a consequence of this approach, the second event extended beyond 5 hours (330 minutes). A total number of 78 challenges were available in this hackathon.

First Hackathon			Second Hackathon			Third Hackathon		
#	Topic	Duration	#	Topic	Duration	#	Topic	Duration
1	Introduction	30'	1	Introduction	30'	1	Introduction	30'
2	Dark Web Monitor	60'	2	Easy Challenges	90'	2	Easy Challenges	60'
3	Visual Analytics and Ordainsare	90'	3	Luckp47 UC	120'	3	Luckp47 UC	60'
4	GraphSense	60'	4	Hard Challenges	90'	4	Multiple UCs	60'
5	Medium/Hard Challenges	60'	5	Award Ceremony	-	5	Mobile Challenges	60'
6	Award Ceremony	-	-	-	-	6	Award Ceremony	-
	Total	300'		Total	330'		Total	270'

Figure 1: Agenda first, second and third hackathon events.

Table 1: Examples of challenges for each category of Madrid, The Hague, and Vienna events.

Id	Tool	Category	Description/Context	Task
A	Visual Analytics	Easy	While browsing the existing dataset, you encounter an image depicting a gun over an orange background (see attachment).	**What is the prediction accuracy of the Top Concept (e.g. Glock)?**
B	GraphSense	Hard	Look at the US DoJ Statement of Facts in the Bitfinex arrest: https://www.justice.gov/opa/pressrelease/file/1470186/download.	**Based on the diagram on page 11, use GraphSense to determine the identity (the label/tag) of VCE4.**
C	Ordainsare	Hard	The attached file contains several addresses labelled as AlQueda activities.	**How many addresses are in the .csv? How many of them are correctly classified by Ordainsare? Among the classified, which is the most predominant LAST behaviour?**

Id	Tool	Category	Description/Context	Task
D	GraphSense	Luckp47 UC	Besides finding out who controls the funds, we may also be interested in learning more about the people who fund Luckp47.	**How many transactions were done directly from coinbase.com to the cluster containing the address "329NN882qvm69….LcXsh"?**
E	-	Multiple UCs	You have come across the Guns"R"Us webshop.	**Which exchange did the seller use to cash out?**
F	-	Multiple UCs	The BOAK has been known for attacking Russian military commissariats and telecommunication since 2022. Gathering information about this group, 2 Bitcoin addresses can be found.	**The first usage for one of the addresses (a1) was on 15/06/2020 at 01:52:02, and for the second one (a2) was on 29/09/2021 at 04:44:24. Which is the total amount that a1 has received? And a2?**
G	-	Mobile	Following some criminal investigations in the dark web, several suspicious addresses encoded in QR format are found.	**Which behaviour showed the address in its third appearance, and what classification score did it get?**

In the third hackathon, a *free-tool* strategy was implemented in order to remove constraints during the learning process. However, the first sessions, i.e., numbers 2 and 3 (Figure 1), were practically the same as sessions 2 and 3 of The Hague event, but with a reduced duration. In fact, these two sessions were used to assist participants in refreshing their tool knowledge and acquiring fundamental domain understanding. In session 4, new realistic challenges were implemented based on Guns'R'us and Arms Complex, two shops that allow the use of cryptos for buying weapons (similar to *Luckp47*). Users were asked to analyse the transactions of the addresses related to these two shops. At the same time, tasks related to "*Combat Organization of Anarcho-Communists*" (or *BOAK*) UC were implemented. *BOAK* is a militant anarcho-communist organization in Eastern Europe (Alexey Rozhkov, 2023), which often asks for donations for their purposes (CrimethInc., 2022). They accept Bitcoin donations, and several addresses are directly linked to known Exchanges. Nevertheless, following the free-tool strategy in the new task definitions, there was no indication of the tools to be used for completing the investigation, as shown by entries E and F in Table 1. The same approach was followed for creating the challenges of session 5, in which tasks were designed to show the tools' responsiveness and ability to adapt themselves to tablets and smartphones. These challenges required the usage of the device camera for taking pictures, converting images to text, scanning QR codes, etc, as shown by the entry G in Table 1. On this occasion, following user feedback gathered in the previous events, the overall duration of the hackathon was reduced to 270 minutes, and each session lasted 60 minutes. An overall number of 113 challenges were available in this hackathon.

3.4 Evaluation Metrics

Two evaluation frameworks are used for collecting feedback from the hackathon participants, one based on the common state-of-the-art *(a) learning schemes* and the other based on *(b) objective metrics*. In the *(a)* case, a survey with 35 questions is designed. This questionnaire is created following two distinct learning schemes: the System Usability Scale (SUS) (Peres, et al., 2013) and the Kirkpatric Model (Smidt, et al., 2009). The SUS is composed of 10 standardised questions used to assess the usability of a wide range of systems. These questions are rated on a five-point scale ranging from *Strongly Disagree* (1) to *Strongly Agree* (5). The questions cover a variety of factors that contribute to the overall usability, such as ease of use, efficiency, learnability, and satisfaction. On the other hand, the survey is improved with 25 (five-point Likert scale and open) questions based on the Kirkpatric model. This model comprises four criteria levels: Reaction, Learning, Behaviour, and Results (Smidt, et al., 2009). In the *(b)* case, regarding objective metrics, data and logs are directly extracted from the FBCtF platform and analysed in order to evaluate the trends and statistics of each participant as well as their engagement level. This analysis gives us an overview of the difficulties and problems encountered by each participant, and, at the same time, it helps us to determine the engagement level at each step. Yet, the results allow us to fill the gap between the perception of trainees about their learning process and their actual performance. For the sake of simplicity and also for the relevance of this work, just the results gathered from the objective metrics are reported and discussed in the next section. In fact, the survey results do not directly influence the presentation of the methodology's strengths and weaknesses.

4. Validation

4.1 Results

In the Madrid event, 16 participants attended the hackathon, 15 were in The Hague event, and 13 were in Vienna. Figure 2 reports the distribution of the participants' expertise in the three events. The figures show that, in all the events, the number of officers that work directly on real investigations (operational level) overwhelms the number of strategic ones. In fact, operational officers represent about 80% of the attendees. These outcomes align with expectations, as the AFT objective is to showcase the effectiveness of innovative tools for detecting terrorism financing primarily intended for operational officers' usage. Furthermore, we always had more LEAs rather than FIU officers.

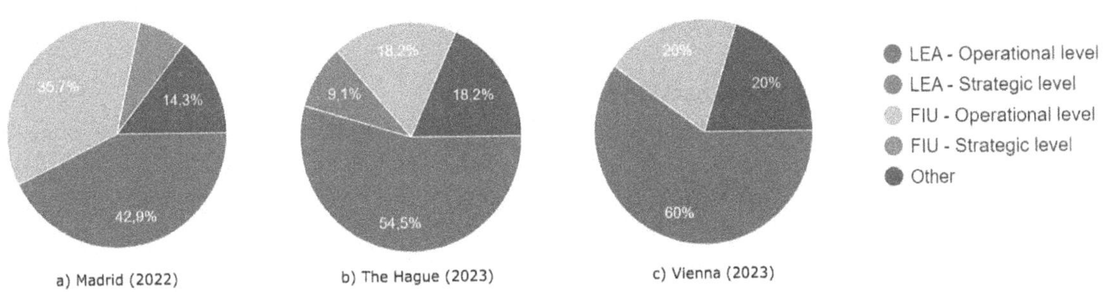

Figure 2: AFT users and external stakeholders' distribution in the first (a), second (b) and third (c) events.

The Madrid event showed a fairly consistent progress level among the participants, i.e., they were able to earn points without getting stuck for a long time. In fact, Figure 4 shows that four players (25%) achieved extraordinary scores of more than 2,000 points, and the other eight players (twelve in total, 75% of participants) achieved more than 1,425 points (black dotted line in Figure 4). Yet, two more players reached at least 1,000 points, whereas only two were below this last threshold. On average, the participants reached 1640 points out of the 2,850 available (red dotted line in Figure 4). On the other hand, Figure 3 shows that in The Hague event, the progress level was not as homogenous as in the first hackathon. In fact, despite the good feedback and comments gathered with the survey, only one player completed all the tasks and nearly attained the highest possible score, while six other additional players (less than 50% of the attendees) were able to reach at least half of the maximum score (black dotted line in Figure 3). In this event, the average score was 2,576 out of 4,350 available. Finally, as shown in Figure 5, more than 50% of the participants (7 out of 13) reached more than 3,000 points during the Vienna event. In particular, it is interesting that 11 out of 13 users, about 85%, reached scores higher than the average ones performed in The Hague and Madrid events and drawn as blue and black dotted lines in Figure 5, respectively. Therefore, the average score on this event was 3,496 points (green dotted line in Figure 5) out of 7,530 available (red dotted line). The participant's ability to achieve higher scores over successive events suggests a positive learning trajectory and potential knowledge retention. Furthermore, data indicate a progressive development of skills in using AI tools for terrorism financing investigations. Ultimately, the variation in performance levels shown in the different events suggests areas where the learning program could be refined for a more consistent and impactful training experience.

4.2 Discussion and Limitations

In general, the proposed methodology was shown to be suitable for training LEA and FIU officers and resulted in an improvement in the participant learning skills, as demonstrated by the increasing trend of average scores obtained in all the pilots. While one might question the significance of these improvements, considering that various challenges were previously addressed in past events, it's important to highlight that participants should recall how to use different tools even after extended periods (at least 6 months). At the same time, the improvements could also be related to a major number of challenges available in each newest hackathon. However, these concerns can be refuted considering that in the third hackathon, the overall event duration was reduced to 30 minutes and 60 minutes with respect to the first and second hackathons, respectively, and that information about the tool to be used in each task was removed. This confirms that, at this final stage, participants reached total autonomy and the highest level of tool and domain knowledge.

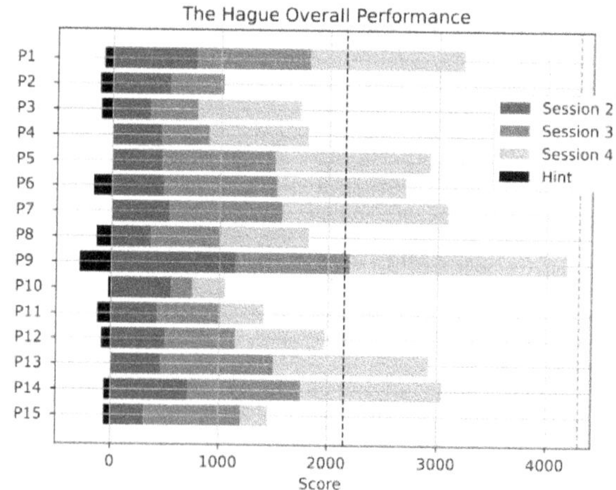

Figure 3: Participant score in the second hackathon

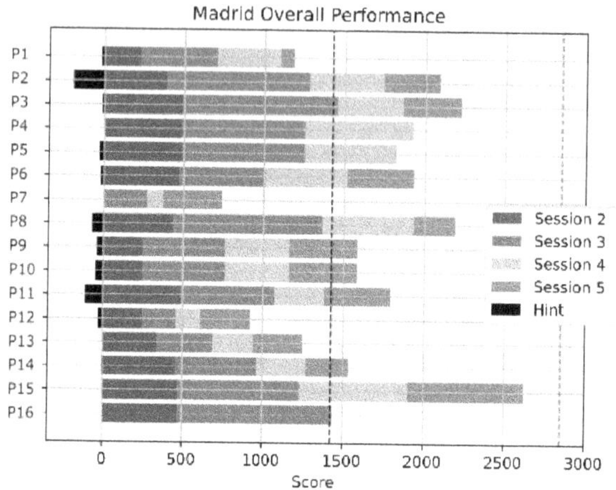

Figure 4: Participant score in the first hackathon

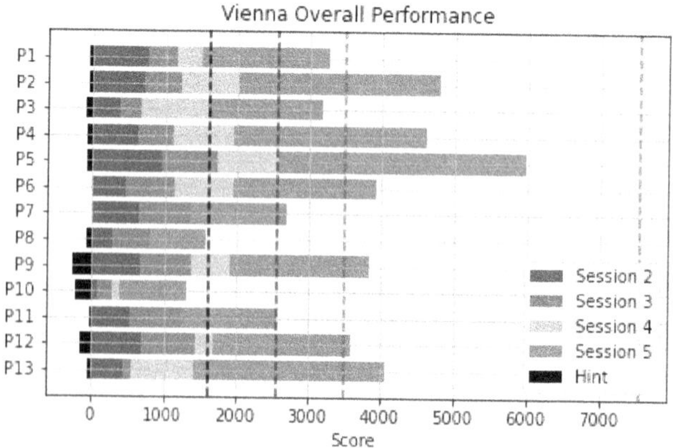

Figure 5: Participant score in the third hackathon

5. Conclusion

This paper describes a framework for training Law Enforcement Agencies and Financial Investigation Units to enhance their ability to use emergent technologies and complex pipelines to reveal financing activities of terrorism. The proposed approach used gamification techniques, such as Capture-the-Flag exercises, to engage the participants and to teach them how to use novel tools in their (realistic) investigations. The methodology was evaluated in three events held in Madrid (2022), The Hague (2023), and Vienna (2023) for training LEOs and FIUs in terrorism financing investigations. The overview of the results presented in Section 5 shown a satisfactory level of engagement among the participants in all the hackathon events, as well as an incremental improvement in the acquired domain and technical knowledge.

Despite the positive results obtained, as a lesson learned, technical partners need to spend more time understanding the day-to-day needs of the agents to improve tool functionalities and adapt them to real investigations. At the same time, European Agencies and Commissions should keep working on trying to provide new ideas to foster cooperation and share knowledge and experiences on key challenges like new crypto-threats, financing trends and terrorism *modus operandi*. In this way, it will be possible to create a more homogeneous community, in which LEAs and FIUs can take inspiration for sharing experiences about new learning methodologies, realistic training/games and new tools/products useful for their investigations.

Acknowledgement

This work was partially funded by the European Union's Internal Security Fund — Police as a part of the Anti-FinTer project (grant agreement No. 101036262).

References

Alexey Rozhkov, C. A. D. P. F. C., 2023. *theanarchistlibrary.org.* [Online] Available at: https://en.wikipedia.org/wiki/Combat_Organization_of_Anarcho-Communists [Accessed 20 12 2023].

Anti-FinTer, 2022. *Versatile artificial intelligence investigative technologies for revealing online cross-border financing activities of terrorism.* [Online] Available at: https://anti-finter.eu/ [Accessed 20 12 2023].

ASGARD, 2016. *Analysis System for Gathered Raw Data.* [Online] Available at: https://www.asgard-project.eu/ [Accessed 20 12 2023].

Barrows, H., 2022. Is it truly possible to have such a thing as dPBL?. *Distance Education,* Volume 23, pp. 119-122.

Boopathi, K. S. S. a. B. A., 2015. Learning cyber security through gamification. *Indian Journal of Science and Technology,* Volume 8, pp. 642-649.

CFLW, 2023. *cflw.com.* [Online] Available at: https://cflw.com/dwm/ [Accessed 20 12 2023].

CrimethInc., 2022. *theanarchistlibrary.org.* [Online] Available at: https://theanarchistlibrary.org/library/crimethinc-russia-the-anarcho-communist-combat-organization [Accessed 20 12 2023].

CTC, 2023. *Cut The Cord.* [Online] Available at: https://ctc-project.eu/ [Accessed 20 12 2023].

CYCLOPES, 2021. *Fighting Cybercrime – Law Enforcement Practitioners' Network.* [Online] Available at: https://www.cyclopes-project.eu/ [Accessed 13 02 2024].

DANTE, 2018. *Detecting and Analysing Terrorist-Related Online Contents and Financing Activities.* [Online] Available at: https://www.h2020-dante.eu/ [Accessed 13 13 2024].

Eagle, C. & Clark, J. L., 2004. *Capture-the-flag: Learning computer security under fire,* s.l.: s.n.

ENISA, 2021. *All you need to know about Capture the Flag competitions.* s.l., s.n.

Europol, 2021. *Internet Organised Crime Threat Assessment (IOCTA).* s.l., s.n.

Europol, 2022. *European Union Terrorism Situation and Trend Report, Publications Office of the European Union.* s.l., s.n.

Harkin, D. a. W. C., 2022. Perceptions of police training needs in cyber-crime. *International Journal of Police Science & Management,* Volume 24, pp. 66-76.

Haslhofer, B., Stütz, R., Romiti, M. & King, R., 2021. GraphSense: A General-Purpose Cryptoasset Analytics Platform. *Arxiv pre-print.*

Huang, H., Ding, J., Zhang, W. & Tomlin, C. J., 2011. *A differential game approach to planning in adversarial scenarios: A case study on capture-the-flag.* s.l., s.n., p. 1451–1456.

i-LEAD, 2017. *innovation - Law Enforcement Agency's Dialogue.* [Online] Available at: https://cordis.europa.eu/project/id/740685 [Accessed 20 12 2023].

Jiang, C., Foye, J., Broadhurst, R. & Ball, M., 2021. Illicit firearms and other weapons on darknet markets. *Trends and Issues in Crime and Criminal Justice [electronic resource],* p. 1–20.

Kilger, M. & Choo, K.-K. R., 2022. *Do Dark Web and Cryptocurrencies Empower Cybercriminals?.* s.l., s.n., p. 277.

Klingberg, S., 2022. Countering Terrorism: Digital Policing of Open Source Intelligence and Social Media Using Artificial Intelligence. In: *Artificial Intelligence and National Security.* s.l.:Springer, p. 101–111.

Leune, K. & Petrilli Jr, S. J., 2017. *Using capture-the-flag to enhance the effectiveness of cybersecurity education.* s.l., s.n., p. 47–52.

Maher, D., 2017. Can artificial intelligence help in the war on cybercrime?. *Computer Fraud & Security,* Volume 2017, p. 7–9.

McDaniel, L., Talvi, E. & Hay, B., 2016. *Capture the flag as cyber security introduction.* s.l., s.n., p. 5479–5486.

Peres, S. C., Pham, T. & Phillips, R., 2013. *Validation of the system usability scale (SUS) SUS in the wild.* s.l., s.n., p. 192–196.

Prinetto, P., Roascio, G. & Varriale, A., 2020. *Hardware-based capture-the-flag challenges.* s.l., s.n., p. 1–8.

Smidt, A., Balandin, S., Sigafoos, J. & Reed, V. A., 2009. The Kirkpatrick model: A useful tool for evaluating training outcomes. *Journal of Intellectual and Developmental Disability,* Volume 34, p. 266–274.

Švábenskỳ, V., Čeleda, P., Vykopal, J. & Brišáková, S., 2021. Cybersecurity knowledge and skills taught in capture the flag challenges. *Computers & Security,* Volume 102, p. 102154.

Werther, J., Zhivich, M., Leek, T. & Zeldovich, N., 2011. *Experiences in cyber security education: The MIT Lincoln laboratory capture-the-flag exercise.*. s.l., s.n.

Zola, F., Eguimendia, M., Bruse, J. L. & Urrutia, R. O., 2019. *Cascading machine learning to attack bitcoin anonymity.* s.l., s.n., p. 10–17.

PhD Research Papers

Addressing the Digital Resilience Challenge in the Electricity Sector in Nigeria: From Risk to Resilience

Pius M Achuama
Coventry University, Priory Street Coventry, United Kingdom
achuamap@coventry.ac.uk

Abstract: The electricity sector in Nigeria stands at the crossroads of an ever-evolving digital landscape and the pressing need for resilience in the face of dynamic challenges. This paper explores Nigeria's electricity sector, navigating its evolving digital landscape with a focus on resilience amid growing challenges. Shifting from risk reduction to resilience building, the study utilizes stakeholder interviews to assess cyber resilience. Unveiling technological advancements, it addresses interdependencies, vulnerabilities, and cyber threats in the connected grid. The study discusses some enabling practices to solve these issues including the role of policy and regulatory frameworks in fostering a culture of resilience and collaboration among various stakeholders. Amid the digital revolution, it advocates readiness, responsiveness, and rehabilitation for Nigeria's electricity sector. The study serves as a strategic roadmap for public and private decision-makers to tackle digital resilience challenges.

Keywords: Digital Resilience, Electricity Sector, Risk Mitigation, Cyber Resilience.

1. Introduction

The implementation of technological innovations has caused revolutionary opportunities and new challenges in Nigeria's electricity sector, which is characterized by a dynamic landscape. The convergence of digitalization and electricity systems gains prominence as the country endeavors to achieve sustainable electricity provision. Electricity generation in Nigeria traces back to 1896 in Lagos, with the first power plant installed in 1929 (Awosope, 2014). The sector saw slow development until 1999, marked by minimal investment and deteriorating infrastructure, leading to a drastic decrease in installed capacity from 5,600MW to an average of 1,750MW (Onuoha, 2010), (Adedeji, 2017). The industry's dire state prompted significant reforms. The Electricity Corporation of Nigeria (ECN) was established in 1951, followed by the formation of the Niger Dams Authority (NDA) in 1962, eventually merging into the National Electric Power Authority (NEPA) in 1972 (Nwaiwu, 2021). NEPA took on the integrated responsibilities of electricity generation, transmission, and distribution in Nigeria. One of the document highlights how susceptible the Nigeria's electricity sector is prone to cyberattacks, especially when it comes to new digital systems and outdated equipment. Cyberthreats that affect generation, transmission, and distribution systems, and attacks that happened like phishing, malware, and data breaches, present serious hazards (Ogundari, 2020).

The current electricity sector situation in Nigeria reflects significant technological innovations for enhanced service delivery. The sector has deployed technological solutions in improving electricity supply and enhancing their service delivery. For instance, in billing and accounting, the use of accounting software and electronic billing, demonstrates modernization efforts. The use of advanced Metering Infrastructure (AMI) facilitates remote meter connection for operational insights while. Communication and marketing tools have been integrated making it easier to have wider and quicker reach to employees in various locations and customers. Customer Relationship Management (CRM) tools streamline customer management, while Geographic Information System (GIS) aids in asset mapping and real-time location tracking. Monitoring systems like SCADA and ETAP contribute to proactive system security and management though only one distribution company in Nigeria can afford SCADA system at the moment. These organizations have tried to build some digital resilience measures to cater for the prevalent issues with technological adoption such as include building redundancy through backup servers and diverse hosting. Strict authorized access controls, multiple communication channels, collaboration with multiple internet service providers, and the implementation of security features such as firewalls contribute to system resilience. Skilled human resources, smart monitoring with devices like smart meters, and comprehensive training programs for all users further enhance the sector's digital resilience.

Generally, Nigeria's electricity sector showcases technological advancements for enhanced service delivery and operational resilience. From the adoption of advanced metering infrastructure to the integration of communication tools and digital resilience measures, organizations are proactively modernizing their operations. Despite these efforts, ongoing investments in scalable solutions, collaboration with service providers, and workforce skill development remain imperative for sustaining progress and effectively navigating future challenges. By prioritizing innovation and resilience-building initiatives, the sector can fortify its position to meet the evolving demands of the nation's energy landscape and drive sustainable growth. This study undertakes a thorough investigation and a critical evaluation of the problems of digital resilience in the context of Nigeria's electricity sector.

2. Literature Review

It is impossible to overestimate the role that energy plays in promoting economic development in countries like Nigeria (Oyedepo, 2014). Today, technology is essential to both socioeconomic advancement and worldwide operations. Digital technologies are being used by critical infrastructure sectors increasingly to improve their services, yet this dependence creates vulnerabilities. Improving legislative and regulatory measures' cybersecurity and resilience in the electricity sector is becoming increasingly important on a global scale (Heymann, 2022). Like many other critical infrastructure companies, the Nigerian electricity sector uses technology for both power generation and distribution. Cybercriminals, however, pose a threat to cybersecurity due to the fact that they strive to get access to its digital infrastructure (Rothrock, 2018). The Nigerian power sector has changed and faced many difficulties throughout the years, reflecting the country's larger dynamics (Alley, 2016). The Nigerian power industry has adopted digital technology to enhance operations, much like other sectors. Cybercriminals have been regarded as a major threat to the industry, therefore there are cybersecurity issues associated with this increased reliance on digital technology (Mbamaluikem, 2016). Any human organization must effectively manage risk, which is defined as the possibility of undesirable events. In order to reduce risks and react positively to their effects, resilience is crucial as the future is dynamic and unpredictable. As per (Rehak, 2020) findings, the process of organizational innovation holds considerable importance in strengthening the resilience of essential infrastructure components. In article by (Nwaiwu, 2021) that focuses on the African location, the digitization of energy systems is investigated, and technologies like blockchain, digital platforms, and smart grids for enabling sustainable energy transitions are critically evaluated. The implementation of intelligent grids has resulted in increased power system efficiency; nevertheless, it also poses security risks related to natural disasters, cyberattacks, and physical attacks. Blackouts, privacy violations, and infrastructure failure can result from these attacks (Otuoze, 2018). While a number of studies have attempted to offer analyses of resilience definitions, evaluation standards, and improvement techniques, the works by (Gholami, 2018), (Jufri, 2019), (Hussain, 2019)) primarily concentrate on reviews and definitions of engineering and ecological resilience. Cybersecurity solutions must progress in tandem with the sector's continuous technological breakthroughs to tackle the escalating threats and vulnerabilities (Tagarev, 2021). The majority of the research on energy system resilience and how it intersects with energy security focuses on particular kinds of threats (Chandramowli, 2014) (Pryor, 2010), (Cadini, 2016), (Li). By detecting possible threats to the business, Business Continuity Management (BCM) is a complete process designed to enhance resilience and ensure effective response to protect the interests of key stakeholders, reputation, brand, and value-creating activities (Ekaette, 2006). Robust protection against cyberthreats must be put in place to address digital resilience in the electricity sector. A thorough cybersecurity plan should be based on standards like ISO/IEC 27001 or the NIST Cybersecurity Framework (Shen, 2014). The sector makes use of drills, training, and exercises to pinpoint assets that require reliability enhancements and to hone crisis response plans. While strategies differ according to resources and region, companies use comparable techniques to train staff for increased resilience (Berkeley, 2010. Based on a literature review (Poonen, 2018), (Jasiunas, 2021), the digital resilience of the electricity industry relies on crucial determinant factors vital for safeguarding power systems against potential threats and disruptions. Thus, the infrastructure management, organizational strategies, and cybersecurity system management are critical for maintaining digital resilience, according to literature insights and factors found.

3. Methodology

This paper adopts a pragmatic approach, relying on qualitative research methods to assess digital resilience in Nigeria's electricity sector. The research design includes stakeholder interviews to perform a survey as the primary data collection method, aligning with an ontological focus on real events and an epistemological belief in knowledge derived from human activities. A convergent mixed method design enhances the assessment depth. The primary data collection involves interviews with key stakeholders in the Nigerian electricity sector. Participants include senior officers from Electricity Distribution Companies (Discos) in Nigeria, and data is analysed using Nvivo 12 software. It was specifically used to investigate the themes and subthemes that emerged from the information gathered from questionnaire responses and stakeholder interviews. The qualitative data was analyzed using the thematic analysis approach, which made it possible to find patterns, trends, and insights on digital resilience in Nigeria's electrical industry. This method made it easier to comprehend the intricate problems relating to digital resilience and made it possible to draw insightful conclusions. The questionnaire, refined through a pilot study, is administered on senior employees of electricity sector in Nigeria.

4. Results Discussion

In the dynamic landscape of Nigeria's electricity sector, technological adoption emerges as a critical catalyst for operational advancement and service optimization. However, this transition is not devoid of challenges, as stakeholders encounter a spectrum of obstacles inherent in the assimilation of new technologies. The journey towards technological integration is rife with complexities. Furthermore, the sector contends with the nuanced nuances of regulatory frameworks, infrastructural deficiencies, and the looming spectre of cybersecurity threats. Therefore, it becomes imperative to contextualize these challenges within the broader narrative of sectoral transformation, acknowledging their multifaceted impacts on operational efficacy and strategic planning. Interviews with stakeholders in the power industry have shown a number of obstacles to advancement in technology and efficiency in operations as shown in Table 3.1.

These issues come in many forms, such as poor communication between stakeholders that impedes effective information exchange. Furthermore, there is a clear reluctance to adopt new technologies, as evidenced by the widespread preference for human operations over automated ones. Additionally, there is a noticeable lack of IT proficiency among industrial workers, which hinders their capacity to handle and understand new technology. Concerns about cybersecurity have also surfaced, as incidences of fraudulent activity and illegal access have been reported, jeopardizing the security of the system and the financial integrity of the clients.

In addition, insufficient IT infrastructure and irregular internet connectivity in rural regions present formidable obstacles to the effective assimilation and application of novel technology. Patent rights for software used in the industry have also been a source of concern. This has resulted in longer wait times for software upgrades and maintenance, which has limited organizational control over software assets. The issues are made worse by inadequate training and awareness initiatives, which deprive staff of the essential knowledge on cyber dangers and appropriate software usage.

The dynamic nature of customer demands introduces an additional level of intricacy, necessitating prompt adaptation and response from the sector in order to maintain competitiveness. Furthermore, because physical and cyber infrastructure are integrated, there is an increased risk of external threats, which calls for strong cybersecurity measures. In addition to these difficulties, poor data management techniques have been found, which lead to inadequate decision-making procedures and lost chances for organizational expansion.

The lack of a well-defined approach to technology adoption and business planning exacerbates these issues, posing challenges for firms to successfully align their goals and leverage technological improvements. Employee satisfaction and sector performance are further hampered by a lack of specialized IT skills. Lastly, a major barrier to the sector's ability to safely and successfully use cutting-edge technologies for operational development and expansion is the absence of comprehensive industry and government policies around technology integration.

Table 3.1 : Identified challenges in the Electricity sector by the participants

Identified Challenge	Participant 1	Participant 2	Participant 3	Participant 4	Participant 5
Communication Breakdown		✓			
Technology-Related Fear	✓	✓			
Inadequate IT Skills			✓	✓	
Cyber Fraud Incidents			✓		✓
Lack of IT Infrastructure					✓
Lack of Internet Access		✓	✓	✓	
Lack of Patent Rights			✓		✓
Lack of Training and Awareness		✓			✓
Evolving Customer Needs			✓		
Increased Threats	✓			✓	

Ineffective Data Management		✓	✓		
Lack of a Defined Strategy				✓	✓
Lack of Dedicated IT Skills		✓		✓	
Lack of Policies			✓		✓

5. Approaches to Promote the Electricity Sector: Suggestions and Perspectives by the Participants

In order to effectively manage technical issues, the participants emphasized the vital need of having a highly skilled staff in the electric power industry. They stressed how important it is to have knowledgeable staff members who can identify, address, and anticipate technical challenges that the industry may face. A compelling recommendation was also made for the establishment of a strategy roadmap to address challenges in the electrical power sector. This plan should include early detection and quick fixes for problems, utilizing digitalization to expedite the process of identifying issues. It is believed that successfully navigating the quickly changing technical landscape in the electrical power industry requires a proactive and strategic strategy.

The necessity of ongoing training and retraining programs for human resources was emphasized because of how rapidly modern technologies are evolving. The adoption of continuing education programs to guarantee staff competency in using new technology was supported by the participants. In addition, they suggested adding certificates of participation and refresher courses to reward and acknowledge staff members who complete training.

Participants suggested an integrated approach to strengthen the security of systems within the energy power industry against cyber threats. Deploying programs with cutting-edge security features, such multifactor authentication modules and enterprise-wide digital security solutions, is part of this all-encompassing strategy. Other recommended actions included the use of SCADA systems for real-time monitoring and the identification and prevention of energy meter tampering in smart meters. It was highlighted that SMART Grid Security should be integrated with reporting sensors for power and electrical infrastructures in order to provide strong cybersecurity measures such authentication, tampering prevention, real-time monitoring, and strategic zoning.

Participants promoted cross-departmental cooperation in order to foster a security-conscious culture while addressing operational and geographic imbalances. They recommended industry-wide avenues for dissemination and emphasized the significance of good communication and technological understanding for issue resolution. It was also decided that creating a culture that could change with technology would be crucial, meaning that cooperation between the energy sector's stakeholders would be required to change perceptions about tech integration.

In addition, participants stressed the importance of giving priority to the deployment of customer-centric technologies in order to improve productivity and customer satisfaction. They advocated for the use of user-friendly technology and a "customer-first" approach, demonstrating a commitment to technical innovations that address the requirements and experiences of customers. In order to successfully integrate technology, participants emphasized the value of working as a team and integrating all relevant parties. It was determined that industry-wide cooperation was essential to maintaining IT and operational technology networks as well as real-virtual link protection.

Participants emphasized the need of regulatory oversight and the function that rules and regulations enforced by regulatory bodies play in guaranteeing thorough data gathering and knowledgeable advice. They also supported disruptive digital technology as a means of satisfying consumer needs and expanding markets, but they stressed that its implications for the electrical industry should be carefully considered. In order to lower risks in the ever-changing digital ecosystem, participants recommended proactive security measures and strategic intelligence on threats. To ensure cybersecurity resilience in the electrical power industry, it was determined that security considerations needed to be incorporated into choices about infrastructure and expansion.

6. Conclusion and Future Directions

This paper investigates the digital resilience landscape within Nigeria's electricity sector. The sector's strides in adopting advanced technologies for service delivery are commendable, yet the persistence of challenges such as communication breakdowns, cyber fraud, and technological hesitancy underscores the complexity of the digital transformation journey. These findings contribute to advancing understanding in the fields of digital resilience, cybersecurity, and organizational management by highlighting the nuanced interplay between technological adoption and resilience-building efforts.

Practical implications of the research findings are manifold, calling for strategic planning, investment in human resources, and robust cybersecurity measures. Addressing digital challenges, including evolving customer needs and insufficient IT skills, necessitates a holistic approach that encompasses human resource availability, targeted training initiatives, strategic roadmaps, and secure technology use.

Moving forward, recommendations for improvement encompass awareness strategies, customer-focused technology adoption, fostering a culture change, industry-wide collaboration, regulatory measures, and reflection on disruptive digital technology. Embracing digital resilience is pivotal for the sustainability and efficiency of Nigeria's electricity sector, offering opportunities for growth and innovation amidst challenges. Future research endeavours could explore the long-term impact of these measures, analyze global best practices, and assess economic implications, thus further enriching the scholarly discourse on digital resilience in the context of the electricity sector.

References

Adedeji, A. O. (2017). Privatisation and performance of electricity distribution companies in Nigeria. *Journal of Public Administration and Governance, 7,* 190--203.

Alley, I. a. (2016). Electricity supply, industrialization and economic growth: evidence from Nigeria. *International Journal of Energy Sector Management, 10,* 511--525.

Awosope, C. A. (2014). Nigeria electricity industry: issues, challenges and solutions. *Covenant University Public Lecture Series, 3,* 5--36.

Cadini, F. a. (2016). A Bayesian Monte Carlo-based algorithm for the estimation of small failure probabilities of systems affected by uncertainties. *Reliability Engineering \& System Safety,* 15--27.

Chandramowli, S. N. (2014). Impact of climate change on electricity systems and markets--A review of models and forecasts. *Sustainable Energy Technologies and Assessments, 5,* 62--74.

(2015). *CYBERCRIME ACT.*

Ekaette, E. U.-L. (2006). Risk analysis in radiation treatment: application of a new taxonomic structure. *Radiotherapy and Oncology, 80,* 282--287.

Gholami, A. a. (2018). Toward a consensus on the definition and taxonomy of power system resilience. *IEEE Access, 6,* 32035--32053.

Heymann, F. e. (2022). Cybersecurity and resilience in the swiss electricity sector: Status and policy options. *Utilities Policy, 79,* 101432.

Hussain, A. a.-H.-M. (2019). Microgrids as a resilience resource and strategies used by microgrids for enhancing resilience. *Applied energy, 240,* 56--72.

Jasiunas, J. a. (2021). Energy system resilience--A review. *Renewable and Sustainable Energy Reviews,* 111476.

Jufri, F. H. (2019). tate-of-the-art review on power grid resilience to extreme weather events: Definitions, frameworks, quantitative assessment methodologies, and enhancement strategies. *Applied energy, 239,* 1049--1065.

Li, Y. a. (n.d.). Influence of cyber-attacks on longitudinal safety of connected and automated vehicles. *Accident Analysis \& Prevention, 121,* 148--156.

Mbamaluikem, P. a. (2016). *AN OVERVIEW OF SMART GRID: A NECESSARY SYSTEM FOR NIGERIAN TODAY AND FUTURE ELECTRICITY.*

Nwaiwu, F. (2021). Digitalisation and sustainable energy transitions in Africa: assessing the impact of policy and regulatory environments on the energy sector in Nigeria and South Africa. *Energy, Sustainability and Society, 11,* 1--16.

Onuoha, K. C. (2010). The electricity industry in Nigeria: What are the challenges and options available to improve the sector? *Available at SSRN 1664788.*

Otuoze, A. O. (2018). Journal of Electrical Systems and Information Technology. *Smart grids security challenges: Classification by sources of threats.,* 468-483.

Oyedepo, S. O. (2014). Towards achieving energy for sustainable development in Nigeria. *Renewable and sustainable energy reviews , 34,* 255--272.

Poonen, J. a. (2018). Application of cyber resilience review to an electricity company. In *ECCWS 2018: proceedings of the 17th European conference on cyber warfare and security* (pp. 380--389).

Pryor, S. C. (2010). Climate change impacts on wind energy: A review. *Renewable and sustainable energy reviews, 14.*

Rehak, a. D. (2020). Assessing and strengthening organisational resilience in a critical infrastructure system: Case study of the Slovak Republic. *Safety Science, 123*, 104573.
Rothrock, R. A. (2018). *Digital Resilience: What You can Do—now.* Amacom.
Shen, L. (2014). The NIST cybersecurity framework: Overview and potential impacts. *Scitech Lawyer, 10*, 16.
Tagarev, T. (2021). Understanding hybrid influence: emerging analysis frameworks. *Digital Transformation, Cyber Security and Resilience of Modern Societies*, 449--463.

Miss the piece of Europe Multilateral Cooperation

Shu-Jui Chang[1], Jen-Fu Wang[2], Tim Waton[1] and Iain Phillips[1]
[1]Loughborough University, UK
[2]Yuan-Ze University, Taoyuan, Taiwan

s.chang@lboro.ac.uk
Fisher2023@saturn.yzu.edu.tw
tim.watson@lboro.ac.uk
i.w.phillips@lboro.ac.uk

Abstract: The research emphasises the importance of European multinational cooperation in addressing cyber threats. Countries cannot combat these threats in isolation; instead, they must engage in collaborative efforts that leverage shared resources, intelligence, and expertise. The study highlights the unique challenges and opportunities Asian countries face, frequently targeted by sophisticated cyber threats, particularly from state actors like China. Despite these challenges, many Asian countries have developed substantial expertise in cyber threat response and mitigation. By participating in multinational cyber exercises and sharing their knowledge, these countries can contribute significantly to the collective resilience of the global cyber defence network. This integration would not only enhance the security capabilities of the individual countries but also foster stronger international relationships, building trust and cooperation that are essential in the fight against cyber adversaries. In conclusion, this study underscores the imperative of multinational cooperation in Europe and beyond, with Asian countries playing a crucial role in enhancing global cybersecurity through their expertise and strategic positions.

Keywords: Cyber Conflict, Cyber Resilience, Multinational Cooperation, Cyber Exercise.

1. Introduction

China's cyber threat approach is more strategic and long-term oriented. China's academic discussion of cyber warfare started in the 1990s when it was called "information warfare"(Jinghua, 2019). They view cyberspace as a critical domain for national power and are actively working to dominate the digital infrastructure and information flow. Since 2004, Hu Jintao has advocated for a "warfare with information principle" due to his deep understanding of how information played an essential role in wars like the Kosovo War (1999), the Afghan War (2001) and the Iraq War (2003). Xi Jinping, the current President of the People's Republic of China, still adheres to the "information-oriented principle" today (中央网安全和信息化委, 2021). Furthermore, realising how information can get an advantage at the initial stage, President Xi applies the intelligence systems to manage and control the flow of information effectively (防研究所, 2021) and the purpose of "accelerating the transformation towards in- formationised warfare, with the beginnings of intelligent warfare." mentioned in the 2019 National Defence white paper (丁, 2019).

Under General Secretary Xi Jinping, China's strategic vision for cyberspace is viewed as the strategic warfare of the information age by Chinese military analysts, paralleling the role of nuclear warfare in the 20th century (Jinghua, 2019). Xi's emphasis on the interconnectedness of cybersecurity and informatisation reflects China's ambition to become a "cyber superpower" (Kania et al., 2017). This ambition focuses on technological advancement and strategically leverages cyber capabilities for information operations and espionage.

Cyber espionage, orchestrated by state-sponsored actors, including government agencies, military units, and affiliated hacker groups, is a critical tool for China. These actors gather intelligence, steal intellectual property, and pursue economic, military, and political objectives (Rugina, 2023). Their activities are designed to give China a competitive edge in various domains, reinforcing its position as a rising global power in cyberspace.

China's cyber espionage or information collection efforts have increasingly become a global concern, with operations targeting various countries across different continents for a long time. These operations often involve state-sponsored hackers or cybercriminal groups with ties to the Chinese government. Below are several case studies detailing China's cyber espionage activities targeting countries around the world (Center for Strategic & International Studies, 2024):

- United States: China's cyber espionage action could be traced back to 2003 when Naval Air Weapons Station China Lake was exfiltrated, including nuclear weapons information and aircraft data. Later, companies like Google and Adobe were compromised without saying that a wide range of U.S. industries, including aerospace, energy, and technology, are also in China's target list.

- United Kingdom: The earliest reported case indicating China's cyber espionage activities targeting the UK dates back to September 2007. British authorities reported that hackers believed to be associated with China's People's Liberation Army had penetrated the network of the UK's Foreign Office and other key government departments. This incident highlights China's initiation of cyber espionage activities against the UK, at least by this time.
- Europe: While the US and UK have long faced Chinese cyber espionage, Europe emerged as a later target. Evidence suggests China's European focus began around 2007, with France's Secretary General of National Defence uncovering Chinese infiltration attempts. This was followed by accusations of direct network breaches in Belgium just months later, highlighting a more aggressive approach. Suspicions of Chinese collaboration also arose during this period, with some speculating that German intelligence may have been involved in hacking Afghanistan while potentially aiding China. These incidents showcase the breadth of China's European cyber espionage, targeting diverse sectors and government institutions and solidifying China's persistent threat to European security.
- Asia: China's cyber espionage activities extend beyond Europe to target Asian countries. In May 2008, China mapped India's official networks, indicating an interest in disrupting networks during potential conflicts. Additionally, South Korean officials reported Chinese attempts to hack into Korean Embassy and military networks in January 2008.
- Africa: China's attention towards Africa has developed more recently than in other areas. It is reported that Chinese cyber operatives began espionage against African telecom companies in 2023. However, some experts believe this group has been active since approximately 2014, focusing on pro-democracy individuals and groups. Their operations might include gathering various data types, from capturing keystrokes to recording audio.

In summary, China's strategy to become a cyber superpower is multifaceted, leveraging its cyber capabilities in the grey zone. The strategy includes developing a comprehensive framework encompassing awareness, modelling, response, mitigation phases, and general governance to maintain control. Analysing China's tactics and techniques can enhance awareness and modelling efforts.

2. Literature Review

The definition of cyberspace has been hotly debated since 1982 when the first term of cyberspace was coined by a science fiction author, Wiliam Gibson. It has been discussed over decades without a clear conclusion because it encompasses abstract and concrete elements and engages academics, practitioners, and governments, complicating efforts to arrive at a precise, scientific definition (Garvey, 2021).

Starodubtsev et al. (2020) highlight the heterogeneous interpretations of the concept of cyberspace despite the large number of research works dedicated to it. In the paper, definitions of cyberspace are listed, demonstrating that till in recent years, cyberspace is still hard to define, and it is hard to have an efficient basis for theoretical and practical development in politics, economics, social status and society (Starodubtsev et al., 2020).

The diverse concept of cyberspace has been defined and interpreted by various scholars. Ning et al. (2018) introduce the concept of reshaped General Cyberspace, emphasising the interconnectedness of physical, social, and thinking spaces through ubiquitous convergence. In the AJP-3.20, the NATO document defines cyberspace as the global domain consisting of all interconnected communications, information technology and other electronic systems, networks and their data, including those separated or independent, which process, store or transmit data (ORGANISATION, 2020). This perspective extends beyond traditional notions of physical or virtual domains to encompass the integration of cyber elements into various aspects of human activity, including cognitive processes (Ning et al., 2018). Conversely, Ormrod et al. (2016) propose a definition within the Cyber Conceptual Framework, emphasising the complexity of cyberspace and its integration into existing military doctrine. Their model, nested within the National Security Domain, delineates cyberspace into physical and virtual domains, highlighting its significance across political, economic, and military spheres. This comprehensive approach underscores the multifaceted nature of cyberspace and its evolving role in contemporary security landscapes (Ormrod and Turnbull, 2016). The two perspectives of viewing cyberspace are like an analogy of "Cyber 9/11" and "Cyber Pearl Harbor". The nature of adversaries is non-state versus state, and the target is civilian in the former. Adversaries are the military versus military, and the target is the military in the latter (Council et al., 2010).

On top of the US-led cyberspace definition, Russia assumes it differently as the information-centred area considers the Information Sphere, which is a set of information objects of information, information systems and websites in the information and telecommunication network, etc., whose activities affect the formation and information processing, from individual to public relations mechanisms (publication of legal acts, unknown).

The key takeaway for cyberspace is that it is multi-dimensional beyond the logical but physical aspect. It even transcends the psychological aspect with the golden thread of data and information flow connecting and interacting virtual and reality, digit and physical. There are other characteristics of this space, such as the private sector having more control in this area as its usage and ownership, the offence has more dominated than the defence, and it is fraught with uncertainty (Council et al., 2010).

The classification of activities in cyberspace, whether as cyber conflict, cyber operations, or the US-led term cyber war, has been the subject of extensive debate, with no clear-cut consensus reached. However, one undeniable fact is the inclusion of cyberspace in military doctrine, signalling the increasing military engagement in this domain. Consequently, this has led to a dominance of military involvement in cyberspace exercises and cooperation initiatives. The shift towards military dominance underscores modern warfare's evolving nature and cyberspace's growing significance as a theatre of conflict and cooperation.

3. Methodology

This paper is divided into two main parts. The first part involves participation in the Locked Shields exercise and a subjective analysis of the exercise itself. The second part comprises objective feedback from Taiwan subject matter experts (SMEs).

Based on Taiwan's Cybersecurity National Security Strategy Version 2, the cybersecurity ecosystem is established around six key organisations: the National Security Council coordinates cybersecurity matters, offering strategic guidance in policy development, international cooperation, and incident response, Ministry of Digital Affairs tasks with propelling Taiwan's digital progress, this ministry fosters connectivity between citizens and technology, enhances industry and security, and addresses evolving threats, National Security Bureau is responsible for collecting and analysing intelligence related to cyber threats from diverse sources, including human intelligence, signals intelligence, and open-source intelligence, Ministry of National Defence supports safeguarding critical information infrastructures and military networks from cyberattacks while developing counter-cyber capabilities to deter and neutralise cyber threats against Taiwan's military, Ministry of Justice investigates cybercrimes, encompassing tasks such as identifying and apprehending cybercriminals, collecting evidence, and prosecuting offenders, and Ministry of Investigation Bureau conducts criminal investigations nationwide, with the 9th Division specifically handling cybercrime investigations.

Six SMEs from the organisation mentioned above were interviewed to gather diverse perspectives. Each interviewee held management or high-administrative positions within government-related sectors. Their invaluable insights contributed significantly to identifying the challenges and opportunities of integrating Asian countries into the NATO-dominated Locked Shields exercise. These insights are crucial for this research, providing real-world perspectives on bridging the gap between Asia and the NATO member-dominated cyber exercises.

The combination of direct participation in the exercise and in-depth interviews with key experts ensures a comprehensive understanding of the current landscape and future possibilities. This methodology captures the experiential aspects of Locked Shields. It grounds the analysis in practical, expert-driven viewpoints, offering a holistic view of the potential for broader international cooperation in cyber defence exercises.

4. Multinational Cooperation in Cyberspace

Among those cyber exercises, the NATO CCDCOE takes the lead in hosting prominent Locked Shields (LS), which focuses on offensive tactics, while LS emphasises defensive capabilities. LS typically takes place at the end of April and is the larger of the two exercises, involving over 4000 participants from 40 nations. Initiated in 2010, it was a small European exercise with experimental scenario-building. It pioneered the investigation of the nature of cyber conflict (Smeets, 2022), and the exercise has grown both in scope and participation.

The exercises operate under the scenario around two fictional islands: Berylia (BER) and Crimson (CRI), long-standing regional adversaries in the northern Atlantic Ocean and revolves nations. Although both BER and CRI are members of the UN, neither belongs to NATO. BER is portrayed as a democracy, while CRI is depicted as a weak parliamentary democracy. To simulate real-world dynamics and foster meaningful discussions, a neutral role, Revalia (REV), is introduced in LS but not CS. Under these actors' settings, the exercise focuses on realistic cyber incident scenarios, leveraging cutting-edge technologies to simulate real-world cases by taking the piece of new trends of the form of conflict into the following year's scenario within a cyber range. This platform has evolved to enable strategic decision-makers, legal experts, and technical professionals to hone their skills.

In the LS scenario, participants primarily take on the role of Blue Teams (BT), embodying the defenders from the BER responsible for thwarting and addressing attacks instigated by the CRI. While both technical and non-technical tracks exist within the same framework to receive new incidents or tasks, there is a disconnect in information sharing. Specifically, the situational reports generated at the technical level by the BT do not adequately inform discussions at the legal and strategic levels despite all being part of the same exercise framework. In short, there is a gap between the technical and strategy levels.

In a nutshell, the annual event brings countries together, pooling their resources and manpower for a united exercise, thus fostering collaboration at the technical level, facilitating legal and strategic responses, promoting learning, strengthening trust networks within the security community, and enhancing skills and cyber situational awareness annually.

5. Asia's Challenges and Opportunities

Russia's threat can potentially unite NATO mainly members for the LS exercise, an efficient platform for multinational collaboration. Through LS, participating nations can strengthen their cyber resilience, build trust among allies, and standardise strategic and operational approaches. Meanwhile, China's increasing cyber threat landscape extends beyond Asia to a global scale.

Despite not having formal diplomatic recognition from European Union member states, Asian countries maintain extensive informal relations and cooperation with Europe across various sectors. However, Asian countries face significant challenges, including identity issues and the need for increased collaboration and development.

However, why does the cyber status of Asian countries matter to European countries? Geopolitically, the strategic locations of Asian countries in key regions highlight the potential global economic consequences of any conflict or blockade. Economically, Asian countries play vital roles in global supply chains and trade networks. Politically, the successful democratisation processes in many Asian countries carry significant implications for regional stability and democracy promotion.

The subsequent section delves into the role of Asian countries in multinational cooperation, examining their challenges and opportunities in light of the evolving cyber threat landscape.

5.1 Challenges

5.1.1 *Complicated International Political Issues*

Diplomatic coercion and pressure from China are prevalent, particularly concerning countries and international organisations aligned with nations in Asia. While Russia's political influence tactics are less overt, China actively exerts its power to sway nations away from supporting Asian countries.

China's methods of exerting pressure extend beyond diplomatic channels. For instance, it consistently blocks Asian countries' participation in international organisations, denying them access to vital information and resources, especially during global crises. Economic coercion is evident, with China imposing sanctions on these nations after certain political events or policy decisions, targeting various industries and sectors.

The pressure exerted on the international stage significantly impedes Asian countries' participation in multinational cyber exercises. Organisers and participant countries face considerable pressure from China, discouraging them from engaging with other nations. Unlike Russia's pressure tactics, which may focus on geopolitical interests, China's stance on Asian countries is often treated as a binary issue. Establishing friendly relations with them is viewed by China as aligning against its interests, effectively designating their allies as adversaries of China.

Given these circumstances, many international organisations and countries prefer to maintain a friendly facade towards Asian countries, avoiding any explicit recognition or support that could provoke China. The question of their identity becomes a delicate balancing act, where expressing support risks inviting China's ire and potential retaliation. As a result, despite underlying goodwill towards these nations, most nations and international bodies opt to keep a cautious distance when their status is questioned.

5.1.2 *Scattered Diplomatic Issues*

In NATO, the structure is characterised by a united and multilateral framework where member countries collectively address security issues, coordinate military strategies, and conduct joint exercises under a cohesive organisational umbrella. This unified approach allows for streamlined decision-making processes, shared resources, and strong solidarity among member states. The integrated command structure and common strategic objectives facilitate a coordinated response to global security challenges, exemplifying the strength of a united defence alliance. In contrast, security cooperation in Asia primarily operates on a bilateral basis rather than through a comprehensive multilateral organisation. The US, for instance, maintains separate security alliances with South Korea, Japan, and Taiwan. These alliances are vital for regional stability but lack the overarching framework characterising NATO. Consequently, each bilateral relationship functions independently, with distinct agreements, military commitments, and strategic goals tailored to the specific needs of each partnership.

This bilateral nature of cooperation in Asia presents several challenges. Firstly, there is no unified command structure or formalised mechanism for joint decision-making across these partnerships. This can lead to fragmented responses to regional threats and a lack of cohesion in addressing broader security issues. Secondly, the absence of a multilateral defence organisation means there are limited opportunities for collective training, resource-sharing, and joint military exercises that include all these partners simultaneously. This can result in inefficiencies and missed opportunities to strengthen regional cybersecurity through collaborative efforts. Lastly, lacking a formal multilateral cyber security organisation in Asia can complicate diplomatic efforts. Each bilateral relationship must be managed separately, requiring significant diplomatic resources and often leading to inconsistent policies. Additionally, the absence of a unified Asian security organisation can make it more challenging to present a cohesive front in negotiations with major powers like China.

In summary, while NATO benefits from a united organisational structure that enhances collective security and coordinated action in cyber exercise, Asia's cooperation, predominantly based on bilateral relationships, faces challenges in achieving the same level of cohesion and strategic integration.

5.1.3 *Complicated Geo-Political Issues*

Asia's geo-political terrain is a mosaic of historical legacies, strategic manoeuvres, and economic entanglements, rendering it among the most intricate regions globally.

China's actions in the South China Sea epitomise this complexity. China employs a multifaceted approach by constructing and fortifying artificial islands, establishing administrative frameworks, and deploying coast guard vessels and maritime militia. Furthermore, it enforces fishing regulations and conducts resource extraction, bolstering territorial claims while projecting power without direct military engagement. This assertive stance puts pressure on nations like the Philippines, Vietnam, Malaysia, and Brunei, which are facing encroachments on their territories. Such tactics, distinct from subtler approaches, make uniting Asian nations against Chinese influence a formidable task.

The Taiwan Strait adds another layer of complexity. China's escalating pressure on Taiwan raises the potential military conflict involving the US and its allies. These tensions are exacerbated by the strategic rivalry between global powers like the US and China, extending across economic, technological, and military domains. Consequently, smaller regional players find their policies and alliances influenced by these dynamics.

In this milieu, fostering regional cooperation becomes increasingly challenging, especially for nations directly impacted by China's ambitions.

5.2 Opportunities

5.2.1 *Information-Centered Focus*

The AJP-3.20 Applied Joint Doctrine outlines three distinct layers for cyberspace operations: the cyber persona layer, logic, and physical layer (Organisation, 2020). China's approach has focused towards the cyber-persona layer, prioritising intelligence and information gathering.

When designing multinational cyber exercises, it is crucial to define the objectives clearly, aims, and scope from the outset (Concepts and Centre, 2023). While EU or US-centric exercises emphasise incident response, particularly in scenarios involving cyber disruptions to critical infrastructure, Asian-focused exercises may prioritise risk management and prevention strategies against social engineering, intelligence collection, and cyber espionage. The evolving tactics of major cyber actors like Russia and China influence this distinction.

The current situation, with ongoing kinetic warfare in Ukraine involving Russia, underscores Russia's focus on traditional warfare methods. Conversely, China's approach appears more information-oriented. Therefore, when designing cyber exercises tailored to the Asian context, it would be apt to emphasise intelligence-gathering and information-centric strategies, reflecting the unique cyber landscape and tactics prevalent in the region.

From insights drawn from LS, it is assumed that there is a lack of sufficient discussion and practice on information sharing and intelligence gathering. LS primarily focuses on preparing for potential threats in the physical and logical layers.

Asia countries stand to benefit from filling the gaps in discussions and practices observed in exercises like LS, particularly given the looming threats from China. While the exercises do not explicitly name potential adversaries, the geopolitical and political context suggests that exercises held in Europe primarily aim to counter threats from Russia. Asian countries participating in these exercises are gearing up to confront threats from China.

5.2.2 *Information Sharing*

Enhancing collaborative defence efforts and strengthening cyber resilience can be significantly augmented by integrating Information Sharing and Analysis Centers (ISACs) into cybersecurity exercises. ISACs serve as collaborative forums facilitating the sharing of cybersecurity information and best practices among members within specific sectors or industries, thereby promoting information sharing, threat intelligence exchange, and coordinated incident response among organisations, government agencies, and stakeholders. Considering the emphasis on multi-nation cooperation in exercises like LS, incorporating ISACs becomes crucial for effective practice.

In the context of cyber exercises, involving ISACs in scenarios can simulate real-world collaboration and coordination among participants facing common cyber threats. Through ISAC platforms, participants can share real-time threat intelligence, tactics, and mitigation strategies, enhancing situational awareness and enabling more effective response actions.

One of the key benefits of integrating ISACs into exercises is the opportunity to test and refine information-sharing protocols and procedures. Participants can practice exchanging threat intelligence and incident data, evaluate the effectiveness of communication channels and mechanisms, and identify areas for improvement in collaborative information-sharing processes. This iterative approach enables organisations to strengthen their collective defence capabilities, build trust, and improve information-sharing efficiency among members.

Moreover, involving ISACs fosters a culture of collaboration and cooperation among participants, overcoming traditional barriers to information sharing, such as confidentiality concerns and competitive advantage. By focusing on defending against cyber threats and mitigating potential impacts on critical infrastructure and essential services, organisations can work together within the framework of an ISAC.

Additionally, integrating ISACs into cyber exercises provides valuable cross-sector learning and knowledge exchange opportunities. Participants from different industries can share insights, lessons learned, and best practices, enriching their understanding of emerging threats and effective defence strategies. This collaborative approach enables organisations to leverage the collective expertise and experiences of the broader cybersecurity community, enhancing their ability to adapt and respond to evolving cyber threats.

Asia countries have practised a great success of ISAC systems. Take Taiwan's National Cyber Security Program (2021-2024) exemplifies the effectiveness of integrated defence systems through the establishment of Security Operation Centers (SOCs), Computer Emergency Response Teams (CERTs), and ISACs across multiple critical infrastructure domains. Coordinated by the Executive Yuan, these domains connect with CI providers to ensure cybersecurity protection and conduct united defence efforts across different sectors, contributing to national security through robust information-sharing practices and standard intelligence exchange formats.

In conclusion, including ISACs in cybersecurity exercises like LS offers numerous benefits for enhancing collaborative defence, information sharing, and incident response capabilities. Taiwan's expertise in implementing information-sharing systems serves as a valuable example for other nations, highlighting the pivotal role of ISACs in strengthening cyber resilience and mitigating the impact of cyber threats on critical infrastructure and organisations.

5.2.3 *Joining Existing Fraternity or Establishing a New One*

Under China's influence, Asian countries face challenges in joining existing multinational cyber cooperation organisations or establishing platforms to attract NATO members. Despite this pressure, there has been some progress in fostering multinational cooperation.

For instance, in the 2024 LS, Asia countries such as Korea, Japan, and Singapore successfully collaborated with NATO member states, participating in the BT. Moreover, their efforts in supporting Red Team operations, White Team coordination, and Green Team infrastructure setup have been commendable, showcasing practical cooperation.

However, nations like Taiwan, which are confronting more acute challenges, encounter political and diplomatic hurdles in participating in exercises dominated by NATO members. In response, Taiwan is exploring alternative avenues, such as hosting its exercises and inviting NATO members to participate.

The Taiwan Administration for Cyber Security, MODA, hosted Cyber offensive and Defensive Exercises for years to promote global cooperation in cyber security defence. In 2023, the event attracted participation from 18 international cybersecurity organisations working in one of the critical infrastructures - water resources sectors to build a simulated cyber range. Unlike the rule in the LS, in which all BTs are representative of BER, Taiwan's water company served as the BT. At the same time, the RT consisted of countries like the US and the Czech Republic, joint teams from government agencies, and award-winning participants from Taiwan in international hacking competitions.

In addition to the technical-level exercise, the non-technical part is hosted in the conference format - The Advanced Cybersecurity Exploration Conference (ACE), which brought together scholars, industry representatives, and government officials worldwide to focus on two major cybersecurity issues: critical infrastructure security and risk management for emerging technologies. The ACE conducted an in-depth analysis of recent cyber security threats to Taiwan and corresponding strategies. Other speakers from Estonia, Australia, Albania, and other countries in the field of cyber security shared insights on topics such as geopolitical dynamics and emerging threats, the importance of cyber security, and risk management policies (李昱緯, 2023).

In conclusion, Japan, Korea, and Singapore, among others, strive to integrate into the Western sphere of cyber activities and cooperation, a pursuit that has yielded good progress. Their dedication to aligning with Western standards and practices reflects their commitment to global cybersecurity efforts. Meanwhile, Taiwan's endeavours to participate in NATO-led initiatives have faced obstacles, yet it has proactively engaged in alternative strategies, such as hosting exercises and inviting Western participation. These approaches demonstrate innovative thinking and determination in bridging gaps and fostering collaboration with strengths.

6. Conclusion

Europe has established a robust framework for multinational cooperation in cybersecurity, marked by regular exercises and strategic partnerships, significantly bolstering the collective cyber defence capabilities of nations across the continent. Key exercises like NATO's CMX and Cyber Coalition have played pivotal roles in cultivating trust, improving communication, and nurturing a sense of camaraderie among participating countries.

Given the persistent cyber threats faced by various Asian countries, their integration into the European cyber community could yield substantial benefits. Drawing upon their extensive experience in dealing with cyber threats, these Asian nations could offer valuable insights, enriching the resilience of the European cyber defence network. By actively participating in European cyber-security exercises and sharing their expertise, countries stand to contribute to and gain from the collective strength of these partnerships.

Furthermore, becoming part of the European cyber community would enable Asian countries to forge stronger international relationships, fostering trust and cooperation on a global scale. This integration could facilitate the development of joint strategies, shared resources, and a unified approach to countering cyber threats. In an increasingly interconnected world where cyber threats transcend geographical boundaries, the participation of Asian countries in European cybersecurity initiatives would not only bolster their defences but also contribute to the broader global endeavour to uphold secure and resilient cyberspace.

Acknowledgements

I want to express my sincere gratitude to the NATO Cooperative Cyber Defence Centre of Excellence (CCDCOE) for their invaluable support. The expertise, resources, and guidance provided by CCDCOE were instrumental in completing this work.

References

CSIS Center for Strategic & International Studies. Significant cyber incidents, 2024.

The Development Concepts and Doctrine Centre. Influence Wargaming Handbook. UK Ministry of Defence, 2023.

National Research Council, Global Affairs, Division on Engineering, Physical Sciences, Computer Science, Telecommunications Board, Committee on Deterring Cyberattacks, Informing Strategies, and Developing Options for US Policy. Proceedings of a Workshop on Deterring Cyberattacks: Informing Strategies and Developing Options for US Policy. National Academies Press, 2010.

Myles D Garvey. A philosophical examination on the definition of cyberspace. In Cyber Security and Supply Chain Management: Risks, Challenges, and Solutions, pages 1–11. World Scientific, 2021.

Lyu Jinghua. What are China's cyber capabilities and intentions?, 2019. URL https://carnegieendowment.org/2019/04/01/what-are-china-s-cyber-capabilities-and-intention [Accessed:19/04/2024].

Elsa Kania, Samm Sacks, Paul Triolo, and Graham Webster. China's strategic thinking on building power in cyberspace, 2017. URL https://www.newamerica.org/cybersecurity-initiative/blog/chinas-strategic-thinking-buildin Accessed: 19/04/2024.

Huansheng Ning, Xiaozhen Ye, Mohammed Amine Bouras, Dawei Wei, and Mahmoud Daneshmand. General cyberspace: Cyberspace and cyber-enabled spaces. IEEE Internet of Things Journal, 5(3):1843–1856, 2018.

North Atlantic Treaty Organisation. Allied Joint Publication-3.20 Allied Joint Doctrine for Cyberspace Operations. UK Ministry of Defence, 2020.

NORTH ATLANTIC TREATY ORGANISATION. AJP-3.20 ALLIED JOINT DOCTRINE FOR CYBERSPACE OPERATIONS. NATO STANDARDISA- TION OFFICE (NSO), 2020.

David Ormrod and Benjamin Turnbull. The cyber conceptual framework for developing military doctrine. Defence Studies, 16(3):270–298, 2016.

Official publication of legal acts. Presidential decree of 12.5.2016 number 646 "on approval of the doctrine of the russian federation information security, unknown. URL http://publication.pravo.gov.ru/Document/GetFile/0001201612060002?type=pdf [Accessed:25/05/2024].

Juma Mdimu Rugina. Economic cyber espionage: The us-china dilemma. Ulus- lararası I ̇li¸skiler C¸ alı¸smaları Dergisi, 3(2):77–90, 2023.

Max Smeets. The role of military cyber exercises: A case study of locked shields. In 2022 14th International Conference on Cyber Conflict: Keep Mov- ing!(CyCon), volume 700, pages 9–25. IEEE, 2022.

Yu I Starodubtsev, EG Balenko, EV Vershennik, and VH Fedorov. Cyberspace: terminology, properties, problems of operation. In 2020 International Multi- Conference on Industrial Engineering and Modern Technologies (FarEast-Con), pages 1–3. IEEE, 2020.

丁. 《新代的中防》白皮全文, 2019. http://www.mod.gov.cn/gfbw/fgwx/bps/4846424.html [Accessed: 20/09/2023].

中央网 安全和信息化委. "十四五" 家信息化 划, 2021. URL ttps://www.gov.cn/xinwen/2021-12/28/5664873/files/1760823a103e4d75ac681564fe481af4.pdf [Accessed: 08/04/2024].

李昱緯. 18國資安專家匯聚code 2023活動展現台灣資安戰力, 2023. URL https://moda.gov.tw/ACS/press/news/press/8583 [Accessed: 7/5/2024].

防研究所. Nids china security report 中安全略告2021 新代的中事略. Technical report, 防研究所, 2021.

Towards a Framework for Analysing Complex Interdependence in Digital Espionage Markets

Ahana Datta
University College London, UK

ahana.datta.20@ucl.ac.uk

Abstract: Cyber power indices have dominated discourse in recent years as measuring the relative power of nation-states in cyberspace to exercise their cyber capabilities for offensive and defensive purposes. These indices adapt a variety of methodologies, but their effectiveness in mobilising cyber power remains limited. Indices based on dynamic systems frameworks explain power consolidation arising from network-effects, but are too broad to implement due to complexity. In this article, we analyse cyber power through access to digital espionage capabilities, using the theory that states weaponise complex interdependence of information flows. Instead of proposing an index, we set up a case study contrasting the Chinese system, where the state mediates technology vulnerabilities, with the Five Eyes system, where vulnerability disclosures are a common occurrence. The Chinese system exhibits a "chokepoint" effect, in contrast to the Five Eyes' "panopticon" mediation of information flows. Extant cyber espionage analyses range over themes such as economic vis-a-vis open and closed vulnerability markets; legal, in relation to the circulation of tools like spyware; or strategic and case-based. Given this confluence, we posit a framework of information flows between ecosystems of actors. Exploit vendors, state-backed offensive operators, nation-states, and tech platforms are networked through interdependent information flows, consolidating power in private actors. The political economy of a nation-state provides useful heuristics in articulating strategic aims behind its espionage activities, as well as its approach in controlling the flow of knowledge of vulnerabilities between the private actors of which the state may be a customer. In highlighting this tension between nation-states' political economies defining their roles as both mediator and customer, we offer security scholars nuanced considerations in theorising cyber power. We conclude that while this tension amplifies private power, policymakers must intervene to reshape interdependent networks that influence and counter it.

Keywords: Cyber Power, Complex Interdependence, Cyber Espionage, Vulnerability Disclosure

1. Introduction

In over two decades of literature aiming to define, theorise, score, or evaluate national cyber power, some points of consensus emerge. Firstly, that a nation's cyber power projects on to both cyberspace in itself, as well as as an auxiliary instrument to gain leverage in domains outside cyberspace, such as the military. Second, that international relations scholars converge either towards rationalising "cyber power" through longstanding normative theories of power and war in the vein of (Nye, 2010), (Rid, 2013), (Betz and Stevens, 2011) in recent years, (Kuehl, 2009) or (Starr, 2009) before Stuxnet, or through qualitative methods that ultimately set up a scoreboard of cyber capabilities between nation-states.

As such, the first sets up a lens through which cyber power must be appraised more and more comprehensively, covering as many aspects as possible of offensive and defensive domains, revised after any political event of note where cyber-means play a pivotal role. Comparisons of indices are based against supposedly more comprehensive cybersecurity standards, such as NIST (Cifci, 2022). Each successive cyber power model vies for greater comprehensiveness. On the other hand, the second sets up outcomes that typically favour metrics accuracy with little impact on mobilisation (Inkster, 2017) or theoretical consistency at the cost of exposing biases in analysing a strategic competitor's approach. Typical examples are seen in the sample analytical questions that constitute the scoring mechanism, such as those posed by the Belfer Centre index (Voo et. al, 2020), or the more sophisticated IISS version (International Institute for Strategic Studies, 2021): questions such as whether a nation adopts "a whole of society" approach in its cyber governance, or when national documents first mention "cyber" appear to omit political, national security, and cultural considerations in nation-states like Russia, China or North Korea. For example, China and Russia do not linguistically differentiate between information influence and cyber operations; North Korea's disproportionate offensive cyber power belies its economic weaknesses. Furthermore, nation-states such an Iran compensate for the lack of a sophisticated passive surveillance capability through investment in offensive cyber operations; for many states, investing in cyber defence instead is an opportunity cost. This skews the results of any "comprehensive" index, as the analysis is constrained by limited observability of empirical data, attribution, and national perspective.

The divergences in literature, however, show nuanced conclusions. Analyses of mobilising cyber power recognise that non-state actors play a significant role, and any leverage in cyberspace depends on a state's ability to influence and coerce them (Klimburg, 2011). Dynamic systems models of cyber power illustrate nuances such as an actor's evolving capability, the conception of the state as an actor within a dynamic environment, as well as access to vulnerabilities and capabilities to mature them (Mattila, 2021). A structural analysis demonstrates how the political economy of a bloc like the EU decentralises power over cyber capability to member states, whilst centralising institutional power through common policies, standards and regulatory obligations (Dunn Cavelty, 2018).

This article presents cyber power as a relative phenomenon in a wider ecosystem of actors, each of which act to accrue, consolidate, diffuse or disperse it. In the digital espionage ecosystem, the promise of achieving political, economic, trade, or innovation-based strategic objectives can lead nation-states to exert significant resources and capabilities in acquiring, developing, deploying, and storing offensive cyber capabilities. Depending on a nation-state's strategic objectives, this may well outweigh the priority placed on defensive cyber capabilities or the resilience of institutions that maintain its security, which motivates our scrutiny on crucial offensive cyber capabilities. Our research process adopts as an analytic tool the theory of 'new structuralism', which argues that states entrench power asymmetries by weaponising complex interdependence of information flows. We use a single, interpretive case study, where recent Chinese legislation requiring technology platforms to report vulnerabilities in their systems to the government within days of discovery acts as a break point, allowing us to present the Chinese system as a global "chokepoint" of vulnerabilities, in contrast to the Five Eyes, where vulnerability disclosures are more common. Our sourcing relies on a synthesis of government documents, news reports, peer-reviewed literature such as journal articles, researcher reports, and testimony of actor perspectives in the form of blogs or interviews.

We construct an ecosystem of four types of actors, namely, nation-states; tech platforms; third-party offensive cyber groups (often called mercenaries, proxies, etc) who may act independently, or on behalf of a state. Third-party cyber groups are sometimes indistinguishable from the state, as seen in the case of many Advanced Persistent Threat groups, who are linked to state security and intelligence agencies but not directly employed. Finally, we include a fourth actor in the form of exploit vendors on the legitimate or illegitimate vulnerability market, who may also assist nation-states or mercenaries with offensive cyber operations when such actors need to procure and develop offensive cyber tools. Each actor is connected by a demand-supply relationship with another for a service that provides or develops a capability. We discuss how the interdependence of information flows between these actors entrench established power dynamics, by consolidating two types of private power: that accumulated by tech platforms, and that exercised by exploit vendors. To do so, we turn to weaponised complex interdependence of information flows described by (Farrell and Newman, 2019) and (Oatley, 2018). Given demand and supply relationships between public, private, and "in between" actors in the vulnerability market, coercive power within private actors grows. Political economies of states that help reshape these information flows, or states that have the capability to exercise coercion over private power are most able to mobilise cyber power. (Betz, 2012) and (Maurer, 2018) use actor-network models to appraise coercive power in mercenary hackers, (Harvey and Moore, 2023) analyse Meta's statecraft-like private power.

In Section 2, we justify using digital espionage as an angle to theorise cyber power; in Section 3, we introduce the ecosystem of actors, connectivity and the complex interdependence framework of information flows, and outline the case study; in Section 4, we discuss implications of private power and its coercive abilities on states and other actors, and vice versa; in Section 5 we present concluding remarks on translating digital espionage into strategic advantage for states, and future directions for policymakers considering reshaping private power.

2. Digital Espionage as an Angle For Analysing Cyber Power

Cyber espionage has been defined as "an attempt to penetrate an adversarial computer network system ... for the purpose of extracting sensitive information" (Rid, 2013). Natural questions arise: who does it, why, and how? Some perspectives deal mainly with intelligence operations conducted by states for political objectives (Lindsay, 2021), but absent the effect of mercenaries' independent actions, the analyses can seem incomplete. Many IR scholars may point out that political and commercial espionage are perceived differently, particularly in legal terms, but the targets of alleged Chinese state-sponsored espionage transcend such distinctions in terms of technical methodologies, for example, the Volt Typhoon advisory (Joint Cybersecurity Advisory with Microsoft Threat Intelligence, 2023). When we speak of digital espionage markets, we are concerned with the capabilities — the tools and services — offered on open or closed markets to any customer, regardless of the customer's objective as a strategic actor — at least in the first instance.

To avoid confusion with combined methods such as HUMINT, we speak of digital espionage as espionage conducted by digital means on digital targets. Extracting sensitive information may not entail information exfiltration from a computer network, merely passive surveillance; we look at services and technologies used to establish surveillance and/or computer network exploitation (CNE) as the main methods of digital espionage. Surveillance may help establish CNE, and vice-versa, but unlike CNE, surveillance need not be covert. Further, the type of digital target motivates the tactics, techniques, and processes (TTPs) engaged for penetration. For example, in telecommunications and Internet service providers (ISPs), intelligence sharing networks such as the Five Eyes have established passive surveillance capabilities (SIGINT). In contrast, mass market technology endpoints, such as smartphones can be penetrated by exploiting a vulnerability in the application layer, operating systems, firmware and/or hardware. A canonical example is the spyware Pegasus, aimed at exploiting a vast number of iPhone firmware versions for full access at 0-click target engagement.

Espionage and counterespionage may be intended for offensive or defensive cyber operations. State may use intelligence about adversarial cyber capabilities, obtained from surveillance or CNE or other sources, to develop counter capabilities of their own, to deter the adversary by disclosing their capabilities, or to patch their own high-risk vulnerabilities. As a precursor to meeting a political or commercial strategic objective — which scholars may find hard to deduce and study until some instance of public attribution — the act of mounting an espionage operation itself can be indicative of adversarial cyber power. Factors include how much the adversary invests in the cybersecurity of its digital assets, its purchasing power in accessing sophisticated capabilities, and the resources required to acquire, develop, stage or deploy an exploit. The same questions that analysts in a state's intelligence agency must answer in mounting a digital espionage operation are then necessary in evaluating its offensive cyber power.

Throughout the planning and execution stages of an operation, answers to operational questions are indicative of some facet of cyber power: Are the targets (adversary's digital assets) connected to the Internet; is the target a proprietary technology or mass-market, and if so, are exploits already available on the market or in-house for vulnerabilities in the target; has the state developed its own exploits, or does it have already established relationships with third-party vendors who might be able to provide such capabilities, and at what cost; can the state afford to acquire and develop these exploits, and turn them into "intelligence equities" (Ben-Gad and Finkelstein, 2022); is it best for the state's strategic objective to deploy the equity on to the target (and risk discovery, closure of that attack vector, and rebuttal) or to disclose the equity to the tech platform that can patch the underlying vulnerability or to trade the equity with an intelligence ally for some other utility; how long must penetration be maintained after initial CNE, and is that affordable resource-wise and strategically; how quickly the target reacts to discovering the CNE, if at all; how viable are other attack vectors to the target and for how long.

This is by no means an exhaustive list of the analyst's considerations, but illustrative that in large part, the business of conducting digital espionage is just that — a business. This is the key economic dimension that many cyber power narratives omit. Like any business, the state actor's relationships with other actors in the ecosystem, such as tech platforms, mercenaries, exploit vendors, and intelligence allies are rooted in the ability to negotiate, control, or influence; such forms of coercion is the source of its power. This ability is derived from the political economy of the state itself, which determines its response to private actors, as well as who it views as an ally or adversary (in some contexts, both). Given its relationships and political economy, the state can take on the role of intermediary, consumer, regulator, or some combination of those roles in the vulnerability market. In liberal democracies, the state has lower control over private enterprises in market-based economies, with some ability to regulate information flows in the market, in contrast to more authoritarian systems, where the state acts as an effective ceiling to accrued private power. The UK, as a member of the Five Eyes, for example, admits that its preference towards handling intelligence equities is disclosure wherever possible, and subject to internal governance (Levy, 2018), and this is also reflected in United States policy (Trump White House Archives, 2017).

We are not suggesting that this implies that authoritarian systems must be disproportionately large consumers in the vulnerability market, however, current empirical data suggests quite the opposite — democratic countries appear to be the biggest buyers of spyware globally (Feldstein and Kot, 2023). The aim of interdependence is to discuss the extent of control that states can or cannot exert over private power — for offensive or defensive purposes — which form much of its cyber capability, even as they might play the roles of customers and mediators simultaneously.

3. Complex Interdependence and a Case Study

Weaponised interdependence argues that networks, as sociological structures that place limits on an actor's agency, tend to entrench and amplify existing asymmetries in power relationships over time. Where power is initially centralised, network effects of interdependence such as globalisation will ensure power is only further centralised as these structures evolve, and networks become "highly resistant to change", best visualised as hub-and-spoke models. In particular, Farrell and Newman characterise weaponisation in the guise of "chokepoints" and "panopticons": the former is an actor's ability to limit the access of other actors to an information hub; and the latter is an actor's ability to observe information flows passing through key hubs. In the case of globalised, interdependent information networks, such as the Internet, they observe that American institutions such as ICANN and policies of tech self-regulation allowed online business models to extract and monetise user content, thus first enabling, then entrenching centralised power over digital markets in tech platforms such as Google, Amazon and Facebook. Platform monopolies and the national security apparatus force a disproportionate amount of global Internet traffic to pass through an American hub such as in Virginia. Through the PRISM programme, the US government was able to then exploit this "panopticon" setup and weaponise its dominance over Internet traffic hubs to create extensive surveillance capabilities in cooperation with private partners and intelligence allies such as the Five Eyes.

As a theoretical tool, 'new structuralism' has been applied to other areas of security analyses. (Farrell and Newman, 2019) adapt weaponised complex interdependence to privacy, surveillance, and its governance.(Segal, 2021) applies weaponised interdependence to the 5G rivalry between the US and China, arguing that the exclusion of ZTE from the US supply chain eventually led to ZTE's exclusion from Western tech supply chains, and through restrictions on Huawei, controlling the critical chokepoint of the advanced semiconductors design and manufacturing market, the US prevented Huawei from leveraging diversified markets. (Tusikov, 2021) contextualises states coercing tech platforms into enacting chokepoints for Internet services globally, noting that states need to have considerable structural, legal and economic capacity to coerce the private sector, not just domestically but internationally. She contrasts US weaponisation of its tech platforms' international influence with their Chinese counterparts expanding to catch up and fulfil China's political economy objectives with the state overseeing industrial expansion; China's weaponisation of chokepoints is highlighted in suggested future work, which adds to our motivation.

We use a similar network construction to discuss the case of offensive cyber capability. Our framework consists of actors such as nation-states and tech platforms, but also exploit vendors, and hackers groups, mercenaries, or proxies. Each actor operates in its own 'ecosystem' (Adner, 2017), with tech platforms such as Alibaba, Meta, Amazon, Alphabet, etc offering the most visible examples of multiple product offerings that keeps their customers information walled in. On the other hand, the Lighthouse and Haaretz investigations into exploit vendors also suggest an ecosystem of actors working towards each stack of the technology they target and build offensive capabilities from (Lighthouse Reports, 2022). Each actor interacts with another within its own ecosystem, or in another ecosystem, through information buying and selling relationships. On the other hand, ecosystems are not always cleanly differentiated. Even in the digital espionage ecosystem construct, it is not always possible to distinguish an offensive cyber operation led and owned solely by the nation-state, as opposed to a joint or sponsored effort with a mercenary, enabled by a trusted vendor, or in concert with other intelligence allies, but rather, it depends on what role the actor takes vis-a-vis its requirement to buy or sell a service.

However, to conduct CNE, the offensive actor needs access to a specific information commodity, namely, vulnerabilities in the digital target, the knowledge or use of which may be bought and sold with any degree of technological sophistication, ranging from digital footprints on databases, to exploits that must be used in concert in a wider attack (spearphishing for network penetration, then malware lateral movement is a common example), to packaged and point-and-deploy malware such as Predator or Pegasus. Given the range of expertise and resources needed to facilitate discovery of vulnerabilities and their development into commoditised offensive tools or weapons, the exploit vendors operate in an ecosystem of their own, with different actors focusing on different technology stacks or business development, for example. Vulnerabilities don't necessarily have to be 0-days; simply identifying that the target is vulnerable and an exploit can be made available in fulfilling a broader objective. Each actor has a specific role in the circulation of these commodities over the Internet. Tech platforms produce digital endpoints such as smartphone software or hardware, server and network infrastructures that inevitably have security vulnerabilities, and at the same time must detect and patch these vulnerabilities in a timely manner. The resulting window between any actor detecting such a vulnerability in digital targets and its closure allows actors such as exploit vendors, mercenary groups, and nation-states to develop CNE and data exfiltration capabilities.

The offensive security researcher Maor Schwartz provides a look into exploit vendor actors and the wider industry (Schwartz, 2023). As tech platforms have invested more into the cybersecurity of their products, the availability of an arsenal of vulnerabilities has become rarer and more expensive, reshaping the supply pool. Offensive security researchers have overcome the difficulty of selling the vulnerabilities they do find by establishing trust-based relationships with nation-states through middlemen such as brokers, or by being employed to "end-to-end companies". Schwartz asserts that the market peaked before 2020 with many competing vendors selling the same vulnerabilities, but dipped between 2020-2021 due to a combination of increased media coverage, export control laws on spyware, new regulatory paradigms on cybersecurity, the economic shock of the pandemic, and legal challenges brought by tech platforms to vendors exploiting their products. After 2021, vendors sought R&D investments from nation-states and private equity directly, and recouped their costs by selling the same vulnerabilities to multiple states. In particular, nation-states that appear on US sanctions lists have no legal or affordable purchasing power from vendors supplying to the Five Eyes due to export control and price discrimination, and such states struggle to develop similar capabilities in-house. They must seek alternatives domestically, or amongst their allies and their markets. It is evident that the domestic institutional power, norms, and jurisdictions that form a necessary condition for weaponising complex interdependence in Farrell and Newman's theory are also present in the case of the Five Eyes, and particularly the US, in accessing part of the digital espionage market and isolating adversaries from it. This "panopticon" role is an evolution of the same structural and topological asymmetry as information flows vis-a-vis Internet traffic and surveillance capabilities.

In contrast, China has its own network architecture, derived from and in service to its political economy, that routes information flows in its own favour. Former FBI agent Adam Kozy notes in his testimony to the US-China Economic and Security Review Commission that a part of the Chinese Ministry of State Security (MSS) has been "getting early access to software vulnerabilities for twenty years". In September 2021 vulnerability disclosure by tech platforms and wider industry to the databases of the Ministry of Industry and Information Technology (MIIT) was made legally mandatory within 2 days of discovery, isolating foreign platforms from knowledge of vulnerabilities in mass technology, ostensibly adding to Chinese offensive cyber capability. The Atlantic Council (Cary and Del Rosso, 2023) uses the Chinese CERT data as a primary source to report the role of the MIIT as an intermediary for vulnerability disclosure. The report indicates that new, post-regulation information flows leverage academia, tech platforms, national infrastructure such as telecoms, and the state in bolstering China's offensive cyber capability. They cite the increase in high-severity vulnerabilities reported on its central database as evidence of regulatory success. This apparent sharp increase in the hoarding of 0-days since 2021 is corroborated by Microsoft as well as Recorded Future's reports into the rise of China as a "leading global cyber power," finding that 85% of digital targets were public, Internet-facing appliances (Insikt Group, 2023). They imply that Chinese digital espionage has expanded to mass-market consumer tech products, from firewalls to email infrastructure. The report also describes China's cyber capability evolution as rapid, scaled up, focused, and aligned "...with China's military, political, economic, and domestic security priorities." Formalising the 2021 regulation, coercing industry and cornering the vulnerability market turned an existing norm into legal leverage, with the Chinese state weaponising vulnerabilities and centralising access to an ever-growing database, at the exclusion of foreign tech platforms, as a "chokepoint". As Farrell and Newman observe, "... states that fear they will be targeted ... reshape networks so as to minimise their vulnerabilities."

Restrictions on the availability of, and access to, vulnerabilities and exploits in globally used tech products impact the creation and development of intelligence equities. In turn, this affects the ability to mount espionage campaigns, and so the ability to exert cyber power for strategic leverage. The asymmetric relationship between decentralised disclosures led by industry in the Five Eyes case, and centralised mediation by the state in the Chinese case, on what are likely similar vulnerabilities in underlying tech platforms, is reflective of their respective political economies. Liberal democracies must simultaneously welcome scrutiny and answer to the same institutions that enable them levers such as mobilising and exerting cyber power; autocracies have no such checks and balances. The authoritarian state has a bigger threat than an international adversary to contend with, in the form of domestic dissent. The investment in mitigating internal threat through increased surveillance, or other digital means — including the role of "domestic panopticon" through a vast national firewall — will be as much, if not more, of a priority than foreign and economic policy initiatives outlined in the Belt and Road Initiative, for example. Simply collecting more vulnerabilities than a strategic adversary is not the final word in a nation-state's digital espionage capabilities, or the extent of its "cyber power". Vulnerability markets represent one of the key hubs to which privileged states need sustained access, in order to maintain structural dominance, as well as institutional power that enables them to weaponise these interdependences, fostered by the dominant tech platforms' products and the topology of the Internet. Coercing the tech platform private actor directly (using regulatory or legislative levers, or by targeting its customers) or indirectly (by targeting its products and forcing vulnerability remediation) then requires partnership with other private actors such as exploit vendors and mercenaries.

4. Private Power and State Coercion

In order to weaponise complex interdependence to any sustained degree structurally — by controlling chokepoints that are critical to offensive cyber capability, amplifying data flows through new and existing surveillance hubs, and creating legal and regulatory frameworks that entrench these power asymmetries — the nation-state must coerce to its advantage three types of private power: that of tech platforms, hacker groups, and exploit vendors.

These so-called private actors operate in ecosystems of their own. Hacker groups' relationship with the state, for example, may be semi-private: ideological proxies can form trust-based relationships with the state until a desirable political inertia lasts. Economically motivated mercenaries may act of their own agency, mounting subversive ransomware attacks. Public attribution can muddy the waters. Hacker groups are at times useful for the nation-states' deniability of an offensive operation, but also a potential nuisance or deterrent when acting upon their own initiative — their power, only semi-private where funded by the state, shapes the digital espionage market by leveraging unsophisticated cyber attacks, or burning vulnerabilities. (Sheldon and McReynolds, 2015) assess the policy implications of civil-military integration in Chinese "information warfare militias", and their predictions of the Chinese state leveraging academia and industry in contributing to espionage campaigns, targeting telecommunications and global supply chains have been proved correct. The vast literature on hacker groups and mercenaries does not reach a consensus on the entrenched power in the longer term of any single group, even of any particular Advanced Persistent Threat; in the aftermath the US Office of Personnel Management 2014 breach, for example, APT-1 was publicly attributed. Identified individuals, rather than the state, were sanctioned by the US. The effectiveness of such sanctions as a deterrent to espionage campaigns is debatable, but has remained the one of the few legitimate ripostes where political attribution is fruitless.

Where power is even more private, nearly opaque, in the case of exploit vendors for example, states struggle to create lasting coercive instruments due to complex domiciles and overlapping incentives. As alluded to previously, the joint Lighthouse-Haaretz reportage identifies the vendor of the Predator spyware, Intellexa, and its European connections with the Israeli spy firm; Haaretz also notes in a separate report the involvement of a Swiss actor enabling spyware firms rout regulations through vulnerabilities in the international mobile system (Black and Benjakob, 2023). The scandal of the Pegasus spyware, proliferation and use in EU member states, and legal frameworks on "dual-use" has been covered extensively elsewhere. Additionally, the US Executive Order strengthening export control laws on spyware through a moratorium has drawn criticism at its ability to protect the free press from surveillance, and if this instead strengthens American offensive cyber capability. On the other hand, given its political economy, the Chinese state uses its legal chokepoint to leverage its offensive cyber ecosystem in systematic ways — as seen in researchers' analysis of the recent Anxun ('I-Soon') leaks — which suggest, through new insight these leaks reveal about the group APT-41, that the offensive cyber ecosystem in China is similar to that of its Western counterparts (Bernsen, 2024).

Tech platform power, exploitation, and digital market monopolies are extensively covered in academic literature where 'private power' is invoked; the phrase applies much less to power accrued by exploit vendors and other third-parties. However, nation-states' coercive strategies are now aimed at securing and manipulating private power to build resilience in, or conversely spy on, global supply chains. To achieve meaningful coercion, states must leverage security policies that apply to every actor in the ecosystem both internationally and domestically, and tech platforms can be an obvious target. The US Securities and Exchange Commission response to alleged Russian espionage, resulting in the 2020 SolarWinds breach, has triggered legal action against SolarWinds company staff. Targeting platforms provides easy access into any global supply chain, given increased dependence on cloud infrastructure. Leveraging platform vulnerabilities, such as the 2024 targeting of senior Microsoft leadership by Russian-sponsored Midnight Blizzard, appears to be an emerging pattern in the competition for control of global supply chains (UK National Cyber Security Centre, 2024). The Five Eyes in particular, have suggested policies to "de-risk" their critical infrastructure from that of its strategic competitors, but have to overcome the realities of complex interdependence for this to work.

5. Conclusion

Any strategic leverage derived from digital espionage is not homogenous (Devanny et al, 2021). We have argued that it may depend on several factors such as structural advantages, national objectives, political economies, proportional responses, and legal instruments available to the state. By taking a political economy approach to digital espionage markets, we have constructed a framework of actor ecosystems and their interplay. We identify, in particular, two forms of private power vis-a-vis the role of the state: exploit vendors, where the state may act as a consumer; and tech platforms, where the state acts as regulator. Yet, at the nexus of these actors, the state strives to be an intermediary, and the resulting tension creates an area of future scrutiny. There is growing momentum in cyber espionage literature for such analyses that juxtapose the state's assumed rôle versus its political, economic and security objectives; a recent example highlights the difficulty in establishing espionage norms between Russia, China and the West due to conflicts in this juxtaposition (Harnisch and Zettl-Schabath, 2023). Our proposed approach for theorising cyber power using 'new structuralism' as an analytical tool, states consolidate cyber power by weaponising the complex interdependence of information flows online, exploiting structural asymmetries in accessing digital espionage markets and coercing private actors. Our case study compares the Chinese and Five Eyes approaches to vulnerability disclosures to show how structural asymmetries are embedded using levers of state power.

Even one aspect of mobilising cyber power, in the form of access to offensive tooling needed to conduct digital espionage, is a dynamic and interdependent phenomenon, and comprehensive indices forego nuances. The digital espionage case illustrates that in future models of cyber power, each selection criterion must be considered in both absolute and relative terms; for example, interdependences that affect defending a state's digital assets, or within its civil society vis-a-vis incident response preparedness, and other interdependences.

Digital espionage is mostly motivated by a desire to decrease information asymmetries, and counter-espionage is motivated by maintaining or even increasing them. Its methods originate from, and are a response to, technological innovation that primarily arise from private actors. Future research on factors that increase or limit innovation in an era of systemic competition would be beneficial in understanding the persistence of national cyber power. In particular, while authoritarian systems have greater coercive capabilities on private actors, democratic systems may enable innovation through freer markets. Emerging risks must also be factored into policymakers models aiming to reshape network interdependence. (Tusikov, 2021) points out, for example, that the network structure of the Internet is shifting towards the Pacific due to increased private power in tech platforms serving the BRICS nations. A plausible shift in the global political economy away from democratic capitalist systems will change the nature of interdependent information flows; particularly in the capacity for weaponisation, and thus, cyber power. Future policy frameworks analysing cyber power must be sensitive to these dynamics.

Finally, we posit to the cyber power theory community that the capability of a state to mobilise its cyber capabilities to enhance its "national power" is not merely limited to its absolute technological, institutional, and structural advantages. It is equally a test of it arbitrates and conducts domestic and foreign trust relationships in the long term, and the quality of leadership that decides how best to project it.

Acknowledgments

Thanks to Madeline Carr and David Pym for their feedback. This work was supported by EPSRC grant EP/S022503/1.

References

Adner, R. (2017). Ecosystem as Structure: An Actionable Construct for Strategy. Journal of Management, 43(1), 39-58.

Ben-Gad, M., Finkelstein, A. (2022) 'On Intelligence Equities'. Draft. (0.9.1)

Bernsen, W. (2024) Same Same, but Different, Margin Research. Available at: https://margin.re/2024/02/same-same-but-different/.

Betz, D. (2012) 'Cyberpower in Strategic Affairs: Neither Unthinkable nor Blessed', Journal of Strategic Studies, 35(5), pp. 689–711.

Betz, D.J. (2017) 'Cyberspace and the State: Towards a Strategy for Cyber-Power'. Routledge.

Black, C. and Benjakob, O. (2023) 'How a Secretive Swiss Dealer Is Enabling Israeli Spy Firms', Haaretz.

Cary, D. and Del Rosso, K. (2023) 'Sleight of hand: How China weaponizes software vulnerabilities', Atlantic Council, 6 September.
Cifci, H. (2022) 'Comparison of National-Level Cybersecurity and Cyber Power Indices: A Conceptual Framework' pre-print (2022).
Devanny, J., Martin, C. and Stevens, T. (2021) 'On the strategic consequences of digital espionage', Journal of Cyber Policy, 6(3), pp. 429–450.
Dunn Cavelty, M. (2018) 'Europe's cyber-power', European Politics and Society, 19(3), pp. 304–320.
Farrell, H. and Newman, A.L. (2019) 'Of Privacy and Power: The Transatlantic Struggle over Freedom and Security', in Of Privacy and Power. Princeton University Press.
Farrell, H. and Newman, A.L. (2019) 'Weaponized Interdependence: How Global Economic Networks Shape State Coercion', International Security, 44(1), pp. 42–79.
Harnisch, S. and Zettl-Schabath, K. (2023) 'Secrecy and Norm Emergence in Cyber-Space. The US, China and Russia Interaction and the Governance of Cyber-Espionage', Democracy and Security, 19(1), pp. 82–110.
Harvey, C.J. and Moore, C.L. (2023) 'Cyber statecraft by net states: the case of Meta, 2016–2021', Journal of Cyber Policy, 0(0), pp. 1–21.
IISS. (2021), 'A methodology for assessing the cyber power of states'. Available at: https://www.iiss.org/research-paper/2021/06/cyber-power-methodology/
Inkster, N. (2017) 'Measuring Military Cyber Power', Survival, 59(4), pp. 27–34.
Insikt Group. (2023) 'Charting China's Climb as a Leading Global Cyber Power' , Recorded Futures.
Klimburg, A. (2011) 'Mobilising Cyber Power', Survival, 53(1), pp. 41–60.
Kot, S.F., Brian (Chun Hey) (2023) Why Does the Global Spyware Industry Continue to Thrive? Trends, Explanations, and Responses, Carnegie Endowment for International Peace.
Levy, I. (2018) 'Equities Process'. Available at https://www.ncsc.gov.uk/blog-post/equities-process
Lighthouse Reports (2022), 'Flight of the Predator'. Available at: https://www.lighthousereports.com/investigation/flight-of-the-predator/
Lindsay, J.R. (2021) 'Cyber Espionage', in P. Cornish (ed.) The Oxford Handbook of Cyber Security. Oxford University Press.
Lindsay, J.R., Cheung, T.M. and Reveron, D.S. (2015) China and Cybersecurity: Espionage, Strategy, and Politics in the Digital Domain. Oxford University Press.
Miller, S. (2016) 'Cyberattacks and "Dirty Hands": Cyberwar, Cybercrime, or Covert Political Action?', in F. Allhoff, A. Henschke, and B.J. Strawser (eds) Binary Bullets: The Ethics of Cyberwarfare. Oxford University Press.
Mattila, J.K. (2022) 'A Model for State Cyber Power: Case Study of Russian Behaviour', European Conference on Cyber Warfare and Security, 21(1), pp. 188–197.
Maurer, T. (2018) Cyber Mercenaries. Cambridge University Press.
Oatley, T. (2019) 'Toward a political economy of complex interdependence', European Journal of International Relations, 25(4), pp. 957–978..
Rid, T. (2013) Cyber War Will Not Take Place. Oxford, UNITED STATES: Oxford University Press, Incorporated.
Segal, A. (2021) 'Huawei, 5G, and Weaponized Interdependence', in D.W. Drezner, H. Farrell, and A.L. Newman (eds) The Uses and Abuses of Weaponized Interdependence. Brookings Institution Press, pp. 149–166.
Sheldon, R. and McReynolds, J. (2015) 'Civil-Military Integration and Cybersecurity: A Study of Chinese Information Warfare Militias', in J.R. Lindsay, T.M. Cheung, and D.S. Reveron (eds) China and Cybersecurity: Espionage, Strategy, and Politics in the Digital Domain. Oxford University Press.
Shwartz, M. (2023) 'The boom, the bust and the adjust', Medium, 20 June. Available at: https://medium.com/@maor_s/the-boom-the-bust-and-the-adjust-ea443a120c6.
Trump White House (2017) Vulnerabilities Equities Policy and Process for the United States Government.
Tusikov, N. (2021) Internet Platforms Weaponizing Chokepoints. In D. Drezner, H. Farrell, and A. Newman, eds. The Uses and Abuses of Weaponized Interdependence. (pp. 133-148). Washington, DC: Brookings Institute Press.
UK National Cyber Security Centre. (2024) SVR cyber actors adapt tactics for initial cloud access. Available at: https://www.ncsc.gov.uk/news/svr-cyber-actors-adapt-tactics-for-initial-cloud-access.
Voo, J. et al. (2020) 'National Cyber Power Index 2020: Methodology and Analytical Considerations', China Cyber Policy Initiative Reports [Preprint].

Efficiency Divide: Comparative Analysis of Human & Neural Network Algorithm Development

Petr Gallus, Tomáš Ráčil and Tomáš Šlajs
University of Defence, Brno, Czech Republic

petr.gallus@unob.cz
tomas.racil@unob.cz
tomas.slajs@unob.cz

Abstract: The paper delves into a comparative analysis between human and artificial intelligence (AI) capabilities in algorithm development, with a specific focus on the challenges presented in the "Advent of Code." The research thoroughly investigates the performance of Generative Pre-trained Transformers (GPTs), such as ChatGPT and Bard, in solving intricate algorithmic problems and benchmarks these results against those achieved by human participants. A sizeable portion of the study is dedicated to understanding the nuances of prompt engineering in AI and how it affects the problem-solving process, alongside exploring the choice of programming languages used by both AI and humans. The methodology of the research is extensive, involving the participation of both AI models and human subjects, who vary in their levels of programming expertise. This approach allows for a comprehensive evaluation of the correctness and efficiency of solutions, along with the time taken to resolve the given problems. The results from this study reveal intriguing insights. While AI models like GPTs demonstrate an impressive speed in problem resolution, they often fall short in accuracy when compared to human problem-solvers, particularly in tasks demanding deeper contextual understanding and creative reasoning. Furthermore, the study delves into the impact of time constraints on the effectiveness of problem-solving strategies employed by both AI and humans. It finds that under strict time constraints, AI models can quickly generate solutions, but these solutions may lack the depth and accuracy found in those devised by human participants. This aspect of the research highlights the trade-off between speed and precision in AI-driven problem solving. The research extends its implications beyond mere performance comparison. It suggests the potential for a synergistic approach where the computational efficiency and rapid problem-solving abilities of AI can be effectively combined with the nuanced understanding and creative problem-solving skills inherent in humans. This hybrid approach could redefine the future landscape of programming and algorithm development. The study not only provides a critical analysis of the capabilities of AI in the realm of algorithmic problem-solving but also paves the way for future exploration into the collaborative dynamics of human-AI interaction in programming. It highlights the evolving role of AI in programming and underscores the importance of balancing AI's computational prowess with human creativity and adaptability in solving complex, real-world problems.

Keywords: Human Intelligence, Artificial Intelligence, Algorithm Development, Large Language Models, Comparative Analysis, Problem-Solving Efficiency

1. Introduction

In the rapidly evolving landscape of software development, the intersection of human ingenuity and artificial intelligence (AI) is creating new frontiers in algorithm development. This paper explores this intersection by delving into the "Advent of Code," a unique platform that presents a series of coding challenges known for their complexity and requirement for innovative approaches. The "Advent of Code," created by Eric Wastl, stands out due to its intricately designed puzzles that often demand creative problem-solving strategies. The difficulty of these challenges is highlighted by the fact that in the latest competition, out of 231,994 participants, only 3,047 were able to complete the final algorithmic task [1]. This not only underscores the complexity of the tasks but also sets a rigorous benchmark for assessing coding proficiency.

The advent of Generative Pre-trained Transformers (GPTs) like ChatGPT and Bard has ushered in a new era in programming. These AI models are not only revolutionizing the landscape of code generation but are also expanding their reach across various domains. Their potential to assist in software development raises pivotal questions about the future role of human programmers. This paper aims to investigate whether these advanced neural networks can tackle complex algorithmic problems, akin to those found in the "Advent of Code," and what implications this may have for the programming community.

An integral aspect of this exploration is the role of prompts in directing the functionality of GPTs. Traditionally, the efficacy of a GPT's response heavily relies on the quality of the prompt provided. This study seeks to understand whether intricate prompt engineering is essential for solving complex algorithmic tasks or if GPTs can effectively operate with minimal guidance. This has significant implications for the usability of LLMs (Large Language Models) by individuals without programming expertise.

Furthermore, the choice of programming language is a crucial factor in the realm of software development. In the current scenario, where the emphasis is on delivering efficient and rapid solutions, the selection of a programming language is often dictated by these goals. This research aims to juxtapose the algorithmic solutions provided by university students on the "Advent of Code" platform with those generated by the latest LLMs. This comparison seeks to evaluate the potential of LLMs to solve complex tasks autonomously, which could signify a change in basic assumptions in the role of programmers, reducing it to system architects or requirements specifiers.[2]

This study is not just an academic exercise; it is a foray into the potential future trajectories of programming as a profession. By examining the capabilities of LLMs in contrast to human problem-solving skills in a challenging environment like the "Advent of Code," we aim to uncover insights that could shape the future direction of software development and the role of human programmers in it.

2. Methodology

This study embarked on a comprehensive examination of algorithmic problem-solving skills, juxtaposing human capabilities against advanced neural networks. The primary platform for this investigation was the "Advent of Code" 2023 challenges, a well-known series of programming puzzles that escalate in complexity.

2.1 Selection of Challenges and Participants

The research was bifurcated into two distinct phases. Initially, a broad assessment was conducted on the first six tasks of the "Advent of Code" which is a digital event during the Christmas season each year, where participants are presented with daily coding challenges suitable for various skill levels and can be tackled using any programming language. This inclusive initiative is widely utilized for diverse purposes including interview preparation, company training, university coursework, and as a competitive speed contest.[2]

These six tasks were followed by an extended evaluation up to day 15, ceasing when human participants were unable to progress further. A total of 23 participants, ranging from first-semester undergraduates to doctoral candidates with 1 to 10 years of programming experience, were enlisted. Additionally, 27 first-year students participated in a time-bound challenge, attempting to solve as many tasks as possible from the first six within a 90-minute time limit.

2.2 Neural Networks Usage

The neural networks employed were Bard, ChatGPT 3.5, ChatGPT 4.0 and custom GPT. For ChatGPT 4.0 and custom GPT, complete tasks from the "Advent of Code" website were inputted along with the respective data. Due to input length limitations with ChatGPT 3.5 and Bard, only essential parts of the tasks were extracted for generating Python code, which was then tested against the provided data. Each LLM had up to three attempts to generate a correct solution before moving to the next task.

2.3 Custom configured GPT

The "Own GPTs" feature of ChatGPT represents a groundbreaking advancement in customizable AI technology. It allows users to create and tailor their custom GPT models to cater to specific needs and tasks. A notable example of this innovation is "Adventer", a custom GPT developed specifically to tackle coding challenges from the renowned Advent of Code event. Adventer [Figure 1] is designed to excel in understanding and solving complex programming problems, making it an invaluable tool for programmers participating in these challenges. By analysing code structures, algorithms, and logic, Adventer assists in deciphering and solving intricate puzzles, highlighting the versatility and adaptability of custom GPTs in specialized fields.[4]

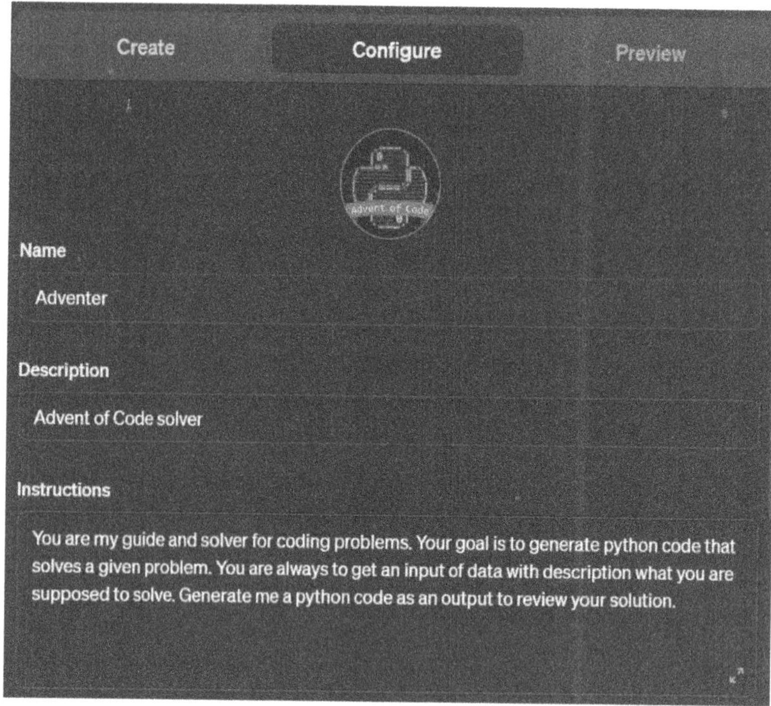

Figure 1: Custom GPTs default configuration. Source: [own]

2.4 Prompt Importance

Prompts play a pivotal role in the functionality of Generative Pre-trained Transformers (GPTs). They serve as the primary interface through which users communicate their requests or tasks to these language models. Prompts are input sentences or questions that guide the GPT to generate specific outputs. The effectiveness of a prompt influences the quality of the GPT's response. This is because the language model relies on the context provided by the prompt to generate relevant and accurate information.[5]

In the realm of coding, particularly when solving coding challenges with GPT models, the role of prompts becomes even more crucial. A well-crafted prompt can effectively direct the GPT to analyse a coding problem, provide solutions, or even write and debug code snippets. The importance of prompts in this context lies in their ability to transform abstract coding challenges into specific tasks that the GPT can understand and execute. The prompt not only provides context but also sets the scope and limitations within which the GPT operates, making it an indispensable tool in leveraging GPTs for coding challenges.[6]

2.5 Algorithmization and Programming Languages

Algorithms are fundamental to the field of computer science and play a crucial role in solving coding challenges. An algorithm is a set of well-defined instructions or rules designed to perform a specific task or solve a problem. In programming, algorithms are implemented using a programming language, which serves as a tool to express these instructions in a form that a computer can execute. The choice of algorithm and programming language significantly impacts the efficiency and effectiveness of the solution to a coding challenge. For example, pseudocode is often used in teaching problem-solving skills in programming, emphasizing the development of an algorithmic solution before coding it in a specific language.[7]

2.6 Comparison Criteria and Data Collection

The primary focus of comparison has been the correctness of solutions and the time taken to solve the problems. Notably, when the LLMs provided correct solutions, they do so at a speed unattainable by human programmers. Data collection for human participants involves two approaches: extracting data from a private leaderboard on the "Advent of Code" site and using a custom-built testing website. The website enables more precise tracking of the number of attempts and the time taken to solve each task.

2.7 Ethical Considerations

Ethical integrity was maintained throughout the study. Participant data were anonymized, and all individuals were informed about the purpose of their participation and the use of collected data.

2.8 Limitations and Assumptions

The study acknowledges several limitations. For the first group of participants, uninterrupted problem-solving was not feasible due to the time-consuming nature of the tasks and their academic obligations. The second phase limited students to a 90-minute window time limit, which, while sufficient for initial tasks, was restrictive for later challenges. The potential for more extended testing was curtailed by logistical constraints and the availability of participants.

2.9 Reproducibility

To ensure the reproducibility of our experiments, we meticulously detail our methodology, emphasizing the configurations of various neural network models such as ChatGPT 3.5, ChatGPT 4.0, Bard, and our tailored GPT setup. Our experimental design includes selecting coding challenges from the "Advent of Code" and engaging participants across a spectrum of programming expertise. While we strive for precision in the technical setup, we acknowledge the inherent variability in human performance due to differences in education, experience, and regional influences, which may affect the development of relevant skills.

Our comprehensive data collection strategy, utilizing both a private leaderboard and a custom testing platform, was designed to capture a wide array of data points, including solution correctness and problem-solving speed. Ethical integrity was maintained throughout the study, with a focus on participant anonymity and transparent data usage. This approach ensures that our findings are both reliable and replicable, notwithstanding the natural variance in human participant abilities.

Replicating this study requires adherence to our detailed setup and acknowledgment of the human element's variability. This variability underscores the complexity of drawing comparisons between human and AI problem-solving capabilities. By providing clear guidelines on our experimental configuration and participant selection, we aim to enable other researchers to validate our results and further explore the dynamic interaction between humans and AI in solving complex challenges, while recognizing the unique factors influencing human performance.

3. Results

In the context of the 'Advent of Code' challenges, the study provides a nuanced understanding of the performance of human participants compared to AI models, including ChatGPT 4.0, 3.5, and Bard.

3.1 Correctness Analysis of Task Performance

3.1.1 LLMs (Large Language Models) Performance

The LLMs demonstrated a consistent level of correctness, averaging between 16.67 % and 33.33 %. Its performance shows a degree of stability across the tasks, albeit with a lower correctness rate. This consistency might indicate the models' uniform approach to problem-solving, regardless of the task complexity.

3.1.2 Human Participants – Limited Time Limit

This group displayed a significant drop in correctness after the initial tasks, with correctness rates of 9.26 % and 3.70 % for the first two tasks and 0 % for subsequent tasks. The data suggests a struggle in coping with the complexity or specific requirements of the later challenges within the limited time limit.

3.1.3 Human Participants – Unlimited Time Limit

Exhibiting higher correctness rates, this group achieved 88.64 % and 86.36 % in the first two tasks. The rates gradually decreased in the subsequent tasks but remained notably higher than the other groups. This trend highlights their ability to adapt and apply effective problem-solving strategies, especially when not constrained by time.

3.1.4 Task-wise Correctness Comparison

The plot comparing correctness rates (Figure X) across tasks illustrates these trends vividly. LLMs maintain a flat line of moderate success, while the unlimited time limit group shows a descending curve, indicating higher success in initial tasks. The limited time limit group's curve sharply declines after the first two tasks.

3.1.5 Implications of Correctness Analysis

The correctness analysis underscores the distinct strengths and limitations of each group. While LLMs offer a consistent but limited accuracy, human participants, particularly with an unlimited time limit, demonstrate a higher degree of adaptability and accuracy, especially in tasks in which understanding context and applying creative solutions are crucial.

These findings suggest the potential of combining the computational efficiency of LLMs with the creative and adaptive problem-solving skills of humans, particularly in scenarios where accuracy and understanding of complex problems are vital.

Table 1: LLMs and Human Participants Correctness Analysis. Source: [own]

Group	Task 1	Task 2	Task 3	Task 4	Task 5	Task 6
LLMs	16.67% (std: 0.41)	33.33% (std: 0.52)	0.0%	33.33% (std: 0.52)	16.67% (std: 0.41)	16.67% (std: 0.41)
Human Participants – Limited time limit	9.26% (std: 0.29)	3.70% (std: 0.19)	0.0%	0.0%	0.0%	0.0%
Human Participants – Unlimited time limit	88.64% (std: 0.32)	86.36% (std: 0.35)	63.64% (std: 0.49)	75.0% (std: 0.44)	54.55% (std: 0.50)	52.27% (std: 0.51)

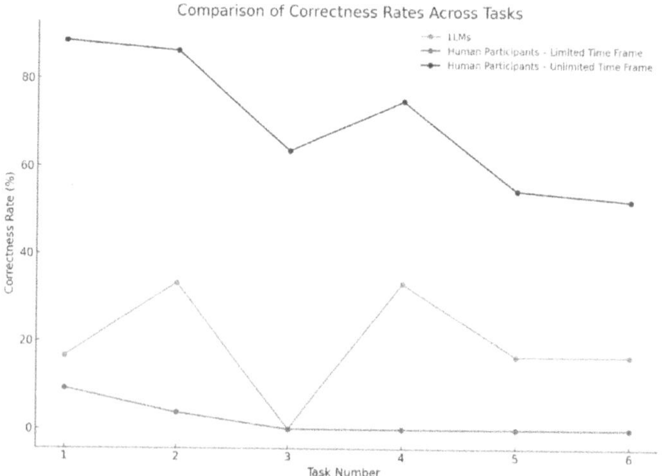

Figure 2: LLMs and human participants Correctness Analysis Graph. Source: [own]

The plot above [*Figure 2*] visually compare the correctness rates of the three groups – LLMs (Large Language Models), Human Participants with a Limited time limit, and Human Participants with an Unlimited time limit – across the first six tasks of the 'Advent of Code' challenges.

Key Observations:

- LLMs show a consistent correctness rate, averaging around 16.67% to 33.33%, with some variability in tasks 2 and 4.
- Human Participants with a Limited Time Limit exhibit lower correctness rates, particularly in tasks beyond the first two, where the rate drops to 0%.

- Human Participants with an Unlimited Time Limit demonstrate higher correctness rates, especially in the initial tasks, with a gradual decrease in later tasks but still maintaining high rates of correctness. [*Table 1*]

3.2 Time Efficiency Analysis

The time spent on tasks reveals striking differences between AI models and human participants:

3.2.1 *LLMs*

Exhibited consistent and rapid task completion, with an average time ranging from 34 to 544 seconds for various tasks. The standard deviation, where applicable, was low, indicating a uniform approach across tasks. [*Table 2*]

3.2.2 *Human Participants – Limited Time Limit*

Showed considerable investment in time, with an average of about 18.74 minutes for Task 1 and 15.16 minutes for Task 2. The high standard deviation suggests a wide variation in time spent among participants. [*Table 2*]

3.2.3 *Human Participants – Unlimited Time Limit*

This group had a much broader range of time spent, with averages from 14 to 85 hours for different tasks. The notably high standard deviation indicates a diverse set of strategies and time investments among these participants. [*Table 2*]

Table 2: LLMs and Human Participants Time Spent Analysis Table. Source: [own]

Group	Task 1	Task 2	Task 3	Task 4	Task 5	Task 6
LLMs	34 sec	38 sec (std: 4.24 sec)	-	52.5 seconds (std: 7.78 sec)	544 sec	53 sec
Human Participants – Limited time limit	1124.47 sec (~18.74 min	909.66 sec (~15.16 min)	-	-	-	-
Human Participants – Unlimited time limit	50874.85 sec (~14.13 h)	229329.71 sec (~63.70 h)	118959.93 sec (~33.04 h)	308699.52 sec (~85.75 h)	148960.75 sec (~41.38 h)	164948.74 sec (~45.82 h)

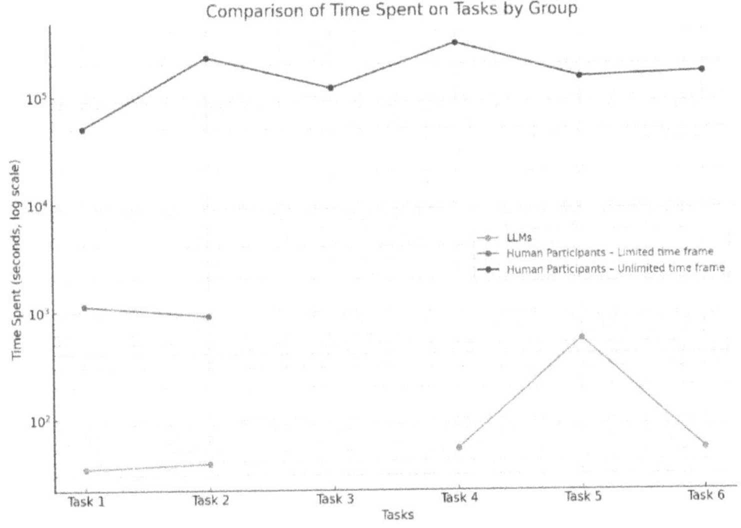

Figure 3: LLMs and Human Participants Time Spent Analysis. Source: [own]

The logarithmic chart above [*Figure 3*] compare the time spent on each task by the separate groups: LLMs (Large Language Models), Human Participants with a Limited time limit, and Human Participants with an Unlimited time limit.

Key Observations:

- The time spent by LLMs is consistently lower across tasks, illustrating their rapid problem-solving capabilities.
- Human Participants with a Limited time limit show a notable increase in time spent on the first two tasks but do not extend to the subsequent tasks.
- Human Participants with an Unlimited time limit demonstrate a significant increase in time spent, especially on the later tasks, indicating the increased complexity and the considerable effort invested in solving these challenges.

3.3 Comprehensive Comparison Across All 15 Tasks

The analysis for all 15 tasks for the groups LLMs and Human Participants with an Unlimited time limit provides a detailed comparison in terms of correctness and time efficiency.

3.3.1 Correctness Analysis

LLMs (Large Language Models)

Exhibited a moderate level of correctness, with rates ranging from 0 % to 33.33 %. The consistency in correctness across various tasks suggests a stable but limited capability in accurately solving the tasks.

Human Participants – Unlimited Time Limit

Demonstrated significantly higher correctness rates, especially in the initial tasks, with rates starting at 88.64% for Task 1 and gradually decreasing in the subsequent tasks. This trend indicates a strong ability to solve the initial tasks accurately, with a decline in success as tasks become more complex.

3.3.2 Time Efficiency Analysis

LLMs

Maintained a consistent and low time spent across tasks, with times ranging from 34 to 544 seconds. The low variance in time spent indicates a uniform approach to problem-solving regardless of task complexity.

Human Participants – Unlimited Time Limit

Showed a significant variance in time spent, with averages ranging from 14.13 to 85.75 hours for different tasks. The wide range in time spent and high standard deviation reflect the diverse strategies and considerable effort invested by participants in solving these challenges.

3.3.3 Comparative Insights

The correctness analysis reveals a clear distinction in problem-solving accuracy between LLMs and human participants. While LLMs maintain a consistent but moderate level of correctness, human participants, given unlimited time, exhibit a higher capability to solve tasks correctly, especially in the earlier challenges. However, as the tasks progress in complexity, their correctness rates decline, yet they remain higher than those of LLMs.

In terms of time efficiency, LLMs demonstrate rapid problem-solving, while human participants exhibit a wide range in time investment, indicating diverse problem-solving approaches and the complexity of the tasks.

3.3.4 Implications

These findings highlight the strengths and limitations of both LLMs and human problem-solving in coding challenges. LLMs offer speed and consistency but lack the higher accuracy rates seen in humans, particularly in complex tasks. The results suggest the potential for a synergistic approach, combining the rapid processing of LLMs with the nuanced and adaptive problem-solving of humans, especially in scenarios requiring high accuracy and understanding of complex problems.

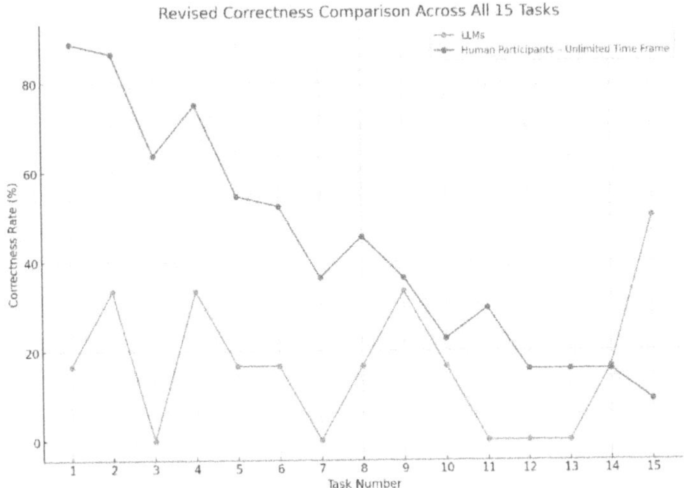

Figure 4: Revised Correctness Comparison Across All 15 Tasks. Source: [own]

The revised plot above [*Figure 4*] present an accurate comparison of the correctness rates for LLMs (Large Language Models) and Human Participants with an Unlimited time limit across all 15 tasks of the 'Advent of Code' challenges.

Key Observations:

- LLMs display a variability in correctness rates across the 15 tasks. The plot shows their performance on the tasks they attempted, with some tasks demonstrating higher correctness rates.
- Human Participants with an Unlimited Time Limit exhibit higher correctness rates in several tasks, with notable performance in the initial tasks as well as some of the later ones. This indicates their ability to solve a range of tasks with varying complexity.

3.4 AI Model Specific Analysis

3.4.1 *GPT-4.0 and Custom GPT*

- Correctness: Demonstrated a range of correctness from 0 % to 100 % across the 15 tasks, showing a higher level of problem-solving capability with a peak correctness rate of 100 % on several tasks.
- Time Efficiency: The time spent on tasks varied, with an average of 85 seconds for Task 1 and going up to 644.5 seconds for Task 5, indicating an efficient problem-solving time.

3.4.2 *GPT-3.5*

- Correctness: Displayed a lower correctness rate, with most tasks showing 0 % correctness and a peak of 50 % correctness only on Task 15.
- Time Efficiency: Generally spent less time on tasks compared to GPT-4.0, with times ranging from 7.34 to 16.54 seconds across tasks, suggesting quicker but less accurate responses.

3.4.3 *Bard*

- Correctness: Like GPT-3.5, Bard also had most tasks at 0 % correctness, apart from 50 % correctness on Task 15.
- Time Efficiency: Time spent was comparable to GPT-3.5, ranging from 4.66 to 21.91 seconds, indicating rapid task completion.

3.4.4 *Summary*

GPT-4.0 and Custom GPT stand out as the most capable in terms of correctness, handling a wider range of tasks effectively, though taking longer to respond in some cases.

Both GPT-3.5 and Bard showed limited problem-solving abilities with lower correctness rates, although they were quicker in responding.

3.5 Insights on Problem-Solving Strategies

An interesting observation from the study was the diversity in problem-solving strategies. Students employed a range of approaches, from methodical to innovative, adapting their strategies as required. AI models, while consistent in their approach, lacked the adaptability and creative problem-solving exhibited by human participants.

3.6 Implications of Findings

3.6.1 Synergy Between Human Creativity and AI Efficiency

In the realm of coding challenges like the 'Advent of Code', our study reveals critical insights into the interplay between human intelligence and AI models. The findings shed light on the distinct strengths and limitations inherent in both approaches, suggesting a path towards a more integrated and synergistic problem-solving paradigm.

3.6.2 Balancing Strengths and Limitations:

The performance of AI models, particularly the advanced LLMs such as GPT-4.0, is characterized by rapid processing and a consistent approach to problem-solving. However, they often fall short in achieving high correctness rates in complex tasks, where nuanced understanding and contextual interpretation are key. In contrast, human participants, especially with the luxury of unlimited time, demonstrate remarkable adaptability and creativity. They excel in tasks that demand a deeper comprehension of context, highlighting an ability to devise solutions that are not only correct but also innovative.

3.6.3 The Role of Time Constraints:

Our analysis underlines the significant impact of time constraints on problem-solving effectiveness. Participants with limited time limits struggled to maintain high correctness rates, particularly as tasks grew in complexity. This highlights the importance of time as a resource in achieving optimal problem-solving efficacy, especially in environments where accuracy is as crucial as speed.

3.6.4 Potential for Hybrid Problem-Solving Models:

The contrasting capabilities of humans and AI models pave the way for a collaborative approach in coding challenges. By amalgamating the computational efficiency of AI with the nuanced, adaptive problem-solving of humans, it becomes possible to achieve solutions that are both efficient and highly accurate. Such a hybrid model would be particularly valuable in scenarios demanding a blend of speed, accuracy, and creative insight.

3.6.5 Advancements in AI Models:

The progression from GPT-3.5 to GPT-4.0 illustrates ongoing enhancements in AI's problem-solving abilities. Nevertheless, the need for human-like creativity and contextual understanding remains a vital aspect that AI has yet to fully replicate.1

3.6.6 Future Research Directions:

This study not only elucidates the current capabilities of AI and human intelligence in algorithmic challenges but also sets the stage for future explorations. Investigating the collaborative potential of human and AI intelligence can lead to groundbreaking solutions that capitalize on the strengths of both. It opens new avenues in programming and algorithm development, where the creative problem-solving capabilities of humans are synergized with the relentless efficiency of AI.

4. Conclusion

The research embarked on a journey to explore the dynamic interplay between human intelligence and artificial intelligence (AI) in the sphere of algorithm development. Through a meticulous examination of the 'Advent of Code' challenges, insightful contrasts in the problem-solving approaches and efficiencies of human participants and neural network models have been uncovered, including the latest iterations of Large Language Models such as GPT-4.0, GPT-3.5, and Bard.

The analysis revealed that while AI models, particularly GPT-4.0, exhibit remarkable computational speed and consistency, they often fall short in achieving high correctness rates, especially in tasks that demand a deeper contextual understanding and creative reasoning. On the other hand, human participants, particularly those not constrained by time, demonstrated a superior ability to adapt and apply more effective problem-solving strategies, achieving higher accuracy in solving complex challenges.

The study illuminates the unique strengths and limitations of both human and AI-driven algorithm development. It underscores the potential of a synergistic approach that harnesses the computational prowess of AI with the creative and adaptive problem-solving skills of humans. Such a collaborative model could significantly enhance efficiency and accuracy in algorithmic challenges, paving the way for innovative solutions in various technological and scientific fields.

The research not only contributes to the understanding of the current capabilities of AI-assisted programming but also opens avenues for future exploration into the untapped potential of human-AI collaboration. It sets a foundation for further investigations into hybrid problem-solving models where the ingenuity of human intelligence is augmented by the relentless efficiency of AI.

In conclusion, the "Efficiency Divide" study highlights the evolving narrative of programming and algorithm development in the modern era, highlighting the complementary roles of human creativity and AI's computational efficiency. As we progress further into the age of AI, the fusion of human and machine intelligence stands as a promising frontier for future innovations.

References

Advent of Code. (2023). Stats - Advent of Code 2023. Accessed on: January 24, 2024 [Online]. Available at: https://adventofcode.com/2023/stats

Lee M., Srivastava M., Hardy A., Thickstun J., Durmus E., Paranjape A., ... & Liang P. (2022). Evaluating human-language model interaction. Accessed on: January 17, 2024 [Online]. Available at: https://arxiv.org/abs/2212.09746

Advent of Code. (2023). About - Advent of Code 2023. Accessed on: January 05, 2024 [Online]. Available at: https://adventofcode.com/2023/about

OpenAI. (2024). Introducing GPTs. OpenAI Blog. Accessed on: January 22, 2024 [Online]. Available at: https://openai.com/blog/introducing-gpts

Arora, S., Narayan A., Chen M.F. (2022). Ask me Anything: A Simple Strategy for Prompting Language Models. Accessed on: January 12, 2024 [Online]. Available at: https://arxiv.org/abs/2210.02441

Si Ch., Gan Z., Yang Z. (2022). Prompting GPT-3 To Be Reliable. Accessed on: January 14, 2024 [Online]. Available at: https://www.researchgate.net/publication/364438038_Prompting_GPT-3_To_Be_Reliable

Olsen, A.L. (2005). Using Pseudocode to Teach Problem Solving. Accessed on: January 14, 2024 [Online]. Available at: https://www.researchgate.net/publication/234778626_Using_pseudocode_to_teach_problem_solving

Complexity of Contemporary Indicators of Compromise

Raymond Andre Hagen and Kirsi Helkala
Norwegian University of Science and Technology, Norway
Norwegian Defence College, Norway
raymohag@stud.ntnu.no
Khelkala@mil.no

Abstract. The cybersecurity landscape has undergone substantial transformation, especially in the sphere of Advanced Persistent Threats (APT). These evolving threats, marked by increased sophistication, scale, and impact, require the critical revaluation of traditional security models and the development of more advanced defensive strategies. This study offers a comprehensive analysis of the progress in APT attack methodologies over the past 30 years, focused on the evolving nature of compromise (IoCs) and their role in shaping future predictive and defensive mechanisms. Using a rigorous methodological approach, this survey systematically reviewed 21 significant APT incidents that span three decades. This includes integrating data from various sources such as academic journals, specialised cybersecurity blogs, and media reports. Using comparative and analytical methods, this study dissects each incident to provide an intricate understanding of the APT landscape and the evolution of IoCs. Our findings indicate a notable change in thinking from isolated hacker activities to organised state-sponsored APT operations driven by complex motives such as political espionage, economic disruption, and national security interests. Advancements in APTs are characterised by sophisticated persistence mechanisms, innovative attack vectors, advanced lateral movement within networks, and more covert data exfiltration and evasion methods. This study emphasises the difficulties in detecting advanced persistent threat (APT) activities due to their sophisticated and secretive nature. This stresses the importance of thoroughly investigating the evidence of such activities and highlights the need for a dynamic and initiative-cybersecurity approach. This study also highlights the crucial role of integrating IoC understanding into AI-driven predictive models and frameworks to predict potential APT. This integration is essential for the development of pre-emptive defence strategies. This study provides valuable information on the evolving dynamics of cyber threats and emphasises the urgent need for forward-thinking adaptive cybersecurity strategies. It offers a framework for understanding the complexities of modern APTs and guides the development of more effective AI-enhanced defence mechanisms against emerging cyber threats.

Keywords: State Actors, APT, IoC, Threats

1. Introduction

Cybersecurity has changed significantly in the past three decades, as malicious actors have refined their strategies and tactics. This evolution has ushered in an era where threats are not only more sophisticated but also highly targeted, leveraging a mix of technological prowess and strategic planning to breach defense. Advanced Persistent Threats (APTs) are among the most formidable. APTs are specialized cyber operation collectives that are primarily associated with nation-state entities or, in some instances, organized crime groups. These entities are characterized by their high level of sophistication, significant resources, and persistent focus on specific targets. Their operations are typically aimed at espionage, data theft, or disruption, leveraging a wide array of tactics, techniques, and procedures (TTPs) over prolonged periods to achieve their objectives.

The identification and analysis of IoCs is an integral aspect of understanding and mitigating the risks posed by APTs involves the identification and analysis of Indicators of Compromise (IoCs). IoCs are observable artefacts or behaviors in a network or system that, alone or aggregated with other IoCs, can suggest a successful cyberattack. These indicators can range from simple indicators, such as known malicious IP addresses or domain names, to more complex patterns of behavior that suggest unauthorized access or data exfiltration. Recognizing IoCs is pivotal for the early detection of cybersecurity breaches, enabling timely response and mitigation actions to limit damage and prevent future attacks.

This study aims to improve and optimize defensive cyber strategies by examining cyber incidents, particularly their IoCs. By dissecting and understanding the nature of APTs and IoCs that characterize their attacks, cybersecurity professionals can enhance their defensive measures. This entails not only deploying technical solutions but also adopting a more strategic approach to defense, considering the sophisticated nature of APT actors and their campaigns. A thorough understanding of APTs and their IoCs is crucial for fortifying the defense against ever-evolving cyber threats. Through detailed analysis and strategic implementation of defense mechanisms, it is possible to build resilience against these advanced adversaries and protect critical information and infrastructure from compromises.

2. Methodology

This chapter describes our systematic research methodology for investigating the development of APTs over the past 30 years. Our approach guarantees transparency and thoroughness, thereby ensuring the empirical validity of the APT observations.

2.1 Evolving Indicators of Advanced Persistent Threats in Cybersecurity

The survey focused on understanding advanced persistent threats (APTs) within the ever-evolving realm of cybersecurity. This addresses the following critical question.

"Dynamic Indicators of APT Incursions: What are the predominant indicators of an APT attack, and how have these indicators evolved to adapt to the changing cybersecurity environment?"

2.2 Research Design

We use a strategic framework to examine the intricate nature of advanced persistent threats (APTs) during a designated period. Therefore, we applied a combination of comparative and analytical methods.

Selection Criteria We conducted a thorough parameter selection process to identify a wide range of standard parameters. We then reviewed each and removed any redundant or challenging information that could be obtained, with the Norwegian Cybersecurity Centre (NCSC) providing valuable input to help us make our final decision. We selected 21 APT attacks that spanned more than three decades, with diversity and importance as the main criteria. Furthermore, we analysed each incident against twenty carefully selected parameters to create a complete dataset. This allowed us to take a multifaceted look at the APT dynamics.

2.3 Data Collection, Database Selection, and Search Strategy

We sourced our primary data from Oria, a renowned academic database. We adopted a strategic approach, using search terms such as 'Moonlight Maze', 'APT', 'hacking', 'cyberattacks', and 'attribution of APT.' Information search was conducted using traditional search engines and new AI tools, as specified in the references.

2.4 Inclusion of Non-Traditional Sources

Recognising the rapid evolution of cyberattacks, we have expanded our research beyond traditional academic sources. This included insights from YouTube channels, such as True Spies, Kaspersky, Darknet Diaries, authoritative security blogs, and prompt press releases. Although these sources may deviate from academic norms, their relevance in supplying the current cyber-threat perspectives is crucial. We carefully reviewed each for credibility, ensuring that they complemented our research with practical insight. This approach bridges the gap between academic research and the dynamic cyber landscape, offering a comprehensive understanding of the cyberattack ecosystem. Readers are encouraged to consider these diverse sources holistically from a well-rounded perspective.

2.5 Data Analysis

Comparative analysis. We use comparative analysis as a methodological approach to qualitative research. The goal is to name patterns, similarities, and variances between events and cases. Furthermore, our aim was to figure out the broader patterns and their unique deviations.

Procedure:

Data Categorisation: Data were sorted according to year, type of attack, affected entities, and methods.

Event-by-Event Comparison: Each event was contrasted with others to find similarities and differences.

Thematic Extraction: Emerging themes were documented during these events.

2.6 Analytical Approach

The data were subjected to more in-depth comparative analysis. This stage distils the findings to reveal the changing sides of the APTs throughout the study period. This study aimed to uncover information on the evolution and transformation of APTs.

2.7 Limitations and Mitigation

Although every methodological approach has intrinsic limitations, conscious steps were taken to minimise their potential impact on our research.

Subjectivity: Different researchers interpret the same dataset differently. However, by defining our research question and selecting the parameters, we proved a structured framework that reduced the scope of various interpretations. Furthermore, cross-verification of findings from multiple researchers can further dilute individual biases.

2.8 Overemphasis on Commonalities

Although focusing on standard parameters might lead to overlooking outliers or unique events, these were conscious decisions to ensure a consistent data comparison. However, we know of the potential loss of insight from individual cases. To address this, our analytical approach was designed to be vigilant for significant deviations or outliers with different implications.

To keep the credibility of our research, we used a standardised survey that systematically collected identical data points across the board. This method speeded up the data collection process and significantly minimised the likelihood of introducing inconsistencies or errors in our analysis. Our overarching goal was to support the precision and authenticity of our findings and to accurately reflect the genuine dynamics of APT.

2.9 Ethical Considerations

Finding who is behind cyber threats, particularly those linked to the government, is challenging. We conducted our research cautiously to recognise advanced persistent threat actors and have been transparent about our sources, while considering their limitations. We focus intensely on being explicit to ensure the correctness of our findings.

2.10 Limitations of the Survey

Our research was based on 21 well-known attacks in the cybersecurity community. Although these cases supply valuable information, other APT activities that can reveal various aspects of APT capabilities have not yet been investigated. A more extensive or added set of attacks can lead to varying conclusions, emphasising the need for continuous and diverse studies in this field.

3. Comparative Analysis of APT Attacks Over Two Decades

We comprehensively examined twenty-one major APT attacks over the past two decades.

Table 1: Table 1 of the 8 of the comparative analysis

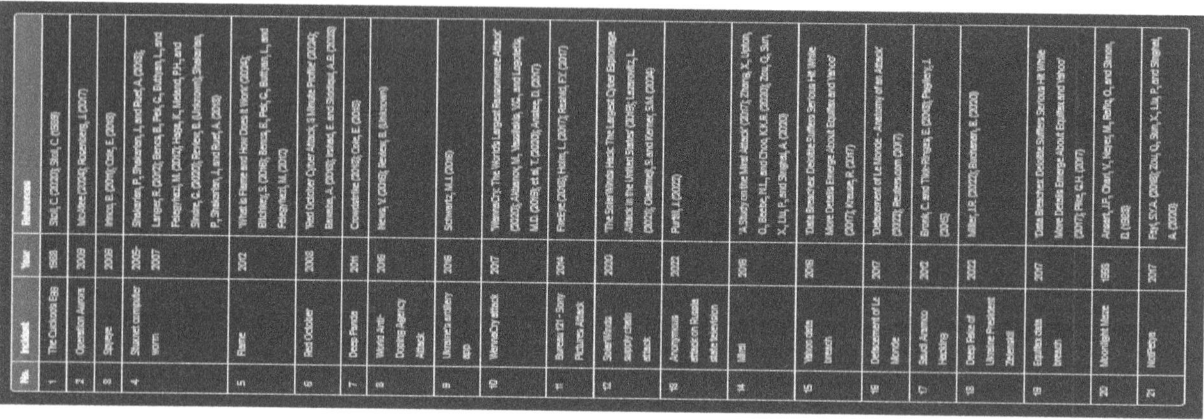

No.	Incident	Year	References
1	The Cuckoo's Egg	1988	Stoll, C. (2020); Stoll, C. (1989)
2	Operation Aurora	2009	McAfee (2024); Rosenberg, J. (2017)
3	[illegible]	2008	[illegible] (2019); Cole, E. (2008)
4	Stuxnet computer worm	2005-2007	Shakarian, P., Shakarian, J., and Ruef, A. (2013); Langner, R. (2013); Bencsáth, B., Pék, G., Buttyán, L., and Felegyhazi, M. (2012); Hoga, K., Melland, P.H., and Shaw, C. (2020); Fenton, E. (Unknown); Shakarian, P., Shakarian, J., and Ruef, A. (2013)
5	Flame	2012	'What is Flame and How Does It Work' (2024); Bitchley, S. (2016); Bencsáth, B., Pék, G., Buttyán, L., and Felegyhazi, M. (2012)
6	Red October	2008	'Red October' Cyber Attack: 5 Minute Profile (2024); Baraka, A. (2013); Ishaq, E. and Siddiqui, A.B. (2023)
7	Deep Panda	2011	Crowdstrike (2013); Cole, E. (2013)
8	World Anti-Doping Agency Attack	2016	Nena, V. (2016); Fenton, B. (Unknown)
9	Ukraine's artillery app	2016	Schwartz, M.J. (2016)
10	WannaCry attack	2017	'WannaCry: The World's Largest Ransomware Attack' (2023); Akbanov, M., Vassilakis, V.G., and Logothetis, M.D. (2019); et al, T. (2020); Avelar, D. (2017)
11	Bureau 121 - Sony Pictures Attack	2014	FireEye (2016); Haller, L. (2017); Recard, F.X. (2017)
12	SolarWinds supply chain attack	2020	'The SolarWinds Hack: The Largest Cyber Espionage Attack in the United States' (2021); Lazarovitz, L. (2021); Oladimeji, S. and Kerner, S.M. (2024)
13	Anonymous attack on Russia state television	2022	Purtill, J. (2022)
14	Mirai	2016	'A Study on the Mirai Attack' (2017); Zhang, X., Upton, O., Beebe, N.L., and Choo, K.K.R. (2020); Zou, Q., Sun, X., Liu, P., and Singhal, A. (2020)
15	Yahoo data breach	2016	'Data Breaches: Deloitte Suffers Serious Hit While More Details Emerge About Equifax and Yahoo' (2017); Krause, R. (2017)
16	Defacement of Le Monde	2017	'Defacement of Le Monde - Anatomy of an Attack' (2022); Reuters.com (2017)
17	Saudi Aramco Hacking	2012	Bronk, C. and Tikk-Ringas, E. (2013); Pagliery, J. (2015)
18	Deep Fake of Ukraine President Zelenskij	2022	Miller, J.P. (2022); Bachmann, E. (2022)
19	Equifax data breach	2017	'Data Breaches: Deloitte Suffers Serious Hit While More Details Emerge About Equifax and Yahoo' (2017); Pike, G.H. (2017)
20	Moonlight Maze	1998	Ansari, J.P., Chan, V., Nazer, M., Rafiq, O., and Simon, D. (1998)
21	NotPetya	2017	Fayi, S.Y.A. (2018); Zou, Q., Sun, X., Liu, P., and Singhal, A. (2020)

Table 1b: Table 1b of the 8 of the comparative analysis

No.	Incident	Year	References
16	Defacement of Le Monde	2017	'Defacement of Le Monde - Anatomy of an Attack' (2022); Reuters.com (2017)
17	Saudi Aramco Hacking	2012	Bronk, C. and Tikk-Ringas, E. (2013); Pagliery, J. (2015)
18	Deep Fake of Ukraine President Zelenskii	2022	Miller, J.R. (2022); Buchanan, B. (2020)
19	Equifax data breach	2017	'Data Breaches: Deloitte Suffers Serious Hit While More Details Emerge About Equifax and Yahoo' (2017); Pike, G.H. (2017)
20	Moonlight Maze	1998	Ansart, J.P., Chari, V., Neyer, M., Rafiq, O., and Simon, D. (1983)
21	NotPetya	2017	Fayi, S.Y.A. (2018); Zou, Q., Sun, X., Liu, P., and Singhal, A. (2020)

Table 2: Table 2 of 8 of the comparative analysis

No.	Aspect	Description
1	Confidentiality	German hacking group that broke into American universities, government, and military computer systems.
2	Confidentiality	A series of attacks on around 30 large companies.
3	Confidentiality	Malware that uses different methods to steal credentials.
4	Availability	Worm used to stop Iran's nuclear program.
5	Availability and Confidentiality	A highly sophisticated tool that allows for customization-based tools in relation to the attacker's needs.
6	Confidentiality	Espionage programmed.
7	Confidentiality	Espionage programmed.
8	Confidentiality	APT hacked into WADA and accessed information about WADA athletes that leaked to the media.
9	Availability	Russian APT managed to change a target calculating app for howitzers that allowed GPS coordinates to be sent to Russia, Ukraine lost 60% of howitzers in one day.
10	Availability	Using zero-day exploits, the ransomware spread around the world in 18 hours.
11	Availability	Due to the Hollywood movie "The Interview," where the North Korean leader was depicted in a nonflattering way, DPRK launched a cyberattack on Sony Pictures.
12	Confidentiality and Integrity	Supply chain attack where the popular SolarWinds Orion Software update server was compromised, giving the attackers access to more than 18,000 systems.
13	Integrity	Hacktivism group 'Anonymous' got access to Russian state television and sent a pro-Ukraine video.
14	Availability	A massive botnet took advantage of insecure IoT devices.
15	Confidentiality	The largest data breach in history up to that point.
16	Integrity	Attack that killed several French media outlets.
17	Integrity	35,000 computers from the world's largest oil company were wiped out.
18	Integrity	A deep fake trying to claim Zelenskiy wanted Ukraine to surrender.
19	Confidentiality	The credit bureau was breached.
20	Confidentiality	Different US government agencies, defence contractors, and research institutions were compromised.
21	Confidentiality and Availability	NonPetya was a destructive malware attack on 27 June 2017. Although disguised as a ransomware attack similar to the notorious Petya ransomware, it was identified as a more damaging wiper attack designed to cause destruction.

Table 3: Table 3 of 8 of the comparative analysis

Nr	Duration	Aggressor	Who did Attribution?
1	3 years	(Group of countries / APT) KGB by proxy of a West-German hacker group	The parties involved in the case
2	2 years	China	Google
3	3 years	Russia	USA
4	5 years	USA	Several public and private IT-security companies
5	1994-2012	USA / Israel / China	The Washington Post
6	2008 - 2012	China	Russia / England
7	2008-dd	China	CrowdStrike
8	2016	Russia	FireEye / Mandiant
9	2016	Russia	Armed forces of Ukraine
10	2 days	North Korea	USA
11	1 month	North Korea	USA
12	6 months	Russia	USA
13	2 hours	Anonymous hacking collective	Russia
14	Constantly adjusted; ongoing in some form	USA	USA
15	22.09.2016	Russia	USA
16	2017	Russia	France
17	6 months	The group "Cutting sword of justice"	Saudi Arabia
18	1 day	Russia	Ukraine
19	3 months	China	USA
20	3 years	Russia	USA
21	From a few hours up to six months	Russia	ESET, Kaspersky, and Microsoft

Table 4: Table 4 of 8 of the comparative analysis

Nr	Country that was attacked	Time to Mitigate Attack	Method Used
1	USA	3.5 years	Credential stealing
2	USA	1.5 years until Microsoft had a patch ready	Exploiting operating systems vulnerability
3	USA, Canada, UK, India, Mexico	Six months	Credential stealing
4	Primary objective Iran, but the worm spread worldwide	2 years	Custom malware to attack Siemens SCADA systems
5	Different Countries in the World, Middle East and Africa	Shortly after attack	Modular-based malware
6	Global attack	2012	Error in the MS Office file format
7	American companies, most famous Adobe Breach	2 years	Custom malware
8	Canada	1 month	Custom malware
9	Ukraine	Instantly	Custom malware
10	500,000 companies around the world	18 hours	Custom malware
11	Japan	2 days	Custom malware
12	Global attack	Ongoing	Custom supply chain attack malware
13	Russia	2 hours	Intrusion of broadcast system
14	Global attack	Estimate 1 day for each attack	Password hacking, HTTP flooding, wipers and other malware from infected IoT devices
15	USA	4 months	Hackers got access to Yahoo's main site user database
16	France	6 months	Phishing emails
17	Saudi Arabia	6 months	Phishing emails
18	Ukraine	1 day	Deep fake video (AI GAN method)
19	USA, UK, and Canada	76 days	Exploiting nonpatched systems
20	USA	3 years	Social Engineering and Exploitation vulnerabilities
21	Ukraine initially and then globally	Short-lived due to destructive operation	Wiper malware hidden as ransomware

Table 5: Table 5 of the 8 of the comparative analysis

Nr	Complexity Assessment	Attack Surface	Targeted or Random (Opportunistic)
1	Low	Software vulnerability	Targeted
2	High	Operating system	Targeted
3	Medium	Internet Browsers	Targeted
4	High	PLC controllers of Siemens SCADA systems	Targeted
5	High	Rootkits	Targeted
6	High	Exploits	Random
7	High	Exploits	Targeted
8	High	Exploits	Targeted
9	Medium	Exploits	Targeted
10	High	Exploits	Random
11	High	Destructive malware	Targeted
12	High	Update server	Targeted
13	Medium	Exploits	Targeted
14	Medium	IoT devices	Random
15	Medium	Exploits	Targeted
16	Low	Exploits	Targeted
17	Low	Exploits	Targeted
18	High	Video and social networks	Targeted
19	High	Apache Struts framework	Targeted
20	High	Exploits and social manipulation	Targeted
21	High	Malware	Targeted

Table 6: Table 6 of 8 of the comparative analysis

Nr	Motivation	Consequence	Specially Adapted Malware
1	Bragging rights	KGB got access to some US systems, but very little data was stolen.	Yes
2	Political	Several high-value targets got exposed and lost data	Yes
3	Economic gain	Further development of the malware used in this attack	Yes
4	Political	Managed to negotiate the Iran nuclear treaty	Yes
5	Political	Espionage	Yes
6	Research and development	Espionage	Yes
7	Political	Espionage	Yes
8	Political / Show of force	Hacktivism	Yes
9	Political / War	State actor	Yes
10	Economic gain	Many billions to restore and fix the attack, many Eastern European companies went down	Yes
11	Political	Show of force	Yes
12	Persistent access and stealing of data	18,000 companies were infected	Yes
13	Hacktivism	Tried to create civil unrest due to the Russian war in Ukraine	Yes
14	Hacktivism	Have been used in state actors to try and stop root DNS servers, tough attack to negotiate	Yes
15	Economic gain	The market value of Yahoo was severely reduced	Yes
16	Hacktivism	Le Monde had to rebuild their entire IT system infrastructure, no cost has been publicly disclosed	Yes
17	Hacktivism	Cost of rebuilding and protecting the infrastructure	Yes
18	Political / War	None	Yes
19	Economic gain / Political	Lost a lot of sensitive data	Yes
20	Political	Loss of sensitive information and showed vulnerabilities in national infrastructure	Yes
21	Political	Parties were hit. The initial spread was in Ukraine, affecting much of the Ukrainian infrastructure	Yes

Table 7: Table 7 of 8 of the comparative analysis

Nr	Total Number of Users Affected?	Social Engineering Used?	How Was the Attack Discovered?
1	Estimate of 15 companies attacked by the group	No	A billing error in the accounting system
2	More than 20 companies	No	McAfee discovered zero days
3	Unknown	No	Security Companies
4	200,000 companies worldwide	Yes	A company was hired to do an audit and found the malware
5	1,000 computers	No	Kaspersky Labs, Iranian National CERT and CrySYS investigated Iranian systems on behalf of the UN
6	Around 300 systems had the trojan	No	Cybersecurity files
7	Unknown	No	Security Companies
8	Unknown	No	Observed data were extracted from WADA servers
9	Unknown	No	70% of the Ukrainian howitzers were destroyed in one day
10	500,000 at least	Unknown	Security companies
11	Unknown	No	Leaked documents
12	Unknown	No	Mandiant (FireEye) investigated their breach and found a modified DLL that was used
13	Unknown	No	N/A
14	Unknown	No	Instantly
15	Between 500 million and 3 billion user accounts	No	No public information suggested that management knew about the attack for four months before publishing it
16	N/A	Yes (Phishing)	Employees noticed the system acted "abnormal"
17	N/A	Yes	N/A
18	N/A	Yes. Played on feelings	It was a terrible job and it was easy to see that it was fake
19	160 million users	No	Equifax disclosed the breach themselves
20	Several hundred systems, classified and unclassified networks	Yes	The US DoD discovered the attack and alerted the different targets
21	Unknown	No	The malware was so destructive that the impact was imminent

Table 8: Table 8 of 8 of the comparative analysis

No.	Political Situation at the Time of the Attack (Both Local and Global)
1	Cold War and a divided Germany
2	Tensions between the United States and China
3	Normal
4	Global worry over Iran getting nuclear weapons
5	The "normal" tensions between different states in the Middle East
6	Normal
7	Normal
8	Normal, but there was some tension when WADA decided not to let Russian athletes compete internationally
9	At the start of the still ongoing war between Russia and Ukraine
10	Normal, North Korea was looking for cash due to sanctions
11	North Korea was under pressure to stop their rocket and missile tests
12	A part of the ongoing tensions between Russia and the USA
13	Full-scale war in Ukraine
14	This has become a tool of different groups; amongst others, the Russian-affiliated APT group "Killnet" used a derived version towards countries that help Ukraine in their ongoing war with Russia
15	Normal
16	Some social tension in France at the time before the attack
17	Some protests against the Royal Family of Saudi Arabia
18	War in Ukraine
19	Some protests against the US financial system. Most famous was the "Occupy Wall Street" movement
20	Several regional conflicts and evolving security threats, including cyber
21	The attack was considered part of the ongoing war between Russia and Ukraine, which began in 2014

Working with the Norwegian Cybersecurity Centre (NCSC), we carefully selected these attacks to ensure their relevance to cybersecurity. To understand the dynamics of APTs, we collected data from various sources, including academic databases, blogs, and media outlets. This approach supplies a detailed exploration of this topic.

3.1 Observations from Notable APT Attacks

During the past two and a half decades, the post-Cold War era and aspirations for technological dominance have prompted a significant increase in cyberattacks, reshaping the cyber warfare landscape. The digital age, while empowering, has allowed governments to conduct secret operations, making it challenging to assign definitive blame for online assaults. This anonymity, especially the use of zero-day vulnerabilities and deceptive tactics by APT groups, complicates the attribution process (Tables 3 and 5).

APT groups vary in their motivations: Chinese factions are linked to industrial espionage, Russian groups to military objectives, and US entities to political cyber activities. Countries such as India, Pakistan, and North Korea also demonstrate APT capabilities, with North Korea focusing on national pride and financial gains (see Table 6).

Since the late 1980s, the evolution of individual hackers into state-sponsored APT entities has become notable. The Mandiant identification of China Unit 61398 and the activities of the Equation Group and Russia APT29 illustrate this change (Table 6).

3.2 Categorising the Attacks

Attacks can be classified according to their motivation and consequences. We divide the attacks into four categories.

Early Espionage: These attacks prove the development of cyber espionage, which focuses on obtaining confidential data and the growth of state-sponsored cyber operations. Examples include Cuckoo's Egg incident (1986), Operation Aurora (2009), Flame (2012), Red October (2007-2013), and Moonlight Maze (mid-1990s), which illustrate the stages of collecting classified information and increasing participation in state-sponsored cyber activities (see relevant citations).

Economic Infiltration: This category looks at cyberattacks that have significantly affected global financial systems, highlighting the economic weaknesses of these incidents. Examples of such attacks include SpyEye (2009-2011), Yahoo Data Breach (2013-2014), Equifax Data Breach (2017), and Saudi Aramco Hacking (2012), all of which have had considerable monetary impacts on the world economy (see relevant citations).

Political Disruption: These examples demonstrate the increasing prevalence of cyber warfare in political disputes, with incidents such as the Stuxnet Worm (2010), WADA Hack (2016), SolarWinds Attack (2020), Anonymous Attack on Russian State TV (2022), Le Monde Newspaper Defacement (2015), Deep Panda Operations (2014), and NotPetya Attack (2017) serving as evidence. Cyberattacks have been used to disrupt political processes and institutions, highlighting the growing importance of cyber warfare in geopolitical conflicts (see citations).

Unique Cases: This wide range of cyberattacks encompass various methods and targets, displaying various threats and creative tactics in the cyber world. Examples include the WannaCry attack (2017), Bureau 121 Sony Pictures attack (2014), Deep Fake Attack on President Zelensky (2022), Mirai attack (2016), and 2014 Russian cyberattack on a Ukrainian artillery app, each of which proves distinct threats and approaches (see the respective citations).

4. Results

This section explores the dynamic and constantly evolving domain of cybersecurity, with an emphasis on advanced persistent threats (APTs). Our study focused on the expansion and transformation of the indicators of compromise (IoC) associated with these threats.

An analysis of 21 different APT attacks revealed that APT activity is more complex and sophisticated. This development in IoCs reflects the increasing skill and sophistication of attackers. APTs are "a group involved in specialised cyber operations, often linked to national-state entities or organised crime." As outlined below, a transition in IoCs has been seen from the primary signs of persistence and stealth to more intricate strategic behaviour.

Enhanced Persistence: APT groups show a persistent effort to keep access to target networks, evident in repeated infiltration attempts and continuous communication with command-and-control centres.

Advanced Attack Methods: These threats employ sophisticated tactics, including zero-day exploits, custom malware, and complex multi-tier strategies, providing a detailed understanding of the vulnerabilities of their targets.

Lateral Movement: Indicators such as unusual network activities, unanticipated privilege increases, and system interconnection exploitation suggest APT strategies to navigate within systems for increased control or access to critical data.

Strategic data exfiltration: APTs are characterised by unauthorised data transfers that involve abnormal data movement to unknown IP addresses or at unusual times.

Evasion Techniques: APTs use advanced techniques to avoid detection, including hidden network traffic, encrypted communications, and alterations in system logs.

APT Group-Specific IoCs: Certain IP addresses, domain names, malware signatures, or known tactics, techniques, and procedures can be used to propose APT.

Unusual User Activities: Signs such as logging in during odd hours, multiple failed access attempts, or unauthorised data access can indicate APT activities.

Resource utilisation: Abnormal system resource usage, such as increased CPU activity, unexpected network traffic, or sudden disk space consumption, may indicate an APT incident.

Detection of APTs is challenging because of their sophisticated and covert nature. Although these IoCs supply crucial information, they do not offer definitive proof of the presence of APT. Therefore, a complete and thorough investigation is essential when these signs are detected. A comprehensive and initiative-based approach for detection and analysis is necessary to counteract the covert and complex activities of APTs effectively.

5. Conclusions

This study extensively examines the development of advanced persistent threat actors (APT) over the past three decades. Studies have shown these actors have become increasingly complex and influential in cybersecurity. The transformation from isolated cyberattacks to well-structured state-sponsored operations, fuelled by a complex interplay of geopolitical, economic, and security interests, has led to a growing concern that traditional cybersecurity approaches are becoming less effective against the evolving tactics of APT actors.

Our analysis of twenty-one major APT incidents revealed a worrisome trend: changing tactics outpaced traditional cybersecurity strategies. Our findings emphasise the need for a dynamic and initiative-taking approach to cybersecurity that can adapt to constantly evolving threats posed by APTs. This includes enhancing indicators of compromise (IoCs) to be more responsive to advanced tactics, such as stealthy network infiltration, sophisticated data exfiltration techniques, and evasive manoeuvres that challenge conventional detection frameworks.

The increasing complexity and stealth of APTs require an equally sophisticated and vigilant cybersecurity posture. Organisations must adopt a multifaceted approach, focusing on detecting and mitigating attacks while emphasising preventive measures through continuous learning and adaptation. As APTs evolve, strategies must be developed to defend against them and ensure that cybersecurity measures are dynamic and resilient to threats they seek to combat.

The identification of Indicators of Compromise (IoCs) for advanced persistent threats (APTs) in this study significantly contributes to cybersecurity measures in the era of Artificial Intelligence (AI) and machine learning. This study catalogues and analyses IoCs associated with APT attacks by supplying a dataset that can be used to train AI systems. Understanding IoCs enables the development of more sophisticated AI-driven security tools capable of recognising subtle patterns and anomalies indicative of APT activities. Given the evolving nature of APTs, which often employ complex and stealthy strategies, AI and machine learning algorithms trained on comprehensive IoC data can adapt and improve over time, improving their ability to predict, detect, and respond to APT incidents with greater precision and speed. Integrating these IoCs into AI models transforms cybersecurity from reactive to initiative-taking, equipping systems with the foresight needed to thwart advanced threats before they manifest full-blown attacks. Thus, the study's insights into IoCs are not just retrospective analyses but are instrumental in shaping a more resilient and dynamic defense against future cyber threats.

In conclusion, our analysis of Compromise Indicators (IoCs) in the context of Advanced Persistent Threats (APTs) has yielded valuable insights into cybersecurity strategies. This research provides a robust dataset that can enhance the effectiveness of AI and machine-learning algorithms in threat detection and response. Our study provides a nuanced understanding of IoCs, enabling advanced technologies to identify and respond to the complex patterns associated with APT activities. As APTs continue to employ sophisticated tactics, integrating AI-driven tools informed by our findings is essential. These tools are expected to evolve and enhance predictive accuracy and responsiveness to appearing threats. We contribute to advancing cybersecurity from a reactive approach to a more initiative-taking and adaptive framework. Using the power of AI and machine learning, we can remain ahead of APTs, ensuring that our defense mechanisms are as sophisticated and dynamic as those of the adversaries.

Acknowledgments

I extend my deepest gratitude to Professor Lasse Øverlier at Norwegian University of Science and Technology for his invaluable guidance and inspiration throughout my research. His expertise and encouragement have been pivotal in shaping my work, offering both challenges and support in equal ways.

Similarly, my sincere thanks go to Professor Kirsi Helkala at Norwegian Defence College, whose critical insights and contributions have significantly enriched my research. Her thoughtful feedback and encouragement were instrumental in pushing the boundaries of my work.

Together, Professors Øverlier and Helkala guided my academic path and profoundly impacted my professional development and personal growth. Their mentorship is the cornerstone of my journey, for which I am eternally grateful. As part of my ongoing research, this article is a testament to their invaluable support and belief in my potential.

References

Akbanov, M., Vassilakis, V.G. and Logotetis, M.D. (2019) 'Ransomware Detection and Mitigation Using Software-Defined Networking - The Case of WannaCry', Computers Electrical Engineering.

Ansart, J.P., Chari, V., Neyer, M., Rafiq, O. and Simon, D. (1983) 'Description, Simulation and Implementation of Communication Protocols Using PDIL', Computer Communication Review, 13(2), pp. 112-120.

Anstee, D. (2017) 'The Great Threat Intelligence Debate', Computer Fraud Security, 2017(9), pp. 14-16.

Bawaba, A. (2013) ''Red October' Cyber Espionage Network Discovered', InformationWeek.

Bencs, B., Pek, G., Buttyan, L. and Felegyhazi, M. (2012) 'The Cousins of Stuxnet: Duqu, Flame, and Gauss'. Available at: www.mdpi.com/journal/futureinternet [Accessed 5 January 2024].

Bitchkey, S. (2016) 'The Yahoo Data Breach and Its Repercussions'. Available at: https://hitachi-systems-security.com/the-yahoo-data-breach-and-its-repercussions/ [Accessed 5 January 2024].

Bronk, C. and Tikk-Ringas, E. (2013) 'The Cyber Attack on Saudi Aramco', Survival.

Buchanan, B. (2020) The Hacker and the State, Cambridge: Harvard University Press.

Cole, E. (2013) 'Author Biography', in Advanced Persistent Threat, Boston: Syngress, p. xiii. Available at: https://doi.org/10.1016/B978-1-59-749949-1.00018-8 [Accessed 5 January 2024].

Crowdstrike (2013) 'Deep Panda - Intelligence Team Report Ver 1.0'.

Fayi, S.Y.A. (2018) 'What Petya/NotPetya Ransomware Is and What Its Remediations Are', in Latifi, S. (ed.) Information Technology - New Generations, Cham: Springer International Publishing, pp. 93-100.

FireEye (2018) 'APT38: Un-usual Suspects'. Available at: https://www.fireeye.com/blog/threat-research/2018/10/apt38-details-on-new-north-korean-regime-backed-threat-group.html [Accessed 5 January 2024].

Haga, K., Meland, P.H. and Sindre, G. (2020) 'Breaking the Cyber Kill Chain by Modelling Resource Costs', in Graphical Models for Security, Lecture Notes in Computer Science, vol. 12419, Cham: Springer International Publishing, pp. 111-126.

Holm, L. (2017) 'Cyber Attacks Coercion in the Digital Era - A Qualitative Case Analysis of the North Korean Cyber Attack on Sony Pictures'.

Irinco, B. (2011) 'Trend Micro Researchers Uncover SpyEye Operation'. Available at: https://www.trendmicro.com/vinfo/us/threat-encyclopedia/web-attack/87/trend-micro-researchers-uncover-spyeye-operation [Accessed 5 January 2024].

Irshad, E. and Siddiqui, A.B. (2023) 'Cyber Threat Attribution Using Unstructured Reports in Cyber Threat Intelligence', Egyptian Informatics Journal, 24(1), pp. 43-59. Available at: https://doi.org/10.1016/j.eij .2022.11.001 [Accessed 5 January 2024].

Krause, R. (2017) 'Verizon Surprise - Yahoo Data Breach Hit All 3 Billion Accounts'. Available at: https://www.investors.com/news/technology/verizon-surprise-yahoo-data-breach-hit-all-3-billion-accounts/ [Accessed 5 January 2024].

Langer, R. (2012) Robust Control System Networks - How to Achieve Reliable Control After Stuxnet, New York: Momentum Press.

Lazarovitz, L. (2021) 'Deconstructing the SolarWinds Breach', Computer Fraud Security, 2021(6), pp. 17-19. Available at: https://doi.org/10.1016/S1361-3723(21)00065-8 [Accessed 5 January 2024].

Lemay, A., Calvet, J., Menet, F. and Fernandez, J.M. (2018) 'Survey of Publicly Available Reports on Advanced Persistent Threat Actors', Computers Security, 72, pp. 26-59. Available at: https://doi.org/10.1016/j.cose.2017.08.005 [Accessed 5 January 2024].

McAfee (2024) 'Operation Aurora Overview'. Available at: https://www.youtube.com/watch?v=AEVbd5thokU [Accessed 5 January 2024].

Miller, J.R. (2022) 'Deepfake Video Shows Volodymyr Zelensky Telling Ukrainians to Surrender'. Available at: https://nypost.com/2022/03/17/deepfake-video-shows-volodymyr-zelensky-telling-ukrainians-to-surrender/ [Accessed 5 January 2024].

News, V. (2016) 'Wada Confirms Cyberattack by Russian Hackers'. Available at: www.voanews.com [Accessed 5 January 2024].

Oladimeji, S. and Kerner, S.M. (2024) 'SolarWinds Hack Explained: Everything You Need to Know'. Available at: https://www.techtarget.com/whatis/feature/SolarWinds-hack-explained-Everything-you-need-to-know [Accessed 5 January 2024].

Pagliery, J. (2015) 'CNN Business'. Available at: https://money.cnn.com/2015/08/05/technology/aramco-hack/index.html [Accessed 5 January 2024].

Pike, G.H. (2017) 'Equifax - Yet Another Data Breach', Information Today.

Purtill, J. (2022) 'Hacker Collective Anonymous Declares 'Cyber War' Against Russia, Disables State News Website: Hackers Launch Cyber Attacks Against Russian Government Websites, Including State-Controlled Russia Today, in Response to the Ukraine Crisis', ABC Science Online.

Rashid, F.Y. (2017) 'Old Attack Code is New Weapon for Russian Hackers', InfoWorld.com.

Research, C.P. (2018) 'APT37: Inside the Laziest Yet Most Effective North Korean APT Group'. Available at: https://blog.checkpoint.com/security/twisted-panda-check-point-research-unveils-a-chinese-apt-espionage-campaign-against-russian-state-owned-defense-institutes/ [Accessed 5 January 2024].

Review, B. (Unknown) 'Breaking the Cyber Kill Chain by Modelling Resource Costs'.

Rosenberg, J. (2017) 'Operation Aurora - Security in Embedded Systems', Rugged Embedded Systems.

Schwartz, M.J. (2016) 'Russian DNC Hackers Tied to Ukrainian Artillery App Hack', Bankinfosecurity.

Shakarian, P., Shakarian, J. and Ruef, A. (2013) 'Chapter 13 - Attacking Iranian Nuclear Facilities: Stuxnet', in Advanced Persistent Threat, USA: Syngress, 1st ed.

Shakarian, P., Shakarian, J. and Ruef, A. (2013) 'Chapter 8 - Duqu, Flame, Gauss, the Next Generation of Cyber Exploitation', in Introduction to Cyber-Warfare, Boston: Syngress, pp. 159-170. Available at: https://doi.org/10.1016/B978-0-12-407814-7.00008-7 [Accessed 5 January 2024].

Stoll, C. (1989) The Cuckoo's Egg: Tracking a Spy Through the Maze of Computer Espionage, USA, 1st ed.

Stoll, C. (2020) The Cuckoo's Egg, New York: Gallery Books.

Willett, M. (2021) 'Lessons of the SolarWinds Hack', Survival.

Zhang, X., Upton, O., Beebe, N.L. and Choo, K.K.R. (2020) 'IoT Botnet Forensics: A Comprehensive Digital Forensic Case Study on Mirai Botnet Servers', Forensic Science International: Digital Investigation, 32, 300926. Available at: https://doi.org/10.1016/j.fsidi.2020.300926 [Accessed 5 January 2024].

Zou, Q., Sun, X., Liu, P. and Singhal, A. (2020) 'An Approach for Detection of Advanced Persistent Threat Attacks', Computer, 53(12), pp. 92-96. Available at: https://doi.org/10.1109/MC.2020.302154 [Accessed 5 January 2024].

Eight Principles for Intelligence Sharing: A Holistic and Strategic Approach

Gazmend Huskaj[1,2]
[1]Geneva Centre for Security Policy (GCSP), Geneva, Switzerland
[2]Department of Computer and Systems Sciences, Stockholm University, Kista, Sweden
g.huskaj@gcsp.ch

Abstract: This paper reviews the strategic use of warning intelligence to pre-emptively address threats in complex geopolitical scenarios through rapid intelligence sharing. Specifically, the paper reviews the question How, based on research and experience, can a set of principles be applied by states to enhance situational awareness and tackle threat actors through a holistic and collaborative approach to intelligence sharing? The paper examines historical and contemporary alliances like the Five Eyes and reviews a Signals Intelligence Alliance as a case in point, highlighting the importance of collaborative approaches to enhance situational awareness and tackle threat actors. The study, grounded in the philosophical paradigm of interpretivism, adheres to the principles for transparent science when researchers use tools such as large-language-models as grammar editors or research assistants. The paper also acknowledges limitations such as the generalisability of the SIGINT model and the need for continuous adaptation of intelligence sharing practices. The results discuss policy, process, and people challenges to intelligence sharing. The paper concludes that successful intelligence sharing should follow eight general principles. Future research directions include exploring the impact of emerging technologies, human aspects of intelligence sharing, and context-based intelligence sharing alliances.

Keywords: Intelligence Sharing Principles; Strategic Warning Intelligence; SIGINT Alliance

[1]*The views expressed in this research product are only those of the author, and do not represent the Geneva Centre for Security Policy (GCSP), nor the Department of Computer and Systems Sciences, or any other party.*

1. Introduction

The current geopolitical security situation can be summarised by increased uncertainty and a shift from the traditional world order toward an indeterminate future (European Commission, 2023; Lazard, 2023). Threat actors are actively engaging in offensive cyberspace operations (Huskaj & Axelsson, 2023a) and cyber-enabled disinformation campaigns (Huskaj & Axelsson, 2023b) to achieve their tactical, operational, and strategic objectives. These activities include ransomware attacks, cyber-espionage, sabotage, destruction, and the employment of artificial intelligence (AI), such as deepfakes, to manipulate the perceived realities of societies by targeting individuals' fears and sowing distrust (Huskaj, 2024). Mitigating such attacks is crucial, and one effective approach involves the use of indicators and warnings—an intelligence-driven process that entails the identification of threat actors, along with their intentions and capabilities (Grabo, 2002).

How can the intent and capabilities of threat actors be discerned in a complex environment like today's geopolitical landscape, where state actors utilise their full arsenal? According to Meyer and Otto (2016), as cited in Rietjens (2020), "The idea of warning is that it enables a timely response so that harm is prevented or at least reduced by appropriate action. Effectively communicating the warning to decision-makers or the population at large is therefore of great importance. From Warner's perspective, key communication requirements include source credibility, message content, and mode of communication." Cynthia Grabo (2002) notes that strategic warning is a post-World War II innovation, developed in response to the perceived threats from the Soviet Union and other communist states to the security and interests of the "Free World" during the Cold War—actions that could potentially lead to unexpected conflict or direct aggression. In summary, the strategic application of warning intelligence aims to pre-emptively address threats in complex geopolitical scenarios through rapid sharing of intelligence.

The research question is: How, based on research and experience, can a set of principles be applied by states to enhance situational awareness and tackle threat actors through a holistic and collaborative approach to intelligence sharing?

Answering this question necessitates a short review of the literature on intelligence sharing and an understanding of past and current intelligence alliances. These alliances and partnerships include the Five Eyes, AUKUS, and the Signals Intelligence Alliance.

The Five Eyes (FVEY) alliance is one of the oldest and most comprehensive intelligence-sharing partnerships in the world. It consists of Australia, Canada, New Zealand, the United Kingdom, and the United States. Originating from World War II cooperative efforts, FVEY was formalized in the aftermath of the war through the UKUSA

Agreement in 1946 (Farrell, 2013; NSA, n.d.). This alliance focuses primarily on Signals Intelligence (SIGINT) and involves extensive sharing of intelligence gathered by each member's respective intelligence agencies. The unique strength of FVEY lies in its members' shared language, legal systems, and strong historical ties, which facilitate seamless collaboration (Corbett & Danoy, 2022). The geographical spread of the FVEY partners also enhances their global intelligence collection capabilities, providing access to diverse regions and intelligence sources that would be challenging for any single country to achieve alone.

AUKUS is a trilateral partnership announced in September 2021 between Australia, the United Kingdom, and the United States (U.S. DoD, n.d.). While it primarily focuses on enhancing Australia's naval capabilities through the acquisition of nuclear-powered submarines, AUKUS also encompasses broader aspects of defence and security cooperation, including cyber capabilities, artificial intelligence, quantum technologies, and additional undersea capabilities (Australian Government, 2022). This partnership signifies a strategic effort to strengthen security and stability in the Indo-Pacific region, addressing emerging threats and fostering greater interoperability among the three nations' defence forces. The AUKUS agreement underscores the shared commitment of its members to uphold international norms and maintain a balance of power in a region marked by increasing geopolitical competition (The White House, 2022).

The Signals Intelligence Alliance, as described by Bart Jacobs (2020), involves Denmark, France, Germany, the Netherlands, and Sweden. Initiated by Denmark in 1976, the alliance was formed to collaboratively address the challenges posed by signals intelligence, particularly with the advent of satellite communications. Germany and Sweden joined Denmark initially, followed by the Netherlands in 1978 and France in 1985. This alliance focuses on two main areas: signals analysis and cryptanalysis. Signals analysis involves coordinating interception mechanisms and sharing intercepted messages, which are discussed in multilateral meetings. Cryptanalysis, on the other hand, is handled bilaterally, with each country responsible for decrypting the messages it intercepts. The alliance is characterized by strong personal ties among its members and a high level of technical and cryptanalytical expertise, making it a successful model for intelligence sharing.

The main contributions of this research product can be summarised as follows:

- A set of principles for successful intelligence sharing (Section 4);
- A case study analysis of how the U.S. Intelligence Community can increase its intelligence sharing with allies, and based on this identified framework, review the SIGINT Alliance as a successful case, which leads to a set of principles for successful intelligence sharing (Section 3);
- A discussion on technological advancements, like AI and ML, and their impact on intelligence sharing (Section 3).

The remainder of this research product is organised as follows: Section 2 describes the methods and materials, Section 3 presents the results, while Section 4 presents the discussion. Finally, the conclusions are in Section 5.

2. Methods and Materials

This research is founded on the philosophical paradigm of interpretivism (Oates, 2005; Saunders et al., 2016). Interpretivism, a qualitative approach, posits that "the primary focus of research undertaken within this paradigm is the way we as humans attempt to make sense of the world around us" (Saunders et al., 2016, p. 134). Therefore, it can be argued that understanding intelligence sharing is influenced by examining the subjective interpretations and motivations of individuals.

The base of this research product is a systematic review of the scientific literature on intelligence sharing using Elsevier's Scopus abstract database. Scopus was selected due to its extensive coverage of peer-reviewed journals across various disciplines, ensuring a wide range of relevant articles. The search strategy was using a search query designed to capture articles related to intelligence sharing. The search query in Scopus was {intelligence sharing}. The curly bracers force the search engine to only provide research articles having both words in sequence. The results included many articles that were beyond the scope of this research, such as blockchain. Therefore, the decision to use additional sources was taken. Alongside the Scopus database, professional sources such as government reports, policy papers, and white papers were incorporated to provide a practical perspective on intelligence sharing. Notable sources included publications from the U.S. Department of Defence, NATO, various intelligence agencies, and books. The references section provides a list of relevant sources.

Although many instances of intelligence sharing are introduced in the initial section, only two cases are examined in depth: the enhancement of intelligence sharing by the U.S. Intelligence Community (Corbett & Danoy, 2022), and the SIGINT Alliance (2020) as a successful example. The challenges and opportunities of intelligence sharing are analysed and discussed in the discussion section, from which a set of general principles for successful intelligence sharing is deduced and presented.

Additionally, this research aligns with the principles of transparent science as upheld by Nature and Springer Nature journals, utilising tools such as ChatGPT (Nature, 2023). In this study, ChatGPT4 has been employed both as a grammar editor and a research assistant. The editorial in Nature posits that trust in science is founded on researchers' transparency regarding their methods and materials—a position with which this author concurs. Moreover, the author believes that leveraging technological advancements is essential for enhancing information collection, processing, analysis, synthesis, production, and dissemination. Researchers who neglect to utilise these technologies risk falling behind, as discussed thoroughly by Mortenson & Vidgen (2016) in their discussion section.

This research has limitations. While the study describes a successful intelligence sharing strategy exemplified by the SIGINT Alliance, inherent limitations must be considered. First, the generalizability of the SIGINT model may be constrained by unique historical, geopolitical, and cultural contexts absent in other intelligence sharing environments. Additionally, while the focus on technical and cryptanalytical skills is beneficial, it could overshadow other crucial aspects such as human intelligence and open-source intelligence, which are equally vital to a comprehensive intelligence sharing strategy.

Moreover, the reliance on strong personal ties and leadership commitment can be a double-edged sword; while these factors enhance trust and efficiency, they may also introduce vulnerabilities if key individuals depart or if there is a shift in political priorities. Additionally, although technological interoperability is ideal, it often confronts practical challenges such as funding disparities, differing technical standards, and the rapid pace of technological changes, which might surpass the adaptability of alliances. Finally, while streamlined processes can reduce bureaucracy, they may compromise thorough oversight and accountability, potentially leading to ethical and legal dilemmas. These limitations highlight the imperative for continuous evaluation and adaptation of intelligence sharing practices to ensure their efficacy and relevance to evolving circumstances.

3. Results

The first case to review is the U.S. intelligence community. According to former Director of National Intelligence Lt. Gen. James Clapper, "Governments quite rightly protect their intelligence sources, methods, and collection capabilities as critical national assets." However, "this must be balanced against the need to share high-quality intelligence with allies and partners to ensure a compelling and united imperative to act" (Clapper, as cited by Corbett & Danoy, 2022).

Sean Corbett and James Danoy (2022) state that "the Ukraine crisis and the US-led counterterrorist response to 9/11 have both demonstrated an ability to surge intelligence sharing, even with non-traditional partners, where political will exists at the highest level, and it is imperative to address a serious contemporary security challenge. This indicates that restrictive information-sharing practices and policies are not immutable but rather self-imposed and malleable." According to them, the Five Eyes alliance is considered the optimum model for intelligence sharing. The reason for this is "predominantly due to shared values, standards, national interests, and language, but also because the muscle memory already exists—the FVEY relationship has developed over a considerable period." Additionally, "The geographical spread of the FVEY partners also facilitates greater access to intelligence collection opportunities not readily available to all." However, as challenges increase, there is a need to share intelligence with individual nations and coalitions beyond the Five Eyes, depending on security requirements and levels of trust.

The challenges to intelligence sharing stem from various factors, including policy, legal issues, security concerns, processes, technology, and people, as well as institutional and organisational culture. For instance, Jeffery Richelson (2016) highlights the complexity of coordinating multiple agencies within the U.S. intelligence community, which can hinder timely intelligence sharing. Additionally, the complexity of intelligence alliances increases with the number of entities involved: more participants in an alliance make it more difficult to share intelligence and heighten the associated risks. In coalition environments, when individuals become aware of exclusive small group meetings, feelings of exclusion can lead to hurt and a loss of trust (Corbett & Danoy, 2022).

According to Corbett and Danoy (2022), the policy challenges include a federated authority and decentralised control, where the authority to share intelligence is distributed among various bodies within the Intelligence Community and the Department of Defence. Furthermore, numerous intelligence community directives and other policy documents govern intelligence sharing, often leading to policy overlap and sometimes contradictory mandates. This is compounded by a prevalent culture of risk aversion, which prioritises information security over sharing.

Policies that default to non-disclosure unless explicitly authorised perpetuate a cultural bias towards restricting the flow of information. Additionally, approval processes are complex, requiring multiple approvals and interagency coordination, which can be time-consuming and impact time-sensitive actions (Corbett & Danoy, 2022). Some policies also need to be updated to reflect the current operational environment or technological advancements. Moreover, there is always a balance to be struck between security and sharing—the need to protect intelligence, sources, and methods versus the benefits of sharing them.

One way to address the policy challenge is to shift from a default of "NOFORN" to the Australian model, which adopts a default classification of "Releasable FVEY," as noted by Corbett & Danoy (2022). Another approach could involve granting dual citizenship to staff serving in each country's intelligence services during their tenure. Furthermore, policy could be framed to default to stating that information sharing should occur at the broadest possible level with coalition and approved partner countries, and intelligence products should be drafted with a presumption of release to allies, coalitions, and international organisations (Corbett & Danoy, 2022).

Some challenges related to processes and technology include complex approval and coordination chains across different agencies and bodies, often resulting in delays and inefficiencies. For instance, a multi-source intelligence agency, such as the Defense Intelligence Agency, would need to contact each single-source agency to authorise the release of intelligence (Corbett & Danoy, 2022). Additionally, inconsistencies across agencies, with varying comfort levels and policies regarding intelligence sharing, complicate efforts to standardise sharing processes. The technological challenges arise because organisational structures and existing technologies do not keep pace with advancements in artificial intelligence (AI) and machine learning (ML). Moreover, while applying AI and ML can help streamline processes, these technologies cannot be applied to sensitive intelligence, making sharing a significant challenge (Corbett & Danoy, 2022).

The challenge of intelligence sharing related to people includes a cultural trait of risk aversion and fears of potential repercussions, such as criminal, civil, and administrative sanctions, which discourage proactive intelligence sharing. Additionally, workplace and institutional cultures must be integrated and aligned with policies and processes that encourage sharing; otherwise, overall effectiveness is reduced (Herman, 1996). Encouraging sharing also necessitates education and training for staff that highlights the mutual benefits of intelligence sharing and increased situational awareness. Finally, effective intelligence sharing requires strong support from leadership at all levels, who must align policies, processes, and cultural elements and be willing to assume risks on behalf of their teams (Zegart, 2009; Zegart, 2011).

The second case to review is the signals intelligence sharing alliance between Denmark, France, Germany, the Netherlands, and Sweden, as described by Bart Jacobs (2020) in his research article. According to Jacobs (2020), the alliance was initiated by Denmark in 1976, with Germany and Sweden joining initially. The Netherlands was invited to join in 1977 and formally did so in 1978, while France requested to join in 1983, received an invitation in 1984, and became a member in 1985.

The motivations for establishing broader cooperation were twofold. Firstly, the advent of signals intelligence via satellites necessitated substantial investment. Secondly, there was a need to address technical interception challenges and exchange methods collaboratively. The strategy was to combine forces and divide tasks to reduce costs and enhance effectiveness. The cooperation encompassed both cryptanalysis and signals analysis (Jacobs, 2020).

The signals analysis component focused on coordinating interception mechanisms and efforts to exchange intercepted (encrypted) messages. This aspect of the work was discussed in multilateral meetings involving the entire SIGINT Alliance (Jacobs, 2020). Cryptanalysis, in contrast, was addressed only bilaterally, with each participating country responsible for its own decryption efforts. According to Jacobs (2020), maintaining such division is common practice within the intelligence community to prevent the dissemination of manipulated information.

In essence, the intelligence alliance between these five countries was founded on close contacts among leading figures; the cooperation was bottom-up and relied on close personal ties and a shared high level of technical and cryptanalytical skills. Jacobs (2020) notes that certain countries were deliberately excluded from joining because they were considered to lack the relevant signal or crypto-analytical expertise and/or experience.

4. Discussion

The answer to the research question—How, based on research and experience, can a set of principles be applied by states to enhance situational awareness and tackle threat actors through a holistic and collaborative approach to intelligence sharing—comprises a set of eight general principles. These principles were derived from a detailed analysis of the SIGINT Alliance and challenges faced by the U.S. intelligence community, supported by various sources.

4.1 Policy Challenges

Regarding policy challenges, the SIGINT Alliance was formed based on close contacts between leading figures and close personal ties. A second important aspect is the skill set: these countries share a high level of technical and cryptanalytical skills. Additionally, these close ties likely streamlined policies through bilateral discussions and agreements, establishing a framework that accommodated the specific requirements of each country. An example of this framework, as suggested, focuses the cooperation on two parts: signals analysis and cryptanalysis. While signals analysis was discussed in multilateral meetings, cryptanalysis and decryption were the responsibility of each participating country and were discussed only bilaterally. Thus, it is plausible that shared classification protocols were developed to facilitate intelligence sharing, while cryptanalysis, discussed only bilaterally, suggests a security protocol based on the sensitivity of decryption methods. Finally, considering how the alliance was developed, the collaborative approach likely led to a distribution of decision-making authority that was aligned through common goals and regular communication.

4.2 Process Challenges

The SIGINT Alliance's small size and focused membership likely facilitated quicker consensus-building and decision-making processes. The alliance likely benefited from streamlined approval processes, enabled by the trust and operational compatibility developed among the members. The alliance probably invested in compatible technology platforms for sharing intelligence. It is reasonable to suggest that the SIGINT Alliance emphasised technological interoperability and possibly the joint development of tools, which would reduce disparities and enhance real-time data exchange. The SIGINT Alliance was almost certainly focused on efficiency, likely minimising bureaucratic overhead through simplified processes, particularly in secure communications and data handling.

4.3 People Challenges

The shared professional culture of cryptology and SIGINT among the member states likely helped align risk management strategies and operation security, thereby reducing the excessive risk aversion typically seen in larger and more diverse intelligence communities. It is conceivable that a culture of shared risk and mutual benefit was promoted to encourage more open-sharing practices. Given the technical nature of the alliance's work, the SIGINT Alliance likely placed a strong emphasis on specialised training and professional development to ensure that all members were well-versed in the tools and protocols necessary for collaboration. The alliance might have developed a recognition system that acknowledged contributions and successful collaborations, thereby fostering a more proactive sharing environment. This would likely involve clear communication of the benefits of sharing, such as enhanced collective security. Strong leadership and committed support from all levels of the participating intelligence agencies are likely factors in the alliance's success. Leadership possibly played a critical role in maintaining focus on the alliance's objectives and ensuring that operational priorities were aligned.

4.4 The Eight General Principles for Successful Intelligence Sharing

Based on all of the above, the following general principles can be deduced for successful intelligence sharing:

1. Establish strong personal and institutional ties—Build an alliance based on strong personal relationships and close contacts between key figures. This helps streamline decision-making and enhance trust among the members.
2. Develop compatible and streamlined policies—Create mutually agreed-upon frameworks that cater to the specific needs and security requirements of each member country, with shared

classification protocols that allow for seamless intelligence sharing. Policies should be clear, consistent, and as much as possible free from contradictions.

3. Emphasise technical and analytical skills - Encourage developing and sharing high-level technical and cryptanalytical skills within the alliance and provide continuous training and professional development to keep pace with advancements in technology and analytical methods.
4. Foster technological interoperability and joint tool development - Invest in compatible technology platforms that facilitate secure and efficient data exchange and collaborate on developing joint tools and technologies that enhance the capabilities of all members, thereby reducing technological disparities.
5. Streamline processes to reduce bureaucracy - Minimise bureaucratic overhead by simplifying approval processes and enhancing operational compatibilities and develop efficient protocols for secure communications and data handling to prevent delays and ensure timely sharing of intelligence.
6. Cultivate a culture of shared risk and benefit—Promote a culture where risk management strategies are aligned, there is a collective responsibility for security and sharing outcomes and encourage a perspective that values intelligence sharing as beneficial for the collective security and success of all members.
7. Implement incentives and recognition systems - Develop recognition systems that acknowledge and reward successful collaborations and contributions to the alliance's objectives and clearly communicate the benefits of sharing intelligence, such as enhancing collective security and operational effectiveness.
8. Ensure strong and committed leadership—Secure committed support and leadership at all levels within the participating agencies. Leadership should actively maintain the focus on the alliance's objectives and ensure that operational priorities are synchronized and met.

5. Conclusions & Future Research

In conclusion, successful intelligence sharing in the current geopolitical security situation hinges on strategic collaboration that efficiently circumvents common barriers associated with policy, process, and people. The SIGINT Alliance exemplifies a model where close personal ties, a high degree of technical and cryptanalytical expertise, and a concerted effort towards streamlined operational processes effectively enhance intelligence sharing capabilities among member states. This alliance underscores the importance of mutual trust and the alignment of strategic goals across different national entities, facilitated by an agreed framework that accommodates the varied requirements and security protocols of each country.

By focusing on creating a conducive environment for intelligence sharing through compatible technological platforms, minimised bureaucratic processes, and a shared professional culture, intelligence sharing alliances can likely manage to mitigate the risks associated with complex intelligence sharing. These efforts are supported by strong leadership, continuous training, and a clear understanding of the shared benefits of collaboration, which are crucial for maintaining the operational integrity and effectiveness of intelligence operations.

The general principles derived from the SIGINT Alliance provide a first step for other intelligence sharing initiatives. These principles advocate for the establishment of strong foundational relationships, the development of cohesive and flexible policy frameworks, and the cultivation of a supportive operational culture. Together, these strategies empower intelligence communities to respond more dynamically and effectively to emerging global threats, thereby enhancing international security and cooperation.

Future research can explore several areas to further understand and enhance intelligence sharing, such as a potential prioritisation between the sharing principles. While this study mentions the Five Eyes and the AUKUS, these are not covered here. As the Five Eyes intelligence sharing alliance has worked to date, the AUKUS trilateral partnership highlights how an intelligence sharing alliance is established based on a specific context (the Indo-Pacific), and with specific capabilities (e.g. submarines, nuclear power and propulsion). Future research can include these intelligence sharing alliances as well as military operations. Next, the impact of emerging technologies should be examined, focusing on the impact of AI and ML. Additionally, ethical, legal and security implications should be reviewed. Additional areas may include cultural and organisational structures and how they influence trust-building, risk perception and cooperation among allies.

The role of policy evolution and harmonisation within a rapidly changing geopolitical security situation may be further investigated. Studies focusing on how policies are adapted and harmonised among diverse international partners are crucial, particularly in responding to emergent threats such as malicious cyber operations and disinformation. Additionally, there is a significant need to delve into the human aspects of intelligence sharing. Future research may explore the impact of training programs, personnel exchanges, and establishing a common linguistic and professional standard among allies. Understanding how these factors either facilitate or impede effective intelligence sharing could offer valuable insights into enhancing collaborative intelligence sharing. A good start could be to review the NATO standardisation agreements (STANAG).

Longitudinal research is also essential to gauge the long-term efficacy of intelligence sharing agreements. Such studies could provide a deeper understanding of the sustainability and adaptability of these agreements to evolving threats. They may track the progression and outcomes of intelligence sharing initiatives over time, offering a comprehensive view of their effectiveness.

Moreover, incorporating quantitative methods can augment research of intelligence sharing. By applying empirical data to evaluate aspects such as response times to threats, the accuracy of shared intelligence, and the cost-effectiveness of cooperative operations, research can provide data-driven conclusions.

Finally, comparative studies can provide additional understanding of different intelligence sharing frameworks and agreements. Researchers can identify best practices and common challenges by comparing and contrasting various alliances, including those that are, for example, military-led versus civilian-led. These comparisons may highlight effective intelligence sharing strategies and help recognise areas that require improvement or adjustment to better meet contemporary security demands.

References

Australian Government, Department of the Prime Minister and Cabinet. (2022). FACT SHEET: Implementation of the Australia – United Kingdom – United States Partnership (AUKUS). Retrieved from: https://pmtranscripts.pmc.gov.au/sites/default/files/AUKUS-factsheet.pdf.

Corbett, S., & Danoy, J. (2022). Beyond NOFORN: Solutions for increased intelligence sharing among allies. Atlantic Council. Retrieved from: https://www.atlanticcouncil.org/in-depth-research-reports/issue-brief/beyond-noforn-solutions-for-increased-intelligence-sharing-among-allies/.

Defence Research and Development Canada. (2020). Standards for Evaluating Source Reliability and Information Credibility in Intelligence Production. Retrieved from: https://cradpdf.drdc-rddc.gc.ca/PDFS/unc351/p812555_A1b.pdf.

Department of the Army. (2006). Human intelligence collector operations (FM 2-22.3 [FM 34-52]). Retrieved from: https://irp.fas.org/doddir/army/fm2-22-3.pdf.

European Commission. (2023). Shift in the geopolitical landscape. Retrieved from: https://knowledge4policy.ec.europa.eu/foresight/shift-geopolitical-landscape_en.

Grabo, C. M. (2002). Anticipating Surprise: Analysis for Strategic Warning. ISBN: 0-9656195-6-7.

Farrell, P. (2013). History of 5-Eyes – explainer. The Guardian. Retrieved from: https://www.theguardian.com/world/2013/dec/02/history-of-5-eyes-explainer.

Herman, M. (1996). Intelligence Power in Peace and War. Cambridge University Press.

Huskaj, G., & Axelsson, S. (2023a). A state-of-the-art of scientific research on disinformation. Proceedings of the 22nd European Conference on Cyber Warfare and Security, 22(1).

Huskaj, G., & Axelsson, S. (2023b). A whole-of-society approach to organise for offensive cyberspace operations: The case of the smart state Sweden. Proceedings of the 22nd European Conference on Cyber Warfare and Security, 22(1).

Huskaj, G. (2024). Future Elections and AI-Driven Disinformation. The Defence Horizon Journal. https://doi.org/10.5281/zenodo.11140806.

Jacobs, B. (2020). Maximator: European signals intelligence cooperation, from a Dutch perspective. Intelligence and National Security, 35(5), 659-668. https://doi.org/10.1080/02684527.2020.1743538.

Lazard. (2023). The Global Geopolitical Landscape in 2023. Retrieved from: https://www.lazard.com/research-insights/the-global-geopolitical-landscape-in-2023/.

Mortenson, M. J., & Vidgen, R. (2016). A computational literature review of the technology acceptance model. International Journal of Information Management, 36(6), 1248–1259. https://doi.org/10.1016/j.ijinfomgt.2016.07.007.

Nature. (2023). Tools such as ChatGPT threaten transparent science; here are our ground rules for their use. Nature. Retrieved from: https://www.nature.com/articles/d41586-023-00191-1.

NSA-National Security Agency/Central Security Service. (n.d.). UKUSA Agreement Release. Retrieved from: https://www.nsa.gov/Helpful-Links/NSA-FOIA/Declassification-Transparency-Initiatives/Historical-Releases/UKUSA/.

North Yorkshire. (2020). Intelligence Sharing Guide for the Partnership Information Sharing Form. Retrieved from: https://www.safeguardingchildren.co.uk/wp-content/uploads/2020/02/NYSCP-NYCSP-Intel-sharing-OMG-2020-06-15.pdf.

Oates, B. J. (2005). Researching Information Systems and Computing. Sage Publications, Inc.

Richelson, J.T. (2016). The U.S. Intelligence Community (7th ed.). Routledge. Retrieved from: https://doi.org/10.4324/9780429494321.

Rietjens, S. (2020). A warning system for hybrid threats – is it possible? Hybrid CoE. Retrieved from: https://www.hybridcoe.fi/wp-content/uploads/2020/06/Strategic-Analysis_22_WarningSystem-1.pdf.

Saunders, M. N. K., Lewis, P., & Thornhill, A. (2016). Research Methods for Business Students. Financial Times/Prentice Hall.

U.S. Department of Defense. (2016). Evaluation of U.S. intelligence and information sharing with coalition partners in support of Operation Inherent Resolve. Retrieved from: https://media.defense.gov/2020/Aug/07/2002472951/-1/-1/1/DODIG-2016-081.PDF (Report No. DODIG-2016-081).

The White House. (2022). FACT SHEET: Implementation of the Australia – United Kingdom – United States Partnership (AUKUS). Retrieved from: https://www.whitehouse.gov/briefing-room/statements-releases/2022/04/05/fact-sheet-implementation-of-the-australia-united-kingdom-united-states-partnership-aukus/.

Zegart, A. (2009). Spying Blind: The CIA, the FBI, and the Origins of 9/11. Princeton University Press.

Zegart, A. (2011). Implementing Change: Organizational Challenges. In Fischhoff, B., In Chauvin, C., & National Research Council (U.S.). Intelligence analysis: Behavioral and social scientific foundations. Washington, DC: National Academies Press.

Leveraging Gamification for Cyber Threat Intelligence for Resilience in Satellite Cyber Supply Chains

Mona Kriesten, Mamello Thinyane and David Ormrod
University of South Australia, Adelaide, Australia

mona.kriesten@mymail.unisa.edu.au
mamello.thinyane@unisa.edu.au
dave.ormrod@unisa.edu.au

Abstract: Cyber Threat Intelligence (CTI) is collected threat information put in context to enhance decision-making before, during and after an attack. The application of CTI is widely limited to the reactive field of cybersecurity. The evolving cyber threat landscape requires a shift to an anticipatory and adaptable approach that addresses the complex and changing cybersecurity environment. CTI has the potential to support this shift to proactive threat handling towards a more resilient cybersecurity posture. This research is part of a project that aims to enhance the use of CTI for satellite cyber supply chain resilience through gamification. Cybersecurity games are established tools to raise security awareness and train security staff in red and blue team exercises. However, there is a lack of research on how gamification and serious games can be used to improve the application of CTI and enable training for security staff, even though existing literature points out the beneficial effects of gamification. Building on the gamification approach in cybersecurity, the research focuses on creating a gamified experience that simulates a cyber-attack derived from real-world examples and the utilisation of CTI to handle the simulated cyber-attack. The scenario addresses the need for informed decision-making throughout a cyber-attack by focusing on the utilisation of CTI in the context of satellite cyber supply chain security as the domain of application. This paper takes stock of the recent developments in CTI towards improving cyber resilience and presents gamification for cybersecurity and CTI to highlight the benefits of the approach. Further, it discusses the potential of gamification as an effective tool for CTI and describes the approach that is used to build a gamification solution inspired by real-world events. This paper contributes to the nascent research on gamification of CTI to strengthen cyber resilience in the context of increasingly frequent and sophisticated cyber threats, especially against space systems.

Keywords: Cyber Threat Intelligence, Gamification, Cyber Resilience, Satellite Supply Chain Security, Cybersecurity

1. Introduction

Global reliance on space systems has increased in recent years, providing numerous services including positioning, navigation, and timing (PNT), communications and earth observation. This increased reliance has occurred across civilian and defence contexts. In the civilian context, space systems are an integral part of critical societal infrastructure; and in the defence context, space systems have become a domain of ongoing militarisation and geopolitical contestation (Falco 2018; Pavur and Martinovic 2022). The increasing complexity of the space ecosystem, the growing satellite cyber supply chain (SCSC) attack surface, and several prominent attacks against satellite systems, including the Viasat KA-SAT cyber-attack linked to the Ukraine conflict (Viasat, Inc. 2022) and the non-malicious demonstrator hack of the Moonlighter satellite at DEFCON 31 in 2023 (Vasquez 2023), have highlighted the vulnerability of these systems and heightened the need for adaptable and proactive approaches towards strengthening the cyber resilience (CR) of space systems (Manulis et al, 2021).

Cyber threat intelligence (CTI) has shown the potential to improve cybersecurity and the handling of cyber-attacks, by facilitating informed decision-making and creating an adaptable environment for the vastly evolving threat landscape (Yeboah-Ofori et al, 2021). While CTI is currently predominantly used in reactive contexts, this research is oriented towards enhancing the proactive use of CTI for SCSC resilience (Samtani et al, 2017). The specific approach explored in this research towards this goal is gamification, which has effectively been used in different areas to improve cybersecurity outcomes.

The primary line of inquiry and the key question addressed in this paper is "How can gamification enhance the use of CTI towards CR in general and resilient SCSC in particular?" To address this question, the paper first explores the current literature across four focus areas in this project: (1) satellite supply chain security (SSCS), (2) CR, (3) CTI, and (4) gamification. This is followed by a mapping of the role of CTI across the CR phases to highlight the associated affordances and opportunities. Next, the development approach and scenario that form the basis for the gamification solution implemented in this project are presented. The paper concludes by discussing the significance of gamification, as a user-centred approach, to amplify the performance of human defenders towards the resilience of the complex SCSC socio-technical systems.

2. Literature Review

This research is undertaken at the intersection of space systems security, CR, CTI, and gamification. Prior research in these domains is presented and synthesized as the basis for the solutions developed in this research and presented in the paper.

2.1 Satellite Supply Chain Security

Space systems are vulnerable to many types of cyber threats targeting elements within the ground, space, or user segments. One of the vectors that is exploited in satellite attacks which is the focus of this research, is the SCSC – the set of entities, resources, and processes supported by digital technologies to establish an effective value chain in the production and delivery of space system (Kim and Im 2014). This has become an important vector for space systems security due to the increased commercialisation of the space industry, the popularity of commercial-of-the-shelf (COTS) components, and the growing number of third-party service providers involved in the industry (Falco 2018). Further, as evidenced in recent high-profile supply chain incidents, cyber supply chains can increase the risk exposure and degrade the cybersecurity posture of organisations and their systems (Linton, Boyson and Aje 2014).

Satellite supply chain security builds on the body of work on supply chain security and applies it to the space systems domain. The SSCS cuts across the ground, space and user segment and the extension of supporting units including software, hardware manufacturing, tools and cloud infrastructure (Burch 2020; Manulis et al, 2021). The research in the field identifies the following five categories of measures to address threats to the SCSC: network management, identification and authentication, system management, general security and incident prevention and response (Fleming, Reith and Henry 2023). While these are formulated from the cybersecurity perspective, there is an evolution in perspectives towards strengthening the CR of space systems.

2.2 Cyber Resilience

Cyber Resilience is a system's ability to prepare (or anticipate), absorb (or withstand), recover and adapt (or evolve) amid adverse cyber incidents (Bodeau and Graubart 2011; Kott and Linkov 2019). In contrast to the goal of operating fail-safe systems, the goal of CR is to operate systems that are safe to fail, and that can maintain critical functioning in the face of cyber-attacks. There are frameworks and models that operationalize the CR goals, such as the Cyber Resiliency Engineering Framework by Bodeau and Graubart (2011) or the CR model by the U.S. Department of Defense (2011). These provide guidance on how to engineer resilient environments across many domains such as industrial network supply chains and the space industry (Burch 2020; Gajek, Lees and Jansen 2021). Beyond the traditional technocentric notions of CR, there is an increasing recognition of the need for a socio-technical systems perspective towards resilience. The socio-technical perspective includes human and organisational factors that contribute to the overall CR posture. Human defenders play a critical role across the CR phases, leveraging CTI to inform decisions and responses to cyber threats. A mapping of the role of CTI across the CR phases has been developed and is presented later in the paper.

2.3 Cyber Threat Intelligence

CTI originates from the military notion of Threat Intelligence (TI). In the military, TI is used to warn of threats and indicate adversary action. CTI applies this military perspective to cyberspace; it provides analysed and correlated data about past, present, and emerging threats to inform decision-making and action. The three types of CTI; strategic, operational and tactical; can assist different organisational levels, from management to system administration, to improve their cybersecurity practice (Ainslie et al, 2023). CTI can be used both from a reactive and a proactive perspective, with the former representing efforts to respond to cyber-attacks and the latter representing an anticipatory action before the onset of the cyber threats. Research suggests that proactive approaches have a higher potential to increase a system's resilience (Samtani et al, 2017). However, despite this potential, the main challenges in the CTI field are handling the large amount of threat data that must be analysed, correlated, and structured; establishing sharing standards to overcome interoperability challenges between platforms; and defining consistent quality measures. Apart from the challenges with the management of CTI, developments in cyber-attacks and the shift to more evasive methods on the attacker side, affect the life-span and validity of CTI (Sahrom Abu et al, 2018).

Efforts have been made to define ontologies as a basis for a uniform understanding of CTI and to derive quality dimensions and metrics for CTI (Schlette et al, 2021; Yeboah-Ofori and Islam 2019). Recommendations have been provided on how to effectively implement CTI, such as considering a knowledge base with a threat repository, applying detection models including AI approaches and utilising visualisation tools for monitoring and measurement purposes (Saeed et al, 2023). There are knowledge databases shared across the industry, such as MITRE ATT&CK (The MITRE Cooperation 2024). However, much of the research on CTI focuses on the technology-driven perspective like sharing standards and technical implementation approaches, whereas the benefit of CTI is to support better-informed decision-making. This research focuses on the need for user-centric and proactive approaches that enable defenders to use CTI to inform and improve their decision-making and response in dealing with cyber threats. Gamification is proposed as a user-centred approach towards enhancing the use of CTI to improve the CR of SCSC.

2.4 Gamification

Gamification is the process of using game elements in non-game contexts (Deterding et al, 2011) to improve learning, increase motivation and influence a positive outcome in users (Abdul Rahman et al, 2018), and to simplify real-world problems and make problem-solving more approachable (Schell 2019). Gamification approaches are employed within serious games, which are defined as games developed for purposes that go beyond entertainment (eds Ritterfeld, Cody and Vorderer 2009). While gamification and serious games are predominately linked to educational and training purposes, serious games analytics focuses on the analytical side to measure and assess performance through gamification (Loh, Sheng and Ifenthaler 2015).

One of the major benefits of gamification for cybersecurity is the creation of a safe environment that simulates real-world conditions to practice, train and test certain operations (Wolfenden 2019). Common examples of gamification approaches in cybersecurity include red teaming and blue teaming exercises and Capture The Flag (CTF) challenges. Research has been undertaken to test the benefits of gamification for cybersecurity. For example, tabletop exercises were used to identify skill gaps in the field and to find solutions to close the skills gaps using gamified experiences (McClaskey 2022). Further, cybersecurity games in the category of serious games were designed to investigate the differences in effectiveness between common video games and cybersecurity games with a focus on behavioural elements (van Steen and Deeleman 2021). In general game-based learning has been found to be most effective for the engagement of humans (Thompson et al, 2022). In the context of research on first responder's cybersecurity training, positive effects and learning outcomes were noted from introducing a gamified solution (Coull et al, 2017).

While existing research points to the broad effectiveness of gamification within the cybersecurity domain, there is a dearth of research on the gamification of CTI specifically for SCSC resilience. This gap is addressed in this research by mapping the possibilities of CTI for SCSC and by demonstrating an approach to gamify SSCS.

3. Mapping the Role of CTI Across Cyber Resilience Phases

CTI provides knowledge and insights about cyber threats and threat actors to security roles across organisations for better decision-making and practice at many levels from the technical to the strategic (Ainslie et al, 2023). Due to the versatility of CTI, it has emerged as a critical component in organisations' cybersecurity arsenal (Kant 2022). The resilience-creating ability originates from the CTI process of obtaining, processing, analysing, and distributing threat information and risk assessment that affects an organisation's cybersecurity. Organisations are able to employ risk and threat information to proactively decide on measures to mitigate risk and be better prepared against cyber threats. Protection, detection and response functions can be improved through the enrichment of CTI towards improved CR (Saeed et al, 2023).

Cyber resilience is enacted across different phases in the attack lifecycle. The order and number of phases vary depending on the model referenced, for example, Burch (2020) uses a modified model from the U.S. Department of Defense (2011) that defines the resilience phases as avoidance, robustness, reconstitution, and recovery. Whereas a publication from the MITRE Corporation defines resilience goals as anticipate, withstand, recover and evolve (Bodeau and Graubart 2011). For this research, the CR lifecycle that builds on the presented approaches was developed. It combines the approaches and defines the resilience phases as Anticipation, Avoidance, Robustness, Recovery, Reconstitution, and Evolution – as in Figure 1.

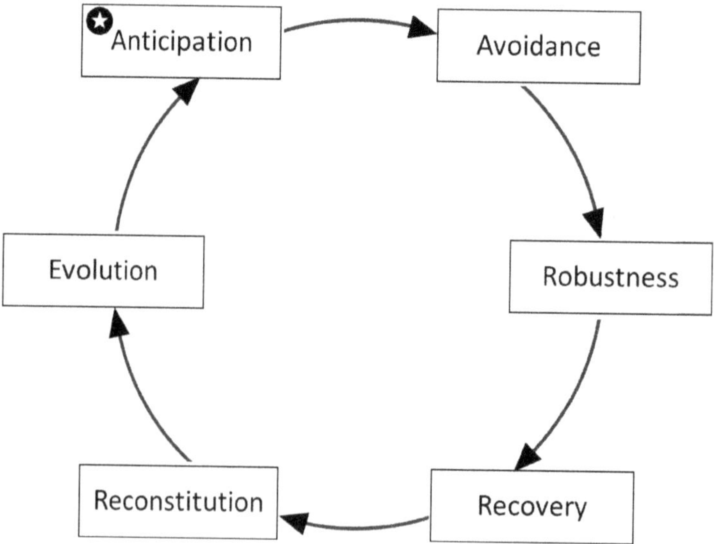

Figure 1: Cyber Resilience Lifecycle

Based on the literature on CR and CTI, a mapping of the role of CTI for each of the CR phases has been developed, starting with the *Anticipation* phase – as illustrated in Figure 1:

- *Anticipation* has the purpose of maintaining a state of informed readiness to prevent the impairment of functions through evolving threats (Bodeau and Graubart 2011). CTI is used for proactive situational awareness without any indication of an intrusion. In this context, CTI data must be continuously collected, updated, and analysed to predict threats and help security staff develop countermeasures against potential threats.
- *Avoidance* refers to the ability to evade and reduce risk. Accordingly, *Avoidance* includes the prevention and preparation for a cyber-attack (Burch 2020). As with Anticipation, CTI information must be collected continuously. However, at this stage, there is already a suspicion or a threat has been identified, for which information is collected in a targeted manner.
- *Robustness* describes the situation when a cyber-attack is detected, and the attacked infrastructure must be defended. It allows a system to withstand an attack by continuing mission-critical operations and constraining the attack's impact (U.S. Department of Defense 2011). Here, CTI provides information about adversarial tactics, techniques, and procedures (TTPs), reducing the effectiveness of the cyber-attack and increasing the probability of detection.
- *Recovery* aims to stop the attack, provide damage assessments and restore functions and capabilities to an acceptable level of operation (Burch 2020). In this phase, CTI enhances the prevention of lateral movement by isolating the threat and blocking attack vectors, enabling a return to mission-critical operation.
- *Reconstitution*, which occurs after a successful defence against and isolation of the threat, re-establishes the full operation of capabilities and functions. The objective is to get back to the status quo of operation (Burch 2020). CTI information enables threat hunting which eliminates persistence, identifies backdoors, and evicts the adversary. At this stage, the attack was successfully stopped, and attack residues were removed.
- *Evolve* contains the steps of transforming and re-architecting the infrastructure. It represents the lessons learned stage of the lifecycle (Bodeau and Graubart 2011). CTI supports the response to environmental change and the evolving threat landscape, including updates to the threat model and changes to TTPs. Gathered attack information can be incorporated and analysed to improve the security posture. Finally, further hardening activities of the infrastructure and continuous CTI updates should be undertaken.

From this mapping, it is apparent that CTI plays an important role towards CR. The critical element of this process is that high-quality CTI should be used, which among others means CTI that is timely, specific, and actionable. Assessing the quality of CTI is a key component of the gamification solution in this project, but this is beyond the scope of this paper.

4. Gamifying Cyber Threat Intelligence for Satellite Cyber Supply Chain Resilience

CTI has been identified as another potential area where gamification has beneficial effects from a training as well as an analytical perspective. Due to the dearth of prior work on the gamification of CTI in the SCSC contexts, a relevant approach and methodology to tackle the problem had to be developed. This was synthesized from existing gamification approaches in cybersecurity, and iterative and human-centred design methodologies. An output of this process along with the SCSC attack scenario are presented hereafter.

4.1 Gamification Design Approach

The overall approach for the development of the gamification solution is based on the design science methodology. This methodology employs three cycles. The relevance cycle connects the design process to the SCSC security context. The design cycle is outworked through an iterative build and evaluate cycle. The rigour cycle grounds the work in relevant domain expertise including cybersecurity frameworks and models (see Figure 2). Inspirations for this approach include iterative build and evaluate cycles aligned to the Rapid Application Development processes and the framing of the design in terms of the Mechanics, Dynamics and Aesthetics (MDA) components from gamification methods (Hevner 2007). The approach features influence from participatory design (PD) and User-Centred Design (UCD). By collecting feedback from experts who are potential users of the product, features of the game can be tested while they are developed to improve the user experience (Lowdermilk 2013).

The specific method to engage users in this process is primarily through Delphi. In Delphi, expert's opinions are collected to generate common sense during a decision-making process to find consensus and receive controlled feedback (Dietz 1987). Traditionally, Delphi covers three decision rounds. Each round builds on the previous one and a new iteration is updated based on the received feedback (Brady 2015). For the game development, the traditional process was virtualised allowing for a regular cadence of engagement with experts framed around identifying requirements (within the relevance cycle), evaluating and receiving feedback on key game artifacts such as the MDA components and the CTI (within the design cycle), and lastly leveraging their experience and expertise (within the rigour cycle) – see Figure 2. The expertise of the recruited participants ranges across cybersecurity, CTI, space systems engineering and game design domains. The variety of expertise and experience allows for a broad coverage of topics relevant to the game. Thus, not only MDA components are considered, but more importantly for this research, the SCSC attack scenario and the associated CTI are also evaluated.

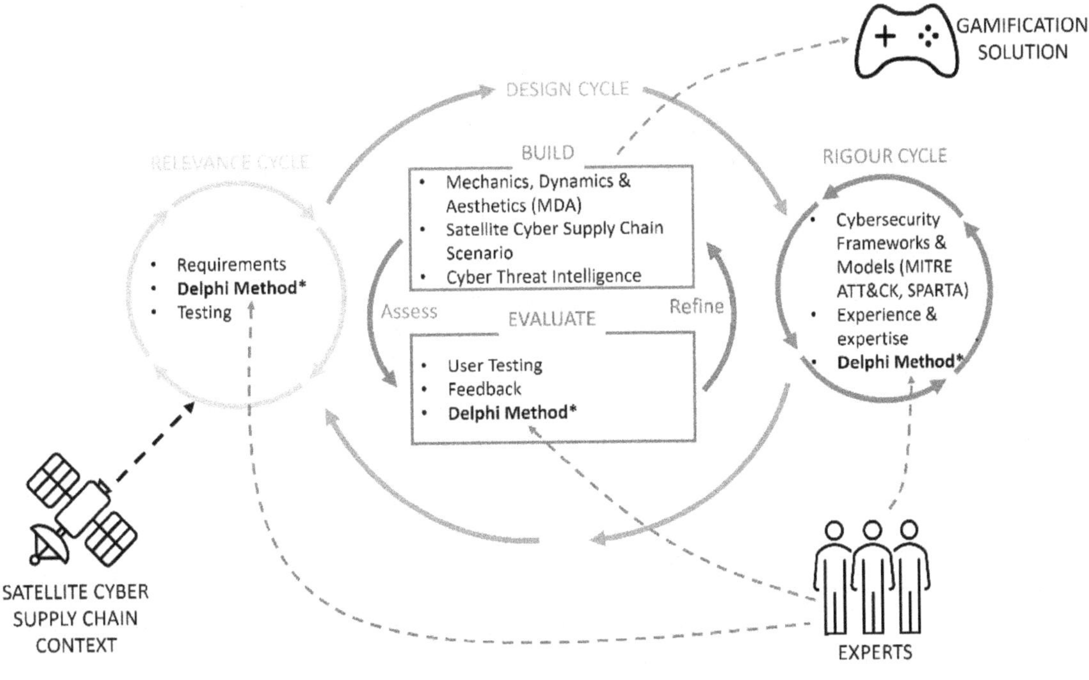

Figure 2: Game Development Process aligned to Delphi

4.2 Satellite Cyber Supply Chain Attack Scenario

A hypothetical SCSC cyber-attack scenario has been constructed to capture the core elements and key decision points as the attack unfolds (see Figure 3). References from real-world examples were used that covered a cyber supply chain attack and one targeting a satellite service provider. The SolarWinds attack from 2020 was used as the inspiration for the supply chain elements in the scenario (Willett 2021). This was combined with elements of the ViaSat KA-SAT cyber-attack from 2022 where attackers were able to access satellite modems and interrupt the satellite communication causing multiple service disruptions (Viasat, Inc. 2022).

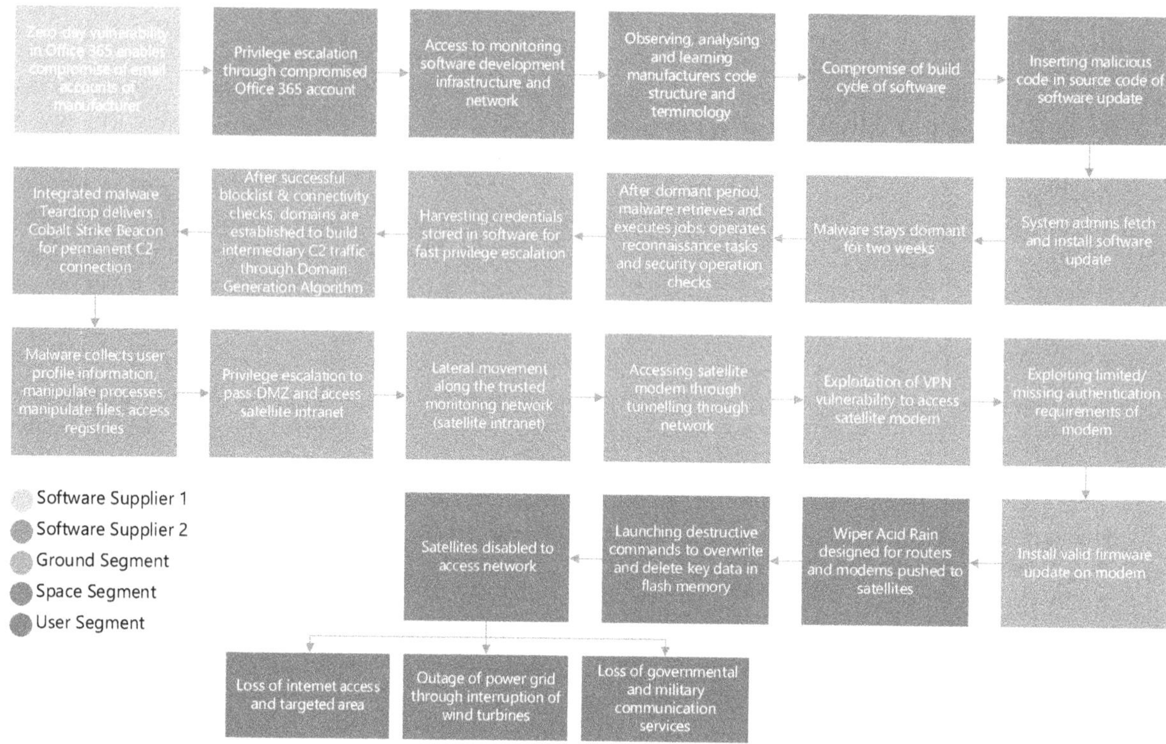

Figure 3: Hypothetical Satellite Cyber Supply Chain Attack

The phases of the attack were divided into the different SCSC components (which are marked by different colours). The proposed cyber-attack was then reviewed and refined through the participant's feedback. After the attack drafting, the attack steps were used to assign CTI to enable the simulation of the decision-making process based on CTI information. The CTI information is synthesised from real-world examples and based on knowledge databases like MITRE ATT&CK (The MITRE Cooperation 2024) and SPARTA. SPARTA, similar to MITRE ATT&CK, is a TTP database specifically for space system TTPs (The Aerospace Corporation 2022). The collected CTI data was then divided into strategic, operational, and tactical intelligence to enable a differentiated analysis of the player's decision-making process. Based on the underlying goal of improving SCSC resilience, the generated CTI is also considered in terms of the mapping to CR phases as presented in Section 3.

The development of this SCSC attack scenario and the associated CTI has benefited from the iterative build and evaluate (i.e., feedback) cycle discussed in the approach above. The initial game prototypes were also developed to test the MDA components and feedback from the participants was collected to improve the design iteratively.

5. Discussion and Conclusion

There is an opportunity to enhance SCSC resilience by leveraging gamification to improve the use of CTI in these contexts. The research presented in this paper shows that CTI can be beneficial across each CR phase and can be shaped to inform decisions and response action along each step of the SCSC cyber-attack scenario. The suggested gamification solution that encapsulates real-life inspired SCSC scenarios and that has been developed with input from domain experts can help to better analyse and improve decision-making processes as well as the use of CTI to support these decisions. This can have an impact on the effectiveness of dealing with actual SCSC attacks. The approach involves the end user in the development phase, enabling feedback and adjustments to be made at an early stage of development. A game has the potential to test different scenarios, enables adjustments to analyse the human decision-making processes, and can be adapted into an educational or training version.

This paper has presented three key elements from the research: an analysis of the benefits of CTI for improving cyber resilience, a CTI gamification approach, and a SCSC scenario that forms the basis of the gamification solution. The synthesis of a CR lifecycle, from existing CR models, and the mapping of the role that CTI can play for CR demonstrates the utility of CTI and has provided a foundation for the gamification solution. These benefits include additional information during each CR lifecycle phase to better inform sense-making and decision-making about the cyber-attack. The SCSC scenario is an example of how real cyberattacks can be incorporated and used for hypothetical simulations. Further, the gamification approach provides the use case for such a simulation that can be leveraged for analysis, educational or training purposes. Finally, the gamification of CTI provides a platform for further research on human-centred cybersecurity scenarios. The developed scenario and associated CTI provide a refined (i.e., by domain experts) and rigorously developed knowledge base of ideal decision-making and action towards addressing SCSC attacks.

There are, however, a few limitations and constraints to consider. First, the involvement of experts with different backgrounds does not eliminate personal bias. Hence, the need for broader testing and validation of the SCSC scenario, the CTI, and the game MDAs is necessary. Second, the scope of the scenario is informed by a small set of real-world cases and has a narrowly defined focus. A broader context could be reached by creating multiple cyber-attack versions which can be considered in future versions and further research in this field.

Future activities in this project will focus on the quality of CTI to integrate other metrics, such as trustworthiness, reliability, and timeliness, into the game design. In addition, different difficulty levels, associated with the complexity of the decision-making process, will be generated. Further, the CTI information will be presented to have a balanced distribution of information across the CR lifecycle. This will enable observations of how CTI can be used to enhance CR in the SCSC context.

In summary, this research presents an interactive approach to tackle the challenges of applying CTI to enhance CR and create resilient SCSC. The gamification approach enables the integration of the human factor and the possibility of adapting scenarios depending on the research focus for future use cases. Multi-player versions and different cyber-attack examples can extend on the given example.

References

Abu, M.S., Selamat, S.R., Ariffin, A. and Yusof, R. (2018), "Cyber Threat Intelligence – Issue and Challenges", *Indonesian Journal of Electrical Engineering and Computer Science*, Vol. 10, No. 1, p 371. Available at: https// 10.11591/ijeecs.v10.i1.pp371-379.

Ainslie, S., Thompson, D., Maynard, S. and Ahmad, A. (2023), "Cyber-threat intelligence for security decision-making: A review and research agenda for practice", *Computers & Security*, Vol. 132, p 103352. Available at: https://10.1016/j.cose.2023.103352.

Bodeau, D.J. and Graubart, R. (2011), "Cyber Resiliency Engineering Framework, MTR110237", [online], September, The MITRE Corporation, Bedford, Massachusetts, www.mitre.org/sites/default/files/pdf/11_4436.pdf, [Accessed 13.10.2022].

Brady, S.R. (2015), "Utilizing and Adapting the Delphi Method for Use in Qualitative Research", *International Journal of Qualitative Methods*, Vol. 14, No. 5, p 160940691562138. Available at: https://10.1177/1609406915621381.

Burch, R.W. (2020), Resilient space systems design: an introduction, CRC Press, Boca Raton.

Coull, N., Donald, I., Ferguson, I., Keane, E., Mitchell, T., Smith, O.V., Stevenson, E., Tomkins, P. (2017), "The Gamification of Cybersecurity Training", in F. Tian, C. Gatzidis, A. El Rhalibi, W. Tang and F. Charles (eds), *E-Learning and Games*, Vol. 10345, Springer International Publishing, Cham, pp 108–111.

Deterding, S., Sicart, M., Nacke, L., O'Hara, K. and Dixon, D. (2011), "Gamification. using game-design elements in non-gaming contexts", in *CHI EA'11 Proceedings of the 2011 annual conference extended abstracts on Human factors in computing systems*, p 2425-2428. Available at: https://10.1145/1979742.1979575.

Dietz, T. (1987), "Methods for analyzing data from Delphi panels: Some evidence from a forecasting study", *Technological Forecasting and Social Change*, Vol. 31, No. 1, pp 79–85. Available at: https: 10.1016/0040-1625(87)90024-2.

Falco, G. (2018), "The Vacuum of Space Cyber Security", in *2018 AIAA SPACE and Astronautics Forum and Exposition*, p 5275. Available at: https://10.2514/6.2018-5275.

Fleming, C., Reith, M. and Henry, W. (2023), "Securing Commercial Satellites for Military Operations: A Cybersecurity Supply Chain Framework", *International Conference on Cyber Warfare and Security*, Vol. 18, No. 1, pp 85–92. Available at: https:// 10.34190/iccws.18.1.1062.

Gajek, S., Lees, M. and Jansen, C. (2021), "IIoT and cyber-resilience: Could blockchain have thwarted the Stuxnet attack?", *AI & SOCIETY*, Vol. 36, No. 3, pp 725–735. Available at: https://10.1007/s00146-020-01023-w.

Hevner, A. (2007), "A Three Cycle View of Design Science Research", *Scandinavian Journal of Information Systems*, Vol. 19, No. 2, pp 87–92.

Kant, N. (2022), "How Cyber Threat Intelligence (CTI) Ensures Cyber Resilience Using Artificial Intelligence and Machine Learning", in J. Om Prakash, H.L. Gururaj, M.R. Pooja and S.P. Pavan Kumar (eds), *Advances in Information Security, Privacy, and Ethics*, IGI Global, pp 65–96.

Kim, K.-C. and Im, I. (2014), "Research letter: Issues of cyber supply chain security in Korea", *Technovation*, Vol. 34, No. 7, pp 387–388. Available at: https:// 10.1016/j.technovation.2014.01.003.

Kott, A. and Linkov, I (2019), "Fundamental Concepts of Cyber Resilience: Introduction and Overview" in A. Kott and I. Linkov (eds), *Cyber Resilience of Systems and Networks*, Springer International Publishing, Cham.

Linton, J.D., Boyson, S. and Aje, J. (2014), "The challenge of cyber supply chain security to research and practice – An introduction", *Technovation*, Vol. 34, No. 7, pp 339–341. Available at: https:// 10.1016/j.technovation.2014.05.001.

Loh, C.S., Sheng, Y. and Ifenthaler, D. (2015), "Serious Games Analytics: Theoretical Framework", in C.S. Loh, Y. Sheng and D. Ifenthaler (eds), *Serious Games Analytics*, Springer International Publishing, Cham, pp 3–29.

Lowdermilk, T. (2013), *User-centered design: a developer's guide to building user-friendly applications*, First edition, O'Reilly, Beijing.

Manulis, M., Bridges, C.P., Harrison, R., Sekar, V. and Davis, A. (2021), "Cyber security in New Space: Analysis of threats, key enabling technologies and challenges", *International Journal of Information Security*, Vol. 20, No. 3, pp 287–311. Available at: https:// 10.1007/s10207-020-00503-w.

McClaskey, T.M. (2022), "Tabletop Exercises: Gamification in Cybersecurity", [online], Master Thesis, Utica University, www.proquest.com/docview/2665552356/74B62B4D8B3F402FPQ/1?accountid=14649, [Accessed 17.04.2023].

Pavur, J. and Martinovic, I. (2022), "Building a launchpad for satellite cyber-security research: lessons from 60 years of spaceflight", *Journal of Cybersecurity*, Vol. 8, No. 1, p tyac008. Available at: https:// 10.1093/cybsec/tyac008.

Rahman, M.H.A., Yusuf Panessai, I., Noor, A.Z.M. and Salleh, N.S.M. (2018), "Gamification Elements and their Impacts on Teaching and Learning - A Review", *The International Journal of Multimedia & Its Applications*, Vol. 10, No. 06, pp 37–46. Available at: https:// 10.5121/ijma.2018.10604.

Ritterfeld, U., Cody, M.J. and Vorderer, P. (eds) (2009), *Serious games: mechanisms and effects*, Routledge, New York.

Saeed, S., Suayyid, S.A., Al-Ghamdi, M.S., Al-Muhaisen, H. and Almuhaideb, A.M. (2023), "A Systematic Literature Review on Cyber Threat Intelligence for Organizational Cybersecurity Resilience", *Sensors*, Vol. 23, No. 16, p 7273. Available at: https:// 10.3390/s23167273.

Samtani, S., Chinn, R., Chen, H. and Nunamaker, J.F. (2017), "Exploring Emerging Hacker Assets and Key Hackers for Proactive Cyber Threat Intelligence", *Journal of Management Information Systems*, Vol. 34, No. 4, pp 1023–1053. Available at: https:// 10.1080/07421222.2017.1394049.

Schell, J. (2019), *The art of game design: a book of lenses*, Third edition, Taylor & Francis, CRC Press, Boca Raton.

Schlette, D., Böhm, F., Caselli, M. and Pernul, G. (2021), "Measuring and visualizing cyber threat intelligence quality", *International Journal of Information Security*, Vol. 20, No. 1, pp 21–38. Available at: https:// 10.1007/s10207-020-00490-y.

The Aerospace Corporation (2022), "Space Attack Research & Tactic Analysis (SPARTA)", [online], *SPARTA*, www.sparta.aerospace.org, [Accessed 04.11.2022].

The MITRE Cooperation (2024), "MITRE ATT&CK", [online], *ATT&CK Matrix for Enterprise*, www.attack.mitre.org, [Accessed 25.10.2022].

Thompson, L., Melendez, N., Hempson-Jones, J. and Salvi, F. (2022), "Gamification in Cybersecurity Education: The RAD-SIM Framework for Effective Learning", *European Conference on Games Based Learning*, Vol. 16, No. 1, pp 562–569. Available at: https:// 10.34190/ecgbl.16.1.504.

U.S. Department of Defense (2011), *FACT SHEET: Resilience of Space Capabilities*, www.dod.defense.gov/Portals/1/features/2011/0111_nsss/docs/DoD%20Fact%20Sheet%20-%20Resilience.pdf, [Accessed 19.01.2024].

van Steen, T. and Deeleman, J.R.A. (2021), "Successful Gamification of Cybersecurity Training", *Cyberpsychology, Behavior, and Social Networking*, Vol. 24, No. 9, pp 593–598. Available at: https:// 10.1089/cyber.2020.0526.

Vasquez, C. (2023), "First in space: SpaceX and NASA launch satellite that hackers will attempt to infiltrate during DEF CON", [online], *Cyberscoop*, www.cyberscoop.com/moonlighter-hack-a-sat-defcon, [Accessed 19.12.2023].

Viasat, Inc. (2022), "KA-SAT Network cyber attack overview", [online], *Viasat News*, www.news.viasat.com/blog/corporate/ka-sat-network-cyber-attack-overview, [Accessed 19.12.2023].

Willett, M. (2021), "Lessons of the SolarWinds Hack", *Survival*, Vol. 63, No. 2, pp 7–25. Available at: https:// 10.1080/00396338.2021.1906001.

Wolfenden, B. (2019), "Gamification as a winning cyber security strategy", *Computer Fraud & Security*, Vol. 2019, No. 5, pp 9–12. Available at: https:// 10.1016/S1361-3723(19)30052-1.

Yeboah-Ofori, A. and Islam, S. (2019), "Cyber Security Threat Modeling for Supply Chain Organizational Environments", *Future Internet*, Vol. 11, No. 3, p 63. Available at: https:// 10.3390/fi11030063.

Yeboah-Ofori, A., Ismail, U.M., Swidurski, T. and Opoku-Boateng, F. (2021), "Cyberattack Ontology: A Knowledge Representation for Cyber Supply Chain Security", in *2021 International Conference on Computing, Computational Modelling and Applications (ICCMA)*, IEEE, Brest, France, pp 65–70. Available at: https:// 10.1109/ICCMA53594.2021.00019.

State of Research: Relevance of Computer Emergency Response Teams in Operational Technology

Asiye Öztürk
University of Wuppertal, Germany
Clavis Institute for Information Security

Asiye.oeztuerk@hs-niederrhein.de

Abstract: The increasing integration of Information Technology (IT) and Operational Technology (OT) in industrial environments has led to increased vulnerability to cyber threats. This article examines the need for a dedicated Computer Emergency Response Team (CERT) for OT to ensure the security, integrity, and resilience of critical infrastructure, particularly in the energy sector. OT is subject to specific challenges that differ from those in traditional IT networks. Cyberattacks on OT systems can not only cause financial losses, but also have a significant impact on physical security and the environment. A specific CERT for OT is necessary to address the unique characteristics of these environments. This requires expertise in industrial protocols, control systems and SCADA systems. The CERT for OT should be able to respond quickly to security incidents, perform forensic analysis and implement effective countermeasures to ensure business continuity. Research shows that implementing a specialized CERT for OT leads to improved threat detection, faster response, and more effective defense against attacks. In addition, this article emphasizes the importance of collaboration and communication between IT and OT security teams to ensure comprehensive system resilience. The following article provides a detailed literature analysis that comprehensively examines the current state of research on CERTs in the context of OT. The analysis of the relevant literature highlights the increasing threat to OT systems and emphasizes the specific requirements arising from the integration of IT and OT. By identifying research gaps and summarizing current findings, this article provides a comprehensive overview of the existing literature on this topic.

Keywords: Computer Emergency Response Teams, CERT, CRITIS, OT, Information security, Energy

1. Introduction

With the structural change in the electrical energy supply, numerous supply-related processes and procedures are increasingly being modified. The structural and technical modification of the future electricity supply affects the two fields of action of the electricity grid. The primary field of action can be characterized by the term "system" or "grid" and includes the predominantly electrotechnical and information technology functions that serve to ensure a secure energy supply and are used, among other things, in the context of grid operation and grid management. The secondary field of action "market" specifies the energy industry processes, which focus on the definition of products, business models, players, and roles. As a result of structural change, these latter fields of action are growing closer together. The interaction between the supply and demand of electrical energy will therefore be networked and regulated in future through the exchange of information at all grid levels.

One of the fundamental characteristic aspects of the energy transition is the paradigm shift triggered by the Renewable Energy Sources Act and the Paris Climate Protection Agreement towards the decentralization of electricity generation using renewable energy sources within the "grid" field of action. During the paradigm shift, nuclear and fossil primary energy sources are gradually being replaced by renewable energies. Offshore plants (wind farms) at sea and photovoltaic plants are the new large-scale producers that are connected directly to the extra-high voltage grid and are increasingly forcing conventional large-scale power plants off the grid. These feed the electricity they generate into the extra-high-voltage grid and transmit it over long distances to the high-voltage grid, where large, intensive industrial consumers are connected. Medium-sized energy generation plants are connected to the medium-voltage grid as producers and medium-sized consumers (e.g. hospitals), which feed in or draw their electricity from here.

Small producers such as biogas consumers who use animal and plant materials to generate energy are connected to the low-voltage grid and thus to the last level of the electrical distribution grid. End consumers who install photovoltaic systems on their roofs to generate electricity by converting solar energy are also connected. The gradual decentralization of electrical energy generation and the grid expansion required for this are placing new demands on electrical engineering and information and communication technology processes.

For example, the so-called transmission system operators (TSOs) and distribution system operators (DSOs), which act as active players in the energy supply, must reckon with new intelligent instances, the integration of which entails an increase in complexity. The second characteristic aspect of the energy transition is therefore the increasing degree of complexity (Dai et al, 2020, p. 565).

On the generation side, in addition to the actors described above, the TSOs and DSOs, there are numerous decentralized energy generation systems, which are currently estimated at around 3.7 million solar systems in Germany (CIO, 2024). This will result in the integration of volatile energy generation based on renewable energies, which means that the comprehensive installation and operation of intelligent monitoring and control systems on the generation side will play a key role. Furthermore, decentralization provides for the integration of so-called prosumers (producer + consumer), whose behaviour as "energy producers and energy consumers" no longer corresponds to the conventional passive role definition (BMWi, 2018, p. 107). This shows that in the future energy supply structure, a traditional separation between producers and consumers no longer seems appropriate and the typical producer-consumer image is increasingly disappearing. Accordingly, the increasing number of energy producers, energy consumers and grid users are equivalent to the increasing degree of complexity and can therefore be declared as the third characteristic of the energy transition.

A logical conclusion from the increasing number of grid users is the proportional increase in interfaces. With a manageable number of members, many grid users, market users and multidirectional interfaces, the energy supply system, which has been labeled obsolete, now defines new requirements that require additional dynamic system control and system monitoring. Another characteristic of future system interfaces is sector coupling, which contributes to the transfer of electrical energy to other sectors and can create synergy effects through efficient energy distribution (BMWi, 2018, p. 25).

To cope with the increasing level of complexity and thus ensure a safe and trouble-free power supply, new concepts and system structures must first be configured and implemented. This novelty must also be able to handle intelligent and dynamic monitoring and control of the multidirectional energy supply structure. The fourth aspect of the energy transition can thus be characterized under the term "digitalization". Digitalization addresses a broad spectrum of modifications that affect the following fields of application, among others:

- Electrical engineering
- Information technology
- Communication technology

Control technology networks electrical and physical signals, such as electrical voltage currents, with information technology hardware and software components. This allows physical signals and attributes in the form of logical measured values and system states (information technology) to be exchanged bidirectionally within a network via specific protocols (communication technology). Data is exchanged here between the central monitoring and control units (e.g. grid control center) and the decentralized field components (e.g. substations and transformer stations).

The focus of the future grid is therefore on the smart grid integration of producers, consumers and grid users, the aim of which is to ensure a sustainable, economical, and secure electricity supply. Similarly, Scheffler (2016, p. 13) defines the goal of the future energy supply system as the "networking and control of intelligent generators, storage facilities, consumers and grid equipment in energy transmission and distribution grids with the help of information and communication technology (ICT). The aim is to ensure a sustainable and environmentally friendly energy supply based on transparent, energy- and cost-efficient, safe, and reliable system operation".

The use of networked information technology and the increasing digitalization of the electrical supply structure thus serve to simultaneously ensure an intelligent, environmentally friendly, trouble-free, and secure power supply. While ICT processes are becoming more efficient with the use of ICT, the potential for ICT dependency is increasing at the same time.

2. Relevance of Information Security

An efficient energy supply is of crucial importance. An outage of electricity and gas would quickly have serious consequences, as public life and vital services would be affected. At the same time, the functionality of the energy supply is closely linked to well-functioning operational technology (OT). The increasing integration of interfaces in industrial environments (OT) has led to increased vulnerability to cyber threats.

In its policy brief "IT security in the energy industry" (2019, p. 3), the Virtual Institute Smart Energy (VISE) states that "the challenge posed by the convergence of process and control technology with information and communication technology systems (...) increases the potential threat of cyber-attacks. The fact that hardware systems in water or nuclear power plants, for example, have a very long service life and cannot simply be replaced with more modern, more secure components for cost reasons, among others, does not improve the conditions".

Considering the increasing number of participants in the electricity grid of the future, this increased number of people involved, i.e. centralized and decentralized energy producers, energy suppliers and consumers, grid operators, metering point operators and service providers as well as customers in a grid, can be regarded as potential attack vectors for cyberattacks (VISE, 2019, p. 2).

The importance of information security is also reflected in the current legal landscape, which, following the introduction of the IT Security Act 2.0 (IT-SA) (July 2021), the publication of the Federal Office for Information Security Criticism Ordinance Part I (May 2016) and Part II (June 2017) and Section 11 (1a) of the Energy Industry Act, calls for the successive optimization and achievement of a minimum security level for Critical Infrastructure (CRITIS) in Germany, especially for the energy sector (FMI, 2016, p. 1).

The IT-SA refers to Section 11 (1a) of the Energy Industry Act and classifies network operators as operators of critical infrastructures. This classification is independent of the defined values set out in the Federal Office for Information Security Critical Infrastructure Ordinance. This type of consideration also implies the maintenance and safeguarding of information technology components that are used as part of grid operation and grid management.

The classification of the energy sector as a CRITIS explicitly emphasizes the importance of these entities as an active member of the German electrical energy system, particularly in the interest of compliance with electrotechnical and IT security. The primary focus is on securing and maintaining the energy supply and thus on the availability of electricity, which equivalently also requires the availability of electrotechnical and IT systems due to the technical interlocking. One of the key elements in ensuring the availability of OT systems (hardware and software components) is the effective cooperation and coordination of system administrators and IT managers. In addition, active monitoring of system behaviour is also part of this, as structured and organized processes enable a proactive and responsive approach to information security incidents. This approach is the reaction to dealing with the IT security incidents of the "Morris" cyber worm, which attacked a wide range of global OT systems in 1988. As a result of the serious cyberattack, the first Computer Emergency Response Team (CERT) approaches were conceived, which still exist today in different forms and variations (ENISA 2006, p. 8).

This research paper is dedicated to an in-depth examination of the current state of research in the field of Computer Security Incident Response Teams (CSIRTs) or CERT particularly regarding the energy sector. The terms CERT and CSIRT are used as synonyms in this paper. As already explained in the first chapter, the energy sector is characterized by increased procedural and technical interfaces, the effective management of which is of crucial importance in practice.

The importance of CERTs in the context of cyber security is becoming increasingly clear, especially in view of the growing complexity and frequency of cyber-attacks on critical infrastructures such as energy supply systems. These systems are characterized by a multitude of interfaces that include both procedural and technical aspects. Understanding and managing these interfaces is crucial to maintaining business continuity and minimizing risks.

By analyzing the current state of research and identifying best practices, the aim is to gain insights that can help improve the effectiveness and efficiency of CERTs in the energy sector. This is crucial to ensure the safety and reliability of the energy infrastructure and minimize the potential impact of cyber-attacks.

3. State of Research: Computer Emergency Response Team in the Energy Industry

A CERT is a team of IT security experts or specialists whose core process is to manage computer security breaches for a selected target group by offering preventive, reactive, and detective services. Preventive, reactive and detective services offered support the achievement of objectives. Preventive services provide support and information to prepare for attacks, problems, or events in advance. Reactive services are divided into two main core components:

- In the form of alerts or remote support processes aimed at identifying concepts for resolving incoming security incidents (analysis, coordination)
- In the form of on-site support processes or remote sessions (response, resolution).

Detective services support the continuous improvement processes. These include awareness-raising and training units, security audits and certifications, analyses (business continuity management and risk and vulnerability analyses).

A CERT can be established in various organizations or sectors, including government agencies, businesses, educational institutions, and critical infrastructure such as the energy sector. These teams can operate internally within an organization or externally as a service provider shared by multiple organizations.

The European Union Agency for Cybersecurity (ENISA) regularly publishes the CERT-Map, also known as the "European Union's National and governmental CSIRTs and their cooperation with ENISA", on its website and other relevant platforms (Öztürk, 2023, S. 78). The CERT Map provides an overview of the various CERTs and comparable institutions in the member states of the European Union. A current examination of this map shows, when selecting the energy sector, that as of the update 31.01.2024 there are a total of four CERTs that are specifically geared towards the energy sector (ENISA, 2024).

Italy
Enel CERT
https://www.enel.com/
cert@enel.com
Energy
Italy
TERNA-CERT
https://www.terna.it
cert@terna.it
Energy
Portugal
CSIRT EDP
http://edp.pt/
csirt@edp.pt
Energy

Figure 1: CSIRT – Intentory: Selection of sector energy (ENISA 2024)

However, the list is not exhaustive. A general search for CERTs for the energy sector has shown that in Austria the so-called Austrian Energy Cert, which provides specific services for the energy sector (Cert.at).

The following section examines the current state of research on the topic of CERT for network operators and members of the electrical power supply. The answer to this question is based on a comprehensive research analysis that focuses on written works. This includes primary and secondary literature, scientific papers, technical articles, and studies. Table 1 presents the results of this research: The list is the result of a thorough analysis of different databases combined with different keywords.

Table 1: Literature analysis with databases

Results table work package								
Database	**Absolute number of works recorded**	**Percentage share**	**Absolute number of eliminated shares**	**Percentage share**	**Reason for selection**	**Absolute number of selected works**	**Percentage share**	**Key words**
ACM	49	100%	15	31%	Duplicates	34	69%	Computer Emergency Response Team
AIS	100	100%	56	56%	Duplicates	44	44%	Cert
IEEE	169	100%	83	49%	Duplicates	86	51%	Computer Security Incident Response Team
EBSCO	12	100%	1	8%	Duplicates	11	92%	CSIRT
SPRINGER E	64	100%	9	14%	Duplicates	55	86%	Incident Response Team
WISO	1	100%	0	0%		1	100%	IRT
SPRINGER D	4	100%	0	0%		4	100%	Security Operations Center
ECONBIZ	8	100%	4	50%	Duplicates	4	50%	SOC
								Cyber Defense Model (Modell)
SUM	**407**		**168**			**239**		

Keywords were also combined with "concept, model + energy"

After selecting the duplicate files, a total of 239 papers containing the combination of keywords in their abstract were selected for analysis.

In the next step, these papers were analyzed in more detail, so that a total of 29 papers were selected that were classified as "relevant" and subjected to a semantic analysis in the next step.

As part of the content analysis, the following 31 research papers were examined in greater depth for the specific characteristics of CERTs in the energy sector.

Table 2: Research paper on CERTs in the energy sector

Index	Author	Year	Title
1	ENISA	2016	Report on Cyber Security Information Sharing in the Energy Sector
2	NIS Policy 2.0	2023	Network and information security policy 2.0
3	NIS Policy	2016	Network and information security policy 1.0

Index	Author	Year	Title
4	Holzleitner et al.	2017	European provisions for cyber security in the smart grid – an overview of the NIS-directive
5	ISO/IEC 27019	2018	Information technology - Security procedures -Information security measures for the energy supply
6	Skopik et al.	2018	Cyber situational awareness in Public-Private-Partnerships
7	Martins et al.	2019	Specialized CSIRT for Incident Response Management in Smart Grids
8	CMU/SEI	2003	Handbook for Computer Security Incident Response Teams (CSIRTs)
9	CMU/SEI	2004	Steps for Creating National CSIRTs
10	ENISA	2006	Setting up a CSIRT step by step
11	CMU/SEI	2006	Action List for Developing a Computer Security Incident Response Team (CSIRT)
12	ENISA	2007	A basic collection of good practices for running a CSIRT
13	CMU/SEI	2011	Best Practices for National Cyber Security: Building a National Computer Security Incident Management Capability V. 2.0
14	Huber et al.	2018	Introduction of an SME CERT in Austria
15	BSI	2008	National response plans: IT-Crisis Response in Germany
16	BMVIT	2013 - 2015	KIRAS project: Research Security. CERT communication model II
17	Huber	2015	Security in cyber networks. Computer Emergency Response Teams and their communication
18	New America	2015	National CSIRTs and Their Role in Computer Security Incident Response
19	CMU/SEI	2016	WHAT SKILLS ARE NEEDED WHEN STAFFING YOUR CSIRT?
20	Huber et al.	2016a	Knowledge sharing and trust among Computer Emergency Response Teams - a European challenge
21	Huber et al.	2016b	Study CERT Communication
22	Pospisil et al.	2017	Cyber security strategies - realizing goals through cooperation
23	ENISA	2011	CERT Operational Gaps and Overlaps
24	Hoyer et al.	2006	Critical success factors for a Computer Emergency Response Team (CERT) using the example of CERT-Niedersachsen
25	CMU/SEI	2011	Best Practices for National Cyber Security: Building a National Computer Security Incident Management Capability V.2.0
26	Dartmouth College	2017	IMPROVING CYBERSECURITY INCIDENT RESPONSE TEAM (CSIRT) SKILLS, DYNAMICS, AND EFFECTIVENESS
27	ENISA	2019	Maturity Evaluation Methodology for CSIRTs
28	Energy Community	2019	Final Report - Study on cyber security in the energy sector of the Energy Community
29	ENISA	2020	SECTORAL CSIRT CAPABILITIES Status and Development in the Energy and the Air Transport sector

Index	Author	Year	Title
30	CMU/SEI	2021	The Sector CSIRT Framework Developing Sector-Based Incident Response Capabilities
31	Daniel Núñez-Agurto et al.	2022	Design of an academic CSIRT – A proposal based on strategic planning principles

The works listed in 2 (see Table 2, indices 1 - 7) do not represent conceptual approaches or methods for CERT structures in the energy supply. In some points they merely underline the importance of this topic regarding the challenges to be expected in the energy transition.

In the "Report on Cyber Security Information Sharing in the Energy Sector", ENISA provides an insight into the development of CERTs, Information Sharing Analysis Centers (ISACs) and relevant initiatives for sharing information on cyber security incidents in the energy sector. Basically, ENISA analyzes existing regulations and functioning of the energy sector to derive how information sharing regarding CERTs can be improved in the future. The report is for informational purposes and does not present any specific methods or concepts that show how the exchange of information for CERTs could possibly look based on the results (ENISA 2016, p. 43).

A further examination of the works shows that there are various approaches to setting up CERT organizations (see Table 2, indices 8 - 14). However, no explicit conceptual process model for a CERT could be identified within the scope of the study that is either sector-specific or specifically addresses energy suppliers. The works listed above present procedures that enable the establishment of a CERT step by step. A closer examination illustrates that general and national institutions as well as SMEs are declared as the target group for the integration of the CERT organizational structure.

It also shows that ENISA is increasingly focusing on the establishment of new CERTs with the mission of securing the European information society by raising awareness of network and information security throughout Europe with the help of handbooks.

An analysis of the communication and cooperation models of CERTs illustrates that the topic of communication and cooperation plays an eminent role in the activities of CERTs, as, on the one hand, the increasing complexity means that an efficient and secure exchange of information and communication between the players in the digital supply infrastructure must be guaranteed and, on the other hand, incidents cannot always be resolved locally, so that the involvement of other units is required (Huber 2015, p. 54).

The listed theoretical works (see Table 2, indices 15 - 21) address the topic of communication and cooperation among CERT units for effective response, detection, and prevention of security incidents and present both empirical and conceptual approaches. Essentially, these works deal with efficient communication and cooperation between CERT units and emphasize the importance of this regarding the large number of actors that are generally required in the event of incidents. Fundamentally, this shows that there is currently no CERT that covers all services, meaning that the handling of security incidents requires different CERT units with different services (ENISA 2006, p.13).

According to Huber (2015, p. 55), "[t]he clear objective of cooperation for CERTs (...) is to obtain the support they need for their work". None of these works show a targeted discussion of the CERT communication structure regarding the energy sector.

The GÉANT network's TRANSITS funding program (see Table 2, Index 16), which is also listed, supports the establishment and further training of CERT structures. It supports the training and further education of CERT employees and is sponsored by European associations such as ENISA and Forum of Incident Response and Security Teams (FIRST). The courses take place twice a year and are aimed at individuals or organizations (Huber 2015, p. 56).

Some of the literary works (see Table 2, indices 22 - 28) deal with increasing the quality of existing CERT structures and present best practices for continuous improvement processes and maturity models. Among other things, these works focus on the perspective of better CERT structures, success factors for setting up and operating a CERT and optimization options that are essential for the successful establishment of CERTs.

The last two papers (29 and 30) deal with studies on CERTs in the energy sector, but do not represent methods or research projects.

The paper in 31 deals with the development of an organizational model to support security processes in academic institutions during computer incidents. It includes a systematic literature review to identify relevant organization types, services, infrastructures, and procedures for the development of academic CSIRTs. Guidelines from ENISA and FIRST and principles of the Strategic Planning Process are applied to develop an organizational model, operational proposals for the CSIRT and research areas.

In addition to the theoretical research, existing empirical concepts and research models/projects will now be examined to answer the second sub-question.

Table 3: Research projects and concepts on CERTs in the energy sector

Index	Association/authority/institute	Period	Research project?
1	Federal Ministry for Economic Affairs and Energy	2000 - 2023	No
2	Federal Ministry of Education and Research	2000 - 2023	No
3	Federal Network Agency	2000 - 2023	No
4	Fraunhofer Communication, Information Processing and Ergonomics (FKIE)	2000 - 2023	No
5	Fraunhofer Secure Information Technology	2000 - 2023	No
6	German Energy Agency	2000 - 2023	No
7	Network Technology/Network Operation Forum (FNN within the VDE)	2000 - 2023	No
8	Federal Office for Information Security	2000 - 2023	No
9	Research Power Grids	2000 - 2023	No
10	European Network and Information Security Agency	2000 - 2023	No
11	DFN-CERT	2000 - 2023	No

Overall, it can be seen (Table 2, indices 1 - 11) that none of the bodies examined deal with the topic of CERT for network operators in their research projects. A review of the Federal Ministry for Economic Affairs and Energy Hanover Technical Information Library shows that the topics of CERT, the energy sector, virtual power plants and CRITIS are dealt with, but that no specific organizational model or research project is being carried out in this regard.

This result is also fundamentally reflected in the other sources. According to Huber (2015, p. 58), one possible reason for this could be that CERTs for CRITIS operators are still in the process of being developed, but that this development is difficult in practice because "ICT security considerations are very different for commercial IT systems and industrial control systems" (Huber 2015, p. 58). Actions carried out by the system operator in the control center, for example, usually require immediate action.

These actions can be, for example, shutting down or starting up certain systems, controlling the power supply and switching capacities and loads on and off. Traditional two-factor authentication methods usually fail here, as immediate action cannot be guaranteed.

4. Conclusion

In summary, the literature review shows that there are no dedicated research projects or approaches that specifically address the alignment of CERT services to the energy sector. Although there are general approaches to increasing information security in the energy sector, there is a lack of preventive, reactive and detective measures geared towards this sector. This is significant given the complexity and specificity of OT systems in this sector, which require special measures and expertise. The existing gap in research suggests that there is an urgent need to develop specific modeling approaches to ensure the safety and resilience of OT systems in the energy sector. The development of such approaches requires a comprehensive examination of the unique challenges and threats faced by OT systems in the energy sector, as well as close collaboration between researchers, industry representatives and regulators.

Nevertheless, there is an urgent need for such projects in this sector. The energy sector is technically different from other sectors and therefore requires specific considerations in terms of information security. This industry operates complex infrastructures that are spread over wide geographical areas and include different types of energy sources and distribution systems. The integration of renewable energy sources and smart grid technology further increases the complexity and potential for attacks.

In addition, many assets and systems in the energy industry are highly outdated and may not be adequately protected against modern cyber threats. Therefore, it is crucial to conduct research projects that consider the unique technical aspects of the energy sector and aim to develop customized security solutions.

These projects should focus on identifying and addressing vulnerabilities in specific energy systems, developing security standards and guidelines for the industry, and training professionals in the unique challenges of energy security. Such targeted efforts can strengthen the energy sector's resilience to cyber-attacks and minimize the risk of serious impacts on society.

References

BMWi (2018) "Sixth monitoring report on the energy transition. The energy of the future", Federal Ministry for Economic Affairs and Energy, Germany, pp 1-190.

CIO (2024) *"How the promotion of solar energy will continue in 2024"*, [online] https://www.cio.de/a/wie-es-mit-der-foerderung-von-solarenergie-2024-weitergeht,3726505.

CMU/SEI (2021): "The Sector CSIRT Framework: Developing Sector-Based Incident Response Capabilities", 1-74.

CMU/SEI (2016): "WHAT SKILLS ARE NEEDED WHEN STAFFING YOUR CSIRT?" REV-03.18, pp 1-17.

CMU/SEI (2011): "Best Practices for National Cyber Security: Building a National Computer Security Incident Management Capability, Version 2.0" pp 1-40.

CMU/SEI (2006): "Action List for Developing a Computer Security Incident Response Team (CSIRT) ", Carnegie Mellon, Software Engineering Institute, pp 1-9.

CMU/SEI (2004): "Steps for Creating National CSIRTs", Carnegie Mellon, Software Engineering Institute, pp 1-26.

CMU/SEI (2003): "Handbook for Computer Security Incident Response Teams (CSIRTs)", Carnegie Mellon, Software Engineering Institute, pp 1-223.

Dai, J., Li, Y., Zhang, T., Zheng, S., Zhou, X. (2020) *"Research on Optimal Decision-Making of Power Grid Flexible Reserve under New Situation"*, IEEE Sustainable Power and Energy Conference (iSPEC), Chengdu, China, pp 565-571.

Dartmouth College (2017): "IMPROVING CYBERSECURITY INCIDENT RESPONSE TEAM (CSIRT) SKILLS, DYNAMICS AND EFFECTIVENESS", pp 1-17.

CERT.at (n. d.): "Mission Statement", [online] https://cert.at/de/.

ENISA (2024): "CSIRTs by Country – Interactive map" [online] https://www.enisa.europa.eu/topics/incident-response/csirt-inventory/certs-by-country-interactive-map.

ENISA (2020): "Sectoral CSIRT Capabilities - Energy and Air Transport", 1-62.

ENISA (2019): "ENISA Maturity Evaluation Methodology for CSIRTs", pp 1-42.

ENISA (2016): "Report on Cyber Security Information Sharing in the Energy Sector", European Union Agency for Cybersecurity, V. 1.1, pp 1-71.

ENISA (2011): "CERT Operational Gaps and Overlaps", pp 1-73.

ENISA (2007): "PART I: A basic collection of good practices for running a CSIRT", European Union Agency for Cybersecurity, pp 1-82.

ENISA (2006): "A step-by-step approach on how to set up a CSIRT", European Union Agency for Cybersecurity, pp 1-86.

EU (2022): "NIS 2 Directive", Official Journal of the European Union, 27.12.2022.

FMI (2016) *Ordinance on the Determination of Critical Infrastructures under the BSI Act (BSI Criticism Ordinance - BSI-KritisV)*, Federal Ministry of the Interior.

Hoyer, S., Pomes, R., Wohlers, G., Breitner, H. M., (2006): Critical success factors for a Computer Emergency Response Team (CERT) using the example of CERT-Niedersachsen, Germany, pp 1-51.

Huber, E., Pospisil, B., Hellweig, O., Rosenkranz, W. (2018): "Introduction of an SME CERT in Austria", in: P. Schartner - N. Pohlmann (Eds.) - D-A-CH Security 2018 – syssec, pp 142-150.

Huber, E., Hellwig, O., Quirchmayr, G., Donko-Huber, M. (2016b): Study CERT Communication", in: In: BMVIT Research Security, KIRAS Study volume 3, Vienna, pp 1-12.

Huber, E., Hellwig, O. (2016a): Knowledge sharing and trust among Computer Emergency Response Teams - a European challenge", in: Data protection and data security, pp 163-167.

Huber, E. (2015): "Security in cyber networks: Computer Emergency Response Teams and their communication", Springer VS; 2015th edition, Germany.

ISO/IEC 27019:2020-08, Information technology - Security procedures - Information security measures for energy supply (ISO/IEC 27019:2017, corrected version 2019-08).

Martins, R.J., Knob, L.A.D., da Silva, E.G. et al. (2019): Specialized CSIRT for Incident Response Management in Smart Grids. J Netw Syst Manage 27, pp 269–285.

New America (2015): "National CSIRTs and Their Role in Computer Security Incident Response", pp 1-36.

Núñez-Agurto, D. et al. (2022): "Design of an Academic CSIRT – A Proposal Based on Strategic Planning Principles", in: Botto-Tobar, M., Cruz, H., Díaz Cadena, A., Durakovic, B. (eds) Emerging Research in Intelligent Systems. CIT 2021. Lecture Notes in Networks and Systems, vol 405. Springer, Cham.

Öztürk, A. (2023): Shared Service Processes for the Information Security in the Smart Grid of the Future, International Journal of Engineering and Technology, Vol. 15, No. 3, August 2023, pp 76-80.

Pospisil, B./Gusenbauer, M./Huber, E./Hellwig, O. (2017) Cyber security strategies - implementing goals through cooperation.

Scheffler, J. (2016) *Distribution grids on the way to an area power plant, legal framework, generators, grids*, Springer Publishing Berlin Heidelberg.

Skopik, F., Wurzenberger, M., Settani, G., Fiedler, R. (2015): Building national cyber situational awareness through incident information clustering. In: Proceedings of the International Conference on Cyber Situational Awareness, Data Analytics and Assessment (CyberSA), London, UK, pp 1-8.

VISE (2019) Virtual Institute Smart Energy: "Policy Brief January 2019, IT security in the energy industry" Germany, pp 1-13.

A Review of IoMT Security and Privacy Related Frameworks.

Ramadhan M. Rajab, Mabrouka Abuhmida, Ian D. Wilson and Richard P. Ward
University of South Wales, Pontypridd, United Kingdom

ramadhan.rajab@southwales.ac.uk
mabrouka.abuhmida@southwales.ac.uk
ian.wilson@southwales.ac.uk
richard.ward@southwales.ac.uk

Abstract: This paper reviews current IoMT security and privacy frameworks, highlighting their contributions towards addressing the challenges in the rapidly evolving domains of IoT and IoMT. It examines the role of international standardisation efforts and evaluates the effectiveness of existing frameworks in enhancing interoperability and ensuring secure, reliable medical data communication. It begins by contextualising IoT within the broader spectrum of Ubiquitous Computing and Machine-to-Machine communications, underscoring its transformative potential. The paper delves into specific IoT frameworks, like the Open IoT Framework by Sun and Memon (2017), which emphasises microservices architecture for scalable and interoperable platforms. Additionally, it covers unique IoMT frameworks, including the SaYoPillow for stress and sleep analysis and the EMRI framework for secure healthcare data communication.

Keywords: IoT (Internet of Things), IoMT (Internet of Medical Things), Interoperability, Frameworks

1. Introduction

The development and implementation of the Internet of Things (IoT) and Internet of Medical Things (IoMT) frameworks have the potential to revolutionise various industries, including healthcare (Maskeliūnas et al., 2019). The integration of artificial intelligence (AI) and IoT technologies has led to radical transformations in the healthcare industry, creating what is known as the Intelligent IoMT. Furthermore, the emergence of IoMT-based healthcare monitoring systems has enabled medical practitioners to remotely monitor and analyse real-time health data. However, despite the numerous benefits and advancements in IoT and IoMT frameworks, challenges still need to be addressed. For instance, there is often a lack of interoperability and coordination between different systems and stakeholders in the healthcare sector. The fragmentation and inadequate linkage between the Ministry of Information and Communications Technology and healthcare providers can hinder the effective implementation of IoT and IoMT frameworks (Pelekoudas-Oikonomou et al., 2022). Additionally, the lack of standardised protocols and interoperable functionalities in existing electronic medical record systems limits the exchange of patient data between healthcare facilities. As a result, there is a need for comprehensive and standardised frameworks that address these challenges and ensure the secure and efficient integration of IoT and IoMT technologies in the healthcare industry. To address these challenges, it is crucial to establish robust cybersecurity measures and protocols to protect patient data and ensure the privacy and confidentiality of sensitive healthcare information.

2. Literature Review

Existing IoMT frameworks and standards discussed in the literature include the E-Health Big Data Architecture (E-HBDA) (Villegas-Ch & García-Ortiz, 2023), the cov-AID framework (Hamid et al., 2022), and the Digital Forensic Investigation Framework (DFIF) (Hassan et al., 2022). The E-HBDA framework focuses on collecting, storing, and analysing data generated by IoMT devices, using Hadoop and Spark for data processing and analysis (Lin et al., 2022). The cov-AID framework is designed for remote monitoring, diagnosis, and prevention of COVID-19, utilising IoMT sensors and extensive data analysis (Hassan et al., 2022). The DFIF framework is used for digital forensic investigation in the IoT environment, addressing challenges in IoT security and providing solutions and strategies. These frameworks differ in their specific objectives and applications, with E-HBDA and cov-AID focusing on healthcare and COVID-19, respectively, while DFIF addresses digital forensic investigation in the IoT environment.

Existing IoMT frameworks and standards have evolved to address the challenges of heterogeneity, interoperability, and security in the healthcare sector. These frameworks provide functionalities such as data collection, storage, analysis, and decision-making based on machine learning models. They aim to improve the accuracy, reliability, and productivity of electronic equipment in healthcare. The frameworks also focus on ensuring the safety and transparency of data usage, as well as backtracking decisions made by medical professionals. Standardisation is crucial to increase trust and enable the integration of devices from different vendors. The frameworks emphasise the need for common functionalities, interoperability standards, and network protocols across sectors. They also highlight the importance of openness, support for various applications, and the creation of healthy ecosystems in the IoT community (Mahalakshmi S.and Desai, 2022).

There are other proposed IoT frameworks that have been previously developed within the past decade. A previous instance is the Open IoT Framework by Sun et. al. (2017), that is based on Microservices Systems Architecture, that offers more scalable, extensive, interoperable, and maintainable platforms, that can accommodate heterogenous objects, and easily achieve application integration using automation, geo service intelligence and Big Data (Sun et al., 2017). This proposed framework coined the concept "Internet of Infinite Things", a vision where everything in the world may communicate with each other (Sun et al., 2017).

The upcoming section will present architectures related to the Internet of Medical Things (IoMT) and outline several well-established frameworks.

3. IoMT Architectures and Frameworks

3.1 Microservice-Based Architectures for IoMT Scalability and Interoperability

Microservice architecture has emerged as a potential approach to enable scalable and interoperable systems for IoMT applications. In contrast to traditional monolithic architectures, microservices decompose a large system into a suite of independently deployable modular services. As discussed by Sun and Memon (2017), this brings key benefits for IoMT platforms that need to integrate heterogeneous devices, data, systems, and user interfaces. A microservice oriented IoMT platform implements functionalities as discrete services, and core capabilities are implemented in a central microservice.

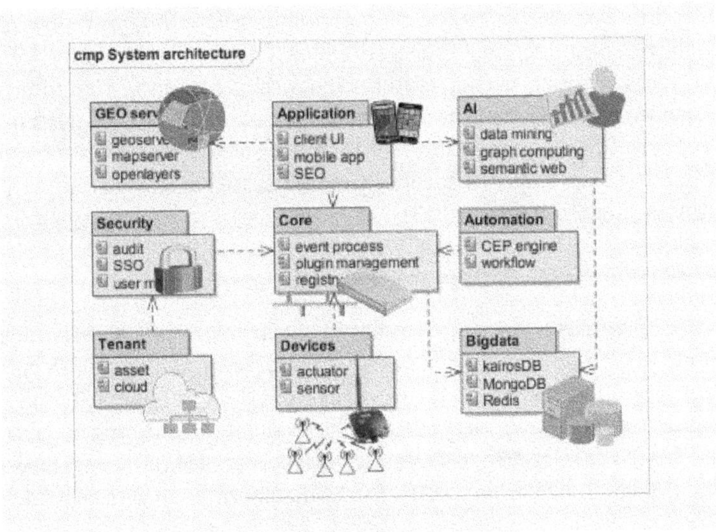

Figure 1: Microservice Based IoT Framework (Sun and Memon, 2017)

Sun and Memon (2017) propose a conceptual Open IoT microservice-oriented architecture for IoMT platforms, where specialised concerns such as geospatial capabilities, application modules, big data analytics, and machine learning are delegated to surrounding microservices. This approach enables independent development of various services in optimal languages with suitable data models, facilitating flexibility within the IoMT environment. Standard web interfacing architectures like the Representational State Transfer (REST) facilitate data exchange among services, while containerisation frameworks like Docker support testing and simulation of operational environments for individual microservices (Sun et al., 2017, p. x). **Figure 1** highlights the proposed architecture, which is composed of eight different microservices that are integrated to facilitate a flexible and interoperable IoT platform. It also has extensive features that may allow it to accommodate more of these microservices.

A key issue to be addressed here is distinguishing between IoT and IoMT application development architectures and frameworks, where application frameworks are shell abstractions that provide optimal solutions to software challenges (Mnkandla, 2009), as application architectures are sets of structures that formulate the disciplines and methods of developing applications (Perry & Wolf, 1992).

The SaYoPillow is an IoMT framework proposed by Rachakonda *et al.* (2021), that aims to understand the relationship between stress and sleep through an IoT edge device. The framework provides statistically monitored analysis to determine if the user has achieved sufficient and complete sleep in a day. **Figure 2** highlights specialised microservices for key functions. Note that it also monitors and controls psychological stress during the sleep period and in relation to food habits. The framework addresses several major issues identified by Rachakonda *et al.* (2021):

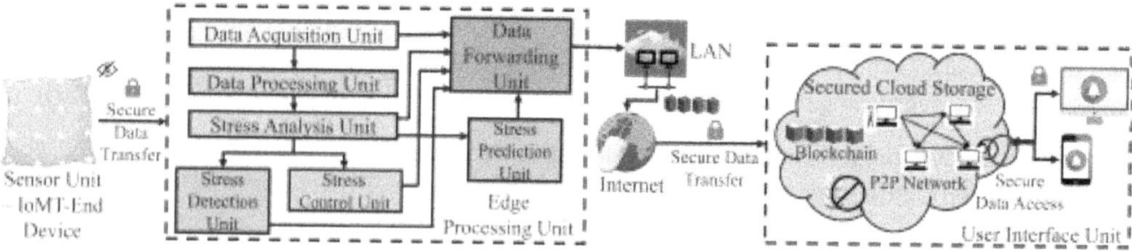

Figure 2: SaYoPillow Architecture (Rachakonda et al.,2021)

The SaYoPillow framework integrates a non-wearable device for stress monitoring during sleep, processing edge device data securely stored in the cloud. It enables stress detection, prediction, and user privacy in IoT cloud storage (Rachakonda et al., 2021. The cloud setup includes an EC2 Admin node, a miner, and two peers, with Geth clients on end-user devices accessing physiological data. Policy smart contracts on the admin node control user access, while RSA key encryption managed by a key system ensures secure client interactions. Prior to encryption, irreversible digests are generated using SHA-256 hashing, with digital signatures for data integrity (Rachakonda et al., 2021).

Ghubaish *et al.* (2020) proposed a security framework for mitigating various known physical and network related attacks. It was developed with reference to a four-layered IoMT system architecture, i.e., the sensor, gateway, cloud, and visualisation layers. It adopts certain features that provide three key functions, i.e. secure collection, transmission, and storage of data, based on the exploration, assessment, and analysis of the available security techniques, and how resilient they are against the IoMT attack surface, upon their findings indicating that no single technique can provide comprehensive security to IoMT systems against fourteen known IoMT physical and network related attacks (Ghubaish et al., 2020).

3.2 Blockchain Frameworks for IoMT Data Privacy and Security

Mallick and Sharma (2021) propose a Blockchain-based Electronic Medical Record Infrastructure (EMRI), facilitating secure communication and preserving patient data privacy. EMRI enables remote access to patient reports, addressing centralised Internet of Medical Things (IoMT) limitations. It employs smart contracts for privacy policy maintenance and Proof of Work (PoW) for block validation, ensuring decentralisation and reducing single points of failure. Smart contracts grant limited transaction access to non-trusted participants based on predefined policy terms. (Malick and Sharma, 2021). The EMRI algorithm occurs as follows:

- Doctor must be from a healthcare institution.
- Doctor must be a registered EMRI system user.
- Doctor logs in with user credentials.
- Smart contract is automatically executed.
- Patient provides Personal Identifiable Information (PII) for inputting medical data.
- Doctor provides treatment with reference to patient medical data.

According to the smart contract terms, validated user credentials, and verified PII, diagnostic centers add patient clinical records to a blockchain database, stored in decentralized ledger blocks validated by minor nodes. Hospitals operating these systems must adhere to regulatory authority guidelines, with registered practitioners. Smart contracts define terms for decentralized authentication of non-trusted parties. EMRI offers transparency and data integrity without modification, leveraging decentralized architecture for scalability, security, and privacy (Mallick & Sharma, 2021).

Golosova and Romanovs (2018) identified challenges in implementing blockchain technology in Emergency Medical Response Initiatives (EMRI), such as high energy consumption for real-time ledger maintenance, cryptographic complexities in signature verifications, and network instability from chain splits. Balancing node numbers and user costs remains problematic, with high rewards incentivizing nodes but potentially slowing transaction processing. Node capacity limitations may compromise blockchain immutability and transparency, leading to centralization and security risks. Additionally, while smart contracts are immutable, they lack flexibility for necessary annulments, particularly in dynamic ecosystems. Concerns also arise regarding contractual secrecy and privacy breaches in public ledger environments.

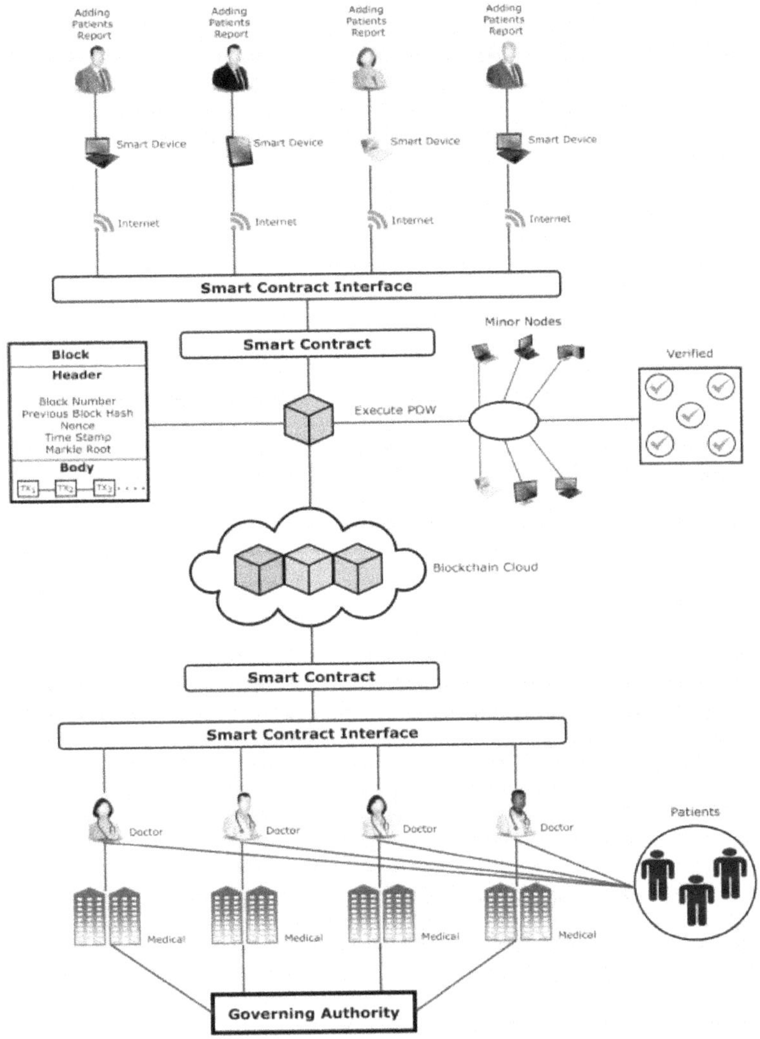

Figure 3: Process of Blockchain Smar Contracts (Rahmani et al.,2022)

The integration of secure protocols ensures transactional anonymity and guards against unauthorized access in blockchain systems. Legal adjudications encounter challenges in enforcing smart contract terms, particularly in the Internet of Medical Things (IoMT). Ongoing research focuses on trust management, cloud computing, and improving malware detection in IoMT devices. Innovations include energy-efficient solutions, merging 6G with 5G, integrating blockchain with edge computing and machine learning, and developing quantum-computing-based IoMT technologies (Nzuva, 2019 ; Rahmani et al., 2022). **Figure 3** depicts the proposed blockchain smart contract process (Rahmani et al., 2022).

4. IoMT Standards and Regulations

4.1 HL7 FHIR Standard for Healthcare Interoperability

Health Level 7 (HL7) is a non-profit organization accredited by the American National Standards Institute (ANSI), formulating ISO-accredited standards for exchanging electronic health information (HL7org, 2023). These standards provide a standardized framework crucial for clinical and medical management, outlining linguistic, structural, and typological requirements (HL7org, 2023). HL7's international presence involves affiliates dedicated to adapting standards globally, while in the United States, it operates through the U.S. Realm Steering Committee (HL7org, 2023). HL7 hosts 40 workgroups across healthcare sectors, overseen by elected co-chairs and divided into four steering divisions, managed by the Technical Steering Committee and the HL7 Board of Directors (HL7org, 2023). The HL7 standards' categorization is detailed in Table 1 (McKenzie & Peters, 2022).

Table 1: HL7 Sections

HL7 SECTION		SECTION NAME
Section 1		Primary Standards
	Section 1a	Clinical Documentation Architecture (CDA)
	Section 1b	Electronic Health Records (EHR)
	Section 1c	Fast Healthcare Interoperability Resources (FHIR)
	Section 1d	Version 2 (V2)
	Section 1e	Version 3 (V3)
	Section 1f	Arden Syntax
	Section 1g	Clinical Context Management Specification (CCOW)
	Section 1h	Cross-paradigm/Domain Analysis Models
Section 2		Clinical and Administrative Domains
Section 3		Implementation Guides
Section 4		Rules and References

The HL7 standardization process typically involves a 2-year timeline for a specification to achieve "Standard Trial for Use" status, followed by 3 or more years for it to become normative, reflecting ANSI standards and maintaining backward compatibility through upgrades (McKenzie, 2022). Basic interactions like those outlined in **Table 2** are complemented by advanced interactions such as Batch/Transaction (CRUD operations), VRead, Patch, and Capabilities, along with operational interactions enabling actions like RPC paradigms. Additionally, endpoints encompass validation and documentation entities (Kryszyn et al., 2023).

Table 2: HL7 FHIR Process Commands

NAME	INTERACTION
Create	Create new resource with server id. = POST url/(resourceType)
Read	Reading current resource status. = GET url/{resourceType}/{id}
Update	Update an existing resource by id (or create new one). = PUT url/{resourceType}/{id}
Delete	Delete resource. = DELETE url/{resourceType}/{id}
Search	Search/filtering resources. = GET url/{resourceType}? Search parameters
History	Get the change history for specific resource. = GET url/{resourceType}/{id}/history

Kryszyn et al. (2023) suggests that the functionality of a server depends on its capabilities, leading to varying sets of interactions and resources to manage. Standard specifications facilitate extensions and resource profiles tailored to local requirements, particularly in data authorisation, access, and encryption scenarios.

4.2 Benefits of HL7 Standards

The benefits that HL7 brings into healthcare sector are as follows (McKenzie, 2022):

- Processes to help in forming communities, perform reviews and performing both testing and a balanced, objective review of specifications.
- A community of stakeholders with expertise in healthcare and data sharing technologies.
- A community with interests in technology to improve the flow of healthcare information.
- Processes at the outset of projects to ensure the scope is well defined, awareness of intended work propagated across the entire HL7 and external communities.
- Technical infrastructure to support communication, and knowledge sharing.
- Formal methodologies that guide creativity of consistent, good quality specifications.
- Regular connectivity, shared registries, and testing environments to support ongoing validation of specifications upon their development.

- Mechanisms to solicit review widely based on knowledgeable experts and processes to coordinate responses to adaptation and providing feedback.
- Management process to coordinate committee efforts and facilitate community processes.
- Governance process to ensure all stakeholders have an opportunity to express their opinions and specifications are developed collaboratively in due consensus.
- Regional affiliations and fostered partnerships with other standards-related organisations, regulatory authorities, and key stakeholders.

4.3 Limitations of HL7 Standards

There are limitations to HL7 standards which must be considered (McKenzie & Peters, 2022):

- Both the standards and implementer communities have finite bandwidth towards fulfilling project objectives, timelines, pending regulations, funding, and other critical considerations.
- While communal resources aim to be fairly allocated across work products, volunteers and funded members will only develop and review content that reflects their own interests.
- The difficult and time-consuming efforts towards the standards process is not the technical artifacts but working with the people.
- There are no guarantees in the outcomes, stability, timing, and adoption of the standard process.
- Standards contribute towards limited expectations. Significant change management is often needed to shift market incentives, business practices, professional cultures and habits, and regulations in ways that befit the benefits that are to be achieved by a specification.
- Considering that better outcomes are to be achieved gradually and incrementally, it takes a lot of effort and time to fulfil them.
- There are challenges in some respects towards HL7 interoperability with other organisational standards.

The Fast Healthcare Interoperability Resources (FHIR) framework prioritizes robust security and privacy measures. This includes encryption of communications, prevention of information leaks, mitigation against script injections, and establishment of audit trails. FHIR integrates NIST mobile device security and OWASP Top 10 and other standardised security frameworks. It also facilitates communication of individual preferences via standardised protocols, resource tagging for data sensitivity, and data access record sharing for disclosure accountability (HL7, 2011; Pulivarti, 2023).

Some common use cases and approaches towards implementing security and privacy controls using HL7 FHIR are highlighted in **Table 3**:

Table 3: HL7 FHIR Use Cases

FHIR USE CASE	DESCRIPTION
Authorisation and Access Control	Defined a security label infrastructure that supports access control management.
User Identity and Access Context	Implemented using OAuth and HL7 Smart App Launch.
Audit Logging and Provenance	Audit logs are essential when investigating system security related events with reference to their timestamps. Provenance records are essential in checking and auditing user activities within the system.
Privacy Consent	This is essential in legally and ethically directing the collection, use and disclosure of the health data of an individual.
Digital Signatures	These are provided and exist in reserved locations.
De-Identification, Pseudonymization and Anonymization	These data processes reduce privacy risks by modifying and eliminating elements to fit a specific use-case. This follows access control decisions allowing a form of de-identification of diagnostic test results for the requesting client, based on ISO/IEC 20889:2018 guidelines.
Labels	Provided to affect the handling of resources.
Data Management Policies	Defined set of data exchange capabilities that are appropriate and of legal use to ensure that regulations and requirements are met.
Narrative	This should be undertaken with care when extracted from FHIR resources.

FHIR USE CASE	DESCRIPTION
Input Validation	This received input of data must be acceptable and correct to ensure that it does not have content that may corrupt system operations.
Event Reporting	There should exist Legal and ethical obligations which must provide means of reporting security incidents.

A production FHIR system also has a security subsystem for user administration, authentication an authorisation that fits into a) the consumer using the healthcare system, b) the client application, c) the security system and d) a clinical/healthcare repository (HL7, 2023-b).

In the UK, particularly within England, NHS institutions have largely integrated HL7 standards, primarily driven by initiatives spearheaded by INTEROpen since 2018 (INTEROpen, 2023). INTEROpen, in collaboration with HL7 UK and FHIR stakeholders, introduced the Care Connect API approach to foster open standards for interoperability in healthcare and social care sectors (NHS England, 2021). The Care Connect API approach facilitates data communication and exchange across clinical centers at a national level, as outlined in the detailed development and deployment guideline provided in **Figure 4** (Care Connect, 2019).

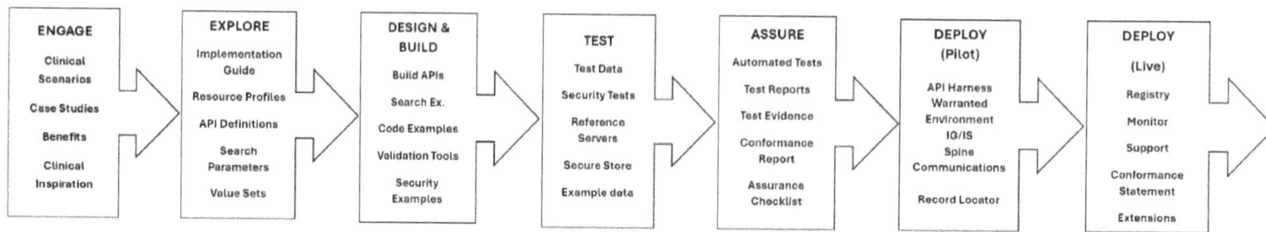

Figure 4: Guideline into developing a Care Connect API (Care Connect, 2019)

As from September 2021, the NHS Digital had strategized to adopt HL7 FHIR Release 4 to formulate a unified approach at UK National Level (N. H. S. England, 2019). The strategies move towards interoperability focuses upon:

- Working with services to identify strategic business needs.
- Developing priority use cases for interoperability to justify local business investment and development of supporting systems.
- Providing development support tools and guidance for interoperability to local institutions
- Developing electronic transfer standards for discharge from inpatient care and mental health.
- Accidental and Emergency attendance.
- Outpatient clinic letters.

According to the NHS England (2015), the interoperability of systems can be considerably achieved using two problematic approaches:

- **Technical interoperability** – This involves inter-systems processing of data based on the orchestration of reliable delivery of information (i.e., the *"how"*)
- **Semantic interoperability** – This involves processing each system to ensure it understands and interprets the information it is processing without ambiguity, by use of specific coding and messaging schemes at the core of integrating health and social care (i.e., the *"what"*)

As an approach to ensure the HL7 FHIR, and other key open standards that are implemented within public healthcare systems under NHS England, the National Information Board Interoperability Strategy was formed to develop Open APIs, as a requirement by the UK health and social care economy to self-assess the progress of its digital roadmap by April 2016 using a *Digital Maturity Index.* The key priority elements that were to be addressed by the Systems Interoperability strategy are the *NHS Number for every UK Citizen, Prescribed Medications for patients, NHS Medical Staff ID Numbers, Dates and Scheduling of Medical Appointments, Basic Observations on Patients upon their treatment, Basic Pathology* and *Diagnostic Coding* respectively (NHS England, 2015-b).

4.4 EU Regulations on Medical Device Safety and Security

The EU Medical Device Regulation (EU MDR), enacted in 2017, introduces stringent regulations, including expanded scope to diagnostic devices, higher risk classifications, and cybersecurity measures for IoMT devices.

Compliance challenges include complex approval processes, increased documentation, and costs affecting AI-based medical devices. IoMT devices face transitional issues adapting to the new regulations. While enhancing patient safety and device performance, the EU MDR poses challenges for manufacturers, impacting costs and product availability. It signals a significant shift in IoMT device security and AI development, prompting the need for more efficient clinical research methodologies and standardized protocols. (Vergani & Barrios, 2023;Melvin, 2022; Niemiec, 2022; Yu, 2021).

5. Challenges and Implications Around Security and Privacy of IoMT systems

In the current era of smart technology and IoT, securing IoMT devices in healthcare against cyber threats is crucial. Cybersecurity incidents, often due to human error, jeopardize patient data security, with diverse attack frequencies observed in the U.S. (Cartwright, 2023;Jiang & Bai, 2019). Notable incidents like the 2012 WannaCry attack underscore healthcare systems' vulnerability (Cartwright, 2023). Despite NHS efforts, ransomware attacks persist (Penfold, 2023). Legal frameworks like HIPAA, GDPR, and UK Data Protection Act emphasize robust cybersecurity (Memmi, 2023). Cyberattacks not only compromise patient safety but also raise ethical and financial concerns (Grably, 2022;Poulsen et al., 2021), with medical data fetching high values on the dark web (Sulleyman, 2017).

In Kenya, IoMT proliferation surpasses policy reforms, heightening ethical and security issues (Maina & Murungi, 2023). Inadequate national security standards exacerbate risks in E-Health (Raburu, 2021). Urgent regulatory actions are required (Maina & Murungi, 2023;Munyolo, 2021). Blockchain exploration faces regulatory hurdles, alongside challenges in EMR systems' interoperability and data confidentiality (Kamau et al., 2018). Collaborative efforts are essential to address IoMT cybersecurity risks and safeguard healthcare data integrity (Ondiek & Onyango, 2023). **Table 4** below comparatively summarises the challenges and implications in securing and assuring privacy in IoMT that are discussed in this section.

Table 4: Summary of the Challenges and Implications around IoMT security and privacy

IoMT Geographical Scope(s)	IoMT Challenge(s) Description	Implication to Challenge(s)	Author(s)
United States of America (USA)	Statistical investigations indicate diverse occurrences of cyber-attacks in healthcare, encompassing theft of Patient Health Data (41%), unauthorized access or disclosure (25%), hacking incidents (20%), data loss (10%), and improper disposal of records (3.4%).	Healthcare cyberattacks impact approximately 182 million patients.	Cartwright, 2023
		Breach frequency surged by 40% between 2018-2019, potentially exposing health data records.	Jiang & Bai, 2019
	Ransomware attack at Springhill Medical Centre in Alabama in 2019 affected a pregnant woman in labour.	cyberattack lead to the death of her baby nine months later.	Memmi, 2023; Poulsen et al., 2021
	There were 18 data breaches reported to the US Department of Health and Human Services Office for Civil Rights, rising to 368 by 2018, and 500 more data breaches in 2019, 347 more attacks in 2022.	Cyberattacks in healthcare pose significant risks to patient safety, particularly with patient-dependent Internet of Medical Things (IoMT) devices and systems.	Memmi, 2023; Poulsen et al., 2021
		Confirmation of 314,063,186 healthcare records were lost or stolen between 2009 and 2021.	Memmi, 2023
United Kingdom (UK)	Healthcare data, including Patient Health Information (PHI), is highly sensitive and regulated by laws like HIPAA, GDPR, and the UK Data Protection Act (2018) to ensure secure storage and access.	PHI's unique nature not only makes it a target for cyberattacks but also drives the development of cybersecurity solutions due to its critical role in patient care.	Memmi, 2023

IoMT Geographical Scope(s)	IoMT Challenge(s) Description	Implication to Challenge(s)	Author(s)
	NHS patient data can be traded on the dark web for financial ransom.	Data exfiltration, theft and exposure of healthcare data being traded at 10 times the value of bank data on the dark web.	Cartwright, 2023
	The WannaCry ransomware, affecting NHS 111 service and other systems.	This resulted into 20,000 cancelled medical appointments and operations, costing £92 million and jeopardising patient health, and affected MS Windows Computers in 80 NHS organizations.	Cartwright, 2023; Penfold, 2023
The Republic of Kenya	AI technologies were utilised to address service delivery challenges amid Covid-19 pandemic lockdowns.	There was limited digital preparedness due to financial constraints and infrastructural gaps raised ethical concerns regarding digital access.	Ondiek & Onyango, 2023
		Despite obstacles, Kenya deployed IoMT devices for Covid-19 monitoring, yet faced privacy issues due to insufficient implementation of proximity tracking, underscoring the necessity for ethical governance, privacy and transparency.	
	Cyberattacks on the E-Health in the Public Sector.	A loss of approximately $2 billion annually in revenue.	Raburu, 2021
	The technological progress has not standardized national security techniques. Healthcare faces challenges like manual processes, data quality issues, and inadequate security measures, hampering decision-making.	Challenges in the healthcare sector include manual processes, poor data quality, and insufficient data security measures, impeding effective decision-making.	Kamau et al., 2018
	The rapid growth of the Internet of Medical Things (IoMT) outpaces policy reforms, posing ethical and security risks and Stakeholder discrepancies hinder effective IoT policy engagement.	E-Health cyberthreats exceed defense mechanisms, jeopardising sensitive data.	Maina & Murungi, 2023; Munyolo, 2021
		There is limited access to healthcare forensics data from Kenya National Cybersecurity Incidence Response Team, which complicates the addressing of cyber-attacks.	
European Union (EU)	Corbeil-Essonnes Hospital in France was breached by Russian hackers and exfilrated healthcare data, exposing it on Google and the dark web, demanding a ransom of 10 million euros, later reduced to 1 million euros, which the hospital refused to pay.	Invested 2 million euros in system security and 5 million euros in cybersecurity upgrades, which is an incurring loss of revenue.	Memmi, 2023; Grably, 2022

6. Conclusion

This paper confirms that the examined frameworks pertaining to the IoMT exhibit certain identified flaws such as lack of scalability and immutability that impede their practical implementation into the real world. This is especially evident in the case of both the EMRI and SaYoPillow frameworks. Consequently, this justifies the need for further research with the aim of exploring more sophisticated approaches to developing scientifically agreeable and standardised technical security frameworks for IoMT, aside from relying on blockchain as a fundamental technical mechanism. There is also a crucial need to develop specific research, standards, and policies for ensuring cybersecurity and data privacy in the IoMT. Collaboration among healthcare, government, and technology stakeholders is essential to establish effective regulations and best practices. The vulnerability of the healthcare sector, attributed to legacy devices and disjointed data systems, emphasises the necessity for robust security risk assessment models to address challenges imposed within the rapidly evolving IoMT.

References

Cartwright, A. J. (2023). The elephant in the room: cybersecurity in healthcare. *Journal of Clinical Monitoring and Computing*, 1–10. https://doi.org/10.1007/s10877-023-01013-5

Connect, C. (2019). *Introduction to Care Connect API*. https://nhsconnect.github.io/CareConnectAPI/

England, N. (2023). *NHS England » Interoperability*. https://www.england.nhs.uk/digitaltechnology/connecteddigitalsystems/interoperability/

England, N. H. S. (2015-a). *NHS England » Interoperability Handbook*. https://www.england.nhs.uk/publication/interoperabilty-handbk/

England, N. H. S. (2023-b). *NHS England » Procurement framework strategy recommendations*. https://www.england.nhs.uk/nhs-commercial/central-commercial-function-ccf/procurement-framework-strategy-recommendations/#minimum-standards

Ghubaish, A., Salman, T., Zolanvari, M., Unal, D., Al-Ali, A., & Jain, R. (2020). Recent Advances in the Internet-of-Medical-Things (IoMT) Systems Security. *IEEE Internet of Things Journal*, *8*(11), 8707–8718. https://doi.org/10.1109/JIOT.2020.3045653

Grably, R. (2022). 'Cyberattaque à l'hôpital de Corbeil-Essonnes: les données volées étaient accessibles par une simple...,'. *BFMTV*. https://www.bfmtv.com/tech/cybersecurite/cyberattaque-a-l-hopital-de-corbeil-essonnes-les-donnees-volees-etaient-accessibles-par-une-simple-recherche-google_AN-202210050374.html

Hamid, S., Bawany, N. Z., Sodhro, A. H., Lakhan, A., & Ahmed, S. (2022). A Systematic Review and IoMT Based Big Data Framework for COVID-19 Prevention and Detection. In *Electronics (Switzerland)* (Vol. 11, Issue 17). MDPI. https://doi.org/10.3390/electronics11172777

Hassan, M. A., Samara, G., & Fadda, M. A. (2022). IoT Forensic Frameworks (DFIF, IoTDOTS, FSAIoT): A Comprehensive Study. *International Journal of Advances in Soft Computing and Its Applications*, *14*(1), 72–86. https://doi.org/10.15849/IJASCA.220328.06

HL7. (2023-a). *FHIR Security*. https://www.hl7.org/fhir/security.html

HL7. (2023-b). *FHIR Security and Privacy Module*. https://www.hl7.org/fhir/secpriv-module.html

HL7org. (2023). *Introduction to HL7 Standards | HL7 International*. https://www.hl7.org/implement/standards/index.cfm?ref=nav

Jiang, J. X., & Bai, G. (2019). Evaluation of causes of protected health information breaches. *JAMA Internal Medicine*, *179*(2), 265–267. https://doi.org/10.1001/jamainternmed.2018.5295

Kamau, G., Boore, C., Maina, E., & Njenga, S. (n.d.). May. Blockchain technology: Is this the solution to emr interoperability and security issues in developing countries? *2018 IST-Africa Week Conference (IST-Africa*, 1. https://ieeexplore.ieee.org/abstract/document/8417357

Kryszyn, J., Smolik, W. T., Wanta, D., Midura, M., & Wróblewski, P. (2023). Comparison of OpenEHR and HL7 FHIR Standards. *International Journal of Electronics and Telecommunications*, 47–52. https://doi.org/10.24425/ijet.2023.144330

Lin, C., Zhuang, J., Feng, J., Li, H., Zhou, X., & Li, G. (2022). Adaptive Code Learning for Spark Configuration Tuning. *Proceedings - International Conference on Data Engineering*, *2022-May*, 1995–2007. https://doi.org/10.1109/ICDE53745.2022.00195

Mahalakshmi S. and Desai, K. (2022). IoT Framework, Architecture Services, Platforms, and Reference Models. In J. M. and S. S. Nandan Mohanty Sachi and Chatterjee (Ed.), *Internet of Things and Its Applications* (pp. 37–59). Springer International Publishing. https://doi.org/10.1007/978-3-030-77528-5_2

Maina, A., & Murungi, D. (2023). The Health Policy Implications of Social Representations of the Internet of Things in Kenya. *Academy of Management Proceedings (Vol. 2023*, *1*, 15849. https://doi.org/10.5465/AMPROC.2023.15849abstract

Mallick, S. R., & Sharma, S. (2021). EMRI: A scalable and secure Blockchain-based IoMT framework for healthcare data transaction. *19th OITS International Conference on Information Technology (OCIT*, 261–266. https://doi.org/10.1109/OCIT53463.2021.00060

Maskeliūnas, R., Damaševičius, R., & Segal, S. (2019). A review of internet of things technologies for ambient assisted living environments. *Future Internet*, *11*(12), 259.

McKenzie, L. (2022). *Understanding the standards Process" - HL7 - confluence (2022.* https://confluence.hl7.org/display/HL7/Understanding+the+Standards+Process

McKenzie, L., & Peters, M. (2020). *Participating in HL7 - HL7 - confluence - 2020".* https://confluence.hl7.org/display/HL7/Participating+in+HL7

Melvin, T. (2022). The European Medical Device Regulation–What Biomedical Engineers Need to Know. *IEEE Journal of Translational Engineering in Health and Medicine*, *10*, 1–5. https://doi.org/10.1109/JTEHM.2022.3194415

Memmi, G. (2023). Cyber-attacks in healthcare: why they matter and how to defend against them. *British Journal of Healthcare Management*, *29*(1), 8–11. https://doi.org/10.12968/bjhc.2022.0134

Mnkandla, E. (2009). About software engineering frameworks and methodologies. In *AFRICON 2009* (pp. 1–5). IEEE. https://doi.org/10.1109/AFRCON.2009.5308117

Munyolo, G. N. O. (2021). *Cyber-security in E-health: a Critical Analysis of the Regulatory Framework in Kenya.* http://erepository.uonbi.ac.ke/bitstream/handle/11295/157251/Munyolo_Cyber-security%20in%20E-health.pdf?sequence=1

Navakauskas, D., Romanovs, A., Plonis, D., (2018) Institute of Electrical and Electronics Engineers. Lithuania Section, Institute of Electrical and Electronics Engineers. Latvia Section, Vilniaus Gedimino technikos universitetas, Rīgas Tehniskā universitāte, Institute of Electrical and Electronics Engineers. Lithuania Section. Education Society Chapter, & Institute of Electrical and Electronics Engineers. (2018). *2018 IEEE 6th Workshop on Advances in Information, Electronic and Electrical Engineering (AIEEE) : proceedings of the 6th IEEE workshop : November 8-10, 2016, Vilnius, Lithuania.*

Niemiec, E. (2022). Will the EU Medical Device Regulation help to improve the safety and performance of medical AI devices? *Digital Health*, *8*, 20552076221089080. https://doi.org/10.1177/20552076221089079

Nzuva, S. (2019). Smart contracts implementation, applications, benefits, and limitations. *Journal of Information Engineering and Applications*, *9*(5), 63–75. https://doi.org/10.7176/JIEA

Ondiek, J. O., & Onyango, G. (2023). Ethical Dilemmas in Public Innovations and ICT Solutions During COVID-19 in Kenya". In G. Onyango (Ed.), *Public Policy and Technological Transformations in Africa. Information Technology and Global Governance*. Palgrave Macmillan. https://doi.org/10.1007/978-3-031-18704-9_16

Pelekoudas-Oikonomou, F., Zachos, G., Papaioannou, M., Ree, M., Ribeiro, J. C., Mantas, G., & Rodriguez, J. (2022). Blockchain-based security mechanisms for IoMT Edge networks in IoMT-based healthcare monitoring systems. *Sensors*, *22*(7), 2449. https://doi.org/10.3390/s22072449

Penfold, J. (2023). The growing risk of cyber-attacks in the NHS. *British Journal of Healthcare Management*, *29*(1), 5–7. https://doi.org/10.12968/bjhc.2022.0132

Perry, D. E., & Wolf, A. L. (1992). Foundations for the study of software architecture. *ACM SIGSOFT Software Engineering Notes*, *17*(4), 40–52. https://doi.org/10.1145/141874.141884

Poulsen, K., McMillan, R., & Evans, M. (2021). *A hospital hit by hackers, a baby in distress: the case of the first alleged ransomware death.* https://www.wsj.com/articles/ransomware-hackers-hospital-first-alleged-death-11633008116?mod=hp_lead_pos5

Pulivarti, R. (2023). *Cybersecurity of Genomic Data.* https://doi.org/10.6028/NIST.IR.8432

Raburu, E. E. (2021). A Cybersecurity Model for the Health Sector: A Case Study of Hospitals in Nairobi, Kenya. http://erepo.usiu.ac.ke/11732/6742

Rachakonda, L., Bapatla, A. K., Mohanty, S. P., & Kougianos, E. (2021). SaYoPillow: Blockchain-Integrated Privacy-Assured IoMT Framework for Stress Management Considering Sleeping Habits. *IEEE Transactions on Consumer Electronics*, *67*(1), 20–29. https://doi.org/10.1109/TCE.2020.3043683

Rahmani, M. K. I., Shuaib, M., Alam, S., Siddiqui, S. T., Ahmad, S., Bhatia, S., & Mashat, A. (2022). Blockchain-based trust management framework for cloud computing-based internet of medical things (IoMT): a systematic review. *Computational Intelligence and Neuroscience*. https://doi.org/10.1155/2022/9766844

Statement, Interopen. (2022). *United Kingdom.* https://www.intersystems.com/uk/resources/interopen-statement/

Sulleyman, A. (2017). 'NHS cyber-attack: Why stolen medical information is so much more valuable than financial data | The Independent,'. *The Independent*. https://www.independent.co.uk/tech/nhs-cyber-attack-medical-data-records-stolen-why-so-valuable-to-sell-financial-a7733171.html

Sun, L., Li, Y., & Memon, R. A. (2017). An open IoT framework based on microservices architecture. *China Communications*, *14*(2), 154–162. https://doi.org/10.1109/CC.2017.7868163

Vergani, T., & Barrios, C. F. M. (2023). *Needs, Challenges, and Obstacles in the Implementation of the EU Medical Device Regulation.* https://www.iicj.net/subscribersonly/23june/iicj1jun-regulation-tancredivergan-obelis-belgium.pdf

Villegas-Ch, W., & García-Ortiz, J. (2023). Toward a Comprehensive Framework for Ensuring Security and Privacy in Artificial Intelligence. *Electronics (Switzerland)*, *12*(18). https://doi.org/10.3390/electronics12183786

Yu, H. (2021). Digital health technologies under the new EU Medical Devices Regulation: monitoring and governing intended versus actual use. *BMJ Innovations*, *7*(4). https://doi.org/10.1136/bmjinnov-2021-000713

A Comprehensive Analysis of Narratives within NATO's Doctrines

Dominic Saari, Teemu Häkkinen and Panu Moilanen
University of Jyväskylä, Finland

dobejosa@jyu.fi
teemu.hakkinen@jyu.fi
panu.moilanen@jyu.fi

Abstract: The 2022 Russian invasion of Ukraine reshaped global security norms, challenging the West with a strategy known as hybrid warfare. Rooted in Russia's military doctrine, this approach integrates both military and non-military means, labelled hybrid warfare in the West and non-linear warfare in Russia. Prioritizing psychological and cognitive influence, the New Generation Warfare emphasizes soft power. NATO responded by investing in strategic communications and exploring cognitive warfare as a potential sixth domain of war. Adversaries use intricate methods to manipulate civilian cognitive processes, relying on persuasive narratives. Like business corporations, nation-states now craft strategic narratives to shape political and military thinking, employing various narrative levels in information and cognitive warfare, including counter-narratives against hostile stories. This article provides a comprehensive review of the different perspectives on the role of narratives within defence and security strategies and doctrines of NATO. The qualitative methodology employed in this study focuses on understanding how narratives are perceived within the strategies of the alliance. The approach involves a comprehensive examination and comparison of narrative practices to uncover the evolution of NATO's narrative concepts. The sources for this study encompass a range of materials, including official NATO strategy and doctrine papers. This article reveals that, over the period spanning from the 2003 to 2024, narratives have gained increasing significance for NATO. Initially regarded merely as a means to depict events in a preferred manner, narratives have evolved to play a pivotal role in shaping the alliance's strategy. They have transcended their initial role, now exerting influence on military operations and taking precedence at every level of NATO, from headquarters to the boots on the ground. It is highlighted in this article that NATO endeavours to align its actions with its values, aiming to establish credibility and legitimacy. NATO perceives a robust, multi-levelled, and ever-evolving narrative as an effective safeguard against hostile information and cognitive warfare.

Key Words: Information Warfare, NATO, Strategic Narratives, Narrative Strategies, Qualitative Research

1. Introduction

Traditionally, narratives served as a way to tell stories. In modern times, they are acknowledged as a crucial aspect of warfare, representing the transformation of the narrative concept into a powerful tool that profoundly impacts the surrounding world. Conflict-related narratives are now a key component in war, shifting the battleground into the cognitive domain (Kvernbekk & Bøe-Hansen 2017).

In 2013, the Russian Chief of General Staff, General Valery Gerasimov (2013) held his famous speech, in which he described the changes in contemporary warfare. The main message of Gerasimov was that "the role of non-military means of achieving political and strategic goals has grown, and, in many cases, they have exceeded the power of force of weapons in their effectiveness (....)". In the model presented by Gerasimov, the only set of operations spanning over all stages of military conflict, are information operations. Later Gerasimov (2016, 20) also referred to hybrid methods stating them to include e.g. "informational and psychological influence". While the cognitive dimension was embraced in Russian thinking, NATO was compelled to adapt as well. NATO echoed this by investing heavily in strategic communications and the research of cognitive warfare. As part of NATO's Warfare Development Agenda, the organization's Warfare Development Imperative is set to publish its Cognitive Warfare Concept later in 2024 (NATO, 2024).

Dr. Andreas Krieg (2023) defines narratives as stories that structure realities, shape identity, and provide meaning. He emphasizes their pivotal role in fostering social cohesion and consensus. Environmental scientist Braden Allenby (2017) extends this, asserting narratives as versatile and widely adaptable strategic tools. Allenby underscores their flexibility as strategic instruments applicable in various contexts, highlighting the adaptability of those who use them by integrating knowledge from diverse fields. Going beyond storytelling, Allenby stresses the power of narratives as influential frameworks shaping identities, meaning, and exercising manipulative influence over individuals. Narrative strategist Ajit Maan (2018) takes it further, stating, "Through narrative, we co-construct our personal and cultural identities. Ideas and beliefs result from those identities, and actions follow."

This research article aims to reveal the role of narrative in the thinking of the North Atlantic Treaty Organization (NATO). As a prominent military alliance, NATO holds a leading position in the Western context, forming a coalition where nations mutually defend each other, serving as a significant deterrent against foreign aggression toward any member state. Notably, NATO functions as a nuclear alliance with the capacity to undertake diverse missions under the overarching themes of peace and security.

Information plays a crucial role in NATO operations, and our empirical section will explore this aspect. However, understanding how NATO operates, particularly in the cognitive domain and the role of narratives, remains partially unclear. This poses a research problem: what is the role of narratives in NATO's thinking, especially at the doctrinal level, and what insights can a better understanding provide regarding their importance in modern military and strategic thinking? This article focuses on NATO as a single entity, recognizing the varied interests of other actors within the organization. Our goal is to outline NATO's thinking and how narratives are portrayed in different doctrines.

We will outline our research approach, present empirical analysis findings, and conclude with a comprehensive discussion and conclusion.

2. Methods and Selected Sources

To delve into the comprehension of narratives within the alliance, this article adopts a qualitative approach, focusing on textual analysis of sources and contextualizing our findings. Our methodology draws on an understanding of history, where the significance of narratives and storytelling has traditionally played a pivotal role, aligning with an empiricist approach (Munslow 2007). Viewing NATO as an entity, we recognize the role of narratives as providing insight into the historical thinking within the organization or the lack thereof. The portrayal of narratives, both as contemporary and historical phenomena, sheds light on the organization and offers clues about potential future directions.

We utilized official NATO reports, toolkits, and strategy papers, primarily sourced from NATO's online archives. After an extensive search, we carefully selected 32 documents, with eleven identified as crucial for this article's context. Covering the period from 2003 to 2024, these documents highlight a notable shift in NATO's attention towards narratives. While earlier psychological operations doctrines vaguely mention stories and persuasion, they lack additional context, definitions, or methods.

After compiling data, we employed qualitative analysis software, specifically Atlas.ti, for coding and categorizing our findings using keywords such as "narrative" and "story." The categories—narrative as a tool, NATO's brand building and storytelling, and narratives as part of military operations leadership—were chosen based on the context of the quote. These categories summarize key themes present in the empirical sources and are grounded in empiricism. This method facilitated the precise identification of patterns, allowing us to understand how various NATO doctrine and policy papers conceptualize the narrative concept.

The research reveals a clear evolution of this concept throughout modern times, providing a historical understanding of the role of narrative in NATO thinking with both strategic and operational implications. We discuss its significance for the organization and potential implications for the future.

3. NATO and the Emergence of the Cognitive Domain

The role of narratives in the history of warfare is intertwined with long-term trends, where the dissemination of information has played a crucial role in various war-related activities. This includes maintaining or undermining morale and informing the public about war-related events and activities. Particularly since the First World War, propaganda has held a key position, connecting modern advertising and information dissemination to purposeful efforts in shaping the ideas and understanding of target audiences (Taylor 2003; Jowett & O'Donnell 2012).

Since the Gulf War and the emergence of the "information war", Western thinking has focused on waging war based on information dominance. This approach stems from the changing nature of international crises, shifting from inter-state wars to more intra-state conflicts. The need to revise doctrines related to defence arises as more powerful and globalized communication means become ever-present on the battlefield (Taylor 2003, 298-314).

In the early 2000s, as NATO's attention turned to the Middle East and the war on terror, member states, particularly the United States, re-evaluated psychological warfare capabilities and strategies. However, in a post-Cold War political environment, Psychological Operations (PSYOPS) faced criticism for being perceived as a "black art" focused solely on lies and deception (Collins 2002). In an attempt to rebrand PSYOPS, terms like information campaigns and influence operations took the centre stage. The U.S., for instance, introduced the concept of Military Information Support Operations (MISO) (JCS JP 3-13.2). Despite its tarnished reputation, PSYOPS would still have its place within NATO to this very day. In NATO's Military Policy on Psychological Operations, PSYOPS were defined as planned activities using communication methods to influence approved audiences, shaping perceptions, attitudes, and behaviour to achieve political and military objectives. In 2007 NATO published its Allied Joint Doctrine for Psychological Operations (AJP-3.10.1(A)). Here, Psychological Operations (PSYOPS) were viewed as a component of a broader Information Operations (INFO OPS/IO), described as strategic actions to influence adversaries and approved parties in line with Alliance objectives by manipulating information, processes, and systems, while safeguarding one's own interests. (AJP-3.10.1(A) 2007). Despite attempts to clarify, more confusion followed as, in US military thinking, INFO OPS and PSYOPS were often at odds, leading to overlapping responsibilities and significant confusion (Munoz, 2012).

Symbolizing the shift in NATO's attention, the 2008 Bucharest Summit Declaration called for appropriate, timely, accurate, and responsive communication regarding NATO's policies and engagement in international operations (Bucharest Summit Declaration 2008). This sentiment was reiterated in the Strasbourg / Kehl Summit Declaration the following year, emphasizing the need for better strategic communication (Strasbourg / Kehl Summit Declaration 2009). In 2009 NATO defined strategic communication as a coordinated use of all NATO's communications capabilities such as Public Diplomacy and Affairs, IO and PSYOPS in order to advance NATO's interests (NATO Strategic Communications Policy 2009). In the same year, NATO also published its Allied Joint Doctrine for Information Operations, indicating the rising understanding of the new threat (AJP-3.10 2009).

For NATO, another watershed moment occurred in 2014 following Russia's intense hybrid warfare against Ukraine, especially after the Euromaidan Revolution. During the 2016 Warsaw Summit, the alliance committed to countering hybrid threats and building resilience (Warsaw Summit Communiqué 2016). Additionally, Russian disinformation campaigns played a role in popularizing the term "information warfare" as we know it in the West (Giles 2016). In the Brussels Summit of 2021, these disinformation campaigns were singled out as one of the main Russian hybrid actions against NATO (Brussels Summit Communiqué 2021).

In the following years within NATO, concerns about cognitive threats led to the emergence of the concept of cognitive warfare in 2020 (Du Cluzel 2020). This concept has since been actively developed by NATO-backed scientists and military personnel, with the aim of publishing it in 2024 (NATO 2024). According to NATO cognitive warfare blends cyber, information, psychological, and social engineering to influence, protect, or disrupt cognition for strategic advantage. It targets rationality, exploits vulnerabilities, and weakens defences, shaping perceptions and behaviours at individual, group, and societal levels (NATO 2023,2024; Bernal et al 2020; Claverie & du Cluzel 2022)).

4. Empirical Findings

4.1 Crafting a NATO Story

Multiple earlier NATO papers underscore the significance of "telling the NATO story". In 2011, NATO's Public Diplomacy Division (PDD) highlighted that narrating and showcasing the NATO story is a key mission, providing guidance to practitioners on imagery and platforms for effective message dissemination (NATO Military Public Affairs Policy 2011). In 2017, NATO's Brand Guide identified the alliance's most crucial challenge as establishing an emotional bond with unfamiliar citizens, conveying its identity, purpose, and significance (NATO Brand Guide 2017). The guide outlined a clear brand promise—NATO guarantees freedom and security—integrated into external communications to evoke desired emotions and understanding about the organization. The brand narrative unfolds in three key chapters—political, military, and change—with the overarching goal of strengthening the grand narrative. In the political chapter, there is a commitment to cooperative efforts aimed at bolstering security through consensus decision-making and advocating for the crucial role of women in peace and security. The Military chapter highlights NATO's formidable military capabilities, placing a strong emphasis on the dedication to safeguarding civilians, particularly through the application of NATO's Article 5. Finally, the Change chapter assures a commitment to innovation, adaptation, and scientific advancements. The storytelling objective is to build legitimacy and showcase shared values, referencing NATO's history and core principles established in The North Atlantic Treaty of 1949 (NATO Brand Guide 2017; The North Atlantic Treaty, 1949; AJP-10, 2023).

Published in 2023, NATO's official Allied Joint Doctrine for Strategic Communications reinforces the idea, that The North Atlantic Treaty of 1949 serves as a core tenet of NATO's institutional narrative (AJP-10, 2023). All NATO activities, including public affairs, strategic communications, psychological operations, information operations, and kinetic military actions, are grounded in this narrative, aiming to provide meaning and unify the Alliance under a clear, easily understandable narrative. This institutional or grand narrative not only serves as a tool for building support and legitimacy but is also viewed as a defensive asset against hostile information operations, disinformation, and propaganda (NATO FFAO 2018). Within the alliance, there is a concern that failing to convey NATO's story effectively could leave room for others to shape the narrative, posing a potential threat to the alliance's brand (NATO Brand Guide 2017).

4.2 Towards a Unified Approach

Despite its growing importance, the concept of narratives was initially unclear within NATO and its member states. In 2014, the Allied Joint Doctrine for Psychological Operations provided one of the earliest clear definitions of narratives, stating it as "the translation of an organization's mandate and vision into a fundamental persistent story of who the organization is, what its guiding principles are, and what it aspires to achieve" (AJP 3.10.1). To ensure a unified approach, an agreed-upon definition was officially approved in 2020 and incorporated into the NATO Terminology: "A spoken or written account of events and information arranged in a logical sequence to influence the behaviour of a target audience" (NATOTerm).

According to NATO StratCom, narratives convey the purpose and desired outcomes of activities, fostering understanding, support, and legitimacy. These brief and memorable story arcs help contextualize strategic planning, enhance organizational cohesion, and enable culturally relevant communication to reach target audiences and promote objectives (AJP-10 2023). NATO Counter-Insurgency Doctrines state that narrative is the central mechanism through which ideologies are mobilized and expressed (AJP-3.4.4 2011; AJP-3.27 2023).

After the general approval of the concept, NATO delved deeper into its understanding. The terminology evolved, unifying terms like 'grand narrative,' 'master narrative,' and 'brand narrative' under the term 'institutional narrative' after 2020. In 2023, NATO StratCom divided the narrative into three levels (AJP-10 2023). The first is the institutional narrative, which naturally forms during an entity's establishment and emerges implicitly through words, actions, and communication within the information environment. NATO roots its core institutional narrative in the 1949 North Atlantic Treaty, projecting itself as a democratic multinational alliance with a strong capability to protect its borders. According to StratCom, institutional narratives are enduring but may evolve based on the organization and the operational environment (AJP-10 2023). The 2022 Allied Joint Doctrine described institutional narratives as enduring narratives supporting enduring campaigns, promoting predictability and consistency in the organization's actions (AJP-01 2022). NATO's institutional narrative, outlined in four key building blocks, signals dedication to collective defence, commitment to cooperative security and stability, and showcases solidarity among member states and shared values (AJP-01 2022). The institutional narrative communicates the NATO story and why NATO does what it does.

Below the institutional level are strategic narratives, defined by NATO StratCom as the means to reveal an organization's reasoning behind its actions and strategic objectives. Unlike institutional narratives that develop naturally, strategic narratives are deliberately crafted and must be driven from the top, executed by commanders on all levels of mission command (AJP-10, 2023). Within NATO, strategic narratives are viewed as dynamic and alterable, with military action amplifying them. These narratives must be credible, and all military actions should align within them (AJP-3.27 2023).

While NATO's official definitions emphasize the importance of strategic narratives, scholars like Professor Alister Miskimmon describe them as instruments for political entities to create shared understanding and influence the behavior of other actors (Miskimmon et al. 2013). Strategic narratives are also seen as captivating storylines that rally support, diminish opponents' influence, and connect strategy and narrative (Lieffers 2014; Laity 2015). They serve as a useful tool to influence different audiences, building legitimacy, shaping perceptions, and provoking cognitive and psychological responses (Wellings et al., 2018; Hoyle et al., 2024; Hoyle et al., 2023).

Strategic narratives can be categorized into three types: identity, issue, and system narratives (Miskimmon et al., 2017). Identity narratives aim to alter perceptions and promote a specific self-image. For example, NATO's identity narrative is rooted in the North Atlantic Treaty of 1949, portraying NATO as a strong shield of democracy. Issue narratives, on the other hand, seek to influence specific policy decisions by shaping the entire discursive environment. NATO's commitment to conflict-related sexual- and gender-based violence (CRSGBV) is cited as an example of an issue narrative, promoting awareness, and presenting NATO as a champion of the Women, Peace, and Security (WPS) agenda (Wright, Rosamond, 2021). System narratives focus on portraying how the international system functions, and from a NATO perspective, this could mean emphasizing the alliance's commitment to the rule-based world order.

Most sources emphasize the importance of strategic narratives, with various NATO doctrines providing guidance on how NATO should employ and modify its strategic narrative. The strategic narrative is designated as the principal context for all planning and should remain unaltered for specific audiences (AJP-10, 2023). According to the Allied Joint Doctrine, strategic narratives for certain operations should be developed by NATO Headquarters in collaboration with joint force commanders (AJP-01 2022). All NATO operations, whether military or non-military, must be compatible with the strategic narrative, while the supporting information operations are tailored for specific audiences (AJP-10, 2023).

Another level mentioned by StratCom is micro-narratives, which, unlike institutional and strategic narratives focused on supporting long-term goals, support mid- or short-term tactical objectives and activities (AJP-01 2022). Micro-narratives are considered versatile and dynamic, crafted to suit diverse audiences and various situations (AJP-10 2023). NATO StratCom emphasizes the importance of coherence between micro-narratives and broader institutional and strategic narratives. Constructing micro-narratives at the relevant level, seeking approval from Joint Force Command Commander or Joint Task Force Commander with the backing of J-10 StratCom, is recommended (AJP-10 2023). Micro-narratives can be used locally at a tactical level and to counter opposition narratives. However, NATO's concepts regarding micro-narratives are less clear compared to the emphasis on strategic narratives, possibly due to considerations of operational secrecy when crafting tactical-level narratives.

The Allied Joint Doctrine specifies that institutional narratives are political, while strategic and micro-narratives can support military operations. The institutional narrative provides guidelines for all NATO operations, ensuring that all actions and sub-narratives align with it, thereby granting NATO legitimacy and credibility, allowing it to portray itself as a beacon of stability and security (AJP-01 2022).

4.3 Narrative-led Execution

After 2022, numerous NATO doctrines underscore the pivotal role of narratives in information warfare, particularly evident in the 2022 Allied Joint Doctrine (AJP-01 2022). Serving as a capstone document providing strategic guidance for all Allied joint operations, it caters to NATO commanders and their staff. Narratives are recognized as versatile tools applicable in every facet of NATO's public diplomacy, strategic communication, and information and psychological operations. The document highlights narratives as a battleground within the information instrument, emphasizing their importance by mentioning the word 'narrative' 83 times, surpassing mentions of 'terrorism' at 53 times.

Practical insights into crafting and mobilizing narratives are evident in NATO's counter-insurgency operation doctrine, AJP-3.27 (2023). To achieve narrative supremacy, planners should construct a concise, easily comprehensible, and adaptable multilevel narrative tested on selected populations. This narrative portrays the enemy negatively, garners support for the operation, and legitimizes governments on the ground. It must remain flexible in changing strategic and operational situations and be supported on the ground with tangible actions, including addressing local grievances to dismantle insurgent narratives. For example, according to NATO's Allied Joint Doctrine for Information Operations (2023), even engagements at the soldier level need to adhere to the Alliance's narratives. Soldiers and NATO civilians, regardless of rank, also need to be aware of the narratives employed and how their actions impact them (AJP-10.1. 2023). Interestingly, the 2023 Allied Joint Doctrines for Strategic Communications and Information Operations provide practical tools, such as how to build effective narratives and analyse target audiences.

Narratives become intricately linked with NATO's operational objectives and planning, leading to the concept of narrative-led execution. Defined by NATO StratCom, this concept sees the narrative serving as an overarching expression of the whole-of-Alliance strategy, influencing audiences and providing context to the campaign, operation, or situation (AJP-10 2023). Narrative-led execution ensures consistent alignment of actions with words to minimize vulnerabilities adversaries could exploit (AJP-10.1. 2023). It unifies strategic intent across the Alliance on all operational levels, enabling decentralized execution to converge multiple effects on targeted audiences. The 2022 NATO Allied Joint Doctrine emphasizes a "behaviour-centric approach," acknowledging the pivotal role of people's attitudes and behaviours in achieving the end state. Narrative-led execution focuses beyond the 'enemy or adversary' to a broader audience segmented into three categories: public, stakeholder, and actor (AJP-01 2022). Commanders at every level are expected to be aware of institutional and strategic narratives, adjusting their plans accordingly to align with them.

5. Discussion

Naval British officer Steve Tatham suggested in 2008 (Tatham, 9) that "Narratives are the foundation of all strategy. They are the organizing framework for policy and the definitive reference for how events are to be argued and described." The discussion on narratives has not emerged from a vacuum, as empirical analysis has already illustrated, showing a gradual expansion in NATO thinking related to the role of narratives. The conflicts related to the War on Terror since the 9/11 terrorist attacks in the United States have had particular importance. Especially, the conflict in Afghanistan was a conflict about narratives and the legitimacy of particular actors taking part in the conflict.

Oleg Svet (2010, 2) argued in his campaign assessment of the US-led coalition's psychological and information operations that the aspect of narrative was among the themes that experienced failures. Claims of strategic coherence and a lack of resonance in messaging targeted to the Afghan population highlight shortcomings in how narratives were created and reflected in the coalition's activities. Similarly, Emile Simpson (2012, 192-197) developed the idea further and emphasized the need to accept and understand the role of emotions in war, as well as the moral factors associated with emotions. At the core of such thinking was the need to have the legitimacy to wage war, to act in a potentially foreign country, and create a context-bound strategy that could win the support of the population, thus linking the aims and means of war to emotional factors.

NATO papers illustrate an organization that has tried to learn from such experiences and pay more attention not only to having a legitimate role in the conflict but also to conveying a message that reflects and supports that legitimacy. This thinking takes place while the organization acknowledges the role of the information environment, a rather abstract context in which actors, processes, and messages are dynamic.

6. Conclusion

In this article, we have explored how NATO perceives narratives. Our research question aimed to uncover the role of narratives in NATO doctrine and understand how NATO's narrative thinking has evolved over time. Based on the analysis of empirical sources, we have observed a growing significance placed on narratives by NATO. Narratives not only allow us to tell stories but also influence audiences and serve as vessels for political ideology, shaping personal and cultural identities.

NATO's narrative concept has undergone a transformation, progressing from a mere description of activities to a defining strategy where all actions must align with the Alliance's institutional and strategic narratives. In achieving cohesion across all levels, the narrative takes precedence, potentially even surpassing tactical realities. From the top-down, NATO's narrative is constructed, and adherence to this narrative is expected from the Joint Force Command down to the individuals serving in NATO's missions.

A consistent narrative strategy enables NATO to craft a robust public image and establish legitimacy. This legitimacy is considered a crucial factor in the contemporary landscape of cognitive and information warfare, where it may provide an advantage against adversaries whose primary weapon is disinformation. In this case, both legitimacy and storytelling also aim to portray NATO as stronger, more capable, and more united. This, in turn, can create deterrence in the face of a threat. The growing importance of NATO's Strategic Communications underscores the significance of narrative in this context.

In an ever more clustered and challenging information environment with hostile actors trying to sway public opinion, NATO recognizes the imperative to garner public approval. NATO relies on narrative as a valuable asset and as a shield against hostile information and cognitive warfare aimed at disrupting the Alliance's unity. Overall, NATO has adopted a history-bound and value-bound approach to create and sustain its narrative. By placing its values, rooted in the North Atlantic Treaty of 1949, at the forefront of its activities, it can be anticipated that the role of narratives and values will continue to expand in future international conflicts.

References

Primary Sources

Joint Chiefs of Staff. Joint Publication 3-13.2. Military Information Support Operations. Available at: https://www.esd.whs.mil/Portals/54/Documents/FOID/Reading%20Room/Joint_Staff/Military_Information_Support_Operations.pdf (21.1.2024)

NATO ACO/ACT (2020) Public Affairs Handbook.

NATO (2022) AJP-01 The Allied Joint Doctrine (Edition F Version 1).

NATO (2009) AJP-3.10 Allied Joint Doctrine for Information Operations.

NATO (2007) AJP-3.10.1(A) Allied Joint Doctrine for Psychological Operations.

NATO (2015) AJP-3.10.1 Allied Joint Doctrine for Psychological Operations.

NATO (2023) AJP-3.27 Allied Joint Doctrine for Counter-Insurgency Edition A, Version 2.

NATO (2011) AJP-3.4.4 Allied Joint Doctrine for Counter-insurgency.

NATO (2023) AJP-10 Allied Joint Doctrine for Strategic Communications.

NATO (2023) AJP-10.1 Allied Joint Doctrine for Information Operations.

NATO (2017) Brand Guide.

NATO (2008) Bucharest Summit Declaration. Available at: https://www.nato.int/cps/en/natohq/official_texts_8443.htm (19.1.2024)

NATO (2021) Brussels Summit Communiqué. Available at: https://www.nato.int/cps/en/natohq/official_texts_156624.htm (2.3.2024)

NATO (2023) Cognitive Warfare: Strengthening and Defending the Mind Available at: https://www.act.nato.int/article/cognitive-warfare-strengthening-and-defending-the-mind/ (2.3.2024)

NATO (2018) Framework for Future Alliance Operations (FFAO).

NATO (2024) Happening in 2024: Advancements in Cognitive Warfare, Multi-Domain Operations, Future Operating Environments, Sweden's Accession to NATO. Available at: https://www.act.nato.int/article/happening-in-2024-cognitive-warfare-mdo-future-operating-environments-sweden/ (25.1.2024).

NATO (2003) Military Policy on Psychological Operations.

NATO (2011) Military Public Affairs Policy.

NATO (1949) North Atlantic Treaty.

NATO (2009) Strategic Communications Policy.

NATO (2009) Strasbourg / Kehl Summit Declaration. Available at: https://www.nato.int/cps/en/natohq/news_52837.htm (19.1.2024)

NATOTerm, the official NATO Terminology Database. Accessed 20.1.2024: https://nso.nato.int/natoterm

NATO (2016) Warsaw Communiqué. Available at: https://www.nato.int/cps/en/natohq/official_texts_133169.htm. (2.3.2024)

Literature

Allenby, B. R. (2017) 'The Age of Weaponized Narrative or, Where Have You Gone, Walter Cronkite?' Issues in Science and Technology, 33(4), pp. 65–70. Available at: http://www.jstor.org/stable/44577336.

Bernal, A., Carter, C., Singh, I., Cao, K., & Madreperla, O. (2020). Cognitive warfare: An attack on truth and thought. NATO and Johns Hopkins University: Baltimore MD, USA.

Claverie, B., & du Cluzel, F. (2022). The Cognitive Warfare Concept. Innovation Hub Sponsored by NATO Allied Command Transformation, 2022-02.

Collins, S. (2002) 'NATO and Strategic PSYOPS: Policy Pariah or Growth Industry?' Journal of Information Warfare, 1(3), pp. 72–78. Available at: https://www.jstor.org/stable/26504105.

Du Cluzel, F. (2020) Cognitive Warfare. NATO Innovation Hub.

Gerasimov, V. (2013) "Ценность науки в предвидении - Новые вызовы требуют переосмыслить формы и способы ведения боевых действий" Военно-промышленный курьер, 8:476, 1–2

Gerasimov, V. (2016) "Организация обороны Российской Федерации вусловиях применения противником «традиционных» и «гибридных» методов ведения войны" Вестник Академии военных наук, 2:55, 19–23

Giles, K. (2016) Handbook of Russian Information Warfare. NATO Defense College.

Hoyle, A., Wagnsson, C., Powell, T. E., van den Berg, H., & Doosje, B. (2024) 'Life through grey-tinted glasses: how do audiences in Latvia psychologically respond to Sputnik Latvia's destruction narratives of a failed Latvia?', Post-Soviet Affairs, 40(1), pp. 1-18. DOI: 10.1080/1060586X.2023.2275507.

Hoyle, A., Wagnsson, C., van den Berg, H., Doosje, B., & Kitzen, M. (2023) 'Cognitive and emotional responses to Russian state-sponsored media narratives in international audiences', Journal of Media Psychology: Theories, Methods, and Applications, 35(6), pp. 362–374. DOI: 10.1027/1864-1105/a000371.

Jowett, G. S., & O'Donnell, V. (2012) Propaganda & persuasion (5th ed.). SAGE.

Krieg, A. (2023) Subversion: The strategic weaponization of narratives. Washington, DC: Georgetown University Press.

Kvernbekk, T., & Bøe-Hansen, O. (2017) 'How to Win Wars: The Role of the War Narrative', in Olmos, P. (ed.) Narration as Argument. Argumentation Library, vol 31. Springer, Cham. DOI: 10.1007/978-3-319-56883-6_12.

Laity, M. (2015) 'NATO and the Power of Narrative', BEYOND PROPAGANDA | SEPTEMBER 2015 Information at War: From China's Three Warfares to NATO's Narratives.

Lieffers, E. (2014) '"We answered the call": Strategic Narrative in NATO's Public Diplomacy for Operation Unified Protector'. Carleton University, Ottawa, Ontario.

Maan, A. K. (2018) Narrative warfare. Narrative Strategies Ink.

Miskimmon, A., O'Loughlin, B., & Roselle, L. (Eds.). (2017) Forging the World: Strategic Narratives and International Relations. University of Michigan Press. DOI: 10.3998/mpub.6504652.

Miskimmon, A., O'Loughlin, B., & Roselle, L. (2013) Strategic Narratives: Communication Power and the New World Order (1st ed.). Routledge. DOI: 10.4324/9781315871264.

Munoz, A. (2012) U.S. Military Information Operations in Afghanistan: Effectiveness of Psychological Operations 2001-2010. RAND Corporation.

Munslow, A. (2007) Narrative and history. Palgrave Macmillan.

Simpson, E. (2012) War From the Ground Up. Twenty-first Century Combat as Politics. London: Hurst & Company.

Svet, O. (2010, September 12) 'Fighting for a Narrative. A Campaign Assessment of the US-led Coalition's Psychological and Information Operations in Afghanistan', Small Wars Journal. Available at: https://smallwarsjournal.com/blog/journal/docs-temp/537-svet.pdf.

Tatham, S. (2008) Strategic Communication: A Primer. Advanced Research and Assessment Group, Special Series 08/28. Defence Academy of the United Kingdom. Available at: https://www.files.ethz.ch/isn/94411/2008_Dec.pdf.

Wellings, B., S., Kelly, S., Wilson, B., Burton, J., & Holland, M. (2018) 'Narrative Alignment and Misalignment: NATO as a Global Actor as Seen from Australia and New Zealand', Asian Security, 14(1), pp. 24-37. DOI: 10.1080/14799855.2017.1361731.

Analysing Multidimensional Strategies for Cyber Threat Detection in Security Monitoring

Palvi Shelke[1] and Timo Hamalainen[2]
Faculty of Information Technology, University of Jyvaskyla, Finland

vidya.palvi0211@gmail.com
timo.t.hamalainen@jyu.fi

Abstract: The escalating risk of cyber threats requires continuous advances in security monitoring techniques. This survey paper provides a comprehensive overview of recent research into novel methods for cyber threat detection, encompassing diverse approaches such as machine learning, artificial intelligence, behavioral analysis and anomaly detection. Machine learning plays a central role in cyber threat detection, highlighting the effectiveness of deep neural networks in identifying evolving threats. Their adaptability to changing attack patterns is emphasized, underlining their importance for real-time security monitoring. In parallel, ensemble learning is explored, combining multiple models to improve overall detection accuracy and create a robust defense against a spectrum of cyber threats. The literature reviewed highlights the importance of behavioral analysis, with a novel approach that integrates user behaviour profiling with anomaly detection. This has proven effective in identifying suspicious activity within a network, particularly insider threats and stealthy attacks. Another behavioral framework using User and Entity Behavior Analytics (UEBA) is presented for enhanced anomaly detection, highlighting the importance of context-aware monitoring in improving threat detection accuracy. Collaborative defense mechanisms emerge as a major focus of the research papers reviewed, exploring the potential of sharing threat information between organisations to enhance collective security monitoring. Their findings underscore the importance of a collaborative approach to staying ahead of rapidly evolving cyber threats. Some types of cyber-attacks are also analysed in the context of a security operations centre (SOC) monitoring environment using a security information and event management (SIEM) tool - Splunk. In conclusion, this survey paper synthesizes recent advances in cyber threat detection methods in security monitoring that integrate machine learning, behavioral analysis, and collaborative defense strategies. As cyber threats continue to evolve, these novel methods provide valuable insights for researchers, practitioners, and organisations seeking to strengthen their cybersecurity defenses. This concise overview emphasises the multi-dimensional approach required to secure digital ecosystems, providing a concise yet comprehensive guide to modern cyber threat detection strategies.

Keyword(s): SIEM and Splunk Monitoring, Security Monitoring, Machine Learning, Behavioral Analysis, Anomaly Detection, Threat Intelligence

1. Introduction:

In the ever-evolving landscape of digital technology, the escalating risk of cyber threats poses a formidable challenge to the security and integrity of information systems. Protecting digital assets in this dynamic environment requires constant innovation in security monitoring techniques. This survey paper serves as a comprehensive guide to recent research efforts dedicated to advancing cyber threat detection methodologies.

Exploring a wide range of approaches, from machine learning and artificial intelligence to behavioral analysis and anomaly detection, this survey consolidates key findings from studies at the forefront of security monitoring. The role of machine learning is highlighted, emphasising the adaptability of deep neural networks in real-time security monitoring. At the same time, the paper explores ensemble learning techniques, advocating the integration of multiple models to improve overall detection accuracy and strengthen defenses against a wide range of cyber threats.

Behavioral analysis emerges as a focal point, with novel approaches combining user behaviour profiling and anomaly detection. This is proving to be a key method for identifying suspicious activity within networks, particularly in the case of insider threats and stealthy attacks. The importance of context-aware monitoring is highlighted, refining the accuracy of threat detection through a behavioural framework that leverages User and Entity Behavior Analytics (UEBA).

Collaborative defense mechanisms such as threat intelligence sharing between organisations are also explored, emphasising the importance of a community-driven approach to proactively countering rapidly evolving cyber threats.

In conclusion, this survey paper synthesizes recent advances in cyber threat detection methods in security monitoring, including machine learning, behavioral analysis, and collaborative defense strategies. As organisations and practitioners seek to strengthen their cybersecurity defenses, these innovative methods offer valuable insights into the multidimensional approach required to secure digital ecosystems. This introduction provides the framework for a detailed exploration of contemporary cyber threat detection strategies.

2. Background and Literature Review

The primary objective of the Security Operations Centre (SOC) is to safeguard the organization against cyber breaches and attacks while ensuring the protection of valuable assets like data, applications, and infrastructure. Operating around the clock (Palo Alto Networks, 2020), the SOC aims to maintain the organization's normal operations. As defined by the SANS Institute (2018), the SOC represents a harmonious integration of individuals, processes, and technology, all dedicated to preserving the integrity of an organization's information systems. This involves proactive measures such as system setup and configuration, continuous monitoring for anomalies, early identification of unintended actions or unfavourable conditions, and timely mitigation of any undesirable effects.

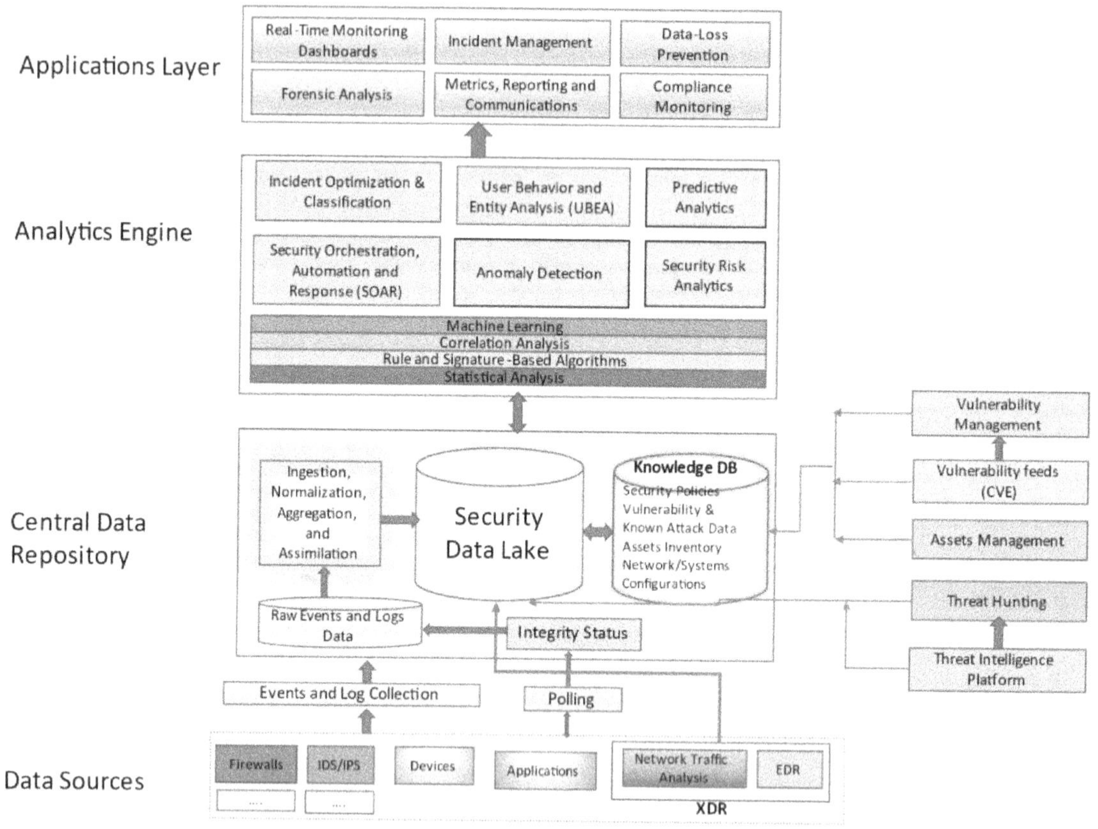

Figure 1: Security Architecture for the SOC (Mohammad A. Islam, 2023)

The Security Operations Centre (SOC) technology stack relies on the analytics engine as its core component for detecting, responding to, and recovering from cyber events and intrusions. This engine is based on machine learning, correlation analysis, rule-based algorithms and statistical analysis. It facilitates correlation analysis across the enterprise to detect intrusions or malicious activity. Anomaly detection, a machine learning algorithm within the analytics engine, identifies anomalous patterns in network traffic or user behaviour, using historical data to detect unknown threats and minimise false positives. In addition, user behaviour and entity analysis tools use advanced analytics and machine learning algorithms to detect anomalous user behaviour and potential insider threats. SOAR (Security Orchestration, Automation, and Response) automates incident response processes, including incident triage and response, threat hunting, and vulnerability scanning, streamlining workflows and eliminating false positives. In addition, predictive analytics, another machine learning model, can be trained to predict the likelihood of a security incident based on historical data (Mohammad A. Islam, 2023).

Alison Smith-Renner et al. (2019) provide an overview of anomaly detection using DAART (Detection of Anomalous Activity in Real Time) systems. Data enters the system from various sensor feeds and sensor features are extracted. These features feed the multimodal anomaly detection component along with user-defined ranges. A normalcy model is trained to represent normal behaviour against which new, potentially anomalous, behaviour is compared. Identified anomalies are presented to the user by the active learning threat classification component, which assists the user in validating or rejecting anomalous alerts as threats, as well as specifying the threat class.

Md Faisal Ahmed et al (2023) explored the strategies, processes and mechanisms required to achieve cyber resilience in the face of emerging security risks in today's complex digital landscape. Within the domain of cyber resilience, they introduced an innovative conceptual cyber resilience model that encompasses both information security and cybersecurity considerations. The future scope of this research has been proposed to be extended to the areas of personal, network and organisational cyber security management. The foundational conceptual model of cyber resilience is of paramount importance, as it serves as a conduit for incorporating knowledge and subsequently improving the efficiency and effectiveness of cyber security and cyber defense processes. The aim is to reduce the prevalence of 'unknown unknowns' and gradually transform them into 'known unknowns' and 'known knowns'.

Junhong Kim et al. (2019) studied insider threats and applied anomaly detection algorithms and their combinations to detect malicious activities. They constructed three structured datasets to train the anomaly detection algorithms. Given the different nature of the three datasets - comprising a user's daily activity, an email's topic distribution and a user's weekly email communication - individual anomaly detection models are trained independently for each dataset. Effectively integrating the diverse results from these different anomaly detection models could potentially improve overall insider threat detection performance. Second, they built the insider threat detection model based on a specific unit of time, such as a day. In other words, this approach can detect malicious behaviour based on the batch process, but not in real time. Therefore, there may be value in developing a sequential insider threat detection model that can handle real-time streaming data. In addition, while the presented model relied solely on data-driven approaches, integrating domain expert expertise with a purely data-driven machine learning model has the potential to improve insider threat detection performance in the security domain.

Rasheed Yousef and Mahmoud Jazzar (2021) presented a real-time experiment to measure the effectiveness of user and entity behavior analytics for insider threat prevention, illustrating the impact of UEBA on false positives. The experiment demonstrated the effectiveness of UEBA in detecting insider threats and reducing false positives. However, the use of metadata, cloud and user privacy are still issues to be considered in future deployments.

Thomas D. Wagner et al. (2018) analysed 30 threat sharing platforms with respect to anonymity. Their work focused on implementing and evaluating the anonymity prototype as a proof of concept for automating the processes involved in real time. The study included the collection of Indicator of Compromise (IOC) activity data, advanced persistent threat (APT) analysis, and the development of a threat intelligence platform (TIP).

Yonghe Guo et al. (2015) mention cybersecurity as a challenging issue in smart grid implementation. They discuss the model of Distributed Denial of Service (DDoS) attack in Advanced Metering Infrastructure (AMI) system. In their study, they analysed the difference between the DDoS attack in AMI system and the Internet version. The future scope insists on focusing on developing effective defense approaches against DDoS attack in AMI system. The intrusion detection system has shown its potential in defending against various cyber-threats, but still needs to be improved to handle more advanced attacks.

3. Current and Evolving Challenges of SIEM and SOC:

The current and evolving challenges have been summarised based on literature reviews and published reports from several reputable security technology vendors, including Splunk, Microfocus, IBM, Veracode, Trend Micro, Rapid7, Exabeam, LogRhythm, CrowdStrike, Trellix, etc. SOC tools have been described as primarily defensive in nature, passively monitoring and reacting (InfosecMatter, 2020). Challenges such as manual investigation, alert prioritisation and the use of threshold-based correlation rules persist in many organisations (Kaliyaperumal, 2021).

Ongoing challenges in Security Operations Centres have been identified in four main areas: people (lack of skilled individuals, monotonous tasks, collaboration skills, integration of domain knowledge), processes (lack of standard procedures, adaptation of generic IT processes to the SOC), technologies (increased complexity, variety of tools, visualisation capabilities, insufficient level of automation), and governance and compliance (effective measurement of SOC performance, lack of best practices and standards, privacy regulations) (Microfocus, n.d.; Vielberth et al., 2020). While organisations lacked skilled individuals, determined and highly skilled attackers were able to use the latest tools and technologies, including artificial intelligence and machine learning, to launch sophisticated attacks against organisations (Microfocus, n.d.). Even Tier 3 or Tier 4 SOC analysts found it difficult to investigate incidents when sophisticated attackers had removed their digital footprint (IIoT World, 2022).

Enormous amounts of data from network traffic and logs from devices, applications and networks need to be processed by the security operations centre. Parsing and ingesting data into the data lake and then identifying malicious activity in real time was identified as a challenge. Alert fatigue could result from numerous anomaly alerts without context or intelligence. A machine learning-based tool corroborates and correlates with contextual data across the enterprise, minimising false positives and generating a prioritised list of alerts and incidents. Zero-day attack vectors can be challenging due to lack of threat intelligence and undiscovered vulnerabilities. Behavioral analytics embedded in machine learning can detect unusual behaviour and unknown attacks (Microfocus, n.d.).

In some organisations, the CISO/CIO has chosen a best-of-breed set of security tools and software from multiple vendors. The use of too many security tools from multiple vendors without a unified framework, integration architecture, and sometimes disconnected work in silos could lead to duplicate, overlapping and conflicting alerts and recommendations (Microfocus, n.d.).

Many organisations lacked a complete inventory of their digital infrastructure, with different teams managing different components. Sometimes full configuration details, firewall rules and network diagrams were not available to the SOC. Naming conventions for infrastructure components may not be standardised across many organisations (InfosecMatter, 2020).

Some organisations may not subscribe to a threat intelligence platform and lack indicators of compromise (IOC) data. IOC data is essential to defend against advanced persistent threats (APTs) and determined malicious actors (InfosecMatter, 2020).

4. Security Attacks and Splunk Monitoring:

Live threat identification for cloud-based systems is performed using Splunk (Ananthapadmanabhan, 2022). Identification of cyber-attacks in the cloud involves the application of threat modelling and threat intelligence. Detection of malicious DNS behaviour, including spam, phishing, malware and botnet activity, is performed using the Splunk machine learning toolkit (Cersosimo, 2022). Cyber-attacks and suspicious user activity are identified using Splunk Enterprise 6.4.2 (Zhao, 2022). Network anomalies are detected in the Security Operation Centre (SOC) through a proactive threat hunting model and digital footprint analysis using Splunk (Prakash, 2022). Cyber-attacks on cyber-physical systems (CPS) will be detected using Splunk Enterprise Security software (Saraf, 2020), and predictive analysis of CPS cyber-attacks will be performed using Splunk (Saraf, 2022). Securing a contactless tachometer-based brushless DC motor involves a combination of lightweight cryptographic algorithms and Splunk (Saraf, 2021).

Monitoring for different types of cyber-attacks, including zero-day, eavesdropping, DDoS and brute force attacks, in Splunk involves configuring the platform to collect and analyse relevant log data (Saraf, 2023). Here is how to set up monitoring for each of these attack types in Splunk:

4.1 Zero-Day Attack Monitoring:

Steps:

- Behavioral Analytics: Use Splunk's Machine Learning Toolkit (MLTK) to build models that identify anomalous behaviour that could indicate a zero-day attack. Train the models on historical data to establish a baseline of normal activity.
- Threat Intelligence Integration: Integrate threat intelligence feeds into Splunk to stay on top of new vulnerabilities and threats. This can include indicators of compromise (IOCs) associated with zero-day attacks.
- Correlation searches: Implement correlation searches in Splunk to connect seemingly unrelated events that may indicate a zero-day attack. Correlation can help identify patterns that traditional signature-based detection may miss.
- Real-time alerting: Configure real-time alerts to notify security teams when suspicious activity or patterns indicative of a zero-day attack are detected.

- Threat hunting queries: Engage in threat hunting by creating specific queries and searches to proactively look for signs of zero-day attacks in Splunk.

4.2 Monitor for Eavesdropping Attacks:

Steps:

- Network traffic analysis: Monitor network traffic logs in Splunk to detect unusual patterns or unauthorised access that could indicate an eavesdropping attack.
- Encryption monitoring: Track the effectiveness of encryption protocols with Splunk. Ensure that communication channels are adequately encrypted to protect against eavesdropping.
- Alerts for unusual activity: Configure alerts in Splunk to notify administrators of any suspicious or unauthorised access to sensitive communication channels.

4.3 Monitoring DDoS Attacks:

Steps:

- Traffic Analysis: Analyse network traffic logs in Splunk to identify sudden spikes in traffic that could indicate a DDoS attack.
- Threshold Based Alerts: Configure alerts based on predefined network traffic thresholds. Any abnormal increase in traffic can trigger alerts.
- Anomaly detection: Leverage Splunk's machine learning capabilities to detect anomalies in traffic patterns that may indicate a DDoS attack.

4.4 Monitor for Brute Force Attacks:

Steps:

- Monitor login activity: Monitor authentication and login activity logs in Splunk to detect multiple failed login attempts that may indicate a brute force attack.
- Threshold Based Alerts: Set up alerts based on thresholds for failed login attempts. Unusual patterns or high numbers of failed attempts can trigger alerts.
- User behavior analytics: Implement user behavior analytics in Splunk to detect anomalous login patterns or suspicious user activity associated with brute force attacks.
- IP reputation analytics: Integrate threat intelligence feeds to assess the reputation of IP addresses attempting to log in. Identify and block IP addresses associated with malicious activity.

By implementing these monitoring strategies, organisations can improve their ability to detect and respond to different cyber threats and tailor their approach to the specific characteristics of each type of attack. Regularly review and update monitoring configurations to adapt to the evolving threat landscape.

5. Research Methodology and Implementation Guidelines:

The following is an in-depth analysis of the implementation of the SIEM solution, focusing on Splunk and its integral role in Security Operations Centre (SOC) monitoring:

1. The skills and training of SOC analysts play a critical role in influencing the effectiveness of threat detection and response supported by security information and event management (SIEM) systems. How does the expertise of SOC analysts impact the effectiveness of SIEM tools in identifying and responding to potential cybersecurity threats?
2. In time-critical scenarios, the design of user interfaces and visualisations in SIEM tools becomes critical in facilitating optimal decision making by Security Operations Centre (SOC) analysts. How can the layout and presentation of information in SIEM tools be customised to improve the decision-making process for SOC analysts, especially when rapid response is essential?

5.1 The Impact of SOC Analyst Training on SIEM-based Threat Detection:

The impact of SOC analyst training on the effectiveness of SIEM-based threat detection is significant and multi-faceted. Well-trained SOC analysts play a critical role in maximising the benefits of SIEM systems. Here are some key aspects of this impact:

- Detection accuracy: Trained analysts are better able to understand the nuances of security events and alerts generated by SIEM. Their expertise enables them to distinguish between false positives and real threats, reducing the likelihood of missing critical security incidents.
- Incident response efficiency: Trained SOC analysts have the skills to interpret SIEM output quickly and accurately, enabling them to respond quickly to security incidents. Their skills ensure a more efficient incident response process, minimising the time between threat detection and mitigation.
- Optimised rule tuning: Skilled analysts can fine-tune SIEM rules and correlation logic based on their deep understanding of organisational nuances. This optimisation improves the SIEM system's ability to adapt to the organisation's specific threat landscape.
- Contextual analysis: Training enables analysts to add context to SIEM alerts by integrating knowledge of organisational workflows, systems and user behaviour. This contextual analysis enables more informed decision making and reduces the risk of misinterpreting the severity of alerts.
- Continuous improvement: Ongoing training ensures that SOC analysts stay abreast of evolving cyber threats, attack techniques, and updates to SIEM technologies. This continuous learning is critical to maintaining the relevance and effectiveness of SIEM-based threat detection strategies.

5.2 Designing SIEM User Interfaces for Optimal Decision-Making:

The design of user interfaces (UIs) in SIEM tools is critical to supporting optimal decision making by SOC analysts, especially under time-sensitive conditions. Here are UI design considerations:

- Intuitive visualisation: Create visualisations that are intuitive and easy to interpret. Graphs, charts, and dashboards should present complex information in a clear and understandable manner, allowing analysts to quickly grasp security status.
- Prioritisation and alert clustering: Design the UI to prioritise alerts based on severity and relevance. Clustering related alerts and providing a hierarchy of threats can help analysts focus on the most critical issues first, facilitating efficient decision-making in high-pressure situations.
- Interactive and responsive features: Incorporate interactive features that allow analysts to drill down into details, pivot between data views, and dynamically adjust parameters. Responsive interfaces enable rapid exploration of data, enhancing the analyst's ability to make timely decisions.
- Display contextual information: Provide contextual information alongside alerts, such as historical data, threat intelligence, and user behaviour patterns. This additional context helps analysts make more informed decisions by understanding the broader security landscape.
- Customise to analyst preferences: Allows the user interface to be customised to suit different analyst preferences. Features such as customisable dashboards and alert views allow analysts to tailor the interface to their specific needs, improving the overall user experience.
- Real-time monitoring and notification: Implement real-time monitoring capabilities with instant notification of critical events. A responsive user interface that provides real-time updates ensures that analysts are promptly informed of unfolding security incidents, enabling rapid decision-making.

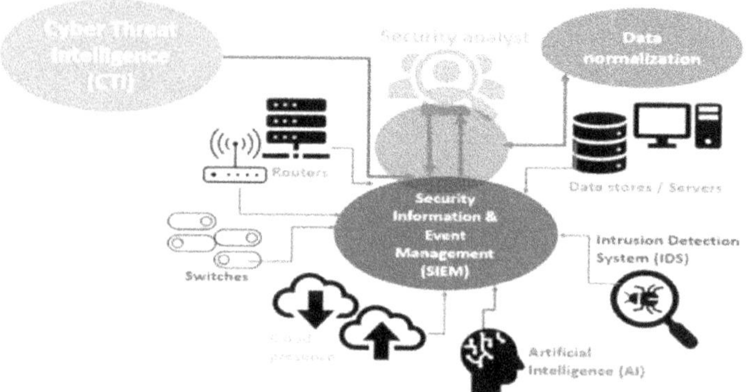

Figure 2: A high-level CompTIA suggested sample SIEM-SOC architecture.

CompTIA (n.d.) has delineated common responsibilities for the Security Operations Centre that include proactive monitoring, incident response and recovery, remediation, compliance monitoring, coordination and contextual understanding. Figure 2 illustrates the high-level overarching structure of a typical SOC (Mohammad A. Islam, 2023). By combining effective SOC analyst training with a well-designed SIEM user interface, organisations can optimise their ability to efficiently detect, respond to and mitigate cybersecurity threats, even in time-sensitive situations.

6. Conclusions and Future Research:

This research has delved into the critical area of cybersecurity, focusing specifically on the monitoring and detection of various cyber threats, including zero-day attacks, eavesdropping attacks, DDoS attacks and brute force attacks. Leveraging the capabilities of Splunk, a robust security information and event management (SIEM) platform, the research highlighted the importance of proactive monitoring and advanced analytics in protecting digital assets.

The study of zero-day attacks highlighted the importance of behavioral analytics, threat intelligence integration and real-time alerting to effectively detect and respond to emerging threats. Eavesdropping attacks were addressed by examining network traffic and the effectiveness of encryption to ensure secure communication channels.

DDoS monitoring involved analysing network traffic patterns, setting up threshold-based alerts and using machine learning to detect anomalies. Monitoring for brute force attacks emphasised user behaviour analysis, IP reputation analysis and real-time alerts based on login activity.

In short, the cybersecurity landscape is dynamic, and ongoing research is critical to staying ahead of sophisticated cyber threats. The future of the field lies in the continuous evolution of strategies, technologies, and collaborative efforts to ensure the resilience and security of digital ecosystems. We have therefore analysed multi-dimensional strategies for cyber threat detection in security monitoring.

Looking ahead to future developments, a key focus is on a more comprehensive understanding of user behaviour. This includes extending analytics to provide nuanced insights for accurate identification of anomalous behaviour and potential insider threats, which will contribute significantly to cybersecurity measures. In addition, it is imperative to adapt security measures to the scale and complexity of extended environments, particularly those rooted in cloud infrastructure. The challenges associated with monitoring in such environments require the development and implementation of security strategies specifically tailored to the unique characteristics of cloud-based systems. In response to emerging threats, there is a need for dedicated platforms that systematically collect, analyse and share information. These platforms aim to remain proactive against evolving vulnerabilities and associated attack methods, improving overall cybersecurity resilience in the face of dynamic challenges.

References:

Alison Smith-Renner, Rob Rua, Mike Colony, (2019) "Towards an Explainable Treat Detection Tool", In Joint Proceedings of ACM IUI 2019 Workshops. ACM, Los Angeles, USA, 20 March 2019

Ananthapadmanabhan A., and Krishnashree Achuthan (2022) "Threat Modelling and Threat Intelligence System for Cloud using Splunk", In 2022 10th International Symposium on Digital Forensics and Security (ISDFS), pp. 1-6. IEEE

Cobb, M. (n.d.), (2023) "SIEM vs. SOAR vs. XDR: Evaluate the differences", TechTarget, Retrieved February 4, 2023, from https://www.techtarget.com/searchsecurity/tip/SIEM-vs-SOAR-vs-XDR-Evaluatethe-differences

Cersosimo, Michelle, and Adrian Lara (2022) "Detecting Malicious Domains using the Splunk Machine Learning Toolkit", In NOMS 2022-2022 IEEE/IFIP Network Operations and Management Symposium, pp. 1-6. IEEE

Crowley, C. and Pescatore, J. (2018) "The definition of SOC-cess? SANS 2018 Security Operations Center Survey", SANS Institute Reading Room, SANS Institute. Retrieved January 28, 2023, from https://assets.extrahop.com/whitepapers/Survey_SOC-2018_ExtraHop.pdf

Exabeam documentation "The SOC, SIEM and other essential SOC tools", Retrieved January 28, 2023, from https://www.exabeam.com/explainers/siem/the-soc-secops-and-siem/

Gustavo González-Granadillo, Susana González-Zarzosa, Rodrigo Diaz (2021) "Security Information and Event Management (SIEM): Analysis, Trends, and Usage in Critical Infrastructures", Sensors 2021, 21, 4759, https://doi.org/10.3390/s21144759

InfosecMatter (2020, 20 September) "Security Operations Centre: Challenges for SOC teams" Retrieved 3 February 2023, from https://www.infosecmatter.com/security-operations-center-challenges-ofsoc-teams/

IIoT World (2022, 28 January) "What is a SOC? Top security operations centre challenges" Retrieved 12 February 2023, from https://www.iiot-world.com/ics-security/cybersecurity/top-challengessoc-are-facing/

Kaliyaperumal, L.N. (2021, 21 October) "The evolution of security operations and strategies for building an effective SOC". ISACA Journal, 5. Retrieved 3 February 2023, from https://www.isaca.org/resources/isaca-journal/issues/2021/volume-5/the-evolution-of-securityoperations-and-strategies-for-building-an-effective-soc

Kundankumar Rameshwar Saraf, P. Malathi (2023) "Splunk-Based Threat Intelligence of Cyber-Physical System: A Case Study with Smart Healthcare", International Journal of Intelligent Systems and Applications in Engineering, IJISAE, 2023, 11(2), 537–549

Kim J, Park M, Kim H, Cho S, Kang P, (2019) "Insider Threat Detection Based on User Behavior Modeling and Anomaly Detection Algorithms", Applied Sciences, 2019; 9(19):4018, https://doi.org/10.3390/app9194018

Md Faisal Ahmed et al (2023) "Advancing Cyber Resilience: Bridging the Divide Between Cyber Security and Cyber Defense", International Journal for Multidisciplinary Research (IJFMR), Volume 5, Issue 6, November-December 2023

Mohammad Anwarul Islam (2023) "Application of artificial intelligence and machine learning in security operations center", Research paper from https://comp.mga.edu/static/media/doctoralpapers/2023_Islam_0516152253.pdf

Microfocus (n.d.) (2023) "What is a Security Operations Center (SOC)?" Retrieved February 3, 2023, from https://www.microfocus.com/en-us/what-is/security-operations-center

Prakash, G., M. Ganeshan, A. Shenbagavalli, M. Satheesh Kumar, K. Srujan Raju, and K. Suthendran (2022) "A Proactive Threat Hunting Model to Detect Concealed Anomaly in the Network" In Smart Intelligent Computing and Applications, Volume 2, pp. 553-565. Springer, Singapore

Rasheed Yousef, Mahmoud Jazzar (2021) "Measuring the Effectiveness of User and Entity Behavior Analytics for the Prevention of Insider Threats", Journal of Xi'an University of Architecture & Technology, Volume XIII, Issue 10, 2021

Saraf, K.R. and Malathi, P. (2020) "Cyber Physical System Security by Splunk" i-Manager's Journal on Communication Engineering and Systems, 9(2), p.41

Saraf Kundan Kumar Rameshwar, and P. Malathi. (2022) "Intelligent Learning Analytics in the Healthcare Sector Using Machine Learning and IoT", In Machine Learning, Deep Learning, Big Data, and Internet of Things for Healthcare, pp. 37-53. Chapman and Hall/CRC

Saraf Kundan Kumar Rameshwar, P. Malathi, and Kailash Shaw (2021) "Security Enhancement of Contactless Tachometer-Based Cyber-Physical System", In Machine Learning Approaches for Urban Computing, pp. 165-187. Springer, Singapore

Splunk documentation "Securing Splunk Enterprise", version 9.0.2, (2022) available: https://docs.splunk.com/Documentation/Splunk/9.0.2/Security/ConfigureS2Sonnewcipher

Splunk documentation "Securing Splunk Enterprise", version 9.0.2, (2022) available: https://docs.splunk.com/Documentation/Splunk/9.0.2/Security/Updates

Thomas D. Wagner et al (2018) "Towards an Anonymity Supported Platform for Shared Cyber Threat Intelligence", Springer International Publishing AG, part of Springer Nature 2018, https://doi.org/10.1007/978-3-319-76687-4_12

Vielberth, M., Böhm, F., Fichtinger, I., & Pernul, G. (2020) "Security Operations Center: A systematic study and open challenges" IEEE Access, 8, 227756-227779

Yonghe Guo, Chee-Wooi Ten, Shiyan Hu, and Wayne W. Weaver (2015) "Modeling Distributed Denial of Service Attack in Advanced Metering Infrastructure", DOI: 10.1109/ISGT.2015.7131828

Zhao, Liguo, Derong Zhu, Wasswa Shafik, S. Mojtaba Matinkhah, Zubair Ahmad, Lule Sharif, and Alisa Craig (2022) "Artificial intelligence analysis in cyber domain: A review", International Journal of Distributed Sensor Networks 18, no. 4: 15501329221084882

Unmasking the Subconscious Fallacies Within Critical Infrastructure Protection

Marion Stephens
American Public University, Charles Town, WV, United States of America

marion.stephens@mycampus.apus.edu

Abstract: Cybersecurity, a vital challenge in today's ever-changing digital world, it has gained prominence with the global shift towards cyber-enabled critical infrastructures. Critical infrastructure protection efforts are fundamental for the continuation of essential services. Traditionally constituted as separate sectors, these infrastructures are increasingly interconnected, leading to potential domino effects during security breaches. For instance, failures within the power grid could have cascading effects on multiple sectors that depend on electricity for their operations, creating large-scale failures that affect functions on which society depends. The multidimensional nature of the infrastructures presents complex challenges for solutions, given their status as long-established legacy systems needing further development and enhancements to withstand the digital world. The lack of a concerted and focused infrastructure enhancement strategy has led to incremental approaches versus a comprehensive revamp to ensure a holistic cyber protection program. A lack of national focus has created inconsistencies that can lead to potentially catastrophic consequences. Understanding the decision-making processes within a complex environment is critical to the mission success. One significant risk is the cognitive roadblocks that have the potential to influence one's judgements as this often outweighs balanced decisions. This study aims to investigate the subconscious biases that arise from a perceived resolution of the problem which can lead to de-prioritization within the decision-making processes. The study employs a convergent parallel mixed methods design to collect and analyse the data. The study then will compare the results allowing for the exploration of various aspects of the research. This approach is aligned to provide a thorough understanding of the challenges associated with protecting the infrastructures and the underlying subconscious fallacies in the digital age, thereby devising effective mitigation strategies, and fostering a more sustainable and resilient critical infrastructure that is useful for a variety of stakeholders, including policymakers, infrastructure owners and operators, cybersecurity professionals, and researchers.

Keywords: Cybersecurity, Critical Infrastructure, Decision-Making, De-prioritization, Subconscious Bias, and Mitigation Strategies

1. Introduction

In the intricate web of modern society, there exist certain threads stronger and more vital than others. These threads are the underlying critical infrastructures that are universally recognized as systems or assets that are indispensable to the functioning of today's societies. However, the specifics of these infrastructures can vary based on each nation's unique needs and perceptions (De Felice et al, 2022). These requirements are governed by what each nation identifies as the fundamental pillars of its social functions. The designation of 'critical' for infrastructure is derived from its impact on the safety, health, and economic well-being of a nation (Mussington, 2021). The interconnected critical infrastructures form the backbone of a functioning society, providing essential services that society has become dependent upon. Given this dependency, it becomes evident that this emphasizes the importance of safeguarding the critical infrastructures. However, the condition of the critical infrastructure is deteriorating across the globe due to factors such as aging, environmental impacts, lack of adequate maintenance, budget constraints, limitations to legacy systems, and an inability to keep up with technological advancements (Zahidi, 2023). In addition to these ongoing challenges, the systems also face heightened risks from natural disasters to cyber-attacks. It is critical to ensure the nation's security and resilience against potential threats. In today's interconnected digital age, these critical infrastructures are not always isolated within national boundaries. They often have global implications. They are intertwined to such an extent that a threat to one can potentially trigger a domino effect of disruptions across multiple infrastructures (De Felice et al, 2022). Despite the variations in the definitions of critical infrastructures across different nations, there is a universal need to safeguard all critical infrastructures. Given the global interconnectedness, this is to prevent any debilitating impacts that could compromise not just a single nation's functioning, but potentially have far-reaching effects on a global scale. A single misguided decision could potentially trigger cascading failures, posing threats from national security to loss of life. The protection of critical infrastructures is thus not just a national concern, but a global one, emphasizing the shared responsibility of all nations in safeguarding the security and resilience of modern society's lifeline.

2. Methodology

This study employed a convergent parallel mixed methods design approach to allow simultaneous collection of qualitative and quantitative data to enhance the understanding of the research problem. The empirical data, constituting as the foundation of the study, was obtained through surveys, focus groups, and observation to generate a comprehensive dataset. The data analysis was conducted through rigorous methodologies such as meta-analysis for quantitative data and thematic analysis for qualitative data, supporting the validity and reliability of the results. Descriptive and inferential statistics were used to interpret the quantitative data, while themes and patterns were identified in the qualitative data. These results were then used to produce the mitigations within this study.

3. Challenges Protecting the Critical Infrastructures

Critical infrastructures are vital to a fully functioning society and economy. Protecting them requires a comprehensive understanding of potential threats, vulnerabilities, and impacts. As the world collaborates to protect the critical infrastructures, various reports have identified national emerging threats and high-risk factors. The Executive Opinion Survey (EOS) by the World Economic Forum (2023) surveyed 121 economies to identify the top emerging risks to critical infrastructures. The most significant potential impacts were identified as the energy supply crisis, cost-of-living crisis, rising inflation, food supply crisis, and cyberattacks (World Economic Forum 2023). However, some risks may not be immediately apparent. KPGM International (2023) adds additional insight into the risks of territorialism, digital transformation, and supply chain disruptions. Upon reflection of recent developments, it becomes evident that the spectrum of risks has broadened. For instance, the 2024 Global Risks Report highlighted the increasing concern over environmental risks due to the more recent extreme weather changes (World Economic Forum 2024). In today's digital world, the threat of cyberattacks is escalating. While certain attacks can be predicted and defended against, others, such as zero-day attacks, necessitate a comprehensive set of protective measures and a robust emergency plan to ensure resilience. The Homeland Threat Assessment by the United States Homeland Security (2024) predicts that both domestic and foreign adversaries will likely target critical infrastructures in the coming year. The resilience of these aging systems is a matter of concern, especially with the increasing focus on the critical infrastructures. A Gartner survey indicated a 38% increase in funds allocated for operational technology protection for critical infrastructures in 2022, with an expected annual increment of 5% (Moore 2021). However, even with this increased investment, the survey also predicted that by 2025, around 30% of critical infrastructures worldwide will have fallen victim to successful cyber breaches (Moore 2021). Analysis suggests that the existing strategies are inadequate to meet the requirements and overcome the challenges posed by the digital era. These figures consider over 14,000 infrastructure projects worldwide, costing more than $14.8 trillion USD (Global Data, 2023). Thus, adding budgetary constraints as another layer of risk. Moreover, Raina (2023) highlights the global shortage of skilled cyber professionals mixed with high rates of employee attrition as another threat to businesses which then adds another layer to the risks. It is estimated globally by 93% of cyber professionals and 86% of business leaders that a catastrophic cyberattack will occur within the next couple of years that will cause global geopolitical instability (Raina 2023). Given these threats, it becomes crucial for the decision-making process to have a comprehensive understanding of the issues at hand. This 360-degree view is essential for making better-informed decisions.

4. Decision Making

Effective decision-making plays a pivotal role in managing risks associated with cybersecurity, a field marked by its complexity and need for specialized knowledge. However, not all decision-makers possess cyber expertise, leading them to rely on simplified explanations or visible security indicators. These indicators are tangible, measurable aspects of a system's security that can be easily understood and monitored such as, the frequency of security patches applied or the status of networked devices. Yet, the simplicity of these metrics does not show the full complexity of the situation. These tendencies, as noted by Villadiego (2020), leads to a preference for more conspicuous solutions, which are typically influenced by the rapid pace of technological change, communication gaps, resource constraints, and the pressure for immediate results. Collectively, these factors shape the decision-making process in cybersecurity. To delve deeper into these factors, it is important to note that the constant evolution of cybersecurity—with new threats and solutions emerging regularly—poses significant challenges for decision-makers occupied with multiple responsibilities. Villadiego (2020) provides further insight into the challenges that decision-makers face due to their lack of cyber expertise by explaining how technical experts, with their deep understanding of the field, often face challenges in conveying complex cybersecurity issues in a manner that decision-makers, who may lack such specialized knowledge, can understand and act upon. This gap can lead to misinterpretations and potentially flawed decision-making. Moreover, implementing a comprehensive approach to cybersecurity can be resource intensive. Decision-makers are tasked with balancing cybersecurity needs with other organizational priorities, which may lead them to opt for less comprehensive, but also less resource-intensive solutions. These solutions often yield immediate, tangible results, making them appear "shiny" or noticeable. In contrast, a holistic approach to cybersecurity is a long-term investment that may not produce immediate visible results, as highlighted by Villadiego (2020).

5. The Subconscious Fallacies

Though it is important to note the reasoning behind every decision, the implementation of decisions is influenced by a myriad of factors, not all of which are easily discernible. To further analyse decision making one must address the psychological aspects of cognitive obstacles. According to cognitive theory, an individual's actions and decisions are influenced by their personality, environment, and thought processes (Erisen 2012). In essence, factors ranging from one's upbringing and accumulated experiences to their present circumstances influence their decision-making. Erisen (2012) further explains that these cognitive biases can lead to a form of heuristics, as shortcuts remain a consistent variable recurring within the decision-making process. This notion corroborates Freud's (1915) theory that human behaviour stems from the unconscious level within the mind. Even though some decisions appear to be well thought out this entails that there can be a biased judgment behind the decision, often unbeknownst to the decision-maker. Within the necessity of the decision processes exists a form of heuristics that often leads to a type of hyper fixation on achieving a goal, and rarely encompasses all potential outcomes causing de-prioritization (Gowda, 1999). In terms of critical infrastructures, this can lead to a subconscious bias that overemphasizes on physical security aspects. These biases can then potentially divert the decision-maker from making a logical choice considering all aspects of the problem. Utilizing cognitive theory allows for an analysis of each subject to understand the individual and the logic behind their decision-making process.

Personality significantly influences decision-making. While there are several frameworks to assess personalities one approach outlines that personality is comprised of six basic needs: certainty/comfort, variety, significance, connection, growth, and contribution (Ciccotti 2014). Certainty and comfort equate to security, variety is the necessary change needed so one does not become stagnate, significance is an actionable result the person requires, a connection is a sense of love, growth is a sense of maturing and expanding, and contribution is an effort that one is putting forth (Ciccotti 2014). These needs intertwine with personal biases and beliefs, which are ingrained as we grow and shape our reactions. Assumptions gathered during this process account for the normalcies within the era and environment. From the point humans are born, information is absorbed, establishing precedents for everything else in their life as biases develop and they independently condition to react in set patterns and mindsets. Schoen (2007) categorizes personality into five traits: neuroticism, extroversion, openness, conscientiousness, and agreeableness. As each person is individually different with a degree of like-mindedness then it is understood that this is true within the personality formed as each trait is varying by a spectrum where the individual would fall into a category. This spectrum within the big five personality traits then falls into the following: in neuroticism, which varies by controlling negative emotions, extraversion is a scale of socialness, openness varies by spontaneous pursuits, conscientiousness is self-disciplined, and agreeableness is trusting (Schoen 2007). Depending on which is the highest driving force of the personality would then depend on the categorization of the individual. This is where predictive behavioural analysis begins as it delves into the inner workings of the personality for then one can work to achieve a greater understanding of the reasoning within the decision formed (Erisen 2012). All decisions involve a choice. This is often based on Maslow's hierarchy of needs: physical needs, safety, love/belonging, self-esteem, and self-actualization (Davies 1963). On the basis of the basic human needs, one develops a type of necessity they want to achieve. By fulfilling these needs, consciously or subconsciously, individuals exert control over their feelings and actions, as explained by the Glasser Institute for Choice Theory (N.D.). In essence, humans exercise autonomy over their influences, making choices based on a complex interplay of personality traits, cognitive biases, and basic needs. Glasser Institute for Choice Theory (N.D.) explains that behaviour consists of feeling, acting, physiology, and thinking and by understanding the control within behaviours one can develop more of a rational mindset versus overreacting. Again, this falls in line with Mercer's (2005) theory that logical decisions are based on a form of emotion. This also gives the rationale that the individual can become empowered by realizing they do not have responsibility for other choices, just their own. However, whatever the choice Winter (2005) explains that the motive is based on one of three choices, achievement, affiliation, or power.

While the theories of Glasser, Mercer, and Winter provide valuable insights into individual behaviour and decision-making based on emotions, achievement, affiliation, or power. However, it is important to consider these concepts in a broader context. As Rathbun (2009) suggests, the principle of realism is more relevant when the shift focuses on the state and international levels of analysis that has a pessimistic overview that leads to the primary concern of survival within the state on the basis of lack of trust or a strategic trust with the international relations. This perspective then emphasizes the imperative demand needed for the critical infrastructures to maintain a higher standard of reliability and security. At this level, the decision-making process considers key factors to the interconnectedness of the infrastructures, shared information and resources, potential threats, and global operations. Emotions, such as fear, could prompt the decision-maker to bolster security measures within their process, while simultaneously managing budgetary needs. Concurrently, one should bear in mind that security, akin to a picture, possesses multiple dimensions. In today's ever-changing environment, the heightened threat of a cyber-attack deepens the need for additional, yet-to-be-conceived strategies for cyber protection. This underscores the idea that unseen threats are still very real and must be accounted for in our security planning.

Transitioning from the discussion of security threats and the need for innovative strategies, another perspective to explore is liberalism. This school of thought offers a more optimistic viewpoint, advocating for a higher degree of trust (Rathbun, 2009). To understand how this concept fits into the decision-making process of critical infrastructures, one can draw parallels with the three levels of analysis in political psychology - individual, state, and international (Jervis, 1976). As each level is subject to the principle of bias, which can influence the decision-making process, the resulting analysis could provide the means to integrate the economic and social considerations into the decision-making process. Building onto this, it is important to note that one's approach can be influenced by both realism and liberalism, depending on the situation. For example, a person who typically leans towards realism might choose to operate based on trust when interacting with someone they feel a strong connection to. Within the context of critical infrastructures, decisions hinge more on overarching personality traits, as these processes frequently prioritize objects. These objects, in turn, impact the individual and serve as a motivational determinant. Nevertheless, is it of importance to state that if the threat is not immediately visible or one does not understand the full spectrum of the threat then this can incur a subconscious bias that leads to a lack of prioritization within the decision-making process. In any decision-making process, leadership is often perceived as the driving force to the most logical decisions (McDermott 2004). Within rational theory, the foundations of any decision are fundamentally based on logic. However, it was Mercer (2005) who established the general concept detailing the generation of logical decisions, suggesting these decisions are formed on top of an emotional response even if at a subconscious level. This idea gains further traction as McDermott (2004) rationalizes that thoughts and beliefs add crucial layers to the decision-making process. This method would be inherent to the decisions based on supply, price, and distribution of which could expand to a final decision built on realism.

While decisions are often tethered to sturdy foundations within the realm of logic and time-honoured principles, the incorporation of the human condition undermines their position with underlying bias (Nielson and Minda 2019). These biases, a natural flaw that intensifies as individuals mature and learn from past experiences, can influence future actions and shape behavioural patterns. These patterns can be a stem from both external influences like digitization and personal experiences like perception (Acciarini et al, 2020). The complexity of decision-making processes relies on roles with both conscious and unconscious thought. Newell and Shanks (2014) explain that judgment for decisions comes from multiple cues, deliberation without attention, and decisions relying on assumptions versus a type of certainty. As the human condition is in opposition to the innate significance of the decisions being selected, each component must be revised and calculated. Analysis suggests that this extra layer of protection would benefit the cyber realm as the act would retrace the decision process and generate a barrier in opposition to blatantly biased suggestions. These considerations must be held with multiple perspectives in mind, allowing the decision-makers to select the most profitable method. It could be theorized that cognitive bias leads to a form of prioritization, although it may not always be suited to deal with the present situation. An analysis might suggest that past events are considered preliminarily in response to the emergence of new threats in a modern era, providing clarity in unfamiliar situations. As the world evolves and unseen threats emerge, this issue may be predisposed based on the assumption that events and threats are judged by their past success. This theory could be further substantiated within the boundaries of positive and negative feedback, extending to the validation that behaviour becomes negotiated (Smith and Postmes 2011). In relation to visible outcomes, actions may be taken more swiftly to achieve immediate gratification. This holds true even for tasks that require more patience, emphasizing the propensity for immediate action. While this could pertain to a task that requires a touch more patience, this still yields true for immediate action. Individuals are far less likely to act when placed within unfavourable conditions and will typically wait until an opportunity presents itself (Smith and Postmes 2011). This behaviour is predominant when information is partially obscured, and the potential threat is not immediately recognized. In this case, sight does not serve as the most effective identifier of information and should, therefore, be excluded from the conclusion.

6. Recommendations for Effective Mitigation

Effective mitigation in the critical infrastructure decision-making process requires a comprehensive strategy. There are various laws, defense-in-depth processes, and regular discussions to create protective measures, all appearing exemplary on paper, but that does not certify their significance in practice as learned from the analysis of the World Economic Forum (2024). Like in chess, where subtle moves can provide a powerful advantage, professional decisions require strategic thinking. Cyber initiatives tend to focus on hardening the infrastructure and security but often neglect the rationale behind decision-making processes Villadiego's (2020) insights, highlights the need to understand decision-making mindsets beyond defense and consider offensive measures. Until this is addressed, offensive measures will remain weak in practice despite appearing strong on paper. To make better, more informed decisions, it is essential to adopt a 360-degree view, considering various perspectives and evaluating potential solutions and their consequences. The demand for updating critical infrastructures and implementing additional protection measures to be implemented is unambiguous, highlighting the need for adaptability. To address these challenges, analysis suggests organizations should prioritize cybersecurity education for decision-makers and promote effective communication between technical experts and leadership. This point is derived from Raina's (2023) work, which highlights the shortage of skilled cyber professionals and high rates of employee attrition. Furthermore, decision-makers should be encouraged to adopt a long-term perspective on cybersecurity, acknowledging that a comprehensive approach can offer more robust protection against threats. Additionally noting that risk assessments are vital, requiring decision-makers to identify potential risks, emphasized by Mussington (2021). This involves fully understanding the nature of the threat, the vulnerability of the infrastructure to the threat, and the potential impact if the threat is realized. This is where the role of heuristics in decision-making and the need for a comprehensive view of decision-making should be acknowledged. While security is important, an overemphasis on it can lead to other aspects being neglected.

As the critical infrastructures span various domains and organizations, developing partnerships with private sectors can enhance efficiency, highlighted by KPGM International (2023). However, the gap between the theoretical strategies and their practical execution requires further discussion. This gap, or discrepancy, can be addressed by continuously monitoring and adjusting strategies based on practical experiences, promoting effective communication between different stakeholders, and fostering a culture of learning and adaptability. Enabling cybersecurity education for decision-makers can foster effective communication between technical experts and leadership. It is important to bridge the gap between technical experts who understand the nuances of the threats and decision-makers who determine the strategic response derived from Riana (2023). Bridging this gap ensures that decisions are informed by both theoretical knowledge and practical insights. Effectively communicating between multiple sectors can lead to efficiency and promote a mutual understanding between these two groups is essential for making informed and effective decisions in cybersecurity.

As these challenges are lessened by interdisciplinary collaboration. This collaborative practice brings together diverse perspectives and skill sets, providing a more comprehensive understanding of the situation and potential threats. Interdisciplinary collaboration is key, evolving into a bipartisan effort that delivers a unified message to all, from lawmakers to the general public advocated by Rathburn (2009). The duality of infrastructures ensures the consideration and cooperation of previously independent entities which could otherwise omit practices resulting in a negative impact on the now opposing counterpart. The key to an enhanced system that can outperform the current infrastructure array is to discover benefits within the public opinion, especially from those who have developed specialized skills within the respective fields necessary to maintain infrastructure. Construction workers pouring the concrete extending to the leaders who make the decisions would incorporate varying skill sets, perspectives, and influences which could better perpetuate an open forum type of conference, the message is well developed and supported. This type of decision would fall under the constructivism theory as it requires a form of knowledge gained and insight learned emphasized by Rathbun (2009). This would contrast with the current standing where a closed conference is held by the few for the many. Instead using constructivism theory there exists a role of learners from where the knowledge of each process is gained and the learning is an active process, that is both contextual and plays a role within the community of users observed by Rathbun (2009). Some examples of this include teams of construction workers that add the structure or physical outreach to the critical infrastructures, the workers on ladders and in trenches spreading communication across the country, and even the teams in offices that demonstrate bureaucratic decision-making processes to ensure the safety of these communicational standards. Each member of each team implements specialized skills to create infrastructures. Together they provide a greater form of trust and communication incorporating a 360 view of the process.

7. Conclusion

While several studies on critical infrastructures focus on making the infrastructure being more sustainable and resilient by security measures, it is the mindset that drives the processes for achieving the innovations necessary to safeguard the critical infrastructures. Despite being meticulously designed, these powerful structures designed with great care from the ground up, have long since been established as obsolete, requiring further development and refinement to compete with the modern era. At the same time, it is the comprehension of such requirements that are not fully understood to properly mitigate the situation (Villadiego 2020). With the lack of awareness, the complexity of the situation, having other priorities, and even matters of cost considerations the decisions can overlook the issues. This situation can give rise to a phenomenon known as 'out of sight, out of mind,' where problems are disregarded because they are not immediately visible or causing pressing issues (Smith and Postumes 2011). It is human nature that is created via precedent, every decision, outcome, and outlier presented in life generating a mentality that guides not only the traditional thought processes that guide any coming decisions but also the outlook on life which generates biases and establishes powerful direction, such as a moral compass. While decision-makers are often entrusted with valuable information to determine pivotal actions, bias, and the human condition are inevitability something that cannot be easily avoided. Even when overcoming the bias for logical decisions, there is still the basis in emotional fundamentals, the human nature, that limits a single person to the quality of performance required in such a strategic decision (Mercer 2005). This mistaken belief in the effectiveness of independent decision-making is challenged when viewed within a team-based framework. In such a framework, a team, composed of different individuals selected independently from the previous panel each time, can offer a variety of perspectives towards each goal. This diversity of viewpoints can enhance the decision-making process, highlighting the limitations of relying solely on one individual's judgment. With a degree of randomization, the conflict of group mentality is minimized, while logic and perspective are quickly held at the forefront of the decision. This panel would provide the consideration and influence of numerous personalities while allowing for the consideration of realism, liberalism, and rational theory to meld in a culmination of logical decisions. This approach exemplifies the application of cognitive biases in decision-making for critical infrastructures.

References

Acciarini, Acciarini, C., Brunetta, F., and Boccardelli, P. (2020) "Cognitive biases and decision-making strategies in times of change: a systematic literature review", Management Decision, Vol 9, No. 4, pp 66–75. ISSN: 0025-1747.

Ciccotti, K. (2014) "The human factor in project management", PMI® Global Congress: Project Management Institute, Available online at: https://www.pmi.org/learning/library/human-factor-project-management-9276.

Davies, J.C. (1963) "You Can't Change Human Nature", John Wiley & Sons Inc, Hoboken, NJ., pp 1-30, Available online at: Doi: HTTP://dx.doi.org.ezproxy2.apus.edu/10.1037/14301-00.

De Felice, F., Baffo, I., and Petrillo, A. (2022) "Critical Infrastructures Overview: Past, Present and Future", Sustainability, Vol 14, No. 4, pp 11-13.

Erisen, E. (2012) "An Introduction to Political Psychology for International Relations Scholars", Perceptions, Vol. 17, No. 3, pp 9-28, Available online at: https://search-proquest-com.ezproxy2.apus.edu/scholarly-journals/introduction-political-psychology-international/docview/1196589032/se-2?accountid=8289.

Freud, S. (1915) "The unconscious", SE, Vol 14, pp 159-204. Available online at: http://dravni.co.il/wp-content/uploads/2014/01/Freud-S.-1915.-The-Unconscious.-.pdf.

Glasser Institute for Choice Theory (N.D.) "What is Choice Theory?" Glasser Institute for Choice Theory, Available online at: https://wglasser.com/what-is-choice-theory/.

Global Data. (2023) "Global Infrastructure Outlook to 2023" Global Data. Available online at: https://www.globaldata.com/store/report/global-infrastructure-outlook-to-2023/.

Gowda, R.M.V. (1999) "Heuristics, Biases, and the Regulation of Risk", Policy Sciences, Vol 32, No. 1, pp 59–78.

Jervis, R. (1976) "Perception and Misperception in International Relations", Princeton University Press.

KPGM International. (2023) "Emerging Trends in Infrastructure", KPGM International. Available online at https://assets.kpmg.com/content/dam/kpmg/xx/pdf/2023/01/emerging-trends-in-infrastructure.pdf.

McDermott, R. (2004) "The Feeling of Rationality: The Meaning of Neuroscientific Advances for Political Science", Political Psychology Vol. 2 No. 4.

Mercer, J. (2005) "Rationality and Psychology in International Politics", International Organization, Vol 59, No. 1, pp 77-106.

Moore, S. (2021) "Gartner Predicts 30% of Critical Infrastructure Organizations Will Experience a Security Breach by 2025", Gartner, Available online at: https://www.gartner.com/en/newsroom/press-releases/2021-12-2-gartner-predicts-30–of-critical-infrastructure-organi.

Mussington, D. (2021) "Securing the Critical National Infrastructure" in Paul Cornish (ed.), The Oxford Handbook of Cyber Security, Oxford Handbooks (2021; online edn, Oxford Academic) Chapter 26, pp 429-446. Available online at: https://doi.org/10.1093/oxfordhb/9780198800682.013.26.

Nielsen, E.G., and Minda, J.P. (2019) "Problem Solving and Decision Making", Psychology, DOI: 10.1093/OBO/9780199828340-0246.

Newell, B. and Shanks, D. (2014) "Unconscious influences on decision making: A critical review," Behavioral and Brain Sciences, Cambridge University Press, Vol 37, No. 1, pp. 1–19. doi: 10.1017/S0140525X12003214.

Rathbun, B.C. (2009) "It Takes all Types: Social Psychology, Trust, and the International Relations Paradigm in our Minds: A Journal of International Politics, Law and Philosophy", International Theory 1 Vol 3, No. 11, pp. 345-380 Available online at: https://search-proquest-com.ezproxy2.apus.edu/scholarly-journals/takes-all-types-social-psychology-trust/docview/217957605/se-2?accountid=8289.

Schoen, H. (2007) "Personality Traits and Foreign Policy Attitudes in German Public Opinion", The Journal of Conflict Resolution Vol. 51, No. 3, pp. 408-430.

Smith, L.G.E., and Postmes, T. (2011) "The Power of Talk: Developing Discriminatory Group Norms through Discussion", British Journal of Social Psychology Vol. 50 No.2, pp. 193–215 doi:10.1348/014466610X504805.

United States Department of Homeland Security (2024) "Homeland Threat Assessment", Office of Intelligence and Analysis, Available online at: https://www.dhs.gov/sites/default/files/2023-09/23_0913_ia_23-333-ia_u_homeland-threat-assessment-2024_508C_V6_13Sep23.pdf.

Villadiego, R. (2020) "Decision Making in Cybersecurity", Lumu Technologies, Available online at https://lumu.io/wp-content/uploads/2020/10/en_wp_decision-making-in-cybersecurity.pdf.

Winter, D.G. (2005) "Measuring the Motive of Political Actors at a Distance", Psychological Assessment of Political Leaders pp. 153-177. Edited by Jerrold Post. Ann Arbor: University of Michigan Press.

World Economic Forum (2023) "Global Risks Report 2023", World Economic Forum, 18th Edition, ISBN-13: 978-2-940631-36-0, Available online at: https://www.weforum.org/publications/global-risks-report-2023/.

World Economic Forum (2024) "Global Risks Report 2024", World Economic Forum, 19th Edition, ISBN- 978-2-940631-64-3, Available online at: https://www.weforum.org/publications/global-risks-report-2024/digest/.

Zahidi, S. (2023) "Global Risks Report 2023", World Economic Forum, 18th Edition, Available online at: https://www.weforum.org/publications/global-risks-report-2023504805

Masters Research Papers

AI-Enhanced VPN Security Framework: Integrating Open-Source Threat Intelligence and Machine Learning to Secure Digital Networks

Mohamad Hasan and Dr Tania Malik
School of Informatics and Cybersecurity, Technological University Dublin, Ireland

b00158228@mytudublin.ie
Tania.Malik@tudublin.ie

Abstract: In today's digital age, ensuring network privacy and integrity is of utmost importance. To address this, our work proposed an advanced VPN security framework that integrates open-source threat intelligence and machine learning (ML) to enhance cyber defences. By combining Wazuh for threat detection and analysis, and pfsense for firewall capabilities, with state-of-the-art ML algorithms, we present a robust VPN security solution to the challenges presented by the evolving landscape of cyber threats, representing a significant advancement in securing digital networks. This framework is strengthened by the integration of four ML algorithms— Gradient Boosted Trees (GBT), Random Forest (RF), K-Nearest Neighbors (KNN), and Dense Deep Learning (DDL)— chosen for their classification efficacy and their ability to process complex security data, thereby improving the efficiency and accuracy of threat detection. Results indicated significant improvements in threat detection accuracy following the integration of ML algorithms. The Random Forest (RF) algorithm, in particular, stood out for its exceptional accuracy and ability to handle various threat scenarios, showcasing its efficacy in identifying sophisticated cyber threats through network traffic pattern analysis. Further performance benchmarking confirmed the feasibility of deploying the advanced VPN security framework, demonstrating minimal impact on network latency and throughput.

Keywords: VPN Security, ML in Cybersecurity, Deep Learning, Encrypted Traffic, VPN Framework

1. Introduction

Network privacy and integrity has become the utmost priority in today's digital world. The internet not only facilitates global communication and access to worldwide events but is increasingly supplanting traditional business practices. With the rise of remote working, there has been a significant shift away from the secure environments of corporate offices, leading individuals and businesses to frequently rely on Virtual Private Networks (VPNs) to access geographically restricted resources. Ensuring the data security and the reliability of networks in such settings is paramount. VPNs create secure tunnels between remote users and networks, protecting data traffic from external threats. However, the security of these tunnels depends on the robustness of the tunneling protocols and the integrity of the network devices. Despite their popularity, VPNs are not immune to vulnerabilities. Current VPN setups often face security challenges that can compromise sensitive data and threaten network integrity (Iqbal, MA and Riadi, I. 2019). These vulnerabilities are intensified by the rapidly evolving and increasingly complex landscape of cyber threats.

Given the vulnerabilities identified in existing VPN configurations and the evolving landscape of cyber threats, there is a pressing need for a more advanced VPN security framework. To address this, we proposed an advanced VPN security framework that integrates open-source threat intelligence and machine learning (ML) to enhance cyber defense. The core objective of our research is to develop a robust VPN security framework that enhances the detection and mitigation of internal network attacks. These attacks typically become evident after remote PCs are connected to the network via a VPN, exposing the network to various security risks. This AI-enhanced VPN security framework aims to deliver a comprehensive solution that secures VPN connections as an integral part of the VPN service, independently of external network security devices. In this advanced framework, we integrate Wazuh for threat detection and analysis, and pfSense for firewall capabilities, along with cutting-edge ML algorithms to create a robust VPN security solution that addresses the challenges posed by the dynamically evolving cyber threat landscape, marking a notable advance in digital network security.

The framework is enhanced by incorporating four algorithms—Gradient Boosted Trees (GBT), Random Forest (RF), K-Nearest Neighbors (KNN), and Dense Deep Learning (DDL). These algorithms were specifically chosen for their high classification efficacy and their ability to process complex security data, significantly improving the efficiency and accuracy of threat detection. The major contribution of this research is the integration of machine learning with open-source threat intelligence and firewalls to create a robust, standalone solution that can be implemented within any network without the need for additional devices to monitor network traffic, all through an integrated VPN solution. To the best of our knowledge, this is the first research effort to apply ML specifically to VPN security, as most previous research has focused only on analyzing encrypted traffic and identifying attack patterns within it. In our study, we also evaluate which model performs best for this specific issue. Our experimental results demonstrate significant improvements in threat detection accuracy following the integration of these ML algorithms. Additionally, our performance benchmarking has confirmed the feasibility of implementing this advanced VPN security framework, demonstrating minimal impact on network latency and throughput.

2. Literature Review

Recent developments in VPN security have increasingly incorporated machine learning techniques to enhance encryption and threat detection capabilities. In this literature review we cover various studies that have significantly contributed to the application of ML in the field of VPN security, particularly focusing on the classification of encrypted traffic and the improvement of security protocols.

Significant efforts have been explored in utilizing traditional ML algorithms to better understand and secure VPN traffic. For instance, Logistic Regression, Support Vector Machine (SVM), and Naive Bayes have been widely used for their ability to classify and predict outcomes based on historical data, which is crucial for identifying anomalous patterns that may indicate security breaches (Zhou, Y. et al. 2023), (Bagui, S. et al.2017). Furthermore, the k-Nearest Neighbors (kNN) algorithm has been applied for its simplicity and effectiveness in classification tasks by comparing new data points with known data points (Bagui, S. et al. 2017). Additionally, ensemble methods such as Random Forest and Gradient Boosted Trees have received attention for their robustness and accuracy in handling complex datasets with multiple input variables. These methods combine multiple decision trees to improve the predictive performance and have proven to be particularly effective in enhancing the detection capabilities within VPN security frameworks (Wang, Z. et al. 2022), (Muliukha, V.A. et al. 2020). These models were compared to determine which could most effectively classify the encrypted network traffic with high accuracy and minimal overfitting. Among the models tested, ensemble methods, particularly Random Forest and Gradient Boosting Trees, were highlighted for their superior performance in terms of accuracy and the ability to handle overfitting (Bagui, S. et al. 2017). Muliukha et al. (2020) discussed the application of machine learning algorithms such as Random Forest and Naive Bayesian for the classification of encrypted network traffic, specifically focusing on SSL sessions and VPN connections. Similarly, Wang et al. (2022) provided a comprehensive analysis of using machine learning to detect encrypted malicious traffic, offering insights into different datasets and the efficacy of various ML algorithms in this context. The importance of robust datasets for training and testing ML models in traffic classification was emphasized by Uğurlu et al. (2021), who developed a new classification method that leverages extreme gradient boosting (XGBoost) and other ML techniques. They reported a high success rate in classifying encrypted traffic, which underscores the potential of ML in enhancing VPN security.

Encrypted traffic analysis has become more sophisticated with the application of deep learning models. Works by Zhou et al. (2023) introduce one-dimensional convolutional neural networks for efficient and accurate traffic classification. Research by Naas and Fesl (2023) introduced a novel dataset for VPN traffic analysis, which could significantly aid in the development of ML models tailored for VPN security. This dataset includes various VPN protocols and is designed to help researchers improve network Quality of Service (QoS) and security features. Several studies have focused on the detection of malicious activities through encrypted traffic. For instance, Wang et al. (2022) and Zhao et al. (2013) have explored machine learning-based approaches for identifying malicious entities within encrypted traffic, which is crucial for preventing security breaches in VPNs. The integration of ML algorithms into network security systems has been proven to significantly reduce false positives, thereby enhancing the operational efficiency of cybersecurity measures. This is particularly relevant in the context of VPN security, where distinguishing between benign and malicious traffic quickly is crucial. However, existing research predominantly focuses on the analysis of encrypted traffic, seeking patterns within this data—a process that is inherently complex. Once a user connects through the VPN gateway, the traffic is decrypted on the internal side, where analyzing it requires substantially lower processing capabilities and allows for much easier implementation with a focus on effective monitoring of internal network traffic.

Our research introduces an integrated framework dedicated to VPN security, based on machine learning and open-source threat intelligence. This framework is designed to monitor any suspicious behaviour of connected users and provide feedback if their actions are deemed malicious. The selection of machine learning algorithms in this study is based on (Bagui, S. et al. 2017) work that compared various ML algorithms used in network traffic analysis, focusing on their performance, accuracy, and precision. This approach facilitates a more efficient and straightforward implementation while maintaining high levels of security and threat detection.

3. Framework Overview

In this section, we discussed in detail the advanced VPN security framework's architecture and its functionality. The framework integrates multiple components—Wazuh, pfSense, and several machine learning (ML) algorithms—to create a robust solution for mitigating the evolving landscape of cyber threats.

3.1 Architectural Design

A Graphic representation of the architecture shown in Figure 1 illustrates how data flows between the threat detection modules, firewall, and ML processing units. This design ensures that each component can operate efficiently while maintaining high security standards across the network. At first, we discuss the specifics of each component within the framework, detailing their roles and contributions to the overall functionality and security capabilities of the system. Each component is crucial for ensuring the robustness and efficiency of our advanced VPN security framework. After that, we describe the implementation detail of the framework and data flow and processing interactions among the components of the framework.

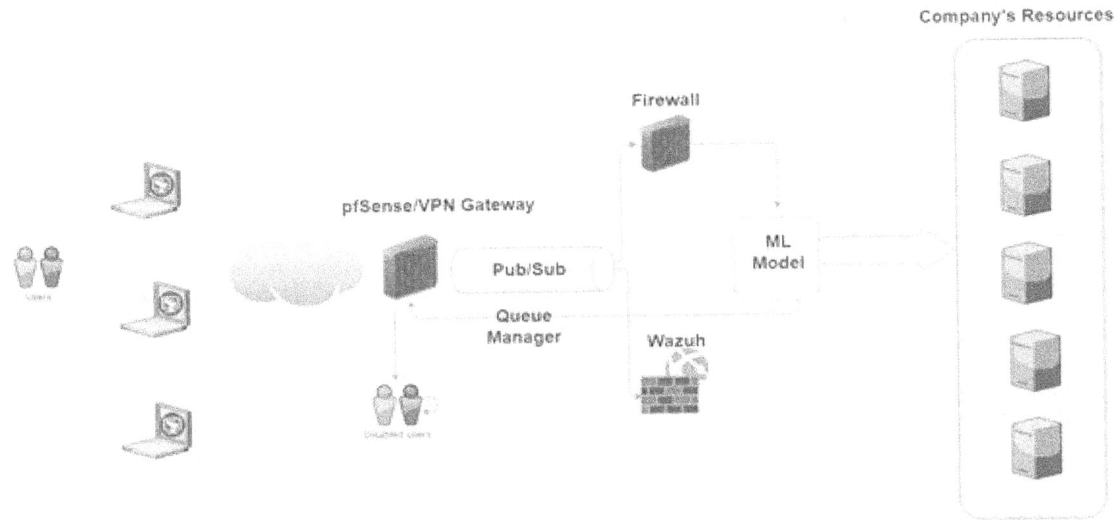

Figure 1: AI-Enhanced VPN Security Framework

3.1.1 Wazuh

Within our VPN security framework, Wazuh acts as a critical component. Wazuh (Asswad A2022) is an open-source security monitoring tool that provide comprehensive protection capabilities and built on the Open-Source Host-based Intrusion Detection System Security (OSSEC) framework, providing features like intrusion detection, log analysis, and file integrity monitoring. Wazuh excels at aggregating logs from various points within the network, including the pfSense/VPN gateway, offering a unified view of the system's activities. Its strength lies in the real-time analysis of collected data, utilizing advanced rule-based threat detection algorithms that can recognize signs of malicious activity, such as intrusion attempts or malware presence. By correlating and analyzing the patterns within the traffic data, Wazuh contributes significantly to the proactive aspect of the framework, enabling early detection of potential threats before they can escalate into breaches. This integration ensures that any abnormal or suspicious behaviours are flagged promptly, strengthening the VPN network's defense against cyber threats and aligning with the framework's goal of maintaining a secure and resilient digital environment for any organization.

3.1.2 pfSense

Another component of the VPN security framework is pfSense which acts as the VPN gateway, and it is therefore the first perimeter of defense. pfSense (Patel, at al 2017) is an open-source and FreeBSD-based firewall and router platform with number of features, among which is the capability for VPN provision. Inside, pfSense is the VPN gateway—managing secure access to the company network and the encrypted/decrypted traffic. This is highly valuable functionality for the framework, which is responsible for steering the flow of data through security checks to the machine-learning models. Also, at the second stage it acts as a firewall where we can use it's Suricata threat detection plugin (Meena, at al 2020) as another layer of protection.

3.1.3 ML Algorithms

This section provides a detailed description of our chosen machine learning algorithms and the rationale behind choosing them.

- Random Forest (RF) - The Random Forest algorithm (Zhou, Y. et al. 2023, Bagui, S. et al. 2017) is an ensemble learning method used for classification tasks, which constructs multiple decision trees during training and outputs the class that is the mode of the classes predicted by individual trees. It aims to improve prediction accuracy and control over-fitting by averaging the results of several trees, each created on randomly selected subsets of the data. Adjusting the number of trees in the forest is key to finding the right bias-variance balance, with more trees leading to better performance. Although less directly interpretable compared to some other methods, Random Forest requires minimal parameter tuning and relies on an understanding of the data to yield effective outcomes, making it a practical and robust choice for predictive analysis.
- Gradient Boosted Trees (GBT) - Gradient Boosting Trees (GBT) (Bagui, S. et al. 2017) is a powerful ensemble learning technique used for both regression and classification problems. Like Random Forest, GBT builds multiple decision trees, but in a sequential manner where each subsequent tree aims to correct the errors of the previous ones. This method combines weak predictive models to create a strong model in a stage-wise fashion, using an optimization algorithm that minimizes a loss function. GBT is particularly effective because it focuses on areas where the previous trees performed poorly, iteratively improving the model's accuracy. The model uses gradient descent to minimize errors, which involves adjusting tree parameters to better predict the outliers and misclassified data points from earlier iterations. The result is a highly accurate prediction model that can handle complex non-linear relationships within the data.
- K-Nearest Neighbors (KNN) - K-Nearest Neighbors (KNN) is a straightforward and widely used classification algorithm (Zhou, Y. et al. 2023, Bagui, S. et al. 2017, Lichy, A. et al. 2022) that predicts the label of a data point by looking at the 'k' closest labeled data points and choosing the most common label among them. This non-parametric method operates by calculating the distance (often Euclidean) between points and aggregating the categories of nearest neighbour data points. KNN is unique in that it doesn't build a model in advance but performs the classification directly at the time of prediction, making it very intuitive and easy to implement. Despite its simplicity, KNN can be highly effective, particularly in cases where the decision boundary is irregular. To enhance performance, the choice of 'k' and the distance metric can be adjusted based on the specific characteristics of the data.
- Dense Deep Learning (DDL) - Dense Deep Learning (DDL) (de Brito Guimarães, L.C. 2023) involves the use of densely connected neural networks, a type of deep learning architecture where each neuron in a layer is connected to every neuron in the next layer, maximizing the potential for learning complex patterns in data. These models are particularly known for their ability to extract features at multiple levels of abstraction, allowing them to capture intricate dependencies and relationships within the data. The strength of DDL lies in its layered structure, which can include hundreds or even thousands of layers, each contributing to a more refined analysis of the input features. This makes Dense Deep Learning highly effective for tasks involving large volumes of data with many variables, such as image and speech recognition, and complex decision-making scenarios in real-time systems.

3.2 Configuration and Implementation

After describing overall architecture and individual components of VPN security framework, we will now discuss the specific configuration steps and detailed implementation of these components within the framework.

Step 1: Configuration and Setup of PfSense as a VPN Gateway

Setting up an OpenVPN server in pfSense involves several key steps to ensure secure and efficient operation. All the components of the framework are setup on virtual box as VM environment and was interfaced together as different components. First, a Certificate Authority (CA) is generated to authenticate the server and client credentials. Next, server and client certificates are created within pfSense's certificate manager. The OpenVPN server configuration is then established, specifying parameters like server mode, cryptographic settings, and tunnel settings. After configuring the server, necessary firewall rules are defined to allow traffic through the specified ports. Lastly, the OpenVPN Client Export Utility is used to generate and distribute client configuration files. This streamlined process ensures that users can securely access their network remotely through the VPN.

Step 2: Wazuh Deployment

Wazuh was implemented as a Docker container on a Linux virtual machine within the VirtualBox environment. Docker was chosen for its ability to simplify the deployment process. The Wazuh container was linked to the network where VPN traffic flows to monitor logs in real-time. Configuration files were tailored to define the specific security rules and alerts relevant to the traffic patterns of the organization. The Wazuh manager was set up to aggregate logs, analyse data, and flag potential security incidents, acting as an SIEM (Security Information and Event Management) system.

Step 3: Setting Up and Configuring a Second pfSense Instance for Enhanced Security

A second pfSense instance was configured to act as a dedicated firewall within the VirtualBox environment. This instance was responsible for filtering incoming and outgoing VPN traffic after the VPN gateway in order to minimize CPU resources usage within the firewall. Network interfaces were carefully configured to establish distinct zones for internal which is connected to a virtual server and external traffic which is coming from the vpn gateway. Firewall rules were set to allow legitimate traffic from a specific subnet dedicated to VPN users and block malicious or unauthorized access. This setup was crucial for creating a strong security layer that would work in parallel with the VPN gateway.

Step 4: Integration of Argus for Network Monitoring

Argus (Audit Record Generation and Utilization System) has been integrated with the audit network tool very methodically, capturing details of network traffic from the internal interface of the firewall. Argus provides a network-wide visibility tool with a fine perspective since it offers a fine-grain perspective on network activity by generating complete flow metrics data. Argus captures the data at the packet level, providing visibility into the details of what type, structure, and behavior of traffic is going by the firewall. It should monitor and report the state of network transactions, systematically logged for analysis.

Step 5: Implementing and Deploying Machine Learning Model

The machine learning component is developed using Python, with scripts written for training and testing the four algorithms: GBT, RF, KNN, and DDL which are described in above section. The Python environment was set up with necessary libraries, we used scikit-learn for algorithm implementation and NumPy for data manipulation. The scripts were executed within a Linux VM hosted on VirtualBox, accessing pre-processed traffic data to train the models. Once trained, the models were tested for performance and accuracy in classifying traffic as benign or malicious. The captured packet data is a vital resource for the machine learning (ML) algorithms at play within the framework. The ML algorithm ingests rich, granular flow data from Argus, including metrics on duration, packet counts, byte counts, and transaction sequences as the traffic data streams in. This data is then used by the algorithm for understanding normal behavior within patterns of the network traffic so that it would then be possible to detect changes, which would in turn show potential security incidents or malicious activity.

3.3 Data Flow and Processing

The VPN security framework begins with a thorough analysis of all potential threats. This involves assessing the threat agents that might be interested in accessing the data protected by the VPN, which is essential for developing an effective threat model. Threat modeling is a complex process that encompasses a broad spectrum of potential threats and vulnerabilities. The general approach includes identifying a structured list of all conceivable threats, envisaging the worst-case scenarios, and devising prevention strategies. This methodology is valuable not only for setting security benchmarks but also for prioritizing threats and vulnerabilities based on their potential impact. Threat modeling is a dynamic process; as new threats emerge; the VPN's design may need to be adjusted. Any modifications to the VPN's design and security policies should be evaluated to determine whether they reduce or exacerbate the risk of threats. Static analysis of the VPN's configuration data can reveal vulnerabilities, while dynamic analysis involves simulating potential attack scenarios and assessing the effectiveness of threat detection and prevention strategies. The outcomes of this analysis could lead to modifications in the VPN's security policy and adjustments in network and security configurations. An ongoing cycle of evaluation and feedback helps enhance the efficacy of the security policy, with mechanisms in place to detect and address any violations or unintended configuration changes, ultimately improving the security policy's quality.

In our advanced VPN security framework, the VPN user connects to the WAN interface of the pfSense firewall and initiates a VPN connection. Once authenticated, all logs are sent to Wazuh for analysis as a syslog server, and the traffic is routed through a Linux server acting as a router. This is facilitated by configuring a third pfSense interface as a SPAN port, which mirrors all traffic from other interfaces. The Linux machine, connected to this virtual interface, runs an ML script on the traffic captured, segmenting it minute-by-minute into a CSV file stored in the "tmp" folder. If malicious activity is detected, the ML script triggers an alert. Meanwhile, another pfSense instance functions as a standard firewall, managing policies that allow VPN users' IP subnet to communicate with servers on the internal network, and preventing these servers from initiating traffic to the WAN interface to enhance protection of internal resources. Wazuh is configured to automatically send an email alert when a threat is detected as shown in Figure 2. This real-time alert system contrasts with the machine learning section's minute-by-minute CSV analysis. For demonstration purposes, two internal servers were set up and connected to the internal interface to illustrate complete traffic flow. The efficacy of the system was tested using two methods: deploying Metasploit from Kali Linux to identify CVEs and utilizing a 7-day demo of Tenable, both of which are reliable tools for vulnerability testing. These tools help to confirm when the traffic is identified as attack traffic by any threat intelligence system.

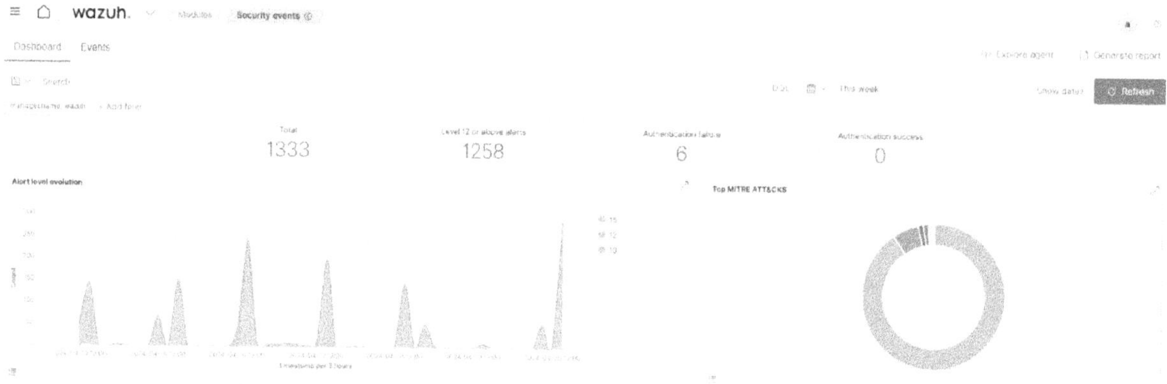

Figure 2: Wazuh Dashboard after simulating attacks

4. Experimental Results

In our study, we have designed two types of experiments: one to evaluate and compare the accuracy and performance of each chosen machine learning model, and another set of experiments to assess the system impact analysis of our VPN security framework. In this section, we will discuss the results of both experiments.

4.1 Performance and Accuracy Experiments

The first set of experiments was conducted to identify the most effective machine learning technique for detecting malicious activities in VPN traffic. Four ML algorithms were chosen for comparison—Gradient Boosted Trees (GBT), Random Forest (RF), K-Nearest Neighbors (KNN), and Dense Deep Learning (DDL). These were primarily selected for their classification efficacy and their ability to process complex security data, thereby enhancing the efficiency and accuracy of threat detection. The goal of these experiments is to evaluate the performance and accuracy of each selected ML model in identifying potential threats separately, to determine which algorithm—or combination of them—yields the best results. This comparison is crucial for optimally designing the security measures for the VPN network to ensure that the chosen model or models achieve the highest possible accuracy in classifying and mitigating cyber threats.

In our supervised learning environment, we were looking for a rich dataset that is big enough to include various types of known attacks such as DOS, Backdoors, Reconnaissance and Worms, also to be recorded over a decent period of time. Our digging came across the UNSW-NB15 Dataset (Moustafa, N. et al. 2015) which contains all of that and more, over a 175k training set and 82k testing set collecting in CSV files and also was captured using Argus so that adjusting the data to match the training data would be a smooth process. A quick check on the Dataset showed that there were some categorical values that needed to be dealt with as well as some feature selections and feature removal to keep only the packets actual data relative features, this all was done using python script and tested to make sure that there will be no problem during either training or testing phases.

The expected impact on learning algorithm performance is important for security data, as we would like threat detection algorithms to not only learn the same pattern with less computation, but also to learn it with increased accuracy. An increased understanding of the relationship between specific optimization methods and algorithm performance could lead to the development of better optimization methods for specific algorithm types and the automatic selection of optimization methods for data sets of a specific type. That's why in our experiments we focused on optimising the features before using each algorithm experiment as well as testing in multiple environments (local and Google Colab cloud environment). The results were consistent across both platforms. We observed that some algorithms outperformed others in terms of accuracy and performance. We believe this performance can be attributed to the process of analyzing packets post-decryption through the internal interface of the firewall, which not only consumes fewer system resources but also enhances the efficiency of the algorithms. Using the DDL algorithm at the first time showed very low accuracy so we had to try several values for Epochs and Batch size during the training phase to get the best accuracy out of it, which occurred at Epoch=10 with batch size =8 and a split of 0.2.

Our findings indicate that in terms of performance, the Random Forest (RF) algorithm surpassed other models, with the Gradient Boosting Trees (GBT) algorithm close behind, performing only 1% lower. The K-Nearest Neighbors (KNN) algorithm ranked third, achieving a score above 80%, as depicted in Figure 3. Regarding accuracy, the RF algorithm again outperformed the rest, with GBT in second place, while KNN displayed the lowest accuracy, as illustrated in Figure 4.

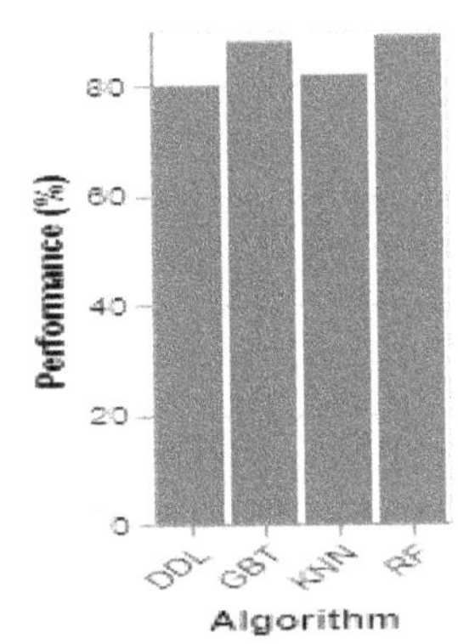

Figure 3: Comparison in terms of Performance

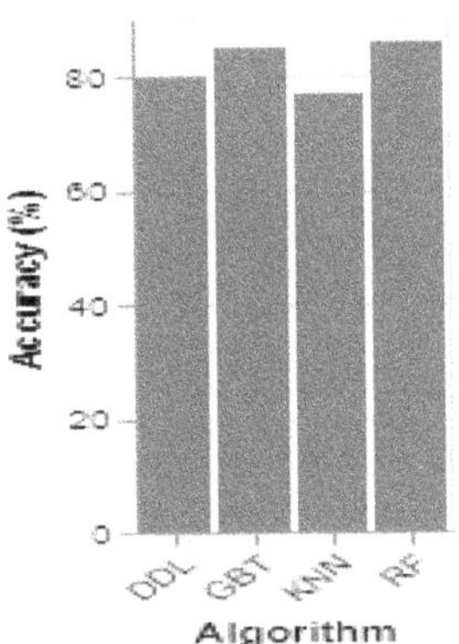

Figure 4: Comparison in terms of Accuracy

The comparison will not only to see how accurate each model is in the prediction but, also to check how each of the models has the capability to adapt and learn from the data. In this scenario, the Random Forest (RF) algorithm becomes one of the more attractive ways to extract great insight into network traffic, which will eventually improve its overall effectiveness with reference to the VPN security system.

4.2 System Impact Analysis

The second set of experiments evaluated the system's impact, first conducted within a VirtualBox environment on a Windows machine equipped with 32 GB of RAM, an Intel Core i7 CPU at 3.2 GHz, and SSD storage. While the overall performance was not considered slow, some delays were noted during the training phases of the KNN and DLL algorithms. However, no performance issues were observed during testing, with traffic type notifications displayed within 3 seconds. Despite this, we opted to transfer the machine learning workload to the Google Collab environment to assess how the models would perform on the cloud, utilizing a T4 GPU and 15 GB of RAM. The tests in this environment mirrored the performance and accuracy observed on the local machine. We theorize that to get the actual system performance impact; it should be deployed in a production environment with significant user traffic. Our findings suggest that the system can smoothly process up to 100 users' traffic, recorded into a CSV file, on an Intel Core i7 CPU without noticeable performance degradation. CPU and memory usage comparisons were conducted in the Google Collab environment using a Tesla T4 GPU, which features a clock speed of 1.59 GHz, 40 cores, and 16 GB of RAM. This GPU, though architecturally similar to a

CPU, offers significantly faster processing speeds. GPU and memory utilization of each algorithm is illustrated in Figure 5 and 6 respectively.

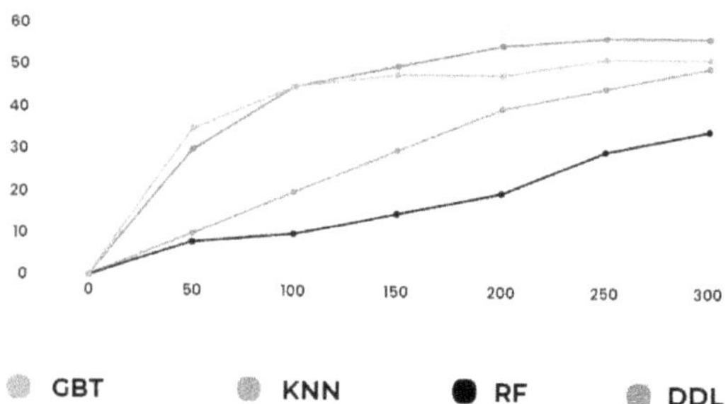

Figure 5: GPU Utilization for each algorithm

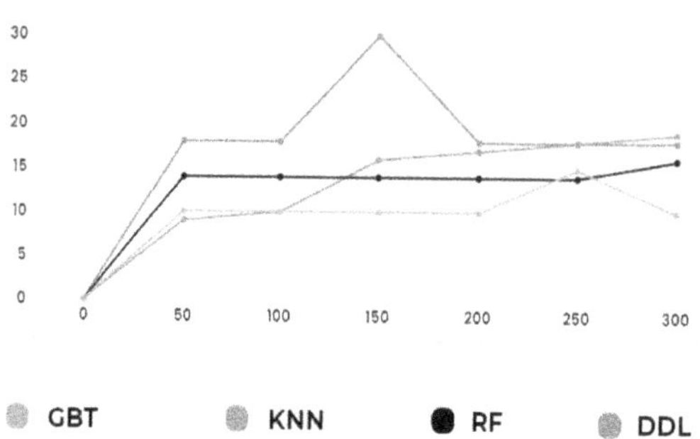

Figure 6: Memory Utilization for each algorithm

The machine learning algorithms GBT, KNN, RF, and DDL exhibit different patterns of GPU and memory utilization due to their varying operational complexities. DDL tends to steadily use more GPU over time because of its complex network layers, whereas RF does not utilize the GPU as much, due to its reliance on multiple decision trees. GBT also experiences high GPU usage, reflecting the computational demands of iterative error correction. KNN maintains moderate GPU and memory usage as it directly operates on the data during prediction. Figure 6 shows trends in memory utilization, suggesting that DDL requires more memory, likely for handling extensive data through its layers, while RF and GBT use memory more consistently—RF for storing multiple trees and GBT for managing tree computations. These trends highlight the inherent balance between algorithm complexity and resource efficiency, which is crucial for selecting algorithms in practice and also demonstrate that accuracy is not always correlated with algorithm complexity.

5. Conclusion

Machine learning (ML) algorithms are reshaping the way complex security data is evaluated. Even though ML methods are not a new concept in computer network defense, they have only recently been applied to the problem of intrusion detection and prevention. Machine learning algorithms have the potential to not only help secure VPN traffic more effectively but also reduce the total cost of ownership of security for an organization. Our work proposed an advanced VPN security framework that integrates open-source threat intelligence and machine learning models to enhance cyber defences. By combining Wazuh for threat detection and analysis, and pfsense for firewall capabilities, with state-of-the-art ML algorithms, we present a robust VPN security solution to the challenges presented by the evolving landscape of cyber threats, representing a significant advancement in securing digital networks. Our experiments demonstrate that these algorithms are highly effective in detecting anomalous behavior within network traffic. Particularly, the Random Forest (RF) algorithm excelled in accuracy and versatility across various threat scenarios, proving its effectiveness in identifying sophisticated cyber threats through analysis of network traffic patterns. Further performance benchmarking confirmed the viability of deploying this advanced VPN security framework with minimal impact on system.

Our future work will focus on integrating the ML component with a web service to enable real-time ML feedback, moving away from recording packet captures with Argus to a fully automated system that provides immediate notifications. Additionally, we plan to integrate the output from the ML algorithms directly into the firewall management process using the pfSense API, allowing for automatic blocking or permitting actions based on whether a traffic is identified as malicious.

References

Iqbal, Muhammad & Riadi, Imam. (2019). Analysis of Security Virtual Private Network (VPN) Using OpenVPN. International Journal of Cyber-Security and Digital Forensics. 8. 58-65.

Zhou, Y., Shi, H., Zhao, Y., Ding, W., Han, J., Sun, H., Zhang, X., Tang, C., Zhang, W. (2023) "Identification of encrypted and malicious network traffic based on one-dimensional convolutional neural network", Journal of Cloud Computing, 12(53).

Wang, Z., Fok, K.W., Thing, V.L.L. (2022) "Machine learning for encrypted malicious traffic detection: Approaches, datasets and comparative study", Computers & Security, 113, p.102542.

Bagui, S., Fang, X., Kalaimannan, E., Bagui, S., Sheehan, J. (2017) "Comparison of machine-learning algorithms for classification of VPN network traffic flow using time-related features", Journal of Cyber Security Technology, 1, pp. 1-19.

Muliukha, V.A., Laboshin, L.U., Lukashin, A.A. (2020) "Analysis and Classification of Encrypted Network Traffic Using Machine Learning", IEEE.

Uğurlu, M., Doğru, I.A., Arslan, R.S. (2021) "A New Classification Method for Encrypted Internet Traffic Using Machine Learning", Turkish Journal of Electrical Engineering & Computer Science.

Naas, M., Fesl, J. (2023) "A Novel Dataset for Encrypted Virtual Private Network Traffic Analysis", Data in Brief.

Sowinski-Mydlarz, V., Li, J., Ouazzane, K., Vassilev, V. (2022) "Threat Intelligence Using Machine Learning Packet Dissection", London Metropolitan University Cyber Security Research Centre.

Lichy, Adi & Bader, Ofek & Dubin, R. & Dvir, Amit & Hajaj, Chen. (2022). When a RF Beats a CNN and GRU, Together -- A Comparison of Deep Learning and Classical Machine Learning Approaches for Encrypted Malware Traffic Classification.

de Brito Guimarães, L.C., 2023. DEEP LEARNING-BASED REAL-TIME BOTNET DETECTION FOR EDGE DEVICES (Doctoral dissertation, Universidade Federal do Rio de Janeiro).

Ndichu, s & Okoth, Sylvester & Okoyo, Henry & Wekesa, Cyrusd. (2023). Detecting Remote Access Network Attacks Using Supervised Machine Learning Methods. International Journal of Computer Network and Information Security. 15. 48-61.

N. Moustafa and J. Slay, "UNSW-NB15: a comprehensive data set for network intrusion detection systems (UNSW-NB15 network data set)," 2015 (MilCIS), Canberra, ACT, Australia, 2015, pp. 1-6.

Asswad, A., 2022. Analysis of attacks and prevention methods in cybersecurity (Doctoral dissertation, University of Brescia).

Patel, K.C. and Sharma, P., 2017. A Review paper on pfsense-an Open-source firewall introducing with different capabilities & customization.

Meena, A.K., Hubballi, N., Singh, Y., Bhatia, V. and Franke, K., 2020, December. Network Security Systems Log Analysis for Trends and Insights: A Case Study. In *2020 IEEE (ANTS)* (pp. 1-6).

OpenArgus, (2024). Documentation. Available at: https://openargus.org/documentation (Accessed: 5 April 2024)

Harmonizing Rights and Rewards: Music NFTs as a Paradigm for Equitable Compensation in the Digital Era

Alexander Pfeiffer[1] and Stephanie Dzihan-Zamagna[2]
[1]Center for Applied Game Studies, Donau-Universität Krems (DUK), Krems, Austria
[2]Independent Researcher, Vienna, Austria

zamagna@gmx.at
alexander.pfeiffer@donau-uni.ac.at

Abstract: This paper provides a critical examination of Music Non-Fungible Tokens (NFTs) within the context of the digital transformation of the music industry, focusing on the implications for equitable artist compensation. As digitalization reshapes consumption and revenue models, the advent of Music NFTs, predicated on blockchain technology, presents a nuanced paradigm for artist-fan interactions and compensation structures. Through an interdisciplinary methodology that integrates literature review and expert interviews, this study scrutinizes the operational mechanisms of Music NFTs, their potential to reconfigure the economics of music production, and the attendant legal and technical challenges. While Music NFTs proffer an innovative approach to direct artist revenue and engagement, this inquiry reveals a complex landscape fraught with legal ambiguities, technological hurdles, and market volatility. The findings underscore the dialectical relationship between the potential benefits of Music NFTs for artists and the prevailing challenges that circumscribe their efficacy.

Keywords: Music Non-Fungible Tokens (NFTs), Blockchain Technology, Digital Music Industry, Artist Compensation, Intellectual Property Rights.

1. Introduction

The music industry has undergone a significant transformation due to digitalization, profoundly affecting how music is consumed and how artists are compensated. The streaming model introduced in 2006 by Daniel Ek exemplifies this change, offering an average payout of about $0.004 per streamed song. However, this amount is often split between the record label and the artist, with the artist typically receiving a smaller portion (Ginsburg, 2022; Dokalik, 2017). This shift towards digitalization and the challenges it presents for equitable artist compensation set the potential stage for the emergence of blockchain technologies, initially conceptualized for financial transactions but increasingly relevant in creative industries like music.

The foundations of today's blockchain technologies are often attributed to the white paper "Bitcoin: A Peer-to-Peer Electronic Cash System" by the pseudonymous author Satoshi Nakamoto in 2008. Bitcoin exemplifies a public blockchain, where a digital record is replicated across many locations (nodes), each managed by different individuals or entities. This decentralized system enables consensus without direct agreement among these parties. While blockchain is adept at providing tamper-proof transaction records, its capacity to verify external information, such as details in an attached text message or token ownership beyond its presence in a legitimate blockchain wallet, is limited. Blockchains continuously produce new data blocks, cryptographically linked, with functionalities varying among different blockchain systems. Some, for instance, enable users to create their own tokens and contracts (Grech & Camilleri, 2017).

In 2021, the rise of Non-Fungible Tokens (NFTs) marked a significant shift, introducing a novel digital music format. These Music NFTs, based on blockchain technology, allow the creation and direct trade of unique digital items between artists and fans. Offering more than just digital files, Music NFTs can include various offerings like songs, collections, albums, exclusive experiences, or merchandise items, thereby expanding the scope of digital music (Fortnow & Terry, 2022).

As described by Pfeiffer et al. (2021), Non-Fungible Tokens (NFTs) are multifaceted in their appearance and function within the blockchain ecosystem, and they can manifest in various forms:

- The most common form involves generating a unique token for each instance, where each token possesses distinct asset properties and metadata. This approach aligns with the widely accepted definition and application of an NFT.
- Alternatively, it is possible to create multiple tokens, starting from two, that share identical asset properties and asset IDs. The differentiation among these tokens lies in their metadata, which varies with each token's transmission.

- A third, more innovative approach is the creation of a token series, drawing inspiration from the serial nature of blockchain-based art (Jutel, 2021). This method represents a hybrid of the first two, where each token is unique but shares certain asset properties with others created at the same time, allowing each to maintain its distinct asset ID.

In all these scenarios, there is a dual-layer structure: on one side, the blockchain-based asset holds legal data and serves as an ownership certificate, and on the other side, the media file resides on an IPFS server. This server utilizes a peer-to-peer hypermedia protocol, allowing users to clone the file with their own IPFS Node.

Music NFTs also present an innovative approach to music financing. Artists can sell shares of their songs, inviting investments in their music. This model promises a larger revenue share for the artists, potentially improving their financial sustainability. Furthermore, the blockchain's ability to trace the origins of these NFTs enables artists to benefit from secondary sales, receiving a predetermined portion from each resale (PwC, 2018). The introduction of Music NFTs represents more than just a new revenue model; it signifies a shift in artist-fan interaction. Through direct sales and diverse communication channels enabled by blockchain technology, artists can establish a closer, more dynamic relationship with their audience.

This study aims to explore the potential and opportunities of Music NFTs in the music industry. It aims to assess whether this innovative model can be successfully integrated into the market and provide fair compensation for artists, marking a significant turn in the digital music landscape.

2. Methodology

The exploration of NFTs in the music industry was grounded in literature research covering key areas such as blockchain technology, Music NFTs, and the structures of the music industry. This theoretical insight set the foundation for validating our understanding through problem-centered expert interviews (Meuser & Nagel, 2009). These interviews aimed to bridge the gap between theoretical knowledge and practical application in the field. A wide spectrum of professionals from the NFT ecosystem was consulted, including NFT artists, lawyers, blockchain specialists, and experts from the music industry and music business research. This approach allowed for cross-validation of theoretical findings with industry insights and assessment of the practical applicability of the concepts. By integrating the insights from literature and expert interviews, this research comprehensively addresses both theoretical and practical aspects. The interviews were conducted individually via Zoom, recorded with the consent of the participants, and subsequently transcribed for analysis. The experts consulted in this study were:

- Expert in Legal Aspects & Blockchain Technology: Offering insights into the legal and taxation aspects related to blockchain and Music NFTs. (NS)
- Legal Expert with a Focus on Copyright Law: Providing a legal perspective on the application of Music NFTs within the broader legal framework. (PK)
- Specialist in Music NFTs: Sharing expertise in the practical implementation of Music NFTs, including successful project launches. (FS)
- Professional in Music Rights and Investments: Offering a unique view on the intersection of music rights, investment, and the role of Music NFTs. (CS)
- Blockchain Technology Expert: Focusing on Ethereum and other blockchain technologies, contributing insights on transaction registers and smart contract development. (JD)
- Music Industry Professional: Bringing an industry viewpoint on artist signing strategies, project management, and the integration of new technologies. (NN)
- Academic with Expertise in Music Economy: Providing an academic perspective on the economic aspects of music and the impact of emerging technologies. (PT)

3. Results

The following chapter explores an expanded scope of critical aspects surrounding NFTs in the industry. It delves into six key areas: the overarching potential of blockchain technology in music and its advantages, the complex legal and technological challenges, the issues of market acceptance and security risks, the importance and challenges of ERC standards, the intricacies of direct artist-fan relationships in a decentralized environment, and the evolving landscape of Music NFTs. This comprehensive exploration aims to offer a deeper understanding of the current state and future potential of Music NFTs, encapsulating a confluence of expert opinions, practical insights, and findings from extensive literature review.

3.1 Potential and Advantages of Blockchain in the Music Industry

The study reveals that blockchain technology is promising for the music industry. Experts JD and CS noted its potential to eliminate intermediaries, create immutability and transparency, shorten distribution channels, and offer unique value-added services like special fan experiences (PwC, 2018). FS emphasized the opportunity for innovative creative pathways, moving beyond traditional music mediums, and forging new fan connections. This aligns with literature indicating blockchain's role in facilitating new forms of music financing through direct license trading, suggesting a shift towards genuine value exchanges in music.

3.2 Legal and Technological Framework Challenges

A significant hurdle for Music NFTs is the legal framework. NS, PK, and NN highlighted the legal grey area surrounding NFTs, echoing literature that questions the clarity of ownership and usage rights associated with digital works (Kaulartz, Schmid, 2021; Hu et al., 2021). The complexity of music copyright law and the necessity for comprehensive legal education were noted as crucial for safely navigating the Music NFT market. McLellan & Leung (2022) support this, suggesting a need for contractual foundations to define these relationships clearly.

3.3 Market Acceptance and Security Risks

The study found that market acceptance and security are major concerns. CS pointed out the impact of several fraud cases and the cryptocurrency crash on the Music NFT market, which has led to significant losses and a decline in market confidence (Hauck, 2022; Smith, 2023; finanzen.net, 2022). This uncertainty has led to a shift in how artists refer to their NFT-based works, moving towards terms like "digital collectibles" and "music shares" to avoid the negative connotations associated with NFTs.

3.4 ERC Standards and Decentralization in Music Industry

A lack of suitable ERC standards for Music NFTs prevents proper metadata integration and automatic royalty distribution, as per FS's observations. CS, however, questioned the necessity of fully automated systems, suggesting that the decentralization principle in the music industry might render such automation less critical. The literature (Hu et al., 2021; Botero et al., 2022) also discusses the need for standards that cater specifically to the metadata of music files to enable efficient management and monetization.

3.5 The Complexity of Direct Artist-Fan Relationships

The elimination of intermediaries, while beneficial, presents challenges for emerging artists who must find ways to connect with their audience. PT highlighted the complexities of self-promotion and market visibility for artists working independently. The possibility of NFT platforms offering solutions for artist visibility, albeit for a fee, suggests a need for careful consideration to ensure artists retain a larger share of profits.

3.6 The Evolving Landscape of Music NFTs

Despite the challenges, the potential of Music NFTs in reshaping the music industry remains significant. The study indicates that legal and technological maturation, market education, and the development of standards tailored to the unique needs of the music industry are crucial for the widespread adoption and success of Music NFTs.

3.7 Future Prospects and Opportunities

Despite existing challenges, the potential of Music NFTs for enhancing artist engagement and creating new revenue models is undeniable. The opportunities for acquiring licenses and benefiting from secondary sales, as discussed by experts and supported by PwC (2018), indicate a promising future for musicians. Yet, the journey to a holistic solution for equitable compensation involves navigating the complex landscape of legal, technical, and public acceptance issues.

Having explored the diverse facets of Music NFTs in the music industry, it becomes evident that while the potential is vast, so are the challenges. The journey ahead in fully harnessing the capabilities of Music NFTs is laden with complexities that demand further exploration. In the following section, we will pivot to future research, outlining the areas that require deeper investigation and the prospects that hold promise for the evolution of Music NFTs and their role in reshaping the music industry landscape.

4. Conclusion, Limitations and Further Research

In this paper, we have delved into the transformative potential of Music Non-Fungible Tokens (NFTs) within the evolving digital landscape of the music industry. By employing a qualitative research methodology that incorporated problem-centered expert interviews, this study aimed to uncover both the promising prospects and the significant challenges Music NFTs present for ensuring fair compensation for artists. The findings of this research underscore the enthusiasm shared by experts regarding the capability of blockchain technology to revolutionize the music industry. These professionals highlighted numerous advantages, such as eliminating intermediaries, enhancing transparency, and offering novel avenues for artist-fan engagement. Expert insights emphasized the innovative nature of Music NFTs, which extend beyond mere digital assets to include exclusive experiences and merchandise, thereby forging deeper connections between artists and their audience.

However, the interviews also shed light on substantial hurdles. Legal uncertainties surrounding the ownership and rights associated with Music NFTs were recurrent themes, with experts stressing the need for a robust legal framework to navigate this new terrain. The technological readiness of blockchain systems for widespread adoption in the music industry was another concern echoed by interviewees, who highlighted the necessity for standards that cater specifically to the music sector. The study also revealed the complexities of direct artist-fan relationships facilitated by Music NFTs. While the decentralization aspect offers greater control and potentially higher revenue for artists, the challenges of self-promotion and establishing visibility in a saturated market remain significant. Experts suggested that despite the removal of traditional intermediaries, new forms of platforms and services might emerge, offering visibility solutions at a cost, thereby emphasizing the need for artists to remain vigilant about the terms of these new relationships.

In conclusion, this paper has highlighted the dualistic nature of Music NFTs in the music industry: their potential to empower artists and transform industry dynamics is significant, yet it is equally matched by a set of formidable challenges that require careful navigation. The integration of expert insights with theoretical perspectives has provided a comprehensive view of the current state and future possibilities of Music NFTs, laying the groundwork for further research to explore the nuanced interplay of legal, technological, and market factors in this emerging domain.

A central limitation of this study is the relatively new domain of Music NFTs, resulting in limited availability of specialized literature. Most sources are online contributions that might only superficially address the topic. Additionally, the technology is constantly evolving, which means new forms of usage or significant developments might emerge post-study. The number of Austrian artists deeply engaged with this technology is relatively limited, allowing for only a few different perspectives to be considered.

Future research should focus on the legal aspects, particularly how copyright law and property rights of Music NFTs can be best regulated to protect both artists and buyers. The need to develop an adequate ERC standard for Music NFTs is crucial to enable correct and comprehensive metadata for music works. Furthermore, the exploration of second-layer solutions to reduce transaction costs and improve blockchain scalability for mass operation is warranted. The decoupling of cryptocurrency in relation to NFTs merits discussion, as it could help lower barriers to mass application. Lastly, enhancing security and protecting against fraud is vital. It is important to identify security gaps and develop structures to ensure the authenticity of Music NFTs.

AI-Disclaimer

This document has utilized the capabilities of ChatGPT Model 4.0, an advanced Artificial Intelligence language model developed by OpenAI, for specific auxiliary purposes. The AI model was employed primarily for spellchecking, grammar correction, and the translation of interviews conducted in non-English languages While ChatGPT Model 4.0 is a sophisticated tool designed to assist with language processing tasks, the final responsibility for the accuracy and integrity of the content in this document rests with the human authors and editors. Any errors or omissions in the text should be attributed to human oversight rather than the AI tool used.

References

Ballhaus, W., Weyßer, M., Perfall, A., Brockmann, S., Siadat, A., Wipper, A., Stallmeier, L., & Schulze Bröring, H. (2018). Nach dem Streaming kommt die Blockchain: Hype oder echte Chance für die Musikindustrie? PricewaterhouseCoopers (PwC) GmbH Wirtschaftsprüfungsgesellschaft.

Botero, A., Amaya, P., & Spielburg, Y. (2022). Splitting the difference: Music and Web3's multiplayer problem. Water & Music. Available at: https://www.waterandmusic.com/splitting-the-difference-music-and-web3s-multiplayer-problem/ [Accessed 1 January 2024].

Dokalik, D., Fischer, P., & Waldingbrett, I. (2017). Musik-Urheberrecht. Österreichisches Urheberrecht für Komponisten, Musiker, Musiknutzer und Produzenten (3rd ed.). NWV Neuer Wissenschaftlicher Verlag.

Fortnow, M., & Terry, Q. (2022). The NFT Handbook: How to create, sell and buy Non-Fungible Tokens. John Wiley & Sons, Inc., Hoboken, New Jersey.

Ginsburg, R. (2022). What is the Metaverse? A Complete Guide to Our Web3 Future. nftnow. Available at: https://nftnow.com/guides/what-is-the-metaverse-a-complete-guide-to-our-web3-future/ [Accessed 1 January 2024].

Grech, A., & Camilleri, A. (2017). Blockchain in Education. Available at: https://doi.org/10.2760/60649 [Accessed January 2020].

Hauck, F. (2022). Krypto-Crash. blockchaincenter.net. Available at: https://www.blockchaincenter.net/krypto-crash/ [Accessed 25 March 2023].

Hu, C., Chatfield, H., Xhjyl, J., Spallone, J., Hughes, G., & Landowski, B. (2021). The state of music/Web3 tools for artists. Water & Music. Available at: https://www.waterandmusic.com/the-state-of-music-web3-tools-for-artists/ [Accessed 1 January 2024].

Jutel, O. (2021). Blockchain imperialism in the Pacific. Big Data & Society, 8(1), 2053951720985249. Available at: https://doi.org/10.1177/2053951720985249.

Kaulartz, M., & Schmid, A. (2021). Rechtliche Herausforderungen sog. Non-Fungible Token (NFTs). Available at: https://www.cmshs-bloggt.de/tmc/rechtliche-herausforderungen-sog-non-fungible-token-nfts/ [Accessed 1 January 2024].

McLellan, J., & Leung, A. (2022). NFT Ownership and Intellectual Property: What Are Your Rights? Available at: https://www.haldanes.com/nft-ownership-and-intellectual-property-what-do-you-own/#_ftn6 [Accessed 25 March 2023].

Meuser, M., & Nagel, U. (2009). The expert interview and changes in knowledge production. In A. Bogner, B. Littig, & W. Menz (Eds.), Interviewing Experts (pp. 17-42). Palgrave Macmillan.

Nakamoto, S. (2008). Bitcoin: A Peer-to-Peer Electronic Cash System. Available at: https://bitcoin.org/bitcoin.pdf [Accessed January 2024].

Pfeiffer, A., Bezzina, S., & Wernbacher, T. (2021). Use of Blockchain Technologies Within the Creative Industry to Combat Fraud in the Production and (Re)Sale of Collectibles. In ECCWS 21 proceedings, https://doi.org/10.34190/EWS.21.055.

Smith, H. (2023). Bitcoin crash: what was behind the crypto collapse? The Times UK. Available at: https://www.thetimes.co.uk/money-mentor/article/is-bitcoin-crash-coming/ [Accessed 1 January 2024].

Using Chia Blockchain Technology for Department of Defense Systems

Ethan Schofield and Mark Reith
Air Force Institute of Technology, Wright Patterson Air Force Base, USA

ethan.schofield.1@au.af.edu
mark.reith.3@au.af.edu

Abstract: The United States faces an escalating cybersecurity challenge, with national assets increasingly vulnerable to sophisticated attacks. The ever-reducing barriers to entry in the cyber realm, coupled with advanced persistent threats, underscore the critical imperative to fortify the defense of U.S. assets. Blockchain technology, pioneered by Satoshi Nakamoto over a decade ago, emerges as a resilient cryptographic solution capable of safeguarding data and assets from threats both within and outside a network. This paper delves into the potential of the Chia blockchain as a strategic ally for the Department of Defense (DoD) in bolstering its cybersecurity measures. Beyond a theoretical exploration, the paper provides tangible use cases that illustrate the practical application of Chia within the DoD framework. Notably, the examination extends to crucial areas such as financial auditing, identification management, and supply chain oversight, showcasing the versatility and efficacy of Chia in addressing multifaceted challenges faced by the DoD.

Keywords: Blockchain, Government, Defense, Chia, Security, Applications

1. Introduction

Cyberspace today is a warfighting domain where actors from around the globe converge. Battles in cyberspace have few barriers to entry, allowing adversaries and threats, ranging from near-peer competitors to economically disadvantaged ones, to harm the United States and its resources. This necessitates the United States and the Department of Defense (DoD) to safeguard its assets with the latest advancements in cryptography and cybersecurity. Blockchain technology, as one of the latest cryptographic techniques, will be explored in this paper. It will delve into the basics of blockchain technology and argue why the Chia blockchain should be a strong candidate for adoption by the DoD. This is due to its ability to leverage the advantages of both public and private blockchains through Virtual Private Blockchains, and its capability to repurpose old Department of Defense data storage into new technological assets. The paper will also present a use case of Chia for DoD supply chain management.

The blockchain was first introduced in 2008 by Satoshi Nakamoto when he published the Bitcoin paper, 'Bitcoin: A Peer-to-Peer Electronic Cash System.' This paper outlines how cryptographic techniques on a peer-to-peer network can create an immutable, decentralized, and secure storage of data (Nakamoto, 2008). This creates data storage that has greater integrity than a traditional database, which after updating could have little to no evidence of any change. An analogy that illustrates how a blockchain works compares it to a small village where villagers traded frequently with one another (Khan, 2021). However, with how much trade was happening, they required a bookkeeper to keep track of all the trades and promises made between parties. After some time, the bookkeeper became corrupt and started accepting bribes to change what was owed. When the village discovered that the bookkeeper was corrupt, they implemented a new way to keep track of all the trades and promises between parties. The proposed solution was for every villager to keep a record. Throughout the day, villagers would meet in the town square to trade and write down what prices were agreed upon. Then, once a week the villagers would meet to check for discrepancies amongst the ledgers. If there were any, all ledgers would be crosschecked and the most frequently entered record would be assumed correct. The blockchain works similarly to every villager keeping a ledger. Every computer or node that is a part of the network keeps a record of what was sent, received, and stored on the blockchain. Generally, every node on the network can see what is on the blockchain but cannot change it without approval from the majority of nodes on the chain.

2. Blockchain Technology Overview

Every blockchain has three layers: consensus, smart contracts, and application. Consensus is how all the nodes on the blockchain decide to agree on the order of transactions submitted by clients in the form of requests (Clavin et al, 2020). In essence, it ensures that only one sequence of transactions is deemed correct. In cases of disagreement among nodes, the consensus method is referenced, and the correct sequence of transactions is selected based on the accumulated information. Next, smart contracts serve as the interface between consensus protocols and application layer-level implementations. This enables developers to create applications to run on the blockchain. Lastly, applications represent the user-facing aspects of the blockchain. Examples of application layers include the Philippine banking system, the Walmart/IBM supply chain initiative, and Malaysia's blockchain city.

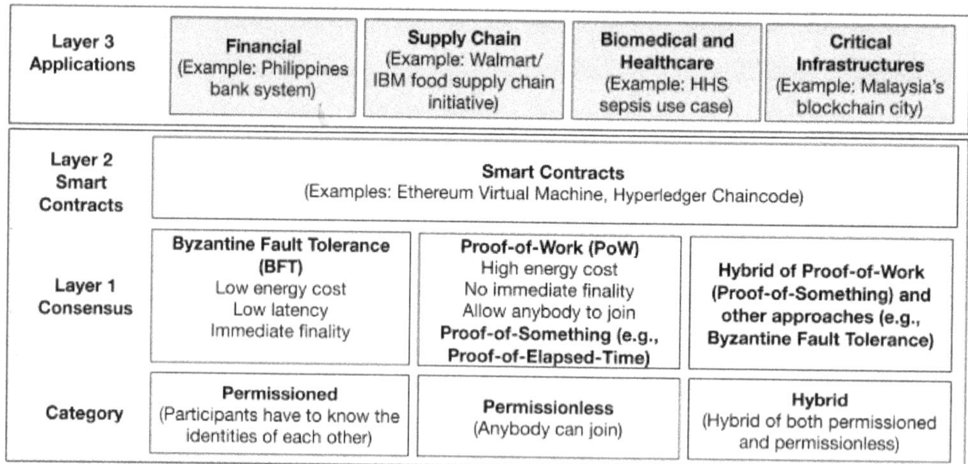

Layer 3 Applications
Financial (Example: Philippines bank system)
Supply Chain (Example: Walmart/ IBM food supply chain initiative)
Biomedical and Healthcare (Example: HHS sepsis use case)
Critical Infrastructures (Example: Malaysia's blockchain city)
Layer 2 Smart Contracts
Smart Contracts (Examples: Ethereum Virtual Machine, Hyperledger Chaincode)
Layer 1 Consensus
Byzantine Fault Tolerance (BFT) Low energy cost Low latency Immediate finality
Proof-of-Work (PoW) High energy cost No immediate finality Allow anybody to join Proof-of-Something (e.g., Proof-of-Elapsed-Time)
Hybrid of Proof-of-Work (Proof-of-Something) and other approaches (e.g., Byzantine Fault Tolerance)
Category
Permissioned (Participants have to know the identities of each other)
Permissionless (Anybody can join)
Hybrid (Hybrid of both permissioned and permissionless)

Figure. 1: Overview of Blockchain Technology with Potential Examples (Clavin et al., 2020)

2.1 Consensus Methods

Consensus or proof methods are how nodes on the blockchain verify that the newly added block is correct. There are various methods of proving that the next block should be added, each with unique attributes, such as power requirements, time to find the next block, and resource intensity. The two most prominent proof methods are proof of work and proof of stake.

The proof of work method is a computationally intensive operation where computer processing time is used to prove the next block on the chain. As explained by Satoshi Nakamoto, "The proof of work involves scanning for a value that when hashed, such as with SHA-256, the hash begins with a number of zero bits" (Nakamoto, 2008). While each blockchain has a specific algorithm that determines valid hash values, the underlying principle remains consistent. The computed value is quick to verify by other nodes as it can be verified by executing a single hash. Upon verification, nodes add the new block to their copy of the blockchain. Rival blockchains are addressed by this proof method, as the copy of the blockchain that is longer and verified by more nodes becomes the accepted or 'master' copy.

Proof of stake is an alternative method of proofing designed to address the 51 percent attack vulnerability inherent in proof of work and reduce overhead energy costs. The 51 percent attack occurs when an attacker gains control of the majority of nodes in a proof of work network, granting them complete control over the acceptance of transactions as correct. Proof of stake mitigates this risk by introducing the concept of 'coin age' (King & Nadal, 2012).

Coin age represents the financial investment in the blockchain and is calculated based on the time a coin is held and the amount held. For instance, if Bob possesses 50 coins held for 100 days, he accumulates 5000 coin-days of coin age. This concept is integral to proof of stake, as it limits the search space for the next hash. Specifically, the search space is constrained to "one hash per unspent walletoutput per second." (King & Nadal, 2012) In other words it is one hash per unit coin age. This is much more efficient than the unlimited search space of proof of work. Consequently, individuals with more coin age possess greater decision-making power, aligning decision influence with investment levels in the blockchain. This strategic integration of coin age in the proofing process enhances the security and efficiency of the proof of stake consensus mechanism.

2.2 Public, Private and Hybrid Blockchains

Public and private blockchains, also known as permissionless and permissioned blockchains, dictate access levels for reading, writing, and editing data on the blockchain. Public blockchains typically allow public access to both read and write data (Lewis, 2015). This openness promotes decentralization, immutability, and a diverse and large participant base. Consensus methods for public blockchains typically take the form of "proof of" models, like proof of work or proof of stake. These consensus methods are ideal for solving disputes on a trustless network and creating confidence in the transactions made on the network. However, challenges for public blockchains such as scalability and transaction speed may arise due to the extensive participation and competition among nodes for block validation.

In a private or permissioned blockchain, every participant on the network must receive approval from a central authority, enabling control over who can view, edit, or publish to the blockchain. For example, specific nodes may have publishing privileges, others may be limited to read-only access, or perhaps only designated nodes can access the blockchain (Yaga et al., 2018). Because all nodes require authorization to participate in the blockchain, a level of trust is established between them. Any misconduct can lead to the revocation of membership in the blockchain. Various consensus models can be employed in a permissioned network, depending on the level of trust among nodes. While both permissioned and permissionless blockchains implement smart contracts and the application layer similarly, the addition of a central authority in private blockchains sacrifices decentralization and immutability in order to ensure only authroized individuals have access to data on the chain.

Hybrid blockchains aim to combine the strengths of both public and private blockchains, seeking to strike a balance between the openness of public networks and the controlled access of private ones. To achieve this, they adopt specific measures to avoid shortcomings and enhance their capabilities. Hybrid blockchains strive to overcome the limitations of both public and private models by implementing a nuanced approach. They often involve integrating public and private elements selectively, tailoring the blockchain to meet specific use cases. Typically hybrid blockchains aim to harness the benefits of public blockchains, like decentralization, while also implementing features like controlled access from private chains for increased efficiency. For example, a hybrid blockchain might employ a public network for broader data access while using private channels for specific transactions or confidential information. Hybrid blockchains are tailored for specific use cases to take advantage of specific traits from public or private chains.

3. Smart Contracts

Smart contracts are coded instructions written into the blockchain, automatically executing when nodes reach consensus. The term "smart contracts" is derived from their resemblance to traditional business contracts, as they fulfill agreements made by multiple parties. The "smart" aspect refers to their seamless execution without disrupting blockchain operations. Developers can write a new smart contract that includes a set of functions. Once the contract is deployed on the blockchain, authorized users can call the contract to use those functions without interrupting other ongoing blockchain services. (Clavin et al, 2020)

However, the introduction of smart contracts also introduces potential vulnerabilities to the blockchain. As noted by J. Clavin, "Since all blockchain transactions are included in the hash chain,and therefore unchangeable,having a bug in the contract,or a flaw that can be exploited, introduces risk into the system. It is also worth noting that the use of smart contracts will likely degrade the performance of the system." (Clavin et al, 2020)

Smart contracts, while powerful and versatile, demand careful consideration and thorough testing to minimize the risk of introducing vulnerabilities to the blockchain system. The immutability of blockchain transactions amplifies the importance of ensuring that smart contracts are error-free and secure before deployment. Researchers have observed that the utilization of smart contracts may impact system performance, underscoring the need for ongoing research and optimization in this critical aspect of blockchain technology (Gueta et al., 2019).

4. Blockchain Applications

Blockchain applications represent the uppermost layer of the blockchain, encapsulating the tangible outcomes and functionalities that the blockchain system aims to achieve. All the underlying layers of consensus, smart contracts, and data structures converge to fulfill these applications. The scope of blockchain applications is broad, spanning critical infrastructure, healthcare, online gaming, and various other domains. Many large-scale blockchain applications are still in their early stages of development. For instance, the Chinese-funded tourist city in Malaysia's Melaka Straits (Property Report, 2019) and Canada's pilot on blockchain digital credentials are notable examples (Leal, 2022). In the Malaysian project, blockchain is employed to enhance the tourism experience and infrastructure, showcasing the versatility of blockchain in real-world applications. Canada's pilot program, on the other hand, explores the use of blockchain for maintaining permanent, independently owned copies of identification credentials by employees. These examples illustrate the diverse range of applications where blockchain technology is being explored and implemented.

5. Chia Blockchain

Chia, founded by Bram Cohen, is a blockchain platform that shares similarities with Bitcoin but distinguishes itself through its consensus model. Chia's consensus mechanism is known as "proof of space and time," a departure from Bitcoin's proof-of-work. This model leverages excess disk space, repurposing old hard drives from data centers to solve proofs for the blockchain (Cohen & Pietrzak, 2019).

While decentralization is a core principle of the Bitcoin blockchain, unintended centralization occurred, with a few large mining companies, such as NiceHash, controlling the majority of block mining on the network (Chia Network, 2021). This concentration of control poses challenges to the trustworthiness of a decentralized network, as increased influence by a single entity can impact decision-making on the blockchain. Proof of space in Chia resembles proof of work but with a new approach to finding the next hash value. Instead of processing various hashes, it involves storing cryptographic hash values on unused disk space. When the blockchain signals the need for a new block, it issues a challenge. Farmers, participants in the network, scan their disks to find the hash closest to the challenge. The probability of a farmer possessing the correct hash is proportional to their share of disk space in the entire network.

Proof of time is coupled with proof of space to enhance security. As proof of space is relatively quick to solve compared to proof of work, there is a risk of attackers with substantial storage creating competing long transaction chains. In most consensus models if there is a discrepancy between two chains the longer of the two is accepted as the correct history and the other is discarded. To address this, proof of time ensures consistent block additions over time, so parties that want to verify their own elections cannot.

Verifiable Delay Functions, (VDFs), are crucial for proof of time and are executed by servers known as "Timelords." These functions prevent fast completion and add assurance that the next block's validator will be chosen unpredictably. The blockchain only requires one trustworthy Timelord because the fastest Timelord will always execute the proof first. In order to help keep Timelord servers trustworthy Chia partnered with Supranational to produce an open-source proof of time VDF. Proof of time further adds confidence that the selection of the next block's validator will be highly unpredictable, reducing the likelihood of a party interested in a specific transaction becoming the next validator (Chia Network, 2021). This combination of proof of space and time establishes a robust and secure consensus mechanism in the Chia blockchain.

6. Why Chia for the DoD

Chia presents itself as a robust candidate for blockchain implementation by the DoD due to several compelling reasons. First, Chia offers a Virtual Private Blockchain. A unique technology native to Chia which combines the strengths of both public and private blockchains. This includes the decentralization of the entire Chia chain, but also allows to be uniquely programmable for the DoD's applications, have central governance over DoD operations and have permissioned access onto DoD applications. The flexibility to have the decentralization offered by a public blockchain, but the central governance and privacy of information of a private blockchain is crucial for DoD applications.

Chia's consensus layer, proof of space and time, is particularly conducive to the DoD. Given the DoD's possession of large quantities of old storage devices, repurposing these devices to support the blockchain is a sustainable and resourceefficient approach. Instead of discarding outdated hardware, the DoD can leverage its existing infrastructure to contribute to the blockchain's functionality.

Decentralization is a key aspect as to why Chia would be so powerful for the DoD. Decentralization offers strong reliability and trust in the information kept on the blockchain, and the applications executed on top of it. With a higher number of participating nodes, it becomes more challenging for malicious actors to gain control over the network and alter data. At the time Chia published their business whitepaper they claimed that they had "already become the most decentralized blockchain by node count ever." (Chia Network, 2021) This strong decentralization would create a trustworthy platform by ensuring data integrity and immutability.

The combination of decentralization and the Virtual Private Blockchain provides a secure and reliable environment for the DoD. Transactions within the Virtual Private Blockchain are verified by nodes on the entire Chia chain, enhancing security and integrity. Additionally, the permissioned access control further safeguards sensitive DoD applications. This unique combination of public and private chains is exactly what the DoD would need to have for blockchain adaption.

Some may suggest that public blockchains like Ethereum or Cardano may be a better choice for DoD use. However, there are several issues with both of these chains for use by the DoD. First, both are proof of stake, this is not ideal for DoD use because an adversary would only need to buy up a large share of the asset to have substantial voting power on the network. An adversary having control over decisions that affect DoD assets would not be secure. Next, Ethereum's smart contract language and programming environment makes it very difficult for projects to scale. (Chia Network, 2021) Projects launched on their network suffer the same security issues all around, making it a familiar attack surface. Finally, Cardano's network consists of only about 6000 nodes, this is relatively small compared to other public chains. For activities involving national security this is not enough decentralization for a blockchain.

Others may suggest that if public blockchains are not ideal, then the DoD should use a private blockchain like Ripple or Stellar. The primary issue around using a private blockchain is it would remove benefits from public blockchains, with the most important being decentralization. If the blockchain is not decentralized, then it is almost the same as storing data and doing transactions on a standard database. Switching from a standard database that is in use today, to a private blockchain would not be worth the taxpayer money, or the time to implement for such a marginal gain.

7. DoD Chia Use Cases

The existing auditing and funding procedures within the DoD, including the Army Financial System, involve multiple stages such as contract awardation, invoices, receipts, and payment requests. This intricate process introduces several vulnerabilities, including the potential for incorrect accounting, embezzlement, or mismanagement of funds. Transitioning to a blockchain-based system offers a transformative solution. By migrating the current system onto a blockchain, the DoD can publish and maintain contracts with the confidence that the data recorded at the contract's inception remains immutable. The blockchain's inherent immutability ensures that once the contract data is stored, it cannot be altered in the future, providing a secure and transparent foundation for auditing and funding processes. This shift holds the promise of minimizing errors, enhancing accountability, and mitigating the risks associated with financial mismanagement within the DoD.

In a thesis exploring blockchain use to track DoD auditing and funding it was determined that a private permissioned blockchain would be the best use for the DoD and its vendors (Prasanna, 2022). Permissionless public blockchains were not ideal because anyone, including foreign adversaries could join and read, write, and edit data. Next, permissioned public blockchains were not chosen over permissioned private blockchains because the Freedom of Information Act Exemption 4 states that trade secrets and financial information between contractor and government agency can be made confidential (Congress, 2016). If all vendors and contractors are added to the same permissioned public chain then all vendors could see contracts between the DoD and other vendors.

Chia's Virtual Private Blockchain can address the challenge posed by the Freedom of Information Act Exemption 4, allowing trade secrets and financial information between the DoD and contractors to remain confidential. By setting up individual virtual private blockchains between each vendor and the DoD, sensitive information can be protected without compromising transparency within the network. This would enable the decentralization benefits of the Chia blockchain at the cost of additional setup.

The implementation of Chia's Virtual Private Blockchain holds significant potential for managing independently owned identification within the Department of Defense (DoD). By incorporating all DoD members into the virtual private blockchain, a robust and verifiable platform for identification verification can be established. This strategic use case not only enhances security measures but also ensures the integrity of identification information by rendering it tamper-proof. Shifting DoD identification onto the blockchain introduces a powerful deterrent against malicious actors attempting to spoof or steal DoD identification cards. The utilization of unique private keys for each individual on the blockchain becomes a crucial security feature. Without possessing the designated private key, unauthorized individuals would be unable to impersonate someone else. This innovative approach not only bolsters the security of military bases but also enhances protection for areas requiring security clearance access. The adoption of Chia's Virtual Private Blockchain in this context reflects a proactive measure to elevate the overall security posture of DoD identification systems.

Supply chain management within the Department of Defense (DoD) can leverage Chia effectively. In addressing concerns raised by the Government Accountability Office in its report to Congress, which highlighted vulnerabilities to counterfeit parts within the DoD supply chain (United States Government Accountability Office, 2016), the implementation of a Chia-powered blockchain becomes crucial. Establishing a virtual private blockchain that involves all relevant vendors enables comprehensive tracking of parts, their conditions, and shipping information. Not only would this blockchain solution allow the DoD to monitor the entire supply chain but it also facilitates accountability, transparency, and honesty on part of the vendors providing what was agreed upon. Specifics that could be monitored by the DoD include, monitoring parts modifications en route, identifying potential breakages during transportation, and ensuring product authenticity (Pun et al., 2018). Chia's blockchain technology emerges as a robust tool to effectively address these challenges and fortify the integrity of the DoD's supply chain.

8. Conclusion

The examination of Chia's applicability in key DoD use cases, such as financial auditing, identification management, and supply chain oversight, underscores its versatility and effectiveness. The Virtual Private Blockchain's integration into these scenarios not only aligns with the DoD's security requirements but also introduces a higher level of transparency and reliability in critical processes. Chia's decentralized architecture, combined with the tailored approach of the Virtual Private Blockchain, positions it as a strong candidate for securing and managing sensitive information within the DoD. While this paper provides insights into the potential applications of Chia's Virtual Private Blockchain, future research could delve deeper into the nuances of its implementation across various use cases. Exploring the intricacies of financial auditing, identification management, and supply chain oversight with Chia's blockchain technology would contribute valuable insights into its real-world efficacy. Understanding how the Virtual Private Blockchain enhances security benefits compared to traditional blockchains and private permissioned blockchains could pave the way for more informed decisionmaking within the DoD. Future investigations can illuminate the specific advantages and considerations of adopting Chia in different DoD contexts, and providing a comprehensive roadmap for its successful integration into the nation's cybersecurity framework.

References

Abraham, I., Gueta, G. G., Grossman, S., Malkhi, D., Pinkas, B., Reiter, M., ... Tomescu, A. (2019). *Sbft: A scalable and decentralized trust infrastructure.*

Chia Network. (2021). *Chia network inc. business whitepaper.*

Clavin, J., Duan, S., Zhang, H., Janeja, V. P., Joshi, K. P., Yesha, Y., ... Li, J. D. (2020). *Blockchains for government. Digital Government: Research and Practice, 1, 1–21.*

Cohen, B., & Pietrzak, K. (2019). *The chia network blockchain.*

Congress, 114th. (2016). *The Freedom of Information Act, 5 U.S.C. § 552, Jun.*

Doherty, N., & Delener, N. (2001). *Chaos Theory: Marketing and Management Implications. Journal of Marketing Theory and Practice, Fall, 9(4), 66–75.*

Khan, D. (2021). *3 analogies that explain how blockchain technology works.*

King, S., & Nadal, S. (2012). *Ppcoin: Peer-to-peer crypto-currency with proof-of-stake. Self-published paper, August, 19(1).*

Leal, N. (2022). *Canada pilots blockchain staff records.*

Lewis, A. (2015). *A gentle introduction to blockchain technology.*

Nakamoto, S. (2008). *Bitcoin: A peer-to-peer electronic cash system.*

Pun, H., Swaminathan, J. M., & Hou, P. (2018). *Blockchain adoption for combating deceptive counterfeits.*

Prasanna, P. (2022). *The use of blockchain to track dod funding and auditing.*

Property Report. (2019). *Malaysia is building Asia's first blockchain city.*

United States Government Accountability Office. (2016). *Dod needs to improve reporting and oversight to reduce supply chain risk report to congressional committees.*

Yaga, D., Mell, P., Roby, N., & Scarfone, K. (2018). *Blockchain technology overview.*

Cyber Operations in Ukraine: Emerging Patterns in Cases

Markus Takamaa and Martti Lehto
University of Jyväskylä, Finland

markus.k.t.takamaa@jyu.fi
martti.j.lehto@jyu.fi

Abstract: The Ukrainian state has been a target of cyber-related incidents since the annexation of Crimea in 2014. Cyberattacks have targeted Ukrainian critical infrastructure, government offices, and several public and private organisations. Sometimes, these cyberattacks have caused significant impacts within the nation's borders. Some of the most well-known cyber-incidents in Ukraine include attacks on the Ukrainian electrical grid, which cut out the power supply for hundreds of thousands of people in 2015 and 2016. Attacks have also targeted presidential election systems and financial entities operating in Ukraine. The majority of attacks within Ukraine's borders have been attributed to Russian-affiliated non-state actors and organisations, and the number of attacks correlates with the escalation of the war in 2022. This implies previous cyberattacks potentially belonging to a series of hybrid operations related to the Ukrainian conflict and the general geopolitical situation since the annexation of Crimea. The paper focuses on this context by examining cyber incidents targeting Ukraine since 2014. We study the unifying factors related to Ukrainian cyber incidents, and we will discuss emerging patterns related to the attacks during the last ten years. This study will uncover the general traits of state-affiliated attacks in Ukraine, which will help uncover emerging patterns. Our particular focus will be cyber-attacks, where the target is the Ukrainian state and its critical infrastructure. We will examine methods of attacks, the attack targets, and the impacts, among other things. With the patterns emerging from our study, we can predict future cyber-attacks targeting Ukraine, providing tools for preparing for future incidents. We can use the information to improve national cyber-defences, where the attacks are likely to happen in the future. Studying the Ukrainian cases may also provide additional insights for improving cyber defences in other nation-states within the parts that apply to these nation-states and their geopolitical contexts.

Keywords: Cyber Warfare, Cyber-Attack, Cyber Incident, Ukrainian Conflict, Digital Warfare

1. Introduction

Numerous cyber-attacks have hit Ukraine since the start of the current conflict. During the last ten years, attacks in Ukraine have targeted the electricity grid, electoral systems, and army organisations, to name a few. Cyber-attacks have been used numerous times throughout the years and have affected Ukrainian organisations in various ways and effects. It is also likely the attacks will continue striking the nation in the future as the conflict continues within different parts of Ukraine.

The goal of this paper is to examine these previous cyber-attacks in Ukraine during the last ten years. We discuss the cases starting from the annexation of Crimea and proceed to study the attacks throughout the current conflict. We aim to explore the methods used and determine the general patterns the most notable attacks follow. The goal is to discover the general nature of the attacks to understand how cyber operations are used as a part of warfare during the conflict. By doing this, we hope to provide information for assessing the general methods by which these cyberattacks may also occur in the future. We also aim to highlight the cases that harness the most attention within the publicly available sources and focus on patterns discovered from these cases.

In this paper, we first examine general aspects related to cyber-operations and discuss their use as part of general warfare. After this, we examine the overall situation in Ukraine and the cases of cyberattacks occurring throughout the years. We further explore the details of these attacks and attempt to make new conclusions based on the results discovered. We further evaluate the results and assess the meaning of the potential discoveries emerging from the cases. Based on the results, we come to our conclusions regarding the long-term situation in Ukraine and bring awareness to how cyberattacks are used as a part of inter-state conflicts.

2. Background

In this chapter, we will first examine cyber operations and their general use within Ukraine based on previously harnessed information.

Cyber operations are actions in or through cyberspace aiming to create effects on the target's actions (Laari, 2019). They can come in various forms and have different goals based on their actor's and target's relationship. Generally, Cyber operations can be divided into offensive and defensive operations based on the objectives.

Offensive cyber operations are cyberattacks used to project power by applying force through cyberspace and are generally aggressive in their nature. Defensive ones, in turn, aim to protect one's cyber-physical environment and can be both passive and active in their actions (Theohary, 2021). The active ones consist of direct defensive actions taken to reduce or nullify the effectiveness of cyber threats, and the passive ones focus more on protecting one's own cyber infrastructure from possible threats (Turunen & Kari, 2020). From offensive and defensive cyber operations, this paper examines the nature of offensive ones, focusing on attacks targeting Ukraine.

Cyber operations may be used with various tools and purposes. For example, they can act as a method for conducting the actions of warfare. In this context, their use as part of military operations may be called cyber warfare. Cyber warfare is a broad term and may refer to several nation-state actions aiming to achieve objectives in or through cyberspace (Goel, 2020).

Cyber warfare can be defined as the use of armed attacks in or through cyberspace to impose a nation-state's political will onto another nation-state (Applegate, 2015). These involve non-kinetic attacks on information data and its collection process aimed at damaging, disrupting or destroying the target's decision-making processes or normal operations. Cyber warfare encompasses using all the digital tools available to paralyse or destroy the other party's ICT-technology-based systems while keeping one's systems operational. (Lehto & Henselmann, 2020). Often, cyber warfare has been categorised as part of hybrid warfare, which refers to using all non-kinetic forms of combat alongside the traditional forms of warfare. These other forms of hybrid warfare can also include, for example, information operations and energy blockades alongside cyber-attacks (Boyte, 2017).

Cyber warfare has been used extensively as part of the ongoing conflict in Ukraine, and they show how cyber-attacks can be used to conduct inter-state conflicts. Some commonly known cases include cyberattacks targeting Ukrainian electrical infrastructure in 2015 and 2016, each paralysing the electrical distribution within different parts of Ukraine (Kostyk & Zhukov, 2019). Cyberattacks targeting Ukraine also intensified during the escalation of the conflict in 2022, when the number of foreign troops increased significantly within the country. Since then, online activities towards Ukraine have been aimed at destroying, disrupting or infiltrating the various governmental bodies and critical infrastructure organisations (Microsoft, 2022).

Between January 2022 and September 2023, the CyberPeace Institute documented a total of 174 incidents against different entities in Ukraine. In this timeframe, their study indicated that DDoS attacks consisted of almost 71,3% of the observed attacks. The public administration was also seen as the most targeted sector between July and September 2022 (Cyber Peace Institute, 2023a). In the analysis made by CSIS (Centre for Strategic & International Studies) in 2022, almost 60 percent of the targets of the cyber-attacks were private non-state actors, just over 30 percent were government nonmilitary actors, and just over 10 percent were government military actors (Mueller et al., 2023).

The operations of 2022 in Ukraine correspond to the principles of the Russian so-called Gerasimov doctrine[1], according to which:

- Reduction of the state's military-economic potential by destroying critically important facilities of their military and civilian infrastructure in a short time.
- Warfare simultaneously in all physical environments and the information space.
- The use of asymmetric and indirect operations.
- Command-and-control of forces and assets in a unified information space.

In exchange for the Western concept of hybrid warfare, Russia has developed its own concept: New Generation Warfare (Russian. Война нового поколения). As part of the doctrine, continuous cyber operations are conducted below the threshold of war beyond the reach of attribution. (Kari, 2019, 54)

Russian doctrines include the concept of information warfare, which consists of two elements:

1. Information Technology-based – The target is critical infrastructure.

---

[1] Gerasimov Doctrine based on General Valery Gerasimov's annual speech and presentation at the Russian Military Academy of Science in March 2013 and interpretations of some Russian analysts.

2. Information Psychology-based – The target in the human mind, the moral and mental world of man, socio-political and psychological orientation, or decision-maker's ability to make decisions.

From a Western point of view, Russia has combined cyber operations and information operations into a single entity, where the goal of the information war is:

- Generating losses on information systems, processes, resources, and critical or other structures.
- Paralysis of political, economic, and social systems.
- Massive psychological surgery to unbalance society and the state.

(Kari, 2016)

As we can notice from the previous information, most of the recent discussion of the situation in Ukraine has focused on the events during and after the escalation of the conflict in 2022, leaving the previous events with less attention. Therefore, to understand the situation regarding the overall progression of the conflict, there is a need to examine and bring awareness of the long-term patterns since the annexation of the Crimean Peninsula by Russia. This study aims to focus on this timeframe in Ukraine since 2014.

However, it should be noted that attributing the cyber-attacks to any nation-state actors has often been challenging in the past. This is due to the natural anonymity as a core part of the internet, which enables state actors to perform their online actions often unnoticed (Goel, 2020). Proper attribution of cyber-attacks is considered to be important in justifying countermeasures against the correct nation-state perpetrator of the attacks (Goel, 2020). Still though, the international law regarding the attribution of cyberattacks has remained undefined for the moment (Banks, 2021). However, the technical tools for attribution have improved in recent years, making states declare the potential actors behind the attack more often (Goel, 2020; Banks, 2021).

3. Research and Methods

Next, we will further examine the use of cyber operations during the current Ukrainian conflict. In our examination, we will attempt to find answers to the following questions:

Q1: Can we uncover patterns from cyber incidents targeting Ukraine since 2014?

Q2; If patterns are uncovered, what kind of patterns are these?

We examine the notable cases during the last ten years in Ukraine, of which we can collect information from public sources. These sources can be journal articles, reports, and other publications for example. We collect information from these sources and examine the details of the previous incidents. We use comparison on the collected information on the cases and examine the potential emerging patterns and trends from the incidents overall. In our study, we especially focus on incidents that have affected normal operations within the Ukrainian state. We collect information from the cases' details, such as the attack methods, the targets, and the overall impacts of the events. Based on the discovered data, we will also subjectively evaluate these incidents' potential goals and objectives.

The cases selected for our study examination are based on the availability of the information. We will start conducting the study by searching for mentions of previous cyberattacks in Ukraine and attempt to find more details by examining more data on each case from the public sources available. We then insert the gathered information on the cases in a table, which helps examine the overall patterns of the observed cases. If only limited information is available on the case, we will leave these unexamined within our study. By collecting all this data, our qualitative study aims to provide the first glimpse into the nature of cyber-attacks in Ukraine in the last ten years. By this, we hope to provide new information on the trends and patterns emerging in these cases.

Due to the issues caused by the attribution problem for evaluating the culprit of these attacks from public sources, we will leave the most likely actors of the incidents unexamined within the scope of our study. It should be noted that within the West, Russia and Russian state-affiliated groups have often been said to have performed previous attacks, especially the cases regarding Ukraine. Also, we will leave espionage and influence operations unexamined within the Ukrainian cyber environment in our study and focus on other cyber incidents affecting normal operations within Ukraine. Further, since the study is based on publicly available sources, those potential cases yet to be brought to public attention are unincluded within the study data.

Our objective in studying previous cyber-attacks is to examine the long-term threats targeting Ukraine in or through cyberspace. By this study, we hope to discover the long-term trends in the nation-state level. The discoveries may be used to forecast the potential attack mechanisms and targets in the future, which can be used to harden the protection of the potential targets' cyber environment before any possible offensive cyber operations occur. The discovered data could be used to pre-emptively improve the security of the it-systems in other nation-states, considering the parts of their practical and geopolitical contexts where they are similar or equal regarding Ukraine now or in the future. In addition, we aim to highlight the cases which are brought to attention in the publicly available sources and have the most visibility within them.

Next, we will examine the cases in detail and evaluate the data available from public sources.

4. Cases Examined in the Study

The following table shows the most important and well-known cyberattacks on Ukraine, which also have publicly available information.

Table 1:

Event	Date	Attack method	Target	Impact	Potential objectives
DDoS attack before the referendum on the status of Crimea (Przetacznik & Tarpova, 2022; Weedon, 2018)	March, 2014	DDoS	Official government and media websites	Sites unavailable for up to multiple hours	Disruption of online services
An attempt to delete the results of the presidential election of 2014 (Weedon, 2015)	May, 2014	Malware	Ukraine's Central Election Commission	Impacts prevented by Ukraine's Security Service (SBU)	Election interference
DDoS attack on Election counting systems (Clayton, 2014)	May, 2014	DDoS	Ukraine's election counting systems	Election counting blocked for 2 hours, delaying the final results of the vote	Election interference
BlackEnergy (Izycki & Vianna, 2021)	December, 2015	Trojan	Ukrainian electricity distribution network	Disruption of energy services for hundreds of thousands of people for 1-6 hours	Disruption of energy services
2016 attack on the Ukrainian power grid (Simons, Danyk & Maliarchuk, 2020)	December, 2016	Malware	Ukrenergo's (Ukraine's national grid operator) network	Disruption of energy services around Kyiv for around an hour	Disruption of energy services
NotPetya (Izycki & Vianna, 2021)	June, 2017	Wiper -attack disguised as ransomware	Various critical infrastructure organizations and companies	destruction of data of close to 10 percent of computers in Ukraine and impacts on various companies globally	Destruction of computers, disruption of normal operations
WhisperGate -attack (Microsoft Digital Security Unit, 2022; Dutta, 2022)	January, 2022	Wiper attack disguised as ransomware	Ukrainian government and IT organizations	destruction of computers	Destruction of data and disabling of normal operations
Attack on the KA-SAT-satellite network (Przetacznik & Tarpova, 2022; Cyber Peace Institute, 2022)	February, 2022	Wiper attack	modems used to communicate with the KA-SAT-satellite network	Communication outages for several thousand people up to two weeks	Disruption of communication services

Event	Date	Attack method	Target	Impact	Potential objectives
DDoS attacks on government websites and Ukrainian bank systems (Regional Cyber Defence Centre, 2023)	February, 2022	DDoS	Web resources of Ukrainian banks and state institutions	Disruption of the availability of web services	Disruption of services
HermeticWiper -attack (Grossman et al., 2023; Lehto, 2022)	February, 2022	Wiper-attack	300 systems, such as dozens of financial, government, energy, information technology, and agricultural organizations	destruction of computers	Destruction of data, disruption of normal operations
Attack on Ukrainian state organization (Cyber Peace Institute, 2023b)	April, 2023	Wiper and BASH script attack	Ukrainian state organisations	Destruction and disabling of computers	Destruction of data and disabling of normal operations
Wiper attack on Ukraine's largest telecom operator, Kyivstar (Antoniuk, 2023; Antoniuk, 2024)	December, 2023	wiper-attack	Telecommunications in Ukraine	Disruption of telecommunication services for days	Disruption of telecommunication services

5. Results

The examination of the cases suggests that the cases available from public sources follow general patterns in Ukraine. In these cases, the most common attack tools have been various forms of malware and DDoS attacks. From the malware types, wiper attacks are most mentioned in the cases. These are malware, whose primary purpose is to wipe out the contents of the infected computer's hard drive, which disables the ability to turn on the computer, making it inoperable. Based on these cases, the goal of the considerable number of examined cases has been to make the infected systems inoperable, thus disrupting the daily operations dependent on these systems. Some cases also seem to have aimed to temporarily slow down the normal operations in Ukraine by using DDoS as a method of attack.

In addition, most target organisations can be considered part of the critical infrastructure in Ukraine, while governmental organisations have also been targeted in some cases. The number of cyber-attacks targeting Ukraine seems to be also correlating with the significant events of the conflict, such as the occupation of Crimea and the escalation of the conflict at the start of 2022. Based on this, there is a clear link between the events of the conflict and the timing of cyber-attacks targeting Ukraine.

6. Conclusions and Discussion

The results examine the various cases targeting Ukraine. Most of these cases seem to be aimed at causing damage to the information systems, preventing everyday actions dependent on these systems, and bringing extra expenses to Ukrainian organisations with repair costs and lost work hours. Many of the attacks seem to have aimed to maximise their impact on Ukrainian society by causing as much of the effects within the nation as possible. NotPetya and Hermaticwiper -cases have been especially aimed at affecting Ukrainian society broadly. This would indicate that the main objective of these cyber operations is to undermine the functioning of Ukrainian society. Based on this, the attack targets, and the observed correlation between cyber-attacks and significant events of the conflict, most of the observed cases follow similar patterns with Russian information warfare strategies and doctrines throughout the years.

It should be noted, however, that the limitations of the study leave some nation-state activities online outside the scope of this study. These activities include espionage and operations targeting the public perception, which have been observed to be very common. More studies can be done to examine these other kinds of online operations in the Ukraine context further.

In addition, since most of the cases observed have had significant impacts on Ukrainian society, these effects might explain their visibility within the publicly available information. This visibility could impact the nature of cases and their patterns observed in the study. The cases with more minor effects may be left with less attention on the public material, making these more challenging to observe throughout the years. Further studies may be conducted to examine the potential correlation between the effects of the attacks and their public visibility.

Overall, the results indicate that offensive cyber operations are aimed at weakening the ability to operate in Ukraine. The results could be used to anticipate techniques, timing, and targets of cyberattacks if future conflicts arise within societies that have integrated IT technology-based solutions into their regular operating capabilities. In these scenarios, utilising technology may become a significant supporting tool for the toolbox of warfare.

References

Antoniuk, S. (2023) *"Ukraine's largest telecom operator shut down after cyberattack",* The Record. December 12th, 2023. Viewed 15.01.2024. https://therecord.media/kyivstar-cyberattack-telecom-shutdown-ukraine

Antoniuk, S. (2024) *"Russian hackers infiltrated Ukrainian telecom giant month before cyberattack",* The Record. January 4th, 2024. Viewed 15.01.2024. https://therecord.media/russians-infiltrated-kyivstar-months-before

Applegate, S. (2015) "Cyber Conflict: Disruption and Exploitation in the Digital age", in Lemieux, F. (eds.), *Current and emerging trends in cyber operations: Policy, Strategy and Practice*. Basigstoke: Palgrave Macmillan. pp. 19-36.

Banks, W. (2021) "Cyber Attribution and State Responsibility", *International Law Studies*, Vol 91, pp 1040-1072.

Boyte, K. (2017) "A Comparative Analysis of the Cyberattacks Against Estonia, the United States, and Ukraine", *International Journal of Cyber Warfare and Terrorism*, Vol 7, No. 2 pp 54-69.

Clayton, M. (2014) *"Ukraine election narrowly avoided 'wanton destruction' from hackers",* The Christian Science Monitor. June 17th, 2014. Viewed 15.01.2024. https://www.csmonitor.com/World/Passcode/2014/0617/Ukraine-election-narrowly-avoided-wanton-destruction-from-hackers

Cyber Peace Institute (2022) *Case Study: Viasat, June 2022*, Cyber Peace Institute. Viewed 22.01.2024. https://cyberconflicts.cyberpeaceinstitute.org/law-and-policy/cases/viasat

Cyber Peace Institute (2023a) *Cyber Dimensions of the Armed Conflict in Ukraine: Quarterly Analysis report Q3 July to September 2023*, Cyber Peace Institute.

Cyber Peace Institute (2023b) *Cyber Dimensions of the Armed Conflict in Ukraine: Quarterly Analysis report Q2 April to June 2023*, Cyber Peace Institute.

Dutta, S. "Cyber Operations Associated with the Ukraine-Russia Conflict: An Open-Source Assessment", in Chauhan, P., Lahiri, D. and Kumar, R. (eds.), *Maritime perspectives 2022: Non-traditional Dimensions of Maritime Security,* New Delhi: National Maritime Foundation. pp 346-361

Goel, S. (2020) "How Improved Attribution in Cyber Warfare Can Help De-Escalate Cyber Arms Race", *Connections*, Winter, Vol 19, No. 1, pp. 87-95.

Grossmann, T., Kaminska, M., Shires, J., and Smeets, M. (2023) The Cyber Dimensions of the Russia-Ukraine war, ECCRI workshop report. The European Cyber Conflict Research Initiative.

Izycki, E. and Vianna, E. (2021) "Critical Infrastructure: A Battlefield for Cyber Warfare?", *Proceedings of the 16th International Conference on Cyber Warfare and Security, ICCWS 2021,* 25 – 26 February 2021. Online. pp. 454–464.

Kari M. (2016) "Cyber fortress under siege - The cyber threat to Russia according to Russian public documents", JYU MSc thesis, University of Jyväskylä 2016

Kari M. (2019) "Russian Strategic Culture in Cyberspace: Theory of Strategic Culture – a tool to Explain Russia´s Cyber Threat Perception and Response to Cyber Threats", JYU academic dissertation 122, University of Jyväskylä

Kostyk, N. and Zhukov, Y. (2019) "Invisible Digital Front: Can Cyber Attacks Shape Battlefield Events?", *Journal of Conflict Resolution,* Vol 63, No. 2, pp 317–347.

Laari, T. (2019*) #Kyberpuolustus, Kyberkäsikirja puolustusvoimien henkilöstölle*, Helsinki: National Defense University.

Lehto, M. (2020) "Cyber warfare: The new game changer in the battlespace", *Cyberwatch magazine*, 2022(2), pp 21-26.

Lehto, M. and Hanselmann, G. (2020) "Non-kinetic warfare – The new game changer in the battle space", *15 th International Conference on Cyber Warfare and Security*, 12-13 March 2020, Old Dominion University, Norfolk, Virginia, USA, pp 316-25.

Microsoft (2022) *Special report: Ukraine – an overview of Russia's cyberattack activity in Ukraine*. Digital Security Unit. 27th April, 2022

Microsoft Digital Security Unit (2022) *"destructive malware targeting Ukrainian organizations,* Microsoft. January 15th, 2021. Viewed 17.01.2024. https://www.microsoft.com/en-us/security/blog/2022/01/15/destructive-malware-targeting-ukrainian-organizations/

Mueller, G., Jensen, B., Valeriano, B., Maness, R, and Macias J. (2023) *Cyber Operations during the Russo-Ukrainian War from Strange Patterns to Alternative Futures*, CSIS report July 2023. https://www.csis.org/analysis/cyber-operations-during-russo-ukrainian-war

Regional cyber defence centre (2023) *Report on Cyber Lessons Learned during the War in Ukraine,* Vilnius: Regional cyber defence centre.

Przetacznik, J. & Tarpova, S. (2022) *Russia's war in Ukraine: Timeline of Cyber-attacks,* Brieffing of the European Parliament, June 2022. European Parliamentary Research Service.

Simons, G., Danyk, Y. and Maliarchuk, T. (2020) "Hybrid war and cyber-attacks: creating legal and operational dilemmas", *Global change, peace & security,* Vol 32, No. 3, pp 337–342.

Theohary, C. (2021) *Defensive primer: Cyberspace operations*, Congressional Research Service report, 1 December.

Turunen, M. and Kari, M. (2020) "Cyber deterrence and Russia's active cyber defensive", *Proceedings of the 19 the European Conference on Cyber Warfare and Security*, 25-26 June 2020, Online, pp 526-532.

Weedon, J. (2015) "Beyond 'Cyber War': Russia's Use of Strategic Cyber Espionage and Information Operations in Ukraine", From Kenneth Geers (Ed.), *"Cyber War in Perspective: Russian Aggression against Ukraine*", Tallinn: NATO CCD COE Publications.

Cyber Game-Based Learning for DoD CEs

Jillian Valente and Mark Reith
Air Force Institute of Technology, Wright-Patterson AFB, USA
jillian.valente.1@au.af.edu
mark.reith.3@au.af.edu

Abstract: Cyber competition and conflict remain an enduring concern for the Department of Defense (DoD). Positive control of cyberspace is crucial across the vast diversity of military operations and supporting activities. People play an important role in cyber prevention, detection, and remediation, but they receive relatively little training outside of the annual Cyber Awareness Challenge. While this gamified training is a reasonable baseline, it primarily addresses cybersecurity from the office worker's perspective. Other career fields within the DoD may benefit from specialized training in cybersecurity, in particular the civil engineering (CE) community supporting critical infrastructure protection. This paper surveys a range of contemporary cyber serious games and assesses each for potential inclusion into CE training. Furthermore, it suggests game elements and characteristics that are likely to benefit the CE community.

Keywords: Cyber, Game-Based Learning, DoD, Cyber Learning, Learning Objectives, Bloom's Taxonomy

1. Introduction

Cyber is critical in today's warfighting domain. Due to its low barrier of entry, it has leveled the playing field between the U.S. and its adversaries. Today, everything from personal addresses, social security numbers, and banking information to the military's intelligence operations, planning, and communication systems are all stored virtually. If an international conflict were to occur, a breach of data could be a contributing factor between success and failure. Due to its importance for maintaining global security, members of the Department of Defense (DoD) must be prepared to defend and respond in this dynamic battlespace. This requires service members to have a strong foundation of cyber skills.

Many methods are available for DoD members to advance their knowledge in cyber. One such way is the Cyber Awareness Challenge taken by all DoD members. This is important because cyber vulnerabilities are often exploited on the cyber-persona layer since human error is often the greatest weakness of cyberspace (USAF, 2023*)*. Another example are the techniques used to teach cyber operators. They use mainly classroom-based discussions and exercises in virtual environments (Galbraith, 2019). Benefits arise from these tactics, yet superior methods exist that can offer more thought-provoking and memorable ways to learn. Serious games offer a promising avenue for enhancing the cyber learning experience for DoD members by engaging them in interactive environments that promote active learning, critical thinking, and skill development. This will ultimately contribute to the readiness and effectiveness of the armed forces in the realm of cybersecurity. The paper focuses on a particular military career field: civil engineering (CE) students at the Air Force Institute of Technology (AFIT) at Wright Patterson AFB. All CE professionals in the Air Force, prior to achieving the rank of Technical Sergeant, must attend the Advanced Control Systems Cybersecurity (WENG 270) program. It is a four-day, thirty-two credit hour course. Topics included in the syllabus are risk management, malicious logic, and basic networking cybersecurity principles (Kulesza, 2023). The course themes are mapped to key domains of Security+ and Certified Information System Security Professional (CISSP) certifications. The curriculum focuses on operational technology (OT) devices such as programmable logic controllers (PLCs), heating, ventilation, and air conditioning (HVAC) systems, and waste management.

OT is an increasingly relevant domain within cybersecurity. Vault Typhoon is the recent surge of malicious activities associated with the People's Republic of China on U.S. critical infrastructure (CISA, 2023). A primary tactic used by the actor is the living off the land (LOTL) attack. It allows the actor to blend in with the system operations to evade detection (CISA, 2023). Vault Typhoon is one of many instances of U.S. critical infrastructure attacks. It demonstrates the urgent need of OT educated workers in the DoD to recognize and defend against these attacks.

This paper merges a variety of survey, hypothesis, and design of experiment papers to answer the following research question:

RQ: What learning concepts are currently represented in modern cyber serious games?

The contribution of this paper is the proposition of using cyber serious games focused on OT devices in the DoD. The paper is organized as follows: Section 2 discusses background research and defines learning and serious games. Section 3 describes different types of serious games used in the DoD. Section 4 proposes a cyber learning game that incorporates OT devices that would be beneficial for DoD CE students. Section 5 concludes the paper and provides information for further research.

2. Background

Cyber knowledge is important to the DoD's ability to function not only in the warfighting domain but also in routine operations. Millions of emails are sent over the DoD network each day, displaying the importance of communication. Cyber is also used to maintain and upgrade the software of everything from fighter jets and satellites to myPay and LeaveWeb. For this reason, DoD members need to be educated on how to prevent the exploitation of these systems. The following subsections will introduce the concepts of learning and serious games, and how these are the basis for increasing cyber learning among DoD members.

2.1 Learning

The rapid onset of technology has not changed the human ability to process information, but it can be used to aid and accelerate the learning process. One of the theoretical perspectives for human learning is cognitivism. This theory considers the different types of memory and how information is encoded into the brain. The three types of memory are sensory, working, and long-term. For working memory to be transferred into long-term memory, it needs to be encoded through visual, auditory, verbal, semantic, or episodic cues (Craig, 2020). The cognitive load theory (CLT) is another key concept in cognitivism. It theorizes that an overload of sensory stimuli can inhibit memory retention in the cognitive system (Craig, 2020). This is important to consider when creating a game framework to ensure that there are not unnecessary components that overload the brain and reduce the learning effect. Learning cyber through the usage of serious games requires a level of self-regulated learning (SRL) (Craig, 2020). Even though it may be mandated as part of a curriculum for DoD members, it takes time to learn the game's structure, rules, and to develop a strategy. SRL is shown to improve learning outcomes, making it another benefit of using serious games as a platform for achieving cyber learning objectives (Craig, 2020). The usage of cyber games within the DoD is meant to be a supplement to the education program, not a replacement. This level of technology implementation is known as augmentation. Its purpose is to improve current learning methods (Craig, 2020).

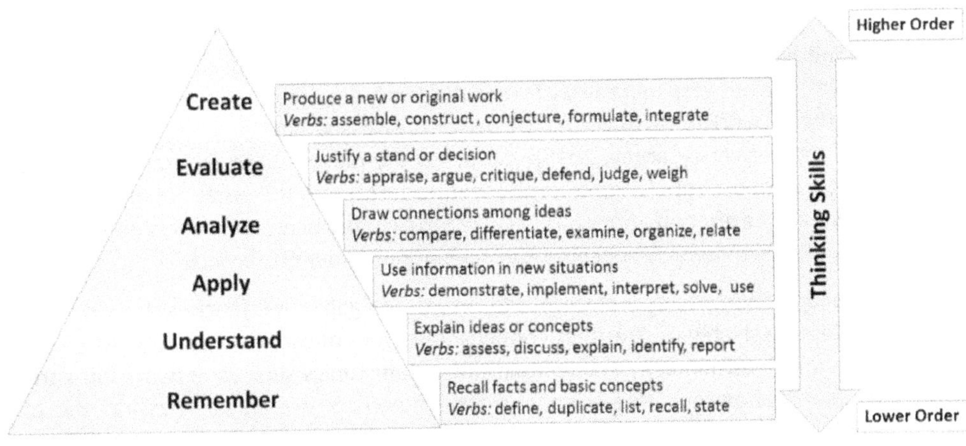

Figure 1: Revised Bloom's Taxonomy of Learning (Ruhl, 2022)

Bloom's Taxonomy of Learning is a model used to categorize learning objectives in increasing complexity. The creator of the model, Benjamin Bloom, discovered during his research that learning is best achieved through a variety of teaching methods and individualized plans (Ruhl, 2022). Using serious games as a learning mechanism diversifies the learning experience and may satisfy many of the hierarchy levels.

2.2 Serious Games

Serious games are developed primarily for educational purposes but are also meant to be an enjoyable and engaging method of learning. The literature suggests that this type of learning is beneficial for long-term knowledge retention as opposed to traditional learning (Flack, 2020). This is likely due to the memorable situations that the player encounters. Games utilizing the serious game framework can develop military members' skills for a particular subject (Flack, 2020). The mission impact of replacing these games in the training pipeline is that it will better equip the DoD to respond to cyber conflicts.

3. Serious Games for Teaching Cyber Concepts

Many serious games are currently employed to teach cyber skills. Studies show that scenario-based games with clear learning objectives are the most beneficial for long-term learning retention (Hendrix, 2016) (Yamin, 2021). A learning gap of OT devices that satisfy the needs of WENG 270 have been identified within these games. The curriculum focuses on programmable logic controllers (PLCs), heating, ventilation, and air conditioning (HVAC) systems, and waste management. Addressing deficiencies is critical in order to best equip the DoD's CEs with the correct cyber resources. The next section describes a variety of serious games that could be used in the CE curriculum. The research method for inclusion of these cyber serious games is all games that teach cyber concepts at a high school to masters-level education, have been found using the IEEE, ACM, or recommended by a DoD research partner, and could potentially fit the requirements and time constraints for a classroom-based learning environment.

3.1 Cyber Serious Games

Battlespace Next (BSN) is a serious game developed to teach wargaming based on objectives valued by the U.S. military. The game contains multi-domain operations that challenge the player to perform within different realms of warfighting (Flack, 2020). Within the cyber domain, it contains themes of attack and defense. It uses learning objectives aligned with Bloom's Taxonomy of Learning to show that all educational standards can be met through this game (Flack, 2020). A cyber serious game must have learning objectives that match the DoD cyber strategy and cyber operation goals. These objectives can also be used to convince senior leadership that the game is worth military resources and time. BSN was evaluated based on a series of survey and open-response questions. The results of the game played by students within an educational environment were largely positive. Most players enjoyed the game and believed that it increased their knowledge of military strategy and concepts (Flack, 2020). Flack was concerned that BSN would be too complicated, but player feedback suggested that it was acceptable. Games with a high learning curve could be a cause of concern when implementing a cyber serious game and should be considered in terms of time commitment and alignment to the WENG 270 curriculum.

Cyber Protect is another serious game used to teach cyber concepts. The premise of the game is for players to create a secure local area network that can withstand randomly generated attacks. Each attack affects a different level or aspect of the network infrastructure. The player is assessed quarterly based on whether the attack was able to penetrate the network (Carney, 2010). It teaches the player about different types of attacks that can occur on a network, what security features can prevent attacks, and the potential motivations behind attacks. The game also gives advice after an attack has occurred to help the player recover their systems. The limitations of the game is that it only teaches IT concepts and does not consider OT devices.

Cyber Threat Defender is a multiplayer physical and virtual card game that teaches students about cybersecurity information and defense strategies. The deck contains four types of cards: Assets, Defense, Event, and Attack. It develops students' cyber terminology and contains important topics such as network infrastructure and cyber attack and defense relationships. The winner is determined by the player that has the best strategy for protecting the network against their opponent (CIAS, 2016).

The U.S. Cyber Games is a yearly capture the flag event (CTF) open to everyone. It includes activities involving cryptography, forensics, reverse engineering, binary exploitation, and exploiting web-based applications. Based on scores, select players are invited to participate in the U.S. Cyber Combine. This experience has virtual learning opportunities, exercises, and competitions during a 2-month time frame. Then, players are drafted by coaches and prepare for the International Cybersecurity Championship via scrimmaging and training camps. This game provides many real-world opportunities for the player to gain cyber knowledge and experience (US Cyber Games, 2024).

The National Cyber League is a collegiate cybersecurity competition. It helps students prepare for a career in cyber or computer science. The primary objective is to promote diversity and inclusion in the cyber industry. Students can prepare and test their skills against cyber challenges that are present in the workforce. These include analyzing forensic data, pentesting, and recovering from ransomware attacks (Cyber Skyline, 2024).

The Cybersecurity Leadership TableTop Simulation was created by a SANS instructor and included in multiple SANS courses. Players improve the state of security for an organization. There are time, money, and resource constraints, all of which mimic real world situations. Events within the game can cause delays or even ruin a planned strategic initiative. Players are scored from 1-5 based on how they performed in the round (Kim, 2022).

TryHackMe is a learning environment that develops skills for players pursuing a cyber career. It teaches skills for all levels through a wide range of lesson modules. Players can choose a structured learning path that suits their needs for a specific job or certification. It contains most topics within the cybersecurity realm. Some of these paths include red teaming, defending a network, security engineering, web fundamentals, hardware components, and offensive pentesting (TryHackMe, 2024).

CyberStart is composed of hacking challenges and puzzles that teach cybersecurity skills. It has over 200 simulations for players to choose from. The game allows the player to acquire a toolkit of industry-recognized skills. Experts help expand the players' knowledge through tutorial videos and walkthrough guides in the Field Manual. CyberStart provides a safe environment to hack into networks and websites legally (CyberStart, 2022).

The Cyber Awareness Challenge is an annual DoD required set of online modules used to teach basic cyber skills. It focuses on threat mitigation and vulnerabilities within DoD information systems to create user awareness of potential consequences that their actions may have (DoD Cyber Exchange, 2024). It highlights aspects within cybersecurity such as phishing attacks, malicious email attachments, using proper security measures when dealing with controlled unclassified information (CUI) and personally identifiable information (PII), and attacks that can occur when physical access to a system is achieved. The module content is considered critical for DoD members and is enforced by Congress, the Office of Management and Budget, the Office of the Secretary of Defense, and the Cyber Workforce Advisory Group (DoD Cyber Exchange, 2024).

CyberCIEGE is a computer and network security-focused video game using a similar model as employed in SimCity™ (Naval Postgraduate School, 2024). Players in the virtual world operate and defend a network. They are able to spend virtual money to enhance the networks and protect them against cyber attacks (Naval Postgraduate School, 2024). The game syllabus contains information for each of the cyber modules. The cyber components listed are information assurance and security policies, identification and authentication, access control, network security, system assurance and certification, applied cryptography, and public key infrastructure. It also teaches the user about a variety of cyber attacks such as trap doors, corrupt insiders, Trojan horses, viruses, denial of service, and exploitation of weakly configured systems (Naval Postgraduate School, 2024). The US Navy, the Naval Education and Training Command, and the Office of Naval Research are a few of the DoD organizations that find this game valuable to implement in an educational environment.

The NICE challenge is composed of a narrative-driven scenario, business environment, and a set of technical objectives and deliverables. These components are used to provide a real-world simulated experience for the player. It also provides ample feedback for the educator or employer about the player's readiness for the cyber workforce (NICE Challenge Project, 2019). The narrative-driven scenario is composed of conversations with fictional co-workers to develop the player's understanding of cyber in the workforce and the challenges that may arise. The business environment is a workspace with functional servers, services, workstation, and networks available to the player to use for solving the challenges. Lastly, there is a set of technical objectives and deliverables that the player must complete in order to finish a challenge (NICE Challenge Project, 2019). The challenges consist of activities such as installing security software, altering running configurations, and remediating errors. The objectives within the challenges match the NIST SP 800-181, the NICE Framework, and the National Centers of Academic Excellence in Cybersecurity Knowledge Units (NICE Challenge Project, 2019).

Circadence™ is a cybersecurity environment that provides training for users across multiple disciplines. The platform provides specific modules for users in academia, enterprise, government, and military sectors (Circadence, 2024). The cybersecurity training engages the user through gamified, cyber-range practice labs. The concepts and skills taught in these games include the cyber kill chain, ports and protocols, Linux basics, Windows fundamentals, PowerShell, and Wireshark, as well as red and blue team lab scenarios.

CyberFire™ is an OT-focused course with a combination of lectures and hands-on cyber exercises. It develops user knowledge of industrial control systems and physical protection systems. It provides a baseline of cybersecurity information related to OT devices and how they are implemented into various operational industries. There is also an opportunity to learn about the OT network topology, the consequences of an OT cyberattack, how field controllers are different from typical PCs, and OT reconnaissance techniques (CyberFire,

2024*)*. The problem with this learning platform is that it takes multiple days to complete and must be done while the online lectures are broadcasted.

Thales™ is an OT cyber defense game available online and on mobile devices. The player's objective is to dodge cyber attacks and respond to OT security questions. It reinforces the idea that OT devices are increasingly vulnerable to cyber attacks and the consequences that may arise. The game is played similarly to Temple Run or Subway Surfer - the player's virtual avatar is physically dodging cyber threats. About every 20 seconds, an OT question is presented to the player. If answered correctly, the player will advance to the next level (Thales, 2021*)*.

3.2 Game Classification Based on Bloom's Taxonomy of Learning

The cyber serious games have been classified into levels based on Bloom's Taxonomy of Learning. Buchanan has identified game elements that relate to a particular level (Buchanan, 2024). It should be acknowledged that there are multiple methodologies for categorizing serious games using Bloom's Taxonomy of Learning, but this paper uses Buchanan's implementation. Most of the games fall within the lower two levels of Bloom's Taxonomy of Learning: Remember and Understand. Some games can be elevated to the Apply level if post-game questions are added to assess a player's knowledge. Games classified within the Remember level demonstrate skills such as remembering ideas and information. The Understand level requires the player to interpret, discuss, and compare their knowledge. In order for a game to be on the Apply level, it must test the player's ability to solve problems or use skills in difficult situations (Buchanan, 2024).

A modified Bloom's Taxonomy of Learning diagram is shown in Figure 2. It maps each game to an associated level. CyberStart, the Cyber Awareness Challenge, Circadence, CyberFire, and Thales are all on the Remember level. These games are all module-focused that require the user to define and recollect information. The following games have been identified under the Understand level: Battlespace Next, Cyber Protect, Cyber Threat Defender, the Cybersecurity Leadership TableTop Simulation, CyberCIEGE, and the NICE Challenge. The games listed are all simulation-focused; the player must interpret their knowledge in a real-world context. The games that are on the Apply level are the U.S. Cyber Games, National Cyber League, and TryHackMe because the player must demonstrate the ability to solve problems in advanced scenarios.

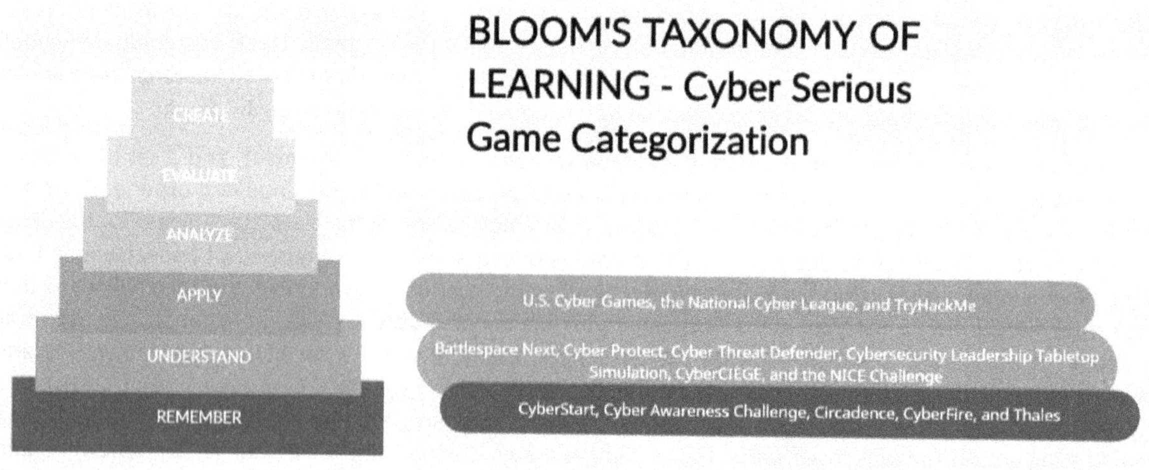

Figure 2: Bloom's Taxonomy of Learning - Cyber Serious Game Categorization

The diagram maps the cyber serious games described in Section 3.1 to a corresponding level.

Remember level criteria: Module-focused. Player defines and recollects information.

Understand level criteria: Simulation-focused. Player interprets knowledge in a real-world context.

Apply level criteria: Player demonstrates ability to solve problems in advanced scenarios.

4. Propositions to Improve Cyber Game-based Learning

Table 1 shows the different domains of cyber that are demonstrated in the games described in Section 3.1. The sub-disciplines of cyber in the "Domain of Cyber" columns were determined according to Cremer et al. (2022),

Karjalainen et al. (2020), and Maalem et al (2020). A clear absence of OT within most cyber learning games is shown. TryHackMe, the Cyber Awareness Challenge, the NICE Challenge, CyberFire, and Thales are the only games that contain a section of critical infrastructure or hardware modules within cybersecurity. As the dependence on OT increases in the CE career field, these learning modules will not be sufficient. An in-depth assessment of each OT game and its applicability to the WENG 270 curriculum is mentioned in the following paragraphs. It would be beneficial to create a game that teaches about OT devices to fill this gap.

Table 1: Popular Cyber-learning Games Mapped to Domains within Cybersecurity

Cyber Game/Domain of Cyber	Networking/Internet Usage	Cyber Attacks	Defense/ Prevention	Recovery Techniques/ Mitigation	Operational Technology/ Hardware/ Infrastructure	Miscellaneous
Battlespace Next		✓	✓			-Multi-domain operations
Cyber Protect	✓	✓	✓	✓		-Motivation
Cyber Threat Defender	✓	✓	✓			-Cyber Terminology
U.S. Cyber Games		✓	✓	✓		
National Cyber League		✓	✓	✓		
Cybersecurity Leadership TableTop Simulation			✓			
TryHackMe	✓	✓	✓	✓	✓	-Linux/Windows fundamentals -Cyber Terminology -Career Paths
CyberStart	✓	✓				
The Cyber Awareness Challenge	✓	✓			✓	-CUI and PII proper security measures
CyberCIEGE	✓	✓	✓			
NICE Challenge	✓				✓	
Circadence	✓	✓	✓			-Cyber Kill Chain -Linux/Windows fundamentals
CyberFire	✓	✓			✓	

Cyber Game/Domain of Cyber	Networking/Internet Usage	Cyber Attacks	Defense/ Prevention	Recovery Techniques/ Mitigation	Operational Technology/ Hardware/ Infrastructure	Miscellaneous
Battlespace Next		✓	✓			-Multi-domain operations
Cyber Protect	✓	✓	✓	✓		-Motivation
Cyber Threat Defender	✓	✓	✓			-Cyber Terminology
U.S. Cyber Games		✓	✓	✓		
Thales					✓	

Limited cyber training resources exist on OT devices. This could be due to the fact that, in the past, OT was much more difficult to attack due to air gapping. It is also important to note that OT devices cannot be protected the same way as IT devices due to their design. Today, these OT devices are often connected to the internet, bridging the gap between OT and IT. A classic example of this is the Stuxnet attack from 2010 that was able to degrade Iran's nuclear centrifuges in an air-gapped system (Yang, 2015). It is even simpler to attack OT devices that are connected to the internet. The Vault Typhoon case study mentioned in the Introduction also demonstrates the relevance of OT in modern cyberwarfare.

The proposition to improve game-based learning for the CE students is to increase the usage of OT devices as opposed to information technology (IT) to make a game that is most relevant to their curriculum. The cyber domains consisting of Networking/Internet usage, Cyber Attacks, Defense/Prevention, and Recovery Techniques/Mitigation are all considered IT. TryHackMe is not sufficient for the CE curriculum because it does not have modules for the OT devices prioritized by the course director. The CyberAwareness Challenge is required for all DoD members, so it is already implemented in the CE curriculum. Also, the OT concepts in this challenge are too basic for the knowledge requirements of CEs. There is potential for the NICE challenge to be modified in order to provide the necessary OT components for the CE curriculum, but further testing is needed. CyberFire is not a feasible option as a game that can be implemented into the WENG 270 curriculum due to the time constraints of the course. Thales is focused on OT technology and asks thought-provoking questions to the user, but does not provide any learning material or feedback for incorrect answers. The game format may also be distracting in a classroom environment. Future research in this field will require the alignment of the WENG 270 course learning objectives and the construction of a cyber learning game that utilizes OT devices.

5. Conclusion

This paper advocates for the enhancement in cyber training within the DOD, emphasizing the crucial role of OT devices. It defines types of learning, Bloom's Taxonomy of Learning, and serious games. Cyber serious games are described and categorized based on a level according to Bloom's. The paper addresses the research question by recognizing the inadequacy of current serious games in covering OT concepts. A focused approach directed at CE students in the DoD is proposed. By addressing the identified learning gaps and integrating OT devices into cyber learning games, CEs will be more equipped to respond in the dynamic realm of cybersecurity.

References

Buchanan, L. (2024). Blending Bloom's Taxonomy and Serious Game Design. *Secure Decisions Division.*
Carney. (2010). *CyberProtect – SGS&C.* Retrieved November 1, 2023, from http://sgschallenge.com/cyber-protect/
CIAS. (2016). *Cyber Threat Defender – The UTSA CIAS.* https://cias.utsa.edu/ctd/
Circadence. (2024). *Gamified Cybersecurity Training Solutions.* Circadence Corporation. https://circadence.com/

CISA. (2023, May 24). *People's Republic of China State-Sponsored Cyber Actor Living off the Land to Evade Detection | CISA.* https://www.cisa.gov/news-events/cybersecurity-advisories/aa23-144a

Craig, S. D., Schroeder, N. L., & Roscoe, R. D. (2020). Science of Learning and Readiness. *U.S. Advanced Distributed Learning (ADL) Initiative.*

Cremer, F., Sheehan, B., Fortmann, M., Kia, A. N., Mullins, M., Murphy, F., & Materne, S. (2022). Cyber risk and cybersecurity: A systematic review of data availability. *The Geneva Papers on Risk and Insurance. Issues and Practice, 47*(3), 698–736. https://doi.org/10.1057/s41288-022-00266-6

CyberFire. (2024). *Cyber Fire Operational Technology*. https://cyberfire.energy.gov/classes/ot/

Cyber Skyline. (2024). *National Cyber League*. https://nationalcyberleague.org/

CyberStart. (2022). *Play fun hacking cyber security games, for free*. https://cyberstart.com/

DoD Cyber Exchange. (2024). *Cyber Awareness Challenge 2024 – DoD Cyber Exchange.* https://public.cyber.mil/training/cyber-awareness-challenge/

Flack, N., Lin, A., Peterson, G., & Reith, M. (2020). Battlespace Next(TM): Developing a Serious Game to Explore Multi-Domain Operations. *International Journal of Serious Games*, *7*(2), Article 2. https://doi.org/10.17083/ijsg.v7i2.349

Galbraith, Jean. U.S. Military Undergoes Restructuring to Emphasize Cyber and Space Capabilities. (2019). *American Journal of International Law, 113*(3), 634–640. https://doi.org/10.1017/ajil.2019.39

Hendrix, M. (2016). Game based cyber security training: Are serious games suitable for cyber security training? *International Journal of Serious Games.*

Karjalainen, M., & Kokkonen, T. (2020). Comprehensive Cyber Arena; The Next Generation Cyber Range. *2020 IEEE European Symposium on Security and Privacy Workshops (EuroS&PW)*, 11–16. https://doi.org/10.1109/EuroSPW51379.2020.00011

Kim, Frank. Cyber42 Cybersecurity Leadership Simulation Games | SANS Institute | Cyber Security Leadership. (2022). https://www.sans.org/blog/cyber42/

Kulesza, N. (2023). *WENG 270 Lesson Objectives*. The Civil Engineer School.

Maalem Lahcen, R. A., Caulkins, B., Mohapatra, R., & Kumar, M. (2020). Review and insight on the behavioral aspects of cybersecurity. *Cybersecurity*, *3*(1), 10. https://doi.org/10.1186/s42400-020-00050-w

Naval Postgraduate School. (2024). *CyberCIEGE - Center for Cybersecurity and Cyber Operations—Naval Postgraduate School*. https://nps.edu/web/c3o/cyberciege

NICE Challenge Project. (2019). *NICE Challenge Project – The Workforce Experience Before the Workforce*. https://nice-challenge.com/

Ruhl, Charlotte. *Bloom's Taxonomy of Learning | Domain Levels Explained*. (2022, November 3). https://www.simplypsychology.org/blooms-taxonomy.html

Thales. (2021). *Launch IT/OT Cyber Defense Game*. https://connect.thalesgroup.com/en/news/lancering-it-ot-cyber-defense-game

TryHackMe. (2024). *TryHackMe | Cyber Security Training.* https://tryhackme.com

USAF. (2023). CYBERSPACE OPERATIONS. *AIR FORCE DOCTRINE PUBLICATION 3-12.*

US Cyber Games. (2024). *https://www.uscybergames.com/*

Yamin, M. M., Katt, B., & Nowostawski, M. (2021). Serious games as a tool to model attack and defense scenarios for cyber-security exercises. *Norwegian University of Science and Technology*.

Yang, J., Liu, X., & Bose, S. (2015). Preventing Cyber-induced Irreversible Physical Damage to Cyber-Physical Systems. *Proceedings of the 10th Annual Cyber and Information Security Research Conference*, 1–4. https://doi.org/10.1145/2746266.2746274

Work in Progress Papers

Deep Graph Neural Networks for Malware Detection Using Ghidra P-Code

Rinaldo Iorizzo and Bo Yuan
Rochester Institute of Technology, USA

rpi1809@g.rit.edu
Bo.Yuan@rit.edu

Abstract: This work examines the effectiveness of using Ghidra P-Code as semantics-based features in a graph neural network-based malware detection system. A preliminary model exhibits a function level precision of ~70% and a recall around ~60%, and a precision and recall of ~55% and ~80% respectively for the program level detection task on a dataset of ~50,000 control flow graphs extracted from functions of malicious and benign programs. Future improvements to this ongoing project include, but are not limited to, collecting dynamic control flow graph information as opposed to static graphs to provide the model with resilience to advanced malware obfuscation and encryption schemes.

Keywords: Malware Detection, Deep Learning, Neural Network, Graph Neural Network, Ghidra

1. Introduction

As malware authors employ ever more sophisticated evasion techniques, it has become apparent that classical approaches such as signature detection leave much to be desired. Malware detection remains difficult in the presence of obfuscation techniques developed by malware authors.

In many cases, deep learning approaches that make use of static features are assumed to fail in the presence of obfuscation techniques. Detection techniques such as those shown in MalIMG (Nataraj et al. 2011) rely upon the bytes of compiled programs, which are easily changed through obfuscation. This has led many researchers to use dynamic features in their malware detection systems, as dynamic features are assumed to be more closely aligned with the behaviour of the program as opposed to the form of the program. By this logic, we extrapolate that the intention of using dynamic features is the alignment of the representation of the samples with the potential behaviour of the sample program. Then, we direct our attention to producing such a representation through the exploration of program representations that avoid over-reliance on the exact form of a given program.

Inspired by vulnerability detection techniques (Cao et al. 2021), we consider the classification of Control Flow Graphs (CFGs) derived from the functions in compiled programs. In this work we explore the relationship and feasibility of the binary classification of function CFGs from malicious and benign software to the task of binary classification on whole programs.

We propose a deep learning malware detection system based on the classification of function control flow graphs with Ghidra P-Code node-level features. Through analysis of our model's performance upon a sample dataset of malicious and benign software under a variety of circumstances we aim to explore the relationship between function classification and malware detection as well as the use of P-Code as a semantic feature for augmenting a GNN malware detection system for resistance to obfuscation techniques.

We have identified several pertinent research questions:

1. How effective is detection at the function level with respect to malware detection at the program level?
2. How does the classification of P-Code derived CFGs for malware detection compare to more traditional malware detection techniques? (Both graph based and otherwise.)
3. Is P-Code suitable for malware detection in the presence of obfuscation?

2. Background and Related Works

2.1 Ghidra and P-Code

Ghidra was selected for decompilation and analysis of programs in this work to make use of Ghidra's internal language for program representation: P-Code. Ghidra internally represents analysed programs using P-Code. P-Code represents computation using registers in a generic way by breaking known instructions on known CPU architectures into one or more P-Code instructions (or P-Code nodes). According to Naus et al. (2023), P-Code is not semantically complete nor executable, however we consider that the application of P-Code to reverse engineering is indicative of the potential for useful representations for deep learning systems.

2.2 Graph Neural Networks

Graph neural networks (GNNs) are a kind of deep learning architecture that takes graphs as input. GNNs have been used across many domains ranging from molecular analysis (Gilmer et al. 2017) to abstract mathematics (Xu et al. 2019) and facilitate tasks on graph data on the node level, edge level, and or whole graph level. GNN models take graph data in the form of matrices of node features, edge features, and an adjacency matrix. In our case, we make use of GNN models for a graph-level classification task where the features of nodes in the input graphs are used to classify the entire graph into one of two classes, malicious or benign.

2.3 Related Works

The following is a discussion of various related works in malware detection. Many of these works informed our decisions made during the creation of our malware detection system. While this work focuses on Windows malware detection, works focused on Android malware detection were also considered.

2.3.1 Static Approaches

Many malware detection systems make use of static features. Examples such as Nataraj's work on the Malimg dataset often make use of machine learning or DL tools from other domains such as image classification (Nataraj et al. 2011). Palma Salas et al. (2023) made use of transfer learning to improve detection on a Malimg based program representation. However, Palma Salas made use of the Microsoft Malware Classification Challenge Dataset for their experiments which does not contain benign software and includes obfuscated samples as a separate class. While their approach was successful, it inherits the vulnerability to obfuscation techniques from their inspiring work, Malimg.

In Pei et al. (2020), the authors used graph representations of android programs to train a malware detection system. While their approach enjoyed high performance, it was not directly applicable to Windows malware detection as Pei's work relies upon Android specific features and obfuscation techniques. Pei's work supports the use of GNNs with semantic attribution at the node level for graph level classification tasks. While Pei's work is demonstrated on obfuscated data, the performance of their approach when only a small portion of the dataset exhibits obfuscation techniques was drastically reduced.

Yan et al. (2019) demonstrated a powerful graph convolution network approach on statically derived CFGs for malware classification. Yan's work supports the creation of CFGs from compiled programs and the attribution of information to nodes in the CFG to retain semantic information. Yan's work strongly supports the use of CFGs for malware detection using static information and provides a basis for future adaptation. However, Yan's work also makes use of the Microsoft Malware Classification Challenge Dataset for one set of their experiments and otherwise does not address obfuscation.

2.3.2 Dynamic Approaches

Dynamic approaches are popular for their ability to capture the behaviour of samples, avoiding obfuscation techniques in the best case. It is common for these approaches to make use of system API calls as in Li et al. (2022), Xiao et al. (2019), and Nguyen et al. (2023). All three of these works make use of a sandbox for the collection of dynamic information, as well as the use of graph structures for representation of their samples. Li's work provides competitive performance with graph convolutional networks, but not to an overwhelming degree. Nguyen's work similarly performs well but not more-so than approaches such as the application of CNNs to Malimg samples. Xiao's work demonstrates the use of stacked auto encoders (SAEs) for eventual classification of graph structured information. However, Xiao's work is intended for use in IoT environments and performs graph compression techniques which may remove structural information. Of these three works, only Nguyen discusses obfuscation at length.

3. Methodology

To address our first research question "How effective is detection at the function level with respect to malware detection at the program level? ", we will compare our GNN model's performance on several datasets and training configurations that differ in their relationship between functions and programs overall.

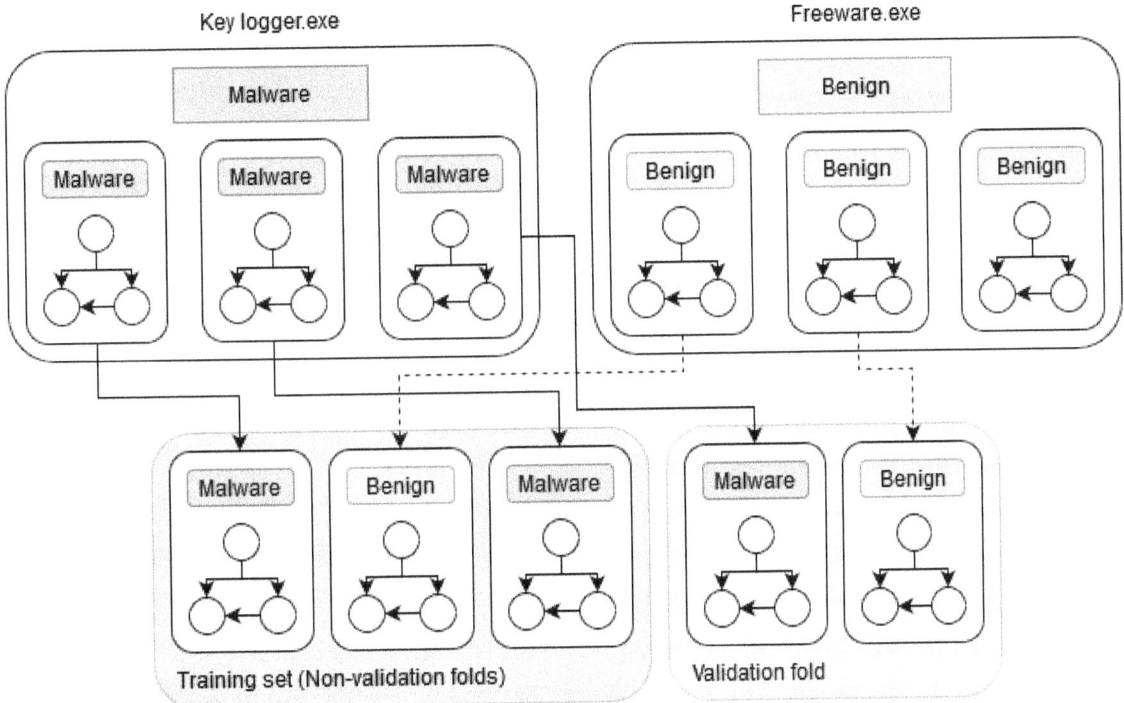

Figure 1: Our first dataset configuration is constructed by selecting function CFGs by sampling the total data generated with Ghidra. Note that not all functions from a program are necessarily selected for inclusion in the dataset.

We first construct several datasets that are balanced with respect to the number of function CFGs from each class (Figure 1). The objective of our model is to predict the class of the program the function CFG originates from. To collect information on program level malware detection, we look at the programs represented in the validation set. If any of a program's functions are considered malicious, we consider the whole program to be malicious.

Next, we create new datasets that are balanced by number of programs from each class and a maximum number of function CFGs (Figure 2). The datasets select programs by their function count and select all functions from each program. We then apply the same training objective and train our model. We account for duplicate programs in this dataset by comparing MD5 hash values. We additionally control for variants of the same malware by considering the number of functions of each program. Programs that have the same number of functions and similar file sizes are considered duplicates. The relationship of program function count to file size can be seen graphically in figure 3. Note the vertical lines and dark points that malware samples form, indicating programs with the same number of extracted functions. Manual analysis of these artifacts indicated that they strongly correlate with variations of the same program through consultation of Virustotal. All malware programs that are not present on Virustotal are excluded from sampling.

Lastly, we consider a similar representation as in the previous datasets where we include all functions from represented programs but do not allow programs to be split between training and validation folds (Figure 4). In doing so, we enforce that the program level detection task is not skewed by partial representation in the validation set. Samples are selected in the same manner as in the previous paragraph.

In this work, we do not provide experimental results to explore our third research question but instead lay the groundwork for doing so. To properly address our third research question, "Is P-Code suitable for malware detection in the presence of obfuscation?" we consider in our future work the extraction of P-Code through dynamic means and the construction of a dataset with known obfuscation techniques. To do this however, it was first necessary to create a proof of concept for P-Code's use in malware detection.

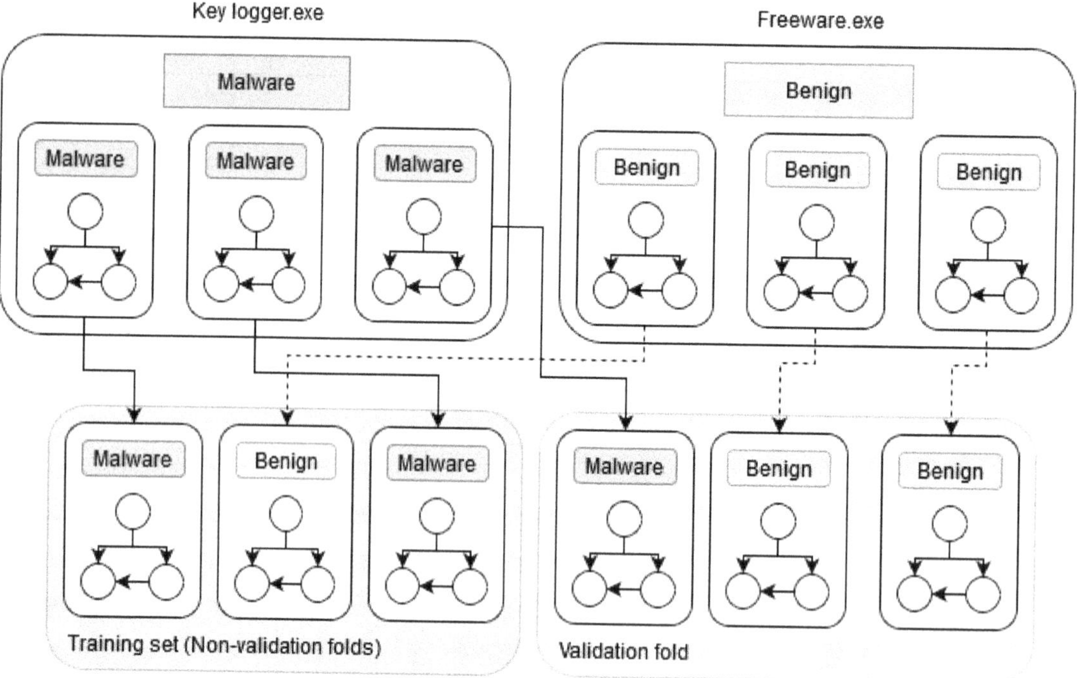

Figure 2: The second configuration enforces that all functions from a program must be included in the total dataset as well as attempts to balance the number of programs and functions from each class.

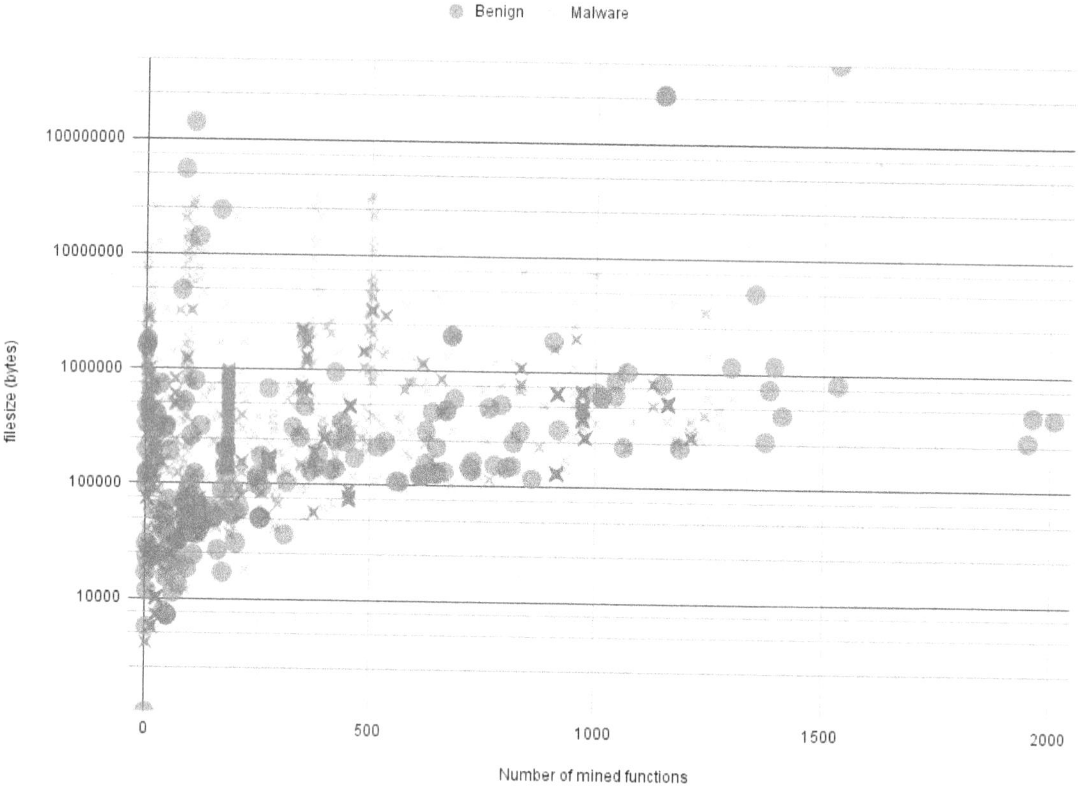

Figure 3: This chart compares the number of mined functions to the file size of the sample program in bytes. The vertical axis is a logarithmic scale due to high disparity in file sizes.

4. Experimental Setup

Spektral was used in tandem with Keras to construct and apply GNN models using Tensorflow as the backend. The system was tested on an Ubuntu Server with a 32 core Xeon E5 2620 CPU and Tesla P100 GPU with 16GB of memory. Our malware detection system was trained on a collection of malware samples from a variety of sources such as Virustotal and Virusshare, and a collection of benign samples from common open-source and freeware projects.

Samples were processed using Ghidra to produce P-Code CFGs for every function of the sample program and were exported as JSON files. The CFG data was processed using node2vec (Grover and Leskovec, 2016) to provide artificial node-level features, and additional features of node degree and P-Code node-kind were concatenated to each node feature vector to complete the initial node representations. Training datasets were created by sampling the total set of programs processed by Ghidra.

A Spektral GeneralGNN model is trained and tested across 10-fold cross validation. Precision and recall are collected for each fold and averaged to obtain performance metrics. This process is performed for each dataset.

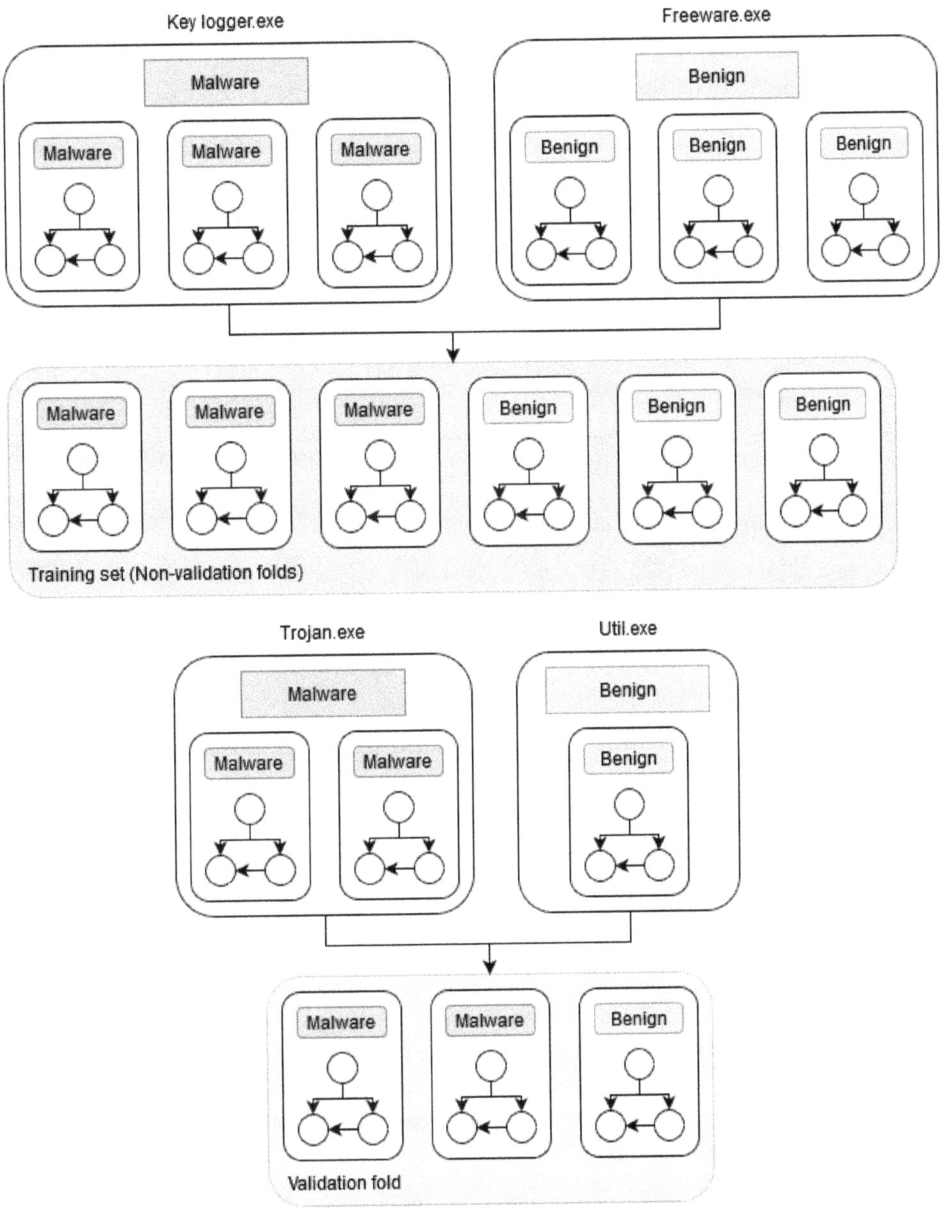

Figure 4: In addition to balancing the number of programs and number of functions from each class in the dataset, we perform train and validation fold splitting along program lines instead of by function count. The fold selection process only considers the number and class of program.

5. Results

The GeneralGNN model was built into the Spektral GNN library and was selected as a general baseline for GNN models. This model was an implementation of the work in You et al. (You, Ying, and Leskovec 2021). Results are shown in table 1. Dataset size indicates maximum number of function CFGs in the dataset. The column "Split on Program" indicates the splitting of training and validation sets on the program level. "Has all Functions?" indicates if all functions from a program are present in the dataset. "Class Weighted" indicates the use of the class weight parameter used by the focal cross entropy loss function. "Pruned" indicates that duplicates are removed. The rows in red reinforce that no pruning has occurred and are derived from the first dataset description in the methodology section.

Table 1: GeneralGNN model results collected across the datasets described in the methodology section.

Dataset Size	Split on Program?	Has all Functions?	Class Weighted	Pruned	Function Precision	Function Recall	Program Precision	Program Recall
10k	no	yes	no	yes	0.79	0.61	0.56	0.70
25k	no	yes	no	yes	0.71	0.58	0.53	0.79
50k	no	yes	no	yes	0.71	0.64	0.55	0.86
10k	yes	yes	no	yes	0.77	0.62	0.66	0.93
25k	yes	yes	no	yes	0.71	0.41	0.61	0.90
50k	yes	yes	no	yes	0.77	0.44	0.61	0.92
10k	no	yes	yes	yes	0.75	0.58	0.55	0.68
25k	no	yes	yes	yes	0.69	0.46	0.52	0.74
50k	no	yes	yes	yes	0.80	0.46	0.54	0.77
10k	yes	yes	yes	yes	0.77	0.53	0.66	0.87
25k	yes	yes	yes	yes	0.70	0.44	0.62	0.94
50k	yes	yes	yes	yes	0.76	0.46	0.60	0.91
10k	no	no	no	no	0.58	0.66	0.71	0.61
25k	no	no	no	no	0.59	0.74	0.81	0.73
50k	no	no	no	no	0.64	0.72	0.85	0.73

6. Discussion

When considering the relationship between function-level prediction and program-level prediction, our results indicate that including entire programs and not splitting them between training and validation sets is beneficial. The low program precision indicates that false positives are likely, but a high recall indicates that our model is unlikely to miss malicious software. This aligns with the intuition that our representation may indicate program behaviour to some degree and that the broad labels applied to the function level task are insufficient to differentiate non-malicious behaviour within malware from non-malicious behaviour in benign software. When considering the red rows present in table 1 that do not include pruning or exclusivity to training/ validation sets, it is important to consider the number of programs represented in the validation set increases with the size of the dataset overall. Therefore, the performance increase shown in program metrics for the red rows falsely indicate high performance in malware detection at the program level.

To address our second research question, "How does the classification of P-Code derived CFGs for malware detection compare to more traditional malware detection techniques? (Both graph based and otherwise.).":

Our model performs better than guessing and achieves a high recall on the program level task when trained on datasets that are controlled for duplicates and include all relevant functions. Models like those in the related works section often boast over 90% precision and recall; our model is far below state of the art at present.

However, if we assume our semantic representation closely aligns with the behaviour of the original program it is possible our results are consistent with the common intuition that malicious software's functions and behaviours may only constitute a small proportion of malware's codebase. If this is true, investigation into characterization of program behaviour from such features may allow for higher performance with labels that are derived from program behaviours. It is an ongoing research. The performance of our model is expected to improve.

Acknowledgements

This work was partially supported by the National Science Foundation under Award 1922169.

References

Cao, S. *et al.* (2021) 'BGNN4VD: Constructing Bidirectional Graph Neural-Network for Vulnerability Detection', *Information and Software Technology*, 136, p. 106576. Available at: https://doi.org/10.1016/j.infsof.2021.106576.

Gilmer, J. *et al.* (2017) 'Neural Message Passing for Quantum Chemistry'. arXiv. Available at: http://arxiv.org/abs/1704.01212 (Accessed: 13 December 2023).

Grover, A. and Leskovec, J. (2016) 'node2vec: Scalable Feature Learning for Networks'. arXiv. Available at: http://arxiv.org/abs/1607.00653 (Accessed: 2 August 2023).

Li, S. *et al.* (2022) 'Intelligent malware detection based on graph convolutional network', *The Journal of Supercomputing*, 78(3), pp. 4182–4198. Available at: https://doi.org/10.1007/s11227-021-04020-y.

Nataraj, L. *et al.* (2011) 'Malware images: visualization and automatic classification', in *Proceedings of the 8th International Symposium on Visualization for Cyber Security. VizSec '11: 2011 International Symposium on Visualization for Cyber Security*, Pittsburgh Pennsylvania USA: ACM, pp. 1–7. Available at: https://doi.org/10.1145/2016904.2016908.

Naus, N. *et al.* (2023) 'A Formal Semantics for P-Code', in A. Lal and S. Tonetta (eds) *Verified Software. Theories, Tools and Experiments.* Cham: Springer International Publishing (Lecture Notes in Computer Science), pp. 111–128. Available at: https://doi.org/10.1007/978-3-031-25803-9_7.

Nguyen, M.T., Nguyen, V.H. and Shone, N. (2023) 'Using deep graph learning to improve dynamic analysis-based malware detection in PE files', *Journal of Computer Virology and Hacking Techniques* [Preprint]. Available at: https://doi.org/10.1007/s11416-023-00505-x.

Pei, X., Yu, L. and Tian, S. (2020) 'AMalNet: A deep learning framework based on graph convolutional networks for malware detection', *Computers & Security*, 93, p. 101792. Available at: https://doi.org/10.1016/j.cose.2020.101792.

Xiao, F. *et al.* (2019) 'Malware Detection Based on Deep Learning of Behavior Graphs', *Mathematical Problems in Engineering*, 2019, p. e8195395. Available at: https://doi.org/10.1155/2019/8195395.

Xu, K., Hu, W., Leskovec, J. and Jegelka, S., 2018. How powerful are graph neural networks?. *arXiv preprint arXiv:1810.00826*.

Yan, J., Yan, G. and Jin, D. (2019) 'Classifying Malware Represented as Control Flow Graphs using Deep Graph Convolutional Neural Network', in *2019 49th Annual IEEE/IFIP International Conference on Dependable Systems and Networks (DSN). 2019 49th Annual IEEE/IFIP International Conference on Dependable Systems and Networks (DSN)*, pp. 52–63. Available at: https://doi.org/10.1109/DSN.2019.00020.

You, J., Ying, R. and Leskovec, J. (2021) 'Design Space for Graph Neural Networks'. arXiv. Available at: http://arxiv.org/abs/2011.08843 (Accessed: 13 December 2023).

LOCKing Patient Safety: A Dynamic Cybersecurity Checklist for Healthcare Workers

Jyri Rajamäki, Kimberley Wood and Benjamin Espada
Laurea University of Applied Sciences, Espoo, Finland

Jyri.Rajamaki@laurea.fi
Kimberley.Wood@student.laurea.fi
Benjamin.Espad@student.laurea.fi

Abstract: Ensuring the cybersecurity of patient data is particularly challenging for healthcare organizations, and healthcare professionals play a key role here. Therefore, they must have the necessary knowledge and skills to be able to identify cybersecurity risks and respond appropriately to them. As part of the CyberSecPro project, this work-in-progress paper aims to provide healthcare professionals with a simple and memorable cybersecurity checklist highlighting important factors to consider. The purpose of the checklist is to support busy healthcare workers in implementing effective cybersecurity measures to secure sensitive information and guarantee patient privacy. The interview method was used to find out the cybersecurity challenges faced by healthcare workers and gather their opinions into a checklist. The mini-mental cybersecurity checklist created in the study, emphasizes the importance of being aware of cyber threats and maintaining secure and reliable information systems. Its name "LOCK" stands for Logging Out every time you leave your computer, Checking e-mails before opening links, and Keeping safe. Keep calm and LOCK on.

Keywords: Cybersecurity, Checklist, Data protection, Digital healthcare, Safeguarding

1. Introduction

Technology is increasingly becoming integral to healthcare facilities in today's healthcare landscape. Technology integration in healthcare offers significant benefits. This also exposes medical devices and healthcare systems to cybersecurity vulnerabilities, making them more vulnerable to cyber threats. Traditional notions of healthcare systems being immune to cyberattacks are no longer valid (Zhuravlev & Blagoveshchenskaya, 2020). The healthcare industry is facing critical cybersecurity issues resulting in patient data breaches (Cartwright, 2023). Delayed detection of cyber threats exacerbates this vulnerability, making it essential to address the issue of inadequate cybersecurity in the healthcare sector (Sabra, 2021). Inadequate investments and training have left the sector vulnerable to cyberattacks. Hacking, mainly through malware and ransomware, compromises patient data and causes disruptions to health services. These breaches lead to financial losses, damage healthcare institutions' reputations, and endanger patient safety (Kandasamy et al., 2022). Therefore, taking immediate action to secure these systems and devices to protect against potential attackers has become crucial. It is crucial to adopt a security-conscious approach integrated with patient care practices.

The CyberSecPro project, funded by the European Union, creates cutting-edge education and training materials and courses to advance competencies and professionalism in EU cybersecurity. Its goal is to strengthen the role of higher education institutions as a provider of practical and working life skills to promote reliable digital change in the critical sectors of health, energy, and transport. CyberSecPro aims to promote cybersecurity education in the following ways: (1) development of material for the development of theoretical and practical skills, (2) training and certification of students and professionals, and (3) promotion of partnerships (CyberSecPro, 2023).

This work-in-progress paper aims to develop material for improving healthcare professionals' theoretical and practical skills in the field of cybersecurity. The paper explores methods for developing a simple and memorable cybersecurity checklist that nurses can use to enhance cybersecurity in the healthcare industry. It also aims to identify the essential factors that should be considered while creating a cybersecurity checklist that is easy and convenient for busy healthcare workers to remember and use efficiently.

2. Methodology

Figure 1 shows how the Design Science Research (DSR) framework (Hevner & Chatterjee, 2010) is applied in this paper. The purpose of the research is to develop a simple and memorable cybersecurity checklist that healthcare professionals can use to enhance cybersecurity. The Relevance Cycle connects the contextual healthcare environment to the design science activities and the research problem of developing material for improving healthcare professionals' theoretical and practical skills in the field of cybersecurity. The healthcare domain consists of people (e.g., healthcare professionals, patients, clients, system operators, and security officers), and organizational and technical systems (e.g., eHealth infrastructure, patient data repositories) that interact to work toward a goal. The Rigor Cycle combines the scientific foundations, experience, and expertise of design science with the Knowledge Base database. The central Design Cycle iterates between the core activities of building and evaluating the design artifacts and processes of the research. In this DSR, the evaluation is done as a desk study.

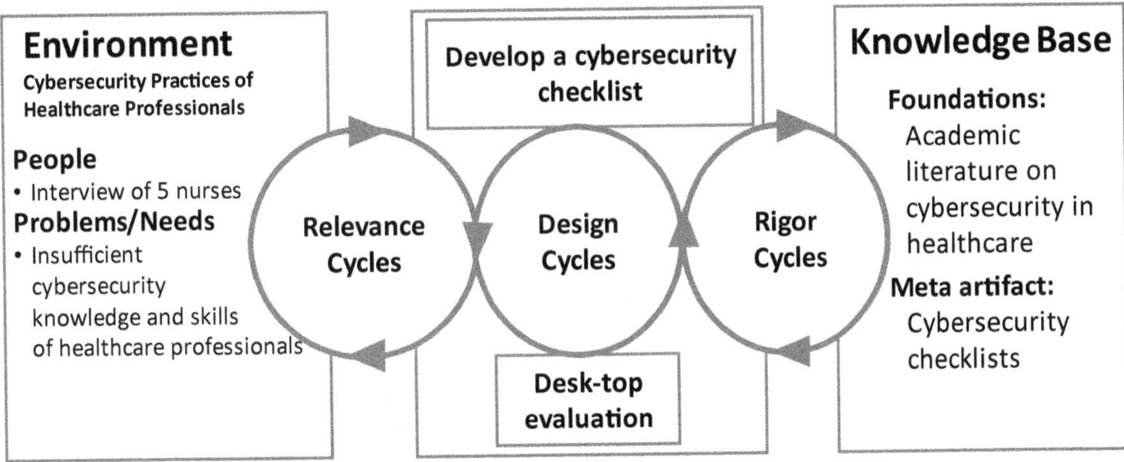

Figure 1: Design Science Research framework of this study

As a part of the relevance cycle, we selected five respondents with expertise in healthcare cybersecurity through convenience sampling. We conducted semi-structured interviews to gain insights into cybersecurity practices, challenges, and strategies. During the rigor cycle, we conducted a literature review that revealed significant risks to patient data and operational continuity in healthcare cybersecurity.

3. Rigor Cycle

3.1 Cybersecurity Practices of Healthcare Professionals

The healthcare industry is a primary target for cyberattacks, resulting in many data breaches. These attacks can be catastrophic for patients, healthcare providers, and the healthcare system. They can cause the loss of sensitive patient data, financial losses, and even patient harm. Although technology integration has led to greater precision in healthcare, cybersecurity measures must advance to keep up with the changes (Pant et al., 2022). On the other hand, only 22.7% of the non-ICT personnel (i.e., doctors, nurses, auxiliary, laboratory, and administrative personnel) felt sufficiently trained in security (Gioulekas et al., 2022).

Healthcare professionals are highly vulnerable to cybersecurity threats as they handle sensitive patient information and rely heavily on technology for various aspects of their work (Pant et al., 2022). The likelihood of medication errors increases if prescription systems do not work (Altamimi, 2022). Among healthcare professionals, nurses are often responsible for collecting and recording patient data, communicating with other healthcare professionals, and accessing electronic health records (Pant et al., 2022). Therefore, they must take proactive measures to implement robust cybersecurity practices to safeguard patient information and prevent data breaches. By doing so, healthcare professionals can ensure that patient data remains secure and prevent unauthorized access or theft of sensitive information.

Identifying phishing messages is crucial. As illustrated by an Italian hospital boasting a workforce of over 6,000 healthcare professionals, conducting an annual phishing simulation is integral to their training and risk assessment protocols (Rizzoni, et al., 2022). Employees play a pivotal role in fortifying the security of both the healthcare organization and patients' privacy by remaining vigilant towards suspicious emails, including scrutinizing links and attachments. Employees must exercise caution with unexpected emails and develop the ability to discern dubious messages, refraining from opening any associated attachments. Indiscriminate opening of email attachments should be strictly avoided. Recognizing one's activities and skills, particularly when under stress, is of paramount importance. The likelihood of human errors rises in demanding conditions and when departing from the established workflow (Sütterlin, et al., 2022). Stressed healthcare professionals are more susceptible to falling victim to phishing emails. Notably, there exists a clear positive correlation between the workload of nurses and the occurrence of opening phishing messages. Regrettably, healthcare personnel may be unaware of the potential consequences of their actions and the associated risks. The staff may not comprehend that their behavior could facilitate the entry of malware into the hospital's system (Rajamäki, Rathod & Kioskli, 2023).

3.2 Cybersecurity Checklist

Preventing cybersecurity breaches in the healthcare industry can be achieved in several ways. One practical approach involves investing in risk management systems that detect and address potential cybersecurity risks. Another crucial aspect of cybersecurity is personnel's cybersecurity awareness (Gioulekas et al., 2022). This can be improved by ensuring that healthcare professionals receive adequate training to recognize and respond to cyber-attacks. These training programs should focus on educating healthcare professionals about the various types of cybersecurity threats they may encounter, how to identify possible signs of an attack, and the appropriate actions to take in response (Nifakos et al., 2021).

Implementing a cybersecurity checklist can significantly reduce the risk of cybersecurity breaches. Studies have shown that checklists can enhance patient safety and minimize errors in healthcare facilities. In addition, utilizing a checklist can ensure that healthcare professionals are adhering to the proper cybersecurity protocols (Wen et al., 2021). A well-defined software update procedure can help ensure systems are regularly patched and safeguarded against known vulnerabilities. Checklists have been successfully implemented in various industries, such as aviation and surgery, and there is potential for them to be utilized in the healthcare sector as well (Rêgo, 2019).

4. Relevance and Design Cycles

The interviews with Nurses A, B, C, D, and E revealed that patient data privacy is their topmost priority in healthcare practice. They all agreed that sensitive patient information should be safeguarded, and phishing emails should be prevented as they pose a common threat to healthcare professionals. When it comes to addressing cybersecurity concerns, Nurses A, B, C, and E mentioned that they rely on hospital-organized training sessions and updates from the IT department. On the other hand, Nurse D emphasized the importance of annual cybersecurity training sessions and online resources provided by the IT department.

All nurses suggested including verifying email sources, creating robust passwords, and identifying suspicious activities on devices in a cybersecurity checklist. They also recommended adding contact information for reporting incidents and an overview of prevalent healthcare-related cybersecurity threats. To make the checklist more engaging and user-friendly, Nurses A, B, D, and E proposed using visual aids and real-life examples. Nurse B suggested implementing regular reminders and easy access through technology such as an app or QR codes. Nurse C suggested enhancing engagement through interactive training sessions.

Despite recognizing time constraints as a significant obstacle, all nurses emphasized the importance of having concise and easily accessible checklists on workstations (Teng et al., 2021). They believe that a checklist would be a handy reminder to follow cybersecurity best practices, especially with busy schedules. These insights highlight the need for accessible, engaging, and concise cybersecurity resources to help healthcare professionals effectively address cybersecurity challenges daily.

The cybersecurity checklist produced in this study, tailored for the healthcare sector, includes the following three key elements:

1. Log Out - Logging out of computer systems and applications is a fundamental practice in cybersecurity. Logging out of users is important as a preventive measure against unauthorized access to patient data. Educating users has a positive effect on improving logout compliance.
2. Check Emails - Phishing attacks are a common entry point for cyber threats. Krause (2017) investigates the effectiveness of email security awareness training in healthcare settings. Their findings reveal that training programs significantly reduce the likelihood of healthcare professionals falling victim to phishing emails, enhancing email security.
3. Keep Safe - Securing devices and data is essential in healthcare cybersecurity. Nifakos et al. (2021) examine the role of encryption in securing patient data on portable devices. Their research underscores the importance of encryption practices and the need for continuous antivirus and anti-malware software updates.

5. Discussion

The purpose of this paper is to investigate ways to create a straightforward and easy-to-remember cybersecurity checklist that healthcare practitioners can use to improve cybersecurity in the healthcare sector. The goal is to determine the key factors to consider when designing a cybersecurity checklist that is user-friendly and convenient for busy healthcare workers to use effectively. By synthesizing information from various sources, we have identified three essential elements that should be included in a cybersecurity checklist for healthcare professionals: proper log-out procedures, email security awareness training, and device and data encryption.

Healthcare professionals should implement a comprehensive cybersecurity checklist specifically tailored to the healthcare industry (Poleto et al., 2021). By incorporating key elements such as logging out of computer systems and applications, checking emails for phishing attacks, and securing devices and data through encryption and regular updates, healthcare professionals can effectively mitigate cyber risks and threats. Moreover, healthcare professionals must be educated about the potential risks associated with cyber threats and the importance of proactively addressing them (Puder et al., 2023). To achieve this, policymakers and healthcare institutions must implement proper measures for cybersecurity, including investing in risk management systems and training employees to recognize and be vigilant against cyberattacks. While these measures may impact the speed of accessing patient information, it is a necessary trade-off to ensure the safety and security of sensitive data.

It is also essential to recognize the significance of ongoing user training programs in reinforcing these cybersecurity practices. Studies have shown promising results in improving compliance rates and reducing vulnerabilities. By prioritizing cybersecurity and integrating these practices into daily routines, healthcare professionals can contribute to developing a robust "human firewall" that safeguards patient information and promotes a culture of cybersecurity within the healthcare industry (Nifakos et al., 2021). Implementing these cybersecurity measures is crucial for protecting the integrity and privacy of patient data and ensuring the continuity and quality of healthcare services. To address the existing gaps in cybersecurity training for healthcare professionals, it is imperative to establish a standardized mode of delivery, a comprehensive curriculum, and clear training assessment criteria.

Using the checklist in healthcare settings can help healthcare professionals understand the importance of cybersecurity and take necessary steps to protect patient data and prevent cyberattacks (Dias et al., 2021). Furthermore, the checklist can serve as a valuable tool for healthcare institutions to assess their current cybersecurity practices and identify areas for improvement.

6. Conclusions

The healthcare industry suffers from a lack of awareness of cyber risks, even though understanding them and recognizing the effects of individual actions contributes significantly to the organization's overall cybersecurity. Nurses play a key role in protecting patients' data privacy. However, they have difficulties in ensuring cybersecurity measures. One significant way to improve cybersecurity in the healthcare industry is to provide nurses with enhanced awareness to practice cybersecurity behaviors. Based on the interviews conducted in this study, a checklist has been developed to provide user input and insights to improve cybersecurity.

In addition to focusing on nurses' cybersecurity practices, the literature emphasizes the importance of identifying the effects of cyber incidents. These effects are far-reaching and affect both the healthcare organization and its patients. Nurses' further training should also focus on dealing with the effects of cyber disruptions.

Acknowledgements

The research conducted in this paper was triggered by the project 'Collaborative, Multi-modal and Agile Professional Cybersecurity Training Program for a Skilled Workforce In the European Digital Single Market and Industries' (CyberSecPro) project. This project has received funding from the European Union's Digital Europe Programme (DEP) under grant agreement No 101083594. Special thanks to the partners of these projects and their contributions.

References

Altamimi, S. (2022) "Investigating and mitigating the role of neutralisation techniques on information security policies violation in healthcare organisations", PhD thesis, University of Glasgow.

Cartwright, A. (2023) "The elephant in the room: cybersecurity in healthcare", *Journal of Clinical Monitoring and Computing,* Vol 1, No. 10.

CyberSecPro (2023) Home. [Online] Available at: https://www.cybersecpro-project.eu/ [Accessed 27 12 2023].

Dias, F., et al. (2021) "Risk management focusing on the best practices of data security systems for healthcare", *International Journal of Innovation,* Vol 9, No. 1, pp. 45-78.

Gioulekas, F., et al. (2022) "A Cybersecurity Culture Survey Targeting Healthcare Critical Infrastructures", *Healthcare,* Vol. 10, 327. pp 1-19.

Hevner, A. & Chatterjee, S. (2010) *Design research in information systems: theory and practice*, New York: Springer Science and Business Media.

Kandasamy, K., Srinivas, S., Achuthan, K. & Rangan, V. (2022) "Digital Healthcare - Cyberattacks in Asian Organizations: An Analysis of Vulnerabilities, Risks, NIST Perspectives, and Recommendations", *IEEE Access*, Vol. 10, pp. 12345-12364.

Kruse, C.S., Smith, B., Vanderlinden, H., et al. (2017) "Security Techniques for the Electronic Health Records", *J Med Syst,* Vol 41, 127.

Nifakos, Sokratis, et al. (2021) "Influence of human factors on cyber security within healthcare organisations: A systematic review", *Sensors* 21.15: 5119.

Pant, K., Bhatia, M., & Pant, R. (2022) "Integrated care with digital health innovation: pressing challenges", *Journal of Integrated Care* 30.4, pp. 324-334.

Poleto, T, et al. (2021) "Fuzzy cognitive scenario mapping for causes of cybersecurity in telehealth services", *Healthcare,* Vol. 9, No. 11.

Puder, A., Henle, J. & Sax, E. (2023) "Threat Assessment and Risk Analysis (TARA) for Interoperable Medical Devices in the Operating Room Inspired by the Automotive Industry", *Healthcare,* Vol. 11, No. 6.

Rajamäki, J., Rathod, P. & Kioskli, K. (2023) "Demand Analysis of the Cybersecurity Knowledge Areas and Skills for the Nurses: Preliminary Findings", *European Conference on Cyber Warfare and Security,* Vol. 22, No. 1.

Rêgo, A. (2019) "WHO Surgical Safety Checklist", *Biomedical Journal of Scientific & Technical Research,* Vol. 20, No. 1, pp. 14815-14816.

Rizzoni, F., Magalini, S., Casaroli, A., Mari, P., Dixon, M., & Coventry, L. (2022) "Phishing simulation exercise in a large hospital: A case study", *Digital Health* 8, 20552076221081716.

Sabra, M. (2021) "Cyberthreats on Implantable Medical Devices", *JISCR*, Vol. 4, No. 1, pp. 36-42.

Sütterlin, S., Knox, B. J., Maennel, K., Canham, M., & Lugo, R. G. (2022) "On the Relationship between Health Sectors' Digitalization and Sustainable Health Goals: A Cyber Security Perspective", *Good Health and Well-Being*, 133.

Teng, Z. et al. (2021) "Checklist Usage in Secure Software Development", In: David C. Wyld et al. (Eds) *Computer Science & Information Technology (CS & IT),* pp. 283-293.

Wen, X., et al. (2021) "Systematic Evaluation of the Effect of Bedside Ward Round Checklist on Clinical Outcomes of Critical Patients", *Journal of Healthcare Engineering* 2021.

Zhuravlev, M. & Blagoveshchenskaya, O. (2020) "Telemedicine: current state and COVID-19 lessons", *Legal Issues in the digital Age* 2: 92-143.

What Culture is ChatGPT's AI?

Juhani Rauhala[1] and Tong Xin[2]
[1]University of Jyväskylä, Jyväskylä, Finland
[2]Queen Mary University of London, London, United Kingdom

juhani.jr.rauhala@jyu.fi
t.xin@qmul.ac.uk

Abstract: Artificial intelligence (AI) is increasingly used in many fields. It is widely perceived as an intelligent system that does not just follow algorithms but can demonstrate independent judgment. AI is especially important in handling complex tasks. The responses from the most popular AI chat interface, Chat Generative Pre-Trained Transformer (ChatGPT), are used for guiding decision-making processes and can provide informative answers or recommendations for a wide variety of scenarios. Such scenarios can include job applicants screening or planning for military strategizing. However, similar to human intelligence, which is characterized by cultural biases affecting thought processes and interactions, AI's outputs may also be influenced by inherent cultural biases, whether programmed or incidental, potentially leading to inappropriate outcomes. Given that AI is often used to assist or replace human decision-making, it is particularly important to examine its potential cultural biases. This study aims to assess the cultural bias of ChatGPT by comparing the responses of ChatGPT with established cultural indices, employing the cultural parameters defined by House et al. (2004) and Hofstede (2001). The methodology involves selecting specific cultural parameters, formulating a set of questions representative of these parameters, and analyzing ChatGPT's responses. By using appropriate statistical methods, this study intends to compare ChatGPT's manifested culture with the known values of existing cultures as defined by the GLOBE and Hofstede parameters.

Keywords: Artificial intelligence, Military Planning, Chatgpt, Cultural Parameters, Societal Implications of Technology

1. Introduction and Background

AI represents a technological development employed across a wide variety of applications. Internet users can interface with AI through the familiar and accessible format of online chat (Hall, 2024). Such popular platforms include Microsoft Copilot, Google Gemini, and the immensely popular ChatGPT (Ortiz, 2024). ChatGPT was the first and some still consider it the best AI chatbot (Dreibelbis & Duffy, 2024; Ortiz, 2024). It is a multimodal generative AI that "learns" by interacting with its users (Naik et al., 2023). Users can apply AI by posing questions and problems to it via chat interfaces, with responses provided by an AI engine. The AI engine used by ChatGPT is OpenAI (Hall, 2024; Schulman et al., 2022).

AI should not be interpreted as "intelligence" in the human sense, including a lifetime's background of experiences, cultural exposures, and empathetic aspects of interaction. The human concept of intelligence is influenced by culture (Sternberg, 2020). Nonetheless, AI, especially in chat formats like GPT, is often interpreted – and sometimes misunderstood – as intelligence through a human lens. Indeed, ChatGPT is designed for human use and to simulate an intelligent human counterpart (Colas et al., 2022). Culture and intelligence (as human-centrically defined) are related in that the definition or recognition of intelligence is dependent on the culture where it is displayed (Sternberg, 2020). This raises the question of how AI, as distinct from intelligence exhibited by humans, through its outputs, may be perceived and applied between cultures. Our work should help to address this issue.

The applications of AI are becoming more and more widespread, from helping employers screen job applications (Kelly, 2024) to alleviating people's loneliness (Broadbent et al., 2023), and even influencing military strategic planning (Flournoy, 2023) and real-time combat situations (Pawlyk, 2020). These applications not only require AI to communicate effectively with humans, whether through assistive robot or interfaces like voice, video, or chat, but also challenge AI's ability to recognize and adapt to different cultural contexts. Such adaptation would be an ability for the AI to exhibit "cultural intelligence," as described by Alifuddin & Widodo (2022). Cultural factors are known to influence human thought and communication (Hwa-Froelich & Vigil, 2004), which is critical to the accuracy of information or advice provided by AI, especially in areas where cultural differences may have significant implications, such as military strategy. Approaches to warfare can vary by culture. Lee (2020) asserts that societal culture plays a role in national militaries' environments and their missions.

Although some attention has been given to cultural aspects of AI, most studies have focused on assessing human responses to AI information rather than directly exploring how AI processes and reflects cultural parameters. Some researchers have noted that the lack of bona fide culture in AI can lead to devaluations of some of its products by consumers (Tubadji et al., 2021).

Additionally, concerns have been raised about bias in AI (Yeh & Clare, 2023). These include controversial ones that have led to contentious discussions in the public domain. The biases include racial (Levin, 2016), gender (Hamilton, 2018), and species (Hagendorff et al., 2023). AI bias in medicine may result in unsuitable treatments (Tejani et al., 2023). Susceptibilities to gender bias in military applications of AI have been studied (Chandler, 2021). Google's Gemini image generator exhibited bias that resulted in inaccurate portrayals of historical figures (Lanum, 2024). A gender bias has been found in a hiring application of AI (Hamilton, 2018). AI bias has also been shown in politics (Baum & Villasenor, 2023) and in public diplomacy (Huang, 2024). Such biases can negatively affect the objectivity or utility of the AI. Therefore, in light of these considerations, understanding AI's performance in cultural adaptability has become both important and urgent, even though this field is still in its infancy.

AI is being anticipated to learn cultures (Colas et al., 2022) and to teach cultures (Johnson & Valente, 2009). Some researchers discuss "the culture of AI" (Elliott, 2019). We ask instead "What culture is ChatGPT's AI?" It not only involves the development of artificial intelligence technology, but also touches on the deep-seated issues of its interaction with human culture. If we can determine the culture of ChatGPT's AI, then we may predict the potential inherent bias in its outputs. The various inquiries, problems, and situations for which such outputs can be applied are limited by the imagination. The outputs could be used for cyberdefense or cyberwarfare purposes. It is not clear whether or how any inherent culture of ChatGPT may result in sub-optimal outputs for cyberdefense or cyberwarfare applications – this merits separate study. Nonetheless, our work should have relevance to such scenarios to the extent that military practitioners, including those engaged in cyberdefense or cyberwarfare, expect or wish to apply their own cultures to their planning or strategies.

Our paper proposes a method to assess ChatGPT's AI using widely accepted cultural paramaters, describes a necessary feasiblity assessment, identifies a potential obstacle, and concludes with a brief summary.

2. Hypothetical Framework and Planned Methods

Our research aims to investigate the cultural dimensions encapsulated by OpenAI's ChatGPT through its conversational interface. If we can determine cultural attributes of the AI by applying established methods and parameters, we may gain knowledge about the cultural bias inherent in its responses. The work is exploratory.

To this end, we will investigate the culture of ChatGPT's AI by posing to it culture-differentiating multiple-choice questions and recording its responses. The questions will be selected from surveys that were used by House et al., (2004) and Hofstede (2001). Hofstede and House et al.'s expansive works on cultural measurements are widely recognized in the research community and have been the basis for numerous studies and for proposals for alternative cultural frameworks (Adamovic, 2023; Javidan et al., 2006; Venaik & Brewer, 2010). The surveys of House et al., (2004) (herein also referred to as the GLOBE study) and Hofstede (2001) contain 199 scale questions that assess several cultural characteristics. The characteristics include individualism, uncertainty avoidance, and assertiveness; some of which may have similarities to the warfare traits of Pitman (2011). (Pitman (2011) describes some warfare traits as aggression, risk taking, ingroup altruism, outgroup xenophobia, dominance and subordination, and territoriality.) Their survey work and their analyses of responses that they acquired resulted in insights into differentiations between cultures of 76 countries. The differentiations were made to varying degrees between characteristics whose presence varied in commonality between respondents of the studied nationalities. Correlations between the parametric survey results of House and Hofstede exist that demonstrate validity of their parameters that are similarly defined.

First, we will choose Hofstede or GLOBE study parameters that not only distinguish cultures effectively but also have relevance to pertinent contexts, including military contexts. Then, we will gather questions from Hofstede's (2001) or House et al.'s (2004) research that match these chosen parameters. For data-gathering, we will interact with OpenAI using ChatGPT.

The AI will be instructed to assume a role as a human being maximally representative of its own processing characteristics for the purpose of answering several questions. The questions would indicate the selected cultural parameters.

Our work will select questions using the following criteria:

1. They must be multiple-choice.
2. They must have maximum relevance.
    a. This will be measured by their influence on the parameters or indices that we deem to be pertinent. The pertinent parameters or indices will be selected based on their similarity or

importance to hypothetical use-cases that we contrive. Such use-cases may include cross-cultural communication, development of military strategy, or methods of adversarial or benign intelligence gathering.

3. Their responses as acquired and analyzed in Hofstede's (2001) and House et al.'s (2004) works should be maximally differentiating between cultures.

We will assess the feasibility of posing the questions as such to ChatGPT. We will then assess the feasibility of obtaining useful responses from ChatGPT. This will be done be analyzing the collected questions for the desired cultural indices. The analysis process will include a judgement of whether a given question could be posed to ChatGPT in its original phrasing with a reasonable expectation of a useful or sensible response. A potential obstacle to such an expectation is that unlike in Hofstede's (2001) and House et al.'s (2004) works, the respondent to the questions is AI.

3. Conclusion

As use of AI increases for a breadth of applications, so does the importance of understanding its potential intrinsic or inherent biases. Because AI communicates and interacts with humans, culture plays some role in its communication process. The ChatGPT interface is simple and very popular, and thus is a reasonable tool for investigating cultural manifestations of AI. Knowledge of the cultural parameters of ChatGPT's AI should help its users assess the suitability of its outputs. Such knowledge may have implications, perhaps profound, when AI is used for security and defense strategizing. Our work may also give insight into the origins of biases it has exhibited, and have implications for the use of AI for simulatory data-gathering.

References

Adamovic, M. (2023). Unlocking the Cultural Mosaic: A Comparison of Hofstede and Modern Cultural Value Frameworks (pp. 181–212). Vernon Press.

Alifuddin, Moh., & Widodo, W. (2022). How Is Cultural Intelligence Related to Human Behavior? Journal of Intelligence, 10(1), 3. https://doi.org/10.3390/jintelligence10010003

Broadbent, E., Billinghurst, M., Boardman, S. G., & Doraiswamy, P. M. (2023). Enhancing social connectedness with companion robots using AI. Science Robotics, 8(80), eadi6347. https://doi.org/10.1126/scirobotics.adi6347

Chandler, K. (2021). Does Military AI Have Gender? Understanding Bias and Promoting Ethical Approaches In Military Applications of AI. United Nations Institute for Disarmament Research. https://doi.org/10.37559/GEN/2021/04

Colas, C., Karch, T., Moulin-Frier, C., & Oudeyer, P.-Y. (2022). Language and culture internalization for human-like autotelic AI. Nature Machine Intelligence, 4(12), 1068–1076. https://doi.org/10.1038/s42256-022-00591-4

Dreibelbis, E., & Duffy, J. (2024, January 8). The Best AI Chatbots for 2024. PCMag.Com. https://www.pcmag.com/picks/the-best-ai-chatbots

Elliott, A. (2019). The Culture of AI: Everyday Life and the Digital Revolution (1st ed.). Routledge. https://doi.org/10.4324/9781315387185

Flournoy, M. A. (2023, December). AI Is Already at War: How Artificial Intelligence Will Transform the Military. Foreign Affairs, 102(6), 56, 58–60, 62–90.

Hagendorff, T., Bossert, L. N., Tse, Y. F., & Singer, P. (2023). Speciesist bias in AI: How AI applications perpetuate discrimination and unfair outcomes against animals. AI and Ethics, 3(3), 717–734. https://doi.org/10.1007/s43681-022-00199-9

Hall, J. (2024, March 9). How Does ChatGPT Work? OpenAI's Groundbreaking Chatbot, Explained. ExtremeTech. https://www.msn.com/en-us/news/technology/how-does-chatgpt-work-openai-s-groundbreaking-chatbot-explained/ar-BB1jBuVM

Hamilton, I. A. (2018, October 10). Amazon built an AI tool to hire people but had to shut it down because it was discriminating against women. Business Insider. https://www.businessinsider.com/amazon-built-ai-to-hire-people-discriminated-against-women-2018-10?op=1&r=US&IR=T

Hofstede, G. H. (2001). Culture's consequences: Comparing values, behaviors, institutions, and organizations across nations (2nd ed). Sage Publications.

House, R. J., Hanges, P. J., Javidan, M., Dorfman, P. W., & Gupta, V. (Eds.). (2004). Culture, leadership, and organizations: The GLOBE study of 62 societies. Sage Publications.

Hwa-Froelich, D. A., & Vigil, D. C. (2004). Three Aspects of Cultural Influence on Communication: A Literature Review. Communication Disorders Quarterly, 25(3), 107–118. https://doi.org/10.1177/15257401040250030201

Javidan, M., House, R. J., Dorfman, P. W., Hanges, P. J., & Sully De Luque, M. (2006). Conceptualizing and measuring cultures and their consequences: A comparative review of GLOBE's and Hofstede's approaches. Journal of International Business Studies, 37(6), 897–914. https://doi.org/10.1057/palgrave.jibs.8400234

Johnson, W. L., & Valente, A. (2009). Tactical Language and Culture Training Systems: Using AI to Teach Foreign Languages and Cultures. AI Magazine, 30(2), 72–83. https://doi.org/10.1609/aimag.v30i2.2240

Kelly, J. (2024, February 20). How AI Helps Employers Screen Candidates, Manage Staff And Make Hiring And Firing Decisions. Forbes.Com. https://www.forbes.com/sites/jackkelly/2024/02/20/how-ai-helps-employers-screen-candidates-manage-staff-and-make-hiring-and-firing-decisions/

Lanum, N. (2024, March 28). Gemini fallout: Former Google employee warns of "terrifying patterns" in company's AI algorithms. Foxbusiness.Com. https://www.foxbusiness.com/media/gemini-fallout-former-google-employee-warns-terrifying-patterns-companys-ai-algorithms

Lee, W. E. (Ed.). (2020). Warfare and culture in world history (Second edition). New York University Press.

Naik, I., Naik, D., & Naik, N. (2023). Chat Generative Pre-Trained Transformer (ChatGPT): Comprehending its Operational Structure, AI Techniques, Working, Features and Limitations. 2023 IEEE International Conference on ICT in Business Industry & Government (ICTBIG), 1–9. https://doi.org/10.1109/ICTBIG59752.2023.10456201

Ortiz, S. (2024, March 18). The best AI chatbots: ChatGPT isn't the only one worth trying. ZDNET.Com. https://www.zdnet.com/article/best-ai-chatbot/

Pawlyk, O. (2020, August 24). Rise of the Machines: AI Algorithm Beats F-16 Pilot in Dogfight. Military.Com. https://www.military.com/daily-news/2020/08/24/f-16-pilot-just-lost-algorithm-dogfight.html

Pitman, G. R. (2011). The Evolution of Human Warfare. Philosophy of the Social Sciences, 41(3), 352–379. https://doi.org/10.1177/0048393110371380

Schulman, J., Zoph, B., Kim, C., Hilton, J., Menick, J., Weng, J., Uribe, J. F. C., Fedus, L., Metz, L., Pokorny, M., Lopes, R. G., Zhao, S., Vijayvergiya, A., Sigler, E., Perelman, A., Voss, C., Heaton, M., Parish, J., Cummings, D., … Hesse, C. (2022, November 30). Introducing ChatGPT. OpenAI. https://openai.com/blog/chatgpt

Sternberg, R. J. (2020). Culture and Intelligence. In R. J. Sternberg, Oxford Research Encyclopedia of Psychology. Oxford University Press. https://doi.org/10.1093/acrefore/9780190236557.013.585

Tejani, A. S., Retson, T. A., Moy, L., & Cook, T. S. (2023). Detecting Common Sources of AI Bias: Questions to Ask When Procuring an AI Solution. Radiology, 307(3), e230580. https://doi.org/10.1148/radiol.230580

Tubadji, A., Huang, H., & Webber, D. J. (2021). Cultural proximity bias in AI-acceptability: The importance of being human. Technological Forecasting and Social Change, 173, 121100. https://doi.org/10.1016/j.techfore.2021.121100

Venaik, S., & Brewer, P. (2010). Avoiding uncertainty in Hofstede and GLOBE. Journal of International Business Studies, 41(8), 1294–1315. https://doi.org/10.1057/jibs.2009.96

Yeh, J., & Clare, C. A. (2023). Women's Health and Artificial Intelligence (AI): Addressing Potential for Bias and Discrimination in AI. Current Women s Health Reviews, 19(4), e010323214222.
https://doi.org/10.2174/157340481904230301140515

Late Submissions

Cyber Social Disruption due to Cyber Attacks

Jorge Barbosa

Coimbra Polytechnic Institute, Portugal

jorge.barbosa@isec.pt

Abstract: We analyze the implications of cyber war actions directed at specific targets, such as critical infrastructures, for modern civil societies that are profoundly dependent on computer systems. These critical infrastructures, whether they are cyber-physical systems or computer systems can be paralyzed or even destroyed if the systems used to directly or remotely manage them are cyber-attacked. Cyber-attacks in the context of cyber war, can generate chaos, which combined with the domino effects caused by the impact on other computer systems, then those directly attacked but indirectly affected, can theoretically lead to major disruptions to the internal order, or even to civil war, due to the scope that such actions may reach. The disturbances caused in civil society as a whole, and in military structures and equipment can go far beyond the local effects on the targets attacked, as would happen in a conventional kinetic war action. The crisis and social disturbance caused may even put the sovereignty of the attacked state at risk. For this specific case of social disruption, which is caused by cyber war actions, we use a concept to describe the situation more adequately, which we call *Cyber Social Disruption*.

Keywords: Cyber Social Disruption, Cyber Dependence, Cyber Warfare, Critical Infra-Structures Protection

1. Introduction

It is considered that in the event of a conventional war, the protection, through conventional kinetic means, of infrastructures is essential. In the event of a cyber war, those structure's protection is also fundamental, due to the local and systemic effects that may indirectly occur on other computer or cyber-physical systems, other than those attacked. Physical protective barriers may be useless in the event of a cyber-war, making cyber barriers indispensable.

Another important aspect, that difficult the establishment of protection against cyber-attacks, is that those protections must be thought out, designed and implemented during peacetime. The speed and unpredictability of a computer attack won't allow time for the cyber protection equipment to be built, put into operation, and used, with the required training. In the case of a conventional kinetic attack, all, or part of the conventional kinetic defences need to be installed close to critical infrastructures, such as the placement of anti-aircraft missile systems next to dams, and may be installed with relatively little advance, due to the fact that kinetic warfare actions are more visible and predictable, through on site-intelligence or remote observation such as satellites, allowing protective actions and defence measures. On the other hand, actions in cyber-war can take place in total secrecy, and be a total surprise for the attacked country.

In the event that a cyber-attack has been launched, it may be too late to implement cyber defence actions, due to the speed and unpredictability of the action. Computerized control systems may immediately be destroyed or rendered unusable, by the deletion or scrambling of database records related to industrial, financial, logistical, or energetically related systems. The result may be the total disruption of energy, including fossil fuels and electricity, food distribution logistics, or even drinking water production and distribution.

Likewise, unlike conventional kinetic protection systems, the effective lack of knowledge of one's own, and the enemy's computer systems, their constant evolution, and the evolution of the cyber techniques affecting them make it very difficult to develop and implement effective protection mechanisms promptly. What is installed today may no longer be effective tomorrow.

2. Scope of this work

The consideration of the cyber actions that we intend to make in this paper does not exactly focus on common cybercrime actions normally carried out by individuals or organizations of individuals against institutions or individuals, in most cases to obtain economic benefits from their actions. These actions are also isolated acts in the sense that they can be triggered simultaneously against several institutions or people but are not usually carried out in a coordinated manner and with the aim of causing a major impact on the society or country attacked as a whole. We will therefore consider actions that are not specifically directed at individuals or institutions in themselves but that actions against these institutions in particular against their computer and/or cyber-physical systems, usually referred to as critical infrastructures, which operate are done in a coordinated and systemic aim having as its objective as a whole and in the coordinated and specific way in which the paralysis of a society or some of its main sectors are triggered through the total or partial destruction of these critical systems or their paralysis and not the obtaining of simple economic benefits but yes with political, economic or military objectives against a country to affect their sovereignty. Therefore, and also taking into account these objectives, this type of cyber-attack is, specifically, called cyber war action. It is assumed that those behind these cyber actions are other countries interested in disturbing the attacked country.

These actions and effects are not new, for some years now reports of actions against computer systems and cyber-physical systems have been made. Many of these reports could not be factually proven as they were mostly secret actions or habitually denied by their likely authors and even by the target countries themselves, strange as it may seem as they cannot or do not want to confirm these attacks that they were targeted in order not to expose secrets or show weakness. These cyber war actions are often launched using techniques commonly used in common cyber-crime, but their final objective is not the same as mentioned above. It is also assumed that they are not perpetuated by individuals or groups of individuals acting on their own, but by organized groups created or at least dependent on the perpetuating countries organized as cyber-attack military corps of those countries, *Cybercorps*. These cybercorps, both cyber defense and cyber-attack, are even considered, given the great importance assigned to them, as the 5th military operational domain designated as *"Cyberspace"* alongside the three more traditional operational domains *"Land"*, *"Sea"* and *"Air"* and the also relatively recent fourth operational domain, the *"Space"*.

As early as 1993 in the RAND Corporation publication *"CyberWar Is Coming!"*, the authors used expressions such as *"As an innovation in warfare, we anticipate that cyberwar may be to the 21st century what blitzkrieg was to the 20th century."* and also *"Netwars are not real wars, traditionally defined. But netwar might be developed into an instrument for trying, early on, to prevent a real war from arising."*, (Arquilla & Ronfeldt, 1993).

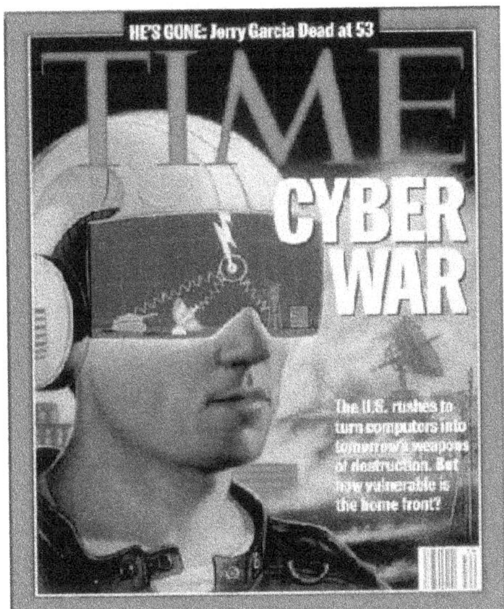

Figure 1 - Cover of TIME magazine of August 21, 1995: Cyber War

Time magazine also dedicated its cover to this topic on August 21, 1995, Figure 1. The advent of Cyberwar was 25 years ago. The USA then created what was considered the first *"Cybercorp"*, the *"Air Force – 1st Cyber Division"*, Figure 2.

Figure 1 - Air Force – 1st cyber division

In addition to this difference in actors participants in the actions that we mentioned and the techniques similar to those of ordinary cyber-crimes, a big difference lies in the fact that these Cybercorps maybe they use more sophisticated means based on computer flaws not yet publicly known and called "Zero Day Vulnerability", ZDV from which they are created cyber-attack software. This software is called Exploit and if it is developed for a ZDV it will be called "Zero Day Exploit", ZDE. ZDEs are the most powerful cyber weapons because as they are based on a computer flaw still unknown to others, there is, a priori, no cyber defense for them.

The approach considered in this work then results from the assumption that it is necessary to go a little further than what is usually considered when addressing common cyber security topics and enter into a broader approach, including considerations related to cyber war because its consequences are much more pernicious.

In other words, the means involved and the possible actions are not simple cyber security acts but much more planned, sophisticated actions, foreseen in advance with a view to possible future use in the aforementioned contexts, these are true acts of war but triggered without being through of the usual kinetic weapons. As such we think that a different framework and importance must be given to acts due to cyber war actions in contrast to that attributed to simple cyber-crime actions, hence the need to systematize concepts in order to be able to perceive more coherently and correctly its results. In particular, we are concerned with making such a systematization in terms of its effects on civil society, namely the social disruptions that it can and we understand that they will cause.

There have been articles for some years now that address this topic of cyber security attacks with possible effects on civil society, for example (Lena Yuryna Connolly, 2020), (Cartwright, 2023), (Erik Schrijvers, 2021), and (V. Palleti, 2021). But from the analysis of these papers that we did, their focus is not on systemic and coordinated actions triggered by countries through their already mentioned organized structures, the Cybercorps or similar, but rather and generally framed in "common" cybercrime actions which alone can also cause social disturbances but with much more limited effects in time and space and much less dangerous.

These possible disruptive actions for civil society caused by these acts of cyber-crime are not in themselves their objective but rather something that in the military context is usually called side effects since the objective of cyber-crime is, as already mentioned, normally the obtaining economic benefits; cyber war actions may have exactly the opposite objective, that is, to cause this disruption of civil society.

Then, such actions, although they can be disruptive, are not or presumably will not be comparable in their effects and disturbances resulting from attacks in the context of cyberwar in which the vector of social disturbance in the society of the attacked country would be one of the main vectors considered and of much greater dimensions and proportions. Since 2018, we have worked in this area of cyber war and its effects at various levels, including social disruption, for example (Barbosa, 2020), (Barbosa, 2022), and (Barbosa, 2020). However, the systematization and definition of concepts, namely those relating to acts arising from actions of cyberwar that affect civil societies is fundamental, given its danger and possibility of being considered in acts of cyberwar. This conceptualization is also necessary to differentiate it from the acts of vulgar cyber-crime.

3. Use of Cyber Weapons

The usage of cyber weapons is possible due to the weaknesses created by the existence of hardware and software vulnerabilities, which, generally, all computer systems have. When those vulnerabilities are known by a restricted group, but not publicly known, then are called *Zero-Day Vulnerabilities* (*ZDV*). *ZDV* can be used with great advantage in the construction of applications called *Exploits*, which if based on *ZDV* will be called *Zero-Day Exploit, ZDE*, which can be used with great success as cyber weapons. These *ZDEs*, by exploiting vulnerabilities in computer systems, can take control or even paralyze systems affected by these vulnerabilities. If those systems are linked to the control of so-called *Critical Infrastructures*, their affectation and even their shutdown or destruction can harm the attacked country and the normal life of society in that country.

The interest in this type of cyber weapons is not only its usage in common cybercrime, but also in war actions between sovereign States against other sovereign States. As this type of actions can compromise the sovereignty of a State, they are called cyber war, instead of cyber security actions, a term used regarding common cybercrime actions.

From industrial process controllers, such as the very well-known SCADA - Supervisory Control and Data Acquisition or the PLC - Programmable Logic Controller which are industrial controllers of legacy systems with consequent deficiencies due to being based on not only old technologies but mainly designed at a time when there were not so many security concerns, particularly at a time when the internet was not yet massively used nor were they originally designed taking into account the necessary security concerns subsequently taken into account. Despite this, these controllers are still widely used today and due to great difficulties if not even impossibility of replacing it and are currently still widely used in critical infrastructure control systems, such as dams, other power generation stations, water treatment and supply systems, transport logistics, fuel logistics, etc., up to sophisticated cyber-physical systems and also sophisticated computer systems linked to databases, whether for customer relationship management or financial systems in banking services, public or private institutions, ATM systems or automatic payment systems, practically everything is based on computer systems, with the known benefits arising from their use. The disruption, destruction, and alteration of those systems can paralyze, or seriously affect modern societies, due to their dependency on them.

The opposite side of this beneficial use is that if such systems are insecure and therefore possibly penetrable, they can result in catastrophic effects, since the disruption of the aforementioned systems, their destruction or alteration can paralyze or seriously affect modern societies. Therefore, this dependence is critical from this point of view and therefore these systems are tangible targets and subject to military actions against them. These military actions can be triggered by conventional kinetic means, but also triggered by computer systems, through so-called cyber weapons. These cyber weapons act directly on the enemy's computer systems, destroying them, paralyzing them or altering them in such a way as to interrupt or interfere with the normal functioning of the equipment they control or manage.

The theoretical possibilities offered by this military option lead a large number of countries, other than conventional powers, to consider its use. Theoretically, the amount of resources needed, human and material, are much lower than those needed to launch conventional military operations. Although the economic and human resources necessary to acquire these technological skills means may be considerable, they are exceptionally lower than those needed to train and equip human resources in conventional kinetic war. The combination of these factors makes this option very desirable and, theoretically, may lead to the proliferation of cyber powers prepared for cyber warfare, as an alternative to kinetic warfare, (Barbosa, 2020).

4. Protection of Cyber-Physical and Digital Critical Services

Concerning cyber protection of services and infrastructures, it must be kept in mind that systems can only be cyber-attacked if they are a priori predisposed to. Flaws must be present in the systems to allow the use of Exploits, which take advantage of those failures, they interfere with the normal functioning of the systems. Therefore, protection actions must be focused on two vectors, (Barbosa, 2019):

1. Eliminate these eventual failures;
2. Obviates the possible use of ZDV.

To protect these vital installations, the Cyber Defence actions necessary for this protection may involve not only direct actions triggered during cyber-attacks but essentially depend on indirect actions that, as already mentioned, were studied, planned and implemented in time.

Three large groups are considered, listed below and we will detail:

4.1 Critical and Essential Conditions for Cyber Defence

1. Legal and Organizational Frameworks
2. The Human Factors
3. Technological Needs

4.2 Cyber-Permeability of Systems and Infrastructures

1. Obsolete Software or Hardware
2. Alarmist
3. System Operators
4. Technical Support Team
5. External Exposure
6. Networks Interconnections
7. Physical Means
8. Physical Access of People

4.3 Commitment to Cyber Means for Cyber Defence

1. Chain of Command
2. Hierarchical Communication Protocols
3. Rapid Integrated Response Teams
4. Replacement Equipment

The first group includes cyber defence actions that all countries must take to protect their critical services and infrastructure. These actions must be general, and not specific for the protection of any particular facility. The creation of possible cyber armies with the mission of triggering defensive and offensive cyber actions, after an attack is initiated, is applicable here. The creation of a cyber-army can be a disincentive to the usage of this type of attack, by other states. Also included at his point, are the equipment and technological resources that allow these cyber armies to carry out cyber defence actions.

In the second group of cyber defence actions for critical services and infrastructures, we consider the equipment itself, that is, the software installed and in use, and the hardware used in the computer systems for command, control, or management of these services and infrastructures. It must be a priority that all software used is fully updated and certified, Periodic routines must be established to check the existence and respective installation of updates for the applications in use, including the basic operating systems or the exploration and control applications themselves. If any of this software is subject to constant updates, this situation should be analyzed and its replacement with other equivalent software should be considered, as constant updates may be a sign of fundamental problems in the software in question. The equipment that is being controlled must also be monitored and analyzed. We must not only specifically focus on the hardware and software of the computer control systems, but also have a more comprehensive perspective including the equipment itself that is being controlled. It may be that problems in these controlled equipment are caused by alteration or physical destruction through the actions of the computer systems that control them.

Special attention should be paid to the operators of these systems, namely by providing them with constant and appropriate training, not only in technical aspects but also in awareness and responsibility. These operators can be the weak party when it comes to the security of these systems and infrastructures. They must be deeply aware of the need to have and adopt a total, integrated and holistic security awareness. Small details about the actions they can take can have major consequences on the overall security of the systems they operate, such as the password policy they must have and use. In this sense, passive and active security protocols must be established and strictly followed.

The technical teams supporting the operation and management of these services and infrastructures must also be aligned with these needs and procedures. Concerns should not only be related to technical aspects, such as maintenance, but on the contrary, they should have a systemic approach.

Exposure to external action should be a major concern. Those external actions can have different origins. Computer networks must be carefully monitored and examined. Connections to networks of any type should not be permitted, except those strictly necessary for the operation of the systems, particularly their remote operation. It should not be forgotten that, as already mentioned, many of these infrastructures still use *SCADA* and *PLC* controllers. These controllers, particularly those from the first generations, were designed at a time when, in addition to security issues being less pressing and known, the systems for which they were designed were not at the time connected to a network, namely to the Internet. For various reasons, most of these systems were subsequently connected to the Internet without themselves and the subsystems they controlled, namely the controllers, having been updated. Whenever possible, there should be a complete separation between public access networks and private access networks to these services and infrastructures.

The physical means used must also be subject to special care. Consideration should be given not only to devices that can be physically connected to systems via computer networks but also to any device, such as pen drives, floppy disks or *CD-ROMs*, that can transfer, purposely or not, harmful applications that interfere with normal functioning of systems. It must also be taken into account that the devices that connect to the IT systems controlling these services and infrastructures must not only be reliable but above all trustworthy. In the literature there are several references to situations in which it is suspected that common computer peripheral equipment, for example printers, have been used to transport *Exploits* to the facilities that later passed into the processing systems, infecting them so that someone from the outside could take over the control of such systems. There are suspicions that the use of such *Exploits* in some cyber wars, for example the attack known as *Stuxnet* or the eventual cyber-attack to interfere, blinding them, with Syrian radar systems before an air attack, was possible using as a gateway input for cyber-attack computer peripherals, (Zetter, 2014), (Carr, 2012) and (Clark & Knake, 2010).

Physical access by unauthorized people to service facilities and critical infrastructures must be prohibited not only to avoid triggering direct actions, even kinetic ones but also because they may intend to install applications that trigger cyber-attacks on the IT systems of these infrastructures and therefore this access should never be allowed.

The speed and unpredictability associated with a possible cyber-attack are not conciliable with the delays in the chains of command of the command structures involved in triggering and conducting defensive cyber actions, whether to minimize effects or launch cyber counter-attacks. Therefore, chains of command and respective communication protocols must be very well defined and established so that there are no failures or delays that could lead to the impossibility of minimizing effects and taking countermeasures. Another aspect to consider is the creation of integrated response centers for cyber warfare actions.

The issue of replacing equipment is one of the most critical aspects of these *Cyber Defence* actions. Considering equipment replacement as an act of *Cyber Defence* is related to the issue of rapid equipment replacement.

This energy replacement can also be considered a defence action because it can allow the effective launch of actions to minimize effects and cyber-attacks, which could be impossible, for example, if there is no energy. However, as mentioned, it is one of the most critical and difficult aspects to achieve.

As can be seen in the simulated example of the destruction of this type of equipment within the scope of *The Aurora Generator Test*, (Clark & Knake, 2010), the eventual physical destruction of electrical generators in a dam is possible. Replacing generators may not be able to be done quickly given the uniqueness and specificity of this type of equipment. Its replacement, if we consider the production time, transportation, and installation time as well as the tests necessary for its effective entry into operational service, can take months. However, the country or a large area of the country may be deprived of electricity from this source. Other similar examples, considering other types of critical equipment, could be considered with the same restrictions.

5. Real Effective Cyber actions against physical targets

There are examples of experimental actions of real physical destruction, simulating software installed remotely on computers that control generators in hydroelectric plants, in which it was relatively easy and quick to physically destroy one of their generators. An example of this is the experience of the *US Department of Energy*, which launched a national *SCADA* testing program in 2003 at the *Idaho National Lab*, *INL*, called the *Aurora Generator Test* and carried out in this laboratory, (Zetter, 2014), (Clark & Knake, 2010).

It was shown in Figure 3, that it was easy and quick (Singer & Friedman, 2014) to destroy a generator similar to those in American dams. In the event of a similar real action, orchestrated as an act of cyber warfare, a country's energy production system, or part of it, could easily be disrupted. In the pictures of Figure 3, we can see that the generator is releasing smoke due to the high rotations to which it is being subjected due to the action that simulates a remote control attack on that generator and ends up self-destructing, (Singer & Friedman, 2014).

Figure 2 - Aurora Generator Test, Idaho National Lab, INL

Another action, not experimental, but real, which became known as *Stuxnet*, the name of the main malware used, was launched against facilities at the *Natanz Nuclear Complex*, in Iran, (Zetter, 2014), (Singer & Friedman, 2014) and (Clark & Knake, 2010). Many authors consider this action as the first real action of an act of cyber warfare. The centrifuge operations of this complex were severely disrupted and some of the centrifuges were physically destroyed. The action was carried out by introducing, into the computers that control the centrifuges *PLC* controllers, an *Exploit* that was later called *Stuxnet*.

On April 27, 2007, cyber actions were launched in the form of violent *DDoS* attacks, which targeted several computer systems in Estonia, namely important websites of the government, parliament, banks and the communications system in general, which resulted in known as the *"Estonian Cyberwar"*. It is assumed that for these *DDoS* attacks, a bot net consisting of 85,000 servers was created, with the attacks lasting three weeks and sixty websites being attacked. These cyber actions have never been officially attributed to any country. However, the Estonian Foreign Minister attributed the attacks to Russia, which has always denied its official participation in them. Russia considered the actions of individuals who acted as *"Patriotic Hackers"*. One of the theories is that they were triggered by the Nashi movement, *"Ours"*. It is believed that this group was organized by supporters of the pro-Putin regime to carry out actions against anti-Motherland forces. Its leader was an advisor to Russian parliamentary leader Sergei Markov (Singer & Friedman, 2014).

These cyber-attacks on Estonia reinforce the conviction that it is difficult to correctly determine the identity of cyber attackers. It is estimated that 25% of the attacks (Singer & Friedman, 2014), presumably originated from computers located in the USA, a country that was an ally of Estonia, and that for this reason and others, theoretically, would have no interest in carrying out such an attack. attack.

At the height of events and due to the near paralysis of its country, the Estonian government requested help from allied countries and organizations, namely NATO, invoking Article 5 of the *Collective Self-Defense Agreement*.

In the 2008 Russia-Georgia War and due to events in Georgia and South Ossetia, cyber-attacks against Georgia occurred. They were highly coordinated among themselves and linked and coincident with invasions by land, sea, and air.

Previously, in the second Russia – Chechnya war that took place between 1997 and 2001, there are reports that the FSB, the Russian Federal Security Service, was responsible for the attack and takedown of Chechen government websites at the time.

Cyberattacks against Ukraine were allegedly launched by Russia in retaliation for that country's actions in Crimea and Donbass. Malware called *Petya* was used and electricity companies, ministries, banks, and newspapers were affected, (Farmer, 2018).

There are suspicions of the Chinese government's involvement in cyberwar actions, disguised as the actions of *"Patriotic Hackers"*. In May 1999, a NATO plane accidentally bombed the Chinese embassy in Belgrade. The Chinese Red Hacker Alliance then launched cyber-attacks against US government websites.

Another action reportedly took place after an accidental collision between an American military plane and a Chinese one in the South China Sea and in protest Chinese hackers launched cyber actions, allegedly in self-defense, against US government websites and institutions. The newspaper The New York Times even classified these actions as those of the First World War via the Web, *"World Wide Web War I"*.

In 2009, North Korea launched cyberwar actions and *DDoS* attacks on a small scale and in specific contexts against the USA on that country's National Day.

Another action attributed to North Korea took place in 2014. Although it is not a cyberwar action, we mention it to highlight and accentuate the scope and the most varied forms in which these attacks can take place. The action was taken against Sony Pictures Entertainment's computer system. The North Koreans felt that their country's honor was offended in the film "The Interview", where the country's leader was allegedly portrayed pejoratively. It will have caused Sony 100 million dollars in losses.

In December 2008, after a military operation launched by Israel, *"Operation Cast Lead"*, several cyberwar actions took place between Israeli and Arab hackers.

Reportedly, there have also been cyber warfare actions in the current conflict between Ukraine and the Russian Federation. However, the cyber-attacks referred to in this paragraph had more the objective of preparing and conditioning the kinetic actions that followed, in what in military strategy is called shaping the theater of operations, than being total cyber war actions, even if inserted in a global action as one of the components of a hybrid war.

6. The Cyber Social Disruption Concept

As far as conventional wars are concerned, on a primary level, the military and political strategists and leaders of a country equate the potential, in the face of a possible and determined enemy, through two factors: the "*Attack Capacity*" and the "*Defence Capacity*" of both their country and that of the enemy country. Considering these capacities, in the case of conventional war between these two countries, infers who, theoretically, can become the winner or the loser.

In the case of a *Cyber War*, these considerations must be different, given the much more complex scenarios.

Mutatis mutandis when considering the strategic analysis of similar factors in a *Cyber War*, the key factors to consider should not only be the two mentioned above, but a total of three, namely: *"Cyber Attack Capability"*, *"Cyber Defence Capacity"* and a third and another factor, concerning conventional war, the *"Cyber Dependency Capacity"* of the countries involved, (Barbosa, 2018).

We consider the *Cyber Dependency Capacity* of a country as the dependence that this country and its society have on IT and the complexity and density of connections and interoperability between its IT systems. The larger the organization, complexity, and density of connections in its IT systems, the greater the country's dependence on IT will be. The greater this dependence, the greater the vulnerability of that country to possible failures in its IT systems. A serious computer failure in an important critical computer system can be a big problem and, in extreme cases, even paralyze the country or many sectors, (Barbosa, 2020).

Modern and developed Western societies, as well as those in some Asian countries, have a very high *Cyber Dependency Capacity* and as such are extremely sensitive to problems in their computer systems, particularly those resulting from *Cyber War*.

Less developed societies are also often underdeveloped in terms of the massive use of information technology in the various organizational aspects of their society. This means that they also have a very low *Cyber Dependency Capacity*. As they do not rely heavily on IT for their daily operations, they are not as sensitive to IT failures and may not even have IT "targets" to attack.

The benefits for civil societies in countries resulting from the massive use of information technology in all aspects of that society, namely service provision, government, central and local administration, banking and finance, transport management, logistics, food, and fuel distribution, etc. it is today an indisputable reality in all minimally developed countries. It can even be said that it is currently no longer possible for these countries to survive without the means and facilities provided by the information society.

Maintaining the information society and the means necessary for its functioning is extremely important. Its alteration or destruction is unthinkable in the current development context. Actions, even relatively small and isolated in their scope and effects, such as the acts of hackers, who, individually or in small groups, trigger cyber actions against individuals or companies, can have relatively serious consequences, (Singer & Friedman, 2014) and (Carr, 2012).

A concern that many security and defence agencies and services have is that such acts do not come from these actors, but are orchestrated and triggered by other actors, namely countries, which, for this purpose, constitute specialized units. If concerted and large-scale actions are carried out against any country, through the exclusive use of IT means, they could profoundly affect the IT systems of that other country, particularly those linked to its critical infrastructures.

This ability of a country's cyber dependence to be directly linked to that country's involvement with information technologies, in particular with the greater or lesser degree of development of its information society, can also transform them into preferential cyber targets.

The combined effects of cyber actions can be so great and disruptive to the experience of civil society in the attacked country that they can lead to serious disruptions in that country. These service dysfunctions, namely the logistics of supplying food, electricity, water, fuel, and other essential goods, banking services, and the impossibility of obtaining money from *ATM* systems or similar, could create not only disruptions in the experience of civil societies but a total disruption. We call this specific type of disruption as *Cyber Social Disruption*.

7. Conclusion

The use of cyber weapons, which allows the launch of *Cyber Wars*, is possible due to vulnerabilities in computer hardware and / or software, which, in general, all computer systems have. When these failures exist in systems more directly related to civil society, for example, critical infrastructures, the consequences of the negative effects of cyber-attacks can be very disruptive to the normal life of civil societies.

In the case of a *Cyber War*, this could lead to a situation that we consider a concept to take into account in *Cyber War* situations and which we call *Cyber Social Disruption*!

Concerns about cyber wars are great because they can be used to totally destroy the target country, both physically and logically. *Cyber Social Disruption* can lead to chaos in modern societies, resulting from the combination of cascading cyber effects, which can consequently cause turbulence and severe disturbances in internal order, and even lead to civil war.

References

Anon, n.d. NATO Cooperative Cyber Defence Centre of Excellence. [Online], s.l.: s.n.

Barbosa, J., 2018. Pequenas potências militares convencionais, Grandes potências militares cibernéticas - Abordagem da utilização de meios informáticos na defesa/ataque militar moderno, Lisboa: Portuguese National Defence Institute, IDN.

Barbosa, J., 2019. The ZDEs as cyber weapons. La Toja, Galicia, Spain, s.n.

Barbosa, J., 2020. Cyber Humanity in Cyber War. Chester, UK, s.n.

Barbosa, J., 2020. Cybernetic Dependency Capacity. In: R. a. others, ed. Developments and Advances in Defence and Security. Smart Innovation, Systems and Technologies. Singapore: Springer.

Barbosa, J., 2020. Is Cyber Warfare an Alternative?. In: Á. R. a. R. P. Pereira, ed. Developments and Advances in Defense and Security, Smart Innovation, Systems and Technologies . Singapore: Springer Nature.

Barbosa, J., 2022. How to Educate to Build an Effective Cyber Resilient Society. In: I. Global, ed. Research Anthology on Advancements in Cybersecurity Education. Hershey(Pennsylvania): Information Resources Management Association, p. 578.

Caldas, A. & Freire, V., 2012. Cibersegurança: das Preocupações à Ação, Lisbon: Portuguese National Defence Institute.

Carr, J., 2012. Inside Cyber Warfare. Second Edition ed. Sebastopol, CA, USA: O'Reilly Media, Inc..

Cartwright, A., 2023. The elephant in the room: cybersecurity in healthcare. Journal of Clinical Monitoring and Computing, Volume 37.

Casimiro, S. d. V., 2018. Quadro Legal para a Cibersegurança e a Ciberdefesa. In: IDN, ed. Contributos para uma Estratégia Nacional de Ciberdefesa. Lisboa: s.n.

Clark, R. A. & Knake, R. K., 2010. Cyber War: the next threat to national security and what to do about. New York: HarperCollins Publishers Inc..

Erik Schrijvers, C. P. ,. R. P., 2021. Preparing for Digital Disruption. s.l.:s.n.

Farmer, B., 2018. Russia was behind 'malicious' cyber attack on Ukraine, Foreign Office says, s.l.: s.n.

Lena Yuryna Connolly, D. S. W. M. L. B. O., 2020. An empirical study of ransomware attacks on organizations: an assessment of severity and salient factors affecting vulnerability. Journal of Cybersecurity, Volume Volume 6, Issue 1.

Ranger, S., 2018. What is cyberwar? Everything you need to know about the frightening future of digital conflict., s.l.: s.n.

Singer, P. W. & Friedman, A., 2014. Cybersecurity and Cyberwar - What everyone needs to know. N. Y,: Oxford University Press.

V. Palleti, S. A. V. M. e. a., 2021. Cascading effects of cyber-attacks on interconnected critical infrastructure. Cybersecur 4, 8.

Zetter, K., 2014. Countdown to Zero Day: Stuxnet and the launch of the world's first digital weapon". N.Y.: Crown Publishers.

An Investigation into the Feasibility of using Distributed Digital Ledger Technology for Digital Forensics for Industrial IoT

Phillip Fitzpatrick and Christina Thorpe
Technological University Dublin, Ireland

Phillip.fitzpatrick@tudublin.ie
Christina.thorpe@tudublin.ie

Abstract: The domain of Digital Forensics for the Industrial Internet of Things (IIoT) and the proposed use of a Distributed Digital Ledger (DDL), has for the most part been theoretical in nature within the current literature. The work in this paper explores the practical feasibility of using DDL technology for Digital Forensics in the IIOT context. We detail a new methodology for testing the performance of writing to and reading from a DDL in an IIOT environment, and present findings on the overhead associated with storing and retrieving IIoT transactions in a DDL. We conclude that while it is possible to build and use a DDL for storing IIoT transactions, there are limitations to the number of sensors that can be supported by a single implementation and the time it takes to retrieve transactions may be too high to be practical for Digital Forensics.

Keywords: Digital Forensics, IIOT, Blockchain, Distributed Digital Ledge, Performance

1. Introduction

Distributed Ledger Technology (DLT) [15, 7] such as Blockchain has garnered significant interest in recent years due to its potential to provide a secure and transparent means of recording and verifying transactions. This has made it a popular choice for applications in various industries, including the Internet of Things (IoT) [8]. In the context of IoT forensics, blockchain can be used to track and verify the actions and events that take place within a connected device network [12]. One key advantage of using blockchain for IoT forensics is its ability to provide an immutable record of events. This means that once a transaction is recorded on the blockchain, it cannot be altered or deleted, providing a tamper-evident record of events. This can be useful in forensic investigations, as it allows investigators to trace the actions of a connected device and determine nature of blockchain technology allows for increased security and resilience against tampering or unauthorized access. This can help to protect the integrity of forensic data and ensure that it is not compromised during an investigation.

The adoption of public cloud has resulted in the establishment of a new domain called Cloud Forensics, which is the application of Digital Forensics in cloud computing. For IIoT devices, the storage of the data that they emit, given the volume of transactions, will typically result in the data being stored in the Cloud. This presents significant challenges for a forensic investigator, as the data from an IIoT device will traverse many networks and devices before being stored in the Cloud. One of the more prominent challenges is that the data from the IIoT device could be altered at many points along the way.

The focus of this work is to investigate whether a Distributed Digital Ledger (DDL) could be used to securely store all transactions relating to Industrial Internet of Things (IIoT) devices, so that they can be later retrieved for the purpose of conducting a digital cloud forensics investigation. There are acceptable processes for Digital Forensics, which are admissible as evidence in a court of law, but this is not the case for Cloud Forensics. Several frameworks and methods have been proposed in the research regarding how DDLs could be used to secure IIoT transactions, but much of this research is theoretical in nature. Any prior research that has moved beyond the theory, has not demonstrated how a proposed approach could scale to support an IIoT implementation.

To the best of our knowledge and as far as can be ascertained in the literature and in the commercial environment, there is no known approach for such a study. So, to comply with a suitable scientific method, a new methodology - the Industrial Internet of Things Simulated Measurement Methodology (IIoT SM-M) - has been devised and employed in this work.

The aim of this paper is to investigate the feasibility of using DDL technology for Digital Forensics for IIoT. Several research questions that were considered for this are:

1. Can a suitable DDL technology platform be built to support Digital Forensics as it applies to IIoT?
2. What, if any, are the challenges with building such a platform and how could these challenges, if applicable, be overcome?
3. What is the overhead with storing encrypted transactions from IIoT devices, when compared to plaintext transactions?
4. What is the overhead with retrieving encrypted transactions from IIoT devices, when compared to plaintext transactions?

5. What is the highest number of IIoT devices that the platform is able to support?

2. Related work

The literature review is aimed at understanding the field of Digital Forensics with a specific focus on its application within the Industrial Internet of Things (IIoT). It critically examines three significant survey papers that provide a comprehensive state-of-the-art review of Digital Forensics in the context of the Internet of Things [2], [13], [5]. The scope of Digital Forensics is extensive, encompassing areas such as disk, mobile, network, wireless, and cloud forensics [6], with particular attention to Cloud Forensics models tailored for IoT and IIoT that utilize Distributed Ledger Technology (DDL).

In terms of Cloud Forensics, it is recognized to include essential elements like the IoT device, the DDL, and the Cloud environment [11]. The focus of this research is on piecing together evidence from these components to create a chronological series of events for forensic analysis.

The discussion extends to several theoretical frameworks and models proposed for storing IoT device data on DDLs, which ensures the integrity of the data through encrypted transactions. Among these, some frameworks have been partially tested using Ethereum, highlighting the secure, decentralized nature of such digital transaction ledgers [17]. However, despite these developments, many models, including a blockchain-based framework for storing IoT communications as transactions [14], and the FIF-IoT framework [10], remain largely theoretical and have not demonstrated scalability or practical implementation in real-world settings.

Additional proposals explored include using DDLs for creating tamper-resistant solutions for audit trails in IoT systems [16], which could later assist in digital forensics. Another notable initiative is the BPIIoT platform for IIoT, which utilizes blockchain technology to enable cloud-based manufacturing. This platform was demonstrated using a single machine prototype, but questions about its scalability remain unanswered [4]. Similarly, the BLOFF IoT forensics model aims to ensure the integrity of forensic evidence but has not been implemented beyond theoretical discussions [1].

Each of these initiatives reflects a growing interest in integrating blockchain and DDL technologies with IoT systems to enhance the security and verifiability of data, crucial for effective forensic investigations in the realm of IIoT. However, the literature indicates a gap in real-world application and evidence of scalability, pointing to areas needing further research and development.

Table 1: Models and Frameworks from the Literature Reviewed.

Models and Frameworks				
Name	Date	Experiment	Ledger	Scaled
	2019	Yes	Ethereum	No
FIF-IoT	2018	Yes	Ethereum	No
Probe-IoT	2018	No	None	No
	2018	No	None	No
BPIIoT	2016	Yes	Ethereum	No
BLOFF	2021	No	None	No

3. Methodology

In order to confirm the aim of this paper, a quantitative research approach needed to be undertaken. To achieve this, two applications were developed using the Python programming language and the integrated development environment for Microsoft Windows, Microsoft Visual Studio. A real-world IIoT transactions dataset, comprising thermostat temperature values, was used to simulate reading IIoT transactions from thermostat sensors and a simulation measurement methodology was devised.

3.1 IIoT SM-Methodology

The Industrial Internet of Things Simulation Measurement Method- ology that was devised for this work contains 5 stages: Platform Installation and configuration, Platform Initialisation, Use Case Experiment Execution, Results Recording, and Results Analysis. Each of these stages are described in relevant subsections below.

3.2 Python Applications

To carry out the quantitative research for this paper, two Python applications were developed (these will be made publicly available if accepted for publication.). One application was used to read and write IIoT transactions from a dataset and process them using the PostgreSQL database, while the other application was used to read and write the same IIoT transactions and process them for the Iroha digital ledger.

3.3 Datasets

For an IIoT implementation, there would be hundreds and, in some cases, thousands of sensors that would be emitting readings every second, 24 hours per day. By way of a simple calculation, for a large manufacturing operation with over 1,000 sensors transmitting every second, over 1.4 million transactions would be emitted in any one twenty-four-hour period. While the size of transactions from such a sensor would be relatively small, it is the volume of transactions needing to be written or read that presents a challenge, particularly as it relates to IIoT and Cloud Forensics. For this paper, several data repositories of different datasets were reviewed, and a suitable data set was identified to execute the experiments. The dataset chosen contains over 400,000 thermostat temperature readings, collected from two building thermostat sensors, reporting every second, over a two-year period (https://tinyurl.com/4d2tsnmt). The dataset was created by the Intelligent Security Group UNSW Canberra, Australia in support of Industry 4.0, [3].

3.4 Use Cases

Each experiment measured the time taken to write or read an IIoT transaction into or from the PostgreSQL database or the Iroha digital ledger. Three use cases were evaluated:

- Use Case 1: Writing or reading an unencrypted IIoT transaction directly to a PostgreSQL database table.
- Use Case 2: Writing or reading an unsigned IIoT transaction into the Iroha digital ledger.
- Use Case 3: Writing or reading a signed IIoT transaction into the Iroha digital ledger.

The experiments were conducted five times for each use case, and the average time was recorded as the result. The types of IIoT transactions tested were:

- Unencrypted IIoT transaction: Directly written or read from the PostgreSQL database without encryption.
- Unsigned IIoT transaction: Written or read from the Iroha digital ledger without a signature.
- Signed IIoT transaction: Written or read from the Iroha digital ledger with a signature, implying encryption.

The results were collated and analysed to identify challenges associated with each use case.

3.5 Database Performance Monitoring

The monitoring of PostgreSQL databases during each experiment was conducted using pgAdmin 4, which features a performance monitoring dashboard. This dashboard provides real-time updates on the health and performance of the database, displaying various statistics such as the number of active database sessions, transactions per second (including commits and rollbacks), tuples processed (inserted, updated, deleted), tuples fetched, and block I/O operations (blocks read from the file system or buffer cache). Key metrics of interest included the transactions per second, which were correlated with the time taken to execute the use cases.

3.6 Iroha Digital Ledger

The DDLs reviewed for this work are hosted by the Hyperledger Foundation, who "support the development of enterprise-grade, cross-industry open platforms for distributed ledgers" (https://www.hyperledger.org/about/join). They include BESU, FABRIC, INDY, IROHA, and SAWTOOTH.

IROHA has been selected for this paper due to its advantageous features for IoT projects requiring distributed ledger technology. Firstly, its simplicity and ease of integration make it highly suitable for such applications. Secondly, IROHA necessitates the use of either a PostgreSQL database or RocksDB as its underlying data repository, aligning with the paper's objectives to analyze and compare read and write times between a DDL and a database. Lastly, IROHA supports a Python library, which facilitates the development of applications that interact with the DDL, further enhancing its utility for this research.

The Iroha digital ledger has a limitation on the type of values that it can store. An Asset, a defined type within the Iroha digital ledger, can only contain a value, which can only be increased or decreased. This presented a challenge for this paper, since value types other than numeric needed to be stored. To overcome this limitation, a User Object was used to store the IIoT transactions, since it is possible to set a value on the User Object of up to 2,048 bytes in size. In the Iroha platform, the setting of this value is achieved in exactly the same way as adding a transaction to the digital ledger. The transaction is signed with a private key and is then written to the Iroha digital ledger.

3.7 Testbed

For this research, a standalone project platform was set up using both commercially available and open-source hardware and software to conduct experiments. The physical infrastructure comprises a single HP ProLiant DL380 Gen10 Intel server running Microsoft Windows Server 2020 R2 and configured with Microsoft Windows

Hyper-V. The server features two Intel Xeon Gold 6130 CPUs at 2.10GHz with 16 cores and 32 logical processors each, 384MB of physical memory, 1.92 TB SSD in RAID 1 for OS internal storage, and 27.8 TB of external storage on an HPE Smart Array P816i-a SR. The logical setup, depicted in Figure 1, includes two virtual instances on Hyper-V: one runs a Microsoft Windows 10 environment with Microsoft Visual Studio (16 virtual processors, 128 MB memory, 1 TB storage), and the other an Ubuntu environment equipped with a Docker setup hosting three containers (12 virtual processors, 128 MB memory, 1 TB storage).

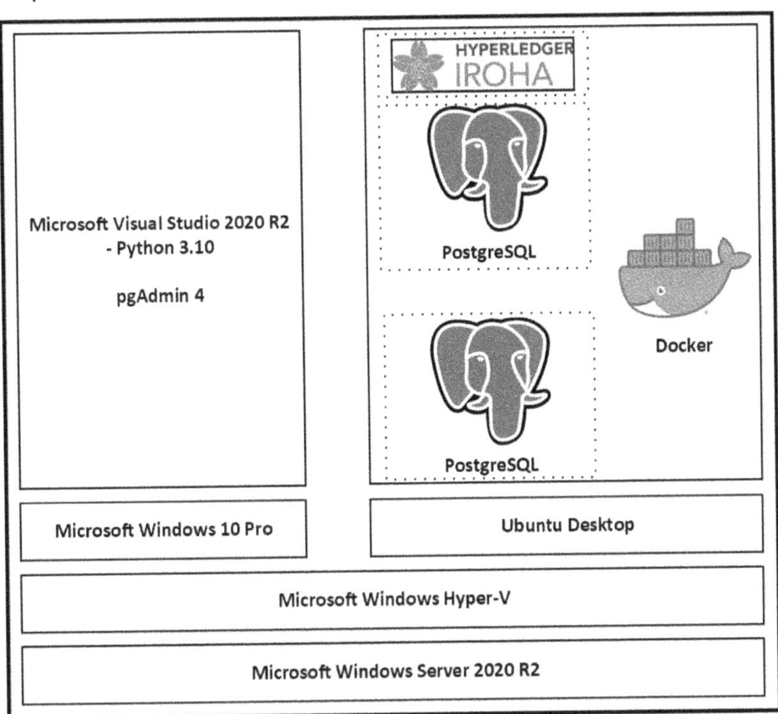

Figure 1: Logical Architecture

The research setup involved deploying various software on an HP ProLiant DL380 Gen10 server. Microsoft Windows Server 2019 Datacenter edition and Microsoft Windows Server 2020 R2 with Hyper-V were installed on the server. Within Hyper-V, Ubuntu Desktop 20.04 was set up, hosting Docker version 20.10.12, which in turn managed three containers. Hyperledger Iroha, utilizing PostgreSQL as its database for storing encrypted IIoT transactions, was deployed on one of these Ubuntu Docker containers. Additionally, two separate PostgreSQL database instances were configured in individual Docker containers—one for Iroha's object store and another for unencrypted IIoT transactions.

On the software development front, Microsoft Windows 10 Pro was installed in another Hyper-V virtual environment, where the Community Edition of Visual Studio and Python 3.10 were set up. This setup was used for programming and running experiments. The psycopg2 and Iroha Python libraries were installed to support database interactions and blockchain functions, respectively. Lastly, pgAdmin 4 version 6.8 was installed on Windows 10 for database creation, configuration, and monitoring.

4. Experiments and results

To achieve the aim of investigating the feasibility of using Distributed Digital Ledger technology for Digital Forensics for Industrial Internet of Things, six experiments were performed on the experimental platform developed for this work. This section details the series of experiments that were executed and records how long it took to write or read unencrypted or encrypted IIoT transactions into or from a PostgreSQL database or the Iroha digital ledger. The IIoT transactions were of various volumes ranging from 100k to over 400k and of varying sizes, ranging from 1k to 4k.

4.1 Experiment Initialisation

Before executing any of the experiments, a series of experiment initialisation steps were performed.

1. **Stop** the Docker containers containing the PostgreSQL databases and the Iroha digital ledger.
2. **Delete** the Docker containers containing the PostgreSQL databases and the Iroha digital ledger.
3. **Run** the Docker container containing the standalone PostgreSQL database.

4. **Run** the Docker container containing the PostgreSQL database for the Iroha digital ledger.
5. **Run** the Docker container containing the Iroha digital ledger.
6. **Confirm** that all containers are up and running.

Performing the above steps before executing any of the experiments ensured that the project platform was clean and stable, that nothing was left behind from a previous experiment and that there was no impact between experiments.

Table 2: Experiment One - Writing, in seconds, 1,000 IIoT Transactions Time.

Use Case	R1	R2	R3	R4	R5	Avg	
1: Unencrypted	0.9		0.94	0.99	1.04	1.25	1.02
2: Unsigned	0.48		0.48	0.44	0.46	0.49	0.47
3: Signed & Encrypted	5.63		5.78	5.56	5.79	5.21	5.59

4.2 Ex1 - Writing 1,000 IIoT Transactions

In an experiment with a baseline of 100 IIoT transactions, a noticeable time difference was observed when writing signed transactions to the Iroha digital ledger. To explore this further, the number of transactions was increased to 1,000, and the experiment involved writing these transactions to both the PostgreSQL database and the Iroha digital ledger. The write times were recorded, and database performance was continuously monitored, showing no anomalies.

Three specific use cases were tested:

- Use Case 1: Unencrypted Transactions - A file with 1,000 IIoT thermostat transactions was processed and written to PostgreSQL. The process was repeated five times to confirm consistent results.
- Use Case 2: Unsigned Transactions - The same file was processed and written unsigned to the Iroha ledger, and similarly repeated for reliability.
- Use Case 3: Signed Transactions - The file was processed, and transactions were signed (thus encrypted) before writing to Iroha, with the process also repeated multiple times.

The results indicated a minor time difference between writing to PostgreSQL and unsigned writing to Iroha. Notably, signed transactions took significantly longer, consistent with the overhead of encryption via private key signing. In a real-world scenario, it is likely that there would be up to a one second time delay between each transaction, but if there were 100 or even 1,000 IIoT devices, all trying to write to the Iroha ledger at the same time, this could become a performance issue for the system. Experiment 4.5 will look at a simulation of 10 IIoT devices, all trying to write 1000 IIoT transactions at the same time to evaluate how the system performs. Experiment 4.5 will simulate writing by 10 IIoT devices simultaneously to assess system performance, exploring potential delays in a real-world scenario.

4.3 Ex2 - Reading 1,000 IIoT Transactions

Being able to read transactions from the Iroha digital ledger is an important requirement in the analysis phase of Cloud Forensics. To investigate this, an experiment was executed to read 1,000 IIoT transactions directly from the PostgreSQL database and from the Iroha digital ledger. The time taken to read the 1,000 IIoT transactions was recorded. For this experiment, there are only two use cases since it is looking to determine whether there may be an overhead when retrieving the signed transactions. The database performance was monitored throughout all experiments and no anomalies were observed. The results are shown in Table 3.

Table 3: Experiment Two - Reading, in seconds, 1,000 IIoT Transactions Time

Use Case	R1	R2	R3	R4	R5	Avg
1: Unencrypted	0.79	0.71	0.74	0.76	0.72	0.74
2: Signed & Encrypted	7.76	7.26	7.61	7.27	7.28	7.44

- Use Case 1: Unencrypted Transactions: A single IIoT transaction from a set of 1,000 thermostat readings was retrieved 1,000 times from the PostgreSQL database. The total processing time was recorded, and the test repeated four times to ensure reliable results, as shown in Figure 3. Throughout the experiment, server performance was monitored via the pgAdmin 4 dashboard to maintain database consistency.

- Use Case 2: Signed Transactions: Similarly, a single IIoT transaction from the Iroha digital ledger was retrieved 1,000 times. The process mirrored Use Case 1, with the total time taken recorded and the test repeated four times for statistical reliability.

The experiment confirmed that both use cases could successfully retrieve transactions from the respective databases. Table 3 details the average time required to retrieve one IIoT transaction 1,000 times for both use cases. There was a noticeable time difference between the two databases; it took just over 1 second in Use Case 1 and more than 7 seconds in Use Case 2 to complete the reads. This time discrepancy is expected due to the decryption required for each transaction in the Iroha ledger. Despite the added time, there were no significant performance issues, suggesting that the Iroha digital ledger could handle the decryption workload without major delays in a real-world scenario.

4.4 Ex3 - Writing varying IIoT Transaction Sizes

The purpose of experiment three was to investigate whether there would be an impact to the overall performance of the Iroha digital ledger for different IIoT transaction sizes. For this experiment, three file sizes, 1k, 2k and 4k were used as the IIoT transaction sizes. The experiment was executed by processing 1,000 IIoT transactions of the three different file sizes and writing them directly into the PostgreSQL database and into the Iroha digital ledger. The time taken to process the 1,000 IIoT transactions was recorded. The database performance for writing the 4k IIoT transaction size was monitored throughout all experiments and no anomalies were observed. The results are shown in Table 4.

Table 4: Experiment Three - Writing, in seconds, different file size IIoT Transactions Time.

Use Case	Size	R1	R2	R3	R4	R5	Avg
1: Unencrypted	1KB	0.95	1.07	0.98	0.88	0.91	0.96
	2KB	0.96	1.04	1	0.99	1.06	1.01
	4KB	0.94	1.09	1.15	1.01	1.02	1.04
2. Unsigned	1KB	0.6	0.56	0.63	0.53	0.57	0.58
	2KB	0.71	0.7	0.72	0.73	0.75	0.72
	4KB	0.99	0.89	0.93	0.89	0.94	0.93
3: S & E	1KB	5.56	5.64	5.74	5.71	5.72	5.69
	2KB	5.78	5.68	5.74	5.65	5.74	5.72
	4KB	6.13	6	5.96	6.09	5.96	6.03

- Use Case 1: Unencrypted Transactions: Files of 1k, 2k, and 4k, each containing a single IIoT transaction, were processed 1,000 times into the PostgreSQL database. The total processing time was recorded and repeated four times for accuracy, with server performance consistently monitored via the pgAdmin 4 dashboard.
- Use Case 2: Unsigned Transactions: The same files were processed 1,000 times into the Iroha digital ledger without signing the transactions. The procedure mirrored Use Case 1, including four repetitions to ensure statistical reliability, with results shown in Table 4.
- Use Case 3: Signed Transactions: The transactions were encrypted through signing and processed similarly in the Iroha ledger, with results also documented in Table 4 after four repetitions.

The experiment validated that all three use cases effectively wrote transactions to both the PostgreSQL and Iroha ledgers, as recorded in Table 4. Time to write transactions was slightly faster in the PostgreSQL database and for unsigned transactions in the Iroha ledger, typically under 1 second. Signed transactions in Iroha took about 6 seconds, regardless of file size. The file size (1k, 2k, or 4k) had minimal impact on processing times across all scenarios, indicating that transaction size would likely not pose significant performance issues in real-world applications.

4.5 Ex4 - IIoT device with Multiprocessing

The purpose of this experiment was to simulate ten IIoT sensors, all writing to the Iroha digital ledger at the same time. This was achieved by using the multiprocessing capabilities within Python and spawning multiple processes to execute in parallel. In experiment one, Section 4.2, the time taken to process 1,000 transactions was recorded. For this experiment, the time taken to process 10,000 transactions was recorded. The experiment then involved comparing the time taken to process 10,000 transactions, with ten parallel processes of 1,000 transactions. The experiment was executed by writing the 10,000 IIoT transactions directly into the PostgreSQL database and into the Iroha digital ledger. The time taken to write the IIoT transactions was recorded. The results are shown in Table 5.

Table 5: Experiment Four - 10 IIoT Sensor Simulation Times. Mode M = Multi and Mode S = Single

Use Case		R1	R2	R3	R4	R5	Avg
1: Unencrypted	S	8.88	8.79	8.16	8.74	8.72	8.66
	M	1.18	1.23	1.23	1.23	1.12	1.20
2. Unsigned	S	4.65	4.59	4.7	4.59	4.59	4.62
	M	0.59	0.68	0.57	0.65	0.55	0.61
3: Signed & Encrypted	S	55.43	55.11	56.71	55.82	55.55	55.72
	M	8.51	7.77	9.05	7.74	8.97	8.41

- Use Case 1: Unencrypted Transactions: Two files containing 10,000 and 1,000 IIoT thermostat transactions were processed into PostgreSQL both individually and as 10 parallel processes. Each round was repeated four times for accuracy, with consistent server performance monitoring via pgAdmin 4 showing no anomalies.
- Use Case 2: Unsigned Transactions: Identical files were processed into the Iroha digital ledger without signatures, also as 10 parallel processes. The processing time was recorded over four repetitions, mirroring the first use case with consistent server performance.
- Use Case 3: Signed Transactions: The same files were processed into Iroha with transactions signed and encrypted, executed as 10 parallel processes. This was repeated four times, with consistent server monitoring and performance.

The experiments confirmed effective transaction writing to both PostgreSQL and Iroha across all use cases, as documented in Table 5. Processing 10,000 IIoT transactions showed a near seven-fold reduction in time when executed in parallel. While there was an expected increase in time for processing signed transactions compared to unsigned, this aligned with previous findings and did not present unexpected anomalies.

4.6 Ex5 - Writing/Reading 400k Transactions

For an IIoT implementation, there will be hundreds, if not thousands, of sensors that would each be sending a transaction at very regular intervals. In some cases, this could be as frequent as every second. In the case of a smart city, there would be tens of thousands of sensors. This experiment was executed to write and read over four hundred thousand transactions into and from the Iroha digital ledger. The time taken to execute the writing and reading was recorded. Since the experiment is only looking to determine whether there is an overhead when retrieving the signed transactions, there are only two use cases. The transactions represent readings from just two IIoT sensors over a two-year period. The results are shown in Table 6.

Table 6: Experiment Five- Writing / Reading, in minutes, 400k IIoT Transactions Time.

Use Case	R1	R2	R3	R4	R5	Avg
1. Writing	41.15	41.1	41.2	41.45	41.2	41.22
2. Reading	43.5	43.3	43.78	43.45	43.35	43.48

- Use Case 1: Written Signed Transactions: A file with over four hundred thousand IIoT thermostat transactions was processed into the Iroha digital ledger, line by line. The processing time was recorded and repeated four times for reliability.
- Use Case 2: Read Signed Transactions: One of the 400,000 IIoT transactions written to Iroha was retrieved 400,000 times. The procedure was identical to Use Case 1, with the time recorded and repeated four times for consistency.

Both use cases successfully wrote to and read from the Iroha ledger, with the results displayed in Table 6 showing the average processing time in minutes for the 400k IIoT transactions. Writing took over 40 minutes, while reading took just under 44 minutes, consistent with previous experiments.

For Cloud Digital Forensics, analysing large numbers of transactions like those from an IIoT sensor—which could generate 1,440 transactions daily—suggests that the Iroha ledger can handle substantial loads without significant performance issues. For instance, processing nearly 13 million transactions from 100 sensors over three months would take about four hours if done serially. Future improvements might involve scaling the Iroha system horizontally to enhance efficiency.

5. Key experimentation findings

A total of six experiments have been successfully executed in order to validate the aim of this research. The key findings are as follows:

1. There is more than a five-fold overhead when comparing the time taken to write an IIoT transaction into the DDL that is encrypted, compared to one that is not.
2. There is almost a ten-fold overhead when comparing the time taken to read an IIoT transaction from the DDL that is encrypted, compared to one that is not.
3. When comparing the time taken to write IIoT transactions of different sizes, allowing for the time difference between encrypted and unencrypted IIoT transactions, the difference is minimal.
4. The number of encrypted transactions that can be written to the platform per second is limited to 170. If the number of IIoT devices emitting data every second was to exceed 170, then a platform backlog would occur.
5. When the number of IIoT transactions was increased to 400k, then the number of supported devices was reduced from 170 to 161.

5.1 Outcomes

The research questions that were considered for this paper and the accompanying answers are:

Q1: This paper has successfully demonstrated that it is possible to build a suitable DDL technology platform for the storage and retrieval of encrypted IIoT transactions, for the purpose of conducting a forensic analysis.

Q2: The methodology section describes the limitation with the Hyperledger Iroha and how this limitation was overcome.

Q3: The execution of experiments demonstrated that there is an overhead when storing encrypted IIoT transactions in the platform. Specifically, there is in excess of a five-fold increase in the time difference for storing transactions, which results in a reduction of processing volume to under 200 transactions per second.

Q4: The execution of experiments demonstrated that there is an overhead when retrieving encrypted IIoT transactions from the platform. Specifically, there is almost a ten-fold increase in the time difference for retrieving transactions which results in a reduction of processing volume to under 135 transactions per second.

Q5: The execution of experiments demonstrated that if the number of IIoT devices was to exceed 170, which is the maximum number of transactions that can be processed per second, then a platform backlog would occur.

6. Conclusions

The aim of this research was to investigate the feasibility of using Distributed Digital Ledger technology for Digital Forensics for Industrial Internet of Things.

The outcome of this work has shown that previously suggested methods and frameworks can be successfully implemented using DDL technology for the storage of encrypted IIoT transactions. These transactions can later be retrieved for the purpose of conducting a forensic investigation. The experimental platform built for this paper and the devised simulated measurement methodology, have proven that it is possible to build and use a DDL, like Hyperledger Iroha, for the purpose of storing IIoT transactions, within certain parameters. Specifically, there is a limit to the number of sensors that could be supported by a single implementation and the time it takes to retrieve IIoT transactions may be too high to be practical for the purpose of Digital Forensics.

References

Promise Agbedanu and Anca Delia Jurcut. "BLOFF: a blockchain-based forensic model in IoT". In: Revolutionary Applications of Blockchain-Enabled Privacy and Access Control. IGI Global, 2021, pp. 59–73.

Ahmed Alenezi et al. "IoT forensics: A state-of-the-art review, challenges and future directions". en. In: Proceedings of the 4th International Conference on Complexity, Future Information Systems and Risk. Heraklion, Crete, Greece: SCITEPRESS - Science and Technology Publications, May 2019.

Abdullah Alsaedi et al. "TON_IoT telemetry dataset: A new generation dataset of IoT and IIoT for data-driven intrusion detection systems". In: IEEE Access 8 (2020), pp. 165130–165150.

Arshdeep Bahga and Vijay K Madisetti. "Blockchain platform for industrial internet of things". In: Journal of Software Engineering and Applications 9.10 (2016), pp. 533–546.

Arafat Al-Dhaqm et al. "Digital Forensics Subdomains: The State of the Art and Future Directions". In: IEEE Access 9 (2021), pp. 152476–152502.

Arafat Al-Dhaqm et al. "Digital Forensics Subdomains: The State of the art and Future Directions". In: IEEE Access (2021).

Nabil El Ioini and Claus Pahl. "A review of distributed ledger technologies". In: OTM Confederated International Conferences" On the Move to Meaningful Internet Systems". Springer. 2018, pp. 277–288.

Bahar Farahani, Farshad Firouzi, and Markus Luecking. "The convergence of IoT and distributed ledger technologies (DLT): Opportunities, challenges, and solutions". In: Journal of Network and Computer Applications 177 (2021), p. 102936.

Mahmud Hossain, Yasser Karim, and Ragib Hasan. "FIF-IoT: A forensic investigation framework for IoT using a public digital ledger". In: 2018 IEEE International Congress on Internet of Things (ICIOT). IEEE. 2018, pp. 33–40.

Md Mahmud Hossain, Ragib Hasan, and Shams Zawoad. "Probe-IoT: A public digital ledger based forensic investigation framework for IoT." In: INFOCOM workshops. 2018, pp. 1–2.

Jianwei Hou et al. "A survey on digital forensics in Internet of Things". In: IEEE Internet of Things Journal 7.1 (2019), pp. 1–15.

Randa Kamal, Ezz El-Din Hemdan, and Nawal El-Fishway. "A review study on blockchain-based IoT security and forensics". In: Multimedia Tools and Applications (2021), pp. 1–32.

Pantaleon Lutta et al. "The complexity of internet of things forensics: A stateof-the-art review". In: Forensic Science International: Digital Investigation 38 (Sept. 2021), p. 301210.

Jung Hyun Ryu et al. "A blockchain-based decentralized efficient investigation framework for IoT digital forensics". In: The Journal of Supercomputing 75.8 (2019), pp. 4372–4387.

Ali Sunyaev. "Distributed ledger technology". In: Internet Computing. Springer, 2020, pp. 265–299.

Magnus Westerlund, Mats Neovius, and Göran Pulkkis. "Providing tamperresistant audit trails with distributed ledger-based solutions for forensics of IOT systems using cloud resources". In: International Journal on Advances in Security 11.3 & 4 (2018).

Gavin Wood et al. "Ethereum: A secure decentralised generalised transaction ledger". In: Ethereum project yellow paper 151.2014 (2014), pp. 1–32.

The Offense-Defense Balance in Cyberspace

Wade Huntley and Timothy Shives

Naval Postgraduate School*, Monterey, California, USA

*(The views expressed here are those of the authors and do not necessarily represent the views of the Naval Postgraduate School, the Department of Defense, or the U.S. Government.)

wlhuntle@nps.edu

timothy.shives@nps.edu

Abstract: The study of cyber strategy and its implications for international security has become increasingly crucial, necessitating an examination of the unique challenges posed by the dynamic and stealthy nature of the cyber domain. This paper addresses whether offensive or defensive strategies prevail in cyberspace, especially in light of evolving technological landscapes and debates over cyber threats. By applying offense-defense theory from international relations, the research explores the nuanced relationship between offensive and defensive operations in cyberspace. Despite prevalent views favoring offense dominance, recent skepticism questions the severity of cyber threats and suggests a possible overemphasis on offensive operations. This paper systematically examines the core concepts, findings, and operational variables of offense-defense theory, providing clarity to the conceptual debates surrounding cyber conflict. Recognizing the unique characteristics of the cyber domain, it urges a careful consideration of biases that may distort judgments about offense dominance. The evolving nature of cyberspace and its potential for redesign introduces caution and underscores the need for a nuanced understanding of the offense-defense balance. The preliminary assessment concludes that the question of whether offense or defense "dominates" in cyberspace is overly simplistic. Given the intricate interactions of cyber capabilities, other coercive means available to states, and the dynamic evolution of cyber technology, this question can only be answered within specific contextual and chronological boundaries. Within such conditions, the state of the offense-defense balance is crucial to tactical and operational decision-making. At the strategic policymaking level, the more coherent question is how cyber technologies are shifting the balance of advantages between offense and defense in the overall military posture of states. In essence, this paper provides valuable insights into the ongoing discourse on cyber strategy, theoretical frameworks, and nuanced analyses to inform policy and strategic decision-making in the face of evolving cyber threats.

Keywords: Cyber Strategy, Offense-Defense Relationship, International Security, Cyber Threats, Offense-Defense Theory

1. Introduction: Offense and Defense in Cyberspace

The paper delves into the intricate realm of cyber strategy, shedding light on the delicate balance between offense and defense in cyberspace. It emphasizes the evolution from traditional information warfare to the contemporary concept of cognitive warfare, reflecting the modern focus on influencing and controlling populations on social, political, and military fronts (Buvarp, 2023). By leveraging established international relations theory, this paper provides clarity to ongoing conceptual debates, advocating for a nuanced understanding of the dynamic nature of cyber threats and the strategic importance of cognitive dimensions.

The question of whether offense or defense holds the upper hand in cyberspace is a central focus within broader discussions of military cybersecurity. However, many of these discussions rely on reasoned yet largely unsubstantiated assertions. Systematic exploration within the framework of existing offense-defense theory has been limited (Lieber, 2014). Furthermore, recent developments suggest that 'cyber' is a tool, not an end, with the ultimate targets being the minds of opponents and allies rather than their digital tools (Meriläinen,; 2023).

This paper addresses this gap by presenting an initial framework for applying the fundamental tenets of offense-defense theory to the cyber domain, while also integrating the principles of cognitive warfare (Canham, et al, 2022; Hiltunen & Huhtinen, 2022; Buvarp, 2023; Murphy, 2023). The goal is to enhance our understanding of the interplay between offensive and defensive capabilities in cyber military conflict and cognitive operations (Nye, 2010). Following a brief overview of representative claims regarding offensive advantage, the section introduces a working definition of "offense" and "defense" in cyberspace. It then applies Jervis' (1978) two principal variables – differentiation and advantage – to the cyber domain. The discussion also explores specific features of cyber conflict relevant to the offense-defense relationship, such as secrecy, geography metaphors, the transient nature of military cyber capabilities, and the emerging focus on cognitive influence and control as noted by Noel, et al, (2021 and Hutchinson (2022).

2. The intuition of offense advantage in cyberspace

Numerous strategists and decision-makers assert that offense holds the upper hand in the cyber domain (Lynn, 2010; Harknett, Callaghan, and Kauffman, 2010; Sterner, 2010; Masters, 2011). Sheldon (2011) provides five reasons supporting the dominance of offense in cyberspace: vulnerability of network defenses, the speed of cyber-attacks, the absence of distance as an inhibiting factor, difficulty in attributing attack sources, and the "target-rich" environment resulting from society's widespread reliance on cyberspace.

Kello (2013) and Krepinevich (2012) also argue in favor of the significant advantage of cyber offense, with a focus on costs. Kello identifies defense costs, including anticipating unpredictable and undetectable cyber-attacks, ensuring the detection of system penetrations, dealing with the "complex defense surface" in terms of hardware and software complexity, managing "defense fragmentation" caused by critical infrastructure ownership by private entities, and ensuring the reliability of supply chains. While acknowledging that cyber-attacks can be expensive, Kello emphasizes that "offensive costs [have] meaning only in reference to the expenses of the defender" (Kello, 2013, pp.27-30). Similarly, Krepinevich (2012) concludes that "the cyber competition appears to be an offense-dominant competition. That is to say, if both the attacker and defender are given equal resources, the attacker will prevail" (p. 40).

These arguments are noteworthy for their consideration of the cost aspect, aligning with one of the two principal aspects of the offense-defense balance identified by Jervis. However, they fall short in not examining the role of this balance in shaping conflict outcomes. Additionally, these formulations neglect the other key variable in determining offensive or defensive advantage: whether capabilities can be differentiated in these terms.

Aucsmith (2012) surveys new features of cyber conflict relevant to both offense and defense. The "compression" of time and space eliminates geography, granting "omnipotent mobility" that empowers the offense to choose when and where to strike. Equally crucial is offensive novelty, defined for cyber weapons as the use of tactics, techniques, or procedures unknown to the defender. The assertion that novelty is the crucial criterion for success in a cyber-attack carries significant implications for the offense-defense balance in cyberspace. If both offense and defense face equivalent costs for achieving novelty, essentially engaging in a "race" to discover vulnerabilities first, neither side gains a clear advantage by this measure.

However, when considering the full picture, even if the unit cost of discovering a relevant vulnerability is the same for both offense and defense, other factors come into play. For instance, the cost of patching vulnerable networks is likely higher than the cost of exploiting discovered vulnerabilities. This suggests that the cumulative costs of defense could still outweigh those of offense. Additionally, the failure of a significant percentage of end-users to implement patches in a timely manner adds further burdens to defense.

Contrary to the prevailing view that offense dominates in cyberspace, Gray (2013) challenges this notion. He contends, "Although it continues to be orthodox to assert that cyberspace is ... friendly to offense, rather than defense, this fashionable belief almost certainly either is wrong, or to be generous, is seriously misleading" (p. 41). Beyond the cost equivalency of offense and defense in identifying vulnerabilities, Gray notes that offense incurs unique costs. For instance, "Detailed up-to-date intelligence literally is essential for successful cyber offense" (Gray, 2013, p.51).

In contrast to traditional domains such as land, sea, air, and space, cyberspace stands out as a humanly created realm. Notably, the medium itself, not just the tools used for projecting force within it, can be modified by human intervention. This inherent quality grants defense a meta-advantage: beyond defending specific targets, those controlling the networks and systems seeking defense could potentially reshape the entire domain to enhance defensive capabilities (Nye, 2010). An illustrative example of this is the impending transition from IPv4 to IPv6, but a more profound instance could involve a comprehensive redesign of basic computer architecture. This redesign might incorporate physically distinct memory locations for data and software instructions, effectively eliminating certain types of malware attacks, such as "buffer overflows," that rely on computers storing instructions and data in the same memory locations.

Gray (2013) underscores the significance of resilience as a defensive advantage. Drawing parallels with the British experience during World War II, where strategic bombing had limited effectiveness, he notes, "Britain prepared to be able to accept damage but to fight on. This is the approach that appears most suitable to the challenge of damage from cyberspace. Cyber offense will register some success, but so what" (Gray, 2013, pp. 41). The emphasis here is on the ability to absorb damage and continue the fight, highlighting resilience as a key defensive strategy in the face of cyber threats.

While the existing analyses of the offense-defense balance in cyberspace offer valuable insights, they fall short of providing a systematic application of the frameworks and variables of offense-defense theory. However, they serve as illuminating and insightful starting points, indicating elements that require more detailed specification for a thorough systematic application. This section identifies key elements essential for such an analysis, which are discussed in the paper:

- Examining differentiation of offensive and defensive weapons in cyberspace
- Calculating costs of offense and defensive capabilities in cyberspace
- Understanding the operational aspect of the offense-defense balance
- Appreciating how the interaction of cyber and non-cyber (physical) forms of conflict shapes judgments of the utility of offensive and defensive cyber capabilities

These identified elements serve as a foundation for a more systematic examination of the offense-defense balance in cyberspace. Further specification and exploration of these components will contribute to a more nuanced understanding of the intricate dynamics within the cyber domain in the era of information warfare and persistent engagement particularly in light of the recent conflicts in Ukraine and the rising threats in Southeast Asia (Goldman & Monarez, 2021; Clarke, et al, 2023; Lehto, 2023; Van Niekerk, 2023)

3. The meanings of "offense" and "defense" in cyberspace

To comprehend the terms "offense" and "defense" in the cyber domain, it's crucial to establish a conceptual framework that aligns with broader international relations scholarship. Nye (2010) provides an insightful foundation, associating these concepts with their wider usage.

Nye begins by defining power as "the ability to affect other people to get the outcomes one wants," highlighting its relational and contextual nature. In cyberspace, power is contextual, dependent on the resources characterizing this unique domain (Nye, 2010). Cyberspace, according to Nye, represents a hybrid regime of physical and virtual properties, encompassing not just networks and software but also informational and identity dimensions. The U.S. Department of Defense similarly recognized the cyberspace domain's layers, including physical network, logical network, and cyber-persona (U.S. Joint Chiefs of Staff, 2013). In the literature this understanding has expanded into the realm of hybrid warfare—that is information warfare and the traditional physical warfare (Saressalo & Huhtinen, 2022; Sheikh, 2022; Ormrod, et al, 2023).

Within this domain, Nye identifies resources of power as infrastructure, networks, software, human skills, and more, enabling the creation, control, and communication of electronic and computer-based information. He defines cyber power as "the ability to obtain preferred outcomes through the use of electronically interconnected information resources of the cyber domain." This definition encompasses achieving outcomes within and outside cyberspace, acknowledging that relevant contexts extend beyond the cyber realm (Ackerman, et al, 2024; Briggs 2023.

By defining cyber power as the ability to obtain preferred outcomes through cyberspace capabilities, a clear distinction emerges between offensive and defensive cyber capabilities:

- *Defensive Cyber Capabilities*: Aim to preserve and protect one's own cyber resources.
- *Offensive Cyber Capabilities*: Aim to penetrate and affect another's cyber resources.

This distinction aligns with most generic notions of offense and defense in cyberspace. Libicki (2012), for instance, defines offensive cyber operations as attempts to exploit information system vulnerabilities to interfere with the ability of victims to carry out military or other tasks. This paper adopts a working definition of cyber offense as actions seeking to exploit vulnerabilities to interfere with adversaries' military or national security-related operations. Cyber defense, in turn, involves actions to thwart adversaries undertaking such offensive actions against oneself.

Understanding these definitions is crucial as they lay the groundwork for analyzing the offense-defense balance in cyberspace. The delineation between offense and defense in cyberspace also encompasses the strategies and tactics used by states and non-state actors to assert power and control within this domain. By exploring these dimensions, the paper contributes to a nuanced understanding of how cyber capabilities are deployed in both offensive and defensive contexts, shaping the broader strategic landscape of international security.

4. Offense-defense differentiation in cyberspace

The task of differentiating offensive and defensive cyber capabilities, as per the preceding definitions, initially seems straightforward. Many specific capabilities can be easily categorized as defensive, such as malware detection and robust user password requirements, while offensive capabilities involve infiltrating target systems and extracting information.

At a basic level, offensive and defensive cyber weapons are distinguishable. However, complications arise, both acknowledged in offense-defense theory and unique to the cyber domain.

4.1 Dual-Use of Offensive Capabilities.

Offensive capabilities may serve defensive functions, and vice versa. For instance, offensive software might be employed to deactivate client computers of an attacking botnet or enhance network protections by detecting threatening malware parameters (Demchak, 2012; Belk and Noyes, 2012). Even the penetration of an adversary's network for intelligence gathering could be construed as essentially defensive, akin to radar or sonar activity. Differentiation in such cases depends on usage and user intentions.

4.2 Concealment in Cyberspace.

A unique challenge in cyberspace is the ease with which offensive capabilities can be concealed. Unlike traditional offense-defense theory, where transparency and time provide early warning of aggressive intentions, offensive cyber capabilities can be developed and deployed almost invisibly. The concealment undermines the benefits of offense-defense differentiation identified by Jervis. States can acquire offensive cyber capabilities without providing early warning to others, eroding the foundational assumption of transparency.

Concealment prevents status quo states from identifying aggressive states or relying on non-acquisition of offensive capabilities as a sign of peaceful intentions. In conditions where offense dominates, even status quo states may feel compelled to acquire offensive capabilities pre-emptively due to the uncertainty caused by the concealed nature of cyber development. In conditions favoring offense, states cannot confidently rely solely on defensive capabilities unless they are certain that all potential adversaries are refraining. The concealment of offensive capabilities heightens the risk of pre-emptive acquisition among status quo states.

These complications necessitate a more nuanced approach to offense-defense differentiation in cyberspace. Traditional markers of offense and defense become blurred, requiring analysts and policymakers to consider intent, context, and the fluidity of cyber operations. Furthermore, the dual-use nature of many cyber capabilities and the inherent difficulty in discerning their true purpose exacerbate the challenge. In response, a robust framework that integrates these complexities is essential for developing effective cyber strategies and ensuring informed decision-making in both national and international security contexts.

5. Offense-defense balance of advantage in cyberspace

The second foundational variable of offense-defense theory focuses on the offense-defense balance of advantage in conflict, considering military costs and operational effectiveness. Jervis identifies these two aspects, and their application in cyberspace further elucidates the dynamics of the offense-defense relationship.

5.1 Cost Variations.

Several analysts, including Libicki, highlight cost variations to argue that offense is advantaged in cyberspace. Libicki's detailed examination of the offense-defense balance emphasizes direct military costs. In a snapshot of circumstances around 2009, he points to U.S. government expenditures on military network security as indicative of offensive advantage. Utilizing Jervis' definition, he notes that "another dollar's worth of offense requires far more than another dollar's worth of defense to restore prior levels of security" (Libicki, 2009, p.32). However, Libicki observes that these cost figures may be influenced by the historical context of relatively low levels of conflict interaction. This highlights the importance of considering the specific circumstances and dynamics prevailing in the cyber domain.

The application of the offense-defense theory to cyberspace involves a nuanced analysis of both cost variations and operational effectiveness. While cost considerations often point to offense advantage, understanding the broader operational effectiveness of offensive and defensive capabilities is essential. The balance in cyberspace is influenced by the intricate interplay between costs, historical context, and the evolving nature of conflict interactions.

5.2 Operational Effectiveness

Beyond cost considerations, operational effectiveness plays a critical role in determining the offense-defense balance. Offense in cyberspace often benefits from the element of surprise, speed, and the ability to exploit vulnerabilities before they are patched. Defensive measures, on the other hand, require constant vigilance, updates, and adaptability to new threats. The dynamic and rapidly evolving nature of cyber threats means that defense must continuously evolve, often at a significant cost.

Libicki's assessment, despite acknowledging the current cost imbalance favouring offense, ultimately concludes that "the best defense is not necessarily a good offense; it is usually a good defense." However, this conclusion is contingent on the "highly problematic" prospects for cyber-deterrence, rather than a steadfast confidence in cyber defense per se (Libicki, 2009, p.176). The rationale is that regardless of offensive capabilities, the United

States is likely to spend more on defense than offense due to the challenges associated with cyber-deterrence (Sakellariadis 2022).

Further, Turner, et al (2024) note that transitional target defense and cyber deception may lead to capabilities that places the advantage towards the defender's side. in cyberspace, the balance of advantage is not static but continuously shifting with technological advancements, new tactics, and evolving threats. Defensive strategies must adapt to not only counter immediate threats but also anticipate future vulnerabilities. Offensive strategies, meanwhile, capitalize on current weaknesses but must also innovate to stay ahead of defensive measures.

In conclusion, while cost variations and operational effectiveness often indicate an offensive advantage in cyberspace, the overall balance is fluid and context-dependent. Effective cyber strategy requires a comprehensive understanding of both offensive and defensive dynamics, continuous adaptation, and the ability to anticipate and counter emerging threats. This nuanced approach is essential for maintaining security and stability in the ever-evolving cyber domain.

6. The geography of cyberspace

Exploring the geography of cyberspace, especially in the context of offense-defense theory, reveals a complex and indeterminate realm. The traditional determinants of advantage in this theory, such as the capacity to "take" or "hold" geographic territory, face challenges in the multifaceted dimensions of cyberspace.

6.1 Metaphorical Mapping.

Cyberspace's physical attributes, including computers, networks, and people, allow for metaphorical geographical mappings. National networks could be considered home terrain, military networks as "key terrain," and malware intrusion as an equivalent to invasion. However, these applications are metaphorical and may not fully capture the virtual dimensions of cyberspace. The virtual dimensions, encompassing information, interaction networks, and identity personas, introduce further complexity. The metaphor of geography becomes both illuminating and misleading, with challenges in applying traditional concepts to the dynamic and rapidly changing nature of cyberspace.

6.2 Borderless and Border-Rich Perspectives

Cyberspace is sometimes referred to as a "borderless" realm, highlighting the ease and speed of information flow globally. The malleability of the "geography" in this context allows for infinite pathways, transcending traditional national borders. Alternatively, a "border-rich" perspective considers the thresholds between owned and unowned cyber capabilities as defining boundaries. In the physical dimension, every system's boundary with the cyber environment constitutes a border. In the virtual aspect, emerging and disintegrating boundaries occur at the speed of thought, challenging traditional concepts of distance.

6.3 Multiplicity of Conceptions

The concept of geography in cyberspace is suggestive but ultimately indeterminate. Constructed through analogy and metaphor, various conceptions of the "lay of the land" exist, each useful for illuminating specific cyber security points. While borders and key terrain may have meaningful applications within specific conflict situations, the multiplicity of potential conceptions makes it challenging to develop a single rigorous framework.

The limitations of the concept of geography in cyberspace pose challenges for the application of offense-defense theory. The essence of offense and defense, as suggested by Jervis, involves the ability to "take" or "hold" territory. However, the viability of these objectives in the diverse conceptions of cyberspace remains uncertain. The impossibility of perfect defense, a concern in cyberspace, is likened to historical battles, emphasizing that challenges in defense are not unique to the digital domain. The main point of this example for cyber conflict is simple: in cyberspace, as in many other forms of conflict, the penetrability of boundaries is not by itself an indication that offense has the advantage. Offense-defense theory points to the importance of grasping strategic consequences holistically and looking to longer-term outcomes as the primary indicators of success and failure in conflict. This holds as a reasonable standard of offensive and defensive efficacy in cyberspace.

7. Perishability and obsolescence

Cyber weapons entail two closely related traits that distinguish them from weapons in other domains. This paper terms these traits perishability and obsolescence. Perishability refers to a weapon becoming ineffective after a single use. Obsolescence refers to a weapon becoming ineffective without being used at all. These traits arise from the reliance of cyber weapons on computer system vulnerabilities, particularly zero-day exploits. These vulnerabilities can be discovered and fixed, rendering the weapon useless.

Perishability induces conservation, as cyber weapons are often saved for crucial moments, especially when exploiting specific vulnerabilities. This conservation contributes to crisis stability and increases the potential for strategic surprise. On the other hand, obsolescence can occur even without using the cyber weapon, as the targeted vulnerability may be removed through system updates or improvements. This potential obsolescence creates incentives for states to use the weapon before it becomes useless, potentially inducing crisis instability. The lack of awareness about impending vulnerability elimination adds a layer of strategic surprise.

Together, perishability and obsolescence impact the behavior of states in an escalating crisis, with the configuration of effects determining the overall stability or instability of the situation. These traits have significant implications for assessing the offense-defense relationship in cyberspace. They emphasize the importance of secrecy, complicating the distinction between offensive and defensive cyber forces. Additionally, perishability and obsolescence incentivize states to discover new vulnerabilities and stockpile a wide range of cyber weapons, leading to a "silent arms race" characterized by aggressive development in both defensive and offensive cyber capabilities. This condition aligns with the security dilemma and reflects the potential dangers of offense-defense indistinguishability and offensive advantage in the cyber domain.

Thus, cyber weapon perishability and obsolescence tend to both obscure the distinguishability of cyber forces and promote cyber capability arms-racing. This condition captures the essence of the security dilemma and approaches the "doubly dangerous" outcome Jervis identified in a world of offense-defense indistinguishability and offensive advantage.

8. Linkages of cyber and physical conflict

Up to this point, applying the basic framework of offense-defense theory to cyberspace suggests indications that trend toward offensive advantage. As discussed above, state incentives to cloak cyber capabilities and the interactivity of cyber and physical capabilities make distinguishing offensive and defensive cyber weapons difficult. Cost considerations – the first of the two aspects of the offense-defense balance—may also favor the offense, and in any event, the principal impact of offensive cost advantage—arms races—also emerges from the unique perishability and obsolescence of cyber weaponry. However, the second aspect of the offense-defense balance – operational effectiveness in shaping the outcomes of conflicts – remains.

Most formulations of offense-defense theory, including Jervis', treat military force posture cumulatively. That is, the offense-defense balance is defined by those military capabilities that would be most likely to determine the overall results of conflict. In this sense, the concept of offense-defense balance applies to the relations of states holistically. That is, the approach directs attention not to how specific types of weapons encounter one another, but to how they change strategies of conflict overall.

The application of offense-defense theory to cyberspace underscores a tendency toward offensive advantage. This assessment takes a holistic view, considering military force posture cumulatively in terms of major state decisions, arms procurement, crisis stability, war initiation, and outcomes. Cyber weapons, while capturing strategic attention, lack the war-deciding quality seen in nuclear or certain conventional weapons. The impact of cyber capabilities in interstate conflict remains uncertain. The strategic implications of cyber weapons are intricately linked to their interaction with physical capabilities in multi-layered conflicts.

Cyber weapons alone cannot fully determine conflict outcomes, as the introduction of other weapons may be driven by circumstantial advantages. There exists the potential for an initially cyber-only conflict to escalate to the use of physical weapons, challenging the concept of an independent "cyber war." Instead, understanding the strategic implications of cyber weapons requires tracing their impacts through all potential forms of coercive interaction and conflict. The interplay of offense and defense in cyberspace is complex, with defense enabling offense and vice versa. The confidence in protecting military computer networks influences decisions related to physical military actions.

Rather than a simplistic assessment of offense or defense dominance in cyberspace, the focus shifts to understanding how cyber capabilities have shifted the broader offense-defense balance between states. Thus, the simple question of whether offense or defense dominates in cyberspace is misleading. The more strategically useful question is whether and how the advent of cyber capabilities has shifted the offense-defense balance between states more broadly. Answers to this question, in turn, depend complexly on the extent and configuration of states' other military capabilities, and on the physical and diplomatic circumstances of their interactions with one another. This observation bounds much of the discussion of the implications of cyber weapons and cyber defenses.

9. Conclusion

Van Evera (1998; 1998/1989) taking seriously the meaningfulness of offense-defense theory to explain state behaviour and international outcomes, offers a stark conclusion. He emphasizes the historical context of offense-defense theory to caution against overestimating offense dominance, noting its rarity and inherent dangers. Exaggerated perceptions of insecurity often lead to bellicose conduct, which can exacerbate national insecurity and precipitate war. While acknowledging genuine cyber threats faced by the United States in the twenty-first century, he urges caution in assessing present and growing cyber threats, citing the potential for misjudgments and biased perceptions. The complexity, opacity, and necessary secrecy inherent in cyberspace magnify the challenges in accurately gauging the offense-defense balance.

The dynamic nature of the cyber domain underscores the need for caution, as cyberspace is a human-created domain with the potential for fundamental shifts in the exercise of power. Unlike other domains with fixed physical properties, cyberspace evolves under the influence of millions of uncoordinated individual actions. This unique dynamic terrain poses challenges in strategizing for the military uses of cyberspace. While understanding warfare patterns in other domains and historical contexts can inform our understanding of cyber warfare, it remains insufficient due to the novel and dynamic character of the cyber domain.

In a broader context, an examination of offense-defense theory and its application to cyberspace reveals significant implications for international relations and security. The historical perspective serves as a cautionary tale, urging careful consideration of the dynamics between offense and defense in the evolving realm of cyberspace. As the cyber domain continues to evolve, the imperative to learn, adapt, and exercise caution becomes increasingly paramount in ensuring the security and stability of the international order.

References

Ackerman, G., Sundelson, A., & Wetzel, A. (2024). 'No-one Likes a Cry-Baby': The Effectiveness of Victimization Narratives in External Information Operations. Journal of Information Warfare, 23(1).

Aucsmith, D. (2012) 'War in Cyberspace: A Theory of War in the Cyber Domain,' *Cyberbelli.com,* May-June 2012.

Belk, R., & Noyes, M. (2012) 'On the Use of Offensive Cyber Capabilities: A Policy Analysis on Offensive US Cyber Policy,' *Belfer Center for Science and International Affairs, Harvard Kennedy School,* March 2012.

Briggs, G. (2023). Desperately Seeking Strategic Alignment: Australia's Response to the Informatic Environment as a Global Security Disruptor. Journal of Information Warfare, 22(4), 40–52.

Buvarp, P. M. H. (2023). The Space of Influence: Developing a New Method to Conceptualise Foreign Information Manipulation and Interference on Social Media. Journal of Information Warfare, 22(2), 31–51.

Clarke, R., Ormrod, D., Lim, Y., & Slay, J. (2023). The Evolution of Chinese Cyber Offensive Operations and Association of Southeast Asian Nations (ASEAN). Journal of Information Warfare, 22(1), 44–60.

Demchak, C. C. (2012) 'Resilience, Disruption, and a 'Cyber Westphalia': Options for National Security in a Cybered Conflict World,' in N. Burns & J. Price (Eds.), *Securing Cyberspace: A New Domain for National Security.* Washington, DC: The Aspen Institute, 2012.

Goldman, E., & Monarez, E. (2021). Persistent Engagement and the Private Sector. Journal of Information Warfare, 20(2), 107–122.

Gray, C. S. (2013) 'Making Strategic Sense of Cyber Power: Why The Sky Is Not Falling,' *Strategic Studies Institute and U.S. Army War College Press,* April 2013.

Harknett, R. J., Callaghan, J. P., & Kauffman, R. (2010) 'Leaving Deterrence Behind: War-Fighting and National Cybersecurity,' *Journal of Homeland Security and Emergency Management,* Vol. 7, No. 1, November 11, 2010.

Hiltunen, E., & Huhtinen, A. (2022). Future of Information Influence Operations: Scifi as a Tool to Imagine the Unthinkable. Journal of Information Warfare, 21(4), 79–99.

Hutchinson, W. (2022). Strategic Cognition War. Journal of Information Warfare, 21(3), 74–83.

Jervis, R. (1978) 'Cooperation under the Security Dilemma,' *World Politics,* 30:2 (January 1978), pp. 167-214.

Kello, L. (2013) 'The Meaning of the Cyber Revolution: Perils to Theory and Statecraft,' *International Security,* 38: 2 (Fall 2013), pp. 7-40.

Krepinevich, A. (2012) 'Cyber Warfare: A 'Nuclear Option'?' *Center for Strategic and Budgetary Assessments,* (2012).

Lehto, M. (2023). Cyber Warfare and War in Ukraine. Journal of Information Warfare, 22(1), 61–75.

Libicki, M. C. (2012) 'Cyberspace Is Not a Warfighting Domain,' *I/S: A Journal of Law and Policy for the Information Society,* 8:2 (Fall 2012), p. 325-340.

Libicki, M. C. (2009) *Cyberdeterrence and Cyberwar.* Santa Monica, CA: RAND, 2009.

Lynn, W. J. III (2010) 'Defending a New Domain,' *Foreign Affairs,* 89:5 (September 2010), pp. 97–108.

Masters, J. (2011) 'Confronting the Cyber Threat,' *Council on Foreign Relations,* May 23, 2011.

Meriläinen, N. (2023). "Information operations do not worry me" – The Role of Credible Information on Digital Platforms. Journal of Information Warfare, 22(4), 93–112.

Murphy, B. (2023). Evaluating the Ambiguous Cognitive Terrain: A Framework to Clarify Disinformation. Journal of Information Warfare, 22(3), 9–27.

Noel, G., & Reith, M. (2021). Cyber Warfare Evolution and Role in Modern Conflict. Journal of Information Warfare, 20(4), 30–44.

Nye, J. S. Jr. (2010) 'Cyber Power,' *Belfer Center for Science and International Affairs,* May 2010.

Sakellariadis, J. (2022). Extending the 'Attribution Problem': Why Who-Based Attribution Is Insufficient to Deterring Cyberattacks. Journal of Information Warfare, 21(2), 64–76.

Saressalo, T., & Huhtinen, A. (2022). Information Influence Operations: Application of National Instruments of Power. *Journal of Information Warfare*, *21*(4), 41–66.

Sheikh, H. (2022). AI as a Tool of Hybrid Warfare: Challenges and Responses. *Journal of Information Warfare*, *21*(2), 36–49.

Sheldon, J. B. (2011) 'Deciphering Cyberpower Strategic Purpose in Peace and War,' *Strategic Studies Quarterly,* Summer 2011.

Sterner, E. (2010) 'Stuxnet and the Pentagon's Cyber Strategy,' Arlington, Va.: George C. Marshall Institute, October 13, 2010.

Turner, B., Ryan, R., Karie, N., & Guidetti, O. (2024). The Theory of Transitional Target Defence: A New Approach to Enhancing Cyber Deception. Journal of Information Warfare, 23(1).

U.S. Joint Chiefs of Staff. (2013) 'Joint Publication 3-12 (R): Cyberspace Operations,' 5 February 2013. [Online] Available at: www.dtic.mil/doctrine/new_pubs/jp3_12R.pdf.

Van Evera, S. (1998/99) 'Correspondence: Taking Offense at Offense-Defense Theory,' *International Security,* 23:3 (Winter, 1998-1999), pp. 195-200.

Van Evera, S. (1998) 'Offense, Defense, and the Causes of War,' *International Security,* 22:4 (Spring, 1998), pp. 5-43.

Van Niekerk, B. (2023). The Evolution of Information Warfare in Ukraine: 2014 to 2022. Journal of Information Warfare, 22(1), 10–31.

A Capability Maturity Model for Benchmarking in Wargames

Mehwish Nasim[1,2,4,*], Adam J. Wilden[1], Peter Williams[3], Timothy Legrand[4] and Patricia A. H. Williams[1]

[1]Flinders University, Adelaide, Australia
[2]The University of Western Australia, Perth, Australia
[3]Defence Science and Technology Group, Adelaide, Australia
[4]The University of Adelaide, Australia

mehwish.nasim@uwa.edu.au
adam.wilden@flinders.edu.au
peter.williams2@defence.gov.au
tim.legrand@adelaide.edu.au
trish.williams@flinders.edu.au

Abstract: This research provides an analysis of maturity models, and insights from specific game studies such as unclassified non-kinetic games, supported by contributions from the wargaming community. By proposing a design framework inspired by capability maturity models used in software development, cyber security, and people management, this research introduces a new benchmark for evaluating wargames, in a reproducible and standardised fashion. This model facilitates the identification of strengths and areas for improvement, offering a structured path to higher maturity levels. It aims to enable wargame designers to assess and compare wargame components systematically, enhancing the ability to validate outcomes, predict gameplay effects, and support decision-making with greater confidence. Such advancements could significantly impact policies and improve disaster resilience, particularly within Defence strategy and capabilities, marking a significant advancement in the academic and practical enhancement of the wargaming field.

Keywords: Validation; Benchmarking; Reproducibility; Wargaming; Maturity Mode

1. Introduction

In our previous research (Wilden et al. 2023), a scoping review on wargaming literature identified a notable lack of standardised methodologies for analysis and benchmarking within the field. The review identified various areas of wargaming research including general and conflict modelling, the use of artificial intelligence in game design, and evaluation practices that highlighted the challenge of replicating studies and validating outcomes due to the lack of uniform standards. Additionally, there is even a distinct lack of standardization in the presentation of information in wargaming Wojtowicz (2019). This level of fragmentation across the wargaming research landscape complicates efforts towards achieving standardisation and reproducibility. While it can be suggested that wargames are more art than science, and developed to be bespoke artifacts for single-use scenarios, research does suggest that there is a methodological definition for wargaming, that can be standardised without losing the artistry, and customisation involved (Banks 2024).

This is a work-in-progress paper. We propose a design framework that draws inspiration from Capability Maturity Models - CMMs (Curtis, Hefley & Miller 2009; Paulk 2009; Rea-Guaman et al. 2017; Silva et al. 2015) that have successfully been applied to domains such as software development, cyber security, and people management. CMM are structured frameworks used to assess and improve the processes of an organization. The proposed model can be used as a benchmark for comparison between wargames. It will enable wargame designers to identify strengths and improvement points and provide a pathway to reach higher maturity levels. Our framework can assess the qualitative positioning of the wargame components in various stages or phases. A standard framework would be a step toward allowing the designers to validate, compare, and predict the effects on gameplay and for decision-makers to draw conclusions with more confidence that could impact policies and disaster resilience for the government's strategies and capabilities.

While there has been a considerable focus and output of academic research in the Software Engineering domain, professional wargaming has had less academic focus and a more fragmented and practical focus concerning design and benchmarking. When considering the history of Capability Maturity Models about software, Paulk (2009) suggests that two key themes emerge. First, there is a definite need for best practice frameworks, and second that said frameworks need to be flexible to accommodate a wide variety of different applications. This need arises from organisational requirements of being able to judge cost-effectiveness, and overall efficiency of software projects, while also being able to adapt to changing software requirements and allow for innovation.

In addition to an overall capability measured by the CMM, there is also the need for a focus on how data is dealt with. To this end, there are data governance maturity models; tools and methodologies used to measure the capability of an organization relating to the acquisition, holding, sharing, use, and exploitation of data (Caballero et al. 2023). Like that of the CMM, categorizing an organization as having mature levels of data governance policies involves all processes that are required to manage, access, and innovate using organizational data. The assessment process for data governance involves the analysis of four core domains (Javaid & Iqbal 2017); People, Technology, Data Management and Process aspects. These four domains are also relatable to the wargaming field.

2. Methodology

To better develop a CMM for wargaming, that would not only be fit for purpose but also consistent with other CMM frameworks, it was decided to use the Australian Energy Sector Cyber Security Framework (AESCSF) (Australian Energy Market Operator (AEMO) 2024) as an inspiration for structuring the wargaming framework (Figure 1).

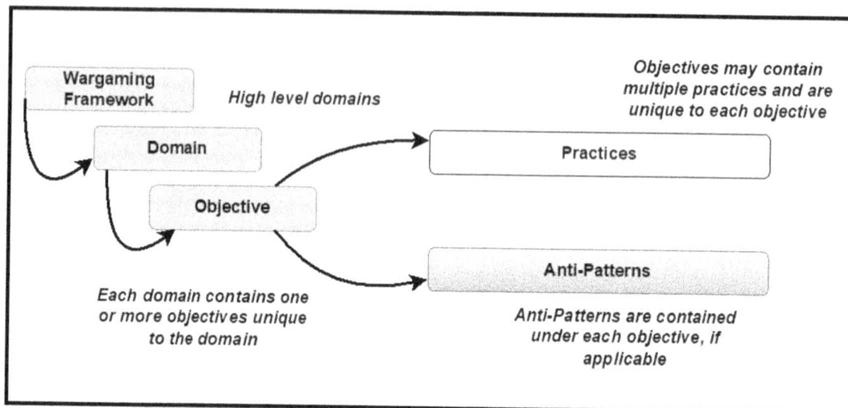

Figure 1 The wargaming framework consisting of domains and objectives

At a lower level, the AESCSF outlines how the practices are benchmarked to judge the maturity of that objective and domain (Figure 2).

As described by the AEMO (2024) in their description of the AESCSF, each of the shown (Figure 2) Practice and Anti-Patterns are assigned a maturity indicator level - MIL (in this case MIL-1, MIL-2 or MIL-3), that describes the level of maturity, and overall implementation of the practice. The AEMO (2024) describe each of these maturity levels and their characteristics that impact the assessment of Practices as follows:

- MIL 1 (Initiated): Initial Practices are performed but may be ad-hoc.
- MIL 2 (Performed): Practices are more complete or advanced than at MIL 1 with the introduction of management characteristics that drive consistency and repeatability.
- MIL 3 (Managed): Practices are more complete or advanced than at MIL 2 with the addition of further management characteristics that drive governance and continuous improvement.

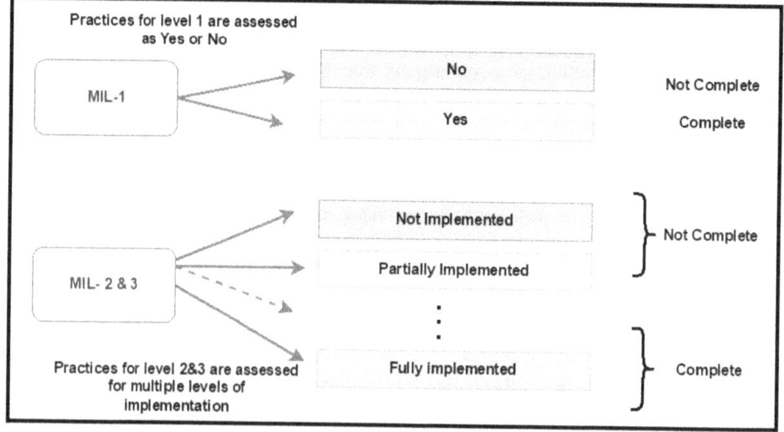

Figure 2 "AESCFS Maturity Levels" AEMO (2024)

While it is not necessary to stick to a three-stage maturity level benchmarking for wargaming (further refinement may necessitate adding levels), this approach can be adopted initially and can be changed without issue later.

The AESCFS scoring model judges the completion of maturity levels using the following guidelines.

- A Practice is "Complete" if it is assessed as "Largely Implemented" or "Fully Implemented".
- A MIL is "Achieved" if all Practices within it are "Complete".
- Scored based on a combination of "Practice implementation" and "Management Characteristics".
- The MILs apply independently to each domain and are cumulative.
- For a participant to gain a MIL in each domain, they must Complete all practices, and not exhibit any Anti-Patterns, at that MIL in that Domain.
- For example, to achieve a MIL-3 the participant would have to perform all Practices and not exhibit any of the Anti-Patterns, in MIL-1, MIL-2, and MIL-3.

These criteria may or may not be appropriate for all wargaming practices, however, it can be initially used as a guide for developing the wargaming CMM. Wargaming maturity levels may end up being considered complete with partially implemented practices, and/or combinations of other complete practices and lack of anti-patterns.

We have modified the AESCFS's definition of anti-pattern in the context of wargaming, as follows:.

- Anti-Patterns are included in the wargame to enable the identification of behaviours/practices that hinder a game from achieving a higher maturity.
- Anti-Patterns are developed in consultation with wargamers and stakeholders.
- In essence, they are 'bad' activities that undermine the effectiveness of an element in a wargame. Therefore, additional focus is given to them to encourage wargamers to fix these behaviours.

For wargaming maturity benchmarking, an anti-pattern could be identified through collaboration with wargaming subject matter experts, and from observations of wargaming activities.

3. Evaluation

The evaluation was conducted on three wargames. Eight wargaming designers conducted the evaluation.

Wargame 1: Notes were taken during the execution of this wargame. This wargame involved three teams (Blue, Orange, Green) with unique units and capabilities, spanning motorised platoons, cyber operations, intelligence networks, electronic warfare, commandos, and local security. Each team's units were designed with specific roles, such as reconnaissance, cyber surveillance, human intelligence, and special operations, reflecting a comprehensive simulation of modern warfare and intelligence-gathering activities. Only one analyst evaluated this wargame.

For the other two wargames, the designers provided the feedback post-wargaming exercise.

Wargame 2: It was a kinetic wargame focused on peer enemies engaged in a conflict with long-range fires and a significant air-sea battle. It used a structured, manual wargaming system and was attended by around 20 people (8 players and 12 analysts/support staff).

Wargame 3: It used a bespoke tabletop system to play an influence scenario where 9 different actors (teams of players) were trying to influence a local population and otherwise positively or negatively affect the other players.

Each wargamer filled out an Excel sheet. A snippet of the Excel sheet is shown in Figure 3. The blank template is available on GitHub (Nasim 2024).

In response to the question, "Can this model be useful for standardizing the wargaming-design process for comparison of wargames and their validation?", all eight wargamers responded *Yes*.

4. Results

We evaluated the agreement between the wargamers for each wargame. The wargamers/analysts independently filled the last column of the Excel sheet (Figure 3). For brevity, we have summarised the results as follows.

Wargame 1: N/A

Wargame 2: There was 90% agreement on the assessment.

Wargame 3: There was 92% agreement on the assessment.

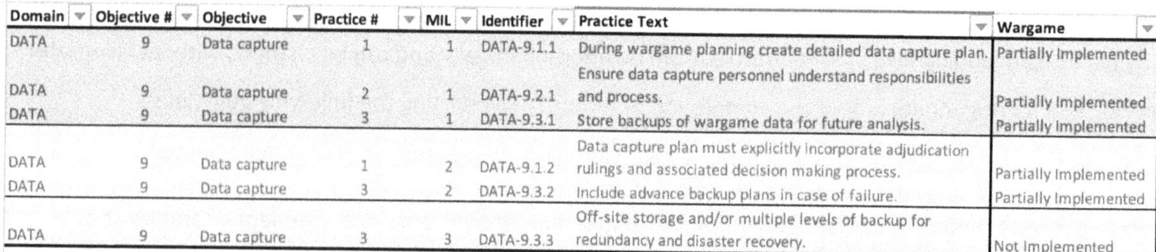

Domain	Objective #	Objective	Practice #	MIL	Identifier	Practice Text	Wargame
DATA	9	Data capture	1	1	DATA-9.1.1	During wargame planning create detailed data capture plan.	Partially Implemented
DATA	9	Data capture	2	1	DATA-9.2.1	Ensure data capture personnel understand responsibilities and process.	Partially Implemented
DATA	9	Data capture	3	1	DATA-9.3.1	Store backups of wargame data for future analysis.	Partially Implemented
DATA	9	Data capture	1	2	DATA-9.1.2	Data capture plan must explicitly incorporate adjudication rulings and associated decision making process.	Partially Implemented
DATA	9	Data capture	3	2	DATA-9.3.2	Include advance backup plans in case of failure.	Partially Implemented
DATA	9	Data capture	3	3	DATA-9.3.3	Off-site storage and/or multiple levels of backup for redundancy and disaster recovery.	Not Implemented

Figure 3 Snippet of the model for Objective # 9 which lies in the data domain

5. Discussion and Future Work

5.1 Conclusions

We presented a capability maturity model for benchmarking wargames. We found the designers have a high level of agreement in rating the objectives and practices in two wargames. In future, we will test the framework on different types of wargames and will expand on objectives relevant to different kinds of scenarios.

Acknowledgment

*This research was supported by the South Australian Defence Innovation Partnership – Collaborative Research Funds, awarded to Dr Mehwish Nasim (2021-2023).

References

Australian Energy Market Operator (AEMO), ACSCA, Cyber and Infrastructure Security Centre (CISC), 2024, *Aescsf Framework and Resources*, Australian Energy Market Operator (AEMO), viewed 25 Mar 2024, <https://aemo.com.au/en/initiatives/major-programs/cyber-security/aescsf-framework-and-resources>.

Banks, DE 2024, 'The Methodological Machinery of Wargaming: A Path toward Discovering Wargaming's Epistemological Foundations', *International Studies Review*, vol. 26, no. 1, p. viae002.

Caballero, I, Gualo, F, Rodríguez, M & Piattini, M 2023, 'A Maturity Model for Data Governance, Data Quality Management, and Data Management', in *Conference on Cloud Computing, Big Data & Emerging Topics*, pp. 157-70.

Curtis, B, Hefley, B & Miller, S 2009, 'People Capability Maturity Model (P-Cmm) Version 2.0', *Software Engineering Institute*, p. 18.

Javaid, MI & Iqbal, MMW 2017, 'A Comprehensive People, Process and Technology (Ppt) Application Model for Information Systems (Is) Risk Management in Small/Medium Enterprises (Sme)', in *2017 International Conference on Communication Technologies (ComTech)*, pp. 78-90.

Nasim, M 2024, *CMM-wargaming*, GitHub, viewed 03 Apr 2024, https://github.com/mehwishnasim/CMM-wargaming.

Paulk, MC 2009, 'A History of the Capability Maturity Model for Software', *ASQ Software Quality Professional*, vol. 12, no. 1, pp. 5-19.

Rea-Guaman, AM, San Feliu, T, Calvo-Manzano, JA & Sanchez-Garcia, ID 2017, 'Comparative Study of Cybersecurity Capability Maturity Models', in *Software Process Improvement and Capability Determination: 17th International Conference, SPICE 2017, Palma de Mallorca, Spain, October 4–5, 2017, Proceedings*, pp. 100-13.

Silva, FS, Soares, FSF, Peres, AL, De Azevedo, IM, Vasconcelos, APL, Kamei, FK & de Lemos Meira, SR 2015, 'Using Cmmi Together with Agile Software Development: A Systematic Review', *Information and Software Technology*, vol. 58, pp. 20-43.

Wilden, AJ, Nasim, M, Williams, P, Legrand, T, Turnbull, BP & Williams, PA 2023, 'On Benchmarking and Validation in Wargames', in *22nd European Conference on Cyber Warfare and Security, ECCWS 2023*, pp. 533-43.

Wojtowicz, N 2019, 'From Sandboxes to Laboratories: Evolution of Wargaming into a Method for Experimental Studies', *International Journal of Scientific and Research Publications*, vol. 9, no. 12, p. 399.

www.ingramcontent.com/pod-product-compliance
Lightning Source LLC
Chambersburg PA
CBHW082303210326
41598CB00028B/4433
* 9 7 8 1 9 1 7 2 0 4 0 6 4 *